ONE TO O

# Bilingual Dictionary

# English-Tigrigna Tigrigna-English Dictionary

Compiled by
**Tsegazeab Hailegebriel**

STAR

**STAR Foreign Language BOOKS**

ISBN : 978 1 912826 60 5



First Edition : 2020

Published by

**STAR Foreign Language BOOKS**

a unit of

**ibs BOOKS (UK)**

56, Langland Crescent

Stanmore HA7 1NG, U.K.

info@starbooksuk.com

www.starbooksuk.com

Printed in India at

Star Print-O-Bind, New Delhi-110 020

# About this Dictionary

Developments in science and technology today have narrowed down distances between countries, and have made the world a small place. A person living thousands of miles away can learn and understand the culture and lifestyle of another country with ease and without travelling to that country. Languages play an important role as facilitators of communication in this respect.

To promote such an understanding, STAR **Foreign Language** BOOKS has planned to bring out a series of bilingual dictionaries in which important English words have been translated into other languages, with Roman transliteration in case of languages that have different scripts. This is a humble attempt to bring people of the word closer through the medium of language, thus making communication easy and convenient.

Under this series of *one-to-one dictionaries*, we have published almost 55 languages, the list of which has been given in the opening pages. These have all been compiled and edited by teachers and scholars of the relative languages.

Publishers

ONE TO ONE

## Bilingual Dictionaries in this Series

| | |
|---|---|
| English-Afrikaans / Afrikaans-English | Abraham Venter |
| English-Albanian / Albanian-English | Theodhora Blushi |
| English-Amharic / Amharic-English | Girun Asanke |
| English-Arabic / Arabic-English | Rania-al-Qass |
| English-Bengali / Bengali-English | Amit Majumdar |
| English-Bosnian / Bosnian-English | Boris Kazanegra |
| English-Bulgarian / Bulgarian-English | Vladka Kocheshkova |
| English-Cantonese / Cantonese-English | Nisa Yang |
| English-Chinese (Mandarin) / Chinese (Mandarin)-Eng | Y. Shang & R. Yao |
| English-Croatian / Croatain-English | Vesna Kazanegra |
| English-Czech / Czech-English | Jindriska Poulova |
| English-Danish / Danish-English | Rikke Wend Hartung |
| English-Dari / Dari-English | Amir Khan |
| English-Dutch / Dutch-English | Lisanne Vogel |
| English-Estonian / Estonian-English | Lana Haleta |
| English-Farsi / Farsi-English | Maryam Zaman Khani |
| English-French / French-English | Aurélie Colin |
| English-Georgian / Georgina-English | Eka Goderdzishvili |
| English-Gujarati / Gujarati-English | Sujata Basaria |
| English-German / German-English | Bicskei Hedwig |
| English-Greek / Greek-English | Lina Stergiou |
| English-Hindi / Hindi-English | Sudhakar Chaturvedi |
| English-Hungarian / Hungarian-English | Lucy Mallows |
| English-Italian / Italian-English | Eni Lamllari |
| English-Japanese / Japanese-English | Miruka Arai |
| English-Korean / Korean-English | Mihee Song |
| English-Latvian / Latvian-English | Julija Baranovska |
| English-Levantine Arabic / Levantine Arabic-English | Ayman Khalaf |
| English-Lithuanian / Lithuanian-English | Regina Kazakeviciute |
| English-Malay / Malay-English | Azimah Husna |
| English-Nepali / Nepali-English | Anil Mandal |
| English-Norwegian / Norwegian-English | Samuele Narcisi |
| English-Pashto / Pashto-English | Amir Khan |
| English-Polish / Polish-English | Magdalena Herok |
| English-Portuguese / Portuguese-English | Dina Teresa |
| English-Punjabi / Punjabi-English | Teja Singh Chatwal |
| English-Romanian / Romanian-English | Georgeta Laura Dutulescu |
| English-Russian / Russian-English | Katerina Volobuyeva |
| English-Serbian / Serbian-English | Vesna Kazanegra |
| English-Sinhalese / Sinhalese-English | Naseer Salahudeen |
| English-Slovak / Slovak-English | Zuzana Horvathova |
| English-Slovenian / Slovenian-English | Tanja Turk |
| English-Somali / Somali-English | Ali Mohamud Omer |
| English-Spanish / Spanish-English | Cristina Rodriguez |
| English-Swahili / Swahili-English | Abdul Rauf Hassan Kinga |
| English-Swedish / Swedish-English | Madelene Axelsson |
| English-Tagalog / Tagalog-English | Jefferson Bantayan |
| English-Tamil / Tamil-English | Sandhya Mahadevan |
| English-Thai / Thai-English | Suwan Kaewkongpan |
| English-Tigrigna / Tigrigna-English | Tsegazeab Hailegebriel |
| English-Turkish / Turkish-English | Nagme Yazgin |
| English-Ukrainian / Ukrainian-English | Katerina Volobuyeva |
| English-Urdu / Urdu-English | S. A. Rahman |
| English-Vietnamese / Vietnamese-English | Hoa Hoang |
| English-Yoruba / Yoruba-English | O. A. Temitope |

STAR

STAR Foreign Language BOOKS

# English - Tigrigna

# A

a *(a.)* ኤ *eh*
aback *(adv.)* ንድሕሪት *ndȟrit*
abandon *(v.t.)* ራሕረሐ *raȟreȟe*
abase *(v.)* ኣዋረደ *'awarede*
abash *(adj.)* ኣሕነኸ *'aȟneḱe*
abate *(v.t.)* ሃድአ *had'e*
abate *(v.t.)* ሃድአ *had'e*
abbey *(n.)* ገዳም *gedam*
abbot *(n.)* ኣበ-ገዳም *'abegedam*
abbreviate *(v.t.)* ኣሕጸረ *'aȟxere*
abbreviation *(n.)* ምሕጻር *mȟxar*
abdicate *(v.t,)* ወረደ *werede*
abdication *(n.)* ምሕዳግ *mȟdag*
abdomen *(n.)* ከብዲ *kebdi*
abdominal *(a.)* ናይ ከብዲ *nay*
*aberration*
abduct *(v.t.)* ጨወየ *čeweye*
abduction *(n.)* ጨወየ *čeweye*
aberrant *(adj.)* ዝንቡል *znbul*
aberration *(n.)* ስሕታን *sȟtan*
abet *(v.)* ኣደፋፈረ *adefafere*
abeyance *(n.)* ዉንዛፈ *wunzafe*
abhor *(v.)* ፈንፈነ *fenfene*
abhorrence *(n.)* ክርሃት *krhat*
abhorrent *(adj.)* ክሩህ *kruh*
abide *(v.i)* ጸንዐ *xen'ë*
abiding *(adj.)* ዘይውዳእ *zeywda'è*
ability *(n.)* ዓቕሚ *'äqmi*
abject *(adj.)* ሕርቱም *ȟrtum*
abjure *(v.)* መሓለ *meȟale*
ablaze *(adv.)*
ዘንጸባርቕ *zenxebarq̈*
able *(adj.)* ክኢላ *k'ila*
ablution *(n.)* ሕጽበት *ȟxbet*
abnormal *(adj.)* ምዝቡል *mzbul*
aboard *(adv.)* ኣብ ልዕሊ *'ab l'ëli*
abode *(n.)* ገዛ *geza*
abolish *(v.t)* ሰረዘ *sereze*
abolition *(v.)* ምውጋድ *mwgad*
abominable *(adj.)* ዚጽላእ *zixla'è*
abominate *(v.)* ጸልአ *xel'e*
aboriginal *(adj.)* ጥንታዊ *ẗntawi*
abort *(v.i)* ተወግረ *tewegre*
abortion *(n.)* ምንጻል *mnxal*
abortive *(adj.)* ውጉር *wgur*
abound *(v.i.)* ፈድፈደ *fedfede*
about *(adv.)* ብዛዕባ *bza'ëba*
about *(prep.)* ኣብ ዙርያ *'ab zurya*
above *(adv.)* ላዕሊ *la'ëli*
above *(prep.)* ብዝያዳ *bzyada*
abrasion *(n.)* ልሕላሐ *lȟlaȟe*
abrasive *(adj.)* ፋሕፋሒ *faȟfaȟi*
abreast *(adv.)* ጎድነ-
ጎድኒ *godnegodni*
abridge *(v.t)* ኣሕጸረ *aȟxere*
abroad *(adv.)* ወጻኢ *wexa'i*
abrogate *(v.)* ሰረዘ *sereze*
abrupt *(adj.)*
ሃንደበታዊ *handebetawi*
abscess *(n.)* ሓገል *ȟagel*
abscond *(v.)* ጸለቖ *xeleq̈Wu*
absence *(n.)* ብኩራት *bkurat*
absent *(adj.)* ብኹር *bḱur*
absentee *(n.)* ትሩፍ *truf*
absolute *(adj.)* ፍጹም *fxum*
absolution *(n.)* ስሬት *sreet*
absolve *(v.)* መሓረ *meȟare*
absorb *(v.)* መጸየ *mexeye*
abstain *(v.)* ተቐጠበ *teq̈eẗebe*
abstinence *(n.)* ዛህዲ *zahdi*
abstract *(adj.)* ረቒቕ *req̈iq̈*
abstruse *(adj.)* ጥሉቕ *ẗluq̈*
absurd *(adj.)* ሃዚል *hazil*
absurdity *(n.)* ትርጉም
ኣልቦነት *trgum 'albonet*

**abundance** ***(n.)*** **ምልኣት** *ml'at*
**abundant** ***(v.t.)*** **ፍድፉድ** *fdfud*
**abuse** ***(v.)*** **ዓመጸ** *ämexe*
**abusive** ***(adj.)*** **ተጻራፊ** *texarafi*
**abut** ***(v.)*** **ተዳወበ** *tedawebe*
**abysmal** ***(adj.)*** **ደልሃመታዊ** *delhametawi*
**abyss** ***(n.)*** **ደልሃመት** *delhamet*
**academic** ***(adj.)*** **ኣካደሚያዊ** *akademiyawi*
**academy** ***(n.)*** **ኣካደሚ** *akademi*
**accede** ***(v.)*** **መጸ** *mexe*
**accelerate** ***(v.)*** **ነሃረ** *nehare*
**accelerator** ***(n.)*** **ኣንሃሪ** *anhari*
**accent** ***(n.)*** **ምጉላሕ** *mgulaȟ*
**accentuate** ***(v.)*** **ኣጉለሐ** *aguleȟe*
**accept** ***(v.)*** **ተቐበለ** *teq̈ebele*
**acceptable** ***(adj.)*** **ተቐባልነት ዘለዎ** *teq̈ebalnet zelewo*
**acceptance** ***(n.)*** **ቅባለ** *qbale*
**access** ***(n.)*** **ኣኽእሎ** *'ak̈'èlo*
**accessible** ***(adj.)*** **ክእቶ ዝከኣል** *k'èto zke'al*
**accession** ***(n.)*** **ብጽሓት** *bxȟat*
**accessory** ***(n.)*** **መሰርሒ** *mesarȟi*
**accident** ***(n.)*** **ሓደጋ** *ȟadega*
**accidental** ***(adj.)*** **ናይ ሓደጋ** *nay ȟadega*
**acclaim** ***(v.)*** **ኣጨብጨበ** *ačebčebe*
**accolade** ***(n.)*** **ሞሳ** *mosa*
**accommodate** ***(v.)*** **ኣጣጥሓ** *'aẗaẗha*
**accommodation** ***(n.)*** **መጣጥሒ** *meẗaẗhi*
**accompaniment** ***(n.)*** **መሰነይቲ** *meseneyti*
**accompany** ***(v.)*** **ዓጀበ** *äjebe*
**accomplice** ***(n.)*** **ግብረ-ኣበር** *gbre'aber*
**accomplish** ***(v.)*** **ፈጸመ** *fexeme*
**accomplished** ***(adj.)*** **ክኢላ** *k'ila*
**accomplishment** ***(n.)*** **ፍጻሜ** *fxamee*
**accord** ***(v.)*** **ውዕል** *- w'ël*
**accordance** ***(n.)*** **ተውህዶ** *tewhdo*
**according** ***(adv.)*** **ብመሰረት** *bmeseret*
**accordingly** ***(adv.)*** **ስለዚ** *slezi*
**accost** ***(v.)*** **ጐነፈ** *gWanefe*
**account** ***(n.)*** **ሕሳብ** *ȟsab*
**accountable** ***(adj.)*** **ተሓታቲ** *teȟatati*
**accountancy** ***(n.)*** **ናይ ተጸባጸቢ ሞያ** *nay texabaxabi moya*
**accountant** ***(n.)*** **ተጸባጸቢ** *texebaxabi*
**accoutrement** ***(n.)*** **ተውሳኸ-ዕጥቂ** *tewsak̈e'ëtqi*
**accredit** ***(v.)*** **ብወግዒ ለኣኸ** *bweg'ï le'ak̈e*
**accredited** ***(adj.)*** **ወግዓዊ** *weg'äwi*
**accretion** ***(n.)*** **ዕብየት** *ëbyet*
**accrue** ***(v.t.)*** **ደለበ** *delebe*
**accumulate** ***(v.)*** **ኣዋህለለ** *awahlele*
**accumulation** ***(n.)*** **ውህለላ** *whlela*
**accurate** ***(adj.)*** **ልክዕ** *lk'ë*
**accusation** ***(n.)*** **ግዚ** *gzi*
**accuse** ***(v.)*** **ከሰሰ** *kesese*
**accused** ***(v.t.)*** **ክሱስ** *ksus*
**accustom** ***(v.)*** **ለመደ** *lemede*
**accustomed** ***(adj.)*** **ልሙድ** *lmud*
**ace** ***(n.)*** **ብልጫዊ** *blčawi*
**acerbic** ***(adj.)*** **ኣረቢክ** *arebik*

**acetate** ***(n.)*** **መጺጽ** *mexix*
**acetone** ***(n.)*** **ነታጉ** *qememawi*
**ache** ***(n.)*** **ቀመማዊ** *nafeq̈e*
**achieve** ***(v.)*** **ተጎናጸፈ** *tegonaxefe*
**achievement** ***(n.)*** **ፍጻሜ** *fxamee*
**acid** ***(n.)*** **መጺጽ** *mexix*
**acidity** ***(n.)*** **መጭቋር** *mečqWAr*
**acknowledge** ***(v.)*** **ተኣመነ** *te'amene*
**acknowledgement** ***(n.)*** **ምቕጻል** *mq̈xal*
**acme** ***(n.)*** **ጫፍ** *čaf*
**acne** ***(n.)*** **ዕንፍሩር** *ënfrur*
**acolyte** ***(n.)*** **ኣናጎንስጤስ** *anagonsẗees*
**acorn** ***(n.)*** **ውጽኢት** *wx'it*
**acoustic** ***(adj.)*** **ምስማዓዊ** *msma'äwi*
**acquaint** ***(v.)*** **ኣፋለጠ** *afaleẗe*
**acquaintance** ***(n.)*** **ሌላ** *leela*
**acquiesce** ***(v.)*** **ተሰማምዐ** *tesemam'e*
**acquiescence** ***(n.)*** **ምስምማዕ** *msmma'e*
**acquire** ***(v.)*** **ረኸበ** *reḱebe*
**acquisition** ***(n.)*** **ቅስመት** *qsmet*
**acquit** ***(v.)*** **ፈትሐ** *feẗhe*
**acquittal** ***(n.)*** **ናጻ ምልቃቕ** *naxa mlqaq̈*
**acre** ***(n.)*** **ኣክር** *'akr*
**acrid** ***(adj.)*** **በዳን** *bedan*
**acrimony** ***(n.)*** **ምረት** *mret*
**acrobat** ***(n.)*** **ኣክሮባት** *akrobat*
**acrobatic** ***(adj.)*** **ን ኣክሮባት** *n 'akrobat*
**across** ***(adv.)*** **ስግር** *sgr*
**acrylic** ***(adj.)*** **ኣክሪሊክ** *'akrilik*
**act** ***(v.)*** **ምግባር** *mgbar*
**acting** ***(n.)*** **ምውሳእ** *mwsa'è*
**acting** ***(adj.)*** **ወኪል** *wekil*
**actinium** ***(n.)*** **ቀመማዊ** *qememawi*
**action** ***(n.)*** **ምግባር** *mgbar*
**actionable** ***(adj.)*** **ዘኽስስ** *zeḱss*
**activate** ***(v.)*** **ኣንጠፈ** *anẗefe*
**active** ***(adj.)*** **ንጡፍ** *nẗuf*
**activist** ***(n.)*** **ምንቅስቓስ** *mnqsq̈as*
**activity** ***(n.)*** **ንጥፈት** *nẗfet*
**actor** ***(n.)*** **ተዋናይ** *tewanay*
**actress** ***(a.)*** **ተዋሳኢት** *tewasa'it*
**actual** ***(adj.)*** **ህሉው** *hluw*
**actually** ***(adv.)*** **ብሓቂ** *bḧaqi*
**actuary** ***(n.)*** **ገምጋሚ** *gemgami*
**actuate** ***(v.)*** **ኣንጠፈ** *anẗefe*
**acumen** ***(n.)*** **ትኩርና** *tkurna*
**acupuncture** ***(n.)*** **ኣኩፓንክቸር** *akupankcher*
**acute** ***(adj.)*** **ንሱር** *nsur*
**adamant** ***(adj.)*** **ተሪር** *terir*
**adapt** ***(v.)*** **ኣልዘበ** *alzebe*
**adaptation** ***(n.)*** **ምውህሃድ** *mwhhad*
**add** ***(v.)*** **ቀጸለ** *qexele*
**addendum** ***(n.)*** **መመላእታ** *memela'èta*
**addict** ***(n.)*** **ተወለፈ** *tewelefe*
**addicted** ***(adj.)*** **ዉሉፍ** *wuluf*
**addiction** ***(n.)*** **ወልፊ** *welfi*
**addition** ***(n.)*** **ወሰኽ** *weseḱ*
**additional** ***(adj.)*** **ተወሳኺ** *tewesaḱi*
**additive** ***(n.)*** **ንምዕቃብ** *nm'ëqab*
**addled** ***(adj.)*** **ዝተናወጸ** *ztenawexe*
**address** ***(n.)*** **ኣድራሻ** *adrasha*
**addressee** ***(n.)*** **ተቐባላይ** *teq̈ebalay*
**adduce** ***(v.)*** **ጠቐሰ** *ẗeq̈ese*

**adept** ***(adj.)*** **ክኢላ** *k'ila*
**adequacy** ***(n.)*** **እኹልነት** *èḱulnet*
**adequate** ***(adj.)*** **እኹል** *èḱul*
**adhere** ***(v.)*** **ሰዓበ** *se'äbe*
**adherence** ***(n.)*** **ምድጋፍ** *mdgaf*
**adhesive** ***(n.)*** **ላጋቢ** *lagabi*
**adieu** ***(n.)*** **ላጋቢደሓን ኩን** *deȟan kun*
**adjacent** ***(adj.)*** **ጐረቤት** *gWarebeet*
**adjective** ***(n.)*** **ቅጽል** *qxl*
**adjoin** ***(v.)*** **ተጋወረ** *tegawere*
**adjourn** ***(v.)*** **ኣቋረጸ** *aqWArexe*
**adjournment** ***(n.)*** **ኣመሓላለፈ** *ameȟalalefe*
**adjudge** ***(v.t.)*** **በየነ** *beyene*
**adjudicate** ***(v.)*** **ፈረደ** *ferede*
**adjunct** ***(n.)*** **ጥብቆ** *ẗbqo*
**adjust** ***(v.)*** **ኣመዓራረየ** *ame'ärareye*
**adjustment** ***(n.)*** **ምውዳድ** *mwdad*
**administer** ***(v.)*** **ኣመሓደረ** *ameȟadere*
**administration** ***(n.)*** **ምምሕዳር** *mmȟdar*
**administrative** ***(adj.)*** **ምምሕዳራዊ** *mmȟdarawi*
**administrator** ***(adj.)*** **ኣመሓዳሪ** *ameȟadari*
**admirable** ***(adj.)*** **ዚነኣድ** *zine'ad*
**admiral** ***(n.)*** **ኣድሚራል** *admiral*
**admiration** ***(n.)*** **ኣድናቖት** *adnaq̈ot*
**admire** ***(v.)*** **ኣድነቐ** *adneq̈e*
**admissible** ***(adj.)*** **ዚፍቀድ** *zifqed*
**admission** ***(n.)*** **ቅበላ** *qbela*
**admit** ***(v.)*** **ተኣመነ** *te'amene*
**admittance** ***(n.)*** **ቅበላ** *qbela*
**admonish** ***(v.)*** **ገሰጸ** *gesexe*
**ado** ***(n.)*** **ሸቐልቀል** *sheq̈elqel*
**adobe** ***(n.)*** **ጥረ-ሕጡብ** *ẗreȟẗub*
**adolescence** ***(n.)*** **ብጽሕና** *bxȟna*
**adolescent** ***(adj.)*** **በጽሒ** *bexȟi*
**adopt** ***(v.)*** **ወሰደ** *wesede*
**adoption** ***(n.)*** **ምርዓም** *mr'äm*
**adoptive** ***(adj.)*** **ረዓሚ** *re'ämi*
**adorable** ***(adj.)*** **ተፈታዊ** *tefetawi*
**adoration** ***(n.)*** **ፍቕሪ** *fq̈ri*
**adore** ***(v.t.)*** **ኣምለኸ** *amleḱe*
**adorn** ***(v.)*** **ኣሰወነ** *asewene*
**adrift** ***(adj.)*** **ፋሉል** *falul*
**adroit** ***(adj.)*** **ጨለ** *čele*
**adsorb** ***(v.)*** **ኣድሰረብ** *adserb*
**adulation** ***(n.)*** **ውዳሰ-ከንቱ** *wdasekentu*
**adult** ***(n.)*** **እኹል** *èḱul*
**adulterate** ***(v.)*** **ኣመራሰሐ** *ameraseȟe*
**adulteration** ***(n.)*** **ምምርሳሕ** *mmrsaȟ*
**adultery** ***(n.)*** **ዝሙት** *zmut*
**advance** ***(v.)*** **ሰጕመ** *segWame*
**advance** ***(n.)*** **ለዓለ** *le'äle*
**advancement** ***(n.)*** **ምምዕባል** *mm'ëbal*
**advantage** ***(v.t.)*** **ብልጫ** *blča*
**advantage** ***(n.)*** **ረብሓ** *rebȟa*
**advantageous** ***(adj.)*** **ጠቓሚ** *ẗeq̈ami*
**advent** ***(n.)*** **ምጽኣት** *mx'at*
**adventure** ***(n.)*** **ዕንደራ** *ëndera*
**adventurous** ***(adj.)*** **ሓደገ'ኛ** *ȟadegeňa*
**adverb** ***(n.)*** **ተወሳከ-ግሲ** *tewesakegsi*
**adversary** ***(n.)*** **ተጻይ** *texay*
**adverse** ***(adj.)*** **ኣሉታዊ** *alutawi*

**adversity** ***(n.)*** **ሽግር** *shgr*
**advertise** ***(v.)*** **ኣፋለጠ** *afaleṫe*
**advertisement** ***(n.)*** **ረክላም** *reklam*
**advice** ***(n.)*** **ምዕዶ** *m'ëdo*
**advisable** ***(adj.)*** **ዝሓሸ** *zḧashe*
**advise** ***(v.)*** **መዓደ** *me'äde*
**advocate** ***(n.)*** **ደጋፊ** *degafi*
**advocate** ***(v.)*** **ተሓላቒ** *teḧalaq̈i*
**aegis** ***(n.)*** **ዑቕባ** *üq̈ba*
**aeon** ***(n.)*** **ኣዩን** *ayun*
**aerial** ***(n.)*** **ሰፋፊ** *sefafi*
**aerobatics** ***(n.)*** **ኣይሮባቲክስ** *ayrobatiks*
**aerobics** ***(n.)*** **ኤሮቢካ** *'eerobika*
**aerodrome** ***(n.)*** **መዓርፎ ነፈርቲ** *me'ärfo neferti*
**aeronautics** ***(n.)*** **ስነ-ምንፋር** *snemnfar*
**aeroplane** ***(n.)*** **ኣይሮፕላን** *ayroplan*
**aerosol** ***(n.)*** **ፍሊት** *flit*
**aerospace** ***(n.)*** **ጠፈረ-ህዋ** *ṫeferehwa*
**aesthetic** ***(adj.)*** **ጽባቐኣዊ** *xbaq̈e'awi*
**aesthetics** ***(n.)*** **ስነ-ጽባቐ** *snexbaq̈e*
**afar** ***(adv.)*** **ንርሑቕ** *nrḧuq̈*
**affable** ***(adj.)*** **ፍሕሹው** *fḧshuw*
**affair** ***(n.)*** **ፍጻሜ** *fxamee*
**affect** ***(v.)*** **ጸለወ** *xelewe*
**affectation** ***(n.)*** **ምስሉይነት** *msluynet*
**affected** ***(adj.)*** **ኣምሳሊ** *amsali*
**affection** ***(n.)*** **ፍትወት** *ftwet*
**affectionate** ***(adj.)*** **ርህሩህ** *rhruh*
**affidavit** ***(n.)*** **ቃለ-ማሕላ** *qalemaḧla*
**affiliate** ***(v.)*** **ተጸግዐ** *texeg'ë*
**affiliation** ***(n.)*** **ምጽጋዕ** *mxga'ë*
**affinity** ***(n.)*** **ተማስሎ** *temaslo*
**affirm** ***(v.)*** **ኣረጋገጸ** *aregagexe*
**affirmation** ***(n.)*** **ምርግጋጽ** *mrggax*
**affirmative** ***(adj.)*** **ኣወንታዊ** *awentawi*
**affix** ***(v.t.)*** **ልቃ'በ** *lqabe*
**afflict** ***(v.)*** **ጐድአ** *gWad'e*
**affliction** ***(n.)*** **ጭንቂ** *čnqi*
**affluence** ***(n.)*** **ሃብቲ** *habti*
**affluent** ***(adj.)*** **ሃብታም** *habtam*
**afford** ***(v.t.)*** **ኣተኻኸለ** *atek̒ak̒ele*
**afforestation** ***(n.)*** **ምግራብ** *mgrab*
**affray** ***(n.)*** **ናዕቢ** *na'ëbi*
**affront** ***(n.)*** **ዘለፈ** *zelefe*
**afield** ***(adv.)*** **ኣብ ርሑቕ** *'ab rḧuq̈*
**aflame** ***(adj.)*** **ዝተቓጸለ** *zteq̈axele*
**afloat** ***(adj.)*** **ዘንሳፍፍ** *zensaff*
**afoot** ***(adv.)*** **ኣብ ምቅርራብ** *'ab mqrrab*
**afraid** ***(adj.)*** **ዝፈርሀ** *zferhe*
**afresh** ***(adv.)*** **እንደገና** *'èndegena*
**African** ***(adj.)*** **ኣፍሪቃ** *afriqa*
**aft** ***(adv.)*** **ንድሕሪት** *ndḧrit*
**after** ***(adv.)*** **ድሕሪ** *dḧri*
**after** ***(conj.)*** **ድሕረ** *dḧre*
**after** ***(prep.)*** **ከም ናይ** *kem nay*
**again** ***(adv.)*** **እንደገና** *'èndegena*
**against** ***(prep.)*** **ኣንጻር** *anxar*
**agate** ***(n.)*** **ተሪር ክቡር እምኒ** *terir kbur 'èmni*
**age** ***(n.)*** **ዕድመ** *ëdme*
**aged** ***(adj.)*** **ሽማግለታት** *shmagletat*
**ageism** ***(n.)*** **dndena 'aregawyan** *dndena 'aregawyan*

**ageless** ***(adj.)*** **ዘይሓርር** *zeyḧarr*
**agency** ***(n.)*** **wanin** *wanin*
**agenda** ***(n.)*** **አጀንዳ** *aĵenda*
**agent** ***(n.)*** **ሰላይ** *selay*
**agglomerate** ***(v.)*** **አከበ** *akebe*
**aggravate** ***(v.)*** **አግደደ** *agdede*
**aggravation** ***(n.)*** **ዘቑጥዕ** *zeq̈uṫ'ë*
**aggregate** ***(n.)*** **ደመረ** *demere*
**aggression** ***(n.)*** **መጥቃዕቲ** *meṫqa'ëti*
**aggressive** ***(adj.)*** **ዓማጺ** *ämaxi*
**aggressor** ***(n.)*** **አጥቃዒ** *aṫqa'ï*
**aggrieve** ***(v.)*** **አቐየመ** *aq̈eyeme*
**aghast** ***(adj.)*** **ዝሰምበደ** *zsembede*
**agile** ***(adj.)*** **ስሉጥ** *sluṫ*
**agility** ***(n.)*** **ሶፕራኖ** *soprano*
**agitate** ***(v.)*** **ቀስቀሰ** *qesqese*
**agitation** ***(n.)*** **ምኽስ** *mḱWas*
**agnostic** ***(n.)*** **ኢፈሊጣዊ** *ifeliṫawi*
**ago** ***(adv.)*** **ይገብር** *ygebr*
**agog** ***(adj.)*** **ርቡጽ** *rbux*
**agonize** ***(v.)*** **ሃወኸ** *haweḱe*
**agony** ***(n.)*** **መሪር ሓዘን** *merir ḧazen*
**agrarian** ***(adj.)*** **መሬታዊ** *mereetawi*
**agree** ***(v.)*** **ተሰማምዐ** *tesemam'ë*
**agreeable** ***(adj.)*** **ዚሰማማዕ** *zisemama'ë*
**agreement** ***(n.)*** **ስምምዕ** *smm'ë*
**agricultural** ***(adj.)*** **ሕርሻዊ** *ḧrshawi*
**agriculture** ***(n.)*** **ሕርሻ** *ḧrsha*
**aground** ***(adj.)*** **ኣብ ባይታ** *'ab bayta*
**ahead** ***(adv.)*** **ኣብ ቅድሚ** - *'ab qdmi*
**aid** ***(n.)*** **ረድኤ** *red'e*
**aide** ***(n.)*** **ደጋፊ** *degafi*
**aids** ***(n.)*** **ረድኢ** *red'i*
**ail** ***(v.)*** **አጨነቐ** *ačeneq̈e*
**ailing** ***(adj.)*** **ኣጨነቐኢ** *ačeneq̈e'i*
**ailment** ***(n.)*** **ሕማም** *ḧmam*
**aim** ***(v.i.)*** **ዕላማ** *ëlama*
**aim** ***(n.)*** **ሽቶ** *shto*
**aimless** ***(adj.)*** **ሰሓተ** *seḧate*
**air** ***(n.)*** **ኣየር** *ayer*
**aircraft** ***(n.)*** **ነፋሪት** *nefarit*
**airy** ***(adj.)*** **ነፋሻ** *nefasha*
**aisle** ***(n.)*** **ኮሪደዮ** *korideyo*
**ajar** ***(adv.)*** **ዝተገፍተነ** *ztegeftene*
**akin** ***(adj.)*** **ዚዛመድ** - *zizamed*
**alacritous** ***(n.)*** **ስሉጥ** *sluṫ*
**alacrity** ***(n.)*** **ቅሩብነት** *qrubnet*
**alarm** ***(n)*** **መጠንቀቕታ** *meṫenqeq̈ta*
**alarm** ***(v)*** **ስግኣት** *sg'at*
**alas** ***(conj.)*** **ዋይ ኣነ** *way 'ane*
**albeit** ***(conj.)*** **ሽሕ'ኳ** *shḧkWa*
**album** ***(n)*** **ኣልቡም** *'album*
**albumen** ***(n.)*** **ኣልቡመን** *albumen*
**alchemy** ***(n.)*** **ኣልከሚ** *alkemi*
**alcohol** ***(n.)*** **ኣልኮል** *alkol*
**alcoholic** ***(adj.)*** **ሰታይ** *setay*
**alcove** ***(n.)*** **ስብሳብ** *sbsab*
**ale** ***(n.)*** **ኣይል=ዓይነት ቢራ** *'ayl'äynet bira*
**alert** ***(adj.)*** **ጥንቁቕ** *ṫnquq̈*
**algebra** ***(n.)*** **ኣልጀብራ** *alĵebra*
**alias** ***(adv.)*** **ሳጓ** *sagWa*
**alias** ***(n.)*** **ልውጠ-ስም** *lwṫesm*
**alibi** ***(n.)*** **መውጽኢ-ነፍሲ** *mewx'inefsi*
**alien** ***(adj.)*** **ba'ëdi** *ባዕዲ*
**alienate** ***(v.i.)*** **ነጸለ** *nexele*
**alight** ***(v.t.)*** **ዚነድድ** *zinedd*
**align** ***(v.)*** **ሰርዐ** *ser'ë*

**alignment** *(n.)* **ኣሳላልፋ** *asalalfa*
**alike** *(adj.)* **ተመሳሳሊ** *temesasali*
**alimony** *(n.)* **ክፍሊት ፍትሒ** *kflit ftḧ*
**alive** *(adj.)* **ህያው** *hyaw*
**alkali** *(n.)* **ኣልካሊ** *alkali*
**all** *(adj.)* **ኩሉ** *kulu*
**allay** *(v.)* **ኣፋኰሰ** *afakWase*
**allegation** *(n.)* **ብህሎ** *bhlo*
**allege** *(v.)* **ኣለ** *ale*
**allegiance** *(n.)* **ተኣማንነት** *te'amannet*
**allegory** *(n.)* **ምስሌኣዊ ዛንታ** *mslee'awi zanta*
**allergen** *(n.)* **ስራይ ድጋም** *sray dgam*
**allergic** *(adj.)* **ተቖጣዒ** *teq̈ota'ï*
**allergy** *(n.)* **ቁጥዐ** *quẗ'ë*
**alleviate** *(v.)* **'aqalele** *ኣቃለለ*
**alleviation** *(n.)* **ምቕላል** *mq̈lal*
**alley** *(n.)* **መሽጐራጉር** *meshgWaragur*
**alliance** *(n.)* **ኪዳን** *kidan*
**allied** *(adj.)* **ተጸግዐ** *texeg'ë*
**alligator** *(n.)* **ዓንጎግ** *ängog*
**alliterate** *(v.)* **ደምሰሰ** *demsese*
**alliteration** *(n.)* **ድግመተ-ኣፈና** *dgmete'afena*
**allocate** *(v.)* **ኣካፈለ** *akafele*
**allocation** *(n.)* **ምምቕራሕ** *mmq̈raḧ*
**allot** *(v.)* **ኣማስሐ** *amasḧe*
**allotment** *(n.)* **ምስሒት** *msḧit*
**allow** *(v.)* **ፈቐደ** *feq̈ede*
**allowance** *(n.)* **መውዕሎ** *mew'ëlo*
**alloy** *(n.)* **ቆርቆሮ** *qorqoro*
**allude** *(v.t.)* **ኣመተ** *amete*
**allure** *(n.)* **ኣወናወነ** *awenawene*
**alluring** *(adj.)* **ኣወናወኒ** *awenaweni*
**allusion** *(n.)* **ኣመት** *amet*
**ally** *(n.)* **ሽርካ** *shrka*
**almanac** *(n.)* **ኣልማናክ** *almanak*
**almighty** *(adj.)* **ኩሉ ዚከኣሎ** *kulu zike'alo*
**almond** *(n.)* **ሉዝ** *luz*
**almost** *(adv.)* **ዳርጋ** *darga*
**alms** *(n.)* **ምጽ'ዋት** *mxwat*
**aloft** *(adv.)* **ዝተሰቕለ** *zteseq̈le*
**alone** *(adv.)* **በይኑ** *beynu*
**along** *(prep.)* **ኣብ ጐድኒ** *ab gWadni*
**alongside** *(prep.)* **ኣብ ጐድነኒ** *ab gWadneh*
**aloof** *(adj.)* **ግሉል** *glul*
**aloud** *(adv.)* **ብዓውታ** *b'äwta*
**alpha** *(n.)* **ኣልፋ** *alfa*
**alphabet** *(n.)* **ፊደል** *fidel*
**alphabetical** *(adj.)* **ብናይ ፊደላት ተርታ** *bnay fidelat terta*
**alpine** *(adj.)* **ከረናዊ** *- kerenawi*
**already** *(adv.)* **ዛጊት** *zagit*
**also** *(adv.)* **ከምኡ'ውን** *kem'uwn*
**altar** *(n.)* **መንበረ-ታቦት** *menberetabot*
**alter** *(v.)* **ጠረጴዛ ቁርባን** *ẗerep̈eeza qurban*
**alteration** *(n.)* **ምልዋጥ** *mlwaẗ*
**altercation** *(n.)* **ቈይቊ** *qWeyqWi*
**alternate** *(v.t.)* **ምርጫ** *mrča*
**alternative** *(adj.)* **ቅያር** *qyar*
**although** *(conj.)* **ምንምኳ** *mnmkWa*
**altitude** *(n.)* **ብራኸ** *brak̈e*
**altogether** *(adv.)* **ኩሉኹሉ** *kulük̈ulu*
**altruism** *(n.)* **ልግስነት** *lgsnet*

**aluminium** *(n.)* አሉሚኒዮም *aluminiyom*
**alumnus** *(n.)* ተማሃራይ ዩኒቨርሲቲ ነበር *yuniversiti neber*
**always** *(adv.)* ኩሉ ግዜ *kulu gzee*
**amalgam** *(n.)* ሕዋስ ባዚቃ *ḧwas baziqa*
**amalgamate** *(v.)* ደብለቐ *debleq̈e*
**amalgamation** *(n.)* ምሕባር *mḧbar*
**amass** *(v.)* አከበ *akebe*
**amateur** *(n.)* አማተር *amater*
**amateurish** *(adj.)* ዘይክኢላ *zeyk'ila*
**amatory** *(adj.)* መስተፋቕር *mestefaqr*
**amaze** *(v.)* አገረመ *agereme*
**amazement** *(n.)* አድናቖት *adnaq̈ot*
**Amazon** *(n.)* አማዘን *amazen*
**ambassador** *(n.)* አምባሳደር=ልኡኽ *ambasaderl'uḱ*
**amber** *(n.)* ዕንዲዳ ጌጽ *ëndida geex*
**ambient** *(adj.)* ዙርያዊ *zuryawi*
**ambiguity** *(n.)* ዘይንጹርነት *zeynxurnet*
**ambiguous** *(adj.)* ዘይንጹር *zeynxur*
**ambit** *(n.)* ደረት *deret*
**ambition** *(n.)* ህርፋን *hrfan*
**ambitious** *(adj.)* ህንጡይ *hnẗuy*
**ambivalent** *(adj.)* ማንታዊ *mantawi*
**amble** *(v.)* ተሳለየ *tesaleye*
**ambrosia** *(n.)* ምቁር *mqur*
**ambulance** *(n.)* አምቡላንስ *ambulans*
**ambush** *(n.)* ድብያ *dbya*
**ameliorate** *(v.)* አመሓየሸ *ameḧayeshe*
**amelioration** *(n.)* ምምሕያሽ *mmḧyash*
**amenable** *(adj.)* ተሓታቲ *teḧatati*
**amend** *(v.)* አመሓየሸ *ameḧayeshe*
**amendment** *(n.pl.)* መአረምታ *me'aremta*
**amiable** *(adj.)* ተፈታዊ *tefetawi*
**amicable** *(adj.)* ምሕዝነታዊ *mḧznetawi*
**amid** *(prep.)* ኣብ መንጎ *'ab mengo*
**amiss** *(adj.)* ግጉይ *gguy*
**amity** *(n.)* ዕርክነት *ërknet*
**ammunition** *(n.)* ተተኳሲ *tetekWasi*
**amnesia** *(n.)* ርሳዕ *rsa'ë*
**amnesty** *(n.)* ምሕረት *mḧret*
**amok** *(adv.)* ብዕብድብድ *b'ëbdbd*
**among** *(prep.)* ኣብ መንጎ *ab mengo*
**amoral** *(adj.)* ብዕሉግ *b'ëlug*
**amorous** *(adj.)* ፍቕራዊ *fq̈rawi*
**amorphous** *(adj.)* ቅርጸ-ኣልቦ *qrxe'albo*
**amount** *(n.)* ማዕረ ኮነ *ma'ëre kone*
**ampere** *(n.)* ኣምፐር *amper*
**ampersand** *(n.)* ፍሉጥ ሰብ *fluẗ seb*
**amphibian** *(n.)* ምድረ-ማያዊ *mdremayawi*
**amphitheatre** *(n.)* ኣምፊትያትር *amfityatr*
**ample** *(adj.)* ሰፊሕ *sefiḧ*
**amplification** *(n.)* ተወሳኺ *tewesaḱi*

**amplifier** *(n.)* **መጉልሒ** *megulḧi*
**amplify** *(v.)* **ኣጉልሐ** *agulḧe*
**amplitude** *(n.)* **ስፍሓት** *sfḧat*
**amulet** *(n.)* **ክታብ** *ktab*
**amuse** *(v.)* **ኣዘናግዐ** *azenag'ë*
**amusement** *(n.)* **ምዝንጋዕ** *mznga'ë*
**an** *(adj.)* **ሓደ** *ḧade*
**anachronism** *(n.)* **ዕለቱ ዝሰሓተ** *ëletu zseḧate*
**anaemia** *(n.)* **ዋሕዲ ደም** *waḧdi dem*
**anaesthesia** *(n.)* **ድንዛዘ** *dnzaze*
**anaesthetic** *(n.)* **መደንዘዚ** *medenzezi*
**anal** *(adj.)* **ቆይቋም** *qoyqWAm*
**analgesic** *(n.)* **ጸረ-ቃንዛ** *xereqanza*
**analogous** *(adj.)* **ተመሳሳሊ** *temesasali*
**analogue** *(adj.)* **ተመሳሳልነት** *temesasalnet*
**analogy** *(n.)* **ተመሳሳልነት** *temesasalnet*
**analyse** *(v.)* **ምትንታን** *mtntan*
**analysis** *(n.)* **ምርምር** *mrmr*
**analyst** *(n.)* **ተንታኒ** *tentani*
**analytical** *(adj.)* **ትንታነኣዊ** *tntane'awi*
**anarchism** *(n.)* **ፋሉልነት** *falulnet*
**anarchist** *(n.)* **ፋሉላዊ** *falulawi*
**anarchy** *(n.)* **ፋሉልነት** *falulnet*
**anatomy** *(n.)* **ስነ-ቅርጺ ኣካል** *sneqrxi 'akal*
**ancestor** *(n.)* **ኣበው** *abew*
**ancestral** *(adj.)* **ውርሻዊ** *wrshawi*
**ancestry** *(n.)* **ኣበው** *abew*
**anchor** *(n.)* **መልህቕ** *melhq̈*
**anchorage** *(n.)* **ተዓሻገ** *te'äshage*
**ancient** *(adj.)* **ጥንታዊ** *ẗntawi*
**ancillary** *(adj.)* **ጽግዕተኛ** *xg'ëteṅa*
**and** *(conj.)* **ድማ** *dma*
**android** *(n.)* **ጽግዕተኛ** *xg'ëteṅa*
**anecdote** *(n.)* **ጽዋ** *xwa*
**anew** *(adv.)* **እንደገና** *èndegena*
**angel** *(n.)* **ፍቱው** *ftuw*
**anger** *(n.)* **ቁጥዐ** *quẗ'ë*
**angina** *(n.)* **ሕማም** *ḧmam*
**angle** *(n.)* **ኩርናዕ** *kurna'ë*
**angry** *(adj.)* **ሕሩቕ** *ḧruq̈*
**anguish** *(n.)* **ጓሂ** *gWahi*
**angular** *(adj.)* **ኩርናዓዊ** *kurna'äwi*
**animal** *(n.)* **እንስሳ** *ènssa*
**animate** *(v.)* **ህያው** *hyaw*
**animated** *(adj.)* **ሕያው** *ḧyaw*
**animation** *(n.)* **ህያውነት** *hyawnet*
**animosity** *(n.)* **ጽልኢ** *xl'i*
**aniseed** *(n.)* **ሸለን** *shelen*
**ankle** *(n.)* **ዓንካር-ዓንካሪቶ** *änkar'änkarito*
**anklet** *(n.)* **ኣንባር** *anbar*
**annals** *(n.)* **መዝገበ-ፍጻሜታት** *mezgebefxameetat*
**annex** *(v.)* **ጎበጠ** *gobeẗe*
**annexation** *(n.)* **ጐበጣ** *gWabeẗa*
**annihilate** *(v.)* **ኣጽነተ** *axnete*
**annihilation** *(n.)* **ድምሰሳ** *dmsesa*
**anniversary** *(n.)* **ዝክረ-ዓመት** *zkre'ämet*
**annotate** *(v.)* **ኣመልከተ** *amelkete*
**announce** *(v.)* **ገለጸ** *gelexe*
**announcement** *(n.)* **መግለጺ** *meglexi*
**annoy** *(v.)* **ሸወዘ** *sheweze*
**annoyance** *(n.)* **ቁጥዐ** *quẗ'ë*

**annual** ***(adj.)*** **በብዓመት** *beb'ämet*
**annuity** ***(n.)*** **በብዓመት** *beb'ämet*
**annul** ***(v.)*** **ሰረዘ** *sereze*
**anode** ***(n.)*** **ኤለትሮድ** *'eeletrod*
**anoint** ***(v.)*** **ቀብአ** *qeb'e*
**anomalous** ***(adj.)*** **ዘይስሩዕ** *zeysru'ë*
**anomaly** ***(n.)*** **ዘይስተ** *zeyst*
**anonymity** ***(n.)*** **ስመ-ስውርነት** *smeswrnet*
**anonymous** ***(adj.)*** **ስመ-ስውር** *smeswr*
**anorexia** ***(n.)*** **ምንማነ** *mnmane*
**another** ***(adj.)*** **ካልእ** *kal'è*
**answer** ***(n.)*** **መልሲ** *melsi*
**answerable** ***(adj.)*** **ኪምለስ ዚከኣል** *kimles zike'al*
**ant** ***(n.)*** **ጻጸ** *xaxe*
**antacid** ***(adj.)*** **ጻጸ መጺጽ** *xaxe mexix*
**antagonism** ***(n.)*** **ተጻራርነት** *texararnet*
**antagonist** ***(n.)*** **ተጻራሪ** *texarari*
**antagonize** ***(v.)*** **ተጻረረ** *texarere*
**Antarctic** ***(adj.)*** **ኣንታርክቲክ** *antarktik*
**antecedent** ***(n.)*** **ቅድመ ፍጻመ** *qdme fxame*
**antedate** ***(v.)*** **ኣቓደመ** *aquadme*
**antelope** ***(n.)*** **ዓጋዜን** *ägazeen*
**antenna** ***(n.)*** **ኣንተና** *antena*
**anthem** ***(n.)*** **ኣንቴማ** *anteema*
**anthology** ***(n.)*** **እኩብ ዛንታታት** *'èkub zantatat*
**anthrax** ***(n.)*** **ነፍሪ** *nefri*
**anthropology** ***(n.)*** **ስነ-ሰብ** *sneseb*
**anti** ***(n.)*** **ጸረ** *xere*
**antibiotic** ***(n.)*** **ጸረ-ነፍሳት** *xerenefsat*
**antibody** ***(n.)*** **ጸረ-ኣካል** *xere'akal*
**antic** ***(n.)*** **ወጀሃላይ** *weĵehalay*
**anticipate** ***(v.)*** **ተጸበየ** *texebeye*
**anticipation** ***(n.)*** **ትጽቢት** *txbit*
**anti-climax** ***(n.)*** **ምንቁልቋል** *mnqulqWAl*
**antidote** ***(n.)*** **ጸረ-መርዚ** *xeremerzi*
**antioxidant** ***(n.)*** **ጸረ-መርዚ** *xeremerzi*
**antipathy** ***(n.)*** **ክርሃት** *krhat*
**antiperspirant** ***(n.)*** **ኩሕለ-ምሕሊ** *kuȟlemȟli*
**antiquarian** ***(adj.)*** **ዘጥንቲ** *zeẗnti*
**antiquated** ***(adj.)*** **ድሑር** *dȟur*
**antique** ***(n.)*** **ጥንታዊ** *ẗntawi*
**antiquity** ***(n.)*** **ጥንቲ** *ẗnti*
**antiseptic** ***(adj.)*** **ጸረ-ረኽሲ** *xerereḱsi*
**antisocial** ***(adj.)*** **ጸረ-ማሕበራዊ** *xeremaȟberawi*
**antithesis** ***(n.)*** **ኣንጻር** *anxar*
**antler** ***(n.)*** **ጭንፋር ቀርኒ** *čnfar qerni*
**antonym** ***(n.)*** **ኣሉታ** *aluta*
**anus** ***(n.)*** **መሃንቱስ** *mehantus*
**anvil** ***(n.)*** **ናውቲ** *nawti*
**anxiety** ***(n.)*** **ጭንቀት** *čnqet*
**anxious** ***(adj.)*** **ሃረርተኛ** *harerteňa*
**any** ***(adj.)*** **ዝኾነ** *zkone*
**anyhow** ***(adv.)*** **ብዘይተገዳስነት** *bzeytegedasnet*
**anyone** ***(pron.)*** **ዝኾነ ሰብ** *zḱone seb*
**anything** ***(pron.)*** **ዝኾነ ነገር** *zḱone neger*
**anywhere** ***(adv.)*** **ዝኾነ ቦታ** *zḱone bota*

**apace** *(adv.)* ብቕልጡፍ *bqlťuf*
**apart** *(adv.)* ዝተፈላለየ *ztefelaleye*
**apartheid** *(n.)* ኣፓርታይድ *apartayd*
**apartment** *(n.)* ክፍሊ-ገዛ *kfligeza*
**apathy** *(n.)* ዘይተገዳስነት *zeytegedasnet*
**ape** *(n.)* ቀዳሒ *qedaḧi*
**aperture** *(n.)* ጭርታ *črta*
**apex** *(n)* ጫፍ *čaf*
**aphorism** *(n.)* ምስላ *msla*
**apiary** *(n.)* መንህብ *menhb*
**aplomb** *(n.)* ርእሰ-ርጉጽነት *r'èserguxnet*
**apocalypse** *(n.)* ራእይ - *ra'èy*
**apologize** *(v.)* ይቕሬታ ሓተተ *qreeta ḧatete*
**apology** *(n.)* ይቕሬታ *yqreeta*
**apoplectic** *(adj.)* ኣፖፐለቲካዊ *apopletikawi*
**apostate** *(n.)* ከሓዲ እምነት *keḧadi 'èmnet*
**apostle** *(n.)* ሃዋርያ *hawarya*
**apostrophe** *(n.)* ጭረት *čret*
**appal** *(v.)* ኣስካሕከሐ - *askaḧkeḧe*
**apparatus** *(n.)* መሳርሒ *mesarḧi*
**apparel** *(n.)* ክዳን *kdan*
**apparent** *(adj.)* ብሩህ *bruh*
**appeal** *(v.t.)* ብሩህ *bruh*
**appear** *(v.)* ተራእየ *tera'èye*
**appearance** *(n.)* ምቕልቃል *mqlqal*
**appease** *(v.)* ኣዝሓለ *azḧale*
**append** *(v.)* መልአ *mel'e*
**appendage** *(n.)* መመላእታ *memela'èta*
**appendicitis** *(n.)* ነድሪ ጥብቆ *nedri ťbqo*
**appendix** *(n.)* መመላእታ *memela'èta*
**appetite** *(n.)* ሸውሃት *shewhat*
**appetizer** *(n.)* ከፋት ሸውሃት *kefat shewhat*
**applaud** *(v.)* ኣጨብጨበ *ačebčebe*
**applause** *(n.)* ጨብጨባ *čebčeba*
**apple** *(n.)* ቱፋሕ *tufaḧ*
**appliance** *(n.)* መሳርያ *mesarya*
**applicable** *(adj.)* ብቑዕ *bqu'ë*
**applicant** *(n.)* ኣመልካቲ *amelkati*
**application** *(n.)* ምሕታት *mḧtat*
**apply** *(v.t.)* ተጠቕመ *teťeqme*
**appoint** *(v.)* ወሰነ *wesene*
**appointment** *(n.)* ቈጸራ *qWexera*
**apportion** *(v.t.)* ጐዘየ *gWazeye*
**apposite** *(adj.)* ዚሰማማዕ *zisemama'ë*
**appraise** *(v.)* ገምገመ *gemgeme*
**appreciable** *(adj.)* እኹል *èḱul*
**appreciate** *(v.)* ተገንዘበ *tegenzebe*
**appreciation** *(n.)* ኣስተያየት *asteyayet*
**apprehend** *(v.)* ተረድአ *tered'e*
**apprehension** *(n.)* ምርዳእ *mrda'è*
**apprehensive** *(adj.)* ዝተሻቐለ *zteshaqele*
**apprentice** *(n.)* ተልመዴን *telmedeen*
**apprise** *(v.)* ኣፍለጠ *afleťe*
**approach** *(v.)* ቀረበ *qerebe*
**appropriate** *(adj.)* ብቑዕ *bqu'ë*
**appropriation** *(n.)* ምንዛዐ *mnza'ë*
**approval** *(n.)* ቅባለ *qbale*
**approve** *(v.)* ተቐበለ *teqebele*

**approximate** *(adj.)* **ዳርጋ** *darga*
**apricot** *(n.)* **ሚሽሚሽ** *mishmishe*
**apron** *(n.)* **ግርምብያለ** *grmbyale*
**apt** *(adj.)* **በሊሕ** *beliḧ*
**aptitude** *(n.)* **ተውህቦ** *tewhbo*
**aquarium** *(n.)* **ጥርሙዝ ፍስቶ** *ẗrmuz fsto*
**aquatic** *(adj.)* **ማያዊ** *mayawi*
**aqueous** *(adj.)* **ማያዊ** *mayawi*
**Arab** *(n.)* **ኣረብ** *areb*
**Arabian** *(n.)* **ኣረቢያን** *arebian*
**Arabic** *(n.)* **ኣረቢክ** *arebik*
**arable** *(adj.)* **ገድላ** *gedla*
**arbiter** *(n.)* **ፈራዲ** *feradi*
**arbitrary** *(adj.)* **ሃውሪ** *hawri*
**arbitrate** *(v.)* **ዳነየ** *daneye*
**arbitration** *(n.)* **ዳኝነት** *daǹnet*
**arbitrator** *(n.)* **ዳኛ** *daǹa*
**arbour** *(n.)* **ዳስ** *das*
**arc** *(n.)* **ቀስቲ** *qesti*
**arcade** *(n.)* **ቀልደዳዊ** *qeldedawi*
**arch** *(n.)* **ቀልደድ** *qelded*
**archaeology** *(n.)* **ስነ ጥንቲ** *sne ẗnti*
**archaic** *(adj.)* **ጥንታዊ** *ẗntawi*
**archangel** *(n.)* **ሊቀ መላእኽት** *liqe mela'èkt*
**archbishop** *(n.)* **ሊቀ-ጳጳሳት** *liqepápasat*
**archer** *(n.)* **መንታጋይ** *mentagay*
**architect** *(n.)* **ስነ-ሃናጺ** *snehanaxi*
**architecture** *(n.)* **ስነ-ህንጻ** *snehnxa*
**archives** *(n.)* **ኣርቺቭ** *archiv*
**Arctic** *(adj.)* **ኣርክቲክ** *arktik*
**ardent** *(adj.)* **ውዕውዕ** *w'ëw'ë*
**ardour** *(n.)* **ብርቱዕ ድሌት** *brtu'ë dleet*
**arduous** *(adj.)* **ኣድካሚ** *adkami*
**area** *(n.)* **ስፍሓት** *sfḧat*
**arena** *(n.)* **መድረኽ** *medreḱ*
**argue** *(v.)* **ተማጎተ** *temagote*
**argument** *(n.)* **መጎተ** *megote*
**argumentative** *(adj.)* **መጎቲና** *megotina*
**arid** *(adj.)* **ኣጻምእ** *axam'è*
**arise** *(v.)* **ተላዕለ** *tela'ële*
**aristocracy** *(n.)* **ኣሪስቶክራሲ** *aristokrasi*
**aristocrat** *(n.)* **ኣሪስቶክራታዊ** *aristokratawi*
**arithmetic** *(n.)* **ቍጽሪ** *quxri*
**arithmetical** *(adj.)* **ቍጽሪና** *quxrina*
**ark** *(n.)* **ታቦት** *tabot*
**arm** *(n.)* **ምናት** *mnat*
**armada** *(n.)* **ኣርመደ** *armede*
**Armageddon** *(n.)* **ኣርማጌዶን** *armagedon*
**armament** *(n.)* **ኣጽዋር** *axwar*
**armistice** *(n.)* **ግዝያዊ ተኹሲ-ዕጾ** *gzyawi teḱusi'ëxo*
**armour** *(n.)* **ድርዒ ሓጺን** *dr'ï ḧaxin*
**armoury** *(n.)* **ድርዒ ሓጺኒ** *dr'ï ḧaxini*
**army** *(n.)* **ሰራዊት** *serawit*
**aroma** *(n.)* **መዓዛ** *me'äza*
**aromatherapy** *(n.)* **መዓዛ -ፍወሳ** *me'äza fwesa*
**around** *(adv.)* **ኣብ ዙርያ** *'ab zurya*
**arouse** *(v.)* **ኣበራበረ** *aberabere*
**arrange** *(v.)* **ሰርዐ** *ser'ë*
**arrangement** *(n.)* **ኣሰራርዓ** *aserar'ä*
**arrant** *(adj.)* **ምሒር** *mḧir*

**array** ***(n.)*** **ተሰለፈ** *teselefe*
**arrears** ***(n.)*** **ተሰለፈን** *teselefin*
**arrest** ***(v.)*** **አሰረ** *asere*
**arrival** ***(n.)*** **እትወት** *ètwet*
**arrive** ***(v.)*** **መጸ** *mexe*
**arrogance** ***(n.)*** **አትሒቱ ረአየ** *'athitu re'aye*
**arrogant** ***(adj.)*** **ትዕቢተኛ** *t'ëbiteňa*
**arrogate** ***(v.)*** **መንዘዐ** *menze'ë*
**arrow** ***(n.)*** **ፍላጻ** *flaxa*
**arsenal** ***(n.)*** **እንዳብረት** *èndabret*
**arsenic** ***(n.)*** **ብርቱዕ ስሚ** *brtu'ë smi*
**arson** ***(n.)*** **ብውሳይ ምቅጻል** *bwsay mqxal*
**art** ***(n.)*** **ጥበብ** *ẗbeb*
**artefact** ***(n.)*** **ጥንቲ** *ẗnti*
**artery** ***(n.)*** **አርተሪ** *arteri*
**artful** ***(adj.)*** **ብልሂ** *blhi*
**arthritis** ***(n.)*** **ሪሕ** *riḧ*
**artichoke** ***(n.)*** **ካርቾፊ** *karchofi*
**article** ***(n.)*** **አቕሓ** *aq̈ḧa*
**articulate** ***(adj.)*** **አነጸረ** *anexere*
**artifice** ***(n.)*** **ክእለት** *k'èlet*
**artificial** ***(adj.)*** **ስኑ'ዕ** *snu'ë*
**artillery** ***(n.)*** **ከቢድ ብረት** *kebid bret*
**artisan** ***(n.)*** **ክኢላ** *k'ila*
**artist** ***(n.)*** **ስነ-ጠቢብ** *sneẗebib*
**artistic** ***(adj.)*** **ስነ-ጥበባዊ** *sneẗbebawi*
**artless** ***(adj.)*** **ባህርያዊ** *bahryawi*
**as** ***(adv.)*** **ከም** *kem*
**asbestos** ***(n.)*** **ማዕድን** *ma'ëdn*
**ascend** ***(v.)*** **ደየበ** *deyebe*
**ascendant** ***(adj.)*** **ደያቢ** *deyabi*
**ascent** ***(n.)*** **ዕርገት** *ërget*
**ascertain** ***(v.)*** **አረጋገጸ** *aregagexe*
**ascetic** ***(adj.)*** **መናን** *menan*
**ascribe** ***(v.)*** **ሃበ** *habe*
**aseptic** ***(adj.)*** **ጽዱይ** *xduy*
**asexual** ***(adj.)*** **ግብረ-ሰዶመኛ** *gbresedomeňa*
**ash** ***(n.)*** **አሽ** *ash*
**ashamed** ***(adj.)*** **ዝሓፈረ** *zḧafere*
**ashore** ***(adv.)*** **መሬት** *mereet*
**Asian** ***(adj.)*** **ኤሽያዊ** *eshiyawi*
**aside** ***(adv.)*** **ገጽ** *gex*
**asinine** ***(adj.)*** **ዓንጃል** *änĵal*
**ask** ***(v.)*** **ሓተተ** *ḧatete*
**askance** ***(adv.)*** **ብጥርጣረ** *bẗrẗare*
**askew** ***(adv.)*** **ዘባል** *zebal*
**asleep** ***(adj.)*** **ጽሙው** *xmuw*
**asparagus** ***(n.)*** **ሻሞት** *shamot*
**aspect** ***(n.)*** **መልክዕ** *melk'ë*
**asperity** ***(n.)*** **ጎነጽ** *gonex*
**aspersions** ***(n.)*** **ምክፋእ** *mkfa'è*
**asphyxiate** ***(v.)*** **ዓበሰ** *äbese*
**aspirant** ***(n.)*** **ደላዪ** *delayi*
**aspiration** ***(n.)*** **ትምኒት** *tmnit*
**aspire** ***(v.)*** **ተመነየ** *temeneye*
**ass** ***(n.)*** **አድጊ** *adgi*
**assail** ***(v.)*** **አጥቀዐ** *aẗqe'ë*
**assassin** ***(n.)*** **ቀታል-ነፍሲ** *qetalnefsi*
**assassinate** ***(v.)*** **ቀተለ** *qetele*
**assassination** ***(n.)*** **ቀተሊ** *qeteli*
**assault** ***(n.)*** **አጥቀዐ** *aẗqe'ë*
**assemblage** ***(n.)*** **ምግጥጣም** *mgẗẗam*
**assemble** ***(v.)*** **አጋጠመ** *agaẗeme*
**assembly** ***(n.)*** **አኼባ** *aḱeeba*
**assent** ***(n.)*** **ስምምዕ** *smm'ë*
**assert** ***(v.)*** **ጸዓደ** *xe'äde*

**assess** *(v.)* **ኣማኻሪ** *amaḱari*
**assessment** *(n.)* **መርመራ** *mermera*
**asset** *(n.)* **ንብረት** *nbret*
**assiduous** *(adj.)* **ጻዕረኛ** *xa'ëreňa*
**assign** *(v.)* **ረተበ** *retebe*
**assignation** *(n.)* **ምደባ** *mdeba*
**assignment** *(n.)* **ምዱብ ስራሕ** *mdub sraȟ*
**assimilate** *(v.)* **ተዋሃደ** *tewahade*
**assimilation** *(n.)* **ተዋህዶ** *tewahdo*
**assist** *(v.)* **ሓገዘ** *ȟageze*
**assistance** *(n.)* **ሓገዝ** *ȟagez*
**assistant** *(n.)* **ረዳት** *redat*
**associate** *(v.)* **ተሓባባሪ** *teȟababari*
**association** *(n.)* **ማሕበር** *maȟber*
**assonance** *(n.)* **ስምምዕ** *smm'ë*
**assorted** *(adj.)* **ዝተፋላለየ** *ztefalaleye*
**assortment** *(n.)* **በብዓይነቱ** *beb'äynetu*
**assuage** *(v.)* **ኣጸናንዐ** *axenan'ë*
**assume** *(v.)* **ገመተ** *gemete*
**assumption** *(n.)* **ግምት** *gmt*
**assurance** *(n.)* **መረጋገጺ** *meregagexi*
**assure** *(v.)* **ኣረጋገጸ** *aregagexe*
**assured** *(adj.)* **ዋሕስ** *waȟs*
**asterisk** *(n.)* **ኣስትሪስክስ** *astrisks*
**asteroid** *(n.)* **ዓለም** *älem*
**asthma** *(n.)* **ኣዝማ** *azma*
**astigmatism** *(n.)* **ነበዐ** *nebe'ë*
**astonish** *(v.)* **ኣደነቐ** *adeneqe*
**astonishment** *(n.)* **ድንጽዉና** *dnxwuna*
**astound** *(v.)* **ኣስደመመ** *asdememe*
**astral** *(adj.)* **ኮኾባዊ** *koḱobawi*
**astray** *(adv.)* **ህዉቱት** *hwtut*
**astride** *(prep.)* **ብምግሕታን** *bmgȟtan*
**astrologer** *(n.)* **ብልጹግ** *blxug*
**astrology** *(n.)* **ቚጸራ ከዋኽብቲ** *qWexera kewaḱbti*
**astronaut** *(n.)* **ጠፈርተኛ** *ẗeferteňa*
**astronomer** *(n.)* **ስነ-ኮኾቢ** *snekoḱobi*
**astronomy** *(n.)* **ስነ-ኮኾብ** *snekoḱob*
**astute** *(adj.)* **ትኩር** *tkur*
**asunder** *(adv.)* **ዝተፈላለየ** *ztefelaleye*
**asylum** *(n.)* **ዑቕባ** *üq̈ba*
**at** *(prep.)* **ኣብ** *ab*
**atavistic** *(adj.)* **የዋህ** *yewah*
**atheism** *(n.)* **ኢዚህርነት** *izihernet*
**atheist** *(n.)* **ኢዚሄራዊ** *iziheerawi*
**athlete** *(n.)* **ስፖርተኛ** *sporteňa*
**athletic** *(adj.)* **ስፖርታዊ** *sportawi*
**atlas** *(n.)* **ኣትላስ** *atlas*
**atmosphere** *(n.)* **ሃዋህው** *hawahw*
**atoll** *(n.)* **ደሴት** *deseet*
**atom** *(n.)* **ኣቶም** *atom*
**atomic** *(adj.)* **ኣቶማዊ** *atomawi*
**atone** *(v.)* **ከሓሰ** *keȟase*
**atonement** *(n.)* **ድሕነት** *dȟnet*
**atrium** *(n.)* **ክፍሊ** *kfli*
**atrocious** *(adj.)* **ኣሰቃቒ** *aseqaq̈i*
**atrocity** *(n.)* **ገፍዐ** *gef'ë*
**attach** *(v.)* **ኣጣበቐ** *aẗabeq̈e*
**attaché** *(n.)* **ኣታሽ** *atash*
**attachment** *(n.)* **ጥብቀት** *ẗbqet*

**attack** ***(v.)*** **አጥቅዐ** *aẗq'ë*
**attain** ***(v.)*** **ምሉእ** *mlu'è*
**attainment** ***(n.)*** **ሰመረ** *semere*
**attempt** ***(v.)*** **ፈተ'ነ** *fetene*
**attempt** ***(v.)*** **ጀመረ** *ĵemere*
**attend** ***(v.)*** **ተኸታተለ** *teḱetatele*
**attendance** ***(n.)*** **ተሳትፎ** *tesatfo*
**attendant** ***(n.)*** **አገልጋሊ** *agelgali*
**attention** ***(n.)*** **አቓልቦ** *aq̈albo*
**attentive** ***(adj.)*** **ጥንቁቕ** *ẗnquq̈*
**attest** ***(v.)*** **አረጋገጸ** *aregagexe*
**attic** ***(n.)*** **ዋልድቢት** *waldbit*
**attire** ***(n.)*** **ልብሲ** *lbsi*
**attitude** ***(n.)*** **አቃጫጭ** *aqačač*
**attorney** ***(n.)*** **ጠበቓ** *ẗebeq̈a*
**attract** ***(v.)*** **ሰሓበ** *seḧabe*
**attraction** ***(n.)*** **ስሕበት** *sḧbet*
**attractive** ***(adj.)*** **ማራኺ** *maraḱi*
**attribute** ***(v.)*** **ባህርይ** *bahry*
**aubergine** ***(n.)*** **ማርጋሪን** *margarin*
**auction** ***(n.)*** **ሓራጅ** *ḧaraĵ*
**audible** ***(adj.)*** **ኪስማዕ ዚከኣል** *kisma'ë zike'a*
**audience** ***(n.)*** **ነባሮ** *nebaro*
**audio** ***(n.)*** **ደሃይ** *dehay*
**audit** ***(n.)*** **ጸብጻብ** *xebxab*
**audition** ***(n.)*** **ምስማዕ** *msma'ë*
**auditorium** ***(n.)*** **አውዲቶርዩም ኣዳራሽ** *'awditoryum 'adarash*
**augment** ***(v.)*** **ወሰኸ** *ወሰኸ*
**August** ***(n)*** **ነሓሰ** *neḧase*
**aunt** ***(n.)*** **ሓትኖ** *ḧatno*
**aura** ***(n.)*** **አኽሊል** *aklil*
**auspicious** ***(adj.)*** **ተስፋኣዊ** *tesfa'awi*
**austere** ***(adj.)*** **ጥብቂ** *ẗbqi*
**Australian** ***(n.)*** **አዎስትራልያ** *awustraliya*
**authentic** ***(adj.)*** **ሓቀኛ** *ḧaqeṅa*
**authenticity** ***(n.)*** **ልክዕነት** *lk'ënet*
**author** ***(n.)*** **ደራሲ** *derasi*
**authoritative** ***(adj.)*** **ምዙዝ** *mzuz*
**authority** ***(n.)*** **መዚ** *mezi*
**authorize** ***(v.)*** **መዘዘ** *mezeze*
**autism** ***(n.)*** **አዉቲዝም** *awutizim*
**autobiography** ***(n.)*** **ርእሰ-ታሪኽ** *r'èsetariḱ*
**autocracy** ***(n.)*** **አውቶክራሲ** *awtokrasi*
**autocrat** ***(n.)*** **ውልቀ-መላኺ** *wlqemelaḱi*
**autocratic** ***(adj.)*** **አውቶክራቲክ** *wlqemelaḱ*
**autograph** ***(n.)*** **ርእሰ-ጽሑፍ** *r'èsexḧuf*
**automatic** ***(adj.)*** **አውቶማቲክ** *awtomatik*
**automobile** ***(n.)*** **አውቶሞቢል=መኪና** *awtomobilm ekina*
**autonomous** ***(adj.)*** **ርእሰ-ምምሕዳራዊ** *r'èsemmḧdarawi*
**autopsy** ***(n.)*** **ምርምረ-ሬሳ** *mrmrereesa*
**autumn** ***(n.)*** **ቀውዒ** *qew'ï*
**auxiliary** ***(adj.)*** **ሓጋዚ** *ḧagazi*
**avail** ***(v.)*** **ተጠቕመ** *teẗeq̈me*
**available** ***(adj.)*** **ክትጥቀመሉ ትኽእል** *ktẗqemelu tk'èl*
**avalanche** ***(n.)*** **መደረጋሕ** *mederegaḧ*
**avarice** ***(n.)*** **ስስዐ** *ss'ë*
**avenge** ***(v.)*** **ሕነ ፈደየ** *ḧne fedeye*
**avenue** ***(n.)*** **ጐደና** *gWadena*

**average** ***(n.)*** **ማእከላይ** *ma'èkelay*
**averse** ***(adj.)*** **ኣንጻር** *anxar*
**aversion** ***(n.)*** **ጽልኣት** *xl'at*
**avert** ***(v.)*** **ኣለየ** *aleye*
**aviary** ***(n.)*** **እንዳ ኣዕዋፍ** *'ènda 'a'ëwaf*
**aviation** ***(n.)*** **ስነ-ምንፋር** *snemnfar*
**aviator** ***(n.)*** **ፓይሎት** *paylot*
**avid** ***(adj.)*** **ህንጡይ** *hnẗuy*
**avidly** ***(adv.)*** **ህንጡዪ** *hnẗuyi*
**avocado** ***(n.)*** **ኣቮካዶ** *avokado*
**avoid** ***(v.)*** **ወገደ** *wegede*
**avoidance** ***(n.)*** **ጉስያ** *gusya*
**avow** ***(v.)*** **ኣመነ** *amene*
**avuncular** ***(adj.)*** **ኣኮኣዊ** *'ako'awi*
**await** ***(v.)*** **ተጸበየ** *texebeye*
**awake** ***(v.)*** **ነቕሐ** *neq̈he*
**awaken** ***(v.)*** **ነቕሐ** *neq̈he*
**award** ***(v.)*** **ሰለመ** *seleme*
**aware** ***(adj.)*** **ገንዘብ** *genzeb*
**away** ***(adv.)*** **ናብ ርሑቕ** *nab rḧuq̈*
**awe** ***(n.)*** **ተምሳጥ** *temsaẗ*
**awesome** ***(adj.)*** **ዘርዕድ** *zer'ëd*
**awful** ***(adj.)*** **ዘስካሕክሕ** *zeskaḧkḧ*
**awhile** ***(adv.)*** **ንሓጺር ግዜ** *nḧaxir gzee*
**awkward** ***(adj.)*** **ጋሕማጥ** *gaḧmaẗ*
**awry** ***(adv.)*** **ብልሽው** *blshw*
**axe** ***(n.)*** **ፋስ** *fas*
**axis** ***(n.)*** **መቐለሲ** *meq̈elesi*
**axle** ***(n.)*** **መቐለስ** *meq̈eles*

# B

**babble** ***(v.)*** **ኣዕዘምዘመ** *a'ëzemzeme*
**babe** ***(n.)*** **ህጻን** *hxan*
**Babel** ***(n.)*** **ዘይምስምማዕ** *zeymsmma'ë*
**baboon** ***(n.)*** **ህበይ** *hbey*
**baby** ***(n.)*** **ህጻን** *hxan*
**bachelor** ***(n.)*** **ቤተ'ልቦ** - *beetelbo*
**back** ***(n.)*** **ዝባን** *zban*
**backbone** ***(n.)*** **ዓንዲ-ሕቖ** *ändiḧq̈o*
**backdate** ***(v.)*** **ሓለፈ** *ḧalefe*
**backdrop** ***(n.)*** **ትዕይንቲ** *t'ëynti*
**backfire** ***(v.)*** **ምጉሳዕ** *mgusa'ë*
**background** ***(n.)*** **ተመኩሮ** *temekuro*
**backhand** ***(n.)*** **ኣሽሙራዊ** *ashmurawi*
**backing** ***(n.)*** **ረድኤ** *red'e*
**backlash** ***(n.)*** **መልሰ-ግብሪ** *melsegbri*
**backlog** ***(n.)*** **መሃዚ** *mehazi*
**backpack** ***(n.)*** **ማህደር** *mahder*
**backside** ***(n.)*** **ብድሕሪት** *bdḧrit*
**backstage** ***(adv.)*** **ዝባን መድረኽ** *zban medrek̗*
**backtrack** ***(v.)*** **ዝባን ኣሰር** *zban aser*
**backward** ***(adj.)*** **ንድሕሪት** *ndḧrit*
**backwater** ***(n.)*** **ዝባን ማይ** *zban may*
**bacon** ***(n.)*** **ቤኮን** *beekon*
**bacteria** ***(n.)*** **ባክተሪያ** *bakteriya*
**bad** ***(adj.)*** **ሕማቕ** *ḧmaq̈*
**badge** ***(n.)*** **ኣርማ** *arma*
**badly** ***(adv.)*** **ብሕማቕ** *bḧmaq̈*

**badminton** *(n.)* **ባድሚንተን** *badminten*
**baffle** *(v.)* **አገረመ** *agereme*
**bag** *(n.)* **መልአ** *mel'e*
**baggage** *(n.)* **ጋዓዝ** *ga'äz*
**baggy** *(adj.)* **ገፍላው** *geflaw*
**baguette** *(n.)* **ሕቡር ስልማት** *ḧbur slmat*
**bail** *(n.)* **ዋሕስ** *waḧs*
**bailiff** *(n.)* **ፖሊስ** *polis*
**bait** *(n.)* **መስሓቢ** *mesḧabi*
**bake** *(v.)* **ደረቐ** *dereq̈e*
**baker** *(n.)* **ሰንካቲ** *senkati*
**bakery** *(n.)* **እንዳ ባኒ** *ènda bani*
**balance** *(n.)* **ተረፍ** *teref*
**balcony** *(n.)* **ሰገነት** *segenet*
**bald** *(adj.)* **በራሕ** *beraḧ*
**bale** *(n.)* **ጥቕላል** *ẗq̈lal*
**ball** *(n.)* **ኩዕሶ** *ku'ëso*
**ballad** *(n.)* **ግጥሚ ወይ ደርፊ** *gẗmi wey derfi*
**ballet** *(n.)* **ባለ** *bale*
**balloon** *(n.)* **ባሉን** *balun*
**ballot** *(n.)* **ምርጫ** *mrča*
**balm** *(n.)* **በለሳን** *belesan*
**balsam** *(n.)* **በለሳን** *belesan*
**bamboo** *(n.)* **አርቃይ** *arqay*
**ban** *(v.)* **ኣገደ** *agede*
**banal** *(adj.)* **ተራ** *tera*
**banana** *(n.)* **ባናና** *banana*
**band** *(n.)* **መእሰሪ** *me'èseri*
**bandage** *(n.)* **መጀነኒ** *meĵeneni*
**bandit** *(n.)* **ሽፍታ ወረበላ** *shfta werebela*
**bane** *(n.)* **መርዚ ስሚ** *merzi smi*
**bang** *(n.)* **ገውታ** *gewta*
**banger** *(n.)* **ገውታት** *gewtat*
**bangle** *(n.)* **በናጅር** *benaĵr*
**banish** *(v.)* **ሓየረ** *ḧayere*
**banishment** *(n.)* **ጥርዝያ** *ẗrzya*
**banisters** *(n.)* **መደንደል** *medendel*
**banjo** *(n.)* **ባንጆ** *banĵo*
**bank** *(n.)* **ባንኪ** *banki*
**banker** *(n.)* **መኰነን** *mekWanen*
**bankrupt** *(adj.)* **ጥፉሽ** *ẗfush*
**bankruptcy** *(n.)* **ጥፈሻ** *ẗfesha*
**banner** *(n.)* **ሰንደቕ** *sendeq̈*
**banquet** *(n.)* **በዓል** *be'äl*
**banter** *(n.)* **ተዋዘየ** *tewazeye*
**baptism** *(n.)* **ጥምቀት** *ẗmqet*
**Baptist** *(n.)* **መጥምቓዊ** *meẗmq̈awi*
**baptize** *(v.)* **ኣጠመቐ** *aẗemeq̈e*
**bar** *(n.)* **መታወር** *metawer*
**barb** *(n.)* **ዓንቃሪቦ** *änqaribo*
**barbarian** *(n.)* **ባርባራዊ** *barbarawi*
**barbaric** *(adj.)* **ባርባራዊ** *barbarawi*
**barbecue** *(n.)* **ጥብሲ ቦታ** *ẗbsi bota*
**barbed** *(adj.)* **ወጋኢ** *wega'i*
**barber** *(n.)* **ቀምቃማይ** *qemqamay*
**bard** *(n.)* **ግጥሚ ወይ ደርፊ** *gẗmi wey derfi*
**bare** *(adj.)* **ጥርሑ** *ẗrḧu*
**barely** *(adv.)* **ብቕሉዕ** *bq̈lu'ë*
**bargain** *(n.)* **ዋጋ ዕዳጋ** *waga 'ëdaga*
**barge** *(n.)* **ባርጅ** *barĵ*
**bark** *(n.)* **ቅራፍ** *qraf*
**barley** *(n.)* **ስገም** *sgem*
**barn** *(n.)* **መኽዘን** *meḱzen*
**barometer** *(n.)* **ባሮሜተር** *baromeeter*

**baron** *(n.)* ባላባት *balabat*
**barrack** *(n.)* ባራካ *baraka*
**barracuda** *(n.)* መሸኒት *meshenit*
**barrage** *(n.)* ግድብ *gdb*
**barrel** *(n.)* በርሚል *bermil*
**barren** *(adj.)* መኻን *meḱan*
**barricade** *(n.)* መደንደል *medendel*
**barrier** *(n.)* ዕንቅፋት *ënqfat*
**barring** *(prep.)* ግድብ *gdb*
**barrister** *(n.)* ጠበቓ *ẗebeq̈a*
**barter** *(v.)* በደላ *bedela*
**base** *(n.)* ሰረተ *serete*
**baseless** *(adj.)* ሰረትኣልቦ *seret'albo*
**basement** *(n.)* ትሕተ-ቤት *tḧtebeet*
**bashful** *(adj.)* ሓፋር *ḧafar*
**basic** *(n.)* ሰረታዊ *seretawi*
**basil** *(n.)* ሪሓን *riḧan*
**basilica** *(n.)* ባዚሊካ *bazilika*
**basin** *(n.)* ስሓኒ *- sḧani*
**basis** *(n.)* ሰረት *seret*
**bask** *(v.)* ተጸልወ *texelwe*
**basket** *(n.)* ዘንቢል *zenbil*
**bass** *(n.)* ባስ ዓይነት ዓሳ *bas 'äynet 'äsa*
**bastard** *(n.)* ድቓላ *dq̈ala*
**baste** *(v.)* ሸለለ *shelele*
**bastion** *(n.)* ዕርዲ *ërdi*
**bat** *(n.)* መንካዕ *menka'ë*
**batch** *(n.)* እኩብ *èkub*
**bath** *(n.)* ምሕጻብ *mḧxab*
**bathe** *(v.)* ኣለኸ *aleḱe*
**bathos** *(n.)* ህውተታ *hwteta*
**batik** *(n.)* ባቲክ *batik*
**baton** *(n.)* በትሪ ፖሊስ *betri polis*
**battalion** *(n.)* ቦጦሎኒ *botöloni*
**batten** *(n.)* ተገዳም *tegedam*
**batter** *(n.)* ከትከተ *ketkete*
**battery** *(n.)* ባተሪ *bateri*
**battle** *(n.)* ውግእ *wg'è*
**bauble** *(n.)* ሕቡር ስልማት *ḧbur slmat*
**baulk** *(v.)* መሰናኸል *mesenaḱl*
**bawl** *(v.)* ወጨጨ *wečeče*
**bay** *(n.)* ፉርዳ *furda*
**bayonet** *(n.)* ሳንጃ *sanĵa*
**bazaar** *(n.)* ባዛር ሹቕ *bazar shuq̈*
**bazooka** *(n.)* ባዙቃ *bazuqa*
**be** *(v.)* ኮነ *kone*
**beach** *(n.)* ገምገም ባሕሪ *gemgem baḧri*
**beacon** *(n.)* መና *mena*
**bead** *(n.)* ዕንቆ *ënqo*
**beady** *(adj.)* ቆርቋር *qorqWAr*
**beagle** *(n.)* ቢግል *bigl*
**beak** *(n.)* መትከብ *metkob*
**beaker** *(n.)* ብርጭቆ *brčqo*
**beam** *(n.)* ገመል *gemel*
**bean** *(n.)* ባልዶንጓ *baldongWa*
**bear** *(v.t)* ድቢ *dbi*
**bear** *(n.)* ተሸከመ *teshekeme*
**beard** *(n.)* ጭሕሚ *čḧmi*
**bearing** *(n.)* ማእዝን *ma'èzn*
**beast** *(n.)* እንስሳ *ènssa*
**beastly** *(adj.)* እንስሳዊ *ènssawi*
**beat** *(v.)* ላጸየ *laxeye*
**beatitude** *(n.)* ደስታ *desta*
**beautician** *(n.)* ላጸየ *laxeye*
**beautiful** *(adj.)* ማራኺ *maraḱi*
**beautify** *(v.)* ኣመልክዐ *amelk'ë*
**beauty** *(n.)* መልክዕ *melk'ë*
**beaver** *(n.)* ቢቨር *biver*
**becalmed** *(adj.)* ኣህድኣ *ahd'e*
**because** *(conj.)* ስለ *sle*

**beck** *(n.)* ምልክት *mlkt*
**beckon** *(v.)* ኣመልከተ *amelkete*
**become** *(v.)* ኮነ *kone*
**bed** *(n.)* መዕረፊ *me'ërefi*
**bedding** *(n.)* መንጸፍ *menxef*
**bedlam** *(n.)* ዕግርግር *ëgrgr*
**bedraggled** *(adj.)* ኣጨፈቐ *ačefeqe*
**bee** *(n.)* ንህቢ *nhbi*
**beech** *(n.)* ዋዕሮ *wa'ëro*
**beef** *(n.)* ስጋ ከብቲ *sga kebti*
**beefy** *(adj.)* ረጕድ *regWid*
**beep** *(n.)* ምልክት *mlkt*
**beer** *(n.)* ቢራ *bira*
**beet** *(n.)* ብንጅር *bnĵr*
**beetle** *(n.)* ማሳ *masa*
**beetroot** *(n.)* ሓምሊ *ħamli*
**befall** *(v.)* ወረደ *werede*
**befit** *(v.)* በቐዐ *beq'ë*
**before** *(adv.)* ቅድሚ *qdmi*
**beforehand** *(adv.)* ኣቐዲሙ *ኣቐዲሙ*
**befriend** *(v.)* መዓደ *me'äde*
**befuddled** *(adj.)* ኣገረመ *agereme*
**beg** *(v.)* ለመነ *lemene*
**beget** *(v.)* ወለደ *welede*
**beggar** *(n.)* ለማኒ *lemani*
**begin** *(v.)* ጀመረ *ĵemere*
**beginning** *(n.)* መጀመርታ *meĵemerta*
**beguile** *(v.)* ኣዘናገዐ *azenage'ë*
**behalf** *(n.)* ኣብ ክንዲ *ab kndi*
**behave** *(v.)* ገበረ *gebere*
**behaviour** *(n.)* ጠባይ *ẗebay*
**behead** *(v.)* ቈረጸ *qWerexe*
**behemoth** *(n.)* ጨካን *čekan*
**behest** *(n.)* ትእዛዝ *t'èzaz*
**behind** *(prep.)* ብድሕሪት *bdħrit*
**behold** *(v.)* ተመልከተ *temelkete*
**beholden** *(adj.)* ኣመስጋኒ *amesgani*
**beige** *(n.)* ፋሕራይ *faħray*
**being** *(n.)* ህላወ *hlawe*
**belabour** *(v.)* ቀጥቀጠ *qeẗqeẗe*
**belated** *(adj.)* ድንጉይ *dnguy*
**belay** *(v.)* ጠመረ *ẗemere*
**belch** *(v.)* ተፍአ *tef'e*
**beleaguered** *(adj.)* ኣጨነቐ *ačeneqe*
**belie** *(v.)* ብጌጋ ኣርኣየ *bgeega 'ar'aye*
**belief** *(n.)* እምነት *èmnet*
**believe** *(v.)* ኣመነ *amene*
**belittle** *(v.)* ኣቈናጸበ *aqWenaxebe*
**bell** *(n.)* ቃጭል *qačl*
**belle** *(n.)* ጽብቕቲ *xbqti*
**bellicose** *(adj.)* ተባኣሳይ *teba'asay*
**belligerent** *(adj.)* ባእሲ ምድላይ *ba'èsi mdlay*
**bellow** *(v.)* ነቀወ *neqewe*
**bellows** *(n.)* መናፍሕ *menafħ*
**belly** *(n.)* ከብዲ *kebdi*
**belong** *(v.)* ተኣሳሰረ *te'asasere*
**belongings** *(n.)* ግላዊ ኣቕሑ *glawi 'aqħu*
**beloved** *(adj.)* ፍቑር *fqur*
**below** *(prep.)* ትሕቲ *tħti*
**belt** *(n.)* ቁልፊ *qulfi*
**bemoan** *(v.)* ኋሃየ *gWahaye*
**bemused** *(adj.)* ኣቃልቦ ኣዘንበለ *'aqalbo 'azenbele*
**bench** *(n.)* ርቦ *rbo*
**bend** *(v.)* ለወየ *leweye*
**beneath** *(adv.)* ትሕቲ *tħti*

**benediction** ***(n.)*** **ቡራኬ** *burakee*
**benefactor** ***(n.)*** **ገቢረ-ሰናይ** *gebiresenay*
**benefice** ***(n.)*** **ገዛ ቀሺ** *geza qeshi*
**beneficent** ***(adj.)*** **ግብረ-ሰናይ** *gbresenay*
**beneficial** ***(adj.)*** **ለዋህ** *lewah*
**benefit** ***(n.)*** **ሓጋዚ** *ĥagazi*
**benevolence** ***(n.)*** **ግብረ-ሰናይ** *gbresenay*
**benevolent** ***(adj)*** **ግብረ-ሰናያዊ** *gbresenayawi*
**benign** ***(adj.)*** **ለዋህ** *lewah*
**bent** ***(adj.)*** **ተውህቦ** *tewhbo*
**bequeath** ***(v.)*** **ኣውረሰ** *awrese*
**bequest** ***(n.)*** **ውርሻ** *wrsha*
**berate** ***(v.)*** **ወቐሰ** *weq̈ese*
**bereaved** ***(v.)*** **ዘረፈ** *zerefe*
**bereavement** ***(n.)*** **ሓዘን** *ĥazen*
**bereft** ***(adj.)*** **ለማኒ** *lemani*
**bergamot** ***(n.)*** **ከውሒ በረድ** *kewĥi bered*
**berk** ***(n.)*** **ደንቆሮ** *denqoro*
**berry** ***(n.)*** **ፍረ** *fre*
**berserk** ***(adj.)*** **ዕብድብድ** *ëbdbd*
**berth** ***(n.)*** **መደቀሲ** *medeqesi*
**beseech** ***(v.)*** **ለመነ** *lemene*
**beset** ***(v.)*** **ኣሸገረ** *ashegere*
**beside** ***(prep.)*** **ኣብ ጥቓ** *ab ẗq̈a*
**besiege** ***(v.)*** **ከበበ** *kebebe*
**besmirch** ***(v.)*** **ኣመራሰሐ** *ameraseĥe*
**besom** ***(n.)*** **መኾስተር** *meḱoster*
**besotted** ***(adj.)*** **ዕኑድ** *ënud*
**bespoke** ***(adj.)*** **ዓውዲ ጸቐጠ** *äwdi xeq̈eẗe*
**best** ***(adj.)*** **ብዝበለጸ** *bzbelexe*
**bestial** ***(adj.)*** **ኣራዊታዊ** *'arawitawi*
**bestow** ***(v.)*** **ሸለመ** *sheleme*
**bestride** ***(v.)*** **ተጋሕተነ** *tegaĥtene*
**bet** ***(v.)*** **ተጣልዐ** *teẗal'ë*
**betake** ***(v.)*** **ከደ** *kede*
**betray** ***(v.)*** **ከድዐ** *ked'ë*
**betrayal** ***(n.)*** **ቅጥፈት** *qẗfet*
**better** ***(adj.)*** **ዝሓሸ** *zĥashe*
**between** ***(adv.)*** **ኣብ መንጎ** *'ab mengo*
**bevel** ***(n.)*** **ስያፍ** *syaf*
**beverage** ***(n.)*** **መስተ** *meste*
**bevy** ***(n.)*** **ኣኼባ** *aḱeeba*
**bewail** ***(v.)*** **ኣልቀሰ** *alqese*
**beware** ***(v.)*** **ጥንቁቕ** *ẗnquq̈*
**bewilder** ***(v.t)*** **ደንጸዎ** *denxewo*
**bewitch** ***(v.)*** **ሰረየ** *sereye*
**beyond** ***(adv.)*** **ክንየው** *knyew*
**bi** ***(comb.)*** **ኣብ ክክልተ** *'ab keklte*
**biannual** ***(adj.)*** **ፍርቂ በብዓመት** *frqi beb'ämet*
**bias** ***(n.)*** **ምቕናን** *mq̈nan*
**biased** ***(adj.)*** **መቕናን** *meq̈nan*
**bib** ***(n.)*** **ሳልቤታ** *salbeeta*
**Bible** ***(n.)*** **መጽሓፍ ቅዱስ** *mexĥaf qdus*
**bibliography** ***(n.)*** **ዝርዝረ-ጽሑፋት** *zrzrexĥufat*
**bibliophile** ***(n.)*** **ፈታው መጽሓፍ** *fetaw mexĥaf*
**bicentenary** ***(n.)*** **ካልኣይ ዘመን** *kal'ay zemen*
**biceps** ***(n.)*** **ጭዋዳምናት** *čwadamnat*
**bicker** ***(v.)*** **ተቛየቔ** *teq̈WAyeq̈We*
**bicycle** ***(n.)*** **ብሽክለታ** *bshkleta*
**bid** ***(v.)*** **ሰመየ** *semeye*
**biddable** ***(adj.)*** **ተሓታቲ** *teĥatati*

**bidder** *(n.)* ስማይ *smay*
**bide** *(v.)* ኣኸበረ *aḱbere*
**bidet** *(n.)* ምምሻጥ *mmshaẗ*
**biennial** *(adj.)* ክልተ ዓመታዊ *klte 'ämetawi*
**bier** *(n.)* ቃሬዛ *qareeza*
**bifocal** *(adj.)* ጽምደ-ትኹረታዊ *xmdetkuretawi*
**big** *(adj.)* ዓቢ *äbi*
**bigamy** *(n.)* ድርብ መርዓ *drb mer'ä*
**bigot** *(n.)* ሕሉ'ፍ *ḧluf*
**bigotry** *(n.)* ምቕናን *mq̈nan*
**bike** *(n.)* ብሽክለታ *bshkleta*
**bikini** *(n.)* ቢኪኒ *bikini*
**bilateral** *(adj.)* ክልተ ጐድናዊ *klte gWadnawi*
**bile** *(n.)* ሓሞት *ḧamot*
**bilingual** *(adj.)* ድርብ-ልሳናዊ *drblsanawi*
**bill** *(n.)* ጎዞሞ *gozomo*
**billet** *(n.)* መኣንገድ ድርጎኛ *me'anged drgoǹa*
**billiards** *(n.)* ቢልያርዶ *bilyardo*
**billion** *(n.)* ቢልዮን *bilyon*
**billionaire** *(n.)* ሃብታም *habtam*
**billow** *(v.)* ዓቢ ማዕበል *'äbi ma'ëbel*
**bin** *(n.)* ቆፎ *qofo*
**binary** *(adj.)* ዕጽፊ *ëxfi*
**bind** *(v.)* ጠመረ *ẗemere*
**binding** *(n.)* መዛዘሚ *mezazemi*
**binge** *(n.)* ፈንጠዝያ *fenẗezya*
**binocular** *(adj.)* በዓል ለዓት መነጽር *be'äl le'ät menexr*
**biochemistry** *(n.)* ስነ-ቅመም ህይወታውያን *sneqmem hywetawyan*
**biodegradable** *(adj.)* ኢኮሎጂ *ikoloĵi*
**biodiversity** *(n.)* ባዮዳይቨርስቲ *bayidayiversiti*
**biography** *(n.)* ሂወት ጽውጽዋይ *hiwet xwxway*
**biologist** *(n.)* ኢኮሎጂ *ikoloĵi*
**biology** *(n.)* ስነ-ህይወት *snehywet*
**biopsy** *(n.)* ምርምረ-ሬሳ *mrmrereesa*
**bipartisan** *(adj.)* ጽምደ-ሰልፋዊ *xmdeselfawi*
**birch** *(n.)* ኮመዲኖ *komedino*
**bird** *(n.)* ዑፍ *üf*
**bird flu** *(n.)* ኢንፍሉወንዛ *influwenza*
**birth** *(n.)* ምውላድ *mwlad*
**biscuit** *(n.)* ብሽኮቲ *bshkoti*
**bisect** *(v.)* ገመሰ *gemese*
**bisexual** *(adj.)* ግብረ-ሰዶመኛ *gbresedomeǹa*
**bishop** *(n.)* ኣቡን *abun*
**bison** *(n.)* ብዕራይ በረኻ *b'ëray bereḱa*
**bit** *(n.)* ልጓም *lgWam*
**bitch** *(n.)* ዋዕሮ *wa'ëro*
**bite** *(v.)* ነኸሰ *neḱese*
**biting** *(adj.)* ወጋኢ *wega'i*
**bitter** *(adj.)* መሪር *merir*
**bizarre** *(adj.)* ፈንጠጋር *fenẗegar*
**blab** *(v.)* ሃተ'ፈ *hatefe*
**black** *(adj.)* ጸሊም *xelim*
**blackberry** *(n.)* ብላክቤሪ *blakberi*
**blackboard** *(n.)* ሰሌዳ *seleeda*
**blacken** *(v.)* ኣጸለመተ *axelemete*
**blacklist** *(n.)* ጸሊም መዝገብ *xelim mezgeb*

**blackmail** *(n.)* **ታህዲደ-ምቕላዕ** *tahdidemq̈la'ë*
**blackout** *(n.)* **ጽልማተ** *xlmate*
**blacksmith** *(n.)* **ሓጓዲ ኣንጠረኛ ሓጺን** *ḧagWadi 'anẗereǹa ḧaxin*
**bladder** *(n.)* **ፍሕኛ** *fḧǹa*
**blade** *(n.)* **ግላዝ** *glaz*
**blain** *(n.)* **ኣብ ከክልተ** *'ab keklte*
**blame** *(v.)* **ከሰሰ** *kesese*
**blanch** *(v.)* **ጻዕደወ** *xa'ëdewe*
**bland** *(adj.)* **ልዙብ** *lzub*
**blank** *(adj.)* **ጥርሑ** *ẗrḧu*
**blanket** *(n.)* **ኮበርታ** *koberta*
**blare** *(v.)* **ድምጺ** *dmxi*
**blarney** *(n.)* **ኣተዓሻሸወ** *ate'äshashewe*
**blast** *(n.)* **ነትጕ** *netgWi*
**blatant** *(adj.)* **ቅሉዕ** *qlu'ë*
**blaze** *(n.)* **ሃልሃልታ** *halhalta*
**blazer** *(n.)* **ጃኬት** *ĵakeet*
**bleach** *(adj.)* **ኣጻዕደወ** *axa'ëdewe*
**bleak** *(adj.)* **ቀዛሒ** *qezaḧi*
**bleat** *(v. i)* **እምቤዕ** *èmbee'ë*
**bleed** *(v.)* **ደመየ** *demeye*
**bleep** *(n.)* **ቃና** *qana*
**blemish** *(n.)* **ኣበር** *aber*
**blench** *(v.)* **ምዩቕ በለ** *myuq̈ bele*
**blend** *(v. t)* **ሓዋወሰ** *ḧawawese*
**blender** *(n.)* **ሕውስ** *ḧws*
**bless** *(v.)* **ባረኸ** *bareḱe*
**blessed** *(adj.)* **ብሩኽ** *bruḱ*
**blessing** *(n.)* **ምርቓ** *mrq̈a*
**blight** *(n.)* **ዋግ** *wag*
**blind** *(adj.)* **ዕዉር** *ëwur*
**blindfold** *(v.)* **ዓመተ** *ämete*
**blindness** *(n.)* **ጉድለት** *gudlet*
**blink** *(v.)* **ሰምሰም ኣበለ** *semsem 'abele*
**blinkers** *(n.)* **ጋራዲ** *garadi*
**blip** *(n.)* **መቓልሕ** *meq̈alḧ*
**bliss** *(n.)* **ታሕጓስ** *taḧgWas*
**blister** *(n.)* **ማይ ምዕጎ** *may m'ëgo*
**blithe** *(adj.)* **ሕጉስ** *ḧgus*
**blitz** *(n.)* **ደቡብ** *debub*
**blizzard** *(n.)* **ህቦብላ ውርጪ** *hbobla wrči*
**bloat** *(v.)* **ነፍሐ** *nefḧe*
**bloater** *(n.)* **ቈንጣ ዓሳ** *qWAnẗa 'äsa*
**blob** *(n.)* **ንጣብ** *nẗab*
**bloc** *(n.)* **ቀጽሪ** *qexri*
**block** *(n.)* **ግላዕ** *gla'ë*
**blockade** *(n.)* **ድንደላ** *dndela*
**blockage** *(n.)* **ዕግታ** *ëgta*
**blog** *(n.)* **ሳይት** *sayit*
**bloke** *(n.)* **ቈንደፈ** *qWendefe*
**blonde** *(adj.)* **ጨዓይ ጸጉሪ ዘለዎ** *če'äy xeguri zelewo*
**blood** *(n.)* **ደም** *dem*
**bloodshed** *(n.)* **ደም ምፍሳስ** *dem mfsas*
**bloody** *(adj.)* **ደማዊ** *demawi*
**bloom** *(v.)* **ዕምባባ** *ëmbaba*
**bloomers** *(n.)* **ስረ-ግትር** *sregtr*
**blossom** *(n.)* **ዕምበባ** *ëmbaba*
**blot** *(n.)* **ንጣብ ቀለም** *nẗab qelem*
**blotch** *(n.)* **ትኳዕ** *tkWa'ë*
**blouse** *(n.)* **ካምቻ** *kamcha*
**blow** *(v.)* **ነፈሰ** *nefese*
**blowsy** *(adj.)* **ቈንደፈ** *qWendefe*
**blub** *(v.)* **ተነኽነኸ** *teneḱneḱe*
**bludgeon** *(n.)* **ጓመድ** *gWamed*

**blue** *(adj.)* ሰማያዊ ሕብሪ *semayawi ḧbri*
**bluff** *(v.)* መጻድፎ *mexadfo*
**blunder** *(n.)* ጠምበርበር በለ *ẗemberber bele*
**blunt** *(adj.)* ጎዲም *godim*
**blur** *(v.)* ጽያቕ *xyaq̈*
**blurb** *(n.)* ትሕዝቶ መጽሓፍ *tḧzto mexḧaf*
**blurt** *(v.)* ኣምለቑ *amleq̈We*
**blush** *(v.)* ሓፈረ *ḧafere*
**blusher** *(n.)* ቀንዲ *qendi*
**bluster** *(v.)* ኣሸምበበ *ashembebe*
**boar** *(n.)* መፍለስ *mefles*
**board** *(n.)* ጣውላ *ẗawla*
**boast** *(v.)* ጃህራ *ĵahra*
**boat** *(n.)* ጃልባ *ĵalba*
**bob** *(v.)* ሓፍ ኮፍ በለ *ḧaf kof bele*
**bobble** *(n.)* ገልተው *geltew*
**bode** *(v.)* ሓበረ *ḧabere*
**bodice** *(n.)* ጅለ-ሰበይቲ *ĵlesebeyti*
**bodily** *(adv.)* ኣካላዊ *akalawi*
**body** *(n.)* ኣካል *akal*
**bodyguard** *(n)* ዘብዐኛ *zeb'ëña*
**bog** *(n.)* ዓዘቕቲ *äzeq̈ti*
**bogey** *(n.)* ጋኔን *ganeen*
**boggle** *(v.)* ተወላወለ *tewelawele*
**bogus** *(adj.)* ሓቂ ዘይብሉ *ḧaqi zeyblu*
**boil** *(v.i.)* ምጉሊ ኣንጮዋ *mguli 'ančwa*
**boiler** *(n.)* መፍልሒ *meflḧi*
**boisterous** *(adj.)* ናውጼን *nawxeen*
**bold** *(adj.)* ተባዕ ደፋር *teba'ë defar*
**boldness** *(n.)* ድምቀት *dmqet*
**bole** *(n.)* ጉንዲ *gundi*
**bollard** *(n.)* ገመል *gemel*
**bolt** *(n.)* መሸጐር *meshegWar*
**bomb** *(n.)* ቦምብ *bomb*
**bombard** *(v.)* ደብደበ *debdebe*
**bombardment** *(n.)* ደብዳብ *debdab*
**bomber** *(n.)* ቦምብር *bomber*
**bona fide** *(adj.)* ሓቀኛ *ḧaqeña*
**bonanza** *(n.)* ኣኸዘ *ak̈eze*
**bond** *(n.)* ውዕል *w'ël*
**bondage** *(n.)* ጊልያነት ከዳሚነት *gilyanet kedaminet*
**bone** *(n.)* ዓጽሚ *äxmi*
**bonfire** *(n.)* መጋርያ *megarya*
**bonnet** *(n.)* ልስሉስ ቆብዕ *lslus qob'ë*
**bonus** *(n.)* መቑሹሽ *meq̈ushush*
**bony** *(adj.)* ዓጻም *äxam*
**book** *(n.)* መጽሓፍ *mexḧaf*
**bookish** *(adj.)* መጽሓፋዊ *mexḧafawi*
**booklet** *(n.)* ንእሽቶ መጽሓፍ *n'èshto mexḧaf*
**booklet** *(n.)* ንእሽቶ መጽሓፍ *n'èshto mexḧaf*
**bookmark** *(n.)* መቓቐር *meq̈aq̈er*
**bookseller** *(n.)* መጽሓፍ ሸያጢት *mexḧaf sheyaẗit*
**boom** *(n.)* ፌሕታ *fiḧta*
**boon** *(n.)* ሕቶ *ḧto*
**boor** *(n.)* ጠገለ-ኣልቦ *ẗegele'albo*
**boost** *(v.)* ምስፋሕ *msfaḧ*
**booster** *(n.)* ሰንካቲ *senkati*
**boot** *(n.)* ነዊሕ ሳእኒ *newiḧ sa'èni*
**booth** *(n.)* ጎጆ *goĵo*
**bootleg** *(adj.)* ኮንትሮባንድ *kontroband*

**booty** *(n.)* **ምርኮ** *mrko*
**border** *(n.)* **ዶብ** *dob*
**bore** *(v.)* **ጐርጐሐ** *gWargWaȟe*
**born** *(adj.)* **ወልደ** *tewelde*
**borough** *(n.)* **ወረደ** *werede*
**borrow** *(v.)* **ተለቅሐ** *teleqȟe*
**bosom** *(n.)* **ሕጽöኒ** *ȟxni*
**boss** *(n.)* **ሓለቓ** *ȟaleq̈a*
**bossy** *(adj.)* **ኣውቶክራት** *'awtokrat*
**botany** *(n.)* **ስነ-ኣትክልቲ** *sne'atklti*
**both** *(adj. & pron.)* **ክልቲኡ** *klti'u*
**bother** *(v.)* **ኣሸገረ** *ashegere*
**bottle** *(n.)* **ጥርሙዝ** *ẗrmuz*
**bottom** *(n.)* **ታሕቲ** *taȟti*
**bough** *(n.)* **ቃራና** *qarana*
**boulder** *(n.)* **ዓረ** *äre*
**boulevard** *(n.)* **ጐደና** *gWadena*
**bounce** *(v.)* **ነጠረ** *neẗere*
**bouncer** *(n. )* **መሰነዪ** *meseneyi*
**bound** *(v.)* **ሓጸረ** *ȟaxere*
**boundary** *(n.)* **ዶብ** *dob*
**boundless** *(adj.)* **ደረት-ኣልቦ** *deret'albo*
**bountiful** *(adj.)* **ለጋስ** *legas*
**bounty** *(n.)* **ልግሲ** *lgsi*
**bouquet** *(n.)* **ሕቍፊ-ዕምባባ** *ȟq̈ufi'ëmbaba*
**bout** *(n.)* **ግጥ'ም** *gẗm*
**boutique** *(n.)* **ባዛር** *bazar*
**bow** *(n.)* **ቀስቲ** *qesti*
**bow** *(v.)* **ሰገደ** *segede*
**bowel** *(n.)* **መዓናጡ** *me'änaẗu*
**bower** *(n.)* **ዳስ** *das*
**bowl** *(n.)* **ጭሖሎ** *čholo*
**box** *(n.)* **ሳንዱቕ** *sanduq̈*
**boxer** *(n.)* **ተጋዳላይ** *tegadalay*
**boxing** *(n)* **ጉስጢ** *gusẗi*
**boy** *(n.)* **ወዲ** *wedi*
**boycott** *(v.)* **ኣደመ** *ademe*
**boyhood** *(n)* **ንእስነት** *n'èsnet*
**bra** *(n.)* **ቢኪኒ** *bikini*
**brace** *(n.)* **ድጋፍ** *dgaf*
**bracelet** *(n.)* **በናጅር** *benaĵr*
**bracket** *(n.)* **መደገፍ** *medegef*
**brag** *(v.)* **ተጀሃረ** *teĵehari*
**Braille** *(n.)* **ብረይል** *breyl*
**brain** *(n.)* **ሓንጎል** *ȟangol*
**brake** *(n.)* **ልጓም** *lgWam*
**branch** *(n.)* **ጨንፈር** *čenfer*
**brand** *(n.)* **ዕላመት** *ëlamet*
**brandish** *(v.)* **ኣንበልበለ** *anbelbele*
**brandy** *(n.)* **ብራንዲ** *brandi*
**brash** *(adj.)* **ደረቐኛ** *dereq̈eǹa*
**brass** *(n.)* **ኣስራዚ** *asrazi*
**brave** *(adj.)* **ተባዕ** *teba'ë*
**bravery** *(n.)* **ትብዓት** *tb'ät*
**brawl** *(n.)* **ቈየቛ** *qWeyeq̈WA*
**bray** *(v.)* **ህላ** *hla*
**breach** *(v.)* **ምጥሓስ** *mẗȟas*
**bread** *(n.)* **እንጀራ** *ènĵera*
**breadth** *(n.)* **ውርዲ** *wrdi*
**break** *(v.)* **ሰበረ** *sebere*
**breakage** *(n.)* **ስብረት** *sbret*
**breakfast** *(n.)* **ቁርሲ** *qursi*
**breast** *(n.)* **ጡብ** *ẗub*
**breath** *(n.)* **ትንፋስ** *tnfas*
**breathe** *(v.)* **ኣተንፈሰ** *atenfese*
**breech** *(n.)* **ዓንቀር ጠበንጃ** *änqer ẗebenĵa*
**breeches** *(n.)* **ስረ-ግትር** *sregtr*
**breed** *(v.)* **ኣራብሐ** *arabhe*
**breeze** *(n.)* **ህዱእ ንፋስ** *hdu'è nfas*

**brevity** *(n.)* ሕጽረት ሓጺርነት *ȟxret ȟaxirnet*
**brew** *(v.)* ጸመቘ *xemeq̈We*
**brewery** *(n.)* እንዳ ቢራ *'ènda bira*
**bribe** *(v. t.)* ጉቦ *gubo*
**brick** *(n.)* ሕጡብ ማቶኒ *ȟẗub matoni*
**bridal** *(adj.)* ናይ መርዓ *nay mer'ä*
**bride** *(n.)* መርዓት *mer'ät*
**bridegroom** *(n.)* መርዓዊ *mer'äwi*
**bridge** *(n.)* ድልድል *dldl*
**bridle** *(n.)* ልጓም *lgWam*
**brief** *(adj.)* ሓጺር *ȟaxir*
**briefing** *(n.)* ሓጺር መግለጺ *ȟaxir meglexi*
**brigade** *(n.)* ጉጅለ *guĵle*
**brigadier** *(n.)* መራሒ ብርጌድ *meraȟ brgeed*
**bright** *(adj.)* ድሙቕ *dmuq̈*
**brighten** *(v.)* ደመቐ በርሀ *demeq̈e berhe*
**brilliance** *(n.)* ብልጫ *blča*
**brilliant** *(adj.)* ድሙቕ *dmuq̈*
**brim** *(n.)* ጫፍ *čaf*
**brindle** *(adj.)* ሓበጀራይ *ȟabeĵeray*
**brine** *(n.)* ማይ ጨው *may čew*
**bring** *(v.)* ኣምጸአ *amxe'e*
**brinjal** *(n.)* ብሪንጃል *birinjal*
**brink** *(n.)* ጠረፍ *ẗeref*
**brisk** *(adj.)* ስሉጥ *sluẗ*
**bristle** *(n.)* ነደ'ረ *nedere*
**British** *(adj.)* ብሪቲሽ *biritish*
**brittle** *(adj.)* ተሰባሪ *tesebari*
**broach** *(adj.)* ኣንኰለ *ankWale*
**broad** *(adj.)* ሰፊሕ *sefiȟ*
**broadcast** *(v. t)* ዘርግሐ *zergȟe*
**brocade** *(n.)* በዘቕዘቕ *bezeq̈zeq̈*
**broccoli** *(n.)* ካውሎ ፍዮሪ *kawlo fyori*
**brochure** *(n.)* መንሹር *menshur*
**broke** *(adj.)* ሰበረ *sebere*
**broken** *(adj.)* ስቡር *sbur*
**broker** *(n.)* ደላ'ላይ *delalay*
**bronchial** *(adj.)* ቃራየ ጉርጉማ *qaraye gurguma*
**bronze** *(n.)* ብሮንዞ *bronzo*
**brood** *(n.)* ጨቓዊት *čeq̈awit*
**brook** *(n.)* ዛራ *zara*
**broom** *(n.)* መኾስተር *mek̍oster*
**broth** *(n.)* መረቕ *mereq̈*
**brothel** *(n.)* እንዳ ኣመንዝራ *ènda 'amenzra*
**brother** *(n.)* ሓው *ȟaw*
**brotherhood** *(n.)* ሕውነት *ȟwnet*
**brow** *(n.)* ሸፋሽፍቲ *shefashfti*
**brown** *(n.)* ቡናዊ *bunawi*
**browse** *(v.)* ገሃጸ *gehaxe*
**browser** *(n.)* ማእረረ *ma'èrere*
**bruise** *(n.)* ስንብራት *snbrat*
**brunch** *(n.)* ኵላሶ *kulaso*
**brunette** *(n.)* ጸሊም ጸጉሪ *xelim xeguri*
**brunt** *(n.)* ቀንዲ ክብደት *qendi kbdet*
**brush** *(n.)* ኣስባስላ *asbasla*
**brusque** *(adj.)* ኣሻኹ *ashak̍Wi*
**brutal** *(adj.)* ዘይምሕር *zeymȟr*
**brute** *(n.)* እንስሳ *ènssa*
**bubble** *(n.)* ዓፍራ *äfra*
**buck** *(n.)* ኮናዕ *kona'ë*
**bucket** *(n.)* መገለል *megelel*
**buckle** *(n.)* መቈለፍ *meq̈Welef*
**bud** *(n.)* ኣጓም *agWam*
**budge** *(v.)* ምንቕ በለ *mnq̈ bele*

**budget** *(n.)* ባጀት *baĵet*
**buffalo** *(n.)* ጎባይ *gobay*
**buffer** *(n.)* ወሓጥ ጉንጺ *weḧaẗ gWanxi*
**buffet** *(n.)* ጉስጢ *gusẗi*
**buffoon** *(n.)* መስሓቕ *mesḧaq̈*
**bug** *(n.)* ትኳን *tḱWan*
**buggy** *(n.)* ካሮሳ *karosa*
**bugle** *(n.)* ጥሩምባ *ẗrumba*
**build** *(v.)* ሃነጸ *hanexe*
**building** *(n.)* ህንጻ *hnxa*
**bulb** *(n.)* ሽጉርቶ *shgurto*
**bulge** *(n.)* ሕበጥ *ḧbeẗ*
**bulimia** *(n.)* ቡሊምያ *bilimiya*
**bulk** *(n.)* ብብዝሒ *bbzḧi*
**bulky** *(adj.)* ደጕላጽ *degWalax*
**bull** *(n.)* ኣርሓ *arḧa*
**bulldog** *(n.)* ገዚፍ ዓይነት ከልቢ *gezif 'äynet kelbi*
**bullet** *(n.)* ዓረር *ärer*
**bulletin** *(n.)* ቡለቲን *buletin*
**bullion** *(n.)* ሕጡብ ወርቂ *ḧẗub werqi*
**bullish** *(adj.)* ኣዛዚ *azazi*
**bullock** *(n.)* ቅጥቁጥ ብዕራይ *qẗquẗ b'ëray*
**bully** *(n.)* ዓላቕ *älaq̈*
**bulwark** *(n.)* ዕርዲ *ërdi*
**bum** *(n.)* መዓኮር *me'äkor*
**bumble** *(v.)* ተዓንቀፈ *te'änqefe*
**bump** *(n.)* ተናጕጸ *tenagWaxe*
**bumper** *(n.)* ዋልጋ ጕንጺ *walga gWanxi*
**bumpkin** *(n.)* ሁጉሬ *huguree*
**bumpy** *(adj.)* ተናጕጸ *tenagWaxe*
**bun** *(n.)* ምቁር ባኒ *mqur bani*
**bunch** *(n.)* ጥማር *ẗmar*
**bundle** *(n.)* ጠቕለለ *ẗeq̈lele*
**bung** *(n.)* ቡሽ *bush*
**bungalow** *(n.)* ሓደ ዝደርቡ ገዛ *ḧade zderbu geza*
**bungle** *(v.)* ገልተው *geltew*
**bunk** *(n.)* ሃደመ *hademe*
**bunker** *(n.)* መኽዘን ነዳዲ ናይ መርከብ *mekźen nedadi nay merkeb*
**buoy** *(n.)* ሓባ'ር መርከብ *ḧabar merkeb*
**buoyancy** *(n.)* ምንስፋፍ *mnsfaf*
**buoyant** *(adj.)* ተንሳፋፊ *tensafafi*
**burble** *(v.)* ጕራዕራዕ በለ *gWara'ëra'ë bele*
**burden** *(n.)* ሸከም *shekem*
**bureau** *(n.)* ሰደቓ *sedeq̈a*
**bureaucracy** *(n.)* ቢሮክራሲ *birokrasi*
**bureaucrat** *(n.)* ቢሮክራታዊ *birokratawi*
**burgeon** *(v.)* ኣጕመ *agWame*
**burger** *(n.)* በርገር *berger*
**burglar** *(n.)* ሰራቒ *seraq̈i*
**burglary** *(n.)* ገበን *geben*
**burial** *(n.)* ቀብሪ *qebri*
**burlesque** *(n.)* ላግጺ *lagxi*
**burn** *(v.)* ምንዳድ *mndad*
**burner** *(n.)* ኣንዳዲ *andadi*
**burning** *(adj.)* ርሱን *rsun*
**burrow** *(n.)* ጉድጓድ *gudgWad*
**bursar** *(n.)* ተሓዝ ገንዘብ *teḧaz genzeb*
**bursary** *(n.)* ሓገዝ *ḧagez*
**burst** *(v.)* ነተጕ *netegWa*
**bury** *(v.)* ቀበረ *qebere*
**bus** *(n.)* ኣውቶቡስ *awtobus*
**bush** *(n.)* ቈጥቋጥ *qWeẗqWAẗ*
**bushy** *(adj.)* ጎፍጓፍ *gofgWaf*

**business** *(n.)* ዋኒን *wanin*
**businessman** *(n.)* ነጋዳይ *negaday*
**bust** *(n.)* ደረት *deret*
**bustle** *(v.)* ኣሽበድበደ *ashbedbede*
**busy** *(adj.)* ተጸምደ *texemde*
**but** *(conj.)* ግን *gn*
**butcher** *(n.)* ሓራድ ስጋ *ḧarad sga*
**butler** *(n.)* ባልጠጂ *balťeĵi*
**butter** *(n.)* ጠስሚ *ťesmi*
**butterfly** *(n.)* ጽምብላሊዕ *xmblali'ë*
**buttock** *(n.)* ዶሶ *doso*
**button** *(n.)* መልጎም *melgom*
**buy** *(v.)* ገዝአ *gez'e*
**buyer** *(n.)* ዓዳጊ *ädagi*
**buzz** *(n.)* ዚዝ በለ *ziz bele*
**buzzard** *(n.)* ሽላ *shla*
**buzzer** *(n.)* ሲረና *sirena*
**by** *(prep.)* ብ *b*
**by-election** *(n.)* ጎድናዊ-ምርጫ *godnawimrča*
**bygone** *(adj.)* ቀደም *qedem*
**by-line** *(n.)* ብ ሕንጻጽ *bḧnxax*
**bypass** *(n.)* ጎድናዊ መንገዲ *godnawi mengedi*
**byre** *(n.)* ደምበ *dembe*
**bystander** *(n.)* ተመልካቲ *temelkati*
**byte** *(n.)* ባይት *bayit*

# C

**cab** *(n.)* ጋቢ'ና *gabina*
**cabaret** *(n.)* ካበረ *kabare*
**cabbage** *(n.)* ካውሎ *kawlo*
**cabin** *(n.)* ጋቢና *gabina*
**cabinet** *(n.)* ከብሒ *kebḧi*
**cable** *(n.)* መዳወር *medawer*
**cacao** *(n.)* ካካው *kakaw*
**cache** *(n.)* ሓብአ *ḧab'e*
**cachet** *(n.)* ክታም *ktam*
**cackle** *(n.)* ቃቓ *qaq̈a*
**cactus** *(n.)* ቈልቋል *qWelqWAl*
**cad** *(n.)* ነውራም *newram*
**cadaver** *(n.)* ሬሳ *reesa*
**cadaver** *(n.)* ሬሳ *reesa*
**caddy** *(n.)* ካዲ *kadi*
**cadet** *(n.)* ካደት *kadet*
**cadmium** *(n.)* ካድምዩም *kadmyum*
**cadre** *(n.)* ኣስከሬን *askereen*
**caesarean** *(n.)* ቄሳር *qeesar*
**cafe** *(n.)* ካፈ *kafe*
**cafeteria** *(n.)* ካፈተርያ *kafeterya*
**cage** *(n.)* ጎብያ *gobya*
**cahoots** *(n.)* ኪዳን *kidan*
**cajole** *(v.)* ሸሓጠ *sheḧaťe*
**cake** *(n.)* ዶልሺ *dolshi*
**calamity** *(n.)* መዓት *me'ät*
**calcium** *(n.)* ካልስዩም *kalsyum*
**calculate** *(v.)* ቀመረ *qemere*
**calculation** *(n.)* ቀመር *qemer*
**calculator** *(n.)* መተሓሳሰቢ *meteḧasasebi*
**calendar** *(n.)* ዓውደ-ኣዋርሕ *äwde'awarḧ*
**calf** *(n.)* ምራኽ *mrak*
**calibrate** *(v.)* ኣተኻኸለ *atekakele*

**calibre** *(n.)* **ውሽጣዊ ሰንጣቒት** *wshťawi senťaqit*
**call** *(v.)* **ደወለ** *dewele*
**calligraphy** *(n.)* **ጽባቐ ጽሕፈት** *xbaqe xḧfet*
**calling** *(n.)* **ሞያ** *moya*
**callous** *(adj.)* **ጽዖታዊ** *x'ötawi*
**callow** *(adj.)* **ጥረ** *ťre*
**calm** *(adj.)* **ህዱእ** *hdu'è*
**calorie** *(n.)* **ካሎሪ** *kalori*
**calumny** *(n.)* **ምጽላም** *mxlam*
**camaraderie** *(n.)* **ብጻይነት** *bxaynet*
**camber** *(n.)* **ጐብጓበ** *gWabgWabe*
**cambric** *(n.)* **ሻሽ** *shash*
**camcorder** *(n.)* **ካምኮርደር** *kamkorder*
**camel** *(n.)* **ገመል** *gemel*
**cameo** *(n.)* **ካምዮ** *kamyo*
**camera** *(n.)* **ካመራ** *kamera*
**camp** *(n.)* **መዓስከር** *me'äsker*
**campaign** *(n.)* **ዘመተ** *zemete*
**camphor** *(n.)* **ካምፎራ** *kamfora*
**campus** *(n.)* **ካምፓስ** *kampas*
**can** *(n.)* **ታኒካ** *tanika*
**can** *(v.)* **ኣብ ታኒካ ሓተመ** *'ab tanika ḧateme*
**canal** *(n.)* **መትረብ** *metreb*
**canard** *(n.)* **ናይ ሓሶት ጸብጻብ** *nay ḧasot xebxab*
**cancel** *(v.)* **ሰረዘ** *sereze*
**cancellation** *(n.)* **ምጥፋእ** *mťfa'è*
**cancer** *(n.)* **መንሽሮ** *menshro*
**candela** *(n.)* **ብራሃን** *brahan*
**candid** *(adj.)* **ግሁድ** *ghud*
**candidate** *(n.)* **ሕጹይ** *ḧxuy*
**candle** *(n.)* **ሽምዓ** *shm'ä*
**candour** *(n.)* **ጋህዲ** *gahdi*
**candy** *(n.)* **ካራመላ** *karamela*
**cane** *(n.)* **ከረዛን** *kerezan*
**canine** *(adj.)* **ከልባዊ** *kelbawi*
**canister** *(n.)* **ሳጹን** *saxun*
**cannabis** *(n.)* **ሀምፕ** *hemp*
**cannibal** *(n.)* **በላዕ ሰብ** *bela'ë seb*
**cannon** *(n.)* **መድፍዕ** *medf'ë*
**canny** *(adj.)* **ጐራሕ** *gWaraḧ*
**canoe** *(n.)* **ታንኳ** *tankWa*
**canon** *(n.)* **ቀኖና** *qenona*
**canopy** *(n.)* **ድባብ** *dbab*
**cant** *(n.)* **ግብዝና** *gbzna*
**cantankerous** *(adj.)* **ሓራቕ** *ḧaraq*
**canteen** *(n.)* **ካንቲና** *kantina*
**canter** *(n.)* **ህዱእ ጋልቢት** *hdu'è galbit*
**canton** *(n.)* **ወረዳ** *wereda*
**cantonment** *(n.)* **ቀዋሚ መዓስከር** *qewami me'äsker*
**canvas** *(n.)* **ጅርባ** *ĵrba*
**canvass** *(v.)* **ብምሉ'እ ተዛተየ** *bmlu'è tezateye*
**canyon** *(n.)* **ዓሚቕ ስንጭሮ** *ämiq snčro*
**cap** *(n.)* **ቈብዕ** *qWeb'ë*
**capability** *(n.)* **ዓቕሚ** *äqmi*
**capable** *(adj.)* **ክኢላ** *k'ila*
**capacious** *(adj.)* **ሰፊሕ** *sefiḧ*
**capacitor** *(n.)* **ካፓሲተር** *kapaciter*
**capacity** *(n.)* **ዓቕሚ** *äqmi*
**caparison** *(v.)* **ሰለመ** *seleme*
**cape** *(n.)* **መንጠሊና** *menťelina*
**capital** *(n.)* **ርእሰ-ማል** *r'èsemal*
**capitalism** *(n.)* **ርእሰ-ማልነት** *r'èsemalnet*

**capitalist** ***(n. &adj.)*** **ርእሰ-ማላዊ** *r'èsemalawi*
**capitalize** ***(v.)*** **ርእሰ-ማል ገበረ** *r'èsemal gebere*
**capitation** ***(n.)*** **ግብሪ** *gbri*
**capitulate** ***(v.)*** **ተምበርከኸ** *temberkeḱe*
**caprice** ***(n.)*** **ቅበጥ** *qbeẗ*
**capricious** ***(adj.)*** **ቀባጥ** *qebaẗ*
**capsicum** ***(n.)*** **ካፕሲከም** *kapsikem*
**capsize** ***(v.)*** **ገልበጠ** *gelbeẗe*
**capstan** ***(n.)*** **ጠምጣሚ መስሕብ** *ẗemẗami meshb*
**capsule** ***(n.)*** **ለቖታ-ፍረ** *leqotafre*
**captain** ***(n.)*** **ግብጣን** *gbẗan*
**captaincy** ***(n.)*** **ግብጣኒ** *gbẗani*
**caption** ***(n.)*** **ኣርእስቲ** *ar'èsti*
**captivate** ***(v.)*** **መሰጠ** *meseẗe*
**captive** ***(n.)*** **ምሩኽ** *mruḱ*
**captivity** ***(n.)*** **ምሩኽነት** *mruḱnet*
**captor** ***(n.)*** **ሓላው ምሩኽ** *ḧalaw mruḱ*
**capture** ***(v.)*** **ኣሰረ** *asere'*
**car** ***(n.)*** **ማኪና** *makina*
**caramel** ***(n.)*** **ካራሜል** *karame' el*
**carat** ***(n.)*** **ካራት** *kara 't*
**caravan** ***(n.)*** **ቃፍላይ** *qaflay*
**carbohydrate** ***(n.)*** **ሽኮር መሰል** *shkor mesel*
**carbon** ***(n.)*** **ሕመት** *hemete*
**carbonate** ***(adj.)*** **ባይካርቦነት** *baykarbonet*
**carboy** ***(n.)*** **ጥርሙዝ** *terimuz*
**carcass** ***(n.)*** **ገምቢ** *ge'mbi*
**card** ***(n.)*** **ካርዲ** *ka'ardi*
**cardamom** ***(n.)*** **ጠጠው ኣቢሉ** *tte'ttew aa'billu*
**cardboard** ***(n.)*** **ካርቶን** *kartoon*
**cardiac** ***(adj.)*** **ናይ ልቢ** *na' ae lebii*
**cardigan** ***(n.)*** **ጎልፎ** *gole 'foo*
**cardinal** ***(n.)*** **ጳጳስ** *papase'*
**cardiograph** ***(n.)*** **ካርድዮግራፍ** *kardyograf*
**cardiology** ***(n.)*** **ካርድዮሎጂ** *kardyoloĵi*
**care** ***(n.)*** **ክንክን** *kinkin*
**career** ***(n.)*** **ስራሕ** *sir'ahh*
**carefree** ***(adj.)*** **ዘይእጅቦ** *they'aa jibo*
**careful** ***(adj.)*** **ጥንቁቅ** *tinkuq*
**careless** ***(adj.)*** **ዘየስተውዕል** *ze yestewu 'el*
**carer** ***(n.)*** **ኣብ** *aa'b*
**caress** ***(v.)*** **ተናኸፈ** *tenahe'fe*
**caretaker** ***(n.)*** **ወኪል** *wekil*
**cargo** ***(n.)*** **ኣብ መርከብ** *aa'b merkeb*
**caricature** ***(n)*** **ምስሊ** *mesili*
**carmine** ***(n.)*** **ቀይሕ ሕብሪ** *qeyiha hib're*
**carnage** ***(n.)*** **ጩፍጨፋ** *Chif'chefa*
**carnal** ***(adj.)*** **ስጋዊ** *segawi*
**carnival** ***(n.)*** **ካርኒቫል** *karnival*
**carnivore** ***(n.)*** **በላዕ ስጋ** *bela'ë sga*
**carol** ***(n.)*** **ደርፊ** *derfi*
**carpal** ***(adj.)*** **ኣዕበርበረ** *zz'ebere bere*
**carpenter** ***(n.)*** **ፀራቢ** *tserabi*
**carpentry** ***(n.)*** **ፅርበት** *tsirbet*
**carpet** ***(n.)*** **መንፀፍ** *mentseff*
**carriage** ***(n.)*** **ባቡር** *babur*
**carrier** ***(n.)*** **ብነፋሪት** *binefarit*
**carrot** ***(n.)*** **ካሮት** *carrot*
**carry** ***(v.)*** **ተሸከመ** *teshekeme*
**cart** ***(n.)*** **ዓረብያ** *arebia*
**cartel** ***(n.)*** **ካርተል** *kartel*

**cartilage** *(n.)* **ቆርጠምጠማ** *qorẗemẗema*
**carton** *(n.)* **ባኮ** *bako*
**cartoon** *(n.)* **ካርቱን** *kartun*
**cartridge** *(n.)* **ቀልሃ** *qeliha*
**carve** *(v.)* **ቀረፀ** *qeretse*
**carvery** *(n.)* **ጠበሰ ስጋ** *ẗebese sga*
**Casanova** *(n.)* **ወዲ** *wedi*
**cascade** *(n.)* **መንጫ ጫዕታ** *mencha chaeta*
**case** *(n.)* **ኩነት** *kunet*
**casement** *(n.)* **መስኮት** *mesekote*
**cash** *(n.)* **ቅርሺ** *qeriishe*
**cashew** *(n.)* **ኦም** *ome*
**cashier** *(n.)* **ተቀባሊት ቅርሺ** *teqebalit qereshi*
**cashmere** *(n.)* **ሱፍ** *suf*
**casing** *(n.)* **ዝተለበጠ** *zetelebte*
**casino** *(n.)* **ህንፀት** *hintsete*
**cask** *(n.)* **ፊስቶ** *fiseto*
**casket** *(n.)* **ሳፁን ሬሳ** *satsun resa*
**casserole** *(n.)* **ምግቢ** *megebi*
**cassock** *(n.)* **ጁባ** *juba*
**cast** *(v.)* **ተመልከተ** *temeleket*
**castaway** *(n.)* **ውጻእ መዓት** *wxa'è me'ät*
**caste** *(n.)* **ማሕበራዊ ደረጃ** *mahiberawi dereja*
**castigate** *(v.)* **ነቀፈ** *neqefe*
**casting** *(n.)* **ደርበየ** *derebye*
**castle** *(n.)* **ቤት ነገስታት** *bete negestat*
**castor** *(n.)* **ወሃብ ቅርጺ** *wehab qrxi*
**castor oil** *(a.)* **ጎማ ዘይት** *goma zeite*
**castrate** *(v.)* **ቀጥቀጥ** *qeteqetw*
**casual** *(adj.)* **ዘይተሓሰበሉ** *zeytehasebelo*
**casualty** *(n.)* **ዝሞተ** *zemote*
**cat** *(n.)* **ድሙ** *demu*
**cataclysm** *(n.)* **መቕዘፍቲ** *meq̈zefti*
**catalogue** *(n.)* **ብስሩዕ መዝገብ** *bsru'ë mezgeb*
**catalyse** *(v.)* **ኣቀፃፀለ** *aqetsatsele*
**catalyst** *(n.)* **ኣቀፃፃሊ** *aqetsatseli*
**cataract** *(n.)* **ሓበላ** *habela*
**catastrophe** *(n.)* **መቕዘፍቲ** *meq̈zefti*
**catch** *(v.)* **ቆበለ** *qobl*
**catching** *(adj.)* **ተላጋቢ** *telagabi*
**catchy** *(adj.)* **ተዛካሪ** *tezakari*
**catechism** *(n.)* **ትምህርተ-ሃይማኖት** *tmhrtehaymanot*
**categorical** *(adj.)* **ፍጹም** *fxum*
**categorize** *(v.)* **ጎጀለ** *goje-le*
**category** *(n.)* **ጉጅለ** *guge-le*
**cater** *(v.)* **ሰርዐ** *sere'aa*
**caterpillar** *(n.)* **ኣባጨጓራ** *aaba'che'guara*
**catharsis** *(n.)* **ምሕራእ** *mḧra'è*
**cathedral** *(n.)* **ደብሪ** *debri*
**catholic** *(adj.)* **ካቶሊክ** *catholic*
**cattle** *(n.)* **ከብቲ** *kebtei*
**catty** *(n.)* **ሓሜተኛ** *hametegna'*
**Caucasian** *(adj.)* **ካውካዝያዊ** *kawkazyawi*
**cauldron** *(n.)* **በራድ** *beradd*
**cauliflower** *(n.)* **ካዉሎ ፍዮሪ** *kawulo fiyorii*
**causal** *(adj.)* **ጠንቃዊ** *ẗenqawi*
**causality** *(n.)* **ጠንቅነት** *ẗenqnet*
**cause** *(n.)* **መንቀሊ** *mneqsi*
**causeway** *(n.)* **ኣዉራ መንገዲ** *awra mnegedeei*
**caustic** *(adj.)* **መፂፅ** *matsiee.e*

**caution** *(n.)* መጠንቀቕታ *metenqekta*
**cautionary** *(adj.)* ኣጠንቀቐ *aa'tenqeqe*
**cautious** *(adj.)* ጥንቁቕ *tenquqk*
**cavalcade** *(n.)* ናይ ፈረሳት *nayei feresat*
**cavalier** *(adj.)* ዘይግደስ *zeyg des*
**cavalry** *(n.)* ፈረሰኛ *fresenga*
**cave** *(n.)* በዓቲ *beaa'ti*
**caveat** *(n.)* መዘካከሪ *mezkakrii*
**cavern** *(n.)* ገፊሕ በዓቲ *gefihe beatii*
**cavernous** *(adj.)* ብጣዕሚ ገፊሕ *betaemi gefihei*
**cavity** *(n.)* ዝጎድጎደ ስኒ *zgodedod sieni*
**cavort** *(v.)* ተሰራሰረ *teserasere*
**cease** *(v.)* ደው ኣበለ *dwuo aabele*
**ceasefire** *(n.)* ተኹሲ ኣቋረጸ *tekusi 'aqWArexe*
**ceaseless** *(adj.)* ዘየቋርጽ *zeyeqWArx*
**cedar** *(n.)* ኦም ሲዳር *oom cidar*
**cede** *(v.)* ኣስተለመ *'asteleme*
**ceiling** *(n.)* ሰንቀ *senqe*
**celandine** *(n.)* ዕምባባ *embaba*
**celebrant** *(n.)* ቀዳሲ *qedasi*
**celebrate** *(v.)* ኣብዓለ *'ab'äle*
**celebration** *(n.)* በዓል *beaal*
**celebrity** *(n.)* ስሙይ ሰብ *semuyei sebe*
**celestial** *(adj.)* ሰማያዊ *semayawii*
**celibacy** *(n.)* ድንግልና *denegelena*
**celibate** *(adj.)* ድንግላይ *denegelaye*
**cell** *(n.)* ዋህዮ *waheyo*
**cell phone** *(n.)* ተንቀሳቃሲ ስልኪ *teneqesaqasi seliki*
**cellar** *(n.)* ናይ እሱራት ክፍሊ *naye esurat kiflii*
**cellular** *(adj.)* ልኡክ ጉጀለ *leuuke gujelle*
**cellulite** *(n.)* ስብሒ *sebehi*
**celluloid** *(n.)* ዝነድድ ረብሓ *zenededei rehehaa*
**cellulose** *(n.)* ሓይሊ ወሃቢ ንጥረ ምግቢ *hayeli wehabi netere megebi*
**Celsius** *(n.)* ሴልሲየስ *celcius*
**Celtic** *(adj.)* ሴልቲክ ቋንቋ *celtik quaniqua*
**cement** *(n.)* ስሚንቶ *seminito*
**cemetery** *(n.)* መካነ መቓብር *mekne mekabir*
**censer** *(n.)* ሸሓነ *shehane*
**censor** *(n.)* መርማሪ *meremari*
**censorious** *(adj.)* ነቃፊ *neqkafi*
**censorship** *(n.)* ቅድመ ምርመራ *qedeme meremra*
**censure** *(v.)* ብርቱዕ ነቀፌታ *beretiee' neqefeta*
**census** *(n.)* ቆፀራ *qoxera*
**cent** *(n.)* ሳንቲም *sanetim*
**centenary** *(n.)* ዝክረ-ዘመን *zkrezemen*
**centennial** *(n.)* ኣብ ርእ *ab reaa'*
**centigrade** *(adj.)* ሙቀት መጠን *muqete metene*
**centimetre** *(n.)* ርቐት መጠን *reqete metene*
**centipede** *(n.)* ዘርኢ ሰብ ዝመሰል *zereii sebe zemsle*
**central** *(adj.)* ኣዉራ/ቀንዲ *aawura/qenedi*

**centralize** *(v.)* **ኣማእከለ** *zamaeekele*
**centre** *(n. )* **ማዕከል** *meee'kele*
**century** *(n.)* **ዘበን** *zbene*
**ceramic** *(n.)* **ጣሳ** *tasa*
**cereal** *(n.)* **ጥራጥረ** *teraterre*
**cerebral** *(adj.)* **ናይ ሓንጎል** *nayei hanegole*
**ceremonial** *(adj.)* **ስነ ስርዓታዊ** *sene sereaa'tawii*
**ceremonious** *(adj.)* **ስነ ስርዓት ዘለዎ** *senei sereat zelewoo*
**ceremony** *(n.)* **በዓል/ፅምብል** *beaal/xeembil*
**certain** *(adj.)* **ርጉፅ** *reguxee*
**certainly** *(adv.)* **ብዘይጥርጥር** *bethzey tiritir*
**certifiable** *(adj.)* **ዕቡድ/ፅሉል** *eebudd/xelule*
**certificate** *(n.)* **ምስክር ወረቐት** *mesekir wereqet*
**certify** *(v.)* **ምስክር ወረቐት ሃበ** *meseker wereqket habe*
**certitude** *(n.)* **ርግፀኛነት** *regexegninet*
**cervical** *(adj.)* **ናይ ክሳድ** *nay ksad*
**cessation** *(n.)* **ምቁራፅ** *mekuraxee*
**cession** *(n.)* **ውህበት** *whbet*
**chain** *(n.)* **ሰንሰለት** *seneselet*
**chair** *(n.)* **ወንበር** *weneber*
**chairman** *(n.)* **ኣቦወንበር** *abo' weneber*
**chaise** *(n.)* **ሰብ ተጓዕዝ** *sebe tegwaeeze*
**chalet** *(n.)* **ባራካ** *barakaa*
**chalice** *(n.)* **ፅዋዕ** *xewaee*
**chalk** *(n.)* **በረቕ** *bereqqe*
**challenge** *(n.)* **ፈተነ** *fetene*
**chamber** *(n.)* **ኣዳራሽ** *adarashe*
**chamberlain** *(n.)* **ኣጋፋሪ** *'agafari*
**champagne** *(n.)* **ሻምፓኝ** *shampagne*
**champion** *(n.)* **ዕዉት/ሰዓራይ** *eewuut/seaarayi*
**chance** *(n.)* **ዕድል** *eedil*
**chancellor** *(n.)* **መራሒ መንግስቲ** *merahi menegeseti*
**Chancery** *(n.)* **ቤት ፅሕፈት** *bete xehifeti*
**chandelier** *(n.)* **ልሻን ሸለመ** *leshane' shelem'e*
**change** *(v.)* **ለወጠ/ተለወጠ** *lewete/telewete*
**channel** *(n.)* **ጣቢያ ጤሌቪዥን** *tabiya television*
**chant** *(n.)* **ዜማ** *zema*
**chaos** *(n.)* **ህዉከት** *hewuuket*
**chaotic** *(adj.)* **ዕግርግር ዘለዎ** *egereger zelewo*
**chapel** *(n.)* **ንእሽተይ ቤተክርስቲያን** *neeshtey betekerestian*
**chaplain** *(n.)* **ካህን** *kahiN'*
**chapter** *(n.)* **ምዕራፍ** *mee'eraf*
**char** *(v.)* **ሓረር/ኣሕረረ** *harer/aaehi'rere*
**character** *(n.)* **ባሕርይ/ፀባይ** *bahereyei/xebayii*
**characteristic** *(n.)* **ባሕርይ** *bahereyei*
**charcoal** *(n.)* **ፋሓም/ሕመት** *fahame/hemeute*
**charge** *(n.)* **ክፍሊት ሓተተ** *kefelit hatete*
**charge** *(v.)* **ክፍሊት** *kefelite*
**charger** *(n.)* **ብርጭቆ መልአ** *bereCheqo melea'a*

**chariot** ***(n.)*** **ዓረብያ/ሰረገላ** *arebiya/seregela*
**charisma** ***(n.)*** **ግርማ ሞገስ** *gerima moges*
**charismatic** ***(adj.)*** **በዓል ሞገስ** *beal moges*
**charitable** ***(adj.)*** **ናይ ገባሪ ሰናይ** *nayei gebari senayei*
**charity** ***(n.)*** **ትካል ገባሪ ሰናይ** *tekaal gebarii senayei*
**charlatan** ***(n.)*** **መምሰሊ** *memeiseli*
**charm** ***(n.)*** **ሰሓባይነት** *sehabayineet*
**charming** ***(adj.)*** **ሰባሓይ/ማራኪ** *sebahaayi/marakii*
**chart** ***(n.)*** **ሰንጠረዥ** *seneterezjj*
**charter** ***(n.)*** **መምርሒ** *memerehii*
**chartered** ***(adj.)*** **ተኮናተረ** *tekonateree*
**chary** ***(adj.)*** **ስግኣት** *segeaa'te*
**chase** ***(v.)*** **አጓየየ** *aaguwayeye*
**chassis** ***(n.)*** **ሞተር** *mote'R'*
**chaste** ***(adj.)*** **ዘየዝሙዉ** *zeyezemuwue*
**chasten** ***(v.)*** **ወቐሰ** *weqqese*
**chastise** ***(v.)*** **ኣደብ** *A'deb*
**chastity** ***(n.)*** **ዘይምዝማዉ** *zeymzemawu*
**chat** ***(v. i.)*** **ኣዕለለ/ኣዉገዐ** *aae'lele/aawugeaa'*
**chateau** ***(n.)*** **ቤት ነገስታት** *bete' negeseta't*
**chattel** ***(n.)*** **ንብረት/ንዋይ** *neberet/newaye*
**chatter** ***(v.)*** **ሃተፈ/ለፈለፈ** *hatefe/lefelefe*
**chauffeur** ***(n.)*** **ኣውቲስታ** *aawutiseta*
**chauvinism** ***(n.)*** **ትምክሕቲ** *temekeheti*
**chauvinist** ***(n. &adj.)*** **ምኩሕ** *mekuhh*
**cheap** ***(adj.)*** **ሕሳር** *hesaree*
**cheapen** ***(v. t.)*** **ኣዋረደ** *aawarede*
**cheat** ***(n.)*** **ኣሕሰረ** *aa'hesere*
**cheat** ***(v.)*** **ኣታለለ** *aatalele*
**check** ***(v.)*** **ኣፃረየ** *axareyee*
**checkmate** ***(n)*** **ዝተዛዘመ** *ziteza'zeme'*
**cheek** ***(n.)*** **ምዕጉርቲ** *meaegurtii*
**cheeky** ***(adj.)*** **ባዕለገ** *bae'leGe'*
**cheep** ***(n.)*** **ጩቅ በለ** *Chuqk' bele*
**cheer** ***(v. t.)*** **ታሕጓስ** *taheGua'ss*
**cheerful** ***(adj.)*** **ወትሩ ሕጉስ** *wetru higus*
**cheerless** ***(adj.)*** **ዘየሕጉስ** *zyehiGus'*
**cheery** ***(adj.)*** **ሕጉስ** *Higus'*
**cheese** ***(n.)*** **ኣጅቦ** *Ajobo*
**cheetah** ***(n.)*** **ጭኮንበሳ** *ChikonbeSa*
**chef** ***(n.)*** **ዋና ከሻኒ** *wana Kesha'ni*
**chemical** ***(adj.)*** **ኬሚካል** *kemikal*
**chemist** ***(n.)*** **ቀማሚ** *Qe'mami*
**chemistry** ***(n.)*** **ቕመም** *qE'mem*
**chemotherapy** ***(n.)*** **ሕክምና** *hikiM'NA*
**cheque** ***(n.)*** **ቸክ** *chek*
**cherish** ***(v.)*** **ኣፍቀረ** *Af'Qere*
**chess** ***(n.)*** **ቹዝ** *Chezz'*
**chest** ***(n.)*** **ኣፍልቢ** *Aflebi*
**chestnut** ***(n.)*** **ሳንዱቕ** *saneduqQ*
**chevron** ***(n.)*** **መለለይ ምልክት** *Me'Leleyei milikit*
**chew** ***(v.)*** **ሓየከ** *HayYeke*
**chic** ***(adj.)*** **ስብቁል** *sbqul*
**chicanery** ***(n.)*** **ሸፍጢ** *Shefe'Ti*

**chicken** ***(n.)*** **ደርሆ** *Dereho*
**chickpea** ***(n.)*** **ዓይኒ ዓተር** *Ayni Ater*
**chide** ***(v.)*** **ነቐፈ** *NeQefe*
**chief** ***(n.)*** **ኣዉራ/ቀንዲ** *Auwra/Qendi'*
**chiefly** ***(adv.)*** **ሓላፊ/ሓለቓ** *Halafi/HaleQa*
**chieftain** ***(n.)*** **መሪሕነት** *MerihNet'*
**child** ***(n.)*** **ቆልዓ** *QoleA'*
**childhood** ***(n.)*** **ቁልዕነት** *Qole'eneT'*
**childish** ***(adj.)*** **ናይ ቆልዓ** *Nayei QoleA'*
**chill** ***(n.)*** **ቁሪ/ቀዝሒ** *Quri/Qezhi*
**chilli** ***(n.)*** **ሽርባ/በርበረ** *Shirba/berebre*
**chilly** ***(adj.)*** **ቆራር** *qorare*
**chime** ***(n.)*** **ሰዓት ደወለት** *seAt' dwle't*
**chimney** ***(n.)*** **ቆንቆር** *QonQkor*
**chimpanzee** ***(n.)*** **ህበይ** *HeBeyei*
**chin** ***(n.)*** **መንከስ** *Menkes'*
**china** ***(n.)*** **በረቕ** *BereqQe'*
**chip** ***(n.)*** **ሽርፍራፍ** *Sherifrafe*
**chirp** ***(v.)*** **ጩቕ በለ** *CchUQ' Bel'le*
**chisel** ***(n.)*** **መንደል** *Mendel*
**chit** ***(n.)*** **ንእሽቶ ቈልዓ** *n'èshto qWel'ä*
**chivalrous** ***(adj.)*** **ድጊ** *dgi*
**chivalry** ***(n.)*** **ዳጌት** *dageet*
**chlorine** ***(n.)*** **ክሎሪን** *kilorin*
**chloroform** ***(n.)*** **መርዚ** *merzi*
**chocolate** ***(n.)*** **ቸኮላታ** *checolata*
**choice** ***(n.)*** **መረፃ** *meretsa*
**choir** ***(n.)*** **መዘምራን** *mezemeran*
**choke** ***(v.)*** **ሓነቐ** *haneqe*
**cholera** ***(n.)*** **ሕማም ሸሮኽ** *hemam sheroke*
**choose** ***(v. t)*** **መረፀ** *meretse*
**chop** ***(v.)*** **ከተፈ** *ketefe*
**chopper** ***(n.)*** **ሴፍ** *sefe*
**chopstick** ***(n.)*** **ጥሕሎ** *telohe*
**choral** ***(adj.)*** **ክፋል መዝሙር** *kefale mezemur*
**chord** ***(n.)*** **ደመርቲ** *dmreti*
**chorus** ***(n.)*** **ተደጋጊሙ ዝዝመር** *tedegagimu zezemre*
**Christ** ***(n.)*** **ክርስቶስ** *keresetos*
**Christian** ***(adj.)*** **ክርስቲያን** *keresitiyane*
**Christianity** ***(n.)*** **ክርስትና ሃይማኖት** *keresetena hayimanot*
**Christmas** ***(n.)*** **በዓል ልደት** *beal lidet*
**chrome** ***(n.)*** **ቀምቀመ** *qemeqme*
**chronic** ***(adj.)*** **ነባር** *nebar*
**chronicle** ***(n.)*** **ዜና መዋልዕ** *zena mewalee*
**chronograph** ***(n.)*** **ሰዓት** *seat*
**chronology** ***(n.)*** **ስነ-ዕለታት** *sne'ëletat*
**chuckle** ***(v.)*** **ክምስ** *kemese*
**chum** ***(n.)*** **ቀረባ ፈታሒ** *qereba fetahi*
**chunk** ***(n.)*** **ቁርማም** *qurmame*
**church** ***(n.)*** **ቤተ ክርስቲያን** *bete kiristian*
**churchyard** ***(n.)*** **መካነ መቓብር** *mekane meqabere*
**churn** ***(v.)*** **ዓምጠቑ** *ameteqku*
**chutney** ***(n.)*** **ፀብሒ** *xebhi*
**cider** ***(n.)*** **ሲደር** *cider*
**cigar** ***(n.)*** **ሲጋር** *sigar*
**cigarette** ***(n.)*** **ሽጋራ** *shegara*
**cinema** ***(n)*** **ቤት ስኒማ** *bet ciniema*
**cinnamon** ***(n.)*** **ቐረፋ** *qerefa*
**circle** ***(n.)*** **ክቢ** *kebi*

**circuit** *(n.)* ዑደት *'üdet*
**circular** *(adj.)* ክቢብ *kbibe*
**circulate** *(v.)* ተሰራጨወ *tsrachew*
**circulation** *(n.)* ዑደት *xudet*
**circumcise** *(v.)* ገረዘ *gereze'*
**circumference** *(n.)* ዶብ *dobe*
**circumscribe** *(v.)* ገደበ *gedebe*
**circumspect** *(adj.)* አዝዩ ጥንቁቕ *azeyu tenequqe*
**circumstance** *(n.)* ሃዋህዉ *hawahewu*
**circus** *(n.)* ሰርከስ *serekse*
**cist** *(n.)* ሳንዱቕ *sanaduqe*
**cistern** *(n.)* ማይ መዋህለሊ *maye mwaheleli*
**citadel** *(n.)* ዕርደ-ከተማ *'ërdeketema*
**cite** *(v.)* ጠቐሰ *tekese*
**citizen** *(n.)* ዜጋ *zega*
**citizenship** *(n.)* ዜግነት *zegenet*
**citric** *(adj.)* ሲትሪክ *citric*
**citrus** *(n.)* ተኽል *tekil*
**city** *(n.)* ከተማ *ketema*
**civic** *(adj.)* ናይ ከተማ *nayei ketema*
**civics** *(n.)* ናይ ስነ ዜጋ ትምሕርቲ *nayei sine zega temehereti*
**civil** *(adj.)* ማሕበረሰባዊ *mahebresebawi*
**civilian** *(n.)* ስቪል ሰብ *sevil sebe*
**civilization** *(n.)* ስልጣነ *seletan*
**civilize** *(v.)* ኣሰልጠነ *aseltene*
**clad** *(adj.)* ዝተኸደነ *zetkdn*
**cladding** *(n.)* ኸዳን *Kedan*
**claim** *(v.)* ሓቂዩ በለ *haqiyu bele*
**claimant** *(n.)* ይግበአኒ በሃላይ *yigbeani behalayi*
**clammy** *(adj.)* ርሁድ *rehude*
**clamour** *(n.)* ብኣዉያት ሓተተ *beawyat hattete*
**clamp** *(n.)* ኣጣበቐ *atabeqe*
**clan** *(n.)* ዓሌት *alet*
**clandestine** *(adj.)* ሕቡእ *hibuea'*
**clap** *(v.)* ኣጣቕዐ *atabeqe*
**clarification** *(n.)* ከለሰ *keles*
**clarify** *(v.)* ኣብራህረሀ *abrahereh*
**clarion** *(adj.)* መልእኽቲ *mleekti*
**clarity** *(n. )* ግልፅነት *geletsinet*
**clash** *(v.)* ባእሲ *baesii*
**clasp** *(v.)* ጨበጠ *chebete*
**class** *(n.)* ክፍሊ *kifeli*
**classic** *(adj.)* ሕሩይ *heruyei*
**classical** *(adj.)* ቀንደኛ *qenedegna*
**classification** *(n.)* ምጉጃል *megujak*
**classify** *(v.)* ጎጀለ *gojele*
**clause** *(n.)* ዓንቀፅ *aneqetse*
**claustrophobia** *(n.)* ኣብ ፀቢብ ቦታ *ab tsebib bota*
**claw** *(n.)* ፅፍሪ *txefri*
**clay** *(n.)* ጭቃ *chiqa*
**clean** *(adj.)* ፅሩይ *tsxeruye*
**cleanliness** *(n.)* ፅሬት *tsxerete*
**cleanse** *(v.)* ሓፀበ *hatsxebe*
**clear** *(adj.)* ንፁር *netsxur*
**clearance** *(n.)* ምእላይ *meaelayi*
**clearly** *(adv.)* ፅሩይ *tsxeruyi*
**cleave** *(v.)* ጨደደ *chedede*
**cleft** *(n.)* ጨዳድ *cdade*
**clemency** *(n.)* ምሕረት *meherte*
**clement** *(adj.)* መሓሪ *mhari*
**Clementine** *(n.)* ክሌምንታይን *klemintaine*
**clench** *(v.)* ነኸሰ *nKes*
**clergy** *(n.)* ካህናት *kahenat'*

**cleric** *(n.)* ካህን *kahin*
**clerical** *(adj.)* ቀሺ *qshi*
**clerk** *(n.)* ፀሓፊ *tsehafi*
**clever** *(adj.)* ብልሂ *bilihi*
**click** *(n.)* ድምጺ ፈጠረ *dimtsi ftre'*
**client** *(n.)* ዓሚል *Amil*
**cliff** *(n.)* ፀድፊ *Tsxdefi*
**climate** *(n.)* ኩነታት ኣየር *kunetat ayer'*
**climax** *(n.)* መዛዘሚ ወሰናይ *mzammi wsanaye*
**climb** *(v.i)* ደየበ *deYebe*
**clinch** *(v.)* ተዓወተ *tAwte'*
**cling** *(v.)* ተለጠፈ *tlTefe'*
**clinic** *(n.)* ክሊኒክ *kliniqk*
**clink** *(n.)* ኣጋጨዉ *agachewu*
**clip** *(n.)* መንቀርቀር *menqerker*
**cloak** *(n.)* መንጠሊና *mentelina*
**clock** *(n.)* ሰዓት *seat'*
**cloister** *(n.)* ናይ ገዳም ሕይወት *nayei gedam hiwot*
**clone** *(n.)* ምድቃል *mdqal*
**close** *(adj.)* ዓፀወ *atsewe*
**closet** *(n.)* ውሸጠ *wushate'*
**closure** *(n.)* ዝተቓረበ *zitqarebe*
**clot** *(n.)* ዝረገአ ደም *ziregeaA' deM'*
**cloth** *(n.)* ክዳን *kidan*
**clothe** *(v.)* ከደነ *kedeNe'*
**clothes** *(n.)* ክዳዉንቲ *kidawunti'*
**clothing** *(n.)* ክዳውንቲ *kdawnti*
**cloud** *(n.)* ደበና *debNa'*
**cloudy** *(adj.)* ዕስለ ኣናሕብ *esil anahib*
**clove** *(n.)* ሸኾና *shekona*
**clown** *(n.)* ኣዘናግእ *azenagiaa*
**cloying** *(adj.)* ኣዝዩ ጥዑም ግን ዝመርር *aziyu teum gin zemrer*
**club** *(n.)* ጋንታ *ganeta*
**clue** *(n.)* ኣፋፍኖት *afafenote*
**clumsy** *(adj.)* ለህዛዝ *lahezaZ'*
**cluster** *(n.)* ዝተኣከቡ ነገራት *ziteakebu negerat*
**clutch** *(v. t.)* ኣጥቢቑ ሓዘ *atbiqu haze'*
**coach** *(n.)* ኣሰልጣኒ *aseltani*
**coal** *(n.)* ሕመት *himet*
**coalition** *(n.)* ሓድነት *hatnet*
**coarse** *(adj.)* ሻሕኻር *shahikar*
**coast** *(n.)* ገምገም ባሕሪ *gemgem bahiriyi*
**coaster** *(n.)* ኣብ ገምገም ባሕሪ ዝርከብ *ab gemgem bahiri zirkeb*
**coat** *(n.)* ጁባ *juba*
**coating** *(n.)* ለፀመ *ltseme'*
**coax** *(v.)* ሸሓረ *shehare*
**cobalt** *(n.)* ኣገደዳሲ ኣካል *agededasi akal'*
**cobble** *(n.)* ኮረት *koret*
**cobbler** *(n.)* ሰራሒ ሳእኒ *serahi saeni'*
**cobra** *(n.)* ኮብራ ተመን *korabe tmN'*
**cobweb** *(n.)* ዓለባ ሳሬት *aleba saret*
**cocaine** *(n.)* ኮኬን *kocain*
**cock** *(n.)* ኩኩናይ መኮንን *kukunai mekonin*
**cockade** *(n.)* ቁፃር *qutsar*
**cockpit** *(n.)* ሰፈር ኣብራሪ ኣየር *sefer abrar ayer*
**cockroach** *(n.)* ድዱዕ *diduee'*
**cocktail** *(n.)* ሕዉስዋስ መስተ *hiwuswas meste*
**cocky** *(adj.)* ዕቡይ *eebuY;*
**cocoa** *(n.)* ክእለት *keeileT*
**coconut** *(n.)* ኮኮናት *coconat*

**cocoon** *(n.)* ኮኩን *cocoon*
**code** *(n.)* ምስጢራዊ ፅሑፍ *mesetirawi tsihuf*
**co-education** *(n. )* ኣወዳትን ኣጓላትን ዝማሃርሉ *awedatin agwalatene zemayarelu*
**coefficient** *(n.)* ቀዋሚ *qewami*
**coerce** *(v.)* ኣገደደ *agedded*
**coeval** *(adj.)* ኣምረሓ *amreha*
**coexist** *(v.)* ተሰነየ ተስማዕሞዖም ነበሩ *tesanY' tesmaemoom neberu*
**coexistence** *(n.)* ሓቢርካ ምንባር *habireka menebare*
**coffee** *(n.)* ቡን *bun*
**coffer** *(n.)* ካዝና *kazina*
**coffin** *(n.)* ሳፁን ሬሳ *satsun resa*
**cog** *(n.)* ቅልጣፈ *qiltafe*
**cogent** *(adj.)* ዘዕግብ *heigib*
**cogitate** *(v.)* ኣስተንተነ *astentene*
**cognate** *(adj.)* ተመሳሳሊ *temesasali*
**cognizance** *(n.)* ግንዛበ *ginizabe*
**cohabit** *(v.)* ከይተመርዓዉ ሓቢሮም ነበሩ *keyitemerawu habirom neberu*
**cohere** *(v.)* ተሰነየ *tesaneyei*
**coherent** *(adj.)* ዝሰነይን ዘእተዋደድን *zisaneyin etewadedin*
**cohesion** *(n.)* ሓድነት *hadinet*
**cohesive** *(adj.)* ሓድነት ዝፈጠረ *hadinet zifetere*
**coil** *(n.)* ዓኹለለ *qkulele*
**coin** *(n.)* ሳንቲም *sanetime*
**coinage** *(n.)* ሳንቲም ሰርሐ *sanetime sereha*
**coincide** *(v.)* ተገጣጠመ *tegetateme*
**coincidence** *(n.)* ተጓንፎ *tegwanefo*
**coir** *(n.)* ዓለባ *aleba*
**coke** *(n.)* ቀፀላይ *qetselayi*
**cold** *(adj.)* ቆራር *qorare*
**colic** *(n.)* ቁርፀት ከብዲ *quretset kebedi*
**collaborate** *(v.)* ተሓባበረ *tehababere*
**collaboration** *(n.)* ትህብብር *tehibiberi*
**collage** *(n.)* ናይ ስራሕ ቦታ *nayei serahe bota*
**collapse** *(v.)* ተደርዓመ *tederame*
**collar** *(n.)* ኳሌታ *kwaleta*
**collate** *(v.)* ኣከበ *akebe*
**collateral** *(n.)* ትሕጃ *tihija*
**colleague** *(n.)* መሳርሕቲ *mesarȟti*
**collect** *(v.)* ኣከበ *akebe'*
**collection** *(n.)* ተዋሕለለ *tewahilwlw*
**collective** *(adj.)* ተጠራቐመ *teteraqeme*
**collector** *(n.)* ኣምፀአ *amtseA'*
**college** *(n.)* ኮሌጅ-ብርኪ ትምህርቲ *co;ege berki temihereti*
**collide** *(v.)* ተጋጨወ *tegachewe*
**colliery** *(n.)* ናይ ማዕድን *nayi maeidin*
**collision** *(n.)* ናይ ምግጫዉ ሓደጋ *nayei megechaw hadega*
**colloquial** *(adj.)* ናይ ዘረባ *nay zereba*
**collusion** *(n.)* ምሽጥራዊ ስምምዕ *mishtirawi simemeeh*
**cologne** *(n.)* ሽቶ *shito*
**colon** *(n.)* ዓብይ መኣንጣ *abiy meanta*

colonel *(n.)* ኮሎኔል *kolonele*
colonial *(adj.)* ባዕዳዊ *baeedawi*
colony *(n.)* ግዝኣት *gz'at*
colossal *(adj.)* ገዚፍ *gezife*
colossus *(n.)* ሓወልቲ *hawelti*
colour *(n.)* ሕብሪ *hibri*
colouring *(n.)* ፅልዋ ኣሕደረ *tsilwa ahdere*
colourless *(n.)* ዝተሕብረ *zitehibri*
column *(n.)* ዓንዲ *anedi*
coma *(n.)* ሕሊና ምስሓት *hilina mesehate*
comb *(n.)* ሚዶ/መመሸጢ *mido/memesheti*
combat *(n.)* ኹናት *kunat*
combatant *(n)* ተዋጋኢ *tewagaei*
combination *(n.)* ጥማር *timar*
combine *(v.)* ፀንበረ *tsenber*
combustible *(adj.)* ነዳዲ *nedadi*
combustion *(n.)* ተቐፃፃላይ *teqetsatsalaye*
come *(v.)* ናዓ *na'ä*
comedian *(n.)* መስሓቕ *meshäq*
comedy *(n)* መስሓቕ *meshäq*
comet *(n.)* ጅራታም ኮኾብ *ĵratam*
comfort *(n.)* ምቾት *mchot*
comfort *(v.)* ጥጣሐ *ẗtahe*
comfortable *(adj.)* ምቹእ *mchu'è*
comic *(adj.)* ተዋዛዪ *tewazayi*
comma *(n.)* ጭሕጋር *čhgar*
command *(v.)* ኣዘዘ *azeze*
commandant *(n.)* ኣዛዚ *azazi*
commander *(n.)* ኮማንደር *komander*
commando *(n.)* ኮማንዶ *komando*
commemorate *(v.)* ኣኽበረ *aḱbere*
commemoration *(n.)* ዝክር *zkr*
commence *(v.)* ጀመረ *ĵemere*
commencement *(n.)* ምጅማር *mĵmar*
commend *(v.)* ነኣደ *ne'ade*
commendable *(adj.)* ዚነኣድ *zine'ad*
commendation *(n.)* ናእዳ *na'èda*
comment *(n.)* ርእይቶ *r'èyto*
commentary *(n.)* ታዕሊቕ *ta'ëliq*
commentator *(n.)* ዓላቒ *älaqi*
commerce *(n.)* ንግድ *ngd*
commercial *(adj.)* ንግዳዊ *ngdawi*
commiserate *(v.)* ራህርሀ *rahrhe*
commission *(n.)* ውክልና *wklna*
commissioner *(n.)* ኮሚሽነር *komishner*
commissure *(n.)* መጋጠሚ *megatmi*
commit *(v.)* ፈጸመ *fexeme*
commitment *(n.)* ሙብጽዓ *mebx'ä*
committee *(n.)* ሽማግለ *shmagle*
commode *(n.)* ተመዛዚ ከብሒ *temezazi kebḧi*
commodity *(n.)* ኣቕሓ *'aqḧa*
common *(adj.)* ሓባራዊ *ḧabarawi*
commoner *(n.)* ሓፋሽ *ḧafash*
commonplace *(adj.)* ልሙድ *lmud*
commonwealth *(n.)* ናይ ሓባር ብልጽግና *nay ḧabar blxgna*
commotion *(n.)* ህውከት *hwket*
communal *(adj.)* ኮማዊ *komawi*
commune *(n.)* ተዋህደ *tewahde*

**communicable** ***(adj.)*** **ተማሓላለፊ** *temaȟalalefi*
**communicant** ***(n.)*** **ቈራቢ** *qWerabi*
**communicate** ***(v.)*** **ሃበሬታ ተለዋወጠ** *habereta*
**communication** ***(n.)*** **ርክብ** *rkb*
**communion** ***(n.)*** **ምክፋል** *mkfal*
**communism** ***(n.)*** **ዴስነት** *deesnet*
**community** ***(n.)*** **ማሕበረ ሰብ** *maȟbere seb*
**commute** ***(v.)*** **ለወጠ** *leweẗe*
**compact** ***(adj.)*** **ጥርኑፍ** *ẗrnuf*
**companion** ***(n.)*** **ብጻይ** *bxay*
**company** ***(n.)*** **መሰነይታ** *meseneyta*
**comparative** ***(adj.)*** **ተነጻጻሪ** *tenexaxeri*
**compare** ***(v.)*** **ኣነጻጸረ** *anexaxere*
**comparison** ***(n.)*** **ምንጽጻር** *mnxxar*
**compartment** ***(n.)*** **ክፍሊ** *kfli*
**compass** ***(n.)*** **ቡሶላ** *busola*
**compassion** ***(n.)*** **ድንጋጸ** *dngaxe*
**compatible** ***(adj.)*** **ተቓዳዊ** *teq̈adawi*
**compatriot** ***(n.)*** **ወዲ ሃገር** *wedi hager*
**compel** ***(v.)*** **ቀሰ'በ** *qesebe*
**compendious** ***(adj.)*** **ቁንጩል** *qunčul*
**compendium** ***(n.)*** **ቁንጩል** *qunčul*
**compensate** ***(v.)*** **ከሓሰ** *keȟase*
**compensation** ***(n.)*** **ካሕሳ** *kaȟsa*
**compère** ***(n.)*** **ኣላ'ላዪ** *alalayi*
**compete** ***(v.)*** **ተቐዳደመ** *teq̈edademe*
**competence** ***(n.)*** **ክእለት** *k'èlet*
**competent** ***(adj.)*** **ክኢላ** *k'ila*
**competition** ***(n.)*** **ምውድዳር** *mwddar*
**competitive** ***(adj.)*** **ውድድራዊ** *wddrawi*
**competitor** ***(n.)*** **ተዋዳዳሪ** *tewadadari*
**compile** ***(v.)*** **ጠርነፈ** *ẗernefe*
**complacent** ***(adj.)*** **ዕጉብ** *ëgub*
**complain** ***(v.)*** **ተጣርዐ** *teẗar'ë*
**complaint** ***(n.)*** **ዝበልዎ ሕራይ ዝብል** *zibeliwo hirayi zibil*
**complaisant** ***(adj.)*** **ምቕሉል** *mq̈lul*
**complement** ***(n.)*** **መልእ** *meleA'*
**complementary** ***(adj.)*** **መላኢ** *mela'i*
**complete** ***(adj.)*** **ምሉእ** *mlu'è*
**completion** ***(n.)*** **ምፍጻም** *mfxam*
**complex** ***(adj.)*** **ዝተሓላለኸ** *zteȟalaleḱe*
**complexion** ***(n.)*** **ወጅሂ** *weĵhi*
**complexity** ***(n.)*** **ሕልኽልኽ** *ȟlḱlḱ*
**compliance** ***(n.)*** **እሺታ** *èshita*
**compliant** ***(adj.)*** **ምቕሉል** *mq̈lul*
**complicate** ***(v.)*** **ሓላለኸ** *ȟalaleḱe*
**complication** ***(n.)*** **ሕልኽልኽ** *ȟlḱlḱ*
**complicit** ***(adj.)*** **ምስ ግበነኛ** *mis gibenegna*
**complicity** ***(n.)*** **ምሽባን** *mshban*
**compliment** ***(n.)*** **ናእዳ** *na'èda*
**compliment** ***(v. i)*** **ናእዳ** *na'èda*
**comply** ***(v.)*** **ተኣዘዘ** *te'azeze*
**component** ***(n.)*** **ክፋል** *kifale*
**comport** ***(v.)*** **ኣኽበረ** *aḱbere*
**compose** ***(v.)*** **ኣቈመ** *aq̈Weme*
**composer** ***(n.)*** **ደራሲ ወራቢ** *derasi werabi*

**composite** *(adj.)* ዝተዋሃሃደ *ztewahahade*
**composition** *(n.)* ምድላው *mdlaw*
**compositor** *(n.)* ለቓም ፊደል *leq̈am fidel*
**compost** *(n.)* ድኹዒ *dḱu'ï*
**composure** *(n.)* ቅሰነት *qsanet*
**compound** *(n.)* ውሁድ *whud*
**comprehend** *(v.)* ተረድአ *tered'e*
**comprehensible** *(adj.)* ኪርዳእ ዚከኣል *kirda'è zike'al*
**comprehension** *(n.)* ምርዳእ *mrda'è*
**comprehensive** *(adj.)* ኣጠቓላሊ *aẗeq̈alali*
**compress** *(v.)* ጨበጠ *čebeẗe*
**compression** *(n.)* ምጭባጥ *mčbaẗ*
**comprise** *(v.)* ሓዘ *ḧaze*
**compromise** *(n.)* ግድድፍ *gddf*
**compulsion** *(n.)* ምግዳ'ድ *mgdad*
**compulsive** *(adj.)* ግዴታዊ *gdeetawi*
**compulsory** *(adj.)* ግድነታዊ *gdnetawi*
**compunction** *(n.)* ስክፍታ *skfta*
**computation** *(n.)* ምቕማር *mq̈mar*
**compute** *(v.)* ቈጸረ *qWexere*
**computer** *(n.)* ኮምፒዩተር *kompyuter*
**computerize** *(v.)* ኣራጠበ *aratebe*
**comrade** *(n.)* ብጻይ *bxay*
**concatenation** *(n.)* ምትእስሳር *mt'èssar*
**concave** *(adj.)* ሃጓም *hagWam*
**conceal** *(v.)* ሓብአ *ḧab'e*
**concede** *(v.)* ኣመነ *amene*
**conceit** *(n.)* ትዕቢት *t'ëbit*
**conceivable** *(adj.)* ተኣማኒ *te'amani*
**conceive** *(v. t)* ተረድአ *tered'e*
**concentrate** *(v.)* ኣጽዓቐ *ax'äq̈e*
**concentration** *(n.)* ምጽዓቕ *mx'äq̈*
**concept** *(n.)* ኣምር *amr*
**conception** *(n.)* ምእማር *m'èmar*
**concern** *(v.)* ተመልከተ *temelkete*
**concerning** *(prep.)* ብዛዕባ *bza'ëba*
**concert** *(n.)* ሙዚቃዊ ምርኢት *muziqawi mr'it*
**concerted** *(adj.)* ውሁድ *whud*
**concession** *(n.)* ሕድገት *ḧdget*
**conch** *(n.)* ዛዕጎል *za'ëgol*
**conciliate** *(v.)* ደገፍ ረኸበ *degef reḱebe*
**concise** *(adj.)* ሓጺርን ብሩህን *ḧaxirn bruhn*
**conclude** *(n.)* ወድአ *wed'e*
**conclusion** *(n.)* መወዳእታ *meweda'èta*
**conclusive** *(adj.)* ደካሊ *dekali*
**concoct** *(v.)* ኣቃመመ *aqameme*
**concoction** *(n.)* ፈጠራ *feẗera*
**concomitant** *(adj.)* መኻይድቲ *meḱaydti*
**concord** *(n.)* ስምምዕ *smm'ë*
**concordance** *(n.)* ስምምዕ *smm'ë*
**concourse** *(n.)* ብሓባር ምኻድ *bḧabar mḱad*
**concrete** *(n.)* ጭቡጥ *čbuẗ*
**concubine** *(n.)* ውሽማ *wshma*
**concur** *(v.)* ተሰማምዐ *tesemam'ë*

**concurrent** *(adj.)* **ተቓዳዊ** *teq̈adawi*
**concussion** *(n.)* **መውቃዕቲ** *mewqa'ëti*
**condemn** *(v.)* **ኰነነ** *kWanene*
**condemnation** *(n.)* **ምዃናን** *mḱunan*
**condense** *(v.)* **ሓፈሰ** *ḧafese*
**condescend** *(v.)* **ተበርጠጠ** *tebertete*
**condiment** *(n.)* **ቀመመ** *qememe*
**condition** *(n.)* **ኩነት** *kunet*
**conditional** *(adj.)* **ኩነታዊ** *kunetawi*
**conditioner** *(n.)* **ኩነታት ጥዕና** *kunetate tiena*
**condole** *(v.)* **ደበ'ሰ** *debese*
**condolence** *(n.)* **ምጽንናዕ** *mxnna'ë*
**condom** *(n.)* **ኮንዶም** *condom*
**condominium** *(n.)* **ሓበራዊ መንበሪ ህንፃ** *haberawi menberi hintsa*
**condone** *(v.)* **መሓረ** *meḧare*
**conduct** *(n.)* **ጠባይ** *ẗebay*
**conduct** *(v.)* **ኣደብ** *adeb*
**conductor** *(n.)* **መራሒ** *meraḧi*
**cone** *(n.)* **ኮኖ** *kono*
**confection** *(n.)* **ሕዋስ ምቁራን** *ḧwas mquran*
**confectioner** *(n.)* **ናይ ዶልሺ** *naydolshi*
**confectionery** *(n.)* **እንዳ-ዶልሺ** *èndadolshi*
**confederate** *(adj.)* **ተሓባባሪ** *teḧababari*
**confederation** *(n.)* **ማሕበር** *maḧber*
**confer** *(v.)* **ዓደለ** *ädele*
**conference** *(n.)* **ዘተ** *zete*
**confess** *(v.)* **ተናዘዘ** *tenazeze*
**confession** *(n.)* **ኑዛዜ** *nuzazee*
**confidant** *(n.)* **ኣማኒት** *amanit*
**confide** *(v.)* **ምስጢር ኣካፈለ** *mstïr 'akafele*
**confidence** *(n.)* **እምነት** *èmnet*
**confident** *(adj.)* **ተኣማማኒ** *te'amamani*
**confidential** *(adj.)* **ምስጢራዊ** *mstïrawi*
**configuration** *(n.)* **ኣሰራርዓ** *aserar'ä*
**confine** *(v.)* **ወሰነ** *wesene*
**confinement** *(n.)* **ማእሰርቲ** *ma'èserti*
**confirm** *(v.)* **ኣረጋገጸ** *aregagexe*
**confirmation** *(n.)* **ምርግጋጽ** *mrggax*
**confiscate** *(v.)* **ወረሰ** *werese*
**confiscation** *(n.)* **ውርሳ** *wrsa*
**conflate** *(v.)* **ፀንበረ** *tsenbere*
**conflict** *(n.)* **ግጭት** *gčt*
**confluence** *(n.)* **መራኽበ** *meraḱbo*
**confluent** *(adj.)* **ሓባሪ** *ḧabari*
**conform** *(v.)* **ተሰማምዐ** *tesemam'ë*
**conformity** *(n.)* **ስምምዕ** *smm'ë*
**confront** *(v.)* **ተጋተረ** *tegatere*
**confrontation** *(n.)* **ቅርሕንቲ** *kiri hinti*
**confuse** *(v.)* **ኣደናገረ** *adenagere*
**confusion** *(n.)* **ዕግርግር** *ëgrgr*
**confute** *(v.)* **ረትዐ** *ret'ë*
**congenial** *(adj.)* **ዚወሃሃድ** *ziwehahad*
**congenital** *(adj.)* **ውርሻዊ** *wrshawi*

**congested** *(adj.)* **ቅጽጽ ዝበለ** *qxx zbele*
**congestion** *(n.)* **ጻዕቂ** *xa'ëqi*
**conglomerate** *(n.)* **ኣኸኸበ** *aḱaḱebe*
**conglomeration** *(n.)* **እኽብካብ** *èḱbkab*
**congratulate** *(v.)* **እንቋዕ ኣሓጐሰካ በለ** *ènqWA'ë 'aḧagWaseka bele*
**congratulation** *(n.)* **መግለጺ ሓጐስ** *meglexi ḧagWas*
**congregate** *(v.)* **ተኣከበ** *te'akebe*
**congress** *(n.)* **ጉባኤ** *guba'ee*
**congruent** *(adj.)* **ዝስማዕማዕ** *zismaemae tsemaexmeaa*
**conical** *(adj.)* **ተሰስማዕመዐ** *tsemaexmeaa*
**conjecture** *(n. &v.)* **ግምታዊ ሓሳብ** *gemetawi hasabe*
**conjugal** *(v.t. & i.)* **መወስበኣዊ** *mewesbo'awi*
**conjugate** *(v.)* **ግጥሚ ኣንበበ** *geTemi anebbb*
**conjunct** *(adj.)* **መስተፃምር** *,mestetsamire*
**conjunction** *(n.)* **ጠራፊ መሳርዕ** *Terafi ms*
**conjunctivitis** *(n.)* **ናይ ቁስለት ዓይኒ** *nay'l qusele't aa'yeni*
**conjuncture** *(n.)* **ዋኒን/ጉዳይ** *maniein/guda'yi*
**conjure** *(v.)* **ምትሃተኛ** *meteha'te'gna*
**conker** *(n.)* **ኮራዕ** *kora'ee*
**connect** *(v.)* **ኣራኸበ** *aara'EH'kebe*
**connection** *(n.)* **ርክብ** *re'KE'be*
**connive** *(v.)* **ተመሻጠረ** *temeSHA'tere*
**conquer** *(v.)* **ወረረ** *were're*
**conquest** *(n.)* **ወረራ** *we're'ra*
**conscience** *(n.)* **ሕሊና** *hi'lina*
**conscious** *(adj.)* **ግንዛበ ዘለዎ** *giniza'be zelewo*
**consecrate** *(v.)* **ቀደሰ** *qede'se*
**consecutive** *(adj.)* **ተኸታታሊ** *teHE'tata'li*
**consecutively** *(adv.)* **ዝተሓተ** *zi'te'hat'ee*
**consensus** *(n.)* **ሓበራዊ ምርድዳእ** *haberawi merederaoo*
**consent** *(v.t.)* **ስምምዕ** *se'memeee*
**consent** *(n.)* **ፍቓድ** *feqa'de*
**consequence** *(n.)* **ሳዕቤን** *saee'bene*
**consequent** *(adj.)* **ውፅኢት** *wutsieiit*
**conservation** *(n.)* **ሓለዋ ተፈጥሮ** *haalewa tefetero*
**conservative** *(adj.)* **ፀረ ለዉጢ** *tsere lewuti*
**conservatory** *(n.)* **ሰርዐ** *sereaa'*
**conserve** *(v. t)* **ብቑጠባ ተጠቐመ** *b'quteba te'teqe'mu*
**consider** *(v.)* **ኣስተንተነ** *aa' seten'tene*
**considerable** *(adj.)* **ብዙሕ** *bezuHi'h*
**considerate** *(adj.)* **ሓሳቢ** *ha'sabi*
**consideration** *(n.)* **ኣብ ግምት ኣእተወ** *hab' gimit aaetewe*
**considering** *(prep.)* **ኣተኩሩ ረኣየ** *aa' tekuru rexayee*
**consign** *(v.)* **ሰንደወ** *senedwwe*

**consignment** *(n.)* ዝተለኣኹ ኣቑሑት *zetelezaaHu aaqkuhut*
**consist** *(v.)* ኣካተተ *aakate'te*
**consistency** *(n.)* ተኸታታሊ *te'KHE'tatali*
**consistent** *(adj.)* ዘይቕየር *zey'qeyer*
**consolation** *(n.)* መፅናዕንዒ *mexenaee'neeeii*
**console** *(v. t.)* ኣፀናንዐ *a'txennea*
**consolidate** *(v.)* ኣሓየለ *ahayl'e*
**consolidation** *(n.)* ፀንበረ *xeneber*
**consonant** *(n.)* ስምምዕ *sememe'*
**consort** *(n.)* ሰብኣይ ንግስቲ *sebeaayi negeseti*
**consortium** *(n.)* ኮንሰርትዮም *konsertyom*
**conspicuous** *(adj.)* ብቕሊሉ ዝረኣይ *beqlilu zereaayii*
**conspiracy** *(n.)* ሻራ *shara*
**conspirator** *(n.)* ዉዲት *wudit*
**conspire** *(v.)* ተመሻጠረ *temeshatere*
**constable** *(n.)* ኮንስታብል *konstablee*
**constabulary** *(n.)* ኮንስታብል ሰብነት *konstable sebenet'*
**constant** *(adj.)* ዘየቋርፅ *zeye'qereXe'*
**constellation** *(n.)* ናይ ከዋኽብቲ *naye kKe'wakib'ti*
**consternation** *(n.)* ድንጋፀ *denegaXE'*
**constipation** *(n.)* ድርቀት *dere'qe'T*
**constituency** *(n.)* ክፋል *kefale*
**constituent** *(adj.)* ኣድማፂ *adma'txi*
**constitute** *(v.)* ተሓሰበ *teha'sebe*
**constitution** *(n.)* ሕገ መንግስቲ *hige mengistii*
**constitutional** *(adj.)* ቅዋማዊ *qwamawi*
**constrain** *(v.)* ኣጋደደ *aagadede*
**constraint** *(n.)* ገደብ *gedbb*
**constrict** *(v.)* ኣፀበበ *axebebbe'*
**construct** *(v.)* ሃነፀ *hanXE'*
**construction** *(n.)* ህንፀት *hintsxet'*
**constructive** *(adj.)* ሃናፂ *hanatxi'*
**construe** *(v.)* ተረደአ *teredeA'*
**consul** *(n.)* ቆንስል *qonesele*
**consular** *(n.)* ቆንፅላ *qonexela*
**consulate** *(n.)* ናይቆንስል ገዛ *nayi qonsele geza*
**consult** *(v.)* ኣማኸረ *aAmaHe're*
**consultant** *(n.)* ኣማኻሪ *amaHa'ri*
**consultation** *(n.)* ተመማኻኸረ *temeHaHere'*
**consume** *(v.)* ተመቐመ *temeQeme'*
**consumer** *(n.)* ሸማቲ *shemati*
**consummate** *(v.)* ምሉ'እ *mlu'è*
**consumption** *(n.)* ምጥቃም *miT; Qqam'*
**contact** *(n.)* ርክብ *rikib*
**contagion** *(n.)* ምልጋብ *milgab*
**contagious** *(adj.)* ተላጋቢ *telagabi*
**contain** *(v.t.)* ሓዘ *haze'*
**container** *(n.)* ኮንቴነር *konte'ner*
**containment** *(n.)* ምዕጋት *meegat*
**contaminate** *(v.)* በከለ *bekele*
**contemplate** *(v.)* ሓሰበ *haseb*

**contemplation** *(n.)* **ኣትኩሩ ረኣየ** *xteKuru reAaye'*
**contemporary** *(adj.)* **እዋናዊ** *eewanawi*
**contempt** *(n.)* **ንዕቐት** *neeeiqet*
**contemptuous** *(adj.)* **ሸለልታ** *shelelta*
**contend** *(v.)* **ተኸራኸረ** *teHerakere*
**content** *(adj.)* **ዝዓገበ** *zea'gebe*
**content** *(n.)* **ትሕዝቶ** *tihizeto*
**contention** *(n.)* **ቅርሕንቲ** *kqir'hinti*
**contentious** *(adj.)* **ዘቀሓሕር** *zeqkeha'hir*
**contentment** *(n.)* **ዕግበት** *qeig'bet*
**contest** *(n.)* **ዉድድር** *wudi'dir*
**contestant** *(n.)* **ተወዳዳሪ** *te'we'dada'Rei*
**context** *(n.)* **ሃዋህው** *hawahewu'*
**contiguous** *(adj.)* **ጥቓንጥቓ** *tQAneTeQA'*
**continent** *(n.)* **ክፍለ ኣለም** *kefele ale'm*
**continental** *(adj.)* **ክፍለ ኣለማዊ** *kefele alemawii*
**contingency** *(n.)* **ወዝቢ** *wezbi*
**continual** *(adj.)* **ተደጋጋሚ** *tedegagami*
**continuation** *(n.)* **ተደጋጋሚ** *tedegagami*
**continue** *(v.)* **ቀፀለ** *qeTsele'*
**continuity** *(n.)* **ዝተቐፃፀለ** *zeteqaTsaTse'le*
**continuous** *(adj.)* **ቀፃላይ** *qetsetay*
**contort** *(v.)* **እስርስር በለ** *esir'sir bele*
**contour** *(n.)* **ወሰናወሰን** *wesena'wesen*
**contra** *(prep.)* **ምፅባዕ** *mitsbaee*
**contraband** *(n.)* **ኮንትሮባንድ** *kontroband*
**contraception** *(n.)* **ምክልኻል ጥንሲ** *meihil'hal tinsi*
**contraceptive** *(n.)* **መከላኸሊ ጥንሲ** *mekelaḱeli ẗnsi*
**contract** *(n.)* **ናይ ዉዕሊ** *nayei wueili'*
**contract** *(n)* **ውዕል** *w'ël*
**contraction** *(n.)* **ኣሕፀረ** *had'e*
**contractor** *(n.)* **ተኸናታሪ** *awarede*
**contractual** *(adj.)* **ዉዕሊ ፈፀመ** *raȟreȟe*
**contradict** *(v.)* **ተፃበአ** *ztegedfe*
**contradiction** *(n.)* **ተፃረረ** *gedam*
**contrary** *(adj.)* **ተቓራኒ** *abegedam*
**contrast** *(n.)* **ኣፈላላይ** *mȟxar*
**contravene** *(v.)* **ሕጊ ጠሓሰ** *werede*
**contribute** *(v.)* **ኣዋፅአ** *mwrad*
**contribution** *(n.)* **ወፈየ** *neqele*
**contrivance** *(n.)* **ኢ-ተኣማኒነት** *ȟamed*
**contrive** *(v.)* **ገበረ** *kebdi*
**control** *(n.)* **ቁፅፅር** *nay kebdi*
**controller** *(n.)* **ተቖፃፃሪ** *zerefe*
**controversial** *(adj.)* **ኣከራኻሪ** *zerefe*
**controversy** *(n.)* **ኽርክር** *mzbul*
**contusion** *(n.)* **ስምብራት** *sȟtan*
**conundrum** *(v. t)* **ሽግር** *adefafere*
**conurbation** *(n.)* **ምኽታ'ም** *mḱtam*

**convene** ***(v.)*** **ኣኼባ ፀወዐ** *fenfene*
**convenience** ***(n.)*** **ምቾት** *krhat*
**convenient** ***(adj.)*** **ምችዊ** *kruh*
**convent** ***(n.)*** **ናይ ደናግል ገዳም** *xen'ë*
**convention** ***(n.)*** **ባህሊ/ልምዲ** *zeywda'è gedam*
**converge** ***(v.)*** **ተኣኻኸበ** *'äqmi*
**conversant** ***(adj.)*** **ፍልጠት ዘለዎ** *ḧrtum zelwo*
**conversation** ***(n.)*** **ወግዒ** *meḧale*
**converse** ***(v.)*** **ኣዋግዐ** *lbu'ë*
**conversion** ***(n.)*** **ምቕያር** *nfu'ë bqu'ë*
**convert** ***(n.)*** **ቀየረ** *me'änatu*
**convert** ***(v.)*** **ተቐየረ** *mzbul*
**convey** ***(v.)*** **ገለፀ** *'ab l'ëli*
**conveyance** ***(n.)*** **አጓጓዘ** *geza*
**convict** ***(n.)*** **ገበነኛ** *'atfe'e*
**convict** ***(v.)*** **ገበነኛ እዩ በለ** *mtfa'è bele eyik*
**conviction** ***(n.)*** **ገበነኛነት** *zixla'è*
**convince** ***(v.)*** **ኣእመነ** *xel'e*
**convivial** ***(adj.)*** **ምሑእ/ደስ ዝብል** *ïntawi*
**convocation** ***(n.)*** **ኣኼባ** *tewegre*
**convoy** ***(n.)*** **ተዓጂበን ብሓባር ዝኸዳ** *mwgad*
**convulse** ***(n.)*** **ኣንቀጥቀጠ** *wgur*
**convulsion** ***(n.)*** **ምንቅጥቃጥ** *fedfede*
**cook** ***(n.)*** **ከሻኒ** *bza'ëba*
**cook** ***(v.)*** **ኣብሰለ** *'ab zurya*
**cooker** ***(n.)*** **ዘበናዊ እቶን** *'ab l'ëli*
**cookie** ***(n.)*** **ኬክ** *bzyada*
**cool** ***(adj.)*** **ዝሑል** *lḧlaḧe*
**coolant** ***(n.)*** **ዛሕሊ** *faḧfaḧi*
**cooler** ***(n.)*** **ዝሕልቱ** *godnegodni*
**cooper** ***(n.)*** **ምሕዳስ** *aḧxere*
**cooperate** ***(v.)*** **ተሓባበረ** *wexa'i*
**cooperation** ***(n.)*** **ትሕብብር** *sereze*
**cooperative** ***(adj.)*** **ተሓጋገዘ** *handebetawi*
**coordinate** ***(v. t)*** **ኣተሓባበረ** *ḧagel*
**coordination** ***(n.)*** **ሓቢሩ ከደ** *xeleqWu*
**cope** ***(v.)*** **ተፃወረ** *bkurat*
**copier** ***(n.)*** **ብማሽን ዝተገልበጠ ቅዳሕ** *bḱur*
**copious** ***(adj.)*** **ኣዝዩ ብዙሕ** *bḱur*
**copper** ***(n.)*** **መዳብ** *fxum*
**copulate** ***(v.)*** **ሰረረ** *sreet*
**copy** ***(n.)*** **ቅዳሕ** *meḧare*
**copy** ***(v.)*** **ናይ ሓንቲ ሓባ** *seteye*
**coral** ***(n.)*** **ደረቕ ተሪር** *teqetebe*
**cord** ***(n.)*** **ፍሕሶ** *zahdi*
**cordial** ***(adj.)*** **ልባዊ** *reqiq*
**cordon** ***(n.)*** **ዝተስለፉ ፖላይስ** *tluq*
**core** ***(n.)*** **ወጢሽጣዊ ኣካ** *trgum 'albo*
**coriander** ***(n.)*** **ተኽሊ ቅመቃ ቕመም** *trgum 'albonet*
**cork** ***(n.)*** **ኮረኪ** *ml'at*
**corn** ***(n.)*** **ሱማ** *fdfud*
**cornea** ***(n.)*** **ፃዕዳ ኣይኒ** *ämexe*
**corner** ***(n.)*** **ኩርናዕ** *texarafi*
**cornet** ***(n.)*** **ዘዛንመሎ** *tedawebe*
**coronation** ***(n.)*** **ስርዓተ ንግስና** *delhametawi*
**coroner** ***(n.)*** **መርማሪ** *delhamet*
**coronet** ***(n.)*** **ኣኽሊል** *akademiyawi*
**corporal** ***(n.)*** **ኣካላዊ** *akademi*
**corporate** ***(adj.)*** **ዓብይ** *mexe*
**corporation** ***(n.)*** **ዓብይ ትካል ንግዲ** *nehare*

**corps** ***(n.)*** **ብርጌድ** *anhari*
**corpse** ***(n.)*** **ሬሳ** *mgulaȟ*
**corpulent** ***(adj.)*** **ሃዝራጥ** *aguleȟe*
**correct** ***(adj.)*** **ልክዕ** *teq̈ebele*
**correct** ***(v.)*** **አረመ** *teq̈ebalnet zelewo*
**correction** ***(n.)*** **እርማት** *qbale*
**corrective** ***(adj.)*** **መቕፃዕቲ** *me'ètewi*
**correlate** ***(v.)*** **ተዛመደ** *kirkeb zike'al*
**correlation** ***(n.)*** **ዝምድና** *bxȟat*
**correspond** ***(v.)*** **ተመሳሰለ** *mesarȟi*
**correspondence** ***(n.)*** **ስምምዕ** *smm'ë*
**correspondent** ***(n.)*** **ፀብፃቢ** *nay ȟadega*
**corridor** ***(n.)*** **ናይ ህንፃ መተሓላለፊ** *ačebčebe*
**corroborate** ***(v.)*** **መረዳእታ አቕረበ** *a'ënewe*
**corrode** ***(v.)*** **አበላሸወ** *selamta*
**corrosion** ***(n.)*** **መበላሸቲ** *tesemam'ë*
**corrosive** ***(adj.)*** **ዝጎድእ** *me'ëref 'agaysh*
**corrugated** ***(adj.)*** **ዕፅፍፃፍ** *meseneyti*
**corrupt** ***(adj.)*** **ግዕዙይ** *äĵebe*
**corrupt** ***(n.)*** **ጋዕዘየ** *gbre'aber*
**corruption** ***(n.)*** **ግዕይዝና** *fexeme*
**cortisone** ***(n.)*** **ኮርቲሶን** *k'ila*
**cosmetic** ***(adj.)*** **መፀባበቒ** *fxamee*
**cosmetic** ***(n.)*** **መፀባበቂ ቕብኣት** *w'ël*
**cosmic** ***(adj.)*** **ምስ ሃዋህዉ** *tewhdo*
**cosmology** ***(n.)*** **ጠፈር ዝተዛመደ** *bmeseret*
**cosmopolitan** ***(adj.)*** **ቆዝሞፖሊታዊ** *qozmopolitawi*
**cosmos** ***(n.)*** **ሃዋህዉ** *gWanefe*
**cost** ***(v.)*** **ዋጋ ኣዉፃኢ** *ȟsab*
**costly** ***(adj.)*** **ክቡር** *teȟatati*
**costume** ***(n.)*** **ክዳን ሰበይቲ** *kdan sebeyti*
**cosy** ***(adj.)*** **ምዉቕን ምቾዊን** *sneẗebib*
**cosy** ***(adj.)*** **ምዉቕን ምቾዊን** *texebaxabi*
**cot** ***(n.)*** **ዓራት ቆልዓ** *bweg'ï le'aḱe*
**cottage** ***(n.)*** **ጐጇ** *bweg'ï le'aḱe*
**cotton** ***(n.)*** **ተኽሊ ጡጥ** *weg'äwi*
**couch** ***(n.)*** **ወንበር** *ëbyet*
**couchette** ***(n.)*** **ዝዝርጋሕ ዓራት** *delebe*
**cough** ***(v.)*** **ሰዓለ** *awahlele*
**council** ***(n.)*** **ቤት ምኽሪ** *whlela*
**councillor** ***(n.)*** **ኣባል ቤት ምኽሪ** *lk'ë*
**counsel** ***(n.)*** **ምኽሪ/ማዕዳ** *gzi*
**counsel** ***(v.)*** **ኣማኸረ** *kesese*
**counsellor** ***(n.)*** **ጠበቃ** *teȟatatnet*
**count** ***(v.)*** **ቆፀረ** *lemede*
**countenance** ***(n.)*** **ገፅ ሰብ** *lmud*
**counter** ***(n.)*** **ባንኮኒ** *ȟade*
**counter** ***(v.t.)*** **መልሲ ሃበ** *arebik*
**counteract** ***(v.)*** **ተጻረረ** *texarere*
**counterfeit** ***(adj.)*** **ተመሳሰሲሉ ዝተሰርሐ** *netagWi*
**counterfoil** ***(n.)*** **ቅዳሕ ቅብሊት** *qdaȟ qblit*
**countermand** ***(v.)*** **ትእዛዝ ለወጠ** *tegonaxefe*
**counterpart** ***(n.)*** **መዘና** *fxamee*

**countless** *(adj.)* መዓት/ማእለያ ሀይብሉ *mexix*
**country** *(n.)* ሃገር/ዓዲ *mečqWAr*
**county** *(n.)* መዲና *amesgene*
**coup** *(n.)* ዕልዋ መንግስቲ *mq̈xal*
**coupe** *(n.)* ሸሓነ *čaf*
**couple** *(n.)* ፅምዲ/ክልተ *ënfrur*
**couplet** *(n.)* ዉሑዳት *anagonsẗees*
**coupon** *(n.)* ኩፖን *fre 'ok nay ḧade 'ok zisme gereb fre*
**courage** *(n.)* ጅግንነት *ms msma'ë zte'asasere*
**courageous** *(adj.)* ጅግና *afaleẗe*
**courier** *(n.)* ኣቐሑ ዘብፅሕ ሰብ *leela*
**course** *(n.)* ዓይነት ትምህርቲ *tesemam'e*
**court** *(n.)* ቤት ፍርዲ/መጋባኣያ *msmma'e*
**courteous** *(adj.)* ምእዙዝ *rekebe*
**courtesan** *(n.)* ፋይቶት *qsmet*
**courtesy** *(n.)* ትሕትና *fetḧe*
**courtier** *(n.)* ተቐባሊ ጋሻ *naxa mlqaq̈*
**courtly** *(adj.)* ኣዝዩ ምእዙዝ *akr*
**courtship** *(n.)* ኣርገፀ/ጀነጀነ *bedan*
**courtyard** *(n.)* ካንሸሎ *mret*
**cousin** *(n.)* ወዲኣኮ/ወዲሓዉቦ *akrobat*
**cove** *(n.)* ዕረፍቲ *bariton*
**covenant** *(n.)* ቃል ኪዳን *sgr*
**cover** *(n.)* መሸፈኒ *zer'ëd*
**cover** *(v.)* ሸፈነ/ከወለ *mgbar*
**covert** *(adj.)* ሕቡእ/ምሸጢራዊ *gzeeyawi fexami*
**covet** *(v.)* ተሃቀወ *mwsa'è*
**cow** *(n.)* ላሕሚ *zefrh*
**coward** *(n.)* ጃጃዊ *mgbar*
**cowardice** *(n.)* ፍርሓት *'ab ḧgawi mesrḧ ze'ètu*
**cower** *(v.)* ተጎንበሓ *anẗefe*
**coy** *(adj.)* ሓፋር *nẗuf*
**crab** *(n.)* ሸርጣን *nẗfet*
**crack** *(n.)* ነቓዕ/ጭዳድ *tewanay*
**crack** *(v.)* ነቐዐ/ጨደደ *tewasa'it*
**cracker** *(n.)* ብሽኩቲ *hluw*
**crackle** *(v.)* ጠራዕራዕ ዝብል ደምፂ *bḧaqi*
**cradle** *(n.)* ዓራት ህፃን *gemgami*
**craft** *(n.)* እደጥበብ *anẗefe*
**craftsman** *(n.)* ጥበበኛ *tkurna*
**crafty** *(adj.)* ለመጭ *meridyan*
**cram** *(v.)* ጠቕጠቐ *nsur*
**cramp** *(n.)* ስትራፖ *terir*
**crane** *(n.)* ሰፍሳፊት *alzebe*
**crank** *(v.)* ዘወረ *mwhhad*
**crash** *(v.)* ተጋጨወ *demere*
**crass** *(adj.)* ተቐባልነት ዘይብሉ *memela'èta*
**crate** *(n.)* ካሳ/ናይ ጥርሙዝ ሳንዱቕ *tewelefe*
**cravat** *(n.)* ክራባት *mwlaf*
**crave** *(v. t)* ተሃንቀወ/ሃረር በለ *welfi*
**craven** *(adj.)* ፈራሕ/ጃጃዊ *mdmar*
**crawl** *(v.)* ታተ በለ *tewesaḱi*
**crayon** *(n.)* ሕብሪ/ኩሩሽ *äqabi*
**craze** *(n.)* ዝምነዉ ድልየት *dngur*
**crazy** *(adj.)* ዓንጃል/ሃላይ *adrasha*
**creak** *(n.)* ፂፅ በለ *teq̈ebali 'èti 'adrasha'u ztexaḧfe seb*
**creak** *(v.)* ፂፅ ዝብል ድምፂ *ẗeq̈ese*
**cream** *(n.)* ላህመት/ላመት *k'ila*

**crease** *(n.)* **ሽምራር** *èkulnet*
**create** *(v.)* **ፈጠረ/ሰርሐ** *èḱul*
**creation** *(n.)* **ምፍጣር** *se'äbe*
**creative** *(adj.)* **መሃዛይ** *mdgaf*
**creator** *(n.)* **ፈጣሪ** *lagabi*
**creature** *(n.)* **ፍጥረት** *deḧan kun*
**crèche** *(n.)* **መዉዓሊ ህፃናት** *gWarebeet*
**credentials** *(n.)* **ብቕዓት፤ ስልጠናን ተመክሮን** *qxl*
**credible** *(adj.)* **እሙን** *texeg'ë 'ab gWadni kone*
**credit** *(n.)* **ኣዉድ** *aqWArexe*
**creditable** *(adj.)* **ተኣማኒነት** *ameḧalalefe*
**creditor** *(n.)* **ኣወፋይ** *beyene*
**credulity** *(adv.)* **ናይ ምእማን ክእለት/ድልየት** *ferede*
**creed** *(n.)* **እምነት** *ïbqo*
**creek** *(n.)* **ፍሰት** *ame'ärareye*
**creep** *(v.)* **መሎቑ** *mwdad*
**creeper** *(n.)* **ሓረግ** *ameḧadere*
**cremate** *(v.)* **ሬሳ ኣቃፀለ** *mmḧdar*
**cremation** *(n.)* **ሬሳ ማቃፀል** *mmḧdarawi*
**crematorium** *(n.)* **ሬሳ ኣቃፀለ ቦታ/ከባቢ** *ameḧadari*
**crescent** *(n.)* **ሓዳሽ ናይ ዝተወለደት ወርሒ ቅርፂ** *zine'ad*
**crest** *(n.)* **ወሳናይ/ዘሐጉስ** *admiral*
**crew** *(n.)* **ሓቢሮም ዝሰርሑ ኪኢላታት** *adnaq̈ot*
**crib** *(n.)* **ዓራ ቖልዓ** *adneq̈e*
**cricket** *(n.)* **ክሪኬት** *zifqed*
**crime** *(n.)* **ገበን** *qbela*
**criminal** *(n.)* **ገበነኛ** *te'amene*
**criminology** *(n.)* **ናይ ገበነኛ መፅናዕቲ** *qbela*
**crimson** *(n.)* **ቀይሕ** *gesexe*
**cringe** *(v.)* **ሸለገ** *sheq̈elqel*
**cripple** *(n.)* **ልሙስ ሰብ** *ïreḧẗub*
**crisis** *(n.)* **ቅልዉላዉ** *bxḧna*
**crisp** *(adj.)* **ተረርን ነቓፅን** *bexḧi*
**criterion** *(n.)* **ረቋሕ መለክዒ** *wesede*
**critic** *(n.)* **ናይ መፅሓፍ ተዋስኦ/ገምጋሚ** *mr'äm*
**critical** *(adj.)* **ነቓፊ** *re'ämi*
**criticism** *(n.)* **ነቐፌታ** *tefetawi*
**criticize** *(v.)* **ነቐፈ** *fq̈ri*
**critique** *(n.)* **ነቓፊ ዝኾነ ሰብ** *amleḱe*
**croak** *(n.)* **ብኽያት** *asewene*
**crochet** *(n.)* **ኹረሽ** *falul*
**crockery** *(n.)* **ብልቃጥ ስራ** *čele*
**crocodile** *(n.)* **ሓርገፀ** *adserb*
**croissant** *(n.)* **ኩራሳ** *wdasekentu*
**crook** *(n.)* **መልቲ** *èkul*
**crooked** *(adj.)* **ቁባዕ** *amerasehe*
**crop** *(n.)* **ዘራእቲ** *mmrsaḧ*
**cross** *(n.)* **መስቀል** *zmut*
**crossing** *(n.)* **ተሰገረ/ሓለፈ** *segWame*
**crotchet** *(n.)* **ቀራፂቶ** *le'äle*
**crouch** *(v.)* **ተኾደመ/ተኾደጨ** *mm'ëbal*
**crow** *(n.)* **ንቅዋ** *blča*
**crowd** *(n.)* **ዝተኣከቡ ሰባት** *rebḧa*
**crown** *(n.)* **ኣኽሊል** *ẗeq̈ami*
**crown** *(v.)* **ኣንገሰ** *mx'at*
**crucial** *(adj.)* **ኣዝዩ ወሳናይ** *ëndera*
**crude** *(adj.)* **ሓፈሻዊ** *ḧadegeḣa*
**cruel** *(adj.)* **ጨካን** *tewesakegsi*

**cruelty** *(adv.)* **ጭካነ** *texay*
**cruise** *(v.)* **ብመርከብ ተጓጓዓዘ** *alutawi*
**cruiser** *(n.)* **መርከብ** *shgr*
**crumb** *(n.)* **ቁራስ ባኒ/ፓስተ** *afaleẗe*
**crumble** *(v.)* **ቆረሰ/መቐለ** *reklam*
**crumple** *(v.)* **ዓምጠረ/ሓምተለ** *m'ëdo*
**crunch** *(v.)* **ፀገም** *zḧashe*
**crusade** *(n.)* **ቃልሲ/ተጋድሎ** *me'äde*
**crush** *(v.)* **ፀቐጠ/ዓምጠረ** *degafi*
**crust** *(n.)* **ላዕለዋይ** *teḧalaq̈i*
**crutch** *(n.)* **ምርኩስ** *üq̈ba*
**crux** *(n.)* **አዉራ ሽግር/ዋኒን** *sefafi*
**cry** *(n.)* **ብኽያት** *ayun*
**cry** *(v.)* **በኸየ** *ayrobatiks*
**crypt** *(n.)* **ሕቡእ** *mariwana*
**crystal** *(n.)* **ዓካር** *me'ärfo neferti*
**cub** *(n.)* **ኩርኩር ኣንበሳ** *snemnfar*
**cube** *(n.)* **ኪዩብ** *ayroplan*
**cubical** *(adj.)* **ኪዩቢካል** *flit*
**cubicle** *(n.)* **ዝተኸፈለ ፀቢብ ክፍሊ** *nay neferti*
**cuckold** *(n.)* **ሰብኣይ** *xbaq̈e'awi*
**cuckoo** *(n.)* **ዒፍ/ርግቢት** *snexbaq̈e*
**cucumber** *(n.)* **ዝኩኒ** *kab rḧuq̈*
**cuddle** *(v.)* **ሓቖፈ** *fḧshuw*
**cuddly** *(adj.)* **ምሕቋፍ** *fxamee*
**cudgel** *(n.)* **ጎመድ** *xelewe*
**cue** *(n.)* **ፍንጪ** *msluynet*
**cuff** *(n.)* **ታሕተዋይ ክፋል እጅገ** *amsali*
**cuisine** *(n.)* **ኣከሻሽና ፀብሒ/ምግቢ** *ftwet*
**culinary** *(adj.)* **ለኽተተ** *rhruh*
**culminate** *(v.)* **ዛዘመ** *qalemaḧla*
**culpable** *(adj.)* **ዝኹነን** *texeg'ë*
**culprit** *(n.)* **ገበነኛ ሰብ** *mxga'ë*
**cult** *(n.)* **ዉሩይ/ፍሉጥ** *temaslo*
**cultivate** *(v.)* **ሓረሰ** *aregagexe*
**cultural** *(adj.)* **ባህላዊ** *mrggax*
**culture** *(n.)* **ባህሊ** *awentawi*
**cumbersome** *(adj.)* **ኣዝዩ ረዚን** *lqabe*
**cumin** *(n.)* **ተኽሊ** *gWad'e*
**cumulative** *(adj.)* **በብእዋኑ ዝዉስኽ** *čnqi*
**cunning** *(adj.)* **ተበላፂ/መታለሊ** *habti*
**cup** *(n.)* **ኩባያ** *habtam*
**cupboard** *(n.)* **ጣዉላ** *atek̇ak̇ele*
**cupidity** *(n.)* **ስስዐ** *mgrab*
**curable** *(adj.)* **ዝሓዊ/ዝፍወስ** *na'ëbi*
**curative** *(adj.)* **ኣረጋግአ** *zelefe*
**curator** *(n.)* **ኣመሓዳሪ** *'ab rḧuq̈*
**curb** *(v. t)* **ተቖፃፀረ/ዓገተ** *zteq̈axele*
**curd** *(n.)* **ኣጅቦ** *zensaff*
**cure** *(v. t.)* **ኣሕወጠ/ፈወሰ** *'ab mqrrab*
**curfew** *(n.)* **ሕላፍ ሰዓት** *zferhe*
**curiosity** *(n.)* **ሃንቀዉታ ፍልጠት** *kem bḧadsh*
**curious** *(adj.)* **ንምፍላጥ ዝህንቀው** *afriqa*
**curl** *(v.)* **ተዓኹለለ** *'ab ritemerkeb*
**currant** *(n.)* **ዘቢብ** *dḧri*
**currency** *(n.)* **ገንዘብ** *dḧre*
**current** *(adj.)* **ናይ ሕጂ/ሎሚ** *dḧri*
**current** *(n.)* **ምንቅስቓስ ባሕሪ/ዉሕጅ** *'èndegena*
**curriculum** *(n.)* **ስርዓተ ትምህርቲ** *anxar*
**curry** *(n.)* **ሕሩጭ** *terir kbur 'èmni*

**curse** *(n.)* **መርገም** *ëdme*
**cursive** *(adj.)* **ናይ ኢድ ፅሑፍ** *shmagletat*
**cursor** *(n.)* **ሽተት ኣበለ** *qdmefrdi*
**cursory** *(adj.)* **ብህፁፅ ዝተሰርሓ** *zel'alemawi*
**curt** *(adj.)* **ሓፂር** *nay wklna tkal*
**curtail** *(v.)* **ዓገተ** *aĵenda*
**curtain** *(n.)* **መጋረጃ** *glul*
**curve** *(n.)* **ጎበጥ** *akebe*
**cushion** *(n.)* **መተርኣስ/መኽዳ** *agdede*
**custard** *(n.)* **መወራረዲ ምቁር ምግቢ** *zeq̈uẗ'ë*
**custodian** *(n.)* **ኣበብ ቀይዲ ምዉዕል ሰብ** *demere*
**custody** *(n.)* **ቅዳሕ ቅብሊት** *qdaȟ qblit*
**custom** *(n.)* **ባህሊ** *ämaxi*
**customary** *(adj.)* **ልሙድ** *aẗqa'ï*
**customer** *(n.)* **ዓሚል** *aq̈eyeme*
**customize** *(v.)* **ለዉጢ ገበረ** *zsembede*
**cut** *(v.)* **ሓረድ/ተለዘ** *sluẗ*
**cute** *(adj.)* **ዉቅብቲ** *soprano*
**cutlet** *(n.)* **ፍረ ነገር** *qesqese*
**cutter** *(n.)* **ምቕምቃም** *mḱWas*
**cutting** *(n.)* **ቁራፅ** *ifeliẗawi*
**cyan** *(n.)* **ሲያን** *ygebr'abilu yḱewn*
**cyanide** *(n.)* **ሲያናይድ** *rbux*
**cyber** *(comb.)* **ሳይበር** *haweḱe*
**cyberspace** *(n.)* **ሳይበርስፔስ** *merir ȟazen*
**cycle** *(n.)* **ብሽክሌታ** *mereetawi*
**cyclic** *(adj.)* **ዑደት** *tesemam'ë*
**cyclist** *(n.)* **ቱግቱግ ሰብ** *zisemama'ë*
**cyclone** *(n.)* **ኣባኸበራ** *smm'ë*
**cylinder** *(n.)* **ሲሊንደር** *ȟrshawi*
**cynic** *(n.)* **ተጠራጣሪ ሰብ** *ȟrsha*
**cynosure** *(n.)* **መስሕብ** *'ab bayta*
**cypress** *(n.)* **ተኽሊ** *'ab qdmi*
**cyst** *(n.)* **ማይ ዝማሃገ ሕብጠት** *red'e*
**cystic** *(adj.)* **ፍሕኛ** *degafi*

# D

**dab** *(v.)* **ለኸየ** *ačeneq̈e*
**dabble** *(v.)* **ተሳተፈ** *ačeneq̈e'i*
**dacoit** *(n.)* **ገበነኛ** *ȟmam*
**dad** *(n)* **ኣቦ** *ëlama*
**daffodil** *(n.)* **ተኽሊ** *shto*
**daft** *(adj.)* **ዓንጃል** *seȟate*
**dagger** *(n.)* **ሰንጢ** *ayer*
**daily** *(adj.)* **ዕለታዊ** *nefarit*
**dainty** *(adj.)* **ንእሽተይን ማራኺን** *nefasha*
**dairy** *(n.)* **ምፍራይ ፀባ** *korideyo*
**dais** *(n.)* **ኣትራኖስ** *ztegeftene*
**daisy** *(n.)* **ኣትራኖሳዊ** *zizamed*
**dale** *(n.)* **ሽንጥሮ** *sluẗ*
**dalliance** *(n.)* **ኣዕጠይጠየ** *meẗenqeq̈ta*
**dally** *(v.)* **ቀሰይ ኢሉ ሰርሐ** *qrubnet*
**dam** *(n.)* **ሓፅቢ** *sg'at*
**damage** *(n.)* **መጉዳእቲ** *way 'ane*
**dame** *(n.)* **ሰበይቲ** *shȟkWa*
**damn** *(v.)* **ኮነነ** *'album*
**damnable** *(adj.)* **ተኮናኛ** *albumen*
**damnation** *(n.)* **ኩነኔ** *alkemi*
**damp** *(adj.)* **ርሑስ/ትርኩስ** *alkol*
**dampen** *(v.)* **ኣጠልቀየ** *setay*
**damper** *(n.)* **ጠየቀ** *sbsab*
**dampness** *(n.)* **ኣዛሕተለ** *'ayl'äynet bira*

**damsel** *(n.)* **ዘይተመርዓወት ጓል** *ẗnquä̈*
**dance** *(v.)* **ሳዕሰዐ** *alĵebra*
**dancer** *(n.)* **መምስዕሳዕ ሰብ** *sagWa*
**dandelion** *(v.)* **ተኽሊ** *lwẗesm*
**dandle** *(v.)* **አሰራሰረ** *aserasere*
**dandruff** *(n.)* **ፎረፎር** *mewx'inefsi*
**dandy** *(n.)* **ስብቁል** *sbqul*
**danger** *(n.)* **ሓደጋ** *zinedd*
**dangerous** *(adj.)* **ሓደገኛ** *ser'ë*
**dangle** *(v. i.)* **ዓንጠልጠለ** *asalalfa*
**dank** *(adj.)* **ርሑስን ቆራርን** *temesasali*
**dapper** *(adj.)* **ፅፉፍ** *kflit fẗh*
**dapple** *(v.)* **ዕንፍሩር** *hyaw*
**dare** *(v.)* **ደፈረ/ተብዐ** *alkali*
**daring** *(adj.)* **ጅግና/ደፋር** *kulu*
**dark** *(adj.)* **ዝፀልመተ** *afakWase*
**darken** *(v.)* **ፀልመተ** *ale*
**darkness** *(n.)* **ፀልማት** *bhlo*
**darling** *(n.)* **መዓረይ** *te'amannet*
**darn** *(v.)* **ለገበ** *mslee'awi zanta*
**dart** *(n.)* **ቀስቲ** *aẗreq̈e*
**dash** *(v.)* **ሽዉ ምባል** *teq̈oẗa'ï*
**dashboard** *(n.)* **ጣዉላ** *quẗ'ë*
**dashing** *(adj.)* **ፅቡቕ** *afakẂase*
**dastardly** *(adj.)* **ፈራሕ** *mq̈lal*
**data** *(n.)* **ሓበሬታ** *meshgWaragur*
**database** *(n.)* **ሓበሬታ** *kidan*
**date** *(n.)* **ዕለት** *texeg'ë*
**date** *(n.)* **እዋን** *ängog*
**datum** *(n.)* **ተምሪ** *demsese*
**daub** *(v.)* **ለመፀ** *dgmete'afena*
**daughter** *(n.)* **ጓል** *akafele*
**daughter-in-law** *(n.)* **ሰበይቲ ወዲ** *mmq̈rah*
**daunt** *(v.)* **ኣፈራረሐ** *amasẖe*

**dauntless** *(adj.)* **ዘይፈርሕ** *msẖit*
**dawdle** *(v.)* **ኣዕጠይጠየ** *feq̈ede*
**dawn** *(n.)* **ወጋሕታ** *mew'ëlo*
**day** *(n.)* **መዓልቲ** *qorqoro*
**daze** *(v.)* **ዝዓዘመ** *amete*
**dazzle** *(v. t.)* **ሕዉዝዉዝ አበለ** *awenawene*
**dead** *(adj.)* **ዝማተ** *awenaweni*
**deadline** *(n.)* **መዕፀዊ ዕለት** *amet*
**deadlock** *(n.)* **ኣብ ስምምዕ ዘይምብፃሕ** *shrka*
**deadly** *(adj.)* **ዝቐትል** *almanak*
**deaf** *(adj.)* **ፀማም** *kulu zike'alo*
**deafening** *(adj.)* **ዘፅምም** *luz*
**deal** *(n.)* **ብዙሕ** *darga*
**deal** *(v. i)* **ጠልዐ ዓደለ** *mxwat*
**dealer** *(n. )* **ነጋዳይ** *zteseq̈le*
**dean** *(n.)* **ሓለቓ ደብሪ** *beynu*
**dear** *(adj.)* **ተፈታዊ/ፍትዊ** *ab gWadni*
**dearly** *(adv.)* **ክቡር** *ab gWadneh*
**dearth** *(n.)* **ዋሕዲ** *glul*
**death** *(n.)* **ሞት** *b'äwta*
**debacle** *(n.)* **ስዕረት** *alfa*
**debar** *(v. t.)* **ኽለከለ** *fidel*
**debase** *(v.)* **ኣርከሰ** *bnay fidelat terta*
**debatable** *(adj.)* **ክትዕ** *kerenawi*
**debate** *(v. t.)* **ተላዘበ** *kem'uwn*
**debate** *(n.)* **ምይይጥ/ዘተ** *zagit*
**debauch** *(v.)* **ዕዋላ** *menberetabot*
**debauchery** *(n.)* **ዕዋላዊ** *ẗerep̈eeza qurban*
**debenture** *(n.)* **ዘመስግን** *mlwaẗ*
**debilitate** *(v.)* **ኣዳኸመ** *qWeyqWi*
**debility** *(n.)* **ማማንማን** *mrča*
**debit** *(n.)* **ዕዳ** *qyar*

**debonair** *(adj.)* ዘበናዊን ብዓርሱ ዝተኣማመንን *mnmkWa*
**debrief** *(v.)* ሓተተ *brake*
**debris** *(n.)* ፈፍርስራስ *kulukulu*
**debt** *(n.)* ዕዳ *lgsnet*
**debtor** *(n.)* ናይ ወፃኢ ሰብ *aluminiyom*
**debunk** *(v.)* ሓሰት ከምዝኾነ ኣርኣየ *yuniversiti neber*
**debut** *(n.)* ናይ መፈለምታ መድረኽ *kulu gzee*
**debutante** *(n.)* ተቓላዒት *teqala'ït*
**decade** *(n.)* ዓሰርተ ዓመት *debleqe*
**decadent** *(adj.)* ጥፋሽ *ïfashe*
**decaffeinated** *(adj.)* ብዘይ ካፈይን *bzey kafeyn*
**decamp** *(v.)* ጠፍአ/መለስ በለ *amater*
**decant** *(v.)* ኣገማድሐ *zeyk'ila*
**decanter** *(n.)* ኣገማድሒ *mestefaqr*
**decapitate** *(v.)* ቀንዘፈ/ሰየፈ *agereme*
**decay** *(v. i)* በስበሰ *adnaqot*
**decease** *(n.)* ሞት *amazen*
**deceased** *(adj.)* ምዉት *'ambasaderl'uk*
**deceit** *(n.)* ቅጥፈት *'ëndida geex*
**deceitful** *(adj.)* መታለሊ *zuryawi*
**deceive** *(v.)* ኣታለለ/ሓበለ *zeynxurnet*
**decelerate** *(v.)* ናህሪ ቀነሰ *zeynxur*
**December** *(n.)* ታሕሳስ *deret*
**decency** *(n.)* ትሕትና *hrfan*
**decent** *(adj.)* ፅቡቕ/ግሩም *hnïuy*
**decentralize** *(v.)* ስልጣኑ ኣካፈለ *mantawi*
**deception** *(n.)* ምትላል *tesaleye*
**deceptive** *(adj.)* መደናገሪ *mqur*
**decibel** *(n.)* ዴሲቤል *ambulans*
**decide** *(v.)* ወሰነ *dbya*
**decided** *(adj.)* ዝተረጋገፀ *amehayeshe*
**decimal** *(adj.)* ዴሲማል *mmhyash*
**decimate** *(v.)* ረፍረፈ *amehayeshe*
**decipher** *(v.)* ትርጉሙ ረኸበ *me'aremta*
**decision** *(n.)* ዉሳነ *tehatati*
**decisive** *(adj.)* ወሳናይ *tefetawi*
**deck** *(n.)* ላዕለዋይ ደብሪ መርከብ *mhznetawi*
**deck** *(n)* ደብሪ *'ab mengo*
**declaim** *(v.)* ዓዉ ኢሉ ተዛረበ *gguy*
**declaration** *(v. t.)* መግለፂ *ërknet*
**declare** *(n)* ኣወጀ *tetekWasi*
**declassify** *(v.)* ዕላዊ *rsa'ë*
**decline** *(v. t.)* ምንቁልቋል/ምንካይ *mhret*
**declivity** *(n.)* ንታሕቲ/ንቑልቑል *b'ëbdbd*
**decode** *(v.)* ትርጉሙ ፈልፈለ *ab mengo*
**decompose** *(n.)* በስበሰ *b'ëlug*
**decomposition** *(v. t)* መቓቕል *fqrawi*
**decompress** *(v.)* ድፍኢት ኣየር ነከየ *qrxe'albo*
**decongestant** *(n.)* ንጥረ ነገር *ma'ëre kone*
**deconstruct** *(v.)* ዘይተሃነፀን *amper*
**decontaminate** *(v.)* ዝተመረዘ ከባቢ/ነገር ኣፅረየ *fluï seb*

**decor** *(n.)* **ኣገያይፃ/ኣሸላልማ** *mdremayawi*
**decorate** *(v.)* **ኣፀባበቐ/ሸለመ** *amfityatr*
**decoration** *(n.)* **ሽልማት** *sefiḧ*
**decorative** *(adj.)* **ኣፀባበቒ** *tewesaḱi*
**decorous** *(adj.)* **ቅቡል** *megulḧi*
**decorum** *(n.)* **ትሕትና** *agulḧe*
**decoy** *(n.)* **መተዓሸሸዊ ሰብ/ነገር** *sfḧat*
**decrease** *(v.)* **ነከየ** *ktab*
**decree** *(n.)* **ኣዋጅ** *azenag'ë*
**decrement** *(v. t.)* **ኣንቆልቆለ** *mznga'ë*
**decrepit** *(adj.)* **ዝቐንቐነ** *ḧade*
**decriminalize** *(v.)* **ሕጋዊ ንክኸዉን ገበረ** *ëletu zseḧate*
**decry** *(v.)* **ኮነነ** *waḧdi dem*
**dedicate** *(v.)* **ወፈየ** *dnzaze*
**dedication** *(n.)* **ዉፉይነት** *medenzezi*
**deduce** *(v.)* **ተገንዘበ** *qoyqWAm*
**deduct** *(v.)* **ቆርፁ ወሰደ** *xereqanza*
**deduction** *(n.)* **ግንዛበ** *temesasali*
**deed** *(n.)* **መግብር** *temesasalnet*
**deem** *(v.)* **ርእይቶ ሓዘ** *temesasalnet*
**deep** *(adj.)* **ዉሽጢ** *mtntan*
**deer** *(n.)* **ዓጋዜን/ርኤም** *mrmr*
**deface** *(v.)* **ፀየቐ** *tentani*
**defamation** *(n.)* **ዝጠቀነ** *tntane'awi*
**defame** *(v.)* **ጠቀነ/ሽም ሰብ ኣጥፈአ** *falulnet*
**default** *(n.)* **ዕዳኻ ዘይምኽፋል** *falulawi*
**defeat** *(v. t.)* **ሰዓረ/ተዓወተ** *falulnet*
**defeatist** *(n.)* **ሰዓሪ** *sneqrxi 'akal*
**defecate** *(v.)* **ሓርኣ/ቀልቀል ወፀ** *abew*
**defect** *(n.)* **ጉድለት/ሕፍቲ** *wrshawi*
**defective** *(adj.)* **ከድዐ** *abew*
**defence** *(n.)* **ምክልኻል** *melhq̈*
**defend** *(v.)* **ተኸላኸለ** *te'äshage*
**defendant** *(n.)* **ተኸሳሲ** *ïntawi*
**defensible** *(adj.)* **ተኸላኸለ ዝሕለፍ** *xg'ëteṅa*
**defensive** *(adj.)* **መከተ** *dma*
**defer** *(v.)* **ኣመሓላለፈ** *xg'ëteṅa*
**deference** *(n.)* **ኽብሪ** *xwa*
**defiance** *(n.)* **እምቢታ** *èndegena*
**deficiency** *(n.)* **ዋሕዲ** *ftuw*
**deficient** *(adj.)* **ዉሑድ** *quẗ'ë*
**deficit** *(n.)* **ክሳራ** *ḧmam*
**defile** *(v. t)* **ኣርኸሰ** *kurna'ë*
**define** *(v.)* **ተርጎመ** *ḧruq̈*
**definite** *(adj.)* **ዝተረጋገፀ** *gWahi*
**definition** *(n.)* **ገለፃ** *kurna'äwi*
**deflate** *(v.)* **ኣንፈሰ** *ènssa*
**deflation** *(n.)* **ኣብ ጥቅሚ ዝዉዕል ናይ ዘንዘብ መጠን ምንካይ** *hyaw*
**deflect** *(v.)* **ኣንፈት ቀየረ**
**deforest** *(v.)* **ዱር ኣብረሰ** *hyawnet*
**deform** *(v.)* **ኣዛበዐ** *xl'i*
**deformity** *(n.)* **ጉድኣት ኣካል** *shelen*
**defraud** *(v.)* **ኣታለለ** *änkar'änkarito*
**defray** *(v.)* **ወፃኢኡ ከኣለ/ሸፈነ** *anbar*
**defrost** *(v.)* **ኣዉዓየ/ወዓየ** *mezgebefxameetat*
**deft** *(adj.)* **ክእለት ዘለዎ** *gobeẗe*

**defunct** ***(adj.)*** **ዝበረሰ/ኣብ ጥቕሚ ዘይዉዕል** *gWabeïa*
**defuse** ***(v.)*** **ዓገተ/ኣለዘበ** *axnete*
**defy** ***(v.)*** **እምቢ በለ** *dmsesa*
**degenerate** ***(v.)*** **ተዳኸመ** *zkre'ämet*
**degrade** ***(v.)*** **ኣራኸሰ** *amelkete*
**degree** ***(n.)*** **መለክዒ ኩርናዕ** *gelexe*
**dehumanize** ***(v.)*** **ሰብኣዊነት ዘጥፍእ** *meglexi*
**dehydrate** ***(v.)*** **ኣፅለለ** *sheweze*
**deify** ***(v.)*** **ኣጥዐወ** *quï'ë*
**deign** ***(v.)*** **ተኣነነ** *beb'ämet*
**deity** ***(n.)*** **ጣኦት** *beb'ämet*
**déjà vu** ***(n.)*** **ሓደ ዓይነት ምኽን** *sereze*
**deject** ***(v.)*** **ኣሕዘነ** *'ah̆zene*
**dejection** ***(n.)*** **ጓሂ/ሕርቃን** *qeb'e*
**delay** ***(v. t)*** **ኣደንጎየ** *zeysru'ë*
**delectable** ***(adj.)*** **መኣዛ ዘለዎ** *zeyst*
**delectation** ***(n.)*** **ራህዋ/ፍስሃ** *smeswrnet*
**delegate** ***(n.)*** **ልኡኽ/ተወካሊ** *smeswr*
**delegation** ***(n.)*** **ልኡኽነት** *mnmane*
**delete** ***(v. i)*** **ደምሰሰ** *kal'è*
**deleterious** ***(adj.)*** **ጉዳኢ** *kimles zike'al*
**deletion** ***(n.)*** **ሰረዘ** *melsi*
**deliberate** ***(adj.)*** **ዝተሃነቀ** *xaxe*
**deliberation** ***(n.)*** **ምኽክር/ዘተ** *xaxe mexix*
**delicacy** ***(n.)*** **ተነቓፊነት** *texararnet*
**delicate** ***(adj.)*** **ተነቓፊ/ተሰባሪ** *texarari*
**delicatessen** ***(n.)*** **ዓብይ ሹቕ** *texarere*
**delicious** ***(adj.)*** **ምቁር/ስፋጥ** *antarktik*
**delight** ***(v. t.)*** **ፍስሃ/ታሕጓስ** *qdme fxame*
**delightful** ***(adj.)*** **ዘሕጉስ** *aquadme*
**delineate** ***(v.)*** **ገለፀ/ኣርኣየ** *ägazeen*
**delinquent** ***(adj.)*** **ገበነኛ/በደለኛ** *antena*
**delirious** ***(adj.)*** **ስሚዒታዊ** *anteema*
**delirium** ***(n.)*** **ዘተሓጎስ** *'èkub zantatat*
**deliver** ***(v.)*** **ኣብፀሐ** *sneseb*
**deliverance** ***(n.)*** **ምርካብ** *nefri*
**delivery** ***(n.)*** **ምርካብ** *xere*
**dell** ***(n.)*** **ሽንጥሮ** *xerenefsat*
**delta** ***(n.)*** **ዴልታ** *xere'akal*
**delude** ***(v.)*** **ኣታለለ** *weĵehalay*
**deluge** ***(n.)*** **ከቢድ ዝናም** *texebeye*
**delusion** ***(n.)*** **ምትላል** *mtlal*
**deluxe** ***(adj.)*** **ኣዝዩ ፅፉፍን ክቡርን** *mnqulqWAl*
**delve** ***(v.)*** **ኣለሽ በለ** *xeremerzi*
**demand** ***(n.)*** **ጥብቂ ሕቶ** *xeremerzi*
**demanding** ***(adj.)*** **ብዙሕ ክእለት /ትዕግስቲ/ፃዕሪ** *krhat*
**demarcation** ***(n.)*** **ምጥራር/ጥሪ** *kuh̆lemh̆li*
**demean** ***(v.)*** **ኣዋረደ** *zeïnti*
**demented** ***(adj.)*** **ዕቡድ/ፅሉል** *dh̆ur*
**dementia** ***(n.)*** **ዝዓበደ** *ïntawi*
**demerit** ***(n)*** **ጌጋ** *ïnti*
**demise** ***(n.)*** **ውድቀት** *xerereḱsi*

**demobilize** *(v.)* ረፈተ *xeremaȟberawi*
**democracy** *(n.)* ዲሞክራሲ *anxar*
**democratic** *(adj.)* ደዲሞክራሲያዊ *čnfar qerni*
**demography** *(n.)* ቁፅራዊ ሐበሬታ *aluta*
**demolish** *(v.)* ኣዕነወ *mehantus*
**demon** *(n.)* ርኹስ መንፈስ *wexeq̈a meter'as nay ziq̈ẗqeẗ ȟaxin*
**demonize** *(v.)* ዘጨንቕ ነገር *čnqet*
**demonstrate** *(v.)* ሰላማዊ ሰልፈኛ *harerteňa*
**demonstration** *(n.)* ሰላማዊ ሰልፊ *zḱone*
**demoralize** *(v.)* ደሃለ *bzeytegedasnet*
**demote** *(v.)* ኣዉረደ *zḱone seb*
**demur** *(v.)* ተቓወመ/ተፃረረ *zḱone neger*
**demure** *(adj.)* ህድእቲ *zḱone bota*
**demystify** *(v.)* ኣብራህረህ *bq̈lẗuf*
**den** *(n.)* ገዛ እንስሳ ዘገዳም *ztefelaleye*
**denationalize** *(v.)* ትካል ሸጠ *apartayd*
**denial** *(n.)* ክሕደት *kȟdet*
**denigrate** *(v.)* ኣናሸወ *zeytegedasnet*
**denomination** *(n.)* ስም *sm*
**denominator** *(n.)* ረቋሒ *črta*
**denote** *(v. t)* ኣመላኸተ *čaf*
**denounce** *(v.)* ኣዉገዘ *msla*
**dense** *(adj.)* ፅዑቕ *menhb*
**density** *(n.)* ፃዕቂ *r'èserguxnet*
**dent** *(n.)* ኣጠንበቐ *ra'èy*
**dental** *(adj.)* ናይ ስኒ *q̈reeta ȟatete*
**dentist** *(n.)* ናይ ስኒ ሓኪም *yq̈reeta*
**denture** *(n.)* ሰብሰርሖ ስኒ *apopletikawi*
**denude** *(v.)* ቀንጠጠ *keȟadi 'èmnet*
**denunciation** *(n.)* ነቐፈ *hawarya*
**deny** *(v. i.)* ኣሉ በለ *čret*
**deodorant** *(n.)* ክሕደት *askaȟkeȟe*
**depart** *(v.)* ነቐለ *mesarȟi*
**department** *(n.)* መምርሒ *kdan*
**departure** *(n.)* መምልቃቕ *bruh*
**depend** *(v.)* ተደረኸ *bruh*
**dependant** *(n.)* ፅግዕተኛ ዝኾነ ቆልዓ *tera'èye*
**dependency** *(n.)* ፅግዕተኛነት *mq̈lqal*
**dependent** *(adj.)* ዉሉፍ *azȟale*
**depict** *(v.)* ሰኣለ *mel'e*
**depilatory** *(adj.)* ኣጥፋእ ጸጉሪ *'aẗfa'è xeguri*
**deplete** *(v.)* ኣዉሓደ *nedri ẗbqo*
**deplorable** *(adj.)* ዘሰቅ ቕ *memela'èta*
**deploy** *(v.)* ኣዋፈረ *shewhat*
**deport** *(v. t)* ጠረዘ *kefat shewhat*
**depose** *(v.)* ኣዉረደ *ačebčebe*
**deposit** *(n.)* ዕቋር *čebčeba*
**depository** *(n.)* ትሕጃ *tufaȟ*
**depot** *(n.)* መኻዚኖ *mesarya*
**deprave** *(v.)* ኣበዕለገ *bq̈u'ë*
**deprecate** *(v.)* ኣናሸወ *amelkati*
**depreciate** *(v.)* ዋግኡ ነከየ *mȟtat*
**depreciation** *(n.)* ድሕሪ እዋን *teẗeq̈me*
**depress** *(v.)* ኣተከዘ *wesene*
**depression** *(n.)* ትካዘ *qWexera*
**deprive** *(v.)* ከልከለ *gWazeye*

**depth** *(n.)* ዕምቈት *zisemama'ë*
**deputation** *(n.)* ተወከልቲ *gemgeme*
**depute** *(v.)* ወከለ *èḱul*
**deputy** *(n.)* ምኽትል *tegenzebe*
**derail** *(v. t.)* ካብ መስመሩ ኣስሓተ *asteyayet*
**deranged** *(adj.)* ኣእምሩኡ ዝተቓወሰ *tered'e*
**deregulate** *(v.)* ካብ ደምቢን ቁፅፅርን ናፃ ገበረ *mrda'è*
**deride** *(v.)* ኣላገፀ *zteshaq̈ele*
**derivative** *(adj.)* መበቆል *telmedeen*
**derive** *(v.)* ረኸበ *afleëte*
**derogatory** *(adj.)* ክብሪ ዝነክአ *qerebe*
**descend** *(v.)* ተሓተ/ወረደ *bq̈u'ë*
**descendant** *(n.)* ትዉልዲ *mnza'ë*
**descent** *(n.)* ጭምት *qbale*
**describe** *(v.)* ገለፀ *teq̈ebele*
**description** *(n.)* ገለፃ *darga*
**desert** *(v.)* ደርበየ *mishmishe*
**deserve** *(v. t.)* ተገነአ *grmbyale*
**design** *(n.)* ኣሰራርሓ *belih̆*
**designate** *(v.)* ሰየመ *tewhbo*
**desirable** *(adj.)* ተደላዪ *tedelayi*
**desire** *(n.)* ድልየት *mayawi*
**desirous** *(adj.)* ህንቁዉ *mayawi*
**desist** *(v.)* አቋረፀ *areb*
**desk** *(n.)* ሰደቓ *arebian*
**desolate** *(adj.)* ፅምዋ ዝኾነ *arebik*
**despair** *(n.)* ቅብፀት ምቁራፅ *gedla*
**desperate** *(adj.)* ቀባፅ ዝቖረፅ *feradi*
**despicable** *(adj.)* ርጉም *hawri*
**despise** *(v.)* ነዓቐ *daneye*
**despite** *(prep.)* እንትርፌ *dan̆net*
**despondent** *(adj.)* ዝጎሃየ *dan̆a*
**despot** *(n.)* ዉልቀ መላኺ መራሒ *das*
**dessert** *(n.)* መወራረዲ ምቁር ምግቢ *qesti*
**destabilize** *(v.)* ቅልዉላዉ ፈጠረ *qeldedawi*
**destination** *(n.)* መብፅሒ ቦታ *qelded*
**destiny** *(n.)* ዕድል *sne ïnti*
**destitute** *(adj.)* ስኡን *ïntawi*
**destroy** *(v.)* ኣዕነወ *liqe mela'èkt*
**destroyer** *(n.)* ኣጥፊአ ሰብ *liqeṕaṕasat*
**destruction** *(n.)* ብርሰት *mentagay*
**detach** *(v.)* ፈለየ *snehanaxi*
**detachment** *(n.)* ዕሽሽታ *snehnxa*
**detail** *(n.)* ዝርዝር *archiv*
**detain** *(v. t)* ኣሰረ *arktik*
**detainee** *(n.)* ናይ ፓለቲካ እሱር *w'ëw'ë*
**detect** *(v.)* ኣሊሹ ረኸበ *brtu'ë dleet*
**detective** *(n.)* መርማሪ ፖሊስ *adkami*
**detention** *(n.)* ማእሰርቲ *sfh̆at*
**deter** *(v.)* ዓቀበ *medreḱ*
**detergent** *(n.)* መሕፀቢ *temagote*
**deteriorate** *(v.)* ተጋደደ *megote*
**determinant** *(n.)* ዉሱንን ንፁርን *megotina*
**determination** *(v. t)* ፅንዓት *axam'è*
**determine** *(v. t)* መርመረ *tela'ële*
**deterrent** *(n.)* መዐቀቢ *aristokrasi*
**detest** *(v.)* ፀልአ *aristokratawi*
**dethrone** *(v.)* ኣዉረደ *quxri*
**detonate** *(v.)* ነተጉ *quxrina*

**detour** *(n.)* **አኳላል መንገዲ** *tabot*
**detoxify** *(v.)* **መርዚ ኣወገደ** *mnat*
**detract** *(v.)* **ኣዛሕተለ** *čfra meraḱb wg'è*
**detriment** *(n.)* **ዕንወት ምስዓብ** *armagedon*
**detritus** *(n.)* **ተረፈ ምህርቲ** *axwar*
**devalue** *(v.)* **ሸርፊ ወፃኢ ነኸየ** *gzyawi teḱusi'ëxo*
**devastate** *(v.)* **ኣባደመ** *dr'ï ḧaxin*
**develop** *(v.)* **ዓበየ** *dr'ï ḧaxini*
**development** *(n.)* **ዕብየት** *serawit*
**deviant** *(adj.)* **ፍሉይ** *me'äza*
**deviate** *(v.)* **ተፈለየ** *me'äza fwesa*
**device** *(n.)* **መሳርሒ** *'ab zurya*
**devil** *(n.)* **ሰይጣን** *aberabere*
**devious** *(adj.)* **ሸፋጢ** *ser'ë*
**devise** *(v.)* **መሃዘ** *aserar'ä*
**devoid** *(adj.)* **ኣልቦ ዘይብሉ** *mḧir*
**devolution** *(n.)* **ውክልና** *wklna*
**devolve** *(v.)* **ሓላፍነት ሃበ** *teselefin*
**devote** *(v.)* **ወፈየ** *asere*
**devotee** *(n.)* **ፈታዊ** *ètwet*
**devotion** *(n.)* **ፍቕሪ** *mexe*
**devour** *(v.)* **ዉሕጥሕጥ ኣበለ** *'atḧitu re'aye*
**devout** *(adj.)* **ሃይማኖተኛ** *t'ëbiteǹa*
**dew** *(n.)* **ዛዕዛዕታ** *menze'ë*
**dexterity** *(n.)* **ናይ ኢድ ጥበብ** *flaxa*
**diabetes** *(n.)* **ሽኮርያ** *èndabret*
**diagnose** *(v.)* **መርሚሩ ፈለጠ** *brtu'ë smi*
**diagnosis** *(n.)* **ምርመራ** *bwsay mqxal*
**diagram** *(n.)* **ሰደቓ** *ẗbeb*
**dial** *(n.)* **መዘወሪ** *ẗnti*
**dialect** *(n.)* **ከባቢያዊ ቋንቋ** *arteri*
**dialogue** *(n.)* **ቃለ ምልልስ** *blhi*
**dialysis** *(n.)* **ሕክምና** *riḧ*
**diameter** *(n.)* **ስፋቲ** *karchofi*
**diamond** *(n.)* **ኣልማዝ** *aq̈ḧa*
**diaper** *(n.)* **ጨርቂ ሽንቲ** *anexere*
**diarrhoea** *(n.)* **ዉፅኣት** *k'èlet*
**diary** *(n.)* **ዕለታዊ ማስታወሻ** *snu'ë*
**Diaspora** *(n.)* **ናይ ኣይሁዳዊያን ስደት** *kebid bret*
**dice** *(n.)* **ሓደገኛ** *k'ila*
**dictate** *(adj.)* **ብልቃ ኣፅሓፈ** *sneẗebib*
**dictation** *(n.)* **ብቓል ምፅሓፍ** *sneẗbebawi*
**dictator** *(n.)* **ዉልቂ መላኺ መራሒ** *bahryawi*
**diction** *(n.)* **ኣነባበብ ቃላት** *kem*
**dictionary** *(n.)* **መዝገበ ቃላት** *mezgebeqalat*
**dictum** *(n.)* **ብሂል** *deyebe*
**didactic** *(adj.)* **ትምሕርታዊ** *deyabi*
**die** *(v.)* **ሞተ** *ërget*
**diesel** *(n.)* **በንዚን** *aregagexe*
**diet** *(n.)* **ምግቢ** *menan*
**dietician** *(n.)* **ዉሱን ምግቢ ተመጋቢ ሰብ** *habe*
**differ** *(v.)* **ተፈላለየ** *xduy*
**difference** *(n.)* **ኣፈላላይ** *gbresedomeǹa*
**different** *(adj.)* **ፍሉይ** *ash*
**difficult** *(adj.)* **ኣሸጋሪ** *zḧafere*
**difficulty** *(n.)* **ሽግር** *'ab gemgem baḧri*
**diffuse** *(v.)* **ዝተጋፍሐ** *eshiyawi*
**dig** *(v.)* **ኮዓተ** *'ab wey nab gWadni*

**digest** *(v.)* ሓቐቐ *änĵal*
**digestion** *(n.)* ምሕቓቕ ምግቢ *ȟatete*
**digit** *(n.)* ቁፅሪ *bïrȉare*
**digital** *(adj.)* ኣፃብዕቲ *zebal*
**dignified** *(adj.)* ግርማ ሞገስ ዘለዎ *xmuw*
**dignify** *(v.)* ኣማዕረገ *shamot*
**dignitary** *(n.)* ሰበ ስልጣን መዚ *melk'ë*
**dignity** *(n.)* ክብሪ *gonex*
**digress** *(v.)* ካብ ኣርእስቲ ወዘ *mkfa'è*
**dilapidated** *(adj.)* ዑና *äbese*
**dilate** *(v.)* ኣግፈሐ *delayi*
**dilemma** *(n.)* ሰንፈላል *tmnit*
**diligent** *(adj.)* ትጉሕ *temeneye*
**dilute** *(v.)* በፅበፀ *adgi*
**dim** *(adj.)* ዘይድሙቕ *aẗqe'ë*
**dimension** *(n.)* መለክዒ *qetalnefsi*
**diminish** *(v.)* ነከየ *qetele*
**diminution** *(n.)* ምንካይ *qeteli*
**din** *(n.)* ጫዉጫዉታ *aẗqe'ë*
**dine** *(v.)* ተደረረ *mgẗtam*
**diner** *(n.)* ተመጋቢ *agaẗeme*
**dingy** *(adj.)* ፀልማትን ረሳሕን *aḱeeba*
**dinner** *(n.)* ድራር *smm'ë*
**dinosaur** *(n.)* ዳይኖሰር *daynoser*
**dip** *(v. t)* ጠምዐ *amaḱari*
**diploma** *(n.)* ዲፕሎማ *diploma*
**diplomacy** *(n.)* ብልሃት *blhat*
**diplomat** *(n.)* ቆንስል *xa'ëreňa*
**diplomatic** *(adj.)* ቆንስላዊ *retebe*
**dipsomania** *(n.)* ሰታይ *mdeba*
**dire** *(adj.)* ጥብቂ *mdub sraȟ*
**direct** *(adj.)* ቀጥታዊ *tewahade*
**direction** *(n.)* ኣንፈት *tewahdo*
**directive** *(n.)* መምርሒ *ȟageze*
**directly** *(adv.)* ቀጥ ዝበለ *ȟagez*
**director** *(n.)* ሓላፊ/ኣመሓዳሪ *redat*
**directory** *(n.)* መሓበሪ *meȟaberi*
**dirt** *(n.)* ረስሓት *maȟber*
**dirty** *(adj.)* ረሳሕ *smm'ë*
**disability** *(n.)* ድኽመት *ztefalaleye*
**disable** *(v.)* ሃሰየ *beb'äynetu*
**disabled** *(adj.)* ዝተሃሰየ *axenan'ë*
**disadvantage** *(n.)* ጉድኣት *gemete*
**disaffected** *(adj.)* ዘይዓገበ *gmt*
**disagree** *(v.)* ተፈላለየ ተረፈ *meregagexi*
**disagreeable** *(adj.)* ዘፅልእ *aregagexe*
**disagreement** *(n.)* ዘይምስምዕማዕ *waȟs*
**disallow** *(v.)* ነፀገ *astrisks*
**disappear** *(v.)* ተኸወለ *älem*
**disappoint** *(v.)* ኣሕዘነ *azma*
**disapproval** *(n.)* ተቓዉሞ *nebe'ë*
**disapprove** *(v.)* ተቓወመ *adeneq̈e*
**disarm** *(v.)* ዕጥቂ ኣፍተሐ *dnxwuna*
**disarmament** *(n.)* ምንካይ ቁፅሪ ሰራዊት ዉግዕ *asdememe*
**disarrange** *(v.)* ኣጋዕዘየ *koḱobawi*
**disarray** *(n.)* ዕግርግር *hwtut*
**disaster** *(n.)* ከቢድ ሓደጋ/መዓት *bmgȟ̈tan*
**disastrous** *(adj.)* ሕማቕ *blxug*

**disband** *(v.)* በተነ *qWexera kewakbti*
**disbelief** *(n.)* ጥርጣረ *ëteferteña*
**disburse** *(v.)* ገንዘብ ዓደለ *snekokobi*
**disc** *(n.)* ዲስክ *snekokob*
**discard** *(v.)* ሰንደወ *tkur*
**discern** *(v.)* ተረደአ *ztefelaleye*
**discharge** *(v.)* ፍቓድ ሃበ *üq̈ba*
**disciple** *(n.)* ተኸታሊ *ab*
**discipline** *(n.)* ስነ ስርዓት *yewah*
**disclaim** *(v.)* ኣሉ በለ/ከሓደ *izihernet*
**disclose** *(v.)* ዕላዊ ገበረ *iziheerawi*
**disco** *(n.)* ዲስኮ *sporteña*
**discolour** *(v.)* ፈሰመ ሃሰሰ *sportawi*
**discomfit** *(v.)* ኣደናገረ *atlas*
**discomfort** *(n.)* ቃንዛ *hawahw*
**disconcert** *(v.)* ኣሕፈረ *deseet*
**disconnect** *(v.)* ነቐለ *atom*
**disconsolate** *(adj.)* ዝጎሃየ *atomawi*
**discontent** *(n.)* መረረት *keḧase*
**discontinue** *(v.)* ኣቋረፀ *dḧnet*
**discord** *(n.)* ቅርሕንቲ *kfli*
**discordant** *(adj.)* ዘይስማማዕ *aseqaq̈i*
**discount** *(n.)* ንካይ *gef'ë*
**discourage** *(v.)* ንምክልኻል ፀዓረ *aẗabeq̈e*
**discourse** *(n.)* መደረ *atash*
**discourteous** *(adj.)* ብዕሉግ *ẗbqet*
**discover** *(v.)* ሓድሽ ነገር ረኸበ *aẗq'ë*
**discovery** *(n.)* ሓበሬታ ረኸበ *mlu'è*
**discredit** *(v.)* ኣዋረደ *semere*
**discreet** *(adj.)* ጠጥንቁቕ *fetene*
**discrepancy** *(n.)* ኣፈላላይ *ĵemere*
**discrete** *(adj.)* ዓርሱ ዝኸኣለ *teketatele*
**discriminate** *(v.)* ፈለየ *tesatfo*
**discursive** *(adj.)* ሃውታቲ *agelgali*
**discuss** *(v.)* ተዛተየ *aq̈albo*
**discussion** *(n.)* ዘተ/ምይይጥ *ẗnquq̈*
**disdain** *(n.)* ንዕቐት *aregagexe*
**disease** *(n.)* ሕማም *waldbit*
**disembark** *(v.)* ወረደ *lbsi*
**disembodied** *(adj.)* ካ ዘይተፈለጠ ቦታ ዝመፀዕ *aqačač*
**disempower** *(v.)* ዝሓይሊ *ẗebeq̈a*
**disenchant** *(v.)* ዝተሰላቸወ *seḧabe*
**disengage** *(v.)* ኣላቐቐ *sḧbet*
**disentangle** *(v.)* መመየ *maraḱi*
**disfavour** *(n.)* ፀልኢ *bahry*
**disgrace** *(n.)* ዉርደት *margarin*
**disgruntled** *(adj.)* ዝተበሳጨ *ḧaraĵ*
**disguise** *(v.)* መልክዑ ቀየረ *kisma'ë zike'a*
**disgust** *(n.)* ፀልኢ *nebaro*
**dish** *(n.)* ሽሓነ *dehay*
**dishearten** *(v.)* ደሃለ *xebxab*
**dishonest** *(adj.)* ሽፋጢ *nay msma'ë fetena*
**dishonour** *(n.)* ዉርደት *'oditoryomme'akebi 'aderash*
**disillusion** *(v.)* እምነት ሰብ ኣፍረሰ *ወሰኸ*
**disincentive** *(n.)* ተስፋ ዘቑርፅ ነገር *neḧase*

**disinfect** *(v.)* ብፀረ ታሕዋሲያን ፀረገ *ḧatno*
**disingenuous** *(adj.)* መምሰሊ *aḱlil*
**disinherit** *(v.)* ንኸይወርስ ከልከለ *tesfa'awi*
**disintegrate** *(v.)* ሓምሸሸ *ẗbqi*
**disjointed** *(adj.)* ዘይተሓሓዝ *awustraliya*
**dislike** *(v.)* ፀልአ *ḧaqeňa*
**dislocate** *(v.)* ቆፀየ *lk'ënet*
**dislodge** *(v.)* ፈንቀለ *derasi*
**disloyal** *(adj.)* ከሓዲ *mzuz*
**dismal** *(adj.)* ዘሕዝን *mezi*
**dismantle** *(v.)* ፈታተሐ *mezeze*
**dismay** *(n.)* ሓዘን *awutizim*
**dismiss** *(v.)* ዕሽሽ በለ *r'èsetariḱ*
**dismissive** *(adj.)* ሰደደ/ፈነወ *awtokrasi*
**disobedient** *(adj.)* እምቢተኛ *wlqemelaḱi*
**disobey** *(v.)* እምቢ በለ *wlqemelaḱ*
**disorder** *(n.)* ሕንፍሽፍሽ *r'èsexḧuf*
**disorganized** *(adj.)* ብደንቢ ዘይተተለመ *awtomatik*
**disorientate** *(v.)* ኣጋገየ *awtomobilmekina*
**disown** *(v.)* ኣግለለ *r'èsemmḧdarawi*
**disparity** *(n.)* ኣፈላላይ *mrmrereesa*
**dispassionate** *(adj.)* ፍትሓዊ *qew'ï*
**dispatch** *(v.)* ለኣኸ *ḧagazi*
**dispel** *(v.)* ስሚዒቱ ኣጥፈአ *teëeq̈me*
**dispensable** *(adj.)* ዘየድሊ *ktẗqemelu tḱ'èl*
**dispensary** *(n.)* ግልጋሎት *mederegaḧ*
**dispense** *(v.)* ኣዉፂኡ ሃበ *ss'ë*
**disperse** *(v.)* ተበታተነ *ḧne fedeye*
**dispirited** *(adj.)* ድሁል *gWadena*
**displace** *(v. t)* ኣመዛበለ *ma'èkelay*
**display** *(v.)* ኣርአየ *anxar*
**displease** *(v.)* ኣበሳጨወ *xl'at*
**displeasure** *(n.)* ሕርቃን *aleye*
**disposable** *(adj.)* ተጠምቒምካሉ ዝድርበ *'ènda 'a'ëwaf*
**disposal** *(n.)* ምእላይ *snemnfar*
**dispose** *(v. t)* ኣመዓራረየ *paylot*
**dispossess** *(v.)* መንጠለ *hnẗuy*
**disproportionate** *(adj.)* ዘይመጣጠን *hnẗuyi*
**disprove** *(v.)* ጌጋ ከምዝኾነ ኣርአየ *avokado*
**dispute** *(v. i)* ክትዕ *wegede*
**disqualification** *(n.)* ብቕዓት-ማጣት *gusya*
**disqualify** *(v.)* ንኸይተሳተፍ ከልከለ *amene*
**disquiet** *(n.)* ንኸይተሳተፍ *'ako'awi*
**disregard** *(v. t)* ሸለል በለ *texebeye*
**disrepair** *(n.)* ዝተበላሸወ ህንፃ ወዘተ *neq̈ḧe*
**disreputable** *(adj.)* መታለሊ *neq̈ḧe*
**disrepute** *(n.)* ንዕቐት *seleme*
**disrespect** *(n.)* ንዕቐት *genzeb*
**disrobe** *(v.)* ክዳኑ ኣዉፀአ *nab rḧuq̈*

**disrupt** *(v.)* አቋረፀ *temsaẗ*
**dissatisfaction** *(n.)* ቅርታ *zer'ëd*
**dissect** *(v.)* በጢሑ ተመራመረ *zeskaȟkȟ*
**dissent** *(v.)* ተፈለየ *nȟaxir gzee*
**dissertation** *(n.)* መመረቒ ፅሑፍ *gaȟmaẗ*
**dissident** *(n.)* ብርቱዕ ተቓዋሚ *blshw*
**dissimulate** *(v.)* ትክክለኛ ስሚዒቱ ሓብአ *fas*
**dissipate** *(v.)* አዳኸመ *meq̈elesi*
**dissolve** *(v. t)* ሓቖቖ *meq̈eles*
**dissuade** *(v.)* ኣታረፈ *'atarefe*
**distance** *(n.)* ርሕቀት *rȟqet*
**distant** *(adj.)* ርሑቕ *a'ëzemzeme*
**distaste** *(n.)* ፅልኢ *hxan*
**distil** *(v.)* ፅረየ *zeymsmma'ë*
**distillery** *(n.)* ኣፅረየ መሻሸሒ *hbey*
**distinct** *(adj.)* ብቐሊሉ ዝስማዕ *hxan*
**distinction** *(n.)* አኣፈላይ/ፍልልይ *beetelbo*
**distinguish** *(v. t)* ፈለየ *zban*
**distort** *(v.)* ኣዛነዐ *ändiȟq̈o*
**distract** *(v.)* ኣቓልቦ ሰብ ሃወኸ *ȟalefe*
**distraction** *(n.)* ዝርብሽ ነገር *t'ëynti*
**distress** *(n.)* ከቢድ ጭንቀት *mgusa'ë*
**distribute** *(v.)* ዓደለ *temekuro*
**distributor** *(n.)* ዕደላ ሰብ *ashmurawi*
**district** *(n.)* ክልል *red'e*
**distrust** *(n.)* ጥርጣረ *melsegbri*
**disturb** *(v.)* ረበሸ *mehazi*
**ditch** *(n. )* መትረብ *mahder*
**dither** *(v.)* ኣመንተወ *bdȟrit*
**ditto** *(n.)* ከምኡ *zban medreḱ*
**dive** *(v.)* ቲፎ ኣተወ *zban aser*
**diverge** *(v.)* ኣንፈቱ ቀየረ *ndȟrit*
**diverse** *(adj.)* ዝተፈላዩ *zban may*
**diversion** *(n.)* ኣንፈት ምቕያር *beekon*
**diversity** *(n.)* ፍልልይ *bakteriya*
**divert** *(v. t)* ኣንፈት ቀየረ *ȟmaq̈*
**divest** *(v.)* ኣዉፀአ *arma*
**divide** *(v.)* መቓለ *bȟmaq̈*
**dividend** *(n.)* ኽፍፍሊ *badminten*
**divine** *(adj.)* ኣምላኻዊ *agereme*
**divinity** *(n.)* ኣምላኽነት *mel'e*
**division** *(n.)* ክፍፍል *ga'äz*
**divorce** *(n.)* ፍትሕ *geflaw*
**divorcee** *(n.)* ዝተፋትሐ *ȟbur slmat*
**divulge** *(v.)* ምሽጥር ነገር *waȟs*
**do** *(v.)* ገበረ *polis*
**docile** *(adj.)* ምእዙዝ *meshȟabi*
**dock** *(n.)* ፋርዳ *dereq̈e*
**docket** *(n.)* ሓጺር ጽሑፍ *ȟaxir xȟuf*
**doctor** *(n.)* ሓኪም *ènda bani*
**doctorate** *(n.)* ደረጃ *dereĵa*
**doctrine** *(n.)* እምነት *segenet*
**document** *(n.)* ሰነድ *beraȟ*
**documentary** *(n.)* ዶኩመንታዊ *dokumentawi*
**dodge** *(v. t)* ተመኹለየ *ku'ëso*
**doe** *(n.)* ኣንስተይቲ ማንቲለ *gẗmi wey derfi*
**dog** *(n.)* ከልቢ *bale*
**dogma** *(n.)* ሕጊ *balun*
**dogmatic** *(adj.)* ሕጋዊ *nay medmexi wereq̈et*
**doldrums** *(n.)* ሓዘን *belesan*
**doll** *(n.)* ባምቡላ *belesan*

**dollar** *(n.)* **ዶላር** *arqay*
**domain** *(n.)* **ዓይነት ፍልጠት** *agede*
**dome** *(n.)* **ጉልላት** *tera*
**domestic** *(adj.)* **ናይ ዉሽጢ ዓዲ** *banana*
**domicile** *(n.)* **አድራሻ** *me'èseri*
**dominant** *(adj.)* **ዓብላላይ** *meĵeneni*
**dominate** *(v.)* **ዓብለለ** *shfta werebela*
**dominion** *(n.)* **ስልጣን** *merzi smi*
**donate** *(v.)* **ለገሰ** *gewta*
**donkey** *(n.)* **አድጊ** *gewtat*
**donor** *(n.)* **ለጋሲ ሰብ** *benaĵr*
**doom** *(n.)* **ሞት** *ḧayere*
**door** *(n.)* **ማዕፆ** *ïrzya*
**dormitory** *(n.)* **መደቀሲ ክፍሊ** *medendel*
**dose** *(n.)* **ዓቐን** *banĵo*
**dossier** *(n.)* **መዝገብ** *banki*
**dot** *(n.)* **ነጥቢ** *mekWanen*
**dote** *(v.)* **አፍቀረ** *ïfush*
**double** *(adj.)* **ድርብ** *ïfesha*
**doubt** *(n.)* **ጥርጣረ** *sendeq̈*
**dough** *(n.)* **ብሒቝ** *be'äl*
**down** *(adv. )* **ኣብ ታሕቲ** *tewazeye*
**downfall** *(n.)* **ዉድቀት** *ïmqet*
**download** *(v.)* **ዝጫነ** *meïmq̈awi*
**downpour** *(n.)* **ዝፈሰሰ** *aïemeq̈e*
**dowry** *(n.)* **ገዝሚ** *metawer*
**doze** *(v. i)* **ሰለም ኣበለ** *änqaribo*
**dozen** *(n.)* **ደርዘን** *barbarawi*
**drab** *(adj.)* **ዘአይስሕብ ዘይብል** *barbarawi*
**draft** *(n.)* **ንድፊ** *ndfi*
**drag** *(v. t)* **ጎተተ** *wega'i*
**dragon** *(n.)* **ሓላዉ** *qemqamay*
**drain** *(v. t)* **ኣፅረረ** *gïmi wey derfi*
**drama** *(n.)* **ተዋስኦ** *ïrḧu*
**dramatic** *(adj.)* **ዘርገም** *bq̈lu'ë*
**dramatist** *(n.)* **ፀሓፊ ተዋስኦ** *waga 'ëdaga*
**drastic** *(adj.)* **ጥብቂ** *tegačewe telag'ë*
**draught** *(n.)* **ንፋስ** *qraf*
**draw** *(v.)* **ሰኣለ** *sgem*
**drawback** *(n.)* **መሰናኽል** *meḱzen*
**drawer** *(n.)* **ትሬቶ** *baromeeter*
**drawing** *(n.)* **ዝወቀለ** *balabat*
**dread** *(v.t)* **ሰግአ** *baraka*
**dreadful** *(adj.)* **ኣዝዩ ሕማቕ** *meshenit*
**dream** *(n.)* **ሕልሚ** *gdb*
**dreary** *(adj.)* **ዘሕዝን** *bermil*
**drench** *(v.)* **ኣጠልቀየ** *meḱan*
**dress** *(v.)* **ተኸደነ** *medendel*
**dressing** *(n.)* **ናይ ሰላጣ መመቀሪ** *ënqfat*
**drift** *(v.)* **ዘገምታ** *gdb*
**drill** *(n.)* **መንደል** *ïebeq̈a*
**drink** *(v. t)* **መስተ ፈሳሲ** *bedela*
**drip** *(v. i)* **ጥብጥብ በለ** *serete*
**drive** *(v.)* **ዘወረ** *seret'albo*
**driver** *(n.)* **ዘዋሪ ማኪና** *tḧtebeet*
**drizzle** *(n.)* **ኣኻፈየ** *ḧafar*
**droll** *(adj.)* **ኣዘናጋዒ** *seretawi*
**droop** *(v.)* **ደነነ** *riḧan*
**drop** *(v.)* **ወደቐ** *bazilika*
**dross** *(n.)* **ዘይረብሕ** *sḧani*
**drought** *(n.)* **ድርቂ** *seret*
**drown** *(v.)* **ጥሒሊ ሞተ ቀተለ** *texelwe*
**drowse** *(v.)* **ተታኸሰ** *zenbil*
**drug** *(n.)* **ሓሸሽ** *bas 'äynet 'äsa*
**drum** *(n.)* **ከበሮ** *dq̈ala*

**drunkard** *(adj.)* ሰኽራም *shelele*
**dry** *(adj.)* ደረቕ *ërdi*
**dryer** *(n.)* ኣድራቒ *menka'ë*
**dual** *(adj.)* ፅምዲ *èkub*
**dubious** *(adj.)* ዘተጠራጠረ *mḧxab*
**duck** *(n.)* ደርሆ ማይ *aleḱe*
**duct** *(n.)* ቱቦ *hwteta*
**dudgeon** *(n.)* ሕርቃን *batik*
**due** *(adj.)* ዝሰዓበ *betri polis*
**duel** *(n.)* ቅልስ *boẗoloni*
**duet** *(n.)* ክልቲ *tegedam*
**dull** *(adj.)* ዘፅልእ *ketkete*
**dullard** *(n.)* ዘይርደእ *'ahadu kebid bret*
**duly** *(adv. )* ብትኽክል *wg'è*
**dumb** *(adj.)* ዓባስ/በሃም *ḧbur slmat*
**dummy** *(n.)* ክዳን መርኣይ ባንቡላ *mesenaḱl*
**dump** *(n.)* ደርበየ *wečeče*
**dung** *(n.)* ዒባ *furda*
**dungeon** *(n.)* ትሕቲ መሬት ዝርከብ ክፍሊ *sanĵa*
**duo** *(n.)* ብሕባር ዝደርፉ ክልተ ሰባት *bazar shuq̈*
**dupe** *(v.)* ኣታለለ *bazuqa*
**duplex** *(n.)* ክልተ *kone*
**duplicate** *(adj.)* ኣብዝሐ *nab dendes 'axege'ë*
**duplicity** *(n.)* ሸፍጢ *mena*
**durable** *(adj.)* ንብዙሕ እዋን ዝፀንሕ *ënqo*
**duration** *(n.)* ዉሱን እዋን *qorqWAr*
**during** *(prep.)* ኣብ እዋን *bigl*
**dusk** *(n.)* ኣጋ ምሸት *metkob*
**dust** *(n.)* ደሮና *brčqo*
**duster** *(n.)* መወልወሊ ጨርቂ *gemel*
**dutiful** *(adj.)* ሰብ መኽበሪ *baldongWa*
**duty** *(n.)* ሓላፍነት *dbi*
**duvet** *(n.)* ኮበርታ *teshekeme*
**dwarf** *(n.)* ደኽዳኽ *čḧmi*
**dwell** *(v.)* ነበረ *ma'èzn*
**dwelling** *(n.)* መንበሪ ቦታ *ènssa*
**dwindle** *(v. t)* ወሓደ/ነኣሰ *ènssawi*
**dye** *(n.)* ቀለም ለኸየ *laxeye*
**dynamic** *(adj.)* ሓያል/ጥንኩር *laxeye*
**dynamics** *(n.)* ሰዓማይ *maraḱi*
**dynamite** *(n.)* ደማሚት *amelk'ë*
**dynamo** *(n.)* ዲናሞ *desta*
**dynasty** *(n.)* ስርወ መንግስቲ *melk'ë*
**dysentery** *(n.)* ሕመም *biver*
**dysfunctional** *(adj.)* ብልሽዊ *ahd'e*
**dyslexia** *(n.)* ዝእንበቢ *mḱnyatu bmknyat*
**dyspepsia** *(n.)* ብቐሊሉ ዘይሓቅቕ ምግቢ *mlkt*

# E

**each** *(adj.)* ሕድሕድ *kone*
**eager** *(adj.)* ህንጡዉ *me'ërefi*
**eagle** *(n.)* ንስሪ *menxef*
**ear** *(n.)* እዝኒ *me'ëqob snkulane'a'èmro*
**earl** *(n.)* ምዕሩግ *ačefeq̈e*
**early** *(adj.)* መጀመርታ *nhbi*
**earn** *(v.)* ሰረሑ ረኸበ *wa'ëro*
**earnest** *(adj.)* ቅኑዕ *sga kebti*
**earth** *(n.)* ዓለም *regWid*

**earthen** *(adj.)* **ብጭቃ ዝተሰርሐ** *mlkt*
**earthly** *(adj.)* **ምድራዊ** *bira*
**earthquake** *(n.)* **ራዕዲ መሬት** *bnĵr*
**ease** *(n.)* **ቅለት** *masa*
**east** *(n.)* **ምብራቕ** *mbraq̈*
**Easter** *(n.)* **ትንሳኤ** *werede 'agaẗeme*
**eastern** *(adj.)* **ኣብ ምብራቕ ዝርከብ** *beq̈'ë*
**easy** *(adj.)* **ቀሊል** *qdmi*
**eat** *(v.)* **በልዐ** *ሳቻዷሙ*
**eatable** *(adj.)* **ዝብላዕ** *agereme*
**eatery** *(n.)* **በቤት ብልዒ** *me'äde*
**ebb** *(n.)* **ዳሕረዋይ** *lemene*
**ebony** *(n.)* **ደረቕ** *welede*
**ebullient** *(adj.)* **ልበ ምሉእ** *lemani*
**eccentric** *(adj.)* **ዘይልሙድ** *ĵemere*
**echo** *(n.)* **መቓልሕ** *meĵemerta*
**eclipse** *(n.)* **ግርደት** *grdet*
**ecology** *(n.)* **ስነ ምሕዳር** *ab kndi*
**economic** *(adj.)* **ቁጠባዊ** *gebere*
**economical** *(adj.)* **ቆጣቢ** *ẗebay*
**economics** *(n.)* **መፅናዕቲ ሃብቲ ቁጠባ** *qWerexe*
**economy** *(n.)* **ሃብቲ ቁጠባ** *čekan*
**ecstasy** *(n.)* **ፍሰሃ** *t'èzaz*
**edge** *(n.)* **ወሰናወሰን** *bdȟrit*
**edgy** *(adj.)* **ቁጡዕ** *temelkete*
**edible** *(adj.)* **ዝብላዕ** *amesgani*
**edict** *(n.)* **ኣዋጅ** *faȟray*
**edifice** *(n.)* **ህንጻ** *hnxa*
**edit** *(v.)* **ንኽሕተም ኣሰናደአ** *qeẗqeẗe*
**edition** *(n.)* **መሰናድኦ** *dnguy*
**editor** *(n.)* **ኣሰናዳኢ** *ẗemere*
**editorial** *(adj.)* **ናይ ኣሰናዳኢ መልእኽቲ** *tef'e*
**educate** *(v.)* **ኣማሃረ** *ačeneq̈e*
**education** *(n.)* **ትምህርቲ** *bgeega 'ar'aye*
**efface** *(v.)* **ኣጥፈአ** *èmnet*
**effect** *(n.)* **ሳዕቤን** *amene*
**effective** *(adj.)* **ዉፅኢታዊ** *aqWenaxebe*
**effeminate** *(adj.)* **ሰበይታይ** *qačl*
**effete** *(adj.)* **ዝተዳኸመ** *xbq̈ti*
**efficacy** *(n.)* **ፈዋሳይነት** *teba'asay*
**efficiency** *(n.)* **ብቕዓት** *ba'èsi mdlay*
**efficient** *(adj.)* **ብቑዕ** *neqewe*
**effigy** *(n.)* **ሓወልቲ** *menafȟ*
**effort** *(n.)* **ፃዕረ** *kebdi*
**egg** *(n.)* **እንቋቑሖ** *te'asasere*
**ego** *(n.)* **ባዕሊ** *ba'ëli*
**egotism** *(n.)* **ተጀሃሪ ዝኾነ ሰብ** *fq̈ur*
**eight** *(adj. & n.)* **ሸሞንተ** *tẗti*
**eighteen** *(adj. & n.)* **ዓሰርተ ሸሞንተ** *qulfi*
**eighty** *(adj. & n.)* **ሰማንያ** *gWahaye*
**either** *(adv.)* **ወይ** *'aqalbo 'azenbele*
**ejaculate** *(v.)* **ኣምነወ** *rbo*
**eject** *(v. t)* **ኣባረረ** *leweye*
**elaborate** *(adj.)* **ዘዝተሓላለኸን ዝርዝርን** *tẗti*
**elapse** *(v.)* **ግዜ ሓለፈ** *burakee*
**elastic** *(adj.)* **ላስቲክ** *gebiresenay*
**elbow** *(n.)* **ኵርናዕ ኢድ** *geza qeshi*
**elder** *(adj.)* **ዓብይ** *gbresenay*
**elderly** *(adj.)* **ኣረጊት/ሽማግሌ** *lewah*
**elect** *(v.)* **መረፀ** *ȟagazi*

**election** *(n.)* **መረፃ** *gbresenay*
**elective** *(adj.)* **ብመረፃ ዝተመረፀ** *gbresenayawi*
**electorate** *(n.)* **መራፂ ህዝቢ** *lewah*
**electric** *(adj.)* **ኮረንቲ ዝጥቀም** *tewhbo*
**electrician** *(n.)* **ኪኢላ ኮረንቲ** *awrese*
**electricity** *(n.)* **ኮረንቲ መብራሕቲ** *wrsha*
**electrify** *(v.)* **ዝለዓለ ስሚዒት** *weq̈ese*
**electrocute** *(v.)* **ብኮረንቲ ኣቑሰለ** *zerefe*
**electronic** *(adj.)* **ኤልክትሮኒክስ** *ḧazen*
**elegance** *(n.)* **ግሩምት** *lemani*
**elegant** *(adj.)* **ግርማ ሞገስ ዘለዎ** *kewḧi bered*
**element** *(n.)* **ኣገዳሲ ኣካል** *denqoro*
**elementary** *(adj.)* **ናይ ቀዳማይ ብርኪ ጀመርቲ** *fre*
**elephant** *(n.)* **ሓርማዝ** *ëbdbd*
**elevate** *(v.)* **ደረጃ ሃበ** *medeqesi*
**elevator** *(n.)* **ናይ ባላሶ መደየቢት** *lemene*
**eleven** *(adj. & n.)* **ዓሰርተ ሓደ** *ashegere*
**elf** *(n.)* **ፀይቂ/ርጉም** *'ab ẗqa*
**elicit** *(v.)* **ሓበሬታ ረኸበ** *kebebe*
**eligible** *(adj.)* **ብቑዕ** *ameraseḧe*
**eliminate** *(v.)* **ኣልገሰ** *meḱoster*
**elite** *(n.)* **እንቋቑሖ መሰል** *'ènqWAq̈uḧo mesel*
**ellipse** *(n.)* **ሞልሟል** *äwdi xeq̈eẗe*
**elocution** *(n.)* **ክእለት ዘረባ** *bzbelexe*
**elongate** *(v.)* **ነዊሕ** *newḧe*
**elope** *(v.)* **ኮብለለ** *sheleme*
**eloquence** *(n.)* **መዳረ ሰብ** *tegaḧtene*
**else** *(adv.)* **ብተወሳኺ** *teïal'ë*
**elucidate** *(v. t)* **ኣብራህረህ** *kede*
**elude** *(v.)* **ተኸወለ** *ked'ë*
**elusion** *(n.)* **ምርካብ** *qẗfet*
**elusive** *(adj.)* **ንምርካብ** *zḧashe*
**emaciated** *(adj.)* **ማሕቋቑ** *'ab mengo*
**email** *(n.)* **መልእኽቲ** *syaf*
**emancipate** *(v. t)* **ሓራ ኣዉፀአ** *meste*
**emasculate** *(v.)* **ኣዳኸመ** *aḱeeba*
**embalm** *(v.)* **በልሰነ** *belsene*
**embankment** *(n.)* **ገምገም** *gemgem*
**embargo** *(n.)* **እገ'ዳ** *'ègeda*
**embark** *(v. t)* **ደየበ** *sereye*
**embarrass** *(v.)* **ኣሕፈረ** *knyew*
**embassy** *(n.)* **ኢምባሲ** *'ab keklte*
**embattled** *(adj.)* **ብሽግር ዝኸበበ** *frqi beb'ämet*
**embed** *(v.)* **ኣጣበቐ** *mq̈nan*
**embellish** *(v.)* **ኣፀባበቐ** *meq̈nan*
**embitter** *(v.)* **ኣበሳጨወ** *salbeeta*
**emblem** *(n.)* **ኣርማ** *mexḧaf qdus*
**embodiment** *(v. t.)* **ኣርኣያ** *zrzrexḧufat*
**embolden** *(v.)* **ኣደፋፈረ** *fetaw mexḧaf*
**emboss** *(v.)* **ኣጉለሐ** *'aguleḧe*
**embrace** *(v.)* **ሓቖፈ** *čwadamnat*
**embroidery** *(n.)* **ጥልፊ** *teq̈WAyeq̈We*
**embryo** *(n.)* **ድቂ** *bshkleta*
**emend** *(v.)* **ኣረመ** *semeye*
**emerald** *(n.)* **ስመራግድ** *teḧatati*

**emerge** *(v.)* ተቐልቐለ *smay*
**emergency** *(n.)* ሓደጋ *aḱbere*
**emigrate** *(v.)* ተሰደደ *mmshaï*
**eminence** *(n.)* ዝና/ክብሪ *klte 'ämetawi*
**eminent** *(adj.)* ስሙይ *qareeza*
**emissary** *(n.)* ልኡኽ *l'uḱ*
**emit** *(v.)* ድምጺ ፈነወ *äbi*
**emollient** *(adj.)* ዘረጋግእ *drb mer'ä*
**emolument** *(n.)* ክስቢ *ḧluf*
**emotion** *(n.)* ብርቱዕ ስሚዒት *mäqnan*
**emotional** *(adj.)* ናይ ስሚዒት *bshkleta*
**emotive** *(adj.)* ስምዒታዊ *sm'ïtawi*
**empathy** *(n.)* ተደናጋጽነት *tedenagaxnet*
**emperor** *(n.)* ሃፀይ *ḧamot*
**emphasis** *(n.)* ጠመተ *drblsanawi*
**emphasize** *(v.)* ጠመተ ሃበ *gozomo*
**emphatic** *(adj.)* ዘየማትእ *zeyemat'è*
**empire** *(n.)* ግዝኣት *bilyardo*
**employ** *(v.)* ቆፀረ *bilyon*
**employee** *(n.)* ሰራሕተኛ *habtam*
**employer** *(n.)* ቖጻሪ *'äbi ma'ëbel*
**empower** *(v.)* ስልጣን ሃበ *qofo*
**empress** *(n.)* ንግስቲ ነገስት *ëxfi*
**empty** *(adj.)* ጥርሑ *ţemere*
**emulate** *(v. t)* ተወዳደረ *tewedadere*
**enable** *(v.)* ኣኽኣለ *fenţezya*
**enact** *(v.)* ሓገገ *be'äl le'ät menexr*
**enamel** *(n.)* ኣናመል *'anamel*
**enamour** *(v. t)* ኣዝዩ ዝፈተወ *ikoloĵi*
**encapsulate** *(v.)* ኣብ ካፕሱላ ዓጸወ *'ab kapsula 'äxewe*
**encase** *(v.)* ሓፀረ ጠቕለለ *tariḱ hywet bkal'è seb ztexaḧfe nay ḧade*
**enchant** *(v.)* ምሒር ማረኸ *ikoloĵi*
**encircle** *(v. t)* ከበበ ሓዘ *snehywet*
**enclave** *(n.)* ከተማ *mrmrereesa*
**enclose** *(v.)* ኢነየ ሰርሐ *xmdeselfawi*
**enclosure** *(n.)* ምኽላል *mḱlal*
**encode** *(v.)* ኣሸፈረ *'ashefere*
**encompass** *(v.)* ብዙሕ ነገር ኣጠቓለለ *influwenza*
**encore** *(n.)* ተወሳኺ ምርኢት *mwlad*
**encounter** *(v.)* ኣጓነፈ ኣጋጠመ *bshkoti*
**encourage** *(v.)* ኣተባብዐ *gemese*
**encroach** *(v.)* በዝበዘ *gbresedomeṅa*
**encrypt** *(v.)* ነዝዐ *abun*
**encumber** *(v.)* ኣፃገመ *b'ëray bereḱa*
**encyclopaedia** *(n.)* **eensayklopidya** ኢንሳይክሎፒድያ
**end** *(n. )* ጫፍ *wa'ëro*
**endanger** *(v.)* ንሓደጋ ኣሳጠሐ *neḱese*
**endear** *(v.)* ስሙይ ገበረ *wega'i*
**endearment** *(n.)* ፍቕሪ መግለጺ ቃል *merir*
**endeavour** *(v.)* ፀዓረ *fenţegar*
**endemic** *(adj.)* በብርቂ *hatefe*
**endorse** *(v.)* ደገፈ *xelim*
**endow** *(v.)* ገንዘብ ወፈየ *blakberi*
**endure** *(v.)* ተፃወረ *seleeda*
**enemy** *(n.)* ፀላኢ *axelemete*

**energetic** *(adj.)* ሓያል *xelim mezgeb*
**energy** *(n.)* ጉልበት *tahdidemqla'ë*
**enfeeble** *(v.)* ኣዳኸመ *xlmate*
**enfold** *(v.)* ሓቖፈ *ḧaq̈ofe*
**enforce** *(v.)* ኣኽበረ *fḧna*
**enfranchise** *(v.)* ለቐቐ *leq̈eq̈e*
**engage** *(v.)* ኣድሕበ *'ab keklte*
**engagement** *(n.)* ሕፀ *kesese*
**engine** *(n.)* ሞተር *xa'ëdewe*
**engineer** *(n.)* መሃንዲስ *lzub*
**English** *(n.)* እንግሊዝኛ *ïrḧu*
**engrave** *(v.)* ፅሑፍ/ቅርፂ ቀረፀ *koberta*
**engross** *(v.)* መሰጠ *dmxi*
**engulf** *(v.)* ወሓጠ *weḧaïe*
**enigma** *(n.)* ምሽጥር *netgWi*
**enjoy** *(v.)* ኣዘዘ *qlu'ë*
**enlarge** *(v.)* ኣዐበየ *halhalta*
**enlighten** *(v.)* ሓበሬታ ሃበ *ĵakeet*
**enlist** *(v.)* ደፋፍአ *axa'ëdewe*
**enliven** *(v.)* ከምዝስሕብ ገበረ *qezaḧi*
**enmity** *(n.)* ፅልኢ *èmbee'ë*
**enormous** *(adj.)* ገዚፍ *demeye*
**enough** *(adj.)* እኹል *qana*
**enquire** *(v.)* ሓተተ *aber*
**enquiry** *(n.)* ምፅራይ *myuq̈ bele*
**enrage** *(v.)* ኣገሃየ *ḧawawese*
**enrapture** *(v.)* ብሓጐስ ፈንጨሐ *bḧagWas fenčeḧe*
**enrich** *(v.)* ኣማዕበለ *bareḱe*
**enrol** *(v.)* ተመዝገበ *bruḱ*
**enshrine** *(v.)* ኣኽበረ *mrq̈a*
**enslave** *(v.)* ባርያ ገበረ ገዝአ *wag*
**ensue** *(v.)* ሰዓበ *ëwur*
**ensure** *(v.)* ኣረጋገፀ *ämete*
**entangle** *(v. t)* ሓለኸ *gudlet*
**enter** *(v.)* ኣተወ *semsem 'abele*
**enterprise** *(n.)* ትካል *garadi*
**entertain** *(v.)* ኣእንገደ *meq̈alḧ*
**entertainment** *(n.)* መዘናግዒ *taḧgWas*
**enthral** *(v.)* መሰጠ *may m'ëgo*
**enthrone** *(v.)* ኣብ ዙፋን ከፍ በለ *ḧgus*
**enthusiasm** *(n.)* ውዕውዕ ስምዒት *w'ëw'ë sm'ït*
**enthusiastic** *(n.)* ኣፍቃሪ *hbobla wrči*
**entice** *(v.)* ኣህረፈ *nefḧe*
**entire** *(adj.)* ሙሉእ *qWAnïa 'äsa*
**entirety** *(n.)* ሙሉእ ብሙሉእ *nïab*
**entitle** *(v.)* መሰል ሃበ *qexri*
**entity** *(n.)* ዓርሱ ዝኸኣለ ነገር *gla'ë*
**entomology** *(n.)* ባልዕ ምርምሪ *dndela*
**entourage** *(n.)* ዓጀብቲ *ëgta*
**entrails** *(n.)* ዛንጡ መዓንጡ *sayit*
**entrance** *(n.)* መእተዊ *qWendefe*
**entrap** *(v. t.)* ሓለኸ *'a'äshewe*
**entreat** *(v.)* ተማሕፀነ *dem*
**entreaty** *(v. t)* ምሕፅንታ *dem mfsas*
**entrench** *(v.)* ኣስረፀ *demawi*
**entrepreneur** *(n.)* ስራህ ፈጣሪ ሰብ *ëmbaba*
**entrust** *(v.)* ሓላፍነት ሃበ *sregtr*
**entry** *(n.)* ምእታዉ *ëmbaba*
**enumerate** *(v. t)* ዘርዘረ *nïab qelem*
**enunciate** *(v.)* ቃላት ኣንበበ *tkWa'ë*
**envelop** *(v.)* ሸፈነ *kamcha*
**envelope** *(n.)* ቡስጣ *nefese*
**enviable** *(adj.)* ዘቕንእ *qWendefe*

**envious** *(adj.)* ቀናእ *qena'è*
**environment** *(n.)* ከባቢ *gWamed*
**envisage** *(v.)* ተንበየ *semayawi ȟbri*
**envoy** *(n.)* ልኡኽ *mexadfo*
**envy** *(n.)* ቅንኣት *ťemberber bele*
**epic** *(n.)* ነዊሕ ግጥሚ *godim*
**epicure** *(n.)* ኣስተማቓሪ *'astemaq̈ari*
**epidemic** *(n.)* ለበዳ ሕማም *tȟzto mexȟaf*
**epidermis** *(n.)* ላዕለዋይ ክፋል ቆርበት *amleq̈We*
**epigram** *(n.)* መባእታ *ȟafere*
**epilepsy** *(n.)* ትግርትያ *tgrtya*
**epilogue** *(n.)* ድሕረ-ጽሑፍ *dȟrexȟuf*
**episode** *(n.)* ፍፃመ/ተዳንፎ *mefles*
**epistle** *(n.)* መልእኽቲ *mel'èkti*
**epitaph** *(n.)* ጽሑፈ-መቓብር *xȟufemeq̈abr*
**epitome** *(n.)* ጽማቖ *xmaq̈Wi*
**epoch** *(n.)* ዘበን *ȟaf kof bele*
**equal** *(adj.)* ማዕረ *geltew*
**equalize** *(v. t)* ማዕረ ገበረ *ȟabere*
**equate** *(v.)* ማዕረ ጌሩ ረአየ *ĵlesebeyti*
**equation** *(n.)* ማዕረ ጌሩ ሃበ *akalawi*
**equator** *(n.)* ንፍቀ ምድሪ መሬት *akal*
**equestrian** *(adj.)* ፈረስ ጋለቢ *zeb'ëna*
**equidistant** *(adj.)* ማዕረ ዝርሕቀቱ *ma'ëre zrȟqetu*
**equilateral** *(adj.)* ማዕረ-ጐድናዊ *ma'ëregWadnawi*
**equilibrium** *(n.)* ሚዛን *tewelawele*
**equip** *(v.)* ኣማልአ *ȟaqi zeyblu*
**equipment** *(n.)* መሳርሒ *mguli 'ančwa*
**equitable** *(adj.)* ሚዛናዊ *meflȟi*
**equity** *(n.)* ፍትሓዊነት *nawxeen*
**equivalent** *(adj.)* ማዕረ *ma'ëre*
**equivocal** *(adj.)* ማንታ ቃል *manta qal*
**era** *(n.)* ዘበን *gundi*
**eradicate** *(v.)* መሓወ *meȟawe*
**erase** *(v.)* ደምሰሰ *demsese*
**erect** *(adj.)* ቅኑዕ ዝበለ *bomb*
**erode** *(v.)* ሸርሸረ *debdebe*
**erogenous** *(adj.)* ኤሮሳዊ *eerosawi*
**erosion** *(n.)* ፍግረት *fgret*
**erotic** *(adj.)* ፍቕራዊ *fq̈rawi*
**err** *(v.)* ተጋገየ *ákeze*
**errand** *(n.)* መልኣኽቲ *w'ël*
**errant** *(adj.)* ግጉይ *gguy*
**erratic** *(adj.)* ዘይስሩዕ *äxmi*
**erroneous** *(adj.)* ግጉይ *gguy*
**error** *(n.)* ጌጋ *geega*
**erstwhile** *(adj.)* ቀደም *qedem*
**erudite** *(adj.)* ምሁር *äxam*
**erupt** *(v.)* ነቶገ *netoge*
**escalate** *(v.)* ኣዕረገ *'a'ërege*
**escalator** *(n.)* ኣደያቢ *'adeyabi*
**escapade** *(n.)* ጽልቋ *xlqWA*
**escape** *(v.i)* ኣምለጠ *mexȟafawi*
**escort** *(n.)* መሰነዪ *meseneyi*
**esoteric** *(adj.)* ናይ ክቲ *nay kti*
**especial** *(adj.)* ዝበለፀ *ȟto*
**especially** *(adv.)* ብፍላይ *ťegele'albo*
**espionage** *(n.)* ስለላ *msfaȟ*

**espouse** *(v.)* ድጋፍ ሃበ *senkati*
**espresso** *(n.)* ስፕሬሶ *newiȟ sa'èni*
**essay** *(n.)* ሓጺር ፅሁፍ *gojo*
**essence** *(n.)* ፍረ ነገር *kontroband*
**essential** *(adj.)* ዝኣዩ ነገር *mrko*
**establish** *(v.)* ኣጣየሽ *dob*
**establishment** *(n.)* ትካል *gWargWaȟe*
**estate** *(n.)* ርስቲ *tewelde*
**esteem** *(n.)* ኽብሪ *werede*
**estimate** *(v. t)* ግምት *teleqȟe*
**estranged** *(adj.)* ነጸለ *nexele*
**et cetera** *(adv.)* ወዘተረፈ *ȟaleq̈a*
**eternal** *(adj.)* ዘልኣለማዊ *zel'alemawi*
**eternity** *(n.)* ዘልኣለማዊነት *sne'atklti*
**ethic** *(n)* ስነ ምግባር *klti'u*
**ethical** *(n.)* ስነ ምግባራዊ *ashegere*
**ethnic** *(adj.)* ናይ ዓሌት *ïrmuz*
**etiquette** *(n. )* ደምቢ *qarana*
**etymology** *(n.)* ፍልቀተ-ቃል *flqeteqal*
**eunuch** *(n.)* ስሉብ *gWadena*
**euphoria** *(n.)* ጦብላሕታ *neťere*
**euro** *(n.)* ገንዘብ *genzeb*
**European** *(n.)* ናይ ኣዉሮፓ *ȟaxere*
**euthanasia** *(n.)* ምሕረተ-ቅትለት *mȟreteqtlet*
**evacuate** *(v.)* ኣልቀቐ *deret'albo*
**evade** *(v. t)* ኣምለጠ *legas*
**evaluate** *(v. i)* ገምገመ *lgsi*
**evaporate** *(v.)* ሃፈፈ *ȟq̈ufi'ëmbaba*
**evasion** *(n.)* ምዝንጋዕ *mznga'ë*
**evasive** *(adj.)* ጉስያዊ *gusyawi*
**eve** *(n.)* ድሮ *qesti*
**even** *(adj.)* ለሚፅ *segede*
**evening** *(n.)* ምሸት *me'änaťu*
**event** *(n.)* ፍፃመ *das*
**eventually** *(adv.)* ኣብ መወዳእታ *čȟolo*
**ever** *(adv.)* ዋላ ሓደሻዕ *sanduq̈*
**every** *(adj.)* ሕድሕድ *tegadalay*
**evict** *(v.)* ኣባረረ *gusťi*
**eviction** *(n.)* ዝባረረ *wedi*
**evidence** *(n.)* መረዳእታ *ademe*
**evident** *(adj.)* ብንፁር *n'èsnet*
**evil** *(adj.)* ጨካን *bikini*
**evince** *(v.)* ብጋህዲ ኣርኣየ *dgaf*
**evoke** *(v.)* ኣዘከረ *benaĵr*
**evolution** *(n.)* ኣዝጋሚ ዕብየት *medegef*
**evolve** *(v.)* ቀስ ብቐስ ዓበየ *teĵehari*
**exact** *(adj.)* ትኽክለኛ *breyl*
**exaggerate** *(v.)* ኣጋነነ *ȟangol*
**exaggeration** *(n.)* ግነት *lgWam*
**exalt** *(v.)* ልዕል ኣበለ *čenfer*
**exam** *(n.)* ፈተና *ëlamet*
**examination** *(n.)* ምርመራ *anbelbele*
**examine** *(v.)* ኣፅነዐ *brandi*
**examinee** *(n.)* ተመርማሪ *dereq̈eȟa*
**example** *(n.)* ኣብነት *asrazi*
**exasperate** *(v.)* ኣበሳጨወ *teba'ë*
**excavate** *(v.)* ኮዓተ *tb'ät*
**exceed** *(v.)* በለፀ *qWeyeq̈WA*
**excel** *(v.)* ነፍዐ *hla*
**excellence** *(n.)* ዝለዓለ ፅሬት *mťȟas*
**Excellency** *(n.)* ክቡር *ènĵera*
**excellent** *(adj.)* ኣዝዩ ፅቡቕ *wrdi*

**except** ***(prep.)*** **ብጀካ** *sebere*
**exception** ***(n.)***
**ተቓውሞ** *teq̈awmo*
**excerpt** ***(n.)*** **ጥቕሲ** *qursi*
**excess** ***(n.)*** **ተረፍ ነገር** *ẗub*
**excessive** ***(adj.)*** **ዕዙዝ ዝበዝሐ** *tnfas*
**exchange** ***(v. t)*** **ልዉዉጥ** *atenfese*
**exchequer** ***(n.)*** **ዓቃቢ ንዋይ** *änqer ẗebenĵa*
**excise** ***(n.)*** **ቀረፅ** *sregtr*
**excite** ***(v.i)*** **ኣሐጎሰ** *arabḧe*
**excitement** ***(n.)*** **ታሕጓስ** *hdu'è nfas*
**exclaim** ***(v.)*** **ኣንሃርሃር** *ḧxret ḧaxirnet*
**exclamation** ***(n.)*** **ኣንሃርሃር ሃበ** *xemeq̈We*
**exclude** ***(v.)*** **ኣትረፈ** *'ènda bira*
**exclusive** ***(adj.)*** **ብሕታዊ** *gubo*
**excoriate** ***(v.)*** **ኣቖጥዐ** *ḧẗub matoni*
**excrete** ***(v.)*** **ምውጻእ** *mwxa'è*
**excursion** ***(n.)*** **ሽርሽር** *mer'ät*
**excuse** ***(v.)*** **ምኽኒት** *mer'äwi*
**execute** ***(v.)*** **ቀተለ** *dldl*
**execution** ***(n.)*** **መቕተልቲ** *lgWam*
**executive** ***(n.)*** **ናይ ምፍጻም** *nay mfxam*
**executor** ***(n.)*** **ወዳኢ** *weda'i*
**exempt** ***(adj.)*** **ምሒር** *mḧir*
**exercise** ***(n.)*** **ምዉስዋስ ኣካላት** *meraḧ brgeed*
**exert** ***(v.)*** **ስልጣኑ ተጠቐመ** *dmuq̈*
**exhale** ***(v.)*** **ኣተንፈሰ** *demeq̈e berhe*
**exhaust** ***(v.)*** **ኣድከመ** *blča*
**exhaustive** ***(adj.)*** **ዝተማልአ** *dmuq̈*
**exhibit** ***(v.)*** **ንህዝቢ ኣርአየ** *čaf*
**exhibition** ***(n.)*** **ምርኢት** *mr'it*
**exhilarate** ***(v.)*** **'aḧagWase** *'aḧagWase*
**exhort**
***(v.)*** **ኣተሓሳሰበ** *'ateḧasasebe*
**exigency** ***(n.)*** **ህፀፅ** *birinjal*
**exile** ***(n.)*** **ስደት** *ẗeref*
**exist** ***(v.)*** **ሃለወ** *sluẗ*
**existence** ***(n. )*** **ህልዉና** *nedere*
**exit** ***(n.)*** **መዉፅኢ በሪ** *biritish*
**exonerate** ***(v.)*** **ተሓታታይ ኣይኮነን በለ** *tesebari*
**exorbitant** ***(adj.)*** **ኣዝዩ ብጣዕሚ ዝለዓለ** *ankWale*
**exotic** ***(adj.)*** **ካብ ካልእ ሃገር** *sefiḧ*
**expand** ***(v.)*** **ገፈሐ** *zergḧe*
**expanse** ***(n.)*** **ለጥ ዝበለ** *bezeq̈zeq̈*
**expatriate** ***(n.)*** **ወዲ ወፃእ** *kawlo fyori*
**expect** ***(v.)*** **ትፅቢት ገበረ** *menshur*
**expectant** ***(adj.)*** **ተፀባይ** *sebere*
**expedient** ***(adj.)*** **ጠቓሚ** *ẗeq̈ami*
**expedite** ***(v.)*** **ኣሳለጠ** *delalay*
**expedition** ***(n.)*** **ወፍሪ** *wefri*
**expel** ***(v. t)*** **ለጎኑ** *bronzo*
**expend** ***(v.)*** **ኣዉፀአ** *čeq̈awit*
**expenditure** ***(n.)*** **ወፃኢ** *zara*
**expense** ***(n.)*** **ወፃኢ** *meḱoster*
**expensive** ***(adj.)*** **ክቡር** *mereq̈*
**experience** ***(n.)*** **ልምዲ** *temekro*
**experiment** ***(n.)*** **ሳይንሳዊ ፈተነ** *ḧaw*
**expert** ***(n.)*** **በዓልሞያ** *ḧwnet*
**expertise** ***(n.)*** **ሞያ** *shefashfti*
**expiate** ***(v.)*** **ዓደየ** *ädeye*
**expire** ***(v.)*** **ወደቐ** *wedeq̈e*

**expiry** *(n.)* **መፈጸምታ** *mefexemta*
**explain** *(v.)* **ኣብራህረህ** *snbrat*
**explicit** *(adj.)* **ንፁር** *kulaso*
**explode** *(v.)* **ነተጕ** *bunawi čeguri 'äyni gex zelewa xa'ëda sebeyti*
**exploit** *(v. t)* **ተበለፀ** *qendi kbdet*
**exploration** *(n.)* **ብዝበዛ** *asbasla*
**explore** *(v.)* **ዳህሰሰ** *ashaḱWi*
**explosion** *(n.)* **ነትጕ** *zeymḧr*
**explosive** *(adj.)* **ነታጕ** *ènssa*
**exponent** *(n.)* **ደጋፊ** *äfra*
**export** *(v. t. )* **ናብ ወፃዕ ለኣኸ** *kona'ë*
**expose** *(v.)* **ኣቃልዐ** *megelel*
**exposure** *(n.)* **ምቅላዕ** *meq̈Welef*
**express** *(v.)* **ገለፀ** *agWam*
**expression** *(n.)* **መግለፂ** *mnq̈ bele*
**expressive** *(adj.)* **ሓሳብ ዝገልፅ** *baîet*
**expropriate** *(v.)* **ሃገረ** *gobay*
**expulsion** *(n.)* **ምብራር** *weḧaẗ gWanxi*
**extant** *(adj.)* **እስካዕ ሕጂ ዘሎ** *gusẗi*
**extend** *(v.)* **ኣንወሐ** *mesḧaq̈*
**extension** *(n.)* **ምስፍሕፋሕ** *tḱWan*
**extent** *(n.)* **ክብደት** *karosa*
**exterior** *(adj.)* **ደገ** *ẗrumba*
**external** *(adj.)* **ግዳማይ ወፃኢ** *hanexe*
**extinct** *(adj.)* **ዝፃነተ** *hnxa*
**extinguish** *(v.)* **ኣጥፈአ** *shgurto*
**extirpate** *(v.)* **ኣልገሰ** *ḧbeẗ*
**extort** *(v.)* **ብሓይሊ ወሰደ** *bḧayli wesede*
**extra** *(adj.)* **ተወሳኺ** *bbzḧi*
**extract** *(v. t)* **ኣወፃፀአ** *degWalax*
**extraction** *(n.)* **መበቆል** *arḧa*
**extraordinary** *(adj.)* **ፍሉይ** *fluy*
**extravagance** *(n.)* **ምሕንሻሽ** *ärer*
**extravagant** *(adj.)* **ሓሻሺ** *buletin*
**extravaganza** *(n.)* **ሸንዳሕዳሕ** *shendaḧdaḧ*
**extreme** *(adj.)* **ምሒር ዝለዓለ** *azazi*
**extremist** *(n.)* **ፅንፈኛ ዝኮነ ሰብ** *qẗquẗ b'ëray*
**extricate** *(v.)* **ኣምለጠ** *älaq̈*
**extrovert** *(n.)* **ሕዉስ** *ërdi*
**extrude** *(v.)* **ደፊኡ ኣዉፀአ** *me'äkor*
**exuberant** *(adj.)* **ዉዕዉዕ** *te'änqefe*
**exude** *(v.)* **ኣርኣየ** *tenagWaxe*
**eye** *(n.)* **ዓይኒ** *walga gWanxi*
**eyeball** *(n.)* **ኩዕሶ ዓይኒ** *huguree*
**eyesight** *(n.)* **ናይ ምርኣይ ዓቕሚ** *nay mr'ay 'äq̈mi*
**eyewash** *(n.)* **እጥበት ዓይኒ** *mqur bani*
**eyewitness** *(n.)* **ምስክር** *ẗmar*

# F

**fable** *(n.)* **ነበረያ** *bush*
**fabric** *(n.)* **እሉም** *èlum*
**fabricate** *(v.)* **ኣለመ** *'aleme*
**fabulous** *(adj.)* **ዘይእመን** *zey'èmen*
**facade** *(n.)* **ገጽ** *gex*
**face** *(n.)* **ገፅ** *ḧabar merkeb*
**facet** *(n.)* **ጐድኒ** *gWadni*
**facetious** *(adj.)* **ናይ ቀልዲ** *mnsfaf*
**facial** *(adj.)* **ናይ ገጽ** *nay gex*
**facile** *(adj.)* **ቀሊል** *qelil*

**facilitate** *(v.)* ኣሳለጠ *sedeq̈a*
**facility** *(n.)* ስሉጥነት *sluẗnet*
**facing** *(n.)* ገፃዊ *birokratawi*
**facsimile** *(n.)* ቅዳሕ *qdaḧ*
**fact** *(n.)* ክውንነት *kwnnet*
**faction** *(n.)* ተቓዉሞ *seraq̈i*
**factitious** *(adj.)* ልብ ወለዳዊ *geben*
**factor** *(n.)* ምኽንያት *qebri*
**factory** *(n.)* ፋብሪካ *lagxi*
**faculty** *(n.)* ክእለት *mndad*
**fad** *(n.)* መሐደሲ *andadi*
**fade** *(v.i)* ሃሰሰ *rsun*
**Fahrenheit** *(n.)* ፋሐረናይት *gudgWad*
**fail** *(v.)* ተረፈ *terefe*
**failing** *(n.)* ድኽመት *ḧagez*
**failure** *(n.)* ዉድቀት *netegWa*
**faint** *(adj.)* ብንፁር ዘይረአ *qebere*
**fair** *(adj.)* ሚዛናዊ *awtobus*
**fairing** *(n.)* ብቕንዕና *bq̈n'ëna*
**fairly** *(adv.)* ብመጠኑ *gofgWaf*
**fairy** *(n.)* ስንድሮ *wanin*
**faith** *(n.)* እምነት *negaday*
**faithful** *(adj.)* ተኣማኒ *deret*
**faithless** *(adj.)* ዘይእመን *ashbedbede*
**fake** *(adj.)* ተምያን *temyan*
**falcon** *(n.)* ሊላ *lila*
**fall** *(v.)* ወደቐ *ḧarad sga*
**fallacy** *(n.)* ግጉይ ሓሳብ *balẗeǯi*
**fallible** *(adj.)* ክጋገ ዝኽእል *ẗesmi*
**fallow** *(adj.)* ቃድራ *xmblali'ë*
**false** *(adj.)* ሓሶት *doso*
**falsehood** *(n.)* ምሕሳዉ *melgom*
**falter** *(v.)* ተዳኸመ *gez'e*
**fame** *(n.)* ዝና *ädagi*
**familiar** *(adj.)* ልሙድ *ziz bele*
**family** *(n.)* ስድራ ቤት *shla*
**famine** *(n.)* ጥሜት *sirena*
**famished** *(adj.)* ኣዝዩ ዝጠመየ *'azyu zẗemeye*
**famous** *(adj.)* ስሙይ *godnawimrča*
**fan** *(n.)* ኣድናቒ *qedem*
**fanatic** *(n.)* ኣፍቃሪ *bḧnxax*
**fanciful** *(adj.)* ሓላሚ *ḧalami*
**fancy** *(n.)* ደለየ *dembe*
**fanfare** *(n.)* ኣርኣየ *temelkati*
**fang** *(n.)* ስኒ ተመን *bayit*
**fantasize** *(v.)* ቀረጸ *qerexe*
**fantastic** *(adj.)* ዘገርም *zegerm*
**fantasy** *(n.)* ትምኒት *kawlo*
**far** *(adv.)* ርሑቕ *gabina*
**farce** *(n.)* መስሓቕ *mesḧaq̈*
**fare** *(n.)* ዋጋ *waga*
**farewell** *(interj. )* ቻዉ *kakaw*
**farm** *(n.)* ሕርሻ *ḧab'e*
**farmer** *(n.)* ሓረስታይ *ktam*
**fascia** *(n.)* መእሰሪ ነገር *qaq̈a*
**fascinate** *(v.)* መሰጠ *qWelqWAl*
**fascism** *(n.)* ፋሽስትነት *fashstnet*
**fashion** *(n.)* ዘበናይነት *reesa*
**fashionable** *(adj.)* ዘበናይ *kadi*
**fast** *(adj.)* ቅልጡፍ *reesa*
**fasten** *(v.)* ቆለፈ *kadet*
**fastness** *(n.)* ጠንካታ ትሕዞ *kadmyum*
**fat** *(n.)* ሃዝራጥ *askereen*
**fatal** *(adj.)* ቀታሊ *qeesar*
**fatality** *(n.)* ሞት *kafe*
**fate** *(n.)* መጨረሽታ *kafeterya*
**fateful** *(adj.)* xḧftawi ጽሕፍታዊ
**father** *(n.)* ኣቦ *kidan*
**fathom** *(n.)* ተረደአ *sheḧaẗe*

**fatigue** *(n.)* ብርቱዕ ድኸም *dolshi*
**fatuous** *(adj.)* ብስለት ዘይብሉ *me'ät*
**fault** *(n.)* ስሕተት *kalsyum*
**faulty** *(adj.)* ፍፁም ዘይኮነ *qemere*
**fauna** *(n.)* እንስሳታት *meteȟasasebi*
**favour** *(n.)* ድጋፍ *qemer*
**favourable** *(adj.)* ቅንዕና ዘለዎ *äwde'awarȟ*
**favourite** *(adj.)* ተፈታዊ *mraḱ*
**fax** *(n.)* ጽሑፍ *xȟuf*
**fear** *(n.)* ፈርሀ *ferhe*
**fearful** *(adj.)* ዝፈረሐ *dewele*
**fearless** *(adj.)* ዘይፈርሕ *xbaq̈e xȟfet*
**feasible** *(adj.)* ክኸውን ዝኽእል *kḱewn zḱ'èl*
**feast** *(n.)* ድግስ *x'ötawi*
**feat** *(n.)* ክእለት *ïre*
**feather** *(n.)* ክንቲት *hdu'è*
**feature** *(n.)* መልክዕ *melk'ë*
**febrile** *(adj.)* ጭኑቕ *mxlam*
**February** *(n.)* ለካቲት *bxaynet*
**feckless** *(adj.)* ዋጋ ዘይብሉ *waga zeyblu*
**federal** *(adj.)* ፌደራላዊ *shash*
**federate** *(v.)* ፎደራ *fodera*
**federation** *(n.)* ፈደረሽን *federeshn*
**fee** *(n.)* ክፍሊት *kamyo*
**feeble** *(adj.)* ድኹም *kamera*
**feed** *(v.)* መገበ *me'äsker*
**feeder** *(n.)* ተመጋቢ *zemete*
**feel** *(v.)* ተሰምዖ *kamfora*
**feeling** *(n.)* ስምዒት *kampas*
**feign** *(v.)* ኣምሰለ *amsele*
**feisty** *(adj.)* መዕለበጢ *me'ëlebeẗi*

**felicitate** *(v.)* ኣዳለወ *'adalewe*
**felicitation** *(n.)* መግለጺ ሓጐስ *meglexi ȟagWas*
**felicity** *(n.)* ፍሰሃ *sereze*
**fell** *(v.)* ኦም ቆረፀ *mẗfa'è*
**fellow** *(n.)* ሰብኣይ *menshro*
**fellowship** *(n.)* ብፃይነት *brahan*
**felon** *(n.)* ገበነኛ *ghud*
**female** *(adj.)* ኣንስታያዊ *anstayawi*
**feminine** *(adj.)* ኣንስታያዊ *'anstayawi*
**feminism** *(n.)* ኣንስታይነት *'anstaynet*
**fence** *(n.)* ሓፁር *karamela*
**fencing** *(n.)* መሕፀሪ *kerezan*
**fend** *(v.)* ዓርሱ ተኸናኸነ *kelbawi*
**feng shui** *(n.)* ፌንግ ሽዊ *saxun*
**fennel** *(n.)* ተኽሊ *hemp*
**feral** *(adj.)* ቀይዲ በተኽ *bela'ë seb*
**ferment** *(v.)* በኹዐ *medf'ë*
**fermentation** *(n.)* ቡኾዕ *gWaraȟ*
**fern** *(n.)* ተክሊ *tankWa*
**ferocious** *(adj.)* ጨካን *qenona*
**ferry** *(n.)* መርከብ *dbab*
**fertile** *(adj.)* ልሙዕ *gbzna*
**fertility** *(n.)* ልሙዕነት *ȟaraq̈*
**fertilize** *(v.)* ኣጽገየ *axgeye*
**fertilizer** *(n.)* ድኹዒ *dḱu'ï*
**fervent** *(adj.)* ውዕውዕ *w'ëw'ë*
**fervid** *(adj.)* ምውቕ *mwq̈*
**fervour** *(n.)* ብርቱዕ ተምሳጥ *brtu'ë temsaẗ*
**fester** *(v.)* ረኾሰ *reḱWase*
**festival** *(n.)* በዓል *ämiq̈ snčro*
**festive** *(adj.)* ናይ በዓል *qWeb'ë*
**festivity** *(n.)* ምድሳት *mdsat*
**fetch** *(v.)* ኣምፀአ *k'ila*

**fete** *(n.)* **ፀንብል** *sefih*
**fetish** *(n.)* **ጣኦት** *kapaciter*
**fettle** *(n.)* **ጥዕና** *äqmi*
**feud** *(n.)* **ቅርሕንቲ** *seleme*
**feudalism** *(n.)* **መስፍንነት** *mesfnnet*
**fever** *(n.)* **ረስኒ** *r'èsemal*
**few** *(adj.)* **ዉሑድ** *r'èsemalnet*
**fey** *(adj.)* **ስሚዒታዊ** *r'èsemalawi*
**fiancé** *(n.)* **ሕፁይ** *r'èsemal gebere*
**fiasco** *(n.)* **ዉድቀት** *gbri*
**fibre** *(n.)* **ቃንጫ** *temberkeḱe*
**fickle** *(adj.)* **ተለዋዋጣይ** *qbeẗ*
**fiction** *(n.)* **ልቢ ወለድ** *qebaẗ*
**fictitious** *(adj.)* **ናይ ምህዞ** *kapsikem*
**fiddle** *(n.)* **ተናኸፈ** *gelbeẗe*
**fidelity** *(adj.)* **ተኣማኒነት** *ẗemẗami mesḧb*
**field** *(n.)* **ግራት** *leq̈otafre*
**fiend** *(n.)* **ጨካን ሰብ** *gbẗan*
**fierce** *(adj.)* **ሓያል** *gbẗani*
**fiery** *(adj.)* **ሓዊ ዝመስል** *ar'èsti*
**fifteen** *(adj. & n.)* **ዓሰርተ ሓሙሽተ** *'äserte ḧamushte*
**fifty** *(adj. & n.)* **ሓምሳ** *ḧamsa*
**fig** *(n.)* **ተኸሊ** *mruḱnet*
**fight** *(v.t)* **ተበኣሰ** *tebe'ase*
**fighter** *(n.)* **ተጋዳላይ** *tegadalay*
**figment** *(n.)* **ምህዞ** *makina*
**figurative** *(adj)* **ምስላዊ** *karame' el*
**figure** *(n.)* **ቁፀሪ** *kara 't*
**figurine** *(n.)* **ንእሽቶ ምስሊ** *n'èshto msli*
**filament** *(n.)* **ቀጢን ስልኪ** *qeẗin slki*
**file** *(n.)* **ፋይል** *fayl*
**filings** *(n.)* **ብራድ** *brad*
**fill** *(v.)* **መልአ** *terimuz*
**filler** *(n.)* **መወተፊ** *ge'mbi*
**filling** *(n.)* **መምልኢ** *meml'i*
**fillip** *(n.)* **ጦፍታ** *ẗofta*
**film** *(n.)* **ፊልሚ** *kartoon*
**filter** *(n.)* **መፅለሊ** *na' ae lebii*
**filth** *(n.)* **ግዕጋዕ** *gole 'foo*
**filtrate** *(n.)* **ዝፀለለ** *papase'*
**fin** *(n.)* **ክንፊ** *knfi*
**final** *(adj.)* **መወዳእታዊ** *meweda'ètawi*
**finalist** *(n.)* **መጨረሻ** *mečeresha*
**finance** *(n.)* **ገንዘብ** *sir'ahh*
**financial** *(adj.)* **ናይ ገንዘብ** *they'aa jibo*
**financier** *(n.)* **ናይ ገንዘብ ሰብ** *tinkuq*
**find** *(v.)* **ረኸበ** *ze yestewu 'el*
**fine** *(adj.)* **ፅቡቕ** *aa'b*
**finesse** *(n.)* **ኣኸእሎ** *tenahe'fe*
**finger** *(n.)* **ኣፃብዕት** *wekil*
**finial** *(n.)* **መጠቓለሊ** *aa'b merkeb*
**finicky** *(adj.)* **መማረፂ** *mesili*
**finish** *(v.)* **ዛዘመ** *qeyiha hib're*
**finite** *(adj.)* **ዉሱን** *Chif'chefa*
**fir** *(n.)* **ተኽሊ** *segawi*
**fire** *(n.)* **ባርዕ** *bar'ë*
**firewall** *(n.)* **ባርዕ ምሕላው** *bar'ë mḧlaw*
**firm** *(adj.)* **ትካል** *derfi*
**firmament** *(n.)* **ሰማይ** *zz'ebere bere*
**first** *(adj. & n.)* **ፈለማ** *tserabi*
**first aid** *(n.)* **ቀዳማይ ረድኤት** *qedamay red'eet*
**fiscal** *(adj.)* **ናይ ግብሪ** *mentseff*
**fish** *(n.)* **ዓሳ** *babur*

**fisherman** *(n.)* ገፋፍ ዓሳ *binefarit*
**fishery** *(n.)* ምርባሕ ዓሳ *carrot*
**fishy** *(adj.)* ኣጠራጣሪ *teshekeme*
**fissure** *(n.)* ቋቑራ *arebia*
**fist** *(n.)* ዕምኹ *'ëmkWa*
**fit** *(adj.)* በቕዐ *beq̈'ë*
**fitful** *(adj.)* ዝተቛራረፀ *bako*
**fitter** *(n.)* ቀዳዳይ *qedaday*
**fitting** *(n.)* ምዕቃን *m'ëqan*
**five** *(adj. & n.)* ሓሙሽተ *qeretse*
**fix** *(v.)* ኣጥበቐ *'aẗbeq̈e*
**fixture** *(n.)* ጥባቕ *ẗbaq̈*
**fizz** *(v.)* ፈጨጭ በለ *kunet*
**fizzle** *(v.)* ድምፂ *mesekote*
**fizzy** *(adj.)* ጋዝ ዘለዎ *qeriishe*
**fjord** *(n.)* ወሽመጥ *ome*
**flab** *(n.)* ለምባእ *lemba'è*
**flabbergasted** *(adj.)* እዝዩ ዝተደነቐ *suf*
**flabby** *(adj.)* ሃጥሃጥ ዝብል *zetelebte*
**flaccid** *(adj.)* ልስሉስን ድኹምን *hintsete*
**flag** *(n.)* ባንዴራ *fiseto*
**flagellate** *(v.)* ብጭጉራፍ ወቕዐ *satsun resa*
**flagrant** *(adj.)* ግሁድ *megebi*
**flair** *(n.)* ተዉህቦ *juba*
**flake** *(n.)* ቅራፍ *temeleket*
**flamboyant** *(adj.)* መብለጭለጪ *meblečleči*
**flame** *(n.)* ነበልባል *ameteqku*
**flammable** *(adj.)* ብቐሊሉ ዝነድድ *xebhi*
**flank** *(n.)* ጎኒ ሕንፃ *cider*
**flannel** *(n.)* ላና *lana*
**flap** *(v.)* ጸፍዐ *xef'ë*
**flapjack** *(n.)* ኬክ *bet ciniema*
**flare** *(n.)* ተወለዐ *qerefa*
**flash** *(v.)* ማሕ በለ *kebi*
**flashlight** *(n.)* ላምባዲና *lampadina*
**flask** *(n.)* ብርጭቆ *kbibe*
**flat** *(adj.)* ፀፊሕ *tsrachew*
**flatten** *(v.t.)* ኣፀፈሐ *xudet*
**flatter** *(v.)* ኣተዓሻሸወ *gereze'*
**flatulent** *(adj.)* ዝተቐብቀበ *dobe*
**flaunt** *(v.)* ተበርጠጠ *gedebe*
**flavour** *(n.)* መቐረት *meq̈eret*
**flaw** *(n.)* ጉድለት *hawahewu*
**flea** *(n.)* ቁንጪ *serekse*
**flee** *(v.)* ሃደመ *sanaduqe*
**fleece** *(n.)* ጸምሪ *xemri*
**fleet** *(n.)* ጭፍራ *čfra*
**flesh** *(n.)* ስጋ *tekese*
**flex** *(v.)* ኣማወቐ *zega*
**flexible** *(adj.)* ተቐያያራይ *zegenet*
**flexitime** *(n.)* እዋን ምርጫ *tekil*
**flick** *(v.)* ነፀገ *citric*
**flicker** *(v.t)* ዉልዕ ጥፍእ በለ *ketema*
**flight** *(n.)* ንፍረት *nfret*
**flimsy** *(adj.)* ምህሙን *mhmun*
**flinch** *(v.)* ሰገጥ በለ *segeẗ bele*
**fling** *(v.)* ሰንደወ *sevil sebe*
**flint** *(n.)* ፅንፅሕለ *seletan*
**flip** *(v.)* ተጠወየ *aseltene*
**flippant** *(adj.)* ደረቐኛ *dereq̈eña*
**flipper** *(n.)* ተጣወቒ *Kedan*
**flirt** *(v.i)* ኣኳሸመ *tenaḱefe*
**flit** *(v.)* ተናፈረ *tenafere*
**float** *(v.)* ተንሳፈፈ *tensafefe*
**flock** *(n.)* መጓሰ *megWase*
**floe** *(n.)* በረድ *atabeqe*
**flog** *(v.)* ገረፈ *alet*
**flood** *(n.)* ዉሕጅ *hibuea'*

**floodlight** *(n.)* ባጴዛ *atabeqe*
**floor** *(n.)* ባይታ ቤት *abrahereh*
**flop** *(v.)* ዘፍ በለ *keles*
**floppy** *(adj.)* ወደቐ *mleekti*
**flora** *(n.)* ተኽልታት *geletsinet*
**floral** *(adj.)* ዕምባባዊ *'ëmbabawi*
**florist** *(n.)* ሸያጢ ዕምበባ *chebete*
**floss** *(n.)* ተኽሊ ጡጥ *kifeli*
**flotation** *(n.)* ሰፈፍ ምበል *heruyei*
**flounce** *(v.)* ቁጡዕ *qenedegna*
**flounder** *(v.)* ሓሰበ *megujak*
**flour** *(n.)* ሕሩጭ *gojele*
**flourish** *(v.)* ደንፈዐ *aneqetse*
**flow** *(v.i)* ፈሰሰ *fesese*
**flower** *(n.)* ዕምባባ *txefri*
**flowery** *(adj.)* ን ፍዮሪ *n fyori*
**flu** *(n.)* ጉንፋዕ *tsxeruye*
**fluctuate** *(v.)* ተለዋዋጢ *telewawaẗi*
**fluent** *(adj.)* መላኽ ቋንቋ *melaḱ qWAnqWA*
**fluff** *(n.)* ልስሉስ *netsxur*
**fluid** *(n.)* ፈሳሲ ነገር *meaelayi*
**fluke** *(n.)* ፍሉክ *fluk*
**fluorescent** *(adj.)* ፍሎረሸንት *floreshent*
**fluoride** *(n.)* ፍሎራይድ *cdade*
**flurry** *(n.)* ጭንቅንቕ *meherte*
**flush** *(v.)* ኣኹርዐ *'aḱur'ë*
**fluster** *(v.)* ኣጨናነቐ *klemintaine*
**flute** *(n.)* ሻምብቆ *nKes*
**flutter** *(v.)* ኣንበልበለ *kahenat'*
**fluvial** *(adj.)* ሩባ *kahin*
**flux** *(n.)* ዋሕዚ *waȟzi*
**fly** *(v.i)* ነፈረ *tsehafi*
**foam** *(n.)* ሰፍነግ *bilihi*
**focal** *(adj.)* ማእኸላይ *dimtsi ftre'*
**focus** *(n.)* ኣድሃበ ገበረ *Amil*
**fodder** *(n.)* ፍሩሽካ ንፋይ *Tsxdefi*
**foe** *(n.)* ድርቂ *xela'i*
**fog** *(n.)* ጸላኢ *gme*
**foil** *(v.)* ኣፈሸለ *deYebe*
**fold** *(v.t)* ዓፀፈ *tAwte'*
**foliage** *(n.)* ኣቑፅልቲ *tlTefe'*
**folio** *(n.)* ቆጽሊ ወረቐት *qoxli wereq̈et*
**folk** *(n.)* ህዝቢ *agachewu*
**follow** *(v.)* ሰዓበ *menqerker*
**follower** *(n.)* ተኸታሊ *mentelina*
**folly** *(n.)* ዕሽነት *seat'*
**fond** *(adj.)* ኣፍቃሪ *'afqari*
**fondle** *(v.)* ደረዘ *dereze*
**font** *(n.)* ጽዋእ *xwa'è*
**food** *(n.)* ምግቢ *wushate'*
**fool** *(n.)* ዓንጃል *zitqarebe*
**foolish** *(adj.)* ዓንጃል *änĵal*
**foolproof** *(adj.)* ዘይጋገ *zeygage*
**foot** *(n.)* መርገጺ እግሪ *kedeNe'*
**footage** *(n.)* ቀረጻ *kidawunti'*
**football** *(n.)* ኩዕሶ እግሪ *ku'ëso 'ègri*
**footing** *(n.)* መርገጺ *debNa'*
**footling** *(adj.)* ርኩብ *esil anahib*
**for** *(prep. )* ን *n*
**foray** *(n.)* ፈተነ *azenagiaa*
**forbear** *(v.)* ወገደ *wegede*
**forbid** *(v.)* ኸልከለ *ganeta*
**force** *(n.)* ሓይሊ *afafenote*
**forceful** *(adj.)* ዘእምን *lahezaZ'*
**forceps** *(n.)* ወረጦ *wereẗo*
**forcible** *(adj.)* ናይ ሓይሊ *nay ȟayli*
**fore** *(adj.)* ቅዲሚ *aseltani*
**forearm** *(n.)* ቅልፅም *himet*
**forebear** *(n.)* ኣያታት *hatnet*
**forecast** *(v.t)* ተንበየ *shahikar*

**forefather** *(n.)* **አቦሓጎ** *'aboȟago*
**forefinger** *(n.)* **አመልካቲቶ** *'amelkatito*
**foregoing** *(adj.)* **ዝሓለፈ** *zȟalefe*
**forehead** *(n.)* **ግንባር** *juba*
**foreign** *(adj.)* **ናይ ወፃኢ** *shehare*
**foreigner** *(n.)* **ባዕዲ** *ba'ëdi*
**foreknowledge** *(n.)* **ብኣጋ አፍልጦ** *b'aga 'aflïto*
**foreleg** *(n.)* **ኢድ** *id*
**foreman** *(n.)* **ሓለቓ** *ȟaleq̈a*
**foremost** *(adj.)* **ብቐዳሚ** *aleba saret*
**forename** *(n.)* **ስዕሚ** *kocain*
**forensic** *(adj.)* **beet frdawi** *ቤት ፍርዳዊ*
**foreplay** *(n.)* **ናይ ፍቕሪ ዛንታ** *nay fq̈ri zanta*
**forerunner** *(n.)* **ተነባዪ** *tenebayi*
**foresee** *(v.)* **ተንበየ** *diduee'*
**foresight** *(n.)* **ሳዛ** *saza*
**forest** *(n.)* **ዱር** *dur*
**forestall** *(v.)* **አበርዓነ** *'aber'äne*
**forestry** *(n.)* **ስነ-ዱር** *snedur*
**foretell** *(v.)* **ተንበየ** *cocoon*
**forever** *(adv. )* **ንዘልኣለም** *nzel'alem*
**foreword** *(n.)* **መቕድም** *meq̈dm*
**forfeit** *(v.)* **አሀገረ** *qewami*
**forge** *(v.t)* **ፀዓረ** *agedded*
**forgery** *(n.)* **temyan** *ተምያን*
**forget** *(v.)* **ረስዐ** *res'ë*
**forgetful** *(adj.)* **ረሳዒ** *resa'ï*
**forgive** *(v.)* **መሓረ** *meȟare*
**forgo** *(v.)* **ሓደገ** *kazina*
**fork** *(n.)* **ፋርኬታ** *farkeeta*
**forlorn** *(adj.)* **ብሕታዊ** *qiltafe*
**form** *(n.)* **ዓይነት** *heigib*
**formal** *(adj.)* **ስሩዕ** *astentene*
**formality** *(n.)* **አገባብ** *temesasali*
**format** *(n.)* **መልኺ** *ginizabe*
**formation** *(n.)* **አቀዋውማ** *'aqewawma*
**former** *(adj.)* **ናይ ቀደም** *tesaneyei*
**formerly** *(adv. )* **ቅድም** *qdm*
**formidable** *(adj.)* **ዘይድፈር** *hadinet*
**formula** *(n.)* **ቅዋመ** *qwame*
**formulate** *(v.)* **ዘመወ** *qkulele*
**forsake** *(v.)* **ሓደገ** *sanetime*
**forswear** *(v.)* **ነጸገ** *nexege*
**fort** *(n. )* **ዕርዲ** *tegetateme*
**forte** *(n.)* **ጨኽት** *tegwanefo*
**forth** *(adv. )* **ቀረባ** *aleba*
**forthcoming** *(adj.)* **ዝስዕብ** *zs'ëb*
**forthwith** *(adv. )* **ቅፅበታዊ** *qorare*
**fortify** *(v.)* **ዓረደ** *'ärede*
**fortitude** *(n.)* **ትብዓት** *tehababere*
**fortnight** *(n.)* **ክልተ ቕነ** *tehibiberi*
**fortress** *(n.)* **ዕርዲ** *'ërdi*
**fortunate** *(adj.)* **ዕድለኛ** *tederame*
**fortune** *(n. )* **ዕድል** *kwaleta*
**forty** *(adj.& n.)* **አርባዓ** *akebe*
**forum** *(n.)* **መድረኽ** *tihija*
**forward** *(adv. &adj.)* **ንቕድሚት** *nq̈dmit*
**fossil** *(n.)* **አሰር ህይወት** *'aser hywet*
**foster** *(v.)* **አጎልበተ** *tewahilwlw*
**foul** *(adj.)* **ጋዕጋዕ** *teteraqeme*
**found** *(v.)* **አጣየሽ** *amtseA'*
**foundation** *(n.)* **መሰረት** *meseret*
**founder** *(n. )* **መስራቲ** *tegachewe*
**foundry** *(n.)* **ቤት ንህበት** *beet nhbet*

fountain *(n.)* ምንጪ *mnči*
four *(adj.& n.)* ኣርባዕተ *'arba'ëte*
fourteen *(adj.& n.)* ዓሰርተ ኣርባዕተ *'äserte 'arba'ëte*
fourth *(adj.& n.)* ራብዓይ *shito*
fowl *(n.)* ዑፍ *abiy meanta*
fox *(n. )* ቦኳርያ *kolonele*
foyer *(n.)* ኣዳራሽ *baeedawi*
fraction *(n. )* ጉዚ *guzi*
fractious *(adj.)* ተኣፋፊ *te'afafi*
fracture *(v.t)* መንቃዕቲ *hawelti*
fragile *(adj.)* ተሰባሪ *anedi*
fragment *(n. )* ስባር *hibri*
fragrance *(n.)* መኣዛ *me'aza*
fragrant *(adj.)* ምዑዝ *zitehibri*
frail *(adj.)* ድኹም *dkum*
frame *(n.)* መቃን *meqan*
framework *(n. )* መዋቅር *kunat*
franchise *(n.)* ፈቓድ *tewagaei*
frank *(adj.)* ግልጺ *timar*
frankfurter *(n.)* ስጋ ክፍቲ *tsenber*
frantic *(adj.)* ህፁፅ *nedadi*
fraternal *(adj.)* ሕውነታዊ *ḧwnetawi*
fraternity *(n.)* ማሕበር *na'ä*
fraud *(n.)* ገበን ሽፍጢ *meshaq̈*
fraudulent *(adj.)* መታለሊ *metaleli*
fraught *(adj.)* ዝተመልአ *ĵratam*
fray *(v.)* ተዘርዘረ *mchot*
freak *(n.)* ፈታዊ *ẗtahe*
freckle *(n.)* ፈፀጋ *mchu'è*
free *(adj.)* ናፃ *tewazayi*
freebie *(n.)* ናጻ *naxa*
freedom *(n.)* ናፅነት *azeze*
freeze *(v.)* ደስከለ *deskele*
freezer *(n.)* መዝሓሊት *mezḧalit*
freight *(n.)* ፅዕነት *komando*
freighter *(n.)* ተጸዓኒት *texe'änit*
French *(adj.)* ናይ ፈረንሳይ *zkr*
frenetic *(adj.)* ዘይተዋደደ *ĵemere*
frenzy *(n.)* ናዕዋ *na'ëwa*
frequency *(n. )* dggm *dggm*
frequent *(adj.)* ተደጋጋሚ *zine'ad*
fresh *(adj.)* ትኩስ *na'èda*
fret *(v.t. )* ተጨናነቐ *r'èyto*
fretful *(adj.)* ዝተጨናነቐ *ta'ëliq̈*
friable *(adj.)* ፍርትት ዝብል *älaq̈i*
friction *(n. )* ፍግፍግ *ngd*
Friday *(n. )* ዓርቢ *'ärbi*
fridge *(n. )* መዝሓሊ *mezḧali*
friend *(n. )* ዓርኪ *wklna*
fright *(n.)* ፍርሒ *komishner*
frighten *(v.)* ኣፍረሐ *megatmi*
frigid *(adj.)* ቆራር *fexeme*
frill *(n. )* ሽንሽን *mebx'ä*
fringe *(n.)* ዘፈር *zefer*
frisk *(v.)* ዓንደረ *'ändere*
fritter *(v.)* ኣባኸነ *'aq̈ḧa*
frivolous *(adj.)* ዘይዕቱብ *zey'ëtub*
frock *(n. )* ቀምሽ *ḧafash*
frog *(n. )* ጭንቁራዕ *lmud*
frolic *(v.i. )* ተጻወተ *texawete*
from *(prep. )* ካብ *hwket*
front *(n.)* ቅድሚት *komawi*
frontbencher *(n.)* ቅድሚት ተሳኣሊ *qdmit tesa'ali*
frontier *(n. )* ዶብ *temaḧalalefi*
frost *(n. )* ዉርጪ *qWerabi*
frosty *(adj.)* ዉርጫም ቆራር *habereta*
froth *(n.)* ዓፍራ *rkb*
frown *(v.i)* ተፀወገ *mkfal*
frowsty *(adj.)* ዳህናዉ *deesnet*
frugal *(adj.)* ጥንቁቕ *ẗnquq̈*

**fruit** *(n.)* ፍሬምረ *leweẗe*
**fruitful** *(adj.)* ዕጨት *ïrnuf*
**frump** *(n.)* ገዋድ *gewad*
**frustrate** *(v.)* ኣበሳጨወ *meseneyta*
**fry** *(v.)* ጠበሰ *tenexaxeri*
**fudge** *(n.)* ሽፋፈነ *anexaxere*
**fuel** *(n.)* ነዳዲ *mnxxar*
**fugitive** *(n. )* ሃዲም *hadim*
**fulcrum** *(n.)* ደገፊ *busola*
**fulfil** *(v.)* ኣዐወተ *dngaxe*
**fulfilment** *(n.)* ናብ ተግባር *teq̈adawi*
**full** *(adj.)* ሙሉእ *wedi hager*
**fulsome** *(adj.)* ሽሕጣን *shȟtan*
**fumble** *(v.)* ባእባእ በለ *qunčul*
**fume** *(n.)* ተበሳጨወ *qunčul*
**fumigate** *(v.)* ዓጠነ *keȟase*
**fun** *(n.)* ታሕጓስ *kaȟsa*
**function** *(n.)* ተግባር *alalayi*
**functional** *(adj.)* ተግባራዊ *tegbarawi*
**functionary** *(n. )* ሓላፊ *k'èlet*
**fund** *(n.)* ገንዘብ *k'ila*
**fundamental** *(adj.)* መሰረታዊ *mwddar*
**funeral** *(n. )* ስርዓት ቀብሪ *wddrawi*
**fungus** *(n. )* ሳባ *tewadadari*
**funky** *(adj.)* ዘበናይ *ïernefe*
**funnel** *(n.)* መንቆርቆር *ëgub*
**funny** *(adj.)* ዘስሕቕ *teïar'ë*
**fur** *(n.)* ጸምሪ *xemri*
**furious** *(adj.)* ኣዝዩ ዝተቖጥዐ *mq̈lul*
**furl** *(v.)* ዓጺፉ ጠቕለለ *meleA'*
**furlong** *(n. )* ራሕቐ *mela'i*
**furnace** *(n.)* መምከኺ ቦታ *mlu'è*
**furnish** *(v.)* ብኣቕሑት ኣማልአ *mfxam*
**furnishing** *(n.)* ኣቕረበ ኣበ *zteȟalaleke*
**furniture** *(n. )* ኣቕሑ ገዛ *ȟlklk*
**furore** *(n.)* ህዝባዊ ቁጠዐ *weĵhi*
**furrow** *(n.)* ትልሚ *èshita*
**further** *(adv.)* ርሑቕ *mq̈lul*
**furthermore** *(adv.)* ብተወሳኺ *ȟalaleke*
**furthest** *(adj.& adv.)* ተወሳኺ *ȟlklk*
**fury** *(n.)* ቁጠዐ *mis gibenegna*
**fuse** *(v.)* ፀንበረ *mshban*
**fusion** *(n. )* ዉህደት *na'èda*
**fuss** *(n.)* ጭንቀት *na'èda*
**fussy** *(adj.)* መማረፂ *te'azeze*
**fusty** *(adj.)* ህድሁድ *kifale*
**futile** *(adj.)* ከንቱ *akbere*
**futility** *(n.)* ብልሹነት *aq̈Weme*
**future** *(n.)* መፃኢ እዋን *derasi werabi*
**futuristic** *(adj.)* ኣዝዩ ዘበናይ *ztewahahade*

# G

**gab** *(v.)* ብዙሕ ምዝራብ *bzuh-mzrab*
**gabble** *(v.t. )* ከየገናዘብካ ብቕልጡፍ ምዝራብ *ke-ye-gena-zebka bkil-tuf m-z-rab*
**gadget** *(n.)* ናይ ኤሌትሪክ መሳርሒ *nay electric me-sar-hi*
**gaffe** *(n.)* ኣብ ኣደባባይ ዝተሰርሐ ዘሕፍር ስሕተት *ab ade-ba-bay z-te-ser-he ze-h-fr se-h-tet*

**gag** *(n.)* **ቅድሚ ተምላስ ዘሎ ናይ ምምላስ ስምዒት** *kidmi temlas zelo nay me-mlas sem-eit*
**gaga** *(adj.)* **ምዕባድ፣ ኣብ ሽማግለታት ናይ ኣእምሮ ዘይምርግጋዕ** *m-ae-bad*
**gaiety** *(n.)* **ሕጉስ ምኳን** *h-gus me-kua-n*
**gaily** *(adv.)* **ኣብ ዓይኒ ዉሽጢ ዝኣትው፣ ሕጉስ፣ ሰሓቒ፣ ተጫዋቲ** *ab ayini wushti z-at-ew*
**gain** *(v.)* **ምትራፍ፣ ዝኾነ ነገር ምርካብ** *m-traf*
**gainful** *(adj.)* **ኣትራፍን ጠቓምን ዝኾነ ነገር** *atraf-en tekami z-kone neger*
**gait** *(n.)* **ኣካይዳ፣ ናይ ፈረስ ኣካይዳ** *akayida*
**gala** *(n.)* **ፅምብል በዓል** *tse-m-bel be-al*
**galaxy** *(n.)* **ናይ ከዋኽብቲ ስብስብ** *nay kewakbti sebseb*
**gale** *(n.)* **ህቦብላ** *h-bo-b-la*
**gall** *(n.)* **ናይ ሰውነት ስቓይ** *nay sewnet se-kay*
**gallant** *(adj.)* **ጀግና** *jegna*
**gallantry** *(n.)* **ጅግንነት** *jegninet*
**gallery** *(n.)* **ኣደራሽ** *adarash*
**gallon** *(n.)* **ናይ ማይ መጠን መለክዒ** *nay ma-y me-ten*
**gallop** *(n.)* **ምግላብ** *m-glab*
**gallows** *(n.)* **ንመሕነቒ ዝጥቀምዎ ዕንጨይቲ** *n-mehneqi z-tkemwo enchei-ti*
**galore** *(adj.)* **ብዙሕ** *bzuh*
**galvanize** *(v.i.)* **ብረት ንከይዝዕግ ብዚንክ ምሸፋን** *bret zkeyiz-eg b-zinc m-shfan*
**gambit** *(n.)* **መመሰስታ ነገር** *memesesta neger*
**gamble** *(v.)* **ቁማር** *kumar*
**gambler** *(n.)* **ቁማር ዝጫወት ሰብ** *kumar z-chawet*
**gambol** *(v.)* **ዓንደረ** *andere*
**game** *(n.)* **ግጥም፣ ፀዋታ** *g-tim*
**gamely** *(adj.)* **ብትብዓት** *b-tb-at*
**gammy** *(adj.)* **ዝተበላሸወ፣ ዘይሰርሕ** *z-tebela-shewe*
**gamut** *(n.)* **ማዕቐፍ** *ma-ekef*
**gang** *(n.)* **ናይ ገበነኛታት፣ሰበት ስብስብ** *nay gebenegnatat sebeseb*
**gangling** *(adj.)* **ቀዉላል** *kewlal*
**gangster** *(n.)* **ገበነኛ** *geben-egna*
**gangway** *(n.)* **መስገር** *mesg-er*
**gap** *(n.)* **ኽፍተት** *k-ftet*
**gape** *(v.)* **ሃነነ** *hane-ne*
**garage** *(n.)* **ጋራጅ** *gara-j*
**garb** *(n.)* **መደናገር** *mede-nager*
**garbage** *(n.)* **ጎሓፍ** *go-haf*
**garble** *(v.)* **ዝተደናገረ** *z-tedenagere*
**garden** *(n.)* **ገደና** *ge-de-na*
**gardener** *(n.)* **ገደና ሰብ** *ge-de-na seb*
**gargle** *(v.)* **ተጉመፅመፅ** *tegume-tse-me-tse*
**garish** *(adj.)* **ኣመና ድሙቕ** *amena dmu-que*
**garland** *(n.)* **ናይ ዕምበባ ጌፅ** *nay embaba ge-tse*
**garlic** *(n.)* **ፃዕዳ ሽጉርቲ** *tsa-e-da sh-gur-ti*
**garment** *(n.)* **ክዳን** *kdan*
**garner** *(v.)* **ኣምፀኣ** *am-tse-a*
**garnet** *(n.)* **ማዕድን** *ma-e-den*
**garnish** *(v.)* **ሸለመ** *she-leme*

**garret** *(n.)* **ንላዕሊ ቀልዐ** *nla-e-li que-le-ea*
**garrulous** *(adj.)* **ዓዛፍ** *a-zaf*
**garter** *(n. )* **ክዳን** *kdan*
**gas** *(n. )* **ሃፉ** *hafu*
**gasket** *(n.)* **ጎማ** *goma*
**gasp** *(v.i)* **ላህለሀ** *lahle-he*
**gastric** *(adj.)* **ከስዓዊ** *kes-a-wi*
**gastronomy** *(n.)* **ስነ-መግቢ** *sin-e meg-bi*
**gate** *(n.)* **በሪ** *beri*
**gateau** *(n.)* **ኬክ** *kek*
**gather** *(v.)* **ኣከበ** *akebe*
**gaudy** *(adj.)* **ምርኡይ** *mruy*
**gauge** *(n.)* **ዓቐን** *aken*
**gaunt** *(adj.)* **ዕባራ** *ebara*
**gauntlet** *(n.)* **ጓንቲ ብረት** *gua-nti bret*
**gauze** *(n.)* **ጋርዘ** *garze*
**gawky** *(adj.)* **ቀዉላል** *kewlal*
**gay** *(adj.)* **ሕጉስ** *hgus*
**gaze** *(v.)* **ኣትኩሩ ረኣየ** *atkuru re-aye*
**gazebo** *(n.)* **መዋቕር** *mewaker*
**gazette** *(n. )* **ጋዜጣ** *gazeta*
**gear** *(n.)* **ማርሽ** *marsh*
**geek** *(n.)* **ደርጋፍ** *dergaf*
**gel** *(n.)* **ዓይነት ቕብኣት** *aynet kibat*
**geld** *(v.)* **ቀጥቀጠ** *ketkete*
**gem** *(n. )* **ክቡር እምኒ** *kbur emni*
**gender** *(n.)* **ስርዓተ ፆታ** *srate tsota*
**general** *(adj.)* **ሓፈሻዊ** *hafeshawi*
**generalize** *(v.)* **ኣጠቓላሊ** *atekalali*
**generate** *(v.)* **ፈጠረ** *fetere*
**generation** *(n. )* **ትዉልዲ** *te-wle-di*
**generator** *(n. )* **ጀነረተር** *generater*
**generosity** *(n.)* **ልግስና** *legesena*
**generous** *(adj.)* **ለጋስ** *legas*
**genesis** *(n.)* **መፈለምታ** *mefelemta*
**genetic** *(adj.)* **ናይ ዘር** *nay zer*
**genial** *(adj.)* **ምእዙዝ** *me-ezuz*
**genius** *(n.)* **ዝለዓለ ፍልጠት** *ze-le-ale feltet*
**genteel** *(adj.)* **ሱቕተኛን ትሑት** *suktegnan tehut*
**gentility** *(n.)* **ግሩም ፀባይ** *gerum tse-bay*
**gentle** *(adj.)* **ህዱእ** *he-du-e*
**gentleman** *(n.)* **ወረጃ ዝኮነ ሰብ** *wereja zekone seb*
**gentry** *(n.)* **ደቀባት** *dekebat*
**genuine** *(adj.)* **ሓቐኛ** *hakegna*
**geographer** *(n.)* **ክኢላ** *k'ila*
**geographical** *(adj.)* **ስፍራ** *sefra*
**geography** *(n.)* **ጀኦግራፍ** *ĵe'ograf*
**geologist** *(n. )* **መርማሪ ሰብ** *mermari seb*
**geology** *(n.)* **ምድር ምርመራ** *meder mermera*
**geometric** *(adj.)* **ጂኦሜትሪክ** *geo-met-eric*
**geometry** *(n. )* **ጂኦሜትሪ** *geo-met-ery*
**germ** *(n.)* **ታሕዋስያን** *tahwas-eyan*
**German** *(n.)* **ጀርመን** *ger-man*
**germane** *(adj.)* **ኣድላይ** *adlay*
**germinate** *(v.)* **በቖለ** *bekole*
**germination** *(n. )* **በቑል ሃበ** *bekul habe*
**gerund** *(n. )* **ቅርጺ** *kirtsi*
**gestation** *(n.)* **ጥንሲ** *tensi*
**gesture** *(n.)* **ወስታ** *westa*

**get** *(v.)* ተቐበለ *tekebele*
**geyser** *(n.)* ዓይኒ ማይ *ayni may*
**ghastly** *(adj.)* ዘሰቅቕ *zesekek*
**ghost** *(n. )* ረቒቕ *rekik*
**giant** *(n.)* ኪኢላ *ki-ila*
**gibber** *(v.)* ብሪውምሪው በለ *briwmriw bele*
**gibe** *(v.)* ኣላገፀ *alagetse*
**giddy** *(adj.)* ዘንፀራረዎ *zentserarewo*
**gift** *(n.)* ዉህብቶ *wuhbto*
**gifted** *(adj.)* ተዉህቦ ዘለዎ *tewuhbo zelewo*
**gigabyte** *(n.)* ምዕቃን *m'ëqan*
**gigantic** *(adj.)* ገዚፍ *gezif*
**giggle** *(v.t. )* ኪርኪር በለ *kir kir bele*
**gild** *(v.)* ኮልዐ *kole'ea*
**gilt** *(adj.)* ደሚቕ ብጫ *demiq bicha*
**gimmick** *(n.)* መተዓሻሸዊ ነገር *m-ete-a-sha-she-wi neger*
**ginger** *(n. )* ዝንጅብል *zenjebel*
**gingerly** *(adv.)* ብዝዓለ ጥንቃቐ *beze-le-a-le tenkake*
**giraffe** *(n. )* ዘራፍ *zeraf*
**girder** *(n. )* ጩራ *chu-ra*
**girdle** *(n.)* ቅናት *qnat*
**girl** *(n.)* ጓል *qede'se*
**girlish** *(adj.)* ናይ ጓል *teHE'tata'li*
**giro** *(n.)* ምምሕልላፍ *mmḧlla*
**girth** *(n.)* ማዕጠቕ *ma'ëteq*
**gist** *(n.)* ጽሚቕ *tsemWaq*
**give** *(v.)* ሃበ *habe*
**given** *(adj.)* የቕረበ *yeqrebe*
**glacial** *(adj.)* በረዳዊ *beredawi*
**glacier** *(n.)* ከውሒ-በረድ *kewḧibered*
**glad** *(adj.)* ሕጉስ *ḧgus*
**gladden** *(v.)* ኣሓጉሰ *'aḧagWase*
**glade** *(n.)* ቃልዕ *qal'ë*
**glamour** *(n. )* ውበት *wbet*
**glance** *(v.i. )* ቍሊሕ በለ *quliḧ bele*
**gland** *(n. )* ጽኪ *tseki*
**glare** *(v.i)* ደጉሐ *deguḧe*
**glass** *(v.t. )* ጥርሙዝ፣ መስተዋት *ṫrmuz*
**glaze** *(v.)* ፈዘዘ *fezeze*
**glazier** *(n. )* ቀበኢ ብሪቕሪቕ *qeba'i briqriq*
**gleam** *(v.)* ጸዳል *tsedal*
**glean** *(v.)* ቀረመ *qereme*
**glee** *(n.)* ደስታ *desta*
**glide** *(v.)* ሰለል በለ *selel bele*
**glider** *(n. )* ሰፋፊቶ *sefafito*
**glimmer** *(v.)* ብልጭ ብልጭ *blč blč*
**glimpse** *(n.)* ቈላሕታ *qWelaḧta*
**glisten** *(v.)* ኣንጸባረቐ *antsebareqe*
**glitch** *(n.)* ኢንታ *'inta*
**glitter** *(v.)* ብልጭልጭ *berhe*
**gloat** *(v.)* ብህርፋን ነፈገ *bhrfan nefege*
**global** *(adj.)* ዓለምለኻዊ *'älemlekawi*
**globalization** *(n.)* ስልጣነ *mrbaḧ*
**globe** *(n. )* ዓለም *glob*
**globetrotter** *(n.)* ዳህሳሲ *dahsasi*
**gloom** *(n.)* ደበንገረ *debengere*
**gloomy** *(adj.)* ጽልሙት *tselmut*
**glorification** *(n.)* ክብሪ *kbr*
**glorify** *(v.)* ኣኽበረ *'akbere*
**glorious** *(adj.)* ምስጉን ክቡር *msgun kbur*
**glory** *(n. )* ዝና ክብሪ *zna kbri*
**gloss** *(n. )* ብሪቕሪቕታ *briqriqta*

**glossary** *(n.)* ማህደረ ቃላት *mahdere qalat*
**glossy** *(adj.)* አስተንታኒ *astentani*
**glove** *(n.)* ጓንቲ *gWanti*
**glow** *(v.)* ጐሃረ *gWahare*
**glucose** *(n. )* ግሉኮዝ *glukoz*
**glue** *(n. )* መጣበቒ *telaḥage*
**glum** *(adj.)* ትኩዝ *tkuz*
**glut** *(n.)* መልአ *mel'e*
**glutton** *(n. )* ውሒጣ *wḥiṭa*
**gluttony** *(n. )* ሃረርታ *harerta*
**glycerine** *(n.)* ግሊሰሪን *gliserin*
**gnarled** *(adj.)* ሓበጥ ጎባጥ *ḥabaṭ gobaṭ*
**gnat** *(n.)* ጽንጽያ *tsentseya*
**gnaw** *(v.)* ገሃጸ *gehatse*
**go** *(v.t)* ኪድ *kede*
**goad** *(v.)* ደፍአ *def'e*
**goal** *(n. )* ዕላማ *ëlama*
**goalkeeper** *(n.)* ሓላዊ ማዕጾ *ḥalawi-ma'ëxo*
**goat** *(n. )* ጤል *ṭeel*
**gob** *(n.)* አፍ *af*
**gobble** *(v.)* ሰነገ *senege*
**goblet** *(n.)* መለኪያ *melekiya*
**god** *(n.)* አምላኽ *amlaḱ*
**godchild** *(n.)* ጓል አቦ አልገ *gWal blgna*
**goddess** *(n.)* አምላኽ *amlḱo*
**godfather** *(n.)* አቦ አልገ *abalge*
**godly** *(adj.)* ሃይማኖተኛ *haymanoteña*
**godmother** *(n.)* አልገ እኖ *'ènolge*
**goggle** *(n. )* ጉልሓጥሓጥ በለ *gulḥaṭḥaṭ bele*
**going** *(n.)* መንገዲ *mengedi*
**gold** *(n.)* ወርቂ *werqi*
**golden** *(adj.)* ወርቃዊ *werqawi*
**goldsmith** *(n. )* ወርቂ ሰሪ *werqi-serri*
**golf** *(n. )* ጎልፍ *golf*
**gondola** *(n.)* ጎንዶላ *gondola*
**gong** *(n.)* ብረታዊ ነጋሪት *bretawi negarit*
**good** *(adj.)* ጽቡቕ *tsebuq̈*
**goodbye** *(excl.)* ደሓን ኩን *deḥan kun*
**goodness** *(n.)* የዋህነት፣ ፅቡቕነት *lewhat*
**goodwill** *(n. )* ፅቡቕ ስራሕ *meftḧ*
**goose** *(n. )* ዓዓ *'ä'ä*
**gooseberry** *(n.)* ክሽምሽ *kshmsh*
**gore** *(n.)* ርጉእ ደም *rgu'è dem*
**gorgeous** *(adj.)* ቖንጆ *dmuq̈*
**gorilla** *(n. )* ህበይ *gorila*
**gory** *(adj.)* ደማዊ *demawi*
**gospel** *(n. )* ወንጌል *wengeel*
**gossip** *(n. )* ሓሜት *ḥmeeta*
**gouge** *(v.)* መንደል *mendel*
**gourd** *(n. )* ሓምሓም *ḥamḥam*
**gourmand** *(n.)* ፈታው መግቢ *fetaw megbi*
**gourmet** *(n.)* ቀማሲ *qemasi*
**gout** *(n.)* ድሌት *dleet*
**govern** *(v.)* ምግዛእ *gez'e*
**governance** *(n. )* አገዛዝኣ *mgza'è*
**governess** *(n. )* መራሒት *'alayt qWel'ä*
**government** *(n. )* መንግስቲ *mengsti*
**governor** *(n. )* መመሓደሪ፣ ገዛኢ *geza'i*
**gown** *(n.)* ቀሚሽ ክዳን *qemish kdan*
**grab** *(v.)* ምሓዝ *m-ha-z*
**grace** *(n.)* ጸጋ *tsega*
**graceful** *(adj.)* ምዕሩግ *m'ërug*

**gracious** *(adj.)* ጥዑም *ṭ'üm*
**gradation** *(n. )* መዓርግ *me'ärg*
**grade** *(n.)* ደረጃ *dereğa*
**gradient** *(n.)* ቀነነ *qenene*
**gradual** *(adj.)* ደፋእታዊ *defa'ètawi*
**graduate** *(n.)* ምምራቕ *temereqe*
**graffiti** *(n. )* ምጽያቕ *mtseyaq*
**graft** *(n.)* ጨንገር ምድ'ቓል *çhenger mdqal*
**grain** *(n.)* እኽሊ *'èkli*
**gram** *(n. )* ግራም *gram*
**grammar** *(n.)* ሰዋስው *sewasw*
**gramophone** *(n.)* ባዚቃ *baziqa*
**granary** *(n.)* ማዕከን *ma'ëken*
**grand** *(adj.)* ኣዝዩ ኣገዳሲ *azyu 'agedasi*
**grandeur** *(n.)* ዕቤት *ëbeet*
**grandiose** *(adj.)* ኣዝዩ ሰፊሕ *azyu sefiḥ*
**grandmother** *(n.)* ዓባይ *'äbay*
**grange** *(n.)* ገዛ ገጠር *geza geṭer*
**granite** *(n.)* ጸሊም እምኒ *tselim 'èmni*
**grant** *(v.)* ሃበ *habe*
**granule** *(n.)* ዓንካር *änkar*
**grape** *(n. )* ወይኒ *fre weyni*
**graph** *(n.)* ስእላዊ መግለጺ *graf*
**graphic** *(adj.)* ስእላዊ *s'èlawi*
**graphite** *(n.)* ፈኲሽ ጸሊም *fekWish tselim*
**grapple** *(v.t. )* ተጠማጠመ *teṭemaṭeme*
**grasp** *(v.)* ተረድአ *tered'e*
**grass** *(n. )* ሳዕሪ *sa'ëri*
**grasshopper** *(n.)* ኩብኩብታ *kubkubta*
**grate** *(v.t)* መንፊት ፈርኔሎ *menfit ferneelo*
**grateful** *(n. )* ኣመስጋኒ *amesgani*
**grater** *(n.)* መፋሕፍሒ *mefaḥfḥi*
**gratification** *(n. )* ምሕጓስ *mḥgWas*
**gratify** *(v.)* ኣሐጎሰ *aḥegWase*
**grating** *(n.)* ማዕጾ ርባ *ma'ëtso rba*
**gratis** *(adv. &adj.)* ብነጻ *bnetsa*
**gratitude** *(n. )* ታሕጓስ *mosa*
**gratuitous** *(adj.)* ብናጻ *bnatsa*
**gratuity** *(n. )* እስትሕጋግ *'èsthgag*
**grave** *(n.)* መቓብር *meqabr*
**gravel** *(n.)* ብጉዑር ሸፈነ *bgu'ür shefene*
**graveyard** *(n.)* መካነ-መቓብር *mekanemeqabr*
**gravitas** *(n.)* ክብረት *kbret*
**gravitate** *(v.)* ተሳሕበ *tesaḥbe*
**gravitation** *(n.)* ናይ ስሕበት ኩነት *sḥbet*
**gravity** *(n.)* ስሕበት *sḥbet*
**gravy** *(n.)* መረቕ *mereq*
**graze** *(v.)* ሳዕሪ ኣብልዐ *sa'ëri 'abl'ë*
**grease** *(n.)* ስብሒ *sbḥi*
**great** *(adj.)* ዓቢ *'äbi*
**greatly** *(adv.)* ኣዝዩ ብብዝሒ *azyu bbzḥi*
**greed** *(n.)* ስስዐ *ses'ë-a*
**greedy** *(adj.)* ሀሩፍ *hruf*
**green** *(adj. & n.)* ቆፃል *qotsal*
**greenery** *(v.t. )* ቈጽለ መጽሊ *qoetsele metseli*
**greengrocer** *(n. )* በዓል ድኳን *be'äl dkWan*
**greet** *(n. )* ሰላም በለ *selam bele*
**greeting** *(n.)* ሰላምታ *selamta*

**grenade** *(a. )* ንእሽቶ ቦምባ *n'èshto bomba*
**grey** *(n. )* ሓሙኽሽታይ *ḥamuḱshtay*
**greyhound** *(n. )* ከልቢ ሃድን *kelbi hadn*
**grid** *(n.)* መስርዕ *mesr'ë*
**griddle** *(n.)* መቑሎ *meq̈Wulo*
**grief** *(n. )* ጓሂ *gWahi*
**grievance** *(n.)* ቅርታ *qrta*
**grieve** *(v.)* ኣጉሃየ *aguhaye*
**grievous** *(adj.)* ዘጉሂ *zeguhi*
**grill** *(v.)* ሚሒ-ጥብሲ *miḥeṭbsi*
**grim** *(adj.)* ጥብቂ *ṭebqi*
**grime** *(n.)* ምርሳሕ *arsḥe*
**grin** *(v.)* ፍሽኽታ *fshḱ bele*
**grind** *(v.)* ምጥሓን *me-tha-n*
**grinder** *(n.)* መጥሐኒ *meṭḥani*
**grip** *(v.)* ጭበጠ *čhebeṭe*
**gripe** *(v.)* ሓዘ *ḧaze*
**grit** *(n.)* ሑጻ *ḥutsa*
**groan** *(v.)* ተኣነነ *te'anene*
**grocer** *(n.)* በዓል ኣስቤዛ *be'äl 'asbeza*
**grocery** *(n. )* ኣስቤዛ *asbeza*
**groggy** *(adj.)* ዘይርጉእ *zeyrgu'è*
**groin** *(n.)* ሽምጢ *shmṭi*
**groom** *(v.)* መርዓዊ *alay feres*
**groove** *(n.)* ፍሓ'ር *fḥar*
**grope** *(v.)* ሃሰው በለ *hasew bele*
**gross** *(adj.)* ዓሰርተ ክልተ ደርዘን፣ ዝቕፍፍ ነገር *äserte klte derzen*
**grotesque** *(adj.)* ዘደንቕ *zedenq̈*
**grotto** *(n.)* በዓቲ *be'äti*
**ground** *(n. )* ባይታ *bayta*
**groundless** *(adj.)* መሰረት ኣልቦ *meseret 'albo*
**group** *(n.)* ጉጅለ *gujele*
**grouping** *(n.)* ምጉጃል፣ ምክፍፋል *mgujal*
**grout** *(n.)* ዘፍታ *zefta*
**grovel** *(v.)* ሰገደ *segede*
**grow** *(v.i. )* ምዕባይ፣ ምምዕባል *denfe'ë ma'ëbele*
**growl** *(v.)* ሕኒን በለ *ḥenin bele*
**growth** *(n.)* ዕቤት *'ëbeet*
**grudge** *(n)* ቂም *qim*
**grudging** *(adj.)* ዘይረደየ *zeyredeye*
**gruel** *(n.)* ቦጅቦጅ *bojboj*
**gruesome** *(adj.)* ዘፈንፍን *zefenfn*
**grumble** *(v.)* ተጣርዐ *teṭar'ë*
**grumpy** *(adj.)* ተነጫናጪ *tenecha na chi*
**grunt** *(v.i.)* ምጉርምራም *mgurmram*
**guarantee** *(v.t)* ተዋሓሰ *tewaḥase*
**guarantor** *(n.)* ዋሕስ *waḥs*
**guard** *(v.)* ዘብዐኛ *zeb-egna*
**guarded** *(adj.)* ዝተሓለወ *ztehalewe*
**guardian** *(n. )* ሓላዊ *halawi*
**guava** *(n. )* ዘይቱን *zeytun*
**gudgeon** *(n.)* ብቐሊሉ ዝታለል ሰብ፣ ኣብ ንእሽተን ማይ ዘሎ ዓሳ *gağeyon*
**guerrilla** *(n. )* ደባይ ኲናት *debay kWinat*
**guess** *(v.i)* ገመተ *gemet*
**guest** *(n. )* ጋሻ *gasha*
**guffaw** *(n.)* ካዕካዕ በለ *ka'ëka'ë bele*
**guidance** *(n.)* ኣመራርሓ *amerarha*

**guide** *(n. )* ሓበሪ፣ መራሒ *ḥabari merahi*
**guidebook** *(n.)* ሓባሪ መፅሓፍ *habari metsehaf*
**guild** *(n. )* ማሕበር *maḥbe*
**guile** *(n. )* ተንኰል *tenkWal*
**guillotine** *(n.)* መቑረጽ ወረቐት *meq̈uretsi wereq̈et*
**guilt** *(n.)* ገበን *geben*
**guilty** *(adj.)* ፀፀት *tse tse t*
**guise** *(n. )* ቅዲ ክዳን *qdi kdan*
**guitar** *(n. )* ጊታር *gitar*
**gulf** *(n. )* ወሽመጥ *weshmeṭ*
**gull** *(n.)* ሮብራ *robra*
**gullet** *(n.)* ጎሮሮ *gororo*
**gullible** *(adj.)* ብቐሊሉ ተጎዳኢ *bkelilu tegoda-ei*
**gully** *(n.)* መትረብ፣ ዝተሸርሸረ መንገዲ *metreb*
**gulp** *(v.)* ወሓጠ *weḥaṭe*
**gum** *(n. )* ድርዓን፣ ድዲ *drtsan*
**gun** *(n. )* ጠበንጃ፣ መሳርሒ *ṭebenja mesarhi*
**gurdwara** *(n.)* ናይ ኣምልኾት ቦታ *nay amlkot bota*
**gurgle** *(v.)* በቕ በቕ ምባል *beq̈beq̈ mbal*
**gust** *(n. )* ሓያል ንፋስ *hayal nefas*
**gut** *(n.)* መዓንጣ *me'änta*
**gutsy** *(adj.)* ጅግና *ĵgna*
**gutter** *(n. )* ንረስሓት መሕለፊ ዝተሰርሐ መንገዲ *ne resahat mehlefi mengedi*
**guy** *(n.)* ወዲ ተባዕታይ *wedi teba-etay*
**guzzle** *(v.)* ብፍጥነት ምብላዕ *b-ftnet mebla-e*
**gymnasium** *(n.)* ናይ ኣካል ብቕዓት እንቅስቃሰ ዝስርሓሉ ቦታ *nay akal bqat enkeskase zserehelu bota*
**gymnast** *(n.)* ናይ ኣካል ብቕዓት እንቅስቃሰ ዝሰርሕ ሰብ *nay akal bqat enkeskase zserh*
**gymnastic** *(n. )* ናይ ኣካል ብቕዓት እንቅስቃሰ *nay akal bqat enkeskase*
**gynaecology** *(n.)* ብዛዕባ ማህፀን ዘፅንዕ ትምህርቲ *bzaeba mahtsen zetsene-e temerti*
**gypsy** *(n.)* ብሌብነት ዝመሓደር ሰብ *blebnet zmehader*
**gyrate** *(v.)* ሕምብሊል በለ *ḥmblil bele*

# H

**habit** *(n.)* ልማድ *le-mad*
**habitable** *(adj. )* ክትነብረሉ ዚበቅዕ *ktnebrelu zibeq'ë*
**habitat** *(n. )* መቓምጦ *meq̈amṭo*
**habitation** *(n.)* ምቕማጥ *mq̈maṭ*
**habituate** *(v.t. )* ኣልመደ *almede*
**hack** *(v.)* ቆረጸ *qoretse*
**hackneyed** *(adj. )* ኣመና ልሙድ *amena lmud*
**haemoglobin** *(n.)* ሀሞግሎቢን *hemoglobin*
**haemorrhage** *(n.)* ድምያ *dmya*
**haft** *(n.)* ለዓት *le'ät*
**hag** *(n.)* ጠንቋሊት *ṭenqWAlit*
**haggard** *(adj. )* ዓዝዓዝ *äz'äz*
**haggle** *(v.)* ተዋገየ *tewageye*

**hail** *(n.)* በረድ ሃረመ *bered hareme*
**hair** *(n.)* ጸጉሪ *tseguri*
**haircut** *(n.)* ምቕሶ *mq̈so*
**hairstyle** *(n.)* ኣመሻሽጣ ጸጉሪ *ameshashťa tseguri*
**hairy** *(adj. )* ጨጓር *čheguar*
**hajji** *(n.)* ዝሓጀጀ *zḧaĵeĵe*
**halal** *(adj. )* ዝተቐደሰ *zteq̈edese*
**hale** *(adj. )* ጪጠለ *çheṭele*
**halitosis** *(n.)* ብስናው *b-snaw*
**hall** *(n. )* ኣደራሽ መጋበእያ *'aderash megabe'èya*
**hallmark** *(n.)* ዕላመት *ëlamet*
**hallow** *(v.)* ባረኸ *bareḱe*
**hallucinate** *(v.)* ኣህተፍተፈ *ahteftefe*
**halogen** *(n.)* ጠባይ *ťebay*
**halt** *(v.)* ጠጠው በለ *ṭeṭew bele*
**halter** *(n.)* መወጠጢ ፈረስ *meweṭeṭi feres*
**halting** *(adj. )* መጠጠው *maṭeṭew*
**halve** *(v.)* ፈረቐ *fereq̈e*
**halyard** *(n.)* ገመድ ባንዴራ *gemed bandeera*
**ham** *(n.)* ሰለፍ ሓሰማ *selef ḥasema*
**hamburger** *(n.)* ሃምበርገር *hamberger*
**hamlet** *(n. )* ንእሽቶ ቁሸት *n'èshto qushet*
**hammer** *(n.)* ማርተሎ *martelo*
**hammock** *(n.)* ሃለለ *halele*
**hamper** *(n.)* ኣሰናኸለ *asenaḱele*
**hamster** *(n.)* ሃምስተር *hamster*
**hamstring** *(n.)* ቁና *quna*
**hand** *(n. )* ኢድ *e-i-d*
**handbag** *(n.)* ቦርሳ ኢድ *borsa e-i-d*
**handbill** *(n. )* ፎልዮ *folyo*
**handbook** *(n. )* ማኑዋል *manuwal*
**handcuff** *(n.)* መቁሕ ኢድ *mequḧ 'id*
**handful** *(n.)* ዕታሮ *ëtaro*
**handicap** *(n.)* ዕንቅፋት ጸገም *ënqfat tsegem*
**handicapped** *(n. )* ዕንቅፋት ጸገም *ënqfat tsegem*
**handicraft** *(n. )* ኢደ-ጥበብ *ideṭbeb*
**handiwork** *(n. )* ኢደ-ስራሕ *idesraḧ*
**handkerchief** *(n. )* መንዲል *mendil*
**handle** *(v.t)* ሓዘ *ḥaze*
**handout** *(n.)* ምምጽዋት *meme tse wat*
**handshake** *(n.)* ሰላምታ ኢድ *selamta 'id*
**handsome** *(adj. )* ምልኩዕ *mlku'ë*
**handy** *(adj. )* ስሉጥ *sluṭ*
**hang** *(v.i. )* ተንጠልጠለ *tenṭelṭele*
**hangar** *(n.)* ሰፈር ነፈርቲ *sefer neferti*
**hanger** *(n.)* መንጠልጠሊ *menṭelṭeli*
**hanging** *(n.)* ምሕናቕ *mḥnaq̈*
**hangover** *(n.)* ቅርሲ *qrsi*
**hank** *(n.)* ጥቕላል ፈትሊ *ṭq̈lal fetli*
**hanker** *(v.)* ብብርቱዕ ሃረፈ *bbrtu'ë harefe*
**haphazard** *(adj. )* ሃንደበታዊ *handebetawi*
**hapless** *(adj. )* ዘይዕድለኛ *zey'ëdleña*
**happen** *(v.)* ኰነ *kone*
**happening** *(n. )* ፍጻመ *ftsame*

**happiness** *(n.)* ሓጎስ *ḥagos*
**happy** *(adj. )* ደስታ *desta*
**harass** *(v.)* ኣጨነቐ *ač̣heneq̈e*
**harassment** *(n. )* መጨነቐ *meč̣heneq̈e*
**harbour** *(n.)* መርሳ *mersa*
**hard** *(adj. )* ብትሪ ብብርታዐ *btri bbrta'ë*
**hard drive** *(n.)* መሰርሒ *mesarḧi*
**hardback** *(n.)* መጥመሪ *meẗmeri*
**harden** *(v.)* ተረረ *terere*
**hardly** *(adv. )* ሳሕቲ *saḥti*
**hardship** *(n.)* ሽግር *shgr*
**hardy** *(adj. )* ጠንካራ *ṭenkara*
**hare** *(n. )* ማንቲለ *mantile*
**harelip** *(n.)* ጎነፌ *gonefe*
**harem** *(n.)* ሓሪም *ḥarim*
**hark** *(v.)* ሰምዐ *sem'ë*
**harlequin** *(n.)* ተዋዛዪ *tewazayi*
**harm** *(n.)* ጉድኣት *gud'at*
**harmful** *(adj. )* ተጓዳኢ *tegoda'i*
**harmless** *(adj. )* ዘይጎድእ *zeygod'è*
**harmonious** *(adj. )* ዝተወሃሃደ *ztewehahade*
**harmonium** *(n. )* ሃርሞኑዮም *harmunyem*
**harmonize** *(v.)* ተወሃሃደ *tewehahade*
**harmony** *(n. )* ውህደት *whdet*
**harness** *(n.)* ስርዒት ፈረስ *sr'ït feres*
**harp** *(n.)* በገና *begena*
**harpy** *(n.)* ጨካን ፍጥረት *čekan ftret*
**harrow** *(n.)* ጨካን ፍጥረት *ç̣ekan fṭret*
**harrowing** *(adj. )* ጨካን ፍጥረት *ç̣ekan fṭret*
**harsh** *(adj. )* ዘይምእሙእ *zeym'èmu'è*
**harvest** *(n. )* ጻማ *tsama*
**harvester** *(n. )* ዓጻዲ *ätsadi*
**hassle** *(n.)* መትከር *metker*
**hassock** *(n.)* መተርኣስ ብርኪ *meter'as brki*
**haste** *(n.)* ሃወኸ *haweḱe*
**hasten** *(v.)* ተሃወኸ *tehaweḱe*
**hasty** *(adj. )* ህውኽ *hwḱ*
**hat** *(n. )* ቆብዕ *qob'ë*
**hatch** *(n.)* ነቒሔ *neq̈uḥe*
**hatchet** *(n. )* ፋስ *fas*
**hate** *(v.t. )* ጸልአ *tsel'e*
**hateful** *(adj. )* ጽሉእ *tselu'è*
**haughty** *(adj. )* ዕቡይ *ëbuy*
**haulage** *(n.)* ምጉዕዓዝ *mgu'ë'äz*
**haulier** *(n.)* ኣጉዓዓዚ *agWa'ä'äzi*
**haunch** *(n.)* ጎሎ *golo*
**haunt** *(v.)* ኣሻቐለ *'ashaq̈ele*
**haunted** *(adj. )* ኣሻቐለ *'ashaq̈ele*
**have** *(v.)* ኣሎዎ... *'alowo*
**haven** *(n. )* መድሕን *medḥn*
**havoc** *(n.)* ዕንወት *ënwet*
**hawk** *(n.)* ተገዳር ሓረስታይ *tegedar ḥarestay*
**hawker** *(n. )* ኣዝዋሪ *azwari*
**hawthorn** *(n. )* ቆጥቋጥ *qoṭqoat*
**hay** *(n. )* ሓሰር *ḥaser*
**hazard** *(n.)* ሓደጋ *ḥadega*
**hazardous** *(adj. )* ድንገተኛ *dngeteña*
**haze** *(n.)* ፈኰስ ግመ *fokis gme*
**hazy** *(adj. )* ግመኣዊ *gme'awi*
**he** *(pron. )* ተባዕታይ *teba'ëtay*
**head** *(n.)* ርእሲ *r'èsi*
**headache** *(n. )* ርእሲ ቃንዛ *r'èsi qanza*

**heading** *(n.)* **አርእስቲ** *ar'èsti*
**headlight** *(n.)* **መኪና ብርሃን** *mekina brhan*
**headline** *(n.)* **አርእስተ-ዜና** *ar'èstezeena*
**headmaster** *(n.)* **ሓለቓ መማህራን** *ḥaleq̈a memahran*
**headphone** *(n.)* **መስምዒ ራድዮ** *mesm'ï radyo*
**headquarters** *(n.)* **ምሉእ ስልጣን** *mlu'è slṫan*
**headstrong** *(adj. )* **ነቓጽ** *neq̈atse*
**heady** *(adj. )* **ነዳሪ** *nedari*
**heal** *(v.)* **ሓከመ** *ḥakeme*
**health** *(n.)* **ጥዕና** *ṭ'ëna*
**healthy** *(adj. )* **ጥዑይ** *ṭ'üy*
**heap** *(n.)* **ከመረ ደበራ** *kemere debera*
**hear** *(v.)* **ሰምዐ** *sem'ë*
**hearing** *(n.)* **ምስማዕ** *msma'ë*
**hearse** *(n.)* **መኪና ቀብሪ** *mekina qebri*
**heart** *(n. )* **ልቢ** *lebi*
**heartache** *(n.)* **ጓሂ** *guahi*
**heartbreak** *(n.)* **ሓዘን** *ḧazen*
**heartburn** *(n.)* **ቀሓር** *qeḧar*
**hearten** *(v.)* **ኣተባብዐ** *'atebab'ë*
**heartening** *(adj. )* **ኣተባብዐ** *'atebab'ë*
**heartfelt** *(adj. )* **ልባዊ** *lebawi*
**hearth** *(n.)* **መጋርያ** *megarya*
**heartless** *(adj. )* **ጨካን** *čhekan*
**hearty** *(adj. )* **ልባዊ** *lebawi*
**heat** *(n.)* **ዋዒ** *wa'ï*
**heater** *(n.)* **መሞቒ** *memoq̈i*
**heath** *(n.)* **ቃድራ** *qadra*
**heathen** *(n.)* **ኣምላኽ ጣኦት** *amlak̇ ṭa'ot*
**heather** *(n.)* **ኮሎና** *koloṅa*
**heating** *(n.)* **መውዓይ** *mew'äy*
**heave** *(v.)* **ኣልዓለ** *'al'äle*
**heaven** *(n.)* **መንግስተ-ሰማያት** *mengstesemayat*
**heavenly** *(adj. )* **ሰማያዊ** *semayawi*
**heavy** *(adj. )* **ከቢድ** *kebid*
**heckle** *(v.)* **ወጠረ** *we-ṭe-re*
**hectare** *(n.)* **ሄክታር** *hektar*
**hectic** *(adj. )* **ዕረፍቲ ዘይብሉ** *'ërefti zeyblu*
**hector** *(v.)* **ኣጉባዕብዐ** *aguba'ëb'ë*
**hedge** *(n.)* **ተኽሊ ሓጹር** *tek̇li ḥatsur*
**hedonism** *(n.)* **ሄዶንነት** *heedonnet*
**heed** *(v.)* **ኣቓልቦ** *'aqalbo*
**heel** *(n.)* **ሸኾና** *shek̇Wana*
**hefty** *(adj. )* **ገዚፍን ብርቱዕን** n *gezifn brtu'ë*
**hegemony** *(n.)* **ዕብላለ** *'ëblale*
**height** *(n.)* **ቁመት** *qumet*
**heighten** *(v.)* **ለዓለ** *le'äle*
**heinous** *(adj. )* **ጭካነኣዊ** *chkane-awi*
**heir** *(n.)* **ወራሲ** *werasi*
**helicopter** *(n.)* **ሄሊኮፕተር** *heelikopter*
**heliport** *(n.)* **መዕረፍ ሄሊኮፕተር** *me'ëref heelikopter*
**hell** *(n. )* **ገሃነም** *gehanem*
**helm** *(n. )* **መዛወሪ መርከብ** *mezaweri merkeb*
**helmet** *(n.)* **ሃልመት** *halmet*
**help** *(v.)* **ሓገዘ ረድአ** *ḥageze red'e*
**helpful** *(adj. )* **ሓጋዚ** *ḥagazi*
**helping** *(n.)* **መኣዲ** *me'adi*
**helpless** *(adj. )* **ሓጋዚ ኣልቦ** *ḥagazi 'albo*

**hem** *(n.)* **ክፉፍ** *kfuf*
**hemisphere** *(n. )* **ንፍቀ-ክቢ** *nfqekbi*
**hen** *(n.)* **ደርሆ** *derho*
**hence** *(adv. )* **ካብዚ** *kabzi*
**henceforth** *(adv. )* **ካብ ሕጂ ንደሓር** *kab ḥğï ndeḥar*
**henchman** *(n.)* **እሙን ደጋፊ** *èmun degafi*
**henpecked** *(adj. )* **ኮረየ** *koreye*
**hepatitis** *(adj. )* **ወይቦ** *weybo*
**heptagon** *(n.)* **ስቡዕ ጐኖ** *sbu'ë guano*
**her** *(pron. )* **ንዓአ** *n'ä'a*
**herald** *(n.)* **ተለኣኣኺ** *tele'a'aki*
**herb** *(n.)* **ንእሽቶ ተኽሊ** *n'èshto tekĺi*
**herculean** *(adj. )* **ንእሽቶ ተኽሊ** *n'èshto tekli*
**herd** *(n. )* **መጓሰ** *meguase*
**here** *(adv. )* **ኣብዚ** *'abzi*
**hereabouts** *(adv. )* **ኣብዚ ከባቢ'ዚ** *abzi kebabizi*
**hereafter** *(adv. )* **ድሕሪ ሕጂ** *dḥri ḥğï*
**hereby** *(adv. )* **በዚ ገይሩ** *bezi geyru*
**hereditary** *(adj. )* **ተወርሶኣዊ** *tewerso'awi*
**heredity** *(n.)* **ዓሌት** *ae-leet*
**heritage** *(n. )* **ውርሲ** *wersi*
**hermetic** *(adj. )* **ኣየር ዘየሕልፍ** *'ayer zeyeḥlf*
**hermit** *(n. )* **ባሕታዊ** *baḥtawi*
**hermitage** *(n. )* **ኣግልሎ** *agllo*
**hernia** *(n. )* **ኤርንያ** *eernya*
**hero** *(n.)* **ጅግና** *jegna*
**heroic** *(adj. )* **ጅግንነታዊ** *jegn-netawi*
**heroine** *(n. )* **ፍርሰት** *frset*
**herpes** *(n.)* **ሕማም** *ḥmam*
**herring** *(n.)* **ገፈፈ** *gefefe*
**hers** *(pron. )* **ናታ** *nata*
**herself** *(pron. )* **ባዕላ** *ba'ëla*
**hesitant** *(adj. )* **ሰጋእ መጋእ በሃሊ** *sega'è mega'è behali*
**hesitate** *(v.)* **ተወላወለ** *tewelawele*
**heterogeneous** *(adj. )* **ዝተፈላለየ** *ztefelaleye*
**heterosexual** *(adj. )* **ልዩ-ጾተኛ** *lyu tsoteña*
**hew** *(v.)* **ቆረጸ** *qoretse*
**hexogen** *(n.)* **ጠባይ** *ṫebay*
**heyday** *(n. )* **ጥዑም ግዜ** *ṭ'üm gzee*
**hibernate** *(v.)* **ነወመ** *neweme*
**hiccup** *(n. )* **ጥዑም ግዜ** *ṭ'üm gzee*
**hide** *(v.t)* **ሓብአ** *ḥab'e*
**hideous** *(adj. )* **ግናይ** *gnay*
**hierarchy** *(n.)* **መስርዕ-መዓርግ** *mesr'ëme'ärg*
**high** *(adj. )* **ላዕሊ** *la'ëli*
**highlight** *(v.)* **ኣጉልሐ** *'agulḥe*
**highly** *(adv. )* **ብዝለዓለ** *bzle'äle*
**Highness** *(n. )* **ልዑልነት** *l'ülnet*
**highway** *(n.)* **ጽርግያ** *tsergya*
**hijack** *(v.)* **ጨውያ** *chewya*
**hike** *(n.)* **ዙረት** *zuret*
**hilarious** *(adj. )* **ካዕካዕታዊ** *ka'ëka'ëtawi*
**hilarity** *(n.)* **ካዕካዕታ** *ka'ëka'ëta*
**hill** *(n. )* **ኮረብታ** *korebta*
**hillock** *(n.)* **ኩጀት** *kujet*
**hilt** *(n.)* **ልዓት-ሴፍ** *le-a-t seef*
**him** *(pron. )* **ንዓኡ** *ne-a-u*
**himself** *(pron. )* **ባዕሉ** *ba-e-lu*

**hinder** *(v.)* ዓንቀጸ *anqe-tse*
**hindrance** *(n. )* ዕንቅፋት *enqefat*
**hindsight** *(n.)* ተረድአ *tered'e*
**hinge** *(n.)* መፍሰል *mefsel*
**hint** *(n.)* ኣንፈት *anfet*
**hip** *(n. )* ምሕኩልቲ *mḥkulti*
**hire** *(v.t)* ተኻረየ *teḱareye*
**hirsute** *(adj. )* ጸጓር *tseguar*
**his** *(adj. )* ናቱ *natu*
**hiss** *(v.i)* ጺጽ በለ *tsi-tse bele*
**histogram** *(n. )* ቍጽራዊ *qutserawi*
**historian** *(n.)* ተራኺ *teraki*
**historic** *(adj. )* ታሪኸኛ *tariḱeña*
**historical** *(adj. )* ታሪኻዊ *tariḱawi*
**history** *(n.)* ታሪኽ *tariḱ*
**hit** *(v.)* ሃረመ *hareme*
**hitch** *(v.)* ቋጸረ *qua-tse-re*
**hither** *(adv. )* ክሳብ ሕጂ *ksab ȟĵi*
**hitherto** *(adv. )* ክሳብ ሕጂ *ksab ḥği*
**hive** *(n.)* ጎጆ ንህቢ *gojo nehbi*
**hoard** *(n.)* ኣከበ *'akebe*
**hoarding** *(n.)* ምዕቋር *me-e-qua-r*
**hoarse** *(adj. )* ላሕታት *laḥtat*
**hoax** *(n.)* ኣዐሸወ *aeshewe*
**hob** *(n.)* መጽሎ *metselo*
**hobble** *(v.)* ደርገፍገፍ በለ *dergefgef bele*
**hobby** *(n.)* ፍሉይ ግዳሰ *fluy gdase*
**hobgoblin** *(n.)* ጋኔን *ganeen*
**hockey** *(n.)* ቃርሳ *qarsa*
**hoist** *(v.)* ሰቐለ *seq̈ele*
**hold** *(v.t)* ሓዘ *ḥaze*
**holdall** *(n.)* ማህደር *mahder*
**hole** *(n.)* ነኳል *neḱual*
**holiday** *(n.)* በዓል *be-al*
**holistic** *(adj. )* መለኮታዊ *melekotawi*
**hollow** *(adj. )* ዘይሓቂ *zeyȟaqi*
**holly** *(n.)* ንኡድ *n'ud*
**holmium** *(n.)* ባእታ *ba'èta*
**holocaust** *(n.)* ህልቂት *hlqit*
**hologram** *(n.)* ብምሳሌ ምጥቃም *bmsalee mẗqam*
**holster** *(n.)* ሰፈር ሽጉጥ *sefer shguṭ*
**holy** *(adj. )* ቅዱስ *qdus*
**homage** *(n.)* ኣኽብሮት *aḱbrot*
**home** *(n.)* ገዛ *geza*
**homely** *(adj. )* ምቕሉል *mq̈lul*
**homeopathy** *(n.)* ኣተሓሕዛ *ateȟaȟza*
**homicide** *(n. )* ቅትለተ-ሰብ *qtleteseb*
**homoeopath** *(n. )* ሕክምናዊ *ȟkmnawi*
**homogeneous** *(adj. )* ባህረ-ሓደ *bahreḥade*
**homogeneous** *(a. )* ባህረ-ሓደ *bahreḥade*
**homophobia** *(n.)* ፈርሀ ግብረ-ሰዶመኛ *ferhe gbresedomeňa*
**homosexual** *(n.)* ግብረ-ሰዶመኛ *gbresedomeña*
**honest** *(adj. )* ቅኑዕ *qnu'ë*
**honesty** *(n. )* ቅንዕና *qn'ëna*
**honey** *(n. )* መዓር *me'är*
**honeycomb** *(n. )* ስፈ ንህቢ *sfe nhbi*
**honeymoon** *(n.)* ሕጽኖት *ḥxnot*
**honk** *(n.)* ድምጺ ደርሆ ማይ *dmxi derho may*
**honorary** *(adj. )* ክብራዊ *kbrawi*
**honour** *(n.)* ክብሪ *kbri*

**honourable** *(adj. )* መዓርግ ዘለዎ *me'ärg zelewo*
**hood** *(n.)* ቆብዕ *qob'ë*
**hoodwink** *(v.)* ኣታለለ *atalele*
**hoof** *(n. )* ሸኾና *shḱona*
**hook** *(n. )* ዓይነት ማዕጺድ *äynet ma'ëxid*
**hooked** *(adj. )* ዓይነት ማዕጺድ *äynet ma'ëxid*
**hooligan** *(n. )* ዕዋላ *ëwala*
**hoop** *(n.)* ዕንክሊል *'ënklil*
**hoopla** *(n.)* ዕዋላ *ëwala*
**hoot** *(n.)* ድምጺ ጉንዃ *dmxi gungWa*
**Hoover** *(n.)* መስመር መኾስተር *mesmer meḱoster*
**hop** *(v.)* ነጠረ ምንጣር *neṭere mnṭar*
**hop** *(v.t. )* ነጠረ ምንጣር *neṭere mnṭar*
**hope** *(n.)* ተስፋ *tesfa*
**hopefully** *(adv. )* ብተስፋ *btesfa*
**hopeless** *(adj. )* ተስፋ ኣልቦ *tesfa 'albo*
**horde** *(n. )* ጬፍራ *č̣fra*
**horizon** *(n. )* ደረት ትርኢት *deret tr'it*
**horizontal** *(adj. )* ጋድም *gadm*
**hormone** *(n.)* ሆርሞን *hormon*
**horn** *(n. )* ጥሩምባ *ṭrumba*
**hornet** *(n.)* ዕኮት *ëkot*
**horoscope** *(n.)* ስነ ከዋክብቲ *sene kewakbti*
**horrendous** *(adj. )* ዘሰንብድ *zesenbd*
**horrible** *(adj. )* ሕማቕ *ḥmaq̈*
**horrid** *(adj. )* ዘስገድግድ *zesgedgd*
**horrific** *(adj. )* ኣፍራሒ *'afraḥi*
**horrify** *(v.)* ኣፍርሐ *'afrḥe*
**horror** *(n. )* ፍርሒ *frḥi*
**horse** *(n. )* ፈረሰኛ *fereseña*
**horsepower** *(n.)* ሓይሊ ፈረስ *ḥayli feres*
**horticulture** *(n. )* እጽዳት *ètsedat*
**hose** *(n. )* ቱቦ ማይ *tubo may*
**hosiery** *(n.)* ሶል ጫማ *sol chama*
**hospice** *(n.)* መዕረፊ *me'ërefi*
**hospitable** *(adj. )* ኣእንጋዲ *'a'èngadi*
**hospital** *(n. )* ሆስፒታል *hospital*
**hospitality** *(n. )* ኣአንጋዲነት *a'engadinet*
**host** *(n. )* ኣአንጋዲ *a'engadi*
**hostage** *(n. )* ጀሆ *ğeho*
**hostel** *(n.)* ሆስተል *hostel*
**hostess** *(n.)* ኣአንጋዲት *a'engadit*
**hostile** *(adj. )* ተጻባኢ *tetsaba'i*
**hostility** *(n.)* ጽልኢ *tsel-ei*
**hot** *(adj. )* ውዑይ *w'üy*
**hotchpotch** *(n. )* ሕንፍጽፋጽ *ḥnftsefatse*
**hotel** *(n. )* ሆቴል *hoteel*
**hound** *(n. )* ከልቢ ሃድን *kelbi hadn*
**hour** *(n.)* ሰዓት *se'ät*
**house** *(n.)* ገዛ *geza*
**housewife** *(n.)* በዓልቲ ሓዳር *bealti hadar*
**housing** *(n.)* መዕቆቢ *me-ekobi*
**hovel** *(n.)* ዑና *üna*
**hover** *(v.)* ዘንበየ *zenbeye*
**how** *(adv. )* ከመይ *kemey*
**however** *(adv. )* ሸሕ'ኳ *she-h-kua*
**howl** *(n.)* ጨደረ *che-dere*
**hub** *(n.)* ሕምብርቲ *h-m-brti*
**hubbub** *(n.)* ዕግርግር *e-gerger*

**huddle** *(v.)* ተደጐለ *tedegole*
**hue** *(n.)* ሕብሪ *he-bri*
**huff** *(n.)* ቁጥዐ *qute-e*
**hug** *(v.)* ሓቖፈ *haqo-fe*
**huge** *(adj. )* ገዚፍ *gezif*
**hulk** *(n.)* ደርጓጉ መርከብ *derguag merkeb*
**hull** *(n.)* ቅርፍቲ *qerefti*
**hum** *(v.)* ዚዝ *ziz*
**human** *(adj. )* ሰብኣዊ *seb'awi*
**humane** *(adj. )* ሕያዋይ *heya-way*
**humanism** *(n.)* ሰብኣውነት *seb'awnet*
**humanitarian** *(adj. )* ሰብኣዊ *seb'awi*
**humanity** *(n.)* ወዲ ሰብ *wedi seb*
**humanize** *(v.)* ሰብኣዊ ኮነ *seb'awi kone*
**humble** *(adj. )* ትሑት *tehut*
**humid** *(adj. )* ርጡብ *retub*
**humidity** *(n.)* ጠሊ *ṭeli*
**humiliate** *(v.)* ኣዋረደ *awarede*
**humility** *(n.)* ትሕትና *tehtena*
**hummock** *(n.)* ኩጀት *kujet*
**humorist** *(n.)* ተዋዛዪ *tewazayi*
**humorous** *(adj. )* መስሓቕ *mesḥaq̈*
**humour** *(n. )* ዋዛ *waza*
**hump** *(n.)* መንጉድ *mengud*
**hunch** *(v.)* ቍራስ ግናድ *mi-eti*
**hundred** *(adj.& n.)* ሚእቲ *mi-eti*
**hunger** *(n.)* ጠመየ *ṭemeye*
**hungry** *(adj.)* ጥሙይ *temuy*
**hunk** *(n.)* ግማ'ድ *gmad*
**hunt** *(v.)* ደወረ *dewere*
**hunter** *(n. )* ሃዳናይ *hadanay*
**hurdle** *(n.)* መሰናኽል *mesenaḱl*
**hurl** *(v.)* ወርወረ *werwere*
**hurricane** *(n.)* ህቦብላ *hebobla*
**hurry** *(v.)* ሃወኽ ኣቐልጠፈ *haweḱe 'aq̈elṭefe*
**hurt** *(v.)* ጎድአ *god'e*
**hurtle** *(v.)* ወንጨፈ *wenchefe*
**husband** *(n. )* በዓል ቤት *beal bet*
**husbandry** *(n)* ሕርሻ *hersha*
**hush** *(v.i)* ኣህድአ *ah-dea*
**husk** *(n.)* ቅቃሕ *qe-qah*
**husky** *(adj.)* ንቑጽ *nequtse*
**hustle** *(v.)* ጐናነጸ *gonanetse*
**hut** *(n.)* ኣጉዶ *agudo*
**hutch** *(n.)* ጋቢያ *gabiya*
**hybrid** *(n.)* ድቓላ *deqala*
**hydrant** *(n.)* ማፋ ማይ *mafa may*
**hydrate** *(v.)* በጽበጸ *betse betse*
**hydraulic** *(adj.)* ሓይለ-ማያዊ *ḥaylemayawi*
**hydrogen** *(n. )* ሃይድሮጅን *haydrogen*
**hyena** *(n.)* ዝብኢ *zeb-ei*
**hygiene** *(n.)* ስነ-ጥዕና *sene te-ena*
**hymn** *(n. )* ማህለት *mahlet*
**hype** *(n.)* ኣምሲልካ ምቕራብ *amsilka mq̈rab*
**hyperactive** *(adj.)* ኣመና ንጡፍ *amena nṫuf*
**hyperbole** *(n. )* ዝተጋነነ መግለጺ *zteganene meglexi*
**hypertension** *(n.)* ጸቕጢ-ደም *tseqti dem*
**hyphen** *(n.)* መፈላለዪ ሕንጸጽ *mefelaleyi hentsatse*
**hypnosis** *(n.)* ዕንዛዘ *ënzaze*
**hypnotize** *(v.)* ኣዕንዘዘ *ae-nzeze*
**hypocrisy** *(n. )* ምስሉይነት *mesluynet*
**hypocrite** *(n.)* ምስሉይ *meslu*

**hypotension** ***(n.)*** **ጸቕጢ-ደም** *tseqti dem*
**hypothesis** ***(n.)*** **ጥንሰ-ሓሳብ** *tebse hasab*
**hypothetical** ***(adj.)*** **ጽንሰ-ሓሳባዊ** *tsnsehasabawi*
**hysteria** ***(n.)*** **ዓበድበድ** *aebedbed*
**hysterical** ***(adj.)*** **ዕቡድ** *ebud*

# I

**I** ***(pron.)*** **ኣነ** *'ane*
**ice** ***(n. )*** **በረድ** *bered*
**iceberg** ***(n.)*** **ከውሒ በረድ** *kewḥi bered*
**ice-cream** ***(n.)*** **በረድ ሽኮር** *bered shkor*
**icicle** ***(n.)*** **ጭራሮ በረድ** *çraro bered*
**icing** ***(n.)*** **መመላኽዒ ኬክ** *memelakh'e cake*
**icon** ***(n.)*** **ምስሊ ቅዱሳን** *msli qdusan*
**icy** ***(n. )*** **በረዳዊ** *beredawi*
**idea** ***(n.)*** **ሓሳብ** *ḥasab*
**ideal** ***(n.)*** **ብ ሓሳብ ደረጃ** *b hasab dereja*
**idealism** ***(n. )*** **ሓሳባዊነት** *hasabawinet*
**idealist** ***(n.)*** **ሓሳባዊ** *hasabawi*
**idealize** ***(v.)*** **ከም ፍጹም ምቑፃር** *kem fxum mqutsar*
**ideally** ***(adv. )*** **ብሓሳብ** *b hasab*
**identical** ***(adj.)*** **ሓደ ዓይነት** *hade aynet*
**identification** ***(n.)*** **መለለዪ** *meleleyi*
**identify** ***(v.)*** **ምልላይ** *mllay*
**identity** ***(n.)*** **ሓደ ምኳን** *ḥade mḱWan*
**ideology** ***(n.)*** **ስነ-ሓሳብ** *sneḥasab*
**idiocy** ***(n. )*** **ዕሽነት** *'ëshnet*
**idiom** ***(n.)*** **ቋንቋኛ** *qWAnqWAgna*
**idiomatic** ***(adj.)*** **ቛንቋኛዊ** *qunquñawi*
**idiosyncrasy** ***(n.)*** **ፍሉይ ጠባይ** *fluy ṭebay*
**idiot** ***(n.)*** **ዓሻ** *'äsha*
**idiotic** ***(adj.)*** **ናይ ዓሻ ስራሕ** *nay ash srah*
**idle** ***(adj.)*** **ዘይ ምስራሕ** *zey msrah*
**idleness** ***(n. )*** **ስንፍነት** *snfnet*
**idler** ***(n. )*** **ሰነፍ** *senef*
**idol** ***(n. )*** **ጣኦት** *ṭa'ot*
**idolatry** ***(n.)*** **ጣኦት ኣምልኾ** *ṭa'ot 'amlḱo*
**idolize** ***(v.)*** **ምምላኽ** *mmlak*
**idyll** ***(n.)*** **ቕሊል** *qhlil*
**if** ***(conj.)*** **እንድሕር** *endhr*
**igloo** ***(n.)*** **ኢግሎ** *'iglo*
**igneous** ***(adj.)*** **እሳተ ጐሞራዊ** *'èsate gWamorawi*
**ignite** ***(v.)*** **ወልዐ** *wel'ë*
**ignition** ***(n.)*** **ምውላዕ** *mwla'ë*
**ignoble** ***(adj.)*** **ዘይውርዙይ** *zeywrzuy*
**ignominious** ***(adj.)*** **ውርደተኛ** *wrdeteña*
**ignominy** ***(n.)*** **ውርደት** *wrdet*
**ignoramus** ***(n.)*** **ደንቆሮ** *denqoro*
**ignorance** ***(n.)*** **ዘይምፍላጥ** *zeymflaṭ*
**ignorant** ***(adj.)*** **ዘይፈልጥ** *zeyfeleṭe*
**ignore** ***(v.)*** **ዘይ ምድማፅ** *zeymdmats*

**ill** ***(adj.)*** **ሕሙም** *ḥmum*
**illegal** ***(adj.)*** **ዘይሕጋዊ** *zeyḥgawi*
**illegibility** ***(n.)*** **ተቕባልነት** *teqhebalnet*
**illegible** ***(adj.)*** **ተቕባልነት ዘለዎ** *teqhbalnet zelewo*
**illegitimate** ***(adj.)*** **ዘይሕጋዊ** *zeyḥgawi*
**illicit** ***(adj.)*** **ዘይሕጋዊ፣ ዘይንቡር** *zeyḥgawi, zeynubur*
**illiteracy** ***(n.)*** **መሃይምነት** *mehaymnet*
**illiterate** ***(n. )*** **መሃይም** *mehaym*
**illness** ***(n.)*** **ሕማም** *ḥmam*
**illogical** ***(adj.)*** **ዘይስነ-መጐታዊ** *zeysnemegWatawi*
**illuminate** ***(v.)*** **ኣብርሀ፣ ግልጺ ገበረ** *abrhe, gltsi gebere*
**illumination** ***(n. )*** **ምብራህ፣ ግልጺ ምግባር** *mbrah, gltsi mgbar*
**illusion** ***(v.t. )*** **መሕላም** *meḥlam*
**illusory** ***(adj.)*** **መሕልማዊ** *meḥlmawi*
**illustrate** ***(n. )*** **ኣረድአ** *'ared'e*
**illustration** ***(n. )*** **መረዳእታ መግለጺ** *mereda'èta meglexi*
**illustrious** ***(adj.)*** **ክቡር** *kbur*
**image** ***(n. )*** **ምስሊ** *msli*
**imagery** ***(n.)*** **ብምሳሌ ምጥቃም** *bmsalee mṭqam*
**imaginary** ***(adj.)*** **ዘይጩቡጥ ፣ ሓሳባዊ** *zeychubut, hasabawi*
**imagination** ***(n.)*** **ምሕሳብ** *mhsab*
**imaginative** ***(adj.)*** **ብልሂ** *blhi*
**imagine** ***(v.t. )*** **ቀረጸ ፣ ሓሰበ** *qerexe, hasebe*
**imbalance** ***(n.)*** **ዘይምምጣን** *zeymmṭan*
**imbibe** ***(v.)*** **ሰተየ** *seteye*
**imbroglio** ***(n.)*** **ኸቢድ ኩነታት** *kebid kuknetat*
**imbue** ***(v.)*** **መልአ** *mel'e*
**imitate** ***(v.)*** **ቀድሐ** *qedḥe*
**imitation** ***(n. )*** **ምቕዳሕ** *mq̈daḥ*
**imitator** ***(n.)*** **ቐዳሒ** *kedahi*
**immaculate** ***(adj.)*** **ፁሩይ** *tsury*
**immanent** ***(adj.)*** **ህልው** *hlw*
**immaterial** ***(adj.)*** **ዘይረብሕ** *zeyrebḥ*
**immature** ***(adj.)*** **ጥረ፣ ዘይ በሰለ** *ṭre, zeybesele*
**immaturity** ***(n.)*** **ቑልዓዊ** *qWel'äwi*
**immeasurable** ***(adj.)*** **ኪዕቀን ዘይክኣል** *ki'ëqen zeyke'al*
**immediate** ***(adj.)*** **ቀጥታዊ፣ ብፍጥነት** *qeṭtawi, b ftnet*
**immemorial** ***(adj.)*** **ኣዝዩ ጥንታዊ** *'azyu ṭntawi*
**immense** ***(adj.)*** **ኣዚዩ ዓቢዩ** *aziyu abyi*
**immensity** ***(n.)*** **ግዝፊ** *gzfi*
**immerse** ***(v.)*** **ኣጥሓለ** *'aṭḥale*
**immersion** ***(n. )*** **ምጥሓል** *mṭḥal*
**immigrant** ***(n.)*** **ፈላሲ** *felasi*
**immigrate** ***(v.)*** **ፈለሰ** *felese*
**immigration** ***(n.)*** **ፍልሰት** *flset*
**imminent** ***(adj.)*** **ስሩብ** *srub*
**immoderate** ***(adj.)*** **ተቖባልነት ዘይብሉ** *teqhbalnet zeyblu*
**immodest** ***(n. )*** **ዕቡ'ይ** *'ëbuy*
**immodesty** ***(a. )*** **ዕቡ'ይ** *'ëbuy*
**immolate** ***(v.)*** **ሰወአ** *sewe'e*
**immoral** ***(adj.)*** **ዘይሞራላዊ** *zeymoralawi*
**immorality** ***(n.)*** **ብዕልግና** *be'älegna*

**immortal** *(adj.)* ዘይርሳዕ፣ ዘይመውት *zeyrsa'ë, zeymewut*
**immortality** *(n.)* ህያውነት *hyawnet*
**immortalize** *(v.)* ህያው ገበረ *hyaw gebere*
**immovable** *(adv. )* ቀዋሚ፣ ዘይቀሳቀስ *qewami, zeynqesaqhes*
**immune** *(adj.)* ዉሑስ *wuhus*
**immunity** *(n.)* ዉሕስነት *wuhsnet*
**immunize** *(v.)* ውሕስነት ሃበ *wuhsnet habe*
**immunology** *(n.)* ስነ-ዉሕስና *sne- wuhsna*
**immure** *(n.)* ሕዋስ *hwas*
**immutable** *(adj.)* ዘይቅየር *zeyqyer*
**impact** *(n.)* ምንካእ *mnka'e*
**impair** *(v.)* ኣድከመ *adkeme*
**impalpable** *(adj.)* ዘይተሓዝ *zeyteḥaz*
**impart** *(v.)* ኣካፈለ *'akafele*
**impartial** *(adj.)* ኣድልዎ ዘይብሉ *'adlwo zeyblu*
**impartiality** *(n.)* ፍትሒ *fthï*
**impassable** *(adj.)* ዘየሕልፍ *zeyeḥlf*
**impasse** *(n. )* ዓጋቲ *'ägati*
**impassioned** *(adj.)* ስምዒታዊ *sm'ïtawi*
**impassive** *(adj.)* ድንዙዝ *dnzuz*
**impatient** *(adj.)* ዘይዕጉስ፣ ችኩል *zey'ëgus, chkul*
**impeach** *(v.)* ጠርጠረ *ṭerṭere*
**impeachment** *(n.)* ክሲ *ksi*
**impeccable** *(adj.)* ኣበር ዘይብሉ *'aber zeyblu*
**impede** *(v.)* ዓንቀፈ *'änqefe*
**impediment** *(n.)* ዕንቅፋት *'ënqfat*
**impel** *(v.)* ኣተባብዐ *'atebab'ë*
**impending** *(adj.)* ሐዚ ዝኾነ ነገር ክፍጠር እዩ ዝብል ስሚዒት *hzi zkone neger kfter eyu zbel smiet*
**impenetrable** *(adj.)* ኸቢድ *khebid*
**imperative** *(n.)* ብጣዕሚ ጠቓሚ *bta'emi tqhami*
**imperfect** *(adj.)* ኣበር ዘለዎ *aber zelewo*
**imperfection** *(n.)* ኣበር ምህላው *aber mhlaw*
**imperial** *(adj.)* ኑጉሳዊ ስሚዒት ዘለዎ *nugusawi smi'et zelewo*
**imperialism** *(n.)* ኑጉሳዊ *nugusawi*
**imperil** *(v.)* ኣብ ሓደጋ ጠሓለ *ab hadega tehale*
**impersonal** *(adj.)* ምሳኻ ርክብ ዘይብሉ ነገር *msakha rkb zeyblu neger*
**impersonate** *(v.)* ምምሳል፣ ዘይኮንካዮ እየ ምባል *mmsal, zeykonkayo eye mbal*
**impersonation** *(n.)* ምምሳል *mmsal*
**impertinence** *(n)* ቅንዕና ዘይብሉ ፀባይ *qhn'ena zeyblu tebay*
**impertinent** *(adj.)* ቑኑዕ ዘይ ምኺን *qhhunu;e zeymkhuan*
**impervious** *(adj.)* ምክልኻል *mklkhal*
**impetuous** *(adj.)* ችኩል ዘየስተውዕል *chkul zeyestew'el*
**impetus** *(n.)* ምፍጣን *mftan*

**impious** *(adj.)* ን ሃይማኖታዊ ነገር ክብሪ ዘይብሉ *n haymanotawi neger kbri zeyblu*
**implacable** *(adj.)* ኸቢድ ቑጠዐ *khbid qhute'e*
**implant** *(v.)* ኣብ ውሽጢ ስውነት መቐማጥ ምቕባር *ab wushti ssewunet m'etaw*
**implausible** *(adj.)* ሓቂ ክኾውን ዘይኽእል *haqi kkha=wun zeykh'el*
**implement** *(n.)* ምትግባር *mtgbar*
**implicate** *(v.)* ምኽሳስ *mkhsas*
**implication** *(n.)* ኽሲ *khsi*
**implicit** *(adj.)* ዝርዝረ-ጽሑፋት *zrzrexhufat*
**implode** *(v.)* ብድንገት ምጨፍላቕ *bdnget mchflak*
**implore** *(v.t. )* ምግዳድ *mgdada*
**imply** *(v.)* ምሕባር *mhbar*
**impolite** *(adj.)* ዘይቑኑዕ *zeyqhunu'e*
**import** *(v.)* ምምፃእ *mmtsa'e*
**importance** *(n.)* ጠቓምነት *teqhamnet*
**important** *(adj.)* ጠቓሚ *teqhami*
**importer** *(n. )* ኣምፃኢ *amtsa'e*
**impose** *(v.)* ምግዳድ *mgdad*
**imposing** *(v.)* ምግዳድ *mgdad*
**imposition** *(n. )* ምግዳድ *mgdad*
**impossibility** *(n.)* ዘይምኽኣል *zeymkh'al*
**impossible** *(adj.)* ዘይከኣል *zeymkh'al*
**imposter** *(n.)* መመሰሊ *memeseli*
**impotence** *(n.)* ስንፈተ ግብረስጋ *snfete gebresga*
**impotent** *(adj.)* ስንፈተ ግብረስጋ ዘለዎ *snfete gebresga zelewo*
**impound** *(v.)* ብሕጊ ምዉራስ *bhgi mwuras*
**impoverish** *(v.)* ምድኻም *mdkham*
**impracticable** *(adj.)* ክትግበር ዘይክእል *ktgeber zeyk'el*
**impractical** *(adj.)* ዘይ ተግበራዊ *zey tegberawi*
**impress** *(v.)* ምድናቕ *mdnaqh*
**impression** *(n.)* ናይ ሰብ ባህሪ ምምሳል *nay sb bahri mmsal*
**impressive** *(adj.)* ዝድነቕ *zeneqh*
**imprint** *(n.)* ዓሸራ *ashara*
**imprison** *(n.)* ምእሳር *m'esar*
**improbable** *(adj.)* ክኾን ዘይኽእል *kkhon zeykh'eal*
**improper** *(adj.)* ኣግባብ ዘይብሉ *agbaba zeyblu*
**impropriety** *(n.)* ኣግባብ ዘይብሉ ፀባይ *agbaba zeyblu tsebay*
**improve** *(v.)* ኣስተኻክል *astekhakl*
**improvement** *(n. )* ምስትኽካል *mstkhkal*
**improvident** *(adj.)* ጠመረ *ëmere*
**improvise** *(v.)* ዘለካ ተጠቒምካ ምስራሕ *zeleka tetqhimka msrah*
**imprudent** *(adj.)* ጥንቃቄ ዘይፈልጥ *tnqaqhie zeyfelt*
**impudent** *(adj.)* ትሕትና ዘይፈልጥ *thtna zeyfelt*
**impulse** *(n.)* ሃንደፍታ *handefta*
**impulsive** *(adj.)* ሁንድፍ *hunduf*
**impunity** *(n.)* ክቕፃዕ ዘለዎ *kqhtsa'e zelewo*
**impure** *(adj.)* ዘይንጹህ *zeynutsuh*
**impurity** *(n.)* ዘይንጹህ *zeynutsuh*
**impute** *(v.)* ኢድ ምጡቋም *ed mtuquam*

**in** *(prep.)* **ዉሽጢ** *wusht.*
**inability** *(n.)* **ብዓቕሚ** *b'aqmi*
**inaccurate** *(adj.)* **ትኽክል ዘይኮነ** *tkhkl zeylone*
**inaction** *(n.)* **ምንም ዘይምግባር** *mnm zetmgbar*
**inactive** *(adj.)* **ኑቑሕ ዘይኮነ** *nuqhuh zeykone*
**inadequate** *(adj.)* **ዘይኣክል** *zeyakl*
**inadmissible** *(adj.)* **ኣብ ቤት ፈርዲ ተቐባልነት ዘይብሉ** *ab bet frdi teqhebalnet zeyblu*
**inadvertent** *(adj.)* **ተይፈልጥኻ ዝግበር** *teyfeltka zgber*
**inane** *(adj.)* **ሃሳስ፣ ደደብ** *hasas, dedeb*
**inanimate** *(adj.)* **ሂወት ዘይብሉ ነገር** *hiwet heyblu neger*
**inapplicable** *(adj.)* **ክትግበር ዘይኽእል** *ktgber zeykh'el*
**inappropriate** *(adj.)* **ኣግባብነት ዘይብሉ** *agbabnet zeyblu*
**inarticulate** *(adj.)* **ምዝራብ ዘይኽእል** *mzrab zeykh'el*
**inattentive** *(adj.)* **ትኹረት ዘይህብ** *tkhret zeyhb*
**inaudible** *(adj.)* **ዘይስማዕ** *zeysma'e*
**inaugural** *(adj.)* **መኽፈቲ መደረ** *mekhfeti medere*
**inaugurate** *(v.)* **ስራሕ ምጅማር** *srah mjmar*
**inauspicious** *(adj.)* **ዘይሳኻዕ** *zeyssakha'e*
**inborn** *(adj.)* **መፋጥርቲ** *mefatrti*
**inbred** *(adj.)* **ድቃል** *dqal*
**incalculable** *(adj.)* **ክስላሕ ዘይኽእል** *kslah zykh'el*
**incapable** *(adj.)* **ዓቕሚ ዘይብሉ** *aqmi zeyblu*
**incapacity** *(n.)* **ብዓቕሚ** *b'aqmi*
**incarcerate** *(v.)* **ምእሳር** *m'esar*
**incarnate** *(adj.)* **ምስለ መልኣኽ** *msle mle'akh*
**incarnation** *(n.)* **ኣፀቢቕካ ምውካል** *atsebiqhka mwukal*
**incense** *(n. )* **ዕጣን** *etan*
**incentive** *(n. )* **መተባበዒ** *metebab'e*
**inception** *(n. )* **መጀመርታ** *mejemerta*
**incest** *(n.)* **ኣብመንጎ ቤተሰብ ዝግበር ግብረ ስጋ** *ab mengo beteseb zgber gbre-sga*
**inch** *(n. )* **ኢንች** *inch*
**incidence** *(n.)* **ናይ ምግላፅ ዕድል** *nay mglatz edl*
**incident** *(n.)* **ብ ኣጋጣሚ ዝፈጠር ሓደጋ** *b agatammi zfter hadega*
**incidental** *(adj.)* **ብ ኣጋጣሚ ዝፈጠር ሓደጋ** *b agatammi zfter hadega*
**incisive** *(adj.)* **ብግልጺ ሓሳብካ ምግላፅ** *b gltsi hasbka mglats*
**incite** *(v.)* **ምድፍፋእ** *mdffa'e*
**inclination** *(n.)* **ግበር ዝብል ስምዒት** *gber zbl smi'et*
**incline** *(v.)* **ምዕፃፍ** *metsaf*
**include** *(v.)* **ምክታት** *mktat*
**inclusion** *(n.)* **ምክታት** *mktat*
**inclusive** *(adj.)* **ኣካታቲ** *akatati*
**incoherent** *(adj.)* **ባዕሉ ንባዕሉ ዘይስማዕማዕ** *ba'elu n ba'elu zeysma'ema'e*
**income** *(n.)* **ኣታዊ** *atawi*
**incomparable** *(adj.)* **ዘይወዳደሩ** *zeywedaderu*

**incompatible** ***(adj.)*** **ዘይስማዕማዑ** *zeysma'ema'u*
**incompetent** ***(adj.)*** **ዓቕሚ ዘይምህላው** *aqhmi zeymhlaw*
**incomplete** ***(adj.)*** **ዘይተወደኤ** *zeytewede'e*
**inconclusive** ***(adj.)*** **መደምደምታ ዘይብሉ** *medemdemta zeyblu*
**inconsiderate** ***(adj.)*** **ብዛዕባ ኻልኦት ዘይሓስብ** *bza'eba kal'ot zeyhasb*
**inconsistent** ***(adj.)*** **ቐፃልነት ዘይብሉ** *qhetsalnet zeyblu*
**inconsolable** ***(adj.)*** **ካብ ዓቐን ብላዕሊ ምሕዛን** *kab aqhen bla'eli mhzan*
**inconspicuous** ***(adj.)*** **ትኹረት ዘይምስሓብ** *tkhuret zeymhsab*
**inconvenience** ***(n.)*** **ችግር ምፍጣር** *chger mftar*
**incorporate** ***(v.)*** **ምክታት** *mktat*
**incorporation** ***(n.)*** **ብምክታት** *bmktat*
**incorrect** ***(adj.)*** **ስሕተት** *s'htet*
**incorrigible** ***(adj.)*** **ክቕየር ዘይኽእል ሕመቕ** *kqhyer zeykh'el hmeqh*
**incorruptible** ***(adj.)*** **ብላዕ ዘይበልዕ** *bla'e zeybel'e*
**increase** ***(v.)*** **ምዉሳኽ** *mwusakh*
**incredible** ***(adj.)*** **ገራሚ** *gerammi*
**increment** ***(n.)*** **ዘዉስኽሉ መጠን** *zwusekhelu metn*
**incriminate** ***(v.i. )*** **ምዉንጃል** *mwunjal*
**incubate** ***(v.)*** **ምብሳል** *mbsal*
**inculcate** ***(v.)*** **ብምድግጋም ምምሃር** *bmdggam mmhar*
**incumbent** ***(adj.)*** **ብዓል ስልጣን** *b'al sltan*
**incur** ***(v.)*** **ዋጋ ስራሕካ ምርካብ** *waga srahka mrkab*
**incurable** ***(adj.)*** **ክድሕን ዘይኽእል** *kdhn zeykh'el*
**incursion** ***(n.)*** **ምጥሓስ** *mthas*
**indebted** ***(adj.)*** **ኣብ ዕዳ ምእታው** *ab eda m'etaw*
**indecency** ***(n.)*** **ፆታዊ ስርዓት ኣልብኛነት** *tsotawi sr'at albegneet*
**indecent** ***(adj.)*** **ፆታዊ ስርዓት ኣልቦ** *tsotawi sr'at albo*
**indecision** ***(n.)*** **ውሳኔ ምዉሳን ዘይምኽኣል** *wusanie mwusan zeykh'el*
**indeed** ***(adv. )*** **ብደንቢ** *bdenbi*
**indefensible** ***(adj.)*** **ካብ መጥቃዕቲ ንምክልኻል ኣፀጋሚ** *kab metka'et nmklkhal zetsgm*
**indefinite** ***(adj.)*** **ግልፂ ዘይኮነ** *gltsi zeykone*
**indemnity** ***(n. )*** **ሓለዋ** *halewa*
**indent** ***(v.)*** **ዉፅእ ኢልካ ምጅማር** *wts'e elka mjmar*
**indenture** ***(n.)*** **ተገዲድካ ንስብ ምስራሕ** *tegedidka nseb msrah*
**independence** ***(n.)*** **ነፃነት** *netanet*
**independent** ***(adj.)*** **ነፃ** *netsa*
**indescribable** ***(adj.)*** **ንምግላፅ ዘፀግም** *nmglats zetsegm*
**index** ***(n.)*** **ኢንዴክስ** *index*
**Indian** ***(n.)*** **ህንዳዊ** *hndawi*
**indicate** ***(v.)*** **ምምልካት** *mmlkat*
**indication** ***(n.)*** **ኣምልካቲ** *amlkati*
**indicative** ***(adj.)*** **ኣምልካቲ** *amlkati*
**indicator** ***(n.)*** **ኣምልካቲ** *amlkati*

**indict** ***(v.)*** **ምጥቋም** *mtkoum*
**indictment** ***(n.)*** **ኽሲ** *khsi*
**indifference** ***(n.)*** **ድልየት ዘይምህላው** *dlyet zeymhlaw*
**indifferent** ***(adj.)*** **ድልየት ዘይምህላው** *dlyet zeymhlaw*
**indigenous** ***(adj.)*** **ናይ ሓደ ሃገር በዓል ዋና** *nay hade hager be'el wana*
**indigestible** ***(adj.)*** **ብቐሊሉ ዘይሓቅቕ** *bqhelilu zwyhaqqh*
**indigestion** ***(n.)*** **ብዘይ ምሕቓቕ ምግቢ ዝመፅእ ቓንዛ ኸብዲ** *bzey mhqaqh mgbi zmets'e qhanza kebdi*
**indignant** ***(adj.)*** **ቑጡዐ** *qhute'e*
**indignation** ***(n. )*** **ቑጡዐ** *qhute'e*
**indignity** ***(n.)*** **ምሕፋር** *mhfar*
**indigo** ***(n.)*** **ፀሊም ሊላዊ ዕንቆዋይ** *tselim lilawi enqoway*
**indirect** ***(adj.)*** **ብተዘዋዋሪ** *btezewawari*
**indiscipline** ***(n.)*** **ስርዓት ዘይተምሃረ** *sr'at zeytemhare*
**indiscreet** ***(adj.)*** **ሕፍረት ዘይብሉ** *hfret zeyblu*
**indiscretion** ***(n.)*** **ሕፍረት ዘይምህላይ** *hfret zeymhlay*
**indiscriminate** ***(adj.)*** **ብዘይ ኣፍላላይ** *bzey afelalay*
**indispensable** ***(adj.)*** **ወሳኒ** *wsani*
**indisposed** ***(adj.)*** **ዘይምህላው** *zeymhlaw*
**indisputable** ***(adj.)*** **ዘየከራኽር** *zeyekerakr*
**indistinct** ***(adj.)*** **ንፁር ዘይኮነ** *ntsur zeykone*
**individual** ***(adj.)*** **ዉልቀ** *wlqe*
**individualism** ***(n.)*** **ዉልቃዊነት** *wlqawinet*
**individuality** ***(n.)*** **ዉልቃዊነት** *wlqawinet*
**indivisible** ***(adj.)*** **ዘይኽፈል** *zeykhfel*
**indolent** ***(adj.)*** **ሰነፍ** *senef*
**indomitable** ***(adj.)*** **ተስፋ ዘይምቑራፅ** *tesfa zeymuqhurats*
**indoor** ***(adj.)*** **ኣብ ውሽጢ ገዛ** *ab wushti geza*
**induce** ***(v.)*** **ምፍጣር ምግባር** *mftr mgbar*
**inducement** ***(n.)*** **መተባብዒ** *metebab'e*
**induct** ***(v.)*** **ስልጣን ወይ ስራህ ምሃብ** *sltan wey srah mhab*
**induction** ***(n.)*** **ስልጣን ወይ ስራህ ምሃብ** *sltan wey srah mhab*
**indulge** ***(v.)*** **ዘደለዮ ንክገብር ምፍቃድ፣ ስዲ ሰዲድዎ** *zdeleyo neger kgebr mfqhad, sdi msdada*
**indulgence** ***(n.)*** **ስዲ ምስዳድ** *sdi msdada*
**indulgent** ***(adj.)*** **ስዲ ምስዳድ** *sdi msdada*
**industrial** ***(adj.)*** **ኢንዱስትርያላዊ** *industryalawi*
**industrious** ***(adj.)*** **ፃዕራም** *tsa'eram*
**industry** ***(n.)*** **ኢንዱስትሪ** *industri*
**ineffective** ***(adj.)*** **ስክዒታማ ዘይኮነ መንግዲ** *sk;etama zeykone megedi*
**inefficient** ***(adj.)*** **ጊዚኡ ብኣግባብ ዘይጥቀም** *gizi'u b agbab zeytkem*
**ineligible** ***(adj.)*** **ብቑዕ ዝይኮነ** *buqhu'e zeykone*

**inequality** ***(n.)*** ኢ_ማዓርነት *e-ma'arnet*
**inert** ***(adj.)*** ዘይስሕብ *zeyshb*
**inertia** ***(n.)*** ኢነርሻ *inertia*
**inescapable** ***(adj.)*** ክምለጥ ዘይክእል *kmlet zyk'el*
**inevitable** ***(adj.)*** ዘይቐሪ ነገር *zeyqheri neger*
**inexact** ***(adj.)*** ትኽክል ዘይኮነ *tkhkl zeykone*
**inexcusable** ***(adj.)*** ተቐባልነት ዘይብሉ *teqhebalnet zeyblu*
**inexhaustible** ***(adj.)*** ዘይውዳእ *zeywda'e*
**inexorable** ***(adj.)*** ክቋረፅ ዘይኽእል *kquarets zeykh'el*
**inexpensive** ***(adj.)*** ርካሽ *rkash*
**inexperience** ***(n.)*** ልምዲ ዘይብሉ *lmdi zeyblu*
**inexplicable** ***(adj.)*** ዘይፍለጥ ምኽንያት *zeyflet mknyat*
**inextricable** ***(adj.)*** ክፈላለዩ ዘይኽእሉ *kfelaleyu zeykh'elu*
**infallible** ***(adj.)*** ተሰሓሒቱ ዘይፈልጥ *tesehahitu zeyfelt*
**infamous** ***(adj.)*** ተፈላጥ *tefelati*
**infamy** ***(n.)*** ተፈላጢ ምኻን *tefelati mkhan*
**infancy** ***(n. )*** ቁልዕነት *qhul'enet*
**infant** ***(n.)*** ዕሸል *eshel*
**infanticide** ***(n.)*** ዕሸል ምቕታል *eshel mqhtal*
**infantile** ***(adj.)*** ቖልዓ *qhol'a*
**infantry** ***(n.)*** እግረኛ ወታደር *egregna wetader*
**infatuate** ***(v.)*** ምፍታው *mftaw*
**infatuation** ***(n.)*** ምፍታው *mftaw*
**infect** ***(v.)*** ምብካል *mbkal*
**infection** ***(n.)*** ብኽለት *bkhlet*
**infectious** ***(adj.)*** ተመሓላለፊ *temhalallefi*
**infer** ***(v.)*** ካብ ዝበሎ ተላዒለ *kab zbelo tela'ele*
**inference** ***(n.)*** ካብ ዝበሎ ተላዒለ *kab zbelo tela'ele*
**inferior** ***(adj.)*** ትሑት *tȟut*
**inferiority** ***(n.)*** ታሕተዋይነት *tahtewaynet*
**infernal** ***(adj.)*** ደስ ዘይብል *deszeyble*
**infertile** ***(adj.)*** መኻን *mkhan*
**infest** ***(v.)*** ብብዝሓት ምህላው *bbzhat mhlaw*
**infidelity** ***(n.)*** ካብ ሕዳርካ ወፃኢ ዝግበር ግብረ ሰጋ *kab hadarka wetsa'e zgber gbre-sga*
**infighting** ***(n.)*** ቃራና *qarana*
**infiltrate** ***(v.)*** እብ ውሽጢ ኣቲኻ ምስላል *ab wshti atikha mslal*
**infinite** ***(adj.)*** ብጣዕሚ ቡዙሕ *bta'emi buzuh*
**infinity** ***(n.)*** ብጣዕሚ ቡዙሕ *bta'emi buzuh*
**infirm** ***(adj.)*** ብሕማም ዝመፅእ ድኻም *b hmam zmets'e hmam*
**infirmity** ***(n.)*** ብሕማም ዝመፅእ ድኻም *b hmam zmets'e hmam*
**inflame** ***(v.)*** ምውዕዋዕ *mw'ewa'e*
**inflammable** ***(adj.)*** ተዋዓዋዒ *tewa'awa'i*
**inflammation** ***(n.)*** ምኩሳሕ *mkusah*
**inflammatory** ***(adj.)*** ተ኿ሳሒ *tekhuasahi*
**inflate** ***(v.)*** ምውሳኽ *mwusakh*
**inflation** ***(n.)*** ወሰኽ ዋጋ *weskh waga*
**inflect** ***(v.)*** ምምልካት *mmlkat*

**inflexible** *(adj.)* **ዘይቕየር ደረቕ** *zyqhyer dereqh*
**inflict** *(v.)* **ክስመዖ ምግባር** *ksme'o mgbar*
**influence** *(n.)* **ተሰማዒነት** *tesema'enet*
**influential** *(adj.)* **ተሰማዒ** *tesema'e*
**influenza** *(n. )* **ኢንፉሉዌንዛ** *influenza*
**influx** *(n.)* **ብበዝሒ ምምፃእ** *bbezhi mmtsa'e*
**inform** *(v.)* **ምሕባር** *mhbar*
**informal** *(adj.)* **ዘይኣግባባዊ** *zeyagbabawi*
**information** *(n.)* **ሓበሬታ** *haberieta*
**informative** *(adj.)* **ኣደመ** *ademe*
**informer** *(n.)* **ሓባሪ** *habari*
**infrastructure** *(n.)* **መሰረተ ልምዓት** *meserete lm'at*
**infrequent** *(adj.)* **ሓሓሊፉ** *hahalifu*
**infringe** *(v.)* **ምጥሓስ** *mthas*
**infringement** *(n.)* **ጥሕሰት** *thset*
**infuriate** *(v.)* **ምቑጣዕ** *mqhuta'e*
**infuse** *(v.)* **ምምላእ** *mmla'e*
**infusion** *(n.)* **ምልኢት** *el'it*
**ingrained** *(adj.)* **ዝፀነሐ** *ztsenehe*
**ingratitude** *(n. )* **ምስጋና ቢስ** *msgana bis*
**ingredient** *(n.)* **ቅመም** *qhmem*
**inhabit** *(v.)* **ይንብር/ሩ** *ynebr/ru*
**inhabitable** *(adj.)* **ንምምባር ዘይኾን** *nmmbar zeykhon*
**inhabitant** *(n.)* **ነበርቲ** *neberti*
**inhale** *(v.)* **ኣየር ምስሓብ** *ayer mshab*
**inhaler** *(n.)* **መተንፈሲ** *btenfesi*
**inherent** *(adj.)* **ካብ ወሎዶ ናብ ወሎዳ ዝመሓላለፈ** *kab welodo nab welodo zmehlalef*
**inherit** *(v.)* **ወረሰ** *werese*
**inheritance** *(n.)* **ውርሲ** *wursi*
**inhibit** *(v.)* **ምክልኻል** *mklkhal*
**inhibition** *(n.)* **ሕፍረት** *hfret*
**inhospitable** *(adj.)* **ክሕከም ዘይኽእል** *khkem zeykh'el*
**inhuman** *(adj.)* **ኢ_ስብኣዊ** *e-sb'awi*
**inimical** *(adj.)* **ዘተባብዕ** *zetebab'e*
**inimitable** *(adj.)* **ፉሉይ** *fuluy*
**initial** *(adj.)* **መጀመርታ** *mejemerta*
**initiate** *(v.)* **ጀምር** *jemr*
**initiative** *(n.)* **ምልዕዓል** *ml'ë'äl*
**inject** *(v.)* **ምውጋእ** *mwga'e*
**injection** *(n.)* **መርፌእ ምውጋእ** *merfi'e mwga'e*
**injudicious** *(adj.)* **ዕሽነት ዝትምሉእ ዉሳኔ** *arabḧe*
**injunction** *(n.)* **ናይ ፍርዲ ቤት ኽልከላ** *nay bet ferdi khlkela*
**injure** *(v.)* **ምጉዳእ** *mguda'e*
**injurious** *(adj.)* **ጎዳኢ** *goda'e*
**injury** *(n.)* **ጉድኣት** *gudu'at*
**injustice** *(n.)* **ኢ_ፍትሓዊ** *e-fthawi*
**ink** *(n.)* **ቐለም** *qhelem*
**inkling** *(n.)* **ምቕላም** *mqhlam*
**inland** *(adj.)* **ሃገራዊ** *hagerawi*
**inmate** *(n.)* **እስረኛ** *esregna*
**inmost** *(adj.)* **ውሽጣዊ** *wshtawi*
**inn** *(n.)* **ኑኡሽተይ ኣረጊት ሆቴል** *nu'eshtey aregit hotel*
**innate** *(adj.)* **ሒዝካዮ እትውልድ ኽእለት** *hizkayo etwled kh'elet*
**inner** *(adj.)* **ውሽጣዊ** *wushtawi*

**innermost** ***(adj.)*** **ውሽጣዊ** *wushtawi*
**innings** ***(n.)*** **ተፃወቲ ክርኬት ኩዑሶ ዝወቕዐሉ ግዘ** *ttsaweti krikate ku'eso zewek'elu gizie*
**innocence** ***(n.)*** **ዘይምፍላጥ ዘይምግባር** *zeymflat zeymegbar*
**innocent** ***(adj.)*** **ዘይፈልጥ ዘይገበረ** *zeyfelt zeygeber*
**innovate** ***(v.)*** **ምፍጣር** *mftar*
**innovation** ***(n.)*** **ፈጠራ** *fetari*
**innovator** ***(n.)*** **ፈጣሪ** *fetari*
**innumerable** ***(adj.)*** **ብዙሕ** *bzuh*
**inoculate** ***(v.)*** **ምኽታብ** *mkhtab*
**inoculation** ***(n.)*** **ኽትባት** *khtbat*
**inoperative** ***(adj.)*** **ዘይሰርሕ** *zeyserh*
**inopportune** ***(adj.)*** **ዘይሙቹ** *zeymuchu*
**inpatient** ***(n.)*** **ድቂሱ ዝሕከም** *dekisu zhkem*
**input** ***(n.)*** **ኣታዊ** *atawi*
**inquest** ***(n.)*** **ናይ ሓደጋ ምርመራ** *nay hadega mrmera*
**inquire** ***(v.)*** **ሓበሬታ ምሕታት** *haberieta mhtat*
**inquiry** ***(n.)*** **ሓበሬታ ንምግናይ ዝሕተት ሕቶ** *haberieta nmgnay zhtet hto*
**inquisition** ***(n.)*** **ፖሊሳዊ ምርመራ** *polisawi mrmera*
**inquisitive** ***(adj.)*** **ሚስጥራት ምምርማር ዘፈቱ** *mistrat mmrmar zefetu*
**insane** ***(adj.)*** **ዑብድ** *ebud*
**insanity** ***(n.)*** **ዕብደት** *ebdt*
**insatiable** ***(adj.)*** **ዓቐን ዘይብሉ ድልየት** *aqhen zeyblu dlyet*
**inscribe** ***(v.)*** **ፁሑፍ ምቕራፅ** *tsuhuf mqhrats*
**inscription** ***(n.)*** **ዝተቐረፀ ፁሑፍ** *zteqhretse tsuhuf*
**insect** ***(n.)*** **ደቖቕቲ እንስሳት** *deqheqhti enssat*
**insecticide** ***(n.)*** **ፀረ_ባልዕ** *tsere-bal'e*
**insecure** ***(adj.)*** **ዘየተኣማምን** *zeyte'amamen*
**insecurity** ***(n.)*** **ዘየተኣማምን** *zeyete'amamn*
**insensible** ***(adj.)*** **ትርጉም ዘይህብ** *trgum zeyhb*
**inseparable** ***(adj.)*** **ዘይነፃፀል** *zeynetsatsel*
**insert** ***(v.)*** **ሰኹዐ** *seḱu'ë*
**insertion** ***(n.)*** **ምስኳዕ** *mskWa'ë*
**inside** ***(n.)*** **ውሽጢ** *wshẗi*
**insight** ***(n. )*** **ስውጠት** *swṭet*
**insignificance** ***(n.)*** **ዘይረብሕ** *zeyrebḥ*
**insignificant** ***(adj.)*** **ዘይረብሕ** *zeyrebḥ*
**insincere** ***(adj.)*** **ናይ ዉሽጡ ዘይዛረብ** *nay wushtu zeyzareb*
**insincerity** ***(adv. )*** **ናይ ውሽጥኻ ዘይምዝራብ** *nay wushtkha zeymzrab*
**insinuate** ***(v.)*** **ሰለኹ** *seleḱWa*
**insinuation** ***(n.)*** **ምስላኽ** *mslakh*
**insipid** ***(adj.)*** **ዘይጥዕም** *zeyt'em*
**insist** ***(v.)*** **ኣትሪሩ ተዛረበ** *- atriru tezarebe*
**insistence** ***(n.)*** **ፅኑዕ** *tsnu'ë*
**insistent** ***(adj.)*** **ተደጋጋሚ** *tedegagami*
**insolence** ***(n.)*** **ዘይምኽባር** *zeymkbar*

**insolent** ***(adj.)*** **ዘይምኽባር** *zeymkbar*
**insoluble** ***(adj.)*** **ዘይሓቅቕ** *zeyḥaqq̈*
**insolvency** ***(n.)*** **ዕዳኻ ንምኽፋል ዓቕሚ ምስኣን** *edaka nmkhfakl akmi ms'an*
**insolvent** ***(adj.)*** **ዕዳኡ ኪኸፍል ዘይክኣለ** *ed'u kkefel zeyke'ale*
**inspect** ***(v.)*** **መርመረ** *mermere*
**inspection** ***(n.)*** **ቊጽጽር** *qutstsr*
**inspector** ***(n.)*** **ተቈጻጻሪ** *teq̈Wetsatsari*
**inspiration** ***(n.)*** **መተባበዒ** *temsaṭ*
**inspire** ***(v.)*** **ኣተባብዐ** *'atebab'ë*
**instability** ***(n.)*** **ዘይቀዋምነት** *zeyqewaminet*
**install** ***(v.)*** **ኣብ ስልጣን ኣደየበ** *'ab slṭan 'adeyebe*
**installation** ***(n.)*** **ቦታ ምሓዝ** *bota mḥaz*
**instalment** ***(n.)*** **ክፋል** *kfal*
**instance** ***(n.)*** **ኣብነት መረዳእታ** *'abnet mereda'èta*
**instant** ***(adj.)*** **ቅፅበት** *qtsbetawi*
**instantaneous** ***(adj.)*** **ቅፅበታዊ** *qtsbetawi*
**instead** ***(adv. )*** **ኣብ ክንዲ** *ab kndi*
**instigate** ***(v.)*** **ቀስቀሰ** *qesqese*
**instil** ***(v.)*** **በብቑሩብ ኣእተወ** *bebq̈urub 'a'ètewe*
**instinct** ***(n.)*** **ባህረት** *bahret*
**instinctive** ***(adj.)*** **ባህረታዊ** *bahretawi*
**institute** ***(n.)*** **ኣቑመ** *'aq̈Weme*
**institution** ***(n.)*** **ተቛም** *tqhuam*
**instruct** ***(v.)*** **መሃረ** *mehare*
**instruction** ***(n.)*** **መምርሒ** *memrhi*
**instructor** ***(n.)*** **መምህር** *memhr*
**instrument** ***(n.)*** **መሳርሒ** *mesarhi*
**instrumental** ***(adj.)*** **መሳርሒያዊ** *mesarhawi*
**instrumentalist** ***(n.)*** **ተጻዋቲ መሳርሒ** *texawati mesarhi*
**insubordinate** ***(adj.)*** **ምሕንጋድ** *mhngad*
**insubordination** ***(n.)*** **ምሕንጋድ** *mḥngad*
**insufficient** ***(adj.)*** **ዘይእኹል** *zey'èḱul*
**insular** ***(adj.)*** **ሓዱሽ ስብ ወይ ሓሳብ ዘይቕበል** *hadish sb wey hasab zeyqqhbel*
**insulate** ***(v.)*** **ካብ ኤልክትሪክ ወይ ካብ ሙቐት ምክልኻል** *kab electric wey muqhet mklkhal*
**insulation** ***(n.)*** **ካብ ኤልክትሪክ ወይ ሙቐት ዝከላኸል ሽፋን** *kab electric wey muqhet zkelakhel shfan*
**insulator** ***(n.)*** **ኤልክትሪክ ወይ ካብ ሙቐት ዘይመሓላልፍ** *electric wey muqhet zeyemehalalf*
**insulin** ***(n.)*** **ኢንሱሊን** *'insulin*
**insult** ***(v.t. )*** **ፀረፈ;ኣዋረደ** *tserefe;awarede*
**insupportable** ***(adj.)*** **ክትጽመሞ ዘይክኣል** *ktsmemo zeyke'al*
**insurance** ***(n.)*** **መድሕን** *medḧn*
**insure** ***(v.)*** **ኣውሓሰ** *'awḧase*
**insurgent** ***(n.)*** **ፀረ ምንግስቲ** *tse-mengsti*
**insurmountable** ***(adj.)*** **ክስተኸኽል ዘይኽእል ፀገም** *kstekhakel zeylh'el tsegem*
**insurrection** ***(n.)*** **ዓምፅ** *ametse*

**intact** ***(adj.)*** **ዘይተጎደአ** *zeytegode'e*
**intake** ***(n.)*** **መምልኢ** *meml'i*
**intangible** ***(adj.)*** **ኪጭበጥ ዘይክኣል** *kičbeť zeyke'al*
**integral** ***(adj.)*** **ዘይንፀል ኣካል** *zeyntsel 'akal*
**integrity** ***(n.)*** **ቅንዕና** *qn'ëna*
**intellect** ***(n.)*** **ሊቅ** *liq*
**intellectual** ***(adj.)*** **ምሁር በሊሕ ሊቅ** *mhur beliȟ liq*
**intelligence** ***(n.)*** **ክእለት; ኣስተውዕሎ** *k'èlet; astew'ëlo*
**intelligent** ***(adj.)*** **ኣስተውዓሊ** *'astew'äli*
**intelligible** ***(adj.)*** **ብሩህ** *bruh*
**intend** ***(v.)*** **ወጠነ** *weťene*
**intense** ***(adj.)*** **ስምዒታዊ** *sm'ïtawi*
**intensify** ***(v.)*** **ፀዓቐ** *tse'äq̈e*
**intensity** ***(n.)*** **ፀዕቂ** *tsa'ëqi*
**intensive** ***(adj.)*** **ፅዑቕ** *ts'üq̈*
**intent** ***(n.)*** **ዕላማ** *ëlama*
**intention** ***(n.)*** **ምውጣን** *mwťan*
**intentional** ***(adj.)*** **ዉጡን** *wutun*
**interact** ***(v.)*** **ምትእትታው** *mt'ettaw*
**intercede** ***(v.)*** **ይቕር ንክብል ምእማን** *yker nkbl m'eman*
**intercept** ***(v.)*** **ኣቋረጸ** *'aqWArexe*
**interception** ***(n.)*** **ምቍራጽ** *mqurats*
**interchange** ***(v.)*** **ተለዋወጠ** *telewaweťe*
**intercom** ***(n.)*** **ውሽጣዊ መዘራረቢ** *wshťawi mezerarebi*
**interconnect** ***(v.)*** **ዝተረኻኸቡ** *ztelkhakhebu*
**intercourse** ***(n.)*** **ግብረ ስጋ** *gbre sga*
**interdependent** ***(adj.)*** **ተማራኺሲ** *temarakWasi*
**interest** ***(n.)*** **ድልየት ወይ ዝንባለ** *dlyet wey znbale*
**interesting** ***(adj.)*** **ማራኺ** *maraḱi*
**interface** ***(n.)*** **ሽርካ** *shrka*
**interfere** ***(v.)*** **ኢዱ ኣእተወ** *'idu 'a'ètewe*
**interference** ***(n.)*** **ኢድ ምእታው** *id m'ètaw*
**interim** ***(n.)*** **ጊዜዊ** *gizawi*
**interior** ***(adj.)*** **ውሽጣዊ** *wshťawi*
**interject** ***(v.)*** **ዝዛረብ ሰብ ኣቋረፀ** *zzareb seb aqaretse*
**interlink** ***(v.)*** **ተኣሳሰረ** *te'asasere*
**interlock** ***(v.)*** **ተገጣጠመ** *tegeťaťeme*
**interlocutor** ***(n.)*** **መዋግዕቲ** *mewag'eti*
**interloper** ***(n.)*** **ጦብሎቕ በሃሊ** *ťobloq̈ behali*
**interlude** ***(n.)*** **ዕረፍቲ** *'ërefti*
**intermediary** ***(n.)*** **መንጎኛ** *mengoȟa*
**intermediate** ***(adj.)*** **ማእከላይ** *ma'èkelay ( ንግዜ ቦታ፣ ደረጃ...ወዘተ)*
**interminable** ***(adj.)*** **መወዳእታ ዘይብሉ** *meweda'èta zeyblu*
**intermission** ***(n.)*** **ዕረፍቲ** *'ërefti*
**intermittent** ***(adj.)*** **ሓሓሊፍ ዝድጋገም** *hahalifu zdegagem*
**intern** ***(v.)*** **ሰልጣኒ** *seltani*
**internal** ***(adj.)*** **ውሽጣዊ** *wshťawi*
**international** ***(adj.)*** **ዓለም-ለኸዊ** *'älemleḱawi*
**interplay** ***(n.)*** **ርክብ** *rkb*
**interpret** ***(v.)*** **ተረጎመ** *teregome*

**interpreter** ***(n.)*** **እስተርጓሚ** *'astergWami*
**interracial** ***(adj.)*** **በየነ-ዓሌታዊ** *beyene'äleetawi*
**interrelate** ***(v.)*** **ተዘማመደ** *tezemamede*
**interrogate** ***(v.)*** **ሓተተ** *ḧatete*
**interrogative** ***(adj.)*** **ናይ ሕቶ ቃል** *nay ḧto qal*
**interrupt** ***(v.)*** **ኣቋረፀ** *aqaretse*
**interruption** ***(n.)*** **ምቁራፅ** *mqurats*
**intersect** ***(v.)*** **ሰንጠቐ** *senẗeqe*
**interstate** ***(n.)*** **በየነ-መንግስታዊ** *beyenemengstawi*
**interval** ***(n.)*** **ካብ እስካብ** *kab eskab*
**intervene** ***(v.)*** **ጣልቃ ኣተወ** *ẗalqa 'atewe*
**intervention** ***(n.)*** **ኢድ ምእታው** *'id m'ètaw*
**interview** ***(n.)*** **ቃለ-መጠይቕ** *qalemeẗeyq̈*
**intestine** ***(n. )*** **መዓንጣ** *me'änẗa*
**intimacy** ***(n.)*** **ምትዕርራኽ** *mt'ërraḱ*
**intimate** ***(adj.)*** **ቀንዲ** *qendi*
**intimidate** ***(v.)*** **ኣፈራረሐ** *aferarehe*
**intimidation** ***(n.)*** **ምፍርራሕ** *mfrrah*
**into** ***(prep.)*** **ናብ** *nab*
**intolerable** ***(adj.)*** **ዘይፅወር** *zeytswer*
**intolerant** ***(adj.)*** **ዘይፅወር** *zeytswer*
**intone** ***(v.)*** **ኣዜመ** *'azeeme*
**intoxicate** ***(v.)*** **መረዘ** *mereze*
**intoxication** ***(n.)*** **ምምራዝ** *mmraz*
**intractable** ***(adj.)*** **ዘይእዱብ ዘይግራሕ** *zey'èdub zeygraḧ*
**intranet** ***(n.)*** **መርበብ** *merbeb*
**intransitive** ***(adj.)*** **ዘይሳገር** *zeysager*
**intrepid** ***(adj.)*** **ተባዕ** *teba'ë*
**intricate** ***(adj.)*** **ክትርድኦ ዘሸግር** *ktrd'o zeshegr*
**intrigue** ***(v.)*** **ምሽባን ምምሽጣር ምድናቕ** *mshban mmshẗar mdnaqh*
**intrinsic** ***(adj.)*** **ባህርያዊ** *bahryawi*
**introduce** ***(v.)*** **ኣፋለጠ ኣላለየ** *'afaleẗe 'alaleye*
**introduction** ***(n.)*** **ምፍላጥ ምልላይ** *mflaẗ mllay*
**introductory** ***(adj.)*** **መፋለጢ** *mefaleẗi*
**introspect** ***(v.)*** **መፈለጢ ሓተታ** *mefelaleti hateta*
**introspection** ***(n.)*** **ነብስኻ ምምርማር** *nebsḱa mmrmar*
**introvert** ***(n.)*** **ግልፂ ዘይኮነ ሰብ** *gltsi zeykone seb*
**intrude** ***(v.)*** **ህሩግ በለ ጠብሎቕ በለ** *hrug bele ẗebloq̈ bele*
**intrusion** ***(n. )*** **ህሩግ ምባል** *hrug mbal*
**intrusive** ***(adj.)*** **ህሩግ በሃሊ** *hrug behali*
**intuition** ***(n.)*** **ገምሪ** *gemri*
**intuitive** ***(n.)*** **ገምራዊ** *gemrawi*
**inundate** ***(v.)*** **ኣዕለቕለቐ** *'a'ëleq̈leq̈e*
**invade** ***(v.)*** **ወረረ** *werere*
**invalid** ***(n.)*** **ምግዱር ኣካለ-ስንኩል** *mgdur 'akalesnkul*
**invalidate** ***(v.)*** **ዘይቅቡል ገበረ ኣፍረሰ** *zeyqbul gebere 'afrese*

**invaluable** *(adj.)* **ኣዝዩ ክቡር ዕዙዝ** *azyu kbur 'ëzuz*
**invariable** *(adj.)* **ዘይለዋወጥ** *zeylewawet̉*
**invasion** *(n. )* **ምውራር** *mwrar*
**invective** *(n.)* **ነውሪ; ፀያፍ** *newri; tsyaf*
**invent** *(v.)* **መሃዘ** *mehaze*
**invention** *(n.)* **ምምሃዝ** *mmhaz*
**inventor** *(n.)* **መሃዚ** *mehazi*
**inventory** *(n.)* **ዝርዝራዊ ፍቕዲ** *zrzrawi fq̈di*
**inverse** *(adj.)* **ግምጡል** *gmt̉ul*
**invert** *(v.)* **ገምጠለ** *gemt̉ele*
**invest** *(v.t. )* **ኣውዓለ** *aw'ale*
**investigate** *(v.)* **ኣፅነዐ መርመረ** *atsn'ë mermere*
**investigation** *(n. )* **መርመራ** *mermera*
**investment** *(n.)* **ምውዓል** *mw'al*
**invigilate** *(adj.)* **ሓለወ** *ḧalewe*
**invigilator** *(n.)* **ሓላዊ** *ḧalawi*
**invincible** *(adj.)* **ዘይስዓር** *zeys'är*
**inviolable** *(adj.)* **ኪጠሓስ ዘይብሉ** *kit̉ehas zeyblu*
**invisible** *(adj.)* **ዘይረአ** *zeyre'e*
**invitation** *(n.)* **መፀዋዕታ** *metsewa'ëta*
**invite** *(v.)* **ፀወዐ ዓደመ** *tsewe'ë ademe*
**inviting** *(adj.)* **ማራኺ** *maraḱi*
**invocation** *(n.)* **ፀሎት** *tselot*
**invoice** *(n.)* **ዝርዝር ናይ ዝተሸጡ ኣቕሑ** *zrzr nay ztesheṫu 'aq̈ḧu*
**invoke** *(v.)* **ብሕጊ መሰረት ገበረ** *b hgi meseret gebere*
**involuntary** *(adj.)* **ዘይእዙዝ** *zey'èzuz*
**involve** *(v.)* **ኣእተወ** *a'ètewe*
**invulnerable** *(adj.)* **ዘይህሰ ዘይድፈር** *zeyhse zeydfer*
**inward** *(adj.)* **ውሽጣዊ** *wshṫawi*
**irate** *(adj.)* **ሓራቕ** *ḧaraq̈*
**ire** *(n.)* **ሕርቃን** *ḧrqan*
**iris** *(n.)* **ጸላም-ዓይኒ** *tselam'äyni*
**irksome** *(v.)* **መናደዲ መሕረቒ** *menadedi mehreqhi*
**iron** *(n.)* **ሓፂን** *ḧatsin*
**ironical** *(adj.)* **ሓጫጪ ኣሽሙረኛ** *ḧačači 'ashmureña*
**irony** *(n.)* **ሕጫጩ ኣሽሙር** *ḧčače 'ashmur*
**irradiate** *(v.)* **ብርሃን ሃበ** *brhan habe*
**irrational** *(adj.)* **መሰረት ዘይብሉ ዘይርትዓዊ** *meseret zeyblu zeyrt'äwi*
**irreconcilable** *(adj.)* **ዘይተዓረቕ** *zeyte'äreq̈*
**irredeemable** *(adj.)* **ዘይስተኻኸል** *zeystekhakel*
**irrefutable** *(adj.)* **ዘይርታዕ** *zeyrta'ë*
**irregular** *(adj.)* **ዘይስሩዕ** *zeysru'ë*
**irregularity** *(n.)* **ዘይስሩዕነት** *zeysru'ënet*
**irrelevant** *(adj.)* **ዘይዛመድ** *zeyzamed*
**irreplaceable** *(adj.)* **ኪትካእ ዘይከኣል** *kitka'è zeyke'al*
**irresistible** *(adj.)* **ይኣኽለኒ ዘይብሃል** *y'akleni zeybhal*
**irresolute** *(adj.)* **ተጠራጣሪ ዘይዉስን** *teṫeraṫari zeywsen*
**irrespective** *(adj.)* **ኣብ ግምት ብዘይምእታው** *'ab gmt bzeym'ètaw*

**irresponsible** ***(adj.)*** **ሓላፍነት ዘይስምዖ** *ḧalafnet zeysm'ö*
**irreversible** ***(adj.)*** **ናብ ዝነበሮ ክምለስ ዘይኽእል** *nab znebro kmles zeyk'el*
**irrevocable** ***(adj.)*** **ዘይልወጥ** *zeylweẗ*
**irrigate** ***(v.)*** **ብመስኖ ማይ ኣስተየ** *bmesno may 'asteye*
**irrigation** ***(n.)*** **መስኖ** *mesno*
**irritable** ***(adj.)*** **ሓራቕ** *ḧaraq̈*
**irritant** ***(n.)*** **ኣትካሪ** *'atkari*
**irritate** ***(v.)*** **ኣትከረ** *'atkere*
**irruption** ***(n.)*** **ፈንጢስካ ምእታው** *fenẗiska m'ètaw*
**Islam** ***(n.)*** **እስልምና** *islmna*
**island** ***(n. )*** **ደሴት** *deseet*
**isle** ***(n. )*** **ደሴት** *deseet*
**islet** ***(n.)*** **ንእሽቶ ደሴት** *n'èshto deseet*
**isobar** ***(n.)*** **ኣይሶባር** *'aysobar*
**isolate** ***(v.)*** **ኣግለለ** *'aglele*
**isolation** ***(n.)*** **ምግላል** *mglal*
**issue** ***(n. )*** **ሃበ** *habe*
**it** ***(pron.)*** **ንሱ ንሳ** *nsu nsa*
**italic** ***(adj.)*** **ኢታሊክ ቄናን** *italik qeenan*
**itch** ***(v.i. )*** **ህርፋን ቀሊል ቃንዛ** *hrfan qelil qanza*
**itchy** ***(adj.)*** **ኣስሓዪ ምሕክኺ** *asḧayi mehkeki*
**item** ***(n. )*** **ኣቕሑ** *aqhhu*
**iterate** ***(v.)*** **ደጋገመ** *degageme*
**itinerary** ***(n)*** **ናይ ጉዕዞ ዉጥን** *nay go'ezo wutn*
**itself** ***(pron.)*** **ንባዕሉ** *nba'ëlu*
**ivory** ***(n.)*** **ስኒ ሓርማዝ** *sni ḧarmaz*
**ivy** ***(n.)*** **ኣይቪ** *ayvi*

# J

**jab** ***(v.)*** **ኣጕረጠ** *'agureṫe*
**jabber** ***(v.)*** **ኣዝዩ ቅልጡፍ ዘረባ** *'azyu qlẗuf zereba*
**jack** ***(n. )*** **መልዓሊ መኪና ዓሻ** *mel'eli mekina 'äsha (ንሰብ)*
**jackal** ***(n. )*** **ከልቢ ዝመስል እንስሳ** *kelbi zmesl 'ènssa*
**jackass** ***(n. )*** **ተባዕታይ ኣድጊ** *teba'ëtay 'adgi*
**jacket** ***(n. )*** **ጃኬት** *ĵakeet*
**jackpot** ***(n. )*** **ዝለዓለ ሽልማት** *zle'ale shlmat*
**Jacuzzi** ***(n.)*** **ጃኩዚ** *ǧakuzii*
**jade** ***(n. )*** **ቖፃል ኹብር እምኒ** *qhotsal khubr emni*
**jaded** ***(adj.)*** **ምድባር** *mdbar*
**jagged** ***(adj.)*** **በሊሕ** *belih*
**jail** ***(n. )*** **ቤት ማእሰርቲ** *beet ma'èserti*
**jailer** ***(n. )*** **ኣላዪ** *'alayi*
**jam** ***(v.t. )*** **ምትዕፅፃይ** *mt'etstsaw*
**jam** ***(n. )*** **ዓገተ** *'ägete (ንድምጺ)*
**jamboree** ***(n.)*** **ፌስታዊ ኣኼባ** *feestawi 'ak̓eeba*
**janitor** ***(n.)*** **ዓቃበ-ህንጻ** *äqabehntsa*
**January** ***(n.)*** **ጥሪ** *ẗri*
**jar** ***(n. )*** **ስልጣንያ** *sltanya*
**jargon** ***(n. )*** **ፋሉይ ቃል** *fuluy kal*
**jasmine** ***(n. )*** **ሓቢ ጸሊም** *ḧabi xelim (ዓይነት ተኽሊ)*
**jaundice** ***(n.)*** **ዓይኒን ቆርበትን ቢጫ ዝገብር ሕማም** *aynen korbetn bicha zgebr hmam*
**jaunt** ***(n.)*** **ጉብኝት** *ḧaxir zuret*
**jaunty** ***(adj.)*** **ክዩፍ በዓል_ዓርሰእምነት** *kyuf*

**javelin** *(n. )* **ነዊሒ ጦር** *čmara*
**jaw** *(n. )* **ምንጋጋ** *mngaga*
**jay** *(n.)* **ናይ ዒፍ ዓይነት** *bzuḧ zzareb*
**jazz** *(n.)* **ያዕያዕታ ጃዝ** *ya'ëya'ëta ĵaz*
**jazzy** *(adj.)* **ሕብራዊ ዘመናዊ** *muziqawi*
**jealous** *(adj.)* **ቀናእ** *qena'è*
**jealousy** *(n. )* **ቅንኣት** *qn'at*
**jeans** *(n.)* **ጂንስ** *ĵins*
**jeep** *(n.)* **መኪና በረኻ** *mekina bereḱa*
**jeer** *(v.)* **ኣባጨወ** *'abačewe*
**jelly** *(n.)* **መለግለጋ** *meleglega*
**jellyfish** *(n.)* **መለግለጋይ ዓሳ** *meleglegay 'äsa*
**jeopardize** *(v.)* **ኣብ ሓደጋ ኣውደቐ** *'ab ḧadega 'awdeq̈e*
**jeopardy** *(n.)* **ግድዓት ኣብ ሓደጋ ምውዳቕ** *gd'ät*
**jerk** *(n.)* **ነው ኣበለ ሃሳስ** *new 'abele*
**jerkin** *(n.)* **እጀገ ኣልቦ** *'èĵege 'albo*
**jersey** *(n.)* **ጎልፎ ማልያ** *golfo*
**jest** *(n.)* **መስሓቕ** *mesḧaq̈*
**jester** *(n.)* **ተዋዛይ** *tewazay*
**jet** *(n. )* **ፍሊልታ** *flilta*
**jet lag** *(n.)* **ንፍረት ሕማም** *ḥmam-nfret*
**jewel** *(n.)* **ገይፂ መጋየፂ** *ĵewhar*
**jeweller** *(n. )* **ገይፂ ፈጣሪ** *ĵewhar feẗari*
**jewellery** *(n. )* **ገይፂ መጋየፂ** *ĵewhar*
**jibe** *(n.)* **ምልጋፀ** *'alagexe*
**jig** *(n.)* **ቅልጡፍ ሳዕስዒት** *qlẗuf sa'ës'ït*
**jiggle** *(v.)* **ሓቘነ** *ḧaq̈Wene*
**jigsaw** *(n.)* **ምጥዋይን ምስሓብን** *mṭwayn msḥabn*
**jingle** *(n.)* **ጫሕጫሕ ኣበለ** *čaḧčaḧ 'abele*
**jinx** *(n.)* **ቑርሱስ** *qruḧ qrsus*
**jitters** *(n.)* **ራዕዲ** *ra'ëdi*
**job** *(n.)* **ስራሕ** *sraḧ*
**jockey** *(n.)* **ብፈረስ ተቐዳደመ** *bferes teq̈edademe*
**jocose** *(adj.)* **ተዋዛዪ** *tewazayi*
**jocular** *(v.t. )* **ተዋዛዪ ተጫዋቲ** *tewazayi*
**jog** *(v.)* **ሳምሶማ ጉያ** *ḧagWaxgWax 'abele*
**joggle** *(v.)* **ተነውነወ** *tenewnewe*
**join** *(v.)* **ኣባል ኮነ** *'abal kone*
**joiner** *(n. )* **ኣግጣሚ** *agẗami*
**joint** *(n.)* **መሓውር መጋጥም** *meḧawr*
**joist** *(n.)* **ሙራለ** *murale*
**joke** *(n.)* **ቀልዲ** *'asḧaq̈e*
**joker** *(n.)* **ቐልዲ** *tewazayi*
**jolly** *(adj.)* **ሕጉስ** *ḧgus*
**jolt** *(v.t. )* **ሓጎፀጎፀ ኣበለ** *ḧagWaxgWax 'abele*
**jostle** *(v.t. )* **ነውነወ** *newnewe*
**jot** *(v.t. )* **ቅንጣብ ፁሑፍ** *qnẗab*
**journal** *(n. )* **ጋዜጣ** *gazeeẗa*
**journalism** *(n.)* **ጋዜጠኛነት** *gazeeẗeǹanet*
**journalist** *(n. )* **ጋዜጠኛ** *gazeeẗeǹa*
**journey** *(n.)* **ጉዕዞ** *gu'ëzo*
**jovial** *(adj.)* **ሑጉስ** *mesḧaq̈*
**joviality** *(adv. )* **ብሓጎስ** *teḥagWase*
**joy** *(n. )* **ደስታ** *desta*
**joyful** *(adj.)* **ሕጉስ** *dsut*
**joyous** *(adj.)* **ሕጉስ** *ḥgus*
**jubilant** *(adj.)* **ሕጉስ** *dsut*

**jubilation** ***(n.)*** **ሓጐስ** *ḧagWas*
**jubilee** ***(n. )*** **ኢዮበልዩ** *iyobelyu*
**judge** ***(n.)*** **ዳኛ** *feradi*
**judgement** ***(n. )*** **ምፍራድ** *mfrad*
**judicial** ***(adj.)*** **ፍርዳዊ** *frdawi*
**judiciary** ***(n.)*** **ፍርዳዊ** *ferado*
**judicious** ***(adj.)*** **መስተውዓሊ** *mestew'äli*
**judo** ***(n.)*** **ጁዶ** *ĵudo (ናይ ምክልኻል ምጥቃዕን ቃልሲ)*
**jug** ***(n.)*** **ብራኳ** *brakWa*
**juggle** ***(v.)*** **ኣደናገረ ካብቲናብቲ ምባል** *'adenagere*
**juggler** ***(n.)*** **ምርኢት ኣቕራቢ** *mr'it 'aq̈rabi*
**juice** ***(n.)*** **ፅማቝ** *xmaq̈Wu*
**juicy** ***(adj.)*** **ጡዑም** *texemaq̈Wi*
**July** ***(n.)*** **ሓምለ** *ḧamle*
**jumble** ***(n.)*** **ድብልቕለቕ** *debaleq̈e*
**jumbo** ***(adj.)*** **ገጅፍ ዝዓይነቱ** *geĵf z'äynetu*
**jump** ***(v.i)*** **ነጠረ ዘለለ** *neẗere*
**jumper** ***(n.)*** **ዘላሊ** *zelali*
**jumper** ***(n.)*** **ጎልፎ** *termin*
**junction** ***(n. )*** **መራኸቢ** *meraḱebi*
**juncture** ***(n. )*** **መራኸቢ** *meraḱebi*
**June** ***(n.)*** **ሰነ** *sene*
**jungle** ***(n.)*** **ጫካ** *čaka*
**junior** ***(adj.)*** **ታሕታዋይ መባእታ** *salsay 'ämet*
**junior** ***(n. )*** **ንኡስ** *n'us*
**junk** ***(n. )*** **ጐሓፍ** *gWaḧaf*
**Jupiter** ***(n. )*** **ጁፒተር** *ĵupiter*
**jurisdiction** ***(n. )*** **ሕጋዊ ስልጣን** *ḧgawi slẗan*
**jurisprudence** ***(n. )*** **ስነ-ሕጊ** *sneḧgi*
**jurist** ***(n. )*** **ክኢላ ሕጊ** *k'ila ḧgi*
**juror** ***(n. )*** **ኣባል ፈራዶ** *daǹa*
**jury** ***(n. )*** **ፈራዶ** *ferado*
**just** ***(adj.)*** **ልክዕ** *lk'ë*
**justice** ***(n.)*** **ፍትሒ** *ftḧi*
**justifiable** ***(adj.)*** **ቑቡል** *bq̈Wu'ë*
**justification** ***(n.)*** **መመኽነይታ** *memeḱneyta*
**justify** ***(v.)*** **ኣረጋገጸ** *'aregagexe*
**jute** ***(n.)*** **ጁት** *ĵut*
**juvenile** ***(adj.)*** **ትሕቲ ዕድመ** *men'èsey*

# K

**kaftans** ***(n.)*** **ካፍታን** *kaftan*
**kaleidoscope** ***(n.)*** **ተቐያያሪ ሕብርታት** *teq̈eyayari ḧbrtat*
**kangaroo** ***(n.)*** **ካንጋሩ** *kangaru*
**karma** ***(n.)*** **ካርማ** *karma*
**kebab** ***(n.)*** **ከቢብ** *kebib*
**keel** ***(n.)*** **ናይ ገልባ ታሕታዋይ ኣካል** *nay jelba tahtaway alkal*
**keen** ***(adj.)*** **ምህንጣይ** *mhntay*
**keenness** ***(n.)*** **ድልየት** *dlyet*
**keep** ***(v.)*** **ሓለወ** *ḧalewe*
**keeper** ***(n.)*** **ሓላዊ** *ḧalawi*
**keeping** ***(n.)*** **ምሕላው** *mhlaw*
**keepsake** ***(n. )*** **መዘከርታ** *mezekerta*
**keg** ***(n.)*** **ንእሽቶ በርሚል** *n'èshto bermil*
**kennel** ***(n. )*** **ጋቢያ ሰፈር ከልቢ** *gabiya sefer kelbi*
**kerb** ***(n.)*** **ናይ እግረኛ መንገዲ ጫፍ** *nay egregna mengedi chaf*
**kernel** ***(n. )*** **ፍረ ዓካት** *fre 'äkat*
**kerosene** ***(n. )*** **ላምባ** *lamba*

**ketchup** *(n. )* **ከቻፕ** *kechap*
**kettle** *(n. )* **በራድ** *berad*
**key** *(n.)* **መፍትሕ** *mefth̩*
**keyboard** *(n. )* **ሰሌዳ መፋትሕ** *seleeda mefath̩*
**keyhole** *(n.)* **ዓይኒ መፍትሕ** *'äyni mefth*
**kick** *(v.)* **ሃረመ ወቐዐ** *hareme weqh'e*
**kid** *(n.)* **ማሕስእ ህፃን** *mah̩s'è htsan*
**kidnap** *(v.)* **ጨወየ** *çewey*
**kidney** *(n.)* **ኩሊት** *kulit*
**kill** *(v.)* **ቀተለ** *qetele*
**killing** *(n.)* **ቅትለት** *qtlet*
**kiln** *(n. )* **እቶን** *'èton*
**kilo** *(n.)* **ኪሎ** *kilo*
**kilobyte** *(n.)* **ኪሎ ባይት** *kilo-byt*
**kilometre** *(n.)* **ኪሎሜተር** *kilomeeter*
**kilt** *(n.)* **ከሽከሽ ቐሚሽ** *keshkesh qhemish*
**kimono** *(n.)* **ጀለብያ ዚመስል ናይ ጃፓን ክዳን** *ğelebya zimesl nay japan kdan*
**kin** *(n. )* **ዘመድ** *zemed*
**kind** *(n.)* **ዓይነት የዋህ** *äynet yewah*
**kindergarten** *(n.)* **ቤት-ትምህርቲ ሕጻናት** *beettmhrti h̩xanat*
**kindle** *(v.)* **ተወለዐ** *tewele'ë*
**kindly** *(adv. )* **ብሕያውነት** *bh̩yawnet*
**kinetic** *(adj.)* **ምንቅስቓሳዊ** *mnqsq̈asawi*
**king** *(n. )* **ንጉስ** *ngus*
**kingdom** *(n. )* **ስርወ መንግስቲ** *srwe-mengsti*
**kink** *(n.)* **ጠዋይ ለዋይ** *ţeway leway*
**kinship** *(n. )* **ዝምድና** *zmdna*
**kiss** *(v.t. )* **ስዕመት** *s'ëmet*
**kit** *(n. )* **መሳርሒ ኣቕሑ** *mesarh̩i 'aq̈h̩u*
**kitchen** *(n. )* **ክሽነ** *kshne*
**kite** *(n. )* **ኣብ ኣየር ዝበርር ናይ መረቀት መፃወቲ** *ab ayer zeberr nay werqet metsaweti*
**kith** *(n. )* **ዓርከይ** *arkey*
**kitten** *(n. )* **ውላድ ድሙ** *wlad dmu*
**kitty** *(n.)* **መዋጮ** *mewacho*
**knack** *(n.)* **ብልሓት** *blh̩at*
**knacker** *(v.)* **ዝኣረጉ ኣፍራስ ዚገዝእን ዚሓርድን ሰብ** *z'aregu 'afras zigez'èn zih̩ardn seb*
**knave** *(n. )* **ዘይቅኑዕ** *zeyqnu'ë*
**knead** *(v.)* **ለወሰ ኣብኮዐ** *lewese abko'e*
**knee** *(n.)* **ብርኪ** *brki*
**kneel** *(v.)* **ተንበርከኸ** *tenberkeḱe*
**knickers** *(n.)* **ናይ ደቂ ኣንስትዮ ስረ ብርኪ** *nay deki- anstyo sre brki*
**knife** *(n. )* **ካራ** *kara*
**knight** *(n.)* **ፈረሰኛ ወተሃደር** *fereseña wetehader*
**knit** *(v.)* **ረከመ** *rekeme*
**knob** *(n.)* **ለዓት** *le'ät*
**knock** *(v.)* **ኳሕኩሐ** *kWah̩kuh̩e*
**knot** *(n.)* **ቍጻር** *quxar*
**knotty** *(adj.)* **ዝተሓላለኸ** *zteh̩alaleḱe*
**know** *(v.)* **ፈለጠ** *feleţe*
**knowing** *(adj.)* **መፍለጥ** *meflet*
**knowledge** *(n. )* **ፍልጠት** *flţet*
**knuckle** *(n.)* **መላግቦ ኣጻብዕቲ** *melagbo 'axab'ëti*
**kudos** *(n.)* **ክብሪ** *kbri*

# L

**label** *(n.)* **ናይ ኣቕሓ መለለይ መንነት** *nay aqha meleleyi mennet*
**labial** *(adj.)* **ከንፈራዊ** *kenferawi*
**laboratory** *(n.)* **ቤተ-ፈተነ** *biete-fetene*
**laborious** *(adj.)* **ኣድካሚ** *'adkam*
**labour** *(n.)* **ዕዮ** *'ëyo*
**labyrinth** *(n. )* **ጥንግንግ** *ţngng*
**lace** *(n.)* **ዘረፍረፍ** *zerefref*
**lacerate** *(v.)* **ተርብዐ** *terb'ë*
**lachrymose** *(adj.)* **ነባዒ** *neba'ï*
**lack** *(n.)* **ምስኣን** *ms'an*
**lackey** *(n.)* **ዓሽከር** *'äshker*
**laconic** *(adj.)* **ቁጡብ ቡዙሕ ዘይዛረብ** *qhutub buzuh zey zareb*
**lacquer** *(n.)* **በርኒሽ** *bernich*
**lacuna** *(n.)* **ዋጋ ዘይብሉ** *waga zeyblu*
**lacy** *(adj.)* **ታንቴላዊ** *tanteelawi*
**lad** *(n. )* **ወዲ** *wedi*
**ladder** *(n.)* **መሳልል** *mesall*
**laden** *(n.)* **ዝተፅዓነ** *ztets'ane*
**ladle** *(n.)* **መንጨለፍ** *menchelef*
**lady** *(n.)* **ወይዘሮ** *weyzero*
**lag** *(v.)* **ዘሓጠ** *zeḧaťe*
**lager** *(n.)* **ፈኰስ ቢራ** *fekWis bira*
**laggard** *(n.)* **ድሕረት ምቕራይ** *dhrit mqhray*
**lagging** *(n.)* **ናይ ቱቦ ሽፋን** *nay tubo shfan*
**lagoon** *(n. )* **ላጉን** *lagun*
**lair** *(n. )* **ሰፈር ኣራዊት** *sefer 'arawit*
**lake** *(n. )* **ቐላይ** *qhelay*
**lamb** *(n.)* **ማሕሲእ** *mahsi'e*
**lame** *(adj.)* **ሓንካስ** *ḧankas*
**lament** *(n.)* **ሓዘን ምግላፅ** *hazen mglats*
**lamentable** *(adj.)* **ዘሕዝን** *zehzn*
**laminate** *(v.)* **ናይ ላስቲክ ሽፋን** *nay lastik shfan*
**lamp** *(n. )* **ፋኑስ** *fanus*
**lampoon** *(v.)* **ቐልዳዊ ወቐሳ** *qheldawi weqhesa*
**lance** *(n.)* **ዓብዪ ጦር** *abyi tor*
**lancet** *(n.)* **ላንሰት ናይ መጥባሕቲ ክልተ ዝኣፉ ካራ** *lanset nay meťbahti klte z'afu kara*
**land** *(n.)* **መሬት** *mereet*
**landing** *(n. )* **ምውራድ ምዕራፍ** *mwrad m'eraf*
**landlady** *(n.)* **በዓልቲ ገዛ** *be'älti geza*
**landlord** *(n.)* **በዓል ገዛ** *be'äl geza*
**landscape** *(n.)* **ስእሊ መሬት** *s'èli mereet*
**language** *(n.)* **ቋንቋ** *qWAnqWA*
**languid** *(adj.)* **ጎታት** *gotat*
**languish** *(v.)* **ማሰነ** *masene*
**lank** *(adj.)* **ለማሽ** *lemash*
**lanky** *(adj.)* **ቐጢን ነዊሕ** *qhetin newih*
**lantern** *(n. )* **ፋኑስ** *fanus*
**lap** *(n.)* **ሽለፍ** *shelef*
**lapse** *(n.)* **ጊዛዊ ሕማቕ ባህሪ** *gizawi hmaqh bahri*
**lard** *(n.)* **ካብ ሓሰማ ዝርከብ ስብሒ** *kab hasama zrkeb sbhi*
**larder** *(n.)* **ክፍሊ መመገቢ ምግቢ** *kfli memegebi mgbi*
**large** *(adj.)* **ገዚፍ** *gezife*
**largesse** *(n. )* **ናይ የዋህነት ተግባር** *nay yewahnet tegbar*
**lark** *(n.)* **ሓመዳዊት ዒፍ** *hamedawit if*

**larva** *(n.)* **ላርቫ** *larva*
**larynx** *(n.)* **ደባዒቶ** *deba'eto*
**lasagne** *(n.)* **ላሳኛ** *lasagna*
**lascivious** *(adj.)* **ናይ ግብረ ስጋ ሉዑል ድልየት ዘለዎ** *nay gbre sga l'eul dlyet zelewo*
**laser** *(n.)* **ናይ ብርሃን ጨረር** *nay brhan cherer*
**lash** *(v.)* **ቕንድብ** *qhndb*
**lashings** *(n.)* **ምግራፍ** *mgraf*
**lass** *(n.)* **ጓል** *gWal*
**last** *(adj.)* **መጨረሻ** *mečeresha*
**lasting** *(adj.)* **ንነዊሕ ግዜ ዝፀንሕ** *nnewi gzie ztsenh*
**latch** *(n.)* **ባልና ሚስት** *balna mist*
**late** *(adj.)* **ምድንጓይ** *mdnguay*
**lately** *(adv. )* **ሐዚታት** *hezitat*
**latent** *(adj.)* **ዘይረአ** *mezemeran*
**lath** *(n. )* **ሓነቐ** *haneqe*
**lathe** *(n. )* **ተርንዮ ማሽን** *hemam sheroke*
**lather** *(n. )* **ምቕባእ** *mqhba'e*
**latitude** *(n. )* **ናይ ምግባር ነፃነት** *nay mgbar netsanet*
**latrine** *(n.)* **ሽንቲ ቤት** *shnti biet*
**latte** *(n.)* **ካብ ፃባ ዝስራሕ ጠንካራ ቡን** *kab tsaba zsrah tenkara bun*
**latter** *(adj.)* **ዳሕራዋይ** *dahraway*
**lattice** *(n.)* **ናይ ዓውዲ ኣካል ውሽጣዊ ቕርፂ** *nay awdi akal wshtawi qhrtsi*
**laud** *(v.)* **ምድናቕ** *mdnaqh*
**laudable** *(adj.)* **ክድነቕ ዝግቦኦ** *kdneqh zgbo'e*
**laugh** *(v.)* **ሰሓቐ** *sehqhe*
**laughable** *(adj.)* **መስሓቒ** *meshaqhi*
**laughter** *(n.)* **ሰሓቕ** *sehqh*
**launch** *(v.)* **ምቱኳስ** *mtukuas*
**launder** *(v.)* **ምሕፃብ** *mhtsab*
**launderette** *(n. )* **ቤት ሕፅቦ** *bet htsbo*
**laundry** *(n. )* **ዝሕፀቡ ክዳውንቲ** *zhtsebu kdawnti*
**laureate** *(n.)* **ናይ ኣርቲስት ሉዑል ማዓርግ** *nay artist lu'ul ma'arg*
**laurel** *(n.)* **ቖፃል ተኽሊ** *qhotsal tekhli*
**lava** *(n.)* **ላቫ** *lava*
**lavatory** *(n. )* **ሽንቲ ቤት** *shnti biet*
**lavender** *(n.)* **ዕንቆዋይ ሊላ ዕንበባ ዘለዎ ተኽሊ** *e'nqhoway lila e'nbaba zelewo tekhli*
**lavish** *(adj.)* **ገራሚ** *gerami*
**law** *(n.)* **ሕጊ** *hgi*
**lawful** *(adj.)* **ሕጋዊ** *hgawi*
**lawless** *(adj.)* **ሕጊ ኣልቦ** *hgi albo*
**lawn** *(n. )* **ኣብ እፍደገ ገዛ ዝርከብ ዝተኸርከመ ሳዕሪ** *ab afdege geza zrkeb ztkhrkeme sa'eri*
**lawyer** *(n.)* **ጠበቓ** *tbeqha*
**lax** *(adj.)* **ፍትሕ ዝበለ** *fth zbele*
**laxative** *(n.)* **ቐልቐል ንክትብል ዝውሰድ መድሓኒ ወይ ምግቢ** *kelkel n ktble zwsed medhanit wey mgbi*
**laxity** *(n.)* **ኸቢድ ቑፅፅር ዘይምህላይ** *khebid kutstsr zymhlaw*
**lay** *(v.)* **ምቕማጥ ምውዳቕ** *mqhmat mwdaqh*
**layer** *(n.)* **ሽፋን** *shfan*
**layman** *(n.)* **ሞያ ዘይብሉ** *moya zeyblu*
**laze** *(v.)* **ምዝንጋዕ** *mznga'e*
**lazy** *(adj.)* **ሰነፍ** *senef*
**leach** *(v.)* **ደፈአ** *defe'e*
**lead** *(n.)* **ምምራሕ** *mmrah*

**lead** *(v.)* መረሐ *meleh*
**leaden** *(adj.)* ደስ ዘይብል *des zeybl*
**leader** *(n.)* መራሒ *merahi*
**leadership** *(n. )* መሪሕነት *merihnet*
**leaf** *(n. )* ቆፅሊ *qhotsli*
**leaflet** *(n.)* ብዛዕባ ዝኾነ ነገር ሓበሬታ ዘሓዘ ንእሽተይ መፅሓፍ *bza'eba zkhone neger haberieta zheze neshtey metshaf*
**league** *(n. )* ሊግ *lig*
**leak** *(v.)* ኣንጠብጢቡ *antebtibu*
**leakage** *(n.)* ምንጥብጣብ *mntbtab*
**lean** *(v.)* ተደጊፉ *tdegifu*
**leap** *(v.)* ምዝላል *mzlal*
**learn** *(v.)* ምምሃር *mmhar*
**learned** *(adj.)* ምምሃር *mmhar*
**learner** *(n. )* ተምሃሪ *temhari*
**learning** *(n. )* ምምሃር *mmhar*
**lease** *(n.)* ናይ ክራይ ስምምዕነት *nay kray smm'enet*
**leash** *(n.)* መእሰሪ ኸልቢ *me'eseri kebi*
**least** *(adj.& pron.)* መወዳእታ *meweda'eta*
**leather** *(n.)* ኣንጋረ *angare*
**leave** *(v.t. )* ኽድ ልቐቕ *khd lqheqh*
**lecture** *(n.)* ትምህርቲ *tmhrti*
**lecturer** *(n. )* መምህር *memhr*
**ledge** *(n.)* ጫፍ *chaf*
**ledger** *(n. )* መዝገብ *mezgeb*
**leech** *(n. )* ኣብ ዉሽጢ ማይ ዝነብር ንኡሽተይ እንስሳ *ab wshti may znebr nu'ushtey enssa*
**leek** *(n.)* ሹንጉርቲ ዝመስል ተኽሊ *sunkurti zmesl tekhli*
**left** *(n.)* ፀጋም *tsegam*
**leftist** *(n.)* ኮሚኒስት *cominist*
**leg** *(n. )* እግሪ *egri*
**legacy** *(n.)* ዉርሲ *wursi*
**legal** *(adj.)* ሕጋዊ *hgawi*
**legality** *(n.)* ሕጋዊነት *hgawnet*
**legalize** *(v.)* ሕጋዊ ምግባር *hgawi mgbar*
**legend** *(n.)* ዛnta *zanta*
**legendary** *(adj.)* ዛንታዊ ተፈላጢ *zantawi teflati*
**leggings** *(n.)* ጥርንቕ ዘብል ስረ *trnqh zble sre*
**legible** *(adj.)* ተነባቢ *tenbabi*
**legion** *(n. )* ብርጌድ *brgied*
**legislate** *(v.)* ሕጊ ኣፀደቐ *hgi atsdqh*
**legislation** *(n.)* ሕጊ ምፅዳቕ *hgi mtsdaqh*
**legislative** *(adj.)* ሕጊ ኣፅዳቒ *higi atzdaqhi*
**legislator** *(n.)* ኣባል ሕጊ ኣፅዳቒ *abal higi atsdaqhi*
**legislature** *(n.)* ሕጊ መፅደቕቲ *hgi metsdeqhti*
**legitimacy** *(n.)* ሕጋዊነት *hgawinet*
**legitimate** *(adj.)* ሕጋዊነት *hgawinet*
**leisure** *(n.)* ትርፊ ግዘ *trfi gize*
**leisurely** *(adj.)* እናተዘናጋዕካ *enatezenag'eka*
**lemon** *(n. )* ለሚን *lemin*
**lemonade** *(n.)* ናይ ለሚን መስተ ወይ ፁማቕ *nay lemin meste wey tsumaqh*
**lend** *(v.)* ምልቃሕ *mlqh'h*
**length** *(n.)* ንውሓት *nwhat*

**lengthy** ***(adj.)*** **ንነዊሕ ግዜ ዝፀንሕ** *nnewih gzie ztsenh*
**leniency** ***(n.)*** **ጡንኩር ዘይኮነ ኣተሓሳስባ** *tunkur zeykone atehasasba*
**lenient** ***(adj.)*** **ጡንኩር ዘይኮነ** *tunkur zeykone*
**lens** ***(n. )*** **ሌንስ** *lienis*
**lentil** ***(n. )*** **ባሎንጓ** *balongua*
**Leo** ***(n.)*** **ሊዮ** *lio*
**leopard** ***(n. )*** **ኣባ ሸማኔ** *aba shemanie*
**leper** ***(n. )*** **ዱዉይ** *dwuy*
**leprosy** ***(n.)*** **ዱውየት** *duwyet*
**lesbian** ***(n.)*** **ኣንስተይቲ ን ኣንተይቲ ፆታዊ ፍትወት** *ansteyti n ansteyti tsotawi ftwet*
**less** ***(adj. & pron.)*** **ቑሩብ** *qhurub*
**lessee** ***(n.)*** **ተኻራዪ** *tekharayi*
**lessen** ***(v.)*** **እናነኣሰ** *enan'ase*
**lesser** ***(adj.)*** **ዝነኣሰ** *zne'ase*
**lesson** ***(n.)*** **ትምህርቲ** *tmhrti*
**lessor** ***(n.)*** **ኣካራዪ** *akarayi*
**lest** ***(conj.)*** **ከይ** *k*
**let** ***(v.)*** **እንበል** *enbel*
**lethal** ***(adj.)*** **ዝቐትል ነገር** *zqhtl neger*
**lethargic** ***(adj.)*** **ምድኻም** *mdkham*
**lethargy** ***(n.)*** **ድኻም** *dkham*
**letter** ***(n. )*** **ድብዳቤ** *dbdabie*
**level** ***(n.)*** **ደረጃ** *dereja*
**lever** ***(n.)*** **14 ሓንዶቓዱቕ** *ȟandoq̈WAduq̈*
**leverage** ***(n. )*** **ትሕጃ** *thja*
**levity** ***(n.)*** **ኣብ ዘይቅለድ ምቕላድ** *ab zeyqhed mqhlad*
**levy** ***(v.)*** **ምኽፋል** *mkhfal*
**lewd** ***(adj.)*** **ፆታዊ ፅያፍ** *tsotawi tsyaf*
**lexical** ***(adj.)*** **ናይ ዝተፈላለዩ ቋንቋታት ቃላት ምዝማድ** *nay ztefelaleyu quanquatat qalt mzmad*
**lexicon** ***(n.)*** **ናይ ዓይነት ቃላት** *nay aynet qalt*
**liability** ***(n.)*** **ጠቕላላ ዕዳ** *tklala eda*
**liable** ***(adj.)*** **ተዓዳዪ** *te'ad'u*
**liaise** ***(v.)*** **ብሓደ ምስራሕ** *bhade msrah*
**liaison** ***(n. )*** **ብሓደ ምስራሕ** *bhade msrah*
**liar** ***(n. )*** **ሓሳዊ** *hasawi*
**libel** ***(n.)*** **ናይ ሓሶት ክሲ** *nay hasot ksi*
**liberal** ***(adj.)*** **ነፃ** *netsa*
**liberate** ***(v.)*** **ነፃ ኣውፀአ** *netsa mwtsa'e*
**liberation** ***(n.)*** **ነፃነት** *netsanet*
**liberator** ***(n. )*** **ነፃ ኣውፃኢ** *netsa awtsa'e*
**liberty** ***(n.)*** **ነፃነት** *netsanet*
**libido** ***(n.)*** **ናይ ፆታዊ ስሚዒት ኣካል** *nay tsotawi smi'et akal*
**Libra** ***(n.)*** **ሊብራ** *lbra*
**librarian** ***(n. )*** **ሓላዊ ቤተ_መፃሕፍቲ** *halwi biete-metsahft*
**library** ***(n. )*** **ቤተ_መፃሕፍቲ** *biete-metsahft*
**licence** ***(n.)*** **ፍቓድ** *fqhad*
**licensee** ***(n.)*** **ዝተፈቐደሉ** *ztefeqhedelu*
**licentious** ***(adj.)*** **ካብ ማሕበረሰብ ዝወፀ ናይ ግበረ_ስጋ ፀባይ** *kab mahbere seb zewetse nay gbre-sga tsebay*

**lick** *(v.)* **ምልሓስ** *mlhas*
**lid** *(n.)* **ኽዳን** *khdan*
**lie** *(v.)* **ሓሱ** *hasu*
**liege** *(n.)* **ጋንታ** *ganta*
**lien** *(n. )* **ትሕጃ ምሓዝ** *thja mhaz*
**lieu** *(prep. )* **ኽንዲ** *khndi*
**lieutenant** *(n.)* **ሌተናንት** *letenant*
**life** *(n.)* **ሂወት** *hiwet*
**lifeless** *(adj.)* **ሂወት ዘይብሉ** *hiwet zeyblu*
**lifelong** *(adj.)* **ሙሉእ ሂወት** *mlu'e hiwet*
**lift** *(v.t. )* **ምልዓል** *ml'al*
**ligament** *(n.)* **ኣዕፅምቲ ዘራኽብ ጠንካራ ቲሹ/ጭዋዳ** *a'etsmti zerakhb tenkara tish/chwada*
**light** *(n.)* **ብርሃን** *brhan*
**lighten** *(v.)* **ብርሀ ምባል** *brh mbal*
**lightening** *(n. )* **መበረቕ እንትበርቕ** *mbreqh entberqh*
**lighter** *(n.)* **መወለዒ** *mwel'e*
**lighting** *(n.)* **መብረቕ** *mbreqh*
**lightly** *(adv. )* **ብቐሊሉ** *bqhelilu*
**lignite** *(n.)* **ምስጢራዊ ፅሑፍ** *mistrawi tsuhuf*
**like** *(prep.)* **ምፍታው** *mftaw*
**likeable** *(adj.)* **ተፈታዊ** *teftawi*
**likelihood** *(n.)* **ናይ ሙኳን ዕድል** *nay mkhuan edl*
**likely** *(adj.)* **ክኾን ትኽእል** *kkhon tkh'el*
**liken** *(v.)* **ተመሳሳሊ** *temesasali*
**likeness** *(n.)* **ተመሳሳሊነት** *temesasalinet*
**likewise** *(adv. )* **ተመሳሰልቲ እዮም** *temesaselti eyom*
**liking** *(n.)* **ምፍታው** *mftaw*
**lilac** *(n. )* **ናይ ዕንበባ ተኽሊ ዓይነት** *nay enbeba tkhli*
**lily** *(n. )* **ናይ ዕንበባ ዓይነት** *nay enbeba aynet*
**limb** *(n.)* **መሓውር** *mehawr*
**limber** *(v.)* **ምሙዋቕ** *mmuwaqh*
**limbo** *(n.)* **እብ መንጎ** *ab mengo*
**lime** *(n.)* **ናይ ካልሲየም ዉሁድ** *nay kalisiom wuhud*
**limelight** *(n. )* **ትኹረት ዝተውሃበሉ** *tkhuret ztwhableu*
**limerick** *(n.)* **በዓል ሓሙሽተ መስመር መስሕቒ ግጥሚ** *be'al hamushte mesmer msheqhi gtmi*
**limit** *(n.)* **ገደብ** *gdeb*
**limitation** *(n.)* **ገደብ** *gdeb*
**limited** *(adj.)* **ዝተገደበ** *ztegedebe*
**limousine** *(n.)* **ናይ መርዓ ንውሕ መኪና** *nay mer'a newih mekina*
**limp** *(v.)* **ምሕንካስ** *mhnkas*
**line** *(n.)* **መስመር** *msmer*
**lineage** *(n. )* **ናይ ትውልዲ መስመር** *nay twlide mesmer*
**linen** *(n.)* **ናይ ክዳን ዓይነት** *nay kdan aynet*
**linger** *(v.)* **ቐሊጢፉ ዘይጠፍእ** *qhlitifu zey tef'e*
**lingerie** *(n.)* **ናይ ድቂ እንስትዮ ክዳን ዉሽጢ** *nay dqi anstyo kdan wushti*
**lingo** *(n.)* **ዘይትርድኦ ቋንቋ** *zeytrd'o quanqua*
**lingua** *(n.)* **ተወሳኺ ቋንቋ** *tewsakhi quanqua*
**lingual** *(n. )* **ኣፋዊ** *afawi*
**linguist** *(adj.)* **ናይ ቋንቋ ሙሁር** *nay quanqua muhur*
**linguistic** *(adj.)* **ናይ ቋንቋ ትምህርቲ** *nay quanqua tmhrti*
**lining** *(n.)* **መራጎዲ ሽፋን** *meragodi shfan*

**link** *(n.)* **መራኸቢ** *mrakhebi*
**linkage** *(n.)* **መራኸቢ** *mreakhebi*
**linseed** *(n.)* **ትሕጃ** *thja*
**lintel** *(n.)* **ኣብ ልዕሊ ማዕፆ ዝግበር ሞራለ** *ab l'eli ma'etso zgber morale*
**lion** *(n. )* **ኣንበሳ** *anbesa*
**lip** *(n.)* **ከንፈር** *kenfer*
**liposuction** *(n.)* **ናይ ቁንጅና ቀዶ ፅገና ሕክምና** *nay qhunjna qhedo tsgena hkmna*
**liquefy** *(v.)* **ምምካኽ** *mwsakh*
**liquid** *(n.)* **ፈሳሲ** *fesasi*
**liquidate** *(v.)* **ንብረት ምሻጥ** *nbret mshat*
**liquidation** *(n. )* **ንብረት ምሻጥ** *nbret mshat*
**liquor** *(n.)* **ናይ ኣልኮል መስተ** *nay alkol meste*
**lisp** *(n.)* **ናይ s እና z ኩልትፍና** *nay s enn z kultfna*
**lissom** *(adj.)* **ምሽጥራዊ ስምምዕ** *mshtrawi smm'e*
**list** *(n.)* **መዝገብ ዝርዝር** *mzgeb zrzr*
**listen** *(v.)* **ምስማዕ** *msma'e*
**listener** *(n.)* **ሰማዒ** *sema'e*
**listless** *(adj.)* **ዱኹም** *dukhum*
**literal** *(adj.)* **ብቐጥታ** *bqhetta*
**literary** *(adj.)* **ብፁሑፍ** *btsuhuf*
**literate** *(adj.)* **ሙሁር** *muhur*
**literature** *(n.)* **ድርሰት** *drset*
**lithe** *(adj.)* **ተዓፃፃፊ** *te'atsatsefi*
**litigant** *(n.)* **ናይ ማሕበራዊ ፍርዲ ቤት ከሳኪ ወይተከሳሲ** *nay mahbeawi frdi biet kesaki wey tekesasi*
**litigate** *(v.)* **ምኽሳስ** *mkhsas*
**litigation** *(n. )* **ክሲ ምክልኻል ኣብ ማሕበራዊ ቤት ፍርዲ** *khsi mklkhal ab mhberawi frdi biet*
**litre** *(n. )* **መዐቐኒ ትሕዝቶ** *m'eqeni thzto*
**litter** *(n.)* **ዝወዳደቐ ጓሓፍ** *zwedeqe guahaf*
**little** *(adj.)* **ኑኡሽተይ** *nu/eshtey*
**live** *(v.)* **ንበር** *nber*
**livelihood** *(n.)* **ናይ ኣታዊ ምንጪ** *nay atawi mnchi*
**lively** *(adj.)* **ሑጉስ ደስተኛ** *hugus destegna*
**liven** *(v.)* **ምድምማቕ** *mdmmaqh*
**liver** *(n. )* **ፀላም ከብዲ** *tselam kebdi*
**livery** *(n.)* **ናይ ገዛ ሰራሕተኛ ዲቢዛ** *nay geza serahtegna dibiza*
**living** *(n.)* **ምንባር** *mnbaar*
**lizard** *(n. )* **ጠበቕ** *tebeqh*
**load** *(n.)* **ኽብደት** *khbdet*
**loaf** *(n.)* **ዓብዪ ሕንባሻ/ባኒ** *abyi hnbash/bani*
**loan** *(n.)* **ልቓሕ** *lqhah*
**loath** *(adj.)* **እምቢ በሃልነት** *embi behalnet*
**loathe** *(v.)* **ብጣዕሚ ምፅላእ** *bta'emi mtsla'e*
**loathsome** *(adj.)* **መፅልኢ** *metsl'e*
**lobby** *(n. )* **ኣፍደገ** *afdege*
**lobe** *(n. )* **ናይ እዝኒ ሉስሉስ ኣካል** *nay ezni luslus akal*
**lobster** *(n.)* **ሎብስተር** *lobster*
**local** *(adj.)* **ናይ እቲ ዓዲ** *nay eti adi*
**locale** *(n.)* **ኑኡሽተይ ቦታ** *nu'ushtey bota*
**locality** *(n.)* **ኣብ ሓድ ሃገር ዝርከብ ቦታ** *ab hade hager zrkeb bota*

**localize** ***(v.)*** **ሃገራዊ ምግባር** *hagerawi mgbar*
**locate** ***(v.)*** **ዘለዎ ቦታ ምፍላጥ** *zelewo bota mflat*
**location** ***(n.)*** **ኣድራሻ** *adrash*
**lock** ***(n.)*** **ቑልፊ** *qhulfi*
**locker** ***(n. )*** **መሽገጥ** *meshget*
**locket** ***(n. )*** **ኣብ ክሳድ ዝእሰር ፎቶ ዝሓዘ መጋይፂ** *ab ksasd zeseer foto zelowo mgayetsi*
**locomotion** ***(n.)*** **ነገራት ሙጉዕዓዝ** *negerat mugu'e'az*
**locomotive** ***(n. )*** **መጓዓዓዚ** *megua'a'azi*
**locum** ***(n.)*** **ተተካኢ ሓኪም** *teteka'e hakim*
**locus** ***(n. )*** **ማእኸል** *ma'ekhel*
**locust** ***(n. )*** **ባርኖስ** *barnos*
**locution** ***(n. )*** **ኮሚሽነር** *komishner*
**lodge** ***(n.)*** **መናፈሻ** *menafesh*
**lodger** ***(n.)*** **ተኻራዩ ገዛ** *tekharayi geza*
**lodging** ***(n. )*** **ጊዜዊ መምበሪ** *gizawi menberi*
**loft** ***(n.)*** **ኣብ ቆርቆሮ ዝስራሕ ክፍሊ** *ab qorqoro zsrah kfli*
**lofty** ***(adj.)*** **ጠቓሚ** *tkami*
**log** ***(n. )*** **ቑራፅ ዕንፀይቲ** *qhurats entseyti*
**logarithm** ***(n. )*** **ሎጋሪዝም** *logarizm*
**logic** ***(n.)*** **ስነ ሞጎት** *sne-mogot*
**logical** ***(adj.)*** **ምኽንያታዊ** *mkhnyatawi*
**logistics** ***(n.)*** **ኣቑሑ** *aqhuhu*
**logo** ***(n.)*** **ኣርማ** *arma*
**loin** ***(n.)*** **ፆታዊ ክፍሊ ኣካል** *tsotawi kfli akal*
**loiter** ***(v.)*** **ብዘይ ምኽንያት ኣብ ሓደ ቦታ ዘወርወር ምባል** *bzey mkhnyat ab hade bota zewerwer mbal*
**loll** ***(v.)*** **ተዝናኒካ ኮፍ ምባል** *teznanika kof mbal*
**lollipop** ***(n.)*** **ለካሌካ** *liekalieka*
**lolly** ***(n.)*** **ለካሌካ** *liekalieka*
**lone** ***(adj.)*** **ብሕታዊ** *bhtawi*
**loneliness** ***(n.)*** **ብሕታዊነት** *bhtawinet*
**lonely** ***(adj.)*** **ብሕታዊ** *bhtawi*
**loner** ***(n.)*** **ብሕትኡ ምኺን ዝመርፅ** *bht'u mukhun zmerts*
**lonesome** ***(adj.)*** **ብሕታዊ** *bhtawi*
**long** ***(adj.)*** **ነዊሕ** *newih*
**longevity** ***(n.)*** **ነዊሕ ሂወት** *niweh hiwet*
**longing** ***(n.)*** **ብምስኣን ዝመፅእ ሓዘን** *bms'an zmets'e hazen*
**longitude** ***(n.)*** **ሎንጊቱደ** *longitud*
**loo** ***(n.)*** **ሽንቲ ቤት** *shnti biet*
**look** ***(v.)*** **ረአ** *re'e*
**look** ***(n)*** **ምርኣይ** *mr'ay*
**lookalike** ***(n.)*** **ምምስሳል** *mmsal*
**loom** ***(n. )*** **ሽመና ማሽን** *shmena mashn*
**loop** ***(n. )*** **ዓንኬል** *ankiel*
**loose** ***(adj.)*** **ሰፊሕ** *sefih*
**loosen** ***(v.)*** **ኣስፈሐ** *asfehe*
**loot** ***(n.)*** **ምስራቕ** *msraqh*
**lop** ***(v.)*** **ምንቃል** *mnqal*
**lope** ***(v.)*** **ምስዳር** *msdar*
**lopsided** ***(adj.)*** **ዘይመጣጠን** *zeymetaten*
**lord** ***(n.)*** **ጎይታ** *goyta*
**lordly** ***(adj.)*** **ብኹርዓት** *bkhur'at*
**lore** ***(n.)*** **ባህላዊ ዛንታ** *bahlawi zanta*

**lorry** *(n.)* **ናይ ፅዕንት መኪና** *nay ts'ent mekina*
**lose** *(v.)* **ምስዓር** *ms'ar*
**loss** *(n. )* **ምስኣን** *ms'an*
**lot** *(pron.)* **ብዙሕ** *bzuh*
**lotion** *(n. )* **ቕብኣት** *qhb'at*
**lottery** *(n. )* **ሎተሪ** *loteri*
**lotus** *(n.)* **ናይ ዕንበባ ዓይነት** *nay enbeba aynet*
**loud** *(adj.)* **ዓው ዝበለ** *aw zbl*
**lounge** *(v.)* **ምዝንጋዕ** *mznga'e*
**lounge** *(n. )* **ማእኸል መዛናግዒ** *ma'ekhel mezanag'e*
**louse** *(n.)* **ናይ ምድሪ ሓሰኻ** *nay mdri hassekh*
**lousy** *(adj.)* **ሱሩሑ ብኣግባብ ዘይሰርሕ** *suruhu b'agbab zeyserh*
**lout** *(n.)* **ብቑጠዐ እና ብ ሓይሊ ዝኣምን** *buqhte'e ena bhayli z'amn*
**Louvre** *(n.)* **ሱሉስ ኩርናዕ ዘለዎ ሞስኮት ወይ ማዕፆ** *sulus kurna'e zelewo moskot wey ma'etso*
**lovable** *(adj.)* **ተፈቃሪ** *tefqari*
**love** *(n.)* **ፍቕሪ** *fqhri*
**lovely** *(adj.)* **ተፈቃሪ** *tefeqari*
**lover** *(n.)* **ኣፍቃሪ** *afqari*
**low** *(adj.)* **ትሑት** *thut*
**lower** *(adj.)* **ትሕት ዝበለ** *tht zbele*
**lowly** *(adj.)* **ታሕተዎት** *tahtaway*
**loyal** *(adj.)* **ኡሙን** *umun*
**loyalist** *(n. )* **ብምትእምማን ዝኣምን** *bmt'eman z'amn*
**lozenge** *(n.)* **ናይ ሰዓል ከረሜላ** *nay se'al keremiela*
**lubricant** *(n.)* **ቕብኣት** *qhb'at*
**lubricate** *(v.)* **ቕብኣት ቐበአ** *qhb'at qhbe'e*
**lubrication** *(n.)* **ቕብኣት** *qhb'at*
**lucent** *(adj.)* **ኣቑመ** *aqhome*
**lucid** *(adj.)* **ብቐሊሉ ዝርዳእ ፁሑፍ ወይ መደረ** *bqhelilu zrda'e tsuhuf wey medere*
**lucidity** *(adv. )* **ብቕሊሉ ክርዳእ ምኽኣል** *bqhlilu krda'e zkh'el*
**luck** *(n.)* **ዕድል** *edl*
**luckless** *(adj.)* **ዕድል ኣልባ** *edl albo*
**lucky** *(adj.)* **ዕድለኛ** *edlegna*
**lucrative** *(adj.)* **ትርፋማ** *trfama*
**lucre** *(n.)* **ብዘይቑንዕ መንገዲ ዝተረኸበ ገንዘብ** *bzey qhunu'e mengedi ztrekhebe genzeb*
**ludicrous** *(adj.)* **ምኽንያታዊ ዘይኮነ** *mkhnyatawi zeykone*
**luggage** *(n.)* **ናይ ጉዕዞ ሻንጣ** *nay gu'ezo shanta*
**lukewarm** *(adj.)* **ለብ ዝበለ ፈሳሲ** *lb zbele fesasi*
**lull** *(v.)* **ፀጥ ዘብለ ግዜ** *tset zbele gzie*
**lullaby** *(n. )* **ናይ ህፃናት መደቀሲ ሙዚቃ** *nay htssanat medeqeesi muziqa*
**luminary** *(n.)* **ብዛዕባ ሓደ ነገር ሰፊሕ ፍልጠት ዘሎዎ** *bza'eba hade neger sefih fltet zelewo*
**luminous** *(adj.)* **መንፀባረቒ** *mntsebareqhi*
**lump** *(n.)* **ኣምፖል** *ampol*
**lunacy** *(n.)* **ሃሳስ** *hasas*
**lunar** *(adj.)* **ወርሓዊ** *werhawi*
**lunatic** *(n.)* **ዕብድ** *ebud*
**lunch** *(n.)* **ምሳሕ** *msah*
**luncheon** *(n.)* **ናይ ምሳሕ ዝግጅት** *nay msah zgjt*
**lung** *(n. )* **ሳምባ** *samba*

**lunge** *(n.)* **ብፍጥነት ኣንፈት ምቕያር** *bftnet anfet mqhyar*
**lurch** *(n.)* **ሃንደፍደፍ** *handefdef*
**lure** *(v.)* **ምትላል** *mtlal*
**lurid** *(adj.)* **ግጭት፣ ግብረ ስጋ እና መደንገጺ ትሕዝቶ ዘካተተ** *gcht, gbre-sga ena medengetsi thzto zekatette*
**lurk** *(v.)* **ተሓቢእካ ምፅባይ** *tehbi'eka mtsbay*
**luscious** *(adj.)* **ስሓቢ** *sehabi*
**lush** *(adj.)* **ደስ ዝብል ኣታክልቲ ዘለዎ ቦታ** *des zbl ataklti zelewo bota*
**lust** *(n.)* **ግብረ ስጋዊ ድልየት** *gbre-sgawi dlyet*
**lustful** *(adj.)* **ግብረ ስጋዊ ድልየት** *gbre-sgawi dlyet*
**lustre** *(n.)* **ድብዝዝ ዘበለ ተንፀባራቒ ብርሃን** *dbzz zbele tentsebaraqhi brhan*
**lustrous** *(adj.)* **ደሚቕ ተንፀባራቒ ብርሃን** *demiqhi tentsebara qhi brhan*
**lusty** *(adj.)* **በዓል ሙሉእ ጥዕና** *beal mulu'e t'ena*
**lute** *(n.)* **ጊታር ዝመስል መሳርሒ ሙዚቃ** *gitar zmesl mesarhi muziqa*
**luxuriant** *(adj.)* **ፁብቕ** *tsubuqh*
**luxurious** *(adj.)* **ቑኑጡ** *qhetinu*
**luxury** *(n.)* **ቑኑጡ** *qhetinu*
**lychee** *(n.)* **ናይ ቻይና ፈረምረ** *nay chayna fremre*
**lymph** *(n.)* **ፃዕዳ ዋህዮ ደም ዘፈጠርሉ ኣካል** *tsa'eda wahyo dem zfterlu akal*
**lynch** *(n.)* **ብዘይ ፍርዲ ሓኒቕካ ምቕታል** *bzey frdi haniqhka mqhtal*
**lyre** *(n.)* **ናይ ገመድ ሙዚቃ መሳርሒ** *nay gemd muziqa mesarhi*
**lyric** *(n.)* **ናይ ሙዚቃ ግጥሚ** *nay muziqa gtmi*
**lyrical** *(adj.)* **ግጥማዊ** *gtmawi*
**lyricist** *(n.)* **ናይ ሙዚቃ ግጥሚ ገጣሚ** *nay muziqa gtmi getami*

# M

**macabre** *(adj.)* **ዘርዕድ** *zer'ëd*
**machine** *(n.)* **መኪና** *mekina*
**machinery** *(n.)* **ተንቀሳቓሲ ኣካል ናይ መኪና መካይን** *tenqesaq̈asi 'akal nay mekina mekayn*
**mackintosh** *(n.)* **ናይ ዝናብ ክዳን** *nay znab kdan*
**mad** *(adj.)* **ፁሉል** *tsulul*
**madam** *(n.)* **ወይዘሮ** *weyzero*
**madcap** *(adj.)* **ዘይሳኽዕ ዉጡን** *zeysakha'e wutun*
**magazine** *(n.)* **መፂሄት** *metsihiet*
**magenta** *(n.)* **ማጀንታ** *maĵenta*
**magic** *(n.)* **ስራሕ ሰራይ** *srah seray*
**magician** *(n.)* **ሰራዪ** *serayi*
**magisterial** *(adj.)* **ሉዑል በዓል ስልጣን** *lu'el be'al sltan*
**magistrate** *(n.)* **ታሕታዋይ ዳኛ** *tahtaway dagna*
**magnanimous** *(adj.)* **ይቕር በሃሊ** *yqhr behali*
**magnate** *(n.)* **ኣዚዩ ሃፍታም** *aziyu haftam*
**magnet** *(n.)* **ማግኔት** *magnet*

**magnetic** *(adj.)* ማግኔታዊ *magnetawi*
**magnetism** *(n.)* ማግኔታዊነት *magnetawinet*
**magnificent** *(adj.)* ብጣዕሚ ፁብቕ *bta'emi tsubqh*
**magnify** *(v.)* ምጉላሕ *mgulaḧ*
**magnitude** *(n. )* ዓቐን *aqhen*
**magpie** *(n. )* ኒዊሕ ጭራ ዘለዋ ዒፍ *newih chra zelewa ef*
**mahogany** *(n. )* ናይ ጣውላ ዕንፀይቲ *nay tawla entseyti*
**mahout** *(n.)* ጠባይ *ëebay*
**maid** *(n. )* ሰራሕተኛ ገዛ *serahtegna geza*
**maiden** *(n.)* መንእሰይ ስብይቲ *men'esey sebyti*
**mail** *(n.)* ፖስታ *posta*
**mail order** *(n.)* ብፖስታ ዝተገዙኡ *bposta ztegez'u*
**maim** *(v.)* ኸብድ መጥቃዕቲ ኣብፀሐ *khebid metqh'eti eabtsehe*
**main** *(adj.)* ዋና *wana*
**mainstay** *(n.)* ዋና ኣካል *wana alkal*
**maintain** *(v.)* ፀገነ *tsegene*
**maintenance** *(n.)* ምፅጋን ምዕራይ *mtsgan m'eray*
**maisonette** *(n.)* ናይ ደገ ማዕፆ ዘለዎ ክፍሊ ገዛ *nay dege ma'etso zelewo kfli geza*
**majestic** *(adj.)* ቆንጆ *qhonjo*
**majesty** *(n.)* ኽብርነትዎ *khbrnetwo(ልኡኣስ ወይ ንግስቲ)*
**major** *(adj.)* ዋና *wana*
**majority** *(n.)* ብዝሓት *bzhat*
**make** *(v.)* ምስራሕ *msrah*
**make-up** *(n.)* ምስራሕ *msrah*
**making** *(n.)* ምስራሕ *msrah*
**maladjusted** *(adj.)* ናይ ኣእምሮ ሑሙም *nay a'emro humum*
**maladministration** *(n. )* ትኽክል ዘይኮነ መሕደራ *tkhkl zeykone mehdra*
**malady** *(n. )* ሕማም *hmam*
**malaise** *(n.)* ቐሊል መፍትሒ ዘይብሉ ናይ ማሕበረ ሰብ ፀገም *qhelil meftihi zeyblu nay mahbere seb tsegem*
**malaria** *(n.)* ዓሶ *aso*
**malcontent** *(n.)* ዘይዓገቡ *zey'agebu*
**male** *(n.)* ተባዕታይ *teba'ëtay*
**malediction** *(n. )* እርግማን *ergman*
**malefactor** *(n.)* ሕጊ ዝጠሓሰ *hgi ztehase*
**malformation** *(n.)* ዝተበላሸየ ቕርፂ ኣካልሰውነት ካብ ትውልዲ ጀሚሩ *ztebelasheye qhrtsi akalsewnet kab teldi jemiru*
**malfunction** *(v.)* ምብሉሻው *mblshaw*
**malice** *(n.)* ምውራድ *mwrad*
**malicious** *(adj.)* ምውራድ *mwrad*
**malign** *(adj.)* ብሕማቕ ምልዓል *bhmaqh ml'al*
**malignant** *(adj.)* ካብ ቑፅፅር ዝወፀ ሕማም መንሽሮ *kab qhutstsr zwets hmam menshro*
**mall** *(n.)* ናይ ዕዳጋ ማእኸል *nay edaga ma'ekhel*
**malleable** *(adj.)* ተዓፃፃፊ *te'atsatsafi*
**mallet** *(n.)* ካብ ዕንፀይቲ ዝተሰረሐ መዶሻ *kab entseyti ztesreh medisha*

**malnutrition** *(n. )* ሕፅረት ምግቢ *htsret mgbi*
**malpractice** *(n. )* ኣግባባ ዘይብሉ ኣሰራርሓ *agbab zeyblu aserarha*
**malt** *(n. )* ጉዑሽ *gu'ush*
**maltreat** *(v.)* ምጉዳእ *mguda'e*
**mammal** *(n.)* መጥበውቲ *mtbeewti*
**mammary** *(adj.)* ምስ ጡብ ዝተተሓሓዘ *ms tub ztetehahaze*
**mammon** *(n. )* ቅርሺ *qhrsh*
**mammoth** *(n.)* ዓብዪ *abiyi*
**man** *(n.)* ሰብኣይ *sb'ay*
**manage** *(v.)* ምምሕዳር *mmhdar*
**manageable** *(adj.)* ክስራሕ ዝኽእል *ksrah zkh'el*
**management** *(n. )* ምምሕዳር *mmhdar*
**manager** *(n.)* ስራሕ ኣፈፃሚ *srah asfetsami*
**managerial** *(adj.)* ምምሕዳራዊ *mmhdarawi*
**mandate** *(n.)* ግዴታ *gdieta*
**mandatory** *(adj.)* ግዴታ *gdieta*
**mane** *(n. )* ጨጉሪ ኣምበሳ ወይ ፈረስ *cheguri ambesa wey feres*
**manful** *(adj.)* ተባዕ *teba'e*
**manganese** *(n. )* ማንጋኔዝ *manganiez*
**manger** *(n.)* መብልዒ እንስሳ ጋቢያ *mbl'e anbesa gabiya*
**mangle** *(v.)* ምጭፍላቕ *mchflaqh*
**mango** *(n.)* ማንጎ *mango*
**manhandle** *(n. )* ምጉስቓል *mgusqhal*
**manhole** *(n. )* መፈተሺ *mefeteshi*
**manhood** *(n.)* ስብኣይነት *sb'aynet*
**mania** *(n. )* ሕማም ጭንቀት *hmam chnqet*
**maniac** *(n. )* ፁሉል *tsulul*
**manicure** *(n.)* ኢድ ወይ ኣፅፋርካ ምክንካን *eid wey atsfarka*
**manifest** *(adj.)* ብግልፂ ዝረአ ሓቒ *gltsi zre'e haqhi*
**manifestation** *(n. )* ዝግለፀሉ መንገዲ *zgletselu mengedi*
**manifesto** *(n.)* ዕላማ እና ፖሊሲ ዝሓዘ ፁሑፍ *elama ena polisi zhaze tsuhuf*
**manifold** *(adj.)* ማኒፎልድ *manifold*
**manipulate** *(v.)* ኣታለለ *atalele*
**manipulation** *(n.)* ምትላል *mtlal*
**mankind** *(n.)* ሰብ *seb*
**manly** *(adj.)* ናይ ሰብኣይ ስራሕ *nay sb'ay srah*
**manna** *(n.)* ኣብቲ ዝተደለየ ግዜ ዝተፈጠረ ፁብቕ ነገር *abti ztedeleye gzie ztetere tsubuqh neger*
**mannequin** *(n. )* ናይ ቡቲክ ኣሻንጉሊት *nay butik ashangulit*
**manner** *(n. )* ስርዓት *sr'at*
**mannerism** *(n.)* ስርዓት *sr'at*
**manoeuvre** *(n.)* ምግናሕ *mgnah*
**manor** *(n.)* ዓብዪ ገዛ *abyi geza*
**manpower** *(n.)* ሓይሊ ሰብ *hayli seb*
**mansion** *(n. )* ዓብዪ ገዛ *abyi geza*
**mantel** *(n.)* ናይ መሞቒ ሓዊ ጠርዚ *nay mmaqhi hawi terzi*
**mantle** *(n.)* ቕርፊት መሬት *qhrfit meriet*
**mantra** *(n.)* ቡዱሂስት እና ሂንዱ ኣብ እዋን ፀሎት ዘደጋግምዎ ቃል *buduhist ena hindu ab ewan tselot zdegagmwo kal*

**manual** ***(adj.)*** **ዝርዝር መስርሕ** *zrzr mesrh*
**manufacture** ***(v.)*** **ምምራት** *mmrat*
**manufacturer** ***(n. )*** **ኣምራቲ** *amrati*
**manumission** ***(n.)*** **ተጻራፊ** *texarafi*
**manure** ***(n.)*** **ዒባ** *eba*
**manuscript** ***(n.)*** **ናይ ፊልሚ ድርሰት** *nay flmi drset*
**many** ***(adj.)*** **ብዝሕ** *buzh*
**map** ***(n.)*** **ካርታ** *karta*
**maple** ***(n.)*** **ሓሙሽተ ጫፍ ዘለዎ ቆፅሊ ዘለዎ ተኽሊ** *hamushte chaf zelwo qhotsli zelwo tekhli*
**mar** ***(v.)*** **ምብሉሻው** *mblshaw*
**marathon** ***(n.)*** **ማራቶን** *maraton*
**maraud** ***(v.)*** **ኣንሃረ** *anhari*
**marauder** ***(n. )*** **ሌያቡ ወይ ቐተልቲ** *lieyabu wey qhetelti*
**marble** ***(n.)*** **እምኒ በረድ** *emni bered*
**march** ***(n.)*** **ወታደራዊ ሰልፊ** *wetaderawi selfi*
**march** ***(v.)*** **ምስዳር** *msdar*
**mare** ***(n. )*** **ዓባይ ተንስተይቲ ፈረስ** *abay tnsteyti feres*
**margarine** ***(n. )*** **ካብ ኣትክልቲ እና ካብ እንስሳ ስብሒ ዝስራሕ ናይ ምግቢ ተስሚ** *kab atklti ena kab enssa sbhi zsrah nay mgbi tesmi*
**margin** ***(n.)*** **ኣብመንጎ ክልተ ቑፅርታት ዘሎ ኣፈላላይ** *ab mengo klte qhutsrtat zelo afelalay*
**marginal** ***(adj.)*** **ኑኡሹተይ** *nu'ushtey*
**marigold** ***(n.)*** **ቢጫ ዕንበባ** *bich enbeba*
**marina** ***(n. )*** **ናይ ኣናእሽተይ ጀልባ መዕረፊ** *nay ana'ushtey jelba me'erefi*
**marinade** ***(n.)*** **ኣብ ስጋ ዝቕባእ ዘይቲ** *ab sga zqhba'e zeyti*
**marinate** ***(v.)*** **ስጋ ኣብ ዝተፈላለዩ ዘይቲ ምቕማጥ** *sga ab ztefelaleye zeyti mqhmat*
**marine** ***(adj.)*** **ባሕረኛ ወታደር** *bahregna wetader*
**mariner** ***(n. )*** **ሓምባሲ** *hambasi*
**marionette** ***(n.)*** **ብገምደ ዝንቀሳቐስ ኣሻንጉሊት** *b gemed znqesaqhes ashangulit*
**marital** ***(adj.)*** **ምስ ሓዳር ዝተተሓሓዘ** *ms hadar ztetehahaze*
**maritime** ***(adj.)*** **ምስ ባሕሪ ዝተተሓሓዘ** *ms bahri ztetehahaze*
**mark** ***(n.)*** **ምልክት** *mlkt*
**marker** ***(n.)*** **ምልክት መግበሪ** *mlkt megberi*
**market** ***(n.)*** **ዕዳጋ** *edega*
**marketing** ***(n.)*** **ስነ ዕዳጋ** *sne edaga*
**marking** ***(n. )*** **ምልክት ምግባር** *mlkt mgbar*
**marksman** ***(n. )*** **ጎበዝ ጨማቲ** *gobez chemati*
**marl** ***(n.)*** **ተውህዶ** *tewhdo*
**marmalade** ***(n. )*** *bmeseret*
**maroon** ***(n.)*** **በዚ ምኽንያት'ዚ** *bezi mḱnyatzi*
**marquee** ***(n.)*** **ጐነፈ** *gWanefe*
**marriage** ***(n.)*** **ሕሳብ** *ȟsab*
**marriageable** ***(adj.)*** **ተሓታቲ** *teȟatati*
**marry** ***(v.)*** **ተመርዓወ** *temer'äwe*
**Mars** ***(n.)*** **ተጸባጸቢ** *texebaxabi*

**marsh** ***(n )*** **ብወግዒ ለአኸ** *bweg'ï le'aḱe*
**marshal** ***(n.)*** **ብወግዒ ለአኸ** *bweg'ï le'aḱe*
**marshmallow** ***(n.)*** **ወግዓዊ** *weg'äwi*
**marsupial** ***(n. )*** **ዕብየት** *ëbyet*
**mart** ***(n. )*** **ደለበ** *delebe*
**martial** ***(adj.)*** **አዋህለለ** *awahlele*
**martinet** ***(n. )*** **ውህለላ** *whlela*
**martyr** ***(n. )*** **ልክዕ** *lk'ë*
**martyrdom** ***(n. )*** **ግዚ** *gzi*
**marvel** ***(v.i)*** **ከሰሰ** *kesese*
**marvellous** ***(adj.)*** **ተሓታትነት** *teḧatatnet*
**Marxism** ***(n.)*** **ለመደ** *lemede*
**marzipan** ***(n.)*** **ልሙድ** *lmud*
**mascara** ***(n.)*** **ሓደ** *ḧade*
**mascot** ***(n.)*** **አረቢክ** *arebik*
**masculine** ***(adj.)*** **ተባዕታይ** *teba'ëtay*
**mash** ***(v.t)*** **ነታጕ** *netagWi*
**mask** ***(n.)*** **ቃንዛ** *qanza*
**masochism** ***(n.)*** **ተጎናጸፈ** *tegonaxefe*
**mason** ***(n. )*** **ፍጻሜ** *fxamee*
**masonry** ***(n. )*** **መጺጽ** *mexix*
**masquerade** ***(n. )*** **መጮቋር** *mečqWAr*
**mass** ***(n.)*** **ኣመስገነ** *amesgene*
**massacre** ***(n.)*** **ምቕጻል** *mq̈xal*
**massage** ***(n. )*** **ጫፍ** *čaf*
**masseur** ***(n.)*** **ዕንፍሩር** *ënfrur*
**massive** ***(adj.)*** **ኣናጎንስጤስ** *anagonsẗees*
**mast** ***(n. )*** **ስኻን** *sḱan*
**master** ***(n.)*** **ኣቦ ገዛ** *abo geza*
**mastermind** ***(n.)*** **ኣፋለጠ** *afaleẗe*
**masterpiece** ***(n. )*** **ሌላ** *leela*
**mastery** ***(n.)*** **ተሰማምዐ** *tesemam'e*
**masticate** ***(v.)*** **ምስምማዕ** *msmma'e*
**masturbate** ***(v.)*** **ረኸበ** *reḱebe*
**mat** ***(n.)*** **ቅስመት** *qsmet*
**matador** ***(n. )*** **ፈትሐ** *fetḣe*
**match** ***(n.)*** **ናጸ ምልቃቕ** *naxa mlqaq̈*
**matchmaker** ***(n. )*** **ኣክር** *akr*
**mate** ***(n.)*** **በዳን** *bedan*
**material** ***(n.)*** **ምረት** *mret*
**materialism** ***(n.)*** **ኣክሮባት** *akrobat*
**materialize** ***(v.)*** **ባሪቶን** *bariton*
**maternal** ***(adj.)*** **ስግር** *sgr*
**maternity** ***(n.)*** **ዘርዕድ** *zer'ëd*
**mathematical** ***(adj.)*** **ምግባር** *mgbar*
**mathematician** ***(n.)*** **ግዜያዊ ፈጻሚ** *gzeeyawi fexami*
**mathematics** ***(n. )*** **ምውሳእ** *mwsa'è*
**matinee** ***(n.)*** **ዘፍርህ** *zefrh*
**matriarch** ***(n.)*** **ምግባር** *mgbar*
**matricide** ***(n.)*** **ቅትለተ-ኣደ** *qtlete'ade*
**matriculate** ***(v.)*** **ኣንጠፈ** *anẗefe*
**matriculation** ***(n.)*** **ንጡፍ** *nẗuf*
**matrimonial** ***(adj.)*** **ስነ-ጠቢብ** *sneẗebib*
**matrimony** ***(n.)*** **ንጥፈት** *nẗfet*
**matrix** ***(n.)*** **ተዋናይ** *tewanay*
**matron** ***(n. )*** **ተዋሳኢት** *tewasa'it*
**matter** ***(n. )*** **ህሉው** *hluw*
**mattress** ***(n.)*** **ብሓቂ** *bḧaqi*
**mature** ***(adj.)*** **ገምጋሚ** *gemgami*
**maturity** ***(n.)*** **ኣንጠፈ** *anẗefe*
**maudlin** ***(adj.)*** **ትኩርና** *tkurna*

**maul** *(v.)* **መሪድያን** *meridyan*
**maunder** *(v.)* **ንሱር** *nsur*
**mausoleum** *(n. )* **ተሪር** *terir*
**maverick** *(n.)* **ኣልዘበ** *alzebe*
**maxim** *(n.)* **ምውህሃድ** *mwhhad*
**maximize** *(v.)* **ደመረ** *demere*
**maximum** *(n.)* **መመላእታ** *memela'èta*
**May** *(n.)* **ተወለፈ** *tewelefe*
**may** *(v.)* **ምውላፍ** *mwlaf*
**maybe** *(adv. )* **ወልፊ** *welfi*
**mayhem** *(n.)* **ምድማር** *mdmar*
**mayonnaise** *(n.)* **ተወሳኺ** *tewesaḱi*
**mayor** *(n. )* **ዓቃቢ** *äqabi*
**maze** *(n.)* **ድንጉር** *dngur*
**me** *(pron.)* **ኣድራሻ** *adrasha*
**mead** *(n. )* **ሸካ** *sheḱa*
**meadow** *(n.)* **ጠቐሰ** *ẗeq̈ese*
**meagre** *(adj.)* **ክኢላ** *k'ila*
**meal** *(n.)* **እኹልነት** *èḱulnet*
**mealy** *(adj.)* **እኹል** *èḱul*
**mean** *(v.)* **ሰዓበ** *se'äbe*
**meander** *(v.)* **ምድጋፍ** *mdgaf*
**meaning** *(n.)* **ላጋቢ** *lagabi*
**means** *(n.)* **ላጋቢደሓን ኩን** *deḧan kun*
**meantime** *(adv. )* **ጐረቤት** *gWarebeet*
**meanwhile** *(adv. )* **ቅጽል** *qxl*
**measles** *(n.)* **ተጸግዐ ኣብ ጐድኒ ኮነ** *texeg'ë 'ab gWadni kone*
**measly** *(adj.)* **ኣቈረጸ** *aqWArexe*
**measure** *(a. )* **በየነ** *beyene*
**measure** *(v.)* **ኣመሓላለፈ** *ameḧalalefe*
**measured** *(adj.)* **ፈረደ** *ferede*
**measurement** *(n. )* **ጥብቆ** *ẗbqo*
**meat** *(n. )* **ኣመዓራረየ** *ame'ärareye*
**mechanic** *(n.)* **ምውዳድ** *mwdad*
**mechanical** *(adj.)* **ኣመሓደረ** *ameḧadere*
**mechanics** *(n.)* **ምምሕዳር** *mmḧdar*
**mechanism** *(n. )* **ምምሕዳራዊ** *mmḧdarawi*
**medal** *(n. )* **ኣመሓዳሪ** *ameḧadari*
**medallion** *(n.)* **ዚነኣድ** *zine'ad*
**medallist** *(v.i. )* **ኣድሚራል** *admiral*
**meddle** *(v.)* **ኣድናቖት** *adnaq̈ot*
**media** *(n.)* **ኣድነቐ** *adneq̈e*
**median** *(adj.)* **ዚፍቀድ** *zifqed*
**mediate** *(v.)* **ቅበላ** *qbela*
**mediation** *(n.)* **ተኣመነ** *te'amene*
**mediation** *(n.)* **ተፈታዊ** *tefetawi*
**medic** *(n.)* **ቅበላ** *qbela*
**medical** *(adj.)* **ገሰጸ** *gesexe*
**medication** *(n.)* **ሸቐልቀል** *sheq̈elqel*
**medicinal** *(adj.)* **ጥረ-ሕጡብ** *ẗreḧẗub*
**medicine** *(n. )* **ብጽሕና** *bxḧna*
**medieval** *(adj.)* **በጽሒ** *bexḧi*
**mediocre** *(adj.)* **ወሰደ** *wesede*
**mediocrity** *(n.)* **ምርዓም** *mr'äm*
**meditate** *(v.)* **ረዓሚ** *re'ämi*
**meditative** *(adj.)* **ፍቕሪ** *fq̈ri*
**Mediterranean** *(adj.)* **ኣምለኸ** *amleḱe*
**medium** *(n.)* **ኣሰወነ** *asewene*
**medley** *(n.)* **ፋሉል** *falul*
**meek** *(adj.)* **ጨለ** *čele*
**meet** *(v.)* **ኣድሶረብ** *adserb*
**meeting** *(n. )* **ውዳሰ-ከንቱ** *wdasekentu*

**mega** *(adj.)* እኹል *èḱul*
**megabyte** *(n.)* ኣመራሰሒ *ameraseḧe*
**megahertz** *(n.)* ምምርሳሕ *mmrsaḧ*
**megalith** *(n.)* ዝሙት *zmut*
**megalithic** *(adj.)* ሰጕመ *segWame*
**megaphone** *(n. )* ለዓለ *le'äle*
**megapixel** *(n.)* ምምዕባል *mm'ëbal*
**melamine** *(n.)* ብልጫ *blča*
**melancholia** *(n.)* ረብሓ *rebḧa*
**melancholy** *(n.)* ጠቓሚ *ťeqami*
**melange** *(n.)* ምጽኣት *mx'at*
**meld** *(n.)* ዕንደራ *ëndera*
**melee** *(n.)* ሓደገ'ኛ *ḧadegeǹa*
**meliorate** *(v.)* ተወሳከ-ግሲ *tewesakegsi*
**mellow** *(adj.)* ተጸይ *texay*
**melodic** *(adj.)* ኣሉታዊ *alutawi*
**melodious** *(adj.)* ሽግር *shgr*
**melodrama** *(n.)* ኣፋለጠ *afaleťe*
**melodramatic** *(adj.)* ረክላም *reklam*
**melody** *(n.)* ምዕዶ *m'ëdo*
**melon** *(n.)* ዝሓሸ *zḧashe*
**melt** *(v.)* መዓደ *me'äde*
**member** *(n.)* ደጋፊ *degafi*
**membership** *(n.)* ተሓላቒ *teḧalaq̈i*
**membrane** *(n.)* ዑቕባ *üq̈ba*
**memento** *(n.)* ሰፋፊ *sefafi*
**memo** *(n.)* ኣዩን *ayun*
**memoir** *(n.)* ኣይሮባቲክስ *ayrobatiks*
**memorable** *(adj.)* ማሪዋና *mariwana*
**memorandum** *(n.)* መዓርፎ ነፈርቲ *me'ärfo neferti*
**memorial** *(n.)* ስነ-ምንፋር *snemnfar*
**memory** *(n.)* ኣይሮፕላን *ayroplan*
**menace** *(n.)* ፍሊት *flit*
**mend** *(v.)* ናይ ነፈርቲ *nay neferti*
**mendacious** *(adj.)* ጽባቐኣዊ *xbaq̈e'awi*
**mendicant** *(adj.)* ስነ-ጽባቐ *snexbaq̈e*
**menial** *(adj.)* ካብ ርሑቕ *kab rḧuq̈*
**meningitis** *(n. )* ፍሕሹው *fḧshuw*
**menopause** *(n.)* ፍጻሜ *fxamee*
**menstrual** *(adj.)* ጸለወ *xelewe*
**menstruation** *(n.)* ምስሉይነት *msluynet*
**mental** *(adj.)* ኣምሳሊ *amsali*
**mentality** *(n.)* ፍትወት *ftwet*
**mention** *(v.)* ርህሩህ *rhruh*
**mentor** *(n. )* ቃለ-ማሕላ *qalemaḧla*
**menu** *(n.)* ተጸግዐ *texeg'ë*
**mercantile** *(adj.)* ምጽጋዕ *mxga'ë*
**mercenary** *(adj.)* ተማስሎ *temaslo*
**merchandise** *(n.)* ኣረጋገጸ *aregagexe*
**merchant** *(n.)* ምርግጋጽ *mrggax*
**merciful** *(adj.)* ኣወንታዊ *awentawi*
**mercurial** *(adj.)* ልቃ'በ *lqabe*
**mercury** *(n. )* ጕድኣ *gWad'e*
**mercy** *(n.)* ጭንቂ *čnqi*
**mere** *(adj.)* ሃብቲ *habti*
**meretricious** *(adj.)* ሃብታም *habtam*

**merge** *(v.)* **ኣተኻኸለ** *ateḱaḱele*
**merger** *(n.)* **ምግራብ** *mgrab*
**meridian** *(n.)* **ናዕቢ** *na'ëbi*
**merit** *(n.)* **ዘለፈ** *zelefe*
**meritorious** *(adj.)* **ኣብ ርሑቕ** *'ab rḧuq̈*
**mermaid** *(n. )* **ዝተቓጸለ** *zteq̈axele*
**merry** *(adj.)* **ዘንሳፍፍ** *zensaff*
**mesh** *(n.)* **ኣብ ምቅርራብ** *'ab mqrrab*
**mesmeric** *(adj.)* **ዝፈርሀ** *zferhe*
**mesmerize** *(v.)* **ከም ብሓድሽ** *kem bḧadsh*
**mess** *(n.)* **ኣፍሪቃ** *afriqa*
**message** *(n.)* **ኣብ ሪተ-መርከብ** *'ab ritemerkeb*
**messenger** *(n.)* **ድሕሪ** *dḧri*
**messiah** *(n.)* **ድሕረ** *dḧre*
**messy** *(adj.)* **ድሕረ** *dḧri*
**metabolism** *(n.)* **እንደገና** *'èndegena*
**metal** *(n.)* **ኣንጻር** *anxar*
**metallic** *(adj.)* **ተሪር ክቡር እምኒ** *terir kbur 'èmni*
**metallurgy** *(n. )* **ዕድመ** *ëdme*
**metamorphosis** *(n. )* **ሽማግለታት** *shmagletat*
**metaphor** *(n.)* **ቅድመ-ፍርዲ** *qdmefrdi*
**metaphysical** *(adj.)* **ዘልኣለማዊ** *zel'alemawi*
**metaphysics** *(n.)* **ናይ ውክልና ትካል** *nay wklna tkal*
**mete** *(v.)* **ኣጀንዳ** *aĵenda*
**meteor** *(n.)* **ግሉል** *glul*
**meteoric** *(adj.)* **ኣከበ** *akebe*
**meteorology** *(n.)* **ኣግደደ** *agdede*
**meter** *(n. )* **ዘቑጥዕ** *zeq̈uẗ'ë*
**method** *(n.)* **ደመረ** *demere*
**methodical** *(adj.)* **መጥቃዕቲ** *meẗqa'ëti*
**methodology** *(n.)* **ዓማጺ** *ämaxi*
**meticulous** *(adj.)* **ኣጥቃዒ** *aẗqa'ï*
**metre** *(n.)* **ኣቐየመ** *aq̈eyeme*
**metric** *(adj.)* **ዝሰምበደ** *zsembede*
**metrical** *(adj.)* **ስሉጥ** *sluẗ*
**metropolis** *(n.)* **ሶፕራኖ** *soprano*
**metropolitan** *(adj.)* **ቀስቀሰ** *qesqese*
**mettle** *(n.)* **ምኳስ** *mḱWas*
**mettlesome** *(n.)* **ኢፈሊጣዊ** *ifeliẗawi*
**mew** *(v.)* **ኛው** *ǹaw*
**mews** *(n.)* **ርቡጽ** *rbux*
**mezzanine** *(n. )* **ሃወኸ** *haweḱe*
**miasma** *(n.)* **መሪር ሓዘን** *merir ḧazen*
**mica** *(n. )* **መሬታዊ** *mereetawi*
**microbiology** *(n.)* **ተሰማምዐ** *tesemam'ë*
**microchip** *(n.)* **ዚሰማማዕ** *zisemama'ë*
**microfilm** *(n. )* **ስምምዕ** *smm'ë*
**micrometer** *(n. )* **ሕርሻዊ** *ḧrshawi*
**microphone** *(n. )* **ሕርሻ** *ḧrsha*
**microprocessor** *(n.)* **ኣብ ባይታ** *'ab bayta*
**microscope** *(n.)* **ኣብ ቅድሚ** *'ab qdmi*
**microscopic** *(adj.)* **ረድአ** *red'e*
**microsurgery** *(n.)* **ደጋፊ** *degafi*
**microwave** *(n.)* **ረድኢ** *red'i*
**mid** *(adj.)* **ኣጨነቐ** *ačeneq̈e*
**midday** *(n.)* **ኣጨነቐኢ** *ačeneq̈e'i*
**middle** *(adj.)* **ሕማም** *ḧmam*
**middleman** *(n.)* **ዕላማ** *ëlama*
**middling** *(adj.)* **ሽቶ** *shto*

**midget** *(n. )* **ሰሓተ** *sehate*
**midnight** *(n.)* **አየር** *ayer*
**midriff** *(n.)* **ነፋሪት** *nefarit*
**midst** *(adj.)* **ነፋሻ** *nefasha*
**midsummer** *(adj.)* **ኮሪደዮ** *korideyo*
**midway** *(adv. )* **ዝተገፍተነ** *ztegeftene*
**midwife** *(n. )* **ዚዛመድ** - *zizamed*
**might** *(v.)* **ስሉጥ** *sluẗ*
**mighty** *(adj.)* **ቅሩብነት** *qrubnet*
**migraine** *(n. )* **መጠንቀቕታ** *meẗenqeq̈ta*
**migrant** *(n.)* **ስግኣት** *sg'at*
**migrate** *(v.)* **ዋይ ኣነ** *way 'ane*
**migration** *(n.)* **ሽሕ'ኳ** *shḧkWa*
**mild** *(adj.)* **ኣልቡም** *'album*
**mile** *(n. )* **ኣልቡመን** *albumen*
**mileage** *(n. )* **ኣልከሚ** *alkemi*
**milestone** *(n. )* **ኣልኮል** *alkol*
**milieu** *(n.)* **ሰታይ** *setay*
**militant** *(adj.)* **ስብሳብ** *sbsab*
**militant** *(n.)* **ኣይል=ዓይነት ቢራ** *'ayl'äynet bira*
**military** *(adj.)* **ጥንቁቕ** *ẗnquq̈*
**militate** *(v.)* **ኣልጀብራ** *alĵebra*
**militia** *(n. )* **ሳጓ** *sagWa*
**milk** *(n.)* **ልውጠ-ስም** *lwẗesm*
**milkshake** *(n.)* **መውጽኢ-ነፍሲ** *mewx'inefsi*
**milky** *(adj.)* **መውጽኢ-ነፍሲ** *mewx'inefsi*
**mill** *(n.)* **ነጸለ** *nexele*
**millennium** *(n. )* **ዚነድድ** *zinedd*
**millet** *(n. )* **ሰርዐ** *ser'ë*
**milligram** *(n.)* **ኣሳላልፋ** *asalalfa*
**millimetre** *(n.)* **ተመሳሳሊ** *temesasali*
**milliner** *(n. )* **ክፍሊት ፍትሕ** *kflit ftḧ*
**million** *(n. )* **ህያው** *hyaw*
**millionaire** *(n. )* **ኣልካሊ** *alkali*
**millipede** *(n. )* **ኩሉ** *kulu*
**mime** *(n.)* **ኣፋኰሰ** *afakWase*
**mime** *(n. )* **ብህሎ** *bhlo*
**mimic** *(n.)* **ኣለ** *ale*
**mimicry** *(n. )* **ተኣማንነት** *te'amannet*
**minaret** *(n.)* **ምስሌኣዊ ዛንታ** *mslee'awi zanta*
**mince** *(v.)* **ኣሕረቐ** *aḧreq̈e*
**mind** *(n.)* **ተቖጣዒ** *teq̈oẗa'ï*
**mindful** *(adj.)* **ቁጥዐ** *quẗ'ë*
**mindless** *(adj.)* **ኣፋ዆ሰ** *afaḱWase*
**mine** *(pron.)* **ምቕላል** *mq̈lal*
**mine** *(n. )* **መሽጐራጉር** *meshgWaragur*
**miner** *(n. )* **ኪዳን** *kidan*
**mineral** *(n.)* **ተጸግዐ** *texeg'ë*
**mineralogy** *(n.)* **ዓንጎግ** *ängog*
**minestrone** *(n.)* **ደምሰሰ** *demsese*
**mingle** *(v.)* **ድግመተ-ኣፈና** *dgmete'afena*
**mini** *(adj.)* **ኣካፈለ** *akafele*
**miniature** *(adj.)* **ምምቕራሕ** *mmq̈raḧ*
**minibus** *(n.)* **ኣማስሐ** *amasḧe*
**minicab** *(n.)* **ምስሒት** *msḧit*
**minim** *(n.)* **ፈቐደ** *feq̈ede*
**minimal** *(adj.)* **መውዕሎ** *mew'ëlo*
**minimize** *(v.)* **ቆርቆሮ** *qorqoro*
**minimum** *(n.)* **ኣመተ** *amete*
**minion** *(n. )* **ኣወናወነ** *awenawene*
**miniskirt** *(n.)* **ኣወናወኒ** *awenaweni*

**minister** ***(n.)*** **አመት** *amet*
**ministerial** ***(adj.)*** **ሽርካ** *shrka*
**ministry** ***(n. )*** **አልማናክ** *almanak*
**mink** ***(n.)*** **ኩሉ ዚከኣሎ** *kulu zike'alo*
**minor** ***(adj.)*** **ሉዝ** *luz*
**minority** ***(n. )*** **ዳርጋ** *darga*
**minster** ***(n.)*** **ምጽ'ዋት** *mxwat*
**mint** ***(n.)*** **ዝተሰቐለ** *zteseq̈le*
**minus** ***(prep.)*** **በይኑ** *beynu*
**minuscule** ***(adj.)*** **ኣብ ጐድኒ** *ab gWadni*
**minute** ***(n.)*** **ኣብ ጐድነኒ** *ab gWadneh*
**minute** ***(adj.)*** **ግሉል** *glul*
**minutely** ***(adv. )*** **ብዓውታ** *b'äwta*
**minx** ***(n.)*** **ኣልፋ** *alfa*
**miracle** ***(n.)*** **ፊደል** *fidel*
**miraculous** ***(adj.)*** **ብናይ ፊደላት ተርታ** *bnay fidelat terta*
**mirage** ***(n. )*** **ከረናዊ** *kerenawi*
**mire** ***(n.)*** **ዛጊት** *zagit*
**mirror** ***(n.)*** **ከምኡ'ውን** *kem'uwn*
**mirth** ***(n.)*** **መንበረ-ታቦት** *menberetabot*
**mirthful** ***(adj.)*** **ጠረጴዛ ቁርባን** *ťerep̈eeza qurban*
**misadventure** ***(n. )*** **ምልዋጥ** *mlwať*
**misalliance** ***(n. )*** **ቈይቈ** *qWeyqWi*
**misapply** ***(v.)*** **ምርጫ** *mrča*
**misapprehend** ***(v.)*** **ቅያር** *qyar*
**misapprehension** ***(n.)*** **ምንም'ኳ** *mnmkWa*
**misappropriate** ***(v.)*** **ብራኸ** *brak̈e*
**misappropriation** ***(v.)*** **ኩሉኹሉ** *kuluk̈ulu*
**misbehave** ***(v.)*** **ልግስነት** *lgsnet*
**misbehaviour** ***(n. )*** **ኣሉሚኒዮም** *aluminiyom*
**misbelief** ***(n.)*** **ተማሃራይ ዩኒቨርሲቲ ነበር** *yuniversiti neber*
**miscalculate** ***(v.)*** **ኩሉ ግዜ** *kulu gzee*
**miscalculation** ***(n.)*** **ሕዋስ ባዚቃ** *ḧwas baziqa*
**miscarriage** ***(n.)*** **ደብለቐ** *debleq̈e*
**miscarry** ***(v.)*** **ምሕባር** *mḧbar*
**miscellaneous** ***(adj.)*** **ኣከበ** *akebe*
**mischance** ***(n.)*** **ኣማተር** *amater*
**mischief** ***(n.)*** **ዘይክኢላ** *zeyk'ila*
**mischievous** ***(adj.)*** **መስተፋቅር** *mestefaqr*
**misconceive** ***(v.)*** **ኣገረመ** *agereme*
**misconception** ***(n.)*** **ኣድናቖት** *adnaq̈ot*
**misconduct** ***(n.)*** **ኣማዘን** *amazen*
**misconstrue** ***(v.)*** **ኣምባሳደር=ልኡኽ** *'ambasaderl'uk̈*
**miscreant** ***(n.)*** **ዕንዲዳ ጌጽ** *'ëndida geex*
**misdeed** ***(n.)*** **ዙርያዊ** *zuryawi*
**misdemeanour** ***(n.)*** **ዘይንጹርነት** *zeynxurnet*
**misdirect** ***(v.)*** **ዘይንጹር** *zeynxur*
**miser** ***(n.)*** **ደረት** *deret*
**miserable** ***(adj.)*** **ህርፋን** *hrfan*
**miserly** ***(adj.)*** **ህንጡይ** *hnťuy*
**misery** ***(n.)*** **ማንታዊ** *mantawi*
**misfire** ***(v.)*** **ተሰለየ** *tesaleye*
**misfit** ***(n.)*** **ምቁር** *mqur*
**misfortune** ***(n.)*** **ኣምቡላንስ** *ambulans*
**misgive** ***(v.)*** **ድብያ** *dbya*

**misgiving** *(n.)* **አመሓየሸ** *amehäyeshe*
**misguide** *(v.)* **ምምሕያሽ** *mmḧyash*
**mishandle** *(v.)* **አመሓየሸ** *amehäyeshe*
**mishap** *(n.)* **መአረምታ** *me'aremta*
**misinform** *(v.)* **ተሓታቲ** *tehätati*
**misinterpret** *(v.)* **ተፈታዊ** *tefetawi*
**misjudge** *(v.)* **ምሕዝነታዊ** *mḧznetawi*
**mislay** *(v.)* **ኣብ መንጎ** *'ab mengo*
**mislead** *(v.)* **ግጉይ** *gguy*
**mismanagement** *(n.)* **ዕርክነት** *ërknet*
**mismatch** *(n. )* **ተተኳሲ** *tetekWasi*
**misnomer** *(n.)* **ርሳዕ** *rsa'ë*
**misplace** *(v.)* **ምሕረት** *mḧret*
**misprint** *(n.)* **ብዕብድብድ** *b'ëbdbd*
**misquote** *(v.)* **ኣብ መንጎ** *ab mengo*
**misread** *(v.)* **ብዕሉግ** *b'ëlug*
**misrepresent** *(v.)* **ፍቕራዊ** *fq̈rawi*
**misrule** *(n. )* **ቅርጸ-ኣልቦ** *qrxe'albo*
**miss** *(n. )* **ኣምፐር** *amper*
**miss** *(v.)* **ማዕረ ኮነ** *ma'ëre kone*
**missile** *(n. )* **ፍሉጥ ሰብ** *fluẗ seb*
**missing** *(adj.)* **ምድረ-ማያዊ** *mdremayawi*
**mission** *(n. )* **ኣምፊትያትር** *amfityatr*
**missionary** *(n.)* **ሰፊሕ** *sefiḧ*
**missive** *(n. )* **ተወሳኺ** *tewesaǩi*
**misspell** *(v.)* **መጉልሒ** *megulḧi*
**mist** *(n. )* **ኣጉልሖ** *agulḧe*
**mistake** *(n.)* **ስፍሓት** *sfḧat*
**mistaken** *(adj.)* **ክታብ** *ktab*
**mistletoe** *(n.)* **ኣዘናግዐ** *azenag'ë*
**mistreat** *(v.)* **ምዝንጋዕ** *mznga'ë*
**mistress** *(n. )* **ሓደ** *ḧade*
**mistrust** *(v.)* **ዕለቱ ዝሰሓተ** *ëletu zsehäte*
**misty** *(adj.)* **ዋሕዲ ደም** *waḧdi dem*
**misunderstand** *(v.)* **ድንዛዘ** *dnzaze*
**misunderstanding** *(n. )* **መደንዘዚ** *medenzezi*
**misuse** *(v.)* **ቆይቋም** *qoyqWAm*
**mite** *(n.)* **ጸረ-ቃንዛ** *xereqanza*
**mitigate** *(v.)* **ተመሳሳሊ** *temesasali*
**mitigation** *(n.)* **ተመሳሳልነት** *temesasalnet*
**mitre** *(n. )* **ተመሳሳልነት** *temesasalnet*
**mitten** *(n.)* **ምትንታን** *mtntan*
**mix** *(v.)* **ምርምር** *mrmr*
**mixer** *(n.)* **ተንታኒ** *tentani*
**mixture** *(n.)* **ትንታነኣዊ** *tntane'awi*
**moan** *(n. )* **ፋሉልነት** *falulnet*
**moat** *(n.)* **ፋሉላዊ** *falulawi*
**mob** *(n.)* **ፋሉልነት** *falulnet*
**mobile** *(adj.)* **ስነ-ቅርጺ ኣካል** *sneqrxi 'akal*
**mobility** *(n.)* **ኣበው** *abew*
**mobilize** *(v.)* **ውርሻዊ** *wrshawi*
**mocha** *(n.)* **ኣበው** *abew*
**mock** *(v.)* **መልሀቕ** *melhq̈*
**mockery** *(n.)* **ተዓሻገ** *te'äshage*
**modality** *(n. )* **ጥንታዊ** *ẗntawi*
**mode** *(n. )* **ጽግዕተኛ** *xg'ëteňa*

**model** *(n.)* ድማ *dma*
**modem** *(n.)* ጽግዕተኛ *xg'ëteṅa*
**moderate** *(adj.)* ጽዋ *xwa*
**moderation** *(n.)* እንደገና *èndegena*
**moderator** *(n.)* ፍቱው *ftuw*
**modern** *(adj.)* ቁጥዐ *quṫ'ë*
**modernism** *(n.)* ሕሩቕ *ḧruq̈*
**modernity** *(n.)* ሕማም *ḧmam*
**modernize** *(v.)* ኩርናዕ *kurna'ë*
**modest** *(adj.)* ጓሂ *gWahi*
**modesty** *(n. )* ኩርናዓዊ *kurna'äwi*
**modicum** *(n. )* እንስሳ *ènssa*
**modification** *(n.)* ህያው *hyaw*
**modish** *(adj.)* ህያውነት *hyawnet*
**modulate** *(v.)* ጽልኢ *xl'i*
**module** *(n.)* ሸለን *shelen*
**moil** *(v.)* ዓንካር-ዓንካሪቶ *änkar'änkarito*
**moist** *(adj.)* ኣንባር *anbar*
**moisten** *(v.)* መዝገበ-ፍጻሜታት *mezgebefxameetat*
**moisture** *(n. )* ጎበጠ *gobeṫe*
**moisturize** *(v.)* ጐበጣ *gWabeṫa*
**molar** *(n.)* ኣጽነተ *axnete*
**molasses** *(n. )* ድምሰሳ *dmsesa*
**mole** *(n.)* ዝክረ-ዓመት *zkre'ämet*
**molecular** *(adj.)* ኣመልከተ *amelkete*
**molecule** *(n.)* ገለጸ *gelexe*
**molest** *(v.)* መግለጺ *meglexi*
**molestation** *(n.)* ሸወዘ *sheweze*
**mollify** *(v.)* ቁጥዐ *quṫ'ë*
**molten** *(adj.)* ምካኽ *mkak*
**moment** *(n.)* በብዓመት *beb'ämet*
**momentary** *(adj.)* ሰረዘ *sereze*
**momentous** *(adj.)* ኣገዳሲ *'agedasi*
**momentum** *(n.)* ቀብአ *qeb'e*
**monarch** *(n. )* ዘይስሩዕ *zeysru'ë*
**monarchy** *(n. )* ዘይስተ *zeyst*
**monastery** *(n.)* ስሙ-ስውርነት *smeswrnet*
**monastic** *(adj.)* ስሙ-ስውር *smeswr*
**monasticism** *(n. )* ምንማነ *mnmane*
**Monday** *(n.)* ካልእ *kal'è*
**monetarism** *(n.)* መልሲ *melsi*
**monetary** *(adj.)* ኪምለስ ዚከኣል *kimles zike'al*
**money** *(n. )* ጻጸ *xaxe*
**monger** *(n. )* ጻጸ መጺጽ *xaxe mexix*
**mongoose** *(n.)* ተጻራርነት *texararnet*
**mongrel** *(n. )* ተጻራሪ *texarari*
**monitor** *(n.)* ተጻረረ *texarere*
**monitory** *(adj.)* ኣንታርክቲክ *antarktik*
**monk** *(n. )* ቅድመ ፍጻመ *qdme fxame*
**monkey** *(n.)* ኣቓደመ *aquadme*
**mono** *(n.)* ዓጋዜን *ägazeen*
**monochrome** *(n.)* ኣንተና *antena*
**monocle** *(n.)* ኣንቴማ *anteema*
**monocular** *(adj.)* እኩብ ዛንታታት *'èkub zantatat*
**monody** *(n. )* ስነ-ሰብ *sneseb*
**monogamy** *(n. )* ነፍሪ *nefri*
**monogram** *(n. )* ጸረ *xere*
**monograph** *(n.)* ጸረ-ነፍሳት *xerenefsat*

**monolatry** *(n. )* ጸረ-አካል *xere'akal*
**monolith** *(n. )* ወጀሃላይ *weĵehalay*
**monologue** *(n. )* ተጸበየ *texebeye*
**monophonic** *(adj.)* ትጽቢት *txbit*
**monopolist** *(n.)* ምንቁልቋል *mnqulqWAl*
**monopolize** *(v.)* ጸረ-መርዚ *xeremerzi*
**monopoly** *(n. )* ጸረ-መርዚ *xeremerzi*
**monorail** *(n.)* ክርሃት *krhat*
**monosyllable** *(n.)* ኩሕለ-ምሕሊ *kuḧlemḧli*
**monotheism** *(n. )* ዘጥንቲ *zeẗnti*
**monotheist** *(n.)* ድሑር *dḧur*
**monotonous** *(adj.)* ጥንታዊ *ẗntawi*
**monotony** *(n.)* ጥንቲ *ẗnti*
**monsoon** *(n. )* ጸረ-ረኽሲ *xerereḱsi*
**monster** *(n.)* ጸረ-ማሕበራዊ *xeremaḧberawi*
**monstrous** *(n. )* ኣንጸር *anxar*
**monstrous** *(adj.)* ጭንፋር ቀርኒ *čnfar qerni*
**montage** *(n.)* ኣሉታ *aluta*
**month** *(n.)* መሃንቱስ *mehantus*
**monthly** *(adj.)* ወርሓዊ *werḧawi*
**monument** *(n.)* ጭንቀት *čnqet*
**monumental** *(adj.)* ሃረርተኛ *harerteňa*
**moo** *(v.)* ዝኾነ *zḱone*
**mood** *(n.)* ብዘይተገዳስነት *bzeytegedasnet*
**moody** *(adj.)* ዝኾነ ሰብ *zḱone seb*
**moon** *(n. )* ዝኾነ ነገር *zḱone neger*
**moonlight** *(n.)* ዝኾነ ቦታ *zḱone bota*
**moor** *(n.)* ብቕልጡፍ *bq̈lẗuf*
**moorings** *(n. )* ዝተፈላለየ *ztefelaleye*
**moot** *(adj.)* ኣፓርታይድ *apartayd*
**mop** *(n.)* ክፍሊ-ገዛ *kfligeza*
**mope** *(v.)* ዘይተገዳስነት *zeytegedasnet*
**moped** *(n.)* ቀዳሒ *qedaḧi*
**moraine** *(n.)* ጭርታ *črta*
**moral** *(adj.)* ጫፍ *čaf*
**morale** *(n. )* ምስላ *msla*
**moralist** *(n. )* መንህብ *menhb*
**morality** *(n.)* ርእሰ-ርጉጽነት *r'èserguxnet*
**moralize** *(v.)* ራእይ - *ra'èy*
**morass** *(n.)* ይቕሬታ ሓተተ *q̈reeta ḧatete*
**morbid** *(adj.)* ይቕሬታ *yq̈reeta*
**morbidity** *(adv. )* ኣፖፕለቲካዊ *apopletikawi*
**more** *(n.)* ከሓዲ እምነት *keḧadi 'èmnet*
**moreover** *(adv. )* ሃዋርያ *hawarya*
**morganatic** *(adj.)* ጭረት *čret*
**morgue** *(n.)* ኣስካሕከሐ - *askaḧkeḧe*
**moribund** *(adj.)* መሰርሒ *mesarḧi*
**morning** *(n. )* ክዳን *kdan*
**moron** *(n.)* ብሩህ *bruh*
**morose** *(adj.)* ብሩህ *bruh*
**morphine** *(n.)* ተራእየ *tera'èye*
**morphology** *(n.)* ምቕልቃል *mq̈lqal*
**morrow** *(n. )* ኣዝሓለ *azḧale*
**morsel** *(n.)* መልአ *mel'e*

**mortal** ***(adj.)***
**መመላእታ** *memela'èta*
**mortality** ***(n.)*** **ነድሪ ጥብቆ** *nedri ẗbqo*
**mortar** ***(n. )***
**መመላእታ** *memela'èta*
**mortgage** ***(n.)*** **ሸውሃት** *shewhat*
**mortgagee** ***(n. )*** **ከፋት ሸውሃት** *kefat shewhat*
**mortgagor** ***(n.)*** **ኣጨብጨበ** *ačebčebe*
**mortify** ***(v.)*** **ጨብጨባ** *čebčeba*
**mortuary** ***(n.)*** **ቱፋሕ** *tufaḧ*
**mosaic** ***(n. )*** **መሳርያ** *mesarya*
**mosque** ***(n. )*** **ብቑዕ** *bq̈u'ë*
**mosquito** ***(n. )*** **ኣመልካቲ** *amelkati*
**moss** ***(n.)*** **ምሕታት** *mḧtat*
**most** ***(n.)*** **ተጠቕመ** *teẗeq̈me*
**mote** ***(n. )*** **ወሰነ** *wesene*
**motel** ***(n. )*** **ቈጸራ** *qWexera*
**moth** ***(n.)*** **ጐዘየ** *gWazeye*
**mother** ***(n. )*** **ገምገመ** *gemgeme*
**mother** ***(n.)***
**ዚሰማማዕ** *zisemama'ë*
**motherboard** ***(n.)*** **እኹል** *èkul*
**motherhood** ***(n.)***
**ተገንዘበ** *tegenzebe*
**mother-in-law** ***(n.)***
**ኣስተያየት** *asteyayet*
**motherly** ***(adj.)*** **ተረድአ** *tered'e*
**motif** ***(n. )*** **ምርዳእ** *mrda'è*
**motion** ***(n.)*** **ዝተሻቐለ** *zteshaq̈ele*
**motionless** ***(adj.)*** **ተልመዴን** *telmedeen*
**motivate** ***(v.)*** **ኣፍለጠ** *afleẗe*
**motivation** ***(n. )*** **ቀረበ** *qerebe*
**motive** ***(n.)*** **ብቑዕ** *bq̈u'ë*
**motley** ***(adj.)*** **ምንዛዐ** *mnza'ë*

**motor** ***(n.)*** **ቅባለ** *qbale*
**motorcycle** ***(n.)*** **ተቐበለ** *teq̈ebele*
**motorist** ***(n. )*** **ዳርጋ** *darga*
**motorway** ***(n.)***
**ሚሽሚሸ** *mishmishe*
**mottle** ***(n.)*** **ግርምብያለ** *grmbyale*
**motto** ***(n. )*** **በሊሕ** *beliḧ*
**mould** ***(n.)*** **ተውህቦ** *tewhbo*
**moulder** ***(v.)*** **ቦኽቦኸ** *boḱboḱe*
**moulding** ***(n.)*** **ማያዊ** *mayawi*
**moult** ***(v.)*** **ማያዊ** *mayawi*
**mound** ***(n. )*** **ኣረብ** *areb*
**mount** ***(v.)*** **ኣረቢያን** *arebian*
**mountain** ***(n. )*** **ኣረቢክ** *arebik*
**mountaineer** ***(n.)*** **ገድላ** *gedla*
**mountaineering** ***(n.)*** **ፈራዲ** *feradi*
**mountainous** ***(adj.)*** **ሃውሪ** *hawri*
**mourn** ***(v.)*** **ዳነየ** *daneye*
**mourner** ***(n. )*** **ዳኘነት** *daṅnet*
**mournful** ***(adj.)*** **ዳኛ** *daṅa*
**mourning** ***(n.)*** **ዳስ** *das*
**mouse** ***(n. )*** **ቀስቲ** *qesti*
**mousse** ***(n.)*** **ቀልደዳዊ** *qeldedawi*
**moustache** ***(n. )*** **ቀልደድ** *qelded*
**mouth** ***(n.)*** **ስነ ጥንቲ** *sne ẗnti*
**mouthful** ***(n.)*** **ጥንታዊ** *ẗntawi*
**movable** ***(adj.)*** **ሊቀ መላእክት** *liqe mela'èkt*
**move** ***(v.)*** **ሊቀ-ጳጳሳት** *liqep̈ap̈asat*
**movement** ***(n. )*** **መንታጋይ** *mentagay*
**mover** ***(n. )*** **ስነ-ሃናጺ** *snehanaxi*
**movies** ***(n.)*** **ስነ-ህንጻ** *snehnxa*
**moving** ***(adj.)*** **ኣርቺቭ** *archiv*
**mow** ***(v.)*** **ኣርክቲክ** *arktik*
**mozzarella** ***(n.)*** **ውዕውዕ** *w'ëw'ë*

**much** *(pron. )* ብርቱዕ ድሌት *brtu'ë dleet*

**mucilage** *(n. )* ኣድካሚ *adkami*

**muck** *(n.)* ስፍሓት *sfħat*

**mucous** *(adj.)* መድረኽ *medreḱ*

**mucus** *(n. )* ተማጎተ *temagote*

**mud** *(n. )* መጎተ *megote*

**muddle** *(v.)* መጎቲና *megotina*

**muesli** *(n.)* ኣጸምእ *axam'è*

**muffin** *(n.)* ተላዕለ *tela'ële*

**muffle** *(v.)* ኣሪስቶክራሲ *aristokrasi*

**muffler** *(n. )* ኣሪስቶክራታዊ *aristokratawi*

**mug** *(n.)* ቍጽሪ *quxri*

**muggy** *(adj.)* ቍጽሪና *quxrina*

**mulatto** *(n. )* ታቦት *tabot*

**mulberry** *(n. )* ምናት *mnat*

**mule** *(n.)* ጭፍራ መራኽብ ውግእ *čfra meraḱb wg'è*

**mulish** *(adj.)* ኣርማጌዶን *armagedon*

**mull** *(v.)* ኣጽዋር *axwar*

**mullah** *(n. )* ግዝያዊ ተኹሲ-ዕጾ *gzyawi teḱusi'ëxo*

**mullion** *(n.)* ድርዒ ሓጺን *dr'ï ħaxin*

**multicultural** *(adj.)* ድርዒ ሓጺኒ *dr'ï ħaxini*

**multifarious** *(adj.)* ሰራዊት *serawit*

**multiform** *(adj.)* መዓዛ *me'äza*

**multilateral** *(adj.)* መዓዛ -ፍወሳ *me'äza fwesa*

**multimedia** *(n.)* ኣብ ዙርያ *'ab zurya*

**multiparous** *(adj.)* ኣበራበረ *aberabere*

**multiple** *(adj.)* ሰርዐ *ser'ë*

**multiplex** *(n. )* ኣሰራርዓ *aserar'ä*

**multiplication** *(n. )* ምሒር *mħir*

**multiplicity** *(n.)* ተሰለፈ *teselefe*

**multiply** *(v.)* ተሰለፈን *teselefin*

**multitude** *(n.)* ኣሰረ *asere*

**mum** *(n.)* እትወት *ètwet*

**mumble** *(v.)* መጸ *mexe*

**mummer** *(n. )* ኣትሒቱ ረኣየ *'athïtu re'aye*

**mummify** *(v.)* ትዕቢተኛ *t'ëbitena*

**mummy** *(n. )* መንዘዐ *menze'ë*

**mumps** *(n.)* ፍላጻ *flaxa*

**munch** *(v.)* እንዳብረት *èndabret*

**mundane** *(adj.)* ብርቱዕ ስሚ *brtu'ë smi*

**municipal** *(adj.)* ብውሳይ ምቅጻል *bwsay mqxal*

**municipality** *(n.)* ጥበብ *ťbeb*

**munificent** *(adj.)* ጥንቲ *ťnti*

**muniment** *(n.)* ኣርተሪ *arteri*

**munitions** *(n.)* ብልሂ *blhi*

**mural** *(n. )* ሪሕ *riħ*

**murder** *(n.)* ካርቾፊ *karchofi*

**murderer** *(n.)* ኣቕሓ *aq̈ha*

**murk** *(n.)* ኣነጸረ *anexere*

**murky** *(adj.)* ክእለት *k'èlet*

**murmur** *(v.)* ስኑዕ *snu'ë*

**muscle** *(n. )* ከቢድ ብረት *kebid bret*

**muscovite** *(n.)* ክኢላ *k'ila*

**muscular** *(adj.)* ስነ-ጠቢብ *sneťebib*

**muse** *(n.)* ስነ-ጥበባዊ *sneťbebawi*

**museum** *(n. )* ባህርያዊ *bahryawi*

**mush** *(n. )* ከም *kem*

**mushroom** *(n. )* ቃንጥሻ *qanťsha*

**music** *(n.)* ደየበ *deyebe*

**musical** *(adj.)* ደያቢ *deyabi*

**musician** *(n. )* **ዕርገት** *ërget*
**musk** *(n. )* **አረጋገጸ** *aregagexe*
**musket** *(n. )* **መናን** *menan*
**musketeer** *(n. )* **ሃበ** *habe*
**Muslim** *(n.)* **ጽዱይ** *xduy*
**muslin** *(v. )* **ግብረ-ሰዶመኛ** *gbresedomeňa*
**mussel** *(n.)* **ኣሽ** *ash*
**must** *(v.)* **ዝሓፈረ** *zȟafere*
**mustang** *(n.)* **ኣብ ገምገም ባሕሪ** *'ab gemgem baȟri*
**mustard** *(n.)* **ኤሽያዊ** *eshiyawi*
**muster** *(v.)* **ኣብ ወይ ናብ ጐድኒ** *'ab wey nab gWadni*
**musty** *(adj.)* **ዓንጃል** *änĵal*
**mutable** *(adj.)* **ሓተተ** *ȟatete*
**mutate** *(v.)* **ብጥርጣረ** *bẗrẗare*
**mutation** *(n.)* **ዘባል** *zebal*
**mutative** *(v.)* **ጽሙው** *xmuw*
**mute** *(adj.)* **ሻሞት** *shamot*
**mutilate** *(v.)* **መልክዕ** *melk'ë*
**mutilation** *(n.)* **ጎነጽ** *gonex*
**mutinous** *(adj.)* **ምክፋእ** *mkfa'è*
**mutiny** *(n.)* **ዓበሰ** *äbese*
**mutter** *(v.)* **ደላዪ** *delayi*
**mutton** *(n.)* **ትምኒት** *tmnit*
**mutual** *(adj.)* **ተመነየ** *temeneye*
**muzzle** *(n.)* **ኣድጊ** *adgi*
**muzzy** *(adj.)* **ኣጥቀዐ** *aẗqe'ë*
**my** *(adj.)* **ቀታል-ነፍሲ** *qetalnefsi*
**myalgia** *(n. )* **ቀተለ** *qetele*
**myopia** *(n.)* **ቀተለሊ** *qeteli*
**myopic** *(adj.)* **ኣጥቀዐ** *aẗqe'ë*
**myosin** *(n. )* **ምግጥጣም** *mgẗẗam*
**myriad** *(n.)* **ኣጋጠመ** *agaẗeme*
**myrrh** *(n.)* **ኣኼባ** *aǩeeba*
**myrtle** *(n.)* **ስምምዕ** *smm'ë*
**myself** *(pron. )* **ጸዓደ** *xe'äde*
**mysterious** *(adj.)* **ኣማኻሪ** *amaǩari*
**mystery** *(n.)* **መርመራ** *mermera*
**mystic** *(n.)* **ንብረት** *nbret*
**mystical** *(adj.)* **ጻዕረኛ** *xa'ëreňa*
**mysticism** *(n.)* **ረተበ** *retebe*
**mystify** *(v.)* **ምደባ** *mdeba*
**mystique** *(n.)* **ምዱብ ስራሕ** *mdub sraȟ*
**myth** *(n.)* **ተዋሃደ** *tewahade*
**mythical** *(adj.)* **ተዋህዶ** *tewahdo*
**mythological** *(adj.)* **ሓገዘ** *ȟageze*
**mythology** *(n.)* **ሓገዝ** *ȟagez*

# N

**nab** *(v.)* **ተሓባባሪ** *teȟababari*
**nabob** *(nabob)* **ማሕበር** *maȟber*
**nacho** *(n.)* **ስምምዕ** *smm'ë*
**nadir** *(n. )* **ዝተፋላለየ** *ztefalaleye*
**nag** *(v.t. )* **በብዓይነቱ** *beb'äynetu*
**nail** *(n.)* **ኣጸናንዐ** *axenan'ë*
**naivety** *(n.)* **ገመተ** *gemete*
**naked** *(adj.)* **ግምት** *gmt*
**name** *(n.)* **መረጋገጺ** *meregagexi*
**namely** *(n. )* **ኣረጋገጸ** *aregagexe*
**namesake** *(n.)* **ዋሕስ** *waȟs*
**nanny** *(n.)* **ኣስትሪስክስ** *astrisks*
**nap** *(n. )* **ዓለም** *älem*
**nape** *(n. )* **ኣዝማ** *azma*
**naphthalene** *(n.)* **ነበዐ** *nebe'ë*
**napkin** *(n. )* **ኣደነቐ** *adeneqe*
**nappy** *(n.)* **ድንጽዉና** *dnxwuna*
**narcissism** *(n.)* **ኣስደመመ** *asdememe*

**narcissus** *(n. )* ኮኾባዊ *koḱobawi*
**narcotic** *(n.)* ህውቱት *hwtut*
**narrate** *(v.)* ብምግሕታን *bmgḧtan*
**narration** *(n. )* ብልጹግ *blxug*
**narrative** *(n.)* ቈጸራ ከዋኽብቲ *qWexera kewak̂bti*
**narrator** *(n.)* ጠፈርተኛ *ẗeferteǹa*
**narrow** *(adj.)* ስነ-ኮኾቢ *snekok̂obi*
**nasal** *(adj.)* ስነ-ኮኾብ *snekok̂ob*
**nascent** *(adj.)* ትኩር *tkur*
**nasty** *(adj.)* ዝተፈላለየ *ztefelaleye*
**natal** *(adj.)* ዑቕባ *üq̈ba*
**natant** *(adj.)* ኣብ *ab*
**nation** *(n.)* የዋህ *yewah*
**national** *(adj.)* ኢዚሀርነት *izihernet*
**nationalism** *(n. )* ኢዚሄራዊ *iziheerawi*
**nationalist** *(n. )* ስፖርተኛ *sporteǹa*
**nationality** *(n. )* ስፖርታዊ *sportawi*
**nationalization** *(n.)* ኣትላስ *atlas*
**nationalize** *(v.)* ሃዋህው *hawahw*
**native** *(n.)* ደሴት *deseet*
**nativity** *(n.)* ኣቶም *atom*
**natty** *(adj.)* ኣቶማዊ *atomawi*
**natural** *(adj.)* ከሓሰ *keḧase*
**naturalist** *(n.)* ድሕነት *dḧnet*
**naturalization** *(n.)* ኣሰቃቒ *aseqaq̈i*
**naturalize** *(v.)* ክፍሊ *kfli*
**naturally** *(adv. )* ገፍዐ *gef'ë*
**nature** *(n.)* ኣጠበቐ *aẗabeq̈e*
**naturism** *(n.)* ኣታሽ *atash*
**naughty** *(adj.)* ጥብቀት *ẗbqet*
**nausea** *(n.)* ኣጥቅዐ *aẗq'ë*
**nauseate** *(v.)* ምሉእ *mlu'è*
**nauseous** *(adj.)* ሰመረ *semere*
**nautical** *(adj.)* ፈተ'ነ *fetene*
**naval** *(adj.)* ጀመረ *ĵemere*
**nave** *(n.)* ተኸታተለ *tek̂etatele*
**navigable** *(adj.)* ተሳትፎ *tesatfo*
**navigate** *(v.)* ኣገልጋሊ *agelgali*
**navigation** *(n.)* ኣቓልቦ *aq̈albo*
**navigator** *(n.)* ጥንቁቕ *ẗnquq̈*
**navy** *(n.)* ኣረጋገጸ *aregagexe*
**nay** *(adv. )* ዋልድቢት *waldbit*
**near** *(v.i. )* ጠበቓ *ẗebeq̈a*
**near** *(adv. )* ልብሲ *lbsi*
**nearby** *(adv. )* ኣቃጫጭ *aqačač*
**nearest** *(adj.)* ሰሓበ *seḧabe*
**nearly** *(adv. )* ስሕበት *sḧbet*
**neat** *(adj.)* ማራኺ *marak̂i*
**nebula** *(n. )* ባህርይ *bahry*
**nebulous** *(adj.)* ማርጋሪን *margarin*
**necessarily** *(adv. )* ሓራጅ *ḧaraĵ*
**necessary** *(adj.)* ኪስማዕ ዚከኣል *kisma'ë zike'a*
**necessitate** *(v.)* ነባሮ *nebaro*
**necessity** *(n. )* ደሃይ *- dehay*
**neck** *(n. )* ጸብጻብ *xebxab*
**necklace** *(n. )* ናይ ምስማዕ ፈተና *nay msma'ë fetena*
**necklet** *(n. )* ጌጽ ወይ ስልማት ናይ ክሳድ *geex wey slmat nay ksad*
**necromancy** *(n.)* ወሰኸ *ወሰኸ*
**necropolis** *(n. )* ነሓሰ *neḧase*
**nectar** *(n.)* ሓትኖ *ḧatno*
**nectarine** *(n.)* ኣኽሊል *ak̂lil*
**need** *(v.)* ተስፋኣዊ *tesfa'awi*
**needful** *(adj.)* ጥብቂ *ẗbqi*

**needle** *(n.)* **አዎስትራልያ** *awustraliya*
**needless** *(adj.)* **ሓቀኛ** *ḧaqeǹa*
**needy** *(adj.)* **ልክዕነት** *lk'ënet*
**nefarious** *(adj.)* **ደራሲ** *derasi*
**negate** *(v.)* **ምዙዝ** *mzuz*
**negation** *(n.)* **መዚ** *mezi*
**negative** *(adj.)* **መዘዘ** *mezeze*
**negativity** *(n.)* **አዉቲዝም** *awutizim*
**neglect** *(v.)* **ርእሰ-ታሪኽ** *r'èsetarik*
**negligence** *(n.)* **ኣውቶክራሲ** *awtokrasi*
**negligent** *(adj.)* **ውልቀ-መላኺ** *wlqemelaki*
**negligible** *(adj.)* **ኣውቶክራቲክ** *wlqemelak*
**negotiable** *(adj.)* **ርእሰ-ጽሑፍ** *r'èsexḧuf*
**negotiate** *(v.)* **ኣውቶማቲክ** *awtomatik*
**negotiation** *(n.)* **ኣውቶሞቢል=መኪና** *awtomobilm ekina*
**negotiator** *(n.)* **ርእሰ-ምምሕዳራዊ** *r'èsemmḧdarawi*
**negress** *(n. )* **ምርምረ-ሬሳ** *mrmrereesa*
**negro** *(n.)* **ቀውዒ** *qew'ï*
**neigh** *(n. )* **ሓጋዚ** *ḧagazi*
**neighbour** *(n. )* **ተጠቕመ** *teẗeq̈me*
**neighbourhood** *(n.)* **ክትጥቀመሉ ትኽእል** *ktẗqemelu tk'èl*
**neighbourly** *(adj.)* **መደረጋሕ** *mederegaḧ*
**neither** *(adj.)* **ስስዐ** *ss'ë*
**nemesis** *(n.)* **ሕነ ፈደየ** *ḧne fedeye*
**neoclassical** *(adj.)* **ጐደና** *gWadena*
**Neolithic** *(adj.)* **ማእከላይ** *ma'èkelay*
**neon** *(n. )* **ኣንጻር** *anxar*
**neophyte** *(n.)* **ጽልኣት** *xl'at*
**nephew** *(n. )* **ኣለየ** *aleye*
**nepotism** *(n. )* **እንዳ ኣዕዋፍ** *'ènda 'a'ëwaf*
**Neptune** *(n. )* **ስነ-ምንፋር** *snemnfar*
**nerd** *(n.)* **ፓይሎት** *paylot*
**Nerve** *(n.)* **ህንጡይ** *hnẗuy*
**nerveless** *(adj.)* **ህንጡዪ** *hnẗuyi*
**nervous** *(adj.)* **ኣቮካዶ** *avokado*
**nervy** *(adj.)* **ወገደ** *wegede*
**nest** *(n.)* **ጉስያ** *gusya*
**nestle** *(v.)* **ኣመነ** *amene*
**nestling** *(n. )* **ኣኮኣዊ** *'ako'awi*
**net** *(n.)* **ተጸበየ** *texebeye*
**nether** *(adj.)* **ነቕሐ** *neq̈ḧe*
**netting** *(n.)* **ነቕሐ** *neq̈ḧe*
**nettle** *(n. )* **ሰለመ** *seleme*
**network** *(n. )* **ገንዘብ** *genzeb*
**neural** *(adj.)* **ናብ ርሑቕ** *nab rḧuq̈*
**neurologist** *(n. )* **ተምሳጥ** *temsaẗ*
**neurology** *(n. )* **ዘርዕድ** *zer'ëd*
**neurosis** *(n.)* **ዘስካሕክሕ** *zeskaḧkḧ*
**neurotic** *(adj.)* **ንሓጺር ግዜ** *nḧaxir gzee*
**neuter** *(adj.)* **ጋሕማጥ** *gaḧmaẗ*
**neutral** *(adj.)* **ብልሽው** *blshw*
**neutralize** *(v.)* **ፋስ** *fas*
**neutron** *(n.)* **መቐለሲ** *meq̈elesi*
**never** *(adv. )* **መቐለስ** *meq̈eles*

**new** *(adj.)* ሓድሽ *ḧadsh*
**newly** *(adv. )* አዕዘምዘመ *a'ëzemzeme*
**news** *(n.)* ህጻን *hxan*
**next** *(adj.)* ዘይምስምማዕ *zeymsmma'ë*
**nexus** *(n.)* ህበይ *hbey*
**nib** *(n.)* ህጻን *hxan*
**nibble** *(v.)* ቤተ'ልቦ *beetelbo*
**nice** *(adj.)* ዝባን *zban*
**nicety** *(n. )* ዓንዲ-ሕቖ *ändiḧqo*
**niche** *(n. )* ሓለፈ *ḧalefe*
**nick** *(n. )* ትዕይንቲ *t'ëynti*
**nickel** *(n. )* ምጉሳዕ *mgusa'ë*
**nickname** *(n.)* ተመኩሮ *temekuro*
**nicotine** *(n. )* ኣሽሙራዊ *ashmurawi*
**niece** *(n. )* ረድአ *red'e*
**niggard** *(n.)* መልሰ-ግብሪ *melsegbri*
**niggardly** *(adj.)* መሃዚ *mehazi*
**nigger** *(n.)* ማህደር *mahder*
**niggle** *(v.)* ብድሕሪት *bdḧrit*
**nigh** *(adv. )* ዝባን መድረኽ *zban medreḱ*
**night** *(n. )* ዝባን ኣሰር *zban aser*
**nightie** *(n. )* ቤኮን *beekon*
**nightingale** *(n.)* ንድሕሪት *ndḧrit*
**nightmare** *(n.)* ዝባን ማይ *zban may*
**nihilism** *(n. )* ባክተሪያ *bakteriya*
**nil** *(n.)* ሕማቕ *ḧmaq̈*
**nimble** *(adj.)* ኣርማ *arma*
**nimbus** *(n.)* ብሕማቕ *bḧmaq̈*
**nine** *(adj. & n.)* ባድሚንተን *badminten*
**nineteen** *(adj. & n.)* ኣገረመ *agereme*
**nineteenth** *(adj. & n.)* መልአ *mel'e*
**ninetieth** *(adj. & n.)* ጋዓዝ *ga'äz*
**ninety** *(adj. & n.)* ሕቡር ስልማት *ḧbur slmat*
**ninth** *(adj. & n.)* ገፍላው *geflaw*
**nip** *(v.)* ዋሕስ *waḧs*
**nipple** *(n.)* ፖሊስ *polis*
**nippy** *(adj.)* መስሓቢ *mesḧabi*
**nirvana** *(n.)* ደረቐ *dereq̈e*
**nitrogen** *(n.)* ሰንካቲ *senkati*
**no** *(adj.)* እንዳ ባኒ *ènda bani*
**nobility** *(n.)* ተረፍ *teref*
**noble** *(adj.)* ሰገነት *segenet*
**nobleman** *(n.)* በራሕ *beraḧ*
**nobody** *(pron. )* ጥቕላል *ẗq̈lal*
**nocturnal** *(adj.)* ኩዕሶ *ku'ëso*
**nod** *(v.)* ግጥሚ ወይ ደርፊ *gẗmi wey derfi*
**node** *(n. )* ባለ *bale*
**noise** *(n.)* ባሉን *balun*
**noisy** *(adj.)* ናይ መድመጺ ወረቐት *nay medmexi wereq̈et*
**nomad** *(n.)* በለሳን *belesan*
**nomadic** *(adj.)* በለሳን *belesan*
**nomenclature** *(n.)* ኣርቃይ *arqay*
**nominal** *(adj.)* ኣገደ *agede*
**nominate** *(v.)* ተራ *tera*
**nomination** *(n.)* ባናና *banana*
**nominee** *(n.)* መእሰሪ *me'èseri*
**non-alignment** *(n. )* መጀነኒ *meǰeneni*
**nonchalance** *(n.)* ሽፍታ ወረበላ *shfta werebela*
**nonchalant** *(adj.)* መርዚ ስሚ *merzi smi*
**nonconformist** *(n.)* ገውታ *gewta*

**none** *(pron. )* ገውት *gewtat*
**nonentity** *(n.)* በናጅር *benaĵr*
**nonetheless** *(a. )* ጥርዝያ *ẗrzya*
**nonpareil** *(adj.)* መደንደል *medendel*
**nonplussed** *(adj.)* ሓየረ *ȟayere*
**nonplussed** *(adj.)* ባንጆ *banĵo*
**nonsense** *(n.)* ባንኪ *banki*
**nonstop** *(adj.)* መኰነን *mekWanen*
**noodles** *(n.)* ጥፉሽ *ẗfush*
**nook** *(n.)* ጥፈሻ *ẗfesha*
**noon** *(n. )* ሰንደቕ *sendeq̈*
**noose** *(n.)* በዓል *be'äl*
**nor** *(conj.&adv.)* ተዋዘየ *tewazeye*
**Nordic** *(adj.)* ጥምቀት *ẗmqet*
**norm** *(n. )* መጥምቓዊ *meẗmq̈awi*
**normal** *(adj.)* ነቐለ ከደ ተሰናበተ *neq̈ele kede tesenabete*
**normalcy** *(n.)* ሓመድ *ȟamed*
**normalize** *(v.)* ከብዲ *kebdi*
**normative** *(adj.)* ናይ ከብዲ *nay kebdi*
**north** *(n.)* ዘረፈ *zerefe*
**northerly** *(adj.)* ዘረፈ *zerefe*
**northern** *(adj.)* ምዝቡል *mzbul*
**nose** *(n.)* ስሒታን *sȟtan*
**nostalgia** *(n. )* ኣደፋፈረ *adefafere*
**nostril** *(n. )* ዉንዛፈ *wunzafe*
**nostrum** *(n.)* ፈንፈነ *fenfene*
**nosy** *(adj.)* ክርሃት *krhat*
**not** *(adv.)* ክሩህ *kruh*
**notable** *(adj.)* ጸንዐ *xen'ë*
**notary** *(n. )* ዘይውዳእ *zeywda'è*
**notation** *(n. )* ዓቕሚ *'äq̈mi*
**notch** *(n. )* ሕርቱም *ȟrtum*
**note** *(n.)* መሓለ *meȟale*
**notebook** *(n.)* ልቡዕ *lbu'ë*
**noted** *(adj.)* ንፉዕ ብቑዕ *nfu'ë bq̈u'ë*
**noteworthy** *(adj.)* መዓናጡ *me'änaẗu*
**nothing** *(pron. )* ምዝቡል *mzbul*
**notice** *(n.)* ኣብ ልዕሊ *'ab l'ëli*
**noticeable** *(adj.)* ገዛ *geza*
**noticeboard** *(n.)* ኣጥፈአ *'aẗfe'e*
**notifiable** *(adj.)* ምጥፋእ *mẗfa'è*
**notification** *(n.)* ዚጽላእ *zixla'è*
**notify** *(v.)* ጸልአ *xel'e*
**notion** *(n.)* ጥንታዊ *ẗntawi*
**notional** *(adj.)* ተወግረ *tewegre*
**notoriety** *(n.)* ምውጋድ *mwgad*
**notorious** *(prep. )* ውጉር *wgur*
**notwithstanding** *(prep. )* ፈድፈደ *fedfede*
**nougat** *(n.)* ብዛዕባ *bza'ëba*
**nought** *(n. )* ኣብ ዙርያ *'ab zurya*
**noun** *(n.)* ኣብ ልዕሊ *'ab l'ëli*
**nourish** *(v.)* ብዝያዳ *bzyada*
**nourishment** *(n.)* ልሕላሐ *lȟlaȟe*
**novel** *(n.)* ፋሕፋሒ *faȟfaȟi*
**novelette** *(n. )* ጎድነ-ጎድኒ *godnegodni*
**novelist** *(n. )* ኣሕጸረ *aȟxere*
**novelty** *(n. )* ወጻኢ *wexa'i*
**November** *(n. )* ሰረዘ *sereze*
**novice** *(n.)* ሃንደበታዊ *handebetawi*
**now** *(adv.)* ሓገል *ȟagel*
**nowhere** *(adv.)* ጸለቑ *xeleq̈Wu*
**noxious** *(adj.)* ብኩራት *bkurat*
**nozzle** *(n.)* ብኹር *bḱur*
**nuance** *(n.)* ብኹር *bḱur*
**nubile** *(a. )* ፍጹም *fxum*

**nuclear** ***(adj.)*** **ስሬት** *sreet*
**nucleus** ***(n.)*** **መሓረ** *meȟare*
**nude** ***(adj.)*** **ሰተየ** *seteye*
**nudge** ***(v.)*** **ተቐጠበ** *teq̈eẗebe*
**nudge** ***(v.)*** **ጥሉቕ** *ẗluq̈*
**nudist** ***(n.)*** **ዛህዲ** *zahdi*
**nudity** ***(n.)*** **ረቒቕ** *req̈iq̈*
**nugatory** ***(adj.)*** **ትርጉም ኣልቦ** *trgum 'albo*
**nugget** ***(n. )*** **ትርጉም ኣልቦነት** *trgum 'albonet*
**nuisance** ***(n.)*** **ምልኣት** *ml'at*
**null** ***(adj.)*** **ፍድፉድ** *fdfud*
**nullification** ***(n.)*** **ዓመጸ** *ämexe*
**nullify** ***(v.)*** **ተጻራፊ** *texarafi*
**numb** ***(adj.)*** **ተዳወበ** *tedawebe*
**number** ***(n.)*** **ደልሃመታዊ** *delhametawi*
**numberless** ***(adj.)*** **ደልሃመት** *delhamet*
**numeral** ***(n. )*** **ኣካደሚያዊ** *akademiyawi*
**numerator** ***(n.)*** **ኣካደሚ** *akademi*
**numerical** ***(adj.)*** **መጸ** *mexe*
**numerous** ***(adj.)*** **ነሃረ** *nehare*
**nun** ***(n.)*** **ኣንሃሪ** *anhari*
**nunnery** ***(n.)*** **ምጉላሕ** *mgulaȟ*
**nuptial** ***(adj.)*** **ኣጉለሐ** *aguleȟe*
**nurse** ***(n.)*** **ተቐበለ** *teq̈ebele*
**nursery** ***(n. )*** **ተቐባልነት ዘለዎ** *teq̈ebalnet zelewo*
**nurture** ***(v.)*** **ቅበለ** *qbale*
**nut** ***(n.)*** **መእተዊ** *me'ètewi*
**nutrient** ***(n.)*** **ኪርከብ ዚከኣል** *kirkeb zike'al*
**nutrition** ***(n.)*** **ብጽሓት** *bxȟat*
**nutritious** ***(adj.)*** **መሰርሒ** *mesarȟi*
**nutritive** ***(adj.)*** **ሓደጋ** *ȟadega*
**nutty** ***(adj.)*** **ናይ ሓደጋ** *nay ȟadega*
**nuzzle** ***(v.)*** **ኣጨብጨበ** *ačebčebe*
**nylon** ***(n. )*** **ኣዕነወ** *a'ënewe*
**nymph** ***()*** **ሰላምታ** *selamta*

# O

**oaf** ***(n.)*** **halay** ሃላይ
**oak** ***(n. )*** **daEro** ዳዕሮ
**oar** ***(n. )*** **nay jelba betri** ናይ ጀልባ በትሪ
**oasis** ***(n. )*** **lmu'E meriet** ለሙዕ መሬት
**oat** ***(n. )*** **Aynet Teremer** ዓይነት ጥረምረ
**oath** ***(n. )*** **meHala** መሓላ
**oatmeal** ***(n.)*** **kab Teremer zsraH Aynet mgbi** ካብ ጥረምረ ዝስራሕ ዓይነት ምግቢ
**obduracy** ***(n.)*** **dfret** ድፍረት
**obdurate** ***(adj.)*** **Kbur** ኽቡር
**obedience** ***(n.)*** **teazaznet** ተኣዛዝነት
**obedient** ***(adj.)*** **m'ezuz** ምእዙዝ
**obeisance** ***(n. )*** **segede** ሰገደ
**obese** ***(adj.)*** **regiud** ረጒድ
**obesity** ***(n.)*** **lEli AQn mizan sebnet** ልዕሊ ዓቐን ሚዛን ሰብነት
**obey** ***(v.)*** **m'ezaz** ምእዛዝ
**obfuscate** ***(v.)*** **Hbu'e** ሕቡእ
**obituary** ***(n. )*** **Hmum** ሕሙም
**object** ***(n.)*** **neger** ነገር
**objection** ***(n.)*** **mqwam** ምቅዋም
**objectionable** ***(adj.)*** **mKHad zK'el** ምኽሓድ ዝኽእል
**objective** ***(adj.)*** **Oe'lama** ዕላማ

**objectively** ***(adv.)*** **zeyedalw** ዘየዳልው
**oblation** ***(n. )*** **meswa'eti** መስዋእቲ
**obligated** ***(v.)*** **tegedede** ተገደደ
**obligation** ***(n.)*** **gdeta** ግዴታ
**obligatory** ***(adj.)*** **gdeta** ግዴታ
**oblige** ***(v.)*** **zegeded** ዘገድድ
**obliging** ***(adj.)*** **Hagazi** ሓጋዚ
**oblique** ***(adj.)*** **zembal** ዘምባል
**obliterate** ***(v.)*** **demsese** ደምሰሰ
**obliteration** ***(n.)*** **mdemsas** ምድምሳስ
**oblivion** ***(n.)*** **Hbu'e** ሕቡእ
**oblivious** ***(adj.)*** **zres'o** ዚረስዕ
**oblong** ***(adj.)*** **zelela** ዘለላ
**obloquy** ***(n.)*** **shem mxfa'e** ስም ምጥፋእ
**obnoxious** ***(adj.)*** **zeyeHegus** ዘየሕጉስ
**obscene** ***(adj.)*** **boalege** በዓለገ
**obscenity** ***(n.)*** **zetsl'e neger** ዘጽልእ ነገር
**obscure** ***(adj.)*** **bruh zeykone** ብሩህ ዘይኮነ
**obscurity** ***(n. )*** **Hebu'e** ሕቡእ
**observance** ***(n.)*** **Kdri** ኽብሪ
**observant** ***(adj.)*** **z'Ezeb** ዝዕዘብ
**observation** ***(n.)*** **t'Ezebti** ትዕዝብቲ
**observatory** ***(n.)*** **mekane-t'Ezebti** መካነ-ትዕዝብቲ
**observe** ***(v.)*** **te'azebe** ተዓዘበ
**obsess** ***(v.)*** **bHasab wehate** ብሓሳብ ወሓጠ
**obsession** ***(n.)*** **chenqet** ጭንቀት
**obsolescent** ***(adj.)*** **zemenawi** ዘመናዊ
**obsolete** ***(adj.)*** **gziu zhalefe** ግዚኡ ዝሓለፈ
**obstacle** ***(n.)*** **Enqfat** ዕንቅፋት
**obstinacy** ***(n)*** **dereqnet** ደረቕነት
**obstinate** ***(adj.)*** **dereq** ደረቕ
**obstruct** ***(v.)*** **Agete** ዓገተ
**obstruction** ***(n.)*** **tsegem** ጸገም
**obstructive** ***(adj.)*** **zAgt** ዝዓግት
**obtain** ***(v.)*** **reKibu** ረኺቡ
**obtainable** ***(adj.)*** **krkeb zKel** ክርከብ ዝኽእል
**obtrude** ***(v.)*** **zteKefle** ዝተኸፍለ
**obtuse** ***(adj.)*** **gaHtat** ጋሕጣጥ
**obverse** ***(n.)*** **m'Ezab** ምዕዛብ
**obviate** ***(v.)*** **zeyntsur** ዘይንጹር
**obvious** ***(adj.)*** **gltsi** ግልጺ
**occasion** ***(n.)*** **agatami** ኣጋጣሚ
**occasional** ***(adj.)*** **halhalifu** ሓልሓሊፉ
**occasionally** ***(adv.)*** **halhalifu** ሓልሓሊፉ
**occident** ***(n.)*** **m'Erab** ምዕራብ
**occidental** ***(adj.)*** **m'Erabawi** ምዕራባዊ
**occlude** ***(v.)*** **dqas** ድቃስ
**occult** ***(n. )*** **menafstawi ftsame** መናፍስታዊ ፍጻመ
**occupancy** ***(n.)*** **mHaz** ምሓዝ
**occupant** ***(n.)*** **tHazay** ተሓዛይ
**occupation** ***(n. )*** **moya** ሞያ
**occupational** ***(adj.)*** **moyawi** ሞያዊ
**occupy** ***(v.)*** **Haze** ሓዘ
**occur** ***(v.)*** **metse** መጸ
**occurrence** ***(n. )*** **kstet** ክስተት
**ocean** ***(n.)*** **wqyanos** ውቅያኖስ

**oceanic** ***(adj.)*** **wqyanosawi** *ውቅያኖሳዊ*
**octagon** ***(n.)*** **shemonte wegen** *ሸሞንተ ወገን*
**octave** ***(n.)*** **ney muziqa 8notatat bebi 2 nota zfelaleyu** *ናይ ሙዚቃ 8ኖታታት በቢ 2 ኖታ ዝፈላለዩ*
**octavo** ***(n.)*** **16 gets zelewo metsHaf** *16 ግፅ ዘለዎ መፅሓፍ*
**October** ***(n.)*** **Tkemti** *ጥቅምቲ*
**octogenarian** ***(n.)*** **kab 80-89 Edme zelewo seb** *ካብ 80-89 ዕድመ ዘለዎ ሰብ*
**octopus** ***(n.)*** **oktapos** *ኦክታፑስ*
**octroi** ***(n.)*** **tsuret** *ጹረት*
**ocular** ***(adj.)*** **emut** *እሙት*
**odd** ***(adj.)*** **zeylmud** *ዘይልሙድ*
**oddity** ***(n.)*** **gasha** *ጋሻ*
**odds** ***(n. )*** **flly** *ፍልላይ*
**ode** ***(n.)*** **bza'Eba Hade neger zzareb gTmi** *ብዛዕባ ሓደ ነገር ዝዛረብ ግጥሚ*
**odious** ***(adj.)*** **mesHaQ** *መስሓቕ*
**odium** ***(n.)*** **tsl'at** *ፅልኣት*
**odorous** ***(adj.)*** **shta** *ሽታ*
**odour** ***(n.)*** **chena** *ጨና*
**odyssey** ***(n.)*** **nay grik gTmi** *ናይ ግሪክ ግጥሚ*
**of** ***(prep. )*** **nay** *ናይ*
**off** ***(adv.)*** **Tefiu** *ጠፊኡ*
**offence** ***(n.)*** **mesenakl** *መሰናኽል*
**offend** ***(v.)*** **bedele** *በደለ*
**offender** ***(n.)*** **bedali** *በዳሊ*
**offensive** ***(adj.)*** **tetsela'i** *ተጻላኢ*
**offer** ***(v.)*** **mQrab** *ምቕራብ*
**offering** ***(n.)*** **meswa'eti** *መስዋእቲ*
**office** ***(n. )*** **biet-tshfet** *ቤት-ጽሕፈት*
**officer** ***(n.)*** **mekonen** *መኮንን*
**official** ***(adj.)*** **be'Al mezi** *በዓል መዚ*
**officially** ***(adv.)*** **b'Eli** *ብዕሊ*
**officiate** ***(v.)*** **mekonen** *መኮንን*
**officious** ***(adj.)*** **fluT** *ፍሉጥ*
**offset** ***(v.)*** **mkeHaHasi** *ምክሓሓሲ*
**offshoot** ***(n. )*** **nkaye** *ንካየ*
**offshore** ***(adj.)*** **gemgem baHri** *ገምገም ባሕሪ*
**offside** ***(adj.)*** **Tf'ategna** *ጥፍኣተኛ*
**offspring** ***(n.)*** **wlad** *ውላድ*
**oft** ***(adv. )*** **tera** *ተራ*
**often** ***(adv.)*** **btedegagami** *ብተደጋጋሚ*
**ogle** ***(v.)*** **gulbet** *ጉልበት*
**oil** ***(n.)*** **zeyti** *ዘይቲ*
**oil** ***(v.)*** **mlkay zeyti** *ምልካይ ዘይቲ*
**oily** ***(adj.)*** **zeyti ztebekele** *ዘይቲ ዝተበከለ*
**ointment** ***(n.)*** **lKay** *ልኽይ*
**okay** ***(adj.)*** **Heray** *ሐራይ*
**old** ***(adj.)*** **aregit** *ኣረጊት*
**oligarchy** ***(n. )*** **hager zemeHadr gujele** *ሃገር ዘመሓድር ጉጅለ*
**olive** ***(n. )*** **awli'E** *ኣውሊዕ*
**Olympic** ***(adj.)*** **olompiyawi** *ኦሊምፒያዊ*
**omelette** ***(n. )*** **omliet** *ኦምሌት*
**omen** ***(n.)*** **fal** *ፋል*
**ominous** ***(adj.)*** **atseyafi** *ኣፀያፊ*
**omission** ***(n.)*** **mgdaf** *ምግዳፍ*
**omit** ***(v.)*** **mgdaf** *ምግዳፍ*
**omnibus** ***(n.)*** **eKbkab** *እኽብካብ*
**omnipotence** ***(n.)*** **kulu mK'al** *ኩሉ ምኽኣል*

**omnipotent** ***(adj.)*** **kulu keali ኩሉ ከኣሊ**
**omnipresence** ***(n.)*** **kab kulu nla'Eli ካብ ኩሉ ንላዕሊ**
**omnipresent** ***(adj.)*** **kab kulu nla'Eli ካብ ኩሉ ንላዕሊ**
**omniscience** ***(n.)*** **kulu mflaT ኩሉ ምፍላጥ**
**omniscient** ***(adj.)*** **kulu felaTi ኩሉ ፈላጢ**
**on** ***(prep. )*** **ab l'Eli ኣብ ልዕሊ**
**once** ***(adv.)*** **Hade gizie ሓደ ግዜ**
**one** ***(n. & adj.)*** **Hade ሓደ**
**oneness** ***(n.)*** **Hadnet ሓድነት**
**onerous** ***(adj.)*** **brtu'E ብርቱዕ**
**oneself** ***(pron. )*** **Arse ዓርሰ**
**onion** ***(n.)*** **shegurti ሽጉርቲ**
**onlooker** ***(n.)*** **temelkati ተመልካቲ**
**only** ***(adv.)*** **Tray ጥራይ**
**onomatopoeia** ***(n. )*** **kab dmtsu zemetse qal ካብ ድምፁ ዝመፀ ቃል**
**onset** ***(n.)*** **mejemerya መጀመርያ**
**onslaught** ***(n.)*** **Tfatat ጥፍኣታት**
**ontology** ***(n.)*** **nay sne hiwet tmrti ናይ ስነ ሂወት ትምርቲ**
**onus** ***(n.)*** **nay Hade seb gdieta ናይ ሓደ ሰብ ግዴታ**
**onward** ***(adv. )*** **nQdmit ንቅድሚት**
**onyx** ***(n.)*** **Aynet ma'Adn ዓይነት ማዓድን**
**ooze** ***(v.i. )*** **Hafis fesasi ሓፊስ ፈሳሲ**
**opacity** ***(n. )*** **brhal albanet ብርሃን-ኣልባነት**
**opal** ***(n.)*** **Aynet ma'Adn ዓይነት ማዓድን**
**opaque** ***(adj.)*** **brhal zeyeHelf ብርሃን ዘየሕልፍ**
**open** ***(adj.)*** **kfut ክፉት**
**opening** ***(n.)*** **kftet ክፍተት**
**openly** ***(adv.)*** **bgahdi ብጋህዲ**
**opera** ***(n.)*** **opiera ኦፔራ**
**operate** ***(v.)*** **zserH ዝሰርሕ**
**operation** ***(n.)*** **mTbaHti tsgena መጥባሕቲ ጽገና**
**operational** ***(adj.)*** **ab sraH zwe'Ale ኣብ ስራሕ ዝወዓለ**
**operative** ***(adj.)*** **tenaHanaHi ተናሓናሒ**
**operator** ***(n.)*** **asraHi ኣስራሒ**
**opine** ***(v.)*** **r'eyto mhab ርእይቶ ምሃብ**
**opinion** ***(n. )*** **r'eyto ርእይቶ**
**opium** ***(n. )*** **Hshsh ሓሽሽ**
**opponent** ***(n.)*** **tenaHanaHi ተናሓናሒ**
**opportune** ***(adj.)*** **mchuw ምቹው**
**opportunism** ***(n. )*** **Edl ዕድል**
**opportunity** ***(n.)*** **Edl ዕድል**
**oppose** ***(v.)*** **teQaweme ተቓወመ**
**opposite** ***(adj.)*** **b'antsaru ብኣንጻሩ**
**opposition** ***(n.)*** **mqwam ምቅዋም**
**oppress** ***(v.)*** **deQose ደቖሰ**
**oppression** ***(n.)*** **cheqona ጨቆና**
**oppressive** ***(adj.)*** **chequani ጨቋኒ**
**oppressor** ***(n.)*** **chequani ጨቋኒ**
**opt** ***(v.)*** **mmrts ምምራፅ**
**optic** ***(adj.)*** **ms Ayni wey mr'ay zmlket ምስ ዓይኒ ወይ ምርኣይ ዝምልከት**
**optician** ***(n. )*** **nay Ayni Hakim ናይ ዓይኒ ሓኪም**

**optimism** ***(n. )*** **awentawi are'a'eya** ኣወንታዊ ኣረኣእያ
**optimist** ***(n.)*** **bruh** ብሩህ
**optimistic** ***(adj.)*** **Qnu'e Hasab zelewo** ቅኑዕ ሓሳብ ዘለዎ
**optimize** ***(v.)*** **mt'eKKal** ምትእኽኻል
**optimum** ***(adj.)*** **eKul** እኹል
**option** ***(n.)*** **amaratsi** ኣማራጺ
**optional** ***(adj.)*** **gdieta zeykone** ግዴታ ዘይኮነ
**opulence** ***(n.)*** **udet** ዑደት
**opulent** ***(adj.)*** **habtam** ሃብታም
**or** ***(conj. )*** **wey** ወይ
**oracle** ***(n.)*** **Tenquali** ጠንቋሊ
**oracular** ***(adj.)*** **mTnqual** ምጥንቋል
**oral** ***(adj.)*** **bQal** ብቓል
**orally** ***(adv.)*** **bQal** ብቓል
**orange** ***(n.)*** **aranshi** ኣራንሺ
**oration** ***(n.)*** **mdlaw** ምድላው
**orator** ***(n.)*** **medalewi** መዳለዊ
**oratory** ***(n. )*** **tsbuQ mKuan** ፅቡቕ ምኳን
**orb** ***(n. )*** **kbawi akal** ክባዊ ኣካል
**orbit** ***(n. )*** **qnate zuret** ቅናት-ዙረት
**orbital** ***(adj.)*** **Udetawi** ዑደታዊ
**orchard** ***(n. )*** **atsede fratat** ኣጸደ-ፍረታት
**orchestra** ***(n.)*** **muziqawi qnat** ሙዚቃዊ ቅናት
**orchestral** ***(adj.)*** **muziqawi qnat** ሙዚቃዊ ቅናት
**orchid** ***(n.)*** **nay Embaba Aynet** ናይ ዕምበባ ዓይነት
**ordeal** ***(n. )*** **mekera** መከራ
**order** ***(n.)*** **mesr'E** መስርዕ
**orderly** ***(adj.)*** **bsr'At** ብስርዓት
**ordinance** ***(n.)*** **dngage** ድንጋገ
**ordinarily** ***(adv.)*** **lmudawi** ልሙዳዊ
**ordinary** ***(adj.)*** **lmud** ልሙድ
**ordnance** ***(n.)*** **nay kuinat mieda** ናይ ኲናት ሜዳ
**ore** ***(n. )*** **ma'Adn** ማዕድን
**organ** ***(n.)*** **akal** ኣካል
**organic** ***(adj.)*** **organik** ኦርጋኒክ
**organism** ***(n.)*** **sne hywet** ስነ ሕይወት
**organization** ***(n.)*** **kubanya** ኩባንያ
**organize** ***(v.)*** **adalew** ኣዳለዉ
**orgasm** ***(n.)*** **Trzi sm'lt** ጥርዚ-ስምዒት
**orgy** ***(n.)*** **tfg'et** ትፍግእት
**orient** ***(n.)*** **bniew mbraQ** ብኔው ምብራቕ
**oriental** ***(adj.)*** **mbraQawi** ምብራቓዊ
**orientate** ***(v.)*** **meteHababeri** መተሓባበሪ
**origami** ***(n.)*** **bjapanawyan zsraH nay wereQet qrtsaqrtsi** ብጃፓናውያን ዝስራሕ ናይ ወረቐት ቅርፃቅርፂ
**origin** ***(n.)*** **felami** ፈላሚ
**original** ***(adj.)*** **Qdamawi** ቀዳማዊ
**originality** ***(n.)*** **mebeqolawinet** መበቖላውነት
**originate** ***(v.)*** **mnchuw** ምንጬው
**originator** ***(n.)*** **mejemeri** መጀመሪ
**ornament** ***(n.)*** **tr'it** ትርኢት
**ornamentation** ***(n.)*** **tr'itawi** ትርኢታዊ
**ornate** ***(adj.)*** **zuret** ዙረት
**orphan** ***(n.)*** **zeKtam** ዘኽታም

**orphanage** ***(n.)*** **meHebHebi zeKtam htsanat** መሓብሓቢ ዘኽታም ህፃናት
**orthodox** ***(adj.)*** **qbul** ቅቡል
**orthodoxy** ***(n.)*** **qbul** ቅቡል
**orthopaedics** ***(n.)*** **Aynet Hkmna** ዓይነት ሕክምና
**oscillate** ***(v.)*** **mzwar** ምዝዋር
**oscillation** ***(n.)*** **zuret** ዙረት
**ossify** ***(v.)*** **nab Atsmi mQyar** ናብ ዓፅሚ ምቕያር
**ostensible** ***(adj.)*** **zeygltsi** ዘይግልፂ
**ostentation** ***(n.)*** **zeygltsi** ዘይግልፂ
**osteopathy** ***(n.)*** **nay Atsmn megeTaTemin Hkmna** ናይ ዓፅምን መግጣጠምን ሕክምና
**ostracize** ***(v.)*** **aglele** ኣግለለ
**ostrich** ***(n.)*** **segen** ሰገን
**other** ***(adj. & pron.)*** **kal'e** ካልእ
**otherwise** ***(adv.)*** **tezeykone gn** ተዘይኮነ ግን
**otiose** ***(adj.)*** **heTeqm** ዘይጠቅም
**otter** ***(n. )*** **Asa zmgb ensesa** ዓሳ ዝምግብ እንስሳ
**ottoman** ***(n. )*** **dkua** ድኳ
**ounce** ***(n.)*** **me'Eqeni fesasi** መዐቀኒ ፈሳሲ
**our** ***(adj.)*** **natna** ናትና
**ourselves** ***(pron. )*** **nHna** ንሕና
**oust** ***(v.)*** **segon** ሰጎገ
**out** ***(adv.)*** **dege** ደገ
**outbid** ***(v.)*** **zle'Ale kflit mQrab** ዝለዓለ ክፍሊት ምቕራብ
**outboard** ***(adj.)*** **kab dege** ካብ ደገ
**outbreak** ***(n. )*** **werershgn** ወረርሽኝ
**outburst** ***(n.)*** **ntuag** ንትጓ
**outcast** ***(n.)*** **ntsug** ንጹግ
**outclass** ***(v.)*** **l'Ul** ልዑል
**outcome** ***(n.)*** **wts'it** ውፅኢት
**outcry** ***(n.)*** **bKyat** ብኽያት
**outdated** ***(adj.)*** **gizie zHalefo** ጊዜ ዝሓለፎ
**outdo** ***(v.)*** **m'Eblal** ምዕብላል
**outdoor** ***(adj.)*** **dege** ደገ
**outer** ***(adj.)*** **degawi** ደጋዊ
**outfit** ***(n.)*** **Kdan** ኽዳን
**outgoing** ***(adj.)*** **tetsawati** ተፃዋቲ
**outgrow** ***(v.)*** **m'Ebay** ምዕባይ
**outhouse** ***(n. )*** **shQaQ** ሽቓቕ
**outing** ***(n.)*** **shrshr** ሽርሽር
**outlandish** ***(adj.)*** **gdamawi** ግዳማዊ
**outlast** ***(v.)*** **b'Edme beletse** ብዕድመ በለፀ
**outlaw** ***(n.)*** **zeyHgawi mgbar** ዘይሕጋዊ ምግባር
**outlay** ***(n.)*** **wetsieu mbal** ወጺኡ ምባል
**outlet** ***(n.)*** **mesheTi** መሸጢ
**outline** ***(n.)*** **ndfi** ንድፊ
**outlive** ***(v.)*** **b'Edme beletse** ብዕድመ በለፀ
**outlook** ***(n.)*** **r'eyot** ርእዮት
**outlying** ***(adj.)*** **wetsieu mbal** ወጺኡ ዝበለ
**outmoded** ***(adj.)*** **bahlawi** ባህላዊ
**outnumber** ***(v.)*** **bQutsri beletse** ብቑፅሪ በለፀ
**outpatient** ***(n.)*** **Arat zeyHaze teHakami** ዓራት ዘይሓዘ ተሓካሚ
**outpost** ***(n. )*** **Erdi** ዕርዲ
**output** ***(n. )*** **wts'it** ውፅኢት
**outrage** ***(n.)*** **Abi wenjel** ዓቢ ወንጀል

**outrageous** ***(adj.)*** **zedengts** ዘደንግጽ
**outrider** ***(n.)*** **Ajabi** ዓጃቢ
**outright** ***(adv.)*** **meweda'eta** መወዳእታ
**outrun** ***(v.)*** **bguya Qedeme** ብጉያ ቀደመ
**outset** ***(n.)*** **mejemeri** መጀመሪ
**outshine** ***(v.)*** **zentsebarq** ዘንፀባርቅ
**outside** ***(n.)*** **dege** ደገ
**outsider** ***(n.)*** **guana** ጓና
**outsize** ***(adj.)*** **Abyi** ዓብዪ
**outskirts** ***(n.)*** **edub gemgem** እዱብ ገምገም
**outsource** ***(v.)*** ካብ ደገ ዕዳጋ ግልጋሎት ምርካብ
**outspoken** ***(adj.)*** **gltsi r'eyto** ግልፂ ርእይቶ **kab dege Edaga glgalot mrkab**
**outstanding** ***(adj.)*** **bTa'Emi tsbuQ** ብጠዕሚ ፅቡቕ
**outstrip** ***(v.)*** **goyKa mQdam** ጎይኻ ምቕዳም
**outward** ***(adj.)*** **nab dege** ናብ ደገ
**outwardly** ***(adv.)*** **degawi** ደጋዊ
**outweigh** ***(v.)*** **bKbdet beletse** ብኽብደት በለፀ
**outwit** ***(v.)*** **btsaweta beletse** ብፃወታ በለፀ
**oval** ***(adj.)*** **nay enquaQuHo qrtsi** ናይ እንቋቕሖ ቅርጺ
**ovary** ***(n.)*** **maHdere enquaQuHo** ማሕደረ እንቋቑሖ
**ovate** ***(adj.)*** **nay enquaQuHo qrtsi** ናይ እንቋቕሖ ቅርጺ
**ovation** ***(n.)*** **dKnet** ድኽነት

**oven** ***(n.)*** **forno** ፎርኖ
**over** ***(prep.)*** **nla'Eli** ንላዕሊ
**overact** ***(v.)*** **l'Eli meTen mtgbar** ልዕሊ መጠን ምትግባር
**overall** ***(adj.)*** **bTeQlala** ብጠቕላላ
**overawe** ***(v.)*** **akenawene** ኣወናወነ
**overbalance** ***(v.)*** **l'Eli mizan** ልዕሊ ሚዛን
**overbearing** ***(adj.)*** **l'El l'El** ልዕል ልዕል
**overblown** ***(adj.)*** **zteleTefe** ዝተለጠፈ
**overboard** ***(adv.)*** **ab merkeb** ኣብ መርከብ
**overburden** ***(v.)*** **sraH abzaHe** ስራሕ ኣብዘሐ
**overcast** ***(adj.)*** **shfan** ሽፋን
**overcharge** ***(v.)*** **trfi kflit** ትርፊ ክፍሊት
**overcoat** ***(n.)*** **mederebi Kdan** መደረቢ ኽዳን
**overcome** ***(v.)*** **se'Are** ሰዓረ
**overdo** ***(v.)*** **l'Eli meTen mTQam** ልዕሊ መጠን ምጥቃም
**overdose** ***(n.)*** **medHanit l'Eli meTen mwsad** መድሓኒት ልዕሊ መጠን ምውሳድ
**overdraft** ***(n.)*** **lQaH** ልቓሕ
**overdraw** ***(v.)*** **kab gbu'e nla'Eli m'emat** ካብ ግቡእ ንላዕሊ ምእማት
**overdrive** ***(n.)*** **kab AQmi nl'Eli msraH** ካብ ዓቕሚ ንላዕሊ ምስራሕ
**overdue** ***(adj.)*** **gizie zeHlefe** ጊዜ ዘሕለፈ
**overestimate** ***(v.)*** **bziH m'emat** ብዙሕ ምእማት

**overflow** ***(v.)*** **bTa'Emi meli'u** ብጣዕሚ መሊኡ
**overgrown** ***(adj.)*** **bTa'emi Abyi** ብጣዕሚ ዓብዪ
**overhaul** ***(v.)*** **mt'Ereray** ምትዕርራይ
**overhead** ***(adv.)*** **kab r'esi nla'Eli** ካብ ርእሲ ንላዕሊ
**overhear** ***(v.)*** **b'agaTami sem'E** ብኣጋጣሚ ሰምዐ
**overjoyed** ***(adj.)*** **kebid Hagos** ከቢድ ሓጎስ
**overlap** ***(v.)*** **chafatu tederarebe** ጫፋቱ ተደራረበ
**overleaf** ***(adv.)*** **bdHrit** ብድሕሪት
**overload** ***(v.)*** **kebit ts'Enet** ከቢድ ፅዕነት
**overlook** ***(v.)*** **mermere** መርመረ
**overly** ***(adv.)*** **kab lk'E nla'eli** ካብ ልክዕ ንላዕሊ
**overnight** ***(adv.)*** **bHade leyti** ብሓደ ለይቲ
**overpass** ***(n.)*** **dldl** ድልድል
**overpower** ***(v.)*** **se'Are** ሰዓረ
**overrate** ***(v.)*** **kab lk'E nla'eli** ካብ ልክዕ ንላዕሊ
**overreach** ***(v.)*** **arkebe** ኣርከበ
**overreact** ***(v.)*** **bTa'emi astemasele** ብጣዕሚ ኣስተማሰለ
**override** ***(v.)*** **Ablele** ዓብለለ
**overrule** ***(v.)*** **teKelkele** ተኸልከለ
**overrun** ***(v.)*** **werere** ወረረ
**overseas** ***(adv.)*** **gdamawi hager** ግዳማዊ ሃገር
**oversee** ***(v.)*** **te'Azebe** ተዓዘበ
**overseer** ***(n.)*** **l'uK** ልኡኽ
**overshadow** ***(v.)*** **antselalewe** ኣንጸላለወ
**overshoot** ***(v.)*** **ambza asrHe** እምብዛ ኣስርሐ
**oversight** ***(n.)*** **znga'E** ዝንጋዐ
**overspill** ***(n.)*** **ksab zfess zmel'e** ክስብ ዝፈስስ ዝምልእ
**overstep** ***(v.)*** **kab meTen nla'eli** ካብ መጠን ንላዕሊ
**overt** ***(adj.)*** **Adakie nla'Eli** ዓዳኺ ንላዕሊ
**overtake** ***(v.)*** **Qedeme** ቐደመ
**overthrow** ***(v.)*** **gelbeTe** ገልበጠ
**overtime** ***(n)*** **tewesaKi se'At** ተወሳኺ ሰዓት
**overtone** ***(n.)*** **Hbu'e trgum zelewo** ሕቡእ ትርጉም ዘለዎ
**overture** ***(n.)*** **Kbri** ኽብሪ
**overturn** ***(v.)*** **mglbaT** ምግልባጥ
**overview** ***(n.)*** **TeQlala r'eyot** ጠቕላላ ርእዮት
**overweening** ***(adj.)*** **kab meTen nla'eli Arse mt'emman** ካብ መጠን ንላዕሊ ዓርሰ ምትእምማን
**overwhelm** ***(v.)*** **chenqi** ጨንቂ
**overwrought** ***(adj.)*** **zKerere** ዝኸረረ
**ovulate** ***(v.)*** **mfTar enquaQHo** ምፍጣር እንቋቕሖ
**owe** ***(n. )*** **m'ewad** ምእዋድ
**owing** ***(adj.)*** **m'ewad** ምእዋድ
**owl** ***(n.)*** **gungua** ጉንጓ
**own** ***(adj. & pron.)*** **mwnan** ምውናን
**owner** ***(n. )*** **wana** ዋና
**ownership** ***(n. )*** **wannet** ዋንነት
**ox** ***(n. )*** **b'Eray** ብዕራይ

**oxide** *(n.)* **oksayd** *ኦክሳይድ*
**oxygen** *(n. )* **oksjn** *ኦክስጅን*
**oyster** *(n.)* **ab may znebr ensesa** *ኣብ ማይ ዝነብር እንስሳ*
**ozone** *(n)* **ozon** *ኦዞን*

# P

**pace** *(n.)* **መተሓላለፊ መንገዲ** *mteȟalalefi mengedi*
**pacemaker** *(n.)* **መራሒ መንገዲ** *meraȟ mengedi*
**pacific** *(n.)* **ሰላማዊ** *selamawi*
**pacifist** *(n.)* **ደጋፊ ሰላም** *degafi selam*
**pacify** *(v.)* **ኣህድእ** *ahd'e*
**pack** *(n.)* **ጽዕነት** *xëinet*
**package** *(n. )* **መጠቕለሊ** *meẗeqleli*
**packet** *(n. )* **ጥቕላል** *ẗqlal*
**packing** *(n. )* **ምጥርናፍ** *mẗrnaf*
**pact** *(n. )* **ምስምማዕ** *msm'maë*
**pad** *(n.)* **ፍርናሽ** *frnash*
**padding** *(v.)* **ኣዘናግዐ** *mesrȟi meteras*
**paddle** *(n.)* **መጀለቢ** *mejelebi*
**paddock** *(n.)* **ጎልጎል ሳዕሪ** *golgol saëri*
**paddy** *(n. )* **ነድሪ** *nedri*
**padlock** *(n.)* **ሊኬቶ** *likieto*
**paediatrician** *(n.)* **ናይ ህጻናት ዶክቶር** *nay hxanat doctor*
**paediatrics** *(n.)* **ጨንፈር ሕክምና ህጻናት** *čenfer ȟkmna hxanat*
**paedophile** *(n.)* **ምስ ህጻናት ጾታዊ ርክብ ምፍጻም ዝማረኽ በጽሒ** *ms hixanat xotawi rkb mfxam zmareḱ bexȟi*
**pagan** *(n.)* **ኣረሜን** *aremien*
**page** *(n.)* **ምዕራፍ** *m'ëraf*
**pageant** *(n. )* **ስነ-ስርዓት በዓል** *sne-srät beäl*
**pageantry** *(n. )* **ሕብራዊ ምረኢት** *ȟbrawi mreit*
**pagoda** *(n. )* **ብውወርቂ ተሰርሐ ሳንቲም** *bwerqi teserȟe santim*
**pail** *(n. )* **ሰንኬሎ** *senkielo*
**pain** *(n.)* **ቃንዛ** *qanza*
**painful** *(adj.)* **ዘቀንዙ** *zeqenzu*
**painkiller** *(n.)* **ቀታሊ ቃንዛ** *qetali qanza*
**painstaking** *(adj.)* **ጥንቁቕ** *ẗnquq̈*
**paint** *(n.)* **ምቅባእ** *mqbaè*
**painter** *(n. )* **ቀበኣይ** *qebeay*
**painting** *(n. )* **ቅብኣ** *qba*
**pair** *(n.)* **ጽምዲ** *xmdi*
**paisley** *(n.)* **ኣበው//////** *abew*
**pal** *(n. )* **መሓዛ** *meȟaza*
**palace** *(n. )* **ቤተ መንግስቲ** *biete mengsti*
**palatable** *(adj.)* **ምቁር** *mqur*
**palatal** *(adj.)* **ናይ ናሕሲ ኣፍ** *nay naȟsi af*
**palate** *(n.)* **ናሕሲ ኣፍ** *naȟsi af*
**palatial** *(adj.)* **ቤተ መንግስታዊ** *biete mengstawi*
**pale** *(adj.)* **ጽምሉው** *xmluw*
**palette** *(n. )* **መስርዕ ሕብርታት ናይ ዝተዋህበ ስራሕ** *msrie hbrtat nay ztewahbe srah*
**paling** *(n.)* **ዝበልሐ ዕንጸይቲ ሓጹር** *zbelhe enxeyti haxur*
**pall** *(n.)* **ግሩም ልብሲ** *grum lbsi*
**pallet** *(n.)* **መሳርሒ ካይላ** *msarhi kayla*

**palm** *(n.)* ስየ *sye*
**palmist** *(n. )* ጠንቋሊ *meqali*
**palmistry** *(n.)* ናይ ጻዕዳ ኢድ ጥንቁልና *nay xaeda eid tnqulna*
**palpable** *(adj.)* ዝጭበጥ *zchbet*
**palpitate** *(v.)* ተደጋጋሚ ምውቃዕ ልቢ *tedagagami mwqae lbi*
**palpitation** *(n.)* ዘይንቡር መውቃዕቲ ልቢ *zeynbur wqaeti lbi*
**palsy** *(n.)* መልመስቲ *melmesti*
**paltry** *(adj.)* ዘይበቅዕ *zeybeqe*
**pamper** *(v.)* ምሕንቃቕ *mhnqaq*
**pamphlet** *(n. )* መንሹር *menshur*
**pamphleteer** *(n. )* ዓዳሊ መንሹር *adali menshur*
**pan** *(n.)* ባዴላ/ድስቲ *badela/dsti*
**panacea** *(n. )* መድሓኒ *mdhani*
**panache** *(n.)* ኳዕናን *kuae'nan*
**pancake** *(n.)* ፓንኬክ *pankek*
**pancreas** *(n.)* ሓሞት *hamot*
**panda** *(n.)* ድቢ *dbi*
**pandemonium** *(n. )* ናዕቢ *naebi*
**pane** *(n. )* ኣንሶላ መስኮት *ansola mskot*
**panegyric** *(n. )* መደረ ዝሀብ *medere zhb*
**panel** *(n.)* ጓዳ *guada*
**pang** *(n. )* ውግኣት *wgat*
**panic** *(n. )* ራዕዲ *raedi*
**panorama** *(n.)* ኣጠቓላሊ ኣቀማምጣ መሬት *ataqalali aqmamta meriet*
**pant** *(v.)* ምልህላህ *mlhlah*
**pantaloons** *(n. )* ፓንታሎኒ *pantaloni*
**pantheism** *(n. )* ኣብ ኩሎም ኣማልኽቲ ምእማን *ab kulom amalkti meman*
**pantheist** *(adj.)* ኣብ ኩሎም ኣማልኽቲ ዝኣምን *ab kulom amalkti zamn*
**panther** *(n. )* ዓባይ ድሙ *abay dmu*
**panties** *(n.)* ኮስትሞታት *kostmotat*
**pantomime** *(n. )* ትያትር ቆልዑ *tyatr qoleu*
**pantry** *(n. )* ከብሒ ክሽነ *kebhi kshne*
**pants** *(n.)* ስረ *sre*
**papacy** *(n.)* ናይ ፓፓስ ኦፊስ *nay papas ofis*
**papal** *(adj.)* ናይ ፓፓስ *nay papas*
**paper** *(n. )* ወረቐት *werqet*
**paperback** *(n.)* ተዓጻጻፊ ገበር ዘለዎ መጽሓፍ *taxaxafi geber zelewo mxhaf*
**par** *(n. )* ማዕርነት ኩነታት *maernet kunetat*
**parable** *(n. )* ሓጺር ትረኻ *haxir traka*
**parachute** *(n. )* ጃንጥላ *jantla*
**parachutist** *(n. )* ብጃንጥላ ዝንቆት *bjantla znqot*
**parade** *(n.)* ሰልፊ *selfi*
**paradise** *(n. )* ገነት *genet*
**paradox** *(n.)* ምግጫው/ስግንጢር *mgchaw/sgntir*
**paradoxical** *(adj.)* ተጋጫዊ/ስግንጢራዊ *tegachawi sgintrawi*
**paraffin** *(n.)* ላምባ *lamba*
**paragon** *(n. )* ካልኣይ/ማዕረ *kaleay/maere*
**paragraph** *(n.)* ዓንቀጽ *anqex*
**parallel** *(n. )* ጎኒጎኒ *gonigoni*

**parallelogram** *(n.)* **ጎኒጎኒ ዝከይድ ጎብጋብ ርቡዕጎናዊ** *gni goni zkeyd gobgab rubue kurnawi*
**paralyse** *(v.)* **ምልማስ** *mlmas*
**paralysis** *(n.)* **ምልምስና** *mlmsna*
**paralytic** *(adj.)* **ብምልምስና ዝሳቐ ሰብ** *bmlmsna zsaqe seb*
**paramedic** *(n.)* **ሓኪም መረጋግኢ ሕሙማት** *hakim meregagi hmumat*
**parameter** *(n.)* **ፐራመተር** *parameter*
**paramount** *(adj.)* **ዝለዓለ** *zleale*
**paramour** *(n.)* **ፍቕራዊ** *fqrawi*
**paraphernalia** *(n. )* **ካብ ገዝሚ ወጻኢ ንብረት መርዓት** *kab gezmi weai nbret mrat*
**paraphrase** *(v.)* **ትርጉም ምንጻር** *trgum mnxar*
**parasite** *(n. )* **ኣብ ነፍሳት ዝነብሩ ፍጥረት** *ab nefsat znebru ftret*
**parasol** *(n.)* **ጽላል** *xlal*
**parcel** *(n.)* **ፓርሰል ደሴት** *parsel deset*
**parched** *(adj.)* **ዝነቐጸ** *zenqexe*
**pardon** *(n. )* **ምሕረት** *mhretawi*
**pardonable** *(adj.)* **ምሕረታዊ** *mhretawi*
**pare** *(v.)* **ቀኒሱ** *qenisu*
**parent** *(n. )* **ወላዲ** *weladi*
**parentage** *(n.)* **ስድራቤት** *sdrabetawi*
**parental** *(adj.)* **ስድራቤታዊ** *sdrabetawi*
**parenthesis** *(n. )* **ቅንፍ** *qnf*
**pariah** *(n.)* **ዝተሰደደ ሰብ** *zteedede seb*
**parish** *(n. )* **ደብሪ** *debri*
**parity** *(n. )* **ማዕርነት/ምንጽጻር ሓይሊ** *maernet/mnxxar hayl*
**park** *(n.)* **መናፍፈሲ ቦታ** *menafesi bota*
**parky** *(adj.)* **ዝሑል** *zhul*
**parlance** *(n. )* **ኣገባብ ኣዘራርባ** *agebab azerarba*
**parley** *(n.)* **ኣኼባ ዕርቂ** *akeba eirqi*
**parliament** *(n. )* **ፓርላማ** *parlma*
**parliamentarian** *(n.)* **ኣባል ፓርላማ** *abal parlama*
**parliamentary** *(adj.)* **ፓርላማዊ** *parlamawi*
**parlour** *(n. )* **መዘናግዒ ክፍሊ(ሳሎን)** *mezenagei kfli*
**parochial** *(adj.)* **ደብራዊ** *debrawi*
**parody** *(n.)* **ጭርቃን** *chrqan*
**parole** *(n.)* **ብዋሕስ ምውጻእ** *bwahs mwxae*
**parricide** *(n. )* **ወለዱ ዝቐተለ** *weledu zqetele*
**parrot** *(n.)* **ፓፓጋሎ** *papagalo*
**parry** *(v.)* **ክትዕ ምውጋድ** *ktie mwgad*
**parse** *(v.)* **ተንቲኑ** *tentu*
**parsimony** *(n.)* **ስስዐ** *ssie*
**parson** *(n. )* **ካህን** *kahn*
**part** *(n.)* **ክፋል** *kfal*
**partake** *(v.)* **ምክፋል** *mkfal*
**partial** *(adj.)* **ዘይምሉእ** *zeymulue*
**partiality** *(n.)* **ምድላው/ምፍታው** *mdlaw/mftaw*
**participant** *(n.)* **ትሳታፋይ** *tsatafay*
**participate** *(v.)* **ተስሳተፈ** *tesatefe*
**participation** *(n.)* **ምስታፍ** *mstaf*
**particle** *(n.)* **ንእሽተይ በቕሊ** *neshtey beqli*

**particular** *(adj.)* ፍሉይ *fluy*
**parting** *(n.)* ምፍልላይ *mfllay*
**partisan** *(n.)* ደጋፊ *degafi*
**partition** *(n.)* ምክፍፋል *mkffal*
**partly** *(adv. )* ፍርቂ *frqu*
**partner** *(n. )* ተሻራኺ *tesharaki*
**partnership** *(n.)* ሽርክነት *shrket*
**party** *(n.)* ውድብ *wdb*
**pass** *(v.)* ምሕላፍ/ምቕባል *mhlaf/mkbal*
**passable** *(adj.)* ተሓላፊ *tehalafi*
**passage** *(n. )* መተሓላለፊ *metehalalefi*
**passenger** *(n. )* ተሳፋሪ *tsafari*
**passing** *(adj.)* ምስጋር *msgar*
**passion** *(n.)* ብርቱዕ ስምዒት *brtue smeit*
**passionate** *(adj.)* ስምዒታዊ/ተምሳጣዊ *smeitawi/temsatawi*
**passive** *(adj.)* ብዘይ ምኽንያት *bzeymknyat*
**passport** *(n.)* ፓስፖርት *pasport*
**past** *(adj.)* ሕሉፍ *hluf*
**pasta** *(n.)* ባስታ *basta*
**paste** *(n.)* ለጠፈ *letefe*
**pastel** *(n. )* ባህላዊ መግቢ ላቲን ኣመሪካ *bahlawi megbi latin amrica*
**pasteurized** *(adj.)* ምውዓይ መግቢ ባክተርያ ንምጥፋእ *mwuay megbi bakteriya nmtfae*
**pastime** *(n.)* ሕሉፍ ሰዓት *hluf seat*
**pastor** *(n.)* ካህን *kahn*
**pastoral** *(adj.)* መንፈሳዊ *menfesawi*
**pastry** *(n.)* ቤት ሕብስቲ *biet hbsti*
**pasture** *(n.)* ግራት መቓለቢ ጥሪት *grat meqlebi trit*
**pasty** *(n.)* ብሑቕ መሰል *bque mesl*
**pat** *(v.)* ፍኩስ ጽፍዒት *fkus xfeit*
**patch** *(n.)* ምልጋብ/ምስፋይ *mlab/msfay*
**patchy** *(adj.)* ልጋባዊ/ስፋይምፋይ *lgabwi/sfaymfay*
**patent** *(n.)* መኽበሪ መሰል ሰነድ *mekberi mesel sened*
**paternal** *(adj.)* ኣቦኣዊ *aboawi*
**paternity** *(n.)* ኣቦነት *abonet*
**path** *(n.)* ኣጋር መንገዲ *agar mengedi*
**pathetic** *(adj.)* ዘደንግጽ *zedengx*
**pathology** *(n.)* ስርዓተ መጽናዕቲ ሕማም *srate mxnaeti hmam*
**pathos** *(n. )* ስምዒት ሓዘን *smeit hazen*
**patience** *(n.)* ትዕግስቲ *tegsti*
**patient** *(n. )* ሕሙም *hmum*
**patient** *(adj.)* ዕጉስ *egus*
**patio** *(n.)* መረባ *mereba*
**patisserie** *(n.)* ቤት ሕብስቲ *biet hbsti*
**patriarch** *(n.)* ዝለዓለ ክፋል ቅሽነት *zleale kfal qshnet*
**patricide** *(n.)* ቅትለተ-ኣቦ *qtlet abo*
**patrimony** *(n. )* ዝተወርሰ መሰል *ztewerse mesel*
**patriot** *(n.)* ሓርበኛ *harbena*
**patriotic** *(adj.)* ሓርበኛዊ *harbenawi*
**patriotism** *(n.)* ሓርበኛነት *harbenanet*
**patrol** *(v.)* ቃፊር/ዋርድያ *qafir/wardiya*
**patron** *(n. )* ዕሚል/ደጋፊ ተኸራኻሪ *amil/degafi tekerakari*
**patronage** *(n.)* ዓማዊል *amawil*

**patronize** *(v.)* ደጋፊ/ዓሚል ሙኳን *degafi/amil mkan*
**pattern** *(n. )* ሓረግ/ቅዲ *hareg/qdi*
**patty** *(n.)* ክቢ *kbi*
**paucity** *(n. )* ምናስ *mnas*
**paunch** *(n.)* ጉስጢ *gusti*
**pauper** *(n. )* ድኻ/በተኽ *dka/betek*
**pause** *(n.)* ሓጺር ዕረፍቲ *haxir erefti*
**pave** *(v.)* ጽሪጉ *xerigu*
**pavement** *(n. )* ምጽራግ *mxrag*
**pavilion** *(n. )* ዳስ *das*
**paw** *(n.)* ግናዕ ኢድ *gnae ide*
**pawn** *(n.)* ትሕጃ ምትሓዝ *thja mthaz*
**pawnbroker** *(n.)* ተሓዚ ትሕጃ *tehazi thja*
**pay** *(v.)* ምኽፋል *mkfal*
**payable** *(n. )* ተኽፋሊ *tekefali*
**payee** *(n. )* ከፋሊ *kefali*
**payment** *(n. )* ክፍሊት *kflit*
**pea** *(n. )* ዓይኒ ዓተር *ayni ater*
**peace** *(n.)* ሰላም *selam*
**peaceable** *(adj.)* ሰላማዊ *selamawi*
**peaceful** *(adj.)* ሰላማዊ *selamawi*
**peach** *(n. )* ኩኽ *kuk*
**peacock** *(n. )* ተባዕታይ ጣዎስ *tabaetay taewa*
**peahen** *(n. )* ኣንስተይቲ ጣዎስ *ansteyti taewa*
**peak** *(n. )* ጥርዚ *trzi*
**peaky** *(adj.)* ጥርዛዊ *trzawi*
**peal** *(n.)* ድምጺ ደወል *dmxi dewel*
**peanut** *(n.)* ፉል *ful*
**pear** *(n. )* ናይ ሜለ ገረብ *nay mele gereb*
**pearl** *(n. )* ሉል *lul*
**peasant** *(n. )* ሃገረሰብ *hagereseb*
**peasantry** *(n. )* ገባሮ *gebaro*
**pebble** *(n. )* ጸጸር *xexer*
**pecan** *(n.)* ፔካን *pekan*
**peck** *(v.i. )* ወጋአ *wge*
**peculiar** *(adj.)* ፍሉይ *fluy*
**pedagogue** *(n. )* መምህር ቆልዑ *memher qoleu*
**pedagogy** *(n.)* ምምህርና *mmhrna*
**pedal** *(n.)* ዝርገጽ መቆጻጸሪ ማሺን *zrgex mekoxaxeri mashen*
**pedant** *(n. )* ሰራዊት *serawit*
**pedantic** *(adj.)* ፈለጥኩ በሃሊ *feletku bhali*
**peddle** *(v.)* ቤላሮባ/እንዳዘረ ዝሸቅጥ *beilaroba*
**pedestal** *(n. )* ናይ ክብሪ ቦታ *nay kbri bota*
**pedestrian** *(n. )* ኣጋር *agar*
**pedicure** *(n.)* ኣላዪ ኣእጋርን ኣጻብዕቲ ኣእጋርን *alayi aearnaxabetn aegarn*
**pedigree** *(n.)* ዝርዝር ዓሌት *zrzr alet*
**pedlar** *(n.)* እንዳዘረ ዝሸቅጥ *enazere zshket*
**pedometer** *(n.)* ርሕቀት ጉዕዞ ዓቃኒት *rhket guezo aqanit*
**peek** *(v.)* ሰረቕካ ምራይ *seriqka mray*
**peel** *(n.)* ምቕላጥ/ምቕራፍ *mqlat/mqrf*
**peep** *(v.)* ሕሹኽሹኽ *hshukshuk*
**peer** *(n.)* መዘና *mzena*
**peer** *(v.)* ቅልቅል ምባል *qlql mbal*
**peerage** *(n.)* ምድብ መዘና *mdb mezena*
**peerless** *(adj.)* መዘና ኣንቦ *mezena albo*

**peg** *(n.)* **ተካባኖ** *tekabano*
**pejorative** *(adj.)* **ኣንነኣኣሲ** *aneaasi*
**pelican** *(n.)* **ዘርኢ ዑፍ** *zrei euf*
**pellet** *(n.)* **ዕኳር** *ekuar*
**pelmet** *(n.)* **መጋረጃ** *megareja*
**pelt** *(v.)* **ቆርበት ወዲ ሰብ** *qorbet wedi seb*
**pelvis** *(n.)* **ጎሎ** *golo*
**pen** *(n.)* **ቢሮ** *biro*
**penal** *(adj.)* **ገበናዊ** *gebenawi*
**penalize** *(v.)* **ምቕጻዕ** *mqxae*
**penalty** *(n. )* **መቕጻዕቲ** *mqxaeti*
**penance** *(n.)* **ንስሓ** *nsha*
**penchant** *(n.)* **ፍትወት/መቀረት** *ftwet/meqeret*
**pencil** *(n.)* **ርሳስ** *rsas*
**pendant** *(n.)* **መንጠልጥሎ** *menteltlo*
**pendent** *(adj.)* **ዝተጠልጠለ** *ztenteltele*
**pending** *(adj.)* **ይጽናሕ ዝተባህለ** *yxnah ztebahle*
**pendulum** *(n.)* **ምንጥልጣል** *mntltal*
**penetrate** *(v.)* **ውሽጢ ምእታው** *wshti metaw*
**penetration** *(n.)* **ንውሽጢ ምእታው** *nwsheti metw*
**penguin** *(n.)* **ውሽጢ ምእታው** *wsheti metaw*
**peninsula** *(n.)* **ወሽመጥ** *weshmt*
**penis** *(n.)* **መሸሊት ወዲ ተባዕታይ** *mesheit nay wedi tebaetay*
**penitent** *(adj.)* **ተናሳሒ** *tenasahi*
**penniless** *(adj.)* **ሳንቲም ዘይብሉ** *santim zeyblu*
**penny** *(n. )* **ሳንቲም** *santim*
**pension** *(n.)* **ኣበል ጥሮታ/መዕረፍ ኣጋይሽ** *abel trota/meref agaysh*
**pensioner** *(n.)* **ጥሮተኛ** *trotena*
**pensive** *(adj.)* **ምትካዝ** *mtkaz*
**pentagon** *(n. )* **በዓል ሓሙሽተ መኣዝን** *beal hamushte meazn*
**penthouse** *(n.)* **ኣፓርታማ ኣብ ዝለዓለ ደርቢ ዝርከብ** *apartama ab zleale derbi*
**penultimate** *(adj.)* **ዳርጋ/ኣብ መወዳእታ** *darga/ab mewedet a*
**people** *(n.)* **ሰባት** *sebat*
**pepper** *(n.)* **ፐፐሮኒ** *peperoni*
**peppermint** *(n.)* **ሜንታ ፐፐሮኒ** *mienta peperoni*
**peptic** *(adj.)* **ሓጋዚ ምሕቃቕ መግቢ** *hagazi mhqaq megbi*
**per** *(prep.)* **ንነፍሲ ወከፍ** *nnefsi wekef*
**perambulate** *(v.t. )* **ጅረሎ** *jerelo*
**perceive** *(v.)* **ምርዳእ** *mrdae*
**percentage** *(n. )* **ሚእታዊት** *mietawit*
**perceptible** *(adj.)* **ዝርዳእ** *zrdae*
**perception** *(n.)* **ርደኢት** *rdeit*
**perceptive** *(adj.)* **ተረዳኢ** *teredaei*
**perch** *(n.)* **ልዕል ዝበለ** *lel zbele*
**percipient** *(adj.)* **መስተውዓሊ** *mestewali*
**percolate** *(v.)* **ልሒኹ** *lhiku*
**percolator** *(n.)* **ዘቛቒት ቡን** *zequaqit bun*
**perdition** *(n.)* **ሴኦል** *sieol*
**perennial** *(adj.)* **ጸናሒ** *xenahi*
**perfect** *(adj.)* **ፍጹም** *fxum*
**perfection** *(n.)* **ፍጹምነት** *fxumnet*
**perfidious** *(adj.)* **መታለሊ** *metaleli*

**perforate** *(v.)* በሳሲዑ *besasieu*
**perforce** *(adv. )* ናይ ንግዲ *nay ngdi*
**perform** *(v.)* ምትግባር *mtgbar*
**performance** *(n.)* ትግባሬ *tgbarie*
**performer** *(n. )* ኣተግባሪ/ምረኢት ኣርኣዪ *ategbari/mreit arayi*
**perfume** *(n.)* ጨና *chena*
**perfume** *(adv. )* ጨና ምልካይ *chena mlkay*
**perfunctory** *(adj.)* ካብ ክሳድ ንላዕሊ *kab ksad nlaeli*
**perhaps** *(adv. )* ምናልባሽ *mnalbash*
**peril** *(n.)* ሓደጋ *hadega*
**perilous** *(adj.)* ሓደገኛ *hadegena*
**period** *(n. )* እዋን/ዘበን *ewan/zeben*
**periodic** *(adj.)* እዋናዊ/ዘበናዊ *ewanawi/zebenawi*
**periodical** *(adj.)* እዋናዊ/ዘበናዊ *ewanawi/zebenawi*
**periphery** *(n.)* ጨጫፍ *chechaf*
**perish** *(v.)* ሞይቱ/መሽሚሹ *moytu/meshmishu*
**perishable** *(adj.)* ተበላሻዋይ *tebalashaway*
**perjure** *(v.)* ብሓሶት ምምስካር *bhasot mmskar*
**perjury** *(n. )* ብሓሶት ምምሓል *bhasot mmhal*
**perk** *(v.)* ምስራሕ *msrah*
**perky** *(adj.)* ንቑሕ *nquh*
**permanence** *(n.)* ቀዋምነት *qewamnet*
**permanent** *(adj.)* ቀዋሚ *qwami*
**permeable** *(adj.)* ማይ ዝወጥጥ *may zwett*
**permissible** *(adj.)* ዝፍቀድ *zfqed*
**permission** *(n.)* ፍቓድ *fqad*
**permissive** *(adj.)* ዝናሕነሐ *znahnehe*
**permit** *(v.)* ኣፍቀደ *afqede*
**permutation** *(n.)* ኣለዋዊጥካ ምቕማጥ *alewawitka mqmat*
**pernicious** *(adj.)* ጠንቂ *tenqi*
**perpendicular** *(adj.)* ቀጥ በለ *qet bele*
**perpetrate** *(v.)* ገበን ምፍጻም *geben mfxam*
**perpetual** *(adj.)* መፈጸምታ ዘይብሉ *mefexemta zeyblu*
**perpetuate** *(v.t. )* ሓሊኻ ምጽናሕ *halika mxnae*
**perplex** *(v.)* ኣደናጊሩ *adenagiru*
**perplexity** *(n.)* ምድንጋር *mdngar*
**perquisite** *(n.)* ካብ መሃያ ወጻኢ ዝርከብ *kab mehaya wexaei zrkeb*
**Perry** *(n.)* ስም ከተማ *sm ketema*
**persecute** *(v.)* ምጽቃጥ *mxqat*
**persecution** *(n. )* ቈጸራ ከዋኽብቲ *qoxera kewakbti*
**perseverance** *(n.)* ድሕር ዘይምባል *dhr zeymbal*
**persevere** *(v.i. )* ንድሕሪት ዘይብል *ndhrit zeybl*
**persist** *(v.)* ጸንዐ *xene*
**persistence** *(n.)* ምጽናዕ *mxnae*
**persistent** *(adj.)* ጽኑዕ *xnue*
**person** *(n. )* ሰብ *seb*
**persona** *(n.)* ገጸ ባህሪ *gexe bahri*
**personage** *(n.)* ህቡብ ሰብ *hbub seb*
**personal** *(adj.)* ብሕታዊ *bhtawi*
**personality** *(n.)* ጠባይ *tebay*
**personification** *(n.)* ኣብነትነት *abnetnet*
**personify** *(v.)* ኣብነታዊ *abnetawi*

**personnel** *(n.)* **ሰራሕተኛታት** *serahtenatat*
**perspective** *(n. )* **ሓሳባት** *hasabat*
**perspicuous** *(adj.)* **ርዱእ** *rdue*
**perspiration** *(n.)* **ርሃጽ** *rhax*
**perspire** *(v.t. )* **ምርሃጽ** *mrhax*
**persuade** *(v.)* **ኣእመነ** *aemene*
**persuasion** *(n.)* **ምእማን** *meman*
**pertain** *(v.)* **ጠቓሚ/ኣባል ሙኳን** *teqami/abal mukuan*
**pertinent** *(adj.)* **ኣድላዪ** *adlayi*
**perturb** *(v.)* **ሃዊኹ** *hawiku*
**perusal** *(n.)* **ብጥንቃቐ ምንባብ** *btnqaqe mnbab*
**peruse** *(v.)* **ብጥንቃቐ ኣንቢቡ** *btnqaqe anbibu*
**pervade** *(v.)* **በኪሉ** *bekilu*
**perverse** *(adj.)* **ህልኽ** *hlk*
**perversion** *(n.)* **ምውራድ** *mwrad*
**perversity** *(n.)* **ህልኸኛ** *hlkena*
**pervert** *(v.)* **መገዲ ምቕያር** *megedi mqyar*
**pessimism** *(n. )* **ቅኑዕ ዘይምሕሳብ** *qnue zeymhsab*
**pessimist** *(n.)* **ቅኑዕ ዘይሓስብ** *qnuo hasab*
**pessimistic** *(adj.)* **ተስፋ ዘይምግባር** *tesfa zeymgbar*
**pest** *(n. )* **ባልዕ** *ble*
**pester** *(v.)* **ምርባሽ** *mrbash*
**pesticide** *(n. )* **ጸረ ባልዕ** *xere ble*
**pestilence** *(n. )* **ተላባዒ** *telabaei*
**pet** *(n.)* **ናይ ገዛ እንስሳ** *nay geza enssa*
**petal** *(n. )* **ክፋል ዕንባባ** *kfal onbaba*
**petite** *(adj.)* **ቀጣን/ነእሽቶ** *qetan/neshto*
**petition** *(n.)* **ጥርዓን** *tran*
**petitioner** *(n. )* **ጠራዓይ** *teraay*
**petrify** *(v.)* **ኣንቂጹ** *anqixu*
**petrol** *(n. )* **በንዚን** *benzin*
**petroleum** *(n. )* **ነዳዲ ዘይቲ** *nedadi zyti*
**petticoat** *(n.)* **ንይ ውሽጢ ክዳን** *nay wshti kdan*
**pettish** *(adj.)* **ሕማቕ ጠባይ** *hmaq tebay*
**petty** *(adj.)* **ዘይረብሕ** *zeyrebh*
**petulance** *(n.)* **ኲራ** *kuara*
**petulant** *(adj.)* **ኮርፋፍ** *korfaf*
**phantom** *(n. )* **ረቂቕ መንፈስ** *reqiq menfes*
**pharmaceutical** *(adj.)* **መድሃኒታዊ** *medhanitawi*
**pharmacist** *(n.)* **ቀማሚ መድሃኒት** *qemami medhanit*
**pharmacy** *(n. )* **ቤት መድሃኒት** *biet medhanit*
**phase** *(n.)* **ደረጃ** *dereja*
**phenomenal** *(adj.)* **ክስተታዊ** *kstetawi*
**phenomenon** *(n. )* **ክስተት** *kstet*
**phial** *(n.)* **ብልቃጥ** *blqat*
**philanthropic** *(adj.)* **ወሃቢ** *wehabi*
**philanthropist** *(n. )* **ግብረ ሰናያዊ** *gbresenayawi*
**philanthropy** *(n.)* **ግብረ ሰናይ** *gbre senay*
**philately** *(n.)* **ቴንብር ዓቃቢ** *tienbr aqabi*
**philological** *(adj.)* **ናይ ዛንታ ስነ ጽሑፍ** *nay zanta sne xhuf*
**philologist** *(n.)* **ስነ ጽሑፋዊ ዛንታ** *sne xhufawi zanta*
**philology** *(n.)* **ስነ ጽሑፍ ዛንታ** *sne xhufawi zanta*

**philosopher** *(n.)* ተፈላሳፊ *tefelasafi*
**philosophical** *(adj.)* ፍልስፍናዊ *flsfnawi*
**philosophy** *(n.)* ፍንስፍና *flsfna*
**phlegmatic** *(adj.)* ግዲ ዘይብሉ *gdi zeyblu*
**phobia** *(n.)* ፍቮያ *fovya*
**phoenix** *(n.)* ፊኒክስ *fneks*
**phone** *(n.)* ስልኪ *seli*
**phonetic** *(adj.)* መጽናዕቲ ድምጺ ልሳን *mexnaeti dmxi lsan*
**phosphate** *(n. )* ፎዝፌት *fozfeyet*
**phosphorus** *(n.)* ናይ ንግሆ ኮኾብ *nay ngho kokob*
**photo** *(n.)* ስእሊ *seli*
**photocopy** *(n.)* ፍቶ ኮፒ *foto kopi*
**photograph** *(n.)* ስእሊ *seli*
**photographer** *(n.)* ሰኣሊ *seali*
**photographic** *(adj.)* ስእላዊ *selawi*
**photography** *(n.)* ጥበብ ስእሊ *tbeb seli*
**photostat** *(n.)* ፎቶ ኮፒ *foto kopi*
**phrase** *(n.)* ሓረግ *hareg*
**phraseology** *(n.)* ኣዘራርባ *azerarba*
**physical** *(adj.)* ኣካላዊ ተፈጥሮ *akalawi tefetro*
**physician** *(n.)* ፈዋሲ *fewasi*
**physics** *(n.)* ፊዚክስ *fizkis*
**physiognomy** *(n.)* ደጋዊ ትረኢት *degawi treit*
**physiotherapy** *(n.)* ፊዝዮተራፒ *fizyoterapi*
**physique** *(n.)* መሸከል *meshekel*
**pianist** *(n.)* ተጻዋታይ ፒያኖ *texawatay piyano*
**piano** *(n.)* ፒያኖ *piyano*
**piazza** *(n.)* በረንዳ *beranda*
**pick** *(v.)* ኣልዓለ *alale*
**picket** *(n.)* ሰላማዊ ሰልፊ ጌሩ *selemawi selfi gieru*
**pickings** *(n. )* ምልዓል *mlal*
**pickle** *(n.)* ከቢድ ኩነታት *kebidkunetat*
**picnic** *(n.)* ኣብ ደገ ዝብላዕ መኣዲ *ab dege zblae meadi*
**pictograph** *(n.)* ስእላዊ መግለጺ *selawi meglexi*
**pictorial** *(adj.)* ንስእሊ ዝምልከት *asali zmlket*
**picture** *(n.)* ስእሊ/ፊልም *seli/filmi*
**picturesque** *(adj.)* ምሩጽ ስእሊ *mrux seli*
**pie** *(n.)* ፓይ *pay*
**piece** *(n.)* ጭራም *chram*
**piecemeal** *(adv. )* በብቁሩብ *bebequrub*
**pier** *(n.)* ናይ ወደብ መድረኽ *nay wedeb mdreke*
**pierce** *(v.)* ሱቕሬን *suqren*
**piety** *(n. )* ሃይማኖተኛ *haymanotena*
**pig** *(n. )* ሓሸማ *hashema*
**pigeon** *(n. )* ርግቢት *rgbit*
**pigeonhole** *(n.)* ናይ ደብዳበ መግለጺ *nay debdabe mglexi*
**piggery** *(n.)* መፍረ ሓሰማ *mfre hasema*
**pigment** *(n.)* ሕብሪ ዋሃዮ *hbri wahiyo*
**pigmy** *(n. )* ድንኪ *dnki*
**pike** *(n.)* ጭማራ *čmara*
**pile** *(n. )* ኩምራ *kumra*
**pilfer** *(v.)* ምስራቕ *msraq*

**pilgrim** *(n. )* ሃይማኖታዊ ቦታታት ዝበጽሕ *haymanotawi botatat zbxh*
**pilgrimage** *(n. )* ንግደት *ngdet*
**pill** *(n. )* ከኒና *kenina*
**pillar** *(n.)* ዓምዲ *amdi*
**pillow** *(n.)* መተርኣስ *meteras*
**pilot** *(n.)* ፓይሎት *paylot*
**pimple** *(n.)* ፈጸጋ *fexega*
**pin** *(n.)* ዓይኒ ዘይብሉ መርፍእ *ayni zeyblu mefe*
**pincer** *(n.)* ወረጦ *wereto*
**pinch** *(v. )* ቆንጠጠ *qontete*
**pine** *(v.)* ሃረፈ *harefe*
**pineapple** *(n. )* ኣናናስ *ananas*
**pink** *(adj.)* ሮዛ *roza*
**pinnacle** *(n. )* ሓፍ ዝበለ ብርኪ *ȟaf zbele brki*
**pinpoint** *(v.)* ብልክዕ ምምልካት *bmelke mmlkat*
**pint** *(n.)* 1/8 ጃሎን *1/8 jalon*
**pioneer** *(n.)* ቀዳምነት ዝሓዘ *qedamnety zhaze*
**pious** *(adj.)* ዘይሰምር *zeysemr*
**pipe** *(n.)* ትቦ *tubo*
**pipette** *(n.)* ምንቅስቓስ ፈሳሲ ዝጠቅም መሳርሒ *mnqsqas fesasi zẗekm mesarȟi*
**piquant** *(adj.)* ሰሓቢ *seȟabi*
**pique** *(n.)* ስምዒት ሕማም *smeit hmam*
**piracy** *(n. )* ኣብ ባሕሪ ስርቂ *ab bahri srqi*
**pirate** *(n.)* ገበንነኛ ኣብ ባሕሪ ዝዝርፍ *gebenǹa ab baȟri zzrf*
**pistol** *(n. )* ሽጉጥ *shguẗ*
**piston** *(n. )* ፒስቶን *piston*
**pit** *(n.)* ጉድጓድ *gudgad*
**pitch** *(n.)* ኣገዳሲ ኣካል *agedasi akal*
**pitcher** *(n.)* የእታዊ *yeètawi*
**piteous** *(adj.)* ዘሕዝን *zeȟzn*
**pitfall** *(n.)* ዘይፍለጥ ጸገም *zeyflet xegem*
**pitiful** *(adj.)* ዘደንግጽ *zedengx*
**pitiless** *(adj.)* ድንጋጸ ዘይብሉ *dngaxe zeyblu*
**pity** *(n.)* ድንጋጸ *dngaxe*
**pivot** *(n.)* ተሽከርኪሩ *teshkerkiru*
**pivotal** *(adj.)* ተሽከርካሪ *teshkerkari*
**pixel** *(n.)* ስእሊ ዝፈጥር ንሽተይ ነጠብጣብ ኣብ ኮምፒተር *sèli zfeẗr nèshtey neẗebẗab nay kompiter*
**pizza** *(n.)* ፒሳ *pisa*
**placard** *(n.)* ሓበሬታ *ȟberieta*
**placate** *(v.)* ምዝሓል *maȟzel*
**place** *(n.)* መንበሪ ቦታ *menberi bot*
**placement** *(n.)* መቀመጢ *meqemeẗ*
**placid** *(adj.)* ሰላማዊ *selamawi*
**plague** *(n.)* ለበዳ *lebeda*
**plain** *(adj.)* ጎልጎል *golgol*
**plaintiff** *(n. )* ከሳሳይ *kesasy*
**plaintive** *(adj.)* ናይ ሓዘን *nay hazen*
**plait** *(n.)* ቁኖ *quno*
**plan** *(n.)* መደብ *medeb*
**plane** *(n.)* ነፋሪት *nefarit*
**planet** *(n.)* ፕላኔት *planiet*
**planetary** *(adj.)* ናይ ፕላኔታት *nay planatan*
**plank** *(n.)* ደጋፊ *degafi*
**plant** *(n. )* ተኽሊ *teǩli*
**plantain** *(n. )* ፕላንተይን *planteyn*

**plantation** ***(n. )*** **ተኽሊ ዝተተኽለሉ ቦታ** *teḱli zteteḱlelu bota*
**plaque** ***(n.)*** **ብእምኒ ዝተቐርጸ መጋየጺ** *bèmni zteq̈erexe megayexi*
**plaster** ***(n.)*** **መለጠፊ** *meleẗfi*
**plastic** ***(n.)*** **ፕላስቲክ** *plastik*
**plate** ***(n.)*** **ቢያቲ** *biyati*
**plateau** ***(n.)*** **ሮራ** *rora*
**platelet** ***(n.)*** **ፕላተሌት** *planiet*
**platform** ***(n.)*** **መድረኽ** *medreḱ*
**platinum** ***(n.)*** **ሕብሪ ሓጺን** *ḧbri ḧxin*
**platonic** ***(adj.)*** **ዘይጾታዊ ርክብ** *zeyxotawi ckb*
**platoon** ***(n. )*** **ሰብ ኣልቦ ተሸከርከርቲ** *seb anbo teshkerkerti*
**platter** ***(n.)*** **ጸፊሕ ሸሓኒ** *xefiḧ sheḧani*
**plaudits** ***(n.)*** **ምንጭብጫብ** *mnčbčab*
**plausible** ***(adj.)*** **ብቑዕ** *bq̈uë*
**play** ***(v.i. )*** **ጸወታ** *xeweta*
**player** ***(n. )*** **ተጻዋታይ** *texawatay*
**playground** ***(n.)*** **መጽጸወቲ ቦታ** *mexaweti bota*
**playwright** ***(n.)*** **ጸሓፊ ቲያትር** *xeḧafi tyatr*
**plaza** ***(n.)*** **ክፉት መአከቢ ቦታ** *kfut makebi bota*
**plea** ***(n.)*** **ምኽንያት** *mḱnyat*
**plead** ***(v.)*** **ምግላጽ ምጉት** *mglax mgut*
**pleasant** ***(adj.)*** **ፍሕሹው** *fḧshuwnet*
**pleasantry** ***(n.)*** **ናይ ቀልዲ ኣዘራርባ** *nay qeldi azerazba*
**please** ***(v.)*** **ብኽብረት** *bḱbret*
**pleasure** ***(n. )*** **ፍስሃ** *fsha*
**pleat** ***(n.)*** **ሸንሸነ** *shenshene*
**plebeian** ***(adj.)*** **ናይ ሓባር ሰብ** *nay ḧabar seb*
**plebiscite** ***(n. )*** **ሪፈረንዶም** *riferendom*
**pledge** ***(n.)*** **ቃል ምእታው** *qal mètaw*
**plenty** ***(n.)*** **ዕጽፊ** *ëxfi*
**plethora** ***(n.)*** **ምልኡነት** *mleunet*
**pliable** ***(adj.)*** **ተዓጻጻፊ** *teëaxaxafi*
**pliant** ***(adj.)*** **ተዓጻፊ** *teëaxaxafi*
**pliers** ***(n.)*** **ፒንሳ** *pinsa*
**plight** ***(n.)*** **ጽቡቕ ጥዕና** *xbuq̈ ẗëna*
**plinth** ***(n.)*** **ሰረት** *seret*
**plod** ***(v.)*** **ዝሑል ምንቅስቓስ** *zḧul mnqsqas*
**plot** ***(n.)*** **ምስእጢራዊ መደብ** *msẗirawi medeb*
**plough** ***(n.)*** **ምሕራስ** *mḧrasq̈a*
**ploughman** ***(n.)*** **ሓረስታይ** *ḧarestay*
**ploy** ***(n.)*** **ስርሒት** *srḧit*
**pluck** ***(v.)*** **መሸጎጥ/ብሓይሊ ምውጻእ** *meshgoẗ /bḧayli*
**plug** ***(n.)*** **ሶኬት** *sokiet*
**plum** ***(n. )*** **ካብ ክንቲት ዝተሰርሐ መጋየጺ** *kab kntit zteserḧe*
**plumage** ***(n.)*** **ክንቲት ዑፍ** *kntit ëuf*
**plumb** ***(v.)*** **ዓረር** *ärer*
**plumber** ***(n.)*** **ድራውሊኮ** *drawliko*
**plume** ***(n.)*** **ሓፋር** *ḧafar*
**plummet** ***(v.)*** **ምንቛት** *mnq̈uat*
**plump** ***(adj.)*** **ረጒድ** *reguied*
**plunder** ***(v.)*** **ዘረፋ** *zerefa*
**plunge** ***(v.)*** **ተደቕደቐ** *tedeq̈deq̈e*
**plural** ***(adj.)*** **ካብ ሓደ ንላዕሊ** *kab ḧde alaëli*

**plurality** *(n.)* **ድራብነት** *drabnet*
**plus** *(n.)* **ተደመሮ** *tedemero*
**plush** *(n.)* **ክቡር** *kbur*
**ply** *(n.)* **ቀጸላ** *qexela*
**pneumatic** *(adj.)* **ኣየር ዝመስል** *ayer zmesl*
**pneumonia** *(n. )* **ነድሪ ሳንቡእ** *nedri sanbuè*
**poach** *(v.)* **ልስሉስ ሙኳን** *lslus mukuan*
**pocket** *(n.)* **ጁባ** *ĵuba*
**pod** *(n. )* **ለቆታ** *leqota*
**podcast** *(n.)* **ፖድካስት** *podkast*
**podium** *(n.)* **መድረኽ** *medreḱ*
**poem** *(n. )* **ግጥሚ** *gẗmi*
**poet** *(n.)* **ገጣሚ** *geẗami*
**poetry** *(n. )* **ፍርያት ግጥሚ** *fryat gẗmi*
**poignancy** *(n.)* **ኣደንጋጽነት** *adengaxnet*
**poignant** *(adj.)* **ስምዒት ዘንቀሳቕስ** *smëit zenqesaqs*
**point** *(n.)* **ነጥቢ/ኣመልክት** *neẗbi/amelkt*
**pointing** *(n.)* **ምምልካት** *mmlkat*
**pointless** *(adj.)* **ትርጉም ዘይብሉ** *trgum zeyblu*
**poise** *(n.)* **ብዘይ ምንቅስቓስ** *bzey mnqsq̈as*
**poison** *(n.)* **መርዚ** *wečeče merzi*
**poisonous** *(adj.)* **መርዛም** *merzam*
**poke** *(v.)* **ምውጋእ** *mwgai*
**poker** *(n. )* **ወጋኢ** *weraei*
**poky** *(adj.)* **ጸቢብ** *xebib*
**polar** *(adj.)* **ናይ ዕንጨይቲ** *nay ënčeyti*
**pole** *(n. )* **ፓሎ/ዕንጨይቲ** *palo/ënčeyti*
**polemic** *(n.)* **ምጉት** *mgut*
**police** *(n. )* **ፖሊስ** *polis*
**policeman** *(n. )* **ፖሊስ** *polis*
**policy** *(n.)* **መምርሒ** *memrḧi*
**polish** *(n.)* **ምውልዋል/ፖላንዳዊ** *mwlwal/polandawi*
**polite** *(adj.)* **ምቕሉል** *mq̈lul*
**politeness** *(n.)* **ምቕልልና** *gemel*
**politic** *(adj.)* **ናይ ፖለቲካ** *nay polotika*
**political** *(adj.)* **ፖለቲካዊ** *polotikawi*
**politician** *(n.)* **ፖለቲከኛ** *poletikeňa*
**politics** *(n.)* **ፖለቲክስ** *poletiks*
**polity** *(n.)* **ፖለቲቻዊ ጥርናፈ** *poletikeňawi ẗrnafe*
**poll** *(n.)* **መምረጺ ቦታ** *memrexi bota*
**pollen** *(n.)* **ጽገ ዕንባባ** *xge ënbaba*
**pollster** *(n.)* **ምርጫ ዘካይድ** *mrča zekayd*
**pollute** *(v.)* **ምብካል** *mbkal*
**pollution** *(n.)* **ብከላ** *bkela*
**polo** *(n.)* **ፖሎ** *palo*
**polyandry** *(n.)* **ብሓደ ግዜ ልዕሊ ሓደ ሰብኣይ ትምርዖ ሰበይቲ** *bḧde gzie lëli ḧade gzie sebay tmräw sebeyti*
**polygamous** *(adj.)* **ብሓደ ግዜ ልዕሊ ሓደ ሰብኣይ/ሰበይቲ ተመርዓዊ** *bḧde gzie lëli ḧade gzie sebay/sebeti temeräwi*
**polygamy** *(n. )* **ብሓደ ግዜ ልዕሊ ሓደ ሰብኣይ/ሰበይቲ ምምርዓው** *bḧde gzie lëli ḧade gzie sebay/sebeti mmräw*
**polyglot** *(adj.)* **ብዙሕ ቋንቋ ዝዛረብ** *bzuḧ quanq̈a zzareb*

**polygraph** *(n.)* ፖሊግራፍ *poligraf*
**polytechnic** *(n. )* ትምህርቲ ቴክኖሎጂ *tmhrti tieknoloĵi*
**polytheism** *(n. )* ንዝዙሓት ኣማልኽቲ ምምላኽ *nbzuḧat amalḱti mmlaḱ*
**polytheistic** *(adj.)* ንብዙሓት ኣማልኽቲ ዘምልኽ *nbzuḧat amalḱti zemlḱ*
**pomegranate** *(n.)* ጸሊም ቀይሕ ሕብሪ *xelim qeyḧ ḧbri*
**pomp** *(n. )* ድሙቕ ውራይ *dmuq̈ wray*
**pomposity** *(n.)* ጃህራ *ĵhra*
**pompous** *(adj.)* ምጅሃር *mĵhar*
**pond** *(n.)* ራህያ *rahya*
**ponder** *(v.)* ኣመዛዚነ *amezazene*
**pontiff** *(n.)* ቀሺ *qeshi*
**pony** *(n.)* ቅንጁብ ፈረስ *qnxub feres*
**pool** *(n.)* ንእሽተይ ቐላይ *mlkt neshtey q̈lay*
**poor** *(adj.)* ድኻ *dḱa*
**poorly** *(adv. )* ዘይእኹል ናብራ *zeyèḱul nabra*
**pop** *(v.)* ተጒ ምባል *tegiue mbal*
**pope** *(n. )* ጳጳስ *ṕapas*
**poplar** *(n. )* ፖፕላር *potlar*
**poplin** *(n. )* ዓይነት ጨርቂ *äynet čerqi*
**populace** *(n.)* ደቀ ባት *deqi bat*
**popular** *(adj.)* ተፈታዊ *tefetawi*
**popularity** *(n.)* ተፈታውነት *tefetawnet*
**popularize** *(v.)* ተፈታዊ ምግባር *tefetawi mgbar*
**populate** *(v.)* ምብዛሕ *mbzaḧ*
**population** *(n.)* ብዝሒ ህዝቢ *bzḧi hzbi*
**populous** *(adj.)* ብዙሕ ህዝቢ ዘለዎ *bzuḧ hzbi zelewo*
**porcelain** *(n.)* ሰራሕ ሸኽላ *sraḧ shḱla*
**porch** *(n.)* በረንዳ *berenda*
**porcupine** *(n.)* ቅንፍዝ *qnfz*
**pore** *(n. )* ናይ ቆርበት ኖኳል *nay qorbet noḱual*
**pork** *(n. )* ስጋ ሓሰማ *sga ḧasema*
**pornography** *(n.)* ፖርኖግራፊ *pornografi*
**porridge** *(n. )* ገዓት *geät*
**port** *(n.)* ወደብ *wedeb*
**portable** *(adj.)* ቀሊል *qelil*
**portage** *(n. )* ፖርቴጅ *portieĵ*
**portal** *(n.)* ኣፍደገ *afdege*
**portend** *(v.)* መጠንቀቒ *meẗenqeq̈i*
**portent** *(n.)* ምልክት *mlkt*
**porter** *(n. )* ረፋዕ *refaë*
**portfolio** *(n. )* መትሓዚ ገንዘብ *metḧazi genzeb*
**portico** *(n.)* መእተዊ ማዕጾ *meètewi maëxo*
**portion** *(n.)* ብጽሒት *bẗḧit*
**portrait** *(n. )* ቅብኣ *qba*
**portraiture** *(n.)* ቅብኣ ምቅባእ *qba mqbaè*
**portray** *(v.)* ቀብአ *qeba*
**portrayal** *(n.)* ምቅባእ *mqbaè*
**pose** *(v.)* ጠጠው ምባል *ẗeẗew mbal*
**posh** *(adj.)* ግሩም *grum*
**posit** *(v.)* ምቕማጥ *mq̈maẗ*
**position** *(n.)* ኣቀማምጣ *aqemamẗ*
**positive** *(adj.)* ኣወንታዊ *awentawi*
**possess** *(v.)* ወነነ *wenene*

**possession** *(n. )* ዋንነት *wannet*
**possessive** *(adj.)* ኣጋናዛቢ *aganazabi*
**possibility** *(n.)* ዝከኣል *zkeal*
**possible** *(adj.)* ተኽእሎ *teḱèlo*
**post** *(n.)* ምልጣፍ *mlẗaf*
**post office** *(n.)* ፖስጣ ቤት *posẗa biet*
**postage** *(n.)* ዋጋ ቴንብር *waga tienbr*
**postal** *(adj.)* ብፖስጣ *bposẗa*
**postcard** *(n.)* ካርተሊና *kartelina*
**postcode** *(n.)* ቁጽሪ ፖስጣ *quxri posẗ*
**poster** *(n. )* ፖስተር *poster*
**posterior** *(adj.)* መቐመጫ *meq̈emeča*
**posterity** *(n.)* ሰዓብቲ ወለዶ *seäabti weledo*
**postgraduate** *(n.)* ሕላፍ መመረቕታ *ḧlaf memereq̈ta*
**posthumous** *(adj.)* ደድሕሪ ሞት *dedḧri mot*
**postman** *(n.)* እንዳ ፖስጣ ዝሰርሕ *ènda posẗ zserḧ*
**postmaster** *(n.)* ምሕደራ እንዳ ፖስጣ *mḧdera ènda posẗa*
**post-mortem** *(n. )* መርመራ ኣስከሬን *mermera askegrien*
**postpone** *(v.)* ኣተሓላሊፉ *ateḧalalifu*
**postponement** *(n. )* ምትሕልላፍ *mtḧllaf*
**postscript** *(n. )* ድሕሪ መወዳእታ ዛንታ *dḧri mewedaèta zanta*
**posture** *(n. )* ኣቃውማ *aqawma*
**pot** *(n .)* ዕትሮ *ëtro*
**potato** *(n. )* ድንሽ *dnsh*
**potency** *(n.)* ዓቕሚ *äq̈mi*
**potent** *(adj.)* ዘተኣማምን *zeteamamn*
**potential** *(adj.)* ዓቕሚ *äq̈mi*
**potentiality** *(n. )* ዝብጻሕ ነገር *zbxaḧ neger*
**potter** *(v.)* ሰራሕ ካይላ *sraḧ kayla*
**pottery** *(n. )* ስርሓት ካይላ *srḧat kayla*
**pouch** *(n. )* ከረጢት *kereẗit*
**poultry** *(n.)* መፍረ ኣዕዋፍ *mefre aëwaf*
**pounce** *(v.)* ሃንደበት ምንጣር *handebet mnẗar*
**pound** *(n.)* ባጤራ እንግሊዝ *baẗiera èngliz*
**pour** *(v.)* ምቕዳሕ *mq̈daḧ*
**poverty** *(n. )* ድኽነት *dḱnet*
**powder** *(n.)* ሕሩጭ *ḧruč*
**power** *(n.)* ሓይሊ *ḧyli*
**powerful** *(adj.)* ሓያል *ḧeyal*
**practicability** *(n.)* ግብራውነት *gbrawnet*
**practicable** *(adj.)* ግብራዊ ዝኾነ *gbrawi zḱone*
**practical** *(adj.)* ግብራዊ *gbrawi*
**practice** *(n.)* ተግባር *tegbar*
**practise** *(v.)* ተላመደ *telamede*
**practitioner** *(n.)* ተላማዲ *telamadi*
**pragmatic** *(adj.)* ብእምነት ዘይኮነ ብኩነታት ዝሰርሕ *bèmnet zeykone bkunetat zserḧ*
**pragmatism** *(n. )* ፕራግማውነት *pragmawnet*
**praise** *(v.t. )* ምስጋና *msgana*
**praline** *(n.)* ፕራላይን *pralayn*
**pram** *(n.)* ጅረሎ *ĵrelo*
**prank** *(n.)* ምዝንጋዕ *mzngaë*
**prattle** *(v.)* ሃተፍተፍ *hateftef*

**pray** ***(v.)*** **ምጽላይ** *mxlay*
**prayer** ***(n.)*** **ጸሎት** *xelot*
**preach** ***(v.)*** **ምስባኽ** *msbaḱ*
**preacher** ***(n.)*** **ሰባኺ** *sebaḱi*
**preamble** ***(n. )*** **መቕድም** *meq̈dm*
**precarious** ***(adj.)*** **ዘየተኣማምን** *zeyeteamamn*
**precaution** ***(n.)*** **ጥንቃቐ** *ïnqaq̈e*
**precautionary** ***(adj.)*** **ጥንቃቓዊ** *ïnqaq̈awi*
**precede** ***(v.)*** **ኣቐዲሙ** *aq̈edimu*
**precedence** ***(n. )*** **ቀዳምነት** *qedemanet*
**precedent** ***(n. )*** **ምሳሌ ዘረኢ** *msalie zereei*
**precept** ***(n. )*** **ምኽሪ** *mḱri*
**precinct** ***(n.)*** **ክልል** *kll*
**precious** ***(adj.)*** **ብርቂ** *brqi*
**precipitate** ***(v.)*** **ኣንከባሊሉ** *ankebalilu*
**precis** ***(n. )*** **ኩምራ ማይን በረድን** *kumra mayn beredn*
**precise** ***(adj.)*** **ልክዕ** *lkë*
**precision** ***(n. )*** **ልክዕነት** *lkënet*
**precognition** ***(n.)*** **ናይ መጻኢ ፍልጠት** *nay mexaei flïet*
**precondition** ***(n.)*** **ቅድመ ኹነት** *qdme kunet*
**precursor** ***(n. )*** **ዘበስር** *zebesr*
**predator** ***(n.)*** **ሃዳኒ እንስሳ** *hadali ènssa*
**predecessor** ***(n. )*** **ናይ ቀደም** *nay qedem*
**predestination** ***(n.)*** **ጽሕፍቶ** *xḧfto*
**predetermine** ***(v.)*** **ቅድመ ውሳነ** *qdme wsane*
**predicament** ***(n. )*** **ኣሸጋሪ ኩነታት** *ashegari kunetat*
**predicate** ***(n.)*** **ኣንቀጸ** *anqexe*
**predict** ***(v.)*** **ተነበየ** *tenebeye*
**prediction** ***(n.)*** **ትንቢት** *tnbit*
**predominance** ***(n.)*** **ቅድመ ዓብላልነት** *qdme äblalnet*
**predominant** ***(adj.)*** **ቅድመ ዓብላላዊ** *qdme äblalawi*
**predominate** ***(v.)*** **ቅድመ ምዕብላል** *qdme mëblal*
**pre-eminence** ***(n.)*** **ብልጫዊ** *blčawi*
**pre-eminent** ***(adj.)*** **ብልጫ** *blča*
**pre-empt** ***(v.)*** **ቀዲሙ ሒዙ** *qedimu ḧizu*
**prefabricated** ***(adj.)*** **ቀዲሙ ዝተሰርሐ** *qedimu zteserḧe*
**preface** ***(n.)*** **መባእታ** *mebaèta*
**prefect** ***(n.)*** **ኮማንደር** *komander*
**prefer** ***(v.)*** **መረጸ** *merexe*
**preference** ***(n.)*** **ምርጫ** *mrča*
**preferential** ***(adj.)*** **ምርጫዊ** *mrčawi*
**preferment** ***(n.)*** **ሹመት** *shumet*
**prefix** ***(n.)*** **ለቀበ** *leqebe*
**pregnancy** ***(n.)*** **ጥንሲ** *ïnsi*
**pregnant** ***(adj.)*** **ጥንስቲ** *ïnsti*
**prehistoric** ***(adj.)*** **ቅድመ ታሪኽ** *qdme tariḱi*
**prejudge** ***(v.)*** **ቅድመ ፍርዲ** *qdme frdi*
**prejudice** ***(n. )*** **ኣገባብ ዘይብሉ ጽለኢ** *agebab zeyblu xlei*
**prejudicial** ***(adj.)*** **ሃሳዪ** *hasayi*
**prelate** ***(n.)*** **ላዕለዋይ ቀሺ** *laëleway qeshi*
**preliminary** ***(adj.)*** **ኣገዳሲ/ኣላላዪ** *agedasi/alalayi*
**prelude** ***(n.)*** **ድሮ** *dro*
**premarital** ***(adj.)*** *qdme merä*

**premature** *(adj.)* **ግዜኡ ዘይበጽሐ** *gzieeu zeybexḧe*

**premeditate** *(v.)* **አቀዲምካ ምሕሳብ** *aqedimka mḧsab*

**premeditation** *(n.)* **ቀዲምካ ምምዳብ** *qedimka mmdab*

**premier** *(adj.)* **ቀዳማይ /ላዕለዋይ** *qedamay/laëleway*

**premiere** *(n. )* **ቀዳማይ ፈነወ ፊልሚ** *qedamay felewe filmi*

**premise** *(n.)* **ኣቐዲሙ ዝተረቑሐ መሰረት ምጉት** *aq̈edimu ztereq̈uḧ meseret mgut*

**premises** *(n.)* **ኣቐዲሞም ዝተረቑሑ መሰረት ምጉት** *aq̈edimom ztereq̈uḧ meseret mgut*

**premium** *(n. )* **ዝለዓለ ሽልማት** *zleäale shlmat*

**premonition** *(n. )* **ሕማቅ ስምዒት** *ḧmaq smëit*

**preoccupation** *(n.)* **ዘሕስብ ነገር** *zeḧsb neger*

**preoccupy** *(v.)* **ምርስሳዕ** *mrssaë*

**preparation** *(n.)* **ምድላው** *mdlaw*

**preparatory** *(adj.)* **ቅድመ ምድላው** *qdme mdlaw*

**prepare** *(v.)* **ኣዳለወ** *adalewe*

**preponderance** *(n.)* **ካብ ኩሉ ዝበለጸ** *kab kulu zbelexe*

**preponderate** *(v.)* **ካብ ኩሉ በሊጹ** *kab kulu belixu*

**preposition** *(n.)* **መስተዋድድ** *mestewadd*

**prepossessing** *(adj.)* **ተፈታዊ** *tefetawi*

**preposterous** *(adj.)* **ዓንጀንጀል** *änĵelĵel*

**prerequisite** *(n.)* **ቅድመ ኹነት** *qdmi ḱunet*

**prerogative** *(n. )* **ስልጣን** *qdme*

**presage** *(v.)* **ከም ዝመጽእ ሓበረ** *kem zmexè ḧbere*

**prescience** *(n.)* **ፍልጠት ቅድመ ፍጻሜ** *flẗet qdme fxamie*

**prescribe** *(v.)* **ኣዘዘ** *azeze*

**prescription** *(n. )* **መአዘዚ መድሃኒት** *meazezi medhanit*

**presence** *(n.)* **ህላዌ** *hlawe*

**present** *(adj.)* **ናይ ሕጂ** *nay ḧĵi*

**present** *(n.)* **ህሉው** *hluw*

**present** *(v.)* **ኣቕረበ** *aq̈rebe*

**presentation** *(n.)* **ምቕራብ** *mq̈rab*

**presently** *(adv. )* **ኣብዚ እዋን** *abzi èwan*

**preservation** *(n. )* **ዕቃበ** *ëqabe*

**preservative** *(n.)* **ዓቃባዊ** *ëqabawi*

**preserve** *(v.)* **ዕቃበ** *ëqabe*

**preside** *(v.)* **ተቆጻጺሩ** *teqoxaxiru*

**president** *(n.)* **ፕረዘንት** *prezent*

**presidential** *(adj.)* **ፕረዘንታዊ** *prezentawi*

**press** *(v.)* **ጸቒጡ** *xeẗiẗu*

**pressure** *(n.)* **ጸቕጢ** *xeq̈iẗu*

**pressurize** *(v.)* **ጸቕጣዊ** *xeq̈ẗawi*

**prestige** *(n.)* **ክብረት/ፍሉጥ** *kbret/fluẗ*

**prestigious** *(adj.)* **ውሩይ** *wruy*

**presume** *(v.)* **ግምት** *gmt*

**presumption** *(n.)* **ግምታዊ** *gmtawi*

**presuppose** *(v.)* **ብግምት ምውሳን** *bgmt mwsan*

**presupposition** *(n.)* **ብግምት ውሳኔ** *bgmt wusalie*

**pretence** *(n.)* ምምሳል *mmsal*
**pretend** *(v.)* ኣምሰሉ *amselu*
**pretension** *(n.)* ኣለኹ ኣለኹ ኢሉ *aleḱu aleḱu eilu*
**pretentious** *(adj.)* ኣምሳሊ *amsali*
**pretext** *(n. )* ምስምስ *msms*
**prettiness** *(n.)* ጽባቐ *xbaq̈*
**pretty** *(adj.)* መልክዐኛ *melkäña*
**pretzel** *(n.)* ጠዋይ *ẗway*
**prevail** *(v.)* ልዕሊ ኹሉ ሙኻን *lëli ḱulu muḱuan*
**prevalence** *(n.)* ኩነታት ልዕሊ ኹሉ ሙኻን *kunetat lëli ḱulu muḱuan*
**prevalent** *(adj.)* ዓብላሊ *äblali*
**prevent** *(v.)* ዓገተ *gete*
**prevention** *(n.)* ምዕጋት *mägat*
**preventive** *(adj.)* ዓጋታዊ *gatawi*
**preview** *(n.)* ፈተነ *fetene*
**previous** *(adj.)* ዝሓለፈ *zḧalefe*
**prey** *(n.)* ተሃዳኒ *tehadani*
**price** *(n.)* ዋጋ *waga*
**priceless** *(adj.)* ተበሃጊ ዘይሸየጥ ብዝኮነ ዋጋ *tebehagi zeyshyeẗ bzkone waga*
**prick** *(v.)* ንእሽቶ ነኺል *nèshto neḱual*
**prickle** *(n.)* ወግአ *wega*
**pride** *(n.)* ሓበን *ḧaben*
**priest** *(n. )* ቀሺ *qeshi*
**priesthood** *(n.)* ቀሽነት *qexri qeshnet*
**prim** *(adj.)* ፈራሒ *feraḧ*
**primacy** *(n.)* ቀዳማይ ምስራዕ *qedamay msraë*
**primal** *(adj.)* ቀዳማይ *qedamay*
**primarily** *(adv. )* ቀዳምነት *qedamnet*
**primary** *(adj.)* መባእታዊ *mebaètawi*
**primate** *(n.)* ሊቀ ፓፓስ *liqe papas*
**prime** *(adj.)* ብግዜ ቀዳማይ *brzie qedamay*
**primer** *(n.)* መጽሓፍ ንጀመርቲ *mexḧaf*
**primeval** *(adj.)* ቀዳማይ ዕድመ *qedamay ëdme*
**primitive** *(adj.)* ናይ ድሕሪት *nay dḧrit*
**prince** *(n.)* ወድ ንጉስ *wedi ngus*
**princely** *(adj.)* ናይ ወዲ ንጉሳዊ *nay wedi ngusawi*
**princess** *(n. )* ጓል ንጉስ *gual ngus*
**principal** *(adj.)* ዳይረክተር *dayrekter*
**principal** *(n.)* ጀማሪ *ĵemari*
**principle** *(n.)* መትከል *metkel*
**print** *(v.)* ሓተመ *ḧateme*
**printer** *(n.)* ሓታሚት *ḧatamit*
**printout** *(n.)* ዝተሓትመ ወረቐት *zteḧatme wereq̈et*
**prior** *(adj.)* ቅድሚ *qdmi*
**priority** *(n.)* ቀዳምነት *qedamnet*
**priory** *(n.)* ገዳም *gedam*
**prism** *(n.)* ፕሪዝም *prizm*
**prison** *(n. )* ቤት ማሕቡስ *biet maḧbus*
**prisoner** *(n. )* እሱር *èsur*
**pristine** *(adj.)* ዘይመጽጽ *zeymexx*
**privacy** *(n.)* ውልቃውነት *wlqawnet*
**private** *(adj.)* ውልቃዊ *wlqawi*
**privation** *(n. )* ድኽነት *dḱnet*
**privatize** *(n. )* መንግስታዊ ምቁጽጻር ናብ ብሕታዊ ምቅያር *mengsatawi mquxxar nab bḧtawi mq̈yar*

**privilege** *(n. )* ሓለፋታት *ḧlefatat*
**privy** *(adj.)* ጃህራ *ḧalefatat*
**prize** *(n.)* ሽልማት *shlmat*
**pro** *(n. )* ጥቕሚ *ẗqmi*
**proactive** *(adj.)* ገልተው *geltew*
**probability** *(n.)* ናይ ሙኳን ዕድል *nay mukuan ëdl*
**probable** *(adj.)* ምናልባት *mnalbat*
**probably** *(adv. )* ምናልባት *mnalbat*
**probate** *(n.)* ኣጣለለ *aẗalele*
**probation** *(n. )* ኣመክሮ *amekro*
**probationer** *(n.)* ኣመኩሮኣዊ *amkuroawi*
**probe** *(n.)* ምቱኳይ *mtukuay*
**probity** *(n.)* ሓቅነት *ḧaqnet*
**problem** *(n.)* ሽርግ *shgr*
**problematic** *(adj.)* ሽርራዊ *shgrawi*
**procedure** *(n.)* ስርዓት *sräat*
**proceed** *(v.)* ንቅድሚት ኣምርሐ *nqdmit amrḧe*
**proceedings** *(n.)* ሜላ ኣሰራርሓ *miela aserarḧa*
**proceeds** *(n.)* ትርፊ ሰልዲ *trfi seldi*
**process** *(n. )* ምድላው *mdlaw*
**procession** *(n.)* ሰልፊ *selfi*
**proclaim** *(v.)* ኣፍሊጡ *afliẗu*
**proclamation** *(n.)* ኣዋጅ *awaĵ*
**proclivity** *(n.)* ዝንባለ *znbalie*
**procrastinate** *(v.)* ኣደናጎየ *adenagueye*
**procrastination** *(n.)* ምድንጓይ *mdnguay*
**procreate** *(v.)* ሓድጊ ገደፈ *ḧdgi gedefe*
**procure** *(v.)* ረኺቡ *reḱibu*
**procurement** *(n.)* ምዕዳግ *mëdag*
**prod** *(v.)* ውግእ ውግእ ኣቢሉ *wgè wgè abilu*
**prodigal** *(adj.)* ኣባኺኑ *abaḱinu*
**prodigious** *(adj.)* ገዚፍ *gezif*
**prodigy** *(n.)* ዘደንጹ *zedenxu*
**produce** *(v.)* ኣፍርዩ *afryu*
**producer** *(n. )* ኣፍራዪ *afrayi*
**product** *(n. )* ፍርያት *fryat*
**production** *(n.)* ምህርቲ *mhrti*
**productive** *(adj.)* ጠቓሚ *ẗeqami*
**productivity** *(n.)* ውጽኢት /ምህርቲ *wxeit/mhrti*
**profane** *(adj.)* ኣርኪሱ *arkisu*
**profess** *(v.)* ኣሚኑ *amilu*
**profession** *(n.)* ሞያ *moya*
**professional** *(adj.)* በዓል ሞያ *beäl moya*
**professor** *(n.)* ፕሮፌሰር *profieser*
**proficiency** *(n.)* ጣቓ *ẗaqua*
**proficient** *(adj.)* ጥቁው *ẗquw*
**profile** *(n.)* ትርፊ *trfi*
**profit** *(n.)* መኽሰብ *meḱseb*
**profitable** *(adj.)* መኽሰባዊ *meḱsebawi*
**profiteering** *(n.)* ሓድሕዳዊ መኽሰብ *ḧadḧdawi mekseb*
**profligacy** *(n.)* ዘይተገዳስነት *zeytegedasnet*
**profligate** *(adj.)* ኣባኻኒ *abaḱani*
**profound** *(adj.)* ከቢድ *kebid*
**profundity** *(n.)* ክብደት *kbdet*
**profuse** *(adj.)* ብጣዕሚ ብዙሕ *bẗaëmi bzuh*
**profusion** *(n.)* ብርካተ *brkate*
**progeny** *(n. )* ትውልዲ *twldi*
**prognosis** *(n.)* ዕድል ናይ ምሕዋይ *ëdl nay mḧway*

**prognosticate** *(v.)* ምትንባይ *mtnbay*
**programme** *(n. )* መደብ *medeb*
**progress** *(n.)* ምምሕያሽ *mmḧyash*
**progressive** *(adj.)* ምምሕያሻዊ *mmḧyashawi*
**prohibit** *(v.)* ኣገደ *agede*
**prohibition** *(n.)* ምእጋድ *mègad*
**prohibitive** *(adj.)* ክቡር *kbur*
**project** *(n.)* ትልሚ *tlmi*
**projectile** *(n.)* ንቅድሚት ተደርበየ *nqdmit tederbeye*
**projection** *(n. )* በሊሕ ነገር *beliḧ neger*
**projector** *(n.)* ፕሮጀክቶር *proĵecter*
**prolapse** *(n.)* ካብ ቦታ ወጻኢ ምንቅስቓስ *kab bot wexaei mnqsq̈as*
**proliferate** *(v.)* ተራብሐ *terabḧe*
**proliferation** *(n.)* ምርባሕ *mrbaḧ*
**prolific** *(adj.)* ፈራዪ *ferayi*
**prologue** *(n.)* መቕድም *meq̈dm*
**prolong** *(v.)* ኣናውሐ *anawḧe*
**prolongation** *(n.)* ምንዋሕ *mnwaḧ*
**promenade** *(n.)* መሸራሸሪ ህዝቢ *mesherasheri hzbi*
**prominence** *(n.)* ጠቓሚ *ẗq̈ami*
**prominent** *(adj.)* በይኑ ዝወጸ *beynu zmexe*
**promiscuous** *(adj.)* ልኽስክስ *lḱsks*
**promise** *(n.)* ምምብጻዕ *mmbxaë*
**promising** *(adj.)* ተስፋ ዝወሃቦ *tesfa zwehabo*
**promote** *(v.)* ሹመት *shumet*
**promotion** *(n.)* ሽመት *shmet*
**prompt** *(v.)* ኣፍሊቑ *afliq̈u*
**prompter** *(n.)* ኣፍላቒ *aflaq̈i*
**promulgate** *(v.)* ኣውጺኡ *awxieu*
**prone** *(adj.)* ዝንባሌ *znbalie*
**pronoun** *(n.)* ኣፍሊጡ *afliẗu*
**pronounce** *(v.)* ኣድመጸ *admexe*
**pronunciation** *(n.)* ኣደማምጻ *ademamxa*
**proof** *(n.)* መረጋገጺ *meregagexi*
**prop** *(n.)* ዳጌፋ *dagiefa*
**propaganda** *(n. )* ስብከት *sbket*
**propagate** *(v.)* ምርብባሕ *mrbaḧ*
**propagation** *(n.)* ምንቅስቓስ ማዕበል *mnqsq̈as*
**propel** *(v.)* ሰደደ *sedede*
**propeller** *(n.)* ሽኽርክሪት *shḱrkrit*
**proper** *(adj.)* ግቡእ *gbuè*
**property** *(n. )* ርስቲ *rsti*
**prophecy** *(n.)* ትንቢት *tnbit*
**prophesy** *(v.)* ተነበየ *tenebeye*
**prophet** *(n.)* ነቢይ *nebie*
**prophetic** *(adj.)* ትንቢታዊ *tnbitawi*
**propitiate** *(v.)* ኣዝሒሉ *azḧilu*
**proportion** *(n.)* ማዕረ ምቅሊት *maëre mqlit*
**proportional** *(adj.)* ማዕራዊ ምቅሊት *maërawi mqlit*
**proportionate** *(adj.)* ብማዕረ *bmaëre*
**proposal** *(n.)* ሓሳብ *ḧsab*
**propose** *(v.)* ሓሳብ ምቕራብ *ḧsab mq̈rab*
**proposition** *(n.)* ሓሳብ *ḧsab*
**propound** *(v.)* ኣቕረቡ *aq̈ribu*
**proprietary** *(adj.)* በዓል ገዛ *beäl geza*
**proprietor** *(n.)* ዋና *wana*

**propriety** *(n.)* ናይ ሰብ ርስቲ *nay seb rsti*
**prorogue** *(v.)* ምንኳል *mnkual*
**prosaic** *(adj.)* ተራ *tera*
**prose** *(n.)* ጽሑፍ *xḧuf*
**prosecute** *(v.)* ናብ ሕጊ ኣቕረቡ *nab ḧgi aq̈ribu*
**prosecution** *(n. )* ናብ ሕጊ ምቕራብ *nab ḧgi mq̈rab*
**prosecutor** *(n.)* ኣኽባር ሕጊ *aḱbar ḧgi*
**prospect** *(n.)* ተስፋዊ *tesfawi*
**prospective** *(adj.)* ትጽቢታዊ *txbitawi*
**prospectus** *(n.)* መዝገብ መግለጺ ሓሳባት *mezgeb meglexi ḧasabat*
**prosper** *(v.)* በልጸገ *belxege*
**prosperity** *(n.)* ብልጽግና *blxgna*
**prosperous** *(adj.)* ብልጽግናዊ *blxgnawi*
**prostate** *(n.)* ፕሮስተይት *prosteyt*
**prostitute** *(n.)* ኣመንዝራ *amenzra*
**prostitution** *(n.)* ምንዝርና *mnzrna*
**prostrate** *(adj.)* ፕሮስተይት *prosteyt*
**prostration** *(n. )* ምሕሳው *mḧsaw*
**protagonist** *(n.)* ቀንዲ ተዋሳኢ *qendi tewasai*
**protect** *(v.)* ተኸላኸለ *teḱlaḱele*
**protection** *(n.)* ምክልኻል *mklḱal*
**protective** *(adj.)* ተኸላኻላይ *teḱelaḱalay*
**protectorate** *(n.)* ተኸላኻሊ *teḱelaḱali*
**protein** *(n. )* ፕሮቲን *protin*
**protest** *(n.)* ተቓውሞ *teq̈awmo*
**protestation** *(n. )* ተቓዋምነት *teq̈awamnet*
**protocol** *(n.)* እኩብ ሕግታት *èkub ḧgtat*
**prototype** *(n.)* መርኣዪ ፈተነ ምድላው *merayi fetene mdlaw*
**protracted** *(adj.)* ንለዊሕ ዝጸንሕ *newiḧ zxeniḧ*
**protractor** *(n.)* ነዊሕ ጸናሒ *newiḧ xenaḧi*
**protrude** *(v.)* ተወጥወጠ *teweẗweẗe*
**proud** *(adj.)* ኩሩዕ *kuruë*
**prove** *(v.)* ኣእመነ *aèmene*
**provenance** *(n.)* ኣውራጃነት *awraĵanet*
**proverb** *(n.)* እተባህለ *tebahle*
**proverbial** *(adj.)* ጽውጽዋይ *xwxway*
**provide** *(v.)* ምምጻእ *amxaè*
**providence** *(n.)* ፍቓድ ኣምላኽ *fq̈d amlaḱ*
**provident** *(adj.)* መስተውዓሊ *mestewäli*
**providential** *(adj.)* ዕድለኛ *ëdleňa*
**province** *(n.)* ኣውራጃ *awraĵa*
**provincial** *(adj.)* ኣውራጃዊ *awraĵawi*
**provision** *(n.)* ኣስነቐ *asneq̈e*
**provisional** *(adj.)* ንእዋኑ ግን ምስ ግዜ ቖዋሚ *nèwanu gn ms gzie q̈owami*
**proviso** *(n.)* ምምጻእ *mmxaè*
**provocation** *(n.)* ሳዕቤን *saäbien*
**provocative** *(adj.)* ሳዕቤናዊ *saäbienawi*
**provoke** *(v.)* ኣስዓበ *asäbe*
**prowess** *(n.)* ብልሓት *blḧat*
**proximate** *(adj.)* ቅርበት *qrbet*
**proximity** *(n. )* ቅርበትነት *qrbetnet*

**proxy** *(n. )* ወኪል *wekil*
**prude** *(n. )* ጉርሒ *gurḧi*
**prudence** *(n.)* ምጉራሕ *mguraḧ*
**prudent** *(adj.)* ጥንቃቐ *mẗnqaq̈*
**prudential** *(adj.)* ጥንቁቕ *ẗnquq̈*
**prune** *(n.)* ዝዘነቐጸ ፕሮኞ *zneq̈eẗe proňo*
**pry** *(v.)* ኣቕሪብካ ምዕዛብ *aqribka mëzab*
**psalm** *(n. )* መዝሙር ዳዊት *mezmur dawit*
**pseudo** *(adj.)* ሓሳዊ *ḧasawi*
**pseudonym** *(n.)* ሳጓ *sagua*
**psyche** *(n. )* መንፈስ ሰብ *menfes seb*
**psychiatrist** *(n. )* ሓኪም ኣእምሮ *ḧakim aèmro*
**psychiatry** *(n.)* ስነ ኣእምሮ *sne aèmro*
**psychic** *(adj.)* ናይ መጸኢ ዝጥንቁል *nay mexaei zẗnqul*
**psychological** *(adj.)* ሳይኮሎጂካል *saykoloĵikal*
**psychologist** *(n.)* ሳይኮሎጂካዊ *saykoloĵikawi*
**psychology** *(n.)* ሳይኮሎጂ *saykoloyĵi*
**psychopath** *(n. )* መደናጋጊ *medenagari*
**psychosis** *(n.)* ኽማም ኣእምሮ *ḧmam aèmro*
**psychotherapy** *(n.)* ፍወሳ ሕማም ኣእምሮ *fwesa ḧmam aèmro*
**pub** *(n.)* ባርን ሬስቶራንትን *barn giestorantn*
**puberty** *(n.)* ግርዝውና *grzwna*
**pubic** *(adj.)* ኣብ ግርዝውና ዝቦቁል ጸጉሪ *ab grzwna zboqul xeguri*
**public** *(adj.)* ህዝባዊ *hzbawi*
**publication** *(n. )* ሕትመት *ḧtmet*
**publicity** *(n.)* ተፈላጥነት *tefelaẗnet*
**publicize** *(v.)* ምፍላጥ *mflaẗ*
**publish** *(v.)* ምሕታም *mḧtam*
**publisher** *(n.)* ሓታሚ *ḧtami*
**pudding** *(n. )* ዝፈልሐ ጠስሚ *zfelḧ ẗesmi*
**puddle** *(n.)* ንእሽተይ ጉድጓድ ማይ *nèshtey gudguad may*
**puerile** *(adj.)* ቁልዕነት *qulënet*
**puff** *(n.)* ምርሽራሽ *mrshrash*
**puffy** *(adj.)* ምንፋሕ *mnfaḧ*
**pull** *(v.)* ሰሓበ *seḧabe*
**pulley** *(n. )* መስሓቢ ማሽን *mesḧabi mashn*
**pullover** *(n. )* ብርእሲ ስሒብካ ዝኽደን ኽዳን *brèsi sḧibka zḱden ḱdan*
**pulp** *(n.)* ልስሉስ ክፋል ስኒ *lslus kfal sni*
**pulpit** *(n.)* መስበኽያ *mesbeḱya*
**pulsar** *(n.)* ዘዋሪ ኮኾብ *zewari koḱob*
**pulsate** *(v.)* ምህራም *mhram*
**pulsation** *(n. )* ትርግታ *trgta*
**pulse** *(n.)* ድምጺ ትርግታ *dmxi trgta*
**pummel** *(v.)* ብተደጋጋሚ ምህራም *btedegagami mhram*
**pump** *(n. )* ምጭንጓዕ *mčnguaë*
**pumpkin** *(n. )* ዱባ *duba*
**pun** *(n.)* ሓይሊ ምጉዳል *ḧayli mgudal*
**punch** *(v.)* ጉስጢ *gusẗi*
**punctual** *(adj.)* ኣብ ሰዓቱ *ab seätu*

**punctuality** *(n.)* **ኣብ ሰዓቱ ዝርከብ** *ab seätu zrkeb*
**punctuate** *(v.)* **ምውሳኽ(")** *mwsaḱ(")*
**punctuation** *(n.)* **ምልክት መግለጺ ትርጉም (")** *mlkt meglexi qal(")*
**puncture** *(n.)* **ብበለሕ ነገር ዝፍጠር ቀዳድ** *bbeli neger zfťer qedad*
**pungency** *(n.)* **ብርቱዕ ጨና ምህላው** *brtuë čena mhlaw*
**pungent** *(adj.)* **ብርቱዕ ጨና** *brtuë čena*
**punish** *(v.)* **ምቕጻዕ** *mq̈xaë*
**punishment** *(n.)* **መቕጻዕቲ** *meq̈xaëti*
**punitive** *(adj.)* **ቕጻዒ** *q̈exaë*
**punter** *(n.)* **ዓሚል ኣመንዝራ** *ämil amenzra*
**puny** *(adj.)* **ድኹም** *dḱum*
**pup** *(n.)* **ንእሽቶ፣ተመኩሮ ዘይብሉ** *neshto,temekuro zeyblu*
**pupil** *(n. )* **ዘኽታም ብመንግስቲ ዝናበ** *zeḱtam bmengsti znabe*
**puppet** *(n. )* **ብነብሱ ዘይምራሕ** *bnebsu zeymraḧ*
**puppy** *(n.)* **ኩርኩር** *kurkur*
**purblind** *(adj.)* **ፍርቂ ዕዉር** *frqi ëwur*
**purchase** *(v.)* **ምዕዳግ** *mëdag*
**pure** *(adj.)* **ንጹህ** *nxuh*
**purgation** *(n. )* **ካብ ሓጥያት ምንጻህ** *kab ḧaẗyat mnxah*
**purgative** *(adj.)* **ካብ ሓጥያት ክነጽህ ኽእል** *kab ḧaẗyat knexh zḱèl*
**purgatory** *(n.)* **ስቓይ ናይ ምድሓን** *sq̈ay nay mdḧan*
**purge** *(v.)* **ካብ ሓጥያት ኣንጸሀ** *kab ḧaẗyat anxehe*
**purification** *(n.)* **ምንጻህ** *mnxah*
**purify** *(v.)* **ኣጻረየ** *axareye*
**purist** *(n.)* **ንጹህነት** *nxuhnet*
**puritan** *(n.)* **ምቕሉል** *mq̈lul*
**puritanical** *(adj.)* **ነተጐ** *netegue*
**purity** *(n.)* **ኣጹህነት** *axuhnet*
**purple** *(n. )* **ሊላ** *lila*
**purport** *(v.)* **ደገፍ** *degef*
**purpose** *(n.)* **ዕላማ** *ëlama*
**purposely** *(adv. )* **ኮነ ኢልካ** *kone eilka*
**purr** *(v.)* **ናይ ደስታ ድምጺ** *nay desta dmxi*
**purse** *(n.)* **ቦርሳ** *borsa*
**purser** *(n.)* **ሰራሕ ቦርሳ** *seraḧ borsa*
**pursuance** *(n.)* **ምድላይ** *mdlay*
**pursue** *(v.)* **ንክጎድእ ሰዓበ** *nkgodè seäbe*
**pursuit** *(n.)* **ንክጎድእ ምስዓብ** *nkgodè msäb*
**purvey** *(v.)* **ምቕራብ** *mq̈rab*
**purview** *(n. )* **ርደኢት** *rdeit*
**pus** *(n.)* **ሙጉሊ** *muguili*
**push** *(v.)* **ደፍአ** *defae*
**pushy** *(adj.)* **ቖራጽነት** *qoraxnet*
**puss** *(n.)* **ንእሽቶ ጓል** *nèshto gual*
**put** *(v.)* **ኣቐመጠ** *aq̈emeť e*
**putative** *(adj.)* **ግምት** *gmt*
**putrid** *(adj.)* **ብልሹው** *blshw*
**puzzle** *(v.t. )* **መስቀላዊ** *mesqelawi*
**pygmy** *(n. )* **ድንኪ** *dnki*
**pyjamas** *(n.)* **ብጃማ** *bĵama*
**pyorrhoea** *(n. )* **ምፍሳስ መጉሊ** *mfsas meguili*
**pyramid** *(n. )* **ፒራሚድ** *piramid*
**pyre** *(n. )* **ዝርዝር ቐብሪ** *zrzr q̈ebri*

**pyromania** *(n.)* ሕማም ሓዊ *ȟmam ȟawi*

**python** *(n.)* ናይ ዓዲ እንግሊዝ ኮሚዳውያን *nay ädi èngliz commiedawyan*

# Q

**quack** *(n)* ጋቢ'ና *gabina*

**quackery** *(n. )* ካባረ *kabare*

**quad** *(n.)* ካውሎ *kawlo*

**quadrangle** *(a. )* ጋቢና *gabina*

**quadrangular** *(n.)* ከብሒ *kebȟi*

**quadrant** *(n.)* መዳወር *medawer*

**quadrilateral** *(n. )* ካካው *kakaw*

**quadruped** *(n.)* ሓብአ *ȟab'e*

**quadruple** *(adj.)* ክታም *ktam*

**quadruplet** *(n. )* ቃቓ *qaq̈a*

**quaff** *(v.)* ቈልቋል *qWelqWAl*

**quail** *(n.)* ነውራም *newram*

**quaint** *(adj.)* ሬሳ *reesa*

**quaintly** *(adv. )* ካዲ *kadi*

**quake** *(v.)* ሬሳ *reesa*

**Quaker** *(n. )* ካደት *kadet*

**qualification** *(n.)* ካድምዩም *kadmyum*

**qualify** *(v.)* አስከሬን *askereen*

**qualitative** *(adj.)* ቄሳር *qeesar*

**quality** *(n. )* ካፈ *kafe*

**qualm** *(n.)* ካፈተርያ *kafeterya*

**quandary** *(n.)* ጎብያ *gobya*

**quango** *(n.)* ኪዳን *kidan*

**quantify** *(v.)* ሸሓጠ *sheȟaẗe*

**quantitative** *(adj.)* ዶልሺ *dolshi*

**quantity** *(n. )* መዓት *me'ät*

**quantum** *(n. )* ካልስዩም *kalsyum*

**quarantine** *(n.)* ቀመረ *qemere*

**quark** *(n.)* መተሓሳሰቢ *meteȟasasebi*

**quarrel** *(n.)* ቀመር *qemer*

**quarrelsome** *(adj.)* ዓውደ-አዋርሕ *äwde'awarȟ*

**quarry** *(n.)* ምራኽ *mraḱ*

**quart** *(n.)* ደረጃታት መጠነ ወይ ሓንጸጸ *dereĵatat meẗene wey ȟanxexe*

**quarter** *(n.)* ውሽጣዊ ሰንጣቒት *wshẗawi senẗaq̈it*

**quarterly** *(adj.)* ደወለ *dewele*

**quartet** *(n.)* ጽባቐ ጽሒፈት *xbaq̈e xȟfet*

**quartz** *(n.)* ሞያ *moya*

**quash** *(v.)* ጽዖታዊ *x'ötawi*

**quaver** *(v.)* ጥረ *ẗre*

**quay** *(n.)* ህዱእ *hdu'è*

**queasy** *(adj.)* ካሎሪ *kalori*

**queen** *(n.)* ምጽላም *mxlam*

**queer** *(adj.)* ብጻይነት *bxaynet*

**quell** *(v.)* ጐብጓበ *gWabgWabe*

**quench** *(v.)* ሻሽ *shash*

**querulous** *(adj.)* ካምኮርደር *kamkorder*

**query** *(n.)* ገመል *gemel*

**quest** *(n.)* ካምዮ *kamyo*

**question** *(n.)* ካመራ *kamera*

**questionable** *(adj.)* መዓስከር *me'äsker*

**questionnaire** *(n. )* ዘመተ *zemete*

**queue** *(n. )* ካምፎራ *kamfora*

**quibble** *(n.)* ካምፓስ *kampas*

**quick** *(adj.)* ታኒካ *tanika*

**quicken** *(v.)* ኣብ ታኒካ ሓተመ *'ab tanika ȟateme*

**quickly** *(adv. )* መትረብ *metreb*

**quid** ***(n.)*** **ናይ ሓሶት ጸብጻብ** *nay ȟasot xebxab*
**quiescent** ***(adj.)*** **ሰረዘ** *sereze*
**quiet** ***(adj.)*** **ምጥፋእ** *mẗfa'è*
**quieten** ***(v.)*** **መንሽሮ** *menshro*
**quietude** ***(n.)*** **ብራሃን** *brahan*
**quiff** ***(n.)*** **ግሁድ** *ghud*
**quilt** ***(n. )*** **ሕጹይ** *ȟxuy*
**quilted** ***(adj.)*** **ሽምዓ** *shm'ä*
**quince** ***(n.)*** **ካራመላ** *karamela*
**quinine** ***(n. )*** **ከረዛን** *kerezan*
**Quinn** ***(n.)*** **ጋህዲ** *gahdi*
**quintessence** ***(n.)*** **ከልባዊ** *kelbawi*
**quip** ***(n.)*** **ሳጹን** *saxun*
**quirk** ***(n.)*** **ሀምፕ** *hemp*
**quit** ***(v.)*** **በላዕ ሰብ** *bela'ë seb*
**quite** ***(adv. )*** **መድፍዕ** *medf'ë*
**quits** ***(adj.)*** **ጐራሕ** *gWaraȟ*
**quiver** ***(v.)*** **ታንኳ** *tankWa*
**quixotic** ***(adj.)*** **ቀኖና** *qenona*
**quiz** ***(n.)*** **ድባብ** *dbab*
**quizzical** ***(adj.)*** **ግብዝና** *gbzna*
**quondam** ***(adj.)*** **ሓራቕ** *ȟaraq̈*
**quorum** ***(n. )*** **ካንቲና** *kantina*
**quota** ***(n. )*** **ህዱእ ጋልቢት** *hdu'è galbit*
**quotation** ***(n.)*** **ወረዳ** *wereda*
**quote** ***(v.)*** **ቀዋሚ መዓስከር** *qewami me'äsker*
**quotient** ***(n.)*** **ጅርባ** *ĵrba*

# R

**rabbit** ***(n. )*** **ዓሚቕ ስንጭሮ** *ämiq̈ snčro*
**rabble** ***(n.)*** **ቈብዕ** *qWeb'ë*
**rabid** ***(adj.)*** **ዓቕሚ** *äq̈mi*
**rabies** ***(n. )*** **ክኢላ** *k'ila*
**race** ***(v.)*** **ካፓሲተር** *kapaciter*
**race** ***(n.)*** **ሰፊሕ** *sefiȟ*
**racial** ***(adj.)*** **ዓቕሚ** *äq̈mi*
**racialism** ***(n.)*** **ሰለመ** *seleme*
**rack** ***(n. )*** **መንጠሊና** *menẗelina*
**racket** ***(n. )*** **ርእሰ-ማል** *r'èsemal*
**racketeer** ***(n.)*** **ርእሰ-ማልነት** *r'èsemalnet*
**racy** ***(adj.)*** **ርእሰ-ማላዊ** *r'èsemalawi*
**radar** ***(n.)*** **ርእሰ-ማል ገበረ** *r'èsemal gebere*
**radial** ***(adj.)*** **ግብሪ** *gbri*
**radiance** ***(n.)*** **ተምበርከኸ** *temberkeḱe*
**radiant** ***(adj.)*** **ቅበጥ** *qbeẗ*
**radiate** ***(v.)*** **ቀባጥ** *qebaẗ*
**radiation** ***(n.)*** **ካፕሲከም** *kapsikem*
**radical** ***(adj.)*** **ገልበጠ** *gelbeẗe*
**radio** ***(n.)*** **ጠምጣሚ መስሕብ** *ẗemẗami mesȟb*
**radioactive** ***(adj.)*** **ለቖታ-ፍረ** *leq̈otafre*
**radiography** ***(n.)*** **ግብጣን** *gbẗan*
**radiology** ***(n.)*** **ግብጣኒ** *gbẗani*
**radish** ***(n. )*** **ኣርእስቲ** *ar'èsti*
**radium** ***(n. )*** **መሰጠ** *meseẗe*
**radius** ***(n. )*** **ምሩኽ** *mruḱ*
**raffle** ***(n.)*** **ምሩኽነት** *mruḱnet*
**raft** ***(n.)*** **ሓላው ምሩኽ** *ȟalaw mruḱ*
**rag** ***(n.)*** **ኣሰረ** *asere'*

**rage** *(n.)* **ማኪና** *makina*
**ragged** *(adj.)* **ካራሜል** *karame' el*
**raid** *(n.)* **ካራት** *kara 't*
**rail** *(n.)* **ሓዲድ** *ḧadid*
**railing** *(n. )* **መደንደል** *medendel*
**raillery** *(n. )* **ሕመት** *hemete*
**railway** *(n.)* **መገዲ ባቡር** *megedi babur*
**rain** *(n)* **ጥርሙዝ** *terimuz*
**rainbow** *(n.)* **ገምቢ** *ge'mbi*
**raincoat** *(n.)* **ካርዲ** *ka'ardi*
**rainfall** *(n.)* **ጠጠው አቢሉ** *tte'ttew aa'billu*
**rainforest** *(n.)* **ካርቶን** *kartoon*
**rainy** *(adj.)* **ናይ ልቢ** *na' ae lebii*
**raise** *(v.)* **ጎልፎ** *gole 'foo*
**raisin** *(n.)* **ጳጳስ** *papase'*
**rake** *(n.)* **ልብ ሓኪም መሳርሒ** *lib hakim mesarehi*
**rally** *(n.)* **ሓኪም ሕመም ልቢ** *hakim himem le'bi*
**ram** *(n.)* **ክንክን** *kinkin*
**ramble** *(v.)* **ስራሕ** *sir'ahh*
**ramification** *(n.)* **ዘይአጅቦ** *they'aa jibo*
**ramify** *(v.)* **ጥንቁቅ** *tinkuq*
**ramp** *(n.)* **ዘየስተውዕል** *ze yestewu 'el*
**rampage** *(v.)* **ኣብ** *aa'b*
**rampant** *(adj.)* **ተናኸፈ** *tenahe'fe*
**rampart** *(n. )* **ወኪል** *wekil*
**ramshackle** *(adj.)* **ኣብ መርከብ** *aa'b merkeb*
**ranch** *(n.)* **ምስሊ** *mesili*
**rancid** *(adj.)* **ቀይሕ ሕብሪ** *qeyiha hib're*
**rancour** *(n.)* **ጬፍጬፋ** *Chif'chefa*
**random** *(adj.)* **ስጋዊ** *segawi*
**range** *(n. )* **ተርታ ኣትሓዘ** *terta 'athaze*
**ranger** *(n. )* **ፎረስታለ** *forestale*
**rank** *(v.)* **ኣዕበርበረ** *zz'ebere bere*
**rank** *(n.)* **ደርፊ** *derfi*
**rankle** *(v.)* **ፀራቢ** *tserabi*
**ransack** *(v.)* **ፅርበት** *tsirbet*
**ransom** *(n.)* **መንፀፍ** *mentseff*
**rant** *(v.)* **ባቡር** *babur*
**rap** *(v.)* **ብነፋሪት** *binefarit*
**rapacious** *(adj.)* **ካሮት** *carrot*
**rape** *(v.)* **ተሸከመ** *teshekeme*
**rapid** *(adj.)* **ዓረብያ** *arebia*
**rapidity** *(n. )* **ፍጥነት** *ftnet*
**rapier** *(n. )* **ልስሉስ ዓፅሚ** *leseluse aa'tsmi*
**rapist** *(n.)* **ባኮ** *bako*
**rapport** *(n.)* **ስኒት** *snit*
**rapprochement** *(n.)* **ቀልሃ** *qeliha*
**rapt** *(adj.)* **ቀረፀ** *qeretse*
**rapture** *(n.)* **ምሳጠ** *msaẗe*
**rare** *(adj.)* **ወዲ** *wedi*
**raring** *(adj.)* **መንጫ ጫዕታ** *mencha chaeta*
**rascal** *(n.)* **ኩነት** *kunet*
**rash** *(adj.)* **መስኮት** *mesekote*
**rasp** *(n.)* **ቅርሺ** *qeriishe*
**raspberry** *(n.)* **ኦም** *ome*
**rat** *(n.)* **ተቀባሊት ቅርሺ** *teqebalit qereshi*
**ratchet** *(n.)* **ሱፍ** *suf*
**rate** *(n. )* **ዝተለበጠ** *zetelebte*
**rather** *(adv. )* **ህንፀት** *hintsete*
**ratify** *(v.)* **ፊስቶ** *fiseto*
**rating** *(n.)* **ሳፁን ሬሳ** *satsun resa*
**ratio** *(n. )* **ምግቢ** *megebi*
**ration** *(n.)* **ጁባ** *juba*

**rational** *(adj.)* **ተመልከተ** *temeleket*
**rationale** *(n.)* **ስነ-መጎታዊ መሰረት** *snemegotawi meseret*
**rationalism** *(n.)* **ማሕበራዊ ደረጃ** *mahiberawi dereja*
**rationalize** *(v.)* **ነቀፈ** *neqefe*
**rattle** *(v.)* **ደርበየ** *derebye*
**raucous** *(adj.)* **ቤት ነገስታት** *bete negestat*
**ravage** *(v.t. )* **ዝሸክርከር ጎማ ወንበር** *zeShekirker goma wenber*
**rave** *(v.)* **ቀጥቀጥ** *qeteqetw*
**raven** *(n. )* **ጎማ ዘይት** *goma zeite*
**ravenous** *(adj.)* **ዘይተሓሰበሉ** *zeytehasebelo*
**ravine** *(n.)* **ዝሞተ** *zemote*
**raw** *(adj.)* **ድሙ** *demu*
**ray** *(n.)* **ብርሰት ዘስዕብ ሓደጋ** *bereset zsee'b hadega*
**raze** *(v.)* **ነንኣብነት መፃሕፍቲ** *nenabinet metsahifti*
**razor** *(n.)* **ኣቀፃፀለ** *aqetsatsele*
**reach** *(v.)* **ኣቀፃፃሊ** *aqetsatseli*
**react** *(v.)* **ሓበላ** *habela*
**reaction** *(n.)* **ከቢድ ሃንደበታዊ ሓደጋ** *kebid hanedbtawi a'adega*
**reactionary** *(adj.)* **ቆበለ** *qobl*
**reactor** *(n.)* **ብቀሊሉ ዝላገብ** *newlilunzehegden beqlilu zezekren*
**read** *(v.)* **ኣንበበ** *'anbebe*
**readily** *(adv. )* **ንፁርን ርጉፅን** *nitsurin regutsin*
**reading** *(n.)* **ጎጀለ** *goje-le*
**readjust** *(v.)* **ጉጅለ** *guge-le*
**ready** *(adj.)* **ሰርዐ** *sere'aa*
**reaffirm** *(v.)* **ኣባጨጓራ** *aaba'che'guara*
**real** *(adj.)* **ናይ ብሓቂ** *nay bḧaqi*
**realism** *(n. )* **ደብሪ** *debri*
**realistic** *(adj.)* **ካቶሊክ** *catholic*
**reality** *(n.)* **ከብቲ** *kebtei*
**realization** *(n.)* **ሓሜተኛ** *hametegna'*
**realize** *(v.)* **ፃዕዳ ዘርኢ ሰብ** *tsaeda' zereei sebe'*
**really** *(adv. )* **በራድ** *beradd*
**realm** *(n.)* **ካዉሎ ፍዮሪ** *kawulo fiyorii*
**ream** *(n.)* **ናይ ምክንያትን ዉፅኢትን** *nayei mikneyatene wutsieitin*
**reap** *(v.)* **ዓጸደ** *'äxede*
**reaper** *(n. )* **መንቀሊ** *mneqsi*
**reappear** *(v.)* **ኣዉራ መንገዲ** *awra mnegedeei*
**reappraisal** *(n.)* **መፂፅ** *matsiee.e*
**rear** *(n. )* **መጠንቀቅታ** *metenqekta*
**rearrange** *(v.)* **ኣጠንቀቀ** *aa'tenqeqe*
**reason** *(n.)* **ጥንቁቅ** *tenquqk*
**reasonable** *(adj.)* **ናይ ፈረሳት** *nayei feresat*
**reassess** *(v.)* **ዘይግደስ** *zeyg des*
**reassure** *(v.)* **ፈረሰኛ** *fresenga*
**rebate** *(n.)* **በዓቲ** *beaa'ti*
**rebel** *(v.)* **መዘካከሪ** *mezkakrii*
**rebellion** *(n.)* **ገፊሕ በዓቲ** *gefihe beatii*
**rebellious** *(adj.)* **ብጣዕሚ ገፊሕ** *betaemi gefihei*
**rebirth** *(n.)* **ዝጎድጎደ ስኒ** *zgodedod sieni*
**rebound** *(v.)* **ብታሕጓስ ዓንደረ** *bitahegwas aanede're*
**rebuff** *(v.)* **ደው ኣበለ** *dwuo aabele*

**rebuild** *(v.)* ተኩሲ ደው ናይ ምግባር ስምምዕ *tekusi dwu nayi megebare sememea 'e*
**rebuke** *(v.t. )* ኦም ሲዳር *oom cidar*
**recall** *(v.)* ሓይሊ/መሰል ሃበ *hailyii/msele habee*
**recap** *(v.)* ሰንቀ/ጣርያ ገዛ *seneqe/tareya geza*
**recapitulate** *(v.)* ዕምባባ *embaba*
**recapture** *(v.)* ቅዳሴ ዝመርሕ ቀሺ *qwedase zemrehe qeshi*
**recede** *(v.)* ኣብዓለ/በዓል ኣከበረ *aab'ale/bea'eal akebere*
**receipt** *(n.)* በዓል *beaal*
**receive** *(v.)* ስሙይ ሰብ *semuyei sebe*
**receiver** *(n.)* ሰማያዊ *semayawii*
**recent** *(adj.)* ድንግልና *denegelena*
**recently** *(adv. )* ድንግላይ *denegelaye*
**receptacle** *(n.)* ዋህዮ *waheyo*
**reception** *(n.)* ናይ እሱራት ክፍሊ *naye esurat kiflii*
**receptionist** *(n.)* ተንቀሳቃሲ ስልኪ *teneqesaqasi seliki*
**receptive** *(adj.)* ልኡክ ጉጀለ *leuuke gujelle*
**recess** *(n. )* ስብሒ *sebehi*
**recession** *(n. )* ዝነድድ ረብሓ *zenededei rehehaa*
**recessive** *(adj.)* ዕብሉል *'ëblul*
**recharge** *(v.)* ሴልሲየስ *celcius*
**recipe** *(n. )* ሴልቲክ ቋንቋ *celtik quaniqua*
**recipient** *(n.)* ስሚንቶ *seminito*
**reciprocal** *(adj.)* መካነ መቓብር *mekne mekabir*
**reciprocate** *(v.)* ሽሓነ *shehane*
**recital** *(n.)* መርማሪ *meremari*
**recite** *(v.)* ቅድመ ምርመራ *qedeme meremra*
**reckless** *(adj.)* ነቓፊ *neqkafi*
**reckon** *(v.t.)* ብርቲዕ ነቀፌታ *beretiee' neqefeta*
**reclaim** *(v.)* ቆፀራ *qoxera*
**reclamation** *(n.)* ሳንቲም *sanetim*
**recline** *(v.)* ተገምበወ *tegembewe*
**recluse** *(n.)* ኣብ ርእ *ab reaa'*
**recognition** *(n.)* ማዕከል *maeekele*
**recognize** *(v.i. )* ሙቀት መጠን *muqete metene*
**recoil** *(v.)* ርቐት መጠን *reqete metene*
**recollect** *(v.)* ዘርኢ ሰብ ዝመሰል *zereii sebe zemsle*
**recollection** *(n.)* ኣዉራ/ቀንዲ *aawura/qenedi*
**recommend** *(v.)* ኣማእከለ *zamaeekele*
**recommendation** *(n.)* ማዕከል *meee'kele*
**recompense** *(v.)* ዘበን *zbene*
**reconcile** *(v.)* ጣሳ *tasa*
**reconciliation** *(n.)* ጥራጥረ *teraterre*
**recondition** *(v.)* ናይ ሓንጎል *nayei hanegole*
**reconsider** *(v.)* ስነ ስርዓታዊ *sene sereaa'tawii*
**reconstitute** *(v.)* ስነ ስርዓት ዘለዎ *senei sereat zelewoo*
**reconstruct** *(v.)* በዓል/ፅምብል *beaal/xeembil*
**record** *(n. )* ርጉፅ *reguxee*
**recorder** *(n.)* ብዘይጥርጥር *bethzey tiritir*

**recount** *(v.)* **ዕቡድ/ፅሉል** *eebudd/xelule*

**recoup** *(v.)* **ምስክር ወረቐት** *mesekir wereqet*

**recourse** *(n.)* **ምስክር ወረቐት ሃበ** *meseker wereqket habe*

**recover** *(v.)* **ርግፀኝነት** *regexegninet*

**recovery** *(n.)* **ምሕዋይ** *mḧway*

**recreate** *(v.)* **ምቁራፅ** *mekuraxee*

**recreation** *(n. )* **ምዝንጋዕ** *mznga'ë*

**recrimination** *(n.)* **ሰንሰለት** *seneselet*

**recruit** *(v.)* **ወንበር** *weneber*

**rectangle** *(n.)* **አቦወንበር** *abo' weneber*

**rectangular** *(adj.)* **ሰብ ተጓዕዝ** *sebe tegwaeeze*

**rectification** *(n.)* **ባራካ** *barakaa*

**rectify** *(v.)* **ፀዋዕ** *xewaee*

**rectitude** *(n.)* **በረቕ** *bereqqe*

**rectum** *(n.)* **ፈተነ** *fetene*

**recumbent** *(adj.)* **አዳራሽ** *adarashe*

**recuperate** *(v.)* **ናይ በዓል ስልጣን** *naye beeal seletane*

**recur** *(v.)* **ሻምፓኝ** *shampagne*

**recurrence** *(n.)* **ዕዉት/ሰዓራይ** *eewuut/seaarayi*

**recurrent** *(adj.)* **ዕድል** *eedil*

**recycle** *(v.)* **መራሒ መንግስቲ** *merahi menegeseti*

**red** *(adj.)* **ቤት ፅሕፈት** *bete xehifeti*

**reddish** *(adj.)* **ልሻን ሸለመ** *leshane' shelem'e*

**redeem** *(v.)* **ለወጠ/ተለወጠ** *lewete/telewete*

**redemption** *(n.)* **ጣቢያ ጤሌቪዥን** *tabiya television*

**redeploy** *(v.)* **ዜማ** *zema*

**redolent** *(adj.)* **ህዉከት** *hewuuke*

**redouble** *(v.)* **ዕግርግር ዘለዎ** *egereger zelewo*

**redoubtable** *(adj.)* **ንእሽተይ ቤተክርስቲያን** *neeshtey betekerestian*

**redress** *(v.)* **ካህን** *kahiN'*

**reduce** *(v.)* **ምዕራፍ** *mee'eraf*

**reduction** *(n.)* **ሓረር/ኣሕረረ** *harer/aaehi'rere*

**reductive** *(adj.)* **ባሕርይ/ፀባይ** *bahereyei/xebayii*

**redundancy** *(n.)* **ባሕርይ** *bahereyei*

**redundant** *(adj.)* **ፋሓም/ሕመት** *fahame/hemeute*

**reef** *(n.)* **ክፍሊት** *kefelite*

**reek** *(v.)* **ክፍሊት ሓተተ** *kefelit hatete*

**reel** *(n.)* **ብርጬቆ መልአ** *bereCheqo melea'a*

**refer** *(v.)* **ዓረብያ/ሰረገላ** *arebiya/seregela*

**referee** *(n.)* **ግርማ ሞገስ** *gerima moges*

**reference** *(n. )* **በዓል ሞገስ/ምዕሩግ** *beal moges/mee'erug*

**referendum** *(n.)* **ናይ ገባሪ ሰናይ** *nayei gebari senayei*

**refill** *(v.)* **ትካል ገባሪ ሰናይ** *tekaal gebarii senayei*

**refine** *(v.)* **መምሰሊ/መታለሊ ሰብ** *memeiseli/metalelei sebe'e*

**refinement** *(n.)* **ሰሓባይነት** *sehabayineet*

**refinery** *(n.)* ሰባሓይ/ማራኪ *sebahaayi/marakii*
**refit** *(v.)* ሰንጠረዥ *seneterezjj*
**reflect** *(v.)* መምርሒ *memerehii*
**reflection** *(n.)* ተኮናተረ *tekonateree*
**reflective** *(adj.)* ስግኣተ *segeaa'te*
**reflex** *(n.)* ኣጓየየ/ኣባረረ *aaguwayeye/aabarere*
**reflexive** *(adj.)* ሞተር *mote'R'*
**reflexology** *(n.)* ዘየዝሙዉ/ዘይትዝሙዉ *zeyezemuwue/zeyitzemuwu*
**reform** *(v.)* ወቐሰ *weqqese*
**reformation** *(n.)* ኣደብ *A'deb*
**reformer** *(n.)* ዘይምዝማዉ *zeymzemawu*
**refraction** *(n.)* ኣዕለለ/ኣዉገዐ *aae'lele/aawugeaa'*
**refrain** *(v.t.)* ቤት ነገስታት *bete' negeseta't*
**refresh** *(v.)* ንብረት/ንዋይ *neberet/newaye*
**refreshment** *(n.)* ሃተፈ/ለፈለፈ *hatefe/lefelefe*
**refrigerate** *(v.)* ኣውቲስታ/ዘዋሪማኪና *aawutiseta/zewarimeckina*
**refrigeration** *(n. )* ትምክሕቲ *temekeheti*
**refrigerator** *(n.)* ምኩሕ *mekuhh*
**refuge** *(n. )* ሕሳር *hesaree*
**refugee** *(n. )* ኣዋረደ *aawarede*
**refulgence** *(adj.)* ኣታለለ *aatalele*
**refulgent** *(adj.)* ኣሕሰረ *aa'hesere*
**refund** *(v.)* ኣፃረየ *axareyee*
**refund** *(v.)* ዝተዛዘመ *ziteza'zeme'*
**refurbish** *(v.)* ምዕጉርቲ *meaegurtii*
**refusal** *(n.)* ባዕለገ *bae'leGe'*
**refuse** *(v.)* ጩቕ በለ *Chuqk' bele*
**refuse** *(n. )* ታሕጓስ *taheGua'ss*
**refutation** *(n.)* ወትሩ ሕጉስ *wetru higus*
**refute** *(v.)* ዘየሕጉስ *zyehiGus'*
**regain** *(v.)* ሕጉስ *Higus'*
**regal** *(adj.)* ኣጅቦ *Ajobo*
**regard** *(v.)* ጭኮንበሳ *ChikonbeSa*
**regarding** *(prep.)* ዋና ከሻኒ *wana Kesha'ni*
**regardless** *(adv. )* ኬሚካል *kemikal*
**regenerate** *(v.)* ቐማሚ *Qe'mami*
**regeneration** *(n.)* ቕመም *qE'mem*
**regent** *(n.)* ሕክምና *hikiM'NA*
**reggae** *(n.)* ናይ ባንኪ ቼክ *naYei banki' Cheqk*
**regicide** *(n. )* ኣፍቀረ *Af'Qere*
**regime** *(n. )* ቼዝ *Chezz'*
**regiment** *(n.)* ኣፍልቢ *Aflebi*
**region** *(n.)* ሳንዱቕ *saneduqQ*
**regional** *(adj.)* መለለይ ምልክት *Me'Leleyei milikit*
**register** *(n.)* ሓየከ *HayYeke*
**registrar** *(n. )* ዘበናይ ሰሓባይን *Zebenayei Sehabayin*
**registration** *(n. )* ሸፍጢ *Shefe'Ti*
**registry** *(n.)* ደርሆ *Dereho*
**regress** *(v.)* ዓይኒ ዓተር *Ayni Ater*
**regret** *(n.)* ነቐፈ *NeQefe*
**regrettable** *(adj.)* ኣዉራ/ቀንዲ *Auwra/Qendi'*
**regular** *(adj.)* ሓላፊ/ሓለቓ *Halafi/HaleQa*
**regularity** *(n.)* መሪሕነት *MerihNet'*
**regularize** *(v.)* ቆልዓ *QoleA'*

**regulate** *(v.)* **ቁልዕነት** *Qole'eneT'*
**regulation** *(n.)* **ናይ ቆልዓ** *Nayei QoleA'*
**regulator** *(n.)* **ቁሪ/ቀዝሒ** *Quri/Qezhi*
**rehabilitate** *(v.)* **ሽርባ/በርበረ** *Shirba/berebre*
**rehabilitation** *(n.)* **ቆራር** *qorare*
**rehearsal** *(n.)* **ሰዓት ደወለት** *seAt' dwle't*
**rehearse** *(v.)* **ቆንቆር** *QonQkor*
**reign** *(v.)* **ሀበይ** *HeBeyei*
**reimburse** *(v.)* **መንከስ** *Menkes'*
**rein** *(n.)* **በረቕ** *BereqQe'*
**reincarnate** *(v.)* **ሽርፍራፍ** *Sherifrafe*
**reinforce** *(v.)* **ጩቕ በሎ** *CchUQ' Bel'le*
**reinforcement** *(n.)* **መንደል** *Mendel*
**reinstate** *(v.)* **ናብ ስልጣን መለሰ** *nab slťan melese*
**reiterate** *(v.)* **ደጋገመ** *degageme*
**reiteration** *(n.)* **ክሎሪን** *kilorin*
**reject** *(v.)* **መርዚ** *merzi*
**rejection** *(n.)* **ቸኮላታ** *checolata*
**rejoice** *(v.)* **መረፃ** *meretsa*
**rejoin** *(v.)* **መዘምራን** *mezemeran*
**rejoinder** *(n.)* **ሓነቐ** *haneqe*
**rejuvenate** *(v.)* **ሕማም ሸሮኽ** *hemam sheroke*
**rejuvenation** *(n.)* **መረፀ** *meretse*
**relapse** *(v.)* **ከተፈ** *ketefe*
**relate** *(v.)* **ሴፍ** *sefe*
**relation** *(n.)* **ጥሕሎ** *telohe*
**relationship** *(n.)* **ክፋል መዝሙር** *kefale mezemur*
**relative** *(adj.)* **ደመርቲ** *dmreti*
**relativity** *(n.)* **ተደጋጊሙ ዝዝመር** *tedegagimu zezemre*
**relax** *(v.)* **ክርስቶስ** *keresetos*
**relaxation** *(n.)* **ክርስቲያን** *keresitiyane*
**relay** *(n.)* **ክርስትና ሃይማኖት** *keresetena hayimanot*
**release** *(v.)* **በዓል ልደት** *beal lidet*
**relegate** *(v.)* **ቀምቀመ** *qemeqme*
**relent** *(v.)* **ነባር** *nebar*
**relentless** *(adj.)* **ዜና መዋልዕ** *zena mewalee*
**relevance** *(n.)* **ርክብ** *rkb*
**relevant** *(adj.)* **ሰዓት** *seat*
**reliable** *(adj.)* **ክምስ/ፍሽክ በለ** *kemese/feshek bele*
**reliance** *(n.)* **ቀረባ ፈታሒ** *qereba fetahi*
**relic** *(n.)* **ቁርማም** *qurmame*
**relief** *(n.)* **ቤተ ክርስቲያን** *bete kiristian*
**relieve** *(v.)* **መካነ መቓብር** *mekane meqabere*
**religion** *(n.)* **ዓምጠቑ** *ameteqku*
**religious** *(adj.)* **ፀብሒ** *xebhi*
**relinquish** *(v.)* **ሲደር** *cider*
**relish** *(v.)* **መቐረት** *meq̈eret*
**relocate** *(v.)* **ሽጋራ** *shegara*
**reluctance** *(n.)* **ቤት ስኒማ** *bet ciniema*
**reluctant** *(adj.)* **ቐረፋ** *qerefa*
**rely** *(v.)* **ክቢ** *kebi*
**remain** *(v.)* **ተረፈ** *terefe*
**remainder** *(n.)* **ከቢብ** *kbibe*
**remains** *(n.)* **ተሰራጨወ** *tsrachew*
**remand** *(v.)* **ዑደት** *xudet*
**remark** *(v.)* **ገረዘ** *gereze'*
**remarkable** *(adj.)* **ዶብ** *dobe*
**remedial** *(adj.)* **ገደበ** *gedebe*

**remedy** *(n.)* **አዝዩ ጥንቁቕ** *azeyu tenequqe*
**remember** *(v.)* **ሃዋህዉ** *hawahewu*
**remembrance** *(n.)* **ሰርከስ** *serekse*
**remind** *(v.)* **ሳንዱቕ** *sanaduqe*
**reminder** *(n.)* **ማይ መዋህለሊ** *maye mwaheleli*
**reminiscence** *(v.)* **ኣስተንትኖ** *'astentno*
**reminiscent** *(adj.)* **ጠቐሰ** *tekese*
**remiss** *(adj.)* **ዜጋ** *zega*
**remission** *(n.)* **ዜግነት** *zegenet*
**remit** *(n.)* **ተኽል** *tekil*
**remittance** *(n.)* **ሲትሪክ** *citric*
**remnant** *(n.)* **ከተማ** *ketema*
**remonstrate** *(v.)* **ናይ ከተማ** *nayei ketema*
**remorse** *(n.)* **ናይ ስነ ዜጋ ትምሕርቲ** *nayei sine zega temehereti*
**remote** *(adj.)* **ማሕበረሰባዊ** *mahebresebawi*
**removable** *(adj.)* **ስቪል ሰብ** *sevil sebe*
**removal** *(n.)* **ስልጣን** *seletan*
**remove** *(v.)* **ኣሰልጠነ** *aseltene*
**remunerate** *(v.)* **ዝተኸደነ** *zetkdn*
**remuneration** *(n.)* **ኽዳን** *Kedan*
**remunerative** *(adj.)* **ሓቂዩ በለ** *haqiyu bele*
**renaissance** *(n.)* **ይግበኣኒ በሃላይ** *yigbeani behalayi*
**render** *(v.)* **ርሁድ** *rehude*
**rendezvous** *(n.)* **ብኣዉያት ሓተተ** *beawyat hattete*
**renegade** *(n.)* **ኣጣበቐ** *atabeqe*
**renew** *(v.)* **ዓሌት** *alet*
**renewal** *(adj.)* **ሕቡእ** *hibuea'*
**renounce** *(v.t. )* **ኣጣቐዐ** *atabeqe*
**renovate** *(n. )* **ኣብራህረሀ** *abrahereh*
**renovation** *(n. )* **ከለሰ** *keles*
**renown** *(n.)* **መልእኽቲ** *mleekti*
**renowned** *(adj.)* **ግልፀነት** *geletsinet*
**rent** *(n.)* **ባእሲ** *baesii*
**rental** *(n.)* **ጨበጠ** *chebete*
**renunciation** *(n.)* **ክፍሊ** *kifeli*
**reoccur** *(v.)* **ሕሩይ** *heruyei*
**reorganize** *(v.)* **ቀንደኛ** *qenedegna*
**repair** *(v.)* **ምጉጃል** *megujak*
**repartee** *(n.)* **ጎጀለ** *gojele*
**repatriate** *(v.)* **ዓንቀፀ** *aneqetse*
**repatriation** *(n.)* **ኣብ ፀቢብ ቦታ** *ab tsebib bota*
**repay** *(v.)* **ፅፍሪ** *txefri*
**repayment** *(n.)* **ጭቃ** *chiqa*
**repeal** *(v.)* **ፅሩይ** *tsxeruye*
**repeat** *(v.)* **ፅሬት** *tsxerete*
**repel** *(v.)* **ሓፀበ** *hatsxebe*
**repellent** *(adj.)* **ንፁር** *netsxur*
**repent** *(v.)* **ምእላይ** *meaelayi*
**repentance** *(n.)* **ፅሩይ** *tsxeruyi*
**repentant** *(adj.)* **ጨደደ** *chedede*
**repercussion** *(n.)* **ጨዳድ** *cdade*
**repetition** *(n.)* **ምሕረት** *meherte*
**replace** *(v.)* **መሓሪ** *mhari*
**replacement** *(n.)* **ክሌምንታይን** *klemintaine*
**replay** *(v.)* **ነኸሰ** *nKes*
**replenish** *(v.)* **ካህናት** *kahenat'*
**replete** *(adj.)* **ካህን** *kahin*
**replica** *(n.)* **ቀሺ** *qshi*
**replicate** *(v.)* **ፀሓፊ** *tsehafi*

**reply** *(v.)* ብልሂ *bilihi*
**report** *(v.)* ድምፂ ፈጠረ *dimtsi ftre'*
**reportage** *(n.)* ዓሚል *Amil*
**reporter** *(n.)* ፀድፊ *Tsxdefi*
**repose** *(n.)* ኩነታት ኣየር *kunetat ayer'*
**repository** *(n.)* መዛዘሚ ወሰናይ *mzammi wsanaye*
**repossess** *(v.)* ደየበ *deYebe*
**reprehensible** *(adj.)* ተዓወተ *tAwte'*
**represent** *(v.)* ተለጠፈ *tlTefe'*
**representation** *(n.)* ክሊኒክ *kliniqk*
**representative** *(adj.)* ኣጋጨዉ *agachewu*
**repress** *(v.)* መንቀርቀር *menqerker*
**repression** *(n.)* መንጠሊና *mentelina*
**reprieve** *(v.)* ሰዓት *seat'*
**reprimand** *(v.)* መግናሕቲ *megnaḧti*
**reprint** *(v.)* እንደገና ሓተመ *'èndegena ḧateme*
**reprisal** *(n.)* ዓፀወ *atsewe*
**reproach** *(v.)* ውሻጠ *wushate'*
**reprobate** *(n.)* ዝተቓረበ *zitqarebe*
**reproduce** *(v.)* ዝረገአ ደም *ziregeaA' deM'*
**reproduction** *(n.)* ክዳን *kidan*
**reproductive** *(adj.)* ከደነ *kedeNe'*
**reproof** *(n.)* ክዳዉንቲ *kidawunti'*
**reprove** *(v.)* ወቐሰ *weq̈ese*
**reptile** *(n.)* ደበና *debNa'*
**republic** *(n.)* ዕስለ ኣናሕብ *esil anahib*
**republican** *(adj.)* ሸኾና *shekona*
**repudiate** *(v.)* ኣዘናግአ *azenagiaa*
**repudiation** *(n.)* ኣዝዩ ጥዑም ግን ዝመርር *aziyu teum gin zemrer*
**repugnance** *(n.)* ጋንታ *ganeta*
**repugnant** *(adj.)* ኣፋፍኖት *afafenote*
**repulse** *(v.)* ላህዛዝ *lahezaZ'*
**repulsion** *(n.)* ዝተኣከቡ ነገራት *ziteakebu negerat*
**repulsive** *(adj.)* ኣጥቢቑ ሓዘ *atbiqu haze'*
**reputation** *(n.)* ኣሰልጣኒ *aseltani*
**repute** *(n.)* ሕመት *himet*
**request** *(n.)* ሓድነት *hatnet*
**requiem** *(n.)* ሻሕኻር *shahikar*
**require** *(v.)* ገምገም ባሕሪ *gemgem bahiriyi*
**requirement** *(n.)* ኣብ ገምገም ባሕሪ ዝርከብ *ab gemgem bahiri zirkeb*
**requisite** *(n. )* ለፀመ *ltseme'*
**requisite** *(adj.)* ጁባ *juba*
**requisition** *(n.)* ሸሓረ *shehare*
**requite** *(v.t. )* ኣገደዳሲ ኣካል *agededasi akal'*
**rescind** *(v.)* ኮረት *koret*
**rescue** *(v.)* ሰራሒ ሳእኒ *serahi saeni'*
**research** *(n.)* ኮብራ ተመን *korabe tmN'*
**resemblance** *(n.)* ዓለባ ሳሬት *aleba saret*
**resemble** *(v.)* ኮኬን *kocain*
**resent** *(v.)* ኩኩናይ መኮንን *kukunai mekonin*
**resentment** *(n.)* ቋፃር *qutsar*
**reservation** *(n.)* ሰፈር ኣብራሪ ኣየር *sefer abrar ayer*
**reserve** *(v.)* ድዱዕ *diduee'*

**reservoir** *(n.)* **ሕዉስዋስ መስተ** *hiwuswas meste*
**reshuffle** *(v.)* **ዕቡይ** *eebuY;*
**reside** *(v.)* **ክእለት** *keeileT*
**residence** *(n.)* **ኮኮናት** *coconat*
**resident** *(n.)* **ኮኩን** *cocoon*
**residential** *(adj.)* **ምስጢራዊ ፅሑፍ** *mesetirawi tsihuf*
**residual** *(adj.)* **ትራፍ** *traf*
**residue** *(n.)* **ቀዋሚ** *qewami*
**resign** *(v.)* **ኣገደደ** *agedded*
**resignation** *(n.)* **ኣምረሓ** *amreha*
**resilient** *(adj.)* **ተመላሲ** *temelasi*
**resist** *(v.)* **ተቓወመ** *teqaweme*
**resistance** *(n.)* **ቡን** *bun*
**resistant** *(adj.)* **ካዝና** *kazina*
**resolute** *(adj.)* **ሳፁን ሬሳ** *satsun resa*
**resolution** *(n.)* **ቅልጣፈ** *qiltafe*
**resolve** *(v.)* **ዘዕግብ** *heigib*
**resonance** *(n.)* **ኣስተንተነ** *astentene*
**resonant** *(adj.)* **ተመሳሳሊ** *temesasali*
**resonate** *(v.)* **ግንዛበ** *ginizabe*
**resort** *(n.)* **ከይተመርዓዉ ሓቢሮም ነበሩ** *keyitemerawu habirom neberu*
**resound** *(v.)* **ተሳነየ** *tesaneyei*
**resource** *(n.)* **ዝሳነይን ዘእተዋደድን** *zisaneyin etewadedin*
**resourceful** *(adj.)* **ሓድነት** *hadinet*
**respect** *(n.)* **ሓድነት ዝፈጠረ** *hadinet zifetere*
**respectable** *(adj.)* **ዓኹለለ** *qkulele*
**respectful** *(adj.)* **ሳንቲም** *sanetime*
**respective** *(adj.)* **ሳንቲም ሰርሐ** *sanetime sereha*
**respiration** *(n.)* **ተገጣጠመ** *tegetateme*
**respirator** *(n.)* **ተጓንፎ** *tegwanefo*
**respire** *(v.)* **ዓለባ** *aleba*
**respite** *(n.)* **ቀፀላይ** *qetselayi*
**resplendent** *(adj.)* **ቆራር** *qorare*
**respond** *(v.)* **ቁርፀት ከብዲ** *quretset kebedi*
**respondent** *(n.)* **ተሓባበረ** *tehababere*
**response** *(n.)* **ትህብብር** *tehibiberi*
**responsibility** *(n.)* **ናይ ስራሕ ቦታ** *nayei serahe bota*
**responsible** *(adj.)* **ተደርዓመ** *tederame*
**responsive** *(adj.)* **ኳሌታ** *kwaleta*
**rest** *(v.)* **ኣከበ** *akebe*
**restaurant** *(n.)* **ትሕጃ** *tihija*
**restful** *(adj.)* **ኣከበ** *akebe'*
**restitution** *(n.)* **ተዋሕለለ** *tewahilwlw*
**restive** *(adj.)* **ተጠራቐመ** *teteraqeme*
**restoration** *(adj.)* **ኣምፀአ** *amtseA'*
**restore** *(v.)* **ኮሌጅብርኪ ትምህርቲ** *co;ege berki temihereti*
**restrain** *(v.)* **ተጋጨወ** *tegachewe*
**restraint** *(n.)* **ናይ ማዕድን** *nayi maeidin*
**restrict** *(n. )* **ናይ ምግጫዉ ሓደጋ** *nayei megechaw hadega*
**restriction** *(n.)* **ቀያዲ** *qeyadi*
**restrictive** *(adj.)* **ምሽጥራዊ ስምምዕ** *mishtirawi simemeeh*

**result** *(n. )* ሽቶ *shito*
**resultant** *(adj.)* ዓብይ መኣንጣ *abiy meanta*
**resume** *(v.)* ኮሎኔል *kolonele*
**resumption** *(n. )* ባዕዳዊ *baeedawi*
**resurgence** *(a. )* ብባእዳዉያን ትግዛዕ ሃገር *bibaedawiyane tegezaze hager*
**resurgent** *(adj.)* ገዚፍ *gezife*
**resurrect** *(v.)* ሓወልቲ *hawelti*
**retail** *(n. )* ዓንዲ *anedi*
**retailer** *(n.)* ሕብሪ *hibri*
**retain** *(v.i. )* ፅልዋ ኣሕደረ *tsilwa ahdere*
**retainer** *(n.)* ዝተሕብረ *zitehibri*
**retaliate** *(v.)* ሕሊና ምስሓት *hilina mesehate*
**retaliation** *(n.)* ሚዶ/መመሸጥ *mido/memesheti*
**retard** *(v.)* ኹናት *kunat*
**retardation** *(n. )* ተዋጋኢ *tewagaei*
**retarded** *(adj.)* ጥማር *timar*
**retch** *(v.)* ፀንበረ *tsenber*
**retention** *(n.)* ነዳዲ *nedadi*
**retentive** *(adj.)* ተቐፃፃላይ *teqetsatsalaye*
**rethink** *(v.)* ናዓ *na'ä*
**reticent** *(adj.)* መስሓቕ *meshaq̈*
**retina** *(n. )* መስሓቕ *meshaq̈*
**retinue** *(n.)* ጅራታም ኮኾብ *ĵratam*
**retire** *(v.)* ምቾት *mchot*
**retirement** *(n.)* ጥጣሐ *ẗtahe*
**retiring** *(adj.)* ምቹእ *mchu'è*
**retort** *(v.)* ተዋዛዪ *tewazayi*
**retouch** *(v.)* ጭሕጋር *čḧgar*
**retrace** *(v.t. )* ኣዘዘ *azeze*
**retract** *(v.)* ኣዛዚ *azazi*
**retread** *(v.)* ኮማንደር *komander*
**retreat** *(v.t. )* ኮማንዶ *komando*
**retrench** *(v.)* ኣኽበረ *aḱbere*
**retrenchment** *(n.)* ዝክር *zkr*
**retrial** *(n.)* ጀመረ *ĵemere*
**retribution** *(n.)* ምጅማር *mĵmar*
**retrieve** *(v.)* ነኣደ *ne'ade*
**retriever** *(n.)* ዚነኣድ *zine'ad*
**retro** *(adj.)* ናእዳ *na'èda*
**retroactive** *(adj.)* ርእይቶ *r'èyto*
**retrograde** *(adj.)* ታዕሊቕ *ta'ëliq̈*
**retrospect** *(n. )* ዓላቒ *älaq̈i*
**retrospective** *(adj.)* ንግድ *ngd*
**return** *(v.)* ንግዳዊ *ngdawi*
**return** *(n.)* ራህርሀ *rahrhe*
**reunion** *(n.)* ውክልና *wklna*
**reunite** *(v.)* ኮሚሽነር *komishner*
**reuse** *(v.)* መጋጠሚ *megatmi*
**revamp** *(v.)* ፈጸመ *fexeme*
**reveal** *(v.)* መብጽዓ *mebx'ä*
**revel** *(v.)* ሽማግለ *shmagle*
**revelation** *(n. )* ተመዛዚ ከብሒ *temezazi kebḧi*
**revenge** *(n.)* ኣቕሓ *'aq̈ḧa*
**revenue** *(n.)* ሓባራዊ *ḧabarawi*
**reverberate** *(v.)* ሓፋሽ *ḧafash*
**revere** *(v.)* ልሙድ *lmud*
**revered** *(adj.)* ናይ ሓባር ብልጽግና *nay ḧabar blxgna*
**reverence** *(n.)* ህውከት *hwket*
**reverend** *(adj.)* ኮማዊ *komawi*
**reverent** *(adj.)* ተዋህደ *tewahde*
**reverential** *(adj.)* ተማሓላለፊ *temaḧalalefi*
**reverie** *(n. )* ቈራቢ *qWerabi*
**reversal** *(n.)* ሃበሬታ ተለዋወጠ *habereta*

**reverse** ***(v.)*** **ርክብ** *rkb*
**reversible** ***(adj.)*** **ምክፋል** *mkfal*
**revert** ***(v.)*** **ዴስነት** *deesnet*
**review** ***(n.)*** **ማሕበረ ሰብ** *maȟbere seb*
**revile** ***(v.)*** **ለወጠ** *leweẗe*
**revise** ***(v.)*** **ጥርኑፍ** *ẗrnuf*
**revision** ***(n. )*** **ብጻይ** *bxay*
**revival** ***(n.)*** **መሰነይታ** *meseneyta*
**revivalism** ***(n.)*** **ተነጻጸሪ** *tenexaxeri*
**revive** ***(v.)*** **ኣነጻጸረ** *anexaxere*
**revocable** ***(adj.)*** **ምንጽጻር** *mnxxar*
**revocation** ***(n.)*** **ክፍሊ** *kfli*
**revoke** ***(v.)*** **ቡሶላ** *busola*
**revolt** ***(v.)*** **ድንጋጸ** *dngaxe*
**revolution** ***(n.)*** **ተቓዳዊ** *teq̈adawi*
**revolutionary** ***(adj.)*** **ወዲ ሃገር** *wedi hager*
**revolutionize** ***(v.)*** **ቀሰ'በ** *qesebe*
**revolve** ***(v.)*** **ቁንጩል** *qunčul*
**revolver** ***(n. )*** **ቁንጩል** *qunčul*
**revulsion** ***(n.)*** **ከሓሰ** *keȟase*
**reward** ***(n.)*** **ካሕሳ** *kaȟsa*
**rewind** ***(v.)*** **ኣላ'ላዪ** *alalayi*
**rhapsody** ***(n.)*** **ተቐዳደመ** *teq̈edademe*
**rhetoric** ***(n.)*** **ክእለት** *k'èlet*
**rhetorical** ***(adj.)*** **ክኢላ** *k'ila*
**rheumatic** ***(adj.)*** **ምውድዳር** *mwddar*
**rheumatism** ***(n.)*** **ውድድራዊ** *wddrawi*
**rhinoceros** ***(n. )*** **ተዋዳዳሪ** *tewadadari*
**rhodium** ***(n.)*** **ጠርነፈ** *ẗernefe*
**rhombus** ***(n.)*** **ዕጉብ** *ëgub*
**rhyme** ***(n.)*** **ተጣርዐ** *teẗar'ë*
**rhythm** ***(n.)*** **ዝበልዎ ሕራይ ዝብል** *zibeliwo hirayi zibil*
**rhythmic** ***(adj.)*** **ምቕሉል** *mq̈lul*
**rib** ***(n. )*** **መልአ** *meleA'*
**ribbon** ***(n. )*** **መላኢ** *mela'i*
**rice** ***(n.)*** **ምሉእ** *mlu'è*
**rich** ***(adj.)*** **ምፍጻም** *mfxam*
**richly** ***(adv. )*** **ዝተሓላለኸ** *zteȟalaleḱe*
**richness** ***(n. )*** **ሕልኽልኽ** *ȟlḱlḱ*
**rick** ***(n. )*** **ወጅሂ** *weĵhi*
**rickets** ***(n.)*** **እሺታ** *èshita*
**rickety** ***(adj.)*** **ምቕሉል** *mq̈lul*
**rickshaw** ***(n.)*** **ሓላለኸ** *ȟalaleḱe*
**rid** ***(v.)*** **ሕልኽልኽ** *ȟlḱlḱ*
**riddance** ***(n.)*** **ምስ ግበነኛ** *mis gibenegna*
**riddle** ***(n.)*** **ምሽባን** *mshban*
**riddled** ***(adj.)*** **ናእዳ** *na'èda*
**ride** ***(v.)*** **ናእዳ** *na'èda*
**rider** ***(n. )*** **ተኣዘዘ** *te'azeze*
**ridge** ***(n.)*** **ክፋል** *kifale*
**ridicule** ***(n. )*** **ኣኽበረ** *aḱbere*
**ridiculous** ***(adj.)*** **ኣቑመ** *aq̈Weme*
**rife** ***(adj.)*** **ደራሲ ወራቢ** *derasi werabi*
**rifle** ***(n.)*** **ዝተዋሃሃደ** *ztewahahade*
**rifle** ***(v.)*** **ምድላው** *mdlaw*
**rift** ***(n.)*** **ለቓም ፊደል** *leq̈am fidel*
**rig** ***(v.)*** **ድኹዒ** *dḱu'ï*
**rigging** ***(n.)*** **ቅሳነት** *qsanet*
**right** ***(adj.)*** **ውሁድ** *whud*
**right** ***(n)*** **ተረድአ** *tered'e*
**righteous** ***(adj.)*** **ኪርዳእ ዚከኣል** *kirda'è zike'al*
**rightful** ***(adj.)*** **ምርዳእ** *mrda'è*
**rigid** ***(adj.)*** **ኣጠቓላሊ** *aẗeq̈alali*
**rigmarole** ***(n.)*** **ጨበጠ** *čebeẗe*

**rigorous** *(adj.)* ምጭበጥ *mčbaẗ*
**rigour** *(n. )* ሓዘ *ḧaze*
**rim** *(n. )* ግድድፍ *gddf*
**ring** *(n.)* ምግዳ'ድ *mgdad*
**ring** *(v.)* ግዴታዊ *gdeetawi*
**ringlet** *(n. )* ግድነታዊ *gdnetawi*
**ringworm** *(n.)* ስክፍታ *skfta*
**rink** *(n.)* ምቕማር *mq̈mar*
**rinse** *(v.)* ቈጸረ *qWexere*
**riot** *(n.)* ኮምፕዩተር *kompyuter*
**rip** *(v.)* ኣራጠበ *aratebe*
**ripe** *(adj.)* ብጻይ *bxay*
**ripen** *(v.)* ምትእስሳር *mt'èssar*
**riposte** *(n.)* ሃጓም *hagWam*
**ripple** *(n.)* ሓብእ *ḧab'e*
**rise** *(v.)* ኣመነ *amene*
**risible** *(adj.)* ትዕቢት *t'ëbit*
**rising** *(n.)* ተኣማኒ *te'amani*
**risk** *(n. )* ተረድአ *tered'e*
**risky** *(adj.)* ኣጽዓቕ *ax'äq̈e*
**rite** *(n. )* ምጽዓቕ *mx'äq̈*
**ritual** *(n.)* ኣምር *amr*
**rival** *(n.)* ምእማር *m'èmar*
**rivalry** *(n.)* ተመልከተ *temelkete*
**rive** *(v.)* ብዛዕባ *bza'ëba*
**river** *(n. )* ሙዚቃዊ ምርኢት *muziqawi mr'it*
**rivet** *(n.)* ውሁድ *whud*
**rivulet** *(n. )* ሕድገት *ḧdget*
**road** *(n.)* ዛዕጎል *za'ëgol*
**roadster** *(n.)* ወድአ *wed'e*
**roadwork** *(n.)* ደገፍ ረኸበ *degef rek̗ebe*
**roadworthy** *(adj.)* ሓጺርን ብሩህን *ḧaxirn bruhn*
**roam** *(v.)* መወዳእታ *meweda'èta*
**roar** *(n.)* ደካሊ *dekali*
**roar** *(v.)* ኣቃመመ *aqameme*
**roast** *(v.)* ፈጠራ *feẗera*
**rob** *(v.)* መኻይድቲ *mek̗aydti*
**robber** *(n. )* ስምምዕ *smm'ë*
**robbery** *(n. )* ስምምዕ *smm'ë*
**robe** *(n.)* ብሓባር ምኻድ *bḧabar mk̗ad*
**robot** *(n.)* ጭቡጥ *čbuẗ*
**robust** *(adj.)* ውሽማ *wshma*
**rock** *(n. )* ተሰማምዐ *tesemam'ë*
**rocket** *(n. )* ተቓዳዊ *teq̈adawi*
**rocky** *(adj.)* መውቃዕቲ *mewqa'ëti*
**rod** *(n. )* ኰነነ *kWanene*
**rodent** *(n. )* ምኹናን *mk̗unan*
**rodeo** *(n.)* ሓፈሰ *ḧafese*
**roe** *(n. )* ተበርጠጠ *tebertete*
**rogue** *(n.)* ቀመመ *qememe*
**roguery** *(n.)* ኩነት *kunet*
**roguish** *(adj.)* ኩነታዊ *kunetawi*
**roister** *(v.)* ኩነታት ጥዕና *kunetate tiena*
**role** *(n. )* ደበ'ሰ *debese*
**roll** *(v.i. )* ምጽንናዕ *mxnna'ë*
**roll** *(n. )* ኮንዶም *condom*
**roll-call** *(n. )* ኣስማት ምጽዋዕ *'asmat mxwa'ë*
**roller** *(n. )* መሓረ *meḧare*
**rollercoaster** *(n.)* ጠባይ *ẗebay*
**romance** *(n.)* ኣደብ *adeb*
**romantic** *(adj.)* መራሒ *meraḧi*
**romp** *(v.)* ኮኖ *kono*
**roof** *(n.)* ሕዋስ ምቁራን *ḧwas mquran*
**roofing** *(n.)* ናይ ዶልሺ *naydolshi*
**rook** *(n.)* እንዳ-ዶልሺ *èndadolshi*
**rookery** *(n.)* ተሓባባሪ *teḧababari*
**room** *(n.)* ማሕበር *maḧber*
**roomy** *(adj.)* ዓደለ *ädele*
**roost** *(n.)* ዘተ *zete*

**rooster** *(n.)* **ተናዘዘ** *tenazeze*
**root** *(n.)* **ኑዛዜ** *nuzazee*
**rooted** *(adj.)* **ኣማኒት** *amanit*
**rope** *(n.)* **ምስጢር ኣካፈለ** *msẗir 'akafele*
**rosary** *(n.)* **እምነት** *èmnet*
**rose** *(n.)* **ተኣማማኒ** *te'amamani*
**rosette** *(n.)* **ምስጢራዊ** *msẗirawi*
**roster** *(n.)* **ኣሰራርዓ** *aserar'ä*
**rostrum** *(n.)* **ወሰነ** *wesene*
**rosy** *(adj.)* **ማእሰርቲ** *ma'èserti*
**rot** *(v.)* **ኣረጋገጸ** *aregagexe*
**rota** *(n.)* **ምርግጋጽ** *mrggax*
**rotary** *(adj.)* **ወረሰ** *werese*
**rotate** *(v.)* **ውርሳ** *wrsa*
**rotation** *(n.)* **ፀንበረ** *tsenbere*
**rote** *(n.)* **ግጭት** *gčt*
**rotor** *(n.)* **መራኽበ** *meraḱbo*
**rotten** *(adj.)* **ሓባረ** *ḧabari*
**rouge** *(n.)* **ተሰማምዐ** *tesemam'ë*
**rough** *(adj.)* **ስምምዕ** *smm'ë*
**roulette** *(n.)* **ተጋተረ** *tegatere*
**round** *(adj.)* **ቅርሕንቲ** *kiri hinti*
**roundabout** *(n.)* **ኣደናገረ** *adenagere*
**rounded** *(adj.)* **ዕግርግር** *ëgrgr*
**roundly** *(adv. )* **ረትዐ** *ret'ë*
**rouse** *(v.)* **ዚወሃሃድ** *ziwehahad*
**rout** *(n.)* **ውርሻዊ** *wrshawi*
**route** *(n.)* **ቅጽጽ ዝበለ** *qxx zbele*
**routine** *(n.)* **ጻዕቂ** *xa'ëqi*
**rove** *(v.)* **ኣኻኸበ** *aḱaḱebe*
**rover** *(n. )* **እኽብካብ** *èḱbkab*
**roving** *(adj.)* **ተንቀሳቓሲ** *tenqesaq̈asi*
**row** *(n.)* **መግለጺ ሓጐስ** *meglexi ḧagWas*
**rowdy** *(adj.)* **ተኣከበ** *te'akebe*
**royal** *(n. )* **ጉባኤ** *guba'ee*
**royalist** *(n. )* **ዝስማዕማዕ** *zismaemae tsemaexmeaa*
**royalty** *(n.)* **ተሰስማዕመዐ** *tsemaexmeaa*
**rub** *(n.)* **ግምታዊ ሓሳብ** *gemetawi hasabe*
**rub** *(v.)* **ፋሕፍሐ** *faḧfḧe*
**rubber** *(n. )* **ግጥሚ ኣንበበ** *geTemi anebbb*
**rubbish** *(n. )* **መስተፃምር** *,mestetsamire*
**rubble** *(n. )* **ጠራፊ መሳርዕ** *Terafi ms*
**rubric** *(n.)* **ናይ ቁስለት ዓይኒ** *nay'l qusele't aa'yeni*
**ruby** *(n.)* **ዋኒን/ጉዳይ** *maniein/guda'yi*
**rucksack** *(n.)* **ምትሃተኛ** *meteha'te'gna*
**ruckus** *(n.)* **ኮራዕ** *kora'ee*
**rudder** *(n.)* **ኣራኽበ** *aara'EH'kebe*
**rude** *(adj.)* **ርክብ** *re'KE'be*
**rudiment** *(n.)* **ተመሻጠረ** *temeSHA'tere*
**rudimentary** *(adj.)* **ወረረ** *were're*
**rue** *(v.)* **ወረራ** *we're'ra*
**rueful** *(adj.)* **ሕሊና** *hi'lina*
**ruffian** *(n.)* **ግንዛበ ዘለዎ** *giniza'be zelewo*
**ruffle** *(v.)* **ቀደሰ** *qede'se*
**rug** *(n.)* **ተኸታታሊ** *teHE'tata'li*
**rugby** *(n.)* **ዝተሓተ** *zi'te'hat'ee*
**rugged** *(adj.)* **ሓበራዊ ምርድዳእ** *haberawi merederaoo*
**ruin** *(n.)* **ፍቓድ** *feqa'de*
**ruinous** *(adj.)* **ስምምዕ** *se'memeee*
**rule** *(n.)* **ሳዕቤን** *saee'bene*

**rule** *(v.)* ውፅኢት *wutsieiit*
**ruler** *(n.)* ሓለዋ ተፈጥሮ *haalewa tefetero*
**ruling** *(n.)* ፀረ ለዉጢ *tsere lewuti*
**rum** *(n.)* ሰርዐ *sereaa'*
**rumble** *(v.)* ብቑጠባ ተጠቕመ *b'quteba te'teqe'mu*
**rumbustious** *(adj.)* ኣስተንተነ *aa' seten'tene*
**ruminant** *(n.)* ብዙሕ *bezuHi'h*
**ruminate** *(v.)* ሓሳቢ *ha'sabi*
**rumination** *(n.)* ኣብ ግምት ኣእተወ *hab' gimit aaetewe*
**rummage** *(v.)* ኣተኩሩ ረኣየ *aa' tekuru rexayee*
**rummy** *(n.)* ሰንደወ *senedwwe*
**rumour** *(n.)* ዝተለኣኹ ኣቑሑት *zetelezaaHu aaqkuhut*
**rumple** *(v.)* ኣካተተ *aakate'te*
**rumpus** *(n.)* ተኸታታሊ *te'KHE'tatali*
**run** *(n.)* ዘይቕየር *zey'qeyer*
**run** *(v.)* መፅናዕንዒ *mexenaee'neeeii*
**runaway** *(adj.)* ኣፀናንዐ *a'txennea*
**rundown** *(adj.)* ኣሐየለ *ahayl'e*
**rung** *(n. )* ስምምዕ *sememe'*
**runnel** *(n.)* ሰብኣይ ንግስቲ *sebeaayi negeseti*
**runner** *(n. )* ጐያዩ *gWayayi*
**runny** *(adj.)* ብቕሊሉ ዝረኣይ *beqlilu zereaayii*
**runway** *(n.)* ፀንበረ *xeneber*
**rupture** *(v.t. )* ሻራ *shara*
**rural** *(adj.)* ዉዲት *wudit*
**ruse** *(n.)* ተመሻጠረ *temeshatere*
**rush** *(v.)* ኮንስታብል *konstablee*
**Rusk** *(n.)* ኮንስታብል ሰብነት *konstable sebenet'*
**rust** *(n.)* ዘየቕርፅ *zeye'qereXe'*
**rustic** *(adj.)* ናይ ከዋኽብቲ *naye kKe'wakib'ti*
**rusticate** *(v.)* ድንጋፀ *denegaXE'*
**rustication** *(n. )* ድርቀት *dere'qe'T*
**rusticity** *(n.)* ክፋል *kefale*
**rustle** *(v.)* ኣድማፂ *adma'txi*
**rusty** *(adj.)* ተሓሰበ *teha'sebe*
**rut** *(n.)* ሕገ መንግስቲ *hige mengistii*
**ruthless** *(adj.)* ኲነታት ጥዕና ውልቀሰብ *kunetat tieiina wulkeseb*
**rye** *(n.)* ኣጋደደ *aagadede*

# S

**Sabbath** *(n. )* ኣፀበበ *axebebbe'*
**sabotage** *(v.)* ሃነፀ *hanXE'*
**sabre** *(n.)* ህንፀት *hintsxet'*
**saccharin** *(n.)* ሃናፂ *hanatxi'*
**saccharine** *(adj.)* ተረደአ *teredeA'*
**sachet** *(n.)* ቆንስል *qonesele*
**sack** *(n.)* ቆንፅላ *qonexela*
**sack** *(v.)* ናይቆንስል ገዛ *nayi qonsele geza*
**sacrament** *(n.)* ኣማኸረ *aAmaHe're*
**sacred** *(adj.)* ኣማኸሪ *amaHa'ri*
**sacrifice** *(n.)* ተመማኸኸረ *temeHaHere'*
**sacrifice** *(v.)* ተመቖመ *temeQeme'*
**sacrificial** *(adj.)* ሸማቲ *shemati*
**sacrilege** *(n.)* ርክብ ግብረ ስጋ ፈፀመ *rekib gibre siga fetxem'e*

**sacrilegious** *(adj.)* **ምጥቓም** *miT; Qqam'*
**sacrosanct** *(adj.)* **ርክብ** *rikib*
**sad** *(adj.)* **ምልጋብ** *milgab*
**sadden** *(v.)* **ተላጋቢ** *telagabi*
**saddle** *(n.)* **ሓዘ** *haze'*
**saddler** *(n.)* **ኮንቴነር** *konte'ner*
**sadism** *(n. )* **ምዕጋት** *meegat*
**sadist** *(n.)* **መራዚ ንጥረ ነገር** *merazi netire negere'*
**safari** *(n.)* **ሓሰበ** *haseb*
**safe** *(adj.)* **ኣትኹሩ ረኣየ** *xteKuru reAaye'*
**safe** *(n. )* **እዋናዊ** *eewanawi*
**safeguard** *(n. )* **ንዕቐት** *neeeiqet*
**safety** *(n. )* **ሸለልታ** *shelelta*
**saffron** *(n.)* **ተኸራኸረ** *teHerakere*
**sag** *(v.)* **ዝዓገበ** *zea'gebe*
**saga** *(n.)* **ትሕዝቶ** *tihizeto*
**sagacious** *(adj.)* **ቅርሕንቲ** *kqir'hinti*
**sagacity** *(n. )* **ዕግበት** *qeig'bet*
**sage** *(n.)* **ዘቀሓሕር** *zeqkeha'hir*
**sage** *(adj.)* **ዉድድር** *wudi'dir*
**sail** *(v.)* **ሃዋህው** *hawahewu'*
**sail** *(n.)* **ተወዳዳሪ** *te'we'dada'Rei*
**sailor** *(n. )* **ጥቓንጥቓ** *tQAneTeQA'*
**saint** *(n.)* **ክፍለ ኣለም** *kefele ale'm*
**saintly** *(adj.)* **ክፍለ ኣለማዊ** *kefele alemawii*
**sake** *(n.)* **ሳክ** *sak*
**salad** *(n. )* **ተደጋጋሚ** *tedegagami*
**salary** *(n. )* **ቀፀለ** *qeTsele'*
**sale** *(n. )* **ዝተቐፃፀለ** *zeteqaTsaTse'le*
**saleable** *(adj.)* **ተደጋጋሚ** *tedegagami*
**salesman** *(n.)* **ቀፃላይ** *qetsetay*
**salient** *(adj.)* **እስርስር በለ** *esir'sir bele*
**saline** *(adj.)* **ወሰናወሰን** *wesena'wesen*
**salinity** *(n.)* **ምፅባዕ** *mitsbaee*
**saliva** *(n.)* **ጥፍጣፍ** *ïftaf*
**sallow** *(adj.)* **ምክልኻል ጥንሲ** *meihil'hal tinsi*
**sally** *(n.)* **ፍንጣሰ** *fnïase*
**salmon** *(n. )* **ናይ ዉዕሊ** *nayei wueili'*
**salon** *(n.)* **ሳሎን** *salon*
**saloon** *(n. )* **ዉዕሊ ፈፀመ** *raȟreȟe*
**salsa** *(n.)* **ተኾናታሪ** *awarede*
**salt** *(n.)* **ኣሕፀረ** *had'e*
**salty** *(adj.)* **ተፃበአ** *ztegedfe*
**salutary** *(adj.)* **ተፃረረ** *gedam*
**salutation** *(n.)* **ተቓራኒ** *abegedam*
**salute** *(n.)* **ኣፈላላይ** *mȟxar*
**salvage** *(v.)* **ሕጊ ጠሓሰ** *werede*
**salvation** *(n.)* **ኣዋፅአ** *mwrad*
**salver** *(n.)* **ወፈየ** *neq̈ele*
**salvo** *(n.)* **ኢ-ተኣማኒነት** *ȟamed*
**Samaritan** *(n.)* **ገበረ** *kebdi*
**same** *(adj.)* **ቁፀፀር** *nay kebdi*
**sample** *(n.)* **ተቖፃፃሪ** *zerefe*
**sampler** *(n. )* **ኣከራኻሪ** *zerefe*
**sanatorium** *(n. )* **ኽርክር** *mzbul*
**sanatorium** *(n.)* **ገበነኛ እዪ በለ** *mïfa'è bele eyik*
**sanctification** *(n.)* **ስምብራት** *sȟtan*
**sanctify** *(v.)* **ሽግር** *adefafere*
**sanctimonious** *(adj.)* **ጭዋ** *wunzafe*
**sanction** *(v.)* **ኣኼባ ፀወዐ** *fenfene*
**sanctity** *(n. )* **ምኞት** *krhat*
**sanctuary** *(n. )* **ምችዊ** *kruh*

**sanctum** *(n.)* ናይ ደናግል ገዳም *xen'ë*
**sand** *(n. )* ባህሊ/ልምዲ *zeywda'è gedam*
**sandal** *(n. )* ተኣኻኸበ *'äqmi*
**sandalwood** *(n. )* ፍልጠት ዘለዎ *ḧrtum zelwo*
**sander** *(n.)* ወግዒ *meḧale*
**sandpaper** *(n.)* ኣዋግዐ *lbu'ë*
**sandwich** *(n.)* ምቕያር *nfu'ë bq̈u'ë*
**sandy** *(adj.)* ቀየረ *me'änaẗu*
**sane** *(adj.)* ተቐየረ *mzbul*
**sangfroid** *(n.)* ገለፀ *'ab l'ëli*
**sanguinary** *(adj.)* ኣዳዓዘ *geza*
**sanguine** *(adj.)* ገበነኛ *'aẗfe'e*
**sanitary** *(adj.)* ገበነኝነት *zixla'è*
**sanitation** *(n.)* ኣእመነ *xel'e*
**sanitize** *(v.)* ምሹእ/ደስ ዝብል *ẗntawi*
**sanity** *(n.)* ኣኼበ *tewegre*
**sap** *(n.)* ተዓጂበን ብሓባር ዝኸዳ *mwgad*
**sapling** *(n.)* ኣንቀጥቀጠ *wgur*
**sapphire** *(n. )* ምንቅጥቃጥ *fedfede*
**sarcasm** *(n.)* ከሻኒ *bza'ëba*
**sarcastic** *(adj.)* ኣብሰለ *'ab zurya*
**sarcophagus** *(n.)* ዘበናዊ እቶን *'ab l'ëli*
**sardonic** *(adj.)* ኬክ *bzyada*
**sari** *(n.)* ዝሑል *lḧlaḧe*
**sartorial** *(adj.)* ዛሕሊ *faḧfaḧi*
**sash** *(n.)* ዝሕልቱ *godnegodni*
**Satan** *(n. )* ምሕዳስ *aḧxere*
**satanic** *(adj.)* ተሓባበረ *wexa'i*
**Satanism** *(n.)* ትሕብብር *sereze*
**satchel** *(n. )* ተሓጋገዘ *handebetawi*
**sated** *(adj.)* ኣተሓባበረ *ḧagel*
**satellite** *(n.)* ሓቢሩ ከደ *xeleq̈Wu*
**satiable** *(adj.)* ተፃወረ *bkurat*
**satiate** *(v.)* ብማሽን ዝተገልበጠ ቅዳሕ *bḱur*
**satiety** *(n.)* ኣዝዩ ብዙሕ *bḱur*
**satin** *(n.)* መዳብ *fxum*
**satire** *(n.)* ሰረረ *sreet*
**satirical** *(adj.)* ቅዳሕ *meḧare*
**satirist** *(n.)* ናይ ሓንቲ ሓበ *seteye*
**satirize** *(v.)* ደረቕ ተሪር *teq̈eẗebe*
**satisfaction** *(n.)* ፍሕሶ *zahdi*
**satisfactory** *(adj.)* ልባዊ *req̈iq̈*
**satisfy** *(v.)* ዝተሰለፉ ፖላይስ *ẗluq̈*
**saturate** *(v.)* ወዉሸጣዊ ኣካ *trgum 'albo*
**saturation** *(n.)* ተኽሊ ቅመቃ ቕመም *trgum 'albonet*
**Saturday** *(n. )* ኮረኪ *ml'at*
**saturnine** *(adj.)* ሱማ *fdfud*
**sauce** *(n. )* ፃዕዳ ኣይኒ *ämexe*
**saucer** *(n.)* ኹርናዕ *texarafi*
**saucy** *(adj.)* ዘዛንመሎ *tedawebe*
**sauna** *(n.)* ስርዓተ ንግስና *delhametawi*
**saunter** *(v.)* መርማሪ *delhamet*
**sausage** *(n.)* ኣኽሊል *akademiyawi*
**savage** *(adj.)* ኣካላዊ *akademi*
**savagery** *(n.)* ዓብይ *mexe*
**save** *(v.)* ዓብይ ትካል ንግዲ *nehare*
**savings** *(n. )* ብርጌድ *anhari*
**saviour** *(n. )* ነቐለ ከደ ተሰናበተ *neq̈ele kede tesenabete*
**savour** *(v.t. )* ሓመድ *ḧamed*
**savoury** *(adj.)* ከብዲ *kebdi*
**saw** *(n.)* ናይ ከብዲ *nay kebdi*

**saw** ***(v.)*** **ዘረፈ** *zerefe*
**sawdust** ***(n.)*** **ዘረፈ** *zerefe*
**saxophone** ***(n.)*** **ምዝቡል** *mzbul*
**say** ***(n. )*** **ስሒታን** *sḧtan*
**saying** ***(n.)*** **ኣደፋፈረ** *adefafere*
**scab** ***(n.)*** **ዉንዛፈ** *wunzafe*
**scabbard** ***(n. )*** **ፈንፈነ** *fenfene*
**scabies** ***(n. )*** **ክርሃት** *krhat*
**scabrous** ***(adj.)*** **ክሩህ** *kruh*
**scaffold** ***(n. )*** **ጸንዐ** *xen'ë*
**scaffolding** ***(n.)***
**ዘይውዳእ** *zeywda'è*
**scald** ***(v.)*** **ዓቕሚ** *'äq̈mi*
**scale** ***(n.)*** **ሕርቱም** *ḧrtum*
**scallop** ***(n.)*** **መሓለ** *meḧale*
**scalp** ***(n.)*** **ልቡዕ** *lbu'ë*
**scam** ***(n.)*** **ንፉዕ ብቑዕ** *nfu'ë bq̈u'ë*
**scamp** ***(n.)*** **መዓናጡ** *me'änaẗu*
**scamper** ***(v.t.)*** **ምዝቡል** *mzbul*
**scan** ***(v.)*** **ኣብ ልዕሊ** *'ab l'ëli*
**scandal** ***(n.)*** **ኣጥፈአ** *'aẗfe'e*
**scandalize** ***(v.)*** **ምጥፋእ** *mẗfa'è*
**scanner** ***(n.)*** **ገዛ** *geza*
**scant** ***(adj.)*** **ዚጽላእ** *zixla'è*
**scanty** ***(adj.)*** **ጸልአ** *xel'e*
**scapegoat** ***(n.)*** **ጥንታዊ** *ẗntawi*
**scar** ***(n.)*** **ተወግረ** *tewegre*
**scarce** ***(adj.)*** **ምውጋድ** *mwgad*
**scarcely** ***(adv.)*** **ውጉር** *wgur*
**scare** ***(v.)*** **ፈድፈደ** *fedfede*
**scarecrow** ***(n.)*** **ብዛዕባ** *bza'ëba*
**scarf** ***(n.)*** **ኣብ ዙርያ** *'ab zurya*
**scarlet** ***(n.)*** **ኣብ ልዕሊ** *'ab l'ëli*
**scarp** ***(n.)*** **ብዝያዳ** *bzyada*
**scary** ***(adj.)*** **ልሕላሐ** *lḧlaḧe*
**scathing** ***(adj.)*** **ፋሕፋሒ** *faḧfaḧi*
**scatter** ***(v.)*** **ጎድን-**
**ጎድኒ** *godnegodni*
**scavenge** ***(v.)*** **ኣሕጸረ** *aḧxere*
**scenario** ***(n.)*** **ወጻኢ** *wexa'i*
**scene** ***(n. )*** **ሰረዘ** *sereze*
**scenery** ***(n.)***
**ሃንደበታዊ** *handebetawi*
**scenic** ***(adj.)*** **ሓገል** *ḧagel*
**scent** ***(n.)*** **ጸለቕ** *xeleq̈Wu*
**sceptic** ***(n.)*** **ብኩራት** *bkurat*
**sceptical** ***(adj.)*** **ብኹር** *bḱur*
**sceptre** ***(n. )*** **ብኹር** *bḱur*
**schedule** ***(n.)*** **ፍጹም** *fxum*
**schematic** ***(adj.)*** **ስሬት** *sreet*
**scheme** ***(n. )*** **መሓረ** *meḧare*
**schism** ***(n. )*** **ሰተየ** *seteye*
**schizophrenia** ***(n.)***
**ተቐጠበ** *teq̈eẗebe*
**scholar** ***(n.)*** **ዛህዲ** *zahdi*
**scholarly** ***(adj.)*** **ረቒቕ** *req̈iq̈*
**scholarship** ***(n.)*** **ጥሉቕ** *ẗluq̈*
**scholastic** ***(adj.)*** **ትርጉም**
**ኣልቦ** *trgum 'albo*
**school** ***(n.)*** **ትርጉም**
**ኣልቦነት** *trgum 'albonet*
**sciatica** ***(n.)*** **ምልኣት** *ml'at*
**science** ***(n.)*** **ፍድፉድ** *fdfud*
**scientific** ***(adj.)*** **ዓመጸ** *ämexe*
**scientist** ***(n.)*** **ተጻራፊ** *texarafi*
**scintillating** ***(adj.)*** **ተዳወበ**
*tedawebe*
**scissors** ***(n.)***
**ደልሃመታዊ** *delhametawi*
**scoff** ***(v.i.)*** **ደልሃመት** *delhamet*
**scold** ***(v.)***
**ኣካደሚያዊ** *akademiyawi*
**scoop** ***(n.)*** **ኣካደሚ** *akademi*
**scooter** ***(n. )*** **መጸ** *mexe*
**scope** ***(n.)*** **ነሃረ** *nehare*
**scorch** ***(v.)*** **ኣንሃረ** *anhari*

**score** *(n.)* ምጉላሕ *mgulaȟ*
**score** *(v.)* ኣጉለሓ *aguleȟe*
**scorer** *(n. )* ተቖበለ *teq̈ebele*
**scorn** *(n.)* ተቖባልነት ዘለዎ *teq̈ebalnet zelewo*
**scornful** *(adj.)* ቅባለ *qbale*
**scorpion** *(n. )* መእተዊ *me'ètewi*
**Scot** *(v.)* ኪርከብ ዚከኣል *kirkeb zike'al*
**scot-free** *(adv.)* ብጽሓት *bxȟat*
**scoundrel** *(n. )* መሳርሒ *mesarȟi*
**scour** *(v.)* ሓደጋ *ȟadega*
**scourge** *(n.)* ናይ ሓደጋ *nay ȟadega*
**scout** *(n.)* ኣጨብጨበ *ačebčebe*
**scowl** *(n. )* ኣዕነወ *a'ënewe*
**scrabble** *(v.)* ሰላምታ *selamta*
**scraggy** *(adj.)* ተሰማምዐ *tesemam'ë*
**scramble** *(v.)* መዕረፍ ኣጋይሽ *me'ëref 'agaysh*
**scrap** *(n. )* መሰነይቲ *meseneyti*
**scrape** *(v.)* ዓጀበ *äǰebe*
**scrappy** *(adj.)* ግብረ-ኣበር *gbre'aber*
**scratch** *(v.t.)* ፈጸመ *fexeme*
**scrawl** *(v.)* ክኢላ *k'ila*
**scrawny** *(adj.)* ፍጻሜ *fxamee*
**scream** *(v.)* ተውህዶ *tewhdo*
**screech** *(n.)* ውዕል - *w'ël*
**screech** *(n.)* ብመሰረት *bmeseret*
**screed** *(n.)* በዚ ምኽንያት'ዚ *bezi mḱnyatzi*
**screen** *(n.)* ጐነፈ *gWanefe*
**screw** *(n.)* ሕሳብ *ȟsab*
**screwdriver** *(n.)* ተሓታቲ *teȟatati*
**scribble** *(v.)* ናይ ተጻባጻቢ ሞያ *nay texabaxabi moya*
**scribe** *(n.)* ተጸባጸቢ *texebaxabi*
**scrimmage** *(n.)* ብወግዒ ለኣኸ *bweg'ï le'aḱe*
**scrimp** *(v.)* ብወግዒ ለኣኸ *bweg'ï le'aḱe*
**script** *(n. )* ወግዓዊ *weg'äwi*
**scripture** *(n. )* ዕብየት *ëbyet*
**scroll** *(n.)* ደለበ *delebe*
**scrooge** *(n.)* ኣዋህለለ *awahlele*
**scrub** *(v.)* ውህለላ *whlela*
**scruffy** *(adj.)* ልክዕ *lk'ë*
**scrunch** *(v.)* ግዚ *gzi*
**scruple** *(n.)* ከሰሰ *kesese*
**scrupulous** *(adj.)* ተሓታትነት *teȟatatnet*
**scrutinize** *(v.)* ለመደ *lemede*
**scrutiny** *(n. )* ልሙድ *lmud*
**scud** *(v.)* ሓደ *ȟade*
**scuff** *(v.)* ኣረቢክ *arebik*
**scuffle** *(n.)* እምባ-ጋሮ *'èmbagaro*
**sculpt** *(v.)* ነታጒ *netagWi*
**sculptor** *(n.)* ቃንዛ *qanza*
**sculptural** *(adj.)* ተጎናጸፈ *tegonaxefe*
**sculpture** *(n.)* ፍጻሜ *fxamee*
**scum** *(n.)* መጺጽ *mexix*
**scurrilous** *(adj.)* መጨቋር *mečqWAr*
**scythe** *(n.)* ኣመስገነ *amesgene*
**sea** *(n. )* ምቕጻል *mq̈xal*
**seagull** *(n.)* ጫፍ *čaf*
**seal** *(n. )* ዕንፍሩር *ënfrur*
**sealant** *(n.)* ኣናጎንስጤስ *anagonsẗees*
**seam** *(n.)* ጮምዳድ *čmdad*
**seamy** *(adj.)* ኣፋለጠ *afaleẗe*
**sear** *(v.)* ሌላ *leela*

**search** *(v.)* **ተሰማምዐ** *tesemam'e*
**seaside** *(n.)* **ምስምማዕ** *msmma'e*
**season** *(n.)* **ረኸበ** *rekébe*
**seasonable** *(adj.)* **ቅስመት** *qsmet*
**seasonal** *(adj.)* **ፈትሐ** *fetȟe*
**seasoning** *(n.)* **ናጻ ምልቃቕ** *naxa mlqaq̈*
**seat** *(n.)* **ኣክር** *akr*
**seating** *(n.)* **በዳን** *bedan*
**secede** *(v.)* **ምረት** *mret*
**secession** *(n. )* **ኣክሮባት** *akrobat*
**seclude** *(v.)* **ባሪቶን** *bariton*
**secluded** *(adj.)* **ስግር** *sgr*
**seclusion** *(n.)* **ዘርዕድ** *zer'ëd*
**second** *(adj.)* **ምግባር** *mgbar*
**secondary** *(adj.)* **ግዜያዊ ፈጻሚ** *gzeeyawi fexami*
**secrecy** *(n.)* **ምውሳእ** *mwsa'è*
**secret** *(adj.)* **ዘፍርሀ** *zefrh*
**secretariat** *(n. )* **ምግባር** *mgbar*
**secretary** *(n.)* **ጸሓፊ** *xeȟafi*
**secrete** *(v.)* **ኣንጠፈ** *anẗefe*
**secretion** *(n.)* **ንጡፍ** *nẗuf*
**secretive** *(adj.)* **ስነ-ጠቢብ** *sneẗebib*
**sect** *(n.)* **ንጥፈት** *nẗfet*
**sectarian** *(adj.)* **ተዋናይ** *tewanay*
**section** *(n.)* **ተዋሳኢት** *tewasa'it*
**sector** *(n.)* **ህሉው** *hluw*
**secular** *(adj.)* **ብሓቂ** *bȟaqi*
**secure** *(adj.)* **ገምጋሚ** *gemgami*
**security** *(n.)* **ኣንጠፈ** *anẗefe*
**sedan** *(n.)* **ትኩርና** *tkurna*
**sedate** *(adj.)* **መሪድያን** *meridyan*
**sedation** *(n.)* **ንሱር** *nsur*
**sedative** *(n.)* **ተሪር** *terir*
**sedentary** *(adj.)* **ኣልዘበ** *alzebe*
**sediment** *(n. )* **ምውህሃድ** *mwhhad*
**sedition** *(n.)* **ደመረ** *demere*
**seditious** *(adj.)* **መመላእታ** *memela'èta*
**seduce** *(v.)* **ተወለፈ** *tewelefe*
**seduction** *(n.)* **ምውላፍ** *mwlaf*
**seductive** *(adj.)* **ወልፊ** *welfi*
**sedulous** *(adj.)* **ምድማር** *mdmar*
**see** *(v.)* **ተወሳኺ** *tewesaḱi*
**seed** *(n.)* **ዓቃቢ** *äqabi*
**seedy** *(adj.)* **ድንጉር** *dngur*
**seek** *(v.i. )* **ኣድራሻ** *adrasha*
**seem** *(v.)* **መሰለ** *mesele*
**seemly** *(adj.)* **ጠቐሰ** *ẗeq̈ese*
**seep** *(v.)* **ክኢላ** *k'ila*
**seer** *(n.)* **እኹልነት** *èḱulnet*
**see-saw** *(n.)* **እኹል** *èḱul*
**segment** *(n.)* **ሰዓበ** *se'äbe*
**segregate** *(v.)* **ምድጋፍ** *mdgaf*
**segregation** *(n.)* **ላጋቢ** *lagabi*
**seismic** *(adj.)* **ላጋቢደሓን ኩን** *deȟan kun*
**seize** *(v.)* **ጐረቤት** *gWarebeet*
**seizure** *(n.)* **ቅጽል** *qxl*
**seldom** *(adv.)* **ሳሕቲ** *saȟti*
**select** *(v.)* **ኣቋረጸ** *aqWArexe*
**selection** *(n.)* **ኣመሓላለፈ** *ameȟalalefe*
**selective** *(adj.)* **በየነ** *beyene*
**self** *(n.)* **ፈረደ** *ferede*
**selfish** *(adj.)* **ጥብቆ** *ẗbqo*
**selfless** *(adj.)* **ኣመዓራረየ** *ame'ärareye*

**self-made** *(adj.)* **ምውዳድ** *mwdad*
**sell** *(v.)* **አመሓደረ** *amehadere*
**seller** *(n. )* **ምምሕዳር** *mmhdar*
**selvedge** *(n.)* **ምምሕዳራዊ** *mmhdarawi*
**semantic** *(adj.)* **አመሓዳሪ** *amehadari*
**semblance** *(n. )* **ዚነኣድ** *zine'ad*
**semen** *(n. )* **ኣድሚራል** *admiral*
**semester** *(n.)* **ኣድናቖት** *adnaqot*
**semicircle** *(n.)* **ኣድነቐ** *adneqe*
**semicolon** *(n.)* **ዚፍቀድ** *zifqed*
**seminal** *(adj.)* **ቅበላ** *qbela*
**seminar** *(n. )* **ተኣመነ** *te'amene*
**Semitic** *(adj.)* **ቅበላ** *qbela*
**senate** *(n. )* **ገሰጸ** *gesexe*
**senator** *(n.)* **ሸቐልቀል** *sheqelqel*
**senatorial** *(adj.)* **ጥረ-ሕጡብ** *ťrehťub*
**send** *(v.)* **ብጽሕና** *bxhna*
**senile** *(adj.)* **በጽሒ** *bexhi*
**senility** *(n.)* **ወሰደ** *wesede*
**senior** *(adj.)* **ምርዓም** *mr'äm*
**seniority** *(n. )* **ረዓሚ** *re'ämi*
**sensation** *(n.)* **ተፈታዊ** *tefetawi*
**sensational** *(adj.)* **ፍቕሪ** *fqri*
**sensationalize** *(v.)* **ኣምለኽ** *amleke*
**sense** *(n.)* **ኣሰወነ** *asewene*
**senseless** *(adj.)* **ፋሉል** *falul*
**sensibility** *(n.)* **ጨለ** *čele*
**sensible** *(adj.)* **ኣድሰረብ** *adserb*
**sensitive** *(adj.)* **ውዳሰ-ከንቱ** *wdasekentu*
**sensitize** *(v.)* **እኹል** *èkul*
**sensor** *(n.)* **ኣመራሰሐ** *amerasehe*
**sensory** *(adj.)* **ምምርሳሕ** *mmrsah*
**sensual** *(adj.)* **ዝሙት** *zmut*
**sensualist** *(n.)* **ሰጐመ** *segWame*
**sensuality** *(n.)* **ለዓለ** *le'äle*
**sensuous** *(adj.)* **ምምዕባል** *mm'ëbal*
**sentence** *(n.)* **ብልጫ** *blča*
**sententious** *(adj.)* **ረብሓ** *rebha*
**sentient** *(adj.)* **ጠቓሚ** *ťeqami*
**sentiment** *(n.)* **ምጽኣት** *mx'at*
**sentimental** *(adj.)* **ዕንደራ** *ëndera*
**sentinel** *(n.)* **ሓደገ'ኛ** *hadegena*
**sentry** *(n.)* **ተወሳከ-ግሲ** *tewesakegsi*
**separable** *(adj.)* **ተጻይ** *texay*
**separate** *(v.)* **ኣሉታዊ** *alutawi*
**separation** *(n.)* **ሽግር** *shgr*
**separatist** *(n.)* **ኣፋለጠ** *afaleťe*
**sepsis** *(n. )* **ረክላም** *reklam*
**September** *(n.)* **ምዕዶ** *m'ëdo*
**septic** *(adj.)* **ዝሓሸ** *zhashe*
**sepulchral** *(adj.)* **መዓደ** *me'äde*
**sepulchre** *(n.)* **ደጋፊ** *degafi*
**sepulchre** *(n.)* **ተሓላቒ** *tehalaqi*
**sequel** *(n. )* **ዑቕባ** *üqba*
**sequence** *(n.)* **ሰፋፊ** *sefafi*
**sequential** *(adj.)* **ኣዩን** *ayun*
**sequester** *(v.)* **ኣይሮባቲክስ** *ayrobatiks*
**serene** *(adj.)* **ማሪዋና** *mariwana*
**serenity** *(n.)* **መዓርፎ ነፈርቲ** *me'ärfo neferti*
**serf** *(n. )* **ስነ-ምንፋር** *snemnfar*
**serge** *(n.)* **ኣይሮፕላን** *ayroplan*
**sergeant** *(n.)* **ፍሊት** *flit*
**serial** *(adj.)* **ናይ ነፈርቲ** *nay neferti*

**serialize** ***(v.)*** **ጽባቐኣዊ** *xbaqe'awi*
**series** ***(n.)*** **ስነ-ጽባቐ** *snexbaqe*
**serious** ***(adj.)*** **ካብ ርሑቕ** *kab rħuq̈*
**sermon** ***(n.)*** **ፍሕሹው** *fħshuw*
**sermonize** ***(v.)*** **ፍጻሜ** *fxamee*
**serpent** ***(n. )*** **ጸለወ** *xelewe*
**serpentine** ***(adj.)*** **ምስሉይነት** *msluynet*
**serrated** ***(adj.)*** **ኣምሳሊ** *amsali*
**servant** ***(n.)*** **ፍትወት** *ftwet*
**serve** ***(v.)*** **ርህሩህ** *rhruh*
**server** ***(n. )*** **ቃለ-ማሕላ** *qalemaħla*
**service** ***(n.)*** **ተጸግዐ** *texeg'ë*
**serviceable** ***(adj.)*** **ምጽጋዕ** *mxga'ë*
**serviette** ***(n.)*** **ተማስሎ** *temaslo*
**servile** ***(adj.)*** **ኣረጋገጸ** *aregagexe*
**servility** ***(n.)*** **ምርግጋጽ** *mrggax*
**serving** ***(n.)*** **ኣወንታዊ** *awentawi*
**sesame** ***(n.)*** **ልቃ'በ** *lqabe*
**session** ***(n.)*** **ጐድአ** *gWad'e*
**set** ***(n)*** **ሃብቲ** *habti*
**set** ***(v.)*** **ጭንቂ** *čnqi*
**settee** ***(n.)*** **ሃብታም** *habtam*
**setter** ***(n.)*** **ኣተኻኸለ** *atekákele*
**setting** ***(n.)*** **ምግራብ** *mgrab*
**settle** ***(v.)*** **ናዕቢ** *na'ëbi*
**settlement** ***(n.)*** **ዘለፈ** *zelefe*
**settler** ***(n.)*** **ኣብ ርሑቕ** *'ab rħuq̈*
**seven** ***(adj. & n.)*** **ዝተቓጸለ** *zteq̈axele*
**seventeen** ***(adj. & n.)*** **ዘንሳፍፍ** *zensaff*
**seventeenth** ***(adj. & n.)*** **ኣብ ምቅርራብ** *'ab mqrrab*
**seventh** ***(adj. & n.)*** **ዝፈርሀ** *zferhe*
**seventieth** ***(adj. & n.)*** **ከም ብሓድሽ** *kem bħadsh*
**seventy** ***(adj. & n.)*** **አፍሪቃ** *afriqa*
**sever** ***(v.)*** **ኣብ ሪተ-መርከብ** *'ab ritemerkeb*
**several** ***(adj. & pron.)*** **ድሕሪ** *dħri*
**severance** ***(n.)*** **ድሕረ** *dħre*
**severe** ***(adj.)*** **ድሕረ** *dħri*
**severity** ***(n.)*** **እንደገና** *'èndegena*
**sew** ***(v.)*** **ኣንጻር** *anxar*
**sewage** ***(n.)*** **ተሪር ክቡር እምኒ** *terir kbur 'èmni*
**sewer** ***(n.)*** **ዕድመ** *ëdme*
**sewerage** ***(n.)*** **ሽማግለታት** *shmagletat*
**sex** ***(n.)*** **ቅድመ-ፍርዲ** *qdmefrdi*
**sexism** ***(n.)*** **ዘልኣለማዊ** *zel'alemawi*
**sexton** ***(n.)*** **ናይ ውክልና ትካል** *nay wklna tkal*
**sextuplet** ***(n.)*** **ኣጀንዳ** *aĵenda*
**sexual** ***(adj.)*** **ግሉል** *glul*
**sexuality** ***(n. )*** **ኣከበ** *akebe*
**sexy** ***(adj.)*** **ኣግደደ** *agdede*
**shabby** ***(adj.)*** **ዘቑጥዕ** *zeq̈uť'ë*
**shack** ***(n.)*** **ደመረ** *demere*
**shackle** ***(n.)*** **መጥቃዕቲ** *meťqa'ëti*
**shade** ***(v.)*** **ኣጥቃዒ** *aťqa'ï*
**shade** ***(n.)*** **ዓማጺ** *ämaxi*
**shadow** ***(a. )*** **ዝሰምበደ** *zsembede*
**shadow** ***(n.)*** **ኣቐየመ** *aq̈eyeme*
**shadowy** ***(adj.)*** **ስሉጥ** *sluť*
**shady** ***(adj.)*** **ሶፕራኖ** *soprano*
**shaft** ***(n.)*** **ቀስቀሰ** *qesqese*
**shag** ***(n.)*** **ምኳስ** *mḱWas*
**shake** ***(v.)*** **ኢፈሊጣዊ** *ifeliťawi*
**shaky** ***(adj.)*** **ድኹም ቀይቃይ** *dḱum qeyqay*

**shall** *(v.)* ርቡጽ *rbux*
**shallow** *(adj.)* ሃወኸ *haweḱe*
**sham** *(n.)* መሪር ሓዘን *merir ḧazen*
**shamble** *(v.)* መሬታዊ *mereetawi*
**shambles** *(n.)* ተሰማምዐ *tesemam'ë*
**shame** *(n.)* ዚሰማማዕ *zisemama'ë*
**shameful** *(adj.)* ስምምዕ *smm'ë*
**shameless** *(adj.)* ሕርሻዊ *ḧrshawi*
**shampoo** *(n.)* ሕርሻ *ḧrsha*
**shank** *(n.)* ኣብ ባይታ *'ab bayta*
**shanty** *(n. )* ኣብ ቅድሚ - *'ab qdmi*
**shape** *(n.)* ረድአ *red'e*
**shapeless** *(adj.)* ደጋፊ *degafi*
**shapely** *(adj.)* ረድኢ *red'i*
**shard** *(n.)* ኣጨነቐ *ačeneq̈e*
**share** *(n.)* ኣጨነቐኢ *ačeneq̈e'i*
**shark** *(n.)* ሕማም *ḧmam*
**sharp** *(adj.)* ዕላማ *ëlama*
**sharpen** *(v.)* ሽቶ *shto*
**sharpener** *(n.)* ሰሓተ *seḧate*
**shatter** *(v.t. )* ኣየር *ayer*
**shattering** *(adj.)* ነፋሪት *nefarit*
**shave** *(v.)* ነፋሻ *nefasha*
**shaven** *(adj.)* ኮሪደዮ *korideyo*
**shaving** *(n.)* ዝተገፍተነ *ztegeftene*
**shawl** *(n.)* ዚዛመድ - *zizamed*
**she** *(pron.)* ስሉጥ *sluẗ*
**sheaf** *(n.)* ቅሩብነት *qrubnet*
**shear** *(v.)* መጠንቀቕታ *meẗenqeq̈ta*
**sheath** *(n.)* ስግኣት *sg'at*
**shed** *(n.)* ዋይ ኣነ *way 'ane*
**sheen** *(n.)* ሽሕ'ኳ *shḧkWa*
**sheep** *(n.)* ኣልቡም *'album*
**sheepish** *(adj.)* ኣልቡመን *albumen*
**sheer** *(adj.)* ኣልከሚ *alkemi*
**sheet** *(n.)* ኣልኮል *alkol*
**shelf** *(n.)* ሰታይ *setay*
**shell** *(n.)* ስብሳብ *sbsab*
**shelter** *(n.)* መጽለሊ *mexleli*
**shelve** *(v.)* ጥንቁቕ *ẗnquq̈*
**shepherd** *(n. )* ኣልጀብራ *alĵebra*
**shield** *(n.)* ሳጓ *sagWa*
**shift** *(v.)* ልውጠ-ስም *lwẗesm*
**shiftless** *(adj.)* ሓከየ *ḧakeye*
**shifty** *(adj.)* ምያ ዘሎዎ *mya zelowo*
**shimmer** *(v.)* ነጸለ *nexele*
**shin** *(n.)* ዚነድድ *zinedd*
**shine** *(v.)* ሰርዐ *ser'ë*
**shingle** *(n.)* ኣሳላልፋ *asalalfa*
**shiny** *(adj.)* ተመሳሳሊ *temesasali*
**ship** *(n.)* ክፍሊት ፍትሕ *kflit fth*
**shipment** *(n.)* ህያው *hyaw*
**shipping** *(n.)* ኣልካሊ *alkali*
**shipwreck** *(n.)* ኩሉ *kulu*
**shipyard** *(n.)* ኣፋኰሰ *afakWase*
**shire** *(n.)* ብህሎ *bhlo*
**shirk** *(v.)* ኣለ *ale*
**shirker** *(n. )* ተኣማንነት *te'amannet*
**shirt** *(n.)* ምስሌኣዊ ዛንታ *mslee'awi zanta*
**shiver** *(v.)* ኣሕረቐ *aḧreq̈e*
**shoal** *(n.)* ተቖጣዒ *teq̈oẗa'ï*
**shock** *(n.)* ቁጥዐ *quẗ'ë*
**shock** *(v.)* ኣፋኾሰ *afaḱWase*
**shocking** *(adj.)* ምቕላል *mq̈lal*
**shoddy** *(adj.)* መሽጐራጉር *meshgWaragur*
**shoe** *(n.)* ኪዳን *kidan*

**shoestring** *(n.)* ተጸግዐ *texeg'ë*
**shoot** *(v.)* ዓንጎግ *ängog*
**shooting** *(n.)* ደምሰሰ *demsese*
**shop** *(n.)* ድግመተ-ኣፈና *dgmete'afena*
**shopkeeper** *(n.)* ኣካፈለ *akafele*
**shoplifting** *(n.)* ምምቕራሕ *mmq̈raḧ*
**shopping** *(n.)* ኣማስሐ *amasḧe*
**shore** *(n.)* ምስሒት *mshït*
**short** *(adj.)* ፈቐደ *feq̈ede*
**shortage** *(n.)* መውዕሎ *mew'ëlo*
**shortcoming** *(n.)* ቆርቆሮ *qorqoro*
**shortcut** *(n.)* ኣመተ *amete*
**shorten** *(v.)* ኣወናወነ *awenawene*
**shortfall** *(n.)* ኣወናወኒ *awenaweni*
**shortly** *(adv. )* ኣመት *amet*
**should** *(v.)* ሽርካ *shrka*
**shoulder** *(n.)* ኣልማናክ *almanak*
**shout** *(v.i. )* ኩሉ ዚከኣሎ *kulu zike'alo*
**shove** *(v.)* ሉዝ *luz*
**shovel** *(n.)* ዳርጋ *darga*
**show** *(v.)* ምጽ'ዋት *mxwat*
**showcase** *(n.)* ዝተሰቕለ *zteseq̈le*
**showdown** *(n.)* በይኑ *beynu*
**shower** *(n. )* ኣብ ጐድኒ *ab gWadni*
**showy** *(adj.)* ኣብ ጐድነኒ *ab gWadneh*
**shrapnel** *(n.)* ግሉል *glul*
**shred** *(n.)* ብዓውታ *b'äwta*
**shrew** *(n.)* ኣልፋ *alfa*
**shrewd** *(adj.)* ፊደል *fidel*
**shriek** *(v.)* ወጨጨ *wečeče*
**shrill** *(adj.)* ከረናዊ *kerenawi*
**shrine** *(n.)* ዛጊት *zagit*
**shrink** *(v.)* ከምኡ'ውን *kem'uwn*
**shrinkage** *(n. )* መንበረ-ታቦት *menberetabot*
**shrivel** *(v.)* ጠረጴዛ ቁርባን *ťerepeeza qurban*
**shroud** *(n.)* ምልዋጥ *mlwaẗ*
**shrub** *(n.)* ቈይቍ *qWeyqWi*
**shrug** *(v.)* ምርጫ *mrča*
**shudder** *(v.)* ቅያር *qyar*
**shuffle** *(v.t. )* ምንም'ኳ *mnmkWa*
**shun** *(v.t. )* ብራኸ *brake*
**shunt** *(v.)* ኩሉኹሉ *kulukulu*
**shut** *(v.)* ልግስነት *lgsnet*
**shutter** *(n. )* ኣሉሚኒዮም *aluminiyom*
**shuttle** *(n.)* መደርብዮ *shuttle*
**shuttlecock** *(n.)* ኩሉ ግዜ *kulu gzee*
**shy** *(adj.)* ሕዋስ ባዚቃ *ḧwas baziqa*
**sibilant** *(adj.)* ደብለቐ *debleq̈e*
**sibling** *(n.)* ምሕባር *mḧbar*
**sick** *(adj.)* ኣከበ *akebe*
**sickle** *(n.)* ኣማተር *amater*
**sickly** *(adj.)* ዘይክኢላ *zeyk'ila*
**sickness** *(n. )* መስተፋቅር *mestefaqr*
**side** *(n.)* ኣገረመ *agereme*
**sideline** *(n.)* ኣድናቖት *adnaq̈ot*
**siege** *(n. )* ኣማዘን *amazen*
**siesta** *(n. )* ሓጺር ድቃስ *ḧaxir dqas*
**sieve** *(n.)* ዕንዲዳ ጌጽ *'ëndida geex*
**sift** *(v.)* ዙርያዊ *zuryawi*
**sigh** *(v.i. )* ዘይንጹርነት *zeynxurnet*
**sight** *(n.)* ዘይንጹር *zeynxur*
**sighting** *(n.)* ደረት *deret*

**sightseeing** *(n.)* **ህርፋን** *hrfan*
**sign** *(n.)* **ህንጡይ** *hnẗuy*
**signal** *(n.)* **ማንታዊ** *mantawi*
**signatory** *(n. )* **ተሳለየ** *tesaleye*
**signature** *(n. )* **ምቁር** *mqur*
**significance** *(n.)* **ኣምቡላንስ** *ambulans*
**significant** *(n. )* **ድብያ** *dbya*
**signification** *(n.)* **ኣመሓየሸ** *amehayeshe*
**signify** *(v.)* **ምምሕያሽ** *mmhyash*
**silence** *(n.)* **ኣመሓየሸ** *amehayeshe*
**silencer** *(n.)* **መኣረምታ** *me'aremta*
**silent** *(adj.)* **ተሓታቲ** *tehatati*
**silhouette** *(n.)* **ተፈታዊ** *tefetawi*
**silicon** *(n.)* **ምሕዝነታዊ** *mhznetawi*
**silk** *(n.)* **ኣብ መንጎ** *'ab mengo*
**silken** *(adj.)* **ግጉይ** *gguy*
**silkworm** *(n.)* **ዕርክነት** *ërknet*
**silky** *(adj.)* **ተተኳሲ** *tetekWasi*
**sill** *(n.)* **ርሳዕ** *rsa'ë*
**silly** *(adj.)* **ምሕረት** *mhret*
**silt** *(n.)* **ብዕብድብድ** *b'ëbdbd*
**silver** *(n.)* **ኣብ መንጎ** *ab mengo*
**similar** *(adj.)* **ብዕሉግ** *b'ëlug*
**similarity** *(n.)* **ፍቕራዊ** *fq̈rawi*
**simile** *(n.)* **ቅርጸ-ኣልቦ** *qrxe'albo*
**simmer** *(v.)* **ማዕረ ኮነ** *ma'ëre kone*
**simper** *(v.)* **ኣምፐር** *amper*
**simple** *(adj.)* **ፍሉጥ ሰብ** *fluẗ seb*
**simpleton** *(n.)* **ምድረ-ማያዊ** *mdremayawi*
**simplicity** *(n.)* **ኣምፊትያትር** *amfityatr*
**simplification** *(n.)* **ሰፊሕ** *sefih*
**simplify** *(v.)* **ተወሳኺ** *tewesaḱi*
**simulate** *(v.)* **መጉልሒ** *megulhi*
**simultaneous** *(adj.)* **ኣጉልሐ** *agulhe*
**sin** *(n.)* **ስፍሓት** *sfhat*
**since** *(prep.)* **ክታብ** *ktab*
**sincere** *(adj.)* **ኣዘናግዐ** *azenag'ë*
**sincerity** *(n.)* **ምዝንጋዕ** *mznga'ë*
**sinecure** *(n.)* **ሓደ** *hade*
**sinful** *(adj.)* **ዕለቱ ዝሰሓተ** *ëletu zsehate*
**sing** *(v.)* **ዋሕዲ ደም** *wahdi dem*
**singe** *(v.)* **ድንዛዘ** *dnzaze*
**singer** *(a. )* **መደንዘዚ** *medenzezi*
**single** *(adj.)* **ቆይቋም** *qoyqWAm*
**singlet** *(n.)* **ጸረ-ቃንዛ** *xereqanza*
**singleton** *(n.)* **ተመሳሳሊ** *temesasali*
**singular** *(adj.)* **ተመሳሳልነት** *temesasalnet*
**singularity** *(n.)* **ተመሳሳልነት** *temesasalnet*
**singularly** *(adv. )* **ምትንታን** *mtntan*
**sinister** *(adj.)* **ምርምር** *mrmr*
**sink** *(n.)* **ትንታነኣዊ** *tntane'awi*
**sink** *(v.)* **ተንታኒ** *tentani*
**sinner** *(n.)* **ፋሉልነት** *falulnet*
**sinuous** *(adj.)* **ፋሉላዊ** *falulawi*
**sinus** *(n.)* **ፋሉልነት** *falulnet*
**sip** *(v.)* **ስነ-ቅርጺ ኣካል** *sneqrxi 'akal*
**siphon** *(n.)* **ኣበው** *abew*
**sir** *(n. )* **ውርሻዊ** *wrshawi*
**siren** *(n. )* **ኣበው** *abew*
**sissy** *(n.)* **መልህቕ** *melhq̈*
**sister** *(n. )* **ተዓሻገ** *te'äshage*
**sisterhood** *(n.)* **ጥንታዊ** *ẗntawi*
**sisterly** *(adj.)* **ጽግዕተኛ** *xg'ëteňa*

**sit** ***(v.)*** **ድማ** *dma*
**site** ***(n. )*** **ጽግዕተኛ** *xg'ëteña*
**sitting** ***(n.)*** **ጽዋ** *xwa*
**situate** ***(v.)*** **እንደገና** *èndegena*
**situation** ***(n., a)*** **ፍቱው** *ftuw*
**six** ***(adj.& n.)*** **ቁጥዐ** *quẗ'ë*
**sixteen** ***(adj. & n.)*** **ሕማም** *ḧmam*
**sixteenth** ***(adj. & n.)*** **ኩርናዕ** *kurna'ë*
**sixth** ***(adj. & n.)*** **ሕሩቕ** *ḧruq̈*
**sixtieth** ***(adj. & n.)*** **ጓሂ** *gWahi*
**sixty** ***(adj. & n.)*** **ኩርናዓዊ** *kurna'äwi*
**size** ***(n.)*** **እንስሳ** *ènssa*
**sizeable** ***(adj.)*** **ህያው** *hyaw*
**sizzle** ***(v.)***
**skate** ***(n.)*** **ህያውነት** *hyawnet*
**skateboard** ***(n. )*** **ጽልኢ** *xl'i*
**skein** ***(n. )*** **ሸለን** *shelen*
**skeleton** ***(n. )*** **ዓንካር-ዓንካሪቶ** *änkar'änkarito*
**sketch** ***(n.)*** **ኣንባር** *anbar*
**sketchy** ***(adj.)*** **ዘይምሉእ** *zeymlu'è*
**skew** ***(v.)*** **ጎበጠ** *gobeẗe*
**skewer** ***(n.)*** **ጐበጣ** *gWabeẗa*
**ski** ***(n.)*** **ኣጽነተ** *axnete*
**skid** ***(v.)*** **ድምሰሳ** *dmsesa*
**skilful** ***(adj.)*** **ዝክረ-ዓመት** *zkre'ämet*
**skill** ***(n. )*** **ኣመልከተ** *amelkete*
**skilled** ***(adj.)*** **ገለጸ** *gelexe*
**skim** ***(v.)*** **መግለጺ** *meglexi*
**skimp** ***(adj.)*** **ሸወዘ** *sheweze*
**skin** ***(n.)*** **ቁጥዐ** *quẗ'ë*
**skinny** ***(adj.)*** **በብዓመት** *beb'ämet*
**skip** ***(v.)*** **በብዓመት** *beb'ämet*
**skipper** ***(n. )*** **ሰረዘ** *sereze*
**skirmish** ***(n.)*** **ግጥም** *gẗm*
**skirt** ***(n.)*** **ቀብአ** *qeb'e*
**skirting** ***(n. )*** **ዘይስሩዕ** *zeysru'ë*
**skit** ***(n. )*** **ዘይስተ** *zeyst*
**skittish** ***(adj.)*** **ስመ-ስውርነት** *smeswrnet*
**skittle** ***(n.)*** **ስመ-ስውር** *smeswr*
**skull** ***(n. )*** **ምንማነ** *mnmane*
**sky** ***(n.)*** **ካልእ** *kal'è*
**skylight** ***(n. )*** **መልሲ** *melsi*
**skyscraper** ***(n.)*** **ኪምለስ ዚከኣል** *kimles zike'al*
**slab** ***(n.)*** **ጻጸ** *xaxe*
**slack** ***(adj.)*** **ጻጸ መጺጽ** *xaxe mexix*
**slacken** ***(v.)*** **ተጻራርነት** *texararnet*
**slag** ***(n.)*** **ተጻራሪ** *texarari*
**slake** ***(v.t. )*** **ተጻረረ** *texarere*
**slam** ***(v.)*** **ኣንታርክቲክ** *antarktik*
**slander** ***(n.)*** **ቅድመ ፍጻመ** *qdme fxame*
**slanderous** ***(adj.)*** **ኣቐደመ** *aquadme*
**slang** ***(n.)*** **ዓጋዜን** *ägazeen*
**slant** ***(v.)*** **ኣንተና** *antena*
**slap** ***(v.t. )*** **ኣንቴማ** *anteema*
**slash** ***(v.)*** **እኩብ ዘንታታት** *'èkub zantatat*
**slat** ***(n.)*** **ስነ-ሰብ** *sneseb*
**slate** ***(n. )*** **ነፍሪ** *nefri*
**slattern** ***(n.)*** **ጸረ** *xere*
**slatternly** ***(adj.)*** **ጸረ-ነፍሳት** *xerenefsat*
**slaughter** ***(n.)*** **ጸረ-ኣካል** *xere'akal*
**slave** ***(n. )*** **ወጀሃላይ** *weĵehalay*
**slavery** ***(n.)*** **ተጸበየ** *texebeye*
**slavish** ***(adj.)*** **ትጽቢት** *txbit*
**slay** ***(v.)*** **ምንቁልቋል** *mnqulqWAl*
**sleaze** ***(n.)*** **ጸረ-መርዚ** *xeremerzi*

**sleazy** *(adj.)* **ጸረ-መርዚ** *xeremerzi*
**sledge** *(n.)* **ክርሃት** *krhat*
**sledgehammer** *(n.)* **ኩሕለ-ምሕሊ** *kuȟlemȟli*
**sleek** *(adj.)* **ዘጥንቲ** *zeẗnti*
**sleep** *(n.)* **ድሑር** *dȟur*
**sleeper** *(n.)* **ጥንታዊ** *ẗntawi*
**sleepy** *(adj.)* **ጥንቲ** *ẗnti*
**sleet** *(n.)* **ጸረ-ረኽሲ** *xerereḱsi*
**sleeve** *(n. )* **ጸረ-ማሕበራዊ** *xeremaȟberawi*
**sleigh** *(n.)* **ኣንጻር** *anxar*
**sleight** *(n. )* **ጭንፋር ቀርኒ** *čnfar qerni*
**slender** *(adj.)* **ኣሉታ** *aluta*
**sleuth** *(n.)* **መሃንቱስ** *mehantus*
**slice** *(n.)* **ጽላት** *xlat*
**slick** *(adj.)* **ጭንቀት** *čnqet*
**slide** *(v.)* **ሃረርተኛ** *harerteňa*
**slight** *(adj.)* **ዝኾነ** *zḱone*
**slightly** *(adv. )* **ብዘይተገዳስነት** *bzeytegedasnet*
**slim** *(adj.)* **ዝኾነ ሰብ** *zḱone seb*
**slime** *(n.)* **ዝኾነ ነገር** *zḱone neger*
**slimy** *(adj.)* **ዝኾነ ቦታ** *zḱone bota*
**sling** *(n.)* **ብቕልጡፍ** *bqlẗuf*
**slink** *(v.)* **ዝተፈላለየ** *ztefelaleye*
**slip** *(v.)* **ኣፓርታይድ** *apartayd*
**slipper** *(n.)* **ክፍሊ-ገዛ** *kfligeza*
**slippery** *(adj.)* **ዘይተገዳስነት** *zeytegedasnet*
**slit** *(v.t. )* **ቀዳሒ** *qedaȟi*
**slither** *(v.)* **ጭርታ** *črta*
**slob** *(n.)* **ጫፍ** *čaf*
**slobber** *(v.)* **ምስላ** *msla*
**slogan** *(n. )* **መንህብ** *menhb*
**slope** *(v.)* **ርእሰ-ርጉጽነት** *r'èserguxnet*
**sloppy** *(adj.)* **ራእይ** - *ra'èy*
**slot** *(n.)* **ይቕሬታ ሓተተ** *q̈reeta ȟatete*
**sloth** *(n.)* **ይቕሬታ** *yq̈reeta*
**slothful** *(adj.)* **ኣፖፕለቲካዊ** *apopletikawi*
**slouch** *(v.)* **ከሓዲ እምነት** *keȟadi 'èmnet*
**slough** *(n.)* **ሃዋርያ** *hawarya*
**slovenly** *(adj.)* **ጭረት** *čret*
**slow** *(adj.)* **ኣስካሕከሐ** - *askaȟkeȟe*
**slowly** *(adv. )* **መሰርሒ** *mesarȟi*
**slowness** *(n.)* **ክዳን** *kdan*
**sludge** *(n.)* **ብሩህ** *bruh*
**slug** *(n.)* **ብሩህ** *bruh*
**sluggard** *(n.)* **ተራእየ** *tera'èye*
**sluggish** *(adj.)* **ምቕልቃል** *mq̈lqal*
**sluice** *(n.)* **ኣዝሓለ** *azȟale*
**slum** *(n.)* **መልአ** *mel'e*
**slumber** *(v.)* **መመላእታ** *memela'èta*
**slump** *(v.)* **ነድሪ ጥብቆ** *nedri ẗbqo*
**slur** *(v.)* **መመላእታ** *memela'èta*
**slurp** *(v.)* **ሸውሃት** *shewhat*
**slush** *(n.)* **ከፋት ሸውሃት** *kefat shewhat*
**slushy** *(adj.)* **ኣጨብጨበ** *ačebčebe*
**slut** *(n.)* **ጨብጨባ** *čebčeba*
**sly** *(adj.)* **ቱፋሕ** *tufaȟ*
**smack** *(n.)* **መሳርያ** *mesarya*
**small** *(adj.)* **ብቑዕ** *bq̈u'ë*
**smallpox** *(n.)* **ኣመልካቲ** *amelkati*
**smart** *(adj.)* **ምሕታት** *mȟtat*
**smarten** *(v.)* **ተጠቕመ** *teẗeq̈me*
**smash** *(v.)* **ወሰነ** *wesene*
**smashing** *(adj.)* **ቈጸራ** *qWexera*

**smattering** *(n.)* ጐዘየ *gWazeye*
**smear** *(v.)*
ዚሰማማዕ *zisemama'ë*
**smell** *(n.)* ገምገመ *gemgeme*
**smelly** *(adj.)* እኹል *èḱul*
**smidgen** *(n.)* ተገንዘበ *tegenzebe*
**smile** *(v.)* አስተያየት *asteyayet*
**smirk** *(v.)* ተረድአ *tered'e*
**smith** *(n. )* ምርዳእ *mrda'è*
**smock** *(n. )* ዝተሻቐለ *zteshaq̈ele*
**smog** *(n. )* ተልመዴን *telmedeen*
**smoke** *(n.)* አፍለጠ *afleṫe*
**smoky** *(adj.)* ቀረበ *qerebe*
**smooch** *(v.)* ብቑዕ *bq̈u'ë*
**smooth** *(adj.)* ምንዛዐ *mnza'ë*
**smoothie** *(n.)* ቅባለ *qbale*
**smother** *(v.)* ተቐበለ *teq̈ebele*
**smoulder** *(v.)* ዳርጋ *darga*
**smudge** *(v.)*
ሚሽሚሸ *mishmishe*
**smug** *(adj.)*
ግርምብያለ *grmbyale*
**smuggle** *(v.)* በሊሕ *beliḧ*
**smuggler** *(n.)* ተውህቦ *tewhbo*
**snack** *(n. )* ጠዓሞት *ṫe'ämot*
**snag** *(n. )* ማያዊ *mayawi*
**snail** *(n. )* ማያዊ *mayawi*
**snake** *(n.)* አረብ *areb*
**snap** *(v.)* አረቢያን *arebian*
**snapper** *(n.)* አረቢክ *arebik*
**snappy** *(adj.)* ገድላ *gedla*
**snare** *(n.)* ፈራዲ *feradi*
**snarl** *(v.t. )* ዳነየ *daneye*
**snarl** *(v.)* ሃውሪ *hawri*
**snatch** *(v.)* ዳኘነት *daǹnet*
**snazzy** *(adj.)* ዳኛ *daǹa*
**sneak** *(v.)* ዳስ *das*
**sneaker** *(n.)* ቀስቲ *qesti*
**sneer** *(n.)* ቀልደዳዊ *qeldedawi*
**sneeze** *(v.i. )* ቀልደድ *qelded*
**snide** *(adj.)* ስነ ጥንቲ *sne ṫnti*
**sniff** *(v.)* ጥንታዊ *ṫntawi*
**sniffle** *(v.)* ሊቀ መላእክት *liqe mela'èkt*
**snigger** *(n.)* ሊቀ-ጳጳሳት *liqep̈apasat*
**snip** *(v.)* መንታጋይ *mentagay*
**snipe** *(v.)* ስነ-ሃናጺ *snehanaxi*
**snippet** *(n.)* ስነ-ህንጻ *snehnxa*
**snob** *(n.)* አርቺቭ *archiv*
**snobbery** *(n.)* አርክቲክ *arktik*
**snobbish** *(adj.)* ውዕውዕ *w'ëw'ë*
**snooker** *(n.)* ብርቱዕ ድሌት *brtu'ë dleet*
**snooze** *(n.)* አድካሚ *adkami*
**snore** *(n.)* ስፍሓት *sfḧat*
**snort** *(n. )* መድረኽ *medreḱ*
**snout** *(n. )* ተማጎተ *temagote*
**snow** *(n.)* መጎተ *megote*
**snowball** *(n.)* መጎቲና *megotina*
**snowy** *(adj.)* አጻምእ *axam'è*
**snub** *(v.)* ተላዕለ *tela'ële*
**snuff** *(v.)* አሪስቶክራሲ *aristokrasi*
**snuffle** *(v.)*
አሪስቶክራታዊ *aristokratawi*
**snug** *(adj.)* ቊጽሪ *quxri*
**snuggle** *(v.)* ቊጽሪና *quxrina*
**so** *(adv. )* ታቦት *tabot*
**soak** *(v.)* ምናት *mnat*
**soap** *(n.)* ሳሙና *samuna*
**soapy** *(adj.)* አርማጌዶን *armagedon*
**soar** *(v.i. )* አጽዋር *axwar*
**sob** *(v.)* ተነኽነኸ *teneḱneḱe*
**sober** *(adj.)* ድርዒ ሓጺን *dr'ï ḧaxin*

**sobriety** ***(n.)*** **ድርዒ ሓጺኒ** *dr'ï ȟaxini*
**soccer** ***(n.)*** **ሰራዊት** *serawit*
**sociability** ***(n.)*** **መዓዛ** *me'äza*
**sociable** ***(adj.)*** **መዓዛ - ፍወሳ** *me'äza fwesa*
**social** ***(adj.)*** **ኣብ ዙርያ** *'ab zurya*
**socialism** ***(n.)*** **ኣበራበረ** *aberabere*
**socialist** ***(n. & adj.)*** **ሰርዐ** *ser'ë*
**socialize** ***(v.)*** **ኣሰራርዓ** *aserar'ä*
**society** ***(n. )*** **ምሒር** *mȟir*
**sociology** ***(n. )*** **ተሰለፈ** *teselefe*
**sock** ***(n.)*** **ተሰለፈን** *teselefin*
**socket** ***(n.)*** **ኣሰረ** *asere*
**sod** ***(n.)*** **እትወት** *ètwet*
**soda** ***(n.)*** **መጸ** *mexe*
**sodden** ***(adj.)*** **ኣትሒቱ ረኣየ** *'atȟitu re'aye*
**sodomy** ***(n.)*** **ትዕቢተኛ** *t'ëbiteňa*
**sofa** ***(n. )*** **መንዘዐ** *menze'ë*
**soft** ***(adj.)*** **ፍላጻ** *flaxa*
**soften** ***(v.)*** **እንዳብረት** *èndabret*
**soggy** ***(adj.)*** **ብርቱዕ ስሚ** *brtu'ë smi*
**soil** ***(n.)*** **ብውሳይ ምቅጻል** *bwsay mqxal*
**sojourn** ***(n.)*** **ጥበብ** *ïbeb*
**solace** ***(n. )*** **ጥንቲ** *ïnti*
**solar** ***(adj.)*** **ኣርተሪ** *arteri*
**solder** ***(n.)*** **ብልሂ** *blhi*
**soldier** ***(n. )*** **ሪሕ** *riȟ*
**sole** ***(n.)*** **ካርቾፊ** *karchofi*
**solely** ***(adv. )*** **ኣቕሓ** *aqȟa*
**solemn** ***(adj.)*** **ኣነጸረ** *anexere*
**solemnity** ***(n.)*** **ክእለት** *k'èlet*
**solemnize** ***(v.)*** **ስኑ'ዕ** *snu'ë*
**solicit** ***(v.)*** **ከቢድ ብረት** *kebid bret*
**solicitation** ***(n.)*** **ክኢላ** *k'ila*
**solicitor** ***(n.)*** **ስነ-ጠቢብ** *sneïebib*
**solicitous** ***(adj.)*** **ስነ-ጥበባዊ** *sneïbebawi*
**solicitude** ***(n.)*** **ባህርያዊ** *bahryawi*
**solid** ***(adj.)*** **ከም** *kem*
**solidarity** ***(n. )*** **ሓድነት** *solidarity*
**soliloquy** ***(n.)*** **ደየበ** *deyebe*
**solitaire** ***(n.)*** **ደያቢ** *deyabi*
**solitary** ***(adj.)*** **ዕርገት** *ërget*
**solitude** ***(n.)*** **ኣረጋገጸ** *aregagexe*
**solo** ***(n.)*** **መናን** *menan*
**soloist** ***(n. )*** **ሃበ** *habe*
**solubility** ***(n.)*** **ጽዱይ** *xduy*
**soluble** ***(adj.)*** **ግብረ-ሰዶመኛ** *gbresedomeňa*
**solution** ***(n.)*** **ኣሽ** *ash*
**solve** ***(v.)*** **ዝሓፈረ** *zȟafere*
**solvent** ***(n.)*** **ኤሽያዊ** *eshiyawi*
**sombre** ***(adj.)*** **ጽልሙት** *xlmut*
**some** ***(adj.)*** **ዓንጃል** *änĵal*
**somebody** ***(pron. )*** **ሓተተ** *ȟatete*
**somehow** ***(adv. )*** **ብጥርጣረ** *bïrïare*
**someone** ***(pron. )*** **ዘባል** *zebal*
**somersault** ***(n.)*** **ጽሙው** *xmuw*
**something** ***(pron. )*** **መልክዕ** *melk'ë*
**somewhat** ***(adv. )*** **ጎነጽ** *gonex*
**somewhere** ***(adv. )*** **ምክፋእ** *mkfa'è*
**somnambulism** ***(n.)*** **ዓበሰ** *äbese*
**somnambulist** ***(n. )*** **ደላዪ** *delayi*
**somnolence** ***(n. )*** **ትምኒት** *tmnit*
**somnolent** ***(adj.)*** **ሻሞት** *shamot*
**somnolent** ***(adj.)*** **ተመነየ** *temeneye*
**son** ***(n. )*** **ኣድጊ** *adgi*

**song** *(n. )* አጥቀዐ *aẗqe'ë*
**songster** *(n.)* ቀታል-ነፍሲ *qetalnefsi*
**sonic** *(adj.)* ቀተለ *qetele*
**sonnet** *(n. )* ቀተለሊ *qeteli*
**sonority** *(n.)* አጥቀዐ *aẗqe'ë*
**soon** *(adv. )* ምግጥጣም *mgẗẗam*
**soot** *(n.)* አጋጠሙ *agaẗeme*
**soothe** *(v.)* አኼበ *aḱeeba*
**sophism** *(n.)* ስምምዕ *smm'ë*
**sophist** *(n.)* ጸዓደ *xe'äde*
**sophisticate** *(n.)* አማኸሪ *amaḱari*
**sophisticated** *(adj.)* መርመራ *mermera*
**sophistication** *(n.)* ንብረት *nbret*
**soporific** *(adj.)* ጻዕረኛ *xa'ëreňa*
**sopping** *(adj.)* ረተበ *retebe*
**soppy** *(adj.)* ምደባ *mdeba*
**sorbet** *(n.)* ምዱብ ስራሕ *mdub sraḧ*
**sorcerer** *(n. )* ተዋሃደ *tewahade*
**sorcery** *(n.)* ተዋህዶ *tewahdo*
**sordid** *(adj.)* ሓገዘ *ḧageze*
**sore** *(adj.)* ሓገዝ *ḧagez*
**sorely** *(adv. )* ረዳት *redat*
**sorrow** *(n.)* ተሓባባሪ *teḧababari*
**sorry** *(adj.)* ማሕበር *maḧber*
**sort** *(n.)* ስምምዕ *smm'ë*
**sortie** *(n.)* ዝተፋላለየ *ztefalaleye*
**sough** *(v.)* በብዓይነቱ *beb'äynetu*
**soul** *(n.)* አጸናንዐ *axenan'ë*
**soul mate** *(n.)* መረጋገጺ *meregagexi*
**soulful** *(adj.)* ገመተ *gemete*
**soulless** *(adj.)* ግምት *gmt*
**sound** *(n.)* አረጋገጸ *aregagexe*
**soundproof** *(adj.)* ዋሕስ *waḧs*
**soup** *(n.)* አስትሪስክስ *astrisks*
**sour** *(adj.)* ዓለም *älem*
**source** *(n.)* አዝማ *azma*
**souse** *(v.)* ነበዐ *nebe'ë*
**south** *(n.)* አደነቐ *adeneq̈e*
**southerly** *(adj.)* ድንጽዉና *dnxwuna*
**southern** *(adj.)* አስደመመ *asdememe*
**souvenir** *(n. )* ኮኾባዊ *koḱobawi*
**sovereign** *(n.)* ህዉቱት *hwtut*
**sovereignty** *(n.)* ብምግሕታን *bmgḧtan*
**sow** *(n.)* ብልጹግ *blxug*
**spa** *(n. )* ቈጸራ ከዋኽብቲ *qWexera kewaḱbti*
**space** *(n.)* ጠፈርተኛ *ẗeferteňa*
**spacious** *(adj.)* ስነ-ኮኾቢ *snekoḱobi*
**spade** *(n.)* ስነ-ኮኾብ *snekoḱob*
**spam** *(n.)* ትኩር *tkur*
**span** *(n.)* ዝተፈላለየ *ztefelaleye*
**Spaniard** *(n. )* ዑቕባ *üq̈ba*
**spaniel** *(n.)* አብ *ab*
**Spanish** *(n. )* የዋህ *yewah*
**spank** *(v.)* ኢዚሀርነት *izihernet*
**spanking** *(adj.)* ኢዚሄራዊ *iziheerawi*
**spanner** *(n.)* ስፖርተኛ *sporteňa*
**spare** *(adj.)* ስፖርታዊ *sportawi*
**sparing** *(adj.)* አትላስ *atlas*
**spark** *(n.)* ሃዋህው *hawahw*
**sparkle** *(v.)* ደሴት *deseet*
**sparkling** *(n. )* አቶም *atom*
**sparrow** *(n.)* አቶማዊ *atomawi*
**sparse** *(adj.)* ከሓሰ *keḧase*
**spasm** *(n.)* ድሕነት *dḧnet*
**spasmodic** *(adj.)* ክፍሊ *kfli*

**spastic** *(adj.)* **አሰቃቒ** *aseqaäi*
**spat** *(n.)* **ገፍዐ** *gef'ë*
**spate** *(n.)* **አጣበቐ** *aẗabeäe*
**spatial** *(adj.)* **አታሽ** *atash*
**spatter** *(v.)* **ጥብቀት** *ẗbqet*
**spawn** *(v.)* **አጥቅዐ** *aẗq'ë*
**spay** *(v.)* **ምሉእ** *mlu'è*
**speak** *(v.)* **ሰመረ** *semere*
**speaker** *(n.)* **ፈተ'ነ** *fetene*
**spear** *(n.)* **ጀመረ** *ĵemere*
**spearhead** *(n.)* **ተኸታተለ** *teḱetatele*
**spearmint** *(n.)* **ተሳትፎ** *tesatfo*
**special** *(adj.)* **አገልጋሊ** *agelgali*
**specialist** *(n.)* **አቓልቦ** *aäalbo*
**speciality** *(n.)* **ጥንቁቕ** *ẗnquä*
**specialization** *(n.)* **አረጋገጸ** *aregagexe*
**specialize** *(v.)* **ዋልድቢት** *waldbit*
**species** *(n.)* **ልብሲ** *lbsi*
**specific** *(adj.)* **አቃጫጭ** *aqačač*
**specification** *(n.)* **ጠበቓ** *ẗebeäa*
**specify** *(v.)* **ሰሓበ** *seḧabe*
**specimen** *(n.)* **ስሕበት** *sḧbet*
**specious** *(adj.)* **ማራኺ** *maraḱi*
**speck** *(n. )* **ባህርይ** *bahry*
**speckle** *(n.)* **ማርጋሪን** *margarin*
**spectacle** *(n.)* **ሓራጅ** *ḧaraĵ*
**spectacular** *(adj.)* **ኪስማዕ ዚክኣል** *kisma'ë zike'a*
**spectator** *(n. )* **ነባሮ** *nebaro*
**spectral** *(adj.)* **ደሃይ** *- dehay*
**spectre** *(n.)* **ጸብጻብ** *xebxab*
**spectrum** *(n.)* **ናይ ምስማዕ ፈተና** *nay msma'ë fetena*
**speculate** *(v.)* **ኦዲቶርዮም** *'oditoryomme'akebi 'aderash*
**speculation** *(n.)* **ወሰኸ** *ወሰኸ*
**speech** *(n.)* **ነሓሰ** *neḧase*
**speechless** *(adj.)* **ሓትኖ** *ḧatno*
**speed** *(n.)* **አኽሊል** *aḱlil*
**speedway** *(n.)* **ተስፋኣዊ** *tesfa'awi*
**speedy** *(adj.)* **ጥብቂ** *ẗbqi*
**spell** *(v.t. )* **አዎስትራልያ** *awustraliya*
**spellbound** *(adj.)* **ሓቀኛ** *ḧaqeǹa*
**spelling** *(n.)* **ልክዕነት** *lk'ënet*
**spend** *(v.)* **ደራሲ** *derasi*
**spendthrift** *(n.)* **ምዙዝ** *mzuz*
**sperm** *(n.)* **መዚ** *mezi*
**sphere** *(n.)* **መዘዘ** *mezeze*
**spherical** *(n. )* **አዉቲዝም** *awutizim*
**spice** *(n.)* **ርእሰ-ታሪኽ** *r'èsetariḱ*
**spicy** *(adj.)* **አውቶክራሲ** *awtokrasi*
**spider** *(n.)* **ውልቀ-መላኺ** *wlqemelaḱi*
**spike** *(n.)* **አውቶክራቲክ** *wlqemelaḱ*
**spiky** *(adj.)* **ርእሰ-ጽሑፍ** *r'èsexḧuf*
**spill** *(v.)* **አውቶማቲክ** *awtomatik*
**spillage** *(n.)* **አውቶሞቢል** *awtomobilmekina*
**spin** *(v.)* **ርእሰ-ምምሕዳራዊ** *r'èsemmḧdarawi*
**spinach** *(n.)* **ምርምረ-ሬሳ** *mrmrereesa*
**spinal** *(adj.)* **ቀውዒ** *qew'ï*
**spindle** *(n.)* **ሓጋዚ** *ḧagazi*
**spindly** *(adj.)* **ተጠቕመ** *teẗeämе*
**spine** *(n.)* **ክትጥቀመሉ ትኽእል** *ktẗqemelu tḱ'èl*
**spineless** *(adj.)* **መደረጋሕ** *mederegaḧ*
**spinner** *(n. )* **ስስዐ** *ss'ë*

**spinster** ***(n. )*** **ሕነ ፈደየ** *ḧne fedeye*
**spiral** ***(adj.)*** **ጐደና** *gWadena*
**spire** ***(n.)*** **ማእከላይ** *ma'èkelay*
**spirit** ***(n.)*** **ኣንጻር** *anxar*
**spirited** ***(adj.)*** **ጽልኣት** *xl'at*
**spiritual** ***(adj.)*** **ኣለየ** *aleye*
**spiritualism** ***(n.)*** **እንዳ ኣዕዋፍ** *'ènda 'a'ëwaf*
**spiritualist** ***(n.)*** **ስነ-ምንፋር** *snemnfar*
**spirituality** ***(n.)*** **ፓይሎት** *paylot*
**spit** ***(n.)*** **ህንጡይ** *hnẗuy*
**spite** ***(n.)*** **ህንጡዪ** *hnẗuyi*
**spiteful** ***(adj.)*** **ኣቮካዶ** *avokado*
**spittle** ***(n. )*** **ወገደ** *wegede*
**spittoon** ***(n.)*** **ጉስያ** *gusya*
**splash** ***(v.)*** **ኣመነ** *amene*
**splatter** ***(v.)*** **ኣኮኣዊ** *'ako'awi*
**splay** ***(v.)*** **ተጸበየ** *texebeye*
**spleen** ***(n.)*** **ነቕሐ** *neq̈he*
**splendid** ***(adj.)*** **ነቕሐ** *neq̈he*
**splendour** ***(n.)*** **ሰለመ** *seleme*
**splenetic** ***(adj.)*** **ገንዘብ** *genzeb*
**splice** ***(v.)*** **ናብ ርሑቕ** *nab rḧuq̈*
**splint** ***(n.)*** **ተምሳጥ** *temsaẗ*
**splinter** ***(n.)*** **ዘርዕድ** *zer'ëd*
**split** ***(v.)*** **ዘስካሕክሕ** *zeskaḧkḧ*
**splutter** ***(v.)*** **ንሓጺር ግዜ** *nḧaxir gzee*
**spoil** ***(v.)*** **ጋሕማጥ** *gaḧmaẗ*
**spoiler** ***(n.)*** **ብልሽው** *blshw*
**spoke** ***(n. )*** **ፋስ** *fas*
**spokesman** ***(n.)*** **መቐለሲ** *meq̈elesi*
**sponge** ***(n.)*** **መቐለስ** *meq̈eles*
**sponsor** ***(n.)*** **ሓላዪ ሰብ** *ḧalayi seb*
**spontaneity** ***(n.)*** **ኣዕዘምዘመ** *a'ëzemzeme*
**spontaneous** ***(adj.)*** **ህጻን** *hxan*
**spool** ***(n.)*** **ዘይምስምማዕ** *zeymsmma'ë*
**spoon** ***(n.)*** **ህበይ** *hbey*
**spoonful** ***(n.)*** **ህጻን** *hxan*
**spoor** ***(n.)*** **ቤተ'ልቦ** - *beetelbo*
**sporadic** ***(adj.)*** **ዝባን** *zban*
**spore** ***(n.)*** **ዓንዲ-ሕቖ** *ändiḧq̈o*
**sport** ***(n.)*** **ሓለፈ** *ḧalefe*
**sporting** ***(adj.)*** **ትዕይንቲ** *t'ëynti*
**sportive** ***(adj.)*** **ምጉሳዕ** *mgusa'ë*
**sportsman** ***(n. )*** **ተመኩሮ** *temekuro*
**spot** ***(n.)*** **ኣሽሙራዊ** *ashmurawi*
**spotless** ***(adj.)*** **ረድኣ** *red'e*
**spousal** ***(n. )*** **መልሰ-ግብሪ** *melsegbri*
**spouse** ***(n. )*** **መሃዚ** *mehazi*
**spout** ***(n.)*** **ማህደር** *mahder*
**sprain** ***(v.t. )*** **ብድሕሪት** *bdḧrit*
**sprat** ***(n.)*** **ዝባን መድረኽ** *zban medreḱ*
**sprawl** ***(v.)*** **ዝባን ኣሰር** *zban aser*
**spray** ***(n.)*** **ንድሕሪት** *ndḧrit*
**spread** ***(v.)*** **ዝባን ማይ** *zban may*
**spreadsheet** ***(n.)*** **ቤኮን** *beekon*
**spree** ***(n.)*** **ባክተሪያ** *bakteriya*
**sprig** ***(n.)*** **ሕማቕ** *ḧmaq̈*
**sprightly** ***(adj.)*** **ኣርማ** *arma*
**spring** ***(v.)*** **ብሕማቕ** *bḧmaq̈*
**sprinkle** ***(v.i. )*** **ባድሚንተን** *badminten*
**sprinkler** ***(n.)*** **ኣገረመ** *agereme*
**sprinkling** ***(n.)*** **መልአ** *mel'e*
**sprint** ***(v.)*** **ጋዓዝ** *ga'äz*
**sprinter** ***(n.)*** **ገፍላው** *geflaw*

**sprout** *(v.)* **ሕቡር ስልማት** *ḧbur slmat*
**spry** *(adj.)* **ዋሕስ** *waḧs*
**spume** *(n.)* **ፖሊስ** *polis*
**spur** *(n.)* **መስሓቢ** *mesḧabi*
**spurious** *(adj.)* **ደረቐ** *dereq̈e*
**spurn** *(v.)* **ሰንካቲ** *senkati*
**spurt** *(v.)* **እንዳ ባኒ** *ènda bani*
**sputum** *(n. )* **ተረፍ** *teref*
**spy** *(n.)* **ሰገነት** *segenet*
**squabble** *(n.)* **በራሕ** *beraḧ*
**squad** *(n. )* **ጥቕላል** *ẗq̈lal*
**squadron** *(n.)* **ኩዕሶ** *ku'ëso*
**squalid** *(adj.)* **ገስረጥ** *gesreẗ*
**squall** *(n.)* **ባለ** *bale*
**squander** *(v.)* **ባሉን** *balun*
**square** *(n.)* **ትርብዒት** *trb'ït*
**squash** *(v.)* **በለሳን** *belesan*
**squat** *(v.i. )* **በለሳን** *belesan*
**squawk** *(v.)* **ኣርቃይ** *arqay*
**squeak** *(n.)* **ኣገደ** *agede*
**squeal** *(n.)* **ተራ** *tera*
**squeeze** *(v.)* **ባናና** *banana*
**squib** *(n.)* **መእሰሪ** *me'èseri*
**squid** *(n.)* **መጀነኒ** *meĵeneni*
**squint** *(v.)* **ሽፍታ ወረበላ** *shfta werebela*
**squire** *(n. )* **መርዚ ስሚ** *merzi smi*
**squirm** *(v.)* **ገውታ** *gewta*
**squirrel** *(n.)* **ገውት** *gewtat*
**squirt** *(v.)* **በናጅር** *benaĵr*
**squish** *(v.)* **ሓየረ** *ḧayere*
**stab** *(v.)* **ጥርዝያ** *ẗrzya*
**stability** *(n. )* **መደንደል** *medendel*
**stabilization** *(n.)* **ባንጆ** *banĵo*
**stabilize** *(v.)* **ባንኪ** *banki*
**stable** *(adj.)* **መኰነን** *mekWanen*
**stable** *(n.)* **ጥፉሽ** *ẗfush*
**stack** *(n.)* **ጥፈሻ** *ẗfesha*
**stadium** *(n. )* **ሰንደቕ** *sendeq̈*
**staff** *(n.)* **በዓል** *be'äl*
**stag** *(n. )* **ተዋዘየ** *tewazeye*
**stage** *(n.)* **ጥምቀት** *ẗmqet*
**stagecoach** *(n.)* **መጥምቓዊ** *meẗmq̈awi*
**stagger** *(v.)* **ኣጠመቐ** *aẗemeq̈e*
**staggering** *(adj.)* **መታወር** *metawer*
**stagnant** *(adj.)* **ዓንቃሪቦ** *änqaribo*
**stagnate** *(v.)* **ባርባራዊ** *barbarawi*
**stagnation** *(n.)* **ባርባራዊ** *barbarawi*
**staid** *(adj.)* **rezin** *rezin*
**stain** *(v.t. )* **ወጋኢ** *wega'i*
**stair** *(n.)* **ቀምቃማይ** *qemqamay*
**staircase** *(n.)* **ግጥሚ ወይ ደርፊ** *gẗmi wey derfi*
**stake** *(n.)* **ጥርሑ** *ẗrḧu*
**stale** *(adj.)* **ብቕሉዕ** *bq̈lu'ë*
**stalemate** *(n. )* **ዋጋ ዕዳጋ** *waga 'ëdaga*
**staleness** *(n.)* **ተጋጨወ ተላገዐ** *tegačewe telag'ë*
**stalk** *(n.)* **ቅራፍ** *qraf*
**stalker** *(n.)* **ስገም** *sgem*
**stall** *(n.)* **መኽዘን** *mek̈zen*
**stallion** *(n.)* **ባሮሜተር** *barometer*
**stalwart** *(adj.)* **ባላባት** *balabat*
**stamen** *(n.)* **ባራካ** *baraka*
**stamina** *(n.)* **መሸኒት** *meshenit*
**stammer** *(v.)* **ግድብ** *gdb*
**stamp** *(n.)* **በርሚል** *bermil*
**stamp** *(v.)* **መኻን** *mek̈an*

**stampede** *(n.)* **መደንደል** *medendel*
**stance** *(n.)* **ዕንቅፋት** *ënqfat*
**stanchion** *(n.)* **ግድብ** *gdb*
**stand** *(v.)* **ጠበቓ** *ťebeq̈a*
**standard** *(n.)* **በደላ** *bedela*
**standardization** *(n.)* **ሰረተ** *serete*
**standardize** *(v.)* **ሰረትኣልቦ** *seret'albo*
**standing** *(n. )* **ትሕተ-ቤት** *tḧtebeet*
**standpoint** *(n. )* **ሓፋር** *ḧafar*
**standstill** *(n. )* **ሰረታዊ** *seretawi*
**stanza** *(n. )* **ሪሓን** *riḧan*
**staple** *(v.)* **ስሓኒ** - *sḧani*
**staple** *(n.)* **ባዚሊካ** *bazilika*
**stapler** *(n.)* **ሰረት** *seret*
**star** *(n.)* **ተጸልወ** *texelwe*
**starch** *(n.)* **ዘንቢል** *zenbil*
**starchy** *(adj.)* **ባስ ዓይነት ዓሳ** *bas 'äynet 'äsa*
**stare** *(v.)* **ድቓላ** *dq̈ala*
**stark** *(adj.)* **ሸለለ** *shelele*
**starlet** *(n.)* **ዕርዲ** *ërdi*
**starry** *(adj.)* **እኩብ** *èkub*
**start** *(v.)* **ምሕጻብ** *mḧxab*
**starter** *(n.)* **ኣለኸ** *aleḱe*
**startle** *(v.)* **ህውተታ** *hwteta*
**startling** *(n.)* **መንካዕ** *menka'ë*
**starvation** *(n.)* **ባቲክ** *batik*
**starve** *(v.)* **በትሪ ፖሊስ** *betri polis*
**stash** *(v.)* **ቦጦሎኒ** *boťoloni*
**state** *(n.)* **ተገዳም** *tegedam*
**stateless** *(adj.)* **ከትከተ** *ketkete*
**statement** *(n.)* **ውግእ** *wg'è*
**statesman** *(n.)* **ሕቡር ስልማት** *ḧbur slmat*
**static** *(adj.)* **መሰናኽል** *mesenaḱl*
**statically** *(adv. )* **ወጨጨ** *wečeče*
**station** *(n.)* **ፋርዳ** *furda*
**stationary** *(adj.)* **ሳንጃ** *sanĵa*
**stationer** *(n. )* **ባዛር ሹቕ** *bazar shuq̈*
**stationery** *(n.)* **ባዙቃ** *bazuqa*
**statistical** *(adj.)* **ኮነ** *kone*
**statistics** *(n. )* **መና** *mena*
**statuary** *(n.)* **ዕንቆ** *ënqo*
**statue** *(n. )* **ቆርቋር** *qorqWAr*
**statuesque** *(adj.)* **ቢግል** *bigl*
**statuette** *(n.)* **መትኮብ** *metkob*
**stature** *(n. )* **ብርጭቆ** *brčqo*
**status** *(n. )* **ገመል** *gemel*
**statute** *(n.)* **ባልዶንጓ** *baldongWa*
**statutory** *(adj.)* **ድቢ** *dbi*
**staunch** *(adj.)* **ተሸከመ** *teshekeme*
**stave** *(n.)* **ጭሕሚ** *čḧmi*
**stay** *(v.)* **ማእዝን** *ma'èzn*
**stead** *(n.)* **እንስሳ** *ènssa*
**steadfast** *(adj.)* **እንስሳዊ** *ènssawi*
**steadiness** *(n.)* **ላጸየ** *laxeye*
**steady** *(adj.)* **ላጸየ** *laxeye*
**steak** *(n.)* **ማራኺ** *maraḱi*
**steal** *(v.)* **ኣመልክዐ** *amelk'ë*
**stealth** *(n.)* **ደስታ** *desta*
**stealthily** *(adv. )* **መልክዕ** *melk'ë*
**stealthy** *(adj.)* **ቢቨር** *biver*
**steam** *(n.)* **ኣህድአ** *ahd'e*
**steamer** *(n. )* **ምኽንያቱ ብምክንያት** *mḱnyatu bmknyat*
**steed** *(n. )* **ምልክት** *mlkt*
**steel** *(n.)* **ኣመልከተ** *amelkete*
**steep** *(adj.)* **ኮነ** *kone*
**steeple** *(n.)* **መዕረፊ** *me'ërefi*

**steeplechase** *(n.)* **መንጸፍ** *menxef*
**steer** *(v.)* **መዕቆብ ስንኩላነ-ኣእምሮ** *me'ëqob snkulane'a'èmro*
**stellar** *(adj.)* **ኣጨፈቐ** *ačefeqe*
**stem** *(n.)* **ንህቢ** *nhbi*
**stench** *(n. )* **ዋዕሮ** *wa'ëro*
**stencil** *(n.)* **ስጋ ከብቲ** *sga kebti*
**stenographer** *(n. )* **ረጉድ** *regWid*
**stenography** *(n. )* **ምልክት** *mlkt*
**stentorian** *(adj.)* **ቢራ** *bira*
**step** *(n.)* **ብንጅር** *bnĵr*
**steppe** *(n. )* **ማሳ** *masa*
**stereophonic** *(adj.)* **ወረደ ኣጋጠመ** *werede 'agaẗeme*
**stereoscopic** *(adj.)* **በቕዐ** *beq̈'ë*
**stereotype** *(n.)* **ቅድሚ** *qdmi*
**sterile** *(adj.)* **ኣቓዲሙ** *ኣቓዲሙ*
**sterility** *(n. )* **መዓደ** *me'äde*
**sterilization** *(n.)* **ኣገረመ** *agereme*
**sterilize** *(v.)* **ለመነ** *lemene*
**sterling** *(n. )* **ወለደ** *welede*
**stern** *(adj.)* **ለማኒ** *lemani*
**sternum** *(n.)* **ጀመረ** *ĵemere*
**steroid** *(n.)* **መጀመርታ** *meĵemerta*
**stertorous** *(adj.)* **ኣዘናገዐ** *azenage'ë*
**stethoscope** *(n. )* **ኣብ ክንዲ** *ab kndi*
**stew** *(n.)* **ገበረ** *gebere*
**steward** *(n. )* **ጠባይ** *ẗebay*
**stick** *(n.)* **ቈረጸ** *qWerexe*
**sticker** *(n. )* **ጨካን** *čekan*
**stickleback** *(n.)* **ትእዛዝ** *t'èzaz*
**stickler** *(n. )* **ብድሕሪት** *bdḧrit*
**sticky** *(adj.)* **ተመልከተ** *temelkete*
**stiff** *(adj.)* **ኣመስጋኒ** *amesgani*
**stiffen** *(v.)* **ፋሕራይ** *faḧray*
**stifle** *(v.)* **ህላወ** *hlawe*
**stigma** *(n.)* **ቀጥቀጠ** *qeẗqeẗe*
**stigmata** *(n.)* **ድንጉይ** *dnguy*
**stigmatize** *(v.)* **ጠመረ** *ẗemere*
**stile** *(n.)* **ተፍአ** *tef'e*
**stiletto** *(n.)* **ኣጨነቐ** *ačeneqe*
**still** *(adj.)* **ብጌጋ ኣርኣየ** *bgeega 'ar'aye*
**stillborn** *(n.)* **እምነት** *èmnet*
**stillness** *(n.)* **ኣመነ** *amene*
**stilt** *(n.)* **ኣቈናጸበ** *aqWenaxebe*
**stilted** *(adj.)* **ቃጭል** *qačl*
**stimulant** *(n.)* **ጽብቕቲ** *xbq̈ti*
**stimulate** *(v.)* **ተባኣሳይ** *teba'asay*
**stimulus** *(n.)* **ባእሲ ምድላይ** *ba'èsi mdlay*
**sting** *(n.)* **ነቀወ** *neqewe*
**stingy** *(adj.)* **መናፍሕ** *menafḧ*
**stink** *(v.)* **ከብዲ** *kebdi*
**stint** *(n.)* **ተኣሳሰረ** *te'asasere*
**stipend** *(n.)* **ግላዊ ኣቕሑ** *glawi 'aq̈ḧu*
**stipple** *(v.)* **ፍቛር** *fq̈ur*
**stipulate** *(v.)* **ትሕቲ** *tḧti*
**stipulation** *(n.)* **ቁልፊ** *qulfi*
**stir** *(v.)* **ጓሃየ** *gWahaye*
**stirrup** *(n.)* **ኣቃልቦ ኣዘንበለ** *'aqalbo 'azenbele*
**stitch** *(v.)* **ለወየ** *leweye*
**stitch** *(n.)* **ርቦ** *rbo*
**stock** *(n.)* **ትሕቲ** *tḧti*
**stockade** *(n.)* **ገቢረ-ሰናይ** *gebiresenay*
**stockbroker** *(n.)* **ቡራኬ** *burakee*
**stocking** *(n. )* **ገዛ ቀሺ** *geza qeshi*

**stockist** ***(n.)*** **ግብረ-ሰናይ** *gbresenay*
**stocky** ***(adj.)*** **ለዋህ** *lewah*
**stoic** ***(n.)*** **ሓጋዚ** *ḧagazi*
**stoke** ***(v.)*** **ግብረ-ሰናይ** *gbresenay*
**stoker** ***(n.)*** **ግብረ-ሰናያዊ** *gbresenayawi*
**stole** ***(n.)*** **ለዋህ** *lewah*
**stolid** ***(adj.)*** **ተውህቦ** *tewhbo*
**stomach** ***(n.)*** **ኣውረሰ** *awrese*
**stomp** ***(n.)*** **ውርሻ** *wrsha*
**stone** ***(n.)*** **ወቐሰ** *weq̈ese*
**stony** ***(adj.)*** **ዘረፈ** *zerefe*
**stooge** ***(n.)*** **ሓዘን** *ḧazen*
**stool** ***(n.)*** **ለማኒ** *lemani*
**stoop** ***(v.)*** **ከውሒ በረድ** *kewḧi bered*
**stop** ***(v.)*** **ደንቆሮ** *denqoro*
**stoppage** ***(n. )*** **ፍረ** *fre*
**stopper** ***(n.)*** **ዕብድብድ** *ëbdbd*
**storage** ***(n. )*** **መደቀሲ** *medeqesi*
**store** ***(n.)*** **ለመነ** *lemene*
**storey** ***(n. )*** **ኣሸገረ** *ashegere*
**stork** ***(n. )*** **ኣብ ጥቓ** *'ab ẗq̈a*
**storm** ***(n.)*** **ከበበ** *kebebe*
**stormy** ***(adj.)*** **ኣመራሰሐ** *ameraseḧe*
**story** ***(n.)*** **መኾስተር** *mek̈oster*
**stout** ***(adj.)*** **ዕኑድ** *ënud*
**stove** ***(n.)*** **ዓውዲ ጸቐጠ** *äwdi xeq̈eẗe*
**stow** ***(v.)*** **ብዝበለጸ** *bzbelexe*
**straddle** ***(v.)*** **ኣራዊታዊ እንስሳዊ ጨካን** *'arawitawi 'ènssawi čekan*
**straggle** ***(v.)*** **ሸለመ** *sheleme*
**straggler** ***(n.)*** **ተጋሕተነ** *tegaḧtene*
**straight** ***(adj.)*** **ተጣልዐ** *teẗal'ë*
**straighten** ***(v.)*** **ከደ** *kede*
**straightforward** ***(adj.)*** **ከድዐ** *ked'ë*
**straightway** ***(adv. )*** **ቅጥፈት** *qẗfet*
**strain** ***(n. )*** **ኣብ መንጎ** *'ab mengo*
**strain** ***(v.)*** **ዝሓሸ** *zḧashe*
**strained** ***(adj.)*** **ስያፍ** *syaf*
**strait** ***(n.)*** **መስተ** *meste*
**straiten** ***(v.i. )*** **ኣኼባ** *ak̈eeba*
**strand** ***(v.)*** **ኣልቀሰ** *alqese*
**strange** ***(adj.)*** **ተጠንቀቕ! ወይልኻ!** *teẗenqeq̈ weylk̈a*
**stranger** ***(n.)*** **ደንጸዎ** *denxewo*
**strangle** ***(v.)*** **ሰረየ** *sereye*
**strangulation** ***(n. )*** **ክንየው** *knyew*
**strap** ***(n.)*** **ኣብ ከክልተ** *'ab keklte*
**strapping** ***(adj.)*** **ፍርቂ በብዓመት** *frqi beb'ämet*
**stratagem** ***(n.)*** **ምቕናን** *mq̈nan*
**strategic** ***(adj.)*** **መቕናን** *meq̈nan*
**strategist** ***(n.)*** **ሳልቤታ** *salbeeta*
**strategy** ***(n.)*** **መጽሓፍ ቅዱስ** *mexḧaf qdus*
**stratify** ***(v.)*** **ዝርዝረ-ጽሑፋት** *zrzrexḧufat*
**stratum** ***(n. )*** **ፈታው መጽሓፍ** *fetaw mexḧaf*
**straw** ***(n. )*** **ዝክረ ክልተ ሚእቲ ዓመት** *zkre klte mi'èti 'ämet*
**strawberry** ***(n.)*** **ጭዋዳምናት** *čwadamnat*
**stray** ***(v.)*** **ተቛየቘ** *teq̈WAyeq̈We*
**streak** ***(n.)*** **ብሽክለታ** *bshkleta*
**streaky** ***(adj.)*** **ሰመየ** *semeye*
**stream** ***(n. )*** **ተሓታቲ** *teḧatati*
**streamer** ***(n.)*** **ስማይ** *smay*
**streamlet** ***(n. )*** **ኣኽበረ** *ak̈bere*
**street** ***(n. )*** **ምምሻጥ** *mmshaẗ*

**strength** *(n.)* **ክልተ ዓመታዊ** *klte 'ämetawi*
**strengthen** *(v.)* **ቃሬዛ** *qareeza*
**strenuous** *(adj.)* **ጽምደ-ትኹረታዊ** *xmdetḱuretawi*
**stress** *(v.t. )* **ድርብ መርዓ** *drb mer'ä*
**stress** *(n.)* **ዓቢ** *äbi*
**stretch** *(n. )* **ምቕናን** *mq̈nan*
**stretch** *(v.)* **ሕሉ'ፍ** *ḧluf*
**stretcher** *(n.)* **ብሽክለታ** *bshkleta*
**strew** *(v.)* **ቢኪኒ** *bikini*
**striation** *(n.)* **ክልተ ጐድናዊ** *klte gWadnawi*
**stricken** *(adj.)* **ሓሞት** *ḧamot*
**strict** *(adj.)* **ድርብ-ልሳናዊ** *drblsanawi*
**strictly** *(adv. )* **ጎዞሞ** *gozomo*
**stricture** *(n.)* **መኣንገድ ድርጎኛ** *me'anged drgoǹa*
**stride** *(v.)* **ቢልያርዶ** *bilyardo*
**strident** *(adj.)* **ቢልዮን** *bilyon*
**strife** *(n.)* **ሃብታም** *habtam*
**strike** *(v.)* **ዓቢ ማዕበል** *'äbi ma'ëbel*
**striker** *(n. )* **ቆፎ** *qofo*
**striking** *(adj.)* **ዕጽፊ** *ëxfi*
**string** *(n.)* **ጠመረ** *ṫemere*
**stringency** *(n.)* **መዛዘሚ** *mezazemi*
**stringent** *(adj.)* **ፈንጠዝያ** *fenṫezya*
**stringy** *(adj.)* **በዓል ለዓት መነጽር** *be'äl le'ät menexr*
**strip** *(v.t.)* **ስነ-ቅመም ህይወታውያን** *sneqmem hywetawyan*
**stripe** *(n.)* **ኢኮሎጂ** *ikoloĵi*
**stripling** *(n.)* **ባዮዳይቨርስቲ** *bayidayiversiti*
**strive** *(v.)* **ኢኮሎጂ** *ikoloĵi*
**strobe** *(n.)* **ስነ-ህይወት** *snehywet*
**stroke** *(n.)* **ምርምረ-ሬሳ** *mrmrereesa*
**stroll** *(v.)* **ጽምደ-ሰልፋዊ** *xmdeselfawi*
**strong** *(adj.)* **ኮመዲኖ** *komedino*
**stronghold** *(n.)* **ዑፍ** *üf*
**strop** *(n.)* **ኢንፍሉወንዛ** *influwenza*
**stroppy** *(adj.)* **ምውላድ** *mwlad*
**structural** *(adj.)* **ብሽኮቲ** *bshkoti*
**structure** *(n.)* **ገመሰ** *gemese*
**strudel** *(n.)* **ግብረ-ሰዶመኛ** *gbresedomeǹa*
**struggle** *(v.)* **ኣቡን** *abun*
**strum** *(v.)* **ብዕራይ በረኸ** *b'ëray bereḱa*
**strumpet** *(n.)* **ልጓም** *lgWam*
**strut** *(n.)* **ዋዕሮ** *wa'ëro*
**Stuart** *(adj.)* **ነኸሰ** *neḱese*
**stub** *(n. )* **ወጋኢ** *wega'i*
**stubble** *(n.)* **መሪር** *merir*
**stubborn** *(adj.)* **ፈንጣጋር** *fenṫegar*
**stucco** *(n.)* **ሃተ'ፈ** *hatefe*
**stud** *(v.)* **ብላክቤሪ** *blakberi*
**stud** *(n.)* **ጸሊም** *xelim*
**student** *(n. )* **ሰሌዳ** *seleeda*
**studio** *(n.)* **ኣጸለመተ** *axelemete*
**studious** *(adj.)* **ጸሊም መዝገብ** *xelim mezgeb*
**study** *(v.)* **ጽልማተ** *xlmate*
**study** *(n.)* **ታህዲደ-ምቕላዕ** *tahdidemq̈la'ë*

**stuff** *(n.)* ሓጓዲ ኣንጠረኛ ሓጺን *ȟagWadi 'anẗereňa ȟaxin*
**stuffing** *(n.)* ፍሕኛ *fȟňa*
**stuffy** *(adj.)* ግላዝ *glaz*
**stultify** *(v.)* ኣብ ከክልተ *'ab keklte*
**stumble** *(v.)* ከሰሰ *kesese*
**stump** *(n.)* ጸዕደወ *xa'ëdewe*
**stun** *(v.)* ልዙብ *lzub*
**stunner** *(n.)* ጥርሑ *ẗrȟu*
**stunning** *(adj.)* ኮበርታ *koberta*
**stunt** *(v.)* ድምጺ *dmxi*
**stupefy** *(v.)* ኣተዓሻሸወ *ate'äshashewe*
**stupendous** *(adj.)* ነትጕ *netgWi*
**stupid** *(adj.)* ቅሉዕ *qlu'ë*
**stupidity** *(n.)* ሃልሃልታ *halhalta*
**stupor** *(n.)* ጃኬት *ĵakeet*
**sturdy** *(adj.)* ኣጸዕደወ *axa'ëdewe*
**stutter** *(v.)* ቀዛሒ *qezaȟi*
**sty** *(n.)* እምቤዕ *èmbee'ë*
**stygian** *(adj.)* ደመየ *demeye*
**style** *(n.)* ቃና *qana*
**stylish** *(adj.)* ኣበር *aber*
**stylist** *(n.)* ምዩቕ በለ *myuq̈ bele*
**stylistic** *(adj.)* ሓዋወሰ *ȟawawese*
**stylized** *(adj.)* መግቢ ሓዋሲ ኣደባላቒ *megbi ȟawasi 'adebalaq̈i*
**stylus** *(n.)* ባረኽ *bareḱe*
**stymie** *(v.)* ብሩኽ *bruḱ*
**styptic** *(adj.)* ምርቓ *mrq̈a*
**suave** *(adj.)* ዋግ *wag*
**sub judice** *(adj.)* ሕጉስ *ȟgus*
**subaltern** *(n.)* ዕዉር *ëwur*
**subconscious** *(adj.)* ዓመተ *ämete*
**subcontract** *(v.)* ጉድለት *gudlet*
**subdue** *(v.)* ሰምሰም ኣበለ *semsem 'abele*
**subedit** *(v.)* ጋራዲ *garadi*
**subject** *(n.)* መቓልሕ *meq̈alȟ*
**subjection** *(n.)* ታሕጓስ *taȟgWas*
**subjective** *(adj.)* ማይ ምዕጎ *may m'ëgo*
**subjugate** *(v.)* በርቃዊ መጥቃዕቲ *berqawi meẗqa'ëti*
**subjugation** *(n.)* ህቦብላ ውርጪ *hbobla wrči*
**subjunctive** *(adj.)* ነፍሒ *nefȟe*
**sublet** *(v.t. )* ቋንጣ ዓሳ *qWanẗa 'äsa*
**sublimate** *(v.)* ንጣብ *nẗab*
**sublime** *(adj.)* ቀጽሪ *qexri*
**subliminal** *(adj.)* ግላዕ *gla'ë*
**submarine** *(n.)* ድንደላ *dndela*
**submerge** *(v.)* ዕግታ *ëgta*
**submerse** *(v.)* ሳይት *sayit*
**submersible** *(adj.)* ቈንደፈ *qWendefe*
**submission** *(n.)* ጨዓይ ጸጉሪ ዘለዎ *če'äy xeguri zelewo*
**submissive** *(adj.)* ደም *dem*
**submit** *(v.)* ደም ምፍሳስ *dem mfsas*
**subordinate** *(adj.)* ደማዊ *demawi*
**subordination** *(n.)* ዕምባባ *ëmbaba*
**suborn** *(v.)* ስረ-ግትር *sregtr*
**subscribe** *(v.)* ዕምባባ *ëmbaba*
**subscript** *(adj.)* ንጣብ ቀለም *nẗab qelem*
**subscription** *(n.)* ትኳዕ *tkWa'ë*
**subsequent** *(adj.)* ካምቻ *kamcha*
**subservience** *(n.)* ነፈሰ *nefese*

**subservient** *(adj.)* ቈንደፈ *qWendefe*
**subside** *(v.)* ተነኽነኸ *teneḱneḱe*
**subsidiary** *(adj.)* ጓመድ *gWamed*
**subsidize** *(v.)* ሰማያዊ ሕብሪ *semayawi ḧbri*
**subsidy** *(n.)* መጻድፎ *mexadfo*
**subsist** *(v.)* ጠምበርበር በለ *ťemberber bele*
**subsistence** *(n. )* ጎዲም *godim*
**subsonic** *(adj.)* ጽያቕ *xyaq̈*
**substance** *(n.)* ትሕዝቶ መጽሓፍ *tḧzto mexḧaf*
**substantial** *(adj.)* ኣምለቼ *amleq̈We*
**substantially** *(adv. )* ሓፈረ *ḧafere*
**substantiate** *(v.)* ቀንዲ *qendi*
**substantiation** *(n.)* ኣሸምበበ *ashembebe*
**substantive** *(adj.)* መፍለስ *mefles*
**substitute** *(n.)* ጣውላ *ťawla*
**substitution** *(n.)* ጃህራ *ĵahra*
**subsume** *(v.)* ጃልባ *ĵalba*
**subterfuge** *(n.)* ሓፍ ኮፍ በለ *ḧaf kof bele*
**subterranean** *(adj.)* ገልተው *geltew*
**subtitle** *(n.)* ሓበረ *ḧabere*
**subtle** *(adj.)* ጅለ-ሰበይቲ *ĵlesebeyti*
**subtlety** *(n.)* ኣካላዊ *akalawi*
**subtotal** *(n.)* ኣካል *akal*
**subtract** *(v.)* ዘብዐኛ *zeb'ëňa*
**subtraction** *(n.)* ዓዘቕቲ *äzeq̈ti*
**subtropical** *(adj.)* ጋኔን *ganeen*
**suburb** *(n.)* ተወላወለ *tewelawele*
**suburban** *(adj.)* ሓቂ ዘይብሉ *ḧaqi zeyblu*
**suburbia** *(n.)* ምጉሊ ኣንጮዋ *mguli 'ančwa*
**subversion** *(n.)* መፍልሒ *meflḧi*
**subversive** *(adj.)* ናውጼን *nawxeen*
**subvert** *(v.i. )* ተባዕ ደፋር *teba'ë defar*
**subway** *(n.)* ድምቀት *dmqet*
**succeed** *(v.)* ጉንዲ *gundi*
**success** *(n.)* መእሰር ናይ መርከብ *me'èser nay merkeb*
**successful** *(adj.)* መሸጐር *meshegWar*
**succession** *(n.)* ቦምብ *bomb*
**successive** *(adj.)* ደብደበ *debdebe*
**successor** *(n.)* ደብዳብ *debdab*
**succinct** *(adj.)* ቦምብር *bomber*
**succour** *(n.)* ሓቀኛ *ḧaqeňa*
**succulent** *(adj.)* ኣኸዘ *ak̈eze*
**succumb** *(v.)* ውዕል *w'ël*
**such** *(adj.)* ጊልያነት ከዳሚነት *gilyanet kedaminet*
**suck** *(v.)* ዓጽሚ *äxmi*
**sucker** *(n.)* መጋርያ *megarya*
**suckle** *(v.)* ልስሉስ ቆብዕ *lslus qob'ë*
**suckling** *(n.)* መቑሹሽ *meq̈ushush*
**suction** *(n.)* ዓጻም *äxam*
**sudden** *(adj.)* መጽሓፍ *mexḧaf*
**suddenly** *(adv. )* ንእሽቶ መጽሓፍ *n'èshto mexḧaf*
**Sudoku** *(n.)* መቓቐር *meq̈aq̈er*

**sue** *(v.t. )* መጽሓፍ ሸያጢት *mexḧaf sheyaẗit*
**suede** *(n.)* መጽሓፋዊ *mexḧafawi*
**suffer** *(v.i. )* ንእሽቶ መጽሓፍ *n'èshto mexḧaf*
**sufferance** *(n.)* ፊሕታ *fiḧta*
**suffice** *(v.)* ሕቶ *ḧto*
**sufficiency** *(n.)* ጠገለ-ኣልቦ *ẗegele'albo*
**sufficient** *(adj.)* ምስፋሕ *msfaḧ*
**suffix** *(n.)* ሰንካቲ *senkati*
**suffocate** *(v.)* ነዊሕ ሳእኒ *newiḧ sa'èni*
**suffocation** *(n.)* ጎጆ *goĵo*
**suffrage** *(n.)* ኮንትሮባንድ *kontroband*
**suffuse** *(v.)* ምርኮ *mrko*
**sugar** *(n.)* ዶብ *dob*
**suggest** *(v.)* ጕርጕሐ *gWargWaḧe*
**suggestible** *(adj.)* ወልደ *tewelde*
**suggestion** *(n.)* ወረደ *werede*
**suggestive** *(adj.)* ተለቅሐ *teleqḧe*
**suicidal** *(adj.)* ሕጽöኒ *ḧxni*
**suicide** *(n.)* ሓለቓ *ḧaleq̈a*
**suit** *(n.)* ምሉእ ክዳን *mlu'è kdan*
**suitability** *(n.)* ስነ-ኣትክልቲ *sne'atklti*
**suitable** *(adj.)* ክልቲኡ *klti'u*
**suite** *(n.)* ኣሸገረ *ashegere*
**suitor** *(n.)* ጥርሙዝ *ẗrmuz*
**sulk** *(v.)* ታሕቲ *taḧti*
**sullen** *(adj.)* ቃራና *qarana*
**sully** *(v.)* ዓረ *äre*
**sulphur** *(n.)* ጐደና *gWadena*
**sultana** *(n.)* ነጠረ *neẗere*
**sultry** *(adj.)* መሰነዪ *meseneyi*
**sum** *(n.)* ሓጸረ *ḧaxere*
**summarily** *(adv. )* ዶብ *dob*
**summarize** *(v.)* ደረት-ኣልቦ *deret'albo*
**summary** *(n.)* ለጋስ *legas*
**summer** *(n. )* ልግሲ *lgsi*
**summit** *(n.)* ሕቑፊ-ዕምባባ *ḧq̈ufi'ëmbaba*
**summon** *(v.)* ግጥ'ም *gẗm*
**summons** *(n.)* ባዛር *bazar*
**sumptuous** *(adj.)* ቀስቲ *qesti*
**sun** *(v.)* መዓናጡ *me'änaẗu*
**sun** *(n.)* ሰገደ *segede*
**sundae** *(n.)* ዳስ *das*
**Sunday** *(n.)* ጮሎ *čḧolo*
**sunder** *(v.)* ሳንዱቕ *sanduq̈*
**sundry** *(adj.)* ተጋዳላይ *tegadalay*
**sunken** *(adj.)* ጉስጢ *gusẗi*
**sunny** *(adj.)* ወዲ *wedi*
**super** *(adj.)* ኣደመ *ademe*
**superabundance** *(adj.)* ንእስነት *n'èsnet*
**superabundant** *(adj.)* ቢኪኒ *bikini*
**superannuation** *(n.)* ድጋፍ *dgaf*
**superb** *(adj.)* በናጅር *benaĵr*
**supercharger** *(n.)* መደገፍ *medegef*
**supercilious** *(adj.)* ተጀሃሪ *teĵehari*
**superficial** *(adj.)* ብረይል *breyl*
**superficiality** *(n.)* ሓንጎል *ḧangol*
**superfine** *(adj.)* ልጓም *lgWam*
**superfluity** *(n.)* ጬንፈር *čenfer*
**superfluous** *(adj.)* ዕላመት *ëlamet*
**superhuman** *(adj.)* ኣንበልበለ *anbelbele*
**superimpose** *(v.)* ብራንዲ *brandi*

**superintend** *(v.)* ደረቐኘ *dereq̈eňa*
**superintendence** *(n. )* ኣስራዚ *asrazi*
**superintendent** *(n.)* ተባዕ *teba'ë*
**superior** *(adj.)* ትብዓት *tb'ät*
**superiority** *(n.)* ቈየቛ *qWeyeq̈WA*
**superlative** *(adj.)* ህላ *hla*
**supermarket** *(n.)* ምጥሓስ *mẗḧas*
**supernatural** *(adj.)* እንጀራ *ènĵera*
**superpower** *(n.)* ውርዲ *wrdi*
**superscript** *(adj.)* ሰበረ *sebere*
**supersede** *(v.)* ምስባር ስባር መስበርቲ *msbar sbar mesberti*
**supersonic** *(adj.)* ቁርሲ *qursi*
**superstition** *(n.)* ጡብ *ẗub*
**superstitious** *(adj.)* ትንፋስ *tnfas*
**superstore** *(n.)* ኣተንፈሰ *atenfese*
**supervene** *(v.)* ዓንቀር ጠበንጃ *änqer ẗebenĵa*
**supervise** *(v.)* ስረ-ግትር *sregtr*
**supervision** *(n.)* ኣራብሐ *arabḧe*
**supervisor** *(n.)* ህዱእ ንፋስ *hdu'è nfas*
**supper** *(n.)* ሕጽረት ሓጺርነት *ḧxret ḧaxirnet*
**supplant** *(v.)* ጸመቜ *xemeq̈We*
**supple** *(adj.)* እንዳ ቢራ *'ènda bira*
**supplement** *(n.)* ጉቦ *gubo*
**supplementary** *(adj.)* ሕጡብ ማቶኒ *ḧẗub matoni*
**suppliant** *(n.)* ናይ መርዓ *nay mer'ä*
**supplicate** *(v.)* መርዓት *mer'ät*
**supplier** *(n.)* መርዓዊ *mer'äwi*
**supply** *(v.)* ድልድል *dldl*
**support** *(n.)* ሓጺር *ḧaxir*
**support** *(v.)* ልጓም *lgWam*
**suppose** *(v.)* ሓጺር መግለጺ *ḧaxir meglexi*
**supposition** *(n.)* ምግማት *mgmat*
**suppository** *(n.)* መራሕ ብርጌድ *meraḧ brgeed*
**suppress** *(v.)* ድሙቕ *dmuq̈*
**suppression** *(n.)* ደመቐ በርሀ *demeq̈e berhe*
**suppurate** *(v.)* ብልጫ *blča*
**supremacy** *(n.)* ድሙቕ *dmuq̈*
**supreme** *(adj.)* ጫፍ *čaf*
**surcharge** *(n.)* ሓበጀራይ *ḧabeĵeray*
**sure** *(adj.)* ማይ ጨው *may čew*
**surely** *(adv. )* ኣምጸአ *amxe'e*
**surety** *(n.)* ብሪንጃል *birinjal*
**surf** *(n.)* ጠረፍ *ẗeref*
**surface** *(n.)* ስሉጥ *sluẗ*
**surfeit** *(n. )* ነደ'ረ *nedere*
**surge** *(n.)* ብሪቲሽ *biritish*
**surgeon** *(n. )* ተሰባሪ *tesebari*
**surgery** *(n. )* ኣንኰለ *ankWale*
**surly** *(adj.)* ሰፊሕ *sefiḧ*
**surmise** *(v.t.)* ዘርግሐ *zergḧe*
**surmount** *(v.)* በዘቕዘቕ *bezeq̈zeq̈*
**surname** *(n.)* ካውሎ ፍዮሪ *kawlo fyori*
**surpass** *(v.)* መንሹር *menshur*
**surplus** *(n. )* ሰበረ *sebere*
**surprise** *(n.)* ስቡር *sbur*
**surreal** *(adj.)* ደላ'ላይ *delalay*

**surrealism** *(n.)* **ቃራየ ጉርጉማ** *qaraye gurguma*
**surrender** *(n.)* **ጨቓዊት** *čeq̈awit*
**surrender** *(v.)* **ብሮንዞ** *bronzo*
**surreptitious** *(adj.)* **ዛራ** *zara*
**surrogate** *(n.)* **መኾስተር** *meḱoster*
**surround** *(v.)* **መረቕ** *mereq̈*
**surroundings** *(n.)* **እንዳ ኣመንዝራ** *ènda 'amenzra*
**surtax** *(n.)* **ሓው** *ḧaw*
**surveillance** *(n. )* **ሕውነት** *ḧwnet*
**survey** *(v.t. )* **ሸፋሽፍቲ** *shefashfti*
**surveyor** *(n. )* **ቡናዊ** *bunawi*
**survival** *(n.)* **ገሃጸ** *gehaxe*
**survive** *(v.)* **ማእረረ** *ma'èrere*
**susceptible** *(adj.)* **ስንብራት** *snbrat*
**suspect** *(v.)* **ኩላሶ** *kulaso*
**suspect** *(n)* **ẗerẗere** *ẗerẗere*
**suspend** *(v.)* **ቀንዲ ክብደት** *qendi kbdet*
**suspense** *(n. )* **ኣስባስላ** *asbasla*
**suspension** *(n.)* **ኣሻኹ** *ashaḱWi*
**suspicion** *(n.)* **ዘይምሕር** *zeymḧr*
**suspicious** *(adj.)* **እንስሳ** *ènssa*
**sustain** *(v.)* **ዓፍራ** *äfra*
**sustainable** *(adj.)* **ኮናዕ** *kona'ë*
**sustenance** *(n.)* **መገለል** *megelel*
**suture** *(n.)* **መቘለፍ** *meq̈Welef*
**svelte** *(adj.)* **ኣጓም** *agWam*
**swab** *(n.)* **ምንቕ በለ** *mnq̈ bele*
**swaddle** *(v.)* **ባጀት** *baĵet*
**swag** *(n.)* **ጎባይ** *gobay*
**swagger** *(v.)* **ወሓጥ ጐንጺ** *weḧaẗ gWanxi*
**swallow** *(v.)* **ጉስጢ** *gusẗi*
**swamp** *(n. )* **መስሓቕ** *mesḧaq̈*
**swan** *(n. )* **ትኺን** *tḱWan*
**swank** *(v.)* **ካሮሳ** *karosa*
**swanky** *(v.)* **ጥሩምባ** *ẗrumba*
**swap** *(v.)* **ሃነጸ** *hanexe*
**swarm** *(n.)* **ህንጻ** *hnxa*
**swarthy** *(adj.)* **ሽጉርቶ** *shgurto*
**swashbuckling** *(adj.)* **ሕበጥ** *ḧbeẗ*
**swat** *(v.)* **ቡሊምያ** *bilimiya*
**swathe** *(n.)* **ብብዝሒ** *bbzḧi*
**sway** *(v.)* **ደጐላጽ** *degWalax*
**swear** *(v.)* **ኣርሓ** *arḧa*
**sweat** *(n.)* **ገዚፍ ዓይነት ክልቢ** *gezif 'äynet kelbi*
**sweater** *(n.)* **ዓረር** *ärer*
**sweep** *(v.)* **ቡለቲን** *buletin*
**sweeper** *(n.)* **ሕጡብ ወርቂ** *ḧẗub werqi*
**sweet** *(n.)* **ቅጥቁጥ ብዕራይ** *qẗquẗ b'ëray*
**sweet** *(adj.)* **ኣዛዚ** *azazi*
**sweeten** *(v.)* **ዓላቕ** *älaq̈*
**sweetener** *(n.)* **ተዓንቀፈ** *te'änqefe*
**sweetheart** *(n.)* **ዕርዲ** *ërdi*
**sweetmeat** *(n.)* **መዓኮር** *me'äkor*
**sweetness** *(n.)* **ተናጐጸ** *tenagWaxe*
**swell** *(n.)* **ሁጉሬ** *huguree*
**swell** *(v.)* **ዋልጋ ጐንጺ** *walga gWanxi*
**swelling** *(n.)* **ተናጐጸ** *tenagWaxe*
**swelter** *(v.)* **ምቁር ባኒ** *mqur bani*
**swerve** *(v.)* **ጥማር** *ẗmar*
**swift** *(adj.)* **ጠቕለለ** *ẗeq̈lele*
**swill** *(v.)* **ቡሽ** *bush*
**swim** *(v.)* **ሓደ ዝደርቡ ገዛ** *ḧade zderbu geza*
**swimmer** *(n.)* **ገልተው** *geltew*

**swindle** *(v.)* ሃደመ *hademe*
**swine** *(n.)* ሓባ'ር መርከብ *ḧabar merkeb*
**swing** *(v.)* ምንስፋፍ *mnsfaf*
**swing** *(n.)* ተንሳፋፊ *tensafafi*
**swingeing** *(adj.)* ጐራዕራዕ በለ *gWara'ëra'ë bele*
**swipe** *(v.)* ሸከም *shekem*
**swirl** *(v.)* ሰደቓ *sedeq̈a*
**swish** *(adj.)* ቢሮክራሲ *birokrasi*
**switch** *(n.)* ቢሮክራታዊ *birokratawi*
**swivel** *(v.)* ኣጐመ *agWame*
**swoon** *(v.)* በርገር *berger*
**swoop** *(v.)* ሰራቒ *seraq̈i*
**sword** *(n. )* ገበን *geben*
**sybarite** *(n.)* ቀብሪ *qebri*
**sycamore** *(n. )* ላግጺ *lagxi*
**sycophancy** *(n.)* ምንዳድ *mndad*
**sycophant** *(n.)* ኣንዳዲ *andadi*
**syllabic** *(adj.)* ርሱን *rsun*
**syllable** *(n. )* ጉድጓድ *gudgWad*
**syllabus** *(n.)* ተሓዝ ገንዘብ *teḧaz genzeb*
**syllogism** *(n.)* ሓገዝ *ḧagez*
**sylph** *(n.)* ነተጐ *netegWa*
**sylvan** *(adj.)* ቀበረ *qebere*
**symbiosis** *(n.)* ኣውቶቡስ *awtobus*
**symbol** *(n.)* ቈጥቋጥ *qWeẗqWAẗ*
**symbolic** *(adj.)* ጎፍጓፍ *gofgWaf*
**symbolism** *(n.)* ዋኒን *wanin*
**symbolize** *(v.)* ነጋዳይ *negaday*
**symmetrical** *(adj.)* ደረት *deret*
**symmetry** *(n.)* ኣሽበድበደ *ashbedbede*
**sympathetic** *(adj.)* ተጸምደ *texemde*
**sympathize** *(v.)* ግን *gn*
**sympathy** *(n.)* ሓራድ ስጋ *ḧarad sga*
**symphony** *(n.)* ባልጠጂ *balẗeĵi*
**symposium** *(n.)* ጠስሚ *ẗesmi*
**symptom** *(n.)* ጵምብላሊዕ *xmblali'ë*
**symptomatic** *(adj.)* ዶሶ *doso*
**synchronize** *(v.)* መልጎም *melgom*
**synchronous** *(adj.)* ገዝእ *gez'e*
**syndicate** *(n.)* ዓዳጊ *ädagi*
**syndrome** *(n.)* ዚዝ በለ *ziz bele*
**synergy** *(n.)* ሽላ *shla*
**synonym** *(n.)* ሲረና *sirena*
**synonymous** *(adj.)* ብ *b*
**synopsis** *(n.)* ጎድናዊ-ምርጫ *godnawimrča*
**syntax** *(n.)* ቀደም *qedem*
**synthesis** *(n.)* ብ ሕንጻጽ *bḧnxax*
**synthesize** *(v.)* ጎድናዊ መንገዲ *godnawi mengedi*
**synthetic** *(adj.)* ደምበ *dembe*
**syringe** *(n.)* ተመልካቲ *temelkati*
**syrup** *(n. )* ባይት *bayit*
**system** *(n.)* ጋቢ'ና *gabina*
**systematic** *(adj.)* ካባረ *kabare*
**systematize** *(v.)* ካውሎ *kawlo*
**systemic** *(adj.)* ጋቢና *gabina*

# T

**tab** *(n.)* **መፈላልጦ** *mefelalťo*
**table** *(n. )* **ጣውላ፣ሰንጠረዥ** *terebeza*
**tableau** *(n.)* **ብዘይ ምንጋር ብዘይ ምንቅስቃስ ዝግበር ዉደደር** *bzey-mangar bzey-manqsqas zgeber wudder*
**tablet** *(n. )* **ክንኒንያ፣** *knnya*
**tabloid** *(n.)* **ኣማሙቅ ጋዘጠግኛ** *amawuq gazitegna*
**taboo** *(n.)* **ዝተኸልከለ ነገር፣ሕማቅ ነገር** *ztekelkele neger*
**tabular** *(adj.)* **ብሰንጠረዥ ዝተሰርሐ** *bsenterez zteserhe*
**tabulate** *(v.)* **ብሰንጠረዥ ኣዘጋጅዩ ተዳልዩ** *bsenterz ztezagajeye*
**tabulation** *(n.)* **ብሰንጠረዥ ምስራሕ ምምዳብ** *bsenterez msrah mzgjay*
**tabulator** *(v.)* **ሰንጠረዥ ዝሰርሕ ሰብ** *kadet*
**tachometer** *(n.)* **ካድምዩም** *kadmyum*
**tacit** *(adj.)* **ሱቅ ኢልካ ምስምዕማዕ** *suq ailka msm'amaa*
**taciturn** *(adj.)* **ሱቅ በሃሊ፣ሕቱም** *su behali,htum*
**tack** *(n.)* **ሓባጠ ጎባጥ ቦታ** *habate gobat bota*
**tackle** *(v.t. )* **ኩዕሾ ምምንጣል** *kuausho mmntal*
**tacky** *(adj.)* **ዘይጥዕም ዘይረብሕ** *zeyt'am zeyrebh*
**tact** *(n.)* **ብልሓት ጥንቃቀ** *blhat tnkak*
**tactful** *(adj.)* **ብልሓት ጥንቃቀ** *blhat tnkak*
**tactic** *(n.)* **ዜዴ ብልሓት** *zede blhat*
**tactical** *(adj.)* **ብሞያ ዝተሓገዘ** *bmoya ztehageze*
**tactician** *(n. )* **በሊሕ መለኛ** *belih melegna*
**tactile** *(adj.)* **ዝድህሰስ ነገር** *zdhses neger*
**tag** *(n.)* **ምልክት ዝልጠፍ ወይ ዝእሰር** *mlkt ztef'o wey z'aser*
**tail** *(n. )* **ጭራ** *chra*
**tailor** *(n.)* **ሰፋዪ ክዳን** *sefayi kdan*
**taint** *(v.)* **ተበኪሉ፣ሸቲቱ** *tebelilu shetitu*
**take** *(v.)* **ምዉሳድ ምሓዝ** *mwusad mhaz*
**takeaway** *(n.)* **ምውሰድ** *mwusad*
**takings** *(n.)* **ትርፊ፣ምህርቲ** *trfi , mhrti*
**talc** *(n.)* **ጵባቖ ጽሒፈት** *tsibuq tsuhuf*
**tale** *(n. )* **ትረኻ** *treka*
**talent** *(n. )* **ሞያ** *moya*
**talented** *(adj.)* **ብዓል ሞያ** *bal moya*
**talisman** *(n.)* **ክታብ** *ktab*
**talk** *(v.)* **ምንጋር** *mnggar*
**talkative** *(adj.)* **ለፍላፊ፣ተናጋሪ** *leflefi, tenagari*
**tall** *(adj.)* **ነዊሕ** *newih*
**tallow** *(n. )* **ኣንግዕ** *angu'a*
**tally** *(n.)* **ተስማዕሚዑ** *tesmaamiu*
**talon** *(n.)* **ጠንካራ ናይ ኣሞራ ጭፍሪ** *tenkara na amora chifri*
**tame** *(adj.)* **ለማዳ እንስሳ** *lemada enssa*
**tamely** *(adv.)* **መዓስከር** *measker*

**tamp** *(v.)* ጠቅጢቁ፣መሊኡ *tnqiqu meliu*
**tamper** *(v.)* ጣልያ *talya*
**tampon** *(n.)* ፐረድ ዝመጽሉ ግዘ *pered zmetselu gze*
**tan** *(n.)* ቆርበት ኣልፊዑ *qorbet alfi'u*
**tandem** *(n.)* ብክልተ ሰብ ትዝወር ሳይክል *bklte seb etzwer siykle*
**tang** *(n.)* ሓያል ሽታ ንኣፍንጫ ዝርብሽ *hayal shta naafncha zrbish*
**tangent** *(n.)* ተጽጊዑ ዝሓልፍ መስመር *tetsegiuzhalf mesmer*
**tangerine** *(n.)* መንደሪኒ *menderini*
**tangible** *(adj.)* ኣካል ዘለዎ ዝጭበጥ *akal zelewo zchbet*
**tangle** *(v.t. )* ኣጠላሊፉ *atalalafi*
**tank** *(n. )* ታንኪ *tanki*
**tanker** *(n. )* ናይ ማይ መትሓዚ ዓብዪ ጎማ *naymay methazi abuyi goma*
**tanner** *(n. )* ቆርበት ፍሓቂ *qorbet fehaqi*
**tannery** *(n.)* ናይ ቆርበት ፋብሪካ *nay qorbet fabrika*
**tantalize** *(v.)* ኣጎምጅዩ፣ኣቁለጭሊጩ *agomjyu aqulech lichu*
**tantamount** *(adj.)* ተመጣጣኒ *temetatani*
**tantrum** *(n.)* ምክንያት ዘይብሉ ቁጥዐ *mknyat zeyblu qutea*
**tap** *(n.)* መኽፈቲ ቡምባ፣ዳንሲ ዓይነት *makfeti bunba,dansi aynet*
**tape** *(v.i. )* ናይ ካሴት ክሪ *nay kaset kri*
**tape** *(n.)* ብላዕሊ ቅርሺ ምሃብ *blaali qrshi mhab*
**taper** *(v.)* ጧፍ *twaf*
**tapestry** *(n. )* ስግዳን *sgdan*
**tappet** *(n.)* ናይ ሞተር መጫወቲ *nay moter mechaweti*
**tar** *(n.)* ኣስፓልት መንገዲ፣ብቦምቢ ዝተሓጸረ መንገዲ *aspalt mengedi,bbonbi ztehasere mengedi*
**tardy** *(adj.)* ፈዛዝ፣ዘገምተግኛ *fezaz,zegemtagna*
**target** *(n. )* ዕላማ *alama*
**tariff** *(n.)* ቀረፅ *qeres*
**tarn** *(n.)* ፈዚዙ *fezizu*
**tarnish** *(v.)* ፈዛዝ *fezaz*
**tarot** *(n.)* ጥንቆላ *tnkola*
**tarpaulin** *(n.)* ናይ ዝናብ ክዳን *nay znab kdan*
**tart** *(n.)* ጥዑም ነገር ዝሓዘ ብያቲ *t'um neger zhaze byati*
**tartar** *(n.)* ምስ ሰብ ክረዳዳእ ዘይክእል ሰብ *ms seb kredadaA zeyekAl seb*
**task** *(n.)* ስራሕ፣ሞያ *srah moya*
**tassel** *(n.)* ምንስናስ *mnsnas*
**taste** *(v.)* ኣማራፂ *amaratsi*
**taste** *(n.)* ጣዕሚ *taami*
**tasteful** *(adj.)* ጥዑም *t'um*
**tasteless** *(adj.)* ጣዕሚ ዘይብሉ *taami zeyblu*
**tasty** *(adj.)* ጥዑም *t'um*
**tattle** *(n.)* ቅርሪታ ኣቅሪቡ *qreta aqribu*
**tattoo** *(n.)* ዉቃጦ *wuqato*
**tatty** *(adj.)* ኣረጊት፣ዝተቀደደ *aregit,zteqdede*
**taunt** *(n.)* ምዝንባል፣ዘንቢሉ *mznbal,zenbilu*

**taut** *(adj.)* **ዝተወጠረ** *ztewetere*
**tavern** *(n. )* **ናይ መሸት ቡና ቤት** *nay mshet buna bet*
**tawdry** *(adj.)* **ብልጭልጭ ርካሽ** *blchlich rkash*
**tax** *(n.)* **ግብሪ** *gbri*
**taxable** *(adj.)* **ግብሪ ዝክፈለሉ** *gbri zkfelelu*
**taxation** *(n.)* **ናይ ግብሪ ኣከፋፍላ** *ney gbri akefafla*
**taxi** *(n.)* **ታክሲ** *taksi*
**taxonomy** *(n.)* **ናይ እንስሳትን ኣትክልትን ዘፅንዕ** *nay enssat atkltn zesn'a*
**tea** *(n.)* **ሻሂ** *shahi*
**teach** *(v.)* **ምምሃር** *mmhar*
**teacher** *(n.)* **መምህር** *memhr*
**teak** *(n. )* **ናይ ሰሊጥ ዘርኢ** *nay selit zer'i*
**team** *(n.)* **ቡዱን** *budun*
**tear** *( n. )* **ንብዕት** *nb'at*
**tear** *(v.)* **ንብዕት** *nb'at*
**tearful** *(adj.)* **መሕዘኒ** *mehzeni*
**tease** *(v.)* **መብሸቂ** *mebsheqi*
**teat** *(n. )* **ናይ እንስሳ ጫፍ ጡብ** *nay anssa chaf tub*
**technical** *(adj.)* **ሞያዊ** *moyawi*
**technician** *(n. )* **በዓል ሞያ** *beal moya*
**technique** *(n.)* **ብልሓት** *blhat*
**technological** *(adj.)* **ብተክኖሎጅይ ዝተሓገዘ** *bteknology ztehageze*
**technologist** *(n. )* **በዓል ሞያ** *beal moya*
**technology** *(n.)* **ሞያዊ ስልጣነ ቴክኖሎጂ** *moyawi sltena teknology*
**tedious** *(adj.)* **መሰልቸዪ** *meselchyi*
**teem** *(v.)* **መሊኡ፣ሸፊኑ** *meliu shefinu*
**teenager** *(n.)* **ወጣት ዕድሚኡ 13-19 ዝኮነ** *wetat admiu kab 13-19 zkone*
**teens** *(adj.)* **ካብ 13-19 ዝርከብ** *kab 13-19 zrkeb*
**teeter** *(v.)* **ተንጎድጊዱ** *tengedagidu*
**teethe** *(v.)* **ስኒ ኣውፂኡ ን ህፃን** *sni awsiau nhsan*
**teetotal** *(adj.)* **ምንም መስተ ዘይሰቲ** *mnm meste zeyseti*
**teetotaller** *(n. )* **ምንም መስተ ዘይሰቲ** *mnm meste zeyseti*
**telecommunications** *(n. )* **ስልኪ፣ቲቪ፣ኢንተርኔት** *slki,tivi,ainternet*
**telegram** *(n. )* **ቴሌግራም** *telegaram*
**telegraph** *(n.)* **ቴሌግራም** *telegaram*
**telegraphic** *(adj.)* **ቴሌግራም ናይ ምኣላክ ሒደት** *telegram nay melak hidet*
**telegraphy** *(n.)* **ቴሌግራም ናይ ምኣላክ ሒደት** *telegram nay melak hidet*
**telepathy** *(n. )* **ናይ መንፈስ(ኣእምሮ) ርክብ** *nay menfes aemro rkb*
**telephone** *(n.)* **ስልኪ** *slki*
**telescope** *(n.)* **ኣቅሪቡ ዘርኢ መነፀር** *aqribu zerai meneser*
**televise** *(v.)* **ብቴሌቪዥን ተሓላሊፉ** *btelevizn tehalalifu*
**television** *(n.)* **ቴሌቪዥን** *televizion*

**tell** *(v.)* **ምንጋር** *mngar*
**teller** *(n. )* **ገንዘብ ከፋሊ** *genzeb kefali*
**telling** *(adj.)* **ዉዒኢታማ** *wusieitama*
**telltale** *(adj.)* **ሚስጥረኛ** *mistregna*
**temerity** *(n.)* **ዘየድሊ ድፍረት** *zeyedli dfret*
**temper** *(n.)* **ተናዳዲ** *tenadadi*
**temperament** *(n.)* **ኣመል** *amel*
**temperamental** *(adj.)* **ቀልጢፉ ቀልጢፉ ዝኩሪ** *qltifu qltifu zkuri*
**temperance** *(n.)* **ንእሽተይ ዝበልዕ** *nashtey zbl'a*
**temperate** *(adj.)* **ወይና ደጋ** *weyna dega*
**temperature** *(n. )* **ሙቀት መጠን** *muqet meten*
**tempest** *(n.)* **ኣዉሎ ንፋስ** *awulo nfas*
**tempestuous** *(adj.)* **ዉዝምበሩ ዝዋፃ** *wuzmbru zwese*
**template** *(n.)* **ዝኮነ ነገር ንምስራሕ ዝተዘጋጀየ ኣቅሓ** *zkone neger nmsrah ztezgajeye aqha*
**temple** *(n.)* **ቤተ መቅደስ** *bet mekdes*
**tempo** *(n.)* **ናይ ሙዚቃ ስልቲ** *ney muzika slti*
**temporal** *(adj.)* **ግዜያዊ** *giziyawi*
**temporary** *(adj.)* **ግዜያዊ** *giziyawi*
**temporize** *(v.)* **ግዜ ንምግናይ ውሳኒኡ ኣደንጉዩ** *gze nmgnay wusanau adenguyu*
**tempt** *(v.)* **ንምፅላእ ምሙካር** *nmslaa mumukar*
**temptation** *(n. )* **ብጣዕሚ ናይ ምድላይ ስሚዒት** *btaami namdlay smiait*
**tempter** *(n.)* **ተፈታታኒ ሰብ** *tefetatani seb*
**ten** *(adj. & adv.)* **ዓሰርተ** *asert*
**tenable** *(adj.)* **ዝተረጋገፀ** *zteregagese*
**tenacious** *(adj.)* **ዘይረብሕ** *zeyrebh*
**tenacity** *(n.)* **ጥንካረ** *tenkara*
**tenancy** *(n.)* **ሓሪፍ ትኮነሉ ግዘ** *harif tkonelu gze*
**tend** *(v.)* **ሃዋህው** *hawahwu*
**tendency** *(n.)* **ዝንባለ** *znbale*
**tendentious** *(adj.)* **ዝንባለ** *znbale*
**tender** *(n.)* **የዋህ** *yewah*
**tender** *(adj.)* **ጨረታ** *chereta*
**tendon** *(n.)* **ናይ ሰዉነት ጅማት** *nay sewunet jmat*
**tenement** *(n.)* **ኣብ ፎቅ ዝካረ ቦታ** *ab foq zkare bota*
**tenet** *(n. )* **መምርሒ** *memrhi*
**tennis** *(n. )* **ናይ ሜዳ ተንስ ጨዋታ** *nay meda tens chewata*
**tenor** *(n.)* **ወዲ ደራፊ ፅብቅ ድምፂ ዘለዎ** *wedi derafi sbuk dmsi zelewo*
**tense** *(adj.)* **ናይ ግዘታት ስብስብ** *nay gizetat sbsb*
**tensile** *(adj.)* **ናይ ዉጥረት ስብስብ** *nay wutret sbsb*
**tension** *(n.)* **ናይ ሓይሊ መብራህቲ መጠን** *nay hayli mebrahti meten*
**tent** *(n.)* **ኬንዳ** *kenda*
**tentacle** *(n.)* **ኣከርካሪ ዘይብሎም እንስሳታት** *akerkari zeyblom anssatat*
**tentative** *(adj.)* **ዘየተኣማምን ገ ዘ ክቅየር ዝክእል** *zeyeteamamn geza kqyer zkal*

**tenterhook** *(n.)* ብጣዕሚ ምህንጣይ *btaami mhntay*
**tenth** *(adj. & n.)* ዓስራይ *asray*
**tenuous** *(adj.)* ቀጢን ብቀሊሉ ዘይስበር *qetin bkelilu zeysber*
**tenure** *(n. )* ናይ ፖሎቲካ ስልጣን ዝሃዘ *nay pletika sltan zhaze*
**tepid** *(adj.)* ብዙሕ ዘይሞቀ ማይ *bzuh zeymoke may*
**term** *(n.)* ናይ ሓደ ክፍለ ግዘ መጀመሪ/መወድ ኢ *nay hadekfle gze mjemeri/mewedei*
**termagant** *(n.)* ነገረኛ ሰበይቲ *negeregna sebeyti*
**terminal** *(adj.)* ና መጨረሻ ደረጃ *na mecheresha dereja*
**terminate** *(v.)* ኣቋሪፁ *aqarisu*
**termination** *(n.)* ትኣጊዱ *t'agidu*
**terminological** *(adj.)* ና ሓደ ስራሕ መረዳድኢ ቋንቋ *na hade srah meredadei kanka*
**terminology** *(n.)* ና ሓደ ስራሕ መረዳድኢ ቋንቋ *na hade srah meredadei kanka*
**terminus** *(n.)* ናይ ኣየር መስተኣናገዲ ቦታ *nay ayer msteanagedi bota*
**termite** *(n.)* ምሰጠ *msat*
**terrace** *(n.)* ዕብዪ መርየት *abyi meret*
**terracotta** *(n.)* ቀይሕ ሓመድ *keyh hamed*
**terrain** *(n.)* ምልክዐ ምድሪ *melka mdri*
**terrestrial** *(adj.)* ናይ የብስ ነባሪ *nay yebs nebari*
**terrible** *(adj.)* ከቢድ ሓዘን *kebid hazen*
**terrier** *(n.)* ና ሃደን ከልቢ *nahaden kelbi*
**terrific** *(adj.)* ከቢድ *kebid*
**terrify** *(v.)* ምስቃቅ *msqay*
**territorial** *(adj.)* ብሂራዊ ጦር ኣባል *bherawi tor abal*
**territory** *(n. )* ግዝኣት *gzat*
**terror** *(n. )* መፍርሒ ሰብ *mefrhi seb*
**terrorism** *(n.)* ሽብርተኝነት *shbrtegnnet*
**terrorist** *(n.)* ሽብርኛ *shbrtegna*
**terrorize** *(v.)* እሸቢሩ *ashebiru*
**terry** *(n.)* ዘርፍ *zerefa*
**terse** *(adj.)* ሕፅር ምጥን ዝበለ *hsr mtn zbele*
**tertiary** *(adj.)* ስኣልሳይ ደረጃ *salsay derja*
**test** *(n.)* ፈተና/ሙኮራ *fetena/mukera*
**testament** *(n. )* ንዛዘ *nzaze*
**testate** *(adj.)* ዘይ ምንዛዝ *zey mnzaz*
**testicle** *(n.)* ፍረ ነብሲ *frenebsi*
**testify** *(v.)* ምምስካር *mmskar*
**testimonial** *(n. )* ናይ ምስክር ወረቀት *ney mskr werket*
**testimony** *(n. )* ናይ ቃል መሓላ *nay kal mehala*
**testis** *(n.)* ፍረ ነብሲ *frenebsi*
**testy** *(adj.)* ተናዳዲ *tenadadi*
**tetchy** *(adj.)* ምግላል *mglal*
**tether** *(v.t. )* ና እንስሳት መእሰሪ ሰንሰለት *naanssat meseri senselet*
**text** *(n.)* ፅሑፍ *shuf*
**textbook** *(n.)* ደፍተር *defter*
**textile** *(n)* ጨርቃ ጨርቅ *cherka cherki*
**textual** *(adj.)* ካብ ፅሑፍ *kab shuf*

**textual** *(adj.)* ካብ ፅሑፍ *kab shuf*
**texture** *(n.)* ኩነታት ናዙ ነገር ሓርፋፍ/ለማፅ *kunetat nazu neger*
**thank** *(v.)* ኣመስጊኑ *amesginu*
**thankful** *(adj.)* ኣመስጋኒ *amesginu*
**thankless** *(adj.)* ዉለታ ቢስ *wuleta bis*
**that** *(pron. & adj.)* እቲ *ati*
**thatch** *(n.)* ኩምር ዝበለ ፀጉሪ *kumur zbele seguri*
**thaw** *(v.)* ሙውቅ ኣየር *muwuq ayer*
**the** *(adj.)* ፋሉጥ ዘኮነ ነገር ንምግላፅ እንጥቀመሉ *flut zkone neger nmflat entkemelu*
**theatre** *(n.)* ተውኒት *tewunet*
**theatrical** *(adj.)* ተውኒታዊ *tewunitawi*
**theft** *(n.)* ስርቂ *srki*
**their** *(adj.)* ናዮም *nayom*
**theism** *(n. )* ብእግዛቢሄር ምንባር ምእማን *magzabher mnbar m'eman*
**them** *(pron. )* እሶም *asom*
**thematic** *(adj.)* ዝተጨበጠ ነገር *ztechebet neger*
**themselves** *(pron.)* ባዕሎም *baalom*
**then** *(adv. )* ብድሕ ሪኡ *bdhriu*
**thence** *(adv. )* ብድሕ ሪኡ *bdhriu*
**theocracy** *(n. )* ብቀሺ ዝምራሕ ዓዲ *bqeshi zmrah adi*
**theodolite** *(n.)* ናይ ቅየሳ መሳርሒ *nay kyesa mesarhi*
**theologian** *(n.)* ናይ ሃይማኖት ጠቢብ *nay haymanot tebib*
**theology** *(n. )* ስነ-ሃይማኖት *sne haymanot*
**theorem** *(n.)* መላ ምት *melamt*
**theoretical** *(adj.)* ብፅሑፍ ዘሎ/ ዘይተሞከረ *bsuhuf zelo/zeytmokere*
**theorist** *(n.)* ሓሳብ ዘመንጪ *hasab zemenchi*
**theorize** *(v.)* ሓሳብ ኣመንጭዩ *hasab amenchiyu*
**theory** *(n.)* ፅንሲ ሓሳብ *tnsi hasab*
**theosophy** *(n.)* ብፆሎት ብምምሳጥ ምስ እግዛቢሄር ብቀጥታምንግጋር *bsolot bmmsat ms egzabher mgnay*
**therapeutic** *(adj.)* ሕማም ናይምድሓን ዕቅሚ *hmam namdhan aqmi*
**therapist** *(n.)* ሓኪም *hakim*
**therapy** *(n.)* ናይ ሕማም መድሓኒ ሕክምና *nahmam medheni hkmna*
**there** *(adv. )* ኣብ ኡ *abuu*
**thermal** *(adj.)* ሙቅ *muk*
**thermometer** *(n.)* ናይ ሙቀት መለክዒ መሳርሒ *nay muket melekai mesarhi*
**thermos** *(n.)* ፔርሙዝ *permuz*
**thermosetting** *(adj.)* ብሙቀት ዝጥንክር ፕላስቲክ *bmuqet ztnker plastik*
**thermostat** *(n.)* ሙቀት መቆፃፀሪ መሳርሒ *muqet meqosaseri meserhi*
**thesis** *(n.)* ና ዲግሪ መማልኢ ፁሑፍ *nadgri memalai shuf*
**they** *(pron.)* እሶም *Asom*
**thick** *(adj.)* ረጊድ *regid*
**thicken** *(v.)* ኣርጊዱ *argidu*

**thicket** ***(n. )*** **በዕቲ** *bati*
**thief** ***(n. )*** **ሰራቂ** *seraqi*
**thigh** ***(n. )*** **ዳንጋ** *dabga*
**thimble** ***(n.)*** **ጓንቲ** *ganti*
**thin** ***(adj.)*** **ቀጢን** *qetin bkelilu zeysber*
**thing** ***(n.)*** **ስም ዝይብሉ ኣቅሓ** *sm zeyblu aqh*
**think** ***(v.)*** **ምሕሳብ** *Mhsab*
**thinker** ***(n.)*** **ሓሳቢ/ፋላስፋ** *hasabi falasfa*
**third** ***(adj.)*** **ሲሶ** *siso*
**thirst** ***(n.)*** **ማይ ምፅማእ** *may msmaa*
**thirsty** ***(adj.)*** **ማይ ምፅማእ** *may msmaa*
**thirteen** ***(adj. & n.)*** **ዕሰር ሰለስተ** *aserte seleste*
**thirteen** ***(adj. & n.)*** **ዕሰር ሰለስተ** *aserte seleste*
**thirteenth** ***(adj. & n.)*** **መበል ዕሰር ሰለስተ** *mebel aserte seleste*
**thirtieth** ***(adj. & n.)*** **መበል ሰላሳ** *mebel selasa*
**thirtieth** ***(adj. & n.)*** **መበል ሰላሳ** *mebel selasa*
**thirty** ***(adj. & n.)*** **ሰላሳ** *selasa*
**thirty** ***(adj. & n.)*** **ሰላሳ** *selasa*
**this** ***(pron.& adj.)*** **ኡዚ** *azi*
**thistle** ***(n.)*** **ሓሸክሾኽ ምባል** *hashekushok mbal*
**thither** ***(adv. )*** **ርሕቅ ዝበለ ቦታ** *rhik zebele bota*
**thong** ***(n.)*** **ናየ ቆዳ መሰርሒ** *nay koda mesrhi*
**thorn** ***(n.)*** **ዕሾክ** *ashok*
**thorny** ***(adj.)*** **ዕሾክ መዉፅኢ** *ashok mewusai*
**thorough** ***(adj.)*** **ጥብቂ** *tebeka*
**thoroughfare** ***(n.)*** **ዋና ጎዳና** *wana godana*
**though** ***(conj.)*** **ዋላካ እንተኮነ** *walaka entekone*
**thoughtful** ***(adj.)*** **ሓሳቢ** *hasbi*
**thoughtless** ***(adj.)*** **ዘይሓስብ** *zeyhasb*
**thousand** ***(adj. & n.)*** **ሽሕ** *shih*
**thrall** ***(n. )*** **ባርነት** *barnet*
**thrash** ***(v.)*** **ገረፉ** *gerefe*
**thread** ***(n.)*** **ክሪ** *kri*
**threat** ***(n.)*** **ፍርሒ** *frhi*
**threaten** ***(v.)*** **ፈሪሑ** *ferisu*
**three** ***(adj. & n.)*** **ሰለስተ** *seste*
**thresh** ***(v.)*** **ስንዳይ ካብ ሓሰሩ ምፍላይ** *snday hasitu mflay*
**threshold** ***(n.)*** **መእተዊ በሪ** *matewi beri*
**thrice** ***(adv. )*** **ሰለስተ ግዜ** *seleste gze*
**thrift** ***(n.)*** **ምቁጣብ** *mqutab*
**thrifty** ***(adj.)*** **ቆጣቢ** *qotabi*
**thrill** ***(n.)*** **ኣነቃቒሑ** *ane kaki hu*
**thriller** ***(n.)*** **ልቢ ሰቃሊ ታሪክ** *lbisekali tarik*
**thrive** ***(v.)*** **ተስፋሕፊሑ** *tesfahfihu*
**throat** ***(n.)*** **ጎሮሮ** *gororo*
**throaty** ***(adj.)*** **ዝተዓፈነ ድምፂ** *zteafene dmsi*
**throb** ***(v.)*** **ልቢ ብፍጥነት ክወቂዑ** *lbu bftnet weqiau*
**throes** ***(n. )*** **ከቢድ ስቃይ** *kebid skay*
**throne** ***(n.)*** **ዙፋን** *zefen*
**throng** ***(n.)*** **ብሓደ ኪዱ ግር ኢሉ** *bhade kidu ger ailu*
**throttle** ***(n.)*** **ሓኒቁ** *hanaki*
**through** ***(prep. &adv.)*** **ነዳዲ መቆፃፀሪ** *naedadi mekosasaeri*

throughout *(prep. )* ሙሉእ ብሙሉእ *mulua bmulua*
throw *(v.)* ደርብዩ/ምድርባይ *derbyu mdrbay*
thrush *(n.)* ሕብሪ ዝበዝሓ ዒፍ *hbri zbezha af*
thrust *(v.)* ምዉጋእ *mwudae*
thud *(n. )* ሃተፈ/ለፈለፈ *hatafe/leflafi*
thug *(n. )* ዓመፀኛ *amesegna*
thumb *(n.)* ዓባይ ኢድ *anay ad*
thunder *(n.)* ነጎድጓድ *negodgad*
thunderous *(adj.)* ነጎድጓዳዊ *negodgadawo*
Thursday *(n.)* ሓሙስ *hamus*
thus *(adv. )* ብዚ ምክንያት *bzi mknyat*
thwart *(v.)* ኣሰናኺሉ/ከልኪሉ *asenakilu/kelkilom*
thyroid *(n.)* ዕብየት ዝቆፃፀር *abyet zqossaser*
tiara *(n. )* ናይ ጳጳስ ዘዉዲ *nay papas zewudi*
tick *(n.)* ጩረት *cherk*
ticket *(n.)* ቲኬት *tket*
ticking *(n.)* ምቁፃር *mksat*
tickle *(v.)* ምኩርካዕ *kurkaa*
ticklish *(adj.)* ኮርኪዕካዮ ዝስሕቕ *korkiakayo zshk*
tidal *(adj.)* ማዕበል *maabel*
tidally *(n.)* ማዕበላዊ *maabelawi*
tide *(n.)* ማዕበል ባሕሪ *maobrl hahi*
tidiness *(n.)* ንፅህና *nshna*
tidings *(n.)* ዜና/ወረ *zena were*
tidy *(adj.)* ዝተስተካከለ *ztekelkele*
tie *(v.)* ካራባታ *karabota*
tie *(n. )* ጠንካራ ግኑኙነት *tenkartatenkara gnugnnet*
tied *(adj.)* ዝተኣሳሰረ *z'atesasere*
tier *(n. )* ብደረጃ ዝተደርደሩ *bdereja ztederaderu*
tiger *(n.)* ነብሪ *nebri*
tight *(adj.)* ሰጢሙ ዝተኣሰረ *setimu zete asere*
tighten *(v.)* ኣስጢሙ ሒዙ *astimu hizu*
tile *(n.)* ሸክላ ቆርቆሮ *shekla qorqoro*
till *(prep.)* እስካብ/ቀደደ *eskab/qdede*
tiller *(n.)* ሓረስታይ፣መቅዘፊ *harestay,mkzefi*
tilt *(v.)* ናብ ሓደ ምዝንባል *nab hade mznbal*
timber *(n. )* ኣዕኒው *as'ainu*
time *(n.)* ሰዓት *seat*
timely *(adj.)* ብሰዓቱ *bseat*
timid *(adj.)* ሓፋር *hafar*
timidity *(n.)* ፍርሒ *hrhi*
timorous *(adj.)* ሓፋር *hafar*
tin *(n.)* ታንኒካ፣ቆርቆሮ *tanika,qorqoro*
tincture *(n.)* ብኣልኮል ዝብፅበፅ መድሓኒት *balkol zbsbes medhanit*
tinder *(n.)* ሓዊ ምቅፅፃል *hawi mks'al*
tinge *(n.)* ንእሽተይ ንምምሳል ምቅባእ *nAshtey nmmsal mkbae*
tingle *(n.)* መጠነኛ ናይ ምዉጋእ ስምዕት *metenegna nay mugae samet*
tinker *(v.)* ንእሽተይ ምዕራይ *nAshtey m'aray*
tinkle *(v.)* ተደዊሉ *tedewilu*
tinsel *(n. )* መጋየዪ ወረቀታት *megayesi werketat*
tint *(n.)* ንእሽተይ ንምምሳል ምቅባእ *n'ashtey nmmsal mkbae*

**tiny** *(adj.)* **ንእሽተይ፣ብጣዕሚ ንእሽተይ** *n'ashtey,btaami n'eshtey*

**tip** *(n.)* **ኣፍሲሱ፣ገልቢጡ** *afsisu,gelbitu*

**tipple** *(v.)* **ኣልኮል መስተ** *alkol meste*

**tipster** *(n.)* **ናፈርስ ዉድድር ቅርሺ ኣናተቀበለ ዝግምት** *naferes wudder qrshi enateqebele zgmt*

**tipsy** *(n. )* **ሞቅ ዝበሎ** *mok zbelo*

**tiptoe** *(v.)* **ብኣፃብዕቲ እግርካ ምካድ** *basabati egrka mkad*

**tirade** *(n.)* **ነዊሕ ጭቅጭቅ ዝተሓወሶ ንግግር** *newih chikchik ztehaweso nggr*

**tire** *(v.)* **ተስፋ ቆረፅ** *taesfa kors*

**tired** *(adj.)* **ድኻም** *dekam*

**tireless** *(adj.)* **ዘይፅዕር** *zeys'r*

**tiresome** *(adj.)* **ኣድካሚ ፣ኣሰልቻዪ** *adkami aselchayi*

**tissue** *(n.)* **ሶፍቲ** *softi*

**titanic** *(adj.)* **ብጣዕሚ ዓቡዪ ኣድላዪ** *btaemi abyi adlayi*

**tithe** *(n. )* **ቃል ሓደ እስረኛ ን ቤተ-ክርስትያን ዝወሃብ** *kal hade esregna nbetekrstyan zwehab*

**titillate** *(v.)* **ን ግብረ ስጋዊ ግኑኝነት ስሚዕት ምልዕዓል** *ngbre ssgawi gnugnunet smiait mlal*

**titivate** *(v.)* **ተቆናጅዩ** *tekonajyu*

**title** *(n.)* **ኣርእስቲ** *arasti*

**titled** *(adj.)* **በዓል መኣርግ** *beal mearg*

**titular** *(adj.)* **ንስም ብቻ ዝወሃብ መኣርግ** *nsm bcha zwehab mearg*

**to** *(prep.)* **ናብ** *nab hade mznbal*

**toast** *(n.)* **ዝተጠበሰ** *ztetbese*

**toaster** *(n. )* **ፎርኖ/ባኒ መብሰሊ ማሺን** *forno/bani mebseli mashion*

**tobacco** *(n.)* **ትምባኮ** *tmbako*

**today** *(adv. )* **ለሞዕንቲ** *lemaanti*

**toddle** *(v.)* **ኣለክሊኩ** *alkliku*

**toddler** *(n.)* **ታተ ዝብለ ህፃን** *tate zble hsan*

**toe** *(n.)* **ዓባይ ኣፃብዕቲ እግሪ** *abay asabati egry*

**toffee** *(n. )* **ካብ ፀባ ዝተሰርሐ ከረሜላ** *kab seba zteserhe kerimela*

**tog** *(n.)* **ዝተፈለየ ናይ በዓል ክዳን ምክዳን** *ztefely nay beal kdan mkdan*

**toga** *(n.)* **ናይ ሮማውያን ና ኣወዳት ጃኪት** *na romawuyan na awedat jaket*

**together** *(adv. )* **ብሓደ** *bhade*

**toggle** *(n.)* **ሞልጎሙ ብዕንጨይቲ ዝኮነ ክዳን** *molgomu bancheyti zteserhe kedean*

**toil** *(v.i. )* **ከቢድ ስራሕ ብርትዐ ዘድልዮ** *kebid srah brtea zdlyo*

**toilet** *(n.)* **ሽቃቅ፣ሽንቲ ቤት** *shqaq ,shnti bet*

**toiletries** *(n.)* **መተሓፃፀቢ ኣቁሑት** *metehasasebi akuhut*

**toils** *(n. )* **ከቢድ ስራሕ ብርትዐ ዘድልዮ** *kebid srah brtea zdlyo*

**token** *(n.)* **ምልክት መስታወሻ** *mlkt mestawesha*

**tolerable** *(adj.)* **ክትዕገሶ ዝካኣል** *ktageso tk'al*

**tolerance** *(n.)* **ትዕግስቲ** *tagsti*

**tolerant** *(adj.)* **ትዕግስተኛ** *tagstegna*

**tolerate** *(v.)* **ታዓጊሱ** *taagisu*

**toleration** *(n.)* ትዕግስተኝነት *t'agstegninet*
**toll** *(n.)* ና ሓዘን ደወል፣ኣብ ኪላ ዝቁራፅ ቀርፅ *nahazen dewel,ab kelazqures qeres*
**tomato** *(n. )* ኮሚደረ *komidere*
**tomb** *(n. )* መቃብር *mekabr*
**tomboy** *(n. )* ፋሉይ ሎቶሪ *fluy loteri*
**tome** *(n. )* ዝዓበየ ና ምርምር መፅሓፍ *zabeye namrmr meshaf*
**tomfoolery** *(n.)* ዕብዳን *abdan*
**tomorrow** *(adv. )* ናጋ/ፅባሕ *naga/sbah*
**ton** *(n.)* ናይ ክብደት መለክዒ *nakbdet melekai*
**tone** *(n.)* ናይ ድምፂ ቃና *na dmsi kana*
**toner** *(n.)* ና ፕሪንተር ቀለም *na printer kelem*
**tongs** *(n.)* መቆንጠጢ *mekonteti*
**tongue** *(n.)* መልሓስ *melhas*
**tonic** *(n. )* ዘነቃቅሕ መድሓኒ *zenekakh medhanit*
**tonight** *(adv. )* ለሞዓንቲ ምሸት *lemoanti mshet*
**tonnage** *(n.)* ናይ መርከብ ፅዕነት ጠቅላላ ክብደት *na merkeb teklala s'anet*
**tonne** *(n.)* ሓደ ሺሕ ኪሎ ግራም *hade shih kilogram*
**tonsil** *(n.)* ቶንሲል *tonsil*
**tonsure** *(n.)* ብቡድሃ ሃይማኖት መላጥ *bbudha haymanot melat*
**too** *(adv. )* ብጣዕሚ፣ድጋሜ *btaemi, dgame*
**tool** *(n.)* ናይ ኢድ መሳርሒ *ḧrtum*
**tooth** *(n. )* ስኒ *sni*
**toothache** *(n.)* ናይ ስኒ ሕማም *nay sni hmm*
**toothless** *(adj.)* ሸራፍ *sheraf*
**toothpaste** *(n. )* ናይ ስኒ ሳሙና *nay sni samuna*
**toothpick** *(n.)* ና ስኒ መጎርገሪ ዕንጨይቲ *nasni megorgori anchyti*
**top** *(n.)* ኣብ ልዕሊ *ab laali*
**topaz** *(n. )* ፋሉጥ *flut*
**topiary** *(n.)* ኣትክልቲ ብመልክዕ ምቁራፅ *atklti bmelka mkuras*
**topic** *(n.)* ኣርእስቲ *are'esti*
**topical** *(adj.)* ወቅታዊ *weqtawi*
**topless** *(adj.)* ካብ መዓንጣ ንልዕሊ ጥራሕካ ምካን *kab meantanlaali trahka mukan*
**topographer** *(n.)* ናይ መሬት ኣቀማምጣ ዝፅንዕ ሙሁር *nay meret akemamta zesna muhur*
**topographical** *(adj.)* ናይ መሬት ኣቀማምጣ ዘርኢ ካርታ *nay meret akemamta zerei karta*
**topography** *(n.)* ናይ መሬት ኣቀማምጣ *nay meret akemamta*
**topping** *(n.)* ብልዕሊ ዝግበር *blaeli zgber*
**topple** *(v.)* ገልቢጡ ካብ ስልጣን *gelbitu kab sltan*
**tor** *(n.)* ና ከዉሒ ጎቦ *na kewuhi gobo*
**torch** *(n. )* ኣቃፂሉ *akasilu*
**toreador** *(n.)* ተመልካቲ *temelkati*
**torment** *(n.)* ከቢድ ስቃይ *kebid skay*
**tormentor** *(n.)* ኣቸጋሪ ሰብ *achegari seb*
**tornado** *(n. )* ብጣዕሚ ሓያል ንፋስ *btaemi hayal nfas*

**torpedo** *(n.)* ብዉሽጢ ማይ ዝጎዓዝ ቦምብ *bwushti may zgoaz bomb*
**torpid** *(adj.)* ፈዛዝ *fezaz*
**torrent** *(n.)* ፅሕፉ፣ዉሑጅ *shfa ,wuhj*
**torrential** *(adj.)* ከቢድ ብጣዕሚ ሓያል *kebid btaami hayal*
**torrid** *(adj.)* ብጣዕሚ ሓያል ፀሎ *kebid btaami hselo*
**torsion** *(n.)* ምጥምዛዝ *mtmzaz*
**torso** *(n.)* ኢድ እግሪ ርእሲ ዘይብሉ ኣካል *aid agri resi zeyblu akal*
**tort** *(n.)* ፍትሒ ን ብሄር ወንጀል *fthi n bher wenjel*
**tortoise** *(n.)* ኣቦ ጋቡየ *abo gabuye*
**tortuous** *(adj.)* ዝተጠምማዘዘ *ztetemazeze*
**torture** *(n.)* ስቃይ *skay*
**toss** *(v.)* ወርዊሩ ኣፈንጢሩ *werwiru afentiru*
**tot** *(n.)* ጠንካራ ና ኣልኮል መስተ *tenkara alkol meste*
**total** *(n.)* ድምር፣ጠቅላላ *dmer,teklala*
**total** *(adj.)* ድምር፣ጠቅላላ *dmer,teklala*
**totalitarian** *(adj.)* ኣምባገነንነት ና ሓደ ፓርቲ መንግስቲ *ambagenennet na hade parti mengsti*
**totality** *(n.)* ብጠቅላላ *bteqlala*
**tote** *(v.)* ብምትሓዝ ዝግነ ቅርሺ *bmthaz zgne qrshi*
**totter** *(v.)* ደኪሙ መንግስቲ ወዲቁ *dekimu mensti wediqu*
**touch** *(v.)* ነኪኡ፣ምንካእ *nekiau mnkae*
**touching** *(adj.)* ልቢ ዝነክእ *lbiznekea*
**touchy** *(adj.)* ተናዳዲ *tenadadi*
**tough** *(adj.)* ጠንካራ *tenkaara*
**toughen** *(v.)* ኣበርቲዑ፣ኣጠንኪሩ *abertiau,atenkiru*
**toughness** *(n.)* ጥንካሬ *tenkara*
**tour** *(n.)* ጉዕዞ *guazo*
**tourism** *(n. )* ጎብነይቲ ምስትእንጋድ *gobneyti mstengad*
**tourist** *(n. )* ጎብናዪ *gobnayi*
**tournament** *(n.)* ዉድድር *wuddr*
**tousle** *(v.)* ዝረስሐ ፀጉሪ *zreshe seguri*
**tout** *(v.)* ኣሻይጡ *ashaytu*
**tow** *(v.)* ስሒቡ፣ጎቲቱ *sihibu gotitu*
**towards** *(prep.)* ናብ፣ብዝምልከት *nab bzmlket*
**towel** *(n.)* ፎጣ *fota*
**towelling** *(n.)* ፎጣ መስርሒ ጨርቂ *fota mesrhi cherki*
**tower** *(n.)* ፎቅ *foq*
**town** *(n.)* ከተማ *ketema*
**toxic** *(adj.)* መርዛማ *merzama*
**toxicology** *(n.)* ናይ መርዚ ፅንዓት *nay merzi snat*
**toxin** *(n.)* መርዛማ *merzama*
**toy** *(n.)* ቧምብላ *bwambula*
**trace** *(v.t. )* ለጢፉ ኮሪጁ፣ተከታቲልካ ምብፃሕ *letifu koriju,teketatilka mhaz*
**traceable** *(adj.)* ምስ ዝተተሓሓዘ ዝመፀ *ms ztetehahaze zmese*
**tracing** *(n.)* ዝተገልበጠ ካርታ *ztegelbete karta*
**track** *(n.)* ዝበፅሕዎ፣ናይ እግሪ መንገዲ *zbeshwo,nay egrimengedi*

**tract** *(n.)* በራሪ ወረቀት *berari wereket*
**tractable** *(adj.)* ብቀሊሉ ክቆፃፀርዎ ዝክእሉ *bqelilu kqosaserwa zk'al*
**traction** *(n. )* ዝንቀሳቀስ ሕይሊ *znqesaqes hyli*
**tractor** *(n. )* ናይ ሕርሻ መኪና *nay hrsha mekina*
**trade** *(n.)* ንግዲ *ngdi*
**trademark** *(n. )* ናይ ንግረ ምልክት *nay ngdimlkt*
**trader** *(n. )* ነጋዴ *negade*
**tradesman** *(n. )* ነጋዴ *negade*
**tradition** *(n.)* ባህሊ፣ልምዲ *bahli,lmdi*
**traditional** *(adj.)* ብህላዊ *bahlawi*
**traditionalist** *(n.)* በዚ ምኽንያት'ዚ *bezimknyat ezi*
**traduce** *(v.)* ኣብሺቁ *abshiqu*
**traffic** *(n.)* ኣብ ሓደ ቦታ ብምንቅስቃስ ዘሎ መኪና *ab hade bota ab mnkskas zelo mekina*
**tragedian** *(n. )* መሕዘኒት ተዋናዪት፣መሕዘኒ ተውኒት *mehzednit tewanayit,mehzeni tewnit*
**tragedy** *(n.)* መሕዘኒ ኩነታት/ድርጊት *mehzeni kunetat/drgit*
**tragic** *(adj.)* መሕዘኒ *mehzeni*
**trail** *(n.)* ተከታቲሉ *teketatilu*
**trailer** *(n.)* ትእስሓቢ መኪና *teshabi mekina*
**train** *(v.)* ኣለማሚዱ፣ምልምማድ *alemamidu,mlmmad*
**train** *(n.)* ደቂኑ *deqinu*
**trainee** *(n.)* ሰልጣኒ *seltani*
**trainer** *(n.)* ኣሰልጣኒ *aseltani*
**training** *(n. )* ስልጠና *sltena*
**traipse** *(v.)* ምንቅርፋፍ *mnkrfaf*
**trait** *(n. )* ባህሪ *bhri*
**traitor** *(n. )* ካሕዳም *kahdam*
**trajectory** *(n.)* ዝንቀሳቀስ ነገር ምልክት ዳሓደገ ዝከድ *znqesaqes neger mlkt na hadege zked*
**tram** *(n.)* ና ከተማ ኤለትሪክ ባቡር *na ketema electric babur*
**trammel** *(v.)* ስራሕ ዝክልክል ነገር *srah zklkl neger*
**tramp** *(v.)* ደፍጢጡ፣ገሊፁ *deftitu,gelisu*
**trample** *(v.)* ተርጋጊፁ *teregagisu*
**trampoline** *(n.)* ጅምናስቲክ መስርሒ ዕራት *jmnastic mesrhi arat*
**trance** *(n.)* ብዕልካ ለይምፍላጥ *baalka zeymflat*
**tranquil** *(adj.)* ፀጥ ዝበለ ነገር *set zbele neger*
**tranquillity** *(n.)* ፀጥታ *settaa*
**tranquillize** *(v.)* ኣረጋጊያም፣ፀጥ ኣቢልዎም *aregagiaom,set abilowom*
**transact** *(v.)* ዕዳጋ ገይሮም፣ትሸዋዊጦም *adaga girom teshewawitom*
**transaction** *(n.)* ናይ ንግዲ ዉዕሊ *nay ngdi wualo*
**transatlantic** *(adj.)* ዉቅያኖስ ዘቋርፅ *wuqyanos zeqars*
**transcend** *(v.)* ሒሹ *hishu*
**transcendent** *(adj.)* ሕሽ ዝበለ ኣተሓሳስባ ዘለዎ *hish zbele atehasasba zelwo*
**transcendental** *(adj.)* ዝሓሸ ኣተሓሰስባ *zhashe atehasasba*

**transcontinental** *(adj.)* ኣህጉር መቋረሲ *ahugur meqaresi*
**transcribe** *(v.)* ብካሊእ ቋንቋ ፂሒፉ *bkakie qanqa sihifu*
**transcript** *(n.)* ፅሑፍ ንንግግር ን ቃለ መጠይቅ *shuf ngger nkale meteyik*
**transcription** *(n.)* ምስምማዕ *msm'emae*
**transfer** *(v.)* ምልኣክ፣ምምሕልላፍ *mleake mmhllaf*
**transferable** *(adj.)* ተመሓላለፊ *temehalalafi*
**transfiguration** *(n.)* ምልክዕ ምቅያር/ምቁንጃይ *melka mkyar mkunjay*
**transfigure** *(v. )* ምልክዑ ቀይሩ/ትቋናጅዩ *melk'u keyru tekoonajyu*
**transform** *(v.)* ልዉጢ፣ናብ ካሊእ ነገር ምቅያር *lewtinab kalia neger mkyar*
**transformation** *(n.)* ምልዋጥ *mlwat*
**transformer** *(n.)* ናይ ኢሌለትሪክ ሓይሊ ዝቅይር መሳርሒ *na eletric hayli zqyir mesarhi*
**transfuse** *(v.)* ደም ምሃብ *dem mhab*
**transfusion** *(n.)* ደም ና ምሃብ ተግባር፣ልኮነ ፈሳሲ ናብ ካሊእ ምግልባጥ *dem na mhab tegbar*
**transgress** *(v.)* ደንቢሩ ጢሒሱ *denbiru thisu*
**transgression** *(n. )* ድንበር ምጥሓስ *dnber mthas*
**transient** *(adj.)* ግዜያዊ/ሓላፊ *gziywi halafi*
**transistor** *(n.)* ንእሽተይ ናይ ኤሊትሪክ ፍሰት መቆፃፀሪ መሳርሒ *nAshtey nay eletric hayli mokosaseri*
**transit** *(n. )* መሸጋገሪ ቦታ *meshegageri bota*
**transition** *(n. )* መሸጋገሪ ፣ናይ ሽግግር ወቅቲ/ግዜ *meshegageri,na mshiggar gze*
**transitive** *(adj.)* ተሻጋሪ ግስ *teshagari gs*
**transitory** *(adj.)* ግዜያዊ *gziyawi*
**translate** *(v.)* ተርጊሙ *tergimu*
**translation** *(n. )* ትርጉም *trgum*
**transliterate** *(v.)* ሓድ ቋንቋ ብካሊእ ቋንቋ ክፀሓፍ ከሎ *hade qnaqa bkalie qanqa ksehaf kelo*
**translucent** *(adj.)* ብርሃን ዘሕልፍ *brhan zehlf*
**transmigration** *(n. )* ናይ ሂወት ካብ ሞት ናብ ህያው ምዝዉዋር *nay hiwet hab mot nab hyab mshiggar*
**transmission** *(n.)* ዝመሓላለፍ ነገር፣ምምሕልላፍ *zmehalalef neger mmhllaf*
**transmit** *(v.)* ኣመሓላሊፉ *amehalalifu*
**transmitter** *(n.)* መመሓላለፊ መሳርሒ *memahalalefi mesarhi*
**transmute** *(v.)* ለዉጢ ቅርፂ ተፈጥሮ *lewuti qrsi tefetro*
**transparency** *(n.)* ብዉሽጢ ኣመሓላሊፍካ ምርኣይ *bwushty amehalalifka mray*
**transparent** *(adj.)* ብዉሽጡ ዘርኢ *bwushti zer,i*

**transpire** *(v.)* ብቆርብት ቀዳድ ርስሓት ምዉጋድ *bkorbet kedda dshat mray*

**transplant** *(v.)* ኣብ ሓደ ቦታ ዝተተከለ ናብ ካሊእ ቦታ ነቂልካ ምትካል *ab hade bota ztetekele nab kalie bota neklka mtkal*

**transport** *(v.)* መጉዑዓዝ *megueaz*

**transportation** *(n. )* መጓዓዝያ *megaazya*

**transporter** *(n.)* መጓዓዝያ *megaazya*

**transpose** *(v.)* ኣለዋዊጡ ፂሒፉ *alewawitu sihifu*

**transsexual** *(n.)* ፆታ ምቅያር *sota mkyar*

**transverse** *(adj.)* ኣግድም ዝተቀመጠ ኣግድማ *agdm ztekemete agdami*

**transvestite** *(n.)* ና ተቅራኒ ክዳን ክክደን ዝፎቲ *na teqarani sota kdan kkden zufoti*

**trap** *(n.)* ምፅመድ *mdmas*

**trapeze** *(n.)* ሸለውሊዋ መጫወቲ ኮፍ መበሊኡ *shelewliwa mechaeti kef mebeliu*

**trash** *(n.)* ጓሓፍ *gahaf*

**trauma** *(n.)* መደንገፂ ተሞክሮ *medengesi temokkuro*

**travel** *(v.)* ጉዕዞ *guazo*

**traveller** *(n. )* ተጉዕዚ *tegaizu*

**travelogue** *(n.)* ስለ ጉዕዞ ዘርኢ ፊልሚ *sleguazo zerai filmi*

**traverse** *(v.)* ተሻጊሩ/ኣቋሪፁ *teshagiru /aqarisu*

**travesty** *(n.)* ብዘስሕቅ መልክዑ ምምሳል *bzeshq melkau mmsal*

**trawler** *(n.)* ጃልባ መትሓዚ ዓሳ *jalba methazi asa*

**tray** *(n.)* ብያቲ፣ሸሓነ *bati,shehanee*

**treacherous** *(adj.)* ብምክሓድ/ብምሽዋድ *bmkhad bmshwad*

**treachery** *(n.)* ክሕደት *khdet*

**treacle** *(n.)* ሓፊስ ፈሳሲ ሹኮር *hafis fesasi sukor*

**tread** *(v.)* ኣካይዳ *akayda*

**treadle** *(n.)* ና ስፈት መኪና ፒዳል *nasfyet mekina pedal*

**treadmill** *(n. )* ኣሰልቻዩ በዓልታዊ ተግባር *aselchyi mealtawi tegbr*

**treason** *(n. )* ሃገር ክሒድካ ምስ ፀላኢ ምሕባር *hager kihidka ms selai mhbar*

**treasure** *(n.)* ሃፍቲ *hafti*

**treasurer** *(n. )* ምቕምማዕ *msmame*

**treasury** *(n.)* ና ንብርት ሓላፊ *nanbret halefi*

**treat** *(v.)* ጋቢዙ *gabigu*

**treatise** *(n. )* ብሓደ ነገር ዘተኮረ ነዊሕ ፁሑፍ *bhade neger zetekore newih suhuf*

**treatment** *(n. )* ሕክምና *hkmna*

**treaty** *(n. )* ናይ ፁሑፍ ስምምዕነት *nay suhuf smm'a*

**treble** *(adj.)* ብሓደ መዓልቲ ሰለስተ ዉድድር ምሽናፍ *bhade mealti seleste gze mshnaf*

**tree** *(n.)* በህርዛፍ፣ጫዓ *baharzaf,chaa*

**trek** *(n. )* ነዊሕ ጉዕዞ ብእግሪ *newih guazo b'ageri*

**trellis** *(n.)* ናሓረግ መደገፊ ዕንጨይቲ *nahareg medegefi anseyti*
**tremble** *(v.)* ተንቀጥቂጡ፣ተዋዛዊዙ *tenqetkitu*
**tremendous** *(adj.)* ብጣዕሚ ቡዙሕ *btaami bzuh*
**tremor** *(n. )* ንእሽተይ መሬት ምንቅጥቃጥ *n'ashtey merit mnqtqat*
**tremulous** *(adj.)* ዘይተርጋገዐ *zeyteregageae*
**trench** *(n.)* ቦይ *boy*
**trenchant** *(adj.)* ግልጺ ዝኮነ ተግሳፅ *glsi zkone tegsas*
**trend** *(n.)* ዝንባለ *znbale*
**trendy** *(adj.)* ብወቅታዊ ፋሽን ዝክተል *bwuqtawi fashn zktel*
**trepidation** *(n.)* ዝሰርሕዎ ስራሕ ምፍራሕ *zserhwo srah mfrah*
**trespass** *(v.)* ሕጊ ጢሒሱ *higi tihisu*
**tress** *(n.)* ንቆርቆሮ ዝኮን ዕንጨይቲ *nqorqoro zkon anseyti*
**trestle** *(n.)* ተነቃሊ ና ጠረቢዛ እግሪ *teneqali naterebiza egri*
**trial** *(n. )* ሙኮራ *mukora*
**triangle** *(n.)* ሰለስተ መኣዝን *seleste meazen*
**triangular** *(adj.)* በዓል ሰለስተ መኣዝን *beal seleste meazn*
**tribal** *(adj.)* ና ጎሳ *nagosa*
**tribe** *(n. )* ጋሳ *gasa*
**tribulation** *(n. )* ላዕሊ ታሕቲይ ቺገር መከራ *laaliy tahty mekera chigr*
**tribunal** *(n. )* ፍሉይ ቤት ፍርዲ *fluy bet frdi*
**tributary** *(n.)* ዝተገደበ ዉሒጅ *ztegedebe wuhj*
**tribute** *(n.)* ናምስጋና ንግግር *namsgana nggr*
**trice** *(n.)* ብፍጥነት *bftnet*
**triceps** *(n.)* ና ማእገር ጨዋዳ *na maager chwada*
**trick** *(n.)* ምሽዋድ፣ምትላል *mshwad mtlal*
**trickery** *(n.)* ተንኮል *tenkol*
**trickle** *(v.)* ጥብ ጥብ ተንጠብጢቡ *tentebtibu*
**trickster** *(n.)* ተንኮለግኛ *tenkolegna*
**tricky** *(adj.)* መሰሓሓቲ *mesahahati*
**tricolour** *(n.)* በዓል ሰለስተ ሕብሪ ባንደራ *beal seleste hbri bandera*
**tricycle** *(n. )* በዓል ሰለስተ ጎማ ሳይክል *beal seleste goma sycle*
**trident** *(n.)* በዓል ሰለስተ እግሪ መሳርሒ *beal seleste agri mesarhi*
**Trier** *(n.)* ፋሕጠርጠር ዝብለ ጎበዝ ሰራሕተኛ *fahterter zble tenkara serahtegna*
**trifle** *(n.)* ኣመል ኮይንዎ *amel koynuwo*
**trigger** *(n.)* መልሓስ ሽጉጥ *melhas shugut*
**trigonometry** *(n.)* ኩርናዓት ዝፅንዐሉ ናይ ሒሳብ ዘርፍ *kurnaat zesnalu na hisab zerfi*
**trill** *(n.)* ናይ ሙዚቃ ድምፂ *namuziqa*
**trillion** *(adj & n.)* ዓሰርተ ክልተ ዜሮ ዘለዋ ቁፅሪ/1,000,000,000,000 *dmsi*
**trilogy** *(n.)* ሰለስተ ተመሳሳሊ ሓሳብ ዘለዎ ነገር ተከታቲሉ

ክመፅእ ከሎ *seleste temesasali hasab zelewom*
**trim** *(v.)* ቆሪፁ *qorisu*
**trimmer** *(n.)* ሸንቃጣ *shenkata*
**trimming** *(n.)* ጌይሲ *geysi*
**trinity** *(n. )* ስላሴ *slasi*
**trinket** *(n.)* ርካሽ ግን ደስ በሃሊ *rkash gn des behali*
**trio** *(n.)* ሰለስቲኦም ሰለስተ ሙዚቃ *selestiaom seleste muziqa*
**trip** *(v.)* ጉዕዞ *guazo*
**tripartite** *(adj.)* ደጋፊ *degafi*
**triple** *(n.)* ሰለስተ ዕፅፊ፣ሰለስተ ጊዘ *seleste asfi,seleste gze*
**triplet** *(n.)* ብሓደ ግዘ ሰለስተ ቆልዑ ምዉላድ *bhade gze seleste kol'u mwulad*
**triplicate** *(adj.)* ሰለስተ ቅድሕታት *seleste kdhtat*
**tripod** *(n.)* ብዓል ሰለስተ እግሪ ጠጠው መበሊ *beal seleste egri tetew mebeli*
**triptych** *(n.)* ብሰለስተ ዕንጨይቲ ዝተስኣለ ስእሊ *bseleste ansyti ztesale seli*
**trite** *(adj.)* ዘይረብሕ *zeyrebh*
**triumph** *(n.)* ናዓወት ደስታ ኩነታት *nawet dsta knetat*
**triumphal** *(adj.)* ናዓወት መዓልቲ *naawet mealti*
**triumphant** *(adj.)* ናዓወት ስሚዒት *naawet smait*
**trivet** *(n.)* ጉልቻ *gulch*
**trivia** *(n.)* ዘየድሊ ትንተና *zeyedli tntena*
**trivial** *(adj.)* ዋጋ ቢስ የማይረባ *waga bis yemayreba*
**trolley** *(n.)* ጋሪ ጠረጴዛ *gari terebiza*
**troop** *(n.)* ብጉሩፕ ዝጓዓዙ ሰባት *bgurup zgaazu sebat*
**trooper** *(n. )* ና ክልል ፖሊስ *nay kll plis*
**trophy** *(n. )* ዋንጫ ሽልማት *wanch shlmat*
**tropic** *(n.)* ሙቀት እና ደርቅ ኣየር *muket ena derq ayer*
**tropical** *(adj.)* ሙቀት እና ደርቅ ኣየር *muket ena derq ayer*
**trot** *(v.)* ጋሊቡ *ebashi/zesqi seb*
**trotter** *(n.)* ግልባ ዝሰልጠነ *glba zseltene*
**trouble** *(n.)* እስቸጋሪ *aschegari*
**trouble-shooter** *(n.)* ሜላ ደላዪ ሰብ *mela delayi seb*
**troublesome** *(adj.)* ረባሺ/ዘሳቂ ሰብ *rebashi/seb zesaki seb*
**trough** *(n.)* ገንዳ/መሕመሲ *genda mehwesi*
**trounce** *(v.)* ኣጉል ቅጸዓት *agul qsat*
**troupe** *(n.)* ትተኣማመነሉ ሰብ *tteamamenelu seb*
**trousers** *(n. )* ስረ *sre*
**trousseau** *(n.)* ሓዳሽ መርዓት ናብ ስብኣያ ትወስዶ ኣቁሑ *hadash merat nab sbaya etwosddo aquhu*
**trout** *(n.)* ልብላዕ ዓሳ *lblaa asa*
**trowel** *(n. )* ና ነዳቂ ማንካ *na nedaqi manka*
**truant** *(n.)* ስርሑ ዘይሰርሕ ሰብ *srhu zeyserh seb*
**truck** *(n.)* ናፅዕነት መኪና *nas'anet mekina*
**trucker** *(n.)* ናፅዕነት መኪና ሹፌር *nas'anet mekina shuifer*
**truculent** *(adj.)* ተብኣሲ ለከፍ *tebaeisu lekef*

**trudge** *(v.)* ሙጉታት ምርማድ *mugutat*
**true** *(adj.)* ትኽክል /ሓቂ *tkkl/haqi*
**truffle** *(n.)* እንጉዳይ *anguday*
**trug** *(n.)* ናኣትክልተኛ ዘምቢል *naatkeltegna zenbil*
**truism** *(n.)* ፍሉጥ ሓቂ ምንጋር ዘየድልዮ *flut haki mngar zeyedlyo*
**trump** *(n. )* ፈጠራ *fetera*
**trumpet** *(n.)* ዓው ኢሉ ተናጊሩ *awu elu tenagiru*
**truncate** *(v.)* ቀንጢቡ *kentibu*
**truncheon** *(n.)* ና ፖሊስ ዱላ *na polis dula*
**trundle** *(v.)* ደፊኡ /ጎቲቱ *defiau/gotitu*
**trunk** *(n. )* ጉንዲ፣ና ሰዉነት ኣካል *gundi,nasewunet akal*
**truss** *(n.)* ድጋፍ *degafi*
**trust** *(n.)* እምነት ምግባር *amnet mgbar*
**trustee** *(n.)* ብዓል ሓደራ *beal hadera*
**trustful** *(adj.)* ኩሉ ዝኣምን *kulu zamn*
**trustworthy** *(adj.)* እምነት ዝግበረሉ *amnet zgberelu*
**trusty** *(adj.)* እሙን እስረኛ *amun esregna*
**truth** *(n.)* ሓቂ *haki*
**truthful** *(adj.)* ሓቀኛ *hakegna*
**try** *(v.)* ሞክር *mokr*
**trying** *(adj.)* ሙኮራ *mukera*
**tryst** *(n. )* ሞካሪ *mokari*
**tub** *(n. )* ጎድጋድ ሽሓነ *godgad shehane*
**tube** *(n. )* ቱቦ *tubo*
**tubercle** *(n.)* ና ሳንባ መንቀርሳ ምልክት *nasanba menkersa mlkt*
**tuberculosis** *(n.)* ና ሳንባ መንቀርሳ *nasanba menkersa*
**tubular** *(adj.)* ብሳንባ መንቀርሳ ዝሳቀ *basanba menkersa zsaqe*
**tuck** *(v.)* ኣእትዩ *aatyu*
**Tuesday** *(n.)* ሰሉስ *selus*
**tug** *(v.)* መንጪቁ/ጎቲቱ *menchiqu/gotitu*
**tuition** *(n.)* ናመምሃሪ ክፍሊት *namemhari kflit*
**tulip** *(n.)* ና ዕንበባ ዓይነት *na anbeba aynet*
**tumble** *(v.)* ሱቅ ኢሉ ወዲቁ *suq ilu wediqu*
**tumbler** *(n. )* ብርጭቆ *brchiqo*
**tumescent** *(adj.)* ኣብ ግብረ ስጋዊ ግኑኙነት ምሕባጥ *ab gbre sgawi gnugnnet mhbat*
**tumour** *(n.)* እጢ *ati*
**tumult** *(n.)* ረበሻ ጫውጫው ዝበለ ቦታ *rebesha chawchaw zbele bota*
**tumultuous** *(adj.)* ዝተረጋግዕ ረበሻ *zteregagea rebesha*
**tun** *(n.)* ና ወይኒ በርሚን *na weyni brmin*
**tune** *(n.)* ዜማ ቅኝት *zema qgnt*
**tuner** *(n. )* መመሓላለፊ ጣብያ *memehalalefe tabya*
**tunic** *(n.)* ና ወታደር ጃኬት *nawetader jaket*
**tunnel** *(n.)* በዓቲ *beati*
**turban** *(n. )* ና ሙስሊም ጥምጥም *na muslim tmtam*
**turbid** *(adj.)* ዘይተዘረገ *zeytzerege*
**turbine** *(n. )* ብኣየር ብማይ ብጋዝ ዝሽክርከር ሞተር *bmay bayer ngaz zshkrker moter*

**turbulence** *(n.)* **ረበሻ ብጥብጥ ብዓና ፖለቲካ** *rebesh btbt bna poletica*
**turbulent** *(adj.)* **ሓድደገግና ነዉፅ ኣየር ባሕሪ** *hdhdna newase ayer bahri*
**turf** *(n. )* **ሳዕሪ ምግባር ምትካል** *saeri mgbar*
**turgid** *(adj.)* **ምንም ዘይርደአካ ቋንቋ** *mnm zeyrdeeka qanqa*
**turkey** *(n.)* **ና ኤሜሪካ ደርሆ** *na america derho*
**turmeric** *(n. )* **ዕርዲ** *ardi*
**turmoil** *(n.)* **ብፅብፅ ዓመፅ** *bsbs ames*
**turn** *(v.)* **ተዓፅፉ** *teasifu*
**turner** *(n. )* **ብ መሳርሒ ቅርፂ ዘዋፅእ** *bmesarhi qrsi zwese*
**turning** *(n.)* **መዕፀፊ ቦታ** *measefi bota*
**turnip** *(n. )* **ቀይ ስር** *key sr*
**turnout** *(n.)* **ብሓደ ኩነታት ዝተራከቡ ሰባት** *bhade kunetat zterakebu sebat*
**turnover** *(n.)* **ብዝተወሰነ ግዘ ዝተሰርሐ ንግዲ** *bztewesene gze zteserhe ngdi*
**turpentine** *(n. )* **ና ቀለም መቅጠኒ ኬሚካል** *qelem meqteni kemikal*
**turquoise** *(n.)* **ቆፃል ድይመንድ** *qosal dymend*
**turtle** *(n. )* **ና ባሕሪ ኣባ ጋዉየ** *nabahri aba gabuye*
**tusk** *(n. )* **ና ሓርማዝ ስኒ** *naharmaz sni*
**tussle** *(n.)* **ንምዉሳድ ምልፋዕ** *nmwusad mlfae*
**tutelage** *(n. )* **ካብ ጎበዝ ተፅጊዕካ ምምሃር** *kab gobez tesegiaka mmhar*
**tutor** *(n.)* **ና ግሊ መምህር** *nagli memhr*
**tutorial** *(n. )* **ና መምህር ኣና ተምሃሪ ና ዉይዪት መፅሓፍ** *na memher ena temhari na wuyyt meshaf*
**tuxedo** *(n.)* **ናድራር ክዳን** *nadrar kdan*
**tweak** *(v.)* **ምምንጨቅ** *mmnchq*
**twee** *(adj.)* **ደካማ ስምዕታዊ ሰባት ዝፈትዉዎ** *dekama smiaitawi sebat zfetwuwo*
**tweed** *(n.)* **ረጊድ ዝንጉርጉር ክዳን** *regid zngurgur kdan*
**tweet** *(v.)* **ና ንእሽተይ ዒፍ ድምፂ** *naneshtey aif dmsi*
**tweeter** *(n.)* **ንእሽተይ ድምፂ መጋዉሒ** *neshtey dmsi megawuhi*
**tweezers** *(n.)* **ወረንጦ** *werento*
**twelfth** *(adj.&n.)* **ጥቅምቲ** *tkmti*
**twelfth** *(adj.&n.)* **ጥቅምቲ** *tkmti*
**twelve** *(adj.&n.)* **ዓሰርተ ክልተ** *aserte klte*
**twentieth** *(adj.&n.)* **መበል ዒስራ** *mebel aisra*
**twentieth** *(adj.&n.)* **መበል ዒስራ** *mebel aisra*
**twenty** *(adj.&n.)* **ዒስራ** *aisra*
**twice** *(adv. )* **ክልተ ግዘ** *glte gze*
**twiddle** *(v.)* **ብዘይ ጥቅሚ ዘዊሩ** *bzey tkmi zewiru*
**twig** *(n.)* **ቅርንጫፍ** *qrnchaf*
**twilight** *(n. )* **ናፀሓይ ምዕራብ** *nasahay marab*
**twin** *(n.)* **ማንታ** *manta*
**twine** *(n.)* **ገመድ** *gemed*

**twinge** *(n.)* ሕማቅ ስምዒት ንሓፅር ግዘ *hmaq smiet nhasir gze*
**twinkle** *(v.)* ኣብለጭሊጩ *ablechlichu*
**twirl** *(v.)* ተሽከርካሪ *teshkerkari*
**twist** *(v.)* ዝተጠምዘዘ *ztetemazeze*
**twitch** *(v.)* ምንቅጥቃጥ *mnktkat*
**twitter** *(v.)* ናይ ኣዕዋፍ ፍፆት *naeawaf fsot*
**two** *(adj.&n.)* ክልተ *klte*
**twofold** *(adj.)* ኣጥፊኡ *atfiu*
**tycoon** *(n.)* ሃፍታም ነጋዴ *haftam negadi*
**type** *(n.)* ዓይነት *aynet*
**typesetter** *(n.)* ኣፋኹሰ *afkisu*
**typhoid** *(n. )* ተሳሒቡ ካብ ምግቢ ዝወፅእ *teshibu kab mgbi zwese*
**typhoon** *(n. )* ኣውሎ ንፋስ *awulo nfas*
**typhus** *(n.)* ተስሓብቲ *tesehabti*
**typical** *(adj.)* ዝተለመደ *ztelemede*
**typify** *(v.)* ምሳሌ ዝኮነ *msale zkone*
**typist** *(n.)* ፀሓፊት *sehafit*
**tyrannize** *(v.)* ጨቂኑ ገዚኡ *chqinu geziau*
**tyranny** *(n. )* ኣምባገነንነት *ambagenennet*
**tyrant** *(n. )* ጨካን ኣምባ ገነን *chekan ambagenen*
**tyre** *(n.)* ናይ መኪና ጎማ *namekina goma*

# U

**ubiquitous** *(adj.)* ፍቖድኡ *fqodeu*
**udder** *(n.)* መውዕሎ *mew'ëlo*
**ugliness** *(n.)* ክፉእ *kfu'e*
**ugly** *(adj.)* ክፉእ *kfu'e*
**ulcer** *(n.)* ቁስሊ *qusli*
**ulterior** *(adj.)* ዝበለፀ *zbeletse*
**ultimate** *(adj.)* መወዳእታ *mewedaeta*
**ultimately** *(adv. )* ብመወዳእታ *b'mewedaeta*
**ultimatum** *(n. )* ናይ መወዳእታ መጠንቀቕታ *nay mewedaeta metenkekta*
**ultra** *(pref.)* ብጣዕሚ *betaemi*
**ultramarine** *(n.)* ማያዊ *mayawi*
**ultrasonic** *(adj.)* ናይ ደምፂ ማዕበል *nay demtsi maebel*
**ultrasound** *(n.)* ኣልትራሳውንድ *sltrasawnd*
**umber** *(n.)* ፀልም ዝበለ *tselm zebele*
**umbilical** *(adj.)* ዕትብቲ *Etbti*
**umbrella** *(n. )* ፅላል *tselal*
**umpire** *(n.)* ዳኛ *dagna*
**unable** *(adj.)* ኣይከኣለን *aykealen*
**unaccountable** *(adj.)* ኣረማዊ *aremawi*
**unadulterated** *(adj.)* ዘይተበረዘ *zetebereze*
**unalloyed** *(adj.)* ዘይተሓወሰ *zeyteHawese*
**unanimity** *(a. )* ዘይምእዛዝ *zeyme'ezaz*
**unanimous** *(adj.)* ሓደ ድምፂ *Hade demtsi*
**unarmed** *(adj.)* ብዘይ ናይ ውግእ መሳርሒ *bzey nay wege'e mesarhi*

**unassailable** *(adj.)* አይሰርሕን *ayserhen*
**unassuming** *(adj.)* ልዙብ *lzub*
**unattended** *(adj.)* ትጽቢት ዘይተገብረሉ *tetsbit zaytegeberelu*
**unavoidable** *(adj.)* ዘይተርፍ *zayteref*
**unaware** *(adj.)* ብሓፈሻ ፍሉጥ ዝኾነ *bhafesha emun zeykone*
**unbalanced** *(adj.)* ኢሚዛናዊ *i'mizanawi*
**unbelievable** *(adj.)* ዘይእመን *zey'emen*
**unbend** *(v.)* ምቅናዕ *mqna'e*
**unborn** *(adj.)* ዘይተወልደ *zeytewelde*
**unbridled** *(adj.)* ዘይተሓዋውሰ *zeyteHawese*
**unburden** *(v.)* ልግስነት *lgsnet*
**uncalled** *(adj.)* ዘይተፀወዐ *zeytetsewe'e*
**uncanny** *(adj.)* ዘይልሙድ *zeylmud*
**unceremonious** *(adj.)* ኩሉ ግዜ *kulu gzee*
**uncertain** *(adj.)* ዘይርግፀኛ *zeyregetsegna*
**uncharitable** *(adj.)* ጥሙይ *tmuy*
**uncle** *(n.)* ኣኮ *ako*
**unclean** *(adj.)* ዘይፅሩይ *zeytseruy*
**uncomfortable** *(adj.)* ዘይምቹ *zeymechu*
**uncommon** *(adj.)* ዘይልሙድ *zeylmud*
**uncompromising** *(adj.)* ደረቕ *derek*
**unconditional** *(adj.)* ብዘይኩነት *bzeykunet*
**unconscious** *(adj.)* ዘይንቑሕ *zeynkuh*
**uncouth** *(adj.)* ኣማዘን *amazen*
**uncover** *(v.)* ምግላፅ *mglats*
**unctuous** *(adj.)* ዕንዲዳ ጌጽ *'ëndida geex*
**undeceive** *(v.)* ሓቂ *Haki*
**undecided** *(adj.)* ዘይወሰን *zeywesun*
**undeniable** *(adj.)* ግልፂ *gltsi*
**under** *(prep. )* ትሕቲ *thti*
**underarm** *(adj.)* ትሕቲ ኢድ *thti id*
**undercover** *(adj.)* ምስጢራዊ *mistrawi*
**undercurrent** *(n.)* ተጻዒኑ *tetsainu*
**undercut** *(v.)* ምቑራፅ *mkurats*
**underdog** *(n.)* ምቁር *mqur*
**underestimate** *(v.)* ነዓቐ *neaqe*
**undergo** *(v.)* ምክዋን *mkwan*
**undergraduate** *(n.)* ተምሃሪ ዩኒቨርስቲ *temhari yuniversty*
**underground** *(adj.)* ትሕቲ መሬት *thti meriet*
**underhand** *(adj.)* ትሕቲ ኢድ *thti id*
**underlay** *(n.)* መኣረምታ *me'aremta*
**underline** *(v.t. )* ኣስመረ *asmere*
**underling** *(n.)* ዝተሰምረ *ztesemere*
**undermine** *(v.)* ነዓቐ *neaqe*
**underneath** *(prep. )* ብትሕቲ *bthti*
**underpants** *(n.)* ሙታንታ *mutanta*
**underpass** *(n.)* መሕለፊ በዓቲ *mehlegi beati*

**underprivileged** *(adj.)* ውፁዕ *wxeu'e*
**underrate** *(v.)* ነዓቐ *neaqe*
**underscore** *(v.)* ኣስመረ *asmere*
**undersigned** *(n.)* ፈረመ *fereme*
**understand** *(v.t. )* ተረድአ *terede'e*
**understanding** *(n.)* ምርደዳእ *mrdeda'e*
**understate** *(v.)* ኣትሓተ *athate*
**undertake** *(v.)* ግዴታ *gdieta*
**undertaker** *(n.)* ማካየዲ ስራሕ *mekayedi srah*
**underwear** *(n. )* ሙታንታ *mutanta*
**underworld** *(n.)* ናይ ለያቡ ዓለም *lay leyabu alem*
**underwrite** *(v.)* ብታሕቲ ፀሓፈ *btahti tsehafe*
**undesirable** *(adj.)* ንፁግ *ntsug*
**undo** *(v.)* ቀልብስ *kelbs*
**undoing** *(n.)* ምቅልባስ *mqlbas*
**undone** *(adj.)* ዝተቀልበሰ *ztekelbese*
**undress** *(v.)* ኣጉልሐ *agulĥe*
**undue** *(adj.)* ዘይርከብ *zeyrekeb*
**undulate** *(v.)* ዘይዕፀፍ *zey'etsef*
**undying** *(adj.)* ዘይመውት *zeymewut*
**unearth** *(v.)* ምኹዓት *mkuat*
**uneasy** *(adj.)* ከቢድ *kebid*
**unemployable** *(adj.)* ዘይቁፀር *zeykutser*
**unemployed** *(adj.)* ሰራሕ ዝፈትሐ *srah zfethe*
**unending** *(adj.)* ዘይወዳአ *zeywedae*
**unequalled** *(adj.)* ዝተፈላለየ *ztefelaleye*
**uneven** *(adj.)* ዘይመጣጠን *zeymetaten*
**unexceptionable** *(adj.)* ቅቡል *qbul*
**unexceptional** *(adj.)* ተመሳሳሊ *temesasali*
**unexpected** *(adj.)* ሃንደበት *handebet*
**unfailing** *(adj.)* ትኽክል *tkkl*
**unfair** *(adj.)* ዘይፍትሓዊ *zeyfethawi*
**unfaithful** *(adj.)* ቅኑዕ ዘይኮነ *qnue zeykone*
**unfit** *(adj.)* ብቑዕ ዘይኮነ *bku zeykone*
**unfold** *(v.)* ምቅልዕ *mqlae*
**unforeseen** *(adj.)* ዘተኣመተ *zeyteamete*
**unforgettable** *(adj.)* ዘይረሳዕ *zeyresae*
**unfortunate** *(adj.)* ዘሕዝን *zehzen*
**unfounded** *(adj.)* ዘይፈለጥ *zeyfelet*
**unfurl** *(v.)* ምግላሕ *mglah*
**ungainly** *(adj.)* ዘይጻወር *zeytsawer*
**ungovernable** *(adj.)* እምቢተኛ *embtegna*
**ungrateful** *(adj.)* ምስጋና ዘይብሉ *msgana zeybelu*
**unguarded** *(adj.)* ዘይሕሎ *zeyhlo*
**unhappy** *(adj.)* ዘይሕጉስ *zeyhgus*
**unhealthy** *(adj.)* ሕሙም *hmum*
**unheard** *(adj.)* ዘይሰማዕ *zeysemae*
**unholy** *(adj.)* ክፉእ *kfue*
**unification** *(n. )* ሓድነት *hadenet*
**uniform** *(adj.)* ተመሳሳሊ *temesasali*

**unify** ***(v.)*** **ሓደ ምግባር** *hade megbar*
**unilateral** ***(adj.)*** **ሓድነት** *hadenet*
**unimpeachable** ***(adj.)*** **ክበሃል ዘይክእል** *kbehal zeykel*
**uninhabited** ***(adj.)*** **ሰብ ዘይብሉ** *seb zeybelu*
**union** ***(n. )*** **ሕብረት** *hbret*
**unionist** ***(n.)*** **ማሕበራት** *mahberat*
**unique** ***(adj.)*** **ፍሉይ** *fluy*
**unisex** ***(adj.)*** **ፆታ ዘይበሉ** *tsota zeybelu*
**unison** ***(n. )*** **ሓድነት** *hadenet*
**unit** ***(n.)*** **ኣሃዱ** *'ahadu*
**unite** ***(v.)*** **ሓደ ምኳን** *hade mekuan*
**unity** ***(n.)*** **ሓድነት** *hadenet*
**universal** ***(adj.)*** **ናይ ዓለም ኣሕባሪ/ሓቛፊ** *nay alem ahbari/haquafi*
**universality** ***(adv. )*** **ዓለምለኻዊነት** *alemlekawinet*
**universe** ***(n.)*** **ኣጽናፈ ሰማይ** *atsenafe semay*
**university** ***(n.)*** **ዩኒቨርስቲ** *yuniversty*
**unjust** ***(adj.)*** **ዘይፍትሓዊ** *zeyfetHawi*
**unkempt** ***(adj.)*** **ጉበጣ** *gWabeẗa*
**unkind** ***(adj.)*** **ርጉም** *rgum*
**unknown** ***(adj.)*** **ዘይፍሉጥ** *zeyflut*
**unleash** ***(v.)*** **ምፍታሕ** *mftah*
**unless** ***(conj.)*** **ተዘይኮነ** *tezeykone*
**unlike** ***(prep. )*** **ዘይኮነ** *zeykone*
**unlikely** ***(adj.)*** **ዘይከውን** *zeykewun*
**unlimited** ***(adj.)*** **ዘይውሱን** *zeywusn*
**unload** ***(v.)*** **ኣራገፈ** *aragefe*
**unmanned** ***(adj.)*** **ሰብ ዘይብሉ** *seb zeybelu*
**unmask** ***(v.)*** **ምቕላዕ** *mqlae*
**unmentionable** ***(adj.)*** **ክበሃል ዘይክእል** *kbehal zeykel*
**unmistakable** ***(adj.)*** **ዘየጋጊ** *zeyegagi*
**unmitigated** ***(adj.)*** **ዘይጻወር** *zeytsawer*
**unmoved** ***(adj.)*** **ዘይፍቶ** *zeyfeto*
**unnatural** ***(adj.)*** **ዘይልሙድ** *zeylmud*
**unnecessary** ***(adj.)*** **ዘየድሊ** *zeyedeli*
**unnerve** ***(v.)*** **ፈርሐ** *ferhe*
**unorthodox** ***(adj.)*** **ዘይቅቡል** *zeyqbul*
**unpack** ***(v.)*** **ምርጋፍ** *mrgaf*
**unpleasant** ***(adj.)*** **ኣፀያፊ** *atseyafi*
**unpopular** ***(adj.)*** **ዘይቅቡል** *zeyqbul*
**unprecedented** ***(adj.)*** **ዘይፅቡይ** *zeytsebuy*
**unprepared** ***(adj.)*** **ዘይድልው** *zeydeluw*
**unprincipled** ***(adj.)*** **ባዕለገ** *baelege*
**unprofessional** ***(adj.)*** **ሞያዊ ዘይኮነ** *moyawi zeykone*
**unqualified** ***(adj.)*** **ብቑዕ ዘይኮነ** *bku zeykone*
**unreasonable** ***(adj.)*** **ደረቕ** *derek*
**unreliable** ***(n)*** **ዘየተኣማምን** *zeyeteamamn*
**unreserved** ***(adj.)*** **ዘይትሑዝ** *zeythuz*
**unrest** ***(n.)*** **ዘይምርግጋዕ** *zeymreggae*

**unrivalled** ***(adj.)*** **ዘይተማልአ** *zeytemale*
**unruly** ***(adj.)*** **ተለዋዋጥነት** *telewawatnet*
**unscathed** ***(adj.)*** **ዘየጎድአ** *zeyg'e*
**unscrupulous** ***(adj.)*** **ውሑድ** *wHud*
**unseat** ***(v.)*** **ወደቐ** *wedeqe*
**unselfish** ***(adj.)*** **ዘይርጉም** *zeyregum*
**unsettle** ***(v.)*** **ተረበሸ** *terebeshe*
**unshakeable** ***(adj.)*** **ዘይነቓነቕ** *zeyneqaneq*
**unskilled** ***(adj.)*** **ዘይክእል** *zeyk'el*
**unsocial** ***(adj.)*** **ምስ ሰብ ዘይቀርብ** *ms seb zeyqerb*
**unsolicited** ***(adj.)*** **ዘይቅቡል** *zeyqbul*
**unstable** ***(adj.)*** **ዘይድልዱል** *zeydeldul*
**unsung** ***(adj.)*** **ዘይተዘመረ** *zeytezemere*
**unthinkable** ***(adj.)*** **ዘይሕሰብ** *zeyhseb*
**untidy** ***(adj.)*** **ብትንትን ዝበለ** *btntn zbele*
**until** ***(prep. )*** **ክሳብ** *ksab*
**untimely** ***(adj.)*** **ዘይጊዝይዊ** *zeygziyawi*
**untold** ***(adj.)*** **ዘይተነግረ** *zeytegebre*
**untouchable** ***(adj.)*** **ዘይትንከፍ** *zeytnkef*
**untoward** ***(adj.)*** **ተለዋዋጥነት** *telewawatnet*
**unusual** ***(adj.)*** **ዘይልሙድ** *zeylmud*
**unutterable** ***(adj.)*** **ክበሃል ዘይክእል** *kbehal zeykel*
**unveil** ***(v.)*** **ምቕልዕ** *mqlae*
**unwarranted** ***(adj.)*** **ፍቓድ ዘይበሉ** *fqad zeyblu*
**unwell** ***(adj.)*** **ዘይፅቡቕ** *zeytsbuq*
**unwilling** ***(adj.)*** **ብዘይድልየት** *bzeydlyet*
**unwind** ***(v.)*** **ዘርገሐ** *zergeḧe*
**unwise** ***(adj.)*** **ጭንቀት** *chenqet*
**unwittingly** ***(adv. )*** **ሃረርተኛ** *harerteṅa*
**unworldly** ***(adj.)*** **ዘይልሙድ** *zeylmud*
**unworthy** ***(adj.)*** **ብቑዕ ዘይኮነ** *bku zeykone*
**up** ***(adv. )*** **ላዕሊ** *la'eli*
**upbeat** ***(adj.)*** **ሕጉስ** *Hgus*
**upbraid** ***(adj.)*** **ዝኾነ ቦታ** *zḱone bota*
**upcoming** ***(adj.)*** **መፃኢ** *metsai*
**update** ***(v.)*** **ግዝያዊ** *gziyawi*
**upgrade** ***(v.)*** **ምምሕያሽ** *mmhyash*
**upheaval** ***(n.)*** **ረብሻ** *rebsha*
**uphold** ***(v.)*** **ምልዓል** *mlal*
**upholster** ***(v.)*** **ኸደነ** *kedene*
**upholstery** ***(n.)*** **ምኽዳን** *mkdan*
**uplift** ***(v.)*** **ኣለዓዓለ** *ale'a'ale*
**upload** ***(v.)*** **ፀዓነ** *tse'anew*
**upper** ***(adj.)*** **ላዕለዋይ** *la'eleway*
**upright** ***(adj.)*** **ቅኑዕ** *qnu'e*
**uprising** ***(n.)*** **ዓመፅ** *amex*
**uproar** ***(n.)*** **ይቕሬታ ሓተተ** *ÿqreeta ḧatete*
**uproarious** ***(adj.)*** **ይቕሬታ** *yÿreeta*
**uproot** ***(v.)*** **ሱር ሰደድ** *surseded*
**upset** ***(v.)*** **ኣቐየመ** *aqyeme*
**upshot** ***(n.)*** **ሃዋርያ** *hawarya*
**upstart** ***(n.)*** **ጭረት** *čret*

**upsurge** *(n.)* ኣስካሕከሐ - *askaȟkeȟe*
**upturn** *(n.)* መሳርሒ *mesarȟi*
**upward** *(adv. )* ንላዕሊ *nlaeli*
**urban** *(adj.)* ከተማ *ketema*
**urbane** *(adj.)* ብሩህ *bruh*
**urbanity** *(n.)* ምኽታም *mKtam*
**urchin** *(n.)* ምቕልቃል *mq̈lqal*
**urge** *(v.)* ኣእመነ *aemene*
**urgent** *(adj.)* ኣግዳሲ *agedasi*
**urinal** *(n.)* መሸኒ *mesheni*
**urinary** *(adj.)* ቱቦ ሽንቲ *tubo shennti*
**urinate** *(v.)* ሸነ *shene*
**urine** *(n.)* ሽንቲ *shnti*
**urn** *(n.)* ሓሞኽሽቲ *hamokshti*
**usable** *(adj.)* ዝጠቅም *zTekem*
**usage** *(n.)* ኣጠቓቕማ *atekakma*
**use** *(v.t. )* ምጥቃም *mtqam'*
**useful** *(adj.)* ጠቓሚ *tekami*
**useless** *(adj.)* ዘይጠቅም *zaytekm*
**user** *(n.)* ተጠቃሚ *teteqami*
**usher** *(n.)* ዓጃቢ *ajai*
**usual** *(adj.)* ልሙድ *lmud*
**usually** *(adv. )* ከም ልሙድ *kem lmud*
**usurp** *(v.)* ቈጸራ *qWexera*
**usurpation** *(n.)* ጐዘየ *gWazeye*
**usury** *(n.)* ዚሰማማዕ *zisemama'ë*
**utensil** *(n.)* ኣቕሓ *aqha*
**uterus** *(n.)* ማህጸን *mahxen*
**utilitarian** *(adj.)* ተገንዘበ *tegenzebe*
**utility** *(n.)* ኣቕሓ *aqha*
**utilization** *(n.)* ኣጠቓቕማ *atekakma*
**utilize** *(v.)* ምጥቃም *mtqam'*
**utmost** *(adj.)* ዝበለፀ *zbeletse*
**utopia** *(n.)* ምቑው *mchuw*
**utopian** *(adj.)* ምቑው *mchuw*
**utter** *(adj.)* ዘረበ *zereba*
**utterance** *(n.)* ዘረበ *zereba*
**uttermost** *(adj. & n.)* ዝተዘርበሩ *ztezerelu*

# V

**vacancy** *(n.)* ሃህታ *hahta*
**vacant** *(adj.)* ጥርሑ *ṭrḥu*
**vacate** *(v.)* ወጸ *wexe*
**vacation** *(n.)* ዕርፍቲ *'ërfti*
**vaccinate** *(v.)* ከተበ *ketebe*
**vaccination** *(n.)* ክታበት *ktabet*
**vaccine** *(n.)* ክታበት *ktabet*
**vacillate** *(v.)* ተወላወለ *tewelawele*
**vacillation** *(n.)* ውልውል ነግ ፈረግ *wlwl neg fereg*
**vacuous** *(adj.)* ዛህላል *zahlal*
**vacuum** *(n. )* ባዶሽ *badosh*
**vagabond** *(n.)* በጋሚዶ *begamido*
**vagary** *(n.)* ፊንታ *finta*
**vagina** *(n.)* መሸኒት *meshenit*
**vagrant** *(n.)* ከርታት *kertat*
**vague** *(adj.)* ዘይንጹር *zeynxur*
**vagueness** *(n.)* ዘይንጹር *zeynxur*
**vain** *(adj.)* ብላሽ *blash*
**valance** *(n.)* መጋረጃ *megareğ*
**vale** *(n.)* ስንጭሮ *snçro*
**valediction** *(n.)* ስንብታ *snbta*
**valentine** *(n.)* ኣፍቃሪ *'afqari*
**valet** *(n.)* ኣላይ ክዳውንቲ *'alay kdawnti*
**valetudinarian** *(n.)* ስልኩይ *slkuy*

**valiant** *(adj.)* **ተባዕ** *teba'ë*
**valid** *(adj.)* **ብቑዕ** *bq̈u'ë*
**validate** *(v.)* **ብቕዓት** *bq̈'ät*
**validity** *(n. )* **ብቕዓት** *bq̈'ät*
**valise** *(n.)* **ባልጃ** *balğa*
**valley** *(n.)* **ስንጭሮ** *snçro*
**valour** *(n.)* **ጅግንነት** *ğgnnet*
**valuable** *(adj.)* **ክቡር** *kbur*
**valuation** *(n. )* **ኣሻንና** *'ashanna*
**value** *(n.)* **ዋጋ** *waga*
**valve** *(n. )* **መፈንቶ** *mefento*
**vamp** *(n.)* **ስውንዋኖ** *swnwano*
**vampire** *(n.)* **ምሎክ** *mlok*
**van** *(n.)* **መኪና** *mekina*
**vandal** *(n.)* **ኣዕናዊ** *'a'ënawi*
**vandalize** *(v.)* **ኣበላሸወ** *'abelashewe*
**vane** *(n.)* **ሓባር ንፋስ** *ḥabar nfas*
**vanguard** *(n.)* **መሪሕ** *meriḥ*
**vanish** *(v.)* **ተሸርበ** *tesherbe*
**vanity** *(n.)* **ትዕቢት** *t'ëbit*
**vanquish** *(v.)* **ሰዓረ** *se'äre*
**vantage** *(n.)* **ብልጫ** *blça*
**vapid** *(adj.)* **ላህዛዝ** *lahzaz*
**vaporize** *(v.)* **ሃፈፈ** *hafefe*
**vapour** *(n.)* **ሃተፍተፍ** *hateftef*
**variable** *(adj.)* **ተቐያያሪ** *teq̈eyayari*
**variance** *(n.)* **ፍልልይ** *flly*
**variant** *(n.)* **ልውጥ** *lwẗ*
**variation** *(n.)* **ፍልልይ** *flly*
**varicose** *(adj.)* **ሕቡጥ** *ḥbuṭ*
**varied** *(adj.)* **ዝተፈላለየ** *ztefelaleye*
**variegated** *(adj.)* **ጉራማይለ** *guramayle*
**variety** *(n.)* **ዓይነት ዓሌት** *'äynet 'äleet*
**various** *(adj.)* **ዝተፈላለየ** *ztefelaleye*
**varlet** *(n.)* **ተፈላለየ** *tefelaleye*
**varnish** *(n.)* **ቫርኒቸ** *varniche*
**vary** *(v.)* **ተፈላለየ** *tefelaleye*
**vascular** *(adj.)* **ናይ ሻምብቆ ኣካል** *nay shambqo 'akal*
**vase** *(n.)* **ባዞ** *bazo*
**vasectomy** *(n. )* **መጥባሕቲ መትረብ ዘርኢ** *meẗbaḧti metreb zer'i*
**vassal** *(n.)* **ጊላ** *gila*
**vast** *(adj.)* **ሰፊሕ** *sefiḥ*
**vaudeville** *(n.)* **ምርኢት** *mr'it*
**vault** *(n. )* **ቀስቲ** *qesti*
**vaunted** *(adj.)* **ቀስቲ** *qesti*
**veal** *(n.)* **ስጋ ምራኽ** *sga mraḱ*
**veer** *(n.)* **ኣንፈት ቀየረ** *'anfet qeyere*
**vegan** *(n.)* **ሓምሊ ዝቐለቡ** *ḧamli zq̈elebu*
**vegetable** *(n. )* **ናይ ኣትክልቲ** *nay 'atklti*
**vegetarian** *(n.)* **በላዕ ሓምሊ** *bela'ë ḥamli*
**vegetate** *(v.)* **ተረፈዐ** *terefe'ë*
**vegetation** *(n. )* **ቡቕሊ** *buq̈li*
**vehement** *(adj.)* **ብርቱዕ** *brtu'ë*
**vehicle** *(n.)* **መሰርያ ምጉዕዓዝ** *mesarya mgu'ë'äz*
**veil** *(n.)* **ጉልባብ** *gulbab*
**vein** *(n. )* **ቨይን** *veyn*
**velocity** *(n. )* **ፍጥነት** *fṭne*
**velour** *(n.)* **ቫሎር** *valor*
**velvet** *(n.)* **ዓለባ ሃሪ** *'äleba hari*
**venal** *(adj.)* **በላዒ** *bela'ï*
**vend** *(v.)* **ሸጠ** *sheṭe*
**vendetta** *(n.)* **ሕነ** *ḥne*
**vendor** *(n.)* **ሸያጢ** *sheyaṭi*

**veneer** *(n.)* **መሸፈን ሉሕ** *meshefen luḥ*
**venerable** *(adj.)* **ዓቢ** *'äbi*
**venerate** *(v.)* **ኣኽበረ** *'aḱbere*
**vengeance** *(n.)* **ፍዳ** *fda*
**vengeful** *(adj.)* **ቂመኛ** *qimeña*
**venial** *(adj.)* **ዕሽሽ ኪበሃል ዚከኣል** *'ëshsh kibehal zike'al*
**venom** *(n.)* **ሕንዚ** *ḥnz*
**venomous** *(adj.)* **ሕንዛም** *ḥnzam*
**venous** *(adj.)* **ናይ ቨይን** *nay veyn*
**vent** *(n.)* **መፈንቶ** *mefento*
**ventilate** *(v.)* **ኣርወሐ** *'arweḥe*
**ventilation** *(n. )* **ርውሓት** *rwḥat*
**ventilator** *(n. )* **መርውሓ** *merwḥa*
**venture** *(n.)* **ፈተነ** *fetene*
**venturesome** *(adj.)* **ዓንዳሪ** *'ändari*
**venue** *(n. )* **መራኸቢ ቦታ** *meraḱebi bota*
**veracious** *(adj.)* **ናይ ብሓቂ** *nay bḥaqi*
**veracity** *(n. )* **ሓቅነት** *ḥaqnet*
**veranda** *(n. )* **በረንዳ** *berenda*
**verb** *(n.)* **ግሲ** *gsi*
**verbal** *(adj.)* **ናይ ቃላት** *nay qalat*
**verbiage** *(n.)* **ቃለ-ድርዳረ** *qaledrdar*
**verbose** *(adj.)* **ቃለ-ድርዳረኣዊ** *qaledrdare'aw*
**verbosity** *(n.)* **ቃለ-ድርዳረነት** *qaledrdarene*
**verdant** *(adj.)* **ለምለም** *lemlem*
**verdict** *(n.)* **ፍርዲ** *frdi*
**verge** *(n. )* **ጥርዚ** *ṭrzi*
**verification** *(n.)* **ኣመሳኸረ** *'amesaḱere*
**verify** *(v.)* **ኣመሳኸረ** *'amesaḱere*
**verily** *(adv. )* **ብሓቂ** *bḥaqi*
**verisimilitude** *(n.)* **ሓቂ መሰልነት** *ḥaqi meselne*
**veritable** *(adj.)* **ሓቀኛ** *ḥaqeña*
**verity** *(n.)* **ሓቅነት** *ḥaqnet*
**vermin** *(n.)* **ኣራዊት** *'arawit*
**vernacular** *(n.)* **ናይታ ሃገር** *nayta hager*
**vernal** *(adj.)* **ጽድያዊ** *xdyawi*
**versatile** *(adj.)* **ዋሓለ** *waḥale*
**verse** *(n.)* **ቤት** *beet*
**versed** *(adj.)* **ክኢላ** *k'ila*
**versify** *(v.)* **ገጠመ** *geṭeme*
**version** *(n.)* **ትርጓም** *trgWam*
**verso** *(n.)* **ጸጋማይ ገጽ** *xegamay gex*
**versus** *(prep. )* **ኣንጻር** *'anxar*
**vertebra** *(n.)* **ገረንገራት** *gerengerat*
**vertebrate** *(n.)* **ገረንገራዊ** *gerengerawi*
**vertex** *(n.)* **ጫፍ** *čaf*
**vertical** *(adj.)* **ዓንዳዊ** *'ändawi*
**vertigo** *(n.)* **መንጸሮር** *menxeror*
**verve** *(n.)* **ውዕውዕ ስምዒት** *w'ëw'ë sm'ït*
**very** *(adv. )* **ኣዝዩ** *'azyu*
**vessel** *(n.)* **መዕቆሪ** *me'ëqori*
**vest** *(n.)* **ጅለ** *ğle*
**vestibule** *(n.)* **ወገፈ** *wegefe*
**vestige** *(n. )* **ኣሰር** *'aser*
**vestment** *(n.)* **ልብሲ** *lbsi*
**vestry** *(n.)* **ቤተ-ልብሲ** *beetelbsi*
**veteran** *(n.)* **ወተሃደር ነበር** *wetehader neber*
**veterinary** *(adj.)* **ንሕማም እንስሳ ዚምልከት** *nḥmam 'ènssa zimlket*
**veto** *(n.)* **ቀውፊ** *qewfi*
**vex** *(v.)* **ኣሕረቐ** *'aḥreq̈e*
**via** *(prep. )* **ብመንገዲ** *bmengedi*

**viable** *(adj.)* **ኪቕጽል ዚኽእል** *kiq̈xl zik'èl*
**viaduct** *(n.)* **ድንድል** *dndl*
**vial** *(n.)* **ብልቃጥ** *blqaṭ*
**viands** *(n.)* **መግቢ** *megbi*
**vibrant** *(adj.)* **ተንዝናዚ** *teneznazi*
**vibrate** *(v.)* **ተንዝነዘ** *tenezneze*
**vibration** *(n. )* **ንዝናዘ** *nznaze*
**vicar** *(n.)* **ቆሞስ** *qomos*
**vicarious** *(adj.)* **በጃ** *beǧa*
**vice** *(n. )* **ሕማቕ ኣመል** *ḥmaq̈ 'ame*
**viceroy** *(n.)* **ምስሌነ** *msleene*
**vice-versa** *(adv. )* **ተቓወመ** *teq̈aweme*
**vicinity** *(n.)* **ቅርበት** *qrbet*
**vicious** *(adj.)* **እከይ** *'èkey*
**vicissitude** *(n.)* **ምቅይያራት** *mqyyarat*
**victim** *(n.)* **ስዋእቲ** *meswa'èti*
**victimize** *(n. )* **ኣደደ** *'adede*
**victor** *(n.)* **መዋኢ** *mewa'i*
**victorious** *(adj.)* **ዕዉት** *ëwut*
**victory** *(n.)* **ዓወት** *'äwet*
**victualler** *(n.)* **ስንቂ** *snqi*
**victuals** *(n.)* **ኣስነቐ** *'asneq̈e*
**video** *(n.)* **ቪድዮ** *vidyo*
**vie** *(v.)* **ተወዳደረ** *tewedadere*
**view** *(n.)* **ምርኣይ** *mr'ay*
**vigil** *(n. )* **ሓለዋ** *ḥalewa*
**vigilance** *(n.)* **ትኩርና** *tkurna*
**vigilant** *(adj.)* **ጥንቁቕ** *ṭnquq̈*
**vignette** *(n.)* **ስልማት ናይ መጽሓፍ** *slmat nay mexḥaf*
**vigorous** *(adj.)* **ዝተማልአ** *ztemal'e*
**vigour** *(n.)* **ብርታዐ** *brta'ë*
**vile** *(adj.)* **ነውራም** *newram*
**vilify** *(v.)* **ኣዋረደ** *'awarede*
**villa** *(n. )* **ቪላ** *vila*
**village** *(n. )* **ቁሸት** *qushet*
**villain** *(n.)* **ገበነኛ** *gebeneña*
**vindicate** *(v.)* **ሓቅነት ኣረጋገጸ** *ḥaqnet 'aregagexe*
**vine** *(n. )* **ተኽሊ ወይኒ** *tekli weyni*
**vinegar** *(n. )* **ኣቸቶ** *'acheto*
**vintage** *(n.)* **ቀውዒ ናይ ወይኒ** *qew'ï nay weyni*
**vintner** *(n.)* **ሸቃጥ ነቢት** *sheqaṭ nebit*
**violate** *(v.)* **ገሃሰ** *gehase*
**violation** *(n. )* **ገበን** *geben*
**violence** *(n.)* **ዓመጽ** *'ämex*
**violent** *(adj.)* **ጎነጻዊ** *gonexawi*
**violet** *(n. )* **ሊላ** *lila*
**violin** *(n. )* **ቫዮሊን** *vayolin*
**violinist** *(n. )* **ስነ-ጡቢብ** *sneṫebib*
**virago** *(n.)* **ናግራም ሰበይቲ** *nagram sebeyti*
**viral** *(adj.)* **ስሙይ** *smuy*
**virgin** *(n.)* **በዱ** *bedu*
**virile** *(adj.)* **ጠንካራ** *ṭenkara*
**virility** *(n.)* **ሰብእነት** *seb'ènet*
**virtual** *(adj.)* **ግብራዊ** *gbrawi*
**virtue** *(n.)* **ውርዝውና** *wrzwna*
**virulent** *(adj.)* **ሓደገ'ኛ ብርቱዕ** *ḥadegeña brtu'ë*
**virus** *(n. )* **ቫይረስ** *vayres*
**visa** *(n.)* **ቪዛ** *viza*
**visage** *(n. )* **ገጽ** *gex*
**viscid** *(adj.)* **ሓፊስ** *ḥafis*
**viscose** *(n.)* **ቪስኮዝ** *viskoz*
**viscount** *(n.)* **መስፍን** *mesfn*
**viscous** *(adj.)* **ሓፊስ** *ḥafis*
**visibility** *(n.)* **ተረኣይነት** *tere'aynet*

**visible** *(adj.)* ኪረአ ዚኽኣል *kire'e zike'al*
**vision** *(n.)* ራእይ *ra'èy*
**visionary** *(adj.)* ራእያዊ *ra'èyawi*
**visit** *(v.)* በጽሐ - *bexḥe*
**visitation** *(n. )* ብጽሖ *bxḥo*
**visitor** *(n. )* በጻሒ *bexaḥi*
**visor** *(n.)* ድርዒ ገጽ *dr'ï gex*
**vista** *(n.)* ትርኢት *tr'it*
**visual** *(adj.)* ርእየታዊ *r'èyetawi*
**visualize** *(v.)* ቀረጸ *qerexe*
**vital** *(adj.)* ምስ ህይወት ዝተኣሳሰረ *ms hywet zte'asasere*
**vitality** *(n.)* ህይወት *hywet*
**vitalize** *(v.)* ህይወት ሃበ *hywet habe*
**vitamin** *(n.)* ቪታሚን *vitamin*
**vitiate** *(v.)* ኣሕመቐ *'aḥmeq̈e*
**viticulture** *(n.)* ኵስኰሳ ወይኒ *kuskWasa weyni*
**vitreous** *(adj.)* ጥርሙዛዊ *ṭrmuzawi*
**vitrify** *(v.)* ናብ ጥርሙዝ ለወጠ *nab ṭrmuz leweṭe*
**vitriol** *(n.)* ቪትርዮል *vitryol*
**vituperation** *(n.)* shnglaẗ mwxa'è ሽንግላጥ ምውጻእ
**vivacious** *(adj.)* ህይወታዊ ንጡፍ *hywetawi nṭuf*
**vivid** *(adj.)* ውዕውዕ *w'ëw'ë*
**vivify** *(v.)* ህይወት መለሰ *hywet melese*
**vixen** *(n. )* ዋዕሮ *wa'ëro*
**vocabulary** *(n.)* ቃላት *qalat*
**vocal** *(adj.)* ድምጻዊ *dmxawi*
**vocalist** *(n. )* ደራፊ *derafi*
**vocation** *(n. )* ሞያ *moya*
**vociferous** *(adj.)* ወጨጪ *weçaçi*
**vogue** *(n. )* ዘመናይ *zemenay*
**voice** *(n.)* ደሃይ *dehay*
**voicemail** *(n.)* ምድራዝ *mdraz*
**void** *(adj.)* ባድም *badm*
**voile** *(n.)* ሻሽ *shash*
**volatile** *(adj.)* በናኒ *benani*
**volcanic** *(adj.)* እሳተ-ጎመራዊ *'èsategomerawi*
**volcano** *(n. )* እሳተ-ጎመራ *'èsategomera*
**volition** *(n. )* ዊንታ *winta*
**volley** *(n.)* መሾምበባ *meshombeba*
**volt** *(n. )* ቮልት *volt*
**voltage** *(n. )* ዓቕን ሓይሊ ኤሌክትሪክ *'äq̈en ḧayli 'eeleektrik*
**voluble** *(adj.)* ክኢላ *k'ila*
**volume** *(n.)* ቅጺ *qxi*
**voluminous** *(adj.)* ሰፊሕ *sefiḥ*
**voluntary** *(adj.)* ወለንታዊ ዊንታዊ *welentawi wintawi*
**volunteer** *(n.)* ወለንተወ ፍቓደኛ ኮነ *welentewe fq̈adeña kone*
**voluptuary** *(n.)* ፈታው ምቾት *fetaw mchot*
**voluptuous** *(adj.)* ስምዒታዊ *sm'ïtawi*
**vomit** *(v.)* ትፋእ *tfa'è*
**voodoo** *(n.)* ቩዱ *vudu*
**voracious** *(adj.)* ሃርጋፍ *hargaf*
**vortex** *(n.)* ዘራጊቶ *zeragito*
**votary** *(n. )* መናኒ *menani*
**vote** *(n.)* ድምጺ ምርጫ *dmxi mrça*
**votive** *(adj.)* መብጻዓዊ *mebxa'äwi*
**vouch** *(v.)* ተዋሓሰ *tewaḥase*
**voucher** *(n.)* ቫውቸር *vawcher*
**vouchsafe** *(v.)* ለገሰ *legese*

**vow** *(n.)* መብጽዓ *mebx'ä*
**vowel** *(n. )* ኣድማጺ *admaxi*
**voyage** *(n.)* ጉዕዞ *gu'ëzo*
**voyager** *(n.)* ገያሺ *geyashi*
**vulcanize** *(v.)* ቨልከነ *velkene*
**vulgar** *(adj.)* ጽዩፍ *xyuf*
**vulgarian** *(n.)* በዓለገ *be'älege*
**vulgarity** *(n.)* መቐረት ዘይብሉ *meq̈eret zeyblu*
**vulnerable** *(adj.)* ተነቃፊ *teneqaf*
**vulpine** *(adj.)* ናይ ወኻርያ *nay wek̍arya*
**vulture** *(n.)* ጋም *gam*

# W

**wacky** *(adj.)* ዘይልሙድ *zeylemud*
**wad** *(n.)* እኩብ *ekub*
**waddle** *(v.)* ተሳለየ *tesaleye*
**wade** *(v.)* ተንፋሕኹ *tenfaḥk̍Wa*
**wader** *(n.)* ዓይነት ዑፍ *'äynet 'üf*
**wadi** *(n.)* ሩባ *ruba*
**wafer** *(n.)* ሕብስተ-ቁርባን *ḥbstequrban*
**waffle** *(v.)* ኣዕጀውጀወ ለፍለፈ *'a'ëğewğewe leflef*
**waft** *(v.)* ኣንሳፈፈ *'ansafefe*
**wag** *(v.)* ኣወጣወጠ *'aweṭaweṭe*
**wage** *(n.)* ደሞዝ ዓስቢ *demoz 'äsbi*
**wager** *(n. & v.)* ተወራረደ *tewerarede*
**waggle** *(v.)* ኣወጣወጠ *'aweṭaweṭe*
**wagon** *(n.)* ባጎኒ *bagoni*
**wagtail** *(n.)* ዑፍ *üf*
**waif** *(n.)* ዘኽታም *zek̍tam*
**wail** *(n.)* በኸየ *bek̍eye*
**wain** *(n. )* ቃፍላይ *qafla*
**wainscot** *(n.)* ምሉእ ዘድሊ *mlu'è zedli*
**waist** *(n. )* መዓጡቕ *me'äṭuq̈*
**waistband** *(n. )* ቅናት *qnat*
**waistcoat** *(n.)* ሰደርያ *sederya*
**wait** *(v.)* ጸንሐ *xenḥe*
**waiter** *(n. )* ኣሰላፊ *'aselafi*
**waitress** *(n.)* ኣሰላፊት *'aselafit*
**waive** *(v.)* ሰሓበ *seḥabe*
**wake** *(v.)* ተንስአ *tens'e*
**wakeful** *(adj.)* ጽን በሃሊ *xn behali*
**waken** *(v.)* ኣለዓዓለ *'ale'ä'äle*
**walk** *(v.)* ተጓዕዘ *tegWa'ëze*
**wall** *(n.)* መንደቕ *mendeq̈*
**wallaby** *(n.)* ንእሽቶ ካንጋሩ *n'èshto kangaru*
**wallet** *(n.)* ማሕፉዳ *maḥfuda*
**wallop** *(v.)* ደከረ *dekere*
**wallow** *(v.)* ኣንገርገረ *'angergere*
**Wally** *(n.)* ሕሉም *ḥlum*
**walnut** *(n. )* ጀዝ *ğez*
**walrus** *(n.)* መጥበዊ *meẗbewi*
**waltz** *(n.)* ቫልስ *vals*
**wan** *(adj.)* ምህሙን *mhmun*
**wand** *(n.)* ከረዛን *kerezan*
**wander** *(v.)* ኮብለለ *koblele*
**wane** *(v.)* እናጠፍአት ከደት *'ènaṭef'et kedet*
**wangle** *(v.)* ሓበለ *ḥabele*
**want** *(v.)* ደለየ *deleye*
**wanting** *(adj.)* ድልየት *dlyet*
**wanton** *(adj.)* ፈኖ *feno*
**war** *(n.)* ኲናት *kWinat*
**warble** *(v.)* ዘመረ *zemere*
**warbler** *(n. )* ስነ-ጠቢብ *sneṭebib*
**ward** *(n.)* ሓለዋ *ḥalewa*

**warden** *(n. )* ሓላፊ *ḥalafi*
**warder** *(n. )* ድጓና *dgWana*
**wardrobe** *(n. )* አርማድዮ ክዳውንቲ *'armadyo kdawnti*
**ware** *(n.)* ስኑዕ ኣቕሑ *snu'ë 'aq̈ḥu*
**warehouse** *(n. )* ካዝና *kazna*
**warfare** *(n.)* ቅዲ ኵናት *qdi kunat*
**warlike** *(adj.)* ፈታው ኵናት *fetaw kunat*
**warm** *(adj.)* ልቡጥ *lbu*
**warmth** *(n.)* ልብጠት *lbṭet*
**warn** *(v.)* ኣጠንቀቐ *'aṭenqeq̈*
**warning** *(n. )* መጠንቀቕታ *meṭenqeq̈ta*
**warp** *(v.)* ደርበየ *derbeye*
**warrant** *(n.)* ፍቓድ *feqad*
**warrantor** *(n.)* ዋሕስ *waḥs*
**warranty** *(n. )* መዝነት *meznet*
**warren** *(n. )* ስፍራ ማናቲለ *sfra manatile*
**warrior** *(n. )* ወተሃደር *wetehader*
**wart** *(n.)* ጡብ ኣድጊ *ṭub 'adgi*
**wary** *(adj.)* ጥንቁቕ *ṭnquq̈*
**wash** *(v.)* ሓጸበ *ḥaxebe*
**washable** *(adj.)* ክሕፀብ ዝኽእል *kHxeb zK'el*
**washer** *(n. )* ሓጻባይ *ḥaxabay*
**washing** *(n.)* ምሕጻብ *mḥxab*
**wasp** *(n.)* ዕኮት *'ëkot*
**waspish** *(adj.)* ሓራቕ *ḥaraq̈*
**wassail** *(n. )* ፈንጠዝያ *fenṭezya*
**wastage** *(n.)* ብኽነት *bḱnet*
**waste** *(v.)* ኣባኸነ *abaKene*
**wasteful** *(adj.)* ሸለልተኛ *shelelteña*
**watch** *(v.)* ተዓዘበ *te'äzebe*
**watchful** *(adj.)* ዝተበራበረ *zteberabere*
**watchword** *(n. )* ቃለ-ምስጢር *qalemsṭir*
**water** *(n. )* ማይ *may*
**water** *(n.)* ማይ *may*
**waterfall** *(n. )* መንጫዕጫዕታ *menĉa'ëĉa'ëta*
**watermark** *(n.)* ሕታም *Htam*
**watermelon** *(n.)* ብርጭቕ *brčq*
**waterproof** *(adj.)* ማይ ዓገት *may 'äget*
**watertight** *(adj.)* ማይሰጠም *mayseṭem*
**watery** *(adj.)* ቀጢን *qeṭin*
**watt** *(n. )* ኣሃዱ ናይ ኤለትሪካዊ ጉልበት *ahadu nay 'eeletrikawi gulbet*
**wattage** *(n.)* ኤለትሪክ -መስፈር *'eeletrik- mesfer*
**wattle** *(n.)* ባዛር ሹቕ *bazar shuq̈*
**wave** *(v.)* ባዙቃ *bazuqa*
**waver** *(v.)* ኮነ *kone*
**wavy** *(adj.)* ናብ ደንደስ ኣጸገዐ *nab dendes 'axege'ë*
**wax** *(n.)* መና *mena*
**way** *(n.)* መገዲ *megedi*
**waylay** *(v.)* ቆርቋር *qorqWAr*
**wayward** *(adj.)* ቢግል *bigl*
**we** *(pron. )* ንሕና *nhna*
**weak** *(adj.)* ድኹም *dKum*
**weaken** *(v.)* ኣድከመ *adkeme*
**weakling** *(n. )* ድኹም *dKum*
**weakness** *(n. )* ድኻም *dKam*
**weal** *(n. )* ተሸከመ *teshekeme*
**wealth** *(n.)* ንብረት *nbret*
**wealthy** *(adj.)* ሃብታም *habtam*
**wean** *(v.)* እንስሳ *ènssa*
**weapon** *(n.)* ክላሽ *klash*
**wear** *(v.)* ተኸድነ *teKedene*
**wearisome** *(adj.)* ድኻም *dkam*

**weary** *(adj.)* ዝደኸመ *zdekeme'*
**weasel** *(n.)* ናይ እንስሳ ሽም *nay nsesa shm*
**weather** *(n.)* ኩነታት ኣየር *kunetat ayer*
**weave** *(v.)* መልክዐ *melk'ë*
**weaver** *(n. )* ቢቨር *biver*
**web** *(n.)* ዓለኣ ሳሬት *aleba sariet*
**webpage** *(n.)* ድሕረ ገፀ *dhde getse*
**website** *(n.)* ድሕረ ገፅ *dhde getse*
**wed** *(v.)* ኣመርዓወ *amerawe*
**wedding** *(n. )* መርዓ *mer'a*
**wedge** *(n.)* መንጸፍ *menxef*
**wedlock** *(n. )* ምርዕውነት *mrewenet*
**Wednesday** *(n. )* ረቡዕ *rebu'e*
**weed** *(n.)* ኣረም *arem*
**week** *(n.)* ሰሙን *semun*
**weekday** *(n.)* መዓልቲ ስራሕ *me'alti srah*
**weekly** *(adj.)* ሰሙናዊ *semunawi*
**weep** *(v.)* በኸየ *beKeye'*
**weepy** *(adj.)* በኻዪ *bekayi*
**weevil** *(n.)* ብንጅር *bnĵr*
**weigh** *(v.)* መዘነ *mezene*
**weight** *(n.)* ክብደት *kbdet*
**weighting** *(n.)* ወረደ ኣጋጠመ *werede 'agaẗeme*
**weightlifting** *(n.)* በቕዐ *beq̈'ë*
**weighty** *(adj.)* ኸቢድ *kebid*
**weir** *(n.)* ግድብ *gdb*
**weird** *(adj.)* ዘይልሙድ *zeylemud*
**welcome** *(n.)* እንኳዕ ብደሓን መፃኻ *enkuae bdehan mexaka*
**weld** *(v.)* ዓጸፈ *axefe*
**welfare** *(n.)* ድሕንነት *dHnenet*
**well** *(n. )* ጨለ *chele*
**well** *(adv.)* ጨለ *chele*
**wellington** *(n.)* መጀመርታ *meĵemerta*
**welt** *(n.)* ኣዘናገዐ *azenage'ë*
**welter** *(n. )* ኣብ ክንዲ *ab kndi*
**wen** *(n. )* ገበረ *gebere*
**wench** *(n.)* ጠባይ *ẗebay*
**wend** *(v.)* ቈረጸ *qWerexe*
**west** *(n.)* ምዕራብ *merab*
**westerly** *(adv. )* ምዕራባዊ *merabawi*
**western** *(adj.)* ምዕራባዊ *merabawi*
**westerner** *(n.)* ምዕራባዊ *meraawi*
**westernize** *(v.)* ምዕራባዊ ምግር *merabawi mgbar*
**wet** *(adj.)* ርሑስ *rhus*
**wetness** *(n.)* ርሑስነት *rhusnet*
**whack** *(v.)* ዘይልሙድ *zeylemud*
**whale** *(n.)* ዓሳ ነባሪ *asa neari*
**whaler** *(n.)* ሃዳኒ ዓሳ ነባሪ *hadani asa neari*
**whaling** *(n.)* ምህዳን ዓሳ ነባሪ *mhdan asa nebari*
**wharf** *(n.)* ፋርጎ *fargo*
**wharfage** *(n.)* ናይ መርከብ መሳርሒ *nay merkeb mesarhi*
**what** *(pron. & adj.)* እንታይ *entay*
**whatever** *(pron.)* ዋላ *wala*
**wheat** *(n.)* ስርናይ *srnay*
**wheaten** *(adj.)* ስርናይ *srnay*
**wheedle** *(v.)* ኣውያት *awyat*
**wheel** *(n.)* መኪና *mekina*
**wheeze** *(v.)* ታሪኽ *tariK*
**whelk** *(n.)* ፈጸጋ *fexega*
**whelm** *(v.)* መናፍሕ *menafH*
**whelp** *(n.)* ከብዲ *kebdi*
**when** *(adv.)* ምዓዝ *meaz*

**whence** *(adv.)* ግላዊ ኣቐሑ *glawi 'aq̈ḧu*
**whenever** *(conj.)* ዝኾነ ግዜ *zKone gzie*
**where** *(adv.)* ኣበይ *abey*
**whereabouts** *(adv.)* ኣበይ ከምዘሎ *abey kemzelo*
**whereas** *(n.)* ተኾነውን *tekonewen*
**whet** *(v.)* ካራ *kara*
**whether** *(conj.)* ርቦ *rbo*
**whey** *(n.)* ለወየ *leweye*
**which** *(pron. & adj.)* ኣየን *ayen*
**whichever** *(pron.)* ዝኾነ ይኹን *zKone yKun*
**whiff** *(n.)* ገቢረ-ሰናይ *gebiresenay*
**while** *(n.)* ክሳብ *ksab*
**whilst** *(conj.)* ክሳብ *ksab*
**whim** *(n.)* ቐልዲ *qeldi*
**whimper** *(v.)* ኣውያት *awyat*
**whimsical** *(adj.)* ተጻዋታይ *texawatay*
**whimsy** *(n.)* ጽዋታ *xewata*
**whine** *(n.)* ብኽያት *bKyat*
**whinge** *(v.)* ኣንጸርጸረ *anxerxere*
**whinny** *(n.)* መንጸርጸሪ *menxerxeri*
**whip** *(n. )* ፈራሕ *ferHe*
**whir** *(n.)* ፋርጎ *fargo*
**whirl** *(v.)* ምዝዋር *mzwar*
**whirligig** *(n. )* ምዝዋር *mzwar*
**whirlpool** *(n. )* መዝወሪ *mezweri*
**whirlwind** *(n.)* መዝወሪ ንፋስ *mezweri nfas*
**whirr** *(v.)* ደንቆሮ *denqoro*
**whisk** *(v.)* ወቐዐ *weqe*
**whisker** *(n. )* ጬሕሚ *cheHmi*
**whisky** *(n.)* ውስኪ *wski*
**whisper** *(v.)* ሕሹኽሹኽ *hshukshuk*
**whist** *(n.)* ንፋስ *nfas*
**whistle** *(n.)* ፋጻ *faxa*
**whit** *(n.)* ንእሽቶ *aeshto*
**white** *(adj.)* ጻዕዳ *xaeda*
**whitewash** *(n.)* መሕጸቢ *meHxei*
**whither** *(adv.)* ጻዕዳ *xaeda*
**whiting** *(n.)* ምጽዕዳው *mxedaw*
**whittle** *(v.)* ጻዕዳ *xaeda*
**whiz** *(v.)* ኣራዊታዊ እንስሳዊ ጨካን *'arawitawi 'ènssawi čekan*
**who** *(pron. )* መን *men*
**whoever** *(pron.)* ማንም ይኹን *manm yekun*
**whole** *(adj.)* ግኡድጓድ *gudguad*
**whole-hearted** *(adj.)* ምሉእ ልቢ *mluelbi*
**wholesale** *(n.)* መሸጣ *mesheta*
**wholesaler** *(n.)* ቅጥፈት *qẗfet*
**wholesome** *(adj.)* ዝሓሸ *zḧashe*
**wholly** *(adv.)* ኣብ መንጎ *'ab mengo*
**whom** *(pron.)* ንመን *nmen*
**whoop** *(n.)* ሓጎስ *hagos*
**whopper** *(n.)* ተሓጓሳይ *tehaguasay*
**whore** *(n.)* ኣመንዝር *amenzer*
**whose** *(pron.)* ናይ መን *naymen*
**why** *(adv.)* ንምንታይ *nmntay*
**wick** *(n.)* ሰረየ *sereye*
**wicked** *(adj.)* ክፋእ *kfue*
**wicker** *(n. )* ሸንጣር *shentar*
**wicket** *(n.)* ፍርቂ በብዓመት *frqi beb'ämet*
**wide** *(adj.)* ገፊሕ *gefiH*
**widen** *(v.)* ኣግፈሐ *agfeHe*
**widespread** *(adj.)* ውሩይ *wruy*

**widow** *(n.)* **ሰብኣያ ዝሞታ** *seaya zemota*
**widower** *(n. )* **ሰብበይቱ ዝሞተቶ** *sebeytu zmoteto*
**width** *(n.)* **ስፍሓት** *sfHat*
**wield** *(v.)* **ምውፃእ** *mwxae*
**wife** *(n. )* **ሰበይቲ** *sebeyti*
**wig** *(n. )* **ሸንጣር** *shentar*
**wiggle** *(v.)* **ምውዝዋዝ** *mwzwaz*
**Wight** *(n. )* **ምስኪን** *mskin*
**wigwam** *(n.)* **ጎጆ** *gjo*
**wild** *(adj.)* **በረኻ** *bereKa*
**wilderness** *(n.)* **በረኻ** *bereKa*
**wile** *(n. )* **ምምሻጥ** *mmshaẗ*
**wilful** *(adj.)* **ሚስጥረኛ** *mistregna*
**will** *(v.)* **ፍቓድ** *fqad*
**willing** *(adj.)* **ፍቓደኛ** *fqadegna*
**willingness** *(adj.)* **ፍቓድ** *fqad*
**willow** *(n.)* **ኦም** *om*
**wily** *(adj.)* **ንፉዕ** *nfu'e*
**wimble** *(n. )* **ምቕናን** *mqnan*
**wimple** *(n.)* **ሻሽ** *shash*
**win** *(v.)* **ሰዓረ** *seare*
**wince** *(v.)* **ቓንዛ** *qanza*
**winch** *(n.)* **ዓረብያ** *arebya*
**wind** *(n.)* **ንፋስ** *nfas*
**windbag** *(n. )* **ተዛራባይ** *tezarabay*
**winder** *(n.)* **ነፋሽ** *nefash*
**windlass** *(n.)* **ሊፍት** *lift*
**windmill** *(n. )* **ዕፍ ንፋስ** *ef nfas*
**window** *(n.)* **መስኮት** *meskot*
**windy** *(adj.)* **ንፋስ** *nfas*
**wine** *(n. )* **ወይኒ** *weyni*
**winery** *(n.)* **ምስራሕ ወይኒ** *msraH weyni*
**wing** *(n.)* **ክንፊ** *knfi*
**wink** *(v.)* **ጠቐሰ** *Teqese*
**winkle** *(n.)* **ሽም እንስሳ** *shm enssa*
**winner** *(n.)* **ተዓዋቲ** *tawati*
**winning** *(adj.)* **ዓወት** *awet*
**winnow** *(v.)* **ንፋስ** *nfas*
**winsome** *(adj.)* **ስዕረት** *seret*
**winter** *(n.)* **ሓጋይ** *ḧagay*
**wintry** *(adj.)* **ኢኮሎጂ** *ikoloĵi*
**wipe** *(v.)* **ኣጽረየ** *axreye*
**wire** *(n.)* **ሽቦ** *shbo*
**wireless** *(adj.)* **መስመር ኣልባ** *mesmer albo*
**wiring** *(n. )* **መስመር** *msmer*
**wisdom** *(n. )* **ጥበብ** *tbeb*
**wise** *(adj.)* **ጠቢብ** *tebib*
**wish** *(v.)* **ትምኒት** *tmnit*
**wishful** *(adj.)* **ትምኒት** *tmnit*
**wisp** *(n.)* **ንእሽቶ** *neshto*
**wisteria** *(n.)* **ዘለፋ** *zelefa*
**wistful** *(adj.)* **ጥንቁቕ** *tnquq'*
**wit** *(n. )* **ቀልዲ** *qeldi*
**witch** *(n.)* **ጠንቋሊት** *tenqualit*
**witchcraft** *(n. )* **ጥንቆላ** *tnqola*
**witchery** *(n.)* **ጥንቆላ** *tnqola*
**with** *(prep. )* **ብ** *b*
**withal** *(adv.)* **ብተወሰኺ** *btewesaKi*
**withdraw** *(v.)* **ምውጻእ** *mwxae*
**withdrawal** *(n.)* **ምውጻእ** *mwxae*
**withe** *(n.)* **ምስ** *ms*
**wither** *(v.)* **ምስ** *ms*
**withhold** *(v.)* **ምሕባእ** *mhbae*
**within** *(prep. )* **ውሽጢ** *wshti*
**without** *(prep. )* **ብዘይ** *bzey*
**withstand** *(v.)* **ምቅዃም** *mqQuam*
**witless** *(adj.)* **ደረቕ** *dereq*
**witness** *(n.)* **ምምስካር** *mmskar*
**witter** *(v.)* **ምብስባስ** *mbsbas*
**witticism** *(n.)* **ቐልዲ** *qeldi*
**witty** *(adj.)* **ባጫ** *bacha*
**wizard** *(n.)* **ጠንቋሊ** *tenquali*

**wizened** *(adj.)* ጻዕደወ *xa'ëdewe*
**woad** *(n.)* ልዙብ *lzub*
**wobble** *(v.)* ጥርሑ *ïrḧu*
**woe** *(n.)* ኮበርታ *koberta*
**woeful** *(adj.)* ድምጺ *dmxi*
**wok** *(n.)* ኣተዓሻሸወ *ate'äshashewe*
**wold** *(n.)* ነትጒ *netgWi*
**wolf** *(n. )* ተኹላ *tekula*
**woman** *(n. )* ሰበይቲ *seeyti*
**womanhood** *(n. )* ሰበይቲ ምኳን *sebeyti mkuan*
**womanize** *(v.)* ሰበይቲ ምኳን *sebeyti mkuan*
**womb** *(n.)* ማህጸን *mahxen*
**wonder** *(v.)* ሓሰበ *hasebe*
**wonderful** *(adj.)* ጽቡቕ *xbuk*
**wondrous** *(adj.)* ቃና *qana*
**wonky** *(adj.)* ኣበር *aber*
**wont** *(n.)* ኣይከውንን *aykewnn*
**wonted** *(adj.)* ሓዋወሰ *ḧawawese*
**woo** *(v.)* ፍቕሪ *fqri*
**wood** *(n.)* ጣውላ *tawla*
**wooded** *(adj.)* ጣውላ *tawla*
**wooden** *(adj.)* ጣውላ *tawla*
**woodland** *(n. )* ጫካ *chaka*
**woof** *(n. )* ምንባሕ *mnbah*
**woofer** *(n.)* ነባሒ *nbahi*
**wool** *(n.)* ሃሪ *hari*
**woollen** *(adj.)* ሃሪ *hari*
**woolly** *(adj.)* ሃሪ *hari*
**woozy** *(adj.)* ደብዛዝ *dbzaz*
**word** *(n.)* ቃል *qal*
**wording** *(n.)* ኣጠቃቅማ ቃል *atekakema qal*
**wordy** *(adj.)* ቓል ዝበዝሖ *qal zbezho*
**work** *(n.)* ስራሕ *srah*
**workable** *(adj.)* ዝስራሕ *zsrah*
**workaday** *(adj.)* ናይ ስራሕ መዓልቲ *nay srah mealti*
**worker** *(n.)* ሰራሕተኛ *serahtegna*
**working** *(n.)* ዝሰርሕ *zserh*
**workman** *(n. )* ሰራሕተኛ *serahtegna*
**workmanship** *(n. )* ሰራሕተኛ *serahtegna*
**workshop** *(n. )* ናይ ስራሕ ቦታ *naysrah bota*
**world** *(n. )* ዓለም *alem*
**worldly** *(adj.)* ዓለማዊ *alemawi*
**worm** *(n. )* ሓሰኻ *haseka*
**worried** *(adj.)* ጭንቀት *chnqet*
**worrisome** *(adj.)* ጭኑቕ *chnuq*
**worry** *(v.)* ተጨነቐ *techeneqe*
**worse** *(adj.)* ዝኸፍአ *zkefe*
**worsen** *(v.)* በኣሰ *bease*
**worship** *(n.)* ምምላኽ *mmlaK*
**worshipper** *(n. )* ኣምላኺ *amlaKi*
**worst** *(adj.)* ዝኸፍአ *zKefe*
**worsted** *(n.)* ኣኽፈአ *aKfe*
**worth** *(adj.)* ዋጋ *waga*
**worthless** *(adj.)* ቈንደፈ *qWendefe*
**worthwhile** *(adj.)* ዋጋ ዘለዎ' *waga zelewo*
**worthy** *(adj.)* ጓመድ *gWamed*
**would** *(v.)* ይኸውን *ykewn*
**would-be** *(adj.)* ይኸውን *ykewn*
**wound** *(n.)* ቆሰለ *qosele*
**wrack** *(n. )* ጻህያይ ባሕሪ *xahyay baḥri*
**wraith** *(n.)* መልኣከ ሞት *mel'ake mot*
**wrangle** *(n. )* ተጎናፈጠ *tegonafeṭe*
**wrap** *(v.)* ጠቕለለ *ṭeqlele*

**wrapper** *(n. )* መጎልበቢ *megolbebi*
**wrath** *(n. )* ቁጠዐ *quṭe'ë*
**wreak** *(v.)* ገለጸ *gelexe*
**wreath** *(n.)* ዓንኬል *'änkeel*
**wreathe** *(v.)* ኣኽበበ *'akbebe*
**wreck** *(n.)* ዕንወት *'ënwet*
**wreckage** *(n. )* ፍራስ *fras*
**wrecker** *(n. )* ቀንጻሊ *qenxali*
**wren** *(n. )* ንእሽቶ ዓይነት ዑፍ *n'èshto 'äynet 'üf*
**wrench** *(v.)* ምጥዋይን ምስሓብን *mṭwayn msḥabn*
**wrest** *(v.)* ጠወየ *ṭeweye*
**wrestle** *(v.)* ተቓለሰ *teq̈alese*
**wrestler** *(n. )* ተቓላሲ *teq̈alasi*
**wretch** *(n.)* ቅርሱስ *qrsus*
**wretched** *(adj.)* ስቅያታዊ *sqyatawi*
**wrick** *(v.)* ቆጸየ *qoxeye*
**wriggle** *(v.)* ኣካይዳ ተመን ከደ *'akayda temen kede*
**wring** *(v.)* ጸመቚ *xemeq̈We*
**wrinkle** *(n. )* ዓጠረ *'äṭere*
**wrinkle** *(n.)* ዓጠረ *'äṭere*
**wrist** *(n. )* ጉንቦ ኢድ *gunbo 'id*
**writ** *(n.)* ኣዛዚ *'azazi*
**write** *(v.)* ጸሓፈ *xeḥafe*
**writer** *(n.)* ጸሓፊ *xeḥafi*
**writhe** *(v.)* ተፋሕሰ *tefaḥse*
**writing** *(n.)* ጽሕፈት *xḥfet*
**wrong** *(adj.)* ግጉይ *gguy*
**wrongful** *(adj.)* ጽዩፍ *xyuf*
**wry** *(adj.)* ጎምጻጽ ጠዋይ *gomxax ṭeway*

# X

**xenon** *(n.)* ከቢድ ጋዝ *kebid gaz*
**xenophobia** *(n.)* ፅልኢ ሓደሽቲ ሰባት *tselei hdeshti sebat*
**Xerox** *(n.)* መባዝሒ ማሽን *mebazHi mashn*
**Xmas** *(n.)* ልደት *ldet*
**x-ray** *(n.)* ራጅ *raj*
**xylophages** *(adj.)* ባልዕ *megarya*
**xylophilous** *(adj.)* ናይ ዕንጨይቲ ነዋሪ *nay encheyti newari*
**xylophone** *(n.)* ናይ ዕንጨይቲ ሙዚቃ መሳርሒ *nay encheyti muzika mesarhi*

# Y

**yacht** *(n.)* ጀልባ *jelba*
**yachting** *(n. )* ናይ ጀልባ ሃበ *nay jelba habe*
**yachtsman** *(n.)* ናይ ጀልባ ሰብ *nay jelba seb*
**yak** *(n.)* ብዕራይ *beray*
**yam** *(n.)* ሽኮር ድንሽ *shkor dnesh*
**yap** *(v.)* ዘረባ *zereba*
**yard** *(n. )* መረባ *mereba*
**yarn** *(n.)* ፈትሊ *fetli*
**yashmak** *(n.)* መሸፈኒ ሻሽ *meshefeni shash*
**yaw** *(v.)* ኣምቧሃቐ *ambuahaqe*
**yawn** *(v.)* ምምቡሃቕ *mmbuhaq*
**year** *(n.)* ዓመት *amet*
**yearly** *(adv. )* ዓመታዊ *ametawi*
**yearn** *(v.)* ሃረር በለ *harer bele*
**yearning** *(n. )* ናፍቖት *nafqot*
**yeast** *(n.)* ለቢቶ *lebito*
**yell** *(n.)* ኣእወየ *aeweye*

**yellow** *(adj.)* ብጫ *bcha*
**yelp** *(n.)* ኣእወየ *aeweye*
**Yen** *(n. )* ሳንቲም *santim*
**yeoman** *(n.)* ዓኳይ *akuay*
**yes** *(excl.)* እወ *ewe*
**yesterday** *(adv. )* ትማሊ *tmali*
**yet** *(adv.)* ሕጂ *Hji*
**yeti** *(n.)* ኣብ ሂማልያ ዝነብር እንስሳ *ab himalya zeneber ensesa*
**yew** *(n.)* ኦም *om*
**yield** *(v.)* ኣፍረየ *afreye*
**yob** *(n.)* ናይ ሰገናት *nay segenat*
**yodel** *(v.)* ምዝማር *mzmar*
**yoga** *(n.)* ዮጋ *yoga*
**yogi** *(n.)* ናይ ዮጋ ሰብ *nay yoga seb*
**yogurt** *(n.)* ርግኦ *rguo*
**yoke** *(n. )* ኣርዑት *arut*
**yokel** *(n.)* ናይ ሃገረሰብ *nay hagereseb*
**yolk** *(n.)* ፃዕዳ ክፋል እንቋቑሖ *tsaeda kfal enquaquho*
**yonder** *(adj.)* ርሑቕ *rhuQ*
**yonks** *(n.)* ዮንክስ *yonks*
**yore** *(n.)* ዘአረገ *ze'erege*
**you** *(pron.)* ንስኻ *nsKa*
**young** *(adj.)* ሰገን *segen*
**youngster** *(n. )* ሰገን *segen*
**your** *(adj.)* ናትካ *natk*
**yourself** *(pron.)* ዓርስኻ *arseka*
**youth** *(n.)* ንእስነት *n'esenet*
**youthful** *(adj.)* መንእሰይ *men'esey*
**yowl** *(n.)* በኸየ *beKeye*
**yummy** *(adj.)* ምቁር *mqur*

# Z

**zany** *(adj.)* ዘይተለመደ *zeytelemde*
**zap** *(v.)* ኮረንቲ ሓዘ *korenti haze*
**zeal** *(n. )* ብርቱዕ ድልየት *brtu'e dlyet*
**zealot** *(n.)* ኣኽራሪ *aKrari*
**zealous** *(adj.)* ኣዝዩ ህንቁዉ *azyu hnquw*
**zebra** *(n. )* ኣድጊ በረኻ *adgi bereKa*
**zebra crossing** *(n.)* ዜብራ መንገዲ *zebra mengedi*
**zenith** *(n. )* ጫፍ *medegef*
**zephyr** *(n. )* ህዱእ *hdu'e*
**zero** *(adj.)* ባዶ *bado*
**zest** *(n.)* ድልየትን ታሕጓስን *dlyetn taHguasn*
**zigzag** *(n.)* ስብርባር ሕንፃፅ *sbrbar Hntsats*
**zilch** *(n.)* ባዶ *bado*
**zinc** *(n. )* ዚንጎ *zingo*
**zing** *(n.)* ድልየት *dlyet*
**zip** *(n.)* ሻርኔራ *sharnira*
**zircon** *(n.)* ማዕድን *maeden*
**zither** *(n.)* ሙዚቃ መሳርሒ *muzika mesarhi*
**zodiac** *(n.)* ሰማያዊ *semayawi*
**zombie** *(n.)* ዘይሞተ መዉት *zeymote muwut*
**zonal** *(adj.)* ክልላዊ *kllawi*
**zone** *(n.)* ክልል *kll*
**zoo** *(n.)* መካነ እንስሳት *makane enssat*
**zoology** *(n. )* ስነ-እንስሳ *sne-enssat*
**zoom** *(v.)* ሸውታ *shewta*

# Tigrigna-English

# ሀ

**ሀምፕ** hemp ***(n.)* Cannabis**
**ሀርፒስ** herpis ***(n.)* Herpes**
**ሁንድፍ** hunduf ***(adj.)* impulsive**
**ሁጉሬ** huguree ***(n.)* bumpkin**
**ሁፕላ** hupla ***(n.)* hoopla**

# ሂ

**ሂለል** hilel ***(n.)* crescent**
**ሂስቶግራም** histogram ***(n. )* histogram**
**ሂወት** hiwet ***(n.)* life**
**ሂወት ዘይብሉ** hiwet zeyblu ***(adj.)* lifeless**
**ሂወት ዘይብሉ ነገር** hiwet heyblu neger ***(adj.)* inanimate**
**ሃህታ** hahta ***(n.)* lacuna**
**ሃህታ** hahta ***(n.)* vacancy**
**ሃለለ** halele ***(v.)* bray**
**ሃለለ** halele ***(n.)* hammock**
**ሃለወ** halewe ***(v.)* exist**
**ሃለዋት** halewat ***(n., a)* situation**
**ሃለውለው** halewlew ***(n.)* blarney**
**ሃለውለው** halewlew ***(n.)* rigmarole**
**ሃለውለው** halewlew ***(n.)* tattle**
**ሃልሃልታ** halhalta ***(n.)* flare**
**ሃልሃልታ** halhalta ***(v.)* spurt**
**ሃልሃልታ** halhalta ***(n.)* blaze**
**ሃልሃል አበለ** halhal abele ***(v.)* inflame**
**ሃላይ** halay ***(adj.)* crass**
**ሃላይ** halay ***(adj.)* fatuous**
**ሃላይ** halay ***(n.)* oaf**
**ሃልመት** halmet ***(n.)* helmet**
**ሃሎጅን** halojn ***(n.)* halogen**
**ሃመንመን ዝበለ** hamenmen zbele ***(adj.)* gaga**
**ሃምስተር** hamster ***(n.)* hamster**
**ሃምበርገር** hamberger ***(n.)* hamburger**
**ሃምባቆቶ** hambaqoto ***(n.)* midriff**
**ሃረመ** hareme ***(v.)* beat**
**ሃረመ** hareme ***(v.)* hit**
**ሃረመ** hareme ***(v.)* kick**
**ሃረር በለ** harer bele ***(v.)* yearn**
**ሃረርተኛ** harerteňa ***(adj.)* anxious**
**ሃረርታ** harerta ***(n. )* gluttony**
**ሃረፈ** harefe ***(v.)* pine**
**ሃሪ** hari ***(n.)* silk**
**ሃሪ** hari ***(n.)* wool**
**ሃሪ ዝመስል** hari zmesl ***(adj.)* silken**
**ሃሪ ዝመስል** hari zmesl ***(adj.)* woollen**
**ሃርሞኑዮም** harmunyem ***(n. )* harmonium**
**ሃርጋፍ** hargaf ***(adj.)* voracious**
**ሃርጋፍ** hargaf ***(n.)* vulture**
**ሃሰሰ** hasese ***(v.i)* fade**
**ሃሰሰ** hasese ***(v.)* tarnish**
**ሃሰው በለ** hasew bele ***(v.)* grope**
**ሃሰየ** haseye ***(v.)* disable**
**ሃሳስ** hasas ***(adj.)* dim**
**ሃሳዪ** hasayi ***(adj.)* prejudicial**
**ሃቀነ** haqene ***(v.)* attempt**
**ሃበ** habe ***(v.)* grant**
**ሃበ** habe ***(v.)* grant**
**ሃበ** habe ***(v.)* give**
**ሃበ** habe ***(v.)* ascribe**
**ሃበሬታ ተለዋወጠ** habereta ***(v.)* communicate**
**ሃብቲ** habti ***(n.)* welt**
**ሃብቲ** habti ***(n.)* affluence**
**ሃብቲ** habti ***(n. )* mammon**
**ሃብታም** habtam ***(adj.)* affluent**

ሃብታም habtam *(adj.)* **opulent**
ሃብታም habtam *(adj.)* **wealthy**
ሃብት habt *(n.)* **wealth**
ሃተ'ፈ hatefe *(v.)* **blab**
ሃተፈ/ለፈለፈ hatefe/lefelefe *(v.)* **chatter**
ሃተፍተፍ hateftef *(v.)* **prattle**
ሃተፍተፍ hateftef *(n.)* **vapour**
ሃተውቀጠው hatew qeẗew *(n.)* **eyewash**
ሃነነ hane-ne *(v.)* **gape**
ሃነጸ hanexe *(v.)* **build**
ሃነፀ hanxe' *(v.)* **construct**
ሃናት hanat *(n.)* **scalp**
ሃናጺ hanaxi *(n.)* **architect**
ሃናፂ hanatxi' *(adj.)* **constructive**
ሃንቀዉታ hanqewta *(n.)* **curiosity**
ሃንደበታዊ handebetawi *(adj. )* **haphazard**
ሃንደበታዊ handebetawi *(adj.)* **abrupt**
ሃንደበት handebet *(adj.)* **random**
ሃንደበት handebet *(adj.)* **sudden**
ሃንደበት handebet *(adj.)* **unexpected**
ሃንደፍታ handefta *(n.)* **impulse**
ሃካይ hakay *(adj.)* **slothful**
ሃወኸ haweke *(v.)* **disconcert**
ሃወኸ haweḱe *(v.)* **hurry**
ሃዋህዉ hawahewu *(n.)* **circumstance**
ሃዋህው hawahewu' *(n.)* **context**
ሃዋህዉ hawahw *(n.)* **cosmos**
ሃዋህው hawahw *(n.)* **atmosphere**
ሃዋርያ hawarya *(n.)* **apostle**
ሃዋሲ hawasi *(n.)* **sensor**
ሃዊኹ hawiku *(v.)* **perturb**
ሃውሪ hawri *(adj.)* **arbitrary**
ሃውተተ hawtati *(adj.)* **adrift**
ሃውታቲ hawtati *(adj.)* **discursive**
ሃውታቲ hawtete *(v.)* **yaw**
ሃያሲ hayasi *(n.)* **critic**
ሃይማኖተኛ haymanotegna *(adj.)* **devout**
ሃይማኖተኛ haymanoteña *(adj.)* **godly**
ሃይማኖተኛ haymanotena *(n. )* **piety**
ሃይማኖተኛ haymanptegna *(adj.)* **religious**
ሃይማኖታዊ haymanotawi *(adj.)* **mystical**
ሃይማኖታዊ ቦታታት ዝበጽሕ haymanotawi botatat zbxh *(n. )* **pilgrim**
ሃይማኖታዊ ፅምብል haymanotawi tsmbl *(n.)* **sacrament**
ሃይማኖት haymanot *(n.)* **religion**
ሃይድሮጅን haydrogen *(n. )* **hydrogen**
ሃዲም hadim *(n. )* **fugitive**
ሃዝረጠ hazreẗe *(v.)* **bloat**
ሃዝራጥ hazraẗ *(adj.)* **corpulent**
ሃደመ hademe *(v.)* **flee**
ሃደነ hadene *(v.)* **hunt**
ሃዳኒ ዓሳ ነባሪ hadani asa neari *(n.)* **whaler**
ሃዳኒ እንስሳ hadali ènssa *(n.)* **predator**
ሃዳናይ hadanay *(n. )* **hunter**
ሃዳዳይ hadaday *(n. )* **steed**
ሃገራት ምብራቕ hagerat mbraq *(n.)* **orient**
ሃገር hager *(n.)* **country**
ሃገር hager *(n.)* **state**
ሃገር ቦቆል hager boqol *(adj.)* **endemic**

ሃገር ክሒድካ ምስ ፀላኢ ምሕባር hager kihidka ms selai mhbar *(n. )* treason

ሃገራዊ hagerawi *(adj.)* inland

ሃገር ዘመሓድር ጉጅለ hager zemehadr gujele *(n. )* oligarchy

ሃጓም hagwam *(adj.)* concave

ሃፀይ haxey *(n.)* emperor

ሃፀፊ hatzfi *(n. )* gust

ሃፈፈ hafefe *(v.)* evaporate

ሃፈፈ hafefe *(v.)* vaporize

ሃፋ hafa *(n.)* steam

ሃፍቲ hafti *(n.)* opulence

ሃፍታም haftam *(nabob)* nabob

ሃፍታም haftam *(adj.)* rich

ሃፍታምነት haftamnet *(n. )* richness

ሃፍታም ነጋዴ haftam negadi *(n.)* tycoon

ሄሊኮፕተር heel *(n.)* cardamom

ሄል heelikopter *(n.)* helicopter

ሄሞግሎቢን hemoglobin *(n.)* haemoglobin

ሄሮይን heeroyn *(n. )* heroine

ሄክታር hluw *(n.)* present


# ህ

ህሉው hektar *(n.)* hectare

ህላወ hlawe *(n.)* entity

ህላወ hlawe *(n.)* survival

ህላወ hlawe *(n.)* being

ህላዌ hlawe *(n.)* presence

ህልቂት hlqit *(n.)* holocaust

ህልከኛ hlkegna *(adj.)* obdurate

ህልከኛ hlkegna *(adj.)* scrappy

ህልኸኛ hlkena *(n.)* perversity

ህልኽ hlk *(n.)* obduracy

ህልኽ hlk *(adj.)* perverse

ህልው hlw *(adj.)* immanent

ህልውና hlwna *(n. )* existence

ህመት hmet *(n.)* moment

ህሩግ ምባል hrug mbal *(n. )* intrusion

ህሩግ በሃሊ hrug behali *(adj.)* intrusive

ህሩግ በለ hrug bele *(v.)* intrude

ህሩድ hrud *(n. )* turmeric

ህሩፍ hruf *(adj.)* lustful

ህሩፍ hruf *(adj.)* greedy

ህርመታዊ hrmetawi *(adj.)* metrical

ህስየት hsyet *(n.)* detriment

ህበይ hbey *(n.)* ape

ህበይ hbey *(n. )* gorilla

ህበይ hbey *(n.)* monkey

ህበይ hebeyei *(n.)* chimpanzee

ህበይ hbey *(n.)* baboon

ህቡብ ሰብ hbub seb *(n.)* personage

ህቦብላ hebobla *(n.)* hurricane

ህቦብላ h-bo-b-la *(n.)* gale

ህቦብላ ውርጪ hbobla wrči *(n.)* blizzard

ህንቁዉ hnquw *(adj.)* desirous

ህንዳዊ hndawi *(n.)* Indian

ህንጡዉ hntuw *(adj.)* eager

ህንጡው hnŭuw *(n.)* alacritous

ህንጡይ hntuy *(adj.)* keen

ህንጡይ hnŭuy *(adj.)* curious

ህንጡይ hnŭuy *(adj.)* avid

ህንጻ hnxa *(n.)* building

ህንጻ hnxa *(n.)* edifice

ህንፀት hintsxet' *(n.)* construction

ህኩይ hkuy *(adj.)* idle

ህኩይ hkuy *(adj.)* shiftless

ህዋ hwa *(n.)* space

ህዋሳዊ hwasawi *(adj.)* sensory

ህዋሳዊ hwasawi *(adj.)* sensuous

ህዋስ hwas *(n.)* sense

**ህውተታ** hwteta ***(n.)*** **bathos**
**ህዉከት** hwuket ***(n.)*** **chaos**
**ህውከተኛ** hwketegna ***(n.)*** **urchin**
**ህውከት** hwket ***(n.)*** **commotion**
**ህውከት** hwket ***(n.)*** **riot**
**ህውከት** hwket ***(n.)*** **rising**
**ህውከት ፈጠረ** hwket fetere ***(v.)*** **rampage**
**ህዉኽ** hwukh ***(adj.)*** **overwrought**
**ህዉኽ** hwuk ***(adj.)*** **raring**
**ህውኽ** hwḱ ***(adj. )*** **hasty**
**ህያብ** hyab ***(n.)*** **fairing**
**ህያው** hyaw ***(adj.)*** **alive**
**ህያውነት** hyawnet ***(n.)*** **immortality**
**ህያው ገበረ** hyaw gebere ***(v.)*** **immortalize**
**ህይሰት** hyset ***(n.)*** **critique**
**ህይወት** hywet habe ***(v.)*** **vitalize**
**ህይወት ሃበ** hywet ***(n.)*** **vitality**
**ህይወት መለሰ** hywet melese ***(v.)*** **vivify**
**ህዝቢ** hzbi ***(n.)*** **folk**
**ህዝባዊ** hzbawi ***(adj.)*** **public**
**ህዱእ** hd'u ***(adj.)*** **quiet**
**ህዱእ** hdu'e ***(adj.)*** **restful**
**ህዱእ** hdu'e ***(adj.)*** **secure**
**ህዱእ** hdu'e ***(adj.)*** **sedate**
**ህዱእ** hdu'è ***(adj.)*** **calm**
**ህዱእ** hdu'e ***(adj.)*** **still**
**ህዱእ** he-du-e ***(adj.)*** **gentle**
**ህዱእ** hdu'e ***(n. )*** **zephyr**
**ህዱእ ናብራ** hdu'e nabra ***(n.)*** **idyll**
**ህዱእ ንፋስ** hdu'è nfas ***(n.)*** **breeze**
**ህዱእ ጋልቢት** hdu'è galbit ***(n.)*** **canter**
**ህድሁድ** hdhud ***(adj.)*** **fusty**
**ህድህድ** h'dh'd ***(adj.)*** **stuffy**
**ህድማ** h'dma ***(n.)*** **stampede**
**ህድሞ** hdmo ***(n.)*** **bunk**
**ህድኣት** hd'at ***(n.)*** **sobriety**
**ህድኣት** hd'at ***(n.)*** **quietude**
**ህገራ** hgera ***(n.)*** **nationalization**
**ህጻን** hxan ***(n.)*** **babe**
**ህጻን** hxan ***(n.)*** **baby**
**ህጻን** hrtsan ***(n.)*** **tot**
**ህፀፅ** hxex ***(n.)*** **exigency**
**ህፁፅ** htzutz ***(adj.)*** **frantic**
**ህፃን** htsan ***(n.)*** **kid**

# ሆ

**ሆልምየም** holmyem ***(n.)*** **holmium**
**ሆሎግራም** hologram ***(n.)*** **hologram**
**ሆምየፓተኛ** homyepategna ***(n. )*** **homoeopath**
**ሆምየፓቲ** homyepati ***(n.)*** **homeopathy**
**ሆርሞን** hostel ***(n.)*** **hostel**
**ሆስፒታል** hormon ***(n.)*** **hormone**
**ሆስተል** hospital ***(n. )*** **hospital**
**ሆባይ** hobay ***(n.)*** **nave**
**ሆቴል** hoteel ***(n. )*** **hotel**

# ለ

**ለሓሰ** lehase ***(v.)*** **lick**
**ለሓኹ** lehake ***(v.)*** **seep**
**ለመም በለ** lemem bele ***(v.)*** **crawl**
**ለመነ** lemene ***(v.)*** **invoke**
**ለመነ** lemene ***(v.)*** **beg**
**ለመነ** lemene ***(v.)*** **beseech**
**ለመጭ** lemec ***(adj.)*** **crafty**
**ለመጭ** lemech ***(adj.)*** **soapy**
**ለመፀ** lemetse ***(v.)*** **daub**
**ለመፀ** lemetse ***(v.)*** **smear**

**ለሚን** lemin ***(n. )*** **lemon**
**ለሚፀ** lemix ***(adj.)*** **even**
**ለማኒ** lemani ***(adj.)*** **mendicant**
**ለማኒ** lemani ***(n.)*** **beggar**
**ለማሽ** lemash ***(adj.)*** **lank**
**ለማዳ እንስሳ** lemada enssa ***(adj.)*** **tame**
**ለምለም** lemlem ***(adj.)*** **lush**
**ለምለም** lemlem ***(adj.)*** **verdant**
**ለምባእ** lemba'è ***(n.)*** **flab**
**ለምባጥ** lembaẗ ***(adj.)*** **floppy**
**ለሞዕንቲ** lemoanti ***(adv. )*** **today**
**ለሞዓንቲ ምሸት** lemoanti mshet ***(adv. )*** **tonight**
**ለቀቀ** leqeqe ***(v.)*** **release**
**ለቆታ** leqota ***(n. )*** **pod**
**ለቓም ፊደል** lebeda ***(n.)*** **epidemic**
**ለቐቐ** leq̈am fidel ***(n.)*** **compositor**
**ለቖታ-ፍረ** leq̈eq̈e ***(v.)*** **enfranchise**
**ለበዳ** leq̈otafre ***(n.)*** **capsule**
**ለበዳ** lebeda ***(n.)*** **plague**
**ለበጠ** lebeẗe ***(v.i. )*** **galvanize**
**ለባም** lebam ***(adj.)*** **magnanimous**
**ለባም** lebam ***(adj.)*** **sage**
**ለባም** lebam ***(adj.)*** **sensible**
**ለኣኸ** le'ake ***(v.)*** **dispatch**
**ለኣኸ** le'ake ***(v.)*** **send**
**ለካሌካ** liekalieka ***(n.)*** **lolly**
**ለካቲት** lekatit ***(n.)*** **February**
**ለኾቶ** lekhoto ***(n.)*** **strop**
**ለወሰ** leweye ***(v.)*** **bend**
**ለወየ** lewese ***(v.)*** **knead**
**ለወጠ** lewete ***(v.)*** **change**
**ለወጠ** lewete ***(v.)*** **shift**
**ለወጠ** lewete ***(v.)*** **transform**
**ለወጠ** lewete ***(v.)*** **transmute**
**ለወጠ** leweẗe ***(v.)*** **commute**
**ለወጠ** leweẗe ***(v.)*** **swap**
**ለውጢ ኣልቦነት** lewẗe albonet ***(n.)*** **monotony**
**ለዉጢ ገበረ** lewẗi gebere ***(v.)*** **customize**
**ለዋህ** lewah ***(adj.)*** **benign**
**ለዓለ** le'äle ***(v.)*** **heighten**
**ለዓት** le'ät ***(n.)*** **haft**
**ለዓት** le'ät ***(n.)*** **knob**
**ለዘየ** lezeye ***(v.)*** **slobber**
**ለይቲ** leyti ***(n. )*** **night**
**ለገመ** legeme ***(v.)*** **shirk**
**ለገበ** legebe ***(v.)*** **darn**
**ለገሰ** legese ***(v.)*** **donate**
**ለገሰ** legese ***(v.)*** **vouchsafe**
**ለጋሚ** legami ***(adj.)*** **grudging**
**ለጋሲ** legasi ***(n.)*** **donor**
**ለጋስ** legas ***(adj.)*** **generous**
**ለጋስ** legas ***(adj.)*** **lavish**
**ለጋስ** legas ***(adj.)*** **munificent**
**ለጋስ** legas ***(adj.)*** **bountiful**
**ለጠፈ** letefe ***(n.)*** **paste**
**ለጥ ዝበለ** leẗ zbele ***(n.)*** **expanse**
**ለፍለፈ** leflefe ***(v.t. )*** **gabble**
**ለፍለፈ** leflefe ***(v.)*** **jabber**
**ለፍላፊ** leflefi ***(adj.)*** **talkative**
**ለፍላፊ** leflafi ***(n. )*** **magpie**
**ለፍዐ** lef'ë ***(v.)*** **moil**

# ሉ

**ሉል** lul ***(n. )*** **pearl**
**ሉዑል በዓል ስልጣን** lu'el be'al sltan ***(adj.)*** **magisterial**
**ሉዝ** luz ***(n.)*** **almond**

# ሊ

ሊሊ lili *(n. )* **lily**
ሊላ lila *(n. )* **lilac**
ሊላ lila *(n.)* **violet**
ሊላ lila *(n. )* **purple**
ሊሎ lilo *(n. )* **kite**
ሊሞዚን limozin *(n.)* **limousine**
ሊቀ መላእክት liqe mela'èkt *(n.)* **archangel**
ሊቀ-ጳጳሳት liqeṕaṕasat *(n.)* **archbishop**
ሊቀ ፓፓስ liqe papas *(n.)* **primate**
ሊቅ liq *(n.)* **intellect**
ሊብራ lbra *(n.)* **Libra**
ሊትሮ litro *(n. )* **litre**
ሊቺ lichi *(n.)* **lychee**
ሊኖ lino *(n.)* **linen**
ሊኬቶ likieto *(n.)* **padlock**
ሊግ lig *(n. )* **league**
ሊፍት lift *(n.)* **windlass**

# ላ

ላህለሀ lahle-he *(v.i)* **gasp**
ላህመት lahmet *(n.)* **cream**
ላሕሚ laḧmi *(n.)* **cow**
ላህማም lahmam *(adj.)* **purblind**
ላህዘዝ በለ lahzez bele *(v.)* **loll**
ላህዛዝ lahzaz *(adj.)* **vapid**
ላህዛዝ lahezaz' *(adj.)* **clumsy**
ላህጃ lahja *(n.)* **dialect**
ላህጃም lahjam *(n.)* **simpleton**
ላሕለሐ laĥleĥe *(v.)* **fray**
ላሕታት lmu'e meriet *(n. )* **oasis**
ላሙዕ መሬት laḥtat *(adj. )* **hoarse**
ላማ lama *(n.)* **blade**
ላማ lama *(n.)* **razor**
ላምባ lamba *(n. )* **kerosene**
ላምባ lamba *(n.)* **paraffin**
ላምባዲና lampadina *(n.)* **flashlight**
ላምብሬታ lambrieta *(n. )* **scooter**
ላምፖነ lampone *(n.)* **raspberry**
ላርቫ larva *(n.)* **larva**
ላሳኛ lasagna *(n.)* **lasagne**
ላቂባ መስመር laqeeba mesmer *(n.)* **by-line**
ላንቃ lanqa *(n.)* **larynx**
ላቲትዩድ latityud *(n. )* **latitude**
ላንጋላንጋ langalanga *(adj.)* **equivocal**
ላዕለዋይ la'eleway *(adj.)* **supreme**
ላዕለዋይ la'eleway *(adj.)* **upper**
ላዕለዋይ laëleway *(adj.)* **premier**
ላዕለዋይ ቤት ፍርዲ la'eleway beet frdi *(n.)* **Chancery**
ላዕለዋይ ቀሺ laëleway qeshi *(n.)* **prelate**
ላዕለዋይ ደብሪ መርከብ la'ëleway debri merkeb *(n.)* **deck**
ላዕሊ la'eli *(adv. )* **up**
ላዕሊ la'ëli *(adj. )* **high**
ላውሮ lawro *(n.)* **laurel**
ላዛ ዘይብሉ laza zeyblu *(adj.)* **bland**
ላጉን lagun *(n. )* **lagoon**
ላግፂ lagtsi *(n. )* **ridicule**
ላግፂ lagxi *(n.)* **mockery**
ላግጺ lagxi *(n.)* **burlesque**
ላግፂ lagtzi *(n.)* **hoax**
ላፀየ latseye *(v.)* **shave**
ላቫ lava *(n.)* **lava**
ላቫንዳ lavanda *(n.)* **lavender**
ሌባ leba *(n. )* **robber**

# ል

ልሕላሐ lḣlaḣe *(n.)* **abrasion**
ልሒኹ lhiku *(v.)* **percolate**
ልመና lmena *(n.)* **request**
ልሙስ lmus *(n.)* **cripple**
ልሙዕ lmu'ë *(adj.)* **fertile**
ልሙዕነት lmu'ënet *(n.)* **fertility**
ልሙዳዊ lmudawi *(adv.)* **ordinarily**
ልሙድ lmud *(adj.)* **ordinary**
ልሙድ lmud *(adj.)* **accustomed**
ልሙድ lmud *(adj.)* **commonplace**
ልሙድ lmud *(adj.)* **customary**
ልሙድ lmud *(adj.)* **familiar**
ልሙድ lmud *(adj.)* **usual**
ልሙድ lmud *(adj.)* **workaday**
ልሙድ ምግቢ lmud mgbi *(n.)* **diet**
ልሙድነት lmudnet *(n.)* **prevalence**
ልሙድ ኮነ lmud kone *(v.)* **prevail**
ልሙፀ lmuts *(adj.)* **sleek**
ልሙፀ lmuts *(adj.)* **slick**
ልሙፀ lmuts *(adj.)* **smooth**
ልሙፀ lmutz *(adj.)* **glossy**
ልማድ le-mad *(n.)* **habit**
ልማድ lmad *(n.)* **routine**
ልማድ lmad *(adj.)* **wont**
ልምሉም lmlum *(adj.)* **supple**
ልምምድ lmmd *(n.)* **exercise**
ልምምድ lmmd *(n.)* **rehearsal**
ልምዲ lmdi *(n.)* **custom**
ልምዲ lmdi *(n.)* **experience**
ልምዲ lmdi *(n. )* **norm**
ልሳናዊ lsanawi *(n. )* **lingual**
ልሳናዊ lsanawi *(adj.)* **linguistic**
ልስሉስ lslus *(adj.)* **flaccid**
ልስሉስ lslus *(adj.)* **lax**
ልስሉስ lslus *(adj.)* **silky**
ልስሉስ lslus *(adj.)* **soft**
ልስሉስ ክፋል ስኒ lslus kfal sni *(n.)* **pulp**
ልቀት lket *(n.)* **removal**
ልቃሕ lqah *(n.)* **credit**
ልቃሕ ትሕጃ lqaḣ tḣja *(n.)* **mortgage**
ልቓሕ lqhah *(n.)* **loan**
ልቓሕ lqah *(n.)* **overdraft**
ልበ ምሉእ lbe mlu'e *(adj.)* **ebullient**
ልቡጥ lbuẗnet *(n.)* **moderation**
ልቡጥነት lbu *(adj.)* **warm**
ልቢ lebi *(n. )* **heart**
ልቢ ምንጥልጣል lbi mntltal *(n. )* **suspense**
ልቢ ሰቐለ lbi seqele *(n.)* **thrill**
ልቢ ወለድ lbi weled *(n.)* **fiction**
ልቢ ዝነክእ lbiznekea *(adj.)* **touching**
ልባዊ lebawi *(adj. )* **heartfelt**
ልባዊ lebawi *(adj. )* **hearty**
ልባዊ lbawi *(adj.)* **cordial**
ልብላዕ ዓሳ lblaa asa *(n.)* **trout**
ልብምና lbmna *(n. )* **sagacity**
ልብሲ lbsi *(n.)* **attire**
ልብሲ lbsi *(n.)* **vestment**
ልብስታት ጎልፎ lbstat golfo *(n.)* **hosiery**
ልብ ወለዳዊ lbe weledawi *(adj.)* **factitious**
ልብጠት lbṭet *(n.)* **warmth**
ልኡላን l'ulan *(n.)* **nobility**
ልኡኻት l'ukat *(n.)* **delegation**
ልኡኽ l'uk *(n.)* **overseer**
ልኡኽ l'uk *(n.)* **agent**
ልኡኽ l'uk *(n.)* **delegate**
ልኡኽ l'uḱ *(n.)* **ambassador**
ልኡኽ l'uḱ *(n.)* **emissary**
ልኡኽ l'uḱ *(n.)* **envoy**
ልኡኽ l'uḱ *(n.)* **errand**
ልክዕ lkë *(adj.)* **precise**

**ልክዕ** lk'ë ***(adj.)* accurate**
**ልክዕ** lk'ë ***(adj.)* just**
**ልክዕ** lk'ë ***(adj.)* right**
**ልክዕ** lk'ë ***(adj.)* correct**
**ልክዕነት** lkënet ***(n. )* precision**
**ልክዕነት** lk'ënet ***(n.)* authenticity**
**ልኹፍ** lkuf ***(adj.)* rabid**
**ልኻይ** lkay ***(n.)* ointment**
**ልኽስክስ** lksks ***(adj.)* promiscuous**
**ልኽፈተ እሳት** lkfete esat ***(n.)* pyromania**
**ልዓት-ሴፍ** le-a-t seef ***(n.)* hilt**
**ልስሉስ ቆብዕ** lslus qob'ë ***(n.)* bonnet**
**ልዕለ ሓያል** l'ele ȟayal ***(n.)* superpower**
**ልዕለ ባህርያዊ** l'elebahryawi ***(adj.)* uncanny**
**ልዕለ ሰብኣዊ** l'ele seb'awi ***(adj.)* superhuman**
**ልዕለ ተፈጥሮኣዊ** l'ele tefetro'awi ***(adj.)* supernatural**
**ልዕለ ዉራቕ** l'ele wuraqhe ***(adj.)* superscript**
**ልዕለ ድምፃዊ** l'ele dmxawi ***(adj.)* supersonic**
**ልዕሊ መጠን ምጥቃም** l'eli meten mtqam ***(v.)* overdo**
**ልዕሊ ዓቕን ሚዛን ሰብነት** leli aqn mizan sebnet ***(n.)* obesity**
**ልዑላውነት** l'ulawnet ***(n.)* sovereignty**
**ልዑል** l'ul ***(adj.)* superior**
**ልዑል** l'ul ***(v.)* outclass**
**ልዑል** l'ül ***(adj.)* extreme**
**ልዑልነት** l'ülnet ***(n. )* Highness**
**ልዕልና** l'elna' ***(n.)* superiority**
**ልዕልና** l'elna' ***(n.)* supremacy**
**ልዕል ዝበለ** lel zbele ***(n.)* perch**
**ልዕበት** l'ëbet ***(n.)* adaptation**
**ልውጢ-ስም** lwïesm ***(n.)* alias**
**ልውጠት** lwïet ***(n. )* metamorphosis**
**ልውጠት** lwïet ***(n.)* mutation**
**ልዙብ** lzub ***(adj.)* affable**
**ልዙብ** lzub ***(adj.)* unassuming**
**ልዝብ** lzb ***(n.)* negotiation**
**ልደት** ldet ***(n.)* nativity**
**ልደት** ldet ***(n.)* Xmas**
**ልዳት** ldat ***(n.)* sill**
**ልግስነት** lgsnet ***(n.)* altruism**
**ልግስና** legesena ***(n.)* generosity**
**ልጓም** lgwam ***(n.)* brake**
**ልጓም** lgwam ***(n.)* bridle**

## ሎ

**ሎብስተር** lobster ***(n.)* lobster**
**ሎተሪ** loteri ***(n. )* lottery**
**ሎንጊ** longi ***(n.)* slush**
**ሎንጊቱድ** longitud ***(n.)* longitude**
**ሎጋሪዝም** logarizm ***(n. )* logarithm**

## ሐ

**ሐራይ** heray ***(adj.)* okay**
**ሑጉስ** hugus ***(adj.)* lively**
**ሑጻ** ḥutsa ***(n.)* grit**
**ሑፃ** hutsa ***(n. )* sand**

## ሒ

**ሒላብ** ȟilab ***(n.)*** **nappy**
**ሒሳባዊ** ȟisabawi ***(adj.)*** **mathematical**
**ሒሳብ** ȟisab ***(n. )*** **mathematics**
**ሒሹ** hishu ***(v.)*** **transcend**
**ሒቅታ** hiqta ***(n. )*** **hiccup**
**ሒእሒእታ** ȟi'eȟi'eta ***(n.)*** **snigger**
**ሒዝካዮ እትውልድ ኽእለት** hizkayo etwled kh'elet ***(adj.)*** **innate**
**ሒደት** hidet ***(adj.)*** **scanty**
**ሒደት** ȟidet ***(adj.)*** **some**

# ሓ

**ሓለቃ ሓምሳ** haleqa hamsa ***(n.)*** **sergeant**
**ሓለቃ መርከብ** ȟaleka merkeb ***(n. )*** **skipper**
**ሓልቃም** halqam ***(adj.)*** **scrawny**
**ሓለቃ ዓሰርተ** ȟleqa 'äserte ***(n.)*** **corporal**
**ሓለቃ ተምሃሮ** ȟaleqa temharo ***(n.)*** **monitor**
**ሓለቓ** ȟaleq̈a ***(n.)*** **boss**
**ሓለቓ** ȟaleq̈a ***(n.)*** **foreman**
**ሓለቓ ደብሪ** haleqa debri ***(n.)*** **dean**
**ሓለፈ** ĥalefe ***(v.)*** **elapse**
**ሓለፋ** ĥalefa ***(n. )*** **privilege**
**ሓላለኸ** ĥalaleke ***(v. t)*** **entangle**
**ሓላለኸ** ȟalaleḱe ***(v.)*** **complicate**
**ሓላሚ** ȟalami ***(adj.)*** **fanciful**
**ሓላኒ** ȟalani ***(n.)*** **aspirant**
**ሓላዊ** halawi ***(n. )*** **guardian**
**ሓላዊ** ȟalawi ***(n.)*** **invigilator**
**ሓላዊ** ȟalawi ***(n.)*** **keeper**
**ሓለወ** halewe ***(v.)*** **tend**
**ሓለወ** ȟalewe ***(adj.)*** **invigilate**
**ሓለወ** ȟalewe ***(v.)*** **keep**
**ሓለዋ** halewa ***(n. )*** **indemnity**
**ሓለዋ** ḥalewa ***(n.)*** **ward**
**ሓለዋ** ḥalewa ***(n. )*** **vigil**
**ሓለዋ ተፈጥሮ** haalewa tefetero ***(n.)*** **conservation**
**ሓለዋ ፅርየት** halewa tsryet ***(n.)*** **sanitation**
**ሓለዋት** halewat ***(n. )*** **toffee**
**ሓለንጊ** halengi ***(n.)*** **scourge**
**ሓለንጋይ** ȟalengag ***(adj.)*** **svelte**
**ሓላዊ ማዕጾ** ḥalawi-ma'ëxo ***(n.)*** **goalkeeper**
**ሓላዊ ቤተ-መፃሕፍቲ** halwi biete-metsahft ***(n. )*** **librarian**
**ሓላዊ ነብሲ** ȟalawi nebsi ***(n)*** **bodyguard**
**ሓላዊ ገረብ** halwi gereb ***(n. )*** **ranger**
**ሓላፊ** halafi ***(n.)*** **chief**
**ሓላፊ** halafi ***(n.)*** **director**
**ሓላፊ** ĥalafi ***(n. )*** **functionary**
**ሓላፊ** ḥalafi ***(n. )*** **warden**
**ሓላፍነት** ĥalafnet ***(n.)*** **duty**
**ሓላፍነት** ĥalafnet ***(n.)*** **responsibility**
**ሓላፍነት ሃበ** ĥalafnet habe ***(v.)*** **entrust**
**ሓላፍነት ዘይስምዖ** ȟalafnet zeysm'ö ***(adj.)*** **irresponsible**
**ሓልሓሊፉ** halhalifu ***(adj.)*** **occasional**
**ሓልሓሊፉ** halhalifu ***(adv.)*** **occasionally**
**ሓልዮተኛ** ĥalyotegna ***(adj.)*** **dutiful**
**ሓልዮት** ȟalyot ***(n.)*** **solicitude**
**ሓሓ** ĥaĥa ***(n.)*** **pelican**
**ሓሓሊፉ** hahalifu ***(adj.)*** **infrequent**
**ሓሓሊፉ ዝርአ** ȟaȟalifu zr'e ***(adj.)*** **sporadic**
**ሓሓሊፍ ዝድጋገም** hahalifu zdegagem ***(adj.)*** **intermittent**
**ሓመሰ** ȟamese ***(v.)*** **swim**

ሓመዳይ hameday *(adj.)* **drab**
ሓመድ ḧamed *(n.)* **soil**
ሓሙስ hamus *(n.)* **Thursday**
ሓሙኽሽታይ ḥamuḱshtay *(n. )* **grey**
ሓምበበ hambebe *(v.)* **whiz**
ሓምባሲ ḧambasi *(adj.)* **natant**
ሓምሳ ḧamsa *(adj. & n.)* **fifty**
ሓምሻሺ ḧamshashi *(adj.)* **smashing**
ሓምሸሸ ḧamsheshe *(v.)* **smash**
ሓሙሽተ ĥamushte *(adj. & n.)* **five**
ሓሙሽተ ማንታ hamušte manta *(n.)* **Quinn**
ሓማሲ ḧamasi *(n.)* **swimmer**
ሓማት ḧamat *(n.)* **mother-in-law**
ሓሜት ḥameet *(n. )* **gossip**
ሓምለ ḧamle *(n.)* **July**
ሓምሊ ዝቐለቡ ḧamli zq̈elebu *(n.)* **vegan**
ሓምሓም ḥamḥam *(n. )* **gourd**
ሓምሾኽ hamxok *(v.)* **scrunch**
ሓምተለ ḧamtele *(v.)* **crumple**
ሓሞት hamot *(n.)* **pancreas**
ሓሞት ḧamot *(n.)* **bile**
ሓሞኩሽቲ ḧamokushti *(n.)* **ash**
ሓሞኹሽቲ ዝዕቆረሉ hamokshti zeqorelu *(n.)* **urn**
ሓረረ harere *(v.)* **char**
ሓረረ harere *(v.)* **sear**
ሓረሰ ḧarese *(v.)* **cultivate**
ሓረስታይ ĥarestay *(n.)* **farmer**
ሓረስታይ harestay *(n.)* **tiller**
ሓረስታይ ĥarestay *(n. )* **peasant**
ሓረስታይ ḧarestay *(n.)* **ploughman**
ሓረስቶት ĥarestot *(n. )* **peasantry**
ሓረቀ ĥareqe *(v.)* **resent**
ሓረደ ḧarede *(v.)* **cut**
ሓረግ hareg *(n.)* **phrase**
ሓረግ ḧareg *(n.)* **creeper**
ሓረጣ hareta *(n.)* **usury**
ሓሪም ḥarim *(n.)* **harem**
ሓራቕ ḧaraq̈ *(adj.)* **irate**
ሓራቕ ḧaraq̈ *(adj.)* **irritable**
ሓራቕ ḥaraq̈ *(adj.)* **waspish**
ሓራጅ ḧaraĵ *(n.)* **auction**
ሓራ ኣዉፀአ ĥara awwxe'e *(v. t)* **emancipate**
ሓርማዝ ĥarmaz *(n.)* **elephant**
ሓርሽ ĥarše *(n. )* **rhinoceros**
ሓርበኛ ḧrbegna *(n.)* **militant**
ሓርበኛ harbena *(n.)* **patriot**
ሓርበኛነት harbenanet *(n.)* **patriotism**
ሓርበኛዊ harbenawi *(adj.)* **patriotic**
ሓርነኽ harnekhe *(n.)* **snore**
ሓርናኺ harnakhi *(adj.)* **stertorous**
ሓርአ ĥar'e *(v.)* **defecate**
ሓርገፀ ḧargex *(n.)* **crocodile**
ሓርገፅ ḧargex *(n.)* **alligator**
ሓርፈፈ ĥarfefe *(v.)* **ruffle**
ሓርፋፍ harfaf *(adj.)* **jagged**
ሓርፋፍ ĥarfaf *(adj.)* **rough**
ሓርፋፍ ĥarfaf *(adj.)* **rugged**
ሓሰማ ḧasema *(n.)* **swine**
ሓሰረ ĥasere *(v.)* **depreciate**
ሓሰር ḥaser *(n. )* **hay**
ሓሰር ḧaser *(n. )* **straw**
ሓሰበ haseb *(v.)* **contemplate**
ሓሰበ hasebe *(v.)* **consider**
ሓሰበ hasebe *(v.)* **think**
ሓሰበ ḧasebe *(v.)* **mean**
ሓሳቢ ha'sabi *(adj.)* **considerate**
ሓሳቢ hasbi *(adj.)* **thoughtful**
ሓሳቢ hasabi *(n.)* **thinker**
ሓሳባት hasabat *(n. )* **perspective**
ሓሳባዊ hasabawi *(adj.)* **imaginary**
ሓሳብ ḧsab *(n.)* **proposal**

ሓሳብ ḧsab ***(n.)*** **proposition**
ሓሳብ ḥasab ***(n.)*** **idea**
ሓሳብ hasab ***(n.)*** **contemplation**
ሓሳብ ምቕራብ ḧsab mq̈rab ***(v.)*** **propose**
ሓሳብ ከለሰ hasab kelese ***(v.)*** **theorize**
ሓሳብ ዘመንጪ hasab zemenchi ***(n.)*** **theorist**
ሓሳብ ዝገልፅ ĥasab zgelx ***(adj.)*** **expressive**
ሓሰኻ haseka ***(n.)*** **insect**
ሓሰኻ haseka ***(n. )*** **worm**
ሓሰኻ ሃሪ ĥaseka hari ***(n.)*** **silkworm**
ሓሰኽሰኽ በለ haseksek bele ***(v.)*** **teem**
ሓሰወ hasewe ***(v.)*** **lie**
ሓሰወ hasewe ***(v.)*** **sneak**
ሓሳዊ hasawi ***(n. )*** **liar**
ሓሶት ĥasot ***(n.)*** **deceit**
ሓሶት ḧasot ***(adj.)*** **spurious**
ሓሶት ĥasot ***(adj.)*** **false**
ሓሶትነት ĥasotnet ***(n.)*** **falsehood**
ሓሸማ hashema ***(n. )*** **pig**
ሓሻሺ ĥashashi ***(adj.)*** **extravagant**
ሓሻሺ ḧashashi ***(n.)*** **spendthrift**
ሓሽሽ hshsh ***(n. )*** **opium**
ሓሸዋማ hashewama ***(adj.)*** **sandy**
ሓቀኛ hakegna ***(adj.)*** **truthful**
ሓቀኛ ḥaqeña ***(adj.)*** **veritable**
ሓቀኛ ḧaqeṅa ***(adj.)*** **authentic**
ሓቀኛ ḧaqeṅa ***(adj.)*** **bona fide**
ሓቀኛ ĥakegna ***(adj.)*** **sincere**
ሓቂ haki ***(n.)*** **truth**
ሓቂ haki ***(v.)*** **undeceive**
ሓቂ መሰልነት ḥaqi meselne ***(n.)*** **verisimilitude**
ሓቂ መሳሊ ḧaqi mesali ***(adj.)*** **specious**
ሓቂ ዘይብሉ ḧaqi zeyblu ***(adj.)*** **bogus**
ሓቂዩ በለ haqiyu bele ***(v.)*** **claim**
ሓቃቂ ḧaqhaqi ***(adj.)*** **soluble**
ሓቃቅነት ḧaqhaqnet ***(n.)*** **solubility**
ሓቐኛ ĥaqegna ***(adj.)*** **genuine**
ሓቐቐ ĥaqeqe ***(v.)*** **digest**
ሓቐቐ ĥaqeqe ***(v. t)*** **dissolve**
ሓቅነት ĥaqnet ***(n. )*** **realism**
ሓቅነት ĥaqnet ***(n.)*** **reality**
ሓቅነት ḧaqnet ***(n.)*** **probity**
ሓቅነት ḥaqnet ***(n. )*** **veracity**
ሓቅነት ḥaqnet ***(n.)*** **verity**
ሓቅነት ኣረጋገጸ ḥaqnet 'aregagexe ***(v.)*** **vindicate**
ሓቅነታዊ ĥaqnetawi ***(adj.)*** **realistic**
ሓቆነ haqone ***(v.)*** **churn**
ሓቆነ haqone ***(v.)*** **shake**
ሓቆፈ ḧaqofe ***(v.)*** **cuddle**
ሓቆፈ ḧaqofe ***(v.)*** **nestle**
ሓቈነ ḧaq̈wene ***(v.)*** **jiggle**
ሓቖፈ ḧaq̈ofe ***(v.)*** **enfold**
ሓቖፈ haqo-fe ***(v.)*** **hug**
ሓቖፈ ĥaqofe ***(v.)*** **embrace**
ሓበለ ḥabele ***(v.)*** **wangle**
ሓበላ habela ***(n.)*** **cataract**
ሓበረ habere ***(v.)*** **imply**
ሓበረ habere ***(v.)*** **inform**
ሓበረ ḧabere ***(v.)*** **bode**
ሓበረ ḧabere ***(v.)*** **suggest**
ሓበራዊ መንበሪ ህንፃ haberawi menberi hintsa ***(n.)*** **condominium**
ሓበራዊ ምርድዳእ haberawi merederaoo ***(n.)*** **consensus**
ሓበሬታ habereeta ***(n.)*** **suggestion**
ሓበሬታ ĥabereta ***(n.)*** **data**
ሓበሬታ ĥabereta ***(n.)*** **datum**
ሓበሬታ ḧberieta ***(n.)*** **placard**

ሓበሬታ haberieta ***(n.)* information**
ሓበሬታ ምሕታት haberieta mhtat ***(v.)* inquire**
ሓበሬታ ረኸበ ȟabereeta rekebe ***(v.)* elicit**
ሓበሬታዊ haberietawi ***(adj.)* informative**
ሓበን ȟaben ***(n.)* pride**
ሓበጠ ȟabeẗe ***(v.)* swell**
ሓበጀራይ ȟabejeray ***(adj.)* motley**
ሓበጀራይ ȟabeĵeray ***(adj.)* brindle**
ሓቢርካ ምንባር habireka menebare ***(n.)* coexistence**
ሓቢ ጸሊም ȟabi xelim ***(n. )* jasmine**
ሓባሊ ȟabali ***(n.)* smoothie**
ሓባሪ habari ***(n.)* informer**
ሓባሪ habari ***(adj.)* suggestive**
ሓባሪ ĥabari ***(n.)* dial**
ሓባሪ ḥabari ***(n. )* guide**
ሓባሪ መፅሓፍ habari metsehaf ***(n.)* guidebook**
ሓባ'ሪ ተንሰፋፋይ ȟabari tensefafay ***(n.)* buoy**
ሓባራዊ ȟabarawi ***(adj.)* common**
ሓባር ንፋስ ḥabar nfas ***(n.)* vane**
ሓባሲ habasi ***(n. )* jailer**
ሓባጠ ጎባጥ ቦታ habate gobat bota ***(n.)* tack**
ሓባጥ habat ***(adj.)* puffy**
ሓባጥ ጎባጥ ĥabaẗ gobaẗ ***(adj.)* gnarled**
ሓብለት ȟablet ***(n. )* necklet**
ሓብሓብ ȟabȟab ***(n.)* melon**
ሓብአ habe ***(v.)* withhold**
ሓብአ ȟab'e ***(v.)* conceal**
ሓብአ ȟab'e ***(v.)* stash**
ሓብአ ḥab'e ***(v.t)* hide**
ሓቦ ȟabo ***(n.)* mettle**
ሓቦ ȟabo ***(n. )* morale**
ሓቦ ȟabo ***(n.)* stamina**
ሓቦኛ ȟabogna ***(n.)* mettlesome**
ሓተላ ሓፂን ĥatela ĥatsin ***(n.)* slag**
ሓተመ ȟateme ***(v.)* print**
ሓተተ ĥatete ***(v.)* debrief**
ሓተተ ĥatete ***(v.)* enquire**
ሓተተ ȟatete ***(v.)* interrogate**
ሓተተ ȟatete ***(v.)* ask**
ሓተታ ȟateta ***(n.)* commentary**
ሓተታ ኣቅራቢ ȟateta aqrabi ***(n.)* commentator**
ሓታል ĥatal ***(adj.)* slushy**
ሓታሚት ȟatamit ***(n.)* printer**
ሓትኖ ȟatno ***(n.)* aunt**
ሓነቐ haneqe ***(v.)* choke**
ሓነቐ haneqe ***(v.)* throttle**
ሓነቐ ȟaneqe ***(v.)* strangle**
ሓናኽ hanak ***(adj.)* timid**
ሓናኽ ĥanak ***(adj.)* prudent**
ሓንከሰ hankese ***(v.)* limp**
ሓንካስ ȟankas ***(adj.)* lame**
ሓንኮለ ĥankole ***(v.)* disrupt**
ሓንጎል ȟangol ***(n.)* brain**
ሓንጀ መንጂ ĥanjemenji ***(n. )* frill**
ሓንፈፀ ȟanfex ***(n. )* mulatto**
ሓከመ ḥakeme ***(v.)* heal**
ሓኪም hakim ***(n.)* therapist**
ሓኪም ĥakim ***(n.)* doctor**
ሓኪም ĥakim ***(n.)* physician**
ሓኪም ȟakim ***(n.)* medic**
ሓኪም ኣእምሮ ȟakim aèmro ***(n. )* psychiatrist**
ሓኮረ hakore ***(v.)* creep**
ሓኳሪ እምባ ȟaḱwari emba ***(n.)* mountaineer**
ሓኸለ hakhele ***(n.)* sternum**
ሓወልቲ hawelti ***(n.)* colossus**
ሓወልቲ ĥawelti ***(n.)* effigy**

**ሓወልቲ** ȟawelti *(n.)* **monument**
**ሓወልቲ** ȟawelti *(n. )* **statue**
**ሓወልታዊ** ȟaweltawi *(adj.)* **statuesque**
**ሓወልትታት** ȟawelt'tat *(n.)* **statuary**
**ሓወሰ** ȟawese *(n.)* **meld**
**ሓወሰ** ȟawese *(v.)* **mix**
**ሓወየ** ȟaweye *(v.)* **recuperate**
**ሓወየ** ȟaweye *(v.)* **revive**
**ሓዊ ምቅፅፃል** hawi mktstsal *(n.)* **tinder**
**ሓዊ ዝመስል** ȟawi zmesl *(adj.)* **fiery**
**ሓዋላ** ȟawala *(n.)* **remittance**
**ሓዋወሰ** ȟawawese *(v.)* **obfuscate**
**ሓዋወሰ** hawawese *(v.)* **scramble**
**ሓዋወሰ** ȟawawese *(v. t)* **blend**
**ሓዋወሰ** ȟawawese *(adj.)* **wonted**
**ሓው** ȟaw *(n.)* **brother**
**ሓውለለ** ȟawlele *(v.)* **squint**
**ሓውሲ** ȟawsi *(adv. )* **somewhat**
**ሓውሲ ትሮፒካዊ** ȟawsi tropikawi *(adj.)* **subtropical**
**ሓዘ** ḥaze *(v.t)* **hold**
**ሓዘ** haze *(v.)* **seize**
**ሓዘ** ȟaze *(v.)* **preoccupy**
**ሓዘ** ḥaze *(v.t)* **handle**
**ሓዘ** haze' *(v.t.)* **contain**
**ሓዘ** ȟaze *(v.)* **comprise**
**ሓዘነ** ȟazene *(v.)* **mourn**
**ሓዘን** ȟazen *(n.)* **doldrums**
**ሓዘን** ȟazen *(n.)* **bereavement**
**ሓዘን** ȟazen *(n.)* **heartbreak**
**ሓዘን** ȟazen *(n.)* **sorrow**
**ሓዘን ምግላፅ** hazen mglats *(n.)* **lament**
**ሓዘንተኛ** ȟazentegna *(n. )* **mourner**
**ሓዘንተኛ** ȟazentegna *(n.)* **mourning**
**ሓዘ** haze *(v.)* **occupy**
**ሐዚታት** hezitat *(adv. )* **lately**
**ሓየለ** ȟayele *(v.)* **strengthen**
**ሓየረ** ȟayere *(v.)* **banish**
**ሓየከ** hayyeke *(v.)* **chew**
**ሓየኸ** ȟayeke *(v.)* **masticate**
**ሓያል** ȟayal *(adj.)* **energetic**
**ሓያል** ȟayal *(adj.)* **fierce**
**ሓያል** ȟayal *(adj.)* **forceful**
**ሓያል** ȟayal *(adj.)* **mighty**
**ሓያል** ȟayal *(adj.)* **swingeing**
**ሓያል** ȟeyal *(adj.)* **powerful**
**ሓያሎ** hyalo *(adj. & pron.)* **several**
**ሓይሊ** ȟyli *(n.)* **power**
**ሓይሊ** ȟayli *(n.)* **force**
**ሓይሊ** ȟayli *(n.)* **strength**
**ሓይሊ ሰብ** hayli seb *(n.)* **manpower**
**ሓይሊ ስሕበት** ȟayli sḥbet *(n.)* **gravitation**
**ሓይሊ ባሕሪ** ȟayli baȟri *(n.)* **navy**
**ሓይሊ ቀነሰ** ȟayli qenese *(v.)* **disempower**
**ሓይሊ ፈረስ** ḥayli feres *(n.)* **horsepower**
**ሓደ** ȟade *(adj.)* **an**
**ሓደ** hade *(n. & adj.)* **one**
**ሓደ ምግባር** hade megbar *(v.)* **unify**
**ሓደ ምኳን** hade mekuan *(v.)* **unite**
**ሓደ ሰብ** hade seb *(pron. )* **someone**
**ሓደ ሺሕ ኪሎ ግራም** hade shih kilogram *(n.)* **tonne**
**ሓደ ወገን** hade wegen *(adj.)* **unilateral**
**ሓደ ዝእዋኑ** ȟade z'ewanu *(adj.)* **synchronous**
**ሓደ ዝደርቡ ገዛ** ȟade zderbu geza *(n.)* **bungalow**
**ሓደገ** ȟadega *(v.)* **retract**
**ሓደገ** hadege *(v.t. )* **leave**
**ሓደገ** ȟadege *(v.)* **forgo**

**ሓደገ** ĥadege ***(v.)*** **forsake**
**ሓደገ** ĥadege ***(v.)*** **quit**
**ሓደገኛ** ĥaadegegna ***(adj.)*** **risky**
**ሓደገኛ** ĥadegegna ***(adj.)*** **dangerous**
**ሓደገኛ** h'degegna ***(adj.)*** **malignant**
**ሓደገኛ** hadegena ***(adj.)*** **perilous**
**ሓደገ'ኛ** ḥadegeña ***(adj.)*** **virulent**
**ሓደገ'ኛ** ĥadegeǹa ***(adj.)*** **adventurous**
**ሓደጋ** hadega ***(n.)*** **peril**
**ሓደጋ** ĥadega ***(n.)*** **danger**
**ሓደጋ** ĥadega ***(n.)*** **emergency**
**ሓደጋ** ĥadega ***(n. )*** **risk**
**ሓደጋ** ḥadega ***(n.)*** **hazard**
**ሓደጋ** ĥadega ***(n.)*** **accident**
**ሓደ ግዜ** hade gizie ***(adv.)*** **once**
**ሓዲድ** ĥadid ***(n.)*** **rail**
**ሓዳር** ĥadar ***(n.)*** **marriage**
**ሓዳሳይ** ĥadasay ***(n.)*** **reformer**
**ሓደ ዓይነት** hade aynet ***(adj.)*** **identical**
**ሓደ ድምፂ** hade demtsi ***(adj.)*** **unanimous**
**ሓዱሽ ኣማኒ** ĥadush amani ***(n.)*** **neophyte**
**ሓዱሽ ክላሲካዊ** ĥadush klasikawi ***(adj.)*** **neoclassical**
**ሓድነት** hadenet ***(n. )*** **unification**
**ሓድነት** hadenet ***(n. )*** **unison**
**ሓድነት** hadenet ***(n.)*** **unity**
**ሓድነት** hadnet ***(n.)*** **coalition**
**ሓድነት** ĥadnet ***(n. )*** **solidarity**
**ሓድነት** hadnet ***(n.)*** **oneness**
**ሓድ ቋንቋ ብካሊእ ቋንቋ ክፀሓፍ ከሎ** hade qnaqa bkalie qanqa ksehaf kelo ***(v.)*** **transliterate**
**ሓድሽ** ĥadsh ***(adj.)*** **new**
**ሓድሽ** ĥadsh ***(n. )*** **novelty**
**ሓጀር** ĥajer ***(n.)*** **ruby**
**ሓጀት** ĥajet ***(n.)*** **accessory**
**ሓገል** ĥagel ***(n.)*** **abscess**
**ሓገዘ** hageze ***(v.)*** **support**
**ሓገዘ** ḥageze ***(v.)*** **help**
**ሓገዘ** ĥageze ***(v.)*** **assist**
**ሓገዝ** ĥagez ***(n.)*** **assistance**
**ሓገዝ** ĥagez ***(n.)*** **backing**
**ሓገዝ** ĥagez ***(n.)*** **support**
**ሓገዝ ገንዘብ** ĥagez genzeb ***(n.)*** **subsidy**
**ሓገገ** ĥagege ***(v.)*** **enact**
**ሓጋያዊ** hagayawi ***(adj.)*** **wintry**
**ሓጋዚ** ĥagazi ***(adj.)*** **auxiliary**
**ሓጋዚ** ḥagazi ***(adj. )*** **helpful**
**ሓጋዚ ምሕቃቕ መግቢ** hagazi mhqaq megbi ***(adj.)*** **peptic**
**ሓጋዚ ኣልቦ** ḥagazi 'albo ***(adj. )*** **helpless**
**ሓጋይ** ĥagay ***(n.)*** **winter**
**ሓጎስ** hagos ***(n.)*** **whoop**
**ሓጎስ** ĥagos ***(n.)*** **gaiety**
**ሓጎደ** ĥagode ***(v.t)*** **forge**
**ሓጎፀጎፀ ኣበለ** ĥagwaxgwax 'abele ***(v.t. )*** **jolt**
**ሓጐስ** ḥagos ***(n.)*** **happiness**
**ሓጐስ** ĥagwas ***(n.)*** **jubilation**
**ሓጥያተኛ** ĥatyategna ***(n.)*** **sinner**
**ሓጥያት** ĥatyat ***(n.)*** **sin**
**ሓጥያት ዝመልኦ** ĥatyat zmel'o ***(adj.)*** **sinful**
**ሓጬጪ** ĥačači ***(adj.)*** **ironical**
**ሓጸረ** ĥaxere ***(v.)*** **bound**
**ሓጸበ** ḥaxebe ***(v.)*** **wash**
**ሓጻባይ** ḥaxabay ***(n. )*** **washer**
**ሓጺር ፅሁፍ** ĥaxir xĥuf ***(n.)*** **essay**
**ሓፁር** ĥaxur ***(n.)*** **fence**
**ሓጺር** ĥaxir ***(adj.)*** **brief**
**ሓጺርነት** ĥaxirnet ***(n.)*** **brevity**

ሓጺርን ብሩህን ȟaxirn bruhn *(adj.)* **concise**
ሓጺር መግለጺ ȟaxir meglexi *(n.)* **briefing**
ሓጺር ትረኻ haxir traka *(n. )* **parable**
ሓጺር ዕረፍቲ haxir erefti *(n.)* **pause**
ሓጺር ጽሑፍ ĥatsir ts'ĥuf *(n.)* **docket**
ሓፀበ ȟaxebe *(v.)* **swill**
ሓፀበ ĥatsebe *(v.)* **rinse**
ሓፀረ ĥaxere *(v.)* **encase**
ሓፁር ȟaxur *(n.)* **cordon**
ሓፂቡ አስታረረ hatzibu astarere *(v.)* **launder**
ሓፂር ȟaxir *(n.)* **compendium**
ሓፂር ኖቨል ȟaxir noveela *(n. )* **novelette**
ሓፂን ȟatsin *(n.)* **iron**
ሓፂር ĥatsir *(adj.)* **short**
ሓፂር ዘረባ ȟaxir zereba *(adj.)* **curt**
ሓፂር ግጥም ĥatsir gtmi *(n.)* **skirmish**
ሓፂር ፈተና ĥatsir fetena *(n.)* **quiz**
ሓፂርን ንፁርን hatsirn ntsurn *(adj.)* **succinct**
ሓፀበ hatsxebe *(v.)* **cleanse**
ሓፅቢ ĥatsbi *(n.)* **dam**
ሓፅቢ ĥatsbi *(n.)* **reservoir**
ሓፈረ hafere *(v.)* **inhibit**
ሓፈረ ȟafere *(v.)* **blush**
ሓፋር hafar *(adj.)* **sheepish**
ሓፋር hafar *(adj.)* **timorous**
ሓፋር ĥafar *(adj.)* **retiring**
ሓፋር ĥafar *(adj.)* **shy**
ሓፋር ȟafar *(adj.)* **coy**
ሓፋር ȟafar *(adj.)* **bashful**
ሓፈሰ ȟafese *(v.)* **condense**
ሓፈሻዊ ĥafeshawi *(adj.)* **general**
ሓፊስ ḥafis *(adj.)* **viscous**
ሓፊስ ḥafis *(adj.)* **viscid**
ሓፊስ ፈሳሲ ሹኮር hafis fesasi sukor *(n.)* **treacle**
ሓፋሽ ȟafash *(n.)* **commoner**
ሓፍቲ ĥaftawi *(adj.)* **sisterly**
ሓፍታዊ ĥafti *(n. )* **sister**
ሓፍ ኮፍ በለ ȟaf kof bele *(v.)* **bob**
ሓፍ ዝበለ ብርኪ ȟaf zbele brki *(n. )* **pinnacle**

# ሕ

ሕሉም ḥlum *(n.)* **Wally**
ሕሉፍ hluf *(adj.)* **past**
ሕሉፍ ሰዓት hluf seat *(n.)* **pastime**
ሕሊና hi'lina *(n.)* **conscience**
ሕሊና ምስሓት hilina mesehate *(n.)* **coma**
ሕላስ ȟlas *(n.)* **spear**
ሕላፍ መመረቕታ ȟlaf memereqta *(n.)* **postgraduate**
ሕላፍ ሰዓት ȟlaf seät *(n.)* **curfew**
ሕልሚ ĥlmi *(n.)* **dream**
ሕልሚ ቀትሪ ĥlmi qetri *(n. )* **reverie**
ሕልማዊ hlmawi *(adj.)* **utopian**
ሕልማዊ ȟlmawi *(adj.)* **surreal**
ሕልኽላኽ hlklak *(adj.)* **intricate**
ሕልኽልኽ ȟlḱlḱ *(n.)* **complexity**
ሕልኽልኽ ȟlḱlḱ *(n.)* **complication**
ሕልናዊ ȟlnawi *(adj.)* **moral**
ሕልና ዘይብሉ hlna zeyblu *(adj.)* **unscrupulous**
ሕልፍን ትርፍን hlfn trfn *(adj.)* **superabundant**
ሕልፍን ትርፍን h'lfn t'rfn *(adj.)* **superabundance**
ሕመት himet *(n.)* **coal**
ሕሙም hmum *(n. )* **patient**
ሕሙም hmum *(adj.)* **unhealthy**
ሕሙም ȟmum *(adj.)* **ailing**

ሕሙም ȟmum **(adj.) morbid**
ሕሙም ḥmum **(adj.) ill**
ሕሙም ĥmum **(adj.) sick**
ሕሙም ĥmum **(adj.) sickly**
ሕማም hmam **(n. ) malady**
ሕማም ĥmam **(n.) disease**
ሕማም ĥmam **(n. ) sickness**
ሕማም ȟmam **(n.) ailment**
ሕማም ȟmam **(adv. ) morbidity**
ሕማም ȟmam **(n.) syndrome**
ሕማም ḥmam **(n.) illness**
ሕማቅ ምሕደራ ȟmaq mȟdera **(n.) mismanagement**
ሕማቅ ስምዒት ንሓፅር ግዘ hmaq smiet nḥasir gze **(n.) twinge**
ሕማቕ hmaq **(adj.) disastrous**
ሕማቕ ḥmaq̈ **(adj. ) horrible**
ሕማቕ ȟmaq̈ **(adj.) bad**
ሕማቕ ሃለዋት ĥmaq halewot **(n.) plight**
ሕቑፊ-ዕምባባ ȟqufi'ëmbaba **(n.) bouquet**
ሕማቕ ጠባይ hmaq tebay **(adj.) pettish**
ሕቋን ፀባ ȟqwan xeba **(n.) milkshake**
ሕማም ምንፍርፋር ĥmam mnfrfar **(n.) epilepsy**
ሕማም ሸሮኽ hemam sheroke **(n.) cholera**
ሕማም ኣእምሮ ĥmam aemro **(n.) psychosis**
ሕማቅነት hmaqnet **(n.) ugliness**
ሕማቅ ኣማሓድራ hmaq ama'hadra **(n. ) maladministration**
ሕማቅ ኣጋጣሚ ȟmaq agaẗami **(n. ) misadventure**
ሕማቅ ዕድል ȟmaq ëdl **(n.) mischance**
ሕማቕ ኣመል ḥmaq̈ 'ame **(n. ) vice**
ሕምሕምታ ፈረስ ȟmȟmta feres **(n. ) neigh**
ሕምባሻ ȟmbasha **(n.) baguette**
ሕምባሻ ȟmbasha **(n.) bread**
ሕምብሊላይ ȟmbililay **(adj.) spiral**
ሕምብሊል በለ ḥmblil bele **(v.) gyrate**
ሕምብርቲ h-m-brti **(n.) hub**
ሕምየት ĥmyet **(n.) rumour**
ሕሩጭ ĥruĉ **(n.) flour**
ሕሩጭ ȟruč **(n.) powder**
ሕሩቕ ȟruq̈ **(adj.) angry**
ሕራነ ĥrane **(n.) rage**
ሕርቃን ĥrqan **(n.) displeasure**
ሕርቃን ĥrqan **(n.) dudgeon**
ሕርቃን ĥrqan **(n.) fume**
ሕርቃን ȟrqan **(n.) ire**
ሕርሻ hersha **(n) husbandry**
ሕርሻ ĥrsha **(n.) farm**
ሕርሻ ȟrsha **(n.) agriculture**
ሕርሻዊ ȟrshawi **(adj.) agricultural**
ሕሰም ȟsem **(n.) misery**
ሕሱም hsum **(adj.) inimical**
ሕሱም ሰብ ĥsum seb **(n.) ruffian**
ሕሱር ĥsur **(adj.) disreputable**
ሕሱር ĥsur **(adj.) shoddy**
ሕሱር ȟsur **(adj.) measly**
ሕሳር hesaree **(adj.) cheap**
ሕሳብ ȟsab **(n.) account**
ሕስረት hsret **(n.) indignity**
ሕስረት ĥsret **(n.) disrepute**
ሕሹክሹክ hshukshuk **(v.) peep**
ሕሹክሹክ hshukshuk **(v.) whisper**
ሕሽኩለኛ ȟshkulegna **(n. ) marsupial**
ሕሽ ዝበለ ኣተሓሳስባ ዘለዎ hish zbele atehasasba zelwo **(adj.) transcendent**
ሕበጥ hbet **(n.) lump**

ሕበጥ ḧbeẗ *(n.)* **bulge**
ሕቡእ hbu'e *(n.)* **oblivion**
ሕቡእ hibuea' *(adj.)* **clandestine**
ሕቡእ hebu'e *(n. )* **obscurity**
ሕቡእ hbu'e *(n.)* **crypt**
ሕቡእ hbu'e *(adj.)* **ulterior**
ሕቡእ ḧbu'e *(n.)* **cache**
ሕቡእ ḧbu'e *(adj.)* **surreptitious**
ሕቡእ ḧbu'e *(adj.)* **covert**
ሕቡእ ምፍርራሕ ḧbu'e mfrraḧ *(n.)* **blackmail**
ሕቡእ ምስጢር ዘለዎ ĥbu'e mistir zelewo *(adj.)* **oracular**
ሕቡእ ትርጉም ዘለዎ hbu'e trgum zelewo *(n.)* **overtone**
ሕቡጥ ḥbuṭ *(adj.)* **varicose**
ሕቢብ በለ hbib bele *(v.)* **whirr**
ሕቢብታ hbibta *(n.)* **whir**
ሕባበት hbabet *(n.)* **scum**
ሕብረ መድያዊ ḧbre medyawi *(n.)* **multimedia**
ሕብረተሰብ hbreteseb *(n. )* **society**
ሕብረት hbret *(n. )* **union**
ሕብሪ hbri *(n.)* **crayon**
ሕብሪ ኣልቦ hbri 'albo *(n.)* **colourless**
ሕብሪ ዋሃዮ hbri wahiyo *(n.)* **pigment**
ሕብራዊ ምረኢት ḧbrawi mreit *(n. )* **pageantry**
ሕብስቲ hbsti *(n.)* **loaf**
ሕብሪ hibri *(n.)* **colour**
ሕብሪ he-bri *(n.)* **hue**
ሕብብር hhbbr *(n.)* **collaboration**
ሕብስተ-ቁርባን ḥbstequrban *(n.)* **wafer**
ሕብጠት hbeẗet *(n.)* **swelling**
ሓታሚ ḧtami *(n.)* **publisher**
ሕታም htam *(n.)* **watermark**
ሕታም ĥtam *(n.)* **edition**

ሕትመት ḧtmet *(n. )* **publication**
ሕቶ hto *(n.)* **inquiry**
ሕቶ hto *(n.)* **query**
ሕቶ hto *(n.)* **question**
ሕነ ĥne *(n.)* **reprisal**
ሕነ ĥne *(n.)* **revenge**
ሕነ ፈደየ ĥne fedeye *(v.t. )* **requite**
ሕነ ፈደየ ĥne fedeye *(v.)* **retaliate**
ሕነ ምፍዳይ ĥne mfday *(n.)* **retaliation**
ሕነ ḥne *(n.)* **vendetta**
ሕኒን በለ ḥenin bele *(v.)* **growl**
ሕናኽ ĥnake *(n.)* **prudence**
ሕንቅሕንቅሊተይ hnqhnqlitey *(v. t)* **conundrum**
ሕንቅሕንቅሊተይ ĥnqlĥnqlitey *(n.)* **riddle**
ሕንዚ ḥnz *(n.)* **venom**
ሕንዚዝ ḧnziz *(n.)* **beetle**
ሕንግድ hngd *(adj.)* **insubordinate**
ሕንግድ ĥngd *(adj.)* **restive**
ሕንጥልጥል hntltl *(n.)* **wattle**
ሕንፍሽፍሽ ĥnfshfsh *(n.)* **disorder**
ሕንፍጽፋጽ ḥnftsefatse *(n. )* **hotchpotch**
ሕክምና hkmna *(n.)* **therapy**
ሕክምና hkmna *(n. )* **treatment**
ሕክምና ማህፀን ĥkmna mahtzen *(n.)* **gynaecology**
ሕክምናዊ hkmnawi *(adj.)* **therapeutic**
ሕክምናዊ ḧkmnawi *(adj.)* **medical**
ሕክምናዊ ḧkmnawi *(n. )* **medicine**
ሕኹራ እምባ ḧḱwura emba *(n.)* **mountaineering**
ሕዙእ ቦታ ĥbu'e bota *(n.)* **reservation**
ሕዋስ ḧwas *(n.)* **mixture**

ሕዋስ ምቁራን ḧwas mquran *(n.)* **confection**
ሕዋስ ባዚቃ ḧwas baziqa *(n.)* **amalgam**
ሕዉስ ĥwus *(n.)* **extrovert**
ሕዉስነት ḧwusnet *(n.)* **sociability**
ሕዉስነት ḧwusnet *(adj.)* **sociable**
ሕውስዋስ ḧwswas *(n.)* **melange**
ሕውስዋስ ḧwswas *(n. )* **mosaic**
ሕዉስዋስ መስተ hiwuswas meste *(n.)* **cocktail**
ሕውነታዊ ḧwnetawi *(adj.)* **fraternal**
ሕውነት ĥwnet *(n.)* **fraternity**
ሕውነት ḧwnet *(n.)* **brotherhood**
ሕውየት ĥwyet *(n.)* **recovery**
ሕዚ ḧzi *(adv.)* **now**
ሕያዋይ ĥyaway *(adj.)* **debonair**
ሕያዋይ ḧyaway *(adj)* **benevolent**
ሕያዋይ ḧyaway *(adj.)* **mild**
ሕያዋይ ḧyaway *(adj.)* **neighbourly**
ሕያዋይ heya-way *(adj. )* **humane**
ሕያዋይ ḧyaway *(adj.)* **nice**
ሕያዋይነት ḧyawaynet *(n.)* **benevolence**
ሕያው ḧyaw *(adj.)* **animated**
ሕዳር ḧdar *(n. )* **November**
ሕዳግ hdag *(n.)* **margin**
ሕድሕድ ĥdĥd *(adj.)* **every**
ሕድሕድ ĥdĥd *(adj.)* **each**
ሕድሳት ĥdsat *(n. )* **renovation**
ሕድገት ḧdget *(n.)* **concession**
ሕገ መንግስቲ hige mengistii *(n.)* **constitution**
ሕጉስ higus' *(adj.)* **cheery**
ሕጉስ ĥgus *(adj.)* **exuberant**
ሕጉስ ḧgus *(adj.)* **glad**
ሕጉስ hgus *(adj. )* **happy**
ሕጉስ hgus *(adj.)* **sportive**
ሕጉስ hgus *(adj.)* **upbeat**
ሕጉስ ĥgus *(adv.)* **gaily**
ሕጉስ ĥgus *(adj.)* **gay**
ሕጉስ ḧgus *(adj.)* **jolly**
ሕጉስ ḧgus *(adj.)* **merry**
ሕጉስ ḧgus *(adj.)* **mirthful**
ሕጉስ ḥgus *(adj.)* **joyous**
ሕጉስ ḧgus *(adj.)* **blithe**
ሕጉስነት hgusnet *(adv. )* **joviality**
ሕጊ hgi *(n.)* **law**
ሕጊ ĥgi *(n.)* **dogma**
ሕጊ ĥgi *(n.)* **rule**
ሕጊ ḧgi *(n.)* **statute**
ሕጊ መፅደቕቲ hgi metsdeqhti *(n.)* **legislature**
ሕጊ ምፅዳቕ hgi mtsdaqh *(n.)* **legislation**
ሕጊ ኣልቦ hgi albo *(adj.)* **lawless**
ሕጊ ኣፅደቐ hgi atsdqh *(v.)* **legislate**
ሕጊ ኣፅዳቒ higi atzdaqhi *(adj.)* **legislative**
ሕጊ ዝጠሓሰ hgi ztehase *(n.)* **malefactor**
ሕጋዊ hgawi *(adj.)* **lawful**
ሕጋዊ hgawi *(adj.)* **legal**
ሕጋዊ hgawi *(adj.)* **legitimate**
ሕጋዊ ĥgawi *(adj.)* **dogmatic**
ሕጋዊ ĥgawi *(adj.)* **rightful**
ሕጋዊ ስልጣን ḧgawi slẗan *(n. )* **jurisdiction**
ሕጋዊነት hgawinet *(n.)* **legitimacy**
ሕጋዊነት hgawnet *(n.)* **legality**
ሕጋዊ ንክኽዉን ገበረ ĥgawi nknkewn gebere *(v.)* **decriminalize**
ሕጋዊ ገበረ hgawi gebere *(v.)* **legalize**
ሕግግ በለ h'g'g bele *(v.t. )* **snarl**
ሕጡብ ማቶኒ ḧẗub matoni *(n.)* **brick**
ሕጡብ ወርቂ ḧẗub werqi *(n.)* **bullion**
ሕጫጩ ḧčače *(n.)* **irony**

**ሕጭጭታ** h'ch'chta ***(n.)* screech**
**ሕጹይ** ȟxuy ***(n.)* candidate**
**ሕጽበት** ȟxbet ***(n.)* ablution**
**ሕጽኒ** ȟxni ***(n.)* bosom**
**ሕጽኖት** ḥxnot ***(n.)* honeymoon**
**ሕፀ** ĥxe ***(n.)* engagement**
**ሕፁይ** ĥxuy ***(n.)* fiancé**
**ሕፂፅታ** htsitsta ***(n.)* screech**
**ሕፀረት** ĥtsret ***(n. )* paucity**
**ሕፀረት** ĥtsret ***(n.)* shortage**
**ሕፀረት ምግቢ** htsret mgbi ***(n. )* malnutrition**
**ሕፀር ምጥን ዝበለ** hsr mtn zbele ***(adj.)* terse**
**ሕፋኖ** hfano ***(n.)* handful**
**ሕፍረት** hfret ***(n.)* inhibition**
**ሕፍረት** hfret ***(n.)* shame**
**ሕፍረት ዘይብሉ** hfret zeyblu ***(adj.)* indiscreet**
**ሕፍረት ዘይምህላይ** hfret zeymhlay ***(n.)* indiscretion**
**ሕፍሰት** hfset ***(n.)* consistency**
**ሓጓዲ** ȟagwadi ***(n.)* blacksmith**
**ሓራድ ስጋ** ȟarad sga ***(n.)* butcher**
**ሕነ ፈደየ** ȟne fedeye ***(v.)* avenge**

# መ

**መተባበዒ** temsaṭ ***(n.)* inspiration**
**ዓኮር** me'äkor ***(n.)* bum**
**መዓልቦ** me'älbo ***(n.)* destination**
**መዓልቲ** me'älti ***(n.)* day**
**መዓልቲ ዕረፍቲ** mealti erefti ***(n. )* Sabbath**
**መዓልቲ ስራሕ** me'alti srah ***(n.)* weekday**
**መዓናጡ** me'änaṫu ***(n.)* bowel**
**መዓንጡ** me'änaṫu ***(n.)* entrails**
**መአንገድ ድርጎኛ** me'anged drgoȟa ***(n.)* billet**
**መዓንጣ** me'änta ***(n.)* gut**
**መዓንጣ** me'änẗa ***(n. )* intestine**
**መዓቀቢ ሬሳ** me'äqebi reesa ***(n.)* morgue**
**መዓር** me'är ***(n. )* honey**
**መአረምታ** me'aremta ***(n.pl.)* amendment**
**መዓርፎ** mearfo ***(n.)* terminus**
**መዓርፎ ነፈርቲ** me'ärfo neferti ***(n.)* aerodrome**
**መዓርግ** me'ärg ***(n. )* gradation**
**መዓርግ ዘለዎ** me'ärg zelewo ***(adj. )* honourable**
**መዕፀፊ ቦታ** measefi bota ***(n.)* turning**
**መዓሸጊ መራኽብ** me'ashegi merakb ***(n.)* wharf**
**መዓስከር** me'äsker ***(n.)* camp**
**መዓት** me'ät ***(adj.)* countless**
**መዓት** me'ät ***(n.)* disaster**
**መዓት** me'ät ***(n.)* multitude**
**መዓት** me'ät ***(n.)* ream**
**መዓት** me'ät ***(n.)* calamity**
**መዐትዐቲ** me'ät'ëti ***(n. )* garter**
**መዓጡቕ** me'äṭuq̈ ***(n. )* waist**
**መአዛ** me'aza ***(n.)* fragrance**
**መአዛ** me'aza ***(n.)* nutrient**
**መዓዛ** me'äza ***(n.)* aroma**
**መዓዛ -ፍወሳ** me'äza fwesa ***(n.)* aromatherapy**
**መአዛ ዘለዎ** me'aza zelewo ***(adj.)* delectable**
**መአዛ ዘለዎ** me'aza zelewo ***(adj.)* nutritious**
**መአዛዊ** me'azawi ***(adj.)* nutritive**

**መአዘዚ መድሃኒት** meazezi medhanit *(n. )* **prescription**
**መብልዒ እንስሳ ጋቢያ** mbl'e anbesa gabiya *(n.)* **manger**
**መባእታ** meba'eta *(adj.)* **elementary**
**መባእታዊ** mebaètawi *(adj.)* **primary**
**መባኹዕቲ** mebakueti *(n.)* **yeast**
**መባዝሒኢ ማሽን** mebazhi mashn *(n.)* **Xerox**
**መበገሲ** mebegesi *(n.)* **premise**
**መበቆል** mebekol *(n.)* **provenance**
**መበል ዒስራ** mebel aisra *(adj.&n.)* **twentieth**
**መበል ዒስራ** mebel aisra *(adj.&n.)* **twentieth**
**መበል ዓሰርተ ሽድሽተ** mebel äserte šdšte *(adj. & n.)* **sixteenth**
**መበል ዓሰርተ ሰለስተ** mebel aserte seleste *(adj. & n.)* **thirteenth**
**መበል ዓሰርተ ትሽዓተ** mebel äserte tsh'äte *(adj. & n.)* **nineteenth**
**መበል ዓሰርተ ሸውዓተ** mebel aserte xew'ate *(adj. & n.)* **seventeenth**
**መበል ዓሰርተ ክልተ** mebel aserteklte *(adj.&n.)* **twelfth**
**መበል ዓሰርተ ክልተ** mebel aserteklte *(adj.&n.)* **twelfth**
**መበል ሰብዓ** mebel seb'a *(adj. & n.)* **seventieth**
**መበል ሰላሳ** mebel selasa *(adj. & n.)* **thirtieth**
**መበል ሰላሳ** mebel selasa *(adj. & n.)* **thirtieth**
**መዓደ** me'äde *(v.)* **advise**
**መዓደ** me'äde *(v.)* **recommend**
**መኣዲ** me'adi *(n.)* **serving**
**መኣዲ** me'adi *(n.)* **helping**
**መበል ስሳ** mebel ssa *(adj. & n.)* **sixtieth**
**መበል ቴስዓ** mebel tees'ä *(adj. & n.)* **ninetieth**
**መበራትዒ** meberat'i *(n.)* **supercharger**
**መበረኽያ** meberekya *(n.)* **rostrum**
**መበፅበፂ** mebexbexi *(n.)* **blender**
**መበፅበፂ** mebexbexi *(n.)* **mixer**
**መብኮሪ** mebkori *(n.)* **truant**
**መብላዕልዒ** mebla'ël'ï *(n.)* **reactor**
**መብለጭለጪ** meblečleči *(adj.)* **flamboyant**
**መብልሒ** meblhi *(n.)* **sharpener**
**መበቆል** meboqol *(n.)* **cradle**
**መብራህርሂ** mebrahrhi *(n.)* **clarification**
**መብረዲ** mebredi *(n.)* **rasp**
**መብሰሊ** mebseli *(n.)* **cooker**
**መብጽዓ** mebx'ä *(n.)* **commitment**
**መብዛሕትኡ** mebza'ht'u *(n.)* **majority**
**መብዛሕቱኡ** mebzaȟt'u *(n.)* **most**
**መጨረሻ** mečeresha *(adj.)* **last**
**መዳጎኒ** medagoni *(n.)* **cage**
**መዳጎኒ** medagoni *(n.)* **limbo**
**መዳልያተኛ** medalyategna *(v.i. )* **medallist**
**መዳቀሊት** medaqelit *(n.)* **copier**
**መዳርግቲ ዘይብሉ** medargti zeyblu *(adj.)* **unrivalled**
**መዳይ** meday *(n.)* **way**
**መደብ** medeb *(n. )* **programme**
**መደብ** medeb *(n.)* **schedule**
**መደብ** medeb *(n.)* **terrace**
**መደብ** medeb *(n.)* **plan**
**መደበ** medebe *(v.)* **mete**
**መደበር** medeber *(n.)* **station**
**መደብለ ባህላዊ** medeble bahlawi *(adj.)* **multicultural**
**መደገፍታ** medegefta *(n.)* **splint**

መደገፍታ medegefta *(n.)* **strut**
መደቀሲ ክፍሊ medekesi kfli *(n.)* **dormitory**
መደሎ medelo *(n.)* **gong**
መደምደምታ medemdemta *(n.)* **closure**
መደምደምታ ዘይብሉ medemdemta zeyblu *(adj.)* **inconclusive**
መደምደምያ medemdemya *(n.)* **epilogue**
መደናገሪ medenageri *(adj.)* **deceptive**
መደናገሪ medenageri *(n. )* **knave**
መደናገሪ medenageri *(n.)* **racketeer**
መደንደል medendel *(n. )* **railing**
መደንደል medendel *(n.)* **banisters**
መደንደል medendel *(n.)* **barricade**
መደንዘዚ medenzezi *(n.)* **anaesthetic**
መደቀሲ medeqesi *(n.)* **berth**
መደርብዮ mederbyo *(n.)* **shuttle**
መደርደሪ mederderi *(n. )* **rack**
መደርደርያ mederderya *(n.)* **shelf**
መደረ medere *(n.)* **discourse**
መደረ medere *(n.)* **speech**
መደረ ናእዳ medere naeda *(n. )* **panegyric**
መደረጋሕ mederegaḧ *(n.)* **avalanche**
መደያይቦ medeyaybo *(n. )* **rung**
መደያይቦ medeyaybo *(n.)* **staircase**
መድያየቢ medeyayebi *(n.)* **escalator**
መደያየቢ medeyayebi *(n. )* **scaffold**
መደየቢ medeyebi *(n.)* **ramp**
መደየቢት medeyebit *(n.)* **elevator**
መድፍዕ medf'ë *(n.)* **cannon**
መድገምያ medgemya *(n.)* **rosary**
መድሓኒት medhanit *(adj.)* **purgative**
መድሓኒት medĥanit *(n.)* **drug**
መድሓኒት medḧanit *(n.)* **medication**
መድሃኒታዊ medhanitawi *(adj.)* **pharmaceutical**
መድሓርሓሪ medĥarĥri *(adj.)* **reactionary**
መድሕን medḧn *(n.)* **insurance**
መድሕን medḥn *(n. )* **haven**
መዲተራንያዊ mediteranyawi *(adj.)* **Mediterranean**
መድመጺ እዝን medmexi ezni *(n.)* **headphone**
መድመይቲ medmeyti *(n.)* **haemorrhage**
መድረኽ medrek *(n.)* **dais**
መድረኽ medrek *(n.)* **forum**
መድረኽ medreḱ *(n.)* **platform**
መድረኽ medreḱ *(n.)* **podium**
መድረኽ medreḱ *(n.)* **arena**
መድረኽ medrekh *(n.)* **stage**
መድረቒ medreqi *(n.)* **dryer**
መዕበዪት me'ëbeyit *(n.)* **nanny**
መዐፈኒ me'ëfeni *(n.)* **silencer**
መዐደሊ መድሓኒት me'ëdeli medhanit *(n.)* **dispensary**
መንቀሊ mneqsi *(n.)* **cause**
መንፀባረቒ mntsebareqhi *(adj.)* **luminous**
መቕጻዕቲ mqxaeti *(n. )* **penalty**
መራኸቢ mrakhebi *(n.)* **link**
መራኸቢ mreakhebi *(n.)* **linkage**
መዐገሲ me'egesi *(n.)* **sedative**
መዕገቲ me'ëgeti *(n.)* **restraint**
መዕገቲ ስኒ me'ëgeti sni *(n.)* **ratchet**
መዐቀቢ me'ëkebi *(n.)* **deterrent**
መዕቆቢ me-ekobi *(n.)* **housing**
መዕለበጢ me'ëlebeẗi *(adj.)* **feisty**
መእለዪ me'eleyi *(n.)* **spur**
መዐቀቢ me'ëqebi *(n.)* **preservative**

**መዐቀብያ** me'eqebya *(n.)* **conservatory**
**መዕቀሊ** me'ëqeli *(n. )* **refuge**
**መዕቀሊ** me'ëqeli *(n.)* **shelter**
**መዕቆቢ** me'eqobi *(n. )* **sanctuary**
**መዕቆሪ** me'ëqori *(n.)* **vessel**
**መዕረፍ ሄሊኮፕተር** me'ëref heelikopter *(n.)* **heliport**
**መዕረፊ** me'ërefi *(n.)* **hospice**
**መዕረፊ ፀማልያታት** me'erefi tsemalyatat *(n. )* **sanatorium**
**መዕረፊ ፀማልያታት** me'erefi tsemalyatat *(n.)* **sanatorium**
**መእሰሪ** me'eseri *(n.)* **strap**
**መእሰሪ ኸልቢ** me'eseri kebi *(n.)* **leash**
**መእሰሪ** me'èseri *(n.)* **band**
**መእተዊ** me'etewi *(n.)* **access**
**መእተዊ** me'etewi *(n.)* **entrance**
**መእተዊ** me'etewi *(n.)* **prelude**
**መዕጠይጠዪ** me'ëteyteyi *(adj.)* **reluctant**
**መዕፀዊ ዕለት** me'ëtsewi ëlet *(n.)* **deadline**
**መባኸኒ** mebakeni *(adj.)* **wasteful**
**መብጽዓ** mebx'ä *(n.)* **vow**
**መብጻዓዊ** mebxa'äwi *(adj.)* **votive**
**መፋሕፍሒ** mefaḥfḥi *(n.)* **grater**
**መፈንቶ** mefento *(n. )* **valve**
**መፈንቶ** mefento *(n.)* **vent**
**መፍሰል** mefsel *(n.)* **hinge**
**መጋረጃ** megareğ *(n.)* **valance**
**መጋርያ** megarya *(n.)* **hearth**
**መግቢ** megbi *(n.)* **viands**
**መጎልበቢ** megolbebi *(n. )* **wrapper**
**መጓሰ** meguase *(n. )* **herd**
**መንጫዕጫዕታ** menča'ëča'ëta *(n. )* **waterfall**
**መንደቅ** mendeq̈ *(n.)* **wall**
**መረቅ** mereq̈ *(n.)* **gravy**
**መስሓቕ** mesḥaq̈ *(adj. )* **humorous**
**መሸኒት** meshenit *(n.)* **vagina**
**መስርዕ-መዓርግ** mesr'ëme'ärg *(n.)* **hierarchy**
**መጥሐኒ** meṭḥani *(n.)* **grinder**
**መወጠጢ ፈረስ** meweṭeṭi feres *(n.)* **halter**
**መዛወሪ መርከብ** mezaweri merkeb *(n. )* **helm**
**መዝነት** meznet *(n. )* **warranty**
**መእ'ዘኒ** me'e'zeni *(n.)* **minaret**
**መፋሓፍሒ ወረቀት** mefahafhi wereqet *(n.)* **sandpaper**
**መፋሓፍሕቲ** mefahafhti *(n.)* **sander**
**መፋለጢ** mefaleṫi *(adj.)* **introductory**
**መፋጥርቲ** mefatrti *(adj.)* **inborn**
**መፈላለዪ ሕንጻጽ** mefelaleyi hentsatse *(n.)* **hyphen**
**መፈለምታ** mefelemta *(n.)* **genesis**
**መፈንቶ** mefento *(n.)* **sluice**
**መፈረሺ** mefereshi *(n.)* **stuffing**
**መፈተሺ** mefeteshi *(n. )* **manhole**
**መፈጸምታ** mefetsmta *(n.)* **termination**
**መፈጸምታ** mefexemta *(n.)* **expiry**
**መፈጸምታ ዘይብሉ** mefexemta zeyblu *(adj.)* **perpetual**
**መፍለስ** mefles *(n.)* **boar**
**መፍልሒ** meflḧi *(n.)* **boiler**
**መፍረ ኣዕዋፍ** mefre aëwaf *(n.)* **poultry**
**መፍተል** meftel *(n.)* **spindle**
**መፍትሕ** mefth *(n.)* **key**
**መፍትሕ ዳዶ** meft'h dado *(n.)* **spanner**
**መጓዓዝያ** megaazya *(n. )* **transportation**

መጓዓዝያ megaazya *(n.)* **transporter**
መጋቢት megabit *(n.)* **march**
መጋብር megabr *(n.)* **deed**
መጋረጃ megareja *(n.)* **curtain**
መጋረጃ megareja *(n.)* **pelmet**
መጋረጃ megareja *(n. )* **shutter**
መጋርያ megarya *(n.)* **bonfire**
መጋጥም megatm *(n.)* **joint**
መጋጠሚ megatmi *(n.)* **commissure**
መጋየጺ ወረቀታት megayesi werketat *(n. )* **tinsel**
መጋየጺ megayetzi *(n.)* **jewel**
መጋየጺ ሰራሒ megayetzi serahi *(n. )* **jeweller**
መጋዝ megaz *(n.)* **saw**
መግዳዕቲ ዘለዎ megda'eti zelewo *(n. )* **handicapped**
መገበ megebe *(v.)* **feed**
መገዲ megedi *(n.)* **course**
መገዲ ባቡር megedi babur *(n.)* **railway**
መገዱ ሰሓተ megedu seȟate *(v.)* **straggle**
መገለል megelel *(n.)* **bucket**
መገጣጠሚ megeẗaẗemi *(n.)* **fitting**
መግፈፊ megfefi *(n.)* **rake**
መግሓጢ meghati *(n.)* **scoop**
መግለፂ megletsi *(n.)* **definition**
መግለጺ megletsi *(n.)* **statement**
መግለጺ meglexi *(n.)* **announcement**
መግለፂ meglexi *(n.)* **expression**
መግለጺ ሓጐስ meglexi ȟagwas *(n.)* **congratulation**
መግለጺ ሓጐስ meglexi ȟagwas *(n.)* **felicitation**
መጎተ megote *(n.)* **argument**
መግረፍቲ megrefti *(n.)* **lashings**
መጉዳእቲ meguda'eti *(n.)* **damage**
መጉዳእቲ meguda'eti *(n. )* **strain**
መጉዑዓዝ megueaz *(v.)* **transport**
ምጉጃል megujak *(n.)* **classification**
መጉልሒ megulȟi *(n.)* **amplifier**
መጉልሒ ድምፂ megulȟi dmxi *(n. )* **megaphone**
መጉረምረሚ meguremremi *(adj.)* **querulous**
መጉየዪ meguyeyi *(n.)* **runway**
መጓሰ megwase *(n.)* **flock**
መሓለ meȟale *(v.)* **swear**
መሃንዲስ mehandis *(n.)* **engineer**
መሃንቱስ mehantus *(n.)* **anus**
መሓንዘፍ mehanzef *(n.)* **scythe**
መሃረ mehare *(v.)* **instruct**
መሃረ mehare *(v.)* **teach**
መሓረ meȟare *(v.)* **forgive**
መሓረ meȟare *(adj.)* **spare**
መሓረ meȟare *(v.)* **condone**
መሓረ meȟare *(v.)* **absolve**
መሃሪ mehari *(n. )* **mentor**
መሓወ meȟawe *(v.)* **eradicate**
መሓወ meȟawe *(v.)* **pluck**
መሓውር mehawr *(n.)* **limb**
መሃያ mehaya *(n.)* **emolument**
መሃይም mehaym *(n. )* **illiterate**
መሃይምነት mehaymnet *(n.)* **illiteracy**
መሓዛ meȟaza *(n. )* **pal**
መሃዛይ mehazay *(adj.)* **creative**
መሃዘ mehaze *(v.)* **contrive**
መሃዘ mehaze *(v.)* **devise**
መሃዘ mehaze *(v.)* **improvise**
መሃዘ mehaze *(v.)* **innovate**
መሃዘ mehaze *(v.)* **invent**
መሃዚ mehazi *(n.)* **inventor**
መሕብኢ meȟb'i *(n.)* **den**
መሐለውታ mehelewta *(n. )* **safeguard**

**መሕንበቢ** meĥenbebi *(n.)* **propeller**
**መሕንገጋ** meĥengega *(n. )* **gag**
**መሕለፊ በዓቲ** mehlegi beati *(n.)* **underpass**
**መሕነን** meȟnen *(n.)* **accelerator**
**መሕረቒ** mehreqhi *(v.)* **irksome**
**መሕረሲ** meȟresi *(n. )* **midwife**
**መሓሰስያ** me'ȟsesya *(n.)* **swab**
**መሕተሚ** mehtemi *(n.)* **sealant**
**መሕፀቢ** meĥtsebi *(n.)* **detergent**
**መሕፀሪ** meĥxeri *(n.)* **fencing**
**መሕዘኒት ተዋናዪት** mehzednit tewanayit *(n. )* **tragedian**
**መሕዘኒ** mehzeni *(adj.)* **tearful**
**መሕዘኒ** mehzeni *(adj.)* **tragic**
**መሕዘኒ ኩነታት** mehzeni kunetat *(n.)* **tragedy**
**መጀመርታ** mejemerta *(n.)* **alpha**
**መጀመርታ** mejemerta *(n. )* **inception**
**መጀመርታ** mejemerta *(adj.)* **initial**
**መጀመርታ** meĵemerta *(n.)* **beginning**
**መጀነኒ** meĵeneni *(n.)* **bandage**
**መቃብር** mekabr *(n. )* **tomb**
**መኻዕታ** meḱa'ëta *(n.)* **mirth**
**መኳለሊ** mekaleli *(n.)* **detour**
**መኻን** meḱan *(adj.)* **barren**
**መካነ መቓብር** mekane meqabere *(n.)* **churchyard**
**መካነ-መቓብር** mekane meq̃abr *(n.)* **graveyard**
**መካነ ሙታን** mekane mutan *(n. )* **necropolis**
**መካኒክ** mekanik *(n.)* **mechanic**
**መካኒካዊ** mekanikawi *(adj.)* **mechanical**
**መካኒክስ** mekaniks *(n.)* **mechanics**
**መካኒክዝም** mekanikzm *(n. )* **mechanism**
**መካር** mekar *(n.)* **sage**
**መካርነት** mekarnet *(n.)* **aphorism**
**መካቲ** mekati *(adj.)* **defensive**
**መኻይድቲ** meḱaydti *(adj.)* **concomitant**
**መኻዚኖ** mekazino *(n.)* **depot**
**መኽበሪ መሰል ሰነድ** mekberi mesel sened *(n.)* **patent**
**መኽዳድንቲ** mekedadnti *(n.)* **furnishing**
**መከሓሐሲ** mekehahesi *(n.)* **weighting**
**መኽኽ** mekeke *(v.)* **thaw**
**መኽኽ** meḱeḱe *(v.)* **melt**
**መከላኸሊ ጥንሲ** mekelaḱeli ẗnsi *(n.)* **contraceptive**
**መከራ** mekera *(n.)* **mire**
**መከራ** mekera *(n. )* **tribulation**
**መቀስ** mekes *(n.)* **scissors**
**መኼት** meket *(n.)* **pariah**
**መኼታይ** meketay *(adj.)* **plebeian**
**መከወል** mekewel *(n.)* **dashboard**
**መኸወሊ** mekeweli *(n.)* **screen**
**መኸወሊ** mekeweli *(n.)* **shield**
**መኻን** mekhan *(adj.)* **sterile**
**መኻንነት** mekhan'net *(n. )* **sterility**
**መኽደኒ** mekhdeni *(n.)* **stopper**
**መኸኸ** mekhekhe *(v.)* **liquefy**
**መኽሰብ** mekhseb *(n.)* **lucre**
**መኽዘን** mekhzen *(n. )* **storage**
**መኽዘን** mekhzen *(n.)* **store**
**መኪና** mekina *(n.)* **machine**
**መኪና** mekina *(n.)* **van**
**መኪና በረኻ** mekina bereḱa *(n.)* **jeep**
**መኪና ቀብሪ** mekina qebri *(n.)* **hearse**
**መኪና** mekina *(n.)* **automobile**

**መካነ መቃብር** mekne mekabir ***(n.)*** **cemetery**
**መቆንጠጢ** mekonteti ***(n.)*** **tongs**
**መኾስተር** meḱoster ***(n.)*** **mop**
**መኾስተር** meḱoster ***(n.)*** **besom**
**መኾስተር** meḱoster ***(n.)*** **broom**
**መኽሰብ** mekseb ***(n.)*** **proceeds**
**መኽሰብ** meḱseb ***(n.)*** **profit**
**መቕፅዒ** mekts'i ***(adj.)*** **punitive**
**መኩሲ** mekusi ***(n.)*** **namesake**
**መኹተምያ** mekutemya ***(n.)*** **template**
**መኳለሚ** mekwalemi ***(n.)*** **bypass**
**መኳንንቲ** mekwannti ***(n.)*** **aristocracy**
**መኽዘን** mekzen ***(n.)*** **depository**
**መኽዘን** mekzen ***(n.)*** **repository**
**መኽዘን** meḱzen ***(n.)*** **bunker**
**መኽዘን ምግቢ** mekzen mgbi ***(n.)*** **larder**
**መኽዘን** meḱzen ***(n.)*** **barn**
**መልአ** mel'a ***(v.)*** **tamp**
**መላግቦ** melagbo ***(adj.)*** **conjunct**
**መላግቦ** melagbo ***(n.)*** **seam**
**መላግቦ ዓፅሚ** melagbo atzmi ***(n.)*** **ligament**
**መላግቦ ኣጻብዕቲ** melagbo 'axab'ëti ***(n.)*** **knuckle**
**መላገቢ** melagebi ***(n.)*** **stapler**
**መላገቢ** melagebi ***(n.)*** **adhesive**
**መላገጺ** melagetsi ***(adj.)*** **quizzical**
**መላኢ** mela'i ***(adj.)*** **complementary**
**መልኣኽ** mel'ak ***(n.)*** **angel**
**መልኣከ ሞት** mel'ake mot ***(n.)*** **wraith**
**መላለዪ** melaleyi ***(n.)*** **showcase**
**መላሚን** melamin ***(n.)*** **melamine**
**መላጥ** melat ***(n.)*** **tonsure**
**መልአ** mel'e ***(v.)*** **append**
**መልአ** mel'e ***(v.)*** **fill**
**መልአ** mel'e ***(v.)*** **fulfil**
**መልአ** mel'e ***(n.)*** **glut**
**መልአ** mel'e ***(v.)*** **imbue**
**መለግለጋ** meleglega ***(n.)*** **jelly**
**መለግለጋይ ዓሳ** meleglegay 'äsa ***(n.)*** **jellyfish**
**መለኛ** melegna ***(n. )*** **tactician**
**መረሐ** meleh ***(v.)*** **lead**
**መለክዒ** melek'i ***(n.)*** **standard**
**መለኪያ** melekiya ***(n.)*** **goblet**
**መለኮታዊ** melekotawi ***(adj.)*** **divine**
**መለኮታዊ** melekotawi ***(adj. )*** **holistic**
**መልእኽተ ሃወርያ** mel'ekte hawerya ***(n.)*** **epistle**
**መለለይ ምልክት** me'leleyei milikit ***(n.)*** **chevron**
**መለለዪ** meleleyi ***(n.)*** **identification**
**መለለዪ ፀባይ** meleleyi xebay ***(n.)*** **characteristic**
**መለሳ ቃል** melesa qal ***(n.)*** **synonym**
**መለሰ** melese ***(v.)*** **react**
**መለሰ** melese ***(v.)*** **refund**
**መለሰ** melese ***(v.)*** **restore**
**መለስለሲ** meleslesi ***(n.)*** **laxative**
**መለጠፊ** meleťfi ***(n.)*** **plaster**
**መለይ** meley ***(a. )*** **nubile**
**መለይ** meley ***(adj.)*** **shapely**
**መለይ** meley ***(adj.)*** **slender**
**መልጎም** melgom ***(n.)*** **stud**
**መልጎም** melgom ***(n.)*** **button**
**መልሓስ** melhas ***(n.)*** **tongue**
**መልሓስ** melĥas ***(n.)*** **repartee**
**መልሓሱ ኣልመፀ** melĥasu almetse ***(v.)*** **slurp**
**መልሕቕ** melḧq̈ ***(n.)*** **anchor**
**መልክዐኛ** melkäňa ***(adj.)*** **pretty**
**መልክዕ** melk'e ***(n.)*** **texture**
**መልክዕ** melk'ĕ ***(n.)*** **feature**

መልክዐ melk'ë *(n.)* **aspect**
መልክዐ melk'ë *(n.)* **beauty**
መልክዐ melk'ë *(n.)* **splendour**
መልኮታዊነት melkotawinet *(n.)* **divinity**
መልእኽተኛ mel'ḱtegna *(n.)* **messenger**
መልክዑ ቀየረ melk'ü keyere *(v.)* **disguise**
መልመለ melmele *(v.)* **induct**
መልመስቲ melmesti *(n.)* **palsy**
መልቀ melqe *(n.)* **fulcrum**
መልቀ melqe *(n.)* **lever**
መልሰ ተግባር ሃበ melse tegbar habe *(v.)* **respond**
መልሰ-ግብሪ melsegbri *(n.)* **backlash**
መልሲ melsi *(n.)* **answer**
መልሲ melsi *(n.)* **response**
መልሲ ሃበ melsi habe *(v.t.)* **counter**
መልሲ ሃበ melsi habe *(v.)* **reply**
መመሓላለፊ መሰርሒ memahalalefi mesarhi *(n.)* **transmitter**
መማረፂ memaretzi *(adj.)* **fussy**
መማረፂ memarexi *(adj.)* **finicky**
መማፅኢ mema'x'i *(n. )* **matchmaker**
መማዪ memayi *(n.)* **censor**
መማዝንቲ memaznti *(adj.)* **equivalent**
መምሰሊ memeiseli *(n.)* **charlatan**
መመኽነይታ memeḱneyta *(n.)* **justification**
መመላእታ memela'eta *(n.)* **complement**
መመላእታ memela'èta *(n.)* **addendum**
መመላእታ memela'èta *(n.)* **appendage**
መመላኽዒ memelak'e *(n.)* **wainscot**
መመላኽዒ ኬክ memelakh'e cake *(n.)* **icing**
መመልሓቂ memelḧeqi *(n.)* **anchorage**
መመልከቲ memelketi *(n.)* **application**
መመልከቲ memelketi *(n.)* **indicator**
መመቀር ኣፍ memeqer af *(n.)* **dessert**
መመቀሪ memeqeri *(n.)* **sweetener**
መምርሒ memerehii *(n.)* **charter**
መመረቒ ፅሑፍ memereqi tsuĥuf *(n.)* **dissertation**
መመሰሊ memeseli *(n.)* **imposter**
መምህር ቆልዑ memher qoleu *(n. )* **pedagogue**
መምህር memhr *(n.)* **instructor**
መምህር memhr *(n. )* **lecturer**
መምህር memhr *(n.)* **teacher**
መምህር ገዛ memhr geza *(n. )* **governess**
መምለጢ ዘይብሉ memleti zeyblu *(adj.)* **inescapable**
መምልኢ meml'i *(n.)* **charger**
መምልኢ meml'i *(n.)* **filler**
መምልኢ meml'i *(n.)* **intake**
መሞገቲ memogeti *(n.)* **muniment**
መሞቒ memoq̈i *(n.)* **heater**
መምርሒ memrĥi *(n.)* **directive**
መምርሒ memrĥi *(n.)* **guidance**
መምርሒ memrĥi *(n. )* **precept**
መምርሒ memrĥi *(n.)* **regulation**
መምርሒ memrḧi *(n.)* **policy**
መምርሒ memrhi *(n.)* **instruction**
መምፀዪት memtseyit *(n.)* **siphon**
መን men *(pron. )* **who**
መናእኣሲ mena'a'asi *(adj.)* **dismissive**
መናዓቢ mena'abk *(adj.)* **seditious**

**መናብር** menabr *(n.)* **seating**
**መናፍፈሲ ቦታ** menafesi bota *(n.)* **park**
**መናፍሕ** menafȟ *(n.)* **bellows**
**መናገድያ** menagedia *(n.)* **turnover**
**መናን** menan *(adj.)* **ascetic**
**መናን** menan *(adj.)* **quixotic**
**መናኒ** menani *(n. )* **votary**
**መናሽዊ** menashewi *(adj.)* **derogatory**
**መንበሪ ቦታ** menberi bota *(n.)* **dwelling**
**መንበሪ ገዛ** menberi geza *(n.)* **residence**
**መንበሪ ገዛ** menberi geza *(adj.)* **residential**
**መንጫ ጫዕታ** mencha chaeta *(n.)* **cascade**
**መንጨለፍ** menchelef *(n.)* **ladle**
**መንደዲ** mendedi *(n.)* **burner**
**መንደፍ** mendef *(n.)* **fang**
**መንደል** mendel *(n.)* **chisel**
**መንደል** mendel *(n.)* **drill**
**መንደል** mendel *(v.)* **gouge**
**መንደሊ መጋዝ** mendeli megaz *(n.)* **jigsaw**
**መንደቅ** mendeq *(n.)* **firewall**
**መንደቅ እምኒ** mendeq emni *(n. )* **masonry**
**መንደሪኒ** menderini *(n.)* **tangerine**
**መንዲል** mendil *(n. )* **handkerchief**
**መንድቃዊ ቅብኣ** mendqawi qb'i *(n. )* **mural**
**መነባብሮ** menebabro *(n.)* **livelihood**
**መነከዪ ዋሕዚ** menekeyi wahzi *(n.)* **damper**
**መነነ** menene *(v.)* **abjure**
**መነቓቕሒ** meneqaqhȟi *(n.)* **stimulus**
**መንእሰይ** men'esey *(adj.)* **youthful**
**መንእሰይ** men'èsey *(adj.)* **juvenile**
**መነስነሲ** menesnesi *(n.)* **sprinkler**
**መንፈስ** menfes *(n. )* **ghost**
**መንፈስ** menfes *(n.)* **mood**
**መንፈስ** menfes *(n.)* **spectre**
**መንፈስ** menfes *(n.)* **spirit**
**መንፈስ ሰብ** menfes seb *(n. )* **psyche**
**መንፈሳዊ** menfesawi *(n.)* **mystic**
**መንፈሳዊ** menfesawi *(adj.)* **pastoral**
**መንፈሳዊ** menfesawi *(adj.)* **spiritual**
**መንፈሳዊነት** menfesawinet *(n.)* **mysticism**
**መንፈሳውነት** menfesawinet *(n.)* **spirituality**
**መንፊት** menfit *(n.)* **sieve**
**መንገፍ** mengef *(n. )* **mote**
**መንገፊ** mengefi *(n.)* **flannel**
**መንጎኛ** mengoȟa *(n.)* **intermediary**
**መንግስታዊ ምቁጽጻር ናብ ብሕታዊ ምቅያር** mengsatawi mquxxar nab bȟtawi mq̈yar *(n. )* **privatize**
**መንግስተ-ሰማያት** mengstesemayat *(n.)* **heaven**
**መንግስቲ** mengsti *(n. )* **government**
**መንግስቲ ኣልቦ** mengsti albo *(adj.)* **stateless**
**መንጉድ** mengud *(n.)* **hump**
**መንህብ** menhb *(n.)* **apiary**
**መንካዕ** menka'ë *(n.)* **bat**
**መንከስ** menkes' *(n.)* **chin**
**መንከስቲ** menkesti *(n.)* **sting**
**መንነት** mennet *(n.)* **identity**
**መኖከሳዊ** menokesawi *(adj.)* **monastic**
**መንቅብ ዘለዎ** menqb zelewo *(adj.)* **faulty**
**መንቀርቀር** menqerker *(n.)* **clip**
**መንቀርቀር** menqerqer *(n.)* **clamp**
**መንቆርቆር** menqorqor *(n.)* **funnel**

መንሸራተቲ menšerateti *(n.)* **skate**
መንሸራተቲ ጣውላ menšerateti tawla *(n. )* **skateboard**
መንሸራተቲ mensherateti *(n.)* **cursor**
መንሸሮ menshro *(n.)* **cancer**
መንሹር menshur *(n. )* **pamphlet**
መንሹር menshur *(n.)* **brochure**
መንሸራተቲ menšrateti *(n.)* **sledge**
መንታጋይ mentagay *(n.)* **archer**
መንተፍተፊ menteftefi *(n.)* **spittoon**
መንጠለ mentele *(v.)* **dispossess**
መንጠለ men'tele *(v.)* **snatch**
መንጠለ men'tele *(v.)* **snipe**
መንጠሊና mentelina *(n.)* **cloak**
መንጠሊና menťelina *(n.)* **cape**
መንጠልጠሊ mențelțeli *(n.)* **hanger**
መንጠልጥሎ menteltlo *(n.)* **pendant**
መንፀፍ mentseff *(n.)* **carpet**
መንጸፍ menxef *(n.)* **bedding**
መንጸሮር menxeror *(n.)* **vertigo**
መንዝዐ menz'e *(v.)* **usurp**
መንዘዐ menzeë *(v.)* **expropriate**
መንዘዐ menze'ë *(v.)* **arrogate**
ምዕቃብ m'ëqab *(n.)* **retention**
መቓብር meqabr *(n.)* **grave**
መቃብር ከውሒ meqabr kewhi *(n.)* **sepulchre**
መቃጨጪ meqačeči *(n.)* **cynic**
መቓልሕ meqalȟ *(n.)* **blip**
መቃልዒ meqali *(n. )* **palmist**
መቃልዒ meqal'i *(adj.)* **inaugural**
መቋመቲ meqamet *(n.)* **scanner**
መቓምጦ meqamțo *(n. )* **habitat**
መቃን meqan *(n.)* **frame**
መቓቐር meqaqer *(n.)* **bookmark**
መቕድም meqdm *(n.)* **preface**
መቕድም meqdm *(n.)* **foreword**
መቕድም meqdm *(n. )* **preamble**
መቕድም meqdm *(n.)* **prologue**
መቀበጣሪ meqebaťeri *(n.)* **sycophant**
መቐለ meqele *(v.)* **divide**
መቐለስ meqeles *(n.)* **axle**
መቐለስያ meqelesya *(n.)* **pivot**
መቀመጫ meqemeča *(n.)* **ass**
መቀመጫ meqemeča *(n.)* **backside**
መቀመጫዊ meqemečawi *(adj.)* **anal**
መቀረ meqere *(v.t. )* **savour**
መቐረት meqeret *(n.)* **flavour**
መቐረት ዘይብሉ meqeret zeyblu *(n.)* **vulgarity**
መቀፀልታ meqexelta *(n.)* **continuation**
መቀያየዲ meqeyayedi *(n. )* **moorings**
መቓቐለ meqhaqhele *(v.)* **sunder**
መቐረት meqheret *(n.)* **sweetness**
መቐየርታ meqhe'yerta *(n.)* **substitute**
መቐየሪ meqhyeri *(n.)* **switch**
መቓልሕ meqlȟ *(n.)* **echo**
መቆምያ meqomya *(n.)* **scaffolding**
መቅረዝ meqrez *(n.)* **candela**
መቅረዝ meqrez *(n.)* **chandelier**
መቑሹሽ meqshush *(v.)* **perk**
መቑሕ እግሪ mequh 'egri *(n.)* **shackle**
መቑሕ ኢድ mequȟ 'id *(n.)* **handcuff**
መቐረጽ ወረቐት meqüretsi wereqet *(n.)* **guillotine**
መቑሪ mequri *(n.)* **probe**
መቑሹሽ meqüshush *(n.)* **bonus**
መቋደሲ meqwadesi *(adj.)* **indulgent**
መቑለፍ meqwelef *(n.)* **buckle**
መቐሎ meqwulo *(n.)* **griddle**
መቕጻዕቲ meqxaëti *(n.)* **punishment**
መቅይሒ meqyȟi *(n.)* **blusher**

መቅይሒ ምዕጉርቲ meqyĥi m'ëgurti *(n.)* **rouge**
መቅዘፊ meqzefi *(n.)* **flipper**
መቕዘፍቲ meq̈zefti *(n.)* **cataclysm**
መቕዘፍቲ meq̈zefti *(n.)* **catastrophe**
መርዓ mer'a *(n. )* **wedding**
መራሕ ብርጌድ meraȟ brgeed *(n.)* **brigadier**
መራሕ መንገዲ meraȟ mengedi *(n.)* **pacemaker**
መራሒ merahi *(n.)* **leader**
መራሒ meraȟi *(n.)* **conductor**
መራሒ መንግስቲ merahi menegeseti *(n.)* **chancellor**
መራሒ ዋኒን meraĥi wanin *(n.)* **entrepreneur**
መራኽቦ meraḱbo *(n.)* **confluence**
መራኸቢ merakebi *(n.)* **rendezvous**
መራኸቢ meraḱebi *(n. )* **junction**
መራኸቢ meraḱebi *(n. )* **juncture**
መራኸቢ ቦታ meraḱebi bota *(n. )* **venue**
መራኸቢ ብዙሓን meraḱebi bzuȟan *(n.)* **media**
መራት merat *(adj.)* **rusty**
መርዓት mer'ät *(n.)* **bride**
መርዓዊ mer'äwi *(v.)* **groom**
መርዓዊ mer'äwi *(n.)* **bridegroom**
መራፀሚ meraxemi *(n.)* **bumper**
መራፆ meraxo *(n.)* **constituency**
መራፆ meraxo *(n.)* **electorate**
ምዕራይ m'ëray *(n.)* **rectification**
መርኣያ mer'aya *(adj.)* **earnest**
መርኣያ mer'aya *(n.)* **epitome**
መርኣያ mer'aya *(n.)* **sample**
መርኣያ መንነት mer'aya mennet *(adj.)* **bespoke**
መርኣዪ ፈተነ ምድላው merayi fetene mdlaw *(n.)* **prototype**
መርብብ merbb *(n.)* **grid**
መርበብ merbeb *(n.)* **intranet**
መርበብ merbeb *(n.)* **mesh**
መርበብ merbeb *(n.)* **net**
መርበብ merbeb *(n.)* **netting**
መረባ mereba *(n.)* **foyer**
መረባ mereba *(n. )* **yard**
መረባ mereba *(n.)* **patio**
መረዳእታ mereda'èta *(n. )* **illustration**
መረዳእታ ኣቕረበ mereda'eta aqrebe *(v.)* **corroborate**
መረዳእታ mered'eta *(n.)* **evidence**
መሬት mereet *(n.)* **land**
መረጋገጺ meregagetsi *(n. )* **testament**
መረጋገጺ meregagexi *(n.)* **assurance**
መረጋገጺ meregagexi *(n.)* **proof**
መረን meren *(n.)* **rein**
መረቕ mereq *(n.)* **minestrone**
መረቕ mereq̈ *(n.)* **broth**
መረቐ mereqe *(v.)* **inaugurate**
ምእረራ m'èrera *(n.)* **browser**
መረሸ mereshe *(v.)* **march**
መረፃ meretsa *(n.)* **poll**
መረፃ meretsa *(n.)* **suffrage**
መረፀ meretse *(v. t)* **choose**
መረፀ meretse *(v.)* **select**
መረፃ merexa *(n.)* **election**
መረፀ merexe *(v.)* **elect**
መረጸ merexe *(v.)* **prefer**
መረዘ mereze *(v.)* **intoxicate**
መርፍእ merf'e *(n.)* **needle**
መርፌእ ምውጋእ merfi'e mwga'e *(n.)* **injection**
መርገም mergem *(n.)* **curse**
መርገጺ mergetsi *(n.)* **stance**
መርገፂ mergetzi *(n.)* **footing**

መርጕ mergwi *(n.)* **stucco**
መርሓ ግብሪ merha gbri *(n.)* **prospectus**
መርሐ merĥe *(v.)* **preside**
መርሐ merḧe *(v.)* **conduct**
መሪድያን meridyan *(n.)* **meridian**
መሪሕ meriḥ *(n.)* **vanguard**
መሪሕነት merihnet *(n. )* **leadership**
መሪሕነት merihnet' *(n.)* **chieftain**
መሪር merir *(adj.)* **bitter**
መሪፁ ዝወስድ meritsu zwesd *(adj.)* **selective**
መርጀን merjen *(n.)* **coral**
መርከብ merkeb *(n.)* **cruiser**
መርከብ merkeb *(n.)* **ferry**
መርከብ merkeb *(n.)* **ship**
መርከብ merkeb *(n.)* **shipping**
መርማሪ mermari *(n.)* **coroner**
መርማሪ ገበን mermari geben *(n.)* **detective**
መርማሪ ገበን mermari geben *(n.)* **sleuth**
መርመራ mermera *(n. )* **investigation**
መርመራ አስከሬን mermera askegrien *(n. )* **post-mortem**
መርመረ mermere *(v.)* **inspect**
መርሚሩ ፈለጠ mermiru felete *(v.)* **diagnose**
መርቅዒ merq'ë *(n.)* **rivet**
መርሳ mersa *(n.)* **harbour**
መርትዖ ኣቕረበ mert'ö *(v.)* **prove**
መርውሓ merwḥa *(n. )* **ventilator**
መርዛም merzam *(adj.)* **noxious**
መርዛም merzam *(adj.)* **poisonous**
መርዛም merzam *(adj.)* **venomous**
መርዛማ merzama *(adj.)* **toxic**
መርዛማ merzama *(n.)* **toxin**
መርዘን merzen *(n. )* **migraine**
መርዚ ኣወገደ merzi awegede *(v.)* **detoxify**
መሳገሪ mesageri *(n.)* **crossing**
መሳገሪ ሓጹር mesageri hatsur *(n.)* **stile**
መስኣሊት mes'alit *(n.)* **camera**
መሳልል mesall *(n.)* **ladder**
መሳርሒያዊ mesarhawi *(adj.)* **instrumental**
መሳርሒ mesarhi *(n.)* **instrument**
መሳርሒ mesarĥi *(n.)* **device**
መሳርሒ mesarĥi *(n.)* **equipment**
መሳርሒ mesarĥi *(n.)* **gadget**
መሳርሒ mesarḧi *(n.)* **apparatus**
መሳርሒ mesarḧi *(n.)* **hard drive**
መሳርሒ mesarḥi *(n. )* **kit**
መሳርሕቲ mesarḧti *(n.)* **colleague**
መሳርያ ምጉዕዓዝ mesarya mgu'ë'äz *(n.)* **vehicle**
መሳሰዪ mesaseyi *(n.)* **accommodation**
መሳጢ mesati *(v.)* **imposing**
መሳጢ mesati *(adj.)* **scenic**
መሳጢ mesaẗi *(n.)* **cynosure**
መስበኽያ mesbeḱya *(n.)* **pulpit**
መሰጋገሪ mesegageri *(n.)* **gangway**
መሰጋገሪ mesegageri *(n. )* **portage**
መሰገድ mesegodi *(n.)* **gasket**
መስኮት mesekote *(n.)* **casement**
መሰልቸዪ meselchyi *(adj.)* **tedious**
መሰለ mesele *(v.)* **purport**
መሰለ mesele *(v.)* **resemble**
መሰለ mesele *(v.)* **seem**
መሰለ mesele *(v.)* **simulate**
መሰናድኢ mesenad'i *(adj.)* **preparatory**
መሰናኽል mesenakl *(n.)* **drawback**
መሰናኽል mesenaḱl *(n.)* **hurdle**

መሰንበድ ኳኽ mesenbed ka'k *(n.)* **scarecrow**
መሰነዪ meseneyi *(n.)* **escort**
መሰነዪ meseneyi *(n. )* **bouncer**
መሰነይታ meseneyta *(n.)* **company**
መሰንገል mesengel *(n. )* **rib**
መሰንቀር mesenqer *(n.)* **chopstick**
መሰንይቲ mesenyti *(n.)* **accompaniment**
መሰረት meseret *(n.)* **foundation**
መሰረት meseret *(n.)* **rudiment**
መሰረት ኣልቦ meseret 'albo *(adj.)* **groundless**
መሰረት ዘይብሉ meseret zeyblu *(adj.)* **unfounded**
መሰረታዊ meseretawi *(adj.)* **essential**
መሰረታዊ meseretawi *(adj.)* **fundamental**
መሰረታዊ ሞገት meseretawi moget *(adj.)* **rudimentary**
መሰረተ ኩርናዕ meserete kurn'ë *(n. )* **milestone**
መሰረተ ልምዓት meserete lm'at *(n.)* **infrastructure**
መሰጠ mesete *(v.)* **impress**
መሰጠ meseẗe *(v.)* **enthral**
መሰጠ meseẗe *(v.)* **fascinate**
መሰጠ meseẗe *(v.)* **captivate**
መሰውያ mesewya *(n.)* **altar**
መሰየሚ meseyemi *(n.)* **denomination**
መስፈዪ mesfeyi *(n.)* **suture**
መስፍን mesfn *(n.)* **viscount**
መስፍንነት mesfnnet *(n.)* **feudalism**
መሽጊ mešgi *(n.)* **slat**
መስጊድ mesgid *(n. )* **mosque**
መስሓቢ ማሽን mesȟabi mashn *(n. )* **pulley**
መስሓቢ mesȟabi *(n.)* **bait**
መስሓቕ mesȟaq̈ *(n.)* **farce**
መስሓቕ mesȟaq̈ *(n.)* **jest**
መስሓቒን meshaqeen *(n.)* **clown**
መስሓቒን mes'haqeen *(adj.)* **ludicrous**
መስሓቒን mesȟaqeen *(n.)* **antic**
መስሓቒን mesȟaq̈een *(n.)* **buffoon**
መስሓቒ meshaqhi *(adj.)* **laughable**
መሸፈን ሉሕ meshefen luḥ *(n.)* **veneer**
መሸፈኒ meshefeni *(n.)* **cover**
መሸፈኒ ሻሽ meshefeni shash *(n.)* **yashmak**
መሸጋገሪ ቦታ meshegageri bota *(n. )* **transit**
መሸጋገሪ ፣ናይ ሽግግር ወቅቲ/ግዜ meshegageri,na mshiggar gze *(n. )* **transition**
መሸጎሪ meshegori *(n.)* **latch**
መሸጐር meshegwar *(n.)* **bolt**
መሸሊት ወዲ ተባዕታይ mesheit nay wedi tebaetay *(n.)* **penis**
መሸከል meshekel *(n. )* **physique**
መሸንበባ በረድ meshenboba bered *(n.)* **hail**
መሸኒ mesheni *(n.)* **urinal**
መሸንቆቋ meshenqoqa *(n.)* **noose**
መሸራሸሪ ህዝቢ mesherasheri hzbi *(n.)* **promenade**
መሸጣ mesheta *(n. )* **sale**
መሸገጥ meshget *(n. )* **locker**
መሸጐራጉር meshgwaragur *(n.)* **alley**
መሸሎኪ meshloki *(n.)* **hatch**
መሸሎቀ meshloqe *(v.)* **scald**
መሾምበባ meshombeba *(n.)* **volley**
መሲሕ mesiȟ *(n.)* **messiah**

**መስከረም** meskerem ***(n.)*** **September**
**መስኮት** meskot ***(n. )*** **pane**
**መስኮት** meskot ***(n.)*** **window**
**መስኮት አፍንጫ** meskot afnča ***(n. )*** **nostril**
**መሽኮት በለ** meškot bele ***(v.)*** **slink**
**መስመር ጎኒ** mesmer goni ***(n.)*** **sideline**
**መስመር መኾስተር** mesmer meḱoster ***(n.)*** **Hoover**
**መስመስታ** mesmesta ***(n.)*** **sheen**
**መስኖ** mesno ***(n.)*** **irrigation**
**መስቀል** mesqel ***(n.)*** **cross**
**መስቀላዊ ዘመተ** mesqelawi zemete ***(n.)*** **crusade**
**መስቆሪቶ** mesqorito ***(n. )*** **lobe**
**መስራቲ** mesrati ***(n. )*** **founder**
**መስርዕ** mesr'e ***(n.)*** **train**
**መስርዕ** mesr'ë ***(n. )*** **queue**
**መስረብያ** mesrebya ***(n.)*** **distillery**
**መሰረታዊ ሞገት** mesretawi moget ***(n.)*** **rationale**
**መስረተ** mesrete ***(v.)*** **situate**
**መስርሕ** mesrĥ ***(n. )*** **process**
**መስርሕ ምርካብ** mesrĥ mrkab ***(n.)*** **procurement**
**መስርኅ ምግቢ** mesrhi mgbi ***(n.)*** **wok**
**መስታ** mesta ***(adj.)*** **coeval**
**መስተ** meste ***(n.)*** **beverage**
**መስተፋቅራዊ** mestefaqrawi ***(adj.)*** **amatory**
**መስተማሰሊ** mestemaseli ***(adj.)*** **maudlin**
**መስተማሰሊ** meste'maseli ***(adj.)*** **sullen**
**መስተንክር** mestenkr ***(adj.)*** **spectacular**
**መስተንክር** mestenkr ***(adj.)*** **swashbuckling**
**መስተርእየት** mester'eyet ***(n.)*** **spectacle**
**መስተዋድድ** mestewadd ***(n.)*** **preposition**
**መስተውዓሊ** mestewali ***(adj.)*** **percipient**
**መስተውዐሊ** mestew'ali ***(adj.)*** **sagacious**
**መስተውዓሊ** mestewäli ***(adj.)*** **provident**
**መስተውዓሊ** mestew'äli ***(adj.)*** **judicious**
**መስተውዓሊ** mestew'äli ***(adj.)*** **reasonable**
**መስተፃምር** mestexamr ***(n.)*** **conjunction**
**መስትዋት** mestwat ***(n.)*** **mirror**
**መስዋእታዊ** meswa'etawi ***(adj.)*** **sacrificial**
**መስዋእቲ** meswa'eti ***(n.)*** **sacrifice**
**መስዋእቲ** meswa'èti ***(n.)*** **victim**
**መጣበቒ** meťabeqi ***(n. )*** **glue**
**መታለሊ** metaleli ***(n.)*** **cheat**
**መታለሊ** metaleli ***(adj.)*** **cunning**
**መታለሊ** metaleli ***(adj.)*** **deceitful**
**መታለሊ** metaleli ***(adj.)*** **fraudulent**
**መታለሊ** metaleli ***(adj.)*** **illusory**
**መታለሊ** metaleli ***(adj.)*** **perfidious**
**መታለሊ** metaleli ***(n.)*** **trickster**
**መታወር** metawer ***(n.)*** **bar**
**መጥባሕቲ** meťbahti ***(n. )*** **surgery**
**መጥባሕቲ መትረብ ዘርኢ** meťbaḧti metreb zer'i ***(n. )*** **vasectomy**
**መጥብሒ** metbhi ***(n.)*** **lancet**
**መተዓሻሸዊ ነገር** m-ete-a-sha-she-wi neger ***(n.)*** **gimmick**
**መተባበዒ** metebab'e ***(n. )*** **incentive**

**መተባብዒ** metebab'e *(n.)* **inducement**
**መተሓበሪ** metehababeri *(n.)* **directory**
**መተሓላለፊ** metehalalefi *(n. )* **passage**
**መተሓፃፀቢ ኣቁሑት** metehasasebi akuhut *(n.)* **toiletries**
**መተሓፃፀቢ** meteĥatsatsebi *(n.)* **sink**
**መተካእታ** metekaeta *(n.)* **replacement**
**መተካእታ** meteka'eta *(n.)* **surrogate**
**መተኮራዊ** metekorawi *(adj.)* **focal**
**መተኮስ ሬሳ** metekos resa *(n. )* **pyre**
**መጠን** meten *(n.)* **proportion**
**መጠን** meten *(n. )* **rate**
**መጠን** meẗen *(n.)* **amount**
**መጠን ድንገት** meten dnget *(n.)* **incidence**
**መጠነ ሓለፍ** meten ḧalef *(n. )* **surfeit**
**መጠን ዝናብ** meten znab *(n.)* **rainfall**
**መጠነኛ** meťenegna *(adj.)* **middling**
**መተንፈሲ** metenfesi *(n.)* **respirator**
**መጠንከርያ** metenkerya *(n.)* **toner**
**መጠንቀቅታ** metenqekta *(n.)* **caution**
**መጠንቀቒ** meťenqeq̈i *(v.)* **portend**
**መጠንቀቕታ** meťenqeq̈ta *(n)* **alarm**
**መጠንቀቕታ** meţenqeq̈ta *(n. )* **warning**
**መጠንጠኒ** meťenťeni *(n.)* **spool**
**መጠቓለሊ** meťeqaleli *(n.)* **summary**
**መጠቅለሊ** meteqleli *(n. )* **roller**
**መጠቕለሊ** meťeq̈leli *(n. )* **package**
**መተርኣስ** meter'as *(n.)* **cushion**
**መተርኣስ** meteras *(n.)* **pillow**
**መተርኣስ ብርኪ** meter'as brki *(n.)* **hassock**
**መተረ** metere *(v.)* **mince**
**መጠርነፍታ** meťernefta *(n.)* **synopsis**
**መጠጠ** meťeťe *(v.)* **stretch**
**መጠይቅ** meteyk *(n. )* **questionnaire**
**መጠፋፍኢ** metfaf'ï *(adj.)* **shifty**
**መጥፍኢ ጸጉሪ** metf'i tseguri *(adj.)* **depilatory**
**መጥሓን** meť'ḧan *(n.)* **mill**
**መትሓዚ** methazi *(n.)* **container**
**መትከል** metkel *(n.)* **principle**
**መትከል** metkel *(n. )* **tenet**
**መትከል** metkel *(n.)* **theorem**
**መትከል ስነ ምግባር** metkel sne mgbar *(n.)* **morality**
**መትከር** metker *(n.)* **hassle**
**መትከር** metker *(n.)* **nuisance**
**መትኮብ** metkob *(n.)* **beak**
**መጥምቓዊ** meťmq̈awi *(n.)* **Baptist**
**መትናዊ** metnawi *(adj.)* **nervous**
**መትኒ** metni *(n.)* **Nerve**
**መጥቃዕቲ** meẗqa'ëti *(n.)* **aggression**
**መጥቃዕቲ** meẗq'ëti *(n.)* **assault**
**መጠራቀሚ** metraqemi *(n.)* **receptacle**
**መትረብ** metreb *(n.)* **canal**
**መትረብ** metreb *(n.)* **channel**
**መትረብ** metreb *(n. )* **ditch**
**መትረብ ፍሳስ** metreb fsas *(n.)* **sewerage**
**መትረብ ግንቢ** metreb g'nbi *(n.)* **moat**
**መፃኢ** metsai *(adj.)* **upcoming**
**መጸንሒ** metsanhi *(adj.)* **tentative**
**መፃረዪ** metsareyi *(n.)* **refinery**
**መፃወዲ** metsawedi *(n.)* **decoy**
**መጽሎ** metselo *(n.)* **hob**
**መፀዋዕታ** metsewa'eta *(n.)* **summons**

መፀዋዕታ metsewa'ëta *(n.)* **invitation**
መጽሓፍ metshaf *(n.)* **textbook**
መፂሄት metsihiet *(n.)* **magazine**
መፂፅ metsits *(adj.)* **sour**
መፅለሊ metsleli *(n.)* **shed**
መፅናዕቲ metsna'eti *(n.)* **study**
መፅናዕቲ metsnaëti *(n.)* **research**
መፅናዕቲ ምዕባለ ቋንቋታት metsnaeti m'ëbale qanqatat *(n.)* **philology**
መፅናንዒ metsna'n'i *(n. )* **solace**
መጽንሒ መልእኽቲ metsnhi melekti *(n.)* **voicemail**
መፅወድያ metswedya *(n.)* **snare**
መጥወዪ meẗweyi *(n.)* **crook**
መፃኢ metza'i *(n.)* **future**
መፀባበቂ metzebabeqi *(n.)* **make-up**
መፀየ metzeye *(v.)* **leach**
መዋጮ mewacho *(n.)* **kitty**
መዋእል mewa'el *(n. )* **standing**
መዋኢ mewa'i *(n.)* **victor**
መዋኽር mewaker *(n.)* **gazebo**
መዋላይ mewalay *(n.)* **financier**
መዋላይ mewalay *(n.)* **sponsor**
መዋኽራዊ mewaqhrawi *(adj.)* **structural**
መዋኽር mewaqr *(n. )* **framework**
መዋቅር mewaqr *(n.)* **machinery**
መዋኽር mewaqr *(n.)* **structure**
መዋቲ mewati *(adj.)* **mortal**
መዋጥር mewatr *(n.)* **dilemma**
መውዓይ mew'äy *(n.)* **heating**
መወዳእታ mewedaeta *(adj.)* **ultimate**
መወዳእታ meweda'èta *(n.)* **conclusion**
መወዳእታ meweda'èta *(adj.)* **final**
መወዳእታ ዘይብሉ meweda'èta zeyblu *(adj.)* **interminable**
መወዳእታ አልቦ meweda'ta albo *(n.)* **infinity**
መወድስ meweds *(n.)* **rhapsody**
መወጅሂ mewejhi *(n.)* **conditioner**
መወቃቀቢ mewekakebi *(n.)* **decor**
መዉዓሊ ህፃናት mew'eli hxanat *(n.)* **crèche**
መውዐሊ ህፃናት mew'ëli hxanat *(n. )* **nursery**
መውዕሎ mew'ëlo *(n.)* **allowance**
መወልወሊ mewelweli *(n.)* **towelling**
መወልወሊ አፍ mewelweli a'f *(n. )* **napkin**
መወናወኒ mewenaweni *(n.)* **allure**
መወስቦአዊ mewesbo'awi *(v.t. & i.)* **conjugal**
መወሰኽታ mewesekhta *(n.)* **supplement**
መውቃዕቲ mewqa'ëti *(n.)* **concussion**
መውቅዒ mewqe *(n. )* **whip**
መውቀጢ mewqeẗi *(n. )* **mortar**
መውስቦአዊ mewsbo'awi *(adj.)* **matrimonial**
መዉፅኢ mewx'i *(n.)* **exit**
መውጽኢ-ነፍሲ mewx'inefsi *(n.)* **alibi**
መጽጸወቲ ቦታ mexaweti bota *(n.)* **playground**
መጸ mexe *(v.)* **accede**
መጸ mexe *(v.)* **arrive**
መፀባበቒ mexebabeqi *(adj.)* **cosmetic**
መፀባበቂ ቅብአት mexebabeqi qb'at *(n.)* **cosmetic**
መፅናዕንዒ mexenaee'neeeii *(n.)* **consolation**

**መፀውዒ** mexew''ï *(n.)* **nomenclature**
**መጸዩ** mexeye *(v.)* **absorb**
**መጽሓፍ** mexḧaf *(n.)* **book**
**መጽሓፍ ንጀመርቲ** mexḧaf *(n.)* **primer**
**መጽሓፍ ቅዱስ** mexḧaf qdus *(n.)* **Bible**
**መጽሓፍ ሸያጢት** mexḧaf sheyaïit *(n.)* **bookseller**
**መፂፅ** mexix *(adj.)* **acerbic**
**መፅለሊ** mexleli *(n.)* **filter**
**መጽናዕቲ ድምጺ ልሳን** mexnaeti dmxi lsan *(adj.)* **phonetic**
**መዛግብቲ** mezagbti *(n.)* **archives**
**መዛዘሚ** mezazemi *(n.)* **finial**
**መዛዘሚ** mezazemi *(n.)* **selvedge**
**መዛዘሚ** mezazemi *(n.)* **binding**
**መዝበብ** mezbeb *(n.)* **spout**
**መዘኻኸሪ** mezekakeri *(n.)* **reminder**
**መዘኻኸሪ** mezeḱakeri *(n.)* **memento**
**መዘኻኸሪ** mezeḱaḱeri *(n.)* **note**
**መዘኻኸሪት** mezeḱaḱerit *(n.)* **notebook**
**መዘከርታ** mezekerta *(n. )* **keepsake**
**መዘከርታ** mezekerta *(n. )* **souvenir**
**መዘክር** mezekr *(n.)* **memo**
**መዘክር** mezekr *(n.)* **memorandum**
**መዘምራን** mezemeran *(n.)* **choir**
**መዘምራን** mezemeran *(adj.)* **latent**
**መዘምራዊ** mezemrawi *(adj.)* **choral**
**መዘና** mezena *(n.)* **counterpart**
**መዘና አንቦ** mezena albo *(adj.)* **peerless**
**መዘና አልቦ** mezena albo *(adj.)* **superlative**
**መዘና ዘይብሉ** mezena zeyblu *(adj.)* **nonpareil**
**መዘናግዒ ክፍሊ(ሳሎን)** mezenagei kfli *(n. )* **parlour**
**መዘናግዒ** mezenag'i *(n.)* **entertainment**
**መዘናግዒ ቦታ** mezenag'ï bota *(n.)* **resort**
**መዘነ** mezene *(v.)* **weigh**
**መዘዘ** mezeze *(v.)* **authorize**
**መዝገብ** mezgeb *(n.)* **dossier**
**መዝገብ** mezgeb *(n. )* **ledger**
**መዝገብ** mezgeb *(n.)* **register**
**መስመር** msmer *(n.)* **line**
**መስመር** msmer *(n. )* **wiring**
**መስርዕ ሕብርታት ናይ ዝተዋህበ ስራሕ** msrie hbrtat nay ztewahbe srah *(n. )* **palette**
**መጥበውቲ** mtbeewti *(n.)* **mammal**
**መዝገብ** mezgeb *(n.)* **trench**
**መዝገበ** mezgebe *(v.t. )* **jot**
**መዝገበ ቃላት** mezgebe kalat *(n.)* **dictionary**
**መዝገበ ቃላት** mezgebe qalat *(n.)* **lexicon**
**መዝገበ-ታሪኽ** mezgebe tarik *(n.)* **annals**
**መዝሓሊ** mezhali *(n.)* **cooler**
**መዝሓሊ** mezḧali *(n. )* **fridge**
**መዝሓሊት** mezḧalit *(n.)* **freezer**
**መዝሓቀ** mezĥaqe *(v.)* **extrude**
**መዚ** mezi *(n.)* **authority**
**መዝሙር** mezmur *(n.)* **anthem**
**መዝሙር** mezmur *(n.)* **chorus**
**መዝሙር ዳዊት** mezmur dawit *(n. )* **psalm**
**መዞሪ** mezori *(n.)* **roundabout**
**መዞሪ** mezori *(n.)* **winder**
**መዝረጊ** mezregi *(n.)* **spoiler**
**መዝረቕ** mezreq *(n.)* **skewer**

**መዝወሪ ንፋስ** mezweri nfas *(n.)* **whirlwind**
**መፍረ ሓሰማ** mfre hasema *(n.)* **piggery**
**መግዛዝእ** mgza'è *(n. )* **governance**
**መሓሪ** mhari *(adj.)* **clement**
**መፀውዒ ሽም** qendi *(n.)* **forename**
**መኻን** mkhan *(adj.)* **infertile**
**መልእኽቲ** ml'kti *(n.)* **message**
**መወለዒ** mwel'e *(n.)* **lighter**
**መዘና** mzena *(n.)* **peer**
**መሓላ** mehala *(n. )* **oath**
**መሐብሐቢ ዘኽታም ህፃናት** mehebhebi zektam htsanat *(n.)* **orphanage**
**መላዘቢ** melazebi *(n.)* **overture**
**መስርዕ** mesr'e *(n.)* **order**
**መስዋእቲ** meswa'eti *(n.)* **offering**
**መርመረ** mermere *(v.)* **overlook**
**መበቁላውነት** mebeqolawinet *(n.)* **originality**
**መከራ** mekera *(n. )* **ordeal**
**መካነ-ትዕዝብቲ** mekane-t'ezebti *(n.)* **observatory**
**መኰነን** mekonen *(n.)* **officer**
**መውጽኢ** mewts'i *(n.)* **outlet**
**መደረ** medere *(n.)* **oration**
**መዳራይ** medaray *(n.)* **orator**
**መድሓኒት ልዕሊ መጠን ምውሳድ** medhanit l'eli meten mwsad *(n.)* **overdose**
**መጀመሪ** mejemeri *(n.)* **originator**
**መጀመሪ** mejemeri *(n.)* **outset**
**መጀመርያ** mejemerya *(n.)* **onset**
**መጥቃዕቲ** metqa'ëti *(n.)* **offence**
**መጸለዪ ክፍሊ** mrtseleyi kfli *(n. )* **oratory**
**መጸባበቒ** metsebabeqi *(n.)* **ornament**

## ሙ

**ሙዚቃዊ ቅናት** muziqawi qnat *(n.)* **orchestra**
**ሙዚቃዊ ቅናት** muziqawi qnat *(adj.)* **orchestral**
**ሙሉእ ሂወት** mlu'e hiwet *(adj.)* **lifelong**
**ሙሉእ** milu'e *(adj.)* **full**
**ሙጉሊ** muguili *(n.)* **pus**
**ሙሁር** muhur *(adj.)* **literate**
**ሙቅ** muk *(adj.)* **thermal**
**ሙቀት እና ደርቅ ኣየር** muket ena derq ayer *(n.)* **tropic**
**ሙኮራ** mukora *(n. )* **trial**
**ሙላህ** mulah *(n. )* **mullah**
**ሙልሳ** mulsa *(n.)* **mousse**
**ሙሉእ** mulu'e *(adj.)* **entire**
**ሙሉእ ብሙሉእ** mulu'e bmulu'e *(prep. )* **throughout**
**ሙሉእ ሓሳብ** mulu'e hasab *(n.)* **sentence**
**ሙምያ** mumya *(n. )* **mummy**
**ሙቀት መቆፃፀሪ ብልሃት** muqet meqosaser blhat *(n.)* **thermostat**
**ሙቀት መጠን** muqet meten *(n. )* **temperature**
**ሙራለ** murale *(n.)* **joist**
**ሙስካ** muska *(n. )* **musk**
**ሙስኪቶ** muskito *(n. )* **musket**
**ሙስኬተኛ** muskitogna *(n. )* **musketeer**
**ሙስሊ** musli *(n.)* **muesli**
**ሙስሊን** muslin *(v. )* **muslin**
**ሙስታንግ** mustang *(n.)* **mustang**
**ሙስቴላ** musteela *(n.)* **mink**
**ሙታንታ** mutanta *(n.)* **underpants**
**ሙታንታ** mutanta *(n. )* **underwear**
**ሙታንቲ** mutanti *(n.)* **panties**

**ሙዝ** muz ***(n.)* banana**
**ሙዛ** muza ***(n.)* muse**
**ሙዚቃ መሰርሒ** muzika mesarhi ***(n.)* zither**
**ሙዚቃ** muziqa ***(n.)* music**
**ሙዚቃዊ** muziqawi ***(adj.)* jazzy**
**ሙዚቃዊ** muziqawi ***(adj.)* musical**
**ሙዚቃዊ ምርኢት** muziqawi mr'it ***(n.)* concert**
**ሙዚቀኛ** muziqegna ***(n. )* musician**

# ሚ

**ሚዛኑ ሰሓተ** mizanu seĥate ***(v.)* overbalance**
**ሚዶ/መመሸጥ** mido/memesheti ***(n.)* comb**
**ሚሽሚሽ** mishmishe ***(n.)* apricot**
**ሚእታዊት** mietawit ***(n. )* percentage**
**ሚእቲ** mi-eti ***(adj.& n.)* hundred**
**ሚሒ** miĥe ***(n.)* matrix**
**ሚላሳ** milasa ***(n. )* molasses**
**ሚትራ** mitra ***(n. )* mitre**
**ሚሊግራም** miligram ***(n.)* milligram**
**ሚሊሜትር** milimeetr ***(n.)* millimetre**
**ሚልየን** milyen ***(n. )* million**
**ሚልየነር** milyener ***(n. )* millionaire**
**ሚና** mina ***(n. )* mine**
**ሚኒባስ** minibas ***(n.)* minibus**
**ሚኒካብ** minikab ***(n.)* minicab**
**ሚኒም** minim ***(n.)* minim**
**ሚኒስከርት** miniskert ***(n.)* miniskirt**
**ሚኒስተር** minister ***(n.)* minister**
**ሚኒስተራዊ** ministrawi ***(adj.)* ministerial**
**ሚርቶ** mirto ***(n.)* myrtle**
**ሚስማር** mismar ***(n.)* nail**
**ሚስጥራዊ** misťirawi ***(adj.)* subtle**
**ሚስጢርነት** misťirnet ***(n.)* subtlety**
**ሚስጥር** misťr ***(n.)* mystery**
**ሚዛን** mizan ***(n.)* scale**
**ሚዛናዊ** mizanawi ***(adj.)* equitable**
**ሚዛናዊ** mizanawi ***(adj.)* fair**

# ማ

**ማዕጠቕ** ma'ëťeq ***(n.)* girth**
**ማህደረ ቃላት** mahdere qalat ***(n.)* glossary**
**ማጀንታ** maĵenta ***(n.)* magenta**
**ማዕከል** meee'kele ***(n. )* centre**
**ማዕበል** maebel ***(n.)* turbulence**
**ማዕበል** ma'ebel ***(n.)* storm**
**ማዕበላዊ** maebelawi ***(adj.)* wavy**
**ማዕበላዊ** ma'ebelawi ***(adj.)* stormy**
**ማዕበላዊ** ma'ebelawi ***(adj.)* tidal**
**ማዕበላዊ** ma'ebelawi ***(n.)* tidally**
**ማዕበለ** ma'ebele ***(v.)* wave**
**ማዕበለ** ma'ëbele ***(v.)* evolve**
**ማዕዳ** ma'ëda ***(n.)* recommendation**
**ማእዳ ዝግበኦ** ma'eda zgbe'o ***(adj.)* meritorious**
**ማዕድን** maeden ***(n.)* zircon**
**ማዕድን** ma-e-den ***(n.)* garnet**
**ማዕድን** ma'edn ***(n.)* talc**
**ማእገር** ma'eger ***(n.)* shoulder**
**ማዕቐፍ** ma-ekef ***(n.)* gamut**
**ማእኸል** ma'eḱel ***(adj.)* midst**
**ማእኸላይ** ma'eḱelay ***(adj.)* median**
**ማእኸላይ** ma'eḱelay ***(n.)* medium**
**ማእኸላይ** ma'eḱelay ***(adj.)* middle**
**ማእከላይ** ma'èkelay ***(adj.)* intermediate**
**ማእኸላይ ሰለዋ** ma'ëḱelay selewa ***(n. )* mezzanine**

**ማእከላይ** ma'èkelay ***(n.)* average**
**ማዕከን** ma'ëken ***(n.)* granary**
**ማዕከን ሓበሬታ** ma'ëken ĥabereta ***(n.)* database**
**ማእኸል** ma'ekhel ***(n. )* locus**
**ማእኸል መዛናግዒ** ma'ekhel mezanag'e ***(n. )* lounge**
**ማዕረ** ma'ere ***(n. )* stalemate**
**ማዕረ** ma'ëre ***(adj.)* equal**
**ማዕረ** ma'ëre ***(adj.)* quits**
**ማዕረ ገበረ** ma'ëre gebere ***(v. t)* equalize**
**ማዕረ ጌሩ ረኣየ** ma'ëre gieru re'aye ***(v.)* equate**
**ማዕረ ዝርሕቀቱ** ma'ëre zrḧqetu ***(adj.)* equidistant**
**ማዕረ-ጐድናዊ** ma'ëregwadnawi ***(adj.)* equilateral**
**ማዕርነት** maernet ***(n. )* parity**
**ማዕርነት ኩነታት** maernet kunetat ***(n. )* par**
**ማእሰርቲ** ma'eserti ***(n.)* bondage**
**ማእሰርቲ** ma'eserti ***(n.)* custody**
**ማእሰርቲ** ma'eserti ***(n.)* detention**
**ማእሰርቲ** ma'èserti ***(n.)* confinement**
**ማዕተብ** ma'ëteb ***(n. )* necklace**
**ማዕፂድ** ma'ëtsid ***(n.)* sickle**
**ማዕፆ** ma'ëtso ***(n.)* door**
**ማዕጾ ርባ** ma'ëtso rba ***(n.)* grating**
**ማእዘር** ma'ezer ***(n. )* spoke**
**ማእዘራይ** ma'ezeray ***(adj.)* radial**
**ማእዝን** ma'èzn ***(n.)* bearing**
**ማፋ** mafa ***(n.)* Louvre**
**ማፋ ማይ** mafa may ***(n.)* hydrant**
**ማፊን** mafin ***(n.)* muffin**

**ምዕጋት** mägat ***(n.)* prevention**
**ማግኔት** magnet ***(n.)* magnet**
**ማግኔታዊ** magnetawi ***(adj.)* magnetic**
**ማግኔታዊነት** magnetawinet ***(n.)* magnetism**
**ማሕ በለ** maĥ bele ***(v.)* flash**
**ማሕበር** maḧber ***(n.)* commune**
**ማሕበር** maḧber ***(n.)* confederation**
**ማሕበር** maḥber ***(n. )* guild**
**ማሕበር ደናግል** maĥber denagl ***(n.)* sisterhood**
**ማሕበር** maḧber ***(n.)* association**
**ማሕበራት** mahberat ***(n.)* unionist**
**ማሕበራዊ** mahberawi ***(adj.)* social**
**ማሕበራዊ ከባቢ** maḧberawi kebabi ***(n.)* milieu**
**ማሕበራዊነት** mahberawinet ***(n.)* socialism**
**ማሕበረ ሰብ** maḧbere seb ***(n.)* community**
**ማሕበረሰብ** ma'hbereseb ***(n. )* sociology**
**ማሕበርነታዊ** mahbernetawi ***(n. & adj.)* socialist**
**ማሕደፍ** maĥdef ***(n.)* rudder**
**ማህደር** mahder ***(n. )* portfolio**
**ማህደር** mahder ***(n. )* satchel**
**ማህደረ ትምህርቲ** mahdere tmhrti ***(n.)* scholarship**
**ማሕበረሰባዊ** mahebresebawi ***(adj.)* civil**
**ማሕፉዳ** maḥfuda ***(n.)* wallet**
**ማሕበራዊ ደረጃ** mahiberawi dereja ***(n.)* caste**
**ማሕለኻ** mahleka ***(n.)* disincentive**
**ማህለት** mahlet ***(n. )* hymn**
**ማሕምም** mahmm ***(n.)* chum**
**ማሕቋቑ** maĥqwaq ***(adj.)* emaciated**
**ማሕረዲ** mahredi ***(n.)* shambles**
**ማሕረሳዊ** maḧresawi ***(adj.)* agrarian**

**ማሕሲእ** mahsi'e ***(n.)*** **lamb**
**ማሕተም** mahtem ***(n. )*** **seal**
**ማሕተም** maḣtem ***(n.)*** **stamp**
**ማህጸን** mahxen ***(n.)*** **uterus**
**ማህጸን** mahxen ***(n.)*** **womb**
**መካነ እንስሳት** makane enssatat ***(n.)*** **zoo**
**ማእኸላይ** ma'ḱelay ***(adj.)*** **moderate**
**ማእኸላይ** ma'ḱelay ***(adj.)*** **neutral**
**ማኪና** makina ***(n.)*** **car**
**ማማ** mama ***(n.)*** **mum**
**ማሞዝ** mamoz ***(n.)*** **mammoth**
**ማና** mana ***(n.)*** **manna**
**ማንጋኔዝ** manganiez ***(n. )*** **manganese**
**ማንጎ** mango ***(n.)*** **mango**
**ማንካ** manka ***(n.)*** **spoon**
**ማንካ ሙሉእ** manka mulu'e ***(n.)*** **spoonful**
**ማንም ይኹን** manm yekun ***(pron.)*** **whoever**
**ማንቋ** manqwa ***(n.)*** **rift**
**ማንታ** manta ***(n.)*** **twin**
**ማንቲለ** mantile ***(n. )*** **hare**
**ማንትለ** mantle ***(n. )*** **rabbit**
**ማንትራ** mantra ***(n.)*** **mantra**
**ማኑዋል** manuwal ***(n. )*** **handbook**
**ማዕበል ባሕሪ** maobrl hahi ***(n.)*** **tide**
**ማራኺ** marakhi ***(adj.)*** **striking**
**ማራኺ** marakhi ***(adj.)*** **sublime**
**ማራኺ** maraki ***(n.)*** **captor**
**ማራኺ** maraki ***(adj.)*** **winsome**
**ማራኺ** maraḱi ***(adj.)*** **attractive**
**ማራኺ** maraḱi ***(adj.)*** **interesting**
**ማራኺ** maraḱi ***(adj.)*** **inviting**
**ማራኺ** maraḱi ***(adj.)*** **beautiful**
**ማራኪ** marakii ***(adj.)*** **charming**
**ማራቶን** maraton ***(n.)*** **marathon**
**ማርጋሪን** margarin ***(n. )*** **margarine**
**ማርጋሪን** margarin ***(n.)*** **aubergine**
**ማርገሪታ** margerita ***(n.)*** **daisy**
**ማሪት** marit ***(n.)*** **superstition**
**ማሪታዊ** maritawi ***(adj.)*** **superstitious**
**ማርክስነት** marksnet ***(n.)*** **Marxism**
**ማርማላታ** marmalade ***(n. )*** **marmalade**
**ማርና** marna ***(n.)*** **marl**
**ማሮን** maron ***(n.)*** **maroon**
**ማርስ** mars ***(n.)*** **Mars**
**ማርሳፓን** marsapan ***(n.)*** **marzipan**
**ማርሽ** marsh ***(n.)*** **gear**
**ማርሻቤዲ** marshabedi ***(n. )*** **pavement**
**ማርሻል** marshal ***(n.)*** **marshal**
**ማርተሎ** martelo ***(n.)*** **hammer**
**ማሰነ** masene ***(v.)*** **languish**
**ማሰኛ** masenya ***(n.)*** **bard**
**ማስኬራ** maskeera ***(n.)*** **mask**
**ማታዶር** mata'dor ***(n. )*** **matador**
**ማይ** may ***(n. )*** **water**
**ማይ** may ***(n.)*** **water**
**ማይ ዓገት** may 'äget ***(adj.)*** **waterproof**
**ማይ ጨው** may čew ***(n.)*** **brine**
**ማይ ጨባ** may cheba ***(n.)*** **whey**
**ማይ ምዕጎ** may m'ëgo ***(n.)*** **blister**
**ማያዊ** mayawi ***(n.)*** **ultramarine**
**ማያዊ** mayawi ***(adj.)*** **aquatic**
**ማያዊ** mayawi ***(adj.)*** **aqueous**
**ማይ መዋህለሊ** maye mwaheleli ***(n.)*** **cistern**
**ማይካ** mayka ***(n. )*** **mica**
**ማይክሮ ባዮሎጂ** maykro bayoloji ***(n.)*** **microbiology**
**ማይክሮ ሰርጀሪ** maykro serjeri ***(n.)*** **microsurgery**

**ማይክሮቺፕ** maykrochip ***(n.)*** **microchip**
**ማይክሮፎን** maykrofon ***(n. )*** **microphone**
**ማይክሮ ሜትር** maykromeetr ***(n. )*** **micrometer**
**ማይክሮስኮፕ** maykroskop ***(n.)*** **microscope**
**ማይክሮዌቭ** maykroweev ***(n.)*** **microwave**
**ማይል** mayl ***(n. )*** **mile**
**ማዮነዝ** mayonez ***(n.)*** **mayonnaise**
**ማዮሲን** mayosin ***(n. )*** **myosin**
**ማይሰጠም** mayseṭem ***(adj.)*** **watertight**
**ማዘርቦርድ** mazerbord ***(n.)*** **motherboard**
**ሜዳ** mieda ***(n.)*** **field**

# ሜ

**ሜላ ኣሰራርሓ** miela aserarȟa ***(n.)*** **proceedings**
**ሜንታ ፐፐሮኒ** mienta peperoni ***(n.)*** **peppermint**
**ሜዳልያ** meedalya ***(n. )*** **medal**
**ሜዳልዮን** meedalyon ***(n.)*** **medallion**
**ሜሎድራማ** meelodrama ***(n.)*** **melodrama**
**ሜሎድራማዊ** meelodramawi ***(adj.)*** **melodramatic**
**ሜማ** meema ***(n.)*** **censorship**
**ሜንታ** meenta ***(n.)*** **mint**
**ሜርኩሪ** meerkury ***(n. )*** **mercury**
**ሜስ** mees ***(n. )*** **mead**
**ሜታቦሊዝም** meetabolizm ***(n.)*** **metabolism**
**ሜታፊዚካ** meetafizika ***(n.)*** **metaphysics**
**ሜታፊዚካዊ** meetafizikawi ***(adj.)*** **metaphysical**
**ሜትር** meetr ***(n. )*** **meter**
**ሜትር** meetre ***(n.)*** **metre**
**ሜትሮኣዊ** meetro'awi ***(adj.)*** **metric**
**ሜትዮር** meetyor ***(n.)*** **meteor**
**ሜትዮሪካዊ** meetyorikawi ***(adj.)*** **meteoric**
**ሜትዮሮሎጂ** meetyoroloji ***(n.)*** **meteorology**
**ሜላ ደላዪ ሰብ** mela delayi seb ***(n.)*** **trouble-shooter**
**ሜጋ ባይት** meega bayt ***(n.)*** **megabyte**
**ሜጋ ሀርዝ** meega herz ***(n.)*** **megahertz**
**ሜጋ ፒክስል** meega piksl ***(n.)*** **megapixel**
**ሜኑ** menu ***(n.)*** **menu**
**ሜዳ በረድ** meda bered ***(n.)*** **rink**

# ም

**ምዕዳግ** mëdag ***(v.)*** **purchase**
**ምውዓል** mw'al ***(n.)*** **investment**
**ምውዳድ** mwdad ***(n.)*** **montage**
**ምውዳድ** mwdad ***(n.)*** **adjustment**
**ምውድዳር** mwddar ***(n.)*** **competition**
**ምውፋር** mwfar ***(n.)*** **sortie**
**ምውጋእ** mwgai ***(v.)*** **poke**
**ምውካስ** mwkas ***(n. )*** **reference**
**ምውላድ** mwlad ***(n.)*** **birth**
**ምውልዋል** mwlwal ***(n.)*** **polish**
**ምውቕ** mwq̈ ***(adj.)*** **fervid**
**ምውራድ** mwrad ***(n.)*** **ebb**
**ምውራድ** mwrad ***(n.)*** **perversion**

ምውራድ mwrad *(n. )* **landing**
ምውራር mwrar *(n. )* **invasion**
ምውዓይ መግቢ ባክተርያ ንምጥፋእ mwuay megbi bakteriya nmtfae *(adj.)* **pasteurized**
ምዉቕ mwuq *(adj.)* **spirited**
ምዉቕ ዝበለ mwuq zbele *(adj.)* **tepid**
ምዉቕን ምችዊን mwuqn mchuwn *(adj.)* **cosy**
ምዉቕን ምችዊን mwuqn mchuwn *(adj.)* **cosy**
ምውሳድ mwusad *(n.)* **takeaway**
ምዉት mwut *(adj.)* **deceased**
ምዉት mwut *(adj.)* **soulless**
ምውጻእ mwxae *(v.)* **withdraw**
ምውጻእ mwxae *(n.)* **withdrawal**
ምጽዓቕ mx'äq *(n.)* **concentration**
ምጽኣት mx'at *(n.)* **advent**
ምፀታይ mxetay *(n.)* **nectarine**
ምጽላም mxlam *(n.)* **calumny**
ምጽላይ mxlay *(v.)* **pray**
ምዝገባ mzgeba *(n. )* **registration**
ምዝማር mzmar *(v.)* **yodel**
ምዝመዛ mzmeza *(n.)* **extraction**
ምዝንጋዕ mzngaë *(n.)* **prank**
ምዝንጋዕ mznga'ë *(n.)* **distraction**
ምዝንጋዕ mznga'ë *(n.)* **evasion**
ምዝንጋዕ mznga'ë *(n. )* **recreation**
ምዝንጋዕ mznga'ë *(n.)* **amusement**
ምዝራብ ዘይኽእል mzrab zeykh'el *(adj.)* **inarticulate**
ምጽናዕ mxnae *(n.)* **persistence**
ምጽንናዕ mxnna'ë *(n.)* **condolence**
ምፅራይ mx'ray *(n.)* **enquiry**
ምፁ mxu *(n.)* **mongoose**
ምጽ'ዋት mxwat *(n.)* **alms**
ምፅያቕ mxyaq *(n.)* **mottle**
ምዩቕ በለ myuq̈ bele *(v.)* **blench**
ምይይጥ myyt *(n.)* **debate**
ምይይጥ myyt *(n.)* **discussion**
ምዝባለ mzbale *(n.)* **deformity**
ምዝባጥ mzbat *(n.)* **smack**
ምዝቡል mzbul *(adj.)* **abnormal**
ምዕዶ m'ëdo *(n.)* **advice**
ምብዓድ mb'ad *(n.)* **sedition**
ምብካል mbkal *(v.)* **pollute**
ምብኻይ mbḱay *(v.)* **blub**
ምብልዕላዕ mbl'ëlaë *(n.)* **reaction**
ምብልሻው mblshaw *(n.)* **blight**
ምብልሻው mblshaw *(n.)* **undoing**
ምብቋል mbqwal *(n. )* **germination**
ምብራድ mbrad *(n. )* **refrigeration**
ምብራህ mbrah *(n. )* **illumination**
ምብርዓን mbr'än *(n.)* **miscarriage**
ምብራቕ mbraq̈ *(n.)* **east**
ምብራቓዊ mbraq̈awi *(adj.)* **eastern**
ምብራር mbrar *(n.)* **expulsion**
ምብራር mbrar *(n.)* **repulsion**
መብረቕ mbreqh *(n.)* **lighting**
መበረቕ mbreqh *(n. )* **lightening**
ምብስባስ mbsbas *(v.)* **witter**
ምብትታን mbttan *(n.)* **rout**
ምቡኳዕ mbukwa'ë *(n.)* **fermentation**
ምብዛሕ mbzah *(n.)* **preponderance**
ምብዛሕ mbzaḧ *(v.)* **populate**
ምብዛሕ mbzaḧ *(n.)* **propagation**
ምጭባጥ mčbaẗ *(n.)* **compression**
ምቾት mchot *(n.)* **comfort**
ምቾት mchot *(n.)* **convenience**
ምቾት mchot *(n.)* **luxury**
ምቹው mchuw *(adj.)* **favourable**
ምቹው mcḥuw *(adj.)* **luxurious**
ምቹው mchuw *(adj.)* **suitable**
ምቹው mchuw *(n.)* **utopia**
ምቹው mchu'w *(adj.)* **comfortable**

ምቹዊ mchuwi *(adj.)* **convenient**
ምቹው mchuwi *(adj.)* **cuddly**
ምእዙዝ me-ezuz *(adj.)* **genial**
ምዕፋን m'efan *(n.)* **suffocation**
ምጉርምራም mgurmram *(v.i.)* **grunt**
ምሓዝ m-ha-z *(v.)* **grab**
ምሕኩልቲ mḥkulti *(n. )* **hip**
ምህሙን mhmun *(adj.)* **wan**
ምሕናቕ mḥnaq̈ *(n.)* **hanging**
ምንቃሕ mnkah *(v.)* **waken**
ምቕዳሕ mq̈daḥ *(n. )* **imitation**
ምቕማጥ mq̈maṭ *(n.)* **habitation**
ምርኢት mr'it *(n.)* **vaudeville**
ምስክር mskr *(n.)* **voucher**
ምስሌነ msleene *(n.)* **viceroy**
ምስሊ msli *(n. )* **image**
ምስማዕ msma'ë *(n.)* **hearing**
ምጽያቕ mtseyaq̈ *(n. )* **graffiti**
ምውላዕ mwla'ë *(n.)* **ignition**
ምሕረት meherte *(n.)* **clemency**
ምቹውነት mchuwnet *(n.)* **suitability**
ምጭንጓዕ mčnguaë *(n. )* **pump**
ምጭራሕ mĉraĥ *(n.)* **exclamation**
ምድብ mdb *(n.)* **rating**
ምድብ መዘና mdb mezena *(n.)* **peerage**
ምደባ mdeba *(n.)* **placement**
ምደባ mdeba *(n.)* **assignation**
ምድፋር mdfar *(n.)* **molestation**
ምድጋፍ mdgaf *(n.)* **adherence**
ምድጋም mdgam *(n.)* **recurrence**
ምድጋም ፍእምተ ቃል mdgam f'emte qal *(v.)* **alliterate**
ምድግጋም mdggam *(n.)* **reiteration**
ምድሓን mdhan *(n.)* **salvation**
መድሓኒ mdhani *(n. )* **panacea**
ምድህላል mdhlal *(n.)* **diversion**
ምድጃ mdja *(n.)* **stove**
ምድላው mdlaw *(n.)* **bias**
ምድላው mdlaw *(n.)* **composition**
ምድላው mdlaw *(n.)* **partiality**
ምድላው mdlaw *(n.)* **preparation**
ምድላይ mdlay *(n.)* **pursuit**
ምድላይ mdlay *(n.)* **quest**
ምፅመድ mdmas *(n.)* **trap**
ምድንጋር mdngar *(n.)* **elusion**
ምድንጋር mdngar *(n.)* **perplexity**
ምድንጋር mdngar *(n.)* **rigging**
ምድንጓይ mdnguay *(n.)* **procrastination**
ምድቃል mdqal *(n.)* **clone**
ምድራዊ mdrawi *(adj.)* **earthly**
ምድራዊ mdrawi *(adj.)* **secular**
ምልክዑ ቀይሩ melk'u keyru *(v. )* **transfigure**
ምእማን meman *(n.)* **persuasion**
ምእማር m'èmar *(n.)* **conception**
ምምጽዋት meme tse wat *(n.)* **handout**
ምዕራብ merab *(n.)* **west**
ምዕራባዊ merabawi *(adj.)* **western**
ምዕራባዊ ምግር merabawi mgbar *(v.)* **westernize**
ምድራዝ mdraz *(n. )* **massage**
ምድረ-ማያዊ mdremayawi *(n.)* **amphibian**
ምድሪ mdri *(n.)* **earth**
ምድሪ ዝንቕንቕ ድምጺ mdri z'nqhn'qh dmtsi *(adj.)* **stentorian**
ምዱብ ስራሕ mdub sraȟ *(n.)* **assignment**
ምድያብ mdyab *(n.)* **accession**
ማዓድን me'ädn *(n.)* **mineral**
ምዕጉርቲ meaegurtii *(n.)* **cheek**
ምእላይ meaelayi *(n.)* **clearance**
ማሕደረ እንቋቑሖ mahdere enquaquho *(n.)* **ovary**

**ማዕድን** ma'adn *(n. )* **ore**
**ምዕጋት** meegat *(n.)* **containment**
**ምዕራፍ** mee'eraf *(n.)* **chapter**
**ምክልኻል ጥንሲ** meihil'hal tinsi *(n.)* **contraception**
**ምኩሕ** mekuhh *(n. &adj.)* **chauvinist**
**ምቁራፅ** mekuraxee *(n.)* **cessation**
**ምእላይ** m'elay *(n.)* **disposal**
**ምልክዐ ምድሪ** melka mdri *(n.)* **terrain**
**ምልክዕ ምቅያር** melka mkyar *(n.)* **transfiguration**
**ምምራፅ** mmrts *(v.)* **opt**
**ምስ ዓይኒ ወይ ምርኣይ ዝምልከት** ms ayni wey mr'ay zmlket *(adj.)* **optic**
**ምስፋር** msfar *(n.)* **occupancy**
**ምቅዋም** mqwam *(n.)* **objection**
**ምቅዋም** mqwam *(n.)* **opposition**
**ምብራቓዊ** mbraqawi *(adj.)* **oriental**
**ምትዕርራይ** mt'ereray *(v.)* **overhaul**
**ምቹው** mchuw *(adj.)* **opportune**
**ምንጩው** mnchuw *(v.)* **originate**
**ምዕራባዊ** m'erabawi *(adj.)* **occidental**
**ምዕራብ** m'erab *(n.)* **occident**
**ምዕባይ** m'ebay *(v.)* **outgrow**
**ምዕብላል** m'eblal *(v.)* **outdo**
**ምእዋድ** m'ewad *(n. )* **owe**
**ምእዋድ** m'ewad *(adj.)* **owing**
**ምእዙዝ** m'ezuz *(adj.)* **obedient**
**ምኽሓድ ዝኽእል** mkhad zk'el *(adj.)* **objectionable**
**ምውናን** mwnan *(adj. & pron.)* **own**
**ምውካል** mwukal *(v.)* **outsource**
**ምዓዝ** meaz *(adv.)* **when**
**ምዕባለ** m'ëbale *(n.)* **advancement**
**ምዕባለ** m'ëbale *(n.)* **progress**
**ምዕቡል** m'ëbul *(adj.)* **futuristic**
**ምዕጥይጣይ** m'ëtytay *(n.)* **reluctance**
**ምእዋጥር** mewatr *(n. )* **jam**
**ምእዛዝ** m'ezaz *(n.)* **submission**
**ምእዙዝ** m'ezuz *(adj.)* **complaisant**
**ምእዙዝ** m'ezuz *(adj.)* **courteous**
**ምእዙዝ** m'ezuz *(adj.)* **docile**
**ምእዙዝ** m'ezuz *(adj.)* **submissive**
**ምፍዳይ** mfday *(n.)* **repayment**
**ምፍሕፋሕ** mfĥfaĥ *(n.)* **rub**
**ምፍኳስ** mfkwas *(n.)* **simplification**
**ምፍላጥ** mflaẗ *(v.)* **publicize**
**ምፍላጥ** mflaẗ *(n.)* **introduction**
**ምፍልላይ** mfllay *(n.)* **parting**
**ምፍልላይ** mfllay *(n.)* **separation**
**ምፍንጫል** mfn'chal *(n. )* **schism**
**ምፍንጫል** mfn'chal *(n. )* **secession**
**ምፍንጃር** mfnjar *(n.)* **explosion**
**ምፍርራሕ** mfrrah *(n.)* **intimidation**
**ምፍርራስ** mfrras *(n.)* **disrepair**
**ምፍሳስ** mfsas *(n.)* **spillage**
**ምፍሳስ ደም** mfsas dem *(n.)* **gore**
**ምፍሳስ መጉሊ** mfsas meguili *(n. )* **pyorrhoea**
**ምፍጣር** mftar *(n.)* **creation**
**ምፍጣጥ** m'fẗaẗ *(v.)* **stare**
**ምፍታው** mftaw *(n.)* **liking**
**ምፍትሕታሕ** mftĥtaĥ *(n.)* **relaxation**
**ምፍጻም** mfxam *(n.)* **completion**
**ምግባር** mgbar *(n.)* **taxation**
**ምግቢ** mgbi *(n.)* **food**
**ምግቢ** mgbi *(n.)* **meal**
**ምግቢ** mgbi *(n.)* **nourishment**
**ምግጫው/ስግንጢር** mgchaw/sgntir *(n.)* **paradox**
**ምግዳድ** mgdad *(v.)* **impose**
**ምግዳድ** mgdad *(n. )* **imposition**
**ምግዳ'ድ** mgdad *(n.)* **compulsion**

**ምግዳፍ** mgdaf ***(n.)* cession**
**ምግላብ** m-glab ***(n.)* gallop**
**ምግላል** mglal ***(n.)* insulation**
**ምግላል** mglal ***(n.)* isolation**
**ምግላፅ** mglats ***(v.)* uncover**
**ምግላጽ ምጉት** mglax mgut ***(v.)* plead**
**ምግናሕ** mgnah ***(n.)* manoeuvre**
**ምግናን** mg'nan ***(n. )* hyperbole**
**ምግንዛብ** mgnzab ***(n.)* acknowledgement**
**ምግታእ** mgta'e ***(n.)* restriction**
**ምግጥጣም** mgẗtam ***(n.)* assemblage**
**ምንፋሕ** m'nfaḧ ***(n.)* spray**
**ምንፍርፋር** mnfrfar ***(n.)* seizure**
**ምንጋፍ** mngaf ***(v.)* rid**
**ምንጋጋ** mngaga ***(n. )* jaw**
**ምንጋር** mnggar ***(v.)* talk**
**ምንካእ** mnka'e ***(n.)* impact**
**ምንካይ** mnkay ***(n.)* deduction**
**ምንካይ** mnkay ***(n.)* diminution**
**ምንካይ** mnkay ***(n.)* reduction**
**ምንካይ ኣፅዋር** mnkay atswar ***(n.)* disarmament**
**ምንቅርፋፍ** mnkrfaf ***(v.)* traipse**
**ምንቅጥቃጥ** mnktkat ***(v.)* twitch**
**ምንኩስና** mnkusna ***(n. )* monasticism**
**ምንም እኳ** mnm ekwa ***(prep.)* despite**
**ምንም መስተ ዘይሰቲ** mnm meste zeyseti ***(adj.)* teetotal**
**ምንም መስተ ዘይሰቲ** mnm meste zeyseti ***(n. )* teetotaller**
**ምንም ዘይምግባር** mnm zetmgbar ***(n.)* inaction**
**ምንም'ኳ** mnmkwa ***(conj.)* although**
**ምንቕ በለ** mnq̈ bele ***(v.)* budge**
**ምንቅስቃስ** mnqsqas ***(n.)* locomotion**
**ምንቅስቃስ** mnqsqas ***(n.)* motion**
**ምንቅስቃስ** mnqsqas ***(n. )* movement**
**ምንቅስቃስ ፈሳሲ ዝጠቅም መሳርሒ** mnqsqas fesasi zẗekm mesarḧi ***(n.)* pipette**
**ምንቅስቓሳዊ** mnqsq̈asawi ***(adj.)* kinetic**
**ምንቅጥቃጥ** mnqtqat ***(n. )* tremor**
**ምንቅጥቃጥ** mnqt'qat' ***(n.)* convulsion**
**ምንቛት** mnq̈uat ***(v.)* plummet**
**ምንስፋፍ** mnsfaf ***(n.)* buoyancy**
**ምንስናስ** mn'snas ***(n.)* sprinkling**
**ምንጥብጣብ** mntbtab ***(n.)* leakage**
**ምንተፋ ድንኳን** mntefa dnkwan ***(n.)* shoplifting**
**ምንጥልጣል** mntltal ***(n.)* pendulum**
**ምንትራኽ** mntrak ***(n.)* quibble**
**ምንጻፍ** mntsaf ***(n.)* underlay**
**ምንፃፍ ምድሪ** mntsaf mdri ***(n.)* rug**
**ምንፅብራቕ** mntsbraq ***(n. )* projection**
**ምንዋሕ** mnwaḧ ***(n.)* prolongation**
**ምንፃፍ** mnxaf ***(n.)* mat**
**ምንፃግ** mnxag ***(n.)* negation**
**ምንጻህ** mnxah ***(n.)* purification**
**ምንጻል** mnxal ***(n.)* abortion**
**ምንጽጻር** mnxxar ***(n.)* comparison**
**ምንዮት** mnyot ***(n.)* fancy**
**ምንዛዐ** mnza'ë ***(n.)* appropriation**
**ምንዝርና** mnzrna ***(n.)* prostitution**
**ምቅባእ** mqbaè ***(n.)* paint**
**ምቅባእ** mqbaè ***(n.)* portrayal**
**ምቅባል** mqbal ***(n.)* acceptance**
**ምቅባል ኣበየ** mqbal abeye ***(v.)* disclaim**

ምቅብጣር mqbťar *(n.)* **sycophancy**
ምቕዳሕ mq̈daȟ *(v.)* **pour**
ምቕሉል m'qhlul *(adj.)* **subservient**
ምቕሉልነት m'qhlulnet *(n.)* **subservience**
ምቕናስ mqhnas *(v.)* **subside**
ምቕናስ m'qhnas *(n.)* **subtraction**
ምቕያር mqhy'yar *(n.)* **substitution**
ምቕልዕ mqlae *(v.)* **unveil**
ምቅላዕ mqla'e *(n.)* **exposure**
ምቅላዕ mqla'ë *(n. )* **revelation**
ምቅላል mqlal *(mitigation)* **mitigation**
ምቕላል mq̈lal *(n.)* **alleviation**
ምቅሊት mqlit *(n.)* **dividend**
ምቕልቃል mq̈lqal *(n.)* **appearance**
ምቕሉል mq̈lul *(adj.)* **compliant**
ምቕሉል mq̈lul *(adj. )* **homely**
ምቕሉል mq̈lul *(adj.)* **polite**
ምቕማር mq̈mar *(n.)* **computation**
ምቕማጥ mq̈maẗ *(v.)* **posit**
ምቅናዕ mqna'e *(v.)* **unbend**
ምቕናን mqnan *(n. )* **wimble**
ምቅዃም mqquam *(v.)* **withstand**
ምቕራብ mqrab *(v.)* **provide**
ምቕራብ mq̈rab *(n.)* **presentation**
ምቕራፍ mqrf *(n.)* **peel**
ምቕሶ mq̈so *(n.)* **haircut**
ምቅታል mqtal *(n.)* **assassination**
ምቁር mqur *(n.)* **ambrosia**
ምቁር mqur *(adj.)* **delicious**
ምቁር mqur *(adj.)* **mellow**
ምቁር mqur *(adj.)* **palatable**
ምቁር mqur *(adj.)* **saccharine**
ምቁር mqur *(adj.)* **succulent**
ምቁር mqur *(n.)* **sweet**
ምቁር mqur *(adj.)* **sweet**
ምቚር mqur *(adj.)* **yummy**
ምቁር ባኒ mqur bani *(n.)* **bun**
ምቍራጽ mqurats *(n.)* **interception**
ምቁራፀ mqurats *(n.)* **interruption**
ምቁራፀ mqurats *(n.)* **severance**
ምቁራጽ mqurats *(n. )* **stoppage**
ምቀረፀ mqurax *(n.)* **excise**
ምቁጣብ mqutab *(n.)* **thrift**
ምቕጻዕ mqxae *(v.)* **penalize**
ምቕጻዕ mq̈xaë *(v.)* **punish**
ምቕያር mqyar *(n.)* **conversion**
ምርዕውነት mrewenet *(n. )* **wedlock**
ምርጋፍ mrgaf *(v.)* **unpack**
ምርግጋእ m'rg'ga'e *(n.)* **stabilization**
ምርግጋጽ mrggax *(n.)* **confirmation**
ምርግጋጽ mrggax *(n.)* **affirmation**
ምርሃጽ mrhax *(v.t. )* **perspire**
ምርኢት mr'it *(n.)* **exhibition**
ምርኢት mr'it *(n.)* **tableau**
ምርኢት ኣጋ ምሸት mr'it aga mshet *(n.)* **matinee**
ምርኢት ኣቕራቢ mr'it 'aq̈rabi *(n.)* **juggler**
ምርካብ mrkab *(n.)* **delivery**
ምርኮ mrko *(n.)* **booty**
ምርኩስ mrkus *(n.)* **crutch**
ምርመራ mrmera *(n.)* **diagnosis**
ምርመራ mrmera *(n.)* **examination**
ምርምረ-ሬሳ mrmre reesa *(n.)* **autopsy**
ምርቓ mrq̈a *(n.)* **blessing**
ምርራውሕ mr'raw *(n. )* **lullaby**
ምርሳዕ ኣበየ mrsa'ë abeye *(v.)* **rankle**
ምርጥራጥ mr'tra't *(n. )* **lurch**
ምሩኽ mruḱ *(n.)* **captive**
ምሩኽነት mruknet *(n.)* **captivity**
ምሩጽ ስእሊ mrux seli *(adj.)* **picturesque**
ምርኡይ mr'uy *(adj.)* **gaudy**

**ምርኡይ** mr'uy ***(adj.)*** **notable**
**ምርኡይ** mr'uy ***(adj.)*** **showy**
**ምርኡይ** mr'uy ***(adj.)*** **snazzy**
**ምስ ባሕሪ ዝተተሓሓዘ** ms bahri ztetehahaze ***(adj.)*** **maritime**
**ምስ ሓዳር ዝተተሓሓዘ** ms hadar ztetehahaze ***(adj.)*** **marital**
**ምስ ህጻናት ጾታዊ ርክብ ምፍጻም ዝማረኸ በጽሒ** ms hixanat xotawi rkb mfxam zmareḱ bexḧi ***(n.)*** **paedophile**
**ምስ ህይወት ዝተኣሳሰረ** ms hywet zte'asasere ***(adj.)*** **vital**
**ምስ ጡብ ዝተተሓሓዘ** ms tub ztetehahaze ***(adj.)*** **mammary**
**ምሳሕ** msah ***(n.)*** **lunch**
**ምሳሕ** msah ***(n.)*** **luncheon**
**ምሳሌ ዝኾነ** msale zkone ***(v.)*** **typify**
**ምሳሌ ዘረኢ** msalie zereei ***(n. )*** **precedent**
**ምስኣን** ms'an ***(n.)*** **lack**
**ምስባኸ** msbaḱ ***(v.)*** **preach**
**ምስዳድ** msdad ***(n.)*** **consignment**
**ምስፋር** msfar ***(n.)*** **settlement**
**ምስፍሕፋሕ** msf̂hfaĥ ***(n.)*** **extension**
**መስጋድ** msgad ***(n. )*** **prostration**
**ምስጋና** msgana ***(n. )*** **gratitude**
**ምስጋና** msgana ***(v.t. )*** **praise**
**ምስጋና ኣልቦነት** msgana albonet ***(n. )*** **ingratitude**
**ምስጋና ዘይብሉ** msgana zeybelu ***(adj.)*** **ungrateful**
**ምስጋና ዘይብሉ** msgana zeyblu ***(adj.)*** **thankless**
**ምስጋር** msgar ***(adj.)*** **passing**
**ምስጉን** msgun ***(adj.)*** **decorous**
**ምስጉን** msgun ***(adj.)*** **glorious**
**ምስጓግ** msgwag ***(n.)*** **eviction**
**ምስጓግ** msgwag ***(n. )*** **persecution**
**ምስጓግ** m'sgwag ***(n.)*** **suspension**
**ምስጓም** m'sgwam ***(n.)*** **step**
**ምሽባን** mshban ***(n.)*** **complicity**
**ምሸት** mshet ***(n.)*** **evening**
**ምስሒት** msḧit ***(n.)*** **allotment**
**ምሽኩንዳር** mshkundar ***(n. )*** **harassment**
**ምሽምቃቕ ጭዋዳ** mshmqaq cwada ***(n.)*** **cramp**
**ምሽጥር** mshẗr ***(n.)*** **enigma**
**ምሽጥር ነገር** mshtr negere ***(v.)*** **divulge**
**ምሽዋድ** mshwad ***(n.)*** **trick**
**ምስክር** mskr ***(n.)*** **eyewitness**
**ምስክር** mskr ***(n. )*** **testimony**
**ምስክር ወረቀት** mskr werket ***(n. )*** **testimonial**
**ምስኳዕ** mskwa'ë ***(n.)*** **insertion**
**ምሰላ** msla ***(n.)*** **proverb**
**ምስላ** msla ***(n.)*** **saying**
**ምስላብ** mslab ***(n.)*** **infatuation**
**ምስላኽ** mslakh ***(n.)*** **insinuation**
**ምስላዊ** mslawi ***(adj)*** **figurative**
**ምስላዊ** mslawi ***(adj.)*** **proverbial**
**ምስሌኣዊ ዛንታ** mslee'awi zanta ***(n.)*** **allegory**
**ምስሌነ** mslene ***(n.)*** **prefect**
**ምስሊ ቅዱሳን** msli qdusan ***(n.)*** **icon**
**ምስሉይነት** msluynet ***(n.)*** **affectation**
**ምስምማዕ** msm'emae ***(n.)*** **transcription**
**ምቅይያራት** mqyyarat ***(n.)*** **vicissitude**
**ምራኽ** mraḱ ***(n.)*** **calf**
**ምጉዕዓዝ** mgu'ë'äz ***(n.)*** **haulage**
**ምጉጃል** mgujal ***(n.)*** **grouping**
**ምጉላሕ** mgulaĥ ***(n.)*** **emphasis**
**ምጉማድ** mgumad ***(n.)*** **mayhem**

ምጉንፋት mgunfat *(n. )* **wrangle**
ምጉስቓል mgusqhal *(n. )* **manhandle**
ምጉት mgut *(n. )* **litigation**
ምጉት mgut *(n.)* **polemic**
ምጓዐዝ mgwa'az *(n.)* **conveyance**
ምሕባር mḧbar *(n.)* **amalgamation**
ምሕባጥ m'hbaẗ *(n.)* **swell**
ምህዳእ mhda'e *(n.)* **stillness**
ምሕዳግ mḧdag *(n.)* **abdication**
ምህዳን ዓሳ ነባሪ mhdan asa nebari *(n.)* **whaling**
ምሕዳስ mĥdas *(adj.)* **renewal**
ምሕዳስ mĥdas *(adj.)* **restoration**
ምሕደራ እንዳ ፖስጣ mḧdera ènda posẗa *(n.)* **postmaster**
ምሒር mĥir *(adj.)* **dire**
ምሒር ማረኸ mĥir mareke *(v.)* **enchant**
ምሒር mḧir *(adj.)* **arrant**
ምሒር mḧir *(adv. )* **sorely**
ምሕላፍ mhlaf *(v.)* **pass**
ምሕላው mhlaw *(n.)* **keeping**
ምሕልዋይ mhlway *(n.)* **jibe**
ምህሙን mhmun *(adj.)* **flimsy**
ምሕናቕ m'ḧnaq *(n. )* **strangulation**
ምሕንዳል m'hndal *(n.)* **malformation**
ምሕንጋድ mḥngad *(n.)* **insubordination**
ምሕንሓን mhnhan *(n.)* **whinny**
ምሕንቃቕ mhnqaq *(v.)* **pamper**
ምህራም mhram *(v.)* **pulsate**
ምሕራስ mḧrasq̈a *(n.)* **plough**
ምሕራይ mhray *(n.)* **selection**
ምሕረት mĥret *(n.)* **remission**
ምሕረት mḧret *(n.)* **abstinence**
ምሕረት mḧret *(n.)* **amnesty**
ምሕረት m'ḧret *(n.)* **mercy**
ምሕረት mhretawi *(n. )* **pardon**
ምሕረታዊ mhretawi *(adj.)* **pardonable**
ምሕረታዊ-ቅትለት mĥretawi qtlet *(n.)* **euthanasia**
ምህርቲ mhrti *(n.)* **production**
ምህርቲ mhrti *(n.)* **takings**
ምሕሳብ mhsab *(n.)* **imagination**
ምሕሳር mĥsar *(n.)* **depreciation**
ምሕታም mḧtam *(v.)* **publish**
ምሕፀና m'ḧtsena *(n.)* **solicitation**
ምሕፃር mhtzar *(n.)* **immure**
ምሁር mhur *(adj.)* **erudite**
ምሁር mhur *(adj.)* **learned**
ምሁር mhur *(n.)* **scholar**
ምሁራዊ mhurawi *(adj.)* **scholarly**
ምሕጻብ mḥxab *(n.)* **washing**
ምሕጻብ mḧxab *(n.)* **bath**
ምሕጻር mḧxar *(n.)* **abbreviation**
ምሕፃር mḧxar *(n.)* **contraction**
ምሕፅንታ mĥxnta *(v. t)* **entreaty**
ምሕያው mḧyaw *(n.)* **animation**
ምሕየሻ mḧyesha *(n.)* **modification**
ምሕዝነታዊ mḧznetawi *(adj.)* **amicable**
ምህዞ mhzo *(n.)* **figment**
ምልጋብ milgab *(n.)* **contagion**
ምኢሳልነት misalnet *(n. )* **idealism**
ምሽጥራዊ ስምምዕ mishtirawi simemeeh *(n.)* **collusion**
ምስጢራዊ mistrawi *(adj.)* **undercover**
ምጥቓም mit; qqam' *(n.)* **consumption**
ምፅባዕ mitsbaee *(prep.)* **contra**
ምጅሃር mĵhar *(adj.)* **pompous**
ምጅማር mĵmar *(n.)* **commencement**
ምርዓም mr'äm *(n.)* **adoption**

ምራን mran *(n.)* **thong**
ምራተ mrate *(n.)* **rust**
ምርኣይ mr'ay *(n)* **look**
ምርኣይ mr'ay *(n.)* **view**
ምርባሕ mrbaĥ *(n.)* **reproduction**
ምርባሕ mrbaĥ *(n. )* **multiplication**
ምርባሕ mrbaĥ *(n.)* **proliferation**
ምርባሕ ዓሳ mrbaĥ äsa *(n.)* **fishery**
ምርጫ mrča *(n.)* **ballot**
ምርጫ mrča *(n.)* **preference**
ምርጫ ዘካይድ mrča zekayd *(n.)* **pollster**
ምርጫዊ mrčawi *(adj.)* **preferential**
ምርጫ mrcca *(n.)* **choice**
ምርዳእ mrdae *(v.)* **perceive**
ምርዳእ mrda'e *(n.)* **fathom**
ምርዳእ mrda'è *(n.)* **comprehension**
ምርዳእ mrda'è *(n.)* **apprehension**
ምርደዳእ mrdeda'e *(n.)* **understanding**
ምቅባእ mkba'e *(n.)* **tinge**
ምቅባር mkbar *(v.)* **whelm**
ምኽዳን mkdan *(n.)* **upholstery**
ምክፋእ mkfa'è *(n.)* **aspersions**
ምክፋል mkfal *(v.)* **partake**
ምኽፋል mkfal *(v.)* **pay**
ምክፍፋል mkffal *(n.)* **partition**
ምኽፋል mkhfal *(n. )* **liquidation**
ምኽኒት mkhnit *(v.)* **excuse**
ምኽንያታዊ mkhnyatawi *(adj.)* **logical**
ምኽትል ኣራታዒ mkhtl arta'i *(v.)* **subedit**
ምኽክር mkkr *(n.)* **deliberation**
ምኽላል mklal *(n.)* **enclosure**
ምክልኻል mklkal *(n.)* **defence**
ምኽልካል mklkal *(n.)* **prohibition**
ምክልኻል mklḱal *(n.)* **protection**
ምክንያት mknyat *(n.)* **reason**
ምኽንያት mḱn'yat *(n.)* **motive**
ምክንያት ዘይብሉ ቁጥዐ mknyat zeyblu qutea *(n.)* **tantrum**
ምኽንያቱ mknyatu *(conj.)* **because**
ምኽሪ/ማዕዳ mkri/ma'ëda *(n.)* **counsel**
ምኽታል mktal *(n.)* **pursuance**
ምኽታም mktam *(n.)* **urbanity**
ምኽታ'ም mḱtam *(n.)* **conurbation**
ምክታት mktat *(n.)* **inclusion**
ምክታት mktat *(v.)* **incorporate**
ምኽትል mktl *(n.)* **deputy**
ምኹምሳዕ mkumsa'ë *(n.)* **rumination**
ምኹናን mḱunan *(n.)* **condemnation**
ምኩርካዕ mkurka'e *(v.)* **tickle**
ምኩሳሕ mkusah *(n.)* **inflammation**
ምኩሻም mkusham *(n.)* **foreplay**
ምልኣተ ጉባኤ ml'ate guba'e *(n. )* **quorum**
ምልበዳ mlbeda *(n.)* **moulding**
ምልእ ዝበለ ml'e zbele *(adj.)* **turgid**
ምልዕዓል ml'ë'äl *(n.)* **initiative**
ምልጋብ mlgab *(n.)* **patch**
ምልጋፀ mlgatz *(n.)* **levity**
ምልህላህ mlhlah *(v.)* **pant**
ምልካይ ሕብሪ mlkay hhbri *(n.)* **colouring**
ምልክት mlkt *(n.)* **crest**
ምልክት mlkt *(n.)* **label**
ምልክት mlkt *(n. )* **notation**
ምልክት mlkt *(n.)* **sign**
ምልክት mlkt *(n.)* **signal**
ምልክት mlkt *(n.)* **symbol**
ምልክት mlkt *(n.)* **token**
ምልክት mlkt *(n.)* **track**
ምልክት mlkt *(n.)* **mark**

ምልክት ሕማም mlkt ȟmam *(n.)* **symptom**
ምልክት ሕማም ዘለዎ mlkt ȟmam zelewo *(adj.)* **symptomatic**
ምልክት ኮነ mlkt kone *(v.)* **symbolize**
ምልክት መግበሪ mlkt megberi *(n.)* **marker**
ምልክት ምግባር mlkt mgbar *(n. )* **marking**
ምልክት ዝልጠፍ ወይ ዝእሰር mlkt zltef wey z'eser *(n.)* **tag**
ምልክት mlkt *(n.)* **beck**
ምልክት mlkt *(n.)* **beep**
ምልክት mlkt *(n.)* **portent**
ምልክታ mlkta *(n. )* **handbill**
ምልክታ mlkta *(n.)* **notice**
ምልክታ mlkta *(n.)* **notification**
ምልክታዊ mlktawi *(adj.)* **symbolic**
ምልኩዕ mlku'ë *(adj. )* **handsome**
ምልላይ mllay *(v.)* **identify**
ምልማስ mlmas *(v.)* **paralyse**
ምልምል mlml *(v.)* **recruit**
ምልምስና mlmsna *(n.)* **paralysis**
ምሎክ mlok *(n.)* **vampire**
ምልሻ mlsha *(n. )* **militia**
ምልስላስ mlslas *(n.)* **harrow**
ምልጣፍ mlťaf *(n.)* **post**
ምልፃይ mltsay *(n.)* **shaving**
ምሉእ mlu'e *(adj.)* **utter**
ምሉእ mlu'e *(adj.)* **whole**
ምሉእ mlu'è *(adj.)* **complete**
ምሉእ mlu'è *(adv.)* **wholly**
ምሉእ ክዳን mlu'e kidan *(n.)* **suit**
ምሉእ ልቢ mluelbi *(adj.)* **whole-hearted**
ምልዋጥ mlwat *(n.)* **transformation**
ምምብጻዕ mmbxaë *(n.)* **promise**
ምምጋል m'mgal *(v.)* **suppurate**
ምምሃር mmhar *(n. )* **learning**
ምምሃዝ mmhaz *(n.)* **invention**
ምምሕዳር mmhdar *(n. )* **management**
ምምሕዳር m'mȟdar *(n. )* **superintendence**
ምምሕዳር ገንዘብ mmĥdar genzeb *(n.)* **finance**
ምምሕዳር ወረዳ mmȟdar wereda *(n.)* **borough**
ምምሕዳር mmȟdar *(n.)* **administration**
ምምሕዳራዊ mmhdarawi *(adj.)* **managerial**
ምምሕዳራዊ mmȟdarawi *(adj.)* **administrative**
ምምሕልላፍ mmhllaf *(v.)* **transfer**
ምምሕልላፍ mmȟllaf *(n.)* **giro**
ምምህርና mmhrna *(n.)* **pedagogy**
ምምሕያሽ mmĥyaš *(n.)* **reformation**
ምምሕያሽ mmȟyash *(n.)* **amelioration**
ምምካን mmkan *(n.)* **sterilization**
ምምኽካር mmkkar *(n.)* **consultation**
ምምላእ mmla'e *(n.)* **filling**
ምምላእ mmla'e *(n.)* **infusion**
ምምላኽ mmlak *(n.)* **worship**
ምምላስ mmlas *(n.)* **return**
ምምላጥ m'mlaẗ *(n.)* **squeak**
ምምልካት mmlkat *(n.)* **indication**
ምምልካት mmlkat *(n.)* **pointing**
ምምንጫው mmn'chaw *(n.)* **secretion**
ምምቕራሕ mmq̈raȟ *(n.)* **allocation**
ምምቅራሕ ስልጣን mmqrah sltan *(n.)* **devolution**
ምምራሕ mmrah *(n.)* **lead**
ምምራቕ mmraq *(n.)* **graduate**
ምምራዝ mmraz *(n.)* **intoxication**
ምምርባብ mmrbab *(n.)* **blog**

ምምርሳሕ mmrsaḧ *(n.)* **sophistication**
ምምርሳሕ mmrsaḧ *(n.)* **adulteration**
ምምሳል mmsal *(v.)* **impersonate**
ምምሳል mmsal *(n.)* **impersonation**
ምምሳል mmsal *(n.)* **pretence**
ምምስኻር mmskar *(n.)* **verification**
ምምስካር mmskar *(n.)* **witness**
ምምጣጥ m'mẗaẗ *(n.)* **suction**
ምምፃእ mmtsa'e *(v.)* **import**
ምናልባሽ mnalbash *(adv. )* **perhaps**
ምናልባት mnalbat *(adv. )* **maybe**
ምናልባት mnalbat *(adj.)* **probable**
ምናልባት mnalbat *(adv. )* **probably**
ምናምን mnamn *(n.)* **mediocrity**
ምናት mnat *(n.)* **arm**
ምንባር mnbaar *(n.)* **living**
ምንባብ mnbab *(n.)* **reading**
ምንባሕ mnbah *(n. )* **woof**
ምንጭብጫብ mnčbčab *(n.)* **plaudits**
ምንጪ mnchi *(n.)* **source**
ምንጪ mnĉi *(n.)* **resource**
ምንጪ mnči *(n.)* **fountain**
ምንዳድ mndad *(v.)* **burn**
ምዝዋር mzwar *(v.)* **oscillate**
ምድምሳስ mdemsas *(n.)* **obliteration**
ምግልባጥ mglbat *(v.)* **overturn**
ምግዳፍ mgdaf *(n.)* **omission**
ምስሉይ meslu *(n.)* **hypocrite**
ምስሉይነት mesluynet *(n. )* **hypocrisy**
ምእታው m'etaw *(n.)* **entry**
ምጥሓን me-tha-n *(v.)* **grind**
ምዕሪት m'ërit *(n.)* **equation**
ምዕሩግ m'ërug *(adj.)* **graceful**
ምዕሩግነት m'ërugnet *(n.)* **grandeur**
ምዕሩይ m'ëruy *(adj.)* **symmetrical**
ምዕሩዩነት m'ëruynet *(n.)* **symmetry**
ምእሳር m'esar *(n.)* **imprison**
ምስክር ወረቐት mesekir wereqet *(n.)* **certificate**
ምዕሻግ m'ëshag *(n.)* **dock**
ምጽብባቕ mtsbbaq *(n.)* **ornamentation**
ምፍጣር እንቋቑሖ mftar enquaqho *(v.)* **ovulate**
ምስምማዕ msmma'e *(n.)* **acquiescence**
ምስምማዕ msm'maë *(n. )* **pact**
ምስምስ msms *(n. )* **pretext**
ምስንባት msnbat *(n.)* **resignation**
ምስራሕ msrah *(n.)* **making**
ምስራሕ ወይኒ msrah weyni *(n.)* **winery**
ምስራቕ msraq *(v.)* **pilfer**
ምስራቕ msraqh *(n.)* **loot**
ምስስል mssl *(n.)* **resemblance**
ምስታፍ mstaf *(n.)* **participation**
ምስጢራዊ mstiawi *(adj.)* **secret**
ምስጢር mstir *(v.t. )* **puzzle**
ምስጢር mstir *(n.)* **secrecy**
ምስጢር msẗir *(n.)* **mystique**
ምስጢር ኣካፈለ msẗir 'akafele *(v.)* **confide**
ምስጢራዊ msẗirawi *(adj.)* **confidential**
ምስጢራዊ msẗirawi *(adj.)* **esoteric**
ምስጢራዊ msẗirawi *(adj.)* **mysterious**
ምስእጢራዊ መደብ msẗirawi medeb *(n.)* **plot**
ምስጢረኛ mstiregna *(adj.)* **secretive**
ምስትኽካል mstkhkal *(n. )* **improvement**
ምስትንፋስ mstnfas *(n.)* **respiration**

ምስትውዓል mstwu'al *(n.)* **sensibility**
ምሱጥ msuť *(n.)* **enthusiastic**
ምስዮናዊ m'syonawi *(n.)* **missionary**
ምትብባዕ mtbba'ë *(n.)* **patronage**
ምጥቧብ mť'bwab *(n.)* **suckling**
ምትእኽኻብ mt'ekkab *(n.)* **reunion**
ምትዕርራኽ mt'ërraḱ *(n.)* **intimacy**
ምትእስሳር mt'essar *(n.)* **affiliation**
ምትእስሳር mt'essar *(n.)* **implication**
ምትእስሳር mt'essar *(n. )* **liaison**
ምትእስሳር mt'es'sar *(n.)* **nexus**
ምትእስሳር mt'èssar *(n.)* **concatenation**
ምትዕፅፃይ mt'etstsaw *(v.t. )* **jam**
ምጥፍፋእ mtffa'e *(n.)* **scam**
ምትግባር mtgbar *(v.)* **perform**
ምትግባር mtgbar *(n.)* **implement**
ምጥሓል mṭḥal *(n. )* **immersion**
ምጥሓስ mẗḧas *(v.)* **breach**
ምትሃታዊ m'thatawi *(adj.)* **spectral**
ምትሃተ ብርሃን mthate br'han *(n.)* **spectrum**
ምትሕብባር mtḧbbar *(n.)* **alliance**
ምትሕብባር mtḧbbar *(n.)* **cooperation**
ምትሕልላፍ mtḧllaf *(n. )* **postponement**
ምትካል እግሪ mtkal egri *(n.)* **flotation**
ምትካዝ mtkaz *(adj.)* **pensive**
ምትኽኻእ mtkh'kha'e *(n.)* **succession**
ምትኳር mtkwar *(n.)* **focus**
ምትላል mtlal *(n.)* **deception**
ምትላል mtlal *(n.)* **delusion**
ምትላል mtlal *(n.)* **manipulation**
ምጥምዛዝ mtmzaz *(n.)* **torsion**
ምትንባህ mtnbah *(n.)* **allusion**
ምትንባይ mtnbay *(v.)* **prognosticate**
ምትንኳስ mtnkwas *(n.)* **provocation**
ምጥቃም mtqam' *(v.t. )* **use**
ምጥቃም mtqam' *(v.)* **utilize**
ምጥራር mtrar *(n.)* **demarcation**
ምጥርናፍ mẗrnaf *(n. )* **packing**
ምፅጋን mtsgan *(n.)* **maintenance**
ምፅላም mtslam *(n.)* **slander**
ምፅማም mtsmam *(n.)* **sufferance**
ምፅቃጥ mtsqat *(n.)* **repression**
ምፅራይ mtsray *(n.)* **refinement**
ምጹጹላይ mtsutsulay *(n.)* **squirrel**
ምጥዋይን ምስሓብን mṭwayn msḥabn *(v.)* **wrench**
ምፅልላው mtzllaw *(n.)* **interplay**
ምፅንባር mtznbar *(n.)* **incorporation**
ምዑዝ m'üz *(adj.)* **fragrant**
ምኡዝ ተኽሊ m'uz teḱli *(n.)* **herb**

# ሞ

ሞዴል modeel *(n.)* **ideal**
ሞባእ moba'e *(n. )* **oblation**
ሞያ moya *(n. )* **occupation**
ሞዴል modeel *(n.)* **model**
ሞደም modem *(n.)* **modem**
ሞደሻ modesha *(n.)* **anvil**
ሞጁል mojul *(n.)* **module**
ሞቅ ዝበሎ mok zbelo *(n. )* **tipsy**
ሞካ moka *(n.)* **mocha**
ሞከረ mokr *(v.)* **try**
ሞለኩዩል molekuyul *(n.)* **molecule**
ሞለኩዩላዊ molekuyulawi *(adj.)* **molecular**
ሞልጎሙ ብዕንጨይቲ ዝኮነ ክዳን molgomu bancheyti zteserhe kedean *(n.)* **toggle**
ሞልሟል molmwal *(n.)* **ellipse**
ሞንጎኛ mongogna *(n.)* **middleman**

**ሞኖ** mono ***(n.)* mono**
**ሞኖዲ** monodi ***(n. )* monody**
**ሞኖግራፍ** monograf ***(n.)* monograph**
**ሞኖግራም** monogram ***(n. )* monogram**
**ሞንሱን** monsun ***(n. )* monsoon**
**ሞራለ** morale ***(n.)* lintel**
**ሞርፊን** morfin ***(n.)* morphine**
**ሞርጋናዊ** morganawi ***(adj.)* morganatic**
**ሞሳ** mosa ***(n.)* accolade**
**ሞሳሬላ** mosareela ***(n.)* mozzarella**
**ሞስኮኣዊ** mosko'awi ***(n.)* muscovite**
**ሞት** mot ***(n.)* death**
**ሞት** mot ***(n.)* decease**
**ሞት** mot ***(n.)* doom**
**ሞት** mot ***(n.)* mortality**
**ሞተ** mote ***(v.)* die**
**ሞቴል** moteel ***(n. )* motel**
**ሞተር** moter ***(n.)* engine**
**ሞተር** moter ***(n.)* motor**
**ሞተር** mote'r' ***(n.)* chassis**
**ሞተር ብሽክሌታ** moter bshkleeta ***(n.)* moped**
**ሞተር ብሽክሌታ** moter bshkleeta ***(n.)* motorcycle**
**ሞተር ሃፋ** moter hafa ***(n. )* steamer**
**ሞተረኛ** moteregna ***(n. )* motorist**
**ሞያ** moya ***(n.)* expertise**
**ሞያ** moya ***(n.)* profession**
**ሞያ** moya ***(n. )* vocation**
**ሞያ ዘይብሉ** moya zeyblu ***(n.)* layman**
**ሞያ** moya ***(n.)* calling**
**ሞያዊ** moyawi ***(adj.)* technical**
**ሞያዊ** moyawi ***(adj.)* utilitarian**
**ሞያዊ ስልጣነ ቴክኖሎጂ** moyawi sltena teknology ***(n.)* technology**
**ሞያዊ ዘይኮነ** moyawi zeykone ***(adj.)* unprofessional**
**ሞይቱ ዝተወልደ** moytu ztewelede ***(n.)* stillborn**
**ሞያዊ** moyawi ***(adj.)* occupational**

# ረ

**ረአየ** re'eye ***(v.)* look**
**ረፋዕ** refaë ***(n. )* porter**
**ረፋዕ በለ** refa'ë bele ***(v.)* slump**
**ረፈተ** refete ***(v.)* demobilize**
**ረፍረፈ** refrefe ***(v.)* decimate**
**ረጌ** rege ***(n.)* reggae**
**ረገጸ** regetse ***(v.)* stamp**
**ረገጸ** regetse ***(v.)* tread**
**ርግፀኛነት** regexegninet ***(n.)* certitude**
**ረጊድ** regid ***(adj.)* thick**
**ረጌድ ዝንጉርጉር ክዳን** regid zngurgur kdan ***(n.)* tweed**
**ረጎደ** regode ***(v.)* thicken**
**ረግራግ** regrag ***(adj.)* slimy**
**ረግረግ** regreg ***(n.)* slime**
**ረግረግ** regreg ***(n.)* sludge**
**ረግረግ** regreg ***(n. )* swamp**
**ረግረግ** reg'reg ***(n )* marsh**
**ረጉድ** reguied ***(adj.)* plump**
**ርጉፅ** reguxee ***(adj.)* certain**
**ረጉድ ጓንቲ** regwid gwanti ***(n.)* mitten**
**ረጉድ** regwid ***(adj.)* beefy**
**ረሃፅ** rehaxe ***(n.)* sweat**
**ረጂቶ** rejeeto ***(n.)* bra**
**ረጂመንት** rejiment ***(n.)* regiment**
**ረኸበ** rekebe ***(v.)* detect**
**ረኸበ** rekebe ***(v.)* discover**
**ረኸበ** rekebe ***(v.)* find**

ረኸበ rekebe *(v.)* **procure**
ርክብ re'ke'be *(n.)* **connection**
ረኸበ reḱebe *(v.)* **acquire**
ረኸበ reḱebe *(v.)* **meet**
ረከመ rekeme *(v.)* **knit**
ረኸበ rekhebe *(v.)* **locate**
ረኺቡ ኣምፀአ rekibu amtse'e *(v.)* **retrieve**
ረክላም reklam *(n.)* **advertisement**
ረኽሳዊ reksawi *(adj.)* **septic**
ረኽሲ reksi *(n.)* **infection**
ረኽሲ reksi *(n. )* **sepsis**
ረኹሰ reḱwase *(v.)* **fester**
ረማስ remas *(n.)* **barge**
ረምቁታ remquta *(n.)* **debacle**
ረምታ remta *(n.)* **barrage**
ረምታ remta *(n.)* **rhythm**
ረምታዊ remtawi *(adj.)* **rhythmic**
ረቋሒ reqahi *(n.)* **denominator**
ረቃቂቶ reqaqito *(n.)* **groin**
ረቂቕ መንፈስ reqiq menfes *(n. )* **phantom**
ረቂቅ ሽፋን reqiq shfan *(n.)* **membrane**
ረቒቕ req̈iq̈ *(adj.)* **abstract**
ረቂቕ reqiqh *(adj.)* **superfine**
ረቋሒ reqwaḧ *(n.)* **criterion**
ረቋሒ reqwaĥi *(n.)* **factor**
ረሳሕ resah *(adj.)* **scruffy**
ረሳሕ resaĥ *(adj.)* **dirty**
ረሳሕ resaĥ *(adj.)* **sleazy**
ረሳሕ resaḧ *(adj.)* **sordid**
ረሳዒ resa'ï *(adj.)* **forgetful**
ረስዐ res'ë *(v.)* **forget**
ረስኒ resni *(n.)* **fever**
ረትዐ ret'ë *(v.)* **confute**
ረተበ retebe *(v.)* **assign**
ረቲና retina *(n. )* **retina**
ረዋዪ rewayi *(adj.)* **satiable**
ረዚን rezin *(adj.)* **leaden**
ረዚን rezin *(adj.)* **staid**
ረይረይ reyrey *(adj.)* **shaky**
ረኺቡ rekibu *(v.)* **obtain**
ረጕድ regiud *(adj.)* **obese**
ረዓመ re'äme *(v.)* **adopt**
ረዓሚ re'ämi *(adj.)* **adoptive**
ረአየ re'aye *(v.)* **see**
ረባሺ rebashi *(adj.)* **troublesome**
ረብሻ rebesha *(n.)* **tumult**
ረብሻ ዘለዎ rebesha zelewo *(adj.)* **tumultuous**
ረበሸ rebeshe *(v.)* **disturb**
ረበሸ rebeshe *(v.)* **pester**
ረበሸ rebeshe *(v.)* **unsettle**
ረብሓ rebha *(n. )* **weal**
ረብሓ rebḧa *(n.)* **benefit**
ረብሓ rebḧa *(n.)* **advantage**
ረብሐ rebḧe *(v.t.)* **advantage**
ረብረበ rebrebe *(v.)* **splash**
ረብሻ rebša *(n.)* **ruckus**
ረብሻ rebsha *(n.)* **upheaval**
ረቡዕ rebu'e *(n. )* **Wednesday**
ረዳኢ reda'i *(adj.)* **beneficial**
ረዳት ሓኪም redat ĥakim *(n.)* **paramedic**
ረዳት redat *(n.)* **assistant**
ረድኤት red'iet *(n.)* **aid**

## ሩ

ሩባ ruba *(n.)* **gully**
ሩባ ruba *(n. )* **river**
ሩባ ruba *(n. )* **stream**
ሩለት rulet *(n.)* **roulette**
ሩር በለ rur bele *(v.)* **purr**
ሩዝ ruba *(n.)* **wadi**

ሩባ ra'èy *(n.)* **vision**
ራእይ r'èsi *(n.)* **head**
ርእሲ robra *(n.)* **gull**
ሮብራ ruz *(n.)* **rice**

## ሪ

ሪፈረንዶም riferendom *(n. )* **plebiscite**
ሪሕ riĥ *(n.)* **gout**
ሪሕ riĥ *(n.)* **arthritis**
ሪሓን riĥan *(n.)* **basil**
ሪኬትስ rikets *(n.)* **rickets**
ርክብ rikib *(n.)* **contact**
ሪክሻ rikša *(n.)* **rickshaw**
ሪፐፕሊክ ripeplic *(n.)* **republic**
ሪፐፕሊካዊ ripeplikawi *(adj.)* **republican**
ሪት rit *(adv.)* **aft**
ሪቮልቨር rivolver *(n. )* **revolver**
ሪዝ riz *(n. )* **moustache**
ራብዓይ rab'äy *(adj.& n.)* **fourth**
ራዳር radar *(n.)* **radar**
ራድየም radyem *(n. )* **radium**
ራድዮግራፊ radyografi *(n.)* **radiography**
ራድዮሎጂ radyologi *(n.)* **radiology**
ራኢ ዘለዎ ra'e zelewo *(adj.)* **visionary**
ራዕደ ዕብጠት ra'ede ebt't *(n.)* **claustrophobia**
ራዕዲ raedi *(n. )* **panic**
ራዕዲ ra'edi *(n. )* **terror**
ራዕዲ ra'ëdi *(n.)* **jitters**
ራዕዲ መሬት raëdi mereet *(n.)* **earthquake**
ራእይ ra'èy *(n.)* **apocalypse**
ራፋኖ rafano *(n. )* **radish**
ራግቢ ragbi *(n.)* **rugby**
ራህዲ rahdi *(adj.)* **sultry**
ራህረሀ rahrehe *(v.)* **sympathize**
ራሕረሐ raĥreĥe *(v.)* **spurn**
ራሕረሐ raĥreĥe *(v.t.)* **abandon**
ራሕሲ rahsi *(n.)* **dampness**
ራሕሲ raĥsi *(n. )* **moisture**
ራህዋ rahwa *(n.)* **delectation**
ራህዋ rahwa *(n.)* **respite**
ራህያ rahya *(n.)* **pond**
ራጅ raj *(n.)* **x-ray**
ራኬት raket *(n. )* **racket**
ራም ram *(n.)* **rum**
ራሚኖ ramino *(n.)* **rummy**
ረይራይ rayray *(adj.)* **rickety**
ራዛ raza *(n. )* **stork**
ሬድዮ redyo *(n.)* **radio**
ሬሳ reesa *(n.)* **corpse**
ሬሳ ኣቃፀለ reesa aqaxele *(v.)* **cremate**
ሬሳ መቃፀሊ ቦታ reesa meqaxeli bota *(n.)* **crematorium**
ሬሳ ምቅፃል reesa mqxal *(n.)* **cremation**
ሬሳ reesa *(n.)* **cadaver**
ሬሳ reesa *(n.)* **cadaver**
ሬክታንግል rektangl *(n.)* **rectangle**
ሬክታንጉላር rektangular *(adj.)* **rectangular**

## ር

ርሁድ rehude *(adj.)* **clammy**
ርእሰ ኸተማዊ r'ese ḱetemawi *(adj.)* **metropolitan**
ርእሰ ኸተማ r'ese ḱtema *(n.)* **metropolis**

ርእሰ መምህር r'ese memhr *(n.)* **headmaster**
ርእሰ ቅትለት r'ese qtlet *(n.)* **suicide**
ርእሰ ቅትለታዊ r'ese qtletawi *(adj.)* **suicidal**
ርእሰ-ማል ገበረ r'èsemal gebere *(v.)* **capitalize**
ርእሰ-ማል r'èsemal *(n.)* **capital**
ርእሰ-ማላዊ r'èsemalawi *(n. &adj.)* **capitalist**
ርእሰ-ማልነት r'èsemalnet *(n.)* **capitalism**
ርእሰምምሕዳራዊ r'èsemmḧdarawi *(adj.)* **autonomous**
ርእሰ-ርጉጽነት r'èserguxnet *(n.)* **aplomb**
ርእሰ-ታሪኽ r'èsetarik *(n.)* **autobiography**
ርእሰ-ጽሑፍ r'èsexhuf *(n.)* **autograph**
ርእሲ ቃንዛ r'èsi qanza *(n. )* **headache**
ርባዕ rba'ë *(n.)* **quadrant**
ርብዒ rb'ï *(n.)* **quarter**
ርቦ rbo *(n.)* **bench**
ርቡዕ ጎናዊ rbu'ë gonawi *(n. )* **quadrilateral**
ርቡዕ ጉጅለ rbuë gujle *(n.)* **quartet**
ርቡዕ ማንታ rbu'ë manta *(n. )* **quadruplet**
ርቡዕ መሓውር rbu'ë meĥawr *(n.)* **quadruped**
ርቡዕ ኩርናዕ rbu'ëkurnaë *(n.)* **quad**
ርቡሽ rbush *(adj.)* **maladjusted**
ርቡፅ rbuts *(adj.)* **rash**
ርቡጽ rbux *(adj.)* **agog**
ርቡፅ rbux *(adj. )* **heady**
ርቒት rwḥat *(n. )* **ventilation**
ርውሓት rchit *(n.)* **squib**
ርደኢት rdeit *(n.)* **perception**
ርደኢት rdeit *(n. )* **purview**
ርዲ rdi *(n.)* **fastness**
ርዱእ rdue *(adj.)* **perspicuous**
ርጡብ retub *(adj. )* **humid**
ርእየት r'eyet *(n.)* **sight**
ርእየታዊ r'èyetawi *(adj.)* **visual**
ርእይቶ ሓዘ r'eyto *(v.)* **deem**
ርእይቶ r'èyto *(n.)* **comment**
ርእይቶ ሃበ r'eyto habe *(v.)* **remark**
ርፍራፍ rfraf *(n.)* **crumb**
ርፍራፍ ምጋዝ rfraf mogaz *(n.)* **sawdust**
ርግኣት rg'at *(n.)* **sangfroid**
ርግኣት rg'at *(n.)* **serenity**
ርግኣት r'g'at *(n. )* **stability**
ርግቢት rgbit *(n.)* **cuckoo**
ርግቢት rgbit *(n. )* **pigeon**
ርጉእ rgo'e *(adj.)* **serene**
ርጉእ r'gu'e *(adj.)* **stable**
ርጉም rgum *(adj.)* **despicable**
ርጉም rgum *(n. )* **scoundrel**
ርጉም rgum *(adj.)* **unkind**
ርግኦ rguo *(n.)* **yogurt**
ርግፀ r'g'x *(adj.)* **sure**
ርግፀነት rgx'net *(n.)* **surety**
ርሃጽ rhax *(n.)* **perspiration**
ርሕቀት ጉዕዞ ዓቃኒት rhket guezo aqanit *(n.)* **pedometer**
ርሆምበስ rhombes *(n.)* **rhombus**
ርሕቀት rĥqet *(n.)* **distance**
ርሕቀት rĥqet *(n. )* **mileage**
ርህራሀ rhrahe *(n.)* **sympathy**
ርህሩህ rhruh *(adj.)* **merciful**
ርህሩህ rhruh *(adj.)* **sympathetic**
ርሁድ rhud *(adj.)* **muggy**
ርሁድ rhud *(adj.)* **sticky**
ርሑቕ rĥuq *(adj.)* **distant**

**ርሑቕ** rĥuq ***(adv.)* far**
**ርሑቕ** rĥuq ***(adv.)* further**
**ርሑቕ** rĥuq ***(adj.)* remote**
**ርሑቕ ግንዛበ** rĥuq gnzabe ***(n.)* foresight**
**ርሑስ** rhus ***(adj.)* damp**
**ርሑስ** rhus ***(adj.)* wet**
**ርሑስነት** rhusnet ***(n.)* wetness**
**ርካሽ** rkash ***(adj.)* inexpensive**
**ርክብ** rkb ***(n.)* relevance**
**ርክብ** rkb ***(n.)* communication**
**ርከሳ** rkesa ***(n.)* gambit**
**ርኻብ** r'khab ***(n.)* stirrup**
**ርኽሰት** rkset ***(n.)* sacrilege**
**ርሳሕ ፈሳሲ** rsah fesasi ***(n.)* sewage**
**ርሳስ** rsas ***(n.)* pencil**
**ረስሓት** rsĥat ***(n.)* dirt**
**ርስሓት** rsĥat ***(n.)* grime**
**ርስሓት** rsĥat ***(n.)* sleaze**
**ርስሓት ወገደ** rsĥat wegede ***(v.)* excrete**
**ርስቲ** rsti ***(n.)* domain**
**ርስቲ** rsti ***(n.)* manor**
**ርሱን** rsun ***(adj.)* burning**
**ርትዓዊ ሓቂ** rt'äwi ĥaqi ***(n.)* fact**
**ርትዓውነት** rt'äwnwt ***(n.)* rationalism**
**ርውየት** rwuyet ***(n.)* satiety**
**ርውየት** rwyet ***(n.)* fulfilment**
**ርውየት** rwyet ***(n.)* indulgence**
**ርእይቶ** r'eyto ***(n. )* opinion**
**ርእይቶ ሃበ** r'eyto hab ***(v.)* opine**
**ርእዮት** r'eyot ***(n.)* outlook**
**ሮቦት** robot ***(n.)* robot**
**ሮብራ** robra ***(n.)* seagull**
**ሮድስተር** rodster ***(n.)* roadster**
**ሮድየም** rodyem ***(n.)* rhodium**
**ሮኬት** roket ***(n. )* rocket**
**ሮለር ኮስተር** roler koster ***(n.)* rollercoaster**
**ሮራ** rora ***(n.)* plateau**
**ሮስተር** roster ***(n.)* roster**
**ሮዛ** roza ***(adj.)* pink**
**ሮዜት** rozet ***(n.)* rosette**

# ሰ

**ሰዓብቲ ወለዶ** seäabti weledo ***(n.)* posterity**
**ሰፋፊ** sefafi ***(n.)* aerial**
**ሰፋፊቶ** sefafito ***(n. )* glider**
**ሰፋራይ** sefaray ***(n.)* settler**
**ሰፋዪ ክዳን** sefayi kdan ***(n.)* tailor**
**ሰፈር** sefer ***(n.)* neighbourhood**
**ሰፈር** sefer ***(n.)* nest**
**ሰፈር አዕዋፍ** sefer aëwaf ***(n.)* roost**
**ሰፈር ኣልቦ** sefer albo ***(adj.)* numberless**
**ሰፈር ኣራዊት** sefer 'arawit ***(n. )* lair**
**ሰፈር ድኻታት** sefer dkatat ***(n.)* slum**
**ሰፈር ኳኽ** sefer kwak ***(n.)* rookery**
**ሰፈር ነፈርቲ** sefer neferti ***(n.)* hangar**
**ሰፈር ሽጉጥ** sefer shguṭ ***(n.)* holster**
**ሰፈረ** sefere ***(v.)* inhabit**
**ሰፈረ** sefere ***(v.)* quantify**
**ሰፈረ** sefere ***(v.)* settle**
**ሰፈርተኛ** sefertegna ***(n.)* resident**
**ሰፈየ** sefeye ***(v.)* sew**
**ሰፈየ** sefeye ***(v.)* stitch**
**ሰፊሕ** sefih ***(adj.)* loose**
**ሰፊሕ** sefiĥ ***(adj.)* elaborate**
**ሰፊሕ** sefiĥ ***(adj.)* roomy**

**ሰፊሕ** sefiḧ *(adj.)* **ample**
**ሰፊሕ** sefiḥ *(adj.)* **vast**
**ሰፊሕ** sefiḥ *(adj.)* **voluminous**
**ሰፊሕ** sefiḧ *(adj.)* **broad**
**ሰፊሕ** sefiḧ *(adj.)* **capacious**
**ሰፍነግ** sefneg *(n.)* **sponge**
**ሰጋእ መጋእ በሃሊ** sega'è mega'è behali *(adj. )* **hesitant**
**ሰጋእጋእ በለ** sega'ega'e bele *(v.)* **falter**
**ሰጋላይ** segalay *(n.)* **astrologer**
**ሰግአ** seg'e *(v.t)* **dread**
**ሰግአ** seg'e *(v.)* **misgive**
**ሰገባ** segeba *(n. )* **scabbard**
**ሰገደ** segede *(v.)* **bow**
**ሰገን** segen *(adj.)* **young**
**ሰገን** segen *(n. )* **youngster**
**ሰገነት** segenet *(n.)* **balcony**
**ሰገጥ በለ** segeẗ bele *(v.)* **flinch**
**ሰጎደ** segode *(v.)* **guzzle**
**ሰጎገ** segoge *(v.)* **dismiss**
**ሰጎመ** segome *(v.)* **stride**
**ሰሓ** seha *(v.i. )* **itch**
**ሰሓበ** seḧabe *(v.)* **attract**
**ሰሓበ** seḧabe *(v.)* **pull**
**ሰብኣይ** sb'ay *(n.)* **man**
**ሰሓቢ** sehabi *(adj.)* **luscious**
**ሰሓቢ** seḧabi *(adj.)* **piquant**
**ሰሓፊት** sehafit *(n.)* **typist**
**ሰሓቒ** seĥaqi *(adj.)* **risible**
**ሰሓተ** seḧate *(v.)* **miss**
**ሰሓተ** seḧate *(v.)* **stray**
**ሰሓቕ** sehqh *(n.)* **laughter**
**ሰሓቐ** sehqhe *(v.)* **laugh**
**ሰኽራም** sekaram *(adj.)* **drunkard**
**ሰክረታርየት** sekretaryet *(n. )* **secretariat**
**ሰኹዐ** seḱu'ë *(v.)* **insert**
**ሰላሕታ** selaḧta *(n.)* **stealth**
**ሰላሊ** selali *(n.)* **spy**
**ሰላም** selam *(n.)* **peace**
**ሰለም ኣበለ** selam abele *(v. i)* **doze**
**ሰላም በለ** selam bele *(n. )* **greet**
**ሰላማዊ** selamawi *(n.)* **pacific**
**ሰላማዊ** selamawi *(adj.)* **peaceable**
**ሰላማዊ** selamawi *(adj.)* **peaceful**
**ሰላማዊ** selamawi *(adj.)* **placid**
**ሰላማዊ ሰልፊ** selamawi selfi *(n.)* **demonstration**
**ሰላምታ** selamta *(n.)* **greeting**
**ሰላምታ** selamta *(n.)* **salutation**
**ሰላምታ** selamta *(n.)* **salute**
**ሰላሳ** selasa *(adj. & n.)* **thirty**
**ሰላሳ** selasa *(adj. & n.)* **thirty**
**ሰላጠ** selaẗe *(n.)* **cove**
**ሰልዲ** seldi *(n.)* **coinage**
**ሰሌዳ መፋትሕ** seleeda mefatḥ *(n. )* **keyboard**
**ሰሌዳ ምልክታ** seleeda mlkta *(n.)* **noticeboard**
**ሰሌዳ** seleeda *(n.)* **blackboard**
**ሰለፍ** selef *(n. )* **thigh**
**ሰለፍ ሓሰማ** selef ḥasema *(n.)* **ham**
**ሰለኹ** seleḱwa *(v.)* **insinuate**
**ሰላማዊ ሰልፊ ጌሩ** selemawi selfi gieru *(n.)* **picket**
**ሰለመ** seleme *(v.)* **stud**
**ሰለመ** seleme *(v.)* **adorn**
**ሰለስተ** seleste *(adj. & n.)* **three**
**ሰናን** senay *(adj.)* **serrated**
**ሰናይ ግብሪ** senay gbri *(n.)* **succour**
**ሰንበደ** senbede *(v.)* **appal**
**ሰንበት** senbet *(n.)* **Sunday**
**ሰንበተ** senbete *(n.)* **sojourn**
**ሰንደል** sendel *(n. )* **sandal**
**ሰንደልደል በለ** sendeldel bele *(v.)* **shamble**

ሰንደቕ sendeq *(n.)* **banner**
ሰንደወ sendewe *(v.)* **discard**
ሰንደወ sendewe *(v.)* **fling**
ሰነ sene *(n.)* **June**
ሰለስተ ዕፅፊ seleste asfi *(n.)* **triple**
ሰለስተ ግዜ seleste gze *(adv. )* **thrice**
ሰለስተ ቅድሕታት seleste kdhtat *(adj.)* **triplicate**
ሰለስተ ማናቱ seleste manatu *(n.)* **triplet**
ሰለስተ መኣዝን seleste meazen *(n.)* **triangle**
ሰለስተ ተመሳሳሊ ሓሳብ ዘለዎ seleste temesasali hasab zelewo *(n.)* **trilogy**
ሰለስተ ወገን seleste wegen *(adj.)* **tripartite**
ስልጣነ seletan *(n.)* **civilization**
ሰለይ በለ seley bele *(v.)* **trudge**
ሰልፊ selfi *(n.)* **array**
ሰታይ setay *(adj.)* **alcoholic**
ሰታይ setay *(n.)* **dipsomania**
ሰልፊ selfi *(n.)* **parade**
ሰልፊ selfi *(n.)* **procession**
ሰልፊ ተወጣሕቲ selfi teweẗahti *(n.)* **cavalcade**
ሰንፈላል senfelal *(n.)* **rut**
ሰንገለ sengele *(v.)* **coax**
ሰንገለ sengele *(v.)* **comfort**
ሰንገወ sengewe *(v.)* **spay**
ሰንካቲ senkati *(n.)* **baker**
ሰንከልከል በለ senkelkel bele *(v.)* **totter**
ሰንከልከል በለ senkelkel bele *(v.)* **wobble**
ሰንከተ senkete *(v.)* **bake**
ሰንኬሎ senkielo *(n. )* **pail**
ሰንቀ senqe *(n.)* **ceiling**
ሰንጣቂት sentaqit *(n.)* **diameter**
ሰንጠቀ senteqe *(v.)* **rive**
ሰንጠቐ senẗeqe *(v.)* **intersect**
ሰንጢ senti *(n.)* **dagger**
ሰንቲግሬድ sentigreed *(adj.)* **centigrade**
ሰንቲሜትር sentimeetr *(n.)* **centimetre**
ሰፒኖሬሎ sepinoreelo *(n.)* **stickleback**
ሰፕራቶ seprato *(n.)* **sprat**
ሰቐለ seqele *(v.)* **hoist**
ሰቀላ seqhela *(n.)* **loft**
ሰራሒ በርሚል serahi bermil *(n.)* **cooper**
ሰራሒ ሳእኒ serahi saeni' *(n.)* **cobbler**
ሰራሕተኛ serahtegna *(n.)* **worker**
ሰራሕተኛ ገዛ serahtegna geza *(n. )* **maid**
ሰራሕተኛ መዓድን serahtegna me'ädn *(n. )* **miner**
ሰራሕተኛታት serahtegnatat *(n.)* **staff**
ሰራሕተኛታት serahtenatat *(n.)* **personnel**
ሰራሕተኛት serahtenyatat *(n.)* **crew**
ሰራቒ seraqi *(n. )* **thief**
ሰራቒ seraqi *(n.)* **burglar**
ሰራዊት serawit *(n.)* **army**
ሰራዊት ፈረሰኛ serawit fresenya *(n.)* **cavalry**
ሰራዪ serayi *(n.)* **magician**
ሰራዝ seraz *(n.)* **stroke**
ሰርዐ ser'ë *(v.)* **align**
ሰርዐ ser'ë *(v.)* **rank**
ሰርዐ ser'ë *(v.)* **arrange**
ሰርዐ ser'ë *(v.)* **systematize**
ሰረገላ seregela *(n.)* **carriage**
ሰረገላ seregela *(n.)* **coupe**

ሰረገላ በረድ seregela bered ***(n.)*** **sleigh**

ሰርከስ serekse ***(n.)*** **circus**

ሰረቀ sereqe ***(v.)*** **rob**

ሰረቐ sereqhe ***(v.)*** **steal**

ሰረቐ sereqhe ***(v.)*** **swipe**

ሰረረ serere ***(v.)*** **copulate**

ሰረት seret ***(n.)*** **plinth**

ሰረት seret ***(n.)*** **basis**

ሰረት አልቦ seret'albo ***(adj.)*** **baseless**

ሰረታዊ seretawi ***(n.)*** **basic**

ሰረተ serete ***(n.)*** **base**

ሰረተ serete ***(v.)*** **embed**

ሰረተ ሓሳብ serete hasab ***(n.)*** **thesis**

ሰረፀ seretze ***(v.)*** **infiltrate**

ሰረየ sereye ***(v.)*** **conjure**

ሰረየ sereye ***(v.)*** **bewitch**

ሰረዘ sereze ***(v.)*** **annul**

ሰረዘ sereze ***(v.)*** **revoke**

ሰረዘ sereze ***(v.)*** **abrogate**

ሰረዘ sereze ***(v.)*** **cancel**

ሰርሐ serhe ***(v.)*** **make**

ሰርሒ መጣምር serhi metamr ***(n.)*** **saddler**

ሰራሕተኛ serȟtegna ***(n.)*** **employee**

ሰሪሑ ረኸበ serîhu rekebe ***(v.)*** **earn**

ሰረቕካ ምራይ seriqka mray ***(v.)*** **peek**

ሰርወ serwe ***(n. )*** **lath**

ስስዐ ses'ë-a ***(n.)*** **greed**

ሳዕሰዐ sëse'ë ***(v.)*** **dance**

ሰሰነ sesene ***(v.)*** **thrive**

ሰዓረ se'are ***(v.)*** **overcome**

ሰዓረ se'are ***(v.)*** **overpower**

ሰገን segen ***(n.)*** **ostrich**

ሰገደ segede ***(n. )*** **obeisance**

ሰጎገ segoge ***(v.)*** **oust**

ሰፋራይ sefaray ***(n.)*** **occupant**

ሰተኖግራፊ setenografi ***(n. )*** **stenography**

ሰተፕ setep ***(n. )*** **steppe**

ሰተየ seteye ***(v. t)*** **drink**

ሰተየ seteye ***(v.)*** **imbibe**

ሰጢሙ ዝተአሰረ setimu zeteasere ***(adj.)*** **tight**

ሰዓበ seäbe ***(v.)*** **ensue**

ሰዓበ se'äbe ***(v.)*** **adhere**

ሰዓበ se'äbe ***(v.)*** **follow**

ሰአለ se'ale ***(v.)*** **depict**

ሰአለ se'ale ***(v.)*** **draw**

ሰዓለ se'äle ***(v.)*** **cough**

ሰኣሊ seali ***(n.)*** **photographer**

ሰዓመ se'ame ***(v.t. )*** **kiss**

ሰዓመ se'ame ***(v.)*** **smooch**

ሰአነ se'ane ***(v.)*** **lose**

ሰዓረ seare ***(v.)*** **win**

ሰዓረ se'äre ***(v. t.)*** **defeat**

ሰዓረ se'äre ***(v.)*** **repeal**

ሰዓረ se'äre ***(v.)*** **surmount**

ሰዓረ se'äre ***(v.)*** **vanquish**

ሰዓት seat ***(n.)*** **chronograph**

ሰዓት seat' ***(n.)*** **clock**

ሰዓት se'ät ***(n.)*** **hour**

ሰዓት ደወል seat' dewel ***(n.)*** **chime**

ሰብአያ ዝሞታ seaya zemota ***(n.)*** **widow**

ሰብ seb ***(n. )*** **person**

ሰብ seb ***(n.)*** **mankind**

ሰበ ስልጣን seb sltan ***(n.)*** **dignitary**

ሰብ ሰራሕ seb sraȟ ***(adj.)*** **synthetic**

ሰብ ዘይብሉ seb zeybelu ***(adj.)*** **uninhabited**

ሰብ ዘይብሉ seb zeybelu ***(adj.)*** **unmanned**

ሰብ ዝሰርሖ ጸጉሪ seb zserho xeguri ***(n. )*** **wig**

ሰብዓ seb'a ***(adj. & n.)*** **seventy**

ሰባበረ sebabere *(v.)* **inflect**
ሰባበረ sebabere *(v.t. )* **shatter**
ሰባኺ sebaḱi *(n.)* **preacher**
ሰባር መርከብ sebar merkeb *(n.)* **shipwreck**
ሰባት sebat *(n.)* **people**
ሰብኣዊ seb'awi *(adj. )* **human**
ሰብኣዊ ኮነ seb'awi kone *(v.)* **humanize**
ሰብኣዊነታዊ seb'awinetawi *(adj. )* **humanitarian**
ሰብኣዊነት ገፈፈ seb'awnet gefefe *()* **dehumanize**
ሰብኣይ ንግስቲ sebeaayi negeseti *(n.)* **consort**
ሰበባ sebeba *(n.)* **moss**
ስብሒ sebehi *(n.)* **cellulite**
ሰበኸ sebeke *(v.)* **sermonize**
ሰብእነት seb'ènet *(n.)* **virility**
ሰበረ sebere *(v.)* **break**
ሰበይታይ sebeytay *(adj.)* **effeminate**
ሰበይቲ sebeyti *(n. )* **woman**
ሰበይቲ ምኻን sebeyti mkuan *(v.)* **womanize**
ሰበይቲ ወዲ sebeyti wedi *(n.)* **daughter-in-law**
ሰበይትነት sebeytnet *(n. )* **womanhood**
ሰበይቱ ዝሞተቶ sebeytu zmoteto *(n. )* **widower**
ሰደደ sedede *(v.)* **consign**
ሰደደ sedede *(v.)* **propel**
ሰደቓ sedeqa *(n.)* **desk**
ሰደቓ sedeqa *(n.)* **diagram**
ሰደረ sedere *(v.)* **lope**
ሰደርያ sederya *(n.)* **waistcoat**
ሰዲድ sedid *(n.)* **footage**
ሰውአ sew'a *(v.)* **sacrifice**
ሰወአ sewe'e *(v.)* **immolate**
ሰውሒ sewhi *(n. )* **lawn**
ሰውሒ sewhi *(n. )* **turf**
ሰውሒ sewḧi *(n.)* **meadow**
ሰውሰወ sewsewe *(v.)* **shrug**
ሰያዒ seya'i *(adj.)* **sexy**
ሰየፈ seyefe *(v.)* **behead**
ሰየፈ seyefe *(v.)* **decapitate**
ሰየመ seyeme *(v.)* **designate**
ሰየመ seb'awnet *(n.)* **humanism**
ሰብኣውነት seḥabe *(v.)* **waive**
ሰሓበ selamta 'id *(n.)* **handshake**
ሰላምታ ኢድ seyeme *(v.)* **nominate**

## ሲ

ሲደር cider *(n.)* **cider**
ሲጋር sigar *(n.)* **cigar**
ሲልፎ silfo *(n.)* **sylph**
ሲሊንደር silinder *(n.)* **cylinder**
ሲንዲካቶ sindikato *(n.)* **syndicate**
ሲረና sirena *(n.)* **buzzer**
ሲሶ siso *(adj.)* **third**
ሲትሩስ sitrus *(n.)* **citrus**
ሲትሩሳዊ sitrusawi *(adj.)* **citric**
ሲያናይድ siyanayd *(n.)* **cyanide**
ሲ si *()* **C**

## ሳ

ሳዕቤን saëbeen *(n.)* **effect**
ሳዕቤን sa'ëben *(n.)* **repercussion**
ሳዕቤናዊ saëbenawi *(adj.)* **resultant**
ሳዕቤን saebien *(n.)* **upshot**
ሳዕቤን saee'bene *(n.)* **consequence**
ሳእኒ ጎማ sa'eni goma *(n.)* **sneaker**
ሳምሶማ ሳምሶማ *(v.)* **jog**

ሳዕሪ sa'ëri *(n. )* **grass**
ሳዕሪ ኣብልዐ sa'ëri 'abl'ë *(v.)* **graze**
ሳዕሳዓይ sa'ëse'ë *(n.)* **dancer**
ሳፋሪ safari *(n.)* **safari**
ሳጓ sagwa *(n.)* **nickname**
ሳሕቲ sahti *(adv.)* **seldom**
ሳሕቲ saḥti *(adv. )* **hardly**
ሳሕቲ ዝርከብ sahti zrkeb *(adj.)* **scarce**
ሳሕቲ ዝርከብ saĥti zrkeb *(adj.)* **rare**
ሳካሪን sakarin *(n.)* **saccharin**
ሳኬቶ sakieto *(n.)* **sachet**
ሳክስፎን saksfon *(n.)* **saxophone**
ሳልቤታ salbeeta *(n.)* **bib**
ሳልፈር salfer *(n.)* **sulphur**
ሳሎን salon *(n.)* **salon**
ሳልሳ salsa *(n.)* **salsa**
ሳልሳይ ደረጃ salsay dereja *(adj.)* **tertiary**
ሳልቬታ salvieta *(n.)* **serviette**
ሳልቮ salvo *(n.)* **salvo**
ሳምባ samba *(n. )* **lung**
ሳምዕተኛ samëtegna *(n. )* **notary**
ሳምራዊ samrawi *(n.)* **Samaritan**
ሳሙና samuna *(n.)* **soap**
ሳንዱቕ sanaduqe *(n.)* **cist**
ሳንባ መንቀርሳ sanba menkersa *(n.)* **tuberculosis**
ሳንዲ sandi *(n.)* **sundae**
ሳንዱች sanduch *(n.)* **sandwich**
ሳንዱቕ sanduq̈ *(n.)* **box**
ሳንቲም sanetim *(n.)* **cent**
ሳንቲም sanetime *(n.)* **coin**
ሳንጃ sanĵa *(n.)* **bayonet**
ሳንቲም santim *(n. )* **penny**
ሳንቲም santim *(n. )* **Yen**
ሳንቲም ዘይብሉ santim zeyblu *(adj.)* **penniless**
ሳሬት sareet *(n.)* **spider**
ሳሪ sari *(n.)* **sari**
ሳቲን satin *(n.)* **satin**
ሳትላይት satlayt *(n.)* **satellite**
ሳፁን ሬሳ satsun resa *(n.)* **casket**
ሳፁን ሬሳ satsun resa *(n.)* **coffin**
ሳውና sawuna *(n.)* **sauna**
ሳይበር sayber *(comb.)* **cyber**
ሳይበርስፔስ sayberspas *(n.)* **cyberspace**
ሳይኮሎጂካል saykoloĵikal *(adj.)* **psychological**
ሳይኮሎጂካዊ saykoloĵikawi *(n.)* **psychologist**
ሳይኮሎጂ saykoloyĵi *(n.)* **psychology**
ሳይንስ sayns *(n.)* **science**
ሳይንሳዊ saynsawi *(adj.)* **scientific**
ሳይንቲስት saynst *(n.)* **scientist**

# ሴ

ሴዳን siedan *(n.)* **sedan**
ሴፍ sief *(n.)* **sabre**
ሴኦል sieol *(n.)* **perdition**
ሴጣን sietan *(n. )* **Satan**
ሴጣናዊ sietanawi *(adj.)* **satanic**
ሴፍ seef *(n. )* **sword**
ሴጋ ገበረ seega gebere *(v.)* **masturbate**
ሴራሚክ seeramik *(n.)* **ceramic**
ሴጋለ segale *(n.)* **rye**
ስጋዊ segawi *(adj.)* **carnal**
ስእላዊ selawi *(adj.)* **photographic**
ስእላዊ መግለፂ s'elawi megletzi *(n.)* **graph**
ስእላዊ መግለጺ selawi meglexi *(n.)* **pictograph**
ሴልሲየስ selcius *(n.)* **Celsius**

ስሙይ ሰብ semuyei sebe *(n.)* **celebrity**
ስነ ከዋክብቲ sene kewakbti *(n.)* **horoscope**
ስነ ስርዓታዊ sene sereaa'tawii *(adj.)* **ceremonial**
ስነ-ጥዕና sene te-ena *(n.)* **hygiene**
ሰነድ sened *(n.)* **document**
ሰነድ ልቓሕ sened lqah *(n.)* **debenture**
ሰነፍ senef *(n. )* **idler**
ሰነፍ senef *(adj.)* **indolent**
ሰነፍ senef *(adj.)* **lazy**
ሰነገ senege *(v.)* **gobble**
ስነ ስርዓት ዘለዎ senei sereat zelewoo *(adj.)* **ceremonious**
ሰንሰለት seneselet *(n.)* **chain**
ሰይጣን seytan *(n.)* **devil**
ሱቕ በሃሊ suq behali *(adj.)* **taciturn**
ሱቖ suqo *(n.)* **gruel**
ሱር sur *(n.)* **root**
ሱር ዝሰደደ sur zsedede *(adj.)* **rooted**
ሱሱዕ susu'ë *(adj.)* **rapacious**
ስእነት s'enet *(n. )* **loss**
ስእነት ዓቕሚ s'enet 'aqmi *(n.)* **incapacity**
ስመ ጽራሕ sme tsrah *(n. )* **onomatopoeia**
ስም ምጥፋእ shem mxfa'e *(n.)* **obloquy**
ስራሕ ኣብዘሐ srah abzahe *(v.)* **overburden**
ስርዐ ser'ë *(v.)* **organize**
ስነ ህላወ sne hlawe *(n.)* **ontology**
ስዉር swr *(n. )* **occult**
ስቪል sevil *(n.)* **civilian**
ስፋይ sfay *(n.)* **stitch**
ስፈ ንህቢ sfe nhbi *(n. )* **honeycomb**
ስፍሓት sfhat *(n.)* **width**
ስፍሓት s'fȟat *(n. )* **stretch**
ስፍሓት sfȟat *(n.)* **amplitude**
ስፍሓት sfȟat *(n.)* **area**
ስፍለት sflet *(n.)* **anomaly**
ስፍራ ባሕተዎት sfra bahtewot *(n. )* **hermitage**
ስፍሪ sfri *(n. )* **quantity**
ስፍሰፋ sfsefa *(n.)* **weightlifting**
ስጋ sga *(n.)* **curry**
ስጋ sga *(n.)* **flesh**
ስጋ sga *(n. )* **meat**
ስጋ በጊዕ sga begi'ë *(n.)* **mutton**
ስጋ ሓሰማ sga ȟasema *(n. )* **pork**
ስጋ ምልበስ sga mlbas *(n.)* **incarnation**
ስጋ ምራኽ sga mraḱ *(n.)* **veal**
ስጋ ሰለወ sga selewe *(v.)* **grill**
ስጋ ዝለበሰ sga zlebese *(adj.)* **incarnate**
ስግኣት sg'at *(n.)* **misgiving**
ስገም sgem *(n.)* **barley**
ስግለት ከዋኽብቲ sglet kewaḱbti *(n.)* **astrology**
ስነ-መግቢ sin-e meg-bi *(n.)* **gastronomy**
ስራሕ sir'ahh *(n.)* **career**
ስቓይ skay *(n.)* **torture**
ስክፍታ skfta *(n.)* **compunction**
ስኽፍታ skfta *(n. )* **premonition**
ስክፍታ skfta *(n.)* **qualm**
ስክፍታ skfta *(n.)* **scruple**
ስኪዞፍረንያ skizofrenia *(n.)* **schizophrenia**
ስኮታዊ skotawi *(v.)* **Scot**
ስኩፍ skuf *(adj.)* **scrupulous**
ስላሴ slasi *(n. )* **trinity**
ስላጣ slata *(n. )* **salad**
ስልበጣ slbeta *(n.)* **recrimination**

ስለ sle *(n.)* **sake**
ስለ ጉዕዞ ዘርኢ ፊልሚ sleguazo zerai filmi *(n.)* **travelogue**
ሰላሕታዊ s'leħatawi *(adj.)* **stealthy**
ስለላ slela *(n.)* **espionage**
ስለመ sleme *(v.)* **caparison**
ስለው ፈለው slew felew *(n.)* **see-saw**
ስለዚ slezi *(adv.)* **accordingly**
ስለዚ slezi *(adv. )* **thus**
ስሊከን sliken *(n.)* **silicon**
ስልኪ slki *(n.)* **telephone**
ስልኪ ኣልቦ slki albo *(adj.)* **wireless**
ስልኩይ slkuy *(n.)* **valetudinarian**
ስልማት ናይ መጽሓፍ slmat nay mexḥaf *(n.)* **vignette**
ስልመ ክንቲት slme kntit *(n.)* **plume**
ስልኪ seli *(n.)* **phone**
ስእሊ seli *(n.)* **photo**
ስእሊ seli *(n.)* **photograph**
ስእሊ s'eli *(n.)* **drawing**
ስእሊ s'eli *(n.)* **picture**
ስእሊ መሬት s'èli mereet *(n.)* **landscape**
ስእሊ ዝፈጥር ንሽተይ ነጠብጣብ ኣብ ኮምፒተር sèli zfeẗr nèshtey neẗebẗab nay kompiter *(n.)* **pixel**
ስልጣን sltan *(n.)* **dominion**
ስልጣን ሃበ slẗan habe *(v.)* **empower**
ስልጣን ዝሃዘ sltan zhaze *(n. )* **tenure**
ስልጣኑ ኣካፈለ sltanu akafele *(v.)* **decentralize**
ስልጣንያ sltanya *(n. )* **jar**
ስልታዊ s'ltawi *(adj.)* **strategic**
ስልጠና sltena *(n. )* **training**
ስልቲ slti *(n.)* **strategy**
ስልቲ s'lti *(n.)* **stratagem**
ስልቲ ዘውጽእ s'lti zewts'e *(n.)* **strategist**
ኣልትራሳውንድ sltrasawnd *(n.)* **ultrasound**
ስልጡን sltun *(adj.)* **urbane**
ስሉብ slub *(n.)* **eunuch**
ስሉም slum *(n. )* **tapestry**
ስሉጥ sluẗ *(adj.)* **agile**
ስሉጥ sluṭ *(adj. )* **handy**
ስሉጥ sluẗ *(adj.)* **brisk**
ስም s'm *(n.)* **noun**
ስም ኣጥፈአ sm atfe'e *(n.)* **denunciation**
ስም ከተማ sm ketema *(n.)* **Perry**
ስም ሰብ ዘፀልም sm seb zetselm *(adj.)* **scurrilous**
ስምዓት sm'ät *(n.)* **audition**
ስምብራት smbrat *(n.)* **contusion**
ሽምደዳ šmdeda *(n.)* **rote**
ስምዒት sm'eit *(n.)* **sensation**
ስምዒት sm'eit *(n.)* **sentiment**
ስምዒት ሓዘን smeit hazen *(n. )* **pathos**
ስምዒት ዘለዎ sm'eit zelewo *(adj.)* **sentient**
ስምዒት ዘንቀሳቕስ smëit zenqesaqs *(adj.)* **poignant**
ስምዒታዊ smeitawi *(adj.)* **passionate**
ስምዒታዊ sm'eitawi *(adj.)* **sentimental**
ስመራግድ smeragd *(n.)* **emerald**
ስመ-ስውር smeswr *(adj.)* **anonymous**
ስመ-ስውርነት smeswrnet *(n.)* **anonymity**
ስምዒ sm'ie *(n.)* **wax**
ስሚዒት sm'ït *(n.)* **emotion**
ስምዒት sm'ït *(n.)* **feeling**
ስምዒት ቀስቀሰ sm'ït qesqese *(v.)* **electrify**

ስምዒት ዝመልኦ sm'it zmel'o *(adj.)* **soulful**
ስምዒት ዝቅስቅስ sm'ït zqsqs *(adj.)* **emotive**
ስምዒታዊ sm'ïtawi *(adj.)* **emotional**
ስምዒታዊ sm'ïtawi *(adj.)* **impassioned**
ስምዒታዊ sm'ïtawi *(adj.)* **intense**
ስምምዕ smm'e *(adj.)* **tacit**
ስምምዕ smm'e *(a. )* **unanimity**
ስምምዕ smm'ë *(n.)* **agreement**
ስምምዕ smm'ë *(n.)* **concord**
ስምምዕ smm'ë *(n.)* **concordance**
ስምምዕ smm'ë *(n.)* **conformity**
ስምምዕ smm'ë *(n.)* **correspondence**
ስምምዕ smm'ë *(n.)* **assent**
ስምረት smret *(n.)* **realization**
ስምስም smsm *(n.)* **sesame**
ስሙይ smuy *(adj.)* **eminent**
ስሙይ smuy *(adj.)* **famous**
ስናፐር snaper *(n.)* **snapper**
ስድስቶ sdsto *(n.)* **sextuplet**
ስባር sbar *(n. )* **fragment**
ስብኣይነት sb'aynet *(n.)* **manhood**
ስብሓት sbĥat *(n.)* **reverence**
ስብሒ sbĥi *(n.)* **fat**
ስብሒ sbḥi *(n.)* **grease**
ስብሒ ምውጋድ sbhi mwgad *(n.)* **liposuction**
ስብከት sbket *(n. )* **parish**
ስብከት sbket *(n. )* **propaganda**
ስብከት sbket *(n.)* **sermon**
ስብቅልነት sbqlnet *(n.)* **elegance**
ስብቆ sbqo *(n.)* **soup**
ስብቁል sbqul *(adj.)* **chic**
ስብቁል sbqul *(n.)* **dandy**
ስብርባር ሕንፃፅ sbrbar hntsats *(n.)* **zigzag**
ስብረት sbret *(n.)* **breakage**
ስቡዕ ጐኖ sbu'ë guano *(n.)* **heptagon**
ስቡር sbur *(adj.)* **broken**
ስድዓት sd'at *(n.)* **seduction**
ስደት sdet *(n.)* **exile**
ስደተኛ sdetegna *(n. )* **refugee**
ስዲ sdi *(adj.)* **impertinent**
ስዲ sdi *(adj.)* **rude**
ስዲ sdi *(adj.)* **unruly**
ስዲ ኸደ sdi kede *(v.)* **misbehave**
ስዲ ንባብ sdi nbab *(n.)* **prose**
ስድነት sdnet *(n.)* **asperity**
ስድነግ sdnet *(n)* **impertinence**
ስድነት sdnet *(n. )* **misbehaviour**
ስድራ sdra *(n.)* **span**
ስድራ ቤት sdra biet *(n.)* **family**
ስድራቤት sdrabetawi *(n.)* **parentage**
ስድራቤታዊ sdrabetawi *(adj.)* **parental**
ስንብራት snbrat *(n.)* **bruise**
ስንጭሮ snčro *(n.)* **vale**
ስነ ኣእምሮ sne aèmro *(n.)* **psychiatry**
ስነ ባህለታዊ sne bahletawi *(adj.)* **semantic**
ስነ-በረራ sne berera *(n.)* **aviation**
ስነ ብሂላዊ sne bhilawi *(adj.)* **mythological**
ስነ ብረት sne bret *(n. )* **metallurgy**
ስነ ዕዳጋ sne edaga *(n.)* **marketing**
ሰነ ሃለዋት sne halewat *(n. )* **statistics**
ስነ ሃለዋታዊ sne halewatawi *(adj.)* **statistical**
ስነ ሓሸራ sne ĥashera *(n.)* **entomology**
ስነ-ሃይማኖት sne haymanot *(n. )* **theology**

ስነ ህይወተኛ sne hywetenya *(n.)* **biologist**
ስነ ህዝቢ sne hzbi *(n.)* **demography**
ስነ ምድረኛ sne mdregna *(n.)* **geologist**
ስነ ምድሪ sne mdri *(n.)* **geology**
ስነ ማዓድን sne me'ädn *(n.)* **mineralogy**
ስነ መትኒ sne metni *(n. )* **neurology**
ስነ መዛርዕ sne mezar'ë *(n.)* **morphology**
ስነ ምግባራዊ sne mgbarawi *(n.)* **ethical**
ስነ ምግባረኛ sne mgbaregna *(n. )* **moralist**
ስነ ምግባሩ ኣመሓየሸ sne mgbaru amehayeshe *(v.)* **moralize**
ስነ ምሕዳር sne mĥdar *(n.)* **ecology**
ስነ ምንቅስቃስ sne mnqskas *(n.)* **dynamics**
ስነ ነፀብራቕ sne netsebraq *(n.)* **reflexology**
ስነ ቃላዊ sne qalawi *(adj.)* **lexical**
ስነ ቕመም sne qe'mem *(n.)* **chemistry**
ስነ ቅርፃቅርፂ sne qrtsaqrtsi *(n.)* **sculpture**
ስነ ቅርፃዊ sne qrtsawi *(adj.)* **sculptural**
ስነ ቁጠባ sne quteba *(n.)* **economics**
ስነ ሴም sne siem *(adj.)* **Semitic**
ስነ ስርዓት sne sr'ät *(n.)* **discipline**
ስነ ስርዓት sne sr'ät *(n.)* **propriety**
ስነ ፅሑፋዊ sne tzhufawi *(adj.)* **literary**
ስነ-ዉሕስና sne- wuhsna *(n.)* **immunology**
ስነ ፅዋ sne xwa *(n.)* **mythology**
ስነ ዜጋ sne zeega *(n.)* **civics**
ስነ-ኣትክልቲ sne'atklti *(n.)* **botany**
ስነ-በረራ sneberera *(n.)* **aeronautics**
ስነ-ዱር snedur *(n.)* **forestry**
ስነ-ዕለታት sne'ëletat *(n.)* **chronology**
ስነ-እንስሳ sne-enssa *(n. )* **zoology**
ስነ-ፈለክ snefelek *(n.)* **astronomy**
ስነ-ሓሳብ sneḥasab *(n.)* **ideology**
ስነ-ሕጊ sneȟgi *(n. )* **jurisprudence**
ስነ-ህንጻ snehnxa *(n.)* **architecture**
ስነ-ህይወት snehywet *(n.)* **biology**
ስነ-ኮኾበኛ snekokobenya *(n.)* **astronomer**
ስነ ሞጎት sne-mogot *(n.)* **logic**
ስነ-ቅመም ህይወታውያን sneqmem hywetawyan *(n.)* **biochemistry**
ስነ-ቅርጺ ኣካል sneqrxi 'akal *(n.)* **anatomy**
ስነ-ሰብ sneseb *(n.)* **anthropology**
ስነ-ስርዓት በዓል sne-srät beäl *(n. )* **pageant**
ስነ-ጥበባዊ snetbebawi *(adj.)* **artistic**
ስነ-ጠቢብ snetebib *(n.)* **artist**
ስነ-ጽባቐ snexbaqe *(n.)* **aesthetics**
ስንፈተ ግብረስጋ snfete gebresga *(n.)* **impotence**
ስንፈተ ግብረስጋ ዘለዎ snfete gebresga zelewo *(adj.)* **impotent**
ስንፍነት snfnet *(n. )* **idleness**
ስኒ sni *(n.)* **cog**
ስኒ sni *(n. )* **tooth**
ስኒ ኣውፂኡ ን ህፃን sni awsiau nhsan *(v.)* **teethe**
ስኒ ሓርማዝ sni ȟarmaz *(n.)* **ivory**
ስኒት snit *(n.)* **chord**
ስኒት snit *(n.)* **rapprochement**
ስኒት snit *(n.)* **rhyme**

ስንቂ መቅረቢ snqi meqrebi *(n.)* **victualler**
ሽንቅጥ šnqt *(adj.)* **slim**
ስኑከር snuker *(n.)* **snooker**
ሶዳ soda *(n.)* **soda**
ሰደመኛዊት sodemegnawit *(n.)* **lesbian**
ሰዶምነት sodomnet *(n.)* **sodomy**
ሶፋ sofa *(n. )* **sofa**
ሶፍቲ softi *(n.)* **tissue**
ሶኬት sokiet *(n.)* **plug**
ሶኬት sokiet *(n.)* **socket**
ሶሎ solo *(n.)* **solo**
ሶኔት soniet *(n. )* **sonnet**
ሰኑይ sonuy *(n.)* **Monday**
ሶርኖ sorno *(n.)* **sinus**
ፆታ ምቅያር sota mkyar *(n.)* **transsexual**
ስፓም spam *(n.)* **spam**
ስፓንየል spanyel *(n.)* **spaniel**
ስፔይናዊ speeynawi *(n. )* **Spaniard**
ስፔይናዊ speeynawi *(n. )* **Spanish**
ስፒናች spinach *(n.)* **spinach**
ስፖርት sport *(n.)* **sport**
ስፖርታዊ sportawi *(adj.)* **athletic**
ስፖርታዊ sportawi *(adj.)* **sporting**
ሰፖርተኛ sportegna *(n. )* **sportsman**
ስፖርተኛ sporteňa *(n.)* **athlete**
ስፖዳ sppoda *(n. )* **rapier**
ስቃይ sqay *(n.)* **affliction**
ስቃይ sqay *(n.)* **bane**
ስቃይ sq̈ay *(n.)* **agony**
ስቅያታዊ sqyatawi *(adj.)* **wretched**
ስርዓት sräat *(n.)* **procedure**
ስራሕ srah *(n.)* **task**
ስራሕ srah *(n.)* **work**
ስራሕ sraḧ *(n.)* **job**
ስራሕ ኣልቦነት sraĥ albonet *(n.)* **redundancy**
ስራሕ ኣፈፃሚ srah asfetsami *(n.)* **manager**
ሰራሕ ካይላ sraḧ kayla *(v.)* **potter**
ሰራሕ ሸኽላ sraḧ shḱla *(n.)* **porcelain**
ስራሕ ዝፈትሐ srah zfethe *(adj.)* **unemployed**
ስራሕ ዝከልክል ነገር srah zklkl neger *(v.)* **trammel**
ስራሕቲ ቅርፂ sraȟti qrxi *(n.)* **carvery**
ስርዓት sr'at *(n. )* **manner**
ስርዓት sr'at *(n.)* **mannerism**
ስርዓት sr'at *(n.)* **system**
ስርዓት ኣልቦ sr'ät 'albo *(n.)* **anarchy**
ስርዓት ኣትሓዘ sr'ät atĥaze *(v.)* **regulate**
ስርዓት ቀብሪ sr'ät qebri *(n. )* **funeral**
ስርዓት ዘይተምሃረ sr'at zeytemhare *(n.)* **indiscipline**
ስርዒታዊ s'rätawi *(adj.)* **systemic**
ስርዓተ መንግስቲ sr'äte mengsti *(n. )* **regime**
ስርዓተ መርበብ sr'äte merbeb *(n. )* **network**
ስርዓተ መጽናዕቲ ሕማም srate mxnaeti hmam *(n.)* **pathology**
ስርዓተ ነጥቢ sr'ate netbi *(n.)* **punctuation**
ስርዓተ ንግስና sr'äte ngsna *(n.)* **coronation**
ስርዓተ ትምህርቲ sräte tmhrti *(n.)* **curriculum**
ስራይ sray *(n.)* **charm**
ስራይ sray *(n. )* **glamour**
ስርበተ ደም srbete dem *(n.)* **plethora**
ስረ sre *(n.)* **pants**
ስረ sre *(n. )* **trousers**

ስረ-ግትር sregtr *(n.)* **bloomers**
ስረ-ግትር sregtr *(n.)* **breeches**
ስሬት sret *(n.)* **deliverance**
ስረዛ sreza *(n.)* **cancellation**
ስረዛ sreza *(n.)* **deletion**
ስረዛ sreza *(n.)* **revocation**
ስርሓት ካይላ srȟat kayla *(n. )* **pottery**
ስርኤል sriel *(n.)* **fairy**
ስሪንጋ sringa *(n.)* **syringe**
ስርዒት ፈረስ sr'ït feres *(n.)* **harness**
ስርቂ srki *(n.)* **theft**
ስርናይ srnay *(n.)* **wheat**
ስርቂ srqi *(n.)* **burglary**
ስርቂ srqi *(n. )* **robbery**
ስርቂ srqi *(n.)* **stole**
ሽርተቴ šrtete *(n.)* **ski**
ስሩብ srub *(adj.)* **imminent**
ስሩዕ sru'ë *(adj.)* **formal**
ስሩዕ sru'ë *(adj.)* **regular**
ስሩዕ መዝገብ sru'ë mezgeb *(n.)* **catalogue**
ስርወ መንግስቲ srwe mengsti *(n.)* **dynasty**
ስርወ መንግስቲ srwe-mengsti *(n. )* **kingdom**
ስርየት sryet *(n.)* **absolution**
ስሳ ssa *(adj. & n.)* **sixty**
ስሳነ ህይወት ssane hywet *(n.)* **biodiversity**
ስስዐ ss'ë *(n.)* **avarice**
ስስዐ sseä *(n.)* **cupidity**
ስሓኒ sȟani *(n.)* **basin**
ስሰና ssena *(n.)* **accretion**
ስስዐ ssie *(n.)* **parsimony**
ስሱዕ ssu'e *(adj.)* **selfish**
ስታድየም stadyem *(n. )* **stadium**
ስቴሮፎኒክ steerofonik *(adj.)* **stereophonic**
ስቴሮስኮፒክ steeroskopik *(adj.)* **stereoscopic**
ስተኖግራፈር stenografer *(n. )* **stenographer**
ስተንስል stensel *(n.)* **stencil**
ስተረዮ steryo *(n.)* **stereo**
ስተተስኮፕ steteskop *(n. )* **stethoscope**
ስቲግማታ stigmata *(n.)* **stigmata**
ስትሮቦ strobo *(n.)* **strobe**
ሰትሮይድ stroyd *(n.)* **steroid**
ስሑው sȟuw *(adj.)* **sparse**
ስሕተት s'htet *(adj.)* **incorrect**
ስሕተት sĥtet *(n.)* **fault**
ስሕተት sȟtet *(n.)* **mistake**
ስቱዲዮ studyo *(n.)* **studio**
ሱላ sula *(n.)* **barbecue**
ሱላ sula *(n.)* **cutlet**
ሱልጣኒት sulẗanit *(n.)* **sultana**
ሕሱም sum *(prep. )* **notorious**
ስኡን s'un *(adj.)* **destitute**
ስውንዋኖ swnwano *(n.)* **vamp**
ስዉእ swu'e *(n. )* **martyr**
ስዉር swur *(adj.)* **disembodied**
ስዉያ swya *(n.)* **personification**
ስውየት swyet *(n.)* **spasm**
ስውየታዊ swyetawi *(adj.)* **spasmodic**
ስያፍ syaf *(n.)* **bevel**
ስየ sye *(n.)* **palm**
ስየማ syema *(n.)* **nomination**
ስዩም s'èlawi *(adj.)* **graphic**
ስእላዊ selel bele *(v.)* **glide**
ሰለል በለ sem'ë *(v.)* **hear**
ሰምዐ sewasw *(n.)* **grammar**
ሰዋስው sfra manatile *(n. )* **warren**
ስፍራ ማናቲለ sḥbet *(n.)* **gravity**
ስሕበት sm'ïtawi *(adj.)* **voluptuous**

ስምዒታዊ snbta *(n.)* **valediction**
ስንብታ snçro *(n.)* **valley**
ስንጭር snu'ë 'aqḥu *(n.)* **ware**
ስኑዕ ኣቕሑ swṭet *(n. )* **insight**
ስውጠት segome *(n.)* **advance**
ሰገመ sne ïnti *(n.)* **archaeology**
ስነ ጥንቲ sga kebti *(n.)* **beef**
ስጋ ከብቲ xete *(v.)* **sell**

# ሸ

ሸጠ xampo *(n.)* **shampoo**
ሻምፖ šadšay *(adj. & n.)* **sixth**
ሻድሻይ xaw'ay *(adj. & n.)* **seventh**
ሻውዓይ xax *(n.)* **shawl**
ሻሽ xew'ate *(adj. & n.)* **seven**
ሸውዓተ xeyati *(n. )* **seller**
ሸያጢ shfta *(n.)* **bandit**
ሽፍታ xfan *(n.)* **sheath**
ሽፋን xto *(n.)* **scent**
ሽቶ xto amezgabi *(n. )* **scorer**
ሽቶ ኣመዝጋቢ sheqaṭ nebit *(n.)* **vintner**
ሸቃጥ ነቢት syum *(n.)* **nominee**
ሽየመ šeyeme *(v.)* **promote**
ሻሂ shahi *(n.)* **tea**
ሻሕኻር shahikar *(adj.)* **coarse**
ሻሕካር shahkar *(adj.)* **scabrous**
ሻለይ shaley *(n.)* **chalet**
ሻምብቆ shamboqo *(n.)* **flute**
ሻምብቆ shambqo *(adj.)* **tubular**
ሻሞት shamot *(n.)* **asparagus**
ሻምፓይን shampayn *(n.)* **champagne**
ሻንቅላ shanqla *(n.)* **nigger**
ሻቅሎት shaqlot *(n.)* **disquiet**
ሻቅሎት shaqlot *(n.)* **agitation**
ሻራ shara *(n.)* **conspiracy**
ሻርቢ sharbi *(n.)* **scarf**
ሻርነት ዘይምህላው sharnet zeymhlaw *(n. )* **non-alignment**
ሻሽ shash *(n.)* **sash**
ሻሽ shash *(n.)* **voile**
ሻሽ shash *(n.)* **wimple**
ሻሽ shash *(n.)* **cambric**
ሻጣራ shatra *(adj.)* **tricky**
ስሕበት sȟbet *(n.)* **attraction**
ሽቦ shbo *(n.)* **wire**
ሽብርተኛ shbrtegna *(n.)* **terrorist**
ሽክና ርእሲ škna r'esi *(n. )* **skull**
ሽልሽል šlšl *(n.)* **remit**
ሽልማት šlmat *(n.)* **reward**
ሽብርተኝነት shbrtegnnet *(n.)* **terrorism**
ሸፋሽፍቲ shefashfti *(n.)* **brow**
ሸፋጢ shefati *(adj.)* **devious**
ሸፈነ shefene *(v.)* **dissimulate**
ሸፈነ shefene *(v.)* **envelop**
ሸፈነ shefene *(v.)* **insulate**
ሸፈነ shefene *(v.)* **suffuse**
ሸፈነ/ከወለ shefene/kewele *(v.)* **cover**
ሽፍጢ shefe'ti *(n.)* **chicanery**
ሽጣራ štara *(n.)* **ruse**
ሽጋራ shegara *(n.)* **cigarette**
ሽጎማኖ shegomano *(n.)* **terry**
ሽሓነ shehane *(n.)* **censer**
ሽሓነ shehane *(n.)* **salver**
ሽሓነ sheȟane *(n.)* **dish**
ሽሓጠ sheȟaïe *(v.)* **cajole**
ሽሕ'ኳ እንተ she-h-kua ente *(adv. )* **however**
ሽክላ shekla *(n.)* **crockery**
ሽተኽበተኽ šetekbetek *(n.)* **raffle**
ሽክላ ቆርቆሮ shekla qorqoro *(n.)* **tile**
ሽክሚ shekmi *(n.)* **burden**

ሸኰና shekẃana *(n.)* **heel**
ሸላጊ shelagi *(n. )* **mortgagee**
ሸለፍ shelef *(n.)* **lap**
ሸለል በለ shelel bele *(v. t)* **disregard**
ሸለል በለ shelel bele *(v.)* **neglect**
ሸለለ shelele *(v.)* **baste**
ሸለልትነት sheleltnet *(n.)* **laxity**
ሸለመ she-leme *(v.)* **garnish**
ሸለመ sheleme *(v.)* **award**
ሸለመ sheleme *(v.)* **bestow**
ሸለን shelen *(n.)* **aniseed**
ሸለውሊዋ መጫወቲ shelewliwa mechaeti *(n.)* **trapeze**
ሸማቲ shemati *(n.)* **consumer**
ሸበጥ šebet *(n.)* **slipper**
ሸፈሕ በለ šefeĥ bele *(v.t. )* **shuffle**
ሸምዳዲ shemdadi *(adj.)* **bookish**
ሸምገለ shemgele *(v.)* **mediate**
ሸሞንተ shemonte *(adj. & n.)* **eight**
ሸምጣጢ shemtati *(adj.)* **sarcastic**
ሸምጢ shemti *(n.)* **loin**
ሸነ shene *(v.)* **urinate**
መሸበረቂ shenkata *(n.)* **trimmer**
ሸንሸነ shenshene *(n.)* **pleat**
ሸቀጥ sheqeẗ *(n.)* **merchandise**
ሸቅሸቅታ sheqsheqta *(n.)* **angina**
ሸራፍ sheraf *(n.)* **dent**
ሸራፍ sheraf *(adj.)* **toothless**
ሸርበጥ sherbeẗ *(n.)* **sorbet**
ሸረፈ sherefe *(v.)* **indent**
ሸረር sherer *(n. )* **whirligig**
ሸርፍራፍ sherifrafe *(n.)* **chip**
ሸርሸረ shershere *(v.)* **erode**
ሸርጣን sherẗan *(n.)* **crab**
ሸታቲ shetati *(adj.)* **smelly**
ሸጠ sheṭe *(v.)* **vend**
ሸሞንተ ወገን shemonte wegen *(n.)* **octagon**
ሽርሽር shrshr *(n.)* **outing**
ሽጠጥ shetet *(n.)* **zip**
ሸወዘ sheweze *(v.)* **annoy**
ሸውሃት shewhat *(n.)* **appetite**
ሸውታ shewta *(v.)* **zoom**
ሸያጣይ sheyatay *(n.)* **salesman**
ሸጠ sheyaṭi *(n.)* **vendor**
ሸያጢ ዕምበባ sheyaẗi ëmbeba *(n.)* **florist**
ሸያጢ ኣሕምልቲ sheyaẗi ĥamli *(n. )* **greengrocer**
ሸያጢ ናውቲ ጽሕፈት sheyaẗi nawti tsĥfet *(n. )* **stationer**
ሸያጢ ቆቢዕ ኣንስቲ sheyaẗi qobi'ë ansti *(n. )* **milliner**
ሹመት shumet *(n.)* **preferment**
ሹቅ shuq *(n. )* **mart**
ሹሻን shushan *(n.)* **lotus**
ሽፋን shfan *(n.)* **casing**
ሽፋን shfan *(n.)* **coating**
ሽፋን shfan *(n.)* **facing**
ሽፋን shfan *(n.)* **layer**
ሽፌር shfer *(n.)* **driver**
ሽፍጢ shfti *(n.)* **duplicity**
ሽፍጢ shfẗi *(n.)* **fraud**
ሽግር shgr *(n.)* **difficulty**
ሽግር shgr *(n.)* **hardship**
ሽግር shgr *(n.)* **problem**
ሽግር shgr *(n.)* **adversity**
ኣሽጋሪ shgrawi *(adj.)* **problematic**
ሽጉጥ shguẗ *(n. )* **pistol**
ሽሕ ዓመት shȟ ämet *(n. )* **millennium**
ሽሕ 'ኳ shȟ ekwa *(prep. )* **notwithstanding**
ሽሕ'ኳ shȟkwa *(conj.)* **albeit**
ሽሕ shih *(adj. & n.)* **thousand**
ሽርባ/በርበረ shirba/berebre *(n.)* **chilli**

ሽቶ shito *(n.)* **cologne**
ሽድሽተ šdšte *(adj.& n.)* **six**
ሽኻል shkal *(n.)* **peg**
ሽኾና shḱona *(n. )* **hoof**
ሽኮር shkor *(n.)* **sugar**
ሽኮር ድንሽ shkor dnesh *(n.)* **yam**
ሽኮራዊ ምግቢ shkorawi mgbi *(n.)* **sweetmeat**
ሽኮረይ shkorey *(n.)* **sweetheart**
ሽኮርያ shkorya *(n.)* **diabetes**
ሽኩዕኩዕ በለ shku'eku'e bele *(v.)* **snuggle**
ሽኹላል shkulal *(n. )* **roll**
ሽላ shla *(n.)* **buzzard**
ሽላ shla *(n.)* **falcon**
ሽልማት shlmat *(n.)* **decoration**
ሽልማት shlmat *(n.)* **prize**
ሽልማት shlmat *(n. )* **trophy**
ሽም shm *(n.)* **name**
ሽም እንስሳ shm enssa *(n.)* **winkle**
ሽም ስድራ shm sdra *(n.)* **surname**
ሽምዓ shm'ä *(n.)* **candle**
ሽማግለ shmagle *(n.)* **committee**
ሽማግሌ shmagle *(adj.)* **elderly**
ሽመና ማሽን shmena mashn *(n. )* **loom**
ሽመት shmet *(n.)* **promotion**
ሽምገላ shmgela *(n.)* **mediation**
ሽምገላ shmgela *(n.)* **mediation**
ሽምራር shmrar *(n.)* **crease**
ሽምጠጣ shmteta *(n.)* **sarcasm**
ሽታሕ በለ šetah bele *(v.)* **skid**
ሽታሕ በለ šetah bele *(v.)* **slide**
ሽታሕታሕ በለ šetaĥtaĥ bele *(v.)* **slither**
ሽንቅላት ምውጻእ shnqlat mwts'e *(n.)* **vituperation**
ሽንቲ shnti *(n.)* **urine**
ሽንቲ ቤት shnti bet *(n.)* **toilet**
ሽንቲ ቤት shnti biet *(n.)* **latrine**
ሽንቲ ቤት shnti biet *(n. )* **lavatory**
ሽንቲ ቤት shnti biet *(n.)* **loo**
ሽንጥሮ shntro *(n.)* **dale**
ሽንጥሮ shntro *(n.)* **dell**
ሽንጥሮ shnẗro *(v.)* **meander**
ሾመ shome *(v.)* **appoint**
ሽራዕ shra'ë *(v.)* **canvass**
ሽራጥ shraẗ *(n.)* **stripe**
ሽርካ shrka *(n.)* **ally**
ሽርካ shrka *(n.)* **interface**
ሽርክነት shrket *(n.)* **partnership**
ሽርክነት shrknet *(n.)* **cahoots**
ሽርሙጣ shrmuẗa *(n.)* **strumpet**
ሽሮቦ shrobo *(n. )* **syrup**
ሽርሽር shrshr *(n.)* **excursion**
ሽርሽር shrshr *(n.)* **jaunt**
ሽርሽር shrshr *(n.)* **picnic**
ሽሻይ shshay *(n.)* **bonanza**
ሽታ shta *(n.)* **smell**
ሽታ shta *(n.)* **spoor**
ሽጣራ shtara *(n. )* **wile**
ሽጣራ sh'ẗara *(n.)* **subterfuge**
ሽቶል shtol *(n.)* **stiletto**
ሽውሓት ኣልቦነት shwḧat 'albonet *(n.)* **anorexia**
ሽምኒት shmnit *(n.)* **octavo**
ሽታ shta *(adj.)* **odorous**
ሽጉርቲ shegurti *(n.)* **onion**
ሹጉሹግ ssgushug *(n.)* **alcove**
ሽፋን shfan *(adj.)* **overcast**
ሽፍታ shfta *(n.)* **outlaw**

# ቀ

ቀባጥ qebaẗ *(adj.)* **capricious**
ቀባፀ qebats *(adj.)* **desperate**
ቀብአ qeb'e *(v.)* **anoint**
ቀበኣይ qebeay *(n. )* **painter**
ቀበረ qebere *(v.)* **bury**
ቀብሪ qebri *(n.)* **burial**
ቀዳድ qedad *(n.)* **slot**
ቀዳዲ ብርሃን qedadi brhan *(n.)* **floodlight**
ቀዳሓይ qedaȟay *(n.)* **mimic**
ቀዳሒ ደም qedaȟi dem *(n.)* **artery**
ቀዳም qedam *(n. )* **Saturday**
ቀዳማይ qedamay *(adj.)* **primal**
ቀዳማይ ፈነወ ፊልሚ qedamay felewe filmi *(n. )* **premiere**
ቀዳማይ መሓውር qedamay meĥawr *(n.)* **foreleg**
ቀዳማይ ምስራዕ qedamay msraë *(n.)* **primacy**
ቀዳማይ ርበኛ qedamay rbogna *(n.)* **frontbencher**
ቀዳማይ ረድኤት qedamay red'eet *(n.)* **first aid**
ቀዳምነት qedamnet *(adv. )* **primarily**
ቀዳምነት qedamnet *(n.)* **priority**
ቀዳምነት ዝሓዘ qedamnety zhaze *(n.)* **pioneer**
ቀዳሲ qedasi *(n.)* **celebrant**
ቀደም qedem *(adj.)* **erstwhile**
ቀደመ qedem *(v.)* **excel**
ቀደም qedem *(n.)* **yore**
ቀዳምነት qedemanet *(n. )* **precedence**
ቀደሰ qede'se *(v.)* **consecrate**
ቀድሐ qedȟe *(v.)* **copy**
ቀድሐ qedḥe *(v.)* **imitate**
ቀዲምካ ምሕሳብ qedimka mĥsab *(n.)* **premeditation**
ቀዲሙ ሒዙ qedimu ȟizu *(v.)* **pre-empt**
ቀዲሙ ዝተሰርሐ qedimu zteserȟe *(adj.)* **prefabricated**
ቄሳራዊ qeesarawi *(n.)* **caesarean**
ቀሓር qeȟar *(n.)* **heartburn**
ዕግበት qeig'bet *(n.)* **contentment**
ቀጀለ qejele *(v.)* **fantasize**
ቀልቡ ኣጥፈአ qelbu aẗfe'a *(v.)* **swoon**
ቀልደድ qelded *(n.)* **arch**
ቀልደዳዊ qeldedawi *(n.)* **arcade**
ቀልዲ qeldi *(n.)* **quip**
ቕልዲ qeldi *(n.)* **whim**
ቀልዲ qeldi *(n. )* **wit**
ቕልዲ qeldi *(n.)* **witticism**
ቀልዐ qel'e *(v.)* **unfold**
ቀልዐ qel'e *(v.)* **unmask**
ቀልዐ qel'ë *(v.)* **reveal**
ቀለቤት qelebet *(n.)* **ring**
ቀለም qelem *(n.)* **dye**
ቀለም qelem *(n.)* **tint**
ና ቀለም መቅጠኒ ኬሚካል qelem meqteni kemikal *(n. )* **turpentine**
ቀለወ qelewe *(v.)* **roast**
ቀልሃ qeliha *(n.)* **cartridge**
ቀሊል qelil *(adj.)* **easy**
ቀሊል qelil *(adj.)* **facile**
ቀሊል qelil *(adj.)* **portable**
ቀሊል qelil *(adj.)* **simple**
ቀልቀል qelqel *(n.)* **stool**
ቀልጠፈ qeltefe *(v.)* **quicken**
ቀልቀል qelqel *(n.)* **outskirts**
ቀደመ qedeme *(v.)* **outstrip**
ቀዳማዊ qdamawi *(adj.)* **original**
ቀማሚ መድሃኒት qemami medhanit *(n.)* **pharmacist**

**ቀማሪት** qemarit *(n.)* **calculator**
**ቀማሲ** qemasi *(n.)* **gourmet**
**ቀመም** qemem *(n.)* **condiment**
**ቀመም** qemem *(n.)* **seasoning**
**ቀመም** qemem *(n.)* **spice**
**ቀመም ዝበዝሖ** qemem zbezĥo *(adj.)* **spicy**
**ቀመር** qemer *(n.)* **formula**
**ቀመር** qemer *(n.)* **calculation**
**ቀመረ** qemere *(v.)* **formulate**
**ቀመረ** qemere *(v.)* **calculate**
**ቀሚሽ** qemish *(n.)* **skirt**
**ቀሚሽ** qemish *(n.)* **gown**
**ቀምቃማይ** qemqamay *(n.)* **barber**
**ቀምቀመ** qemqeme *(v.)* **lop**
**ቀምሽ** qemš *(n.)* **robe**
**ቀምሽ** qemsh *(n. )* **frock**
**ቀምታ** qemta *(n. )* **nap**
**ቀምታ** qemta *(n. )* **siesta**
**ቀናእ** qena'e *(adj.)* **envious**
**ቀናእ** qena'è *(adj.)* **jealous**
**ቀንዲ** qendi *(n.)* **core**
**ቁልቁል ኣፍ ዝተሰጥሐ** kulkul afu ztesethe *(adj.)* **prostrate**
**ቁልቁለት** kulkulet *(n.)* **declivity**
**ቁምነገር** kum neger *(n.)* **plank**
**ቂምታ** kimta *(n.)* **pique**
**ቅልጡፍ** kltuf *(adj.)* **rapid**
**ቅኑስ** knus *(adj.)* **reductive**
**ቅልጣፈ** kltafe *(n. )* **rapidity**
**ቅርሕንቲ** kiri hinti *(n.)* **confrontation**
**ቅድመ ኩነት** kdme kunet *(n.)* **proviso**
**ቅድስተ ቅዱሳን** kdste kdusan *(adj.)* **sacrosanct**
**ቆርበት** korbet *(n.)* **skin**
**ቐዳሒ** kedahi *(n.)* **imitator**
**መፀውዒ ሽም** qendi *(n.)* **forename**
**ቀንዲ** qendi *(adj.)* **intimate**
**ቀንዲ** qendi *(n.)* **principal**
**ቀንዲ** qendi *(n.)* **staple**
**ቀንዲ ክብደት** qendi kbdet *(n.)* **brunt**
**ቀንዲ ተዋሳኢ** qendi tewasai *(n.)* **protagonist**
**ቀንደኛ** qenedegna *(adj.)* **classical**
**ቀንዲ** qenedi *(adj.)* **central**
**ቀነነ** qenene *(n.)* **gradient**
**ቀነነ** qenene *(v.)* **tilt**
**ቀነሰ** qenese *(v.)* **subtract**
**ቀንፈዘው በለ** qenfezew bele *(v.)* **linger**
**ቀንፈዘው በለ** qenfezew bele *(v.)* **loiter**
**ቀኒሱ** qenisu *(v.)* **pare**
**ቀኖና** qenona *(n.)* **canon**
**ቀንጠብጠብ በለ** qentebteb bele *(v.)* **tamper**
**ቀንጠጠ** qentete *(v.)* **denude**
**ቐንጠጠ** qentete *(v.)* **undress**
**ቀንጠወ** qenṫew *(v.)* **nip**
**ቀንፀለ** qentsele *(v.)* **slay**
**ቀንጸሊ** qal'ë *(n.)* **glade**
**ቃልዕ** qaledrdare'aw *(adj.)* **verbose**
**ቃለ-ድርዳረኣዊ** qarsa *(n.)* **hockey**
**ቃርሳ** qdus *(adj. )* **holy**
**ቅዱስ** qesqese *(v.)* **instigate**
**ቀስቀሰ** qeṭin *(adj.)* **watery**
**ቀጢን** qew'ï nay weyni *(n.)* **vintage**
**ቀውዒ ናይ ወይኒ** qoretse *(v.)* **hack**
**ቆረጸ** qosli *(n.)* **wound**
**ቆስሊ** qoṭqoat *(n. )* **hawthorn**
**ቆጥቋጥ** qrsus *(n.)* **wretch**
**ቅርሱስ** qulih bele *(v.i. )* **glance**
**ቍሊሕ በለ** quṭe'ë *(n. )* **wrath**
**ቁጠዐ** qwanqwagna *(n.)* **idiom**
**ቋንቋኛ** qxi *(n.)* **volume**

**ቅጺ** qenxali ***(n. )*** **wrecker**
**ቅእንዘርዘር** q'enzerzer ***(n.)*** **dalliance**
**ቅቃሕ** qe-qah ***(n.)*** **husk**
**ቀቀኖ** qeqeno ***(n. )*** **swan**
**ቀቀብ** qeqheb ***(n.)*** **maple**
**ቀራጺቶ** qeraxito ***(n.)*** **crotchet**
**ቀረበ** qerebe ***(v.i. )*** **near**
**ቀረበ** qerebe ***(v.)*** **approach**
**ቀረፈ** qerefe ***(v.)*** **excoriate**
**ቅርፍቲ** qerefti ***(n.)*** **hull**
**ቀረመ** qereme ***(v.)*** **glean**
**ቀረፀ** qerets ***(n.)*** **tariff**
**ቀረፀ** qeretse ***(v.)*** **carve**
**ቀረጸ** qerexe ***(v.t. )*** **imagine**
**ቀረጸ** qerexe ***(v.)*** **visualize**
**ቅርሺ** qeriishe ***(n.)*** **cash**
**ቀረሸ** qerixe ***(n.)*** **shark**
**ቀርቀብ ኣበለ** qerqeb abele ***(v.)*** **nab**
**ቀርጣፊ** qertafi ***(n. )*** **rodent**
**ቀስ ኢሉ** qes ilu ***(adv. )*** **slowly**
**ቀስ ዝብል** qes zbl ***(adj.)*** **slow**
**ቀስብቀስ** qesbqes ***(adj.)*** **gradual**
**ቀሰ'በ** qesebe ***(v.)*** **compel**
**ቀሰረ** qesere ***(v.)*** **laminate**
**ቀሺ** qeshi ***(n.)*** **pontiff**
**ቀሺ** qeshi ***(n. )*** **priest**
**ቀስቃሲ ስምዒት ክይኑ ቀረበ** qesqasi sm'et koynu qerebe ***(v.)*** **sensationalize**
**ቀስቀሰ** qesqese ***(v.)*** **incite**
**ቀስቀሰ** qesqese ***(v.)*** **motivate**
**ቀስታ** qesta ***(n.)*** **slowness**
**ቀስተ ድመና** qeste demena ***(n.)*** **rainbow**
**ቀስቲ** qesti ***(n. )*** **vault**
**ቀስቲ** qesti ***(n.)*** **arc**
**ቀስቲ** qesti ***(n.)*** **bow**
**ቀስቲ** qesti ***(n.)*** **dart**

**ቀጥ በለ** qet bele ***(adj.)*** **perpendicular**
**ቀጣፊ** qeẗafi ***(adj.)*** **mendacious**
**ቀታሊ** qetali ***(adj.)*** **fatal**
**ቀታሊ ነፍሲ** qetali nefsi ***(n.)*** **murderer**
**ቀታል-ነፍሲ** qetalnefsi ***(n.)*** **assassin**
**ቀተለ** qetele ***(v.)*** **kill**
**ቀተለ** qetele ***(v.)*** **assassinate**
**ቀጠንቲ** qeẗenti ***(adj.)*** **spindly**
**ቀጥቀጥ** qeteqetw ***(v.)*** **castrate**
**ቀጢን** qetin ***(adj.)*** **tenuous**
**ቀጢን** qetin ***(adj.)*** **thin**
**ቀጢን ስልኪ** qeẗin slki ***(n.)*** **filament**
**ቀጥቀጠ** qetqete ***(v.)*** **geld**
**ቀጥቀጠ** qeẗqeẗe ***(v.)*** **belabour**
**ቀጥቀጠ** qeẗqeẗe ***(n.)*** **stomp**
**ቀራፃይ** qetsaray ***(n.)*** **recorder**
**ቀፀላይ** qetselayi ***(n.)*** **coke**
**ቀፀለ** qetsele' ***(v.)*** **continue**
**ቀፃላይ** qetsetay ***(adj.)*** **continuous**
**ቀፀላ** qetsla ***(n.)*** **slab**
**ቀፀላ** qetsla ***(n. )*** **slate**
**ቀፀሪ መርከብ** qetsri merkeb ***(n.)*** **shipyard**
**ቀጥታዊ** qettawi ***(adj.)*** **direct**
**ቀጥታዊ** qeṭtawi ***(adj.)*** **immediate**
**ቀዋሚ** qewami ***(n.)*** **coefficient**
**ቀዋሚ ኣቁሑ** qewami aquĥu ***(n.)*** **fixture**
**ቀዋሚ መዓስከር** qewami me'äsker ***(n.)*** **cantonment**
**ቀዋምነት** qewamnet ***(n.)*** **permanence**
**ቀውፊ** qewfi ***(n.)*** **veto**
**ቀውዒ** qew'i ***(n.)*** **autumn**
**ቀዉላል** qewlal ***(adj.)*** **gangling**
**ቀፃልነት** qexalnet ***(n.)*** **continuity**
**ቀጸላ** qexela ***(n.)*** **ply**

ቀፀረ qexri *(n.)* **cartel**
ቀጽረ qexri *(n.)* **bloc**
ቀሽነት qexri qeshnet *(n.)* **priesthood**
ቀይ ሱር qey sur *(n.)* **beetroot**
ቀያሲ qeyasi *(n. )* **surveyor**
ቀያየረ qeyayere *(v.)* **reshuffle**
ቀይዲ በተኽ qeydi betek *(adj.)* **feral**
ቀይዲበተኽ qeydi betek *(n.)* **rogue**
ቀይድ በተኽ qeydi betek *(adj.)* **unbridled**
ቀየደ qeyede *(v.)* **impound**
ቀየረ qeyere *(v.)* **alter**
ቀየረ qeyere *(v.)* **convert**
ቀይሕ qeyh *(n.)* **crimson**
ቀይሕ qeyĥ *(adj.)* **red**
ቀይሕ qeyĥ *(adj.)* **reddish**
ቀይሕ ፍረ qeyḧ fre *(n.)* **strawberry**
ቀይሕ ሕብሪ qeyiha hib're *(n.)* **carmine**
ቀዛሒ qezaḧi *(adj.)* **bleak**
ቀዛሕዛሕ ዝብል qezaĥzaĥ zbl *(adj.)* **frowsty**
ቂም qim *(n)* **grudge**
ቂመኛ qimegna *(adj.)* **spiteful**
ቂመኛ qimeña *(adj.)* **vengeful**
ቂምታ qimta *(n.)* **acrimony**
ቂምታ qimta *(n.)* **spite**
ቁባ quba *(n.)* **dome**
ቁልዕነት qulënet *(adj.)* **puerile**
ቁልፊ qulfi *(n.)* **belt**
ቁልቁል qulqul *(adj.)* **steep**
ቁም ነገር qum neger *(n.)* **merit**
ቁማል qumal *(n.)* **louse**
ቁመት qumet *(n.)* **height**
ቁመት qumet *(n. )* **stature**
ቁምነገረኛ qumnegeregna *(adj.)* **serious**
ቁንጪ qunĉi *(n.)* **flea**
ቁንጩል qunčul *(adj.)* **compendious**
ቁኒን qunin *(n.)* **reel**
ቁኖ quno *(n.)* **plait**
ቛንቋኛዊ qunquñawi *(adj.)* **idiomatic**
ቁራ qura *(n. )* **raven**
ቁራስ quras *(n.)* **bit**
ቁራፅ qurats *(n.)* **slice**
ቁራፅ qurats *(n. )* **stub**
ቁራፅ ጉንዲ qurats gundi *(n.)* **stump**
ቁራፅ qurax *(n.)* **cutting**
ቁርባን qurban *(n.)* **communion**
ቁርፀት ከብዲ quretset kebedi *(n.)* **colic**
ቁሪ/ቀዝሒ quri/qezhi *(n.)* **chill**
ቁርማም qurmame *(n.)* **chunk**
ቁርሲ qursi *(n.)* **breakfast**
ቈርጠጠ qurtete *(v.)* **tweak**
ቁርፅራፅ qurtsrats *(n.)* **snippet**
ቁሩብ qurub *(adj.)* **meagre**
ቁሩብ qurub *(n. )* **modicum**
ቁሩብ ፍልልይ qurub fl'ly *(n.)* **nuance**
ቁሳውነት qusawnet *(n.)* **materialism**
ቁሸት qushet *(n. )* **village**
ቁስሊ qusli *(n.)* **blain**
ቁስሊ qusli *(n.)* **ulcer**
ቁጥዐ quẗ'ë *(n.)* **annoyance**
ቁጥዐ quẗ'ë *(n.)* **anger**
ቁጠባ quteba *(n.)* **economy**
ቁጠባ quteba *(n.)* **retrenchment**
ቁጠባዊ qutebawi *(adj.)* **economic**
ቁጥዐ qute-e *(n.)* **huff**
ቁጠዐ quẗe'ë *(n.)* **fury**
ቁጥቋጥ qutqwat *(n.)* **heath**
ቁጥቋጥ qutqwat *(n.)* **shrub**
ቍጽጽር qutstsr *(n.)* **inspection**
ቁፀፀር qutstsr *(n. )* **scrutiny**
ቍጻር quxar *(n.)* **knot**

ቍጽራዊ quxrawi *(adj.)* **arithmetical**
ቁፅሪ quxri *(n.)* **figure**
ቁፅሪ quxri *(n.)* **number**
ቁጽሪ ፖስጣ quxri posẗ *(n.)* **postcode**
ቍጽሪ quxri *(n.)* **arithmetic**
ቁፅፅር quxxr *(n.)* **control**
ቁፅፅር qux'xr *(n.)* **supervision**
ቁዘማ quzema *(adj.)* **plaintive**
ቴጸራ qitsra *(n. )* **tryst**
ቃንጫ qhanca *(n.)* **stalk**
ቐደመ qedeme *(v.)* **overtake**
ቃጭል qačl *(n.)* **bell**
ቃዕታ qaeta *(n.)* **click**
ቃፍላይ qafla *(n. )* **wain**
ቃፍላይ qaflay *(n.)* **caravan**
ቅፍታን qaftan *(n.)* **kaftans**
ቀዘፈ mejelebi *(n.)* **paddle**
ቅድመ ፍጻመ qdme fxame *(n.)* **antecedent**
ቃሕታ qahta *(n.)* **whimsy**
ቃል qal *(n.)* **word**
ቃል ኪዳን qal kidan *(n.)* **covenant**
ቃል ክሱስ qal ksus *(n.)* **plea**
ቃል ምእታው qal mètaw *(n.)* **pledge**
ቓል ዝበዝሖ qal zbezho *(adj.)* **wordy**
ቃላት qalat *(n.)* **vocabulary**
ቃለ ምልልስ qale mlls *(n.)* **dialogue**
ቃለ-ድርዳረ qaledrdar *(n.)* **verbiage**
ቃለ-ድርዳረነት qaledrdarene *(n.)* **verbosity**
ቃለ-ማሕላ qalemaȟla *(n.)* **affidavit**
ቃለ-መጠይቕ qalemeẗeyq̈ *(n.)* **interview**
ቃለ-ምስጢር qalemsṭir *(n. )* **watchword**
ቃልቃል በለ qalqal bele *(adj.)* **aflame**
ቃና qana *(adj.)* **wondrous**
ቃናያይ qanayay *(n. )* **tuner**
ቃንጫ qancha *(n.)* **stem**
ቃንጃ qanja *(n.)* **hamstring**
ቃንዛ qanza *(n.)* **ache**
ቃንዛ qanza *(n.)* **pain**
ቃንዛ ጭዋዳ qanza čwada *(n. )* **myalgia**
ቃቓ qaq̈a *(n.)* **cackle**
ቃቐወ qaqhewe *(v.)* **squawk**
ቃራና qarana *(n.)* **bough**
ቃሬዛ qareeza *(n.)* **bier**
ቃሬዛ qareeza *(n.)* **stretcher**
ቃርፋ qarfa *(n.)* **cinnamon**
ቃርማ qarma *(n.)* **beagle**
ቃታ qata *(n.)* **trigger**
ቃፀሎ qaxelo *(n.)* **combustion**
ቃዝኖት qaznot *(n.)* **melancholia**
ቅብኣ qba *(n. )* **portrait**
ቀብአ qb'a *(v.)* **portray**
ቅብኣ qba *(n. )* **painting**
ቅብኣ ምቅባእ qb'a mqbaè *(n.)* **portraiture**
ቅበለ qbale *(n.)* **approval**
ቅብኣት qb'at *(adj.)* **unctuous**
ቅብብል qbbl *(n.)* **relay**
ቅበላ qbela *(n.)* **admission**
ቅበላ qbela *(n.)* **admittance**
ቅበጥ qbeẗ *(n.)* **caprice**
ቅብሊት qblit *(n.)* **receipt**
ቅብፀት qbtset *(n.)* **despair**
ቅቡል qbul *(adj.)* **unexceptionable**
ቅቡል q'bul *(n.)* **stereotype**
ቅጫ qĉa *(n.)* **patty**
ቅጭን qĉn *(adj.)* **elegant**
ቅዳሕ qdah *(n.)* **tracing**
ቅዳሕ qdaȟ *(n.)* **copy**
ቅዳሕ qdaȟ *(n.)* **facsimile**
ቅዳሕ ቅብሊት qdaȟ qblit *(n.)* **counterfoil**

**ቅዳሰ ሙታን** qdase mutan *(n.)* **requiem**
**ቅድድም መሰናኽል** q'd'dm mesenakhl *(n.)* **steeplechase**
**ቅደኛ** qdegna *(n.)* **stylist**
**ቅዲ** qdi *(n.)* **fashion**
**ቅዲ** qdi *(n. )* **pattern**
**ቅዲ** qdi *(n.)* **style**
**ቅዲ ብዝለበሰ** qdi b'zlebese *(adj.)* **stylized**
**ቅዲ ክዳን** qdi kdan *(n. )* **guise**
**ቅዲ ኵናት** qdi kunat *(n.)* **warfare**
**ቅዲ ዘለዎ** qdi zelewo *(adj.)* **stylistic**
**ቅድም** qdm *(adv. )* **formerly**
**ስልጣን** qdme *(n. )* **prerogative**
**ቅድመ ዓብላላዊ** qdme äblalawi *(adj.)* **predominant**
**ቅድመ ዓብላልነት** qdme äblalnet *(n.)* **predominance**
**ቅድመ ኹነት** qdme kunet *(n.)* **precondition**
**ቅድመ ምዕብላል** qdme mëblal *(v.)* **predominate**
**ቅድሚ መርዓ** qdme merä *(adj.)* **premarital**
**ቅድመ ንጡፍ** qdme ntuf *(adj.)* **proactive**
**ቅድመ ስም** qdme sm *(n.)* **prefix**
**ቅድመ ታሪኽ** qdme tariki *(adj.)* **prehistoric**
**ቅድመ ውሰነ** qdme wsane *(v.)* **predetermine**
**ቅድሚ** qdmi *(adj.)* **prior**
**ቅድሚ** qdmi *(adv.)* **before**
**ቅድመ ኹነት** qdmi ḱunet *(n.)* **prerequisite**
**ቅድሚ_ግዘ** qdmi_gze *(adv.)* **ago**
**ቅድሚት** qdmit *(n.)* **front**
**ቅድስና** qdsna *(n. )* **sanctity**
**ቅርሱስ** qrsus *(adj.)* **ominous**
**ቅቡል** qbul *(adj.)* **orthodox**
**ቅናት-ዙረት** qnate zuret *(n. )* **orbit**
**ቅንዕና** qn'ëna *(n.)* **orthodoxy**
**ቅጥዒ ዘይብሉ** qt'ë zeyblu *(adj.)* **outrageous**
**ቅዱስ ፅሑፍ** qdus tshuf *(n. )* **scripture**
**ቐማሚ** qe'mami *(n.)* **chemist**
**ቕብኣት** qhb'at *(n. )* **lotion**
**ቕብኣት** qhb'at *(n.)* **lubricant**
**ቕብኣት** qhb'at *(n.)* **lubrication**
**ቕብኣት ቐበአ** qhb'at qhbe'e *(v.)* **lubricate**
**ቐላይ** qhelay *(n. )* **lake**
**ቐለም** qhelem *(n.)* **ink**
**ቐጢን ነዊሕ** qhetin newih *(adj.)* **lanky**
**ቐፃልነት ዘይብሉ** qhetsalnet zeyblu *(adj.)* **inconsistent**
**ቕመም** qhmem *(n.)* **ingredient**
**ቕንድብ** qhndb *(v.)* **lash**
**ቖፃል ኹብር እምኒ** qhotsal khubr emni *(n. )* **jade**
**ቖፅሊ** qhotsli *(n. )* **leaf**
**ቕርፊት መሬት** qhrfit meriet *(n.)* **mantle**
**ቑቡል** qhubul *(adj.)* **justifiable**
**ቑልዕነት** qhul'enet *(n. )* **infancy**
**ቑልፊ** qhulfi *(n.)* **lock**
**ቑራፅ ዕንፀይቲ** qhurats entseyti *(n. )* **log**
**ቑጡዐ** qhute'e *(adj.)* **indignant**
**ቑጠዐ** qhute'e *(n. )* **indignation**
**ቑጡብ** qhutub *(adj.)* **laconic**
**ቅልስ** qls *(n.)* **duel**
**ቅልጥፍነት** qltfnet *(n.)* **agility**
**ቀልጢፉ ዝኩሪ** qltifu zkuri *(adj.)* **temperamental**

ቅልጡፍ qltuf *(v.)* **prompt**
ቅልጡፍ qltuf ***(adj.)* quick**
ቅልጡፍ qlẗuf ***(adj.)* fast**
ቅልጡፍ qlẗuf ***(adj.)* swift**
ቅልጡፍ ሳዕስዒት qlẗuf sa'ës'ït ***(n.)* jig**
ቅልፅም qltzm ***(n.)* forearm**
ቅሉዕ qlu'ë ***(adj.)* blatant**
ቅልዉላዉ qlwlaw ***(n.)* crisis**
ቅመማዊ ፍወሳ qmemawi fwesa ***(n.)* chemotherapy**
ቅሚጦ qmito ***(n. )* rick**
ቅሚጦ qmiẗo ***(n.)* stack**
ቅሙጥ ገንዘብ qmuẗ genzeb ***(n.)* fund**
ቅናት qnat ***(n.)* girdle**
ቅናት qnat ***(n. )* waistband**
ቅንኣት qn'at ***(n.)* envy**
ቅንኣት qn'at ***(n. )* jealousy**
ቅንዕና qn'ëna ***(n. )* honesty**
ቅንዕና qn'ëna ***(n.)* integrity**
ቅንዕና qn'ëna ***(n.)* rectitude**
ቅንዕና qn'ëna ***(n.)* sincerity**
ቅነሳ qnesa ***(n.)* discount**
ቅንፍ qnf ***(n.)* bracket**
ቅንፍ qnf ***(n. )* parenthesis**
ቅንፍር qnfr ***(n.)* clove**
ቅንፍዝ qnfz ***(n.)* porcupine**
ቅንጦተኛ qnẗotegna ***(n.)* sybarite**
ቅፀበታዊ qxbetawi ***(adj.)* automatic**
ቅጽል qxl ***(n.)* adjective**
ቅጽጽ ዝበለ qxx zbele ***(adj.)* congested**
ቅያ qya ***(n.)* saga**
ቅያኖስ qyanos ***(n.)* cyan**
ቅያር qyar ***(adj.)* alternative**
ቅያዊ ዛንታ qyawi zanta ***(n.)* epic**
ቅየዓ qye'ä ***(n. )* mimicry**

ቅየዓዊ ተዋስኦ qye'äwi tewas'o ***(n.)* mime**
ቅየዓዊ ተዋስኦ qye'äwi tewas'o ***(n. )* mime**
ቅየራ qyera ***(n.)* alteration**
ቕኑዕ ሓሳብ ዘለዎ qnu'e hasab zelewo ***(adj.)* optimistic**
ቅንጥሻራ qnẗshara ***(n. )* mushroom**
ቅኑዕ qnu'e ***(adj.)* upright**
ቅኑዕ qnu'ë ***(adj. )* honest**
ቅኑዕ qnu'ë ***(adj.)* righteous**
ቅኑዕ ዘይኮነ qnue zeykone ***(adj.)* unfaithful**
ቅኑዕ ዘይኮነ qnue zeykone ***(adj.)* unreasonable**
ቅኑዕ ዘይምሕሳብ qnue zeymhsab ***(n. )* pessimism**
ቅኑዕ q'nu'ë ***(adj.)* straight**
ቅኑዕ ዘይሓስብ qnuo hasab ***(n.)* pessimist**
ቅንጹብ ፈረስ qnxub feres ***(n.)* pony**
ቅቅል q'ql ***(n.)* stew**
ቅራፍ qraf ***(n.)* flake**
ቅራፍ qraf ***(n.)* bark**
ቅራረት qraret ***(n.)* runnel**
ቅርዓት qr'ät ***(n.)* concourse**
ቅርበት qrbet ***(n.)* vicinity**
ቅርበት qrbet ***(n. )* proximity**
ቅርዳድ qrdad ***(n.)* shred**
ይቕሬታ ሓተተ q̈reeta ḧatete ***(v.)* apologize**
ቅርፍቲ qrfti ***(n.)* crust**
ቅርፍቲ qrfti ***(n.)* scab**
ቅርሕንቲ qrĥnti ***(n.)* discord**
ቅርሕንቲ qrĥnti ***(n.)* feud**
ቅርሕንቲ qrĥnti ***(n.)* rancour**
ቅርሕንቲ qrḧnti ***(n.)* antipathy**
ቅሪት qrit ***(n.)* fossil**
ቅርንጫፍ qrnchaf ***(n.)* twig**

**ቅርሲ** qrsi *(n.)* **hangover**
**ቅርሲ** qrsi *(n.)* **relic**
**ቅርሱስ** qrsus *(adj.)* **fateful**
**ቅርሱስ ዕድል** qrsus ëdl *(n.)* **misfortune**
**ቅርታ** qrta *(n.)* **discontent**
**ቅርታ** qrta *(n.)* **dissatisfaction**
**ቅርታ** qrta *(n.)* **grievance**
**ቅርታ** qrta *(n.)* **resentment**
**ቅርጥማት** qrtmat *(n.)* **rheumatism**
**ቅርፀ አልቦ** qrtse 'albo *(adj.)* **shapeless**
**ቅርጺ** qrtsi *(n.)* **shape**
**ቅርጺ** qrtzi *(n. )* **gerund**
**ቑርሱስ** qruȟ qrsus *(n.)* **jinx**
**ቅርጸ-አልቦ** qrxe'albo *(adj.)* **amorphous**
**ቅሳነት** qsanet *(n.)* **composure**
**ቅሳነት** qsanet *(n.)* **ease**
**ቅስመት** qsmet *(n.)* **acquisition**
**ቅጥዒ** qẗ'i *(n.)* **format**
**ቅጥዒ ምስኣን** qẗ'i ms'an *(n.)* **superfluity**
**ቅጥዒ ዘይብሉ** qẗ'i zeyblu *(adj.)* **superfluous**
**ቅትለት** qtlet *(n.)* **killing**
**ቅትለት** qtlet *(n.)* **murder**
**ቅትለተ-ኣቦ** qtlet abo *(n.)* **patricide**
**ቅትለተ-ኣደ** qtlet ade *(n.)* **matricide**
**ቅትለት ንጉስ** qtlet ngus *(n. )* **regicide**
**ቅትለተ-ሰብ** qtleteseb *(n. )* **homicide**
**ቅጥቁጥ ብዕራይ** qẗquẗ b'ëray *(n.)* **bullock**
**ቅፅበታዊ** qtsbetawi *(adj.)* **instantaneous**
**ቅፅበት** qtsbetawi *(adj.)* **instant**
**ቅፁዕ** qtsu'ë *(adj.)* **prim**
**ቅፀበታዊ** qtzbetawi *(adv. )* **forthwith**
**ቆብዕ** qob'ë *(n. )* **hat**
**ቆብዕ** qob'ë *(n.)* **hood**
**ቈጽለ መጽሊ** qoetsele metseli *(v.t. )* **greenery**
**ቆፎ ሓሰኻ** qofo haseka *(n.)* **cocoon**
**ቆፎ** qofo *(n.)* **bin**
**ቆለ** qole *(n.)* **craze**
**ቆለ** qole *(n.)* **quirk**
**ቆልዓ** qolea' *(n.)* **child**
**ቆለበ** qolebe *(v.)* **catch**
**ኮልዐ** qole'ea *(v.)* **gild**
**ቈልዕነት** qole'enet' *(n.)* **childhood**
**ቆማል** qomal *(adj.)* **lousy**
**ቆሞስ** qomos *(n.)* **vicar**
**ቆንስል** qonesele *(n.)* **consul**
**ቆንፅላዊ** qonexelawi *(n.)* **consular**
**ቖንጆ** qonjo *(adj.)* **gorgeous**
**ቆንቆር** qonqkor *(n.)* **chimney**
**ቆንቋን** qonqwan *(adj.)* **ramshackle**
**ቆንስል** qonsl *(n.)* **diplomat**
**ቆንስላዊ** qonslawi *(adj.)* **diplomatic**
**ቆንጠጠ** qontete *(v. )* **pinch**
**ቆቃዕ** qoqa'ë *(n.)* **miser**
**ቆራር** qorar *(adj.)* **frigid**
**ቆራር** qorare *(adj.)* **chilly**
**ቆራር** qorare *(adj.)* **cold**
**ቆራፃይ** qoratzay *(n.)* **cutter**
**ቆርበት ጤል** qorbeet ẗeel *(n.)* **suede**
**ቆርበት ኣልፍዐ** qorbet alf'e *(n.)* **tan**
**ቆርበት ፍሓቂ** qorbet fehaqi *(n. )* **tanner**
**ቆረጸ** qoretse *(v.)* **hew**
**ቆረፀ** qoretse *(v.)* **sever**
**ቆሪፁ** qorisu *(v.)* **trim**
**ቆርቆሮ** qorqoro *(n.)* **alloy**
**ቆርቋር** qorqwar *(adj.)* **beady**

ቆርጠመ qorťeme *(v.)* **crunch**
ቆርጠምጠማ qorťemťema *(n.)* **cartilage**
ቆፃል ድይመንድ qosal dymend *(n.)* **turquoise**
ቆጣቢ qotabi *(adj.)* **economical**
ቆጣቢ qotabi *(adj.)* **thrifty**
ቆጣቢ qoẗabi *(adj.)* **sparing**
ቆጠበ qotebe *(v.)* **retrench**
ቖፃል qotsal *(adj. & n.)* **green**
ቆፀየ qotseye *(v.)* **dislocate**
ቖፃሪ qoxari *(n.)* **employer**
ቆፀራ ህዝቢ qoxera hzbi *(n.)* **census**
ቆፀረ qoxere *(v.)* **count**
ቆፀረ qoxere *(v.)* **employ**
ቆጸየ qoxeye *(v.)* **wrick**
ቆይቆይ በለ qoyqoy bele *(v.)* **scrimp**
ቆዝሞፖሊታዊ qozmopolitawi *(adj.)* **cosmopolitan**
ቋጸረ qua-tse-re *(v.)* **hitch**
ቅዋማዊ qwamawi *(adj.)* **constitutional**
ቀዋሚ qwami *(adj.)* **permanent**
ቋንቋ qwanqwa *(n.)* **language**
ቋንጣ ዓሳ qwanẗa 'äsa *(n.)* **bloater**
ቈብዕ qweb'ë *(n.)* **cap**
ቈላሕታ qwelaȟta *(n.)* **glimpse**
ቈልዓዊ qwel'äwi *(n.)* **immaturity**
ቈልቋል qwelqwal *(n.)* **cactus**
ቈራቢ qwerabi *(n.)* **communicant**
ቈጥቋጥ qweẗqwaẗ *(n.)* **bush**
ቈጸራ qwexera *(n.)* **appointment**
ቈጸረ qwexere *(v.)* **compute**
ቈየቛ qweyeq̈wa *(n.)* **brawl**
ቈይቍ qweyqwi *(n.)* **altercation**

# በ

በጃ beğa *(adj.)* **vicarious**
በጋሚዶ begamido *(n.)* **vagabond**
በገና begena *(n.)* **harp**
በጊዕ begi'e *(n.)* **sheep**
በሓጫጨረ beha'cha'chre *(v.)* **scrawl**
በሃም beham *(n.)* **dummy**
በሃም beham *(n.)* **moron**
በሓተ beȟate *(v.)* **monopolize**
ቤላርባ beilaroba *(v.)* **peddle**
ብዕካክ b'ekak *(n.)* **tartar**
ብዕካክ b'ëkak *(n.)* **plaque**
በኻዪ bekayi *(adj.)* **fretful**
በኻዪ bekayi *(adj.)* **weepy**
በኽኽታ bekekta *(n.)* **puff**
በከለ bekele *(v.)* **contaminate**
በከለ bekele *(v.)* **taint**
በኸየ bekeye *(v.)* **bewail**
በኸየ bekeye *(v.)* **cry**
በኸየ bekeye *(n.)* **yowl**
በኸየ bekeye' *(v.)* **weep**
በኸየ bekheye *(v.)* **sob**
በኾኽ አበለ bekok 'abele *(n.)* **whiff**
በኹዐ beku'ë *(v.)* **ferment**
ብኽያት beḱyat *(n.)* **wail**
በላዕ ሰብ bela'ë seb *(n.)* **cannibal**
በላዕ ስጋ bela'ë sga *(n.)* **carnivore**
በላዒ bela'ï *(adj.)* **venal**
በለ bele *(v.)* **allege**
በለ bele *(n. )* **say**
በለስ ጥልያን beles ẗlyan *(n.)* **fig**
በለሳን belesan *(n.)* **balsam**
በለፀ beletze *(v.)* **surpass**
በለፀ belexe *(v.)* **exceed**
በዓል beaal *(n.)* **celebration**
በዓቲ beaa'ti *(n.)* **cave**
በዓል be'äl *(n.)* **festival**

**በዓል ኣስቤዛ** be'äl 'asbeza ***(n.)*** **grocer**
**በዓል ቤት** beal bet ***(n. )*** **husband**
**በዓል ድንኳን** be'äl dnkwan ***(n.)*** **shopkeeper**
**በዓል ገዛ** be'äl geza ***(n.)*** **landlord**
**በዓል ግርማ ሞገስ** beal grma moges ***(adj.)*** **charismatic**
**ብዓል ሓደራ** beal hadera ***(n.)*** **trustee**
**በዓል ሓሙሽተ መኣዝን** beal hamushte meazn ***(n. )*** **pentagon**
**በዓል ሓሙሽተ መስመር መስሕቒ ግጥሚ** be'al hamushte mesmer msheqhi gtmi ***(n.)*** **limerick**
**በዓል ለዓት መነጽር** be'äl le'ät menexr ***(adj.)*** **binocular**
**በዓል ማስኬራ** be'äl maskeera ***(n. )*** **masquerade**
**በዓል መኣርግ** beal mearg ***(adj.)*** **titled**
**በዓል መዚ** be'äl mezi ***(adj.)*** **authoritative**
**በዓል ሞያ** beal moya ***(n. )*** **technician**
**በዓል ሞያ** beal moya ***(n. )*** **technologist**
**በዓል ሞያ** beäl moya ***(adj.)*** **professional**
**በዓል ሙሉእ ጥዕና** beal mulu'e t'ena ***(adj.)*** **lusty**
**በዓል ሰለስተ እግሪ መሳርሒ** beal seleste agri mesarhi ***(n.)*** **trident**
**ብዓል ሰለስተ እግሪ** beal seleste egri ***(n.)*** **tripod**
**በዓል ሰለስተ ጎማ ሳይክል** beal seleste goma sycle ***(n. )*** **tricycle**
**በዓል ሰለስተ ሕብሪ ባንደራ** beal seleste hbri bandera ***(n.)*** **tricolour**
**በዓል ሰለስተ መኣዝን** beal seleste meazn ***(adj.)*** **triangular**
**በዓል ዘመን** be'al zemen ***(n.)*** **upstart**
**በሊሕ** belih ***(adj.)*** **clever**
**በሊሕ** belih ***(adj.)*** **sharp**
**በሊሕ** belih ***(adj.)*** **trenchant**
**በሊሕ** beliĥ ***(adj.)*** **edgy**
**በሊሕ** beliḧ ***(adj.)*** **brilliant**
**በሊሕ** beliḧ ***(adj.)*** **cute**
**በሊሕ** beliȟ ***(adj.)*** **apt**
**በልሰነ** belsene ***(v.)*** **embalm**
**በዓለገ** be'älege ***(adj.)*** **naughty**
**በዓለገ** be'älege ***(n.)*** **vulgarian**
**ብዕልግና** be'älegna ***(n.)*** **immorality**
**በዓልሞያ** be'älmoya ***(n.)*** **expert**
**በዓልቲ ገዛ** be'älti geza ***(n.)*** **landlady**
**በዓልቲ ሓዳር** bealti hadar ***(n.)*** **housewife**
**በኣሰ** bease ***(v.)*** **worsen**
**በዓቲ** beati ***(n.)*** **tunnel**
**በዓቲ** be'äti ***(n.)*** **grotto**
**በብዓይነቱ** beb'äynet ***(adj.)*** **multifarious**
**በብዓይነቱ** beb'äynetu ***(n.)*** **assortment**
**ብዕብድብድ** b'ëbdbd ***(adv.)*** **amok**
**በብቁሩብ** bebequrub ***(adv. )*** **piecemeal**
**በብቑሩብ ኣእተወ** bebq̈urub 'a'ètewe ***(v.)*** **instil**
**በብቑሩብ ሰተየ** bebqurub seteye ***(v.)*** **tipple**
**በናጅር** benaĵr ***(n.)*** **bangle**
**በናጅር** benaĵr ***(n.)*** **bracelet**
**በናኒ** benani ***(adj.)*** **volatile**
**ብእንቡኡ** b'enb'u ***(adv. )*** **shortly**
**በንዚን** benzin ***(n.)*** **diesel**
**በንዚን** benzin ***(n. )*** **petrol**
**በቃቕ** beqaqh ***(adj.)*** **stingy**
**በቅዐ** beq'ë ***(v.)*** **qualify**
**በቕዐ** beq̈'ë ***(v.)*** **befit**
**በቅሊ** beqli ***(n.)*** **mule**

ብቕሊሉ ዝረኣይ beqlilu zereaayii *(adj.)* **conspicuous**
በቖለ beqole *(v.)* **germinate**
በታኒ betani *(adj.)* **improvident**
በታተነ betatene *(v.)* **disintegrate**
ቤተ ክርስቲያን bete kiristian *(n.)* **church**
ቤት መስተ bete meste *(n. )* **saloon**
ቤት መዝገብ bete mezgeb *(n.)* **registry**
ቤት ነገስታት bete' negeseta't *(n.)* **chateau**
ቤት ነገስታት bete negestat *(n.)* **castle**
በተነ betene *(v.)* **disband**
በተነ betene *(v.)* **scatter**
በተነ betene *(v.)* **spread**
በተነ betene *(v.)* **strew**
በጥሐ bet'ĥe *(v.)* **slash**
ብዘይጥርጥር bethzey tiritir *(adv.)* **certainly**
በቲ beti *(prep.)* **along**
በትናሕ betnaĥ *(adj.)* **rancid**
በጥራን beťran *(n.)* **snob**
በጥራን beťran *(adj.)* **snobbish**
በትረ መንግስቲ betre mengsti *(n. )* **sceptre**
በትሪ ፖሊስ betri polis *(n.)* **baton**
በፀበፀ betsbetse *(v.)* **dilute**
በጽበጸ betse betse *(v.)* **hydrate**
በፅሐ bets'he *(v.)* **reach**
በጽሐ - bexḥe *(v.)* **visit**
በጽሒ bexĥi *(adj.)* **adolescent**
በየደ beyede *(v.)* **weld**
በየነ beyene *(v.t.)* **adjudge**
በየነ-ዓሌታዊ beyene'äleetawi *(adj.)* **interracial**
በየነ-መንግስታዊ beyenemengstawi *(n.)* **interstate**
በይነ ዕብለላ beyne ëblela *(n. )* **monopoly**
በይነ ቁርቁር beyne qurqur *(n.)* **soliloquy**
በይነ ተዋስኦ beyne tewas'o *(n. )* **monologue**
በይኑ beynu *(adv.)* **alone**
በራድ berad *(n. )* **kettle**
በራድ beradd *(n.)* **cauldron**
በራሕ beraḣ *(adj.)* **bald**
በረንዳ beranda *(n.)* **piazza**
በራቂቶ beraqito *(n.)* **shin**
በራሪ ወረቀት berari wereket *(n.)* **tract**
ብዕራይ beray *(n.)* **yak**
በርበረ berbere *(n.)* **capsicum**
በረድ bered *(n.)* **floe**
በረድ bered *(n. )* **ice**
በረዳም ዝናብ beredam znab *(n.)* **sleet**
በረዳዊ beredawi *(adj.)* **glacial**
በረኻ bereka *(n.)* **wilderness**
በረንዳ berenda *(n.)* **porch**
በረንዳ berenda *(n. )* **veranda**
በረቕ bereqqe' *(n.)* **china**
በረሰ berese *(n.)* **decompose**
በርጋሞት bergamot *(n.)* **bergamot**
በርገር berger *(n.)* **burger**
በርሀ berhe *(v.)* **shine**
በሪ beri *(n.)* **gate**
በሪኽ berikh *(adj.)* **lofty**
በርሚል bermil *(n.)* **barrel**
በርኒሽ bernich *(n.)* **lacquer**
በርቁቕ berquq *(n. )* **plum**
በሳሲዑ besasieu *(v.)* **perforate**
በስበሰ besbese *(v. i)* **decay**
በስበሰ besbese *(v.)* **rot**
በሰላ besela *(n.)* **scar**
በሰለ besele *(v.)* **ripen**

በዳን bedan *(adj.)* **acrid**
በደል bedel *(n.)* **injustice**
በደል bedel *(n.)* **tort**
በደው bedew *(adj.)* **silly**
በዲዶ bedido *(n.)* **smallpox**
በዱ bedu *(n.)* **virgin**
በለጽ belets *(n. )* **opportunism**
በላዪ belayi *(adj.)* **obsolescent**
ቡጭ አበለ buch abele *(v.)* **squirt**
ቡዱን budun *(n.)* **team**
ቡፌ bufee *(n.)* **buffet**
ቡለቲን buletin *(n.)* **bulletin**
ቡን bun *(n.)* **coffee**
ቡናዊ ሕመት bunawi hmet *(n.)* **lignite**
ቡናዊ ቀይሕ bunawi qeyh *(n. )* **mahogany**
ቡናዊ bunawi *(n.)* **brown**
ቡቅሊ buqhli *(n. )* **malt**
ቡራኬ burakee *(n.)* **benediction**
ቡሽ bush *(n.)* **bung**
ቡሶላ busola *(n.)* **compass**
ቡስጣ busṫa *(n.)* **envelope**
ቡት but *(n.)* **wellington**
ቡቲክ butik *(n.)* **boutique**
ቢ b *( )* **B**
ባቤል babeel *(n.)* **Babel**
ባጫ bacha *(n.)* **taunt**
ባጫ bacha *(adj.)* **witty**
ባዴላ badeela *(n.)* **spade**
ባዴላ badela *(n.)* **shovel**
ባዴላ/ድስቲ badela/dsti *(n.)* **pan**
ባድሚንተን badminten *(n.)* **badminton**
ባዶ bado *(adj.)* **inane**
ባዶ bado *(n.)* **nil**
ባዶ bado *(adj.)* **zero**
ባዶ bado *(n.)* **zilch**
ባዶ ገበረ bado gebere *(v.)* **nullify**
ባእባእ በለ ba'eba'e bele *(v.)* **fumble**
ባእብእ ba'eb'e *(v.)* **stutter**
ባዕዳዊ ba'ëdawi *(adj.)* **exotic**
ባዕዳዊ ba'ëdawi *(adj.)* **foreign**
ባዕዲ ba'ëdi *(adj.)* **alien**
ባዕዲ ba'ëdi *(n.)* **foreigner**
ባዕዳዊ baeedawi *(adj.)* **colonial**
ባዕላ ba'ëla *(pron. )* **herself**
ባዕለገ baelege *(adj.)* **unprincipled**
ባዕለገ bae'lege' *(adj.)* **cheeky**
ባዕለይ ba'ëley *(pron. )* **myself**
ባዕሊ ba'ëli *(n.)* **ego**
ባዕልነት ba'ëlnet *(n.)* **egotism**
ባዕሎም ba'elom *(pron.)* **themselves**
ባዕሉ ንባዕሉ ዘይስማዕማዕ ba'elu n ba'elu zeysma'ema'e *(adj.)* **incoherent**
ባእሲ baesi *(n.)* **tussle**
ባእሲ ba'esi *(n.)* **infighting**
ባእሲ ba'esi *(n.)* **scrimmage**
ባእሲ ba'esi *(n.)* **strife**
ባእታ ba'eta *(n.)* **element**
ብኣፍንጭኡ ደረዘ b'afn'č'u dereze *(v.)* **nuzzle**
ባጎኒ bagoni *(n.)* **wagon**
ባህገኛ bahgenya *(n.)* **idealist**
ባህጊ bahgi *(adj.)* **wistful**
ባሕጎገ baȟgoge *(v.)* **corrode**
ባህላዊ bahlawi *(adj.)* **cultural**
ባህላዊ መግቢ ላቲን ኣመሪካ bahlawi megbi latin amrica *(n. )* **pastel**
ባህላዊ ዛንታ bahlawi zanta *(n.)* **lore**
ባህሊ bahli *(n.)* **culture**
ባህሊ bahli *(n.)* **ritual**
ባህሊ bahli *(n.)* **tradition**
ባህሊ ዝህሉ bahli zhlu *(n.)* **traditionalist**
ባሕረኛ bahregna *(n. )* **mariner**

ባሕረኛ bahregna *(n. )* **sailor**
ባህረት bahret ***(n.)* instinct**
ባህረታዊ bahretawi ***(adj.)* instinctive**
ባሕሪ bahri ***(n. )* sea**
ባህርያዊ bahryawi ***(adj.)* inherent**
ባህርያዊ bahryawi ***(adj.)* intrinsic**
ባሕታዊ baḥtawi ***(n. )* hermit**
ባሕተላይ baḧtelay ***(n.)* bachelor**
ባጀት baĵet ***(n.)* budget**
ባኮ bako ***(n.)* carton**
ባክተሪያ bakteriya ***(n.)* bacteria**
ባላ bala ***(n.)* stake**
ባላ bala ***(n.)* stanchion**
ባላ እግሪ bala egri ***(n.)* stilt**
ባላባት balabat ***(n.)* baron**
ባልዶንጓ baldongwa ***(n.)* bean**
ባልዕ bale ***(adj.)* xylophages**
ባለይ baley ***(n.)* ballet**
ብኣልኮል ዝብፅበፅ መድሓኒት balkol zbtsbets medhanit ***(n.)* tincture**
ባልሳ balsa ***(n.)* balm**
ባልታዊ baltawi ***(adj.)* satirical**
ባልተኛ baltegna ***(n.)* satirist**
ባልጠጂ balťeĵi ***(n.)* butler**
ባልቲ balti ***(n.)* satire**
ብዓልቲ ቤት b'alti beet ***(n. )* wife**
ባምቡላ bambula ***(n.)* doll**
ባንዴራ bandiera ***(n.)* flag**
ባኒ bani ***(n.)* croissant**
ባንጆ banĵo ***(n.)* banjo**
ባንከኛ bankegna ***(n.)* banker**
ባንኪ banki ***(n.)* bank**
ባንኮኒ bankoni ***(n.)* counter**
ብኣንጻሩ bantaru ***(adv. )* vice-versa**
ብኣቕሑት ኣማልአ b'aquĥt amal'e ***(v.)* furnish**
ባራካ baraka ***(n. )* shanty**
ባራካ baraka ***(n.)* barrack**
ባራኩዳ barakuda ***(n.)* barracuda**
ባርባራዊ barbarawi ***(n.)* barbarian**
ባርባራዊ barbarawi ***(adj.)* barbaric**
ባርነት barbebt ***(n.)* slavery**
ባርዕ bar'ë ***(n.)* fire**
ባረኸ bareke ***(v.)* sanctify**
ባረኸ bareḱe ***(v.)* hallow**
ባረኸ bareḱe ***(v.)* bless**
ባርኾት barkot ***(n.)* sanctification**
ባርነት barnet ***(n. )* thrall**
ባርኖስ barnos ***(n. )* locust**
ባሮሜተር baromeeter ***(n.)* barometer**
ባርያ barya ***(n. )* slave**
ባርያ ገበረ barya gebere ***(v.)* enslave**
ባርያዊ baryawi ***(adj.)* slavish**
ባስ bas ***(n.)* bass**
ባስታ basta ***(n.)* pasta**
ባጤራዊ ፖሊሲ baťeerawi polisi ***(n.)* monetarism**
ባተሪ bateri ***(n.)* battery**
ብያቲ bati ***(n.)* tray**
ባጤራ እንግሊዝ baťiera èngliz ***(n.)* pound**
ባቲክ batik ***(n.)* batik**
ብዓውታ b'äwta ***(adv.)* aloud**
ባውዛ bawza ***(n. )* limelight**
ብዓይኒ ዘይረአ b'äyni zeyre'e ***(adj.)* microscopic**
ባዮፕሲ bayopsi ***(n.)* biopsy**
ባይት bayt ***(n.)* byte**
ባይታ bayta ***(n.)* floor**
ባይታ bayta ***(n. )* ground**
ባይቶ bayto ***(n. )* senate**
ባዛር bazar ***(n.)* bazaar**
ባዚሊካ bazilika ***(n.)* basilica**
ባዚቃ baziqa ***(n.)* gramophone**

**ባዜቃዊ** baziqawi *(adj.)* **mercurial**
**ባዝራ** bazra *(n. )* **mare**
**ባዙቃ** bazuqa *(n.)* **bazooka**

# ቤ

**ቤኮን** beekon *(n.)* **bacon**
**ቤላርባ** beelaroba *(n. )* **hawker**
**ቤት ፍርዲ** beet frdi *(n.)* **court**
**ቤት ግምጃ** beet gmja *(n.)* **bursary**
**ቤት ማእሰርቲ** beet ma'èserti *(n. )* **jail**
**ቤት መዘጋጃ** beet mezageja *(n.)* **municipality**
**ቤት ምኽሪ** beet mkri *(n.)* **council**
**ቤት ንህበት** beet nhbet *(n.)* **foundry**
**ቤት ፅሕፈት** beet xȟfet *(n.)* **bureau**
**ቤተ ክህነት** beete khnet *(n. )* **ministry**
**ቤተ መዘክር** beete mezekr *(n. )* **museum**
**ቤተ ፀሎት** beete xelot *(n.)* **chapel**
**ቤት ስኒማ** bet ciniema *(n)* **cinema**
**ቤት ፍርዲ** bet frdi *(n. )* **tribunal**
**ቤት ግምጃ** bet gmja *(n.)* **treasury**
**ቤት ሕፀቦ** bet htsbo *(n. )* **launderette**
**ቤተ መቅደስ** bet mekdes *(n.)* **temple**
**ቤት መስተ** bet meste *(n.)* **pub**
**ቤት ምግቢ** bet mgbi *(n.)* **restaurant**

# ብ

**ብዕልኛ** b'ëlgna *(n.)* **disrespect**
**ብዕልግና** b'ëlg'na *(n.)* **misconduct**
**ብዕልግቲ** b'ëlgti *(n.)* **slut**
**ብዕሊ ክንገር ዝግባእ** bëli knger zgba'e *(adj.)* **notifiable**
**ብ** b *(prep.)* **by**
**ብ** b *(prep. )* **with**
**ብገምደ ዝንቀሳቐስ ኣሻንጉሊት** b gemed znqesaqhes ashangulit *(n.)* **marionette**
**ብሓሳብ** b hasab *(adv. )* **ideally**
**ብ ቫይረስ** b vires *(adj.)* **viral**
**ብዓል ዝና** ba'al zna *(adj.)* **accredited**
**ብኣጋ ኣፍልጦ** b'aga 'aflïo *(n.)* **foreknowledge**
**ብህላዊ** bahlawi *(adj.)* **traditional**
**ብዓል ቤት** b'al biet *(n. )* **spouse**
**ብዓል ጎባን** bäl goban *(n.)* **cuckold**
**ብዓል ሕድሪ** bäl hdri *(n.)* **custodian**
**ብዓል ሞያ** b'äl moya *(n.)* **practitioner**
**ብዓል ንፅል መነፅር** b'äl nxl menexr *(adj.)* **monocular**
**ብዓል ስልጣን** b'al sltan *(adj.)* **incumbent**
**ብባሕሪ ተጓዓዘ** bbahri tegu'aze *(v.)* **sail**
**ብባህሪኡ** bbahri'u *(adv. )* **naturally**
**ብበዝሒ** bbezĥi *(adj.)* **galore**
**ብበዝሒ ምምፃእ** bbezhi mmtsa'e *(n.)* **influx**
**ብብርቱዕ ሃረፈ** bbrtu'ë harefe *(v.)* **hanker**
**ብጭጉራፍ ወቕዐ** bĉguraf weq'ë *(v.)* **flagellate**
**ብጫ** bcha *(adj.)* **yellow**
**ብጫ እምኒ** bcha emni *(n. )* **topaz**
**ብጫ ክፋል እንቋቑሖ** bcha kfal enquaquho *(n.)* **yolk**
**ብጭቃ ዝተሰርሐ** bĉqa zteserĥe *(adj.)* **earthen**
**ብድብድ** bd'bd *(adj.)* **musty**

ብደንቢ bdenbi *(adv. )* **indeed**
ብደቂቃ bdeqiqa *(adv. )* **minutely**
ብድሕሪ bdḧri *(adv.)* **after**
ብድሕረት ሸነኽ bdĥrit shenek *(adj.)* **posterior**
ብድሕረት bdḧrit *(prep.)* **behind**
ብድሕሪኡ bdhriu *(adv. )* **then**
ብድሕሪኡ bdhriu *(adv. )* **thence**
ብድሌት bdliet *(adj.)* **voluntary**
ብድንገት ምጭፍላቕ bdnget mchflak *(v.)* **implode**
ብዱቅስካ ምኻድ bdquska mkhad *(n.)* **somnambulism**
ብድቁሱ ዝኸድ bdqusu zkhed *(n. )* **somnambulist**
ብዕሉግ b'elug *(adj.)* **lewd**
ብዕሉግ b'elug *(adj.)* **licentious**
ብዕሉግ b'elug *(adj.)* **wanton**
ብዕሉግ b'ëlug *(adj.)* **amoral**
ብዕሉግ b'ëlug *(adj.)* **discourteous**
ብዕሉግ b'ëlug *(v.)* **pervert**
ብዕሉግ b'ëlug *(adj.)* **surly**
በልጸገ belxege *(v.)* **prosper**
ብእምነት ዘይኮነ ብኩነታት ዝሰርሕ bèmnet zeykone bkunetat zserḧ *(adj.)* **pragmatic**
ብዕሙር ኣገባብ b'ëmur agbab *(adv. )* **richly**
ብጣዕሚ betaemi *(pref.)* **ultra**
ብጣዕሚ ገፊሕ betaemi gefihei *(adj.)* **cavernous**
ብዝለዓለ ጥንቃቐ beze-le-a-le tenkake *(adv.)* **gingerly**
በዘወ bezewe *(v.)* **mortify**
ብዕዘዛ b'ëzeza *(n. )* **somnolence**
በዚ ገይሩ bezi geyru *(adv. )* **hereby**
ብዙሕ bezuhi'h *(adj.)* **considerable**
ብዕዙዝ bëzuz' *(adj.)* **somnolent**
ብዕዙዝ b'ëzuz *(adj.)* **sleepy**
ብዕዙዝ b'ëzuz *(adj.)* **somnolent**
ብፈሳሲ ዝሰርሕ bfesasi zserh *(adj.)* **hydraulic**
ብፍላይ bflay *(adv.)* **especially**
ብፍቅሪ ሓረረ bfqri ĥarere *(v. t)* **enamour**
ብፍጥነት bftnet *(n.)* **trice**
ብጋኔን ኣትሓዘ bganen at'haze *(v.)* **demonize**
ብግቡእ ኣገባብ bgbu'e agbab *(adv. )* **duly**
ብጌጋ ኣንበበ bgeega anbebe *(v.)* **misread**
ብጌጋ ኣርኣየ bgeega 'ar'aye *(v.)* **belie**
ብጌጋ ፈረደ bgeega ferede *(v.)* **misjudge**
ብጌጋ ፊደል ፀሓፈ bgeega fidel xeḧafe *(v.)* **misspell**
ብጌጋ መርሐ bgeega merḧe *(v.)* **mislead**
ብጌጋ ምርዳእ bgeega mrda'e *(n. )* **misunderstanding**
ብጌጋ ቀመረ bgeega qemere *(v.)* **miscalculate**
ብጌጋ ጠቀሰ bgeega ẗeqese *(v.)* **misquote**
ብጌጋ ተረድአ bgeega terd'e *(v.)* **misunderstand**
ብጌጋ ተጠቀመ bgeega teẗeqeme *(v.)* **misuse**
ብጌጋ ትርጉም ሃበ bgeega trgum habe *(v.)* **misconstrue**
ብጌጋ ምግንዛብ bgeegs mg'nzab *(v.)* **misconceive**
ብጌጋ ምርዳእ bgiega mrda'e *(n.)* **misapprehension**
ብጌጋ ተረደአ bgiega terede'e *(v.)* **misapprehend**

ብግመ ዝተሸፈነ bgme zteshefene *(adj.)* **misty**

ብግምት ምውሳን bgmt mwsan *(n.)* **presupposition**

ብግምት ወሰነ bgmt wesene *(v.)* **presuppose**

ብሓደ bhade *(adv. )* **together**

ብሓደ ኩነታት ዝተራከቡ ሰባት bhade kunetat zterakebu sebat *(n.)* **turnout**

ብሓደ መዓልቲ ሰለስተ ዉድድር ምሽናፍ bhade mealti seleste gze mshnaf *(adj.)* **treble**

ብሓደ ነገር ዘተኮረ ነዊሕ ፁሑፍ bhade neger zetekore newih suhuf *(n. )* **treatise**

ብሓዱሽ bȟadush *(adv. )* **newly**

ብሓጐስ ፈንጨሐ bȟagwas fenčeȟe *(v.)* **enrapture**

ብሃንደበት bhandebet *(adv. )* **suddenly**

ብሓንሳብ bĥansab *(adj.)* **simultaneous**

ብሓቂ bĥaqi *(adv. )* **really**

ብሓቂ bḥaqi *(adv. )* **verily**

ብሓቂ bȟaqi *(adv.)* **actually**

ብሓርኮትኮቱ ዝሃፍተመ bharkorkotu zhafteme *(adj.)* **self-made**

በሃሩር ተሳቐየ bharur tesaqeye *(v.)* **swelter**

ብሓሶት መስከረ bĥasot meskere *(v.)* **perjure**

ብሓሶት ምምስካር bĥasot mmskar *(n. )* **perjury**

ብሓፂሩ bȟatsiru *(adv. )* **summarily**

ብሓይሊ ወሰደ bȟayli wesede *(v.)* **extort**

ብሕቡእ bhbu'e *(adj.)* **underhand**

ብሓደ ግዜ ልዕሊ ሓደ ሰብኣይ ትምርያ ሰበይቲ bȟde gzie lëli ȟade gzie sebay tmräw sebeyti *(n.)* **polyandry**

ብሓደ ግዜ ልዕሊ ሓደ ሰብኣይ/ሰበይቲ ምምርዓው bȟde gzie lëli ȟade gzie sebay/sebeti mmräw *(n. )* **polygamy**

ብሓደ ግዜ ልዕሊ ሓደ ሰብኣይ/ሰበይቲ ተመርዓዊ bȟde gzie lëli ȟade gzie sebay/sebeti temeräwi *(adj.)* **polygamous**

ብሄር bheer *(n.)* **nation**

ብሄራዊ bheerawi *(adj.)* **national**

ብሕጊ ዝተወሰነ bȟgi ztewesene *(adj.)* **statutory**

ብሕጎጋ bȟgoga *(n.)* **corrosion**

ብሓባር ተቀመጠ bhhabar teqemete *(v.)* **cohabit**

ብሂል bhil *(n.)* **dictum**

ብሂል bhil *(n.)* **epigram**

ብሒቑ bĥiq *(n.)* **dough**

ብሀሎ bhlo *(n.)* **allegation**

ብሕማቕ bȟmaq̈ *(adv.)* **badly**

ብህንጥይና bhnẗyna *(adv.)* **avidly**

ብሕቑር bĥqwar *(n.)* **groove**

ባህሪ bhri *(n. )* **trait**

ብሕታዊ bhtawi *(adj.)* **lone**

ብሕታዊ bhtawi *(adj.)* **lonely**

ብሕታዊ bhtawi *(adj.)* **lonesome**

ብሕታዊነት bhtawinet *(n.)* **loneliness**

ብሕትኡ ምኹን ዝመርፅ bht'u mukhun zmerts *(n.)* **loner**

ብሕትውና bȟtwna *(n.)* **celibacy**

ብህፁፅ ዝተሰርሓ bhuxux zteserȟe *(adj.)* **cursory**

ብሕያውነት bḥyawnet *(adv. )* **kindly**

ቢጫ ዕንበባ bich enbeba ***(n.)*** **marigold**
ብኢድ ዝተፃሓፈ b'id ztetzehafe ***(n.)*** **manuscript**
ቢደ bide ***(n.)*** **bidet**
ቤት ብልዒ biet bl'ï ***(n.)*** **eatery**
ቤት ሕብስቲ biet hbsti ***(n.)*** **pastry**
ቤት ሕብስቲ biet hbsti ***(n.)*** **patisserie**
ቤት ማሕቡስ biet maḧbus ***(n. )*** **prison**
ቤት መድሃኒት biet medhanit ***(n. )*** **pharmacy**
ቤት ምግብን መስተን biet mgbn mesten ***(n. )*** **tavern**
ቤተ መንግስታዊ biete mengstawi ***(adj.)*** **palatial**
ቤተ መንግስቲ biete mengsti ***(n. )*** **palace**
ቤተ-ፈተነ biete-fetene ***(n.)*** **laboratory**
ቤተ-መፃሕፍቲ biete-metsahft ***(n. )*** **library**
ቢኪኒ bikini ***(n.)*** **bikini**
ቡሊምያ bilimiya ***(n.)*** **bulimia**
ቢልያርዶ bilyardo ***(n.)*** **billiards**
ቢልዮን bilyon ***(n.)*** **billion**
ቢራ bira ***(n.)*** **ale**
ቢራ bira ***(n.)*** **beer**
ብሪንጃል birinjal ***(n.)*** **brinjal**
ቢሮ biro ***(n.)*** **pen**
ቢሮክራሲ birokrasi ***(n.)*** **bureaucracy**
ቢሮክራት birokrat ***(n.)*** **bureaucrat**
ቢስተካ bisteka ***(n.)*** **steak**
ቢቨር biver ***(n.)*** **beaver**
ቢያቲ biyati ***(n.)*** **plate**
ብጃማ bĵama ***(n.)*** **pyjamas**
ብጃንጥላ ዝንቆት bjantla znqot ***(n. )*** **parachutist**
ብጀካ bjeka ***(prep.)*** **barring**
ብጀካ bjeka ***(prep.)*** **except**
ብኽብረት bḱbret ***(v.)*** **please**
ብከላ bkela ***(n.)*** **pollution**
ብቐሊሉ ዛኣምን bkelilu za'amn ***(adj.)*** **gullible**
ብክልተ ጎኒ ዝርከብ bklte goni zrkeb ***(prep.)*** **astride**
ብኽነት bḱnet ***(n.)*** **wastage**
ብኮፍ ዝግበር bkof zgber ***(adj.)*** **sedentary**
ብኮፍካ ሽመት bkofka šmet ***(n.)*** **sinecure**
ብኮምፒዩተር ኣስረሐ bkompyuter asreh ***(v.)*** **computerize**
ብኮንትሮባንድ ኣእተወ bkontroband a'etewe ***(v.)*** **smuggle**
ብቆርብት ቀዳድ ርስሓት ምዉጋድ bkorbet kedda dshat mray ***(v.)*** **transpire**
ብኮረንቲ ኣቑሰለ bkorenti aqusele ***(v.)*** **electrocute**
ብቑዕ ዘይኮነ bku zeykone ***(adj.)*** **unfit**
ብቑዕ ዘይኮነ bku zeykone ***(adj.)*** **unqualified**
ብቑዕ ዘይኮነ bku zeykone ***(adj.)*** **unworthy**
ብኹሉኹሉ bkulukulu ***(adv. )*** **roundly**
ብኩራት bkurat ***(n.)*** **absence**
ብኳርያ bkwarya ***(n. )*** **fox**
ብኽያት bkyat ***(n.)*** **croak**
ብኽያት bkyat ***(n.)*** **cry**
ብኽያት bkyat ***(n.)*** **whine**
ብላዕ ዘይበልዕ bla'e zeybel'e ***(adj.)*** **incorruptible**
ብልዕሊ ዝግበር blaeli zgber ***(n.)*** **topping**

**ብላክቤሪ** blakberi ***(n.)*** **blackberry**
**ብላሽ** blash ***(n.)*** **fiasco**
**ብላሽ** blash ***(adj.)*** **vain**
**ብላይ** blay ***(adj.)*** **ragged**
**ብልጭ ብልጭ በለ** blč blč bele ***(v.)*** **glimmer**
**ብልጫ** blča ***(adj.)*** **pre-eminent**
**ብልጫዊ** blčawi ***(n.)*** **pre-eminence**
**ብልጭታ** blchta ***(n.)*** **spark**
**ብልጭልጭ በለ** blĉlĉ bele ***(v.)*** **glitter**
**ባልዕ** ble ***(n. )*** **pest**
**ብልዕሊ** bl'ëli ***(prep.)*** **above**
**ብልሓት** blhat ***(n.)*** **technique**
**ብልሓት** blĥat ***(n.)*** **diplomacy**
**ብልሓት** blĥat ***(n.)*** **genius**
**ብልሓት** blḧat ***(n.)*** **contrivance**
**ብልሓት** blhat ***(n.)*** **tact**
**ብልሓት** blḧat ***(n.)*** **prowess**
**ብልሓተኛ** blĥategna ***(adj.)*** **resourceful**
**ብልሓተኛ** bl'ḧategna ***(adj.)*** **methodical**
**ብልሒ** blhi ***(n.)*** **tang**
**ብልሒ ግምቢ** b'lḧi gmbi ***(n.)*** **steeple**
**ብልህነት** blhnet ***(n.)*** **brilliance**
**ቢልዮነር** blilyoner ***(n.)*** **billionaire**
**ብሎን** blon ***(n.)*** **screw**
**ብልቃጥ** blqat ***(n.)*** **phial**
**ብልሹነት** blshunet ***(n.)*** **futility**
**ብልሹው** blshuw ***(adj.)*** **bent**
**ብልሹው** blshuw ***(adj.)*** **dysfunctional**
**ብልሽው** blshw ***(adv.)*** **awry**
**ብልሹው** blshw ***(adj.)*** **putrid**
**ብልጽግና** bltsg'na ***(n.)*** **prosperity**
**ብልፁግ** bltsug ***(adj.)*** **prosperous**
**ብሉፅ** blutz ***(adj.)*** **superb**
**ብሉፅ እዋን** blutz ewan ***(n.)*** **innings**
**ብሉፅ** blux ***(n.)*** **ace**
**ብሉፅ** blux ***(adj.)*** **classic**
**ብሉፅ** blux ***(n.)*** **elite**
**ብሉፅ ዕዮ** blux ëyo ***(n. )*** **masterpiece**
**ብማዕዶ** bma''ëdo ***(adv.)*** **across**
**ብማዕዶ ፈረደ** bma'ëdo ferede ***(v.)*** **prejudge**
**ብማእኸል** bmaekel ***(prep. &adv.)*** **through**
**ብመድሓኒት ምድቃስ** bmedhanit mdqas ***(n.)*** **sedation**
**ብልክዕ ምምልካት** bmelke mmlkat ***(v.)*** **pinpoint**
**ብመንፅር** bmenxr ***(adv.)*** **according**
**ብመቀስ ቆረፀ** bmeqes qoretse ***(v.)*** **snip**
**ብመርከብ ተጓዓዘ** bmerkeb tgwaäze ***(v.)*** **cruise**
**ብመርትዖ ደገፈ** bmert'o degefe ***(v.)*** **substantiate**
**ብመርትዖ ምድጋፍ** bmert'o mdbaf ***(n.)*** **substantiation**
**ብ መሳርሒ ቅርፂ ዘዋፅእ** bmesarhi qrsi zwese ***(n. )*** **turner**
**ብመሰረት** bmeseret ***(n.)*** **accordance**
**ብመስኖ ማይ ኣስተየ** bmesno may 'asteye ***(v.)*** **irrigate**
**ብመጠኑ** bmeťenu ***(adv.)*** **fairly**
**ብመወዳእታ** b'mewedaeta ***(adv. )*** **ultimately**
**ብምክሓድ** bmkhad ***(adj.)*** **treacherous**
**ብምልምስና ዝሳቐ ሰብ** bmlmsna zsaqe seb ***(adj.)*** **paralytic**
**ብምሳሌ ምጥቃም** bmsalee mṭqam ***(n.)*** **imagery**
**ብምስጋእ** bmsga'e ***(conj.)*** **lest**
**ብምትሓዝ ዝግነ ቅርሺ** bmthaz zgne qrshi ***(v.)*** **tote**

ብሙቀት ዝጥንክር ፕላስቲክ bmuqet ztnker plastik *(adj.)* **thermosetting**
ብምዝንባል bmznbal *(adv.)* **astray**
ብነብሱ ዘይምራሕ bnebsu zeymraȟ *(n. )* **puppet**
ብነጻ bnetsa *(adv. &adj.)* **gratis**
ብንፋስ እትጥሕን መኪና bnfas etthn mekina *(n. )* **windmill**
ብንጅር bnĵr *(n.)* **beet**
ብንፁር ዘይረአ bnuxr zeyr'e *(adj.)* **faint**
ብፖስጣ bposẗa *(adj.)* **postal**
ብፖስታ ዝተገዝኡ bposta ztegez'u *(n.)* **mail order**
ብቕዓት bq'at *(n.)* **credentials**
ብቕዓት bqät *(n.)* **efficiency**
ብቅዓት bq'ät *(n.)* **qualification**
ብቕዓት bq̈'ät *(n. )* **validity**
ብቅዓታዊ bq'ätawi *(adj.)* **qualitative**
ብቕዱስ ዝምራሕ ዓዲ bqdus zmrah adi *(n. )* **theocracy**
ብቀሊሉ bqelilu *(adv. )* **readily**
ብቀሊሉ ክቆፃፀርዎ ዝክእሉ bqelilu kqosaserwa zk'al *(adj.)* **tractable**
ብቐሊሉ ተናዳዲ bqelilu tenadadi *(adj.)* **testy**
ብቐሊሉ ዝነድድ bqelilu znedd *(adj.)* **flammable**
ብቀጥታ bqetta *(adv.)* **directly**
ብቅዓት ዘይብሉ bqha'at zeyblu *(adj.)* **ineligible**
ብቐሊሉ bqhelilu *(adv. )* **lightly**
ብቐሊሉ ዝፅሎ ሰብ bqhelilu ztslo seb *(adj.)* **suggestible**
ብቐሊሉ ዘይሓቅቕ bqhelilu zwyhaqqh *(adj.)* **indigestible**
ብቕጽበት b'qhtsbet *(adv. )* **straightway**
ብቅልጡፍ bqltuf *(adv. )* **quickly**
ብቕልጡፍ bq̈ltuf *(n.)* **ado**
ብቕልጡፍ bq̈lẗuf *(adv.)* **apace**
ብቕሉዕ bq̈lu'ë *(adv.)* **barely**
ብቑዕ bqu'ë *(adj.)* **efficient**
ብቑዕ bqu'ë *(adj.)* **eligible**
ብቁዕ bq̈u'ë *(adj.)* **fit**
ብቑዕ bq̈u'ë *(adj.)* **valid**
ብሑቕ መሰል bque mesl *(n.)* **pasty**
ብቑዕ bq̈u'ë *(adj.)* **appropriate**
ብቋልያ bqwalya *(adj.)* **nascent**
ብር በለ br bele *(v.)* **flush**
ብራድ brad *(n.)* **filings**
ብራኽ braḱe *(n.)* **altitude**
ብራኳ brakwa *(n.)* **jug**
ብራኳ brakwa *(n.)* **pitcher**
ብራንዲ brandi *(n.)* **brandy**
ብርጭቆ brchiqo *(n. )* **tumbler**
ብርጭቕ brčq *(n.)* **watermelon**
ብርጭቆ brčqo *(n.)* **beaker**
ብርእሲ ስሒብካ ዝኽደን ኽዳን brèsi sȟibka zḱden ḱdan *(n. )* **pullover**
ብረት bret *(n.)* **metal**
ብረት bret *(n.)* **weapon**
ብረታዊ bretawi *(adj.)* **metallic**
ብረይል breyl *(n.)* **Braille**
ብርጌድ brgied *(n. )* **legion**
ብርግፀ brg'x *(adv. )* **surely**
ብርሃን brhan *(n.)* **light**
ብርሃን ሃበ brhan habe *(v.)* **irradiate**
ብርሃን ሰማይ brhan semay *(n. )* **skylight**
ብርሃን ወሃቢ br'han wehabi *(n.)* **luminary**
ብርሃን ወርሒ brhan werȟi *(n.)* **moonlight**
ብርሃን ዘሕልፍ brhan zehlf *(adj.)* **translucent**
ብሪ bri *(n.)* **silver**
ብርዒ br'i *(n.)* **sty**

ብረጌድ brigeed *(n.)* **brigade**
ብረቕረቕ briqriq *(n. )* **glazier**
ብረቕረቕታ briqriqta *(n. )* **gloss**
ብረጣንያዊ briťanyawi *(adj.)* **British**
ብረውምረው በለ briwmriw bele *(v.)* **gibber**
ብርካተ brkate *(n.)* **abundance**
ብርካተ brkate *(n.)* **profusion**
ብርኩት brkut *(adj.)* **numerous**
ብርለ brle *(n.)* **flask**
ብርለ ነቢት brle nebit *(n.)* **decanter**
ብርኒጎ brnigo *(n.)* **quail**
ብሮንዞ bronzo *(n.)* **bronze**
ብሮት brot *(n.)* **mole**
ብርቃሕ brqaȟ *(n. )* **notch**
ብርቂ brqi *(adj.)* **precious**
ብርሰት brset *(v. t)* **decomposition**
ብርሰት brset *(n.)* **destruction**
ብርስን brsn *(n. )* **lentil**
ብርታዐ brta'ë *(n.)* **vigour**
ብርቱዕ brtu'e *(adj. )* **herculean**
ብርቱዕ brtu'e *(adj.)* **vigorous**
ብርቱዕ brtu'ë *(adj.)* **acute**
ብርቱዕ brtu'ë *(adj.)* **ardent**
ብርቱዕ brtu'ë *(adj.)* **dynamic**
ብርቱዕ ጨና brtuë čena *(adj.)* **pungent**
ብርቱዕ ጨና ምህላው brtuë čena mhlaw *(n.)* **pungency**
ብርቱዕ ድሌት brtu'ë dleet *(n.)* **ardour**
ብርቲዕ ድልየት brtu'e dlyet *(n. )* **zeal**
ብርቱዕ ስምዒት brtue smeit *(n.)* **passion**
ብርቱዕ ተምሰጥ brtu'ë temsaẗ *(n.)* **fervour**
ብርቱዕ brtu'ë *(adj.)* **strong**
ብሩህ bruh *(adj.)* **apparent**
ብሩህ bruh *(adj.)* **intelligible**
ብሩህ bruh *(adj.)* **lucent**
ብሩህነት bruhnet *(adv. )* **lucidity**
ብሩኽ bruḱ *(adj.)* **blessed**
ብግዜ ቀዳማይ brzie qedamay *(adj.)* **prime**
ብፀብፀ ዓመፅ bsbs ames *(n.)* **turmoil**
ብሰዓቱ bseatu *(adj.)* **timely**
ብሰላሕታ bsela'ȟta *(adv. )* **stealthily**
ብሰለስተ ዕንጨይቲ ዝተስኣለ ስእሊ bseleste ansyti ztesale seli *(n.)* **triptych**
ብሰንጠረዥ ምስራሕ ምምዳብ bsenterez msrah mmdab *(n.)* **tabulation**
ብሰንጠረዥ ዝተሰርሐ bsenterez zteserhe *(adj.)* **tabular**
ብሰንጠረዥ ኣዘጋጅዩ bsenterz azegaj'u *(v.)* **tabulate**
ብሽክለታ bshkleta *(n.)* **bicycle**
ብሽክለታ bshkleta *(n.)* **bike**
ብሽክሌተኛ bshkliteenya *(n.)* **cyclist**
ብሽኮቲ bshkoti *(n.)* **biscuit**
ብሽኩቲ bshkuti *(n.)* **cracker**
ብስለት bs'let *(n.)* **maturity**
ብስልኪ፣ቲቪ፣ኢንተርኔት ርክብ bslki,tivi,internet rkb *(n. )* **telecommunications**
ብስምምዕነ ት bsmm'enet *(adv.)* **tamely**
ብስናው b-snaw *(n.)* **halitosis**
ብጣዕሚ ብዙሕ btaami bzuh *(adj.)* **tremendous**
ብጣዕሚ ሓያል btaami hayal *(adj.)* **torrential**
ብጣዕሚ ምህንጣይ btaami mhntay *(n.)* **tenterhook**
ብታዕሚ btaemi *(adv. )* **too**

ብጣዕሚ ዓቢዩ btaemi abyi *(adj.)* **titanic**
ብጣዕሚ ቡዙሕ bta'emi buzuh *(adj.)* **infinite**
ብጣዕሚ ብዙሕ bẗaëmi bzuḧ *(adj.)* **profuse**
ብጣዕሚ ሓያል ንፋስ btaemi hayal nfas *(n. )* **tornado**
ብጣዕሚ ናይ ምድላይ ስሚዒት btaemi namdlay smi'it *(n. )* **temptation**
ብጣዕሚ ፁብቕ bta'emi tsubqh *(adj.)* **magnificent**
ብጣሕ bẗaḧ *(n. )* **nick**
ብትብዓት b-tb-at *(adj.)* **gamely**
ብጥብቂ bẗbqi *(adv. )* **strictly**
ብተደጋጋሚ ምህራም btedegagami mhram *(v.)* **pummel**
ብተኸታታሊ bteketatali *(adv.)* **consecutively**
ብተክኖሎጅይ ዝተሓገዘ bteknology ztehageze *(adj.)* **technological**
ብቴሌቪዥን ተሓላሊፉ btelevizn tehalalifu *(v.)* **televise**
ብተሎ b'telo *(adv. )* **soon**
ብተመሳሳሊ btemesasali *(adv. )* **likewise**
መተንፈሲ btenfesi *(n.)* **inhaler**
ብጠቕላላ bteqlala *(n.)* **totality**
ብተርታ ሰርዐ bterta ser'e *(v.)* **serialize**
ብተስፋ btesfa *(adv. )* **hopefully**
ብተወሳኺ btewesaki *(adv.)* **else**
ብተወሳኺ btewesaki *(adv.)* **furthermore**
ብተወሳኺ btewesaki *(adv.)* **withal**
ብተወሳኺ btewesaḱi *(adv. )* **moreover**
ብጽሒት bẗḧit *(n.)* **portion**
ብትሕቲ bthti *(prep. )* **underneath**
ብጥንቃቐ ኣንቢቡ btnqaqe anbibu *(v.)* **peruse**
ብጥንቃቀ መርመረ btnqaqe mermere *(v.)* **scrutinize**
ብጥንቃቐ ምንባብ btnqaqe mnbab *(n.)* **perusal**
ብትንትን ዝበለ btntn zbele *(adj.)* **untidy**
ብጥራነ bẗrane *(n.)* **snobbery**
ብጥራሽ bẗrash *(adv. )* **never**
ብጥርጣረ ጠመተ bẗrẗare ẗemete *(adv.)* **askance**
ብፀሓይ ዝሰርሕ btseḧay zserh *(adj.)* **solar**
ብፅሒት btshit *(n.)* **share**
ብፅሒት btsĥit *(n. )* **quota**
ብፅሒት btsĥit *(n.)* **quotient**
ብጽሑፍ አስፈረ btshuf asfere *(v.)* **transcribe**
ብፁእተኛ btsu'etegna *(n.)* **puritan**
ብፁእተኛዊ btsu'etegnawi *(adj.)* **puritanical**
ብንፁር bnxur *(adv.)* **clearly**
ቦኽቦኽ boḱboḱe *(v.)* **moulder**
ቦምብ bomb *(n.)* **bomb**
ቦርሳ borsa *(n.)* **bag**
ቦርሳ borsa *(n.)* **purse**
ቦርሳ ኢድ borsa e-i-d *(n.)* **handbag**
ቦታ bota *(n.)* **place**
ቦታ bota *(n. )* **site**
ቦታ ለወጠ bota lewete *(v.)* **relocate**
ቦታ ምሓዝ bota mḥaz *(n.)* **installation**
ቦጦሎኒ boẗoloni *(n.)* **battalion**
ብዙሕ buzuh *(adj.)* **many**
ብዋጋ ዘይትመን bwaga zeytmen *(adj.)* **priceless**
ቧምብላ bwambula *(n.)* **toy**

**ብዋኒን ዝተጸምደ** bwanin ztexemde ***(adj.)* busy**
**ብወግዒ ገሰፀ** bweg'ï gesetse ***(v.)* reprimand**
**ብወግዒ ተሸመ** bweg'ï tesheme ***(v.)* accredit**
**ብወቅታዊ ፋሽን ዝክተል** bwuqtawi fashn zktel ***(adj.)* trendy**
**ብዉሽጢ ማይ ዝጎዓዝ ቦምብ** bwushti may zgoaz bomb ***(n.)* torpedo**
**ብዉሽጡ ዘርኢ** bwushti zer,i ***(adj.)* transparent**
**ብዉሽጢ ኣመሓላሊፍካ ምርኣይ** bwushty amehalalifka mray ***(n.)* transparency**
**ብጸይ** bxay ***(n.)* companion**
**ብፃይ** bxay ***(n.)* fellow**
**ብጸይ** bxay ***(n.)* comrade**
**ብፃይነት** bxaynet ***(n.)* fellowship**
**ብጸይነት** bxaynet ***(n.)* camaraderie**
**ብጽሕና** bxḧna ***(n.)* adolescence**
**ብጽሖ** bxḥo ***(n. )* visitation**
**ብፁእነት** bxu'enet ***(n.)* beatitude**
**ብያቲ** byati ***(n.)* saucer**
**ብዛዕባ** bza'ëba ***(prep.)* about**
**ብዛዕባ** bza'ëba ***(prep.)* concerning**
**ብዛዕባ** bza'ëba ***(prep.)* regarding**
**ብዘስሕቅ መልክዑ ምምሳል** bzeshq melkau mmsal ***(n.)* travesty**
**ብዘይ** bzey ***(adj.)* wanting**
**ብዘይ** bzey ***(prep. )* without**
**ብዘይ ፍርዲ ሓኒቕካ ምቕታል** bzey frdi haniqhka mqhtal ***(n. )* lynch**
**ብዘይ ጉድኣት** bzey gud'at ***(adv.)* scot-free**
**ብዘይ ካፈይን** bzey kafeyn ***(adj.)* decaffeinated**
**ብዘይ ምሕቃቕ ምግቢ ዝመፅእ ቓንዛ ኸብዲ** bzey mhqaqh mgbi zmets'e qhanza kebdi ***(n.)* indigestion**
**ብዘይ ምንቅስቓስ** bzey mnqsq̈as ***(n.)* poise**
**ብዘይ ናይ ውግእ መሰርሒ** bzey nay wege'e mesarhi ***(adj.)* unarmed**
**ብዘይ ታህዋኽ** bzey tahwak ***(adj.)* leisurely**
**ብዘይተገዳስነት** bzey tegedasnet ***(adj.)* unceremonious**
**ብዘይ ጥቅሚ ዘዊሩ** bzey tkmi zewiru ***(v.)* twiddle**
**ብዘይድልየት** bzeydlyet ***(adj.)* unwilling**
**ብዘየግድስ** bzeyegds ***(adv. )* regardless**
**ብዘይፍላጥ** bzeyflat ***(adv. )* unwittingly**
**ብዘይኩነት** bzeykunet ***(adj.)* unconditional**
**ብዘይምንቅስቓስ** bzeymnqsqhas ***(adv. )* statically**
**ብዘይምቁራፅ** bzeymqurax ***(adj.)* nonstop**
**ብዘይተገዳስነት** bzeytegedasnet ***(adv.)* anyhow**
**ብዝሒ** bzĥi ***(n. )* quantum**
**ብዝሒ ህዝቢ** bzḧi hzbi ***(n.)* population**
**ብዝሒ** bzḧi ***(n.)* bulk**
**ብዝለዓለ** bzle'äle ***(adv. )* highly**
**ብዙሕ** bzuh ***(pron.)* lot**
**ብዙሕ** bzuĥ ***(n.)* plenty**
**ብዙሕ** bzuḧ ***(n.)* more**
**ብዙሕ** bzuḧ ***(pron. )* much**
**ብዙሕ** bzu'ḧ ***(adj.)* substantial**
**ብዙሕ** bzuh ***(adj.)* innumerable**

ብዙሕ ህዝቢ ዘለዎ bzuḧ hzbi zelewo ***(adj.)* populous**
ብዙሕ ቅርፁ bzuḧ qrxu ***(adj.)* multiform**
ብዙሕ ቋንቋ ዝዛረብ bzuḧ quanq̈a zzareb ***(adj.)* polyglot**
ብዙሕ ዝዓይነቱ bzuḧ z'äynetu ***(adj.)* multiple**
ብዙሕ ዝጎኑ bzuḧ zgonu ***(adj.)* multilateral**
ብዙሕ ዝሓቆፈ bzuḧ zḧaqofe ***(n. )* multiplex**
ብዙሕ ዝመዳያቱ bzuh zmedayatu ***(adj.)* manifold**
ብዙሕ ዝዛረብ bzuḧ zzareb ***(n.)* jay**
ብዙሕነት bzuĥnet ***(n.)* diversity**
ብዙሕነት bzuḧnet ***(n.)* multiplicity**
ባዶ bado ***(adj.)* void**
ባዶሽ badosh ***(n. )* vacuum**
ባዕሉ ba-e-lu ***(pron. )* himself**
ባህረ-ሓደ baḥreḥade ***(adj. )* homogeneous**
ባህረ-ሓደ baḥreḥade ***(a. )* homogeneous**
ባልጃ balǧa ***(n.)* valise**
ባዞ bazo ***(n.)* vase**
በዓል be-al ***(n.)* holiday**
ቤት beet ***(n.)* verse**
ቤተ-ልብሲ beetelbsi ***(n.)* vestry**
በላዕ ሓምሊ bela'ë ḥamli ***(n.)* vegetarian**
በረዳዊ beredawi ***(n. )* icy**
በጻሒ bexaḥi ***(n. )* visitor**
ብልጫ blç̣a ***(n.)* vantage**
ብልሓት blḥat ***(n.)* knack**
ብልሂ blhi ***(adj.)* imaginative**
ብልቃጥ blqaṭ ***(n.)* vial**
ብመንገዲ bmengedi ***(prep. )* via**
ብርኪ brki ***(n.)* knee**
ብርቱዕ brtu'ë ***(adj.)* vehement**
ብቴሌግራፍ btelegraph ***(n.)* telegraphy**
ቡቕሊ buq̈li ***(n. )* vegetation**
በዓለገ boalege ***(adj.)* obscene**
በዓል መዚ be'al mezi ***(adj.)* official**
በዳሊ bedali ***(n.)* offender**
ቤት-ጽሕፈት biet-tshfet ***(n. )* office**
ብሓሳብ ወሓጠ bhasab wehate ***(v.)* obsess**
ብሓደ ለይቲ bhade leyti ***(adv.)* overnight**
ብስርዓት bsr'at ***(adj.)* orderly**
ብርሃን ዘየሕልፍ brhal zeyehelf ***(adj.)* opaque**
ብርሃን-አልባነት brhal albanet ***(n. )* opacity**
ብቑፅሪ በለፀ bqutsri beletse ***(v.)* outnumber**
ብቓል bqal ***(adj.)* oral**
ብቓል bqal ***(adv.)* orally**
ብቕጽበት bqtsbet ***(adv.)* outright**
ብተደጋጋሚ btedegagami ***(adv.)* often**
ብአንጻሩ b'antsaru ***(adj.)* opposite**
ብአጋጣሚ ሰምዐ b'agatami sem'e ***(v.)* overhear**
ብዕሊ b'eli ***(adv.)* officially**
ብዕልግና b'ëlgna ***(n.)* obscenity**
ብዕራይ b'eray ***(n. )* ox**
ብዕድመ በለፀ b'edme beletse ***(v.)* outlast**
ብዕድመ በለፀ b'edme beletse ***(v.)* outlive**
ብኽብደት በለፀ bkbdet beletse ***(v.)* outweigh**
ብኽያት bkyat ***(n.)* outcry**
ብዙሕ ምእማት bzih m'emat ***(v.)* overestimate**

ብድሕሪት bdhrit ***(adv.)* overleaf**
ብጃፓናውያን ዝስራሕ ናይ ወረቐት ቕርፃቕርፂ bjapanawyan zsrah nay wereqet qrtsaqrtsi ***(n.)* origami**
ብጉያ ቐደመ bguya qedeme ***(v.)* outrun**
ብጋህዲ bgahdi ***(adv.)* openly**
ብጠቕላላ bteqlala ***(adj.)* overall**
ብጣዕሚ መሊኡ bta'emi meli'u ***(v.)* overflow**
ብጣዕሚ አስተማሰለ bta'emi astemasele ***(v.)* overreact**
ብጣዕሚ ዓብዪ bta'emi abyi ***(adj.)* overgrown**
ብጣዕሚ ፅቡቕ bta'emi tsbuq ***(adj.)* outstanding**
ብፍጥነት ምዝዋር b'ëray bereḱa ***(n.)* bison**
ብዕራይ በረኻ bwsay mqxal ***(n.)* arson**
*ብውሳይ ምቅጻል* vals *(n.) **waltz***

# ቨ

ቩዱ bftnet mzwar ***(n.)* overdrive**
ቫልስ varniche ***(n.)* varnish**
ቫርኒቾ vayolin ***(n. )* violin**
ቫዮሊን vayres ***(n. )* virus**
ቫይረስ valor ***(n.)* velour**
ቫሎር velkene ***(v.)* vulcanize**
ቨልከነ veyn ***(n. )* vein**
ቨይን vidyo ***(n.)* video**
ቪድዮ vila ***(n. )* villa**
ቪላ viskoz ***(n.)* viscose**
ቪስኮዝ viskya ***(n.)* mistletoe**
ቪስክያ vitamin ***(n.)* vitamin**
ቪታሚን vitryol ***(n.)* vitriol**
ቪትርዮል viza ***(n.)* visa**
ቪዛ volt ***(n. )* volt**
ቮልት vudu ***(n.)* voodoo**

# ተ

ተመልካቲ temelkati ***(n.)* onlooker**
ተመጣጠረ temetatere ***(v.)* overreach**
ተስፈኛ tesfegna ***(n.)* optimist**
ተራ tera ***(adv. )* oft**
ተቓወመ teqaweme ***(v.)* oppose**
ተናሓናሒ tenahanahi ***(adj.)* operative**
ተናሓናሒ tenahanahi ***(n.)* opponent**
ተአዘዘ te'azeze ***(v.)* obey**
ተዓዘበ te'azebe ***(v.)* observe**
ተዓዘበ te'azebe ***(v.)* oversee**
ተአዛዝነት teazaznet ***(n.)* obedience**
ተደገፈ tdegefe ***(v.)* lean**
ተአፋፊ teafafi ***(adj.)* queasy**
ተአፋፊ te'afafi ***(adj.)* fractious**
ተአፋፊ te'afafi ***(adj.)* sensitive**
ተዓገሰ teagese ***(v.)* tolerate**
ተዓገሰ te'ägese ***(v.)* forbear**
ተአኻኸበ te'akakebe ***(v.)* converge**
ተአከበ te'akebe ***(v.)* congregate**
ተአከበ te'akebe ***(v.)* convene**
ተዓኹለለ teäkulele ***(v.)* curl**
ተአልየ te'alye ***(v.t. )* shun**
ተአማማኒ te'amamani ***(adj.)* confident**
ተአማኒ te'amani ***(adj.)* conceivable**
ተአማኒ te'amani ***(adj.)* faithful**
ተአማኒ te'amani ***(n. )* loyalist**
ተአማኒነት te'amaninet ***(adj.)* fidelity**
ተአማንነት te'amannet ***(n.)* allegiance**
ተአመነ te'amene ***(v.)* acknowledge**

**ተኣመነ** te'amene *(v.)* **admit**
**ተኣምር** te'amr *(n.)* **miracle**
**ተኣምራዊ** te'amrawi *(adj.)* **miraculous**
**ተኣነነ** te'anene *(v.)* **deign**
**ተኣነነ** te'anene *(v.)* **groan**
**ተዓንገለ** te'angele *(v.)* **subsist**
**ተዓንቀፈ** te'änqefe *(v.)* **stumble**
**ተአንጠጠ** teantete *(v.)* **tiptoe**
**ተዓራረኸ** te'ärareke *(v.)* **befriend**
**ተኣሳሰረ** te'asasere *(v.)* **interlink**
**ተኣሳሰረ** te'asasere *(v.)* **belong**
**ተዓፀፉ** teasifu *(v.)* **turn**
**ተዓፃፃፊ** te'atsatsafi *(adj.)* **malleable**
**ተዓፃፃፊ** te'atsatsefi *(adj.)* **lithe**
**ተኣዋዲ** te'awadi *()* **debtor**
**ተዓወተ** te'awete *(v.)* **achieve**
**ተዓወተ** teäwete *(v.)* **succeed**
**ተዓፃፉይ እዋን** teäxafay ewan *(n.)* **flexitime**
**ተዓዛቢ** te'äzabi *(n. )* **spectator**
**ተኣዛዝነት** te'azaznet *(n.)* **subordination**
**ተዓዘብቲ** te'äzebti *(n.)* **audience**
**ተኣዘዘ** te'azeze *(v.)* **comply**
**ተባኣሳይ** teba'asay *(adj.)* **bellicose**
**ተባደለ** tebadele *(v.)* **barter**
**ተባዕ** teba'e *(adj.)* **manful**
**ተባዕ** teba'ë *(adj.)* **intrepid**
**ተባዕ** teba'ë *(adj.)* **nervy**
**ተባዕ** teba'ë *(adj.)* **valiant**
**ተባዕ** teba'ë *(adj.)* **bold**
**ተባዕ** teba'ë *(adj.)* **brave**
**ተብኣሲ** tebaeisu *(adj.)* **truculent**
**ተባዕታይ** teba'ëtay *(n.)* **male**
**ተባዕታይ** teba'ëtay *(adj.)* **masculine**
**ተባዕታይ ኣድጊ** teba'ëtay 'adgi *(n. )* **jackass**
**ተባዕታይ ፈረስ** teba'etay feres *(n.)* **stallion**
**ተባላዒ** tebala'i *(adj.)* **caustic**
**ተባላዒ** tebala'i *(adj.)* **corrosive**
**ጠባቒ መልእኽቲ** ëebaqhi mel'ekhti *(n. )* **sticker**
**ተባራዒ** tebara'i *(adj.)* **inflammable**
**ተባረዐ** tebare'ë *(adv.)* **ablaze**
**ተበኣሰ** tebe'ase *(v.t)* **fight**
**ተበላሸወ** tebelashew *(v.)* **malfunction**
**ተበለፀ** tebelexe *(v. t)* **exploit**
**ተበራበረ** teberabere *(v.)* **rouse**
**ተበርጠጠ** tebertete *(v.)* **condescend**
**ተበታኒ ፅሑፍ** tebetani tzhuf *(n.)* **leaflet**
**ተበታተነ** tebetatene *(v.)* **disperse**
**ተበተነ** tebetene *(v.)* **dissipate**
**ትዕቢት** t'ëbit *(n.)* **arrogance**
**ትዕቢት** t'ëbit *(n.)* **conceit**
**ትዕቢተኛ** t'ëbiteňa *(adj.)* **arrogant**
**ተንበልባሊ** tebnbelbali *(n.)* **streamer**
**ተጨበጠ** tecebet'e *(v.)* **cringe**
**ተጨበጠ** teĉebete *(v.)* **shrink**
**ተጨምደደ** teĉemdede *(v.)* **shrivel**
**ተጨናፈረ** teĉenafere *(v.)* **ramify**
**ተጨናነቐ** teĉenaneqe *(v.t. )* **fret**
**ተጨፍለቐ** techefleqhe *(v.)* **squish**
**ተጨነቐ** techeneqe *(v.t. )* **stress**
**ተጨነቐ** techeneqe *(v.)* **worry**
**ተጨቓጨቒ** techeqhachaqhi *(n.)* **squabble**
**ተደጋጋሚ ምውቃዕ ልቢ** tedagagami mwqae lbi *(v.)* **palpitate**
**ተዳወበ** tedawebe *(v.)* **abut**
**ተደጋጋሚ** tedegagami *(adj.)* **continual**
**ተደጋጋሚ** tedegagami *(adj.)* **frequent**

ተደጋጋሚ tedegagami *(adj.)* **insistent**
ተደገመ tedegeme *(v.)* **recur**
ተደጐለ tedegole *(v.)* **huddle**
ተደግሰ tedegse *(v.)* **relapse**
ተደላያይ tedelayay *(adj.)* **traceable**
ተደላዪ tedelayi *(adj.)* **desirable**
ተደማፂ tedemaxi *(n.)* **consonant**
ተደመሮ tedemero *(n.)* **plus**
ተደናበረ tedenabere *(v.)* **bumble**
ተደናጋጽነት tedenagaxnet *(n.)* **empathy**
ተደናገረ tedenagere *(v.)* **perplex**
ተደቕደቐ tedeqdeqe *(v.)* **plunge**
ተደራቢ tederabi *(n.)* **lagging**
ተደራቢ tederabi *(n.)* **lining**
ተደርዓመ tederame *(v.)* **collapse**
ተደራራቢ tederarabi *(n.)* **spate**
ተደርባዪ tederbayi *(adj.)* **disposable**
ተደሰተ tedesete *(v.)* **revel**
ተዓጻጻፊ teëaxaxafi *(adj.)* **pliable**
ተዓጻፊ teëaxaxafi *(adj.)* **pliant**
ቴስዓ tees'ä *(adj. & n.)* **ninety**
ተፍኦ tef'a *(n.)* **spit**
ተፋሕሰ tefaḥse *(v.)* **writhe**
ተፋረየ tefareye *(v.)* **reproduce**
ተፍአ tef'e *(v.)* **belch**
ተፈዳዳዪ tefedadayi *(adj.)* **reciprocal**
ተፈደረ tefeder *(v.)* **federate**
ተፈላለየ tefelaleye *(v.)* **differ**
ተፈላለየ tefelaleye *(v.)* **disagree**
ተፈላሳፊ tefelasafi *(n.)* **philosopher**
ተፈላጥነት tefelatnet *(n.)* **repute**
ተፈላጥነት tefelaṫnet *(n.)* **fame**
ተፈላጥነት tefelaṫnet *(n.)* **publicity**
ተፈንጨሐ tefenĉeĥe *(v.)* **gloat**
ተፈንጨለ tefen'chele *(v.)* **secede**
ተፈንጠረ tefentere *(v.)* **recoil**
ተፈንጠረ tefenṫere *(v.)* **snap**
ተፈቃሪ tefeqari *(adj.)* **lovely**
ተፈራረቐ teferareqe *(v.t.)* **alternate**
ተፈታታኒ ሰብ tefetatani seb *(n.)* **tempter**
ተፈታተነ tefetatene *(v.)* **lure**
ተፈታዊ tefetawi *(adj.)* **amiable**
ተፈታዊ tefetawi *(adj.)* **favourite**
ተፈታዊ tefetawi *(adj.)* **popular**
ተፈታዊ tefetawi *(adj.)* **prepossessing**
ተፈታዊ ምግባር tefetawi mgbar *(v.)* **popularize**
ተፈታዊ tefetawi *(adj.)* **adorable**
ተፈታውነት tefetawnet *(n.)* **popularity**
ተፈጥሮኣዊኛ tefeṫro'awegna *(n.)* **naturalist**
ተፈጥሮኣዊ tefeṫro'awi *(adj.)* **natural**
ተፈጥሮነት tefeṫroneet *(n.)* **naturism**
ተፈፃምነት ዘለዎ tefexamnet zelewo *(adj.)* **applicable**
ተፈቃሪ tefqari *(adj.)* **lovable**
ተፍታትሐ teftaṫhe *(v.)* **relax**
ተፈታዊ teftawi *(adj.)* **likeable**
ተፈጥሮ tefṫro *(n.)* **nature**
ተጋጨወ tegaccewe *(v.)* **crash**
ተጋጫዊ/ስግንጢራዊ tegachawi sgintrawi *(adj.)* **paradoxical**
ተጋጨወ tegachewe *(v.)* **collide**
ተጋዳላይ tegadalay *(n.)* **fighter**
ተጋደደ tegadede *(v.)* **deteriorate**
ተጋገየ tegageye *(v.)* **err**
ተጋሕተነ tegahtene *(v.)* **bestride**
ተጉዕዘ tegaizu *(n. )* **traveller**
ተጋሳያይ tegasayay *(n.)* **rapist**
ተጋተረ tegatere *(v.)* **confront**

**ተጋጠመ** tegat'me ***(v.)*** **clash**
**ተጋወረ** tegawere ***(v.)*** **adjoin**
**ተጋውሐ** tegawĥe ***(v.)*** **resonate**
**ተግባር** tegbar ***(n.)*** **function**
**ተግባር** tegbar ***(n.)*** **practice**
**ተግባር** tegbar ***(n.)*** **action**
**ተግባራዊ** tegbarawi ***(adj.)*** **functional**
**ተገባበረ** tegebabere ***(v.)*** **interact**
**ተገብአ** tegeb'e ***(v. t.)*** **deserve**
**ተገዳሚ** tegedami ***(adj.)*** **transverse**
**ተገዳር ሓረስታይ** tegedar ḥarestay ***(n.)*** **hawk**
**ተገዳሲ** tegedasi ***(adj.)*** **solicitous**
**ተገልበጠ** tegelbeẗe ***(v.)*** **flip**
**ተገምበወ** tegembewe ***(v.)*** **recline**
**ተገምሰሰ** tegemsese ***(n.)*** **repose**
**ተገናዛይ** tegenazay ***(n.)*** **sadist**
**ተገናዛይነት** tegenazaynet ***(n. )*** **sadism**
**ተገንዘበ** tegenzebe ***(v.)*** **realize**
**ተገንዘበ** tegenzebe ***(v.)*** **appreciate**
**ተገጣጠመ** tegetateme ***(v.)*** **coincide**
**ተገጣጠመ** tegeẗaẗeme ***(v.)*** **interlock**
**ተገየፀ** tegeyetsd ***(v.)*** **simper**
**ተጉ ምባል** tegiue mbal ***(v.)*** **pop**
**ተጓዳኢ** tegoda'i ***(adj. )*** **harmful**
**ተጎድአ** tegod'e ***(v.)*** **strain**
**ተጎላቲ** tegolati ***(n.)*** **monopolist**
**ተጎንባሲ** tegonbasi ***(adj.)*** **servile**
**ተጎንባስነት** tegonbasnet ***(n.)*** **servility**
**ተጎንበሰ** tegonbese ***(v.)*** **stoop**
**ተግሳፅ** tegsats ***(n.)*** **reproof**
**ትዕግስቲ** tegsti ***(n.)*** **patience**
**ትዕግስቲ** t'egsti ***(n.)*** **tolerance**
**ትዕግስቲ** t'ëgsti ***(n.)*** **solitaire**
**ትዕግስቲ** t'egsti ***(n.)*** **toleration**
**ተጉመፅመፀ** tegume-tse-me-tse ***(v.)*** **gargle**
**ተጓዕዘ** tegwa'ëze ***(v.)*** **walk**
**ተጓንፎ** tegwanefo ***(n.)*** **coincidence**
**ተጓነፀ** tegwanetse ***(v.)*** **dash**
**ተጓሳጣይ** tegwasaẗay ***(n.)*** **boxer**
**ተጓያቒ** tegwayaqi ***(adj.)*** **quarrelsome**
**ተጓየየ** tegwayeye ***(v.)*** **race**
**ተጓየየ** tegwayeye ***(v.)*** **rush**
**ተሓባባሪ** teḧababari ***(adj.)*** **confederate**
**ተሓባበረ** tehababere ***(v.)*** **collaborate**
**ተሓብአ** teḧab'e ***(v.)*** **cower**
**ተሓበበረ** tehabere ***(v.)*** **cooperate**
**ተሃዳናይ** tehadanay ***(n.)*** **quarry**
**ተሃዳኒ** tehadani ***(n.)*** **prey**
**ተሃድሶ** tehadso ***(n.)*** **reclamation**
**ተሃድሶ** tehadso ***(n.)*** **renaissance**
**ተሓጎሰ** teĥagose ***(v.)*** **rejoice**
**ተሓላፊ** tehalafi ***(adj.)*** **passable**
**ተሓላቒ** teḧalaq̈i ***(n.)*** **advocate**
**ተሓለቀ** teḧaleq̈e ***(v.)*** **advocate**
**ተሓንበበ** teḧanbebe ***(adj.)*** **swish**
**ተሓንጋጢ መሳርሒ** teḧangati mesarḧi ***(n.)*** **backpack**
**ተሓንጋጢ ሳንጣ** teḧangati santa ***(n.)*** **rucksack**
**ተሃንቀወ** tehanqewe ***(v. t)*** **crave**
**ተሃቀወ** tehaqewe ***(v.)*** **covet**
**ተሓሰበ** teha'sebe ***(v.)*** **constitute**
**ተሓሰመ** teĥaseme ***(v.)*** **rebuff**
**ተሓሰመ** teĥaseme ***(v.)*** **repudiate**
**ተሓታታይ አይኮነን በለ** teĥatatay aykonen bele ***(v.)*** **exonerate**
**ተሓታቲ** tehatati ***(adj.)*** **liable**
**ተሓታቲ** teĥatati ***(adj.)*** **responsible**
**ተሓታቲ** teḧatati ***(adj.)*** **accountable**

ተሓታቲ teȟatati *(adj.)* **amenable**
ተሓታትነት tehatatnet *(n.)* **liability**
ተሓዋወሰ teȟawawese *(v.)* **mingle**
ተሃወኸ tehaweḱe *(v.)* **hasten**
ተሓዝ ገንዘብ teȟaz genzeb *(n.)* **bursar**
ተሓዚ ገንዘብ teĥazi genzeb *(n.)* **purser**
ተሓዚ መዝገብ tehazi mezgeb *(n. )* **registrar**
ተሓዚ ትሕጃ tehazi thja *(n.)* **pawnbroker**
ተኸራኸረ teherakere *(v.)* **contend**
ተኸታታሊ tehe'tata'li *(adj.)* **consecutive**
ትሕተ ምድራዊ ሓዲድ teȟte mdrawi ȟadid *(n.)* **subway**
ትሕትና tehtena *(n.)* **humility**
ትሑት tehut *(adj. )* **humble**
ተጃህረ tejahre *(v.)* **bluff**
ተጃህረ tejahre *(v.)* **swank**
ተጀሃሪ teĵehari *(v.)* **brag**
ኣኽእሎ teka'elo *(n.)* **finesse**
ተኻፋሊ ሚስጢር tekafali mistir *(adj.)* **privy**
ተካል tekal *(adj.)* **dreary**
ተኻረየ teḱareye *(v.t)* **hire**
ተካትዐ tekat'ë *(v. t.)* **debate**
ተክአ tek'e *(v.)* **replace**
ተክአ tek'e *(v.)* **supersede**
ተክአ tek'e *(v.)* **supplant**
ተቀባሊ tekebali *(n.)* **recipient**
ተኽባሲ tekebasi *(adj.)* **reversible**
ተኸደነ tekedene *(v.)* **dress**
ተኸድነ tekedene *(v.)* **wear**
ተከአ teke'e *(v.)* **replenish**
ተኸፋሊ tekefali *(n. )* **payable**
ተኸላኻላይ teḱelaḱalay *(adj.)* **protective**
ተኸላኸለ tekelakele *(v.)* **defend**
ተኽእሎ tek'elo *(n.)* **possibility**
ተኽምበለ tekembele *(v.)* **tumble**
ተኸናኸነ tekenakene *(v.)* **treat**
ተኸሳሲ tekesasi *(n.)* **defendant**
ተኸሳሲ tekesasi *(n.)* **respondent**
ተኸታሊ teketali *(n.)* **follower**
ተኸታሊ teketali *(n. )* **sequel**
ተኸታታሊ teketatali *(adj.)* **serial**
ተኸታተለ teketatele *(v.t. )* **trace**
ተኸታተለ teḱetatele *(v.)* **attend**
ተከታቲሉ teketatilu *(n.)* **trail**
ተኸተለ teketele *(v.)* **pursue**
ተኸወለ tekewele *(v.)* **disappear**
ተኻራዪ tekharayi *(n.)* **lessee**
ተኻራዪ ገዛ tekharayi geza *(n.)* **lodger**
ተኸልከለ tekhelkele *(v.)* **stymie**
ተኽእሎ tekh'elo *(adj.)* **subjunctive**
ተኸታታሊ tekhetatali *(adj.)* **successive**
ተኾርመየ tekhormeye *(v.i. )* **squat**
ተኳሳሒ tekhuasahi *(adj.)* **inflammatory**
ተኸላኸለ teḱlaḱele *(v.)* **protect**
ተክሊ tekli *(n.)* **tree**
ተኽሊ teḱli *(n. )* **plant**
ተኽሊ ወይኒ teḱli weyni *(n. )* **vine**
ተኽሊ ዝተተኽለሉ ቦታ teḱli zteteḱlelu bota *(n. )* **plantation**
ተኽልታት tekltat *(n.)* **flora**
ተኾላተፈ tekolatefe *(v.)* **slur**
ተቆናጅዩ tekonajyu *(v.)* **titivate**
ተኮናነ tekonani *(adj.)* **damnable**
ተኾናታሪ tekonatari *(n.)* **contractor**
ተኾነውን tekonewen *(conj.)* **whereas**
ተኾርመየ tekormeye *(v.)* **crouch**
ተኾርመየ tekormeye *(v.)* **slouch**

ተኮሰ tekose *(v.)* **shoot**
ተኹላ tekula *(n. )* **wolf**
ተኹሲ tekusi *(n.)* **shooting**
ተኹሲ ቁረፀ teḱusi qurexe *(n.)* **ceasefire**
ተኳዕነነ tekwa'ënene *(v.)* **swagger**
ተኳተኸ teḱwatoḱe *(v.)* **nudge**
ተላባዒ telabaei *(n. )* **pestilence**
ተላዕለ tela'ële *(v.)* **arise**
ተላጋቢ telagabi *(adj.)* **catching**
ተላጋቢ telagabi *(adj.)* **contagious**
ተላመደ telamede *(v.)* **practise**
ተላዘበ telazebe *(v.)* **negotiate**
ተለኣኣኻይ tele'a'akay *(n.)* **courier**
ቴሌግራም telegaram *(n. )* **telegram**
ቴሌግራፍ telegaraph *(n.)* **telegraph**
ተለማመደ telemamede *(v.)* **rehearse**
ተለቅሐ teleqḧe *(v.)* **borrow**
ተለጠፈ teletefe' *(v.)* **cling**
ቴሌቪዥን televizion *(n.)* **television**
ተለዋጣይ telewaẗay *(adj.)* **mutable**
ተለዋጢ telewaẗi *(v.)* **mutative**
ተለዋዋጣይ telewawaẗay *(adj.)* **fickle**
ተለዋዋጠ telewawaẗi *(v.)* **fluctuate**
ተለዋወጠ telewaweẗe *(v. t)* **exchange**
ተለዋወጠ telewaweẗe *(v.)* **interchange**
ተለዋይ ጨንገር ዊሊው teleway chenger wiliw *(n. )* **wicker**
ተለወጠ teleweẗe *(v.)* **mutate**
ተለውየ telewye *(v.)* **shear**
ተልእኾ tel'ḱo *(n. )* **mission**
ተልመዴን telmedeen *(n.)* **amateur**
ተልመዴን telmedeen *(n.)* **apprentice**
ተልመዴናዊ telmedeenawi *(adj.)* **amateurish**
ተማእዛዚ tema'ezazi *(adj.)* **biddable**
ተማጎተ temagote *(v.)* **litigate**
ተማጎተ temagote *(v.)* **argue**
ተማጓታይ temagwatay *(n.)* **litigant**
ተማሓላለፊ temaḧalalefi *(adj.)* **communicable**
ተማሃራይ ዩኒቨርሲቲ ነበር temaharay yuniversiti neber *(n.)* **alumnus**
ተማህለለ temahlele *(v.)* **supplicate**
ተማሕፀነ temahtsene *(v.)* **solicit**
ተማሕፀነ temahtzene *(v.t. )* **implore**
ተማሕፀነ temaĥxene *(v.)* **entreat**
ተማሕፀነ temaḧxene *(v.t.)* **appeal**
ተማራኺሲ temaraḱwasi *(adj.)* **interdependent**
ተማስሎ temaslo *(n.)* **affinity**
ተማዛዘንነት temazazannet *(n.)* **equilibrium**
ተምበርካኺ temberkaki *(n.)* **defeatist**
ተምበርከኸ temberkeḱe *(v.)* **capitulate**
ተመጋቢ temegabi *(n.)* **diner**
ተመጋቢ temegabi *(n.)* **feeder**
ተመገበ temegebe *(v.)* **dine**
ተመሓላለፊ temehalalafi *(adj.)* **transferable**
ተመሃራይ temeharay *(n. )* **pupil**
ተመሃራይ temeharay *(n. )* **student**
ተመካቲ temekati *(adj.)* **defensible**
ትምክሕቲ temekeheti *(n.)* **chauvinism**
ተመላላሲ temelalasi *(adj.)* **recurrent**
ተመላለሰ temelalese *(v.)* **retort**
ተመላሲ temelasi *(adj.)* **resilient**

ተመሊስካ ምስትንታን temeliska mstntan *(n. )* **retrospect**
ተመልካቲ temelkati *(n.)* **toreador**
ተመልካቲ temelkati *(n.)* **bystander**
ተመልከተ temelkete *(v.)* **revere**
ተመልከተ temelkete *(v.)* **concern**
ተመልከተ temelkete *(v.)* **behold**
ተመልሰ temelse *(v.)* **return**
ተመልሰ temelse *(v.)* **revert**
ተመን temen *(n.)* **snake**
ተመነየ temeneye *(v.)* **aspire**
ተመንወ temenwe *(n.)* **pall**
ተመቃላይ temeqalay *(n.)* **numerator**
ተመርዓወ temer'äwe *(v.)* **marry**
ተመርማሪ temermari *(n.)* **examinee**
ተመሳሳሊ temesasali *(adj.)* **alike**
ተመሳሳሊ temesasali *(adj.)* **cognate**
ተመሳሳሊ temesasali *(n.)* **lookalike**
ተመሳሳሊ temesasali *(adj.)* **same**
ተመሳሳሊ temesasali *(adj.)* **similar**
ተመሳሳሊ temesasali *(adj.)* **synonymous**
ተመሳሳሊ temesasali *(adj.)* **analogous**
ተመሳሳሊ temesasali *(adv. )* **unexceptional**
ተመሳሳሊ temesasali *(adj.)* **uniform**
ተመሳሳሊነት temesasalinet *(n.)* **likeness**
ተመሳሳሊነት temesasalinet *(n.)* **similarity**
ተመሳሳልነት temesasalnet *(n.)* **analogy**
ተመሳሰለ temesasele *(v.)* **liken**
ተመሻጠረ temeshatere *(v.)* **conspire**
ተመሻጠረ temesha'tere *(v.)* **connive**
ተመስጦ temesto *(n.)* **impression**
ተመጣጣኒ temetatani *(adj.)* **proportional**
ተመጣጣኒ temetatani *(adj.)* **proportionate**
ተመጣጣኒ temetatani *(adj.)* **tantamount**
ተመጣጣሪ temeẗaẗari *(adj.)* **ambitious**
ተመጣጢ temetati *(adj.)* **elastic**
ተመፃደቂ temetsadaqi *(adj.)* **sanctimonious**
ተመዛበለ temezabele *(v.)* **deform**
ተመዛዛይ temezazay *(n.)* **drawer**
ተመዛዚ ከብሒ temezazi kebḧi *(n.)* **commode**
ተመዝገበ temezgebe *(v.)* **enrol**
ተመሓላለፊ temhalallefi *(adj.)* **infectious**
ተምሃረ temhare *(v.)* **learn**
ተምሃሪ temhari *(n. )* **learner**
ተምሃሪ ዩኑቨርስቲ temhari yuniversty *(n.)* **undergraduate**
ተሞርከሰ temorkese *(v.)* **depend**
ተሞርከሰ temorkese *(v.)* **rely**
ተዉህቦ twhbo *(n.)* **flair**
ተሰራጨወ tsrachew *(v.)* **circulate**
ቱቦ tubo *(n.)* **duct**
ቱቦ tubo *(n.)* **pipe**
ቱቦ tubo *(n. )* **tube**
ቱቦ ፍሳስ tubo fsas *(n.)* **sewer**
ቱቦ ማይ tubo may *(n. )* **hose**
ቱፋሕ tufaḧ *(n.)* **apple**
ትእምርተ እግሪ t'emrete egri *(adj.)* **subscript**
ትእምርትነት t'emrtnet *(n.)* **symbolism**
ተምሳል temsal *(n. )* **semblance**
ተምሳሌት temsaleet *(n.)* **metaphor**
ተምሳጥ temsaẗ *(n.)* **awe**

ተናዳዲ tenadadi ***(n.)*** **temper**
ተናዳዲ tenadadi ***(adj.)*** **touchy**
ተናእደ tena'ede ***(v.)*** **acclaim**
ተናፈረ tenafere ***(v.)*** **flit**
ተናኸፈ ንምዕራይ tenakefe nm'eray ***(v.)*** **tinker**
ተናሳሒ tenasaĥi ***(adj.)*** **repentant**
ተናሳሒ tenasahi ***(adj.)*** **penitent**
ተናስሐ tenaŝhe ***(v.)*** **repent**
ተናጠረ tenaẗere ***(v.)*** **splatter**
ተናዘዘ tenazeze ***(v.)*** **avow**
ተናዘዘ tenazeze ***(v.)*** **confess**
ተናዘዘ tenazeze ***(v.)*** **profess**
ተነባቢ tenbabi ***(adj.)*** **legible**
ተንበልበለ tenbelbele ***(v.)*** **flaunt**
ተንበርከኸ tenberkeke ***(v.)*** **kneel**
ተንበየ tenbeye ***(v.)*** **envisage**
ተንበየ tenbeye ***(v.t)*** **forecast**
ተንበየ tenbeye ***(v.)*** **foresee**
ተንበየ tenbeye ***(v.)*** **foretell**
ተንበየ tenbeye ***(v.)*** **presage**
ተንደልሃፀ tendelhatse ***(v.)*** **slip**
ተነባዪ tenebayi ***(n.)*** **forerunner**
ተነበየ tenebeye ***(v.)*** **predict**
ተነበየ tenebeye ***(v.)*** **prophesy**
ተነጫናጪ tenecha na chi ***(adj.)*** **grumpy**
ተነፋሒት ጀልባ tenefaĥit jelba ***(n.)*** **raft**
ተነቃፊ teneqaf ***(adj.)*** **vulnerable**
ተነቃፊ teneqafi ***(adj.)*** **delicate**
ተነቃፊነት teneqafinet ***(n.)*** **delicacy**
ተንቀሳቃሲ ስልኪ teneqesaqasi seliki ***(n.)*** **cell phone**
ተነቖተ teneqhte ***(v.)*** **swoop**
ተነፃሊ tenetsali ***(n.)*** **separatist**
ተነውነወ tenewnewe ***(v.)*** **joggle**
ተነጻጻሪ tenexaxeri ***(adj.)*** **comparative**

ተነዝሐ tenezhe ***(v.)*** **pervade**
ተነዝነዘ tenezneze ***(v.)*** **vibrate**
ተንፈኽፈኸ tenfekfeke ***(v.)*** **simmer**
ተንጎድጊዱ tengedagidu ***(v.)*** **teeter**
ተንከባለለ tenkebalele ***(v.i. )*** **roll**
ተንኮል tenkol ***(n.)*** **malice**
ተንኮል tenkol ***(n.)*** **mischief**
ተንኮል tenkol ***(n.)*** **ploy**
ተንኮል tenkol ***(n.)*** **trickery**
ተንኮለኛ tenkolegna ***(adj.)*** **disingenuous**
ተንኮለኛ tenkolegna ***(adj.)*** **malicious**
ተንኮለኛ tenkolegna ***(adj.)*** **mischievous**
ተንኮለኛ tenkolenya ***(n.)*** **catty**
ተንኮሰ tenkose ***(v.)*** **provoke**
ተንኰል tenkwal ***(n. )*** **guile**
ተንቀሳቃሲ tenqesaqasi ***(n. )*** **locomotive**
ተንቀሳቃሲ tenqesaqasi ***(adj.)*** **mobile**
ተንቀሳቃሲ tenqesaqasi ***(adj.)*** **movable**
ተንቀሳቃሲ tenqesaqasi ***(adj.)*** **moving**
ተንቀሳቃሲ tenqesaqasi ***(adj.)*** **roving**
ተንቀሳቃስነት tenqesaqasnet ***(n.)*** **mobility**
ተንቀሳቀሰ tenqesaqese ***(v.)*** **move**
ተንቀጥቀጠ tenqetqete ***(v.)*** **quake**
ተንሳፋፊ tensafafi ***(adj.)*** **buoyant**
ተንሳፈፈ tensafefe ***(v.)*** **float**
ተንሳተተ tensatete ***(v.)*** **scud**
ተንስአ tense'e ***(v.)*** **rise**
ጥንሲ ẗensi ***(n.)*** **gestation**
ተንታኒ tentani ***(n.)*** **analyst**
ተንጠብጢቡ tentebtibu ***(v.)*** **trickle**
ተንጠልጠለ tenṭelṭele ***(v.i. )*** **hang**
ተንተነ tentene ***(v.)*** **analyse**

ተንቲኑ tentu *(v.)* **parse**
ተቃብሐ teqabhe *(v.)* **clinch**
ተቓዳዊ teq̈adawi *(adj.)* **compatible**
ተቓዳዊ teq̈adawi *(adj.)* **concurrent**
ተቓላዕነት teqala'enet *(n.)* **subjection**
ተቓላዒት teqala'ït *(n.)* **debutante**
ተቓላሲ teq̈alasi *(n. )* **wrestler**
ተቓለሰ teq̈alese *(v.)* **wrestle**
ተቃልዖ teqal'ö *(n.)* **debut**
ተቃፃዊ teqatsawi *(a. )* **shadow**
ተቓዋሚ teqawami *(n.)* **dissident**
ተቃዋሚ teqawami *(adj.)* **resistant**
ተቓዋምነት teq̈awamnet *(n. )* **protestation**
ተቓወመ teqaweme *(v.)* **demur**
ተቓወመ teqaweme *(v.)* **disapprove**
ተቃወመ teqaweme *(v.)* **dissent**
ተቃወመ teqaweme *(v.)* **militate**
ተቃወመ teqaweme *(v.)* **remonstrate**
ተቓወመ teqaweme *(v.)* **resist**
ተቓዉሞ teqawmo *(n.)* **disapproval**
ተቓውሞ teqawmo *(n.)* **exception**
ተቃውሞ teqawmo *(n.)* **resistance**
ተቓውሞ teq̈awmo *(n.)* **protest**
ተቛያቕት ሰበይቲ teqayaqit sebeyti *(n.)* **termagant**
ተቐባላይ teq̈ebalay *(n.)* **addressee**
ተቀባሊ teqebali *(n.)* **receiver**
ተቀባሊ teqebali *(adj.)* **receptive**
ተቀባሊ ጋሻ teqebali gaša *(n.)* **receptionist**
ተቀባሊት ቅርሺ teqebalit qereshi *(n.)* **cashier**
ተቐባልነት ዘለዎ teq̈ebalnet zelewo *(adj.)* **acceptable**
ተቐበለ teqebele *(v.)* **get**
ተቀበለ teqebele *(v.)* **receive**
ተቐበለ teq̈ebele *(v.)* **approve**
ተቐበለ teq̈ebele *(v.)* **accept**
ተቐዳደመ teq̈edademe *(v.)* **compete**
ተቐልቀለ teqelqele *(v.)* **emerge**
ተቐጠበ teq̈eṫebe *(v.)* **abstain**
ተቐያያራይ teqeyayaray *(adj.)* **flexible**
ተቐያያሪ teq̈eyayari *(adj.)* **variable**
ተቐያያሪ ሕብርታት teq̈eyayari ḧbrtat *(n.)* **kaleidoscope**
ተቓለሰ teqhalese *(v.)* **struggle**
ተቓጻዊ teqhatsawi *(n.)* **stalker**
ተቐባልነት ዘይብሉ teqhbalnet zeyblu *(adj.)* **immoderate**
ተቐባልነት ዘይብሉ teqhebalnet zeyblu *(adj.)* **inexcusable**
ተቅማጥ teqmat *(n.)* **dysentery**
ተቆጠበ teqotebe *(v.t.)* **refrain**
ተቆፃፃሪ teqotsatsari *(n.)* **regulator**
ተቖፃፃሪ teqoxaxari *(n.)* **controller**
ተቆፃፃሪ teqoxaxari *(adj.)* **monitory**
ተቖፃፃራይ teqoxaxari *(n.)* **supervisor**
ተቖፃፀረ teqoxaxere *(v. t)* **curb**
ተቖፃፃረ teqoxaxere *(v.)* **supervise**
ተቛየቔ teq̈wayeq̈we *(v.)* **bicker**
ተቜጸጸሪ teq̈wetsatsari *(n.)* **inspector**
ተራ tera *(adj.)* **mediocre**
ተራ tera *(adj.)* **prosaic**
ተራ tera *(n.)* **rota**
ተራ tera *(adj.)* **banal**
ተራብሐ terabḧe *(v.)* **proliferate**
ተራድኣዊ terad'awi *(adj.)* **cooperative**
ተራእየ tera'èye *(v.)* **appear**
ተራኺቢ terakabi *(adj.)* **confluent**
ተራኸበ terakebe *(v.)* **liaise**
ተራቓቓይ teraqaqay *(n. )* **pedant**
ተጠርጣሪ teraṫari *(n)* **suspect**

**ተርባይን** terbayn ***(n. )*** **turbine**
**ተርብዐ** terb'ë ***(v.)*** **lacerate**
**ተርበዐ** terbe'ë ***(v.)*** **rip**
**ተረበሸ** terebeše ***(v.)*** **rattle**
**ተረዳኢ** teredaei ***(adj.)*** **perceptive**
**ተረድአ** tered'e ***(v.)*** **grasp**
**ተረድአ** tered'e ***(v.)*** **comprehend**
**ተረድአ** tered'e ***(v. t)*** **conceive**
**ተረድአ** tered'e ***(v.)*** **apprehend**
**ተረደአ** teredea' ***(v.)*** **construe**
**ተረድአ** terede'e ***(v.t. )*** **understand**
**ተረፍ** teref ***(n.)*** **remainder**
**ተረፍ ዕጻድ** teref ëtsad ***(n.)*** **stubble**
**ተረፍ መረፍ ኣራረየ** teref meref arareye ***(v.)*** **scavenge**
**ተረፍ** teref ***(n.)*** **balance**
**ተረፈ** terefe ***(v.)*** **fail**
**ተረፍ** terefe ***(n. )*** **surplus**
**ተረፍመረፍ** terefmeref ***(n.)*** **remnant**
**ተረፍመረፍ** terefmeref ***(n. )*** **scrap**
**ተርጋጊሱ** teregagisu ***(v.)*** **trample**
**ተረጎመ** teregome ***(v.)*** **interpret**
**ተረካቢ ይዕደዮ** terekabi y'edeyo ***(n.)*** **scapegoat**
**ተረኸ** tereke ***(v.)*** **recount**
**ተረቅራቂ ሉሕ** tereqraqi luḧ ***(n.)*** **batten**
**ፀረር ዝብል** terer zbl ***(adj.)*** **runny**
**ተርእዮ** ter'eyo ***(n.)*** **scenario**
**ተርጎመ** tergome ***(v.)*** **translate**
**ተሪር** terir ***(adj.)*** **crisp**
**ተሪር** terir ***(adj.)*** **drastic**
**ተሪር** terir ***(adj.)*** **firm**
**ተሪር** terir ***(adj. )*** **hard**
**ተሪር** terir ***(adj.)*** **incisive**
**ተሪር** terir ***(adj.)*** **rigid**
**ተሪር** terir ***(adj.)*** **rigorous**
**ተሪር** terir ***(adj.)*** **solid**
**ተሪር** terir ***(adj.)*** **stiff**
**ተሪር** terir ***(adj.)*** **stringent**
**ተሪር** terir ***(adj.)*** **sturdy**
**ተሪር ክቡር እምኒ** terir kbur 'èmni ***(n.)*** **agate**
**ተሪር ሽፋን** terir shfan ***(n.)*** **hardback**
**ተሪር** terir ***(adj.)*** **adamant**
**ተሪር** terir ***(adj.)*** **scathing**
**ተርከሰ** terkese ***(v.)*** **moisten**
**ጎልፎ** termin ***(n.)*** **jumper**
**ተሮግሮግ በለ** terogrog bele ***(v.)*** **crackle**
**ተርታ** terta ***(n.)*** **row**
**ተርታ** terta ***(n.)*** **sequence**
**ተርታ** terta ***(n.)*** **series**
**ተርታዊ** tertawi ***(adj.)*** **sequential**
**ተርተረ** tertere ***(v.t. )*** **slit**
**ተሳፋፋይ** tesafafay ***(adj.)*** **navigable**
**ተሳሕበ** tesaḥbe ***(v.)*** **gravitate**
**ተሳኽዐ** tesak'ë ***(v.)*** **materialize**
**ተሳለየ** tesaleye ***(v.)*** **amble**
**ተሳለየ** tesaleye ***(v.)*** **waddle**
**ተሳናዪ** tesanayi ***(adj.)*** **coherent**
**ተሳነየ** tesaneyei ***(v.)*** **cohere**
**ተሳነየ ተስማዕሞዖም ነበሩ** tesany' tesmaemoom neberu ***(v.)*** **coexist**
**ተሳቀየ** tesaqeye ***(v.)*** **afflict**
**ተሳቀየ** tesaqeye ***(v.)*** **agonize**
**ተሳተፈ** tesatefe ***(v.)*** **indulge**
**ተስሳተፈ** tesatefe ***(v.)*** **participate**
**ተሳትፎ** tesatfo ***(n.)*** **attendance**
**ተሰበረ** tesbere ***(v.t)*** **fracture**
**ተሰብአ** teseb'a ***(v.)*** **personify**
**ተሰባሪ** tesebari ***(adj.)*** **fragile**
**ተሰባሪ** tesebari ***(adj.)*** **brittle**
**ተሰደደ** tesedede ***(v.)*** **emigrate**
**ተሰሓሒቱ ዘይፈልጥ** tesehahitu zeyfelt ***(adj.)*** **infallible**

ተሰካሚ tesekami *(n.)* **carrier**
ተሰልበጢ teselbati *(adj.)* **reflexive**
ተሰልበ teselbe *(v.)* **infatuate**
ተሰልበጠ teselbete *(v.)* **backfire**
ተሰልበጠ teselbete *(v.)* **rebound**
ተሰማዒ tesema'e *(adj.)* **influential**
ተሰማዒነት tesema'enet *(n.)* **influence**
ተሰማምዐ tesemam'e *(v.)* **acquiesce**
ተሰማምዐ tesemam'ë *(v.)* **agree**
ተሰማምዐ tesemam'ë *(v.)* **concur**
ተሰማምዐ tesemam'ë *(v.)* **conform**
ተሰምዖ tesem'ö *(v.)* **feel**
ተሰናበተ tesenabete *(v.)* **resign**
ተሰነፈ tesenefe *(v.)* **succumb**
ተሰቀለ teseqele *(v.)* **mount**
ተሰራሰረ teserasere *(v.)* **cavort**
ተሰርጓጒት tesergwagwit *(n.)* **submarine**
ተስፋ tesfa *(n.)* **prospect**
ተስፋ ኣልቦ tesfa 'albo *(adj.)* **hopeless**
ተስፋ ሃበ tesfa habe *(v. t.)* **cheer**
ተስፋ ዘይብሉ tesfa zeyblu *(adj.)* **forlorn**
ተስፋ ዘይምግባር tesfa zeymgbar *(adj.)* **pessimistic**
ተስፋ ዝህብ tesfa zhb *(adj.)* **prospective**
ተስፋ ዝቆረፀ tesfa zqoretse *(adj.)* **despondent**
ተስፋ ዝወሃቦ tesfa zwehabo *(adj.)* **promising**
ተስፋኣዊ tesfa'awi *(adj.)* **auspicious**
ተስፋሕፈሐ tesfahfehe *(adj.)* **widespread**
ተስፈኛ tesfegna *(adj.)* **sanguine**
ተስፈኛ ተዋሳኢት tesfegna tewasa'it *(n.)* **starlet**
ተሻበነ teshabene *(v.)* **intrigue**
ተስሓቢ tes'ĥabi *(n.)* **reptile**
ትእስሓቢ መኪና teshabi mekina *(n.)* **trailer**
ተሻጋሪ teshagari *(adj.)* **transitive**
ተሻጊሩ teshagiru *(v.)* **traverse**
ተሻራኺ tesharaki *(n. )* **partner**
ተሸገረ teshegere *(v.)* **beset**
ተሸካሚ teshekami *(n.)* **trestle**
ተሸኸለ teshekele *(v.)* **dive**
ተሸከመ teshekeme *(n.)* **bear**
ተሸከመ teshekeme *(v.)* **carry**
ተሸምቀቐ teshemqeqe *(v.)* **wince**
ተሸራሸረ tesherashere *(v.)* **stroll**
ተሽከርካሪ teshkerkari *(v.)* **twirl**
ተሽከርካሪ teshkerkari *(n.)* **wheel**
ተሽከርከረ teshkerkere *(v.)* **swivel**
ተሽከርካሪ teškerkari *(adj.)* **rotary**
ተሽከርካሪ teškerkari *(n.)* **rotor**
ተስማምዐ tesmam'e *(v.)* **stipulate**
ተሰማምዕ tesmam'ë *(v.)* **correspond**
ተሰናዪ መደምደምታ tesnayi medemdemta *(n.)* **syllogism**
ተሰቐየ tesqeye *(v.i. )* **suffer**
ተስተብሃሊ testebhali *(adj.)* **noticeable**
ተጣዕሰ teta'ëse *(n.)* **regret**
ተታኸሰ tetakese *(v.)* **drowse**
ተጣላዓይ tetala'äy *(n.)* **punter**
ተጣላዒ teťala'ï *(n. )* **gambler**
ተጣልዐ teťal'ë *(v.)* **gamble**
ተጣልዐ teťal'ë *(v.)* **bet**
ተጣራጣሪ tetaratari *(adj.)* **dubious**
ተጣርዐ teṭar'ë *(v.)* **grumble**
ተታተየ tetateye *(v.)* **toddle**

**ተተካኢ ሓኪም** teteka'e hakim ***(n.)* locum**
**ተተኮስቲ** tetekosti ***(n.)* ammunition**
**ተጠንቀቕ** teťenqeq̈ ***(v.)* beware**
**ተጠቃሚ** teteqami ***(n.)* user**
**ተጠቐመ** teteqeme ***(v.)* wield**
**ተጠቐመ** teťeqeme ***(v.)* exert**
**ተጠቕመ** teťeq̈me ***(v.)* avail**
**ተጣራጣሪ** teteratari ***(n.)* sceptic**
**ተጣራጣሪ** teteratari ***(adj.)* sceptical**
**ተጠራጣሪ** teťeraťari ***(adj.)* irresolute**
**ተጠራጠረ** teťeraťere ***(v.)* suspect**
**ተጠወየ** teťeweye ***(v.)* swerve**
**ተትሓሓዚ ተኽሊ** tethahazi tekli ***(n.)* wisteria**
**ተጻዋታይ ቫየሊን** tetsawatay vayelin ***(n. )* violinist**
**ተጽጊዑ ሓልፍመስመር** tetsegiuzhalf mesmer ***(n.)* tangent**
**ተፀላኢ** tetsela'i ***(adj.)* disagreeable**
**ተፀንበረ** tetsenbere ***(v.)* socialize**
**ተፀናተወ** tetzenatewe ***(v.)* lurk**
**ተፀወገ** tetzewege ***(v.i)* frown**
**ተዋዳዳሪ** tewadadari ***(n.)* competitor**
**ተዋጋኢ** tewagaei ***(n)* combatant**
**ተዋገየ** tewageye ***(n.)* bargain**
**ተዋገየ** tewageye ***(v.)* haggle**
**ተዋሃደ** tewahade ***(v.)* assimilate**
**ተዋሓሰ** tewaḥase ***(v.t)* guarantee**
**ተዋሓሰ** tewaḥase ***(v.)* vouch**
**ተዋላዋሊ** tewalawali ***(adj.)* ambivalent**
**ተዋሳኢ** tewasa'i ***(n.)* actor**
**ተዋሳኢት** tewasa'it ***(a.)* actress**
**ተዋስኦ** tewas'o ***(n.)* acting**
**ተዋስኦ** tewas'o ***(n.)* drama**
**ተወዛወዘ** tewazaweze ***(v.)* swing**
**ተዋዛይ** tewazay ***(n.)* jester**
**ተዋዛዪ** tewazayi ***(n.)* comedian**
**ተዋዛዪ** tewazayi ***(adj.)* comic**
**ተዋዛዪ** tewazayi ***(adj.)* jocose**
**ተዋዛዪ** tewazayi ***(v.t. )* jocular**
**ተዋዘየ** tewazeye ***(n.)* joker**
**ተዋዘየ** tewazeye ***(n.)* banter**
**ተወዳዳራይ** tewedadaray ***(n.)* rival**
**ተወዳዳሪ** te'we'dada'rei ***(n.)* contestant**
**ተወዳደረ** tewedadere ***(v. t)* emulate**
**ተወዳደረ** tewedadere ***(v.)* vie**
**ተወፋራይ** tewefaray ***(n. )* serf**
**ተወሃሃበ** tewehahabe ***(v.)* reciprocate**
**ተወካሊ** tewekali ***(adj.)* representative**
**ተወካልነት** tewekalnet ***(n.)* representation**
**ተወከለ** tewekele ***(v.)* represent**
**ተወላዲ** teweladi ***(n.)* descendant**
**ተወላዲ** teweladi ***(adj.)* indigenous**
**ተወላዒ** tewela'ï ***(adj.)* fluorescent**
**ተወላወለ** tewelawele ***(v.)* boggle**
**ተወልደ** tewelde ***(adj.)* born**
**ተወለዐ** tewele'ë ***(v.)* kindle**
**ተወንጫፊ** tewenčafi ***(n. )* missile**
**ተወንጨፈ** tewenĉefe ***(v.)* rifle**
**ተወንጨፈ** tewenchfe ***(v.)* whirl**
**ተወቃሲ** teweqasi ***(adj.)* culpable**
**ተወራዛዪ** tewerazayi ***(adj.)* sententious**
**ተወራዛይነት** tewerazaynet ***(n.)* sophism**
**ተወርሰ** tewerese ***(v.)* devolve**
**ተወርሶኣዊ** tewerso'awi ***(adj. )* hereditary**
**ተወሳኺይ** tewesakay ***(n.)* additive**
**ተወሳከ-ግሲ** tewesakegsi ***(n.)* adverb**

**ተወሳኺ** tewesakhi ***(adj.)*** **subsidiary**
**ተወሳኺ** tewesakhi ***(adj.)*** **supplementary**
**ተወሳኺ** tewesaki ***(n.)*** **adjunct**
**ተወሳኺ** tewesaki ***(adj.)*** **extra**
**ተወሳኺ** tewesaḱi ***(adj.)*** **additional**
**ተወሳኺ** tewesaḱi ***(n.)*** **amplification**
**ተወሳወሰ** tewesawese ***(v.)*** **limber**
**ተወታፊ ፈውሲ** tewetafi fewsi ***(n.)*** **suppository**
**ተወጣሓይ** tewetaĥay ***(n. )*** **rider**
**ተወጣሪ** tewetari ***(adj.)*** **tensile**
**ተወጥሐ** tewet̓ĥe ***(v.)*** **ride**
**ተወጥወጠ** teweẗweẗe ***(v.)*** **protrude**
**ተወዛወዘ** tewezaweze ***(v.)*** **nod**
**ተወዛወዘ** tewezaweze ***(v.)*** **wiggle**
**ተውሓሰ** tewhase ***(v.)*** **underwrite**
**ተውህቦ** tewhbo ***(n.)*** **aptitude**
**ተውህቦ** tewhbo ***(n. )*** **talent**
**ተውላጠ ስም** tewlate sm ***(n.)*** **pronoun**
**ትዉልዲ** te-wle-di ***(n. )*** **generation**
**ተውሳኸ-ዕጥቂ** tewsaḱe'ëtqi ***(n.)*** **accoutrement**
**ተወሳኺ ግብሪ** tewsakhi gbri ***(n.)*** **surtax**
**ተወሳኺ ቋንቋ** tewsakhi quanqua ***(n.)*** **lingua**
**ተውሳስ** tewsas ***(n.)*** **ringworm**
**ተዉህቦ ዘለዎ** tewuhbo zelewo ***(adj.)*** **gifted**
**ተውኒት** tewunit ***(n.)*** **theatre**
**ተውኒታዊ** tewunitawi ***(adj.)*** **theatrical**
**ተፃበአ** texab'e ***(v.)*** **contradict**
**ተጻራፊ** texarafi ***(adj.)*** **abusive**
**ተጻራሪ** texarari ***(n.)*** **antagonist**
**ተፃራሪ** texarari ***(n.)*** **antithesis**
**ተፃራሪ** texarari ***(n.)*** **antonym**
**ተፃራሪ ቃል** texarari qal ***(n.)*** **contradiction**
**ተጻራርነት** texararnet ***(n.)*** **antagonism**
**ተጻረረ** texarere ***(v.)*** **antagonize**
**ተፃረረ** texarere ***(v.)*** **contravene**
**ተጻረረ** texarere ***(v.)*** **counteract**
**ተጻዋታይ** texawatay ***(n. )*** **player**
**ተጻዋታይ** texawatay ***(adj.)*** **whimsical**
**ተጻዋታይ ፒያኖ** texawatay piyano ***(n.)*** **pianist**
**ተፃወረ** texawere ***(v.)*** **cope**
**ተፃወረ** texawere ***(v.)*** **endure**
**ተጻወተ** texawete ***(v.i. )*** **frolic**
**ተጻይ** texay ***(n.)*** **adversary**
**ተጻዓኒት** texe'änit ***(n.)*** **freighter**
**ተጸባጻቢ** texebaxabi ***(n.)*** **accountant**
**ተፀባይ** texebayi ***(adj.)*** **expectant**
**ተጸበየ** texebeye ***(v.)*** **anticipate**
**ተጸበየ** texebeye ***(v.)*** **await**
**ተጸግዐ** texeg'ë ***(v.)*** **affiliate**
**ተጸልወ** texelwe ***(v.)*** **bask**
**ተፀንበረ** texenbere ***(v.)*** **merge**
**ተይፈልጥኻ ዝግበር** teyfeltka zgber ***(adj.)*** **inadvertent**
**ትዕይንቲ** t'eynti ***(n.)*** **locale**
**ተዛካሪ** tezakari ***(adj.)*** **catchy**
**ተዛምዶነት** tezamdonet ***(n.)*** **relativity**
**ተዛመደ** tezamede ***(v.)*** **correlate**
**ተዛራባይ** tezarabay ***(n. )*** **windbag**
**ተዛራቢ** tezarabi ***(n.)*** **speaker**
**ተዛረበ** tezarebe ***(adj.)*** **dictate**
**ተዛረበ** tezarebe ***(v.)*** **speak**
**ተዛታያይ** tezatayay ***(n.)*** **negotiator**
**ተዛታዪ** tezatayi ***(n.)*** **interlocutor**
**ተዛተየ** tezateye ***(v.)*** **discuss**
**ተዛወረ** tezawere ***(v.)*** **ramble**

**ትእዛዝ** tezaz ***(n.)* writ**
**ትእዛዝ** t'ezaz ***(n.)* imperative**
**ትእዛዝ** t'ezaz ***(n.)* mandate**
**ትእዛዝ** t'ezaz ***(n.)* requisition**
**ትእዛዝ ለወጠ** t'ezaz leweẗe ***(v.)* countermand**
**ትእዛዝ** t'èzaz ***(n.)* behest**
**ተዛዘመ** tezazeme ***(v.)* culminate**
**ተዘክሮ** tezekro ***(n.)* memory**
**ተዘክሮ** tezekro ***(n.)* recollection**
**ተዘማመደ** tezemamede ***(v.)* interrelate**
**ተዘርግሐ** tezerghe ***(v.)* unfurl**
**ተዘዋዋሪ** tezewawari ***(adj.)* indirect**
**ተዘይኮነ** tezeykone ***(n.)* winner**
**ተዓዋቲ** tawati ***(n.)* paperback**
**ተዓጻጻፊ ገበር ዘለዎ መጽሓፍ** taxaxafi geber zelewo mxhaf ***(v.)* watch**
**ተዓዘበ** te'äzebe ***(adj.)* vibrant**
**ተነዝናዚ** teneznazi ***(v.)* wade**
**ተፍአ** tef'è ***(v.)* vomit**
**ተፈላለየ** tefelaleye ***(v.)* vary**
**ተኽሊ ሓጹር** teḱli ḥatsur ***(n.)* hedge**
**ተለኣኣኺ** tele'a'aḱi ***(n.)* herald**
**ተንስአ** tens'e ***(v.)* wake**
**ተረኣይነት** tere'aynet ***(n.)* visibility**
**ተረፈዐ** terefe'ë ***(v.)* vegetate**
**ተረረ** terere ***(v.)* harden**
**ተስፋ** tesfa ***(n.)* hope**
**ተሸርበ** tesherbe ***(v.)* vanish**
**ተጠማጠመ** teṭemaṭeme ***(v.t. )* grapple**
**ተጻባኢ** tetsaba'i ***(adj. )* hostile**
**ተዋዛዪ** tewazayi ***(n.)* harlequin**
**ተዋዛዪ** tewazayi ***(n.)* humorist**
**ተወሃሃደ** tewehahade ***(v.)* harmonize**
**ተወላወለ** tewelawele ***(v.)* hesitate**
**ተወላወለ** tewelawele ***(v.)* vacillate**
**ተወራረደ** tewerarede ***(n. & v.)* wager**
**ተጻዋቲ መሳርሒ** texawati mesarhi ***(n.)* instrumentalist**
**ተስፋ ቆረፀ** taesfa kors ***(v.)* tire**
**ታዕታዕ ዘብዝሕ** taëtaë zebzh ***(adj.)* rowdy**
**ትዕግስተኛ** tagstegna ***(adj.)* tolerant**

# ታ

**ታሕጓስ** tahguasn ***(n.)* zest**
**ታሕጓስ** taĥgwas ***(n.)* festivity**
**ታሕጓስ** taĥgwas ***(n.)* fun**
**ታሕጓስ** taḥgwas ***(n. )* gratification**
**ታሕጓስ** taȟgwas ***(n.)* bliss**
**ታሕጓስ** taĥhgwas ***(n.)* excitement**
**ታሕሳስ** tahsas ***(n.)* December**
**ታሕታዋይ ዳኛ** tahtaway dagna ***(n. )* magistrate**
**ታሕታይ** taȟtay ***(adj.)* nether**
**ታሕታዋይ** tahteway ***(adj.)* junior**
**ታሕተዋይ** taȟteway ***(adj.)* subordinate**
**ታሓትዋይ መዓርግ** taȟteway me'arg ***(n.)* subaltern**
**ታሕተዋይነት** tahtewaynet ***(n.)* inferiority**
**ታህዋኽ** tahwaḱ ***(n.)* haste**
**ታሕዋስያን** tahwas-eyan ***(n.)* germ**
**ታኬላ** takela ***(n.)* slough**
**ታክሲ** taksi ***(n.)* cab**
**ታክሲ** taksi ***(n.)* taxi**
**ታምፖን** tampon ***(n.)* tampon**
**ታንኒካ** tanika ***(n.)* tin**
**ታኒካ** tanika ***(n.)* can**
**ታኒካ** tanika ***(n.)* canister**

**ታንኪ** tanki ***(n. )*** **tank**
**ታንኳ** tankwa ***(n.)*** **canoe**
**ታንቴላዊ** tanteelawi ***(adj.)*** **lacy**
**ታሪኽ** tarik ***(n.)*** **history**
**ታሪኽ ሂወት** tarik hiwet ***(n.)*** **memoir**
**ታሪክ ህይወት** tarik hywet ***(n.)*** **biography**
**ታሪኻዊ** tarikawi ***(adj. )*** **historic**
**ታሪኻዊ** tarikawi ***(adj. )*** **historical**
**ታሽዓይ** tash'äy ***(adj. & n.)*** **ninth**
**ታተ ዝብለ ህፃን** tate zble hsan ***(n.)*** **toddler**

# ት

**ትብዓት** tb'ät ***(n.)*** **boldness**
**ትብዓት** tb'ät ***(n.)*** **fortitude**
**ትብዓት** tb'ät ***(n.)*** **bravery**
**ትዕቢት** t'ëbit ***(n.)*** **vanityትኽክል ዘይኮነ** tkhkl zeykone ***(adj.)*** **inexact**
**ትኩዝ** tkuz ***(adj.)*** **glum**
**ትርጓም** trgwam ***(n.)*** **version**
**ትርኢት** tr'it ***(n.)*** **vista**
**ትዕዝምቲ** t'ëzmti ***(n.)*** **rapture**
**ተዝናነየ** teznaneye ***(v.)*** **lounge**
**ትፍንያታዊ** tfn'yatawi ***(adj.)*** **subjective**
**ትፍስህቲነት** tfshtinet ***(n.)*** **hedonism**
**ትፍታፍ** tftaf ***(n. )*** **spittle**
**ትግባሬ** tgbarie ***(n.)*** **performance**
**ትግበራ** tgbera ***(n.)*** **attainment**
**ትጉሕ** tguh ***(adj.)*** **diligent**
**ትከግመ** theg'me ***(n. )*** **smog**
**ትሕጃ ምሓዝ** thja mhaz ***(n. )*** **lien**
**ትሕጃ ምትሓዝ** thja mthaz ***(n.)*** **pawn**
**ትሕት ዝበለ** tht zbele ***(adj.)*** **lower**
**ትሕተ ምድራዊ** tȟte mdrawi ***(adj.)*** **subterranean**
**ትሕተ ውኖኣዊ** tȟte wno'awi ***(adj.)*** **subconscious**
**ትሕተ-ቤት** tȟtebeet ***(n.)*** **basement**
**ትሕቲ** thti ***(prep. )*** **under**
**ትሕቲ መሬት ዝርከብ ክፍሊ** tĥti meret zrkeb kfli ***(n.)*** **dungeon**
**ትሕቲ መሬት** thti meriet ***(adj.)*** **underground**
**ትሕቲ** tȟti ***(prep.)*** **below**
**ትሕቲ** tȟti ***(adv.)*** **beneath**
**ትሕትና** tĥtna ***(n.)*** **decorum**
**ትሕትና** tȟtna ***(n. )*** **modesty**
**ትሕትና ዘይፈልጥ** thtna zeyfelt ***(adj.)*** **impudent**
**ትሕትና** tȟtna ***(n.)*** **courtesy**
**ትሑት** thut ***(adj.)*** **low**
**ትሑት** thut ***(adj.)*** **lowly**
**ትሑት** thut ***(n.)*** **underling**
**ትሑት** tȟut ***(adj.)*** **inferior**
**ትሑት** tȟut ***(adj.)*** **modest**
**ተሳፋሪ** tsafari ***(n. )*** **passenger**
**ተቛም** tqhuam ***(n.)*** **institution**
**ትንታነኣዊ** tntane'awi ***(adj.)*** **analytical**
**ትንተና** tntena ***(n.)*** **analysis**
**ትራፊክ** trafic ***(n.)*** **traffic**
**ትርቢዒት** trbi'ët ***(a. )*** **quadrangle**
**ትርቢዒታዊ** trbi'ëtawi ***(n.)*** **quadrangular**
**ትርብዒት** t'rb'it ***(n.)*** **square**
**ትረኻ** treka ***(n. )*** **tale**
**ትርፋማ** trfama ***(adj.)*** **lucrative**
**ትርፊ** trfi ***(n.)*** **excess**
**ትርፊ ግዘ** trfi gize ***(n.)*** **leisure**
**ትርፍራፍ** trfraf ***(n.)*** **remains**
**ትርግታ** trgta ***(n. )*** **pulsation**

ትርግታ trgta *(v.)* **throb**
ትርጉም trgum *(n.)* **meaning**
ትርጉም trgum *(n. )* **translation**
ትርጉም አልቦ trgum albo *(adj.)* **senseless**
ትርጉም አልቦ trgum albo *(n.)* **signification**
ትርጉም አልቦ trgum 'albo *(adj.)* **absurd**
ትርጉም አልቦነት trgum 'albonet *(n.)* **absurdity**
ትርጉም ምንጻር trgum mnxar *(v.)* **paraphrase**
ትርጉም ዘይብሉ trgum zeyblu *(n.)* **nonsense**
ትርጉም ዘይብሉ trgum zeyblu *(adj.)* **pointless**
ትርጉም ዘይህብ trgum zeyhb *(adj.)* **insensible**
ትርጉሙ ፈልፈለ trgumu felfele *(v.)* **decode**
ትሪግኖሜትሪ trignomietry *(n.)* **trigonometry**
ትሕዝቶ ፅሑፍ tȟzto xȟuf *(n.)* **suppliant**
ትሮፒካዊ muket ena derq ayer *(adj.)* **tropical**
ቴማ tiema *(adj.)* **thematic**
ቴንብር ዓቃቢ tienbr aqabi *(n.)* **philately**
ቲፎ ሕማም tifo hmam *(n.)* **typhus**
ትሕጃ tihija *(n.)* **collateral**
ትሕዝቶ tihizeto *(n.)* **content**
ቲኬት tikiet *(adj.)* **careful**
ትካል tkal *(n.)* **agency**
ትካል tkal *(n.)* **enterprise**
ትካል tkal *(n.)* **establishment**
ትካል tkal *(n.)* **institute**
ትካዊ tkawi *(adj.)* **smoky**
ትኻዋንነት tkawnet *(n.)* **symbiosis**
ትካዘ tkaze *(n.)* **depression**
ትካዘ tkaze *(n.)* **melancholy**
ትኽክል tk'ekl *(adj.)* **true**
ትኻስ tkhas *(n.)* **snooze**
ትኽክል ዘይኮነ tkhkl zeylone *(adj.)* **inaccurate**
ትኹረት ዘይህብ tkhret zeyhb *(adj.)* **inattentive**
ትኪ tki *(n.)* **smoke**
ትኽክል tkkl *(adj.)* **unfailing**
ትኽክለኛ tkklennya *(n.)* **parcel**
ትኽሎኣዊ tkloawi *(v.)* **perpetrate**
ትኹል tkul *(adj.)* **vertical**
ትኩር tkur *(adj.)* **astute**
ትኩርና tkurna *(n.)* **vigilance**
ትኩርና tkurna *(n.)* **acumen**
ትኩስ tkus *(adj.)* **fresh**
ትኩዝ tkuz *(adj.)* **morose**
ትኳዕ tkwa'ë *(n.)* **blotch**
ትኳዕ t'kwa'ë *(n.)* **speckle**
ት኿ን tḱwan *(n.)* **bug**
ትልሚ tlmi *(n.)* **project**
ትማሊ tmali *(adv. )* **yesterday**
ትምባኮ tmbako *(n.)* **tobacco**
ትምህርታዊ tmhrtawi *(adj.)* **didactic**
ትምህርታዊ tmhrtawi *(adj.)* **scholastic**
ትምህርተ-ሃይማኖት tmhrtehaymanot *(n.)* **catechism**
ትምህርቲ tmhrti *(n.)* **education**
ትምህርቲ tmhrti *(n.)* **lecture**
ትምህርቲ tmhrti *(n.)* **lesson**
ትምህርቲ ቤት tmhrti bet *(n.)* **school**
ትምህርቲ ቴክኖሎጂ tmhrti tieknoloĵi *(n. )* **polytechnic**
ትምኒት tmnit *(n.)* **fantasy**
ተመነየ tmnit *(v.)* **wish**
ትምኒት tmnit *(adj.)* **wishful**

ትምኒት tmnit ***(n.)*** **ambition**
ትምኒት tmnit ***(n.)*** **aspiration**
ትምየና tmyena ***(n.)*** **forgery**
ትምዩን tmyun ***(adj.)*** **counterfeit**
ትንባሃዊ tnbahawi ***(adj.)*** **syllabic**
ትንባሀ tnbahe ***(n. )*** **syllable**
ትንበያ tnbeya ***(n.)*** **prescience**
ትንቢት tnbit ***(n.)*** **prediction**
ትንቢት tnbit ***(n.)*** **prophecy**
ትንቢታዊ tnbitawi ***(adj.)*** **prophetic**
ትንፋስ tnfas ***(n.)*** **breath**
ትንግርቲ tngrti ***(n.)*** **feat**
ትንግርቲ tn'grti ***(adj.)*** **splendid**
ትንሳአ tnsa'e ***(n.)*** **revival**
ትንሳኤ tnsa'ie ***(n.)*** **Easter**
ተከሰተ tekesete ***(v.)*** **occur**
ተወሳኺ ሰዓት tewesaki se'at ***(n)*** **overtime**
ተዘይኮነ ግን tezeykone gn ***(adv.)*** **otherwise**
ተገደደ tegedede ***(v.)*** **obligated**
ተፃዋቲ tetsawati ***(adj.)*** **outgoing**
ቱርኪዊ turkwawi ***(n. )*** **ottoman**
ተባዕታይ ጣዎስ tabaetay taewa ***(n. )*** **peacock**
ታቦት tabot ***(n.)*** **shrine**
ታቦት tabot ***(n.)*** **ark**
ታህዋስያን tahwasyan ***(n.)*** **organism**
ትርፊ ክፍሊት trfi kflit ***(v.)*** **overcharge**
ትዕዝብቲ t'ezebti ***(n.)*** **observation**
ትፍግእት tfg'et ***(n.)*** **scenery**
ትርኢት tr'it ***(n.)*** **riposte**
ትርኽ trk ***(n.)*** **bauble**
ትርኪምርኪ ስልማት trkimrki slmat ***(adj.)*** **moist**
ትርኩስ trkus ***(adj.)*** **soppy**
ትርኩስ trkus ***(n.)*** **daffodil**
ትሮምቦኖ trombono ***(n.)*** **absentee**
ትሩፍ truf ***(n.)*** **participant**
ትሳታፋይ tsatafay ***(n.)*** **tonsil**
ትጽቢት txbit ***(n.)*** **anticipation**
ትፀቢት ገበረ txbit gebere ***(v.)*** **expect**
ትያትር ቆልዑ tyatr qoleu ***(n. )*** **pantomime**
ትዝታ tzta ***(v.)*** **reminiscence**
ትዝታዊ tztawi ***(adj.)*** **reminiscent**
ትዋሕታ twahta ***(n.)*** **hoot**
ትውልዲ twldi ***(n.)*** **descent**
ቶንሲል tonsil ***(n. )*** **lathe**
ቶርንዮ tornyo ***(n.)*** **orgy**

# ቸ

ቸሊዶንያ chelidonya ***(n.)*** **celandine**
ቸርቻሪ ĉerĉari ***(n.)*** **retailer**
ቸንዳ chenda ***(n.)*** **marquee**
ቸክ chek ***(n.)*** **cheque**
ቻርት chart ***(n.)*** **chart**
ቼዝ chezz' ***(n.)*** **chess**
ቸግር chger ***(n.)*** **inconvenience**
ቸኩል chkul ***(adj.)*** **impetuous**
ቾክ chok ***(n.)*** **chalk**

# ነ

ነዝዐ nez'ë ***(v.i. )*** **ooze**
ነገር neger ***(n.)*** **object**
ነጸገ netsege ***(v.)*** **overrule**
ነቐዐ neq'ä ***(v.)*** **crack**
ነቃዕ neqa'ë ***(n.)*** **fissure**
ነቓዕ neqa'ë ***(n.)*** **crack**
ነቃፀ neqax ***(adj.)*** **mulish**
ነቓጽ neqax ***(adj.)*** **wayward**
ነቀፈ neqefe ***(v.)*** **castigate**
ነቐፈ neqefe ***(v.)*** **chide**

**ነቐፈ** neqefe *(v.)* **criticize**
**ነቀፈ** neqefe *(v.)* **revile**
**ነቐፌታ** neqefeeta *(n.)* **criticism**
**ነቐለ** neqele *(v.)* **depart**
**ነቐለ** neqele *(v.)* **disconnect**
**ነቐለ** neqele *(v.)* **trip**
**ነቐለ** neqele *(v.)* **uproot**
**ንዕቀት** n'eqet *(n.)* **contempt**
**ንዕቀት** n'eqet *(n.)* **scorn**
**ንዕቐት** n'ëqet *(n.)* **disdain**
**ንዕቀት ዘለዎ** n'eqet zelewo *(adj.)* **scornful**
**ነቀወ** neqewe *(v.)* **bellow**
**ነቐጸ** neqexe *(v.)* **wither**
**ነቓፀ** neqhats *(adj.)* **stubborn**
**ነቕሐ** neq̈he *(v.)* **awake**
**ነቕሐ** neq̈he *(v.)* **awaken**

# ን

**ንቑጽ** nequtse *(adj.)* **husky**
**ንእስነት** n'esenet *(n.)* **youth**
**ንእሽተይ** n'eshtey *(adj.)* **mini**
**ንእሽተይ** n'eshtey *(adj.)* **small**
**ንእሽተይ** n'eshtey *(adj.)* **tiny**
**ንእሽተይ በደል** n'eshtey bedel *(n.)* **misdemeanour**
**ንእሽተይ ድምፂ መጋዉሒ** neshtey dmsi megawuhi *(n.)* **tweeter**
**ንእሽተይ ጋዜጣ** n'eshtey gazieta *(adj.)* **tabloid**
**ንእሽተይ ምኽሪ ሃበ** n'eshtey mkri habe *(n.)* **tipster**
**ንእሽተይ ናይ ኤሌትሪክ ፍሰት መቆፃፀሪ መሳርሒ** n'eshtey nay eletric hayli mokosaseri *(n.)* **transistor**
**ንእሽተይ ስርቂ** n'eshtey srki *(n. )* **pickings**
**ንእሽተይን ማራኺን** n'eshteyn marakin *(adj.)* **dainty**
**ንእሽትሊት** n'eshtlit *(adj.)* **miniature**
**ንእሽቶ** neshto *(n.)* **wisp**
**ንእሽቶ** n'eshto *(adj.)* **petite**
**ንእሽቶ** n'eshto *(n.)* **smidgen**
**ንእሽቶ በርሚል** n'èshto bermil *(n.)* **keg**
**ንእሽቶ ደሴት** n'èshto deseet *(n.)* **islet**
**ንእሽቶ ፊደል** n'eshto fidel *(adj.)* **minuscule**
**ንእሽቶ ሓወልቲ** n'eshto ḧawelti *(n.)* **statuette**
**ንእሽቶ ካንጋሩ** n'èshto kangaru *(n.)* **wallaby**
**ንእሽቶ መጽሓፍ** n'èshto mexḧaf *(n.)* **booklet**
**ንእሽቶ መጽሓፍ** n'èshto mexḧaf *(n.)* **booklet**
**ንእሽቶ ምስሊ** n'èshto msli *(n.)* **figurine**
**ንእሽቶ ነኳል** nèshto nekual *(v.)* **prick**
**ንእሽቶ ቁሸት** n'èshto qushet *(n. )* **hamlet**
**ንእሽቶ ቈልዓ** n'èshto qwel'ä *(n.)* **chit**
**ንእሽቶ ወሓዚ** n'eshto weḧazi *(n. )* **streamlet**
**ንእሽቶ ዝሓበጠት** neshto zhabetet *(n. )* **wen**
**ነስነሰ** nesnese *(v.i. )* **sprinkle**
**ንእስነት** n'èsnet *(n)* **boyhood**
**ንእሽቶ** n'ešto *(adj.)* **slight**
**ነታጒ** netagwi *(adj.)* **explosive**
**ነፃነት** netanet *(n.)* **independence**
**ነጥቢ** netbi *(n.)* **dot**

**ነጥቢ** netbi ***(n.)*** **spot**
**ነጥቢ** neẗbi ***(n.)*** **point**
**ነትዐ** net'ë ***(v.t. )*** **rupture**
**ነተጉ** netege ***(v.)*** **explode**
**ነተጐ** netegwa ***(v.)*** **burst**
**ነጠረ** neẗere ***(v.i)*** **jump**
**ነጠረ** neẗere ***(v.)*** **bounce**
**ነትጉ** netgwi ***(n.)*** **blast**
**ነተጉ** netigu ***(v.)*** **detonate**
**ነቲሕ** netiḧ ***(n.)*** **miasma**
**ነቲሕ** netiḧ ***(n. )*** **stench**
**ነቶገ** netoge ***(v.)*** **erupt**
**ነፃ** netsa ***(adj.)*** **independent**
**ነፃ** netsa ***(adj.)*** **liberal**
**ነፃ ኣውፃኢ** netsa awtsa'e ***(n. )*** **liberator**
**ነፃ ኣውፀአ** netsa mwtsa'e ***(v.)*** **liberate**
**ነፃነት** netsanet ***(n.)*** **liberation**
**ነፃነት** netsanet ***(n.)*** **liberty**
**ነፀብራቅ** netsebraq ***(n.)*** **radiance**
**ነፀብራቅ** netsebraq ***(n.)*** **reflection**
**ነጸፈት** netsefet ***(v.)*** **wean**
**ነፀገ** netsege ***(v.)*** **reject**
**ነፀላ** netsela ***(v.)*** **seclude**
**ንፁር** netsxur ***(adj.)*** **clear**
**ነፀብራቅ** netzebrqh ***(n.)*** **lustre**
**ነወመ** neweme ***(v.)*** **hibernate**
**ነዉሐ** newĥe ***(v.)*** **elongate**
**ነዊሕ** newih ***(adj.)*** **lengthy**
**ነዊሕ** newih ***(adj.)*** **long**
**ነዊሕ** newih ***(adj.)*** **tall**
**ነዊሕ ጭቅጭቅ ዝተሓወሰ ንግግር** newih chikchik ztehaweso nggr ***(n.)*** **tirade**
**ነዊሕ ጉዕዞ ብእግሪ** newih guazo b'ageri ***(n. )*** **trek**
**ነዊሕ ካልሲ** newiḧ kalsi ***(n. )*** **stocking**
**ነዊሕ ልበወለድ** newiḧ lbeweled ***(n.)*** **novel**
**ነዊሕ ሳእኒ** newiḧ sa'èni ***(n.)*** **boot**
**ነዊሒ ጦር** newih tor ***(n. )*** **javelin**
**ነዊሕ ፀጉሪ** newih tseguri ***(n.)*** **tress**
**ነዊሕ ጸናሒ** newiḧ xenaḧi ***(n.)*** **protractor**
**ንለዊሕ ዝጸንሕ** newiḧ zxeniḧ ***(adj.)*** **protracted**
**ነውነወ** newnewe ***(v.t. )*** **jostle**
**ነውነውታ** newnewta ***(n.)*** **jerk**
**ነውራም** newram ***(adj.)*** **indecent**
**ነውራም** newram ***(adj.)*** **nasty**
**ነውራም** newram ***(adj.)*** **vile**
**ነውራም** newram ***(n.)*** **cad**
**ነውሪ** newri ***(adj.)*** **immoral**
**ነውሪ** newri ***(n.)*** **indecency**
**ነውጺ** newtsi ***(n.)*** **shock**
**ነዉጺ** newtsi ***(adj.)*** **turbulent**
**ነውሪ** newuri ***(n.)*** **scandal**
**ነውጺ መትኒ** newxi metni ***(n.)*** **neurosis**
**ነጸገ** nexege ***(v.)*** **forswear**
**ነፀገ** nexege ***(adj.)*** **pseudo**
**ናይ ሓሶት** nay ĥasot ***(adj.)*** **terrestrial**
**ናይ መሬት** nay meriet ***(adj.)*** **vascular**
**ናይ ሻምብቆ ኣካል** nay shambqo 'akal ***(adj.)*** **telegraphic**
**ናይ ቴሌግራፍ** nay telegram ***(adj.)*** **venous**
**ናይ ቨይን** nay veyn ***(pron. )*** **him**
**ንዓኡ** ne-a-u ***(adj. )*** **headstrong**
**ነቓጽ** neq̈atse ***(n. )*** **wren**
**ንእሽቶ ዓይነት ዑፍ** n'èshto 'äynet 'üf ***(a. )*** **grenade**
**ንእሽቶ ቦምባ** n'èshto bomba ***(v.)*** **hop**

**ነጠረ** neṭere ***(v.t. )* hop**
**ነጠረ** neṭere ***(n.)* underworld**
**ናይ ለያቡ ዓለም** lay leyabu alem ***(n. )* hemisphere**
**ንፍቀ-ክቢ** nfqekbi ***(v.)* negate**
**ናይ ሙዚቃ ስልቲ** ney muzika slti ***(n.)* tempo**
**ንፋስ** nfas ***(n.)* draught**
**ንፋስ** nfas ***(n.)* wind**
**ንፋስ** nfas ***(adj.)* windy**
**ንፍቀ ምድሪ** nfqe mdri ***(n.)* equator**
**ንፍራ** nfra ***(n.)* flight**
**ንፉዕ** nfu'e ***(adj.)* smart**
**ንፉዕ** nfu'e ***(adj.)* wily**
**ንፉዕ** nfu'ë ***(adj.)* able**
**ንፍዮ** nfyo ***(n.)* measles**
**ን ግብረ ስጋዊ ግኑኝነት ስሚዕት ምልዕዓል** ngbre ssgawi gnugnunet smiait ml'eal ***(v.)* titillate**
**ንግዳዊ** ngdawi ***(adj.)* commercial**
**ንግዳዊ** ngdawi ***(adj.)* mercantile**
**ንግደት** ngdet ***(n. )* pilgrimage**
**ንግዲ** ngdi ***(n.)* commerce**
**ንግዲ** ngdi ***(n.)* trade**
**ንግሆ** ngho ***(n. )* morrow**
**ንግስና** ngsna ***(n. )* monarchy**
**ንግስቲ** ngsti ***(n.)* queen**
**ንግስቲ ነገስት** ngsti negest ***(n.)* empress**
**ንጉደት ስምዒት** ngudet smi'it ***(n.)* catharsis**
**ንጉሆ** nguho ***(n. )* morning**
**ንጉስ** ngus ***(n. )* king**
**ንጉስ** ngus ***(n. )* monarch**
**ንጉስ** ngus ***(n.)* sovereign**
**ንጉሳዊ** ngusawi ***(adj.)* regal**
**ንጉሳዊነት** ngusawi ***(n.)* royalty**
**ንሓደጋ ኣሳጠሐ** nĥadega asaẗeeĥe ***(v.)* endanger**
**ንሓጺር ግዜ** nĥaxir gzee ***(adv.)* awhile**
**ንህቢ** nhbi ***(n.)* bee**
**ንሕማም እንስሳ ዚምልከት** nḥmam 'ènssa zimlket ***(adj.)* veterinary**
**ንሕማቅ ነገር አውዓለ** nĥmaq neger aw'äle ***(v.)* misapply**
**ንሕና** nhna ***(pron. )* we**
**ንህዝቢ ኣርአየ** nhzbi ar'aye ***(v.)* exhibit**
**ኒከል** nikel ***(n. )* nickel**
**ኒኮቲን** nikotin ***(n. )* nicotine**
**ኒርቫና** nirvana ***(n.)* nirvana**
**ነዊሕ ሂወት** niweh hiwet ***(n.)* longevity**
**ኒውትሮን** niwtron ***(n.)* neutron**
**ኒዮሊቲክ** niyolitik ***(adj.)* Neolithic**
**ኒዮን** niyon ***(n. )* neon**
**ነኸሰ** nkes ***(v.)* clench**
**ንከያ** nkeya ***(n.)* deflation**
**ንከያ** nkeya ***(n.)* rebate**
**ንኽይወርስ ከልከለ** nkeywers kelkele ***(v.)* disinherit**
**ንላዕሊ** nlaeli ***(adv. )* upward**
**ንላዕሊ ምዛር** nlaeli mzar ***(n.)* upturn**
**ንመሕነቒ ዝጥቀምዎ ዕንጨይቲ** n-mehneqi z-tkemwo enchei-ti ***(n.)* gallows**
**ንመን** nmen ***(pron.)* whom**
**ንመገዲ ብቁዕ ዝኮነ** nmengedi bqu'ë kone ***(adj.)* roadworthy**
**ንምግላፅ ዘፀግም** nmglats zetsegm ***(adj.)* indescribable**
**ንምምባር ዘይኾን** nmmbar zeykhon ***(adj.)* inhabitable**
**ንምንባብ ምፅጋም** nmnbab mtzgam ***(n.)* illegibility**
**ንምንታይ** nmntay ***(adv.)* why**

ንነፍሲ ወከፍ nnefsi wekef *(prep.)* **per**
ንነዊሕ ግዜ ዝፀንሕ nnewi gzie ztsenh *(adj.)* **lasting**
ነከዩ ሸጠ mkurats *(v.)* **undercut**
ንእሽተይ ቐላይ mlkt neshtey q̈lay *(n.)* **pool**
ናይ ኢድ መሳርሒ ȟrtum *(n.)* **tool**
ናይ ሓሶት ጸብጻብ nay ȟasot xebxab *(n.)* **canard**
ኖራ nora *(n.)* **lime**
ኖራ nora *(n.)* **whitewash**
ኖርደታይ nordetay *(adj.)* **Nordic**
ንቅድሚት nqdmit *(adv.)* **ahead**
ንቕድሚት nq̈dmit *(adv. &adj.)* **forward**
ንቅድሚት ኣምርሐ nqdmit amrȟe *(v.)* **proceed**
ንቅድሚት ተደርበየ nqdmit tederbeye *(n.)* **projectile**
ንቅሎ nqlo *(n.)* **departure**
ንቁሕ nquh *(adj.)* **dashing**
ንቑሕ nquh *(adj.)* **perky**
ብቑሩብ nqurub *(adv. )* **slightly**
ንርሑቕ nrȟuq̈ *(adv.)* **afar**
ንሳ nsa *(pron. )* **her**
ንሳ nsa *(pron.)* **she**
ንስሓ nsha *(n.)* **penance**
ንስሓ nsĥa *(n.)* **repentance**
ንሽሙ nshmu *(adj.)* **nominal**
ንፅህና nshna *(n.)* **tidiness**
ንስኻ nska *(pron.)* **you**
ንስም ብቻ ዝወሃብ መኣርግ nsm bcha zwehab mearg *(adj.)* **titular**
ንስሪ nsri *(n.)* **eagle**
ንሱ nsu *(pron. )* **he**
ንሱ ንሳ nsu  nsa *(pron.)* **it**
ንሱ ድማ nsu dma *(n. )* **namely**
ንጣብ ቀለም nẗab qelem  *(n.)* **blot**
ንጣብ nẗab *(n.)* **blob**
ንጣር n'ẗar *(n. )* **speck**
ንጥፈት nẗfet *(n.)* **activity**
ነጥረ ነገር ntre neger *(n.)* **particle**
ንጥረ ነገር n'ẗre neger *(n.)* **substance**
ንፀገት ntsget *(n.)* **rejection**
ንፅህና nts'hna *(n.)* **purity**
ንፀል ntsl *(adj.)* **single**
ንፀል ntsl *(adj.)* **singular**
ንፀልነት ntslnet *(n.)* **singularity**
ንፀልታ ntslta *(n.)* **singlet**
ንፀፀር ntstsr *(n.)* **simile**
ንፁግ ntsug *(adj.)* **undesirable**
ንፁር ntsur *(adj.)* **decided**
ንፁር ntsur *(adj.)* **specific**
ንፁር ዘይኮነ ntsur zeykone *(adj.)* **indistinct**
ንጡፍ nẗuf *(adj.)* **spry**
ንጡፍ nṭuf *(adj.)* **vivacious**
ንጡፍ nẗuf  *(adj.)* **active**
ንፁር ntzur *(adj.)* **lucid**
ንፁር ntzur *(adj.)* **manifest**
ንኡድ n'ud *(adj.)* **excellent**
ኑኡሽተይ nu'eshtey *(adj.)* **little**
ኑኡሽተይ ኣረጊት ሆቴል nu'eshtey aregit hotel *(n.)* **inn**
ኑጋት nugat *(n.)* **nougat**
ኑጉሳዊ nugusawi *(adj.)* **imperial**
ኑጉሳዊነት nugusawinet *(n.)* **imperialism**
ኑክልየስ nuklyes *(n.)* **nucleus**
ኑክልየሳዊ nuklyesawi *(adj.)* **nuclear**
ኑቑሕ ዘይኮነ nuqhuh zeykone *(adj.)* **inactive**
ንኡስ n'us *(n. )* **junior**
ንኡስ n'us *(adj.)* **minor**
ንኡስ ኣርእስቲ n'us ar'esti *(n.)* **subtitle**
ንኡስ ድምር n'us dmr *(n.)* **subtotal**

ንኡስ ውዕል ገበረ n'us w'el gebere *(v.)* **subcontract**
ኑኡሹተይ nu'ushtey *(adj.)* **marginal**
ኑዛዜ nuzazee *(n.)* **confession**
ንወሲብ ዘወናውን nwesib zewenawn *(adj.)* **sensual**
ንውሓት nwhat *(n.)* **length**
ንውሽጢ ምእታው nwsheti metw *(n.)* **penetration**
ንውሽጢ ኣስተንፈሰ nwshti astenfese *(v.)* **inhale**
ንዉፅ ኣእምሮ nwux a'emro *(adj.)* **neurotic**
ንፅፈ ፃግን nxfe xag'n *(n.)* **menopause**
ንፅፍ ፃግናዊ nxfe xag'nawi *(adj.)* **menstrual**
ንፅል ኣምልኾ nxl amlḱo *(n. )* **monolatry**
ንፅል ድምፃዊ nxl dmxawi *(adj.)* **monophonic**
ንፅል ሃዲድ nxl hadid *(n.)* **monorail**
ንፅል ከውሒ nxl kewḧi *(n. )* **monolith**
ንፅል መነፅር nxl menexr *(n.)* **monocle**
ንፅል መውስቦ nxl mewsbo *(n. )* **monogamy**
ንፅል ሲላበል nxl silabel *(n.)* **monosyllable**
ንፅል ዝሕብሩ nxl zḧbru *(n. )* **monochrome**
ንጹህ nxuh *(adj.)* **pure**
ንጹህነት nxuhnet *(n.)* **purist**
ንፁር nxur *(adj.)* **articulate**
ንፁር nxur *(adj.)* **clarion**
ንፁር nxur *(adj.)* **evident**
ንፁር nxur *(adj.)* **explicit**
ንፅፅር nxxr *(n.)* **contrast**
ንየው nyew *(adv.)* **afield**
ንዘልኣለም nzel'alem *(adv. )* **forever**
ንዝናዘ nznaze *(n. )* **vibration**
ን n *(prep. )* **for**
ን ኣሰናዳኢ መልእኽቲ n asenada'i mel'ekti *(adj.)* **editorial**

# ና

ናይ ኢሌትሪክ ሓይሊ ዝቅይር መሳርሒ na eletric hayli zqyir mesarhi *(n.)* **transformer**
ናይ ልቢ na' ae lebii *(adj.)* **cardiac**
ና ኤሜሪካ ደርሆ na america derho *(n.)* **turkey**
ና ዕንበባ ዓይነት na anbeba aynet *(n.)* **tulip**
ናይ ድምፂ ቃና na dmsi kana *(n.)* **tone**
ና ሓደ ስራሕ መረዳድኢ ቛንቋ na hade srah meredadei kanka *(adj.)* **terminological**
ና ሓደ ስራሕ መረዳድኢ ቛንቋ na hade srah meredadei kanka *(n.)* **terminology**
ና ከተማ ኤለትሪክ ባቡር na ketema electric babur *(n.)* **tram**
ና ከዉሒ ጎቦ na kewuhi gobo *(n.)* **tor**
ና መጨረሻ ደረጃ na mecheresha dereja *(adj.)* **terminal**
ናይ መርከብ ፀዕነት ጠቅላላ ክብደት na merkeb teklala s'anet *(n.)* **tonnage**
ና ነዳቂ ማንካ na nedaqi manka *(n. )* **trowel**

**ና ፖሊስ ዱላ** na polis dula ***(n.)*** **truncheon**
**ናይ ሮማውያን ና ኣወዳት ጃኬት** na romawuyan na awedat jaket ***(n.)*** **toga**
**ና ተቅራኒ ክዳን ክክደን ዝፎቲ** na teqarani sota kdan kkden zufoti ***(n.)*** **transvestite**
**ና ወይኒ በርሚን** na weyni brmin ***(n.)*** **tun**
**ናዓ** na'ä ***(v.)*** **come**
**ናዓወት መዓልቲ** naawet mealti ***(adj.)*** **triumphal**
**ናዓወት ስሚዒት** naawet smait ***(adj.)*** **triumphant**
**ናብ** nab ***(prep.)*** **into**
**ናብ** nab ***(prep.)*** **to**
**ናብ** nab ***(prep.)*** **towards**
**ናብ ብሕቲ መለሰ** nab bĥti melese ***(v.)*** **denationalize**
**ናብ ደቡብ** nab debub ***(adj.)*** **southerly**
**ናብ ሓደ ገጽ** nab ȟade gex ***(adv.)*** **aside**
**ናብ ሕጊ ኣቅረቡ** nab ȟgi aq̈ribu ***(v.)*** **prosecute**
**ናብ ሕጊ ምቕራብ** nab ȟgi mq̈rab ***(n. )*** **prosecution**
**ናብ ርሑቕ** nab rȟuq̈ ***(adv.)*** **away**
**ናብ ሰሜን** nab semeen ***(adj.)*** **northerly**
**ናብ ስልጣን መለሰ** nab sltan melese ***(v.)*** **reinstate**
**ናብ ጥርሙዝ ለወጠ** nab ţrmuz leweţe ***(v.)*** **vitrify**
**ናብ ወፃዕ ለኣኸ** nab wexa'i le'ake ***(v. t. )*** **export**
**ናብ ዩኒቨርሲቲ ኣተወ** nab yuniversiti atewe ***(v.)*** **matriculate**
**ናብ ዝነበሮ ክምለስ ዘይኽእል** nab znebro kmles zeyk'el ***(adj.)*** **irreversible**
**ናብ/ካብ ምዕራብ** nab/kab m'erab ***(adv. )*** **westerly**
**ና ባሕሪ ኣባ ጋዉየ** nabahri aba gabuye ***(n. )*** **turtle**
**ናባያይ** nabayay ***(n.)*** **carer**
**ናባዪ** nabayi ***(n.)*** **caretaker**
**ናበይ** nabey ***(adv.)*** **whither**
**ናብኡ ሸነኽ** nab'u shenek ***(adv. )*** **thither**
**ናብዚ** nabzi ***(adv. )*** **hither**
**ናቾ** nacho ***(n.)*** **nacho**
**ናድራር ክዳን** nadrar kdan ***(n.)*** **tuxedo**
**ናይ ኣዕዋፍ ፍፆት** naeawaf fsot ***(v.)*** **twitter**
**ናዕቢ** na'ëbi ***(n.)*** **affray**
**ናዕቢ** na'ëbi ***(n.)*** **subversion**
**ናዕቢ** naebi ***(n. )*** **pandemonium**
**ናእዳ** na'èda ***(n.)*** **commendation**
**ናእዳ** na'èda ***(n.)*** **compliment**
**ናዕናዕ** na'ena'e ***(n.)*** **spearmint**
**ናዕዋ** na'ëwa ***(n.)*** **frenzy**
**ናፍቆት** nafqot ***(n.)*** **longing**
**ናፍቆት** nafqot ***(n. )*** **nostalgia**
**ናፍቖት** nafqot ***(n. )*** **yearning**
**ናፍጣ** nafťa ***(n.)*** **naphthalene**
**ና ግሊ መምህር** nagli memhr ***(n.)*** **tutor**
**ና ጎሳ** nagosa ***(adj.)*** **tribal**
**ናግራም ሰበይቲ** nagram sebeyti ***(n.)*** **virago**
**ና ሃደን ከልቢ** nahaden kelbi ***(n.)*** **terrier**
**ናሓረግ መደገፊ ዕንጨይቲ** nahareg medegefi anseyti ***(n.)*** **trellis**

**ና ሓርማዝ ስኒ** naharmaz sni ***(n. )*** **tusk**

**ና ሓዘን ደወል** nahazen dewel ***(n.)*** **toll**

**ናህሪ** nahri ***(n.)*** **momentum**

**ናህሪ ቀነሰ** nahri kenese ***(v.)*** **decelerate**

**ናሕሲ** naĥsi ***(n.)*** **roof**

**ናሕሲ ኣፍ** naȟsi af ***(n.)*** **palate**

**ናሕሲ ምስራሕ** naĥsi msraĥ ***(n.)*** **roofing**

**ናይ ክብደት መለክዒ** nakbdet melekai ***(n.)*** **ton**

**ናይ መኪና ጎማ** namekina goma ***(n.)*** **tyre**

**ናመምሃሪ ክፍሊት** namemhari kflit ***(n.)*** **tuition**

**ናምስጋና ንግግር** namsgana nggr ***(n.)*** **tribute**

**ናሙና** namuna ***(n.)*** **specimen**

**ና ንእሽተይ ዒፍ ድምፂ** naneshtey aif dmsi ***(v.)*** **tweet**

**ናርቺዞ** narchizo ***(n. )*** **narcissus**

**ናፀሓይ ምዕራብ** nasahay marab ***(n. )*** **twilight**

**ናፅዕነት መኪና** nas'anet mekina ***(n.)*** **truck**

**ናፅዕነት መኪና ሹፈር** nas'anet mekina shuifer ***(n.)*** **trucker**

**ና ስፈት መኪና ፒዳል** nasfyet mekina pedal ***(n.)*** **treadle**

**ና ስኒ መጎርገሪ ዕንጨይቲ** nasni megorgori anchyti ***(n.)*** **toothpick**

**ናስትሮ** nastro ***(n. )*** **ribbon**

**ናስትሮ** nastro ***(n.)*** **tape**

**ናታ** nata ***(pron. )*** **hers**

**ናተይ** natey ***(pron.)*** **mine**

**ናተይ** natey ***(adj.)*** **my**

**ናትካ** natk ***(adj.)*** **your**

**ናፃ ለቀቀ** natsa leqeqe ***(v.)*** **deregulate**

**ናቱ** natu ***(adj. )*** **his**

**ናፃ** natza ***(adj.)*** **free**

**ናጻ** natza ***(n.)*** **freebie**

**ናጻ** natza ***(adj.)*** **gratuitous**

**ናፃ ምካድ** natza mkad ***(n.)*** **impunity**

**ናፀነት** natzanet ***(n.)*** **freedom**

**ናፀነት** natzneg ***(n.)*** **manumission**

**ና ወታደር ጃኬት** nawetader jaket ***(n.)*** **tunic**

**ናውቲ ጽሕፈት** nawti tsȟfet ***(n.)*** **stationery**

**ናውጼን** nawxeen ***(adj.)*** **boisterous**

**ናጻ ምልቃቕ** naxa mlqaq̈ ***(n.)*** **acquittal**

**ናይ ኣደ** nay ade ***(adj.)*** **maternal**

**ናይ ኣደ** nay ade ***(adj.)*** **motherly**

**ናይ ኣእምሮ** nay a'emro ***(adj.)*** **mental**

**ናይ ኣፍንጫ** nay afnča ***(adj.)*** **nasal**

**ናይ ዓሌት** nay äleet ***(adj.)*** **ethnic**

**ናይ ኣልኮል መስተ** nay alkol meste ***(n.)*** **liquor**

**ናይ ኣመጋግባ ኪኢላ** nay amegagba ki'ila ***(n.)*** **dietician**

**ናይ ኣምልኾት ቦታ** nay amlkot bota ***(n.)*** **gurdwara**

**ናይ ኣናእሽተይ ጀልባ መዕረፊ** nay ana'ushtey jelba me'erefi ***(n. )*** **marina**

**ናይ ዓንዲ ሑቀ** nay ändi ȟuqe ***(adj.)*** **spinal**

**ናይ ኣትክልቲ** nay 'atklti ***(n. )*** **vegetable**

**ናይ ዓፅሚ ጉንቦ ኢድ** nay äxmi gunbo id ***(adj.)*** **carpal**

**ናይ ባሕሪ** nay bahri ***(adj.)*** **marine**

ናይ ባሕሪ ውግእ nay bahri wg'e *(adj.)* **naval**
ናይ ባይቶ nay bayto *(adj.)* **senatorial**
ናይ በዓል nay be'äl *(adj.)* **festive**
ናይ ቤት መዘጋጃ nay beet mezageja *(adj.)* **municipal**
ናይ ፍርዲ ቤት ኽልከላ nay bet ferdi khlkela *(n.)* **injunction**
ናይ ብሓቂ nay bḥaqi *(adj.)* **veracious**
ናይ ብርሃን ጨረር nay brhan cherer *(n.)* **laser**
ናይ ቡቲክ ኣሻንጉሊት nay butik ashangulit *(n. )* **mannequin**
ናይ ደብዳበ መግለጺ nay debdabe mglexi *(n.)* **pigeonhole**
ናይ ደገ ማዕፆ ዘለዎ ክፍሊ ገዛ nay dege ma'etso zelewo kfli geza *(n.)* **maisonette**
ናይ ደቂ ኣንስትዮ ስረ ብርኪ nay deki- anstyo sre brki *(n.)* **knickers**
ናይ ደምፂ ማዕበል nay demtsi maebel *(adj.)* **ultrasonic**
ናይ ደናግል ገዳም nay denagl gedam *(n.)* **convent**
ናይ ዶልሺ ሰራሒ nay dolshi serahi *(n.)* **confectioner**
ናይ ድቂ እንስትዮ ክዳን ዉሽጢ nay dqi anstyo kdan wushti *(n.)* **lingerie**
ናይ ዱር nay dur *(adj.)* **sylvan**
ናይ ዕዳጋ ማእኸል nay edaga ma'ekhel *(n.)* **mall**
ናይ እግረኛ መንግዲ nay egregna mengedi *(n.)* **kerb**
ናይ ዕልቋቅ nay 'elqaq *(adj.)* **seminal**
ናይ ዕምበባ ጌፀ nay embaba ge-tse *(n.)* **garland**
ናይ ዕንጨይቲ ሙዚቃ መሳርሒ nay encheyti muzika mesarhi *(n.)* **xylophone**
ናይ ዕንጨይቲ ነዋሪ nay encheyti newari *(adj.)* **xylophilous**
ናይ እንቃቁሖ ፃዕዳ nay enqaquho xa'eda *(n.)* **albumen**
ናይ እንስሳ ጫፍ ጡብ nay enssa chaf tub *(n. )* **teat**
ናይ እንስሳትን ኣትክልትን ዘፅንዕ nay enssat atkltn zesn'a *(n.)* **taxonomy**
ናይ ዕንፀይቲ nay entseyti *(adj.)* **wooden**
ናይ ፋንጋይ ሕማም nay fangay hmam *(n.)* **thrush**
ናይ ፈረንሳይ nay ferensay *(adj.)* **French**
ናይ ጋማ nay gama *(adj.)* **nuptial**
ናይ ግብረ ስጋ ሉዑል ድልየት ዘለዎ nay gbre sga l'eul dlyet zelewo *(adj.)* **lascivious**
ናይ ግብሪ nay gbri *(adj.)* **fiscal**
ናይ ግድን nay gdn *(adv. )* **necessarily**
ናይ ገባሪ ሰናይ nay gebari senay *(adj.)* **charitable**
ናይ ገበነኛታት፣ሰባት ስብስብ nay gebenegnatat sebeseb *(n.)* **gang**
ናይ ገበነኛ መፅናዕቲ nay gebenenya mexna'eti *(n.)* **criminology**
ናይ ገጠር nay geter *(adj.)* **rural**
ናይ ገጽ nay gex *(adj.)* **facial**
ናይ ገዛ እንስሳ nay geza enssa *(n.)* **pet**
ናይ ጉዕዞ ዉጥን nay go'ezo wutn *(n)* **itinerary**
ናይ ግጥሚ ቤት nay gtmi biet *(n. )* **stanza**

ናይ ጉዕዞ ሻንጣ nay gu'ezo shanta *(n.)* **luggage**
ናይ ጉጅለ nay gujle *(adj.)* **collective**
ናይ ጉልበት ሰራሕተኛ nay gulbet serahtegna *(n. )* **workman**
ናይ ጓል nay gwal *(adj.)* **girlish**
ናይ ሓባር nay ȟabar *(adj.)* **mutual**
ናይ ሓባር ብልጽግና nay ȟabar blxgna *(n.)* **commonwealth**
ናይ ሓደጋ nay ȟadega *(adj.)* **accidental**
ናይ ሓደጋ ምርመራ nay hadega mrmera *(n.)* **inquest**
ናይ ሃገረሰብ nay hagereseb *(n.)* **yokel**
ናይ ሓሶት nay hasot *(adj.)* **snide**
ናይ ሓሶት nay ȟasot *(adj.)* **fake**
ናይ ሓሶት ክሲ nay hasot ksi *(n.)* **libel**
ናይ ሓሶት ሽም nay ȟasot šm *(n.)* **pseudonym**
ናይ ሓይሊ nay ȟayli *(adj.)* **forcible**
ናይ ሃይማኖት ጠቢብ nay haymanot tebib *(n.)* **theologian**
ናይ ሒሳብ ኪኢላ nay ȟisab ki'ila *(n.)* **mathematician**
ናይ ሂወት ካብ ሞት ናብ ህያው ምዝዉዋር nay hiwet hab mot nab hyab mshiggar *(n. )* **transmigration**
ናይ ሕጂ nay ȟĵi *(adj.)* **present**
ናይ ህንፃ መተሓላለፊ nay hnxa meteȟalalefi *(n.)* **corridor**
ናይ ሕርሻ መኪና nay hrsha mekina *(n. )* **tractor**
ናይ ሕቶ ቃል nay ȟto qal *(adj.)* **interrogative**
ናይ ህዋ nay hwa *(adj.)* **spatial**
ናይ ህጻናት ዶክቶር nay hxanat doctor *(n.)* **paediatrician**
ናይ ኢድ nay 'id *(adj.)* **manual**
ናይ ኢድ ጨዋዳ nay 'id ciwada *(n.)* **triceps**
ናይ ጃጃዊ nay jajawi *(adj.)* **craven**
ናይ ጀልባ ሃበ nay jelba habe *(n. )* **yachting**
ናይ ጀልባ ሰብ nay jelba seb *(n.)* **yachtsman**
ናይ ጀልባ ታሕታዋይ ኣካል nay jelba tahtaway alkal *(n.)* **keel**
ናይ ካህናት nay kahnat *(adj.)* **clerical**
ናይ ክዳውንቲ nay kdawunti *(adj.)* **sartorial**
ናይ ከብዲ nay kebdi *(a.)* **abdominal**
ናይ ከዋኽብቲ ስብስብ nay kewakbti sebseb *(n. )* **galaxy**
ና ክልል ፖሊስ nay kll plis *(n. )* **trooper**
ናይ ኮንትራት nay kontrat *(adj.)* **contractual**
ናይ ክራይ nay kray *(n.)* **rental**
ናይ ክራይ ስምምዕነት nay kray smm'enet *(n.)* **lease**
ናይ ክሳድ nay ksad *(adj.)* **cervical**
ናይ ቅየሳ መሳርሒ nay kyesa mesarhi *(n.)* **theodolite**
ናይ ለይቲ nay leyti *(adj.)* **nocturnal**
ናይ ማእኸላይ ዘመን nay ma'ekelay zemen *(adj.)* **medieval**
ናይ ሜዳ ተኒስ ጨዋታ nay meda tenis chewata *(n. )* **tennis**
ናይ መገጣጥም nay megetatm *(adj.)* **rheumatic**
ናይ መጀመርታ nay mejemerta *(adj.)* **early**
ናይ መጀመርያ nay mejemerya *(adj.)* **preliminary**
ናይ ሜለ ገረብ nay mele gereb *(n. )* **pear**

**ናይ መንፈስ(ኣእምሮ) ርክብ** nay menfes aemro rkb *(n. )* **telepathy**
**ናይ መቓብር** nay meqabr *(adj.)* **sepulchral**
**ናይ መርዓ** nay mer'ä *(adj.)* **bridal**
**ናይ መራኽብ** nay merakb *(adj.)* **nautical**
**ናይ መሬት ኣቀማምጣ** nay meret akemamta *(n.)* **topography**
**ናይ መሬት ኣቀማምጣ ዘርኢ ካርታ** nay meret akemamta zerei karta *(adj.)* **topographical**
**ናይ መሬት ኣቀማምጣ ዝፅንዕ ሙሁር** nay meret akemamta zesna muhur *(n.)* **topographer**
**ናይ መርዚ ፅንዓት** nay merzi snat *(n.)* **toxicology**
**ናይ መሰረት** nay meseret *(adj.)* **radical**
**ናይ መጥባሕቲ ሓኪም** nay meẗbahti ḧakim *(n. )* **surgeon**
**ናይ መትኒ** nay metni *(adj.)* **neural**
**ናይ መወዳእታ መጠንቀቕታ** nay mewedaeta metenkekta *(n. )* **ultimatum**
**ናይ መውስቦ** nay mewsbo *(n. )* **spousal**
**ናይ መጻኢ ፍልጠት** nay mexaei flẗet *(n.)* **precognition**
**ናይ መጻኢ ዝጥንቁል** nay mexaei zẗnqul *(adj.)* **psychic**
**ናይ ምህዞ** nay mhzo *(adj.)* **fictitious**
**ናይ ሙኳን ዕድል** nay mkhuan edl *(n.)* **likelihood**
**ናይ ምንቅጥቃጥ መሬት** nay mnqtqat meriet *(adj.)* **seismic**
**ናይ ምንጎ ግዜ** nay mongo gzee *(adv. )* **meantime**
**ናይ ሞተር መንቀሳቐሲ** nay moter menqesaqesi *(n.)* **tappet**
**ናይ ምቅልቓል ባህረ ኣበው** nay mqlqal bahre 'abew *(adj.)* **atavistic**
**ናይ ምርኣይ ዓቕሚ** nay mr'ay 'äqmi *(n.)* **eyesight**
**ናይ ምርባሕ** nay mrbaĥ *(adj.)* **reproductive**
**ናይ ሙቀት መለክዒ መሰርሒ** nay muket melek'e mesarhi *(n.)* **thermometer**
**ናይ ሙኳን ዕድል** nay mukuan ëdl *(n.)* **probability**
**ናይ ሙዚቃ ግጥሚ** nay muziqa gtmi *(n.)* **lyric**
**ናይ ሙዚቃ ግጥሚ ገጣሚ** nay muziqa gtmi getami *(n.)* **lyricist**
**ናይ ናሕሲ ኣፍ** nay naȟsi af *(adj.)* **palatal**
**ናይ ንግዲ ዉዕሊ** nay ngdi wualo *(n.)* **transaction**
**ናይ ንግረ ምልክት** nay ngdimlkt *(n. )* **trademark**
**ናይ እንስሳ ሽም** nay nsesa shm *(n.)* **weasel**
**ናይ ፓፓስ** nay papas *(adj.)* **papal**
**ናይ ጳጳስ ዘዉዲ** nay papas zewdi *(n. )* **tiara**
**ናይ ፕላኔታት** nay planatan *(adj.)* **planetary**
**ናይ ፖለቲካ** nay polotika *(adj.)* **politic**
**ናይ ቃላት** nay qalat *(adj.)* **verbal**
**ናይ ቅድሚት** nay qdmit *(adj.)* **fore**
**ናይ ቅድሚት መብራህቲ** nay qdmit mebrahti *(n.)* **headlight**
**ናይ ቀደም** nay qedem *(adj.)* **former**
**ናይ ቀደም** nay qedem *(n. )* **predecessor**

ናይ ቀደም nay qedem *(adj.)* **quondam**
ናይ ቀልዲ nay qeldi *(adj.)* **facetious**
ናይ ቀልዲ ኣዘራርባ nay qeldi azerazba *(n.)* **pleasantry**
ናይ ቀረባ እዋን nay qereba ewan *(adj.)* **recent**
ናይ ቆርበት ፋብሪካ nay qorbet fabrika *(n.)* **tannery**
ናይ ቆርበት ኖኳል nay qorbet nokual *(n. )* **pore**
ናይ ቋንቋ ሙሁር nay quanqua muhur *(adj.)* **linguist**
ናይ ርብዒ ዓመት nay rb'ï amet *(adj.)* **quarterly**
ናይ ሰብኣይ nay sb'ay *(adj.)* **manly**
ናይ ሰዓል ከረሜላ nay se'al keremiela *(n.)* **lozenge**
ናይ ሰገናት nay segenat *(n.)* **yob**
ናይሰለስተ ሙዚቃ nay seleste muziqa *(n.)* **trio**
ናይ ሰዉነት ጅማት nay sewunet jmat *(n.)* **tendon**
ናይ ሻምቦቆ ኣየር nay shamboqo ayer *(adj.)* **bronchial**
ናይ ሸንቲ nay shennti *(adj.)* **urinary**
ናይ ስኒ nay sni *(adj.)* **dental**
ናይ ስኒ ሓኪም nay sni ĥakim *(n.)* **dentist**
ናይ ስኒ ሕማም nay sni hmm *(n.)* **toothache**
ናይ ስኒ ሳሙና nay sni samuna *(n. )* **toothpaste**
ናይ ፁሑፍ ስምምዕነት nay suhuf smm'a *(n. )* **treaty**
ናይ ጣቋ ዘረባ nay takwa zereba *(adj.)* **rhetorical**
ናይ ቲፎ nay tifo *(n. )* **typhoid**
ናይ ፅዕንት መኪና nay ts'ent mekina *(n.)* **lorry**
ናይ ትሽትሽ nay tshtsh *(adj.)* **underarm**
ናይ ፆታዊ ርክብ ድሌት nay tsotawi rkb dliet *(n.)* **libido**
ናይ ውድድር ምርኢት nay wddr mr'it *(n.)* **rodeo**
ናይ ወደብ መድረኽ nay wedeb mdreke *(n.)* **pier**
ናይ ወዲ ንጉሳዊ nay wedi ngusawi *(adj.)* **princely**
ናይ ወዲ ስም nay wedi s'm *(adj.)* **Stuart**
ናይ ወኻርያ nay wekarya *(adj.)* **vulpine**
ናይ ውግእ nay wg'e *(adj.)* **martial**
ናይ ውልቀ nay wlqe *(adj.)* **solitary**
ናይ ውንዘፋ ጠለብ nay wnzefa teleb *(n.)* **caveat**
ናይ ዉሽጢ ዓዲ nay wshti ädi *(adj.)* **domestic**
ንይ ውሽጢ ክዳን nay wshti kdan *(n.)* **petticoat**
ናይ ውልቀ መምህር nay wulqe memher *(adj)* **tutorial**
ናይ ውሽጥኻ ዘይምዝራብ nay wushtkha zeymzrab *(adv. )* **insincerity**
ናይ ዉሽጡ ዘይዛረብ nay wushtu zeyzareb *(adj.)* **insincere**
ናይ ጻዕዳ ኢድ ጥንቁልና nay xaeda eid tnqulna *(n.)* **palmistry**
ናይ ፅዋ nay xwa *(adj.)* **mythical**
ናይ የዋህነት ተግባር nay yewahnet tegbar *(n. )* **largesse**
ናይ ዮጋ ሰብ nay yoga seb *(n.)* **yogi**
ናይ ዘርኢ nay zer'i *(adj.)* **genetic**

**ንዓይ ዘይብል** n'ay zeybl ***(adj.)*** **selfless**
**ናይ ዝናብ ክዳን** nay znab kdan ***(n.)*** **tarpaulin**
**ናይ ዝናብ ክዳን** nay znab kdan ***(n.)*** **mackintosh**
**ናይ ሓንጎል** nayei hanegole ***(adj.)*** **cerebral**
**ናይ ቆልዓ** nayei qolea' ***(adj.)*** **childish**
**ናይ ማዕድን ከሰል** nayi maeidin kesel ***(n.)*** **colliery**
**ናይ ቆንስል ገዛ** nayi qonsele geza ***(n.)*** **consulate**
**ናይሎን** naylon ***(n. )*** **nylon**
**ናይ ማይ መትሓዚ ዓብዪ ጎማ** naymay methazi abuyi goma ***(n. )*** **tanker**
**ናይ መን** naymen ***(pron.)*** **whose**
**ናዮም** nayom ***(adj.)*** **their**
**ናይ ስራሕ ቦታ** naysrah bota ***(n. )*** **workshop**
**ናይታ ሃገር** nayta hager ***(n.)*** **vernacular**
**ናይትሮጅን** naytrojn ***(n.)*** **nitrogen**
**ንባዕሉ** nba'ëlu ***(pron.)*** **itself**
**ነባሒ** nbahi ***(n.)*** **woofer**
**ንብዓት** nb'at ***( n. )*** **tear**
**ንበይኑ** nbeynu ***(adv. )*** **solely**
**ንብረት** nbret ***(n.)*** **asset**
**ንቡር** nbur ***(adj.)*** **normal**
**ንቡር ኩነት** nbur kunet ***(n.)*** **normalcy**
**ንዝዙሓት ኣማልኽቲ ምምላኽ** nbzuȟat amalḱti mmlaḱ ***(n. )*** **polytheism**
**ንብዙሓት ኣማልኽቲ ዘምልኽ** nbzuȟat amalḱti zemlḱ ***(adj.)*** **polytheistic**
**ንጨብ** n'cha'b ***(n.)*** **swag**
**ንደገ** ndege ***(adv. )*** **forth**
**ንደገ ኣተንፈሰ** ndege atenfese ***(v.)*** **exhale**
**ንድፋዊ** ndfawi ***(adj.)*** **schematic**
**ንድፊ** ndfi ***(n.)*** **design**
**ንድፊ** ndfi ***(n.)*** **draft**
**ንድፊ** ndfi ***(n. )*** **scheme**
**ንድፊ** ndfi ***(n.)*** **sketch**
**ንድሕሪት** ndȟrit ***(adv.)*** **aback**
**ንድሕሪት ተመልሰ** ndȟrit temelse ***(v.)*** **reverse**
**ንድሕሪት ዛኣንፈቱ** ndȟrit z'anfetu ***(adj.)*** **retrograde**
**ንድሕሪት ዘይብል** ndhrit zeybl ***(v.i. )*** **persevere**
**ንድሕሪት ዝጥምት** ndȟrit ztmt ***(adj.)*** **retrospective**
**ንድሕሪት** ndȟrit ***(adj.)*** **backward**
**ነኣደ** ne'ade ***(v.)*** **commend**
**ነኣደ** ne'ade ***(v. i)*** **compliment**
**ነዓቐ** neaqe ***(v.)*** **underestimate**
**ነዓቐ** neaqe ***(v.)*** **undermine**
**ነዓቐ** neaqe ***(v.)*** **underrate**
**ነዓቐ** ne'äqe ***(v.)*** **despise**
**ነዓቒ** ne'aqi ***(adj.)*** **contemptuous**
**ነብዐ** neb'a ***(v.)*** **tear**
**ነባዒ** neba'ï ***(adj.)*** **lachrymose**
**ነባር** nebar ***(adj.)*** **chronic**
**ነበልባል** nebelbal ***(n.)*** **flame**
**ነበረ** nebere ***(v.)*** **dwell**
**ነበረ** nebere ***(v.)*** **live**
**ነበረ** nebere ***(v.)*** **reside**
**ንብረት/ንዋይ** neberet/newaye ***(n.)*** **chattel**
**ነበርቲ** neberti ***(n.)*** **inhabitant**
**ነብሐ** nebhe ***(v.)*** **yap**
**ነቢይ** nebie ***(n.)*** **prophet**
**ነብሪ** nebri ***(n.)*** **tiger**

ነብስኻ ምምርማር nebska mmrmar *(n.)* **introspection**
ነብስኻ ምቍጽጻር nebska mqutstsar *(n.)* **temperance**
ነብሱ መርመረ nebsu mermere *(v.)* **introspect**
ነቡላ nebula *(n. )* **nebula**
ነዳድ nedad *(adj.)* **apoplectic**
ነዳድ nedad *(adj.)* **cantankerous**
ነዳዲ nedadi *(adj.)* **combustible**
ነዳዲ nedadi *(n.)* **fuel**
ነዳዲ ዘይቲ nedadi zyti *(n. )* **petroleum**
ነዳ'እ ሓርማዝ neda'e harmaz *(n.)* **mahout**
ነዳቃይ nedaqay *(n. )* **mason**
ነዲ nedi *(n.)* **rubric**
ነድሪ nedri *(n. )* **paddy**
ነድሪ ጭራምዑት nedri čram'ut *(n.)* **appendicitis**
ነድሪ ኮንጃንክቲቫ nedri konjanktiva *(n.)* **conjunctivitis**
ነድሪ ሳንቡእ nedri sanbuè *(n. )* **pneumonia**
ኔክታር neektar *(n.)* **nectar**
ኔፕትዩን neeptyun *(n. )* **Neptune**
ነፋሪት nefarit *(n.)* **aeroplane**
ነፋሪት nefarit *(n.)* **aircraft**
ነፋሪት nefarit *(n.)* **plane**
ነፋሻ nefasha *(adj.)* **airy**
ነፋጺ nefatsi *(adj.)* **skittish**
ነፈረ nefere *(v.i)* **fly**
ነፈሰ nefese *(v.)* **blow**
ነፈየ nefeye *(v.)* **sift**
ነፍሐ nefhe *(v.)* **inflate**
ነፍሐ nefȟe *(v.)* **blare**
ነፍሪ nefri *(n.)* **anthrax**
ነፍሲ nefsi *(n.)* **soul**
ነጋዳይ negaday *(n. )* **dealer**
ነጋዳይ ኣክስዮን negaday aksyon *(n.)* **stockbroker**
ነጋዳይ negaday *(n.)* **businessman**
ነጋዴ negade *(n. )* **trader**
ነጋዴ negade *(n. )* **tradesman**
ነጋዲ negadi *(n.)* **merchant**
ነገራት negerat *(n.)* **stuff**
ነገረ negere *(v.)* **tell**
ነገረኛ negeregna *(adj.)* **provocative**
ነገረኛ negerenya *(adj.)* **belligerent**
ነገሰ negese *(v.)* **reign**
ነግሒ neĥi *(n.)* **furrow**
ነጎድጓድ negodgad *(n.)* **thunder**
ነጎድጓዳዊ negodgadawi *(adj.)* **thunderous**
ነግራም negram *(n.)* **shrew**
ነግራም negram *(adj.)* **strident**
ነሃባይ nehabay *(n. )* **smith**
ነሃባይ ወርቂ nehabay werqi *(n. )* **goldsmith**
ነሓሰ neȟase *(n)* **August**
ነሓሲ neȟasi *(n.)* **copper**
ነኳል nekal *(n.)* **puncture**
ነኸሰ neḱese *(v.)* **bite**
ነከየ nekeye *(v.)* **decrease**
ነከየ nekeye *(v.)* **diminish**
ነከየ nekeye *(v. t)* **dwindle**
ነከየ nekeye *(v.)* **reduce**
ነኪኡ nekiau *(v.)* **touch**
ነኧል nekual *(n.)* **hole**
ንዕለቱ ኣቀደመ n'ëletu 'aqedeme *(v.)* **backdate**
ናብ ዓፅሚ ምቕያር nab atsmi mqyar *(v.)* **ossify**
ናብ ደገ nab dege *(adj.)* **outward**
ናትና natna *(adj.)* **our**
ናይ nay *(prep. )* **of**
ናይ ሓደ ሰብ ግዴታ nay hade seb gdieta *(n.)* **onus**

ናይ ሙዚቃ 8ኖታታት በቢ 2 ኖታ ዝፈላለዩ ney muziqa 8notatat bebi 2 nota zfelaleyu ***(n.)*** **octave**
ናይ ዓይኒ nay ayni ***(adj.)*** **ocular**
ናይ ዓይኒ ሓኪም nay ayni hakim ***(n. )*** **optician**
ናይ ዓፅምን መግጣጠምን ሕክምና nay atsmn megetatemin hkmna ***(n.)*** **osteopathy**
ናይ ዕምበበ ዓይነት nay embaba aynet ***(n.)*** **orchid**
ናይ እንቋቕሖ ቅርጺ nay enquaquho qrtsi ***(adj.)*** **oval**
ናይ እንቋቕሖ ቅርጺ nay enquaquho qrtsi ***(adj.)*** **ovate**
ናይ ጀልባ በትሪ nay jelba betri ***(n. )*** **oar**
ንሕና nhna ***(pron. )*** **ourselves**
ንላዕሊ nla'eli ***(prep.)*** **over**
ንቕድሚት nqdmit ***(adv. )*** **onward**
ንትጓ ntuag ***(n.)*** **outburst**
ንድፊ ndfi ***(n.)*** **outline**
ንጹግ ntsug ***(n.)*** **outcast**

# አ

አብ ስልጣን አደየበ 'ab slṭan 'adeyebe ***(v.)*** **install**
አበር ዘይብሉ 'aber zeyblu ***(adj.)*** **impeccable**
አብነት 'abnet ***(n.)*** **instance**
አብዚ 'abzi ***(adv. )*** **here**
አቸቶ 'acheto ***(n. )*** **vinegar**
አደራሽ 'aderash ***(n. )*** **hall**
አድልዎ ዘይብሉ 'adlwo zeyblu ***(adj.)*** **impartial**
አዕናዊ 'a'ënawi ***(n.)*** **vandal**
አእንጋዲ 'a'èngadi ***(adj. )*** **hospitable**
አፍቃሪ 'afqari ***(n.)*** **valentine**
አፍራሒ 'afraḥi ***(adj. )*** **horrific**
አፍርሐ 'afrḥe ***(v.)*** **horrify**
አጉልሐ 'agulḥe ***(v.)*** **highlight**
አሓጉሰ 'aȟagwase ***(v.)*** **gladden**
አሕመቐ 'aḥmeq̈e ***(v.)*** **vitiate**
አካይዳ ተመን ከደ 'akayda temen kede ***(v.)*** **wriggle**
አኽበበ 'aḱbebe ***(v.)*** **wreathe**
አኽበረ 'aḱbere ***(v.)*** **venerate**
አኽበረ 'aḱbere ***(v.)*** **glorify**
አልዓለ 'al'äle ***(v.)*** **heave**
አላይ ክዳውንቲ 'alay kdawnti ***(n.)*** **valet**
አሎዎ... 'alowo ***(v.)*** **have**
አመሳኸረ 'amesaḱere ***(v.)*** **verify**
አምለጠ amleṫe ***(v.i)*** **escape**
አነ 'ane ***(pron.)*** **I**
አንፈት ቀየረ 'anfet qeyere ***(v.)*** **veer**
አንገርገረ 'angergere ***(v.)*** **wallow**
አቕሓ 'aq̈ȟa ***(n.)*** **commodity**
አራዊት 'arawit ***(n.)*** **vermin**
አረድአ 'ared'e ***(n. )*** **illustrate**
አርማድዮ ክዳውንቲ 'armadyo kdawnti ***(n. )*** **wardrobe**
አሰላፊት 'aselafit ***(n.)*** **waitress**
አሰር 'aser ***(n. )*** **vestige**
አሻንና 'ashanna ***(n. )*** **valuation**
አሻቐለ 'ashaq̈ele ***(v.)*** **haunt**
አተባብዐ 'atebab'ë ***(v.)*** **hearten**
አተባብዐ 'atebab'ë ***(v.)*** **inspire**
አጠንቀቐ 'aṭenqeq̈ ***(v.)*** **warn**
አዋረደ 'awarede ***(v.)*** **vilify**
አወጣወጠ 'aweṭaweṭe ***(v.)*** **waggle**
አየር ዘየሕልፍ 'ayer zeyeḥlf ***(adj. )*** **hermetic**
አዝዩ 'azyu ***(adv. )*** **very**
ኤለትሪክ -መስፈር 'eeletrik- mesfer ***(n.)*** **wattage**

እኽሊ 'èḱli *(n.)* **grain**
እናጠፍአት ከደት 'ènațef'et kedet *(v.)* **wane**
እሳተ-ጎመራ 'èsategomera *(n. )* **volcano**
እስትሕጋግ 'èsthgag *(n. )* **gratuity**
ኣብ ምቅርራብ 'ab mqrrab *(adv.)* **afoot**
ኣብ ዙርያ 'ab zurya *(adv.)* **around**
ኣሕነኽ 'aȟneḱe *(adj.)* **abash**
ኣኮኣዊ 'ako'awi *(adj.)* **avuncular**
ኣባጨጓራ aaba'che'guara *(n.)* **caterpillar**
ኣዕለለ/ኣዉገዐ aae'lele/aawugeaa' *(v. i.)* **chat**
ኣገደደ aagedede *(v.)* **constrain**
ኣጓየየ aaguwayeye *(v.)* **chase**
ኣካተተ aakate'te *(v.)* **consist**
ኣማኸረ aamake're *(v.)* **consult**
ኣእንገደ a'anged *(v.)* **entertain**
ኣራኸበ aara'eh'kebe *(v.)* **connect**
ኣታለለ aatalele *(v.)* **cheat**
ኣእትዩ aatyu *(v.)* **tuck**
ኣዋረደ aawarede *(v. t.)* **cheapen**
ኣውቲስታ aawutiseta *(n.)* **chauffeur**
ኣብ ኤስያ ዝርከብ ቤተ ጸሎት ab asya zrkeb bete tselot *(n. )* **pagoda**
ኣብ ባሕሪ ስርቂ ab bahri srqi *(n. )* **piracy**
ኣብ ባይታ 'ab bayta *(adj.)* **aground**
ኣብ ድሕረ መድረኽ ab dȟre medreḱ *(adv.)* **backstage**
ኣብ ዕዳ ዛኣተወ ab eda z'atewe *(adj.)* **indebted**
ኣብ እዋን ab ewan *(prep.)* **during**
ኣብ ፎቅ ዝካረ መንበሪ ab foq zkare menberi *(n.)* **tenement**
ኣብ ገበን ምሽራኽ ab geben mshrak *(adj.)* **complicit**
ኣብ ገምገም ab gemgem *(adv.)* **ashore**
ኣብ ገምገም ባሕሪ ዝርከብ ab gemgem bahiri zirkeb *(n.)* **coaster**
ኣብ ግምት ብዘይምእታው 'ab gmt bzeym'ètaw *(adj.)* **irrespective**
ኣብ ግርዝውና ዝቦቁል ጸጉሪ ab grzwna zboqul xeguri *(adj.)* **pubic**
ኣብ ጐድኒ ab gwadni *(prep.)* **alongside**
ኣብ ሓደ ቦታ ዝተተከለ ናብ ካሊእ ቦታ ነቂልካ ምትካል ab hade bota ztetekele nab kalie bota neklka mtkal *(v.)* **transplant**
ኣብ ሓደጋ ኣውደቐ 'ab ȟadega 'awdeq̈e *(v.)* **jeopardize**
ኣብ ሓደጋ ጠሓለ ab hadega tehale *(v.)* **imperil**
ኣብ ሂማልያ ዝነብር እንስሳ ab himalya zeneber ensesa *(n.)* **yeti**
ኣብ ካፕሱላ ዓጸወ 'ab kapsula 'äxewe *(v.)* **encapsulate**
ኣብ ክክልተ 'ab keklte *(comb.)* **bi**
ኣብ ክክልት ዓመት ab keklte 'ämet *(adj.)* **biannual**
ኣብ ክንዲ ab kndi *(n.)* **behalf**
ኣብ ክንዲ ab kndi *(adv. )* **instead**
ኣብ ክንዲ ab kndi *(n.)* **stead**
ኣብ ክሳድ ዝእሰር ፎቶ ዝሓዘ መጋይፂ ab ksasd zeseer foto zelowo mgayetsi *(n. )* **locket**
ኣብ ኩሎም ኣማልኽቲ ምእማን ab kulom amalkti meman *(n. )* **pantheism**
ኣብ ኩሎም ኣማልኽቲ ዝኣምን ab kulom amalkti zamn *(adj.)* **pantheist**
ኣብ ኩሉ ህልዊ ab kulu hlwi *(adj.)* **omnipresent**

ኣብ ኩሉ ምህላው ab kulu mhlaw *(n.)* omnipresence

ኣብ ልዕሊ ab la'eli *(n.)* top

ኣብ ላዕሊ ab la'ëli *(adv.)* above

ኣብ ልዕሊ ab l'eli *(prep. )* on

ኣብ ልዕሊ 'ab l'ëli *(adv.)* aboard

ኣብ ማይ ዝነብር እንስሳ ab may znebr ensesa *(n.)* oyster

ኣብ መንጎ ab mengo *(prep.)* among

ኣብ መንጎ 'ab mengo *(prep.)* amid

ኣብ መንጎ 'ab mengo *(adv.)* between

ኣብመንጎ ቤተሰብ ዝግበር ግብረ ስጋ ab mengo beteseb zgber gbre-sga *(n.)* incest

ኣብ መርከብ ab merkeb *(adv.)* overboard

ኣብ መወዳእታ ab meweda'ta *(adv.)* eventually

ኣብ ሞንጎ ab mongo *(adv. )* midway

ኣብ መንጎ መፀ ab mongo mexe *(v.)* supervene

ኣብ ነፍሳት ዝነብሩ ፍጥረት ab nefsat znebru ftret *(n. )* parasite

ኣብ ቀረባ ab qereba *(adv. )* nigh

ኣብ ቀረባ እዋን ab qereba ewan *(adv. )* recently

ኣብ ሰዓቱ ab seätu *(adj.)* punctual

ኣብ ሰዓቱ ዝርከብ ab seätu zrkeb *(n.)* punctuality

ኣብ ስጋ ዝቕባእ ዘይቲ ab sga zqhba'e zeyti *(n.)* marinade

ኣብ ስምምዕ ዘይምብፃሕ ab smmë zeymbtsah *(n.)* deadlock

ኣብ ስራሕ ዘወዓለ ab srah zwe'ale *(adj.)* operational

ኣብ ታሕቲ ab tahti *(adv. )* down

ኣብ ጥቓ ab ṭqa *(adv. )* near

ኣብ ጥቓ ab ṭqa *(prep.)* beside

ኣብ ፀሑፍ ዝሰፈረ ab tshuf zsefere *(n.)* transcript

ኣብ ወሰን ዝርከብ ab wesen zrkeb *(adj.)* outlying

ኣብ ዉሽጢ ab wushti *(prep.)* in

ኣብ ውሽጢ ገዛ ab wushti geza *(adj.)* indoor

ኣብ ዘይቦቱኡ ኣቀመጠ ab zey bot'u aqemeë *(v.)* misplace

ኣብ ዘይቲ ኣለኸ ab zeyti aleke *(v.)* marinate

ኣብ ዝኾነ ዘይርከብ ab zkone zeyrkeb *(adv.)* nowhere

ኣብ ዝቅፀል ab zqxl *(prep.)* after

ኣብ ዙርያ ab zurya *(adv.)* about

ኣብ ab *(prep.)* at

ኣባ ሸማኔ aba shemanie *(n. )* leopard

ዓብዓበ äb'äbe *(v.)* swaddle

ኣባጨው 'abačewe *(v.)* jeer

ኣባጨው aba'chewe *(v.i.)* scoff

ኣባደመ abademe *(v.)* devastate

ኣባዕለገ aba'ëlege *(v.)* deprave

ኣባኻኒ abakani *(adj.)* prodigal

ኣባኻኒ abaḱani *(adj.)* profligate

ኣባኸነ abakene *(v.)* fritter

ኣባኸነ abakene *(v.)* waste

ኣባኸነ aba'khene *(v.)* squander

ኣባኮበራ abakobera *(n.)* cyclone

ኣባል abal *(n.)* member

ኣባል ባይቶ abal bayto *(n.)* senator

ኣባል ቤት ምኽሪ abal beet mkri *(n.)* councillor

ኣባል ፈራዶ abal ferado *(n. )* juror

ኣባል ሕጊ ኣፀዳቒ abal higi atsdaqhi *(n.)* legislator

ኣባል ኮነ 'abal kone *(v.)* join

ኣባል ምንቅስቓስ abal mnqsäas *(n.)* activist

**አባል ፓርላማ** abal parlama ***(n.)*** **parliamentarian**
**አብዓለ** 'ab'äle ***(v.)*** **celebrate**
**አባለተ** abalete ***(v.)*** **satirize**
**አባልገ** abalge ***(n.)*** **godfather**
**አባልገ** abalge ***(n.)*** **godmother**
**አባልነት** abalnet ***(n.)*** **membership**
**አባረረ** abarere ***(v.)*** **dispel**
**አባረረ** abarere ***(v. t)*** **eject**
**አባረረ** abarere ***(v.)*** **evict**
**አባረረ** abarere ***(v. t)*** **expel**
**አባረረ** abarere ***(v.)*** **repulse**
**አባረረ** abarere ***(v.)*** **sack**
**አባዝሖ** abazĥe ***(v.)*** **propagate**
**አበጋሲ** abegasi ***(n.)*** **setter**
**አበ-ገዳም** 'abegedam ***(n.)*** **abbot**
**አበሃህላ** abehahla ***(n. )*** **jargon**
**አበላሸወ** abelashewe ***(v.)*** **mar**
**አበላሸወ** abelashewe ***(v.)*** **spoil**
**አበላሸወ** abelashewe ***(v.)*** **undo**
**አበላሸወ** 'abelashewe ***(v.)*** **vandalize**
**አበር ምህላው** aber mhlaw ***(n.)*** **imperfection**
**አበር ዘለዎ** aber zelewo ***(adj.)*** **imperfect**
**አበር ዘውፅእ** aber zewx'e ***(adj.)*** **censorious**
**አበር** aber ***(n.)*** **blemish**
**አበራበረ** aberabere ***(v.)*** **liven**
**አበራበረ** aberabere ***(v.)*** **arouse**
**አበረኛ** aberegna ***(adj.)*** **defective**
**አበረኸ** abereke ***(v.)*** **elevate**
**አበርትዐ** aberte'ë ***(v.)*** **reinforce**
**አበሳጨወ** abesaĉewe ***(v.)*** **embitter**
**አበሳጨወ** abesaĉewe ***(v.)*** **exasperate**
**አበሳጨወ** abesaĉewe ***(v.)*** **frustrate**
**አበው** abew ***(n.)*** **ancestor**
**አበው** abew ***(n.)*** **paisley**

**አበዋት** abewat ***(n.)*** **ancestry**
**አበዋዊ** abewawi ***(adj.)*** **ancestral**
**አበይ** abey ***(adv.)*** **where**
**አበይ ከምዘሎ** abey kemzelo ***(adv.)*** **whereabouts**
**አበየ** abeye ***(v.)*** **refuse**
**አብለጭሊጩ** ablechlichu ***(v.)*** **twinkle**
**አብለሐ** ableh ***(v.)*** **sharpen**
**አብለሐ** ablehe ***(v.)*** **whet**
**አብነት** abnet ***(n.)*** **example**
**አብነት** abnet ***(n.)*** **quintessence**
**አብኖስ** a'bnos ***(n.)*** **ebony**
**አቦ** abo ***(n)*** **dad**
**አቦ** abo ***(n.)*** **father**
**አቦ ጋቡየ** abo gabuye ***(n.)*** **tortoise**
**አቦወንበር** abo' weneber ***(n.)*** **chairman**
**አቦአዊ** aboawi ***(adj.)*** **paternal**
**አቦሓጎ** 'aboḧago ***(n.)*** **forefather**
**አቦነት** abonet ***(n.)*** **paternity**
**አብራህረሀ** abrahereh ***(v.)*** **clarify**
**አብራህረሀ** abrahrehe ***(v.)*** **demystify**
**አብራህረሀ** abrahrehe ***(v. t)*** **elucidate**
**አብራህረሀ** abrahrehe ***(v.)*** **explain**
**አብረሀ** abrehe ***(v.)*** **lighten**
**አብረሰ** abrese ***(v.t. )*** **ravage**
**አብርሀ** abrhe ***(v.)*** **illuminate**
**አብሰለ** absele ***(v.)*** **cook**
**አብሺቁ** abshiqu ***(v.)*** **traduce**
**አብቲ ማዕዶ** abti maedo ***(adj.)*** **yonder**
**አብፀሐ** abtseĥe ***(v.)*** **deliver**
**አብኡ** ab'u ***(adv. )*** **there**
**አቡን** abun ***(n.)*** **bishop**
**አቡቐለም** abuqhelem ***(n.)*** **squid**
**አብዮታዊ** abyotawi ***(adj.)*** **revolutionary**

ኣብዚ እዋን abzi èwan *(adv. )* **presently**

ኣብዚ ከባቢ'ዚ abzi kebabizi *(adv. )* **hereabouts**

ኣብዚሕካ ገንዘብ ምውጻእ abzîĥka genzeb mwtsas'e *(v.)* **overdraw**

ኣጨብጨበ ačebčebe *(v.)* **applaud**

ኣጨፈቐ ačefeq̈e *(adj.)* **bedraggled**

ኣጨናነቐ acenaneqe *(v.)* **fluster**

ኣጨነቐ ačeneq̈e *(v.)* **ail**

ኣጨንገፈት ačengefet *(v.)* **miscarry**

ኣቻዮ achayo *(n.)* **steel**

ኣቸጋሪ ሰብ achegari seb *(n.)* **tormentor**

ኣጨነቐ ač̣heneq̈e *(v.)* **harass**

ኣጭለምለመ aĉlemleme *(v.t)* **flicker**

ኣዳኸመ adakeme *(v.)* **debilitate**

ኣዳኸመ adakeme *(v.)* **emasculate**

ኣዳኸመ adakeme *(v.)* **enfeeble**

ኣዳላዊ ቐብሪ adalawi qebri *(n.)* **undertaker**

ኣዳለወ adalewe *(v.)* **discriminate**

ኣዳለወ adalewe *(v.)* **prepare**

ኣዳመፀ adametze *(v.)* **listen**

ኣድቀለ adaqele *(v.)* **replicate**

ኣደራሽ adarash *(n. )* **gallery**

ኣዳራሽ መቃብር adarash meqabr *(n. )* **mausoleum**

ኣዳራሽ adarashe *(n.)* **chamber**

ኣደ ade *(n. )* **mother**

ኣደበ adebe *(v.)* **chasten**

ኣደዳ adeda *(n. )* **victimize**

ኣደፋፈረ adefafere *(v.)* **abet**

ኣደፋፈረ adefafere *(v.)* **embolden**

ኣደሃሀረ adehahere *(v.)* **enliven**

ኣደኽደኸ adekhdekhe *(v.)* **stunt**

ኣደማምጻ ademamxa *(n.)* **pronunciation**

ኣደመ ademe *(v.)* **revolt**

ኣደመ ademe *(v.)* **boycott**

ኣደናገረ adenagere *(v.)* **confuse**

ኣደናገረ adenagere *(v.)* **discomfit**

ኣደናገረ adenagere *(v.)* **rig**

ኣደናገረ 'adenagere *(v.)* **juggle**

ኣደናጎየ adenagoye *(v.)* **prorogue**

ኣደናጎየ adenagueye *(v.)* **procrastinate**

ኣደነት adeneet *(n.)* **motherhood**

ኣደነቐ adeneq̈e *(v.)* **astonish**

ኣደንጋጽነት adengaxnet *(n.)* **poignancy**

ኣደንጎየ adengoye *(v. t)* **delay**

ኣደንጎየ adengoye *(v.)* **reprieve**

ኣደንጎየ adengoye *(v.)* **temporize**

ኣደንዛዚ adenzazi *(adj.)* **lethargic**

ኣደንዛዚ adenzazi *(adj.)* **stunning**

ኣደንዛዚ ነገር adenzazi neger *(n.)* **narcotic**

ኣደንዘዘ adenzeze *(v.)* **stun**

ኣደንዘዘ adenzeze *(v.)* **stupefy**

ኣደቃሲ adeqasi *(adj.)* **soporific**

ኣድጊ በረኻ adgi bereka *(n. )* **zebra**

ኣድጊ adgi *(n.)* **donkey**

ኣድሓነ adhane *(v.)* **salvage**

ኣድሓነ adhane *(v.)* **save**

ኣድሓነ adĥane *(v.)* **redeem**

ኣድሓነ adĥane *(v.)* **rescue**

ኣድሓኒ adhani *(n. )* **saviour**

ኣድሓርሓረ adĥarĥare *(v.t. )* **retreat**

ዓዲ ወዓለ ädi weale *(v.)* **retire**

ዓዲ ውዒልነት ädi wealnet *(n.)* **retirement**

ኣድካሚ 'adkam *(adj.)* **laborious**

ኣድካሚ adkami *(adj.)* **menial**

ኣድካሚ adkami *(adj.)* **strenuous**

ኣድካሚ adkami *(adj.)* **tiresome**

ኣድካሚ adkami *(adj.)* **trying**

አድካሚ adkami *(adj.)* **arduous**
አድከመ adkeme *(v.)* **exhaust**
አድከመ adkeme *(v.)* **impair**
አድከመ adkeme *(v.)* **weaken**
አድከየ adkeye *(v.)* **impoverish**
አድላይ adlay *(adj.)* **germane**
አድላዪ adlayi *(adj.)* **necessary**
አድላዪ adlayi *(adj.)* **pertinent**
አድላዪ adlayi *(adj.)* **requisite**
አድላዪ adlayi *(n. )* **significant**
አድላዪ ነገር adlayi neger *(n. )* **requisite**
አድላዪነት adlaynet *(n. )* **necessity**
አድላይነት adlaynet *(n.)* **significance**
አድለየ adleye *(v.)* **necessitate**
አድማ adma *(n.)* **mutiny**
አድማዒነት adma'ïnet *(n.)* **efficacy**
አድማሳዊ admasawi *(adj.)* **cosmic**
አድማፂ admatsi *(n.)* **revolution**
አድማፂ adma'txi *(adj.)* **constituent**
አድማጺ admaxi *(n. )* **vowel**
አድመፀ admexe *(v.)* **enunciate**
አድመጸ admexe *(v.)* **pronounce**
አዳሚ admi *(adj.)* **mutinous**
አድሚራል admiral *(n.)* **admiral**
አድናቆት adnakot *(n.)* **wonder**
አድናቒ adnaqi *(n.)* **fan**
አድናቖት adnaqot *(n.)* **admiration**
አድነቐ adneqe *(v.)* **admire**
አድንቆ adnqo *(n.)* **astonishment**
አድራሽ adrash *(n.)* **location**
አድራሻ adrasha *(n.)* **domicile**
አድራሻ adrasha *(n.)* **address**
አድሪ adri *(n.)* **mustard**
አዕበየ aëbeye *(v.)* **enlarge**
አዕበየ a'ëbeye *(v.)* **nurture**
አዕደየ a'edeye *(v.)* **levy**
አዕገበ a'egebe *(v.)* **satisfy**
አዐገሰ a'ëgese *(v.)* **relieve**
አዕጀውጀወ ለፍለፈ 'a'ëğewğewe leflef *(v.)* **waffle**
አዕጎምጎመ a'ëgomgome *(v.)* **mutter**
አእካል ዝበልዕ aekal zibel'e *(n.)* **weevil**
አእላፍ aelaf *(n.)* **aeon**
አዕለቕለቐ 'a'ëleqleqe *(v.)* **inundate**
አእመነ aemene *(v.)* **persuade**
አእመነ aemene *(v.)* **urge**
አእመነ a'emene *(v.)* **convince**
አእምሮ a'emro *(n.)* **mind**
አእምሮአዊ a'emro'awi *(adj.)* **intellectual**
አዕሚቑ ዝሓስብ a'ëmuqu zhasb *(adj.)* **reflective**
አዕናዊ a'ënawi *(n.)* **destroyer**
አዕነወ aenewe *(v.)* **zap**
አዕነወ a'ënewe *(v.)* **demolish**
አዕነወ a'ënewe *(v.)* **destroy**
አእንጋዲ a'engadi *(n. )* **host**
አእንጋዲነት a'engadinet *(n. )* **hospitality**
አእንጋዲት a'engadit *(n.)* **hostess**
አዐንዘዘ ae-nzeze *(v.)* **hypnotize**
አዐንዘዘ a'ënzeze *(v.)* **mesmerize**
አዕረፈ a'ërefe *(v.)* **rest**
አዕረገ 'a'ërege *(v.)* **escalate**
አዐረየ a'ërye *(v.)* **rectify**
አዐርዩ ተዓዘበ aëryu teäzebe *(v.)* **peer**
አዕጠቀ a'ëteqe *(v.)* **equip**
አዕጠይጠየ aëteteye *(v.)* **dally**
አእተወ a'etewe *(v.)* **implant**
አእተወ a'etewe *(v.)* **infuse**
አእተወ a'ètewe *(v.)* **involve**
አዕጠይጠየ a'ëteyteye *(v.)* **dawdle**
አዕወልወለ a'ëwelwele *(v.)* **nauseate**
አእወየ aeweye *(n.)* **yell**

**አይዋይ** aeweye ***(n.)* yelp**
**ኣእወየ** a'eweye ***(v.)* scream**
**ኣእወየ** a'eweye ***(v.i. )* shout**
**ኣእወየ** a'eweye ***(v.)* shriek**
**ኣዕዛዚ** a'ëzazi ***(n.)* booster**
**ኣዕዘምዘመ** a'ëzemzeme ***(v.)* babble**
**ኣዕዘዘ** a'ëzeze ***(v.)* boost**
**ኣዕዘዘ** a'ëzeze ***(v.)* maximize**
**ኣፍ** af ***(n.)* gob**
**ኣፍ** a'f ***(n.)* mouth**
**ኣፍ ጡብ** a'f ťub ***(n.)* nipple**
**ኣፍ ቱቦ** af tubo ***(n.)* nozzle**
**ኣፋፍኖት** afafenote ***(n.)* clue**
**ኣፋኾሰ** afakose ***(v.)* simplify**
**ኣፋኰሰ** afakwase ***(v.)* allay**
**ኣፋለጠ** afaleťe ***(v.)* acquaint**
**ኣፋለጠ** afaleťe ***(v.)* introduce**
**ኣፋለጠ** afaleťe ***(v.)* advertise**
**ዓፋን ድምጺ** äfan dmxi ***(n. )* muffler**
**ኣፍደገ** afdege ***(n. )* lobby**
**ኣፍደገ** afdege ***(n.)* portal**
**ኣፍደገ** afdege ***(n.)* threshold**
**ኣፈ ሙዝ** afe muz ***(n.)* muzzle**
**ኣፈዳድላ** afedadla ***(n.)* spelling**
**ኣፈላላይ** afelalay ***(n.)* difference**
**ኣፈላላይ** afelalay ***(n.)* discrepancy**
**ኣፈላላይ** afelalay ***(n.)* disparity**
**ኣፈላላይ** afelalay ***(n.)* segregation**
**ኣፈራረሐ** aferarehe ***(v.)* intimidate**
**ኣፈራርሐ** aferarhe ***(v.)* threaten**
**ኣፈሸለ** afeshele ***(v.)* foil**
**ኣፍቀረ** afkere ***(v.)* dote**
**ኣፍኮሰ** afkose ***(v.)* slacken**
**ኣፍላቒ** aflaqi ***(n.)* prompter**
**ኣፍልቢ** aflebi ***(n.)* chest**
**ኣፍለጠ** aflete ***(v.)* proclaim**
**ኣፍለጠ** afleťe ***(v.)* apprise**
**ኣፍልጦ** aflto ***(n.)* recognition**
**ኣፍንጫ** afnča ***(n.)* nose**
**ኣፍቃዲ** afqadi ***(adj.)* permissive**
**ኣፍቃሪ** afqari ***(n.)* lover**
**ኣፍቃሪ** afqari ***(n.)* soul mate**
**ኣፍቀደ** afqede ***(v.)* permit**
**ኣፍቀረ** afqere ***(v.t.)* adore**
**ኣፍቀረ** af'qere ***(v.)* cherish**
**ኣፍራዪ** afrayi ***(n. )* producer**
**ኣፍራይነት** afraynet ***(n.)* productivity**
**ኣፍረሐ** afreĥe ***(v.)* frighten**
**ኣፍረሰ** afrese ***(v.)* rescind**
**ኣፍረየ** afreye ***(v.)* generate**
**ኣፍርየ** afreye ***(v.)* produce**
**ኣፍረየ** afreye ***(v.)* synthesize**
**ኣፍረየ** afreye ***(v.)* yield**
**ኣፍርሐ** afrhe ***(v.)* unnerve**
**ኣፍሪካዊ** afrikawi ***(adj.)* African**
**ኣፍሸለ** afšele ***(v.)* refute**
**ኣፍሰሰ** a'fsese ***(v.)* spill**
**ኣፍሸለ** afshele ***(v.)* disprove**
**ኣፍጠጠ** aftete ***(v.)* ogle**
**ኣጋ ምሸት** aga mshet ***(n.)* dusk**
**ኣጋዕዘየ** aga'ëzeye ***(v.)* disarrange**
**ኣጋፋሪ** 'agafari ***(n.)* chamberlain**
**ኣጋገየ** agageye ***(v.)* disorientate**
**ኣጋገየ** agageye ***(v.)* garble**
**ኣጋገየ** agageye ***(v.)* misdirect**
**ኣጋገየ** agageye ***(v.)* misguide**
**ኣጋላባይ** agalabay ***(n.)* jockey**
**ኣጋነነ** aganene ***(v.)* exaggerate**
**ኣጋነነ** aganene ***(v.)* overact**
**ኣጋር** agar ***(n. )* pedestrian**
**ኣጋር መንገዲ** agar mengedi ***(n.)* path**
**ኣጋጣሚ** agatami ***(n.)* incident**
**ኣጋጣሚ** agatami ***(n.)* occasion**
**ኣጋዋሒ** agawaĥi ***(adj.)* resonant**
**ኣጋውሐ** agawĥe ***(v.)* reverberate**

**አግባባ ዘይብሉ አሰራርሓ** agbab zeyblu aserarha ***(n. )*** **malpractice**
**አግባብ ዘይብሉ** agbaba zeyblu ***(adj.)*** **improper**
**አግባብ ዘይብሉ ፀባይ** agbaba zeyblu tsebay ***(n.)*** **impropriety**
**አግባብነት ዘይብሉ** agbabnet zeyblu ***(adj.)*** **inappropriate**
**አግደደ** agdede ***(v.)*** **aggravate**
**አገባብ** agebab ***(n)*** **ethic**
**አገባብ** agebab ***(n.)*** **formality**
**አገባብ** agebab ***(n.)*** **means**
**አገባብ** agebab ***(n.)*** **method**
**አገባብ** agebab ***(n. )*** **mode**
**አገባብ አዘራርባ** agebab azerarba ***(n. )*** **parlance**
**አገባብ ዘይብሉ ጽለኢ** agebab zeyblu xlei ***(n. )*** **prejudice**
**አገባባዊነት** agebabawineet ***(n. )*** **modality**
**አገዳዲ** agedadi ***(adj.)*** **obliging**
**አገዳሲ** agedasi ***(adj.)*** **noteworthy**
**አገዳሲ** agedasi ***(adj.)*** **pivotal**
**አገዳሲ** agedasi ***(adj.)*** **salient**
**አግዳሲ** agedasi ***(adj.)*** **urgent**
**አገዳሲ** 'agedasi ***(adj.)*** **momentous**
**ናይ ስፖርት ሜዳ** agedasi akal ***(n.)*** **pitch**
**አገደደ** agedded ***(v.)*** **coerce**
**አገደ** agede ***(v.)*** **prohibit**
**አገደ** agede ***(v.)*** **ban**
**አገላገለ** agelagela ***(v.)*** **extricate**
**አገላትዐ** agelat'e ***(v.)*** **maltreat**
**አገላትዐ** agelat'ë ***(v.)*** **mishandle**
**አገልጋሊ** agelgali ***(n.)*** **attendant**
**አገልጋሊ** agelgali ***(n.)*** **servant**
**አገልጋሊ** agelgali ***(n.)*** **varlet**
**አገልጋሊ ቤተክርስትያን** agelgali bete krstyan ***(n.)*** **sexton**
**አገልገለ** agelgele ***(v.)*** **serve**
**አገልግሎት** agelglot ***(n.)*** **service**
**አገረመ** agereme ***(v.)*** **amaze**
**አገረመ** agereme ***(v.)*** **baffle**
**አገጣጣማይ** ageẗaẗamay ***(n.)*** **fitter**
**አገጣጠመ** ageẗaẗeme ***(v.)*** **assemble**
**አግፈሐ** agfehe ***(v.)*** **dilate**
**አግሃደ** aghade ***(v.)*** **declassify**
**አግሃደ** aghade ***(v.)*** **evince**
**አግለለ** aglele ***(v.)*** **ostracize**
**አግለለ** 'aglele ***(v.)*** **isolate**
**አጎደ** agode ***(v.)*** **stoke**
**አጎልበተ** agolbete ***(v.)*** **foster**
**አጎምጅዩ** agomjyu ***(v.)*** **tantalize**
**አግሪፎልዮ** agrifolyo ***(n.)*** **holly**
**አግጣሚ** agẗami ***(n. )*** **joiner**
**አጉባዕብዐ** aguba'ëb'ë ***(v.)*** **hector**
**አጉደለ** agudele ***(v.)*** **deduct**
**አጉዶ** agudo ***(n.)*** **hut**
**አጉሃየ** aguhaye ***(v.)*** **grieve**
**አጉል** agul ***(adj.)*** **neuter**
**አጉሌ** agule ***(n.)*** **truffle**
**አጉለሐ** agulehe ***(v.)*** **magnify**
**አጉለሐ** 'aguleḧe ***(v.)*** **emboss**
**አጉለሐ** aguleḧe ***(v.)*** **accentuate**
**አጉልሐ** agulḧe ***(v.)*** **amplify**
**አጉረምረመ** aguremreme ***(v.)*** **gripe**
**አጉረምረመ** aguremreme ***(v.)*** **mumble**
**አጉረምረመ** aguremreme ***(v.)*** **murmur**
**አጉረምረመ** aguremreme ***(v.)*** **whimper**
**አጉረጠ** 'agureẗe ***(v.)*** **jab**
**አጐዓዓዚ** agwa'ä'äzi ***(n.)*** **haulier**
**አጓዲ** agwadi ***(n.)*** **stoker**
**አጓም** agwam ***(n.)*** **bud**
**አጐመ** agwame ***(v.)*** **burgeon**

ኣጓነፈ agwanefe *(v.)* **encounter**
ኣጓነየ agwaneye *(v.i.)* **alienate**
ኣህደአ ahad'e *(v.t.)* **abate**
ኣህደአ ahad'e *(v.t.)* **abate**
ኣሓደሰ aĥadese *(n. )* **renovate**
ኣሃዱ 'ahadu *(n.)* **unit**
ኣሃዱ ኣምላኽኛ ahadu amlaḱegna *(n.)* **monotheist**
ኣሃዱ ኣምላኽነት ahadu amlaḱnet *(n. )* **monotheism**
ኣሃዱ ናይ ኤለትሪካዊ ጉልበት ahadu nay 'eeletrikawi gulbet *(n. )* **watt**
ኣሓጎሰ 'aħagwase *(v.)* **exhilarate**
ኣሐየለ ahayl'e *(v.)* **consolidate**
ኣሃዝ ahaz *(n.)* **digit**
ኣሃዝ ahaz *(n. )* **numeral**
ኣሃዛዊ ahazawi *(adj.)* **digital**
ኣሃዛዊ ahazawi *(adj.)* **numerical**
ኣሕበረ a'ḧbere *(v.)* **stir**
ኣህድአ ahd'e *(v.)* **pacify**
ኣህድአ ah-dea *(v.i)* **hush**
ኣህደአ ahde'e *(v.)* **defuse**
ኣህደአ ahde'e *(v.)* **lull**
ኣህደአ ahde'e *(v.)* **mollify**
ኣህደአ ahde'e *(v.)* **quieten**
ኣህደአ ahde'e *(v.)* **soothe**
ኣሐደሰ ahdese *(v.)* **recondition**
ኣሐደሰ aĥdese *(v.)* **renew**
ኣሐደሰ ahedese *(v.)* **refresh**
ኣሐደሰ aĥedese *(v.)* **recreate**
ኣሀገረ ahegere *(v.)* **nationalize**
ኣሐጎሰ aĥegose *(v.i)* **excite**
ኣሐጎሰ aḥegwase *(v.)* **gratify**
ኣሀለኸ aheleke *(v.)* **knacker**
ኣሐንጠሰ aħentëse *(v.i. )* **sneeze**
ኣህፈፈ ahfefe *(v.)* **defrost**
ኣሕፈረ aĥfere *(v.)* **embarrass**
ኣሓጎሰ aĥgose *(v. t.)* **delight**
ኣህላኺ ahlaki *(adj.)* **demanding**
ኣሕለፈ ahlefe *(v.)* **undergo**
ኣሕቃቒ aḧqaqi *(n.)* **solvent**
ኣህረፈ ahrefe *(v.)* **entice**
ኣሕረቐ aĥreqe *(v.)* **displease**
ኣሕረቐ 'aḥreq̈e *(v.)* **vex**
ኣሕረረ ahrere *(v.)* **scorch**
ኣሕረረ aĥrere *(v.)* **singe**
ኣሕሰረ aĥsere *(v.)* **degrade**
ኣህተፍተፈ ahteftefe *(v.)* **hallucinate**
ኣህተፍተፈ ahteftefe *(v.)* **rave**
ኣሕፀረ aĥtsere *(v.)* **shorten**
ኣህጉር መቛረፂ ahugur meqaresi *(adj.)* **transcontinental**
ኣሕዋት aĥwat *(n.)* **sibling**
ኣሕወየ aĥweye *(v.)* **reimburse**
ኣሕጸረ aḧxere *(v.t)* **abridge**
ኣሕጸረ 'aḧxere *(v.t.)* **abbreviate**
ኣሕየወ ahyewe *(v.)* **animate**
ኣሕዛኒ aḧzani *(adj.)* **mournful**
ኣሕዘነ ahzene *(v.)* **sadden**
ኣሕዘነ aĥzene *(v.)* **deject**
ኣሕዘነ aĥzene *(v.)* **disappoint**
ኢድ እግሪ ርእሲ ዘይብሉ ኣካል aid agri resi zeyblu akal *(n.)* **torso**
ኣጅቦ ajbo *(n.)* **curd**
ኣጀንዳ aĵenda *(n.)* **agenda**
ኣጅቦ ajobo *(n.)* **cheese**
ኣካባቢ akababi *(n.)* **surroundings**
ኣካቢ akabi *(n.)* **collector**
ኣካደሚ akademi *(n.)* **academy**
ኣካደሚያዊ akademiyawi *(adj.)* **academic**
ኣካፍአ akaf'a *(v.)* **stigmatize**
ኣካፈለ 'akafele *(v.)* **impart**
ኣኻፈየ akafeye *(n.)* **drizzle**
ኣካጁ akaju *(n.)* **cashew**
ኣካል akal *(n.)* **organ**

አካል ዕምበባ akal ëmbeba ***(n.)*** **stamen**
አካል akal ***(n.)*** **body**
አካላዊ ተፈጥሮ akalawi tefetro ***(adj.)*** **physical**
አካላዊ akalawi ***(adv.)*** **bodily**
አኽኣለ ak'ale ***(v.)*** **enable**
አቃልዐ akal'ë ***(v.)*** **debunk**
አካለ ጎደሎ ገበረ akale godelo gebere ***(v.)*** **mutilate**
አካለ-ስንኩል akalesnkul ***(n.)*** **invalid**
አካል ምጉዳል akam mgudal ***(n.)*** **mutilation**
አካራዪ akarayi ***(n.)*** **lessor**
አካረየ akareye ***(v.t. )*** **sublet**
አካታቲ akatati ***(adj.)*** **inclusive**
አካትዒ akat'ë ***(adj.)*** **debatable**
አካተተ akatete ***(v.)*** **include**
አካየደ akayede ***(v.)*** **officiate**
አካይዳ akayida ***(n. )*** **gait**
አኽባር ሕጊ aḱbar ḧgi ***(n.)*** **prosecutor**
አኽባሪ akbari ***(adj.)*** **respectful**
አኽባሪ akbari ***(adj.)*** **reverent**
አኽበረ aḱbere ***(v.)*** **commemorate**
አኽበረ aḱbere ***(v.)*** **comport**
አኽበረ aḱbere ***(v.)*** **bide**
አኽብሮት aḱbrot ***(n.)*** **homage**
አኼባ akeba ***(n.)*** **rally**
አኼባ ዕርቂ akeba eirqi ***(n.)*** **parley**
አከባቢ akebabi ***(n.)*** **setting**
አከበ akebe ***(v.)*** **agglomerate**
አከበ akebe ***(v.)*** **amass**
አከበ akebe ***(v.)*** **collate**
አከበ akebe ***(v.)*** **gather**
አከበ akebe ***(v.)*** **muster**
አከበ akebe' ***(v.)*** **collect**
አከዳድና akedadna ***(n.)*** **dressing**
አኼባ akeeba ***(n.)*** **convocation**
አኼባ aḱeeba ***(n.)*** **assembly**
አኼባ aḱeeba ***(n. )*** **meeting**
አከፋፈለ akefafele ***(v.)*** **dispense**
አከሓሓሰ akeḧaḧase ***(v.)*** **offset**
አከላበተ akelabete ***(v.)*** **maul**
አኸለ akele ***(v.)*** **suffice**
አከራኻሪ akerakari ***(adj.)*** **controversial**
አከርካሪ ዘይብሎም እንስሳታት akerkari zeyblom anssatat ***(n.)*** **tentacle**
አከሻሽና akešašna ***(n. )*** **recipe**
አከሻሽና akeshashna ***(n.)*** **cuisine**
አክፈለ akfele ***(v.)*** **charge**
አኽሊ a'khali ***(n.)*** **sufficiency**
አኽበረ akhbere ***(v.)*** **solemnize**
አኽሊል aklil ***(n.)*** **coronet**
አኽሊል aklil ***(n.)*** **crown**
አኽሊል ብርሃን aḱlil brhan ***(n.)*** **aura**
አኮ ako ***(n.)*** **uncle**
አኾምሳዒ akomsa'ï ***(n.)*** **ruminant**
አኾምሰዐ akomse'ë ***(v.)*** **ruminate**
አኾምሰዐ aḱomse'ë ***(v.)*** **munch**
አኽራሪ akrari ***(n.)*** **zealot**
አክሪሊክ 'akrilik ***(adj.)*** **acrylic**
አክሮባስያዊ akrobasyawi ***(adj.)*** **acrobatic**
አክሮባት akrobat ***(n.)*** **acrobat**
አኽሳቢ aksabi ***(adj.)*** **gainful**
አክስዮን ak'syon ***(n.)*** **stock**
አክቲኒየም aktiniyem ***(n.)*** **actinium**
አኩፓንክቸር akupankcher ***(n.)*** **acupuncture**
አኩስቲካዊ akustikawi ***(adj.)*** **acoustic**
አቋራጭ akwaraĉ ***(n.)*** **shortcut**
አኳርየም akwaryem ***(n.)*** **aquarium**
አኳሸመ akwasheme ***(v.i)*** **flirt**
አላገበ alagebe ***(v.)*** **interconnect**

አላገበ alagebe *(v.)* **staple**
አላገፀ alagetse *(v.)* **deride**
አላገፀ alagetse *(v.)* **gibe**
አላገፀ alagetse *(n.)* **sneer**
አላገጸ alagetse *(v.)* **tease**
አላገፀ alagexe *(v.)* **mock**
አላ'ላዪ alalayi *(n.)* **compère**
አልዓለ alale *(v.)* **pick**
አልዓለ al'ale *(v.t. )* **lift**
አልዐለ al'äle *(v.)* **raise**
አላማይ alamay *(n. )* **weaver**
አላቐቐ alaqeqe *(v.)* **disengage**
አላይ ሕሙም alay ȟmum *(n.)* **nurse**
አላዪ አአጋርን አጻብዕቲ አአጋርን alayi aearnaxabetn aegarn *(n.)* **pedicure**
አላዛቢ alazabi *(n.)* **moderator**
አልቦ albo *(adj.)* **devoid**
አልቦነት albonet *(n. )* **nihilism**
አልቡም 'album *(n)* **album**
አለዓዓለ ale'a'ale *(v.)* **uplift**
አለዓዓለ ale'ä'äle *(v.)* **precipitate**
አለኸ aleḱe *(v.)* **bathe**
አለኹ አለኹ ኢሉ aleḱu aleḱu eilu *(n.)* **pretension**
አለለየ aleleye *(v.)* **discern**
አለማመደ alemamede *(v.)* **accustom**
አለማሚዱ alemamidu *(v.)* **train**
አለመ aleme *(v.)* **weave**
አለመ 'aleme *(v.)* **fabricate**
አለቀሐ aleqehe *(v.)* **lend**
አለርጂ alerji *(n.)* **allergy**
አለርጂነት alerjinet *(adj.)* **allergic**
አለስለሰ aleslese *(v.)* **soften**
አለዋዊጥካ ምቕማጥ alewawitka mqmat *(n.)* **permutation**
አለዋዊጡ ጺሒፉ alewawitu sihifu *(v.)* **transpose**
አለሸ alexe *(v.)* **scour**
አለየ aleye *(v.)* **avert**
አልገበ algebe *(v.t.)* **affix**
አልገሰ algese *(v.)* **eliminate**
አልገሰ algese *(v.)* **extirpate**
አልገሰ algese *(v.)* **remove**
አልገሰ algese *(v.)* **obviate**
አልጀብራ alĵebra *(n.)* **algebra**
አልካሊ alkali *(n.)* **alkali**
አልከሚ alkemi *(n.)* **alchemy**
አልኮል alkol *(n.)* **alcohol**
አልማናክ almanak *(n.)* **almanac**
አልማዝ almaz *(n.)* **diamond**
አልመደ almede *(v.t. )* **habituate**
አልቀቐ alqeqe *(v.)* **evacuate**
አልተያ alteya *(n.)* **marshmallow**
አሉሚኒዮም aluminiyom *(n.)* **aluminium**
አሉታ aluta *(adj.)* **negative**
አሉታዊ alutawi *(adj.)* **adverse**
አሉታውነት alutawinet *(n.)* **negativity**
አማእክለ zamaeekele *(v.)* **centralize**
አማዕበለ ama'ëbele *(v.)* **enrich**
አማዕደወ ama'edewe *(v.)* **scan**
አማዕረገ ama'ërege *(v.)* **dignify**
አማጓቲ amagwati *(adj.)* **argumentative**
አማጓቲ amagwati *(adj.)* **moot**
አመሓዳሪ amaȟadari *(n.)* **curator**
አማሃረ amahare *(v.)* **educate**
አማኻሪ amaha'ri *(n.)* **consultant**
አመሓየሸ amahayeshe *(v.)* **adapt**
አማሓየሸ amaȟayeshe *(v.)* **meliorate**
አማሓደረ ama'hdere *(v.)* **manage**
አማኸሪ amakari *(n.)* **counsellor**
አማካሪ amakari *(n.)* **courtier**
አማኸረ amakere *(v.)* **counsel**
አማኒት amanit *(n.)* **confidant**

አማራፂ amaratsi ***(n.)* option**
አማስሖ amasȟe ***(v.)* allot**
አማወቐ amaweqe ***(v.)* flex**
አማዞን amazon ***(n.)* Amazon**
አምባገነንነት ambagenennet ***(adj.)* totalitarian**
አምባገነንነት ambagenennet ***(n. )* tyranny**
አምቡላንስ ambulans ***(n.)* ambulance**
አምዐ am'ё ***(n. )* nettle**
አመዓራረየ ame'ärareye ***(v. t)* dispose**
አመዓራረየ ame'ärareye ***(v.)* adjust**
አመጋግባ amegagba ***(n.)* nutrition**
አመሓደረ ameȟadare ***(v.)* superintend**
አመሓዳሪ ameȟadari ***(n.)* superintendent**
አመሓዳሪ ameȟadari ***(adj.)* administrator**
አመሓደረ ameȟadere ***(v.)* administer**
አመሓላለፈ ameĥalalefe ***(v.)* defer**
አመሓላለፈ ameĥalalefe ***(v.)* refer**
አመሓላሊፉ amehalalifu ***(v.)* transmit**
አመሓየሸ ameĥayeše ***(v.)* reform**
አመሓየሸ ameĥayeše ***(v.)* retouch**
አመሓየሸ amehayeshe ***(v.)* upgrade**
አመሓየሸ ameȟayeshe ***(v.)* ameliorate**
አመሓየሸ ameȟayeshe ***(v.)* amend**
አመኬላ amekiela ***(n.)* thistle**
አመክሮ amekro ***(n.)* parole**
አመክሮ amekro ***(n. )* probation**
አመል amel ***(n.)* temperament**
አመል ኮይኑዎ amel koynuwo ***(n.)* trifle**
አመላኸተ amelakete ***(v. t)* denote**
አመልካቲ amelkati ***(n.)* applicant**
አመልካቲቶ 'amelkatito ***(n.)* forefinger**
አመልክዐ amelk'ë ***(v.)* beautify**
አመልከተ amelkete ***(v.)* annotate**
አመልከተ amelkete ***(v.t.)* apply**
አመልከተ amelkete ***(v.)* indicate**
አመልከተ amelkete ***(v.)* notify**
አመልከተ amelkete ***(v.)* signify**
አመልከተ amelkete ***(v.)* beckon**
አመና a'mena ***(adj.)* super**
አመና ድሙቕ amena dmu-que ***(adj.)* garish**
አመና ልሙድ amena lmud ***(adj. )* hackneyed**
አመና ንጡፍ amena nťuf ***(adj.)* hyperactive**
አመንጨወ amenĉewe ***(v.)* derive**
አመንጨወ amen'chewe ***(v.)* secrete**
አመነ amene ***(v.)* concede**
አመነ amene ***(v.)* believe**
አመንዝር amenzer ***(n.)* whore**
አመንዝራ amenzra ***(n.)* prostitute**
አመንዝራዊ amenzrawi ***(adj.)* meretricious**
አመቀረ ameqere ***(v.)* sweeten**
አመራስሐ ameraseȟe ***(v.)* adulterate**
አመራስሐ ameraseȟe ***(v.)* besmirch**
አመራስሖ amerasȟe ***(n.)* sophisticate**
አመርዓወ amerawe ***(v.)* wed**
አመስጋኒ amesgani ***(n. )* grateful**
አመስጋኒ amesgani ***(adj.)* beholden**
አመስገነ amesgene ***(v.)* thank**
አመሻሽጣ ጸጉሪ ameshashťa tseguri ***(n.)* hairstyle**
አመስከረ ameskere ***(v.)* certify**

**አመስጠረ** amesẗere *(v.)* **encrypt**
**አመተ** amete *(v.t.)* **allude**
**አመዛበለ** amezabele *(v. t)* **displace**
**አመዛዛኒ** amezazani *(adj.)* **rational**
**አመዛዘነ** amezazene *(v.)* **ponder**
**አመዛዘነ** amezazene *(v.)* **rationalize**
**አመዝገበ** amezgebe *(v.)* **score**
**አምፊትያትር** amfityatr *(n.)* **amphitheatre**
**ኣሚዶ** amido *(n.)* **starch**
**ኣሚዶኣዊ** amido'awi *(adj.)* **starchy**
**ኣምከነ** amkene *(v.)* **sterilize**
**ኣመኩሮኣዊ** amkuroawi *(n.)* **probationer**
**አምላኽ ምእማን** amlak m'eman *(n. )* **theism**
**ኣምላኽ ጣኦት** amlaḱ ṭa'ot *(n.)* **heathen**
**አምላኻዊ አስተምህሮ** amlakawi astemhro *(n.)* **theosophy**
**ኣምላኺ መናፍስቲ** amlakhi menafsti *(n.)* **spiritualist**
**ኣምላኺ** amlaki *(n. )* **worshipper**
**አምለከ** amleke *(v.)* **idolize**
**ኣምለቈ** amleq̈we *(v.)* **blurt**
**ኣምለሰ** amlese *(v.)* **regain**
**ኣምለሰ** amlese *(v.)* **retch**
**ኣምለጠ** amlete *(v.)* **elude**
**ኣምለጠ** amleẗr *(v. t)* **evade**
**ኣምልካቲ** amlkati *(adj.)* **indicative**
**ኣምልኾተ መናፍስቲ** amlkhote menafsti *(n.)* **spiritualism**
**ኣምልኾ** amlko *(n.)* **cult**
**ኣምልኾ** amlḱo *(n.)* **adoration**
**ኣምልኾተ ሴጣን** amlkote sietan *(n.)* **Satanism**
**እምነት ምግባር** amnet mgbar *(n.)* **trust**
**እምነት ዝግበረሉ** amnet zgberelu *(adj.)* **trustworthy**
**ኣምፐር** amper *(n.)* **ampere**
**ኣምፑል** ampul *(n.)* **bulb**
**ኣምር** amr *(n.)* **concept**
**ኣምራቲ** amrati *(n. )* **manufacturer**
**ኣምረተ** amrete *(v.)* **manufacture**
**ኣምርሐ** amrhe *(v.)* **wend**
**ኣምሳሊ** amsali *(adj.)* **pretentious**
**ኣምሳሊ** amsali *(adj.)* **affected**
**ኣምሰለ** amsele *(v.)* **feign**
**ኣምለሰ** amsele *(v.)* **reclaim**
**ኣምሰሉ** amselu *(v.)* **pretend**
**ኣምሰሉ** amselu *(n.)* **sham**
**ኣምሲልካ ምቕራብ** amsilka mq̈rab *(n.)* **hype**
**ኣምፃኢ** amtsa'e *(n. )* **importer**
**ኣምፀአ** am-tse-a *(v.)* **garner**
**ኣምፀአ** amxe'e *(v.)* **fetch**
**ኣምጸአ** amxe'e *(v.)* **bring**
**ኣናደደ** anadede *(v.)* **infuriate**
**ኣናደየ** anadeye *(v.)* **search**
**ኣናደየ** anadeye *(v.i. )* **seek**
**ኣናጎንስጢስ** anagonsẗees *(n.)* **acolyte**
**ኣናናስ** ananas *(n. )* **pineapple**
**ኣናሸወ** anashewe *(v.)* **decry**
**ኣናሸወ** anashewe *(v.)* **denigrate**
**ኣናሸወ** anashewe *(v.)* **lampoon**
**ኣናወፀ** anawetse *(v.)* **destabilize**
**ኣናውሐ** anawhe *(v.)* **prolong**
**ኣንባር** anbar *(n.)* **anklet**
**ኣንበበ** anbebe *(v.)* **read**
**ኣንበበ** anbebe *(v.t. )* **spell**
**ኣንበልበለ** anbelbele *(v.)* **brandish**
**ኣንበረ** anbere *(v.)* **lay**
**ኣንበርከኸ** anberkeke *(v.)* **quell**
**ኣንበሳ** anbesa *(n.)* **Leo**

**አንበሳ** anbesa ***(n. )*** **lion**
**አንጬበረቐ** anĉebareqe ***(v.)*** **dabble**
**አንጭዋ** anĉwa ***(n.)*** **rat**
**አንጭዋ** ančwa ***(n. )*** **mouse**
**አንድሮይድ** androyd ***(n.)*** **android**
**አነ** a'ne ***(pron.)*** **me**
**አነዓዓቢ** ane'ä'äbi ***(adj.)*** **subversive**
**አነኣኣሰ** ane'a'ase ***(v.)*** **devalue**
**አንነኣኣሲ** aneaasi ***(adj.)*** **pejorative**
**አነዓበ** ane'äbe ***(v.i. )*** **subvert**
**አነፍነፈ** anefnefe ***(v.)*** **snuffle**
**አነነት** anenet ***(n.)*** **narcissism**
**አነቓቕሐ** aneqaqh'he ***(v.)*** **stimulate**
**አነቓቓሒ** aneqhaqhahi ***(n.)*** **stimulant**
**አነፀረ** anetsere ***(v.)*** **specify**
**አነወረ** anewere ***(v.)*** **scandalize**
**አነጻጸረ** anexaxere ***(v.)*** **compare**
**አንፈሰ** anfese ***(v.)*** **deflate**
**አንፈት** anfet ***(n. )*** **direction**
**አንፈት** anfet ***(n.)*** **hint**
**አንፈት ቀየረ** anfet qeyere ***(v.)*** **deflect**
**አንፈት ቀየረ** anfet qeyere ***(v. t)*** **divert**
**አንፈጥፈጠ** anfetfete ***(v.)*** **quaver**
**አንፈጥፈጠ** anfetfete ***(v.)*** **shudder**
**አንፈቱ ቀየረ** anfetu qeyere ***(v.)*** **diverge**
**አንፊ** anfi ***(n. )*** **snout**
**አንጋረ** angare ***(n.)*** **leather**
**አንገብገበ** angebgebe ***(v.)*** **flap**
**አንገሰ** angese ***(v.)*** **crown**
**አንገሰ** angese ***(v.)*** **enthrone**
**አንጉዕ** angu'e ***(n. )*** **tallow**
**አንጓዕ** angwa'ë ***(n. )*** **node**
**አንሃረ** anhare ***(v.)*** **accelerate**
**አንከባለለ** ankebalwle ***(v.)*** **trundle**
**አንቀጥቀጠ** anketkete ***(v.)*** **dither**
**አንቆልቆለ** ankolkole ***(v. t.)*** **decrement**
**አንኰለ** ankwale ***(adj.)*** **broach**
**አንቀሔ** anqeĥe ***(n. )*** **mover**
**አንቀሳቓሲ** anqesaqasi ***(adj.)*** **spastic**
**አንቀጥቃጢ** anqetqati ***(v.)*** **quiver**
**አብ ምቕርራብ** 'ab mqrrab ***(adv.)*** **afoot**
**አብ ዙርያ** 'ab zurya ***(adv.)*** **around**
**አሕነኸ** 'aĥneke ***(adj.)*** **abash**
**አኮኣዊ** 'ako'awi ***(adj.)*** **avuncular**

# ከ

**ከቢድ** kebid ***(adj.)*** **onerous**
**ከቢድ ሓጎስ** kebid hagos ***(adj.)*** **overjoyed**
**ከቢድ ፅዕነት** kebit ts'enet ***(v.)*** **overload**
**ከፈለ** kefle ***(v.)*** **obtrude**
**ኩሉ ምፍላጥ** kulu mflat ***(n.)*** **omniscience**
**ኩሉ ከኣሊ** kulu keali ***(adj.)*** **omnipotent**
**ኩሉ ፈላጢ** kulu felati ***(adj.)*** **omniscient**
**ካልእ** kal'e ***(adj. & pron.)*** **other**
**ካብ 80-89 ዕድመ ዘለዎ ሰብ** kab 80-89 edme zelewo seb ***(n.)*** **octogenarian**
**ካብ ልክዕ ንላዕሊ** kab lk'e nla'eli ***(adv.)*** **overly**
**ካብ ልክዕ ንላዕሊ** kab lk'e nla'eli ***(v.)*** **overrate**
**ካብ መስመር ወጻኢ** kab mesmer wetsa'i ***(adj.)*** **offside**
**ካብ መጠን ንላዕሊ** kab meten nla'eli ***(v.)*** **overstep**

ካብ መጠን ንላዕሊ ዓርሰ ምትእምማን kab meten nla'eli arse mt'emman *(adj.)* **overweening**

ካብ ርእሲ ንላዕሊ kab r'esi nla'eli *(adv.)* **overhead**

ካብ ጥረምረ ዝስራሕ ዓይነት ምግቢ kab teremer zsrah aynet mgbi *(n.)* **oatmeal**

ካቦት kabot *(n.)* **overcoat**

ኬላ kela *(n. )* **outpost**

ክስብ ዝፈስስ ዝምልእ ksab zfess zmel'e *(n.)* **overspill**

ክስተት kstet *(n. )* **occurrence**

ክርከብ ዝኽእል krkeb zkel *(adj.)* **obtainable**

ክባዊ ኣካል kbawi akal *(n. )* **orb**

ክፉት kfut *(adj.)* **open**

ክፍተት kftet *(n.)* **opening**

ኮረችያ koretya *(n. )* **oak**

ካርዲ ka'ardi *(n.)* **card**

ካብ kab ***(prep. )*** **from**

ካብ kab ***(prep.)*** **since**

ካብ 13-19 ዝርከብ kab 13-19 zrkeb *(adj.)* **teens**

ካብ ኣርእስቲ ወፀ kab ar'esti wetse *(v.)* **digress**

ካብ ቦታ ወጻኢ ምንቅስቓስ kab bot wexaei mnqsq̈as *(n.)* **prolapse**

ካብ ደረቕ ናብ ሃፋ kab dereq nab hafa *(v.)* **sublimate**

ካብ ዕንፀይቲ ዝተሰረሐ መዶሻ kab entseyti ztesreh medisha *(n.)* **mallet**

ካብ እስካብ kab eskab *(n.)* **interval**

ካብ ገዝሚ ወጻኢ ንብረት መርዓት kab gezmi weai nbret mrat *(n. )* **paraphernalia**

ካብ ሃገር ወጻኢ kab hager wexa'i *(adv.)* **abroad**

ካብ ሃሪ ዝተሰርሐ kab hari zterhe *(adj.)* **woolly**

ካብ ሓሰማ ዝርከብ ስብሒ kab hasama zrkeb sbhi *(n.)* **lard**

ኣፅረየ kab ȟaẗyat anxehe *(v.)* **purge**

ካብ ሓጥያት ምንጻህ kab ȟaẗyat mnxah *(n. )* **purgation**

ካብ ሓደ ንላዕሊ kab ȟde alaëli *(adj.)* **plural**

ካብ ሕጂ ንደሓር kab ḩğì ndeḩar *(adv. )* **henceforth**

ካብ ሕልሚ ኣላቀቀ kab ĥlmi alaqeqe *(v.)* **disenchant**

ካብ ኢድ ናብ ኣፍ kab id nab a'f *(n. )* **subsistence**

ካብ ክሳድ ንላዕሊ kab ksad nlaeli *(adj.)* **perfunctory**

ካብ መዓንጣ ንልዕሊ ጥራሕካ ምካን kab meantanlaali trahka mukan *(adj.)* **topless**

ካብ መሃያ ወጻኢ ዝርከብ kab mehaya wexaei zrkeb *(n.)* **perquisite**

ካብ መስመር ዝወጸ kab mesmer zwetse *(n.)* **straggler**

ካብ መስመሩ ኣስሓተ kab mesmeru as'ĥate *(v. t.)* **derail**

ካብ መጥቃዕቲ ንምክልኻል ኣፀጋሚ kab metka'et nmklkhal zetsgm *(adj.)* **indefensible**

ካብ ፅሑፍ kab shuf *(adj.)* **textual**

ካብ ፅሑፍ kab shuf *(adj.)* **textual**

ካብ ስርናይ ዝተሰርሐ kab srnay zteserhe *(adj.)* **wheaten**

ካብ ፃባ ዝስራሕ ጠንካራ ቡን kab tsaba zsrah tenkara bun *(n.)* **latte**

ካባረ kabare *(n.)* **cabaret**

ከበይ kabey *(adv.)* **whence**
ከብስትኖ kabstno *(n.)* **capstan**
ከብ ሕጂ kabz hji *(adv. )* **hence**
ካቻቪተ ka'chavite *(n.)* **screwdriver**
ካደት kadet *(n.)* **cadet**
ካዲ kadi *(n.)* **caddy**
ካድምዩም kadmyum *(n.)* **cadmium**
ካድረ kadre *(n.)* **cadre**
ካዕካዕ ka'ëka'ë *(n.)* **nut**
ካዕካዕታ ka'ëka'ë bele *(n.)* **guffaw**
ካዕካዕታ ka'ëka'ëta *(n.)* **hilarity**
ካዕካዕታዊ ka'ëka'ëtawi *(adj. )* **hilarious**
ካዕካዓዊ ka'ëka'ëwi *(adj.)* **nutty**
ካፋ kafa *(n. )* **shower**
ካፌ kafee *(n.)* **cafe**
ካፊተርያ kafiterya *(n.)* **cafeteria**
ካሓዲ kaĥadi *(n.)* **renegade**
ካሕዳም kahdam *(n. )* **traitor**
ካህናት kahenat' *(n.)* **clergy**
ካህን kahin *(n.)* **cleric**
ካህን kahin' *(n.)* **chaplain**
ካህን kahn *(n. )* **parson**
ካህን kahn *(n.)* **pastor**
ካህን kahn *(adj.)* **reverend**
ካሕሳ kahsa *(n.)* **restitution**
ካሕሳ kaȟsa *(n.)* **atonement**
ካሕሳ kaȟsa *(n.)* **compensation**
ካካው kakaw *(n.)* **cocoa**
ካካው kakaw *(n.)* **cacao**
ካልኣዋይ kal'away *(adj.)* **secondary**
ካልኣይ kal'ay *(adj.)* **second**
ካልእ kal'è *(adj.)* **another**
ካልኣይ/ማዕረ kaleay/maere *(n. )* **paragon**
ካሊእ ሽሙ kali'e shmu *(adv.)* **alias**
ካሎሪ kalori *(n.)* **calorie**
ካልሲ kalsi *(n.)* **sock**
ካልስዩም kalsyum *(n.)* **calcium**
ካምቻ kamcha *(n.)* **blouse**
ካምፎራ kamfora *(n.)* **camphor**
ካምኮርደር kamkorder *(n.)* **camcorder**
ካምፓስ kampas *(n.)* **campus**
ካምሻ kamša *(n.)* **shirt**
ካሙን kamun *(n.)* **cumin**
ካምዮ kamyo *(n.)* **cameo**
ካንጋሩ kangaru *(n.)* **kangaroo**
ካንሸሎ kanshelo *(n.)* **courtyard**
ካንቲና kantina *(n.)* **canteen**
ካፓሲተር kapaciter *(n.)* **capacitor**
ካራ kara *(n. )* **knife**
ካራት kara 't *(n.)* **carat**
ካራሜል karame' el *(n.)* **caramel**
ካርቦሃይድሬት karbohaydreet *(n.)* **carbohydrate**
ካርቦን karbon *(n.)* **carbon**
ካርቦኔት karboneet *(adj.)* **carbonate**
ካርቾፊ karchofi *(n.)* **artichoke**
ካርድዮግራፍ kardyograf *(n.)* **cardiograph**
ካርድዮሎጂ kardyoloĵi *(n.)* **cardiology**
ካሪካቸር karikacher *(n)* **caricature**
ካርማ karma *(n.)* **karma**
ካርኒቫል karnival *(n.)* **carnival**
ካሮሳ karosa *(n.)* **chaise**
ካሮሳ karosa *(n.)* **buggy**
ካርታ karta *(n.)* **map**
ካርተሊና kartelina *(n.)* **postcard**
ካርቶን kartoon *(n.)* **cardboard**
ካርቱን kartun *(n.)* **cartoon**
ካርያ karya *(n.)* **pecan**
ካሳ kasa *(n.)* **crate**
ካሽሚር kashmir *(n.)* **cashmere**
ካስታኖ kastano *(n.)* **chestnut**

ካስታርድ kastard *(n.)* **custard**
ካተድራል katedral *(n.)* **cathedral**
ካትራመ katrame *(n.)* **tar**
ካውካዝያዊ kawkazyawi *(adj.)* **Caucasian**
ካውሎ ፍዮሪ kawlo fyori *(n.)* **broccoli**
ካውሎ kawlo *(n.)* **cabbage**
ካዉሎ ፍዮሪ kawulo fiyorii *(n.)* **cauliflower**
ካዝና kazina *(n.)* **coffer**
ካዚኖ kazino *(n.)* **casino**
ካዝና kazna *(n. )* **safe**
ካዝና kazna *(n. )* **warehouse**
ክባር kbar *(adj.)* **costly**
ክባር kbar *(adj.)* **expensive**
ክባዊ kbawi *(n. )* **spherical**
ክብድብድ ምባል kbd'bd mbal *(n.)* **malaise**
ክብደት kbdet *(n.)* **mass**
ክብደት kbdet *(n.)* **profundity**
ክብደት kbdet *(n.)* **weight**
ክበሃል ዘይክእል kbehal zeykel *(adj.)* **unmentionable**
ክበሃል ዘይክእል kbehal zeykel *(adj.)* **unutterable**
ክቢ kbi *(n.)* **sphere**
ክቢብ kbibe *(adj.)* **circular**
ክቦሳ kbosa *(n.)* **cuff**
ክብረት kbret *(n.)* **gravitas**
ክብረት kbret *(n.)* **prestige**
ኽብሪ kbri *(n.)* **deference**
ክብሪ kbri *(n.)* **dignity**
ኽብሪ kbri *(n.)* **esteem**
ክብሪ kbri *(n.)* **glorification**
ክብሪ kbri *(n.)* **kudos**
ክብሪ kbri *(n.)* **majesty**
ክብሪ kbri *(n.)* **reputation**
ክብሪ kbri *(n.)* **respect**
ክብሪ kbri *(n. )* **glory**
ክብሪ ዝረከበ kbri zrekebe *(n.)* **laureate**
ክብሰት kbset *(n.)* **reversal**
ክቡብ kbub *(n.)* **enclave**
ክቡር kbur *(adj.)* **dear**
ክቡር kbur *(n.)* **Excellency**
ክቡር kbur *(adj.)* **illustrious**
ክቡር kbur *(n.)* **plush**
ክቡር kbur *(adj.)* **respectable**
ክቡር kbur *(n.)* **treasure**
ክቡር kbur *(adj.)* **valuable**
ክቡር እምኒ kbur emni *(n. )* **gem**
ክዳን kdan *(n.)* **apparel**
ኽዳን kdan *(n.)* **garb**
ክዳን kdan *(n. )* **garment**
ክዳን ካህን kdan kahn *(n.)* **cassock**
ክዳን ለይቲ kdan leyti *(n. )* **nightie**
ክዳን ሰበይቲ kdan sebeyti *(n.)* **costume**
ክዳኑ ኣዉፅአ kdanu awtse'e *(v.)* **disrobe**
ክዳውንቲ kdawnti *(n.)* **clothing**
ክዳውንቲ መርዓት kdawnti merat *(n.)* **trousseau**
ክድሕን ዘይኽእል kdhn zeykh'el *(adj.)* **incurable**
ክድነቕ ዝግቦኦ kdneqh zgbo'e *(adj.)* **laudable**
ከኣለ ke'ale *(v.)* **can**
ከባብ kebab *(n.)* **kebab**
ከባቢ kebabi *(n.)* **locality**
ከባሂ kebahi *(adj.)* **cloying**
ከብዲ እግሪ kebdi egri *(n.)* **sole**
ከብዲ kebdi *(n.)* **abdomen**
ከብዲ kebdi *(n.)* **belly**
ከበበ kebebe *(v. t)* **encircle**
ከበባ kebebe *(n. )* **siege**
ከበበ kebebe *(v.)* **surround**

ከበበ kebebe *(v.)* **besiege**
ከበሮ kebero ***(n.)* drum**
ከበርቴ kebertee ***(n.)* aristocrat**
ከብሒ ክሽነ kebhi kshne *(n. )* **pantry**
ከብሒ kebȟi ***(n.)* cabinet**
ከቢ kebi ***(n.)* circle**
ከቢብ kebib ***(adj.)* round**
ከቢድ kebid ***(adj.)* profound**
ከቢድ kebid ***(adj.)* terrific**
ከቢድ kebid ***(adj.)* uneasy**
ኸቢድ kebid ***(adj.)* weighty**
ከቢድ ብረት kebid bret ***(n.)* artillery**
ከቢድ ጋዝ kebid gaz ***(n.)* xenon**
ከቢድ ሓዘን kebid hazen ***(adj.)* terrible**
ኸቢድ ኩነታት kebid kuknetat ***(n.)* imbroglio**
ከቢድ ስቃይ kebid skay ***(n. )* throes**
ከቢድ ስቃይ kebid skay ***(n.)* torment**
ከቢድ ኩነታት kebidkunetat ***(n.)* pickle**
ከብቲ kebtei ***(n.)* cattle**
ከቻፕ kechap ***(n. )* ketchup**
ኸዳን kedan ***(n.)* cladding**
ከደ kede ***(v.t)* go**
ከደ kede ***(v.)* betake**
ከድዐ ked'ë ***(v.)* betray**
ኸደነ kedene ***(v.)* upholster**
ከደነ kedene' ***(v.)* clothe**
ከደራይ kederay ***(adj.)* swarthy**
ኬክ keek ***(n.)* cookie**
ከፋሊ kefali ***(n. )* payee**
ከፋት ሽውሃት kefat shewhat ***(n.)* appetizer**
ከፈለ kefele ***(v.)* defray**
ከፈለ kefele ***(v.)* liquidate**
ከፈለ kefele ***(v.)* remunerate**
ካብ ልክዕ ንላዕሊ መኽሰብ ȟadȟdawi meḱseb ***(n.)* profiteering**
ክእለት k'elet ***(n.)* ability**
ኪምለስ ዚከኣል kimles zike'al ***(adj.)* answerable**
ክልተ ዓመታዊ klte 'ämetawi ***(adj.)* biennial**
ክልቲኡ klti'u ***(adj. & pron.)* both**
ክፍለ አለም kefele ale'm ***(n.)* continent**
ክፍለ አለማዊ kefele alemawii ***(adj.)* continental**
ክፍሊት kefelit ***(n.)* charge**
ክግልገል ዝክእል keglgel zk'el ***(adj.)* serviceable**
ከሓደ keĥade ***(v. i.)* deny**
ከሓደ keĥade ***(v.)* disown**
ከሓዲ keĥadi ***(adj.)* disloyal**
ከሓዲ እምነት keȟadi 'èmnet ***(n.)* apostate**
ከሓሰ keĥase ***(v.)* recompense**
ከሓሰ keĥase ***(v.)* recoup**
ከሓሰ keȟase ***(v.)* compensate**
ከሓሰ keȟase ***(v.)* atone**
ኬክ kek ***(n.)* gateau**
ከከም kekem ***(adj.)* respective**
ከልባዊ kelbawi ***(adj.)* canine**
ከልቢ kelbi ***(n.)* dog**
ከልቢ እለሻ kelbi eleša ***(n.)* retriever**
ከልቢ ሃድን kelbi hadn ***(n. )* greyhound**
ከለለ kelele ***(v.)* enclose**
ከለሰ kelese ***(n.)* review**
ከለሰ kelese ***(v.)* revise**
ክእለት k'elet ***(n.)* facility**
ክእለት k'elet ***(n.)* faculty**
ክእለት k'elet ***(n. )* skill**
ክእለት k'èlet ***(n.)* competence**
ክእለት ዘረባ k'elet zereba ***(n.)* elocution**
ክእለት k'èlet ***(n.)* artifice**

ክእለታዊ k'eletawi *(adj.)* **tactical**
ከልካሊ kelkali *(adj.)* **prohibitive**
ኸለከለ kelkele *(v. t.)* **debar**
ከልከለ kelkele *(v.)* **deprive**
ከልከለ kelkele *(v.)* **disallow**
ኸልከለ kelkele *(v.)* **forbid**
ከም kem *(prep.)* **like**
ከም ብሓዱሽ kem bȟadush *(adv.)* **anew**
ከም ፍጹም ምቑፃር kem fxum mqutsar *(v.)* **idealize**
ከም ገለ kem gele *(adv. )* **somehow**
ከም ልሙድ kem lmud *(adv. )* **usually**
ከም ዝፍቀር ገበረ kem zfqer gebere *(v.)* **endear**
ከም kem *(adv.)* **as**
ከመይ kemey *(adv. )* **how**
ኬሚካል kemikal *(adj.)* **chemical**
ከምኡ kem'u *(n.)* **ditto**
ከምኡ kem'u *(adj.)* **such**
ከምኡ'ውን kem'uwn *(adv.)* **also**
ከባቢ kenabi *(n.)* **environment**
ከንበለ kenbele *(v.)* **topple**
ኬንዳ kenda *(n.)* **tent**
ከንፈር kenfer *(n.)* **lip**
ከንፈር ማንቲለ kenfer mantile *(n.)* **harelip**
ከንፈራዊ kenferawi *(adj.)* **labial**
ከኒና kenina *(n. )* **quinine**
ከኒና kenina *(n. )* **pill**
ከንቲባ kentiba *(n. )* **mayor**
ከንቱ kentu *(adj.)* **futile**
ከንቱ kentu *(n.)* **reprobate**
ከርበ kerebe *(n.)* **myrrh**
ከረሜላ keremeela *(n.)* **candy**
ከረናዊ kerenawi *(adj.)* **alpine**
ክርስትና keresetena *(n.)* **Christianity**

ክርስቶስ keresetos *(n.)* **Christ**
ክርስቲያን keresitiyane *(adj.)* **Christian**
ከረጢት kerețit *(n. )* **pouch**
ከረዛን kerezan *(n.)* **wand**
ከርፋሕ kerfaȟ *(adj.)* **miserable**
ከርከስ kerkes *(n.)* **ridge**
ከርታት kertat *(n.)* **vagrant**
ከሳሲ kesasi *(n.)* **suitor**
ከሳሳይ kesasy *(n. )* **plaintiff**
ከስዓዊ kes-ä-wi *(adj.)* **gastric**
ከሰበ kesebe *(v.)* **gain**
ከሰረ kesere *(v.)* **forfeit**
ከሰሰ kesese *(v.)* **accuse**
ከሰሰ kesese *(v.)* **indict**
ከሰሰ kesese *(v.t. )* **sue**
ከሻኒ keshani *(n.)* **cook**
ከሽዐ kesh'ë *(n.)* **stomach**
ከሽከሽ ቐሚሽ keshkesh qhemish *(n.)* **kilt**
ከስከስ keskes *(n.)* **reef**
ከተበ ketebe *(v.)* **enlist**
ከተበ ketebe *(v.)* **inoculate**
ከተበ ketebe *(v.)* **inscribe**
ከተበ ketebe *(v.)* **vaccinate**
ከተፈ ketefe *(v.)* **chop**
ከተማ ketema *(n.)* **city**
ከተማ ketema *(n.)* **town**
ከተማ ketema *(adj.)* **urban**
ከተረ ketere *(v.)* **waylay**
ከተተ ketete *(v.)* **mobilize**
ቀጢን ketin *(adj.)* **shrill**
ክእቶ ዝከኣል k'èto zke'al *(adj.)* **accessible**
ከወለ kewele *(v.)* **shade**
ከውሓዊ kewȟawi *(adj.)* **megalithic**
ከውሒ kewĥi *(n. )* **rock**
ቀይ ስር key sr *(n. )* **turnip**

ቀያዲ keyadi *(adj.)* **restrictive**
ከያፍ keyaf *(n.)* **bristle**
ከየቕለብካሉ እትግንዘቦ keyeqhlebkalu etg'nzebo *(adj.)* **subliminal**
ቀይሕ ሓመድ keyh hamed *(n.)* **terracotta**
ከይሲ keysi *(adj.)* **sly**
ከይሲ keysi *(adj.)* **splenetic**
ከዘራን kezeran *(n.)* **cane**
ክፋእ ዘይብሉ kfa'e zeyblu *(adj.)* **spotless**
ክፋል kfal *(n.)* **instalment**
ክፋል kfal *(n.)* **part**
ክፋል kfal *(n.)* **sector**
ክፋል ዕንባባ kfal onbaba *(n. )* **petal**
ክፋሎ kfalo *(n.)* **segment**
ክፍኣት kf'at *(n.)* **bale**
ክፍኣት kf'at *(n.)* **infamy**
ክፍኣት kf'at *(n.)* **misdeed**
ክፈላለዩ ዘይኽእሉ kfelaleyu zeykh'elu *(adj.)* **inextricable**
ክፍፍል kffl *(n.)* **division**
ክፍፍላዊ kfflawi *(adj.)* **systematic**
ክፍለግዘ kfle gze *(n.)* **session**
ክፍለ ሃገር kfle hager *(n.)* **province**
ክፍለ ሃገራዊ kfle hagerawi *(adj.)* **provincial**
ክፍለ ዝከእል kfle zk'el *(adj.)* **separable**
ክፍሊ kfli *(n.)* **compartment**
ክፍሊ kfli *(n.)* **department**
ክፍሊ kfli *(n.)* **room**
ክፍሊ kfli *(n.)* **section**
ክፍሊት kflit *(n.)* **fee**
ክፍሊት kflit *(n. )* **payment**
ክፍሊት kflit *(n.)* **remuneration**
ክፍሊት ዕሻገ መራኽብ kflit eshage merakb *(n.)* **wharfage**
ክፍሊት ፍትሕ kflit ftḧ *(n.)* **alimony**
ክፍሊት ዝርከቦ kflit zrkebo *(adj.)* **remunerative**
ኽፍተት k-ftet *(n.)* **gap**
ክፉእ kfue *(adj.)* **unholy**
ክፉእ kfue *(adj.)* **wicked**
ክፉእ kfu'e *(adj.)* **infamous**
ክፉእ kfu'e *(adj.)* **malign**
ክፉእ kfu'e *(adj.)* **ugly**
ክፉፍ kfuf *(n.)* **hem**
ክፉት መአከቢ ቦታ kfut makebi bota *(n.)* **plaza**
ክጋገ ዝኽእል kgage zk'el *(adj.)* **fallible**
ኽብደት khbdet *(n.)* **load**
ኽዳን khdan *(n.)* **lid**
ክሕደት khdet *(n.)* **infidelity**
ክሕደት khdet *(n.)* **treachery**
ክሕደት kĥdet *(n.)* **repudiation**
ክሕደት kḧdet *(n.)* **denial**
ኸብድ መጥቃዕቲ ኣብፀሐ khebid metqh'eti eabtsehe *(v.)* **maim**
ኽንዲ khndi *(prep. )* **lieu**
ኽሲ khsi *(n.)* **indictment**
ኽትባት khtbat *(n.)* **inoculation**
ክሕፀብ ዝኽእል khxeb zk'el *(adj.)* **washable**
ኪጭበጥ ዘይከኣል kičbeẗ zeyke'al *(adj.)* **intangible**
ክዳን kidan *(n.)* **cloth**
ክዳዉንቲ kidawunti' *(n.)* **clothes**
ክፋል kifale *(n.)* **component**
ክፍሊ kifeli *(n.)* **class**
ኪኢላ ki'ila *(n.)* **specialist**
ክኢላ ki'la *(adj.)* **talented**
ክኢላ k'ila *(adj.)* **adept**
ኪኢላ k'ila *(adj.)* **skilled**
ክኢላ k'ila *(adj.)* **competent**
ክኢላ ሕጊ k'ila ḧgi *(n. )* **jurist**

ክኢላ ስነ መትኒ k'ila sne metni *(n. )* **neurologist**
ክኢላ k'ila *(adj.)* **accomplished**
ክኢላ k'ila *(n.)* **artisan**
ክኢላ k'ila *(adj.)* **capable**
ክኢላ k'ila *(adj.)* **deft**
ኪሎ kilo *(n.)* **kilo**
ኪሎ ባይት kilo-byt *(n.)* **kilobyte**
ኪሎሜተር kilomeeter *(n.)* **kilometre**
ክሎሪን kilorin *(n.)* **chlorine**
ክንክን kinkin *(n.)* **care**
ኪርኪር በለ kir kir bele *(v.t. )* **giggle**
ኪርዳእ ዚከኣል kirda'è zike'al *(adj.)* **comprehensible**
ኪስማዕ ዚከኣል kisma'ë zike'a *(adj.)* **audible**
ኪጠሓስ ዘይብሉ kiťeȟas zeyblu *(adj.)* **inviolable**
ኪትካእ ዘይከኣል kitka'è zeyke'al *(adj.)* **irreplaceable**
ኪዩብ kiyub *(n.)* **cube**
ኪዩቢካዊ kiyubikawi *(adj.)* **cubical**
ክኸውን ዝኽእል kḱewn zḱ'èl *(adj.)* **feasible**
ክኾን ዘይኽእል kkhon zeykh'eal *(adj.)* **improbable**
ክኾን ዝኽእል kkhon zkh'el *(adj.)* **likely**
ክላክ klak *(n. )* **siren**
ክሌምንታይን klemintaine *(n.)* **Clementine**
ክለቅቅ ዝክእል kleqq zk'el *(adj.)* **removable**
ክለሳ klesa *(n. )* **revision**
ክሊኒክ kliniqk *(n.)* **clinic**
ክልኩል klkul *(adj.)* **inadmissible**
ክልል kll *(n.)* **district**
ክልል kll *(n.)* **region**
ክልል kll *(n.)* **zone**
ክልላዊ kllawi *(adj.)* **regional**
ክልላዊ kllawi *(adj.)* **zonal**
ክሎሮፎርም kloroform *(n.)* **chloroform**
ክልሰ ሓሳብ klse hasab *(n.)* **theory**
ክልሰ ሓሳብ klse ȟasab *(n.)* **notion**
ክልሰ ሓሳባዊ klse hasabawi *(adj.)* **theoretical**
ክልተ klte *(adj.&n.)* **two**
ክልተ ጐድናዊ klte gwadnawi *(adj.)* **bilateral**
ክልተ ፔዳለ ዘለዎ ሳይክል klte piedale zelewo siykle *(n.)* **tandem**
ክልተ ቕነ klte qne *(n.)* **fortnight**
ክምስ በለ kms bele *(v.)* **chuckle**
ክምስ በለ kms bele *(v.)* **smile**
ክንበብ ዘፀግም knbeb zetzegm *(adj.)* **illegible**
ክንፊ knfi *(n.)* **wing**
ክንፊ ዓሳ knfi äsa *(n.)* **fin**
ክንክን አፃብዕቲ kn'kn atzab'eti *(n.)* **manicure**
ክኒንያ፣ knnya *(n. )* **tablet**
ክንቀፍ ዝግባእ knqef zgba'e *(adj.)* **reprehensible**
ክንቲት kntit *(n.)* **feather**
ክንቲት ዑፍ kntit ëuf *(n.)* **plumage**
ክንቲት ዝመልአ kntit zmel'ö *(adj.)* **quilted**
ክንየው knyew *(adv.)* **beyond**
ኮዓተ ko'äte *(v.)* **dig**
ኮዓተ ko'äte *(v.)* **excavate**
ኮባልት kobalt *(n.)* **cobalt**
ኮበርታ koberta *(n.)* **blanket**
ኮብላሊ koblali *(adj.)* **runaway**
ኮብለለ koblele *(v.)* **elope**
ኮብለለ koblele *(v.)* **roam**
ኮብራ ተመን kobra temen' *(n.)* **cobra**

**ኮደብ በለ** kodeb bele *(v.)* **flounce**
**ኮፍ በለ** kof bele *(v.)* **sit**
**ኮፍ መበሊ** kof mebeli *(n.)* **seat**
**ኮካርድ** kokard *(n.)* **cockade**
**ኮኬን** kokeen *(n.)* **cocaine**
**ኮኾብ** kokhob *(n.)* **star**
**ኮኾብ መሳሊ** kokhob mesali *(adj.)* **starry**
**ኮኾባዊ** kokhobawi *(adj.)* **stellar**
**ኮኾባዊ** koḱobawi *(adj.)* **astral**
**ኮላዥ** kolazz *(n.)* **collage**
**ኮሌጅ** koleej *(n.)* **college**
**ኮለፈ** kolefe *(v.)* **punctuate**
**ኮለለ** kolele *(v.)* **revolve**
**ኮሎኛ** koloṅa *(n.)* **heather**
**ኮሎኔል** kolonele *(n.)* **colonel**
**ኮማንደር** komander *(n.)* **commander**
**ኮማንዶ** komando *(n.)* **commando**
**ኮማዊ** komawi *(adj.)* **communal**
**ኮመዲኖ** komedino *(n.)* **birch**
**ኮሚደረ** komidere *(n. )* **tomato**
**ኮሚሽነር** komishner *(n.)* **commissioner**
**ኮምፕዩተር** kompyuter *(n.)* **computer**
**ኮናዕ** kona'ë *(n.)* **buck**
**ኮናዕ** kona'ë *(n. )* **stag**
**ኮንቺልያ** kon'chilya *(n.)* **scallop**
**ኮነ** kone *(conj.&adv.)* **nor**
**ኮነ ኢልካ** kone eilka *(adv. )* **purposely**
**ኮነ** kone *(v.)* **be**
**ኮነ** kone *(v.)* **become**
**ኮነነ** konene *(v.)* **damn**
**ኮኒካዊ** konikawi *(adj.)* **conical**
**ኮኖ** kono *(n.)* **cone**
**ኮንሰርትዮም** konsertyom *(n.)* **consortium**
**ኮንስታብል ሰብነት** konstable sebenet' *(n.)* **constabulary**
**ኮንስታብል** konstablee *(n.)* **constable**
**ኮንትሮባንድ** kontroband *(n.)* **contraband**
**ኮንትሮባንድ መስተ** kontroband meste *(adj.)* **bootleg**
**ኮራዪ** korayi *(adj.)* **tetchy**
**ኮረብታ** korebta *(n. )* **hill**
**ኮረቻ** korecha *(n.)* **saddle**
**ኮረንቲ** korenti *(n.)* **electricity**
**ኮረር** korer *(n.)* **castor**
**ኮረት** koret *(n.)* **cobble**
**ኮረየ** koreye *(adj. )* **henpecked**
**ኮርፋፍ** korfaf *(adj.)* **moody**
**ኮርፋፍ** korfaf *(adj.)* **petulant**
**ኮሪደዮ** korideyo *(n.)* **aisle**
**ኮረኪ** korki *(n.)* **cork**
**ኮርኪዕካዮ ዝስሕቅ** korkiakayo zshk *(adj.)* **ticklish**
**ኮርነት** kornet *(n.)* **cornet**
**ኮርቲሶን** kortison *(n.)* **cortisone**
**ኮስታራይ** kostaray *(n.)* **sweeper**
**ኮስታሪ** kostari *(n.)* **duster**
**ኮስተረ** kostere *(v.)* **sweep**
**ኮኮናት** coconat *(n.)* **coconut**
**ኮንዶም** condom *(n.)* **condom**
**ኮቶኛ** kotogna *(n.)* **quince**
**ኮይከር** koyker *(n. )* **Quaker**
**ኮዝሞሎጂ** kozmoloji *(n.)* **cosmology**
**ክቅየር ዘይኽእል ሕመቕ** kqhyer zeykh'el hmeqh *(adj.)* **incorrigible**
**ክቋረፅ ዘይኽእል** kquarets zeykh'el *(adj.)* **inexorable**
**ክራባት** krabat *(n.)* **cravat**
**ክራባታ** krabata *(n. )* **tie**
**ክራይ** kray *(n.)* **rent**
**ክራይ** kray *(n.)* **tenancy**

ክረምቲ kremti ***(n. )* summer**
ክርሃት krhat ***(n.)* apathy**
ክሪ kri ***(n.)* floss**
ክሪ kri ***(n.)* thread**
ክሪክ krik ***(n. )* jack**
ክሪንኪሕ krinkiḧ ***(adj.)* bumpy**
ክሪኬት krkeet ***(n.)* cricket**
ክርክር krkr ***(n.)* contention**
ኽርክር krkr ***(n.)* controversy**
ክርክራዊ krkrawi ***(adj.)* forensic**
ክርኩር kr'kur ***(adj.)* mealy**
ክሮም krom ***(n.)* chrome**
ክርተና krtena ***(n.)* quarantine**
ክሳብ ksab ***(prep. )* until**
ክሳብ ksab ***(n.)* while**
ክሳብ ksab ***(conj.)* whilst**
ክሳድ ksad ***(n. )* neck**
ክሳራ ksara ***(n.)* deficit**
ክሻ ksha ***(n.)* sack**
ክሽናዊ kshnawi ***(adj.)* culinary**
ክብራዊ kbrawi ***(adj. )* honorary**
ክብሪ kbri ***(n.)* honour**
ከቢድ kebid ***(adj. )* heavy**
ከልቢ ሃድን kelbi hadn ***(n. )* hound**
ከውሒ በረድ kewḥi bered ***(n.)* iceberg**
ከውሒ-በረድ kewḧibered ***(n.)* glacier**
ኪዕቀን ዘይከኣል ki'ëqen zeyke'al ***(adj.)* immeasurable**
ክኢላ k'ila ***(adj.)* versed**
ኪቕጽል ዚኽእል kiqxl zik'èl ***(adj.)* viable**
ኪረአ ዚከኣል kire'e zike'al ***(adj.)* visible**
ኮብለለ koblele ***(v.)* wander**
ኰነ kone ***(v.)* happen**
ክሳብ ሕጂ ksab ḥği ***(adv. )* hitherto**
ክሽምሽ kshmsh ***(n.)* gooseberry**

ክሲ ksi ***(n.)* impeachment**
ኩጀት kujet ***(n.)* hillock**
ኩሊት kulit ***(n.)* kidney**
ኳሕኩሐ kwaḥkuḥe ***(v.)* knock**
ክሽነ kshne ***(n. )* kitchen**
ክሽየጥ ዝኽእል kshyet zk'el ***(adj.)* saleable**
ክሲ ksi ***(n.)* accusation**
ክስላሕ ዘይኽእል kslah zykh'el ***(adj.)* incalculable**
ክስራሕ ዝኽእል ksrah zkh'el ***(adj.)* manageable**
ክስተኽኽል ዘይኽእል ፀገም kstekhakel zeylh'el tsegem ***(adj.)* insurmountable**
ክስተት kstet ***(n. )* phenomenon**
ክስተታዊ kstetawi ***(adj.)* phenomenal**
ክሱስ ksus ***(v.t.)* accused**
ክታብ ktab ***(n.)* amulet**
ክታበት ktabet ***(n.)* vaccination**
ክታበት ktabet ***(n.)* vaccine**
ክታም ktam ***(n.)* cachet**
ክትዕ kt'ë ***(v. i)* dispute**
ክትዕገሶ ዝካኣል kt'egeso zka'al ***(adj.)* tolerable**
ክትግበር ዘይኽእል ktgber zeykh'el ***(adj.)* inapplicable**
ክትዕ ምውጋድ ktie mwgad ***(v.)* parry**
ክትከላኸለሉ ዝከአል ktkelakelelu zkeal ***(adj.)* tenable**
ክትላዘበሉ ትኽእል ktlazebelu tḱ'el ***(adj.)* negotiable**
ክትነብረሉ ዚበቅዕ ktnebrelu zibeq'ë ***(adj. )* habitable**
ክትራ ktra ***(n.)* wicket**
ክትጽመሞ ዘይከኣል ktsmemo zeyke'al ***(adj.)* insupportable**

ክትጥቀመሉ ትኽእል ktẗqemelu tḱ'èl *(adj.)* **available**
ኳዕናን kuae'nan *(n.)* **panache**
ኲራ kuara *(n.)* **petulance**
ኩዕሾ ምምንጣል kuausho mmntal *(v.t. )* **tackle**
ኩባያ kubaya *(n.)* **cup**
ኩባያ kubaya *(n.)* **mug**
ኩዕሾ ውርጪ ku'esho wrchi *(n.)* **snowball**
ኩዕሶ ዓይኒ ku'ëso äyni *(n.)* **eyeball**
ኩዕሶ እግሪ ku'ëso egri *(n.)* **football**
ኩዕሶ እግሪ ku'ëso egri *(n.)* **soccer**
ኩዕሶ ku'ëso *(n.)* **ball**
ኩሕለ-ምሕሊ kuȟlemȟli *(n.)* **antiperspirant**
ኩሕሊ kuȟli *(n.)* **mascara**
ኩጀት kujet *(n.)* **hummock**
ኩኽ kuk *(n. )* **peach**
ኩኩምበር kukumber *(n.)* **cucumber**
ኩኩናይ kukunay *(n.)* **cock**
ኩኩናይ kukunay *(n.)* **rooster**
ኩላሶ kulaso *(n.)* **morsel**
ኩላሶ kulaso *(n.)* **mouthful**
ኵላሶ kulaso *(n.)* **brunch**
ኩለምሉ kulemulu *(n.)* **entirety**
ኩልተፋ kultefa *(n.)* **lisp**
ኩሉ kulu *(adj.)* **all**
ኩሉ ግዜ kulu gzee *(adv.)* **always**
ኩሉ ዝኣምን kulu zamn *(adj.)* **trustful**
ኩሉ ዚከኣሎ kulu zike'alo *(adj.)* **almighty**
ኩሉኹሉ kuluḱulu *(adv.)* **altogether**
ኩምር ዝበለ ፀጉሪ kumr zbele tseguri *(n.)* **thatch**
ኩምራ kumra *(n.)* **heap**
ኩምራ kumra *(n. )* **pile**
ኩምራ ሓመድ kumra ȟamed *(n. )* **mound**
ኩናነ kunane *(n.)* **damnation**
ኹናት kunat *(n.)* **combat**
ኩነት kunet *(n.)* **case**
ኩነት kunet *(n.)* **condition**
ኩነት kunet *(n.)* **fettle**
ኩነታት ኣየር kunetat ayer *(n.)* **weather**
ኩነታት ኣየር kunetat ayer' *(n.)* **climate**
ኩነታዊ kunetawi *(adj.)* **conditional**
ኩፖን kupon *(n.)* **coupon**
ኹረሽ kuresh *(n.)* **crochet**
ኩሪፍ በለ kurif bele *(n. )* **snort**
ኩርኩር kurkur *(n.)* **pup**
ኩርኩር kurkur *(n.)* **puppy**
ኩርኩር kurkur *(n.)* **whelp**
ኩርኩር ኣንበሳ kurkur aanbesa *(n.)* **cub**
ኩርምቲ kurmti *(n.)* **molar**
ኩርናዓዊ kurna'äwi *(adj.)* **angular**
ኩርናዕ kurna'ë *(n.)* **nook**
ኵርናዕ ኢድ kurna'ë id *(n.)* **elbow**
ኩርናዕ kurna'ë *(n.)* **angle**
ኹርናዕ kurna'ë *(n.)* **corner**
ኩሩዕ kuru'e *(adj.)* **lordly**
ኩሩዕ kuruë *(adj.)* **proud**
ካሮት carrot *(n.)* **carrot**
ካቶሊክ catholic *(adj.)* **catholic**
ክትግበር ዘይክእል ktgeber zeyk'el *(adj.)* **impracticable**
ኵስኰሳ ወይኒ kuskwasa weyni *(n.)* **viticulture**
ኳኽ kwak *(n.)* **crow**
ኳኽ kwak *(n.)* **rook**
ኳሌታ kwaleta *(n.)* **collar**
ኰነነ kwanene *(v.)* **condemn**
ኳንጎ kwanka *(n.)* **quango**

ኳርክ kwark ***(n.)* quark**
ኳርት kwart ***(n.)* quart**
ኳርትዝ kwartz ***(n.)* quartz**
ኲናት kwinat ***(n.)* war**
ክዉን kwun ***(adj.)* actual**
ክዉንነት kwunnet ***(n.)* surrealism**
ኵሉ ምኽኣል kulu mk'al ***(n.)* omnipotence**
ኽብሪ kdri ***(n.)* observance**
ኽዳን kdan ***(n.)* outfit**

# ወ

ወረረ werere ***(v.)* overrun**
ወረርሽኝ werershgn ***(n. )* outbreak**
ወቄት weqet ***(n.)* ounce**
ወይ wey ***(conj. )* or**
ወጥዋጥ wetwat ***(adj.)* oblong**
ዋዕሮ wa'ëro ***(n. )* vixen**
ዋሓለ waḥale ***(adj.)* versatile**
ወዲ wedi ***(n. )* lad**
ወገፈ wegefe ***(n.)* vestibule**
ወልዐ wel'ë ***(v.)* ignite**
ወንጌል wengeel ***(n. )* gospel**
ወርቂ werqi ***(n.)* gold**
ውርሲ wersi ***(n. )* heritage**
ወርወረ werwere ***(v.)* hurl**
ወተሃደር ነበር wetehader neber ***(n.)* veteran**
ውህደት whdet ***(n. )* harmony**
ዊንታ winta ***(n. )* volition**
ውልውል ነገ ፈረግ wlwl neg fereg ***(n.)* vacillation**
ውርደተኛ wrdeteña ***(adj.)* ignominious**
ዋጭዋጭታ wachwachta ***(n.)* squeal**
ዋዕላ wa'ela ***(n.)* convention**
ዋዕሮ wa'ëro ***(n.)* bitch**
ዋዕታ wa'eta ***(n.)* sonority**
ዋዕዋዕ waewae ***(adj.)* uproarious**
ዋዕዋዕ wa'ewa'e ***(n.)* clamour**
ዋዕዋዕ wa'ëwa'ë ***(n.)* noise**
ዋዕዋዕ በለ waëwaë bele ***(v.)* roister**
ዋዕዋዕ ዝበዝሖ wa'ëwa'ë zbezȟo ***(adj.)* noisy**
ዋዕዋዕታ waewaeta ***(n.)* uproar**
ዋጋ waga ***(n.)* fare**
ዋጋ waga ***(n.)* price**
ዋጋ waga ***(n.)* value**
ዋጋ waga ***(adj.)* worth**
ዋጋ ኣዉፀአ waga awxe'e ***(v.)* cost**
ዋጋ ቴንብር waga tienbr ***(n.)* postage**
ዋጋ ዘለዎ' waga zelewo ***(adj.)* worthwhile**
ዋጋ ዘይብሉ waga zeyblu ***(adj.)* feckless**
ዋጋ ዘይብሉ waga zeyblu ***(adj.)* worthless**
ዋሕዲ waĥdi ***(n.)* dearth**
ዋሕዲ waĥdi ***(n.)* deficiency**
ዋሕዲ waĥdi ***(n.)* shortfall**
ዋሕዲ ደም waȟdi dem ***(n.)* anaemia**
ዋህዮ waheyo ***(n.)* cell**
ዋህረም wahrem ***(n.)* banger**
ዋህረም wahrem ***(n. )* pudding**
ዋሕስ waḥs ***(n.)* guarantor**
ዋሕስ waḥs ***(n.)* warrantor**
ዋሕስ waȟs ***(n.)* bail**
ዋህዮኣዊ wahyo'awi ***(adj.)* cellular**
ዋሕዚ waĥzi ***(n. )* rivulet**
ዋሕዚ waȟzi ***(n.)* flux**
ዋዒ wa'ï ***(n.)* heat**
ዋላ wala ***(pron.)* whatever**
ዋላ wala ***(conj.)* whether**
ዋላ ሓደ እኳ wala ȟade ekwa ***(adj.)* neither**
ዋላ ሓደ እኳ wala ȟade ekwa ***(pron. )* nobody**

ዋላ ሓደ እኳ wala ȟade ekwa *(pron. )* **none**
ዋላ ሓደሻዕ wala ȟadeshaë *(adv.)* **ever**
ዋላ ሓንቲ wala ȟanti *(pron. )* **nothing**
ዋላካ እንተኮነ walaka entekone *(conj.)* **though**
ዋልድቢት waldbit *(n.)* **attic**
ዋልድቢት waldbit *(n.)* **garret**
ዋልታዊ waltawi *(adj.)* **polar**
ዋና wana *(adj.)* **main**
ዋና wana *(adj.)* **major**
ዋና wana *(n.)* **proprietor**
ዋና ኣእምሮ wana a'emro *(n.)* **mastermind**
ዋና ኣካል wana alkal *(n.)* **mainstay**
ዋና ጎዳና wana godana *(n.)* **thoroughfare**
ዋና ከሻኒ wana kesha'ni *(n.)* **chef**
ዋና ምምሕዳር wana mmhhdar *(n.)* **headquarters**
ዋና ዘይብሉ wana zeyblu *(adj.)* **unattended**
ዋኒን wanin *(n.)* **business**
ዋኒናት waninat *(n.)* **conjuncture**
ዋንነት wannet *(n. )* **possession**
ዋንነታዊ wannetawi *(adj.)* **proprietary**
ዋርድያ wardiya *(v.)* **patrol**
ዋርድያ wardya *(n.)* **sentry**
ዋርዋርታ warwarta *(n. )* **mirage**
ዋይ ኣነ way 'ane *(conj.)* **alas**
ዋዛ waza *(n)* **comedy**
ዋዛ waza *(n. )* **humour**
ዋዛ waza *(n.)* **lark**
ዋዛ waza *(n. )* **raillery**
ውዳሰ-ከንቱ wdasekentu *(n.)* **adulation**
ውድብ wdb *(n.)* **party**
ውድድር wddr *(n.)* **rivalry**
ውድድራዊ wddrawi *(adj.)* **competitive**
ውዲት ኣለመ wdit aleme *(v.)* **sabotage**
ውድቀት wdqet *(n.)* **demise**
ዉድቀት wdqet *(n.)* **downfall**
ዉድቀት wdqet *(n.)* **failure**
ወጫጪ weçaçi *(adj.)* **vociferous**
ወጨጨ wečeče *(v.)* **bawl**
መርዚ wečeče merzi *(n.)* **poison**
ወዳደሰ wedadese *(v.)* **flatter**
ወዳኢ weda'i *(n.)* **executor**
ወድአ wed'e *(n.)* **conclude**
ወድአ wed'e *(v.)* **consume**
ወደብ wedeb *(n.)* **port**
ወደአ wede'e *(v.)* **deplete**
ወደቀ wedeqe *(v. t.)* **decline**
ወደቐ wedeqe *(v.)* **drop**
ወደቐ wedeqe *(v.)* **fall**
ወደቐ wedeq̈e *(v.)* **expire**
ወደሰ wedese *(v.)* **laud**
ወዲ wedi *(n.)* **bloke**
ወዲ ዓበይቲ wedi äbeyti *(n.)* **nobleman**
ወዲ ዓዲ wedi adi *(adj.)* **local**
ወዲ ዓዲ wedi ädi *(n.)* **native**
ወዲኣኮ wedi 'ako *(n.)* **cousin**
ወዲ ደራፊ ፅብቅ ድምፂ ዘለዎ wedi derafi sbuk dmsi zelewo *(n.)* **tenor**
ወዲ ገጠር ኮነ wedi geter kone *(v.)* **rusticate**
ወዲ ገጠር ምኳን wedi geter mkwan *(n. )* **rustication**
ወዲ ሃገር wedi hager *(n.)* **compatriot**
ወዲ ምዕራብ wedi m'erab *(n.)* **westerner**

ወደ መዝሙር wedi mezmur *(n.)* **disciple**
ወድ ንጉስ wedi ngus *(n.)* **prince**
ወዲ ሰብ wedi seb *(n.)* **humanity**
ወዲ ወፃእ wedi wexa'e *(n.)* **expatriate**
ወዲ wedi *(n.)* **boy**
ወዲ ሰብ wediseb *(n. )* **Wight**
ወድወዶ wedwodo *(n. )* **tomboy**
ወፈያ wefeya *(n.)* **contribution**
ወፈየ wefeye *(v.)* **dedicate**
ወፈየ wefeye *(v.)* **devote**
ወፍሪ wefri *(n.)* **expedition**
ወግአ weg'a *(v.)* **pierce**
ወግአ wega *(n.)* **prickle**
ወጋሕታ wegahta *(n.)* **dawn**
ወጋኢ wega'i *(adj.)* **biting**
ወግዓዊ መልእኽቲ weg'äwi mel'eḱti *(n. )* **missive**
ወግዓዊ ምግዳፍ weg'äwi mgdaf *(n.)* **renunciation**
ወግአ weg'e *(v.)* **inject**
ወግአ we'g'e *(v.)* **stab**
ወግዒ weg'ë *(n. )* **rite**
ወገደ wegede *(v.t. )* **renounce**
ወገደ wegede *(v.)* **avoid**
ወገናዊ wegenawi *(adj.)* **sectarian**
ወገንነት wegen'net *(n. )* **nepotism**
ወግዒ weg'i *(n.)* **conversation**
ወግዒ weg'ï *(n. )* **nicety**
ወሃቢ wehabi *(adj.)* **philanthropic**
ወሓደ wehade *(v.)* **lessen**
ወሓጥ ጐንጺ weȟaẗ gwanxi *(n.)* **buffer**
ወሓጠ weȟate *(v.)* **devour**
ወሓጠ weȟaẗe *(v.)* **engulf**
ወሓጠ weȟaẗe *(v.)* **swallow**
ወሓጠ weḥaṭe *(v.)* **gulp**
ወሓዘ weȟaze *(v.)* **drift**
ወሓለ weĥle *(adj.)* **skilful**
ወጃብ wejab *(adj.)* **seedy**
ወጃብ wejab *(n.)* **slob**
ወጃዕጃዕ በሃሊ wejaëjaë behali *(adj.)* **rumbustious**
ወጅሂ weĵhi *(n.)* **complexion**
ወከለ wekele *(v.)* **depute**
ወኪል wekil *(n. )* **proxy**
ውዕል w'el *(n.)* **indenture**
ውዕል w'ël *(n.)* **contract**
ውዕል w'ël *(n)* **contract**
ውዕል w'ël *(n.)* **deal**
ውዕል w'ël *(n.)* **stipulation**
ውዕል w'ël *(n.)* **bond**
ወላድ welad *(n.)* **maternity**
ወላድ welad *(adj.)* **multiparous**
ወላዲ weladi *(n. )* **parent**
ወላዲት weladit *(n.)* **mother**
ወልዳፍ weldaf *(adj. )* **halting**
ወለደ welede *(v.)* **procreate**
ወለደ welede *(v.)* **beget**
ወለዶ weledo *(n. )* **lineage**
ወለዱ ዝቐተለ weledu zqetele *(n. )* **parricide**
ወልፊ welfi *(n.)* **addiction**
ወንበር wenber *(n.)* **couch**
ወንጭፍ wenĉf *(n.)* **sling**
ወንጨፈ wenchefe *(v.)* **hurtle**
ወንበር weneber *(n.)* **chair**
ወነነ wenene *(v.)* **possess**
ወንጀለ wenjele *(v.)* **attribute**
ወንጀለኛ wenjelegna *(adj.)* **guilty**
ወንጀለኛ wenjelegna *(n.)* **miscreant**
ወቐዐ weqe *(v.)* **whisk**
ወቅዐ weq'ë *(v.)* **strum**
ወቀረ weqere *(v.)* **engrave**
ወቀሰ weqese *(v.)* **blame**
ወቀሰ weqese *(v.)* **censure**

ወቀሰ weqese *(v.)* **deprecate**
ወቀሰ weqese *(v.)* **niggle**
ወቀሰ weqese *(v.)* **reproach**
ወቐሰ weqese *(adj.)* **upbraid**
ወቐሰ weq̈ese *(v.)* **berate**
ወቓዓይ weqha'äy *(n. )* **striker**
ወቅታዊ weqtawi *(adj.)* **seasonable**
ወቅታዊ weqtawi *(adj.)* **seasonal**
ወቅታዊ weqtawi *(adj.)* **topical**
ወቅቲ weqti *(n.)* **season**
ወጋኢ weraei *(n. )* **poker**
ወራሪ werari *(n. )* **marauder**
ወራሪ werari *(adj.)* **rampant**
ወራሲ werasi *(n.)* **successor**
ወራሲ werasi *(n.)* **heir**
ወረዳ wereda *(n.)* **precinct**
ወረዳ wereda *(n.)* **canton**
ወረደ werede *(v.t,)* **abdicate**
ወረደ werede *(v.t.)* **alight**
ወረደ werede *(v.)* **befall**
ወረደ werede *(v.)* **descend**
ወረደ werede *(v.)* **disembark**
ወረጃ ዝኮነ ሰብ wereja zekone seb *(n.)* **gentleman**
ወረንጦ werento *(n.)* **tweezers**
ወረቀት ዕዳ wereqet ëda *(n.)* **bill**
ወረራ werera *(n.)* **foray**
ወረራ werera *(n.)* **incursion**
ወረራ werera *(n.)* **raid**
ወረራ we're'ra *(n.)* **conquest**
ወረረ werere *(v.)* **infest**
ወረረ werere *(v.)* **invade**
ወረረ werere *(v.)* **maraud**
ወረረ were're *(v.)* **conquer**
ወረሰ werese *(v.)* **confiscate**
ወረሰ werese *(v.)* **inherit**
ወረጦ wereẗo *(n.)* **forceps**
ወረጦ wereto *(n.)* **pincer**
ወርሓዊ werhawi *(adj.)* **lunar**
ወርሓዊ werḧawi *(adj.)* **monthly**
ወርሒ werḧi *(n.)* **month**
ወርሒ werḧi *(n. )* **moon**
ወሪርካ ምሓዝ werirka m'ḧaz *(n.)* **subjugation**
ወሪሩ ሓዘ weriru ḧaze *(v.)* **subjugate**
ወርቃዊ werqawi *(adj.)* **golden**
ወረቐት werqet *(n. )* **paper**
ወርቀዘቦ werqezebo *(n.)* **brocade**
ወርጠበ werẗebe *(n.)* **stripling**
ወርዊሩ werwiru *(v.)* **toss**
ወሳናይ wesanay *(adj.)* **decisive**
ወሳኒ wesani *(adj.)* **critical**
ወሳኒ wesani *(n.)* **determinant**
ወሳኒ ግጥም wesani gtm *(n.)* **showdown**
ወሰደ wesede *(v.)* **take**
ወሰኽ wesek *(n.)* **increment**
ወሰኸ weseke *(v.)* **augment**
ወሰኸ weseke *(v.)* **increase**
ወሰን wesen *(n.)* **edge**
ወሰን ከተማ wesen ketema *(n.)* **suburb**
ወሰን ከተማ wesen ketema *(adj.)* **suburban**
ወሰን ከተማ wesen ketema *(n.)* **suburbia**
ወሰናወሰን wesena'wesen *(n.)* **contour**
ወሰነ wesene *(v.)* **confine**
ወሰነ wesene *(v. t)* **determine**
ወሰነ wesesne *(v.)* **decide**
ወሽመጥ weshmeẗ *(n.)* **fjord**
ወሽመጥ weshmeṭ *(n. )* **gulf**
ወሽመጥ weshmt *(n.)* **peninsula**
ወሲብ ዘላዓዕል wesib zela'ä'ël *(adj.)* **erotic**

ወሲብ ዝፈቱ wesib zfetu *(n.)* **sensualist**
ወሰኽ ዋጋ weskh waga *(n.)* **inflation**
ወስላት weslat *(n.)* **rascal**
ወስላት weslat *(adj.)* **roguish**
ወስታ westa *(n.)* **gesture**
ወታደር wetader *(adj.)* **military**
ወታደር wetader *(n. )* **soldier**
ወታደራዊ ቤት ማእሰርቲ wetaderawi beet ma'eserti *(n.)* **stockade**
ወታእታእ በለ weta'eta'e bele *(v.)* **splutter**
ወታእታእ በለ weta'eta'e bele *(v.)* **stammer**
ወጣም wetam *(adj.)* **inquisitive**
ወጣም weťam *(adj.)* **nosy**
ወጣት ዕድሚኡ 13-19 ዝኾነ wetat edmiu kab 13-19 zkone *(n.)* **teenager**
ወተፈ wetefe *(v.)* **thrust**
ወተግ weteg *(n. )* **nape**
ወተሃደር wetehader *(n. )* **warrior**
ወጠነ weťene *(v.)* **intend**
ወጠረ we-ṭe-re *(v.)* **heckle**
ወትሩ ሕጉስ wetru higus *(adj.)* **cheerful**
ወፃኢ ገበረ wetsa'i gebere *(v.)* **disburse**
ውዕውዕ w'ëw'ë *(adj.)* **fervent**
ውዕውዕ w'ëw'ë *(adj.)* **vivid**
ውዕውዕ ስምዒት w'ëw'ë sm'ït *(n.)* **enthusiasm**
ውዕውዕ ስምዒት w'ëw'ë sm'ït *(n.)* **verve**
ወፃኢ wexa'i *(n.)* **expenditure**
ወፃኢ wexa'i *(n.)* **expense**
ወጸ wexe *(v.)* **vacate**
ወይ wey *(adv.)* **either**
ወይቦ weybo *(adj. )* **hepatitis**
ወይቦ weybo *(n.)* **jaundice**
ወይና ደጋ weyna dega *(adj.)* **temperate**
ወይናይ weynay *(n. )* **mulberry**
ወይኒ weyni *(n. )* **grape**
ወይኒ weyni *(n. )* **wine**
ወይዘሪት weyzerit *(n. )* **miss**
ወይዘሮ weyzero *(n.)* **dame**
ወይዘሮ weyzero *(n.)* **lady**
ወይዘሮ weyzero *(n.)* **madam**
ወይዘሮ weyzero *(n. )* **matron**
ወዛል wezal *(adj.)* **blowsy**
ወዛል wezal *(adj.)* **shabby**
ወዛል wezal *(adj.)* **slatternly**
ወዝቢ wezbi *(n.)* **contingency**
ወዘተረፈ wezeterefe *(adv.)* **et cetera**
ውፋይነት wfaynet *(n.)* **dedication**
ውግኣት wgat *(n. )* **pang**
ወጋእ wge *(v.i. )* **peck**
ዋንነታዊ aganazabi *(adj.)* **possessive**
ውግእ ውግእ ኣቢሉ wgè wgè abilu *(v.)* **prod**
ውግእ wg'è *(n.)* **battle**
ውህደት whdet *(n.)* **assimilation**
ውህደት whdet *(n.)* **coordination**
ዉህደት whdet *(n. )* **fusion**
ውሒጣ wḥiṭa *(n. )* **glutton**
ዉሕጅ wĥj *(n.)* **flood**
ዉሕጅ wȟj *(n.)* **current**
ውሕጃዊ wĥjawi *(adj.)* **fluvial**
ውህለላ whlela *(n.)* **accumulation**
ውሕልልነት wĥllnet *(n.)* **dexterity**
ውሕልና ኣእዳው wĥlna a'edaw *(n. )* **sleight**
ውህሉል whlul *(n.)* **hoard**
ውሕስነት ዝተወሃቦ wȟsnet ztewehabo *(adj.)* **assured**

ውሁድ whud *(n.)* **compound**
ውሁድ whud *(adj.)* **concerted**
ውሑዳን wḧudan *(n. )* **minority**
ዊን ዝበሎ ዝገብር win zbelo zgebr *(adj.)* **madcap**
ውከላ wkela *(n.)* **deputation**
ውከሳ ሙታን wkesa mutan *(n.)* **necromancy**
ውክልና wklna *(n.)* **commission**
ውልቀኛ wkqegna *(n.)* **maverick**
ውላድ ድሙ wlad dmu *(n. )* **kitten**
ውልደታዊ wldetawi *(adj.)* **natal**
ውልቃዊ wlqawi *(adj.)* **private**
ዉልቃዊነት wlqawinet *(n.)* **individualism**
ዉልቃዊነት wlqawinet *(n.)* **individuality**
ውልቃውነት wlqawnet *(n.)* **privacy**
ዉልቀ wlqe *(adj.)* **individual**
ውልቀ ምልኪ wlqe mlki *(n.)* **autocracy**
ውልቀኛ w'lqegna *(n. )* **soloist**
ውልቀ-መላኺ wlqemelaḱi *(n.)* **autocrat**
ውልውል wlwl *(n.)* **quandary**
ውቅዒት wq'it *(v.)* **strike**
ውርጪ wrchi *(n.)* **snow**
ዉርደት wrdet *(n.)* **disgrace**
ዉርደት wrdet *(n.)* **dishonour**
ውርደት wrdet *(n.)* **ignominy**
ውርዲ wrdi *(n.)* **breadth**
ውረዛ wreza *(n.)* **courtship**
ውሪግሪግ በለ wrigrig bele *(v.)* **shimmer**
ውርሳ wrsa *(n.)* **confiscation**
ውርሻ wrsha *(n.)* **bequest**
ውርሻዊ wrshawi *(adj.)* **congenital**
ውሩይ wruy *(adj.)* **noted**
ውሩይ wruy *(adj.)* **prestigious**
ውርወራ wrwera *(n.)* **lunge**
ውርዝውና wrzwna *(n.)* **virtue**
ዉሳነ wsane *(n.)* **decision**
ውሳነ ህዝቢ wsane hzbi *(n.)* **referendum**
ወሳኒ wsani *(adj.)* **indispensable**
ውሰኸ wseḱa *(n.)* **addition**
ውሻል wshal *(n.)* **wedge**
ውሻጠ wshate *(n.)* **cellar**
ውሽማ wshma *(n.)* **concubine**
ውሽጣዊ wshtawi *(adj.)* **inmost**
ውሽጣዊ wshẗawi *(adj.)* **interior**
ውሽጣዊ wshẗawi *(adj.)* **internal**
ውሽጣዊ wshẗawi *(adj.)* **inward**
ውሽጣዊ መዘራረቢ wshẗawi mezerarebi *(n.)* **intercom**
ውሽጣዊ ሰንጣቒት wshẗawi senẗaqit *(n.)* **calibre**
ውሽጢ wshti *(prep. )* **within**
ውሽጢ wshẗi *(n.)* **inside**
ውሽጢ ምእታው wshti metaw *(v.)* **penetrate**
ውስኪ wski *(n.)* **whisky**
ውሱን wsun *(adj.)* **exclusive**
ውትረት wtret *(n.)* **tension**
ውፅእ እትው ምበል wts'e 'etuw mbal *(n.)* **sally**
ውጽእ እትው wts'e e'tw *(v.)* **undulate**
ውፅኢት wts'it *(n. )* **result**
ዉድድር wuddr *(n.)* **tournament**
ዉድድር wudi'dir *(n.)* **contest**
ዉዲተኛ wuditenya *(n.)* **conspirator**
ዉገዳ wugeda *(n.)* **avoidance**
ውገዳ wugeda *(n.)* **disqualification**
ዉህብቶ wuhbto *(n.)* **gift**
ውህለላ wuhlela *(n. )* **savings**
ውሁሉል wuhlul *(adj.)* **cumulative**
ውሕስነት wuhsnet *(n.)* **security**

**ዉሕስነት** wuhsnet ***(n.)*** **immunity**
**ውሕስነት ሃበ** wuhsnet habe ***(v.)*** **immunize**
**ዉሑድ** wuhud ***(adj.)*** **scant**
**ዉሑድ** wuĥud ***(adj.)*** **few**
**ዉሑጅ** wuhuj ***(n.)*** **torrent**
**ዉሕስ** wuhus ***(adj.)*** **immune**
**ዉሑስ** wuhus ***(adj.)*** **safe**
**ዉላድ** wulad ***(n. )*** **progeny**
**ውልደ ኦም** wulde om ***(n.)*** **sapling**
**ዉሉድ** wulud ***(n. )*** **son**
**ዉሉፍ** wuluf ***(n.)*** **addict**
**ዉሉፍ** wuluf ***(adj.)*** **addicted**
**ዉሉፍ** wuluf ***(adj.)*** **dependent**
**ውንታ** wunta ***(n.)*** **déjà vu**
**ዉንዘፋ** wunzefa ***(n.)*** **abeyance**
**ዉንዙፍ ስራሕ** wunzuf sraḧ ***(n.)*** **backlog**
**ዉቃጦ** wuqato ***(n.)*** **tattoo**
**ዉቅያኖስ ዘቋርፅ** wuqyanos zeqars ***(adj.)*** **transatlantic**
**ዉርጩም** wurĉam ***(adj.)*** **frosty**
**ውርጬዊ** wurchawi ***(adj.)*** **snowy**
**ዉርጪ** wurĉi ***(n. )*** **frost**
**ውርሲ** wursi ***(n.)*** **inheritance**
**ዉርሲ** wursi ***(n.)*** **legacy**
**ውርይነት** wuruynet ***(n.)*** **renown**
**ውሽጠ** wushate' ***(n.)*** **closet**
**ውሽጣዊ** wushtawi ***(adj.)*** **inner**
**ውሽጣዊ** wushtawi ***(adj.)*** **innermost**
**ውሽጣዊ ዋሕዚ** wushtawi wahzi ***(n.)*** **undercurrent**
**ዉሂኢታማ** wusieitama ***(adj.)*** **telling**
**ዉስተዘ** wustez ***(n.)*** **pun**
**ዉሱን** wusun ***(adj.)*** **definite**
**ዉሱን** wusun ***(adj.)*** **finite**
**ዉሱን** wusun ***(n.)*** **term**
**ዉጥሚት** wutmit ***(n.)*** **tab**
**ዉፅኣት** wuts'at ***(n.)*** **diarrhoea**
**ውፅኢት** wutsieiit ***(adj.)*** **consequent**
**ውፅኢት** wuts'it ***(n.)*** **score**
**ውፁእ** wutsu'e ***(adj.)*** **distinct**
**ዉጡን** wutun ***(adj.)*** **intentional**
**ዉዑይ** wu'uy ***(adj.)*** **sprightly**
**ውዑይ** w'üy ***(adj. )*** **hot**
**ዉዝምበሩ ዝዎየ** wuzmbru zwese ***(adj.)*** **tempestuous**
**ውፁዕ** wxeu'e ***(adj.)*** **underprivileged**
**ዉፅኢታዊ** wxi'itawi ***(adj.)*** **effective**
**ዉዝወዛ** wz'waze ***(n.)*** **swing**
**ወጻኢ ገንዘብ** wetsa'i genzeb ***(n.)*** **outlay**
**ዋና** wana ***(n. )*** **owner**
**ዋንነት** wannet ***(n. )*** **ownership**
**ውላድ** wlad ***(n.)*** **offspring**
**ውሻጠ** wshate ***(n. )*** **outhouse**
**ውቅያኖሳዊ** wqyanosawi ***(adj.)*** **oceanic**
**ውቅያኖስ** wqyanos ***(n.)*** **ocean**
**ውደሳ** wudesa ***(n.)*** **ode**
**ውድብ** wudb ***(n.)*** **organization**
**ውፅኢት** wts'it ***(n.)*** **outcome**
**ውፅኢት** wts'it ***(n. )*** **output**
**ዑደት** xudet ***(n. )*** **goose**

# ዓ

**ዓመታዊ** 'ämetawi ***(n.)*** **circulation**
**ዓዓ** 'ä'ä ***(adj.)*** **annual**
**ዓቢ** 'äbi ***(adj.)*** **great**
**ዓጋቲ** 'ägati ***(n. )*** **impasse**
**ዓጀብቲ** äjebti ***(n.)*** **entourage**
**ዓለባ ሃሪ** 'äleba hari ***(n.)*** **velvet**

ዓለምለኻዊ 'älemlekawi *(adj.)* **global**
ዓማል ämal *(adj.)* **fallow**
ዓንቀፈ 'änqefe *(v.)* **impede**
ዓንቀጸ anqe-tse *(v.)* **hinder**
ዓቃቢ ንዋይ äqabi nway *(n.)* **exchequer**
ዓቀበ 'aqebe *(v. t)* **conserve**
ዓርሱ ተኸናኸነ ärsu tekenakene *(v.)* **fend**
ዓጠረ 'äṭere *(n. )* **wrinkle**
ዓጠረ 'äṭere *(n.)* **wrinkle**
ዓይኒ መፍትሕ 'äyni mefth *(n.)* **keyhole**
ዕቤት 'ëbeet *(n.)* **growth**
ዕብላለ 'ëblale *(n.)* **hegemony**
ዕቡ'ይ 'ëbuy *(n. )* **immodest**
ዕቡ'ይነት 'ëbuynet *(a. )* **immodesty**
ዕኮት 'ëkot *(n.)* **wasp**
ዕንደራ ëndera *(n.)* **escapade**
ዕንክሊል 'ënklil *(n.)* **hoop**
ዕረፍቲ ዘይብሉ 'ërefti zeyblu *(adj. )* **hectic**
ዕሽሽ ኪበሃል ዚከኣል 'ëshsh kibehal zike'al *(adj.)* **venial**
ዕዮ 'ëyo *(n.)* **labour**
ዓመታዊ 'ämetawi *(adj.)* **annual**
ዓቀቅ በለ aaqeq bele *(v.)* **creak**
ዓቀቅታ aaqeqta *(n.)* **creak**
ዓራት ቆልዓ aarat qol'aa *(n.)* **crib**
ዓባስ äbas *(adj.)* **dumb**
ዓባስ äbas *(adj.)* **mute**
ዓባሲ äbasi *(adj.)* **styptic**
ዓባይ ኣፃብዕቲ እግሪ abay asabati egry *(n.)* **toe**
ዓባይቶ abayto *(n.)* **thumb**
ዕብዳን abdan *(n.)* **tomfoolery**
ዓበድበድ äbedbed *(n.)* **furore**
ዓበቅ abeq *(n. )* **scabies**
ዓበሰ äbese *(v.)* **muffle**
ዓበጠ äbete *(v.)* **repress**
ዓበጠ äbete *(v.)* **smother**
ዓበየ äbeye *(v.)* **develop**
ዓበየ äbeye *(v.i. )* **grow**
ዓቢ a'bi *(n.)* **whopper**
ዓቢ 'äbi *(adj.)* **venerable**
ዓቢ ድኳን äbi dkhwan *(n.)* **supermarket**
ዓቢ ድኳን äbi dkhwan *(n.)* **superstore**
ዓቢ ማዕበል äbi ma'ëbel *(v.)* **billow**
ዓቢ äbi *(adj.)* **big**
ዓብይ መኣንጣ abiy meanta *(n.)* **colon**
ዓብላላይ äblalay *(adj.)* **dominant**
ዓብላሊ äblali *(adj.)* **prevalent**
ዓብላሊ äblali *(adj.)* **overbearing**
ዓብለለ ablele *(v.)* **override**
ዓብለለ äblele *(v.)* **dominate**
ዓብለለ äblele *(v.)* **overshadow**
ዓብይ ሹቕ äby shuq *(n.)* **delicatessen**
ዓብዪ abyi *(adj.)* **senior**
ዓብዪ abyi *(adj.)* **outsize**
ዓብይ äbyi *(adj.)* **elder**
ዓብዪ äbyi *(adj.)* **grand**
ዓብዪ äbyi *(adj.)* **noble**
ዓብዪ ገዛ abyi geza *(n. )* **mansion**
ዓብዪ ሞደሻ äbyi modeša *(n.)* **sledgehammer**
ዓብዪ ሳንጣ a'byi santa *(n.)* **holdall**
ዓብዪ ጦር abyi tor *(n.)* **lance**
ዓዳጊ ädagi *(n.)* **buyer**
ዓዳላይ ädalay *(n.)* **distributor**
ዓዳሊ መንሹር adali menshur *(n. )* **pamphleteer**
ዓደለ ädele *(v.)* **allocate**
ዓደለ ädele *(v.)* **confer**

ዓደለ ädele *(v. i)* **deal**
ዓደለ ädele *(v.)* **distribute**
ዓደየ ädeye *(v.)* **expiate**
ዓበድበድ aebedbed *(n.)* **hysteria**
ዓሌት ae-leet *(n.)* **heredity**
ዓፈነ äfene *(v.)* **asphyxiate**
ዓፈነ äfene *(v.)* **stifle**
ዓፈነ äfene *(v.)* **suffocate**
ዓፈነ äfene *(v.)* **suppress**
ዓፈረ äfere *(v.)* **fizzle**
ዓፍራ afra *(n. )* **lather**
ዓፍራ äfra *(n.)* **foam**
ዓፍራ äfra *(n.)* **froth**
ዓፍራ äfra *(n.)* **spume**
ዓፍራ äfra *(n.)* **bubble**
ዓገተ agete *(v.)* **obstruct**
ዓገተ ägete *(v.)* **curtail**
ዓገተ ägete *(v.)* **restrain**
ዓገተ ägete *(v.)* **occlude**
ዓጋፎ ägafo *(n.)* **mob**
ዓጋፎ ägafo *(n.)* **rabble**
ዓጋቲ agati *(n.)* **insulator**
ዓጋቲ ägati *(adj.)* **preventive**
ዓጋዜን ägazeen *(n.)* **antelope**
ዓጋዜን ägazen *(n.)* **deer**
ዒስራ aisra *(adj.&n.)* **twenty**
ዓጃቢ ajabi *(n.)* **outrider**
ዓጀበ äĵebe *(v.)* **accompany**
ዓጀብቲ äjebti *(n.)* **retinue**
ዓጀውጀው äjewjew *(n.)* **delirium**
ዓካር akar *(n.)* **tubercle**
ዓካር äkar *(n.)* **crystal**
ዓቐን aken *(n.)* **gauge**
ዓከሰ äkese *(v.)* **misfire**
ዓኽታ äkhta *(n. )* **sputum**
ዓኳይ akuay *(n.)* **yeoman**
ዓላ a'la *(adj.)* **jovial**
ዓላቕ älaq̈ *(n.)* **bully**
ዓለባ aleba *(n.)* **coir**
ዓለባ ሳሬት aleba sareet *(n.)* **cobweb**
ዓለባ ሳሬት aleba sariet *(n.)* **web**
ቀንዲ aleba saret *(adj.)* **foremost**
ዓለም alem *(n. )* **world**
ዓለም älem *(n. )* **globe**
ዓለም ለኻዊነት älem lekawinet *(n.)* **globalization**
ዓለማዊ alemawi *(adj.)* **worldly**
ዓለማዊ älemawi *(adj.)* **mundane**
ዓለመ aleme *(v.i.)* **aim**
ዓለመኛ ዘይኮነ alemenga zekone *(adj.)* **unworldly**
ዓለምለኻዊ alemlekawi *(adj.)* **universal**
ዓለም-ለኻዊ 'älemlekáwi *(adj.)* **international**
ዓለምለኻዊነት alemlekawinet *(adv. )* **universality**
ዓለቕቲ aleqti *(n. )* **leech**
ዓሌት alet *(n.)* **clan**
ዓሌት älet *(n.)* **race**
ዓሌታዊ äletawi *(adj.)* **racial**
ዓሌታውነት äletawnwt *(n.)* **racialism**
ዓማፂ ämatsi *(adj.)* **dastardly**
ዓማፂ ämatsi *(adj.)* **rebellious**
ዓማጺ ämaxi *(adj.)* **aggressive**
ዓምበበ ämbebe *(v.)* **bloom**
ዓመደ ሙታን ämde mutan *(n. )* **obituary**
ዓምዲ amdi *(n.)* **pillar**
ዓምዲ ሞስኮት ämdi moskot *(n.)* **mullion**
ዓመፀኛ amesegna *(n. )* **thug**
ዓመት amet *(n.)* **year**
ዓመታዊ ametawi *(adv. )* **yearly**
ዓመታዊ መልዕሎ ämetawi mel'ëlo *(n.)* **annuity**
ዓመተ ämete *(v.)* **blindfold**

ዓመፅ ämets *(n.)* **rebellion**
ዓምፅ ametse *(n.)* **insurrection**
ዓመፀ ämetse *(v.)* **rebel**
ዓመፀኛ ämetsgna *(adj.)* **pushy**
ዓመፅ amex *(n.)* **uprising**
ዓመጽ 'ämex *(n.)* **violence**
ዓመጸ ämexe *(v.)* **abuse**
ዓሚል amil *(n.)* **client**
ዓሚል ämil *(n.)* **customer**
ዓሚል ኮነ ämil kone *(v.)* **subscribe**
ዓሚል ሙኳን ämil mkhwan *(n.)* **subscription**
ዓሚቅ ämiq *(adj.)* **deep**
ዓሚቕ ስንጭሮ ämiq sncro *(n.)* **canyon**
ዓምረረ ämrere *(v.)* **pounce**
ዓንዳሪ 'ändari *(adj.)* **venturesome**
ዓንደረ andere *(v.)* **gambol**
ዓንደረ andere *(v.t.)* **scamper**
ዓንደረ ändere *(v.)* **romp**
ዓንደረ 'ändere *(v.)* **frisk**
ዓንዲ ändi *(n. )* **mast**
ዓንዲ ሑቀ ändi ḧuqe *(n.)* **spine**
ዓንዲ-ሕቖ ändiḧqo *(n.)* **backbone**
ዓንዲ anedi *(n.)* **column**
ዓንቀፅ aneqetse *(n.)* **clause**
ዓንቀፀ änqets *(v.)* **remand**
ዓንቀጸ anqetse *(v.)* **thwart**
ዓንቀፀ änqetze *(v.)* **forestall**
ዓንቀጽ anqex *(n.)* **paragraph**
ዓንቀፅ änqex *(n.)* **article**
ዓንገለ ängele *(v.)* **nourish**
ዓንጃል änjal *(adj.)* **daft**
ዓንጃል änjal *(n.)* **fool**
ዓንጃል änjal *(adj.)* **ridiculous**
ዓንጃል änjal *(n.)* **stooge**
ዓንጃል änĵal *(adj.)* **foolish**
ዓንጃል änĵal *(adj.)* **asinine**

ዓንካር änkar *(n.)* **granule**
ዓንካር-ዓንካሪቶ änkar'änkarito *(n.)* **ankle**
ዓንኬል 'änkeel *(n.)* **wreath**
ዓንኬል ankiel *(n. )* **loop**
ዓንቃሪቦ änqaribo *(n. )* **hook**
ዓንቃሪቦ änqaribo *(n.)* **barb**
ዓንቀር ጠበንጃ änqer ẗebenĵa *(n.)* **breech**
ዓቃበ-ህንጻ äqabehntsa *(n.)* **janitor**
ዓቀበ aqebe *(v.)* **maintain**
ዓቀበ aqebe *(v.)* **uphold**
ዓቀበ äqebe *(v.)* **deter**
ዓቀበ äqebe *(v.t. )* **perpetuate**
ዓቀበ äqebe *(v.)* **preserve**
ዓቀበ äqebe *(v.)* **reserve**
ዓቀበ äqebe *(v.i. )* **retain**
ዓቀን äqen *(n.)* **dimension**
ዓቀን ä'qen *(a. )* **measure**
ዓቀን ä'qen *(n. )* **measurement**
ዓቐን ፈውሲ äqen fewsi *(n.)* **dose**
ዓቐን ሓይሊ ኤሌክትሪክ 'äqen ḧayli 'eeleektrik *(n. )* **voltage**
ዓቀናዊ äqenawi *(adj.)* **quantitative**
ዓቀነ ä'qene *(v.)* **measure**
ዓቐን aqhen *(n. )* **magnitude**
ዓቐን ዘይብሉ ድልየት aqhen zeyblu dlyet *(adj.)* **insatiable**
ዓቕሚ ዘይብሉ aqhmi zeyblu *(adj.)* **incompetent**
ዓቅመ ኣዳም ዝበፅሐ äqme adam betzḧe *(adj.)* **marriageable**
ዓቕሚ äqmi *(n.)* **potency**
ዓቕሚ äqmi *(adj.)* **potential**
ዓቕሚ ዘይብሉ aqmi zeyblu *(adj.)* **incapable**
ዓቕሚ äqmi *(n.)* **capability**
ዓቕሚ äqmi *(n.)* **capacity**

ዕሽነት ዝትምሎኦ ዉሳኔ arabḧe *(adj.)* **injudicious**
ዓራት ärat *(n.)* **bed**
ዓራት ቆልዓ ärat qol'ä *(n.)* **cot**
ዓራት ዘይሓዘ ተሓካሚ arat zeyhaze tehakami *(n.)* **outpatient**
ዓርቢ 'ärbi *(n. )* **Friday**
ዓረብ äreb *(n.)* **Arab**
ዓረበታይ ärebetay *(n.)* **Arabian**
ዓረብያ arebia *(n.)* **cart**
ዓረብያ/ሰረገላ arebiya/seregela *(n.)* **chariot**
ዓረብኛ ärebnya *(n.)* **Arabic**
ዓረብያ arebya *(n.)* **winch**
ዓረደ 'ärede *(v.)* **fortify**
ዓረነ ärene *(n. )* **snail**
ዓረነ ärene *(n.)* **slug**
መበየዲ mebeyedi *(n.)* **solder**
ዓረር ärer *(n.)* **bullet**
ቢምቦ bimbo *(v.)* **plumb**
ዓርከይ arkey *(n. )* **kith**
ዓርኪ ärki *(n. )* **friend**
ዓርክ ärki *(n.)* **mate**
ዓርማም ärmam *(adj.)* **raucous**
ዓርሞሸሽ ärmoshesh *(n.)* **giant**
ዓርሰ arse *(pron. )* **oneself**
ዓርስኻ arseka *(pron.)* **yourself**
ዓሳ äsa *(n.)* **fish**
ዓሳ ነባሪ asa neari *(n.)* **whale**
ዓሳ ዝምግብ እንስሳ asa zmgb ensesa *(n. )* **otter**
ዓሳው äsaw *(adj.)* **dank**
ዓሰርተ asert *(adj. & adv.)* **ten**
ዓሰርተ ዓመት äserte ämet *(n.)* **decade**
ዓሰርተ ኣርባዕተ 'äserte 'arba'ëte *(adj.& n.)* **fourteen**
ዓሰርተ ሓደ äserte ĥade *(adj. & n.)* **eleven**
ዓሰርተ ሓሙሽተ 'äserte ḧamushte *(adj. & n.)* **fifteen**
ዓሰርተ ክልተ aserte klte *(adj.&n.)* **twelve**
ዓሰርተ ክልተ ዜሮ ዘለዋ ቁፅሪ aserte klte zero zelewo kqutsri *(adj & n.)* **trillion**
ዓስርተ ሽድሽተ äserte šdšte *(adj. & n.)* **sixteen**
ዓሰርተ ሰለስተ aserte seleste *(adj. & n.)* **thirteen**
ዕሰር ሰለስተ aserte seleste *(adj. & n.)* **thirteen**
ዓሰርተ ሸሞንተ äserte shomonte *(adj. & n.)* **eighteen**
ዓሰርተ ትሽዓተ äserte tsh'äte *(adj. & n.)* **nineteen**
ዓሰርተ ሸውዓተ aserte xew'ate *(adj. & n.)* **seventeen**
ዓሻ asha *(adj.)* **unwise**
ዓሻ asha *(adj.)* **witless**
ዓሻ äsha *(adj.)* **stupid**
ዓሻ 'äsha *(n.)* **idiot**
ዓሸኹ äshakwi *(adj.)* **spiky**
ዓሸራ ashara *(n.)* **imprint**
ዓሽከር äshker *(n. )* **minion**
ዓሽከር 'äshker *(n.)* **lackey**
ዓሶ aso *(n.)* **malaria**
ዓስራይ asray *(adj. & n.)* **tenth**
ዓረብያ garebya *(n.)* **trolley**
ዓጓ ägwa *(n.)* **beige**
ዓፃዳይ ätsaday *(n. )* **reaper**
ዓጻዲ ätsadi *(n. )* **harvester**
ዓፀወ atsewe *(adj.)* **close**
ዓፀወ ätsewe *(v.)* **shut**
ዓፀፋ ምላሽ ätsfa mlaš *(n.)* **rejoinder**
ዓጽሚ ሕቔ ዘለዎ atsmi hqe zelewo *(n.)* **vertebrate**
ዓፅረ ሕቀት ätsre ĥqet *(n.)* **dyspepsia**

**ዓፅረ ንባብ** ätsre nbab ***(n.)*** **dyslexia**
**ዓፀፈ** ätzefe ***(v.t)*** **fold**
**ጠቕለለ** ťeqlele ***(v.)*** **furl**
**ዓዉ ኢሉ ተዛረበ** äw elu tezarebe ***(v.)*** **declaim**
**ዓው ዝበለ** aw zbl ***(adj.)*** **loud**
**ዓዋን** awan ***(adj.)*** **idiotic**
**ዓዋን** awan ***(n.)*** **sap**
**ባስታ መረቕ** basta mereq ***(n.)*** **noodles**
**ዓውደ ፍፃመ** awde ftsame ***(n. )*** **scene**
**ዓውደ መፅናዕቲ** awde metsna'eti ***(n. )*** **seminar**
**ዓውደ መፅናዕቲ** äwde mexna'ëti ***(n.)*** **symposium**
**ዓውደ-ኣዋርሕ** äwde'awarḧ ***(n.)*** **calendar**
**ዓወለ** äwele ***(v.)*** **rove**
**ዓወት** awet ***(n.)*** **achievement**
**ዓወት** awet ***(n.)*** **triumph**
**ዓወት** awet ***(adj.)*** **winning**
**ዓወት** äwet ***(n.)*** **success**
**ዓወት** 'äwet ***(n.)*** **victory**
**ዓፀደ** äxede ***(v.)*** **mow**
**ዓጽሚ** äxmi ***(n.)*** **bone**
**ዓይንዳ** äynda ***(n.)*** **acorn**
**ዓይነ ስዉር** äyne swur ***(adj.)*** **blind**
**ዓይነ ስዉርነት** äyne swurnet ***(n.)*** **blindness**
**ዓይነት** aynet ***(n.)*** **type**
**ዓይነት** äynet ***(n.)*** **form**
**ዓይነት** äynet ***(n.)*** **sort**
**ዓይነት** äynet ***(n.)*** **kind**
**ዓይነት ዓሌት** 'äynet 'äleet ***(n.)*** **variety**
**ዓይነት ባእታ** äynet baeta ***(n.)*** **platinum**
**ዓይነት በሽኩቲ** äynet bškuti ***(n.)*** **pretzel**
**ዓይነት ጨርቂ** äynet čerqi ***(n. )*** **poplin**
**ዓይነት ዶልሺ** äynet dolshi ***(n.)*** **strudel**
**ዓይነት ፍረምረ** äynet fremre ***(n.)*** **pomegranate**
**ዓይነት ሕክምና** aynet hkmna ***(n.)*** **orthopaedics**
**ዓይነት ቕብኣት** aynet kibat ***(n.)*** **gel**
**ዓይነት ማዓድን** aynet ma'adn ***(n.)*** **onyx**
**ዓይነት ማዓድን** aynet ma'adn ***(n.)*** **opal**
**ዓይነት መዓድን** äynet me'ädn ***(n.)*** **phosphorus**
**ዓይነት ንእሽቶ ዓሳ** aynet neshto asa ***(n.)*** **whiting**
**ዓይነት ንእሽቶ ዑፍ** aynet neshto 'uf ***(n. )*** **warbler**
**ዓይነት ጥረምረ** aynet teremer ***(n. )*** **oat**
**ዓይነት ፀወታ** äynet tseweta ***(n.)*** **Sudoku**
**ዓይነት ዑፍ** 'äynet 'üf ***(n.)*** **wader**
**ዓይኒ** äyni ***(n.)*** **eye**
**ዓይኒ ዓተር** ayni ater ***(n.)*** **chickpea**
**ዓይኒ ዓተር** ayni ater ***(n. )*** **pea**
**ዓይኒ ማይ** ayni may ***(n.)*** **geyser**
**ዓይኒ ርግቢ** ayni rgbi ***(n.)*** **lattice**
**ዓይኒ ዘይብሉ መርፍእ** ayni zeyblu mefe ***(n.)*** **pin**
**ዓዛፍ** a-zaf ***(adj.)*** **garrulous**
**ዓዝዓዝ** äz'äz ***(adj. )*** **haggard**
**ዓዘቕቲ** äzeqti ***(n.)*** **bog**

# ዐ

**ዐባሯ** ebara ***(adj.)* scraggy**
**ዐባሯ** ëbara ***(adj.)* gaunt**
**ዐብደት** e'bdet ***(n.)* lunacy**
**ዐብደት** ëbdet ***(n.)* dementia**
**ዐብደት ከልቢ** ëbdet kelbi ***(n. )* rabies**
**ዐብደት** ebdt ***(n.)* insanity**
**ቁጽጽር ዘይብሉ** quxxr zeyblu ***(adj.)* hysterical**
**ስንኩለ-ኣእምሮ** snkule'a'èmro ***(adj.)* insane**
**ጽሉል** xlul ***(n.)* lunatic**
**ዐቡድ** ëbud ***(adj.)* demented**
**ዐቡይ** ëbuy ***(adj. )* haughty**
**ዐቡይ** ëbuy ***(adj.)* supercilious**
**ዐብየት** ebyet ***(n. )* seniority**
**ዐብየት** ëbyet ***(n.)* development**
**ዕዳ** ëda ***(n.)* debit**
**ዕዳ** ëda ***(n.)* debt**
**ዕዳ ንምኽፋል ዓቕሚ ምስኣን** eda nmkhfakl akmi ms'an ***(n.)* insolvency**
**ዕዳ** ëda ***(n.)* arrears**
**ዕዳጋ ገይሮም** edaga girom ***(v.)* transact**
**ዕዳጋ** edega ***(n.)* market**
**ዕደጋ** ëdega ***(n.)* shopping**
**ዕድል** edl ***(n.)* luck**
**ዕድል** edl ***(n.)* opportunity**
**ዕድል** ëdl ***(n. )* fortune**
**ዕድል ኣልቦ** edl albo ***(adj.)* luckless**
**ዕድል ናይ ምሕዋይ** ëdl nay mḧway ***(n.)* prognosis**
**ዕድለኛ** edlegna ***(adj.)* lucky**
**ዕድለኛ** ëdlegna ***(adj.)* fortunate**
**ዕድለኛ** ëdleňa ***(adj.)* providential**
**ዕድመ** ëdme ***(n.)* age**
**ዕድመ** ëdme ***(n.)* duration**
**ዕዳኡ ኪኸፍል ዘይከኣለ** ed'u kkefel zeyke'ale ***(adj.)* insolvent**
**ዕቡድ** eebudd ***(adj.)* certifiable**
**ዕቡይ** eebuy; ***(adj.)* cocky**
**ዕድል** eedil ***(n.)* chance**
**ዕፈና** ëfena ***(n.)* suppression**
**ዕፍሪት** e'frit ***(n.)* crane**
**ዕፉን** ëfun ***(n.)* corn**
**ዕጋት ማይ** ëgat may ***(n.)* backwater**
**ዕግበት** egbet ***(n.)* satisfaction**
**ዕግርግር ዘለዎ** egereger zelewo ***(adj.)* chaotic**
**ዕግርግር** e-gerger ***(n.)* hubbub**
**ዕገታ** ëgeta ***(n.)* obstruction**
**ዕግርግር** ëgrgr ***(n.)* bedlam**
**ድብል-ቕልቕ** dblq̈lq̈ ***(n.)* confusion**
**ብታነ** btane ***(n.)* disarray**
**መንገዲ** mengedi ***(n.)* route**
**ዕግታ** ëgta ***(n.)* blockage**
**ዕጉብ** ëgub ***(adj.)* complacent**
**ቅሱን** qsun ***(adj.)* smug**
**ዕጉስ** egus ***(adj.)* patient**
**ዕኮት** ëkot ***(n.)* hornet**
**ዕኳር** ekuar ***(n.)* pellet**
**ዕኹላል** ekulal ***(n.)* coil**
**ዕኹላል ዛውያ** ëkulal zawya ***(n. )* ringlet**
**ዕኳር ወርቂ** ëkwar werqi ***(n. )* nugget**
**ዕላማ** elama ***(n. )* target**
**ዕላማ** ëlama ***(n. )* goal**
**ዕላማ** ëlama ***(n.)* intent**
**ዕላማ** ëlama ***(n.)* intention**
**ዕላማ** ëlama ***(n.)* purpose**
**ዕላማ** eïama ***(n.)* aim**
**ዕላማ ኣልቦ** eïama albo ***(adj.)* aimless**

**ዕላማ እና ፖሊሲ ዝሓዘ ፁሑፍ** elama ena polisi zhaze tsuhuf *(n.)* **manifesto**
**ዕላመት** ëlamet *(n.)* **hallmark**
**ዕላመት** ëlamet *(n.)* **brand**
**ዕላምኡ ሓለፈ** ëlam'u ȟalefe *(v.)* **overshoot**
**ዕላዊ ገበረ** ëlawi gebere *(v.)* **disclose**
**ዕለት** ëlet *(n.)* **date**
**ዕለታዊ** eletawi *(adj.)* **daily**
**ዕለታዊ ማስታወሻ** ëletawi mastawesha *(n.)* **diary**
**ዕለቱ ዝሰሓተ** ëletu zseȟate *(n.)* **anachronism**
**ዕልቋቅ** elqaq *(n. )* **semen**
**ዕስለ** else *(n.)* **troop**
**ዕልዋ መንግስቲ** ëlwa mengsti *(n.)* **coup**
**ዕማም** ëmam *(n.)* **stint**
**ዕምባባ** ëmbaba *(n.)* **blossom**
**ዕምበባዊ** ëmbababawi *(adj.)* **flowery**
**ዕምባባዊ** 'ëmbababawi *(adj.)* **floral**
**ዕምባባ** ëmbeba *(n.)* **flower**
**ዕምበባ ኒል** embeba nil *(n.)* **woad**
**ዕምኹ** ëmkwa *(n.)* **fist**
**ዕምቈት** ëmqet *(n.)* **depth**
**ዕንጨይቲ** ëncheyti *(n.)* **stick**
**ዕንዲዳ ጌጽ** ëndida geex *(n.)* **amber**
**ዕነ** ëne *(n.)* **muck**
**ዕንፍሩር** ënfrur *(v.)* **dapple**
**ዕንጓል** ëngwal *(adj.)* **mucous**
**ዕንቅፋት** enqefat *(n. )* **hindrance**
**ዕንቅፋት** enqfat *(n.)* **obstacle**
**ዕንቅፋት ጸገም** 'ënqfat xegem *(n.)* **handicap**
**ዕንቅፋት** ënqfat *(n. )* **snag**
**ዕንቅፋት** 'ënqfat *(n.)* **impediment**
**ዕንቅፋት** ënqfat *(n.)* **barrier**
**ዕንቆ** ënqo *(n.)* **bead**
**ዕንቅርቢት** enqrbit *(n. )* **scorpion**
**ዕንፀይቲ** entseyti *(n.)* **wood**
**ዕንጨይቲ ሰንደል** entseyti sendel *(n. )* **sandalwood**
**ዕኑድ** ënud *(adj.)* **besotted**
**ዕንወት** ënwet *(n.)* **havoc**
**ዕንወት** ënwet *(n.)* **ruin**
**ዕንወት** 'ënwet *(n.)* **wreck**
**ዕንዛዘ** enzaze *(n.)* **trance**
**ዕንዛዘ** ënzaze *(n.)* **hypnosis**
**ዕንዚራ** e'nzira *(n.)* **lyre**
**ዕቋር** ëqar *(n.)* **deposit**
**ዕቀባ** ëqeba *(n. )* **preservation**
**ዕቅን** e'qn *(adj.)* **snug**
**ዕቅን ዘይኮነ** ëqn zeykone *(n.)* **misfit**
**ዕቁን** ë'qun *(adj.)* **measured**
**ዕቑር ዓቕሚ** ëqur äqmi *(n. )* **potentiality**
**ዕራቆት** ëraqot *(n.)* **nudity**
**ዕራቆተኛ** ëraqotegna *(n.)* **nudist**
**ዕራቁ** ëraqu *(adj.)* **nude**
**ዕርደ-ከተማ** 'ërdeketema *(n.)* **citadel**
**ዕርዲ** ërdi *(n. )* **fort**
**ዕርዲ** ërdi *(n. )* **rampart**
**ዕርዲ** 'ërdi *(n.)* **fortress**
**ዕርዲ** ërdi *(n.)* **bastion**
**ዕርዲ** ërdi *(n.)* **bulwark**
**ዕረፍቲ** ërefti *(n.)* **adjournment**
**ሃጓፍ መንደቕ** hagwaf mendeq *(n. )* **recess**
**ዕረፍቲ መንጎ** ërefti mengo *(n.)* **interlude**
**ዕረፍቲ** 'ërefti *(n.)* **intermission**
**ዕርፍቲ** 'ërfti *(n.)* **vacation**
**ዕርገት** ërget *(n.)* **ascent**
**ዕርክነት** ërknet *(n.)* **amity**
**ዕርቂ** erqi *(n.)* **sciatica**
**ዕርቂ** ërqi *(n.)* **reconciliation**

**ዕርቆቱ** ërqotu ***(adj.)*** **naked**
**ዕሩድ** ërud ***(adj.)*** **embattled**
**ዕሳው** ësaw ***(n.)*** **mould**
**ዕስለ** ësel ***(n.)*** **melee**
**ዕሰል** ësel ***(n.)*** **bevy**
**ዕሸል** eshel ***(n.)*** **infant**
**ዕሸል ምቕታል** eshel mqhtal ***(n.)*** **infanticide**
**ዕሸላዊ** e'shelawi ***(adj.)*** **infantile**
**ዕሽነት** ëshnet ***(n.)*** **folly**
**ዕሽነት** ëshnet ***(n.)*** **stupidity**
**ዕሽነት** 'ëshnet ***(n. )*** **idiocy**
**ዕሾክ** eshok ***(n.)*** **thorn**
**ዕሽሽታ** ëshshta ***(n.)*** **negligence**
**ዕስለ** ësle ***(n.)*** **shoal**
**ዕስለ** ësle ***(n.)*** **swarm**
**ዕሽሽ በለ** ëšš bele ***(v.)*** **relent**
**ዕሱብ** ësub ***(adj.)*** **mercenary**
**ዕጣን** etan ***(n. )*** **incense**
**ዕትብቲ** etbti ***(adj.)*** **umbilical**
**ዕጥቂ ኣፍተሓ** ëtki afteȟe ***(v.)*** **disarm**
**ዕትሮ** ëtro ***(n .)*** **pot**
**ዕቱብ** e'tub ***(adj.)*** **solemn**
**ዕቱብነት** e'tubnet ***(n.)*** **solemnity**
**ዕጡቕ** ë'ťuq ***(adj.)*** **militant**
**ዑደት** ëudet ***(n.)*** **cycle**
**ዑደታዊ** ëudetawi ***(adj.)*** **cyclic**
**ዕዋላ** ëwala ***(n. )*** **hooligan**
**ኮብላሊ** koblali ***(n. )*** **rover**
**ዕወጃ** eweja ***(v.t. )*** **illusion**
**ዕውልና** ëwlna ***(n.)*** **debauchery**
**ዕውልውል ምባል** ëwlwl mbal ***(n.)*** **nausea**
**ዕዉት** ëwut ***(adj.)*** **fruitful**
**ዕዉት** ëwut ***(adj.)*** **successful**
**ዕዉት** ëwut ***(adj.)*** **victorious**
**ዕፃድ ቦታ** ëxad bota ***(n.)*** **swathe**
**ዕፀፍፃፍ** ëxfxaf ***(adj.)*** **corrugated**
**ዕያግ ጎቦ** eyag gobo ***(n.)*** **tarn**
**ዕያገነዳ** e'yageneda ***(n.)*** **lymph**
**ዕዮ ፅርግያ** ëyo tsrgya ***(n.)*** **roadwork**
**ዕዙም** ëzum ***(adj.)*** **spellbound**
**ዒባ** ïba ***(n.)*** **dung**
**ዒባሩ** ïbara ***(adj.)*** **skinny**
**ዒፍ ያሬድ** ïf yared ***(n.)*** **nightingale**
**ዒላ** ila ***(n. )*** **well**
**ዕላማ** oe'lama ***(adj.)*** **objective**
**ዑደት** üdet ***(n.)*** **sightseeing**
**ዑደት** 'üdet ***(n.)*** **circuit**
**ዑደታዊ** udetawi ***(adj.)*** **orbital**
**ዑፍ** üf ***(n.)*** **fowl**
**ዑፍ** üf ***(n.)*** **bird**
**ዑና** üna ***(adj.)*** **dilapidated**
**ዑና** üna ***(n.)*** **hovel**
**ዑቕባ** üqba ***(n.)*** **aegis**
**ዑቕባ** üqba ***(n.)*** **asylum**

# ዘ

**ዘምባል** zembal ***(adj.)*** **oblique**
**ዘቓይም** zeqeym ***(adj.)*** **offensive**
**ዘኽታም** zektam ***(n.)*** **orphan**
**ዝዓበየ ና ምርምር መፅሓፍ** zabeye namrmr meshaf ***(n. )*** **tome**
**ዛብያ** zabya ***(n.)*** **axis**
**ዛብያ** zabya ***(n.)*** **pike**
**ዛብያ** zabya ***(n.)*** **shaft**
**ዛዕጎል** zaëgol ***(n.)*** **shell**
**ዛዕጎል** za'ëgol ***(n.)*** **conch**
**ዛዕዛዕታ** za'ëza'ëta ***(n.)*** **dew**
**ዝዓገበ** z'agebe ***(adj.)*** **sated**
**ዛጊት** zagit ***(adv.)*** **already**
**ዝሓበረ** zaȟabere ***(adj.)*** **corporate**
**ዛሕተለ** zaȟtele ***(v.)*** **stagnate**
**ዛሕዛሕ ዝበለ** zaȟ'zaȟ zbele ***(n.)*** **mess**

ዝዓነወ z'änewe *(adj.)* **rundown**
ዛንታ zanta *(n.)* **narrative**
ዛንታ zanta *(n.)* **story**
ዛንታ ፍቅሪ zanta fqri *(n.)* **romance**
ዛራ zara *(n.)* **brook**
ዛርቲ zarti *(n.)* **elf**
ዛወነ zawene *(v.)* **saunter**
ዘይጠቅም zaytekm *(adj.)* **useless**
ዘይተርፍ zayteref *(adj.)* **unavoidable**
ዛዛሚ zazami *(n.)* **finalist**
ዛዘመ zazeme *(v.)* **finish**
ዝባሕተወ zbaȟtewe *(adj.)* **celibate**
ዝባን zban *(n.)* **surface**
ዝባን ኢድ zban 'id *(n.)* **backhand**
ዝባን zban *(n.)* **back**
ዝበደነ zbedene *(adj.)* **defunct**
ዝበለፀ zbeletse *(adj.)* **deluxe**
ዝበለፀ zbeletse *(adj.)* **utmost**
ዝበለጸ zbelexe *(adj.)* **best**
ዝበልሐ ዕንጸይቲ ሓጹር zbelhe enxeyti haxur *(n.)* **paling**
ዘበን zbene *(n.)* **century**
ዝበቅዕ zbeqe *(adj.)* **worthy**
ዝበረሰ zberese *(adj.)* **decadent**
ዝበስበሰ zbesbese *(adj.)* **rotten**
ዝበሰለ zbesele *(adj.)* **ripe**
ዝበዝሐ zbezhe *(v.)* **preponderate**
ዝብላዕ zblaë *(adj.)* **edible**
ዝብላዕ zbla'ë *(adj.)* **eatable**
ዝቦኾረ zboḱore *(adj.)* **absent**
ዝብስብስ zbsbs *(adj.)* **biodegradable**
ዝጨኑ zĉenu *(adj.)* **redolent**
ዝጭበጥ zchbet *(adj.)* **palpable**
ዝጭበጥ zchbet *(adj.)* **tangible**
ዝደኸመ zdekeme' *(adj.)* **weary**
ዝደቀሰ zdekese *(adj.)* **quiescent**
ዝደሊ zdeli *(adj.)* **needful**
ዝደንፀዎ zdenxewo *(adj.)* **nonplussed**
ዝደንፀዎ zdenxewo *(adj.)* **nonplussed**
ዝድህሰስ ነገር zdhses neger *(adj.)* **tactile**
ዘየስተውዕል ze yestewu 'el *(adj.)* **careless**
ዝዓገበ zea'gebe *(adj.)* **content**
ዘብዐኛ zeb'agna *(n.)* **sentinel**
ዘባህርር ሕልሚ zebahr'r ȟlmi *(n.)* **nightmare**
ዘባል zebal *(adv.)* **askew**
ዘበበ zebebe *(v.)* **slope**
ዘዕበድብድ zëbedbd *(adj.)* **berserk**
ዘብዐኛ zeb-egna *(v.)* **guard**
ዝብኢ zeb-ei *(n.)* **hyena**
ዘበለ zebele *(v.)* **slant**
መዋእል mewa'èl *(n.)* **epoch**
ዘበን zeben *(n.)* **era**
ዘበን አምፀኦ zeben amxe'o *(n.)* **fad**
ዘበናዊ zebenawi *(adj.)* **fashionable**
ዘበስር zebesr *(n. )* **precursor**
ዘበተ zebete *(v.)* **trounce**
ዘቢብ zebib *(n.)* **currant**
ዘቢብ zebib *(n.)* **raisin**
ዘብለጭልጭ zeblechlch *(adj.)* **tawdry**
ዘብለጭልጭ zeble'chl'ch *(adj.)* **scintillating**
ዘብለጭልጭ zebleĉlĉ *(adj.)* **shiny**
ዜብራ መንገዲ zebra mengedi *(n.)* **zebra crossing**
ዘጨንቕ zechenq *(adj.)* **tense**
ዘደንግጽ zedengx *(adj.)* **pathetic**
ዘደንግጽ zedengx *(adj.)* **pitiful**
ዘደንጹ zedenxu *(n.)* **prodigy**
ዘደንዝዝ zedenz'z *(n.)* **stunner**
ዘዕግብ ze'egb *(adj.)* **satisfactory**

ዜግነት zeeg'net *(n. )* **nationality**
ዜግነት ሃበ zeegnet habe *(v.)* **naturalize**
ዜግነት ምሃብ zeeg'net mhab *(n.)* **naturalization**
ዜግነታዊ zeegnetawi *(adj.)* **civic**
ዘዕግብ ze'eigib *(adj.)* **cogent**
ዘዕጀውጅው ze'ëjewjw *(adj.)* **delirious**
ዜማዊ zeemawi *(adj.)* **melodic**
ዜማዊ zeemawi *(adj.)* **melodious**
ዜማዊ zeemawi *(n.)* **melody**
ዜና zeena *(n.)* **news**
ዘዕኑ ze'ënu *(adj.)* **ruinous**
ዘዐንዝዝ ze'ënzz *(adj.)* **mesmeric**
ዜሮ zeero *(n. )* **nought**
ዘዕወልውል ze'ëwelwl *(adj.)* **nauseous**
ዘፍ በለ zef bele *(v.)* **flop**
ዘፈፍታ zefefta *(n.)* **residue**
ዘፈንፍን zefenfn *(adj.)* **repulsive**
ዘፈር zefer *(n.)* **fringe**
ዘፍራን zefran *(n.)* **saffron**
ዘፍታ zefta *(n.)* **grout**
ዘፍጣጥ zeftat *(n.)* **paunch**
ዘፍዘፈ zefzefe *(v.)* **souse**
ዜጋ zega *(n.)* **citizen**
ዘግድድ zegdd *(adj.)* **compulsive**
ዘገዳማዊ zegedamawi *(adj.)* **wild**
ዘገምተኛ zegemtegna *(adj.)* **tardy**
ዜግነት zegenet *(n.)* **citizenship**
ዘገርም zegerm *(adj.)* **fantastic**
ዘጉሂ zeguhi *(adj.)* **deplorable**
ዘጉሂ zeguhi *(adj.)* **grievous**
ዘጉሂ zeguhi *(adj.)* **rueful**
ዘጓጥጥ zegwatẗ *(n.)* **menace**
ዘሓጠ zehaẗe *(v.)* **lag**
ዘሓጢ zeĥati *(adj.)* **recessive**

ዘሕፍር zehfr *(adj.)* **shameful**
ዘሕጉስ zeĥgus *(adj.)* **delightful**
ዘሕስብ ነገር zeȟsb neger *(n.)* **preoccupation**
ዘሕዝን zehzen *(adj.)* **unfortunate**
ዘሕዝን zeĥzn *(adj.)* **dismal**
ዘሕዝን zehzn *(adj.)* **lamentable**
ዘሕዝን zeȟzn *(adj.)* **piteous**
ዘይቲ ጉልዒ zeiti gul'i *(a.)* **castor oil**
ዘከረ zekere *(v.)* **recall**
ዘከረ zekere *(v.)* **recollect**
ዘከረ zekere *(v.)* **remember**
ዘኽስብ zeksb *(adj.)* **profitable**
ዘኽስስ zeḱss *(adj.)* **actionable**
ዘልኣለማዊ zel'alemawi *(adj.)* **eternal**
ዘልኣለማዊነት zel'alemawinet *(n.)* **eternity**
ዘላሊ zelali *(n.)* **jumper**
ዘላን zelan *(n.)* **nomad**
ዘላናዊ zelanawi *(adj.)* **nomadic**
ዘላቒ zelaqi *(adj.)* **sustainable**
ዘለኣለማዊ zele'alemawi *(adj.)* **monumental**
ዘለፋ zelefa *(n.)* **affront**
ዘለለ zelele *(v.)* **leap**
ዘለለ zelele *(v.)* **skip**
ዜማ zem *(n.)* **tune**
ዜማ zema *(n.)* **chant**
ዘማ zema *(n. )* **nephew**
ዘማዓሪ zema'äri *(adj.)* **normative**
ዘምበዐ zembe'ë *(v.)* **deviate**
ዘምበየ zembeye *(v.i. )* **soar**
ዘመድ zemed *(n. )* **kin**
ዘመድ zemed *(adj.)* **relative**
ዝእመን z'emen *(adj.)* **plausible**
ዘመን ኣምፀኦ zemen amxe'o *(adj.)* **modish**
ዘመናዊ zemenawi *(adj.)* **modern**

ዘመናዊ zemenawi *(adj.)* **stylish**
ዘመናዊ አረኣእያ zemenawi are'a'eya *(n.)* **modernism**
ዘመናውነት zemenawnet *(n.)* **modernity**
ዘመረ zemere *(v.)* **warble**
ዘመስግን zemesgn *(adj.)* **thankful**
ዘይመጣጠን zemetaten *(adj.)* **disproportionate**
ዘመተ zemete *(n.)* **campaign**
ዜና zena *(n.)* **tidings**
ዜና መዋልዕ zena mewalee *(n.)* **chronicle**
ዘምቢል zenbil *(n.)* **trug**
ዘንቢል zenbil *(n.)* **basket**
ዘነኣእስ zene'a'es *(adj.)* **sardonic**
ዘነቃቅሕ መድሓኒ zenekakh medhanit *(n. )* **tonic**
ዝድነቕ zeneqh *(adj.)* **impressive**
ዘንጊ zengi *(n. )* **rod**
ዝንጅብል zenjebel *(n. )* **ginger**
ዘንቀትቅት zenqetqt *(adj.)* **tremulous**
ዝነቐጸ zenqexe *(adj.)* **parched**
ዘንሳፈፈ zensafefe *(adj.)* **afloat**
ዘንሰፋለለት zensefalelet *(adj.)* **becalmed**
ዘንፀባርቅ zentsebarq *(adj.)* **refulgent**
ዘንፀባርቅ zentsebarq *(n. )* **sparkling**
ዘንፀራረዎ zentserarewo *(adj.)* **giddy**
ዘቀላ zeqela *(n. )* **skit**
ዘቀመጠሉ ቦታ ረስዐ zeqemeẗelu bota res'ë *(v.)* **mislay**
ዘቀንዙ zeqenzu *(adj.)* **painful**
ዘቀሓሕር zeqkeha'hir *(adj.)* **contentious**
ዘቕንእ zeqn'e *(adj.)* **enviable**
ዘቋቒት ቡን zequaqit bun *(n.)* **percolator**
ዘቑጥዕ zeq̈uẗ'ë *(n.)* **aggravation**
ዘራእቲ zera'eti *(n.)* **crop**
ዘራፍ zeraf *(n. )* **giraffe**
ዘራጊቶ zeragito *(n.)* **vortex**
ዘራጊቶ ማይ zeragito may *(n. )* **whirlpool**
ዘርአ ነገስት zer'e negest *(n. )* **royal**
ዘረባ zereba *(v.)* **gab**
ዘረባ zereba *(n.)* **utterance**
ዘረባ አልቦ ተዋሳኣይ zereba albo tewasa'ay *(n. )* **mummer**
ዘርዕድ zer'ed *(adj.)* **scary**
ዘፍርሀ zefrh *(adj.)* **awesome**
ዘርዕድ zer'ëd *(adj.)* **macabre**
ዘርዕድ zer'ëd *(adj.)* **redoubtable**
ዘረፈ zerefe *(v.)* **plunder**
አስኣነ 'as'ane *(v.)* **bereaved**
ዘረፍረፍ zerefref *(n.)* **lace**
ዘረጋግእ zeregag'e *(adj.)* **emollient**
ዘረገ zerege *(v.)* **muddle**
ዘርገሐ zergeḧe *(v.)* **unwind**
ዘርግሐ zergḧe *(v. t)* **broadcast**
ዘርኢ zer'i *(n.)* **spore**
ዘርኢ ተባዕታይ zer'i teba'etay *(n.)* **sperm**
ዘርዘረ zerzere *(v. t)* **enumerate**
ዘስድዕ zesd'e *(adj.)* **seductive**
ዘስደምም zesdem'm *(adj.)* **staggering**
ዘሰንብድ zesenbd *(adj. )* **horrendous**
ዘሰንብድ zesenbd *(adj.)* **shattering**
ዘሰንብድ zesenbd *(adj.)* **shocking**
ዘሰንብድ zesenbd *(n.)* **startling**
ዘሰቅቕ zeseqq *(adj.)* **ghastly**
ዘስገድግድ zesgedgd *(adj. )* **horrid**
ዘስሕቕ zesĥq *(adj.)* **funny**

ዘስካሕክሕ zeskaĥkĥ *(adj.)* **gruesome**
ዘስካሕክሕ zeskaȟkȟ *(adj.)* **monstrous**
ዘስካሕክሕ zeskaȟkȟ *(adj.)* **awful**
ዘጣዕስ zeta'ës *(adj.)* **regrettable**
ዘተ zete *(n.)* **conference**
ዘተኣማምን zeteamamn *(adj.)* **potent**
ዘተባብዕ zetebab'e *(adj. )* **heartening**
ዘይተበረዘ zetebereze *(adj.)* **unadulterated**
ዘጠንቅቅ zetenqq *(adj.)* **cautionary**
ዘጠራጥር zeteratr *(adj.)* **questionable**
ዘጠጠ zetete *(v.)* **sag**
ዝተኸደነ zetkdn *(adj.)* **clad**
ዘጥንታዊ zeïntawi *(adj.)* **antiquarian**
ዘፅልም zetslm *(adj.)* **slanderous**
ዘፅምም zetsmm *(adj.)* **deafening**
ዘዋራይ zewaray *(adj.)* **voluble**
ዘዋሪ ኮኾብ zewari koḱob *(n.)* **pulsar**
ዘውደኛ zewdegna *(n. )* **royalist**
ዘወንበለ zewenbele *(v.)* **maunder**
ማኒኮ maniko *(v.)* **crank**
ዘወረ zewere *(v.)* **drive**
ዘወረ zewere *(v.)* **steer**
ዘይ ተግበራዊ zey tegberawi *(adj.)* **impractical**
ዘይኣግባባዊ zeyagbabawi *(adj.)* **informal**
ዘይዓገበ zey'ägebe *(adj.)* **disaffected**
ዘይዓገቡ zey'agebu *(n.)* **malcontent**
ዘይኣክል zeyakl *(adj.)* **inadequate**
ዘይኣክል zey'akl *(adv.)* **scarcely**
ዘይዓሚቅ zey'amiq *(adj.)* **shallow**
ዘያኣርግ zey'arg *(adj.)* **durable**
ዘይበላሾ zeybelasho *(adj.)* **foolproof**
ዘይበቅዕ zeybeqe *(adj.)* **paltry**
ዘይ በሰለ zeybesele *(adj.)* **immature**
ዘይብቑዕ zeybqu'e *(adj.)* **inefficient**
ዘይደሃል zeydehak *(adj.)* **dauntless**
ዘይድልዱል zeydeldul *(adj.)* **unstable**
ዘይደሊ zeydeli *(adj.)* **loath**
ዘይድልው zeydeluw *(adj.)* **unprepared**
ዘይድፈር zeydfer *(adj.)* **formidable**
ዘይድንግጽ zeydngts *(adj.)* **unmoved**
ዘየድሊ zeyedeli *(adj.)* **unnecessary**
ዘይዕድለኛ zey'ëdleña *(adj. )* **hapless**
ኣድላዪ ዘይኮነ 'adlayi zeykwane *(adj.)* **dispensable**
ዘየድሊ zeyedli *(adj.)* **needless**
ዘየድሊ zeyedli *(adj.)* **redundant**
ዘይግቡእ zeygbu'è *(adj.)* **undue**
ዘየድሊ ድፍረት zeyedli dfret *(n.)* **temerity**
ዘየድሊ ትንተና zeyedli tntena *(n.)* **trivia**
ዘየድምዕ zeyedm'e *(adj.)* **ineffective**
ዘይእዱብ zey'edub *(adj.)* **impolite**
ዘየእንግድ zeye'engd *(adj.)* **inhospitable**
ዘየጋጊ zeyegagi *(adj.)* **unmistakable**
ዘየግድስ zeyegds *(adj.)* **negligible**
ዘይዕጉስ zey'ëgus *(adj.)* **impatient**
ዘየሕልፍ zeyeḥlf *(adj.)* **impassable**
ዘየከራኽር zeyekerakr *(adj.)* **indisputable**
ዘይእኹል ናብራ zeyèḱul nabra *(adv. )* **poorly**
ዘየማትእ zeyemat'è *(adj.)* **emphatic**
ዘይእመን zey'emen *(adj.)* **faithless**
ዘየእመን zey'emen *(adj.)* **implausible**

**ዘይእመን** zey'emen ***(adj.)*** **unbelievable**
**ዘይእመን** zey'èmen ***(adj.)*** **fabulous**
**ዝእየናሕሲ** zeyenahsi ***(adj.)*** **implacable**
**ዘየናሕሲ** zeyenaĥsi ***(adj.)*** **relentless**
**ዘየቋርፅ** zeyeqarts ***(adj.)*** **perennial**
**ዘየቋርጽ** zeyeqwarx ***(adj.)*** **ceaseless**
**ዘየቋርፅ** zeye'qwerexe' ***(adj.)*** **constant**
**ዘየስርፅ** zeyesrtz ***(adj.)*** **impervious**
**ዘየተኣማምን** zeyeteamamn ***(adj.)*** **precarious**
**ዘየተኣማምን** zeyeteamamn ***(n)*** **unreliable**
**ዘየጠራጥር** zeyeteratr ***(adj.)*** **unimpeachable**
**ዘይዕቱብ** zey'ëtub ***(adj.)*** **frivolous**
**ዘየዝሙዉ** zeyezemuwue ***(adj.)*** **chaste**
**ዘይእዙዝ** zey'èzuz ***(adj.)*** **involuntary**
**ዘይፈለጠ** zeyfelete ***(adj.)*** **unaware**
**ዘይፈልጥ** zeyfeleṭe ***(adj.)*** **ignorant**
**ዘይፈሊ** zeyfeli ***(adj.)*** **indiscriminate**
**ዘይፈርሕ** zeyferĥ ***(adj.)*** **fearless**
**ዘይፍትሓዊ** zeyfethawi ***(adj.)*** **unfair**
**ዘይፍትሓዊ** zeyfethawi ***(adj.)*** **unjust**
**ዘይፍለጥ** zeyflet ***(adj.)*** **inexplicable**
**ዘይፍለጥ ጸገም** zeyflet xegem ***(n.)*** **pitfall**
**ዘይፍሉጥ** zeyflut ***(adj.)*** **unaccountable**
**ዘይፍሉጥ** zeyflut ***(adj.)*** **unknown**
**ዘይግቡእ ኪዳን** zeygbu'e kidan ***(n. )*** **misalliance**
**ዘይግደስ** zeygdes ***(adj.)*** **negligent**
**ዘይግደስ** zeygdes ***(adj.)*** **nonchalant**
**ዘይሓስብ** zeyḧasb ***(adj.)*** **inconsiderate**
**ዘይግደስ** zeygdes ***(adj.)*** **mindless**
**ሃንዳፍ** handaf ***(adj.)*** **reckless**
**ዘየጎድእ** zeyg'e ***(adj.)*** **unscathed**
**ዘይግራሕ** zeygraḧ ***(adj.)*** **intractable**
**ዘይግታእ** zeygta'e ***(adj.)*** **indomitable**
**ዘይጊዜኡ** zeygzi'u ***(adj.)*** **untimely**
**ዘይሓንኽ** zeyhank ***(adj.)*** **shameless**
**ዘይሓቂ** zeyḧaqi ***(adj. )*** **hollow**
**ዘይሓቅቕ** zeyḥaqq̈ ***(adj.)*** **insoluble**
**ዘይሓርር** zeyḧarr ***(adj.)*** **ageless**
**ዘይሓስብ** zeyhasb ***(adj.)*** **thoughtless**
**ዘይሕጋዊ** zeyḥgawi ***(adj.)*** **illegitimate**
**ዘይሕጋዊ** zeyḥgawi ***(adj.)*** **illicit**
**ዘይሕጋዊ** zeyḥgawi ***(adj.)*** **illegal**
**ዘይሕጉስ** zeyhgus ***(adj.)*** **unhappy**
**ዘይሕለል** zeyhlel ***(adj.)*** **sedulous**
**ዘይሕሎ** zeyhlo ***(adj.)*** **unguarded**
**ዘይህሰ** zeyhse ***(adj.)*** **invulnerable**
**ዘይሕሰብ** zeyhseb ***(adj.)*** **unthinkable**
**ዘይቅዱስ** zeykdus ***(adj.)*** **profane**
**ዘይቅዱስ** zeykdus ***(adj.)*** **sacrilegious**
**ዘይክእል** zeyk'el ***(adj.)*** **unskilled**
**ዘይኸውን** zeykewn ***(adj.)*** **preposterous**
**ዘይከውን** zeykewun ***(adj.)*** **unlikely**
**ዘይኸፈል** zeykhfel ***(adj.)*** **indivisible**
**ዘይኮነ** zeykone ***(prep. )*** **unlike**
**ዘይቁፀር** zeykutser ***(adj.)*** **unemployable**
**ዘይልሙድ** zeylemud ***(adj.)*** **wacky**
**ዘይልሙድ** zeylemud ***(adj.)*** **weird**
**ዘይለዋወጥ** zeylewaweẗ ***(adj.)*** **invariable**
**ዘይተራእየ** zeytera'èye ***(adj.)*** **strange**
**ተቓውሞ** teq̈awmo ***(adj.)*** **uncommon**
**ዘይልሙድ** zeylmud ***(adj.)*** **unnatural**
**ዘይልሙድ** zeylmud ***(adj.)*** **unusual**

**ዘይልወጥ** zeylweẗ *(adj.)* **irrevocable**
**ዘይልወጥ** zeylweẗ *(adj.)* **monotonous**
**ዘይ ምድማፅ** zeymdmats *(v.)* **ignore**
**ዘይምቹ** zeymechu *(adj.)* **uncomfortable**
**ዘይምእሙእ** zeym'èmu'è *(adj. )* **harsh**
**ዘይመጣጠን** zeymetaten *(adj.)* **lopsided**
**ዘይመጣጠን** zeymetaten *(adj.)* **uneven**
**ዘይመውት** zeymewut *(adj.)* **immortal**
**ዘይመውት** zeymewut *(adj.)* **undying**
**ዘይምግዳስ** zeymgdas *(n.)* **nonchalance**
**ዘይምሕር** zeymȟr *(adj.)* **brutal**
**ዘይምካኣል** zeymk'al *(n.)* **inability**
**ዘይምኽኣል** zeymkh'al *(n.)* **impossibility**
**ዘይከኣል** zeymkh'al *(adj.)* **impossible**
**ዘይምምጣን** zeymmṭan *(n.)* **imbalance**
**ዘይምኖ** zeymno *(adj.)* **racy**
**ዘይሞተ** zeymote *(n.)* **zombie**
**ዘይምርግጋዕ** zeymreggae *(n.)* **unrest**
**ዘይምርዑውቲ** zeymr'ëwti *(n. )* **spinster**
**ዘይምስምዕማዕ** zeymsm'ëma'ë *(n.)* **disagreement**
**ዘይምትእምማን** zeymt'emman *(n.)* **insecurity**
**ዘይሙቹ** zeymuchu *(adj.)* **inopportune**
**ዘይምሉእ** zeymulue *(adj.)* **partial**
**ዘይምውሳን** zeymwsan *(n.)* **indecision**
**ዘይንቡር** zeynbur *(adv. )* **singularly**
**ዘይንቡር መውቃዕቲ ልቢ** zeynbur wqaeti lbi *(n.)* **palpitation**
**ዘይነቓነቕ** zeyneqaneq *(adj.)* **unshakeable**
**ዘይነፃፀል** zeynetsatsel *(adj.)* **inseparable**
**ዘይንኪ** zeynki *(adj.)* **unmitigated**
**ዘይንቑሕ** zeynkuh *(adj.)* **unconscious**
**ዘይንቀሳቀስ** zeynqesaqes *(adj.)* **motionless**
**ዘይንቀሳቐስ** zeynqesaqhes *(adj.)* **static**
**ቀዋሚ** qewami *(adj.)* **stationary**
**ዘይንፀል ኣካል** zeyntsel 'akal *(adj.)* **integral**
**ዘይንጡፍ** zeyntuf *(adj.)* **passive**
**ዘይንጹህ** zeynutsuh *(adj.)* **impure**
**ዘይንጹህና** zeynutsuhna *(n.)* **impurity**
**ዘይንጹር** zeynxur *(adj.)* **ambiguous**
**ዘይንጹርነት** zeynxurnet *(n.)* **ambiguity**
**ዘይቅቡል** zeyqbul *(adj.)* **unorthodox**
**ዘይቅቡል** zeyqbul *(adj.)* **unpopular**
**ዘይተጠልበ** zeyteẗelbe *(adj.)* **unsolicited**
**ዘይቅቡል ገበረ** zeyqbul gebere *(v.)* **invalidate**
**ዘይቕየር** zey'qeyer *(adj.)* **consistent**
**ዘይቐሪ ነገር** zeyqheri neger *(adj.)* **inevitable**
**ዘይቅኑዕ** zeyqnu'ë *(adj.)* **dishonest**
**ዘይቅኑዕ እምነት** zeyqnu'ë emnet *(n.)* **misbelief**
**ዘይቅየር** zeyqyer *(adj.)* **immutable**
**ዘይርደኦ** zeyrde'o *(n.)* **dullard**
**ሓተላ ብረታት** ȟatela bretat *(n.)* **dross**

**ንኡስ** n'us ***(adj.)*** **petty**
**ዘይረብሕ ሰብ** zeyrebȟ seb ***(n.)*** **scamp**
**ዘይረብሕ** zeyrebh ***(adj.)*** **trivial**
**ንጻይ ጸጉሪ** nxay xeguri ***(n.)*** **fluff**
**ዘይጠቅም** zeyťeqm ***(adj.)*** **nugatory**
**ዘይረብሕ** zeyrebḥ ***(adj.)*** **insignificant**
**ዘይረብሕ ምኽን** zeyrebḥ mkwan ***(n.)*** **insignificance**
**ዘይረአ** zeyre'e ***(adj.)*** **invisible**
**ዘይርግፀኛ** zeyregetsegna ***(adj.)*** **uncertain**
**ዘይርጉም** zeyregum ***(adj.)*** **unselfish**
**ዘይረሳዕ** zeyresae ***(adj.)*** **unforgettable**
**ዘይርጉጽ** zeyrguts ***(adj.)*** **wonky**
**ዘይርኹብ** zeyrḱub ***(adj.)*** **needy**
**ዘይርሳዕ** zeyrsa'ë ***(adj.)*** **memorable**
**ዘይርስዕ** zeyrs'ë ***(adj.)*** **mindful**
**ዘይርታዕ** zeyrta'ë ***(adj.)*** **irrefutable**
**ዘይርትዓዊ** zeyrt'äwi ***(adj.)*** **irrational**
**ዘይሳገር** zeysager ***(adj.)*** **intransitive**
**ዘይሳነ ሽም** zeysane shm ***(n.)*** **misnomer**
**ዘይስዓር** zeys'är ***(adj.)*** **invincible**
**ዘይሰዓቢ** zeyse'äbi ***(n.)*** **nonconformist**
**ዘይሰኽረ** zeysekhere ***(adj.)*** **sober**
**ዘይሰማዕ** zeysemae ***(adj.)*** **unheard**
**ዘይሰምር** zeysemr ***(adj.)*** **pious**
**ዘይሰርሕ** zeyserh ***(adj.)*** **inoperative**
**ዘይስሕብ** zeyshb ***(adj.)*** **inconspicuous**
**ዘይስሕብ** zeyshb ***(adj.)*** **inert**
**ትሕተ-ድምጻው** tȟtedmxaw ***(adj.)*** **subsonic**
**ዘይስማዕ** zeysma'e ***(adj.)*** **inaudible**
**ዘይስማማዕ** zeysma'ëma'ë ***(adj.)*** **discordant**
**ዘይስማዕማዑ** zeysma'ema'u ***(adj.)*** **incompatible**
**ዘይስነ-መጐታዊ** zeysnemegwatawi ***(adj.)*** **illogical**
**ዘይስንገል** zeysngel ***(adj.)*** **inconsolable**
**ዘይፅዕር** zeys'r ***(adj.)*** **tireless**
**ሳሕቲ ዝርኤ** saȟti zr'ee ***(adj.)*** **anomalous**
**ዘይስሩዕ** zeysru'ë ***(adj.)*** **erratic**
**ሓባጥ-ጐባጥ** ȟabaẗgwabaẗ ***(adj.)*** **irregular**
**ዘይስሩዕነት** zeysru'ënet ***(n.)*** **irregularity**
**ዘይሳኽዕ** zeyssakha'e ***(adj.)*** **inauspicious**
**ዘይስተኻኸል** zeystekhakel ***(adj.)*** **irredeemable**
**ዘየተኣማመን** zeyte'amamen ***(adj.)*** **insecure**
**ዘተኣመተ** zeyteamete ***(adj.)*** **unforeseen**
**ዘይተዓረቕ** zeyte'äreq̈ ***(adj.)*** **irreconcilable**
**ዘይተፈርደ** zeyteferde ***(adj.)*** **sub judice**
**ዘይተነግረ** zeytegebre ***(adj.)*** **untold**
**ዘይተገዳስነት** zeytegedasnet ***(n.)*** **profligacy**
**ዘይተጎደኸ** zeytegode'e ***(adj.)*** **intact**
**ዘይተሓረሰ መሬት** zeyteȟarese mereet ***(n.)*** **moor**
**ዘይጠሓስ** zeytehas ***(adj.)*** **impenetrable**
**ዘይተሓስበ** zeyteȟasbe ***(n.)*** **surprise**
**ዘይተሓሰበሉ** zeytehasebelo ***(adj.)*** **casual**

**ዘይተሓወሰ** zeytehawese ***(adj.)*** **unalloyed**
**ዘይተሓዝ** zeyteḥaz ***(adj.)*** **impalpable**
**ዘይተላገበ** zeytelagebe ***(adj.)*** **disjointed**
**ዘይተለምደ** zeytelemde ***(adj.)*** **unsocial**
**ዘይተለመደ** zeytelemde ***(adj.)*** **zany**
**ዘይጥዕም** zeyt'em ***(adj.)*** **insipid**
**ዘይጥዕም** zeyt'em ***(adj.)*** **tacky**
**ዘይተመስገነ** zeytemesgene ***(adj.)*** **unsung**
**ዘይተመጣጣንነት** zeytemeẗaẗannet ***(n. )*** **mismatch**
**ዘይተቐየረ** zeyteqeyere ***(adj.)*** **pristine**
**ዘይጠቅም** zeyẗeqm ***(n.)*** **nonentity**
**ዘይጠቅም ሽልማት** zeyteqm shlmat ***(n.)*** **trinket**
**ዘይተፀወዐ** zeytetsewe'e ***(adj.)*** **uncalled**
**ዘይተዋደደ** zeytewadede ***(adj.)*** **frenetic**
**ዘይተወደአ** zeytewede'e ***(adj.)*** **incomplete**
**ዘይተወልደ** zeytewelde ***(adj.)*** **unborn**
**ዘይተወጠረ** zeytewetere ***(adj.)*** **slack**
**ዘይጥሓስ** zeythas ***(adj.)*** **unassailable**
**ዘይትሑዝ** zeythuz ***(adj.)*** **unreserved**
**ዘይትንከፍ** zeytnkef ***(adj.)*** **untouchable**
**ዘይትርድኦ ቋንቋ** zeytrd'o quanqua ***(n.)*** **lingo**
**ዘይፃወር** zeytsawer ***(adj.)*** **intolerant**
**ዘይፅቡቕ ዝተሰመዖ** zeytsbuq ztesemeo ***(adj.)*** **unwell**
**ዘይፅቡይ** zeytsebuy ***(adj.)*** **unprecedented**
**ዘይፅሩይ** zeytseruy ***(adj.)*** **unclean**
**ዘይፅወር** zeytswer ***(adj.)*** **intolerable**
**ዘይጥዑም** zeyt'um ***(adj.)*** **untoward**
**ዘይቱን** zeytun ***(n. )*** **guava**
**ዘይውዳእ** zeywda'e ***(adj.)*** **inexhaustible**
**ዘይወዳደሩ** zeywedaderu ***(adj.)*** **incomparable**
**ዘይወዳአ** zeywedae ***(adj.)*** **unending**
**ዘይወግዓዊ** zeyweg'awi ***(adj.)*** **colloquial**
**ዘይወሰን** zeywesun ***(adj.)*** **undecided**
**ዘይውልቃዊ** zeywlqawi ***(adj.)*** **impersonal**
**ዘይውርዙይ** zeywrzuy ***(adj.)*** **ignoble**
**ዘይውሱን** zeywusn ***(adj.)*** **unlimited**
**ዘይጾታዊ ርክብ** zeyxotawi ckb ***(adj.)*** **platonic**
**ዘይዛመድ** zeyzamed ***(adj.)*** **irrelevant**
**ዘይዛረብ** zeyzareb ***(adj.)*** **speechless**
**ዘዘንበለ** zezenbele ***(adj.)*** **tendentious**
**ዝፈልጥ ዝመስል** zfelt zmesl ***(adj.)*** **knowing**
**ዝፈርሐ** zferḧe ***(adj.)*** **afraid**
**ዝፍፈት** zffet ***(n.)*** **dialysis**
**ዝፍቀድ** zfqed ***(adj.)*** **permissible**
**ዝፍወስ** zfwes ***(adj.)*** **curable**
**ዝፍውስ** zfws ***(adj.)*** **curative**
**ዝፍውስ** zfws ***(adj.)*** **remedial**
**ዝገርም** zgerm ***(adj.)*** **marvellous**
**ዝግለፀሉ መንገዲ** zgletselu mengedi ***(n. )*** **manifestation**
**ዝግመት** zgmet ***(adj.)*** **putative**
**ዝግናነ** zgnane ***(n.)*** **revulsion**
**ዝጎደሎ** zgodelo ***(prep.)*** **minus**

**ዝጎሃየ** zgohaye ***(adj.)*** **disconsolate**
**ዝግታ** zgta ***(adj.)*** **residual**
**ዝሓፈረ** zḧafere ***(adj.)*** **ashamed**
**ዝሓጀጀ** zḧaĵeĵe ***(n.)*** **hajji**
**ቀደም** qedem ***(adj.)*** **bygone**
**ኣቐዲሙ ዝተገልጸ** 'aq̈edimu ztegelxe ***(adj.)*** **foregoing**
**ዝሓለፈ** zḧalefe ***(adj.)*** **previous**
**ዝሓመመ** zhameme ***(adj.)*** **indisposed**
**ዝሓሸ ኣተሓሰስባ** zhashe atehasasba ***(adj.)*** **transcendental**
**ዝሓሸ** zḧashe ***(adj.)*** **advisable**
**ዝሓሸ** zḧashe ***(adj.)*** **better**
**ዝሓሸ** zḧashe ***(adj.)*** **wholesome**
**ዝሓዘነ** zhazene ***(adj.)*** **sad**
**ዝሓዘነ** zḧazene ***(adj.)*** **sorry**
**ዝሕታለ** zĥtale ***(n. )*** **retardation**
**ዝሕታለ** zḧtale ***(n.)*** **stagnation**
**ዝሕጠት** zĥtet ***(n. )*** **recession**
**ዝሕፀቡ ክዳውንቲ** zhtsebu kdawnti ***(n. )*** **laundry**
**ዝሕቱል** zḧtul ***(adj.)*** **stagnant**
**ዝሑል** zhul ***(adj.)*** **cool**
**ዝሑል** zhul ***(adj.)*** **parky**
**ዝሑል ምንቅስቓስ** zḧul mnqsqas ***(v.)*** **plod**
**ዝሁም** zhum ***(adj.)*** **lukewarm**
**ዝድነቕ** zidneq ***(adj.)*** **wonderful**
**ዜዴ** ziede ***(n.)*** **tactic**
**ዚፍቀድ** zifqed ***(adj.)*** **admissible**
**ዚነኣድ** zine'ad ***(adj.)*** **admirable**
**ዚነኣድ** zine'ad ***(adj.)*** **commendable**
**ዚንጎ** zingo ***(n. )*** **zinc**
**ዝረገአ ደም** ziregeaa' dem' ***(n.)*** **clot**
**ዚሰማማዕ** zisemama'ë ***(adj.)*** **agreeable**
**ዚሰማማዕ** zisemama'ë ***(adj.)*** **apposite**
**ዝስማዕማዕ** zismaemae tsemaexmeaa ***(adj.)*** **congruent**
**ዝተዛዘመ** ziteza'zeme' ***(n)*** **checkmate**
**ዚወሃሃድ** ziwehahad ***(adj.)*** **congenial**
**ዚጽላእ** zixla'è ***(adj.)*** **abominable**
**ዚዝ በለ** ziz bele ***(v.)*** **hum**
**ዚዛመድ** zizamed ***(adj.)*** **akin**
**ዚዝታ** zizta ***(n.)*** **buzz**
**ዘረገ** tserege ***(n.)*** **puddle**
**ዛህላል** zahlal ***(adj.)*** **vacuous**
**ዘጨንቅ** zeç̣enq ***(adj. )*** **harrowing**
**ዘኽታም** zek̗tam ***(n.)*** **waif**
**ዘመናይ** zemenay ***(n. )*** **vogue**
**ዘንበየ** zenbeye ***(v.)*** **hover**
**ዘይእኹል** zey'èkul ***(adj.)*** **insufficient**
**ዘይጎድእ** zeygod'è ***(adj. )*** **harmless**
**ዘይምፍላጥ** zeymflaṭ ***(n.)*** **ignorance**
**ዘይቀሳቀስ** zeynqesaqhes ***(adv. )*** **immovable**
**ዘይንጹር** zeynxur ***(adj.)*** **vague**
**ዘይንጹርነት** zeynxurnet ***(n.)*** **vagueness**
**ዘይቀዋሚነት** zeyqewaminet ***(n.)*** **instability**
**ዘይረብሕ** zeyrebḥ ***(adj.)*** **immaterial**
**ዝተፈላለየ** ztefelaleye ***(adj. )*** **heterogeneous**
**ዝተፈላለየ** ztefelaleye ***(adj.)*** **varied**
**ዝተመረፀ** ztemerxe ***(adj.)*** **elective**
**ዝከኣል** zkeal ***(adj.)*** **possible**
**ዝኸበበ** zkebebe ***(adj.)*** **rounded**
**ዝኸፍእ** zkefe ***(adj.)*** **worse**
**ዝቐትል** zketl ***(adj.)*** **deadly**
**ዝኾነ** zk̗one ***(adj.)*** **any**
**ዝኾነ ቦታ** zk̗one bota ***(adv.)*** **anywhere**

ዝኾነ ግዜ zkone gzie *(conj.)* **whenever**
ዝኾነ ኮይኑ zkone koynu *(a. )* **nonetheless**
ዝኾነ ነገር zḱone neger *(pron.)* **anything**
ዝኾነ ሰብ zḱone seb *(pron.)* **anyone**
ዝኾነ ይኹን zkone ykun *(pron.)* **whichever**
ዝክር zkr *(n.)* **commemoration**
ዝክረ-ዓመት zkre'ämet *(n.)* **anniversary**
ዝክረ-ዘመን zkrezemen *(n.)* **centenary**
ዝክረ ዘመን zkrezemen *(n.)* **centennial**
ዝኽሪ zkri *(n.)* **remembrance**
ዝኽሪ zḱri *(n.)* **memorial**
ዝኽሪ ክልተ ሚኢቲ ዓመት zkri klte mi'iti ämet *(n.)* **bicentenary**
ዝለዓለ zleale *(adj.)* **paramount**
ዝለአለ zleale *(adj. & n.)* **uttermost**
ዝለዓለ zle'äle *(n.)* **maximum**
ዝለዓለ ክፋል ቀሽነት zleale kfal qshnet *(n.)* **patriarch**
ዝለዓለ ሽልማት zle'ale shlmat *(n. )* **jackpot**
ዝማዕበለ zma'ëbele *(adj.)* **mature**
ዝማርኽ zmark *(adj.)* **sensational**
ዝምድና zmdna *(n.)* **correlation**
ዝምድና zmdna *(n. )* **kinship**
ዝምድና zmdna *(n.)* **relation**
ዝምድና zmdna *(n.)* **relationship**
ዝምድና መጠን zmdna meten *(n. )* **ratio**
ዝመሓላለፍ ነገር zmehalalef nege *(n.)* **transmission**
ዝመኸኸ zmeḱeḱe *(adj.)* **molten**
ዝመልአ zmel'e *(adj.)* **replete**
ዝመሳሰል zmesasel *(adj.)* **analogue**
ዝማተ zmote *(adj.)* **dead**
ዝምስገን zmsgen *(adj.)* **creditable**
ዝምስጥ zmst *(adj.)* **thriller**
ዝሙት zmut *(n.)* **adultery**
ዝና zna *(n.)* **eminence**
ዝናብ znab *(n)* **rain**
ዝናብ ዘለዎ znab zelewo *(adj.)* **rainy**
ምቕናን mq̈nan *(n.)* **inclination**
ዝንባለ znbale *(n.)* **tendency**
ዝንባለ znbale *(n.)* **trend**
ዝንባለ znbalie *(n.)* **proclivity**
ዝንበላ znbela *(n.)* **aberration**
ዝንቡል znbul *(adj.)* **aberrant**
ዝነኣሰ zne'ase *(adj.& pron.)* **least**
ዝውሓደ zwḧade *(adj.)* **lesser**
ዝዘነቐጸ ፕሮኞ zneq̈ete proǹo *(n.)* **prune**
ዝንጋዐነት znga'ënet *(n.)* **amnesia**
ዝንቀሳቀስ ሕይሊ znqesaqes hyli *(n. )* **traction**
ዝንቀሳቀስ ነገር ምልክት ዳሓደገ ዝከድ znqesaqes neger mlkt na hadege zked *(n.)* **trajectory**
ዝንተዋ zntewa *(n. )* **narration**
ዞረ zore *(v.)* **rotate**
ዝቀንዐ zqen'ë *(adj.)* **erect**
ዝቀረበ zqerebe *(adj.)* **impending**
ዝቀረበ zqerebe *(adj.)* **nearest**
ዝቐረበ zqerebe *(adj.)* **proximate**
ዝቀውሰ zqewese *(adj.)* **deranged**
ዝቐትል zqhtl *(adj.)* **lethal**
ዝቖንቖነ zqonqone *(adj.)* **decrepit**
ዝቆሰለ zqosele *(adj.)* **sore**
ዝቅፅል zqxl *(adj.)* **next**
ዝራግ zrag *(adj.)* **turbid**
ዝርዳእ zrdae *(adj.)* **perceptible**

ዝረኣየሉ ኣጋጣሚ zre'ayelu agatami *(n.)* **sighting**
ዝረሓቀ zreĥaqe *(adj.& adv.)* **furthest**
ዝረስሐ ፀጉሪ zreshe seguri *(v.)* **tousle**
ዝርጋሐ zrgahe *(n.)* **scope**
ዝርጋሐ zrgaĥe *(n.)* **extent**
ዝርጋሐ zrgaĥe *(n. )* **range**
ዝርገጽ መቆጻጸሪ ማሺን zrgex mekoxaxeri mashen *(n.)* **pedal**
ዝርጉሕ ቀጽላ zrguḧ qetsla *(n.)* **spreadsheet**
ዝሩግ zrug *(adj.)* **murky**
ዝርዝር zrzr *(n.)* **detail**
ዝርዝር zrzr *(n.)* **index**
ዝርዝር zrzr *(n.)* **tally**
ዝርዝር zr'zr *(n.)* **list**
ዝርዝር z'rz'r *(n.)* **specification**
ዝርዝር ዓሌት zrzr alet *(n.)* **pedigree**
ዝርዝራዊ ፍቕዲ zrzrawi fq̈di *(n.)* **inventory**
ዝርዝረ-ጽሑፋት zrzrexḧufat *(n.)* **bibliography**
ዝሳዕረረ zsa'ërere *(adj.)* **rife**
ዝሰዓበ zse'äbe *(adj.)* **due**
ዝስዕብ zs'ëb *(adj.)* **forthcoming**
ዝስዕብ z's'ëb *(adj.)* **subsequent**
ዝሰሓግ zseḧag *(adj.)* **moribund**
ዝሰምበደ zsembede *(adj.)* **aghast**
ዝሰርሕ zserh *(adj.)* **working**
ዝሰርሕዎ ስራሕ ምፍራሕ zserhwo srah mfrah *(n.)* **trepidation**
ዝስማዕማዕ zsma'ëma'ë *(v.)* **accord**
ዝስራሕ zsrah *(adj.)* **workable**
ዝስረዝ zsrez *(adj.)* **revocable**
ዝተዓፈነ ድምፂ zteafene dmsi *(adj.)* **throaty**
ዝተኣሳሰር zte'asaser *(adj.)* **relevant**
ዝተኣሳሰረ zte'asasere *(adj.)* **tied**
ዝተባህለ ztebahle *(n.)* **dictation**
ዝተበላሸወ z-tebela-shewe *(adj.)* **gammy**
ዝተበራበረ zteberabere *(adj.)* **watchful**
ዝተበሳጨወ ztebesaĉewe *(adj.)* **disgruntled**
ዝተበታተነ ztebetatene *(adv.)* **asunder**
ዝተጨነቐ ztečeneq̈e *(adj.)* **beleaguered**
ዝተጨነቐ ztecheneke *(adj.)* **worried**
ዝተዳኸመ ztedakeme *(adj.)* **effete**
ዝተዳለወ ztedalewe *(adj.)* **biased**
ዝተደናገረ ztedenagere *(adj.)* **bemused**
ዝተደርበየ ztederebye *(n.)* **casting**
ዝተፋላለየ ztefalaleye *(adj.)* **assorted**
ዝተፋትሐ ztefat'ĥe *(n.)* **divorcee**
ዝተራሓሓቐ zteraḧaḧaq̈e *(adv.)* **apart**
በብዓይነቱ beb'äynetu *(adj.)* **sundry**
ዝተፈላለየ ztefelaleye *(adj.)* **unequalled**
ዝተፈላለየ ztefelaleye *(adj.)* **various**
ዝተፈላለዩ ztefelaleyu *(adj.)* **diverse**
ዝተፈለየ ናይ በዓል ክዳን ምክዳን ztefely nay beal kdan mkdan *(n.)* **tog**
ዝተፈቐደሉ ztefeqhedelu *(n.)* **licensee**
ዝተጋፍሐ ztegaf̂he *(v.)* **diffuse**
ዝተጋገየ ztegageye *(adj.)* **mistaken**
ዝተጋነነ zteganene *(adj.)* **stilted**
ዝተገደበ ztegedebe *(adj.)* **limited**
ዝተገፍተነ ztegeftene *(adv.)* **ajar**
ዝተገንዘበ ztegenzebe *(adj.)* **aware**

ዝተጎዝጎዘ ztegozgoze *(adv. )* **nearby**
ዝተሃነቀ ztehakene *(adj.)* **deliberate**
ዝተሓላለኸ zteȟalaleǩe *(adj.)* **complex**
ዝተሓላለኸ zteḥalaleǩe *(adj.)* **knotty**
ዝተሓላለኸ ነገር ፈትሐ zteȟalaleke neger fet'he *(v.)* **disentangle**
ዝተሓለወ ztehalewe *(adj.)* **guarded**
ዝተሃሰየ ztehaseye *(adj.)* **disabled**
ዝተሓተ zteȟate *(n.)* **bottom**
ዝተሓተ ቦታ zteȟate bota *(n. )* **nadir**
ዝተሓትመ ወረቐት zteȟatme wereq̈et *(n.)* **printout**
ዝተሓዋወሰ zteȟawawese *(adj.)* **miscellaneous**
ዝተጃህረሉ ztejahrelu *(adj.)* **vaunted**
ፍቱሕ ztekelbese *(adj.)* **undone**
ዝተኸልከለ ነገር ztekelkele neger *(n.)* **taboo**
ዝጠቅም ztekem *(adj.)* **usable**
ዝተከዘ ztekeze *(adj.)* **saturnine**
ዝተላፀየ ztelatseye *(adj.)* **shaven**
ዝተለመደ ztelemede *(adj.)* **typical**
ዝጥዕም ድምፂ zt'ëm dmtsi *(adj.)* **sibilant**
ዝተማሕረ ztemaȟre *(adj.)* **exempt**
ዝተማልአ ztemal'e *(adj.)* **exhaustive**
ዝተሰነየ zteseneye *(adj.)* **fraught**
ዝተመልከ ztemelke *(adj.)* **revered**
ዝተመንጠለ ztementele *(adj.)* **rapt**
ዝተመንወ ztemenwe *(adj.)* **trite**
ዝተመንዘዐ ztemenze'ë *(adj.)* **bereft**
ዝተመራስሐ ztemerasȟe *(adj.)* **sophisticated**
ዝተመስከረሉ ztemeskerelu *(adj.)* **chartered**
ዝተናወጸ ztenawexe *(adj.)* **addled**
ዝተናዘዘ ztenazeze *(adj.)* **testate**
ዝተነፀለ ztenexele *(adj.)* **estranged**
ዝተጠልጠለ ztenteltele *(adj.)* **pendent**
ዝተቓልዐ zteqal'e *(adj.)* **susceptible**
ዝተቓልዐ zteqal'ë *(adj.)* **prone**
ዝተቀደሰ zteqedese *(adj.)* **sacred**
ዝተቐደሰ zteq̈edese *(adj. )* **halal**
ዝተቀናበረ ሙዚቃ zteqenabere muziqa *(n.)* **symphony**
ዝተቐረፀ ፁሑፍ zteqhretse tsuhuf *(n.)* **inscription**
ዝተቖራረፀ zteqorarexe *(adj.)* **fitful**
ዝተራሕረሐ zteraȟreȟe *(n.)* **castaway**
ዝተሳእነ ztesa'ene *(adj.)* **missing**
ዝተሰቕለ ztesehq̈le *(adv.)* **aloft**
ዝተሻቕለ zteshaq̈ele *(adj.)* **apprehensive**
ዝተጠበሰ ztetbese *(n.)* **toast**
ዝተተሓባበሩ zteteȟababeru *(adj.)* **allied**
ዝተጠምማዘዘ ztetemazeze *(adj.)* **tortuous**
ዝተጠምዘዘ ztetemazeze *(v.)* **twist**
ዝተጠቕዐ zteẗeqh'ë *(adj.)* **stricken**
ዝተፅዓነ ztets'ane *(n.)* **laden**
ዝተዋሃሃደ ztewahahade *(adj.)* **composite**
ዝተወሃበ ztewehabe *(adj.)* **given**
ዝተወሃሃደ ztewehahade *(adj. )* **harmonious**
ዝተወርሰ መሰል ztewerse mesel *(n. )* **patrimony**
ዝተወጠረ ztewetere *(adj.)* **riddled**
ዝተወጠረ ztewetere *(adj.)* **taut**
ዝተዘርገ ztezerge *(adj.)* **muzzy**
ዝፀልመተ ztselmete *(adj.)* **dark**
ዝፀነሐ ztsenehe *(adj.)* **ingrained**
ዙፋን zufan *(n.)* **throne**
ዙረት zuret *(n.)* **hike**

ምብርራይ mbrray ***(n.)*** **rotation**

ዙርያ zurya ***(n.)*** **circumference**

ዙርያዊ zuryawi ***(adj.)*** **ambient**

ዝወዳደቐ ጓሓፍ zwedeqe guahaf ***(n.)*** **litter**

ዝወሓደ zwehade ***(adj. & pron.)*** **less**

ዝወሓደ zweḧade ***(adj.)*** **minimal**

ዝወሓደ zweḧade ***(n.)*** **minimum**

ዝወተረ zwetere ***(adj.)*** **tumescent**

ዝፃነተ zxanete ***(adj.)*** **extinct**

ዝፀለለ zxelele ***(n.)*** **filtrate**

ዝፅላእ zxla'e ***(adj.)*** **averse**

ዝያዳ ክፍሊት zyda kflit ***(n.)*** **surcharge**

ዘየሕጉስ zyehigus' ***(adj.)*** **cheerless**

ዝዛረብ ሰብ ኣቋረፀ zzareb seb aqaretse ***(v.)*** **interject**

ዝዝርጋሕ ዓራት zzrgaȟ 'ärat ***(n.)*** **couchette**

ዘየሐጉስ zeyehegus ***(adj.)*** **obnoxious**

ዘየዳልው zeyedalw ***(adv.)*** **objectively**

ዘይልሙድ zeylmud ***(adj.)*** **odd**

ዘይቲ zeyti ***(n.)*** **oil**

ዘይቲ ለኸየ zeyti lekeye ***(v.)*** **oil**

ዘይቲ ዝበዝሖ zeyti zbezho ***(adj.)*** **oily**

ዘይንጹር zeyntsur ***(adj.)*** **obscure**

ዘይግልጺ zeygltsi ***(adj.)*** **ostensible**

ዘይግልጺ zeygltsi ***(n.)*** **ostentation**

ዘይጠቅም heteqm ***(adj.)*** **otiose**

ዙረት zuret ***(n.)*** **oscillation**

ዚረስዕ zres'o ***(adj.)*** **oblivious**

ዝሑሸ ẑheshe ***(adj.)*** **optimum**

ዝሑሸ ገበረ ẑhheshe gebere ***(v.)*** **optimize**

ዝለዓለ ክፍሊት ምቕራብ zle'ale kflit mqrab ***(v.)*** **outbid**

ዝተጋነነ zteganene ***(adj.)*** **overblown**

ዝተጸባበቐ ztetsebabeqe ***(adj.)*** **ornate**

ዝንጋዐ znga'e ***(n.)*** **oversight**

ዝኣረገ z'arege ***(adj.)*** **outmoded**

ዝዓግት zagt ***(adj.)*** **obstructive**

ዝዕዘብ z'ezeb ***(adj.)*** **observant**

ዝያዳ በለጸ zyada blelexe ***(v.)*** **outshine**

ዝገድድ zegeded ***(v.)*** **oblige**

## የ

የማን yeman ***(n)*** **right**

የዋህ yewah ***(n.)*** **tender**

የዋህ yewah ***(adj.)*** **tender**

የዋህነት yewahnet ***(adv.)*** **credulity**

የዋህነት yewahnet ***(n.)*** **goodness**

ያዕያዕታ ya'ëyaëta ***(n.)*** **rumpus**

ያዕያዕታ ya'ëya'ëta ***(n.)*** **jazz**

ይኣኽለኒ ዘይብሃል y'akleni zeybhal ***(adj.)*** **irresistible**

ያታ yata ***(n.)*** **legend**

ያታዊ yatawi ***(adj.)*** **legendary**

ይግባእ ygba'e ***(v.)*** **must**

ይግባእ ygba'e ***(v.)*** **shall**

ይግባእ ygba'e ***(v.)*** **should**

ይግበኣኒ በሃላይ yigbeani behalayi ***(n.)*** **claimant**

ይኽእል yḱ'el ***(v.)*** **might**

ይኽእል y'ḱ'el ***(v.)*** **may**

ይቕር ንክብል ምእማን yker nkbl m'eman ***(v.)*** **intercede**

ይኸውን ykewn ***(adj.)*** **would-be**

ዮጋ yoga ***(n.)*** **yoga**

ዮንክስ yonks ***(n.)*** **yonks**

ይቕሬታ yq̃reeta ***(n.)*** **apology**

ዩኒቨርስቲ yuniversty ***(n.)*** **university**

ዩሮ yuro ***(n.)*** **euro**

**ይጽናሕ ዝተባህለ** yxnah ztebahle *(adj.)* **pending**
**ደምሰሰ** demsese *(v.)* **obliterate**
**ደረቕ** dereq *(adj.)* **obstinate**
**ደረቕነት** dereqnet *(n)* **obstinacy**
**ደገ** dege *(adv.)* **out**
**ደገ** dege *(adj.)* **outdoor**
**ደገ** dege *(n.)* **outside**
**ደጋዊ** degawi *(adj.)* **outer**
**ደጋዊ** degawi *(adv.)* **outwardly**
**ድልድል** dldl *(n.)* **overpass**
**ዳኛ** daagna *(n.)* **referee**
**ዳዶ** dado *(n.)* **dice**
**ዳዕሮ** da'ëro *(n. )* **sycamore**
**ዳፍላ** dafla *(n.)* **quiff**
**ደጋል** dagal *(adj.)* **dingy**
**ዳጌት** dageet *(n.)* **chivalry**
**ዳጌተኛ** dageetenya *(adj.)* **chivalrous**
**ዳገት** daget *(n.)* **quay**
**ዳጊፋ** dagiefa *(n.)* **prop**
**ዳግም ኣሐተመ** dagm aĥeteme *(v.)* **reprint**
**ዳግም ኣሐየለ** dagm aĥeyele *(v.)* **regenerate**
**ዳግም ኣህገረ** dagm ahgere *(v.)* **repatriate**
**ዳግም ኣማዕረገ** dagm amaërege *(v.)* **rehabilitate**
**ዳግም ኣረጋገፀ** dagm aregagetse *(v.)* **reaffirm**
**ዳግም ኣዋፈረ** dagm awafere *(v.)* **redeploy**
**ዳግመ ፍርዲ** dagm frdi *(n.)* **retrial**
**ዳግም ገምገመ** dagm gemgeme *(v.)* **reassess**
**ዳግም ገምገመ** dagm gemgeme *(v.)* **reconsider**
**ዳግም ግምገማ** dagm gmgema *(n.)* **reappraisal**
**ዳግም ጎበዘ** dagm gobeze *(v.)* **rejuvenate**
**ዳግም ጉብዝና** dagm gubzna *(n.)* **rejuvenation**
**ዳግም ሃነፀ** dagm hanetse *(v.)* **rebuild**
**ዳግም ሃነፀ** dagm hanetse *(v.)* **reconstruct**
**ዳግም ሃነፀ** dagm hanetse *(v.)* **revamp**
**ዳግም ሓሰበ** dagm ĥasebe *(v.)* **rethink**
**ዳግም ሓዘ** dagm ĥaze *(v.)* **recapture**
**ዳግመ ሕውየት** dagm ĥwyet *(n.)* **rehabilitation**
**ዳግመ ህያወ** dagm hyawe *(n.)* **revivalism**
**ዳግም ልደት** dagm ldet *(n.)* **rebirth**
**ዳግም መልአ** dagm mel'e *(v.)* **refill**
**ዳግም ምጅማር** dagm mjmar *(n. )* **resumption**
**ዳግም ምኧን** dagm mkwan *(v.)* **reoccur**
**ዳግም ምልዕዓል** dagm ml'ëäl *(a. )* **resurgence**
**ዳግም ምጥጣዕ** dagm mtta'ë *(n.)* **regeneration**
**ዳግም ቀፀለ** dagm qetsele *(v.)* **resume**
**ዳግም ሰርዐ** dagm ser'ë *(v.)* **rearrange**
**ዳግም ሰወለ** dagm sewele *(v.)* **retread**
**ዳግም ስጋ ኣልበሰ** dagm sga albese *(v.)* **reincarnate**
**ዳግም ተለማመደ** dagm telemamede *(v.)* **readjust**
**ዳግም ተራኣየ** dagm tera'aye *(v.)* **reappear**

ዳግም ተፀንበረ dagm testenbere ***(v.)*** **rejoin**
ዳግም ተጠቀመ dagm teteqeme ***(v.)*** **reuse**
ዳግም ወደበ dagm wedebe ***(v.)*** **reconstitute**
ዳግም ወደበ dagm wedebe ***(v.)*** **reorganize**
ዳግም ወነነ dagm wenene ***(v.)*** **repossess**
ዳግም ዝለዓዓል dagm ztela'ääle ***(adj.)*** **resurgent**
ዳግም ኣተንሰአ dagm ztense'e ***(v.)*** **resurrect**
ዳግመ ህግረት dagme hgret ***(n.)*** **repatriation**
ዳግም ተፃወተ dagmtetsawete ***(v.)*** **replay**
ዳኛ dagna ***(n.)*** **umpire**
ዳጎነ dagone ***(v.)*** **intern**
ዳጉሻ dagusha ***(n. )*** **millet**
ደሓነ daĥane ***(v.)*** **recover**
ዳህናው dahnaw ***(adj.)*** **stale**
ዳሕራዋይ dahraway ***(adj.)*** **latter**
ዳሕረዋይ መነፃፀሪ dahreway menetzatzeri ***(n.)*** **hindsight**
ዳህሳሲ dahsasi ***(n.)*** **globetrotter**
ዳህሳሲ dahsasi ***(n.)*** **navigator**
ዳህሳሲ dahsasi ***(n.)*** **scout**
ዳህሰሰ dahsese ***(v.)*** **explore**
ዳህሰሰ dahsese ***(v.t. )*** **survey**
ዳኛ daǹa ***(n.)*** **judge**
ዳኛ daǹa ***(n.)*** **arbitrator**
ዳንደልዮን dandelyon ***(v.)*** **dandelion**
ዳነየ daneye ***(v.)*** **arbitrate**
ዳንጋ danga ***(n.)*** **shank**
ዳንኬራ dankiera ***(n.)*** **fanfare**
ዳኝነት daǹnet ***(n.)*** **arbitration**
ዳርጋ darga ***(adv.)*** **almost**
ዳርጋ darga ***(adv. )*** **nearly**
ዳርጋ darga ***(adv. )*** **rather**
ዳርጋ ኣብ መወዳእታ darga ab mewedet a ***(adj.)*** **penultimate**
ኣጉዶ 'agudo ***(n.)*** **shack**
ኣዳራሽ 'adarash ***(n. )*** **pavilion**
ዳስ das ***(n.)*** **arbour**
ዳስ das ***(n.)*** **bower**
ዳይኖሰር daynoser ***(n.)*** **dinosaur**
ዳይረክተር dayrekter ***(adj.)*** **principal**
ድባብ dbab ***(n.)*** **canopy**
ድብዳቤ dbdabie ***(n. )*** **letter**
ድበት dbet ***(n.)*** **silt**
ድቢ dbi ***(n.)*** **panda**
ድቢ dbi ***(v.t)*** **bear**
ድብልቅልቅ dbl'ql'q ***(n.)*** **medley**
ድብያ dbya ***(n.)*** **ambush**
ደብዛዝ dbzaz ***(adj.)*** **woozy**
ደዓኸ deä'ḱe ***(v.t)*** **mash**
ድብልቕላቕ debaleq̈e ***(n.)*** **jumble**
ደባን deban ***(adj.)*** **dull**
ደበስ debas ***(n.)*** **retribution**
ደባይ ተዋጋኢ debay tewaga'i ***(n. )*** **guerrilla**
ደብዳብ debdab ***(n.)*** **bombardment**
ደብዳቢት debdabit ***(n.)*** **bomber**
ደብደበ debdebe ***(v.)*** **bombard**
ደበና debena ***(n.)*** **nimbus**
ደበና መሰል debena mesel ***(adj.)*** **nebulous**
ደበናማ debenama ***(adj.)*** **cloudy**
ደበንገረ debengere ***(n.)*** **gloom**
ደበ'ሰ debese ***(v.)*** **condole**
ደብለቐ debleq̈e ***(v.)*** **amalgamate**
ደበና debna' ***(n.)*** **cloud**
ደብራዊ debrawi ***(adj.)*** **parochial**
ደብሪ debri ***(n)*** **deck**
ደብሪ debri ***(n.)*** **sanctum**

በርቃዊ መጥቃዕቲ berqawi meťqa'ěti *(n.)* **blitz**
ደቡብ debub *(n.)* **south**
ደቡባዊ debubawi *(adj.)* **southern**
ደብዛዝ debzaz *(adj.)* **sketchy**
ዴሲቤል decibel *(n.)* **decibel**
ዴሲማል decimal *(adj.)* **decimal**
ደድሕሪ ሞት dedȟri mot *(adj.)* **posthumous**
ዴስነት deesnet *(n.)* **communism**
ደፍአ defae *(v.)* **push**
ኣህረረ 'ahrere *(v.)* **tempt**
ደፋፍአ defaf'a *(v.)* **tout**
ደፋፈአ defafe'a *(v.)* **actuate**
ደፋር defar *(adj.)* **daring**
ውዱቕ ፍናን መሽኳት wduq̈ fnan meshkwat *(adj.)* **nerveless**
ደፋር defar *(adj.)* **saucy**
ደፍደፈ defdefe *(v.)* **dab**
ደፍአ def'e *(v.)* **encroach**
ደፍአ def'e *(v.)* **goad**
ደፍአ def'e *(v.)* **hunch**
ደፈነ defene *(n.)* **default**
ደፈረ defere *(v.)* **dare**
ደፈረ defere *(v.)* **molest**
ደፈረ defere *(v.)* **rape**
ደፍጢጡ፣ገሊፁ deftitu,gelisu *(v.)* **tramp**
ደጋፊ degafi *(n.)* **devotee**
ደጋፊ degafi *(n.)* **exponent**
ደጋፊ degafi *(n.)* **partisan**
ደጋፊ degafi *(n. )* **patron**
ደጋፊ ሙኳን degafi mukwan *(v.)* **patronize**
ደጋፊ ሰላም degafi selam *(n.)* **pacifist**
ደጋፊ degafi *(n.)* **aide**
ጥምሮ ïmro *(n.)* **truss**
ደጋገመ degageme *(v.)* **iterate**
ደጋገመ degageme *(v.)* **reiterate**
ደጋዊ degawi *(adj.)* **external**
ደጋዊ ትረኢት degawi treit *(n. )* **physiognomy**
ደገፍ degef *(n.)* **recourse**
ደገፍ degef *(n.)* **reinforcement**
ደገፍ ረኸበ degef rekebe *(v.)* **conciliate**
ደገፈ degefe *(v.)* **endorse**
ደገፈ degefe *(v.)* **sustain**
ብዝርዝር ገለጸ bzrzr gelexe *(v.)* **recite**
ደገመ degeme *(v.)* **recycle**
ደገመ degeme *(v.)* **repeat**
ደጊሙ መልአ degimu mel'e *(v.)* **recharge**
ደጎመ degome *(v.)* **subsidize**
ደጉሐ deguhe *(v. t.)* **dazzle**
ደጉሐ deguȟe *(v.i)* **glare**
ደጓለጽ degwalax *(adj.)* **bulky**
ደሃለ dehale *(v.)* **daunt**
ደሃለ dehale *(v.)* **demoralize**
ደሃለ dehale *(v.)* **discourage**
ደሃለ dehale *(v.)* **dishearten**
ደሓን ኩን deȟan kun *(interj. )* **farewell**
ደሓን ኩን deȟan kun *(n.)* **adieu**
ደሓረ deĥare *(v.)* **regress**
ደሃይ dehay *(n.)* **voice**
ደሃይ dehay *(n.)* **audio**
ደካሊ dekali *(adj.)* **conclusive**
ድኻም dekam *(adj.)* **tired**
ደኽዳኽ dekdak *(n.)* **dwarf**
ደቂሱ ዝሕከም dekisu zhkem *(n.)* **inpatient**
ሚሊሽያ milishya *(n. )* **monger**
ደላ'ላይ delalay *(n.)* **broker**
ደለበ delebe *(v.t.)* **accrue**
ደለል delel *(n. )* **sediment**
ደልየ deleye *(v.)* **need**

**ደለየ** deleye ***(v.)* require**
**ደለየ** deleye ***(v.)* want**
**ደልሃመት** delhamet ***(n.)* murk**
**ደልሃመት** delhamet ***(n.)* abyss**
**ደልሃመታዊ** delhametawi ***(adj.)* abysmal**
**ዴልታ** delta ***(n.)* delta**
**ደም ምፍሳስ** dem mfsas ***(n.)* bloodshed**
**ደም ምሃብ** dem mhab ***(v.)* transfuse**
**ደም ና ምሃብ ተግባር** dem na mhab tegbar ***(n.)* transfusion**
**ደም** dem ***(n.)* blood**
**ደማሚት** demamit ***(n.)* dynamite**
**ብደም ዝተለቕለቐ** bdem zteleq̈leq̈e ***(adj.)* gory**
**ደማዊ** demawi ***(adj.)* sanguinary**
**ደማዊ** demawi ***(adj.)* bloody**
**ደምበ** dembe ***(n.)* stall**
**ደምበ ላሕሚ** dembe laȟmi ***(n.)* byre**
**ደምቢ** dembi ***(n. )* etiquette**
**ደምደመ** demdeme ***(v.)* deduce**
**ደምደመ** demdeme ***(v.)* infer**
**ደመኛ** demegna ***(n.)* nemesis**
**ደመቐ** demeq̈e ***(v.)* brighten**
**ወሰኸ** weseḱe ***(v.)* add**
**ደመየ** demeye ***(v.)* bleed**
**ደሚቕ ብጫ** demiq bicha ***(adj.)* gilt**
**ደሞተራ** demotera ***(n.)* centipede**
**ደሞዝ** demoz ***(n. )* salary**
**ደሞዝ** demoz ***(n.)* stipend**
**ደሞዝ** demoz ***(n.)* wage**
**ደምሰሰ** demsese ***(v. i)* delete**
**ደምሰሰ** demsese ***(v.)* erase**
**ሰረዘ** sereze ***(v.)* quash**
**ደምሰሰ** demsese ***(v.)* raze**
**ሰረዘ** sereze ***(v.t)* abolish**
**ድሙ** demu ***(n.)* cat**
**ደንበ** denbe ***(n.)* ranch**
**ደንቢ** denbi ***(n.)* code**
**ደንቢሩ ጢሒሱ** denbiru thisu ***(v.)* transgress**
**ድንጋፀ** denegaxe' ***(n.)* consternation**
**ደነነ** denene ***(v.)* droop**
**ደንፈዐ** denfe'ë ***(v.)* flourish**
**ደንገፀ** dengexe ***(v.)* commiserate**
**ደንጎላ** dengola ***(n.)* boulder**
**ደንቆሮ** denqoro ***(n.)* ignoramus**
**ደንቆሮ** denqoro ***(n.)* berk**
**ደንፀወ** denxewe ***(v.)* mystify**
**ደንጸዎ** denxewo ***(v.t)* bewilder**
**ደንዘዘ** denzeze ***(adj.)* befuddled**
**ደንዘዘ** denzeze ***(v.)* daze**
**ድቓላ** deqala ***(n.)* hybrid**
**ደቃሲ** deqasi ***(n.)* sleeper**
**ደቀበት** deqebat ***(n.)* gentry**
**ደቀሰ** deqese ***(v.)* slumber**
**ደቀ ባት** deqi bat ***(n.)* populace**
**ደቂቕ** deqiq ***(adj.)* minute**
**ውሑድ ህያብ** wȟud hyab ***(n.)* mite**
**ደቂቕ ፊልሚ** deqiq filmi ***(n. )* microfilm**
**ደቂቃ** deqiqa ***(n.)* minute**
**ደራፊ** derafi ***(a. )* singer**
**ደራፊ** derafi ***(n.)* songster**
**ደራፊ** derafi ***(n. )* vocalist**
**ደራርዕ** derar'ë ***(v.)* nudge**
**ደራረዘ** derareze ***(v.)* caress**
**ደራረዘ** derareze ***(v.)* fondle**
**ደራሲ ወራቢ** derasi werabi ***(n.)* composer**
**ደሓን ኩን** deḥan kun ***(excl.)* goodbye**
**ደከረ** dekere ***(v.)* wallop**
**ደርገፍገፍ በለ** dergefgef bele ***(v.)* hobble**
**ድጓና** dgwana ***(n. )* warder**

ድርዒ ገጽ dr'ï gex *(n.)* **visor**
ደራሲ derasi *(n.)* **author**
ደራዚ deṙazi *(n.)* **masseur**
ደርበየ derbeye *(v.)* **cast**
ምድረበዳ mdrebeda *(v.)* **desert**
ደርበየ derbeye *(v.)* **throw**
ደርበየሉ derbeyelu *(v.)* **pelt**
ደርቢ derbi *(n. )* **storey**
ደርቢ derbi *(n. )* **stratum**
ደርዐ der'ë *(v.)* **recap**
ደረበ derebe *(v.)* **stratify**
ደረበ derebe *(v.)* **superimpose**
ደረፈ derefe *(v.)* **sing**
ደርሆ dereho *(n.)* **chicken**
ደረጃ dereja *(n.)* **grade**
ደረጃ dereja *(n.)* **level**
ብሩህ ክፍሊ ናይ ወርሒ bruh kfli nay werḧi *(n.)* **phase**
ደረጃ dereja *(n.)* **rank**
መሳልል mesall *(n.)* **stair**
ደረጃ dereja *(n. )* **status**
ደረጃ ኣትሓዘ dereja at'ḧaze *(v.)* **standardize**
ደረጃ ምትሓዝ dereja m'tḧaz *(n.)* **standardization**
ደረቕ derek *(adj.)* **uncompromising**
ደረኸ dereke *(v.)* **incline**
ደረቅ dereq *(n.)* **bigot**
ደረቕ dereqe *(adj.)* **dry**
ደረቀኛ dereqegna *(adj.)* **impious**
ደረቖኛ dereq̈eṅa *(adj.)* **flippant**
ደረቖኛ dereq̈eṅa *(adj.)* **brash**
ድርቀት dere'qe't *(n.)* **constipation**
ደረቕ dereqh *(adj.)* **inflexible**
ደረት ትርኢት deret tr'it *(n. )* **horizon**
ደረት deret *(n.)* **bust**
ደረት-ኣልቦ deret'albo *(adj.)* **boundless**

ደረተ derete *(v.)* **localize**
ደርፊ derfi *(n.)* **carol**
መዝሙር mezmur *(n. )* **song**
ደርገፍገፍ በለ dergefgef bele *(v.)* **waver**
ደርጊ ስኒ dergi sni *(n.)* **denture**
ደርጎስታ dergosta *(n.)* **smattering**
ደርጓጉ መርከብ derguag merkeb *(n.)* **hulk**
ደርጓዕጓዕ በለ dergwa'ëgwaë bele *(v.)* **rumble**
ደርሆ derho *(n.)* **hen**
ደርሆ ማይ derho may *(n.)* **duck**
ደሮና derona *(n.)* **dust**
ደርቀኛ ጓል derqegna gwal *(n.)* **minx**
ደርዘን derzen *(n.)* **dozen**
ደስ ብዝብል des bzbl *(adv. )* **quaintly**
ደስ ዝብል des zbl *(adj.)* **quaint**
ደስ ዘይብል des zeybl *(adj.)* **seamy**
ደሴት deseet *(n. )* **island**
ደሴት deseet *(n. )* **isle**
ኣቶል 'atol *(n.)* **atoll**
ደሴታዊ desietawi *(adj.)* **insular**
ደስከለ deskele *(v.)* **freeze**
ደስታ desta *(n.)* **glee**
ደስታ desta *(n. )* **joy**
ደው በለ dew bele *(v.)* **stand**
ደወለ dewele *(v.)* **ring**
ጭልጭል በለ člčl bele *(v.)* **tinkle**
ደወለ dewele *(v.)* **call**
ደያቢ deyabi *(adj.)* **ascendant**
ደየበ deyebe *(v.i)* **climb**
ኣብ መርከብ ተሰቕለ 'ab merkeb teseq̈le *(v. t)* **embark**
ደየበ deyebe *(v.)* **ascend**
ድፍፍእ dff'e *(n.)* **scuffle**
ድፍኢት df'it *(n. )* **motivation**
ደገፈ degefe *(n.)* **favour**

ድጋፍ ሃበ dgaf habe *(v.)* **espouse**
ድጋፍ dgaf *(n.)* **brace**
ድጋም ፍእምተ ቃል dgam f'emte qal *(n.)* **alliteration**
ምቕላሖ mqlaȟe *(n.)* **assonance**
ድግግም dggm *(n. )* **frequency**
ድግማ dgma *(n.)* **repetition**
ድግማ dgma *(n.)* **encore**
ድግስ dgs *(n.)* **banquet**
ድግስ dgs *(n.)* **feast**
ድሕረ ገፅ dhde getse *(n.)* **webpage**
ድሕረ ገፅ dhde getse *(n.)* **website**
ድህናወ d'hnawe *(n.)* **staleness**
ድሕነት dĥnet *(n.)* **redemption**
ድሕንነት dhnnet *(n. )* **safety**
ድሕንነት dhnnet *(n.)* **welfare**
ድሕር ዘይምባል dhr zeymbal *(n.)* **perseverance**
ድሕረ ባይታ dȟre bayta *(n.)* **backdrop**
ድሕረ ባይታ dȟre bayta *(n.)* **background**
ድሑረ ንጡፍ dĥre ntuf *(adj.)* **retroactive**
ድሕረ ጥብቆ d'hre tbqo *(n.)* **suffix**
ድሕሪ dȟri *(conj.)* **after**
ድሕሪ ሕጂ dḥri ḥği *(adv. )* **hereafter**
ድሕሪ መወዳእታ ዛንታ dȟri mewedaèta zanta *(n. )* **postscript**
ድሕሪት dĥrit *(n. )* **rear**
ድሕሪት dĥrit *(adj.)* **retro**
ድሕሪት ምቕራይ dhrit mqhray *(n.)* **laggard**
ድህሰሳ dhsesa *(n.)* **exploration**
ድህሰሳ dhsesa *(n.)* **navigation**
ድሁል dhul *(adj.)* **dispirited**
ድሁል dhul *(adj. )* **haunted**
ድሑር dĥur *(adj.)* **primitive**
ድሑር dȟur *(adj.)* **antiquated**

ድዱዕ diduee' *(n.)* **cockroach**
ዲግሪ digri *(n.)* **degree**
ዲሞክራሲ dimokrasi *(n.)* **democracy**
ዲሞክራሲያዊ dimokrasiyawi *(adj.)* **democratic**
ዲናሞ dinamo *(n.)* **dynamo**
ዲኦድራንት di'odrant *(n.)* **deodorant**
ዲፕሎማ diploma *(n.)* **diploma**
ዲስክ disc *(n.)* **disc**
ዲስኮ disco *(n.)* **disco**
ዲቫኖ divano *(n.)* **settee**
ዲያስፖራ diyaspora *(n.)* **Diaspora**
ድኻ dka *(n. )* **pauper**
ድኻ dḱa *(adj.)* **poor**
ድኻም dkam *(n.)* **debility**
ድኻም dkam *(n.)* **fatigue**
ድኻም dkam *(adj.)* **wearisome**
ድኻም dkham *(n.)* **lethargy**
ምግደራ mgdera *(n.)* **disability**
ጉድለት gudlet *(n.)* **failing**
ድኽመት dkmet *(n.)* **infirmity**
ድኽመት dkmet *(n. )* **weakness**
ድኽነት dḱnet *(n. )* **poverty**
ስእነት s'ènet *(n. )* **privation**
ድኹዒ dḱu'ï *(n.)* **compost**
ድኹዒ dḱu'ï *(n.)* **fertilizer**
ድኹም dkum *(adj.)* **feeble**
ድኹም ሓበ ዘይብሉ dḱum ȟabo zeyblu *(adj.)* **flabby**
ዘይርጉእ zeyrgu'è *(adj.)* **groggy**
ምሱን msun *(adj.)* **infirm**
ውጹዕ wxu'ë *(n.)* **underdog**
ሰንኮፍ senkof *(adj.)* **weak**
ድኹም dḱum *(adj.)* **frail**
ንእሽቶን ድኹምን n'èshton dḱumn *(adj.)* **puny**
ድልድል dldl *(n.)* **bridge**

ደልዳላ ሓያል ብርቱዕ deldala ḧayal brtu'ë *(adj.)* **robust**
ሶርኖ sorno *(n.)* **serge**
ድልዱል dldul *(adj.)* **stout**
ቂምቂም qimqim *(n.)* **ticking**
ድሉው dluw *(adj.)* **ready**
ድልየት dlyet *(n.)* **desire**
ድልየት dlyet *(n.)* **interest**
ድልየት dlyet *(n.)* **zing**
ድልየት ዘይብሉ dlyet zeyblu *(adj.)* **indifferent**
ድልየት ዘይምህላው dlyet zeymhlaw *(n.)* **indifference**
ድማ dma *(n.)* **ampersand**
ድማ dma *(conj.)* **and**
ድምበጃን dmbejan *(n.)* **carboy**
ድምደማ dmdema *(n.)* **induction**
ድምደማ dmdema *(n.)* **inference**
ድምር dmr *(n.)* **aggregate**
ድምር dmr *(adj.)* **gross**
ድምር d'mr *(n.)* **sum**
ድምር ፀዓት dm'r xe'ät *(n.)* **synergy**
ድምሰሳ dmsesa *(v.)* **abolition**
ድምሰሳ dmsesa *(n.)* **annihilation**
ድምፃዊ dmtsawi *(adj.)* **sonic**
ድምፂ dmtsi *(n.)* **sound**
ድምፂ ዘየሕልፍ dmtsi zeyeḧlf *(adj.)* **soundproof**
ድሙቅ dmuq *(adj.)* **lurid**
ድሙቅ dmuq *(adj.)* **refulgence**
ድሙቅ ቀይሕ dmuq qeyh *(n.)* **scarlet**
ድሙቅ ሰማያዊ ሕብሪ dmuq semayawi hbri *(n. )* **sapphire**
ድሙቕ ውራይ dmuq̈ wray *(n. )* **pomp**
ድሙቕ dmuq̈ *(adj.)* **bright**
ድምጻዊ dmxawi *(adj.)* **vocal**
ድምፀት dmxet *(n.)* **accent**
ድምጺ ደርሆ ማይ dmxi derho may *(n.)* **honk**
ድምጺ ደወል dmxi dewel *(n.)* **peal**
ድምጺ ምርጫ dmxi mrça *(n.)* **vote**
ድምጺ ትርግታ dmxi trgta *(n.)* **pulse**
ድንበር ምጥሓስ dnber mthas *(n. )* **transgression**
ድንደላ dndela *(n.)* **blockade**
ድንደና ኣረጋውያን dndena 'aregawyan *(n.)* **ageism**
ድንድል dndl *(n.)* **viaduct**
ድንጋጸ dngaxe *(n.)* **compassion**
ድንጋጸ dngaxe *(n.)* **pity**
ድንጋጸ ዘይብሉ dngaxe zeyblu *(adj.)* **pitiless**
ድንጋዘ dngaze *(n.)* **sloth**
ድንገታዊ dngetawi *(adj.)* **incidental**
ድንገተኛ dngeteňa *(adj. )* **hazardous**
ድንግልና dnglna *(n.)* **chastity**
ድንግርግር dngrgr *(n. )* **welter**
ድንግርግር dn'gr'gr *(n.)* **maze**
ድንጉር dngur *(n. )* **rubble**
ድንጉይ dnguy *(adj.)* **late**
ድንጉይ dnguy *(adj.)* **belated**
ድንጉዝ dnguz *(adj.)* **retarded**
ድንኪ dnki *(n. )* **midget**
ድንኪ dnki *(n. )* **pigmy**
ድንኪ dnki *(n. )* **pygmy**
ድንኩል ሰውሒ dnkul sewhi *(n.)* **sod**
ድንኳን dnkwan *(n.)* **shop**
ድንሽ dnsh *(n. )* **potato**
ድንፃወ dntsawe *(n.)* **disbelief**
ድንዛዘ dnzaẓe *(n.)* **stupor**
ድንዛዘ dnzaze *(n.)* **anaesthesia**
ድንዙዝ dnzuz *(adj.)* **numb**
ኣዳግ 'adag *(adj.)* **stolid**
ድንዙዝ dnzuz *(adj.)* **impassive**
ዶብ dob *(n. )* **frontier**

ዶብ dob *(n.)* **border**
ዶብ dob *(n.)* **boundary**
ዶጭዳጭ dochdach *(n.)* **stockist**
ዶጭዳጭ dochdach *(adj.)* **stocky**
ዶክተርነት doctoret *(n.)* **doctorate**
ዶኩመንታዊ dokumentawi *(n.)* **documentary**
ዶላር dolar *(n.)* **dollar**
ዶልሺ dolshi *(n.)* **flapjack**
ዶልሺ dolshi *(n.)* **cake**
ዶሶ doso *(n.)* **buttock**
ድቃል dqal *(adj.)* **inbred**
ድቃል dqal *(n.)* **replica**
ድቃላ ከልቢ dqala kelbi *(n. )* **mongrel**
ድቓላ dq̈ala *(n.)* **bastard**
ድቃስ dqas *(n.)* **sleep**
ድቀ መሳርሒት dqe mesarȟit *(n.)* **microprocessor**
ድቂ dqi *(n.)* **embryo**
ድቁስ dqus *(adj.)* **asleep**
ድራብነት drabnet *(n.)* **plurality**
ድራጎን dragon *(n.)* **dragon**
ድራማዊ dramawi *(adj.)* **dramatic**
ድራር drar *(n.)* **dinner**
ድራር drar *(n.)* **supper**
ድራውሊኮ drawliko *(n.)* **plumber**
ድርብ drb *(adj.)* **double**
ድርብ drb *(adj.)* **dual**
ድርብ drb *(n.)* **duplex**
ድርብ መርዓ drb mer'ä *(n.)* **bigamy**
ድርብ ጠርጊቶ drb ťergito *(n.)* **biceps**
ድርብ ፆታዊ drb xotawi *(adj.)* **bisexual**
ድርብ-ልሳናዊ drblsanawi *(adj.)* **bilingual**
ድርዳር drdar *(n.)* **sheaf**
ድረታ dreta *(n.)* **limitation**
ድርዕቶ dr'ëto *(n.)* **duvet**
ድርዕቶ dr'ëto *(n. )* **quilt**
ድርዒ ሓጺን dr'ï ȟaxin *(n.)* **armour**
ድርጅት drjt *(n.)* **corporation**
ድርኪት drkit *(n.)* **impetus**
ድሮ d'ro *(n.)* **eve**
ድርቂ drqi *(n.)* **drought**
ድርቅና drqna *(n.)* **bigotry**
ድርቅና drqna *(n.)* **gall**
ድርሰት drset *(n.)* **literature**
ድርፃን drtsan *(n. )* **gum**
ድስቡጣ dsbuta *(n.)* **despot**
ድስቲ dsti *(n.)* **casserole**
ሕጉስ ȟgus *(adj.)* **convivial**
ሕጉስ dsut *(adj.)* **joyful**
ሕጉስ dsut *(adj.)* **jubilant**
ዱባ duba *(n. )* **pumpkin**
ዱብታ dubta *(n. )* **thud**
ዱኹም dukhum *(adj.)* **listless**
ዱኽዒ duk'i *(n.)* **manure**
ድዑል d'ül *(n.)* **ram**
ዱር dur *(n.)* **forest**
ዱር dur *(n.)* **rainforest**
ዱር ኣብረሰ dur abrese *(v.)* **deforest**
ዱውየት duwyet *(n.)* **leprosy**
ድውሶ dwso *(n.)* **batter**
ደው ኣበለ dwuo aabele *(v.)* **cease**
ዱዉይ dwuy *(n. )* **leper**
ድንጋገ dngage *(n.)* **ordinance**
ጀርመን ger-man *(n.)* **German**
ጀነረተር generater *(n. )* **generator**
ጂኦሜትሪ geo-met-ery *(n. )* **geometry**
ጃህራ ĵahra *(v.)* **boast**
ጃጃዊ jajawi *(n.)* **coward**
ጃኬት ĵakeet *(n. )* **jacket**
ጃኬት ĵakeet *(n.)* **blazer**
ጃኬት ዝናብ jaket znab *(n.)* **raincoat**

ጃልባ መትሓዚ ዓሳ jalba methazi asa *(n.)* **trawler**
ጃልባ ĵalba *(n.)* **boat**
ጃምላ jamla *(n.)* **wholesale**
ጃንጥላ jantla *(n. )* **parachute**
ጀብጀ ብ jebjeb *(n.)* **tassel**
ጀግና jegna *(adj.)* **gallant**
ጅግና jegna *(n.)* **hero**
ጅግንነት jegninet *(n. )* **gallantry**
ጅግንነታዊ jegn-netawi *(adj. )* **heroic**
ጀላቲ jelati *(n.)* **ice-cream**
ጀልባ jelba *(n.)* **yacht**
ጀልፋፍ jelfaf *(adj.)* **unkempt**
ጀልጋድ jelgad *(adj.)* **slovenly**
ጀማሊ jemali *(n.)* **wholesaler**
ጀማራይ jemaray *(n.)* **starter**
ጀማሪ jemari *(n.)* **novice**
ጀመረ jemere *(v.)* **launch**
ጀመረ jemere *(v.)* **start**
ጀመረ ĵemere *(v.)* **begin**
ጀምር jemr *(v.)* **initiate**
ጀኦግራፊ ĵe'ografi *(n.)* **geography**
ጀራግዐ jerag'ë *(v.)* **bungle**
ጀርባዶ jerbado *(n.)* **rectum**
ጀርዲን jerdin *(n. )* **garden**
ጅግና jgna *(adj.)* **courageous**
ጅግና ĵgna *(adj.)* **gutsy**
ጅግንነት jgnnet *(n.)* **courage**
ጃህራ ĵhra *(n.)* **pomposity**
ጅምላ ቅጥለት jimla qtlet *(n.)* **massacre**
ጅኢምናስት jimnast *(n.)* **gymnast**
ጅኢምናስቲካዊ jimnastikawi *(n. )* **gymnastic**
ጂምናዝየም jimnazyem *(n.)* **gymnasium**
ጂንስ ĵins *(n.)* **jeans**
ጂኦግራፈኛ ji'ografi'gna *(n.)* **geographer**
ጂኦግራፍያዊ ji'ografiyawi *(adj.)* **geographical**
ጂኦሜትራዊ ji'omeetrawi *(adj.)* **geometric**
ጂፕሲ jipsi *(n.)* **gypsy**
ጅለ-ሰበይቲ ĵlesebeyti *(n.)* **bodice**
ጅምናስቲክ መስርሒ ዕራት jmnastic mesrhi arat *(n.)* **trampoline**
ጅነ jne *(n.)* **quid**
ጅራታም ኮኾብ ĵratam *(n.)* **comet**
ጅርባ ĵrba *(n.)* **canvas**
ጁባ juba *(n.)* **coat**
ጀመረ ĵemere *(v.)* **commence**
ጁባ ĵuba *(n.)* **pocket**
ጁዶ ĵudo *(n.)* **judo**
ጁፒተር ĵupiter *(n. )* **Jupiter**
ጃኩዚ ğakuzii *(n.)* **Jacuzzi**
ጀሆ ğeho *(n. )* **hostage**
ጀለብያ ዚመስል ናይ ጃፓን ክዳን ğelebya zimesl nay japan kdan *(n.)* **kimono**
ጁት ĵut *(n.)* **jute**
ጅግንነት ğgnnet *(n.)* **valour**
ጅለ ğle *(n.)* **vest**
ጅውታ ማይ jwta may *(n.)* **downpour**

## ገ

ገለጸ gelexe *(v.)* **wreak**
ገዛ geza *(n.)* **house**
ገልበጠ gelbete *(v.)* **overthrow**
ገደፈ gedefe *(v.)* **omit**
ገድላዊ ጉዕዞ gedlawi gu'ëzo *(n.)* **odyssey**
ግማ'ድ gmad *(n.)* **hunk**

ጎንዶላ gondola *(n.)* **gondola**
ጎሮሮ gororo *(n.)* **gullet**
ጉድኣት gud'at *(n.)* **harm**
ጉልባብ gulbab *(n.)* **veil**
ጉራማይለ guramayle *(adj.)* **variegated**
ጉዑር gu'ür *(n.)* **gravel**
ገዚፍ ዓይነት ከልቢ gezif 'äynet kelbi *(n.)* **bulldog**
ገፅታ trfi *(n.)* **profile**
ጉንጓ gungua *(n.)* **owl**
ጊዜ ዘሕለፈ gizie zehlefe *(adj.)* **overdue**
ጊዜ ዝሓለፎ gizie zhalefo *(adj.)* **outdated**
ጋሕጣጥ gahtat *(adj.)* **obtuse**
ግልጺ gltsi *(adj.)* **overt**
ንጹር nxur *(adj.)* **obvious**
ግልፂ ርእይቶ gltsi r'eyto *(adj.)* **outspoken**
ግምገም ባሕሪ gemgem bahri *(adj.)* **offshore**
ግርምቢጥ grmbit *(n.)* **oddity**
ግዚኡ ዝሓለፈ gziu zhalefe *(adj.)* **obsolete**
ግዳማዊ gdamawi *(adj.)* **outlandish**
ግዳማዊ ሃገር gdamawi hager *(adv.)* **overseas**
ግዴታ gdeta *(n.)* **obligation**
ግዴታ gdeta *(adj.)* **obligatory**
ግዴታ ዘይኮነ gdieta zeykone *(adj.)* **optional**
ጋዓዝ ga'äz *(n.)* **baggage**
ኮክፒት kokpit *(n.)* **cockpit**
ጋቢያ gabiya *(n.)* **hutch**
ጋቢያ ሰፈር ከልቢ gabiya sefer kelbi *(n. )* **kennel**
ጋብላ gabla *(n.)* **trough**
ጋድም gadm *(adj. )* **horizontal**

ጋእ በለ ga'e bele *(v.)* **baulk**
ጋዕጋዕ gaëgaë *(adj.)* **foul**
ጋዕጋዕ ga'ëgaë *(n.)* **slattern**
ጋእጋእ በለ ga'ega'e bele *(v.)* **flounder**
ጋእታ ga'eta *(n.)* **reflex**
ጋዕዘየ ga'ëzeye *(n.)* **corrupt**
ጋዕዘየ ga'ëzeye *(v.)* **debauch**
ጓሓፍ gahaf *(n.)* **trash**
ጋህዲ gahdi *(adj.)* **real**
ጋሕግሐ gahghe *(v.)* **snarl**
ጋሕማጥ gaĥmat *(adj.)* **disorganized**
ጋሕማጥ gaȟmaẗ *(adj.)* **awkward**
ጋሕር gaĥr *(adj.)* **rocky**
ጋህሲ gahsi *(n.)* **sepulchre**
ጋሌጣ galeta *(n.)* **Rusk**
ጋሎን galon *(n. )* **gallon**
ጋማ gama *(n.)* **matrimony**
ጋኔን ganeen *(n.)* **hobgoblin**
ጋኔን ganeen *(n.)* **bogey**
ጋኔን ganen *(n.)* **demon**
ጋንታ ganeta *(n.)* **club**
ጋንስላ gansla *(n. )* **panther**
ጋንታ ganta *(n. )* **squad**
ጋንታ ወታደራት ganta wetaderat *(n. )* **platoon**
ጓንቲ ganti *(n.)* **thimble**
ጋንፀላ gantsla *(n.)* **sail**
ጋራዲ garadi *(n.)* **blinkers**
ጋራጅ gara-j *(n. )* **garage**
ጋርዘ garze *(n.)* **gauze**
ጓሰሰ gasese *(v.)* **scuff**
ጋሻ gasha *(n. )* **guest**
ጋሻ gasha *(n.)* **stranger**
ጋጽ gats *(n.)* **stable**
ጋውሕታ gawhta *(n. )* **jackal**
ጋዝ gaz *(n. )* **gas**
ጋዜጣ gazeeẗa *(n. )* **journal**

ጋዜጠኛ gazeeťeňa *(n. )* **journalist**
ጋዜጠኛነት gazeeťeňanet *(n.)* **journalism**
ጋዜጣ gazeta *(n. )* **gazette**
ግቢ gbi *(n.)* **premises**
ግብራዊ gbrawi *(adj.)* **practical**
ግብራዊ gbrawi *(adj.)* **virtual**
ግብራዊ ዝኾነ gbrawi zḱone *(adj.)* **practicable**
ግብራውነት gbrawnet *(n.)* **practicability**
ፕራግማትነት pragmatnet *(n. )* **pragmatism**
ግብረ ሰናይ gbre senay *(n.)* **philanthropy**
ግብረ ስጋ gbre sga *(n.)* **intercourse**
ኮርፎ korfo *(n.)* **shag**
ግብረ-ኣበር gbre'aber *(n.)* **accomplice**
ግብረ-ሰዶመኛ gbresedomeña *(n.)* **homosexual**
ግብረ ሰናያዊ gbresenayawi *(n. )* **philanthropist**
ግብሪ gbri *(n.)* **tax**
ግብሪ ዝክፈለሉ gbri zkfelelu *(adj.)* **taxable**
ግብሪ gbri *(n.)* **capitation**
ግብታ gbta *(n.)* **blackout**
ግብጣን gbťan *(n.)* **captain**
ግብጣኒ gbťani *(n.)* **captaincy**
ግብታዊ g'btawi *(adj.)* **spontaneous**
ግብታውነት g'btawinet *(n.)* **spontaneity**
ግቡእ gbuè *(adj.)* **proper**
ግብዝና gbzna *(n.)* **cant**
ግጭት gcct *(n.)* **collision**
ግጭት gčt *(n.)* **conflict**
ግዳማዊ gdamawi *(adj.)* **superficial**
ግዳማዊ ኣደጎ gdamawi adego *(n.)* **epidermis**
ግዳማዊ ትረኢት gdamawi tr't *(n.)* **facade**
ግዳማይ gdamay *(adj.)* **exterior**
ግድዓት gd'ät *(n.)* **jeopardy**
ግድብ gdb *(n.)* **weir**
ግድድፍ gddf *(n.)* **compromise**
ግደ gde *(n. )* **role**
ግዲ ዘይብሉ gdi zeyblu *(adj.)* **phlegmatic**
ግዲ ዘይብሉ gdi zeyblu *(adj.)* **remiss**
ግዴታ gdieta *(adj.)* **mandatory**
ግዴታ gdieta *(v.)* **undertake**
ግድን ምባል gdn mbal *(n.)* **insistence**
ግድነት gdnet *(adv. )* **perforce**
ግድነታዊ gdnetawi *(adj.)* **compulsory**
ግዱስ gdus *(adj.)* **responsive**
ገዓረ ge'äre *(v.)* **rap**
ገዓት geät *(n. )* **porridge**
ገዓት ge'ät *(n. )* **mush**
ገብ ኣበለ geb abele *(v.)* **slam**
ገባር-ሰናይ gebar senay *(adj.)* **beneficent**
ገባሪ ዉሕጅ gebari wuhj *(n.)* **tributary**
ገበል gebel *(n.)* **python**
ገበል gebel *(n. )* **serpent**
ገበላ gebela *(n.)* **portico**
ገበን geben *(n.)* **crime**
ገበን geben *(n.)* **guilt**
ገበናዊ gebenawi *(adj.)* **penal**
ገበነኛ gebenegna *(n.)* **dacoit**
ገበነኛ geben-egna *(n.)* **gangster**
ገበነኛ gebeneña *(n.)* **villain**
ገበነኛ gebenenya *(n.)* **convict**
ገበነኛ gebenenya *(n.)* **criminal**
ገበነኛ gebenenya *(n.)* **culprit**

ገበነኛ gebenenya *(n.)* **felon**
ገበንነኛ ኣብ ባሕሪ ዝዝርፍ gebenǹa ab baȟri zzrf *(n.)* **pirate**
ገበረ gebere *(v.)* **act**
ገበረ gebere *(v.)* **do**
ገበረ gebere *(v.)* **render**
ገበረ gebere *(v.)* **behave**
ገበጣ gebeta *(n.)* **skittle**
ገበተ gebete *(v.)* **sequester**
ገብገብ ኣበለ gebgeb abele *(v.)* **flutter**
ገቢረ-ሰናይ gebiresenay *(n.)* **benefactor**
ገዳም gedam *(n.)* **abbey**
ገዳም gedam *(n.)* **cloister**
ገዳም gedam *(n.)* **minster**
ገዳም gedam *(n.)* **monastery**
ገዳም gedam *(n.)* **nunnery**
ገዛ ኣበምኔት geza 'abemneet *(n.)* **priory**
ገደብ gedbb *(n.)* **constraint**
ገደብ gedeb *(n.)* **limit**
ገደበ gedebe *(v.)* **circumscribe**
ገደፈ gedefe *(v.)* **relinquish**
ገደል gedel *(n.)* **scarp**
ገድላ gedla *(adj.)* **arable**
ጌጋ geega *(n.)* **error**
ጌጋ geega *(n.)* **lapse**
ጌጋ ሓበሬታ ነገረ geega ȟabereeta negere *(v.)* **misinform**
ጌጋ ስልሒት geega slȟit *(n.)* **miscalculation**
ጌጋ ትርጉም ሃበ geega trgum habe *(v.)* **misinterpret**
ጌጋ ፀብፃብ ሃበ geega xebxab habe *(v.)* **misrepresent**
ጌጋ ግንዛበ geege gnzabe *(n.)* **misconception**
ገፋፍ gefaf *(adj.)* **sluggish**
ገፋፍ ዓሳ gefafi äsa *(n.)* **fisherman**
ገፈፈ gefefe *(v.t.)* **strip**
ገፈሐ gefeȟe *(v.)* **expand**
ገፍሐ gefhe *(v.)* **widen**
ገፊሕ gefih *(adj.)* **wide**
ገፊሕ gefiȟ *(adj.)* **spacious**
ገፊሕ በዓቲ gefihe beatii *(n.)* **cavern**
ገፍላው geflaw *(adj.)* **baggy**
ጌጋ gega *(n)* **demerit**
ግዕጋዕ g'ëga'ë *(n.)* **filth**
ሸልቒ shelqwi *(adj.)* **torrid**
ገሃነም gehanem *(n. )* **hell**
ገሃንማዊ gehanmawi *(adj.)* **infernal**
ገሃሰ gehase *(v.)* **violate**
ገሃጸ gehatse *(v.)* **gnaw**
ገሃጸ gehaxe *(v.)* **browse**
ገጅፍ ዝዓይነቱ geĵf z'äynetu *(adj.)* **jumbo**
ገጂፍ gejif *(adj.)* **massive**
ገላፂ ዓንቀፅ gelatsi änqets *(n.)* **predicate**
ገልበጠ gelbeẗe *(v.)* **capsize**
ገልዒ gel'e *(n.)* **shard**
ገለ ቦታ gele bota *(adv. )* **somewhere**
ገለ ነገር gele neger *(pron. )* **something**
ገለ ሰብ gele seb *(pron. )* **somebody**
ገለፈ gelefe *(v.)* **disqualify**
ገለፃ geletsa *(n.)* **description**
ገለፀ geletse *(v.)* **define**
ሓንጸጸ ȟanxexe *(v.)* **delineate**
ገለፀ geletse *(v.)* **describe**
ግልፅነት geletsinet *(n. )* **clarity**
ኣፍለጠ 'afleẗe *(v.)* **announce**
ኣበጻጽሐ 'abexaxȟe *(v.)* **convey**
ገለፀ gelexe *(v.)* **express**
ገልተው geltew *(n.)* **bobble**
ገምቢ ge'mbi *(n.)* **carcass**

**መዳወር** medawer ***(n.)*** **cable**
**ገመድ** gemed ***(n.)*** **rope**
**ገመድ** gemed ***(v.)*** **strand**
**ገመድ** gemed ***(n.)*** **string**
**ድባራ ፍሕሶ** dbara fĥso ***(n.)*** **twine**
**ገመድ ባንዴራ** gemed bandeera ***(n.)*** **halyard**
**ገመድ ገረብ** gemed gereb ***(n.)*** **withe**
**ገመድ መሰል** gemed mesel ***(adj.)*** **stringy**
**ገመድ ሳእኒ** gemed sa'eni ***(n.)*** **shoestring**
**መእሰር ናይ መርከብ** me'èser nay merkeb ***(n.)*** **bollard**
**ገመል** gemel ***(n.)*** **beam**
**ምቕልልና** gemel ***(n.)*** **politeness**
**ገመሰ** gemese ***(v.)*** **bisect**
**ግምታዊ ሓሳብ** gemetawi hasabe ***(n. &v.)*** **conjecture**
**ግምት** gmt ***(v.i)*** **guess**
**ገመተ** gemete ***(v.)*** **presume**
**ቀመረ** qemere ***(v.t.)*** **reckon**
**ገመተ** gemete ***(v.)*** **suppose**
**ገመተ** gemete ***(v.t.)*** **surmise**
**ገመተ** gemete ***(v.)*** **assume**
**ገመተ** gemete ***(v.)*** **speculate**
**ገመየ** gemeye ***(v.t. )*** **sprain**
**ገምጋሚ** gemgami ***(n.)*** **actuary**
**ደንደስ** dendes ***(n.)*** **embankment**
**ገምገም** gemgem ***(n.)*** **shore**
**ገምገም ባሕሪ** gemgem bahiriyi ***(n.)*** **coast**
**ገምገም ባሕሪ** gemgem baĥri ***(n.)*** **beach**
**ገምገመ** gemgeme ***(v.)*** **assess**
**ገምገመ** gemgeme ***(v. i)*** **evaluate**
**ገምገመ** gemgeme ***(v.)*** **appraise**
**ገምራዊ** gemrawi ***(n.)*** **intuitive**
**ገምሪ** gemri ***(n.)*** **fluke**
**ገምሪ** gemri ***(n.)*** **intuition**
**ገምጠለ** gemẗele ***(v.)*** **invert**
**ገንጫር** genchar ***(adj.)*** **stroppy**
**ገነት** genet ***(n. )*** **paradise**
**ገንሐ** genhe ***(v.)*** **scold**
**ገንሐ** genĥe ***(v.t. )*** **rebuke**
**ገንሐ** genĥe ***(v.)*** **reprove**
**ገንዘብ** genzeb ***(n.)*** **currency**
**ገንዘብ** genzeb ***(n. )*** **money**
**ገንዘብ አኽፋሊ** genzeb akfali ***(n. )*** **teller**
**ገንዘብ ሕድሪ ምብላዕ** genzeb ĥdri mbla'ë ***(v.)*** **misappropriation**
**ገንዘብ ሰብ ሓሸሸ** genzeb seb ĥasheshe ***(v.)*** **misappropriate**
**ገንዘብ ወፈየ** genzeb wefeye ***(v.)*** **endow**
**ገንዘባዊ** genzebawi ***(adj.)*** **financial**
**ገንዘባዊ** genzebawi ***(adj.)*** **monetary**
**ገራሚ** gerammi ***(adj.)*** **incredible**
**ገረፈ** gerefe ***(v.)*** **flog**
**ገረፈ** gerefe ***(v.)*** **thrash**
**ገረንገራት** gerengerat ***(n.)*** **vertebra**
**ገረዘ** gereze' ***(v.)*** **circumcise**
**ገርሂ** gerhi ***(adj.)*** **artless**
**ገርሂ** gerhi ***(adj.)*** **innocent**
**ግርማ ሞገስ** gerima moges ***(n.)*** **charisma**
**ገርናው** gernaw ***(adj.)*** **senile**
**ግሩም ፀባይ** gerum tse-bay ***(n.)*** **gentility**
**ስንቀን** snqen ***(v.)*** **snuff**
**ገሰፀ** gesexe ***(v.)*** **chastise**
**ገሰጸ** gesexe ***(v.)*** **admonish**
**ገስጋስ** gesgas ***(adj.)*** **progressive**
**ገሸ** geshe ***(v.t. )*** **perambulate**
**ዘይጽፉፍ** zeyxfuf ***(n.)*** **lout**
**ገስረጥ** gesret ***(adj.)*** **sloppy**
**ገስረጥ** gesreẗ ***(adj.)*** **messy**

**ገጣሚ** geẗami *(n.)* **poet**
**ገታር** getar *(adj.)* **insolent**
**ገታር** getar *(adj.)* **wilful**
**ግእታርነት** getarnet *(n.)* **insolence**
**ዓገተ** gete *(v.)* **prevent**
**ገትእ** get'e *(n. )* **restrict**
**ገጠመ** geṭeme *(v.)* **versify**
**ገጠራዊ** geterawi *(adj.)* **rustic**
**ገጠራዊነት** geterawnet *(n.)* **rusticity**
**ገጽ** gets *(n.)* **page**
**ገፅ ከልእ** gets kel'e *(v.)* **snub**
**ገፀበ** getsebe *(v.)* **spatter**
**ገዋድ** gewad *(n.)* **frump**
**ገውታ** gewta *(n.)* **bang**
**ገፅ** gex *(n.)* **face**
**ገጽ** gex *(n. )* **visage**
**ገፅ ሰብ** gex seb *(n.)* **countenance**
**ገጸ ባህሪ** gexe bahri *(n.)* **persona**
**ገያሺ** geyashi *(n.)* **voyager**
**ገያሺት ሰረገላ** geyashit seregela *(n.)* **stagecoach**
**ጌይፂ** geysi *(n.)* **trimming**
**ገይፂ** geytzi *(n. )* **jewellery**
**ጀዝ** ĵez *(n. )* **walnut**
**ገዛ** geza *(n.)* **abode**
**ገዛ** geza *(n.)* **home**
**ገዛ ገጠር** geza geṭer *(n.)* **grange**
**ገዛ ርእሲ** geza r'esi *(n.)* **self**
**ገዛኢ** geza'i *(n. )* **governor**
**ገዛኢ** geza'i *(n.)* **ruler**
**ገዛኢት እኖ** geza'it eno *(n.)* **matriarch**
**ገዝአ** gez'e *(v.)* **govern**
**ግዝአ** gez'e *(v.)* **rule**
**ዓደገ** 'ädege *(v.)* **buy**
**ገዝገዘ** gezgeze *(v.)* **saw**
**ገዚፍ** gezif *(adj.)* **enormous**
**ገዚፍ** gezif *(adj.)* **gigantic**
**ገዚፍ** gezif *(adj. )* **huge**
**ገዚፍ** gezif *(adj.)* **prodigious**
**ገዚፍ** gezif *(adj.)* **sizeable**
**ገዚፍ** gezif *(adj.)* **stupendous**
**ገዚፍ እንስሳ ባሕሪ** gezif 'ensssa bahri *(n.)* **walrus**
**ገዚፍ ከውሒ** gezif kewḧi *(n.)* **megalith**
**ገዚፍ** gezife *(adj.)* **colossal**
**ገዚፍ** gezife *(adj.)* **large**
**ገዚፍን ብርቱዕን** gezifn brtu'ë *(adj. )* **hefty**
**ግዕዝም** g'ezm *(n.)* **sausage**
**ግዕዝም ጀርመን** g'ëzm jermen *(n.)* **frankfurter**
**ገዝሚ** gezmi *(n.)* **dowry**
**ግዕዙይ** g'ëzuy *(adj.)* **corrupt**
**ግዕይዝና** g'ëzyna *(n.)* **corruption**
**ግፋዕ በረድ** gfa'ë bered *(n.)* **moraine**
**ግፍዒ** gf'i *(n.)* **atrocity**
**ግጉይ** gguy *(adj.)* **amiss**
**ኮብላሊ** koblali *(adj.)* **errant**
**ግጉይ** gguy *(adj.)* **erroneous**
**ግጉይ** gguy *(adj.)* **wrong**
**ግጉይ** gguy *(adj.)* **wrongful**
**ግጉይ ሓሳብ** gguy ĥasab *(n.)* **fallacy**
**ግጉይ ማሕተም** gguy maḧtem *(n.)* **misprint**
**ግህሰት** ghset *(n. )* **violation**
**ግሁድ** ghud *(adj.)* **flagrant**
**ግሁድ** ghud *(adj.)* **candid**
**ጊዲ** gidi *(n.)* **mascot**
**ጊጋባይት** gigabayt *(n.)* **gigabyte**
**ጊላ** gila *(n.)* **vassal**
**ግንዛበ** ginizabe *(n.)* **cognizance**
**ግንዛበ ዘለዎ** giniza'be zelewo *(adj.)* **conscious**
**ጊንጢ** ginti *(adj.)* **eccentric**
**ጊንጢ** ginẗi *(n.)* **freak**

ጊታር gitar *(n. )* **guitar**
ጊታር ዝመስል መሳርሒ ሙዚቃ gitar zmesl mesarhi muziqa *(n.)* **lute**
ጊዮሶ giyoso *(n.)* **gudgeon**
ጊዜዊ gizawi *(n.)* **interim**
ጊዜዊ መምበሪ gizawi menberi *(n. )* **lodging**
ግዜያዊ giziyawi *(adj.)* **temporal**
ግዜያዊ giziyawi *(adj.)* **temporary**
ጎጆ gjo *(n.)* **wigwam**
ግላዕ gla'ë *(n.)* **block**
ግላዕ gla'ë *(n.)* **stave**
ግላዊ glawi *(adj.)* **personal**
ግላዊ አቕሑ glawi 'aq̈hu *(n.)* **belongings**
ግልባ ዝሰልጠነ glba zseltene *(n.)* **trotter**
ግልግል glgl *(n.)* **riddance**
ግሊሰሪን gliserin *(n.)* **glycerine**
ክልተ ግዘ glte gze *(adv. )* **twice**
ግልጺ gltsi *(adj.)* **straightforward**
ግልጺ gltsi *(adj.)* **undeniable**
ግልጺ ዘይኮነ gltsi zeykone *(adj.)* **indefinite**
ግልጺ ዘይኮነ ሰብ gltsi zeykone seb *(n.)* **introvert**
ግልጺ gltzi *(adj.)* **frank**
ግሉኮዝ glukoz *(n. )* **glucose**
ግሉል glul *(adj.)* **aloof**
ግሉል glul *(n.)* **recluse**
ግሉል glul *(adj.)* **secluded**
ግልፅነት glxnet *(n.)* **candour**
ግመ gme *(n.)* **fog**
ግመ gme *(n. )* **mist**
ግመኣዊ gme'awi *(adj. )* **hazy**
ግመል gmel *(n.)* **camel**
ግምገማ gmgema *(n.)* **assessment**
ግምሱስ gmsus *(adj.)* **recumbent**
ግምት gmt *(v. t)* **estimate**
ግምት gmt *(n.)* **supposition**
ግምት g'mt *(n.)* **speculation**
ግምት gmt *(n.)* **presumption**
ግምት ብምሃብ gmt bmhab *(prep.)* **considering**
ግምት gmt *(n.)* **assumption**
ግምታዊ gmtawi *(adj.)* **approximate**
ግምታዊ gmtawi *(adj.)* **notional**
ግምጡል gmtul *(adj.)* **inverse**
ግምየት gmyet *(n.)* **refraction**
ግን gn *(conj.)* **but**
ግናዕ ኢድ gnae ide *(n.)* **paw**
ኛው gnaw *(v.)* **mew**
ግናይ gnay *(adj. )* **hideous**
ግናይ gnay *(adj.)* **ungainly**
ግንባር gnbar *(n.)* **forehead**
ግምባረኛ ነገር gnbaregna neger *(n.)* **talisman**
ግንቦት g'n'bot *(n.)* **May**
ግነት gnet *(n.)* **exaggeration**
ግንፋለ gnfale *(n.)* **upsurge**
ግንፋለ g'nfale *(n.)* **surge**
ጎኒጎኒ ዝከይድ ጎብጋብ ርቡዕጎናዊ gnigoni zkeyd gobgab rubue kurnawi *(n.)* **parallelogram**
ግምጀኛ gnjegna *(n. )* **treasurer**
ግንዮት gnyot *(n.)* **discovery**
ግንዛበ gnzabe *(n.)* **appreciation**
ጎባጥ gobat *(n.)* **curve**
ጎባይ gobay *(n.)* **buffalo**
ጎበጠ gobet'e *(v.)* **warp**
ጎበዝ gobez *(n.)* **guy**
ጎበዝ ጨማቲ gobez chemati *(n. )* **marksman**
ጎብለል goblel *(n.)* **champion**
ጎብናዪ gobnayi *(n. )* **tourist**
ጎብነይቲ ምስትእንጋድ gobneyti mstengad *(n. )* **tourism**
ጎዳኢ goda'e *(adj.)* **injurious**

ጐዳኢ goda'i *(adj.)* **deleterious**
ጎድአ god'e *(v.)* **hurt**
ጎድአ god'e *(v.)* **injure**
ጎደሎ godelo *(adj.)* **deficient**
ጎደና godena *(n. )* **street**
ጎድጋድ ሽሓነ godgad shehane *(n. )* **tub**
ጎድናዊ-ምርጫ godnawimrča *(n.)* **by-election**
ጎድነ-ጎድኒ godnegodni *(adv.)* **abreast**
ጎፍጓፍ gofgwaf *(adj.)* **bushy**
ጎሓፍ go-haf *(n. )* **garbage**
ጎሓፍ goĥaf *(n. )* **refuse**
ጎሓፍ goĥaf *(n. )* **rubbish**
ጎሃየ gohaye *(v.)* **rue**
ጎጀለ gojele *(v.)* **classify**
ጎጀለ goje-le *(v.)* **categorize**
ጋቢና gabina *(n.)* **cabin**
ጎጆ gojo *(n.)* **lodge**
ጎጆ ንህቢ gojo nehbi *(n.)* **hive**
ጎጆ goĵo *(n.)* **booth**
ጐልዓመ golame *(v.)* **truncate**
ጎልፎ gole 'foo *(n.)* **cardigan**
ጎልፍ golf *(n. )* **golf**
ጎልፎ golfo *(n.)* **jersey**
ጎልፎ golfo *(n.)* **sweater**
ጎልጎል golgol *(adj.)* **plain**
ጎልጎል ሳዕሪ golgol saëri *(n.)* **paddock**
ጎልሓጥ golĥaẗ *(adj.)* **gawky**
ጎሎ golo *(n.)* **haunch**
ጎሎ golo *(n.)* **pelvis**
ጎልጠመ golteme *(v.)* **quaff**
ጎማ goma *(n. )* **rubber**
ጎመድ gomed *(n.)* **cudgel**
ጎመድ gomed *(n.)* **bludgeon**
ጎምጠጥ gomẗeẗ *(n.)* **berry**
ጐናነጸ gonanetse *(v.)* **hustle**
ጎነጸ gonetse *(v.)* **shove**
ጎነጻዊ gonexawi *(adj.)* **violent**
ሽምጢ shmẗi *(n.)* **flank**
ጎኒ goni *(n.)* **side**
ጎኒ ባሕሪ goni bahri *(n.)* **seaside**
ጎኒጎኒ gonigoni *(n. )* **parallel**
ጎንፂ gonxi *(n.)* **bump**
ጎራዕራዕ በለ gora'ëraë bele *(v.)* **gurgle**
ጥበበኛ ẗbebeňa *(adj.)* **shrewd**
ጎራሕ gorah̆ *(adj.)* **artful**
ጎረንዳዮ gorandayo *(n. )* **gutter**
ጎረቤት gorebeet *(n. )* **neighbour**
ጎርጎረ gorgore *(v.)* **ransack**
ጎርጎረ gorgore *(v.)* **rummage**
ጎሮሮ gororo *(n.)* **throat**
ወሸፍ weshif *(n.)* **damsel**
ሳዱላ sadula *(n.)* **maiden**
ጓልሕድርትና gwalĥdrtna *(n)* **nymph**
ጎርዞ gorzo *(n.)* **wench**
ጎሳ gosa *(n. )* **tribe**
ጎታት gotat *(adj.)* **languid**
ጎተተ gotete *(v. t)* **drag**
ጎተተ gotete *(v.)* **tow**
መርከብ እትስሕብ ጃልባ merkeb 'ètsh̆b ĵalba *(v.)* **tug**
ጎቲም gotim *(adj.)* **blunt**
ጐያዪ goyayi *(n. )* **runner**
ጎያዪ ኣትለት goyayi atlet *(n.)* **sprinter**
ጎየየ goyeye *(v.)* **run**
ጎይቋ goyqwa *(n.)* **quarrel**
ጎይታ goyta *(n.)* **liege**
ጎይታ goyta *(n.)* **lord**
ጎይታ goyta *(n.)* **master**
ጎይታቲ goytati *(adj.)* **bossy**
ጎይታይ goytay *(n. )* **sir**
ጎዞሞ gozomo *(n.)* **chopper**

ግራጭ grach *(n.)* **spike**
ግራፋይት grafayt *(n.)* **graphite**
ግራም gram *(n. )* **gram**
ግራመ grame *(n.)* **amazement**
ግራት መቐለቢ ጥሪት grat meqlebi trit *(n.)* **pasture**
ግራዘ graze *(n.)* **cubicle**
ግርደት grdet *(n.)* **eclipse**
ግረባ greba *(n.)* **afforestation**
ግርጉርነት grgurnet *(n.)* **notoriety**
ግርህነት grhnet *(n.)* **innocence**
ግርህነት grhnet *(n.)* **naivety**
ተራ ምኽን tera mḱwan *(n.)* **simplicity**
ግርማ ሞገስ ዘለዎ grma moges zelewo *(adj.)* **dignified**
ግርምቢጥ grmbiť *(adj.)* **grotesque**
ግርምብያለ grmbyale *(n. )* **smock**
ግርምብያለ grmbyale *(n.)* **apron**
ግርንውና grnwuna *(n.)* **senility**
ግርሳም grsam *(adj.)* **myopic**
ግርሳመ grsame *(n.)* **myopia**
ግሩም grum *(adj.)* **majestic**
ግሩም grum *(v.i)* **marvel**
ግሩም grum *(adj.)* **posh**
ግርዝውና grzwna *(n.)* **puberty**
ግስጋሰ gsgase *(v.)* **advance**
ግስጋሰ gsgase *(n.)* **going**
ግሲ gsi *(n.)* **verb**
ግስሩጥ gsrut *(adj.)* **squalid**
ግጥም g-tim *(n.)* **game**
ግጥም g'ť'm *(n.)* **match**
ግጥ'ም gẗm *(n.)* **bout**
ግጥማዊ gtmawi *(adj.)* **lyrical**
ግጥሚ ወይ ደርፊ gẗmi wey derfi *(n.)* **ballad**
ግጥሚ gẗmi *(n. )* **poem**
ጓዳ guada *(n.)* **panel**
ጓሂ guahi *(n.)* **heartache**
ጓል gual *(n.)* **puss**
ጓል ንጉስ gual ngus *(n. )* **princess**
ጓንቲ ብረት gua-nti bret *(n.)* **gauntlet**
ጉዕዞ guazo *(n.)* **tour**
ጉዕዞ guazo *(v.)* **travel**
ጉባኤ guba'ee *(n.)* **congress**
ጉቦ gubo *(v. t.)* **bribe**
ጉዳም gudam *(adj.)* **queer**
ጉድኣት gudat *(n.)* **trauma**
ሓደጋ ḧadega *(n.)* **casualty**
ዘይምቹእ ኩነት zeymchu'è kunet *(n.)* **disadvantage**
ጉድኣት gud'at *(n.)* **fatality**
ጉዳይ guday *(n.)* **affair**
ጉዳይ guday *(n. )* **issue**
ጉዳይ guday *(n. )* **matter**
ጉድጓድ gudgad *(n.)* **pit**
ጉድጓድ gudgwad *(n.)* **burrow**
ጉድለት gudlet *(n.)* **defect**
ጉድለት gudlet *(n.)* **flaw**
ሕጽረት ḧxret *(n.)* **shortcoming**
ጉድለት ምሕደራ gudlet mḧdera *(n. )* **misrule**
ጉድለት ተሞክሮ gudlet temokro *(n.)* **inexperience**
ጉድኣት gudu'at *(n.)* **injury**
ጉዕዞ gu'ëzo *(n.)* **journey**
መገሻ megesha *(n.)* **voyage**
ጉጅለ guge-le *(n.)* **category**
ጉሕ guḧ *(n. )* **niche**
ጉሒላ ኣፍቃሪ guḧila afqari *(n.)* **Casanova**
ጉጅለ gujele *(n.)* **group**
ጉጂ guji *(n.)* **cottage**
ዕሙር 'ëmur *(n.)* **cluster**
ጉጅለ gujle *(n.)* **squadron**
ጉጅለ gujle *(n.)* **troupe**

**ጉልባብ** gulbab ***(n.)*** **shroud**
**ጉልበት** gulbet ***(n.)*** **energy**
**ጉልበተኛ** gulbetegna ***(adj.)*** **strapping**
**ጉልቻ** gulcha ***(n.)*** **trivet**
**ጉለ** gule ***(n.)*** **udder**
**ጉልሓጥሓጥ በለ** gulḥaṭḥaṭ bele ***(n. )*** **goggle**
**ጉልተኛ** gultegna ***(n. )*** **squire**
**ምምሕዳር ሰበኻ** mmḧdar sebeḱa ***(n.)*** **benefice**
**ጉልቲ** gulti ***(n.)*** **estate**
**ጉሉሕ** guluĥ ***(adj.)*** **prominent**
**ጉሉሕነት** guluĥnet ***(n.)*** **prominence**
**ጉንቦ ኢድ** gunbo 'id ***(n. )*** **wrist**
**ጉንዲ** gundi ***(n. )*** **timber**
**ጉንዲ** gundi ***(n. )*** **trunk**
**ጉንዲ** gundi ***(n.)*** **bole**
**ጉርሒ** gurḧi ***(n. )*** **prude**
**ጉርዒ** gur'ï ***(n.)*** **ravine**
**ጉርዞ ባሕሪ** gurzo baḧri ***(n. )*** **mermaid**
**ጉስጢ** gusẗi ***(n)*** **boxing**
**ጉስጢ** gusẗi ***(v.)*** **punch**
**ጉስያዊ** gusyawi ***(adj.)*** **evasive**
**ጉያ** guya ***(n.)*** **run**
**ጉያ** guya ***(v.)*** **sprint**
**ጉዚ** guzi ***(n. )*** **fraction**
**ጎደና** gwadena ***(n.)*** **avenue**
**ጎደና** gwadena ***(n.)*** **boulevard**
**ጎድኒ** gwadni ***(n.)*** **facet**
**ጎሓፍ** gwaḧaf ***(n. )*** **junk**
**ጎሃረ** gwahare ***(v.)*** **glow**
**ጓሃየ** gwahaye ***(v.)*** **bemoan**
**ጓሂ** gwahi ***(n. )*** **grief**
**ጓሂ/ሕርቃን** gwahi /ĥrkan ***(n.)*** **dejection**
**ጓሂ** gwahi ***(n.)*** **anguish**
**ጓል** gwal ***(n.)*** **daughter**
**ጓል** gwal ***(n.)*** **girl**
**ፍቕርቲ** fqrti ***(n.)*** **lass**
**ናይ ክርስትና ውላድ** gwal blgna ***(n.)*** **godchild**
**ጓል ሓው** gwal ḧaw ***(n. )*** **niece**
**ጓልጓሎ** gwalgwalo ***(n.)*** **sissy**
**ጓንጓ** gwangwa ***(n.)*** **cavity**
**ጓንቲ** gwanti ***(n.)*** **glove**
**ጎራዕራዕ በለ** gwara'ëra'ë bele ***(v.)*** **burble**
**ጎራሕ** gwaraḧ ***(adj.)*** **canny**
**ጎርጎሐ** gwargwaḧe ***(v.)*** **bore**
**ጓሳ ኣባጊዕ** gwasa abagi'ë ***(n. )*** **shepherd**
**ጓዘመ** gwazeme ***(v.)*** **roar**
**ጎዘየ** gwazeye ***(v.t.)*** **apportion**
**ጎዘየ** gwazeye ***(n.)*** **usurpation**
**ጓዝማ** gwazma ***(n.)*** **roar**
**ጓና** guana ***(n.)*** **outsider**
**ጎፍ በለ** gwof bele ***(v.)*** **accost**
**ግይፅታ** gytsta ***(v.)*** **smirk**
**ግዛዕ** gza'e ***(n.)*** **thing**
**ግዝኣት** gzat ***(n. )*** **territory**
**ግዝኣት** gz'at ***(n.)*** **colony**
**ኣውራጃ** awraĵa ***(n.)*** **county**
**ንግስነት** ngsnet ***(n.)*** **empire**
**ዓውዲ** 'äwdi ***(n.)*** **realm**
**ግዝኣታዊ** gzatawi ***(adj.)*** **territorial**
**ግዝፊ** gzfi ***(n.)*** **immensity**
**ግዝፊ** gzfi ***(n.)*** **size**
**ግዜ** gzie ***(n.)*** **time**
**ግዜኡ ዘይበጽሐ** gzieeu zeybexḧe ***(adj.)*** **premature**
**ግዜያዊ** gziyawi ***(adj.)*** **transitory**
**ግዝያዊ ሓፁር** gziyawi hatzur ***(n.)*** **hoarding**
**ግዜያዊ** gziywi ***(adj.)*** **transient**
**ግዙእ** gzu'e ***(n.)*** **retainer**
**ግዝዋ** gzwa ***(n.)*** **moth**

ግዜያዊ ፈጻሚ gzeeyawi fexami *(adj.)* **acting**
ግዝያዊ gzyawi *(adj.)* **provisional**
ህሞታዊ hmotawi *(adj.)* **momentary**
ግዝያዊ ተኹሲ-ዕጾ gzyawi tekusi'ëxo *(n.)* **armistice**
ጎድናዊ godnawi *(adj.)* **outboard**

# ጠ

ጠርጠረ ṭerṭere *(v.)* **impeach**
ጠቕለለ ṭeqlele *(v.)* **wrap**
ጠንካራ ṭenkara *(adj.)* **virile**
ጠንቋሊ ṭenqwali *(adj.)* **fey**
ጠንቋሊት ṭenqwalit *(n.)* **hag**
ጠሊ ṭeli *(n.)* **humidity**
ጠጥዐ ẗeẗ'e *(v.)* **sprout**
ጠረጴዛ terebeza *(n.)* **table**
ጠርዐ ẗer'ë *(v.)* **complain**
ጠቕጠቐ teqteqe *(v.)* **cram**
ጠራዓይ teraay *(n.)* **petitioner**
ጠወየ ṭeweye *(v.)* **wrest**
ጠባዊ ẗbawi *(n.)* **sucker**
ጠበቓ tbeqha *(n.)* **lawyer**
ጠምበርበር በለ ẗemberber bele *(n.)* **blunder**
ጠዓሞት ẗe'ämot *(n.)* **snack**
ጠዓየ ẗe'aye *(v.)* **survive**
ሰብኣዊ መንነት seb'awi mennet *(n.)* **personality**
ጠባይ ẗebay *(n.)* **conduct**
ቀመማዊ qememawi *(n.)* **hexogen**
ጠባይ ẗebay *(n.)* **behaviour**
ጠበንጃ tebenja *(n.)* **rifle**
ጠበንጃ ṭebenja *(n.)* **gun**
ጠበቃ ẗebeqa *(n.)* **solicitor**
ጠበቓ ẗebeq̈a *(n.)* **attorney**
ጠበቓ ẗebeq̈a *(n.)* **barrister**
ጠበቕ tebeqh *(n.)* **lizard**
ጠባብሐ tebabhe *(v.)* **dissect**
ጠበሰ ẗebese *(v.)* **fry**
ጠቕላላ ርእዮት teqlala r'eyot *(n.)* **overview**
ጠብላቕ teblaq *(adj.)* **officious**
ጠፊኡ tefiu *(adv.)* **off**
ጠኣት ta'ot *(n.)* **oracle**
ጥራይ tray *(adv.)* **only**
ጥርዚ-ስምዒት trzi sm'it *(n.)* **orgasm**
ጥቅምቲ tkemti *(n.)* **October**
ጥፍኣታት tfatat *(n.)* **onslaught**
ጠፍ አበለ ẗef abele *(v.)* **flick**
ጠፍአ tef'a *(v.)* **decamp**
ጠበወ ẗebewe *(v.)* **suck**
ጠብሒ tebhi *(n.)* **sauce**
ጠቢብ tebib *(adj.)* **wise**
ጥንሰ-ሓሳብ tebse hasab *(n.)* **hypothesis**
ጤረር ሞገድ teerer moged *(n.)* **surf**
ጠፋኢ tefa'i *(adj.)* **perishable**
ጠፍሐ tef'e *(v.)* **skim**
ጠፈረ-ህዋ ẗeferehwa *(n.)* **aerospace**
ጠፈርተኛ ẗeferteǹa *(n.)* **astronaut**
ጠፊኡ tefi'u *(v.)* **perish**
ጠፍታ ẗefta *(n.)* **spat**
ጠፍጠፈ ẗefẗefe *(v.)* **spank**
ጠገለ ዝሰኣነ መደረ ẗegele zse'ane medere *(adj.)* **fulsome**
ጠገለ-ኣልቦ ẗegele'albo *(n.)* **boor**
ጠሓለ teĥale *(v.)* **drown**
ጠሓለ teĥale *(v.)* **sink**
ጠሓለ ẗehale *(v.)* **submerge**
ጠሓለ ẗehale *(v.)* **submerse**
ጠሓሊ ẗeȟali *(adj.)* **submersible**
ጠሓሰ tehase *(v.)* **infringe**
ጠሓሰ tehase *(v.)* **trespass**
ጠቓሚ tekami *(adj.)* **useful**
ጠቕላላ teklala *(n.)* **total**

ጠቅላላ teklala *(adj.)* total
ጠማሪ temari *(adj.)* cohesive
ጠልቀየ ẗelqeye *(v.)* soak
ጠማዕ tema'e *(n.)* scrooge
ጥንቁቕ ẗnquq *(adj.)* frugal
በቃቅ beqaq *(adj.)* miserly
ጠማዕ ẗema'ë *(n.)* niggard
ጠማዕ ẗema'ë *(adj.)* niggardly
ኣተወ 'atewe *(v. t)* dip
ጠመረ ẗemere *(v.)* belay
ጠመረ ẗemere *(v.)* bind
ጠመተ temete *(v.)* regard
ጠመተ ሃበ temete habe *(v.)* emphasize
ጠመየ ẗemeye *(v.)* starve
ጠጠመ ẗeẗeme *(v.)* nibble
ጠጠው በለ ẗeẗew bele *(v.)* halt
ጠጠው ምባል ẗeẗew mbal *(v.)* pose
ጠጠው ምባል ẗeẗew mbal *(n. )* standstill
ጉራሕ gwarah *(adj.)* crooked
ጠዋይ ẗeway *(adj.)* wry
ጠዋይ ẗeway *(n.)* kink
ጠስሚ ẗesmi *(n.)* butter
ጠረዘ tereze *(v. t)* deport
ጠርነፈ ẗernefe *(v.)* compile
ጠቕነ ẗeqhene *(n.)* stigma
ጠቅለለ teqlele *(v.)* rewind
ጠቀር ẗeqer *(n.)* soot
ጠቀሰ teqese *(v.)* quote
ጽቅጠት ዓይኒ xqtet 'äyni *(v.)* wink
ጠቀሰ ẗeqese *(v.)* mention
ጠቐሰ ẗeqese *(v.)* adduce
ጠቓሚ teqhami *(adj.)* important
ጠቓምነት teqhamnet *(n.)* importance
መሓጎስ mehagws *(n.)* boon
ጠቓሚ ẗeqami *(adj.)* expedient

ጠቓሚ ሙኳን teqami mukwan *(v.)* pertain
ጠቓሚ ẗeqami *(adj.)* advantageous
ጠቓሚ ẗeqami *(adj.)* productive
ጠርጠረ ẗerẗere *(v.)* mistrust
ጠርጠረ ẗerẗere *(adj.)* suspicious
ጠርዚ ẗerzi *(n.)* striation
ጠረፍ ẗeref *(n.)* brink
ጠንቀሊ tenqali *(n.)* seer
ጠንቃዊ ẗenqawi *(adj.)* causal
ጠንካራ tenkaara *(adj.)* tough
ጠንካራ ẗenkara *(adj. )* hardy
ጠንካራ ዕርዲ ẗenkara ërdi *(n.)* stronghold
ጠንካራ ናይ ኣሞራ ጨፍሪ tenkara nay amora chifri *(n.)* talon
ጠንከረ tenkere *(v.)* toughen
ጠከሰ tekese *(v.)* cite
ጠላዕ telae *(n.)* whist
ጠላዕ ẗela'ë *(n.)* camber
ጠላለፈ telalefe *(v.t. )* tangle
ጠላም telam *(adj.)* slippery
ጠለብ teleb *(n.)* demand
ጠንቛሊ ẗenqwali *(n. )* sorcerer
ጠላብ teleb *(n.)* requirement
ጠንቂ tenqi *(adj.)* pernicious
ጠንቂ ኣለርጂ ẗenqi alerji *(n.)* allergen
ጠንቅነት ẗenqnet *(n.)* causality
ጠንቛሊ tenquali *(n.)* wizard
ጠንቛሊት tenqualit *(n.)* witch
ጡብ ኣድጊ ẗub 'adgi *(n.)* wart
ጡብ ẗub *(n.)* breast
መኣዛዊ me'azawi *(adj.)* savoury
ጥዑም t'um *(adj.)* tasteful
ጥዑም t'um *(adj.)* tasty
ሕያዋይ ጸጋዊ hyaway xegawi *(adj.)* gracious

**ጥዑም ነገር ዝሓዘ ብያቲ** t'um neger zhaze byati *(n.)* **tart**
**ጡንኩር ዘይኮነ** tunkur zeykone *(adj.)* **lenient**
**ጡንኩር ዘይኮነ ኣተሓሳስባ** tunkur zeykone atehasasba *(n.)* **leniency**
**ጡረታ** ẗureta *(n.)* **superannuation**
**ጡጥ** ẗuẗ *(n.)* **cotton**
**ዘይጽሉል** zeyxlul *(adj.)* **sane**
**ጥዑይ** ẗ'uy *(adj. )* **hale**
**ጥውይዋይ** twuyway *(adj.)* **serpentine**
**ጥውይዋይ** twyway *(adj.)* **sinuous**
**ጣኦት** ẗa'ot *(n.)* **fetish**
**ጣልቃ ኣተወ** ẗalqa 'atewe *(v.)* **intervene**
**ጣልያናዊ** talyanawj *(adj.)* **italic**
**ጣሕሸም በለ** taȟšem bele *(v.)* **rustle**
**ጣንጡ** ẗanẗu *(n. )* **mosquito**
**መለኮታዊ ባህርይ** melekotawi bahry *(n.)* **deity**
**ጣኦት** ẗa'ot *(n.)* **goddess**
**ጣኦት** ţa'ot *(n. )* **idol**
**ጣኦት ኣምልኾ** ţa'ot 'amlḱo *(n.)* **idolatry**
**ጣዕሚ** ta'emi *(n.)* **taste**
**ጣዕሚ ዘይብሉ** ta'emi zeyblu *(adj.)* **tasteless**
**ጣዕሳ** ta'ësa *(n.)* **remorse**
**ጣቋ** ẗaq̈ua *(n.)* **proficiency**
**ጣቋ ዘረባ** taqwa zereba *(n.)* **rhetoric**
**ጣፍያ** ẗafya *(n.)* **spleen**
**ጣሻ** tasha *(n. )* **thicket**
**ጣጥያ** tatya *(n.)* **shingle**
**ቲክ** tik *(n. )* **teak**
**ጣውላ** tawla *(adj.)* **wooded**
**ኣርማዲዮ** 'armadiyo *(n.)* **cupboard**
**ጣውላ እግሪ** tawla egri *(n. )* **skirting**
**ጣውላ** ẗawla *(n.)* **board**
**ጤል** ţeel *(n. )* **goat**
**ጥዕና** ţ'ëna *(n.)* **health**
**ጥረ** tre *(adj.)* **uncouth**
**ዘይበሰለ** zeybesele *(adj.)* **crude**
**ጉዕ** gu'ë *(adj.)* **callow**
**ጥረ-ሕጡብ** ẗreȟẗub *(n.)* **adobe**
**ጥሪ** ẗri *(n.)* **January**
**ጥርሑ** ţrḥu *(adj.)* **vacant**
**ጥርሑ** ẗrȟu *(adj.)* **empty**
**ጥርሑ** ẗrȟu *(adj.)* **bare**
**ጥርሑ** ẗrȟu *(adj.)* **blank**
**ጥርዓን** tran *(n.)* **petition**
**ጥርዓን** ẗr'än *(n.)* **complaint**
**ጥርሙዝ** ẗrmuz *(v.t. )* **glass**
**ጥርሙዝ** ẗrmuz *(n.)* **bottle**
**ጥርሙዛዊ** ţrmuzawi *(adj.)* **vitreous**
**ጥርንቕ ዘብል ስረ** trnqh zble sre *(n.)* **leggings**
**ጥርኑፍ** ẗrnuf *(adj.)* **compact**
**ጥራይ** ẗ'ray *(adj.)* **mere**
**ጥሜት** ẗmiet *(n.)* **famine**
**ጥምጥም** tmtam *(n. )* **turban**
**ጥንግንግ** ţngng *(n. )* **labyrinth**
**ጥንቁቕ** ţnquq̈ *(adj.)* **wary**
**ጥቕላል ፈትሊ** ţq̈lal fetli *(n.)* **hank**
**ጥቅሰ ሳምዕ** ẗqse sam'ë *(n.)* **epitaph**
**ጥቕሲ** ẗqsi *(n.)* **excerpt**
**ጥቅላል** ẗqlal *(n.)* **bundle**
**ጥቕላል** ẗq̈lal *(n. )* **packet**
**ጥቅላል ብራና** tqlal brana *(n.)* **scroll**
**ጠቓምነት** ẗeq̈amnet *(n.)* **utility**
**ጥቕሚ** ẗq̈mi *(n. )* **pro**
**ጥቅሚ ዘለዎ** tqmi zelewo *(adj.)* **salutary**
**ጥቅሲ** tqsi *(n.)* **quotation**
**ጥቅሲ** ẗ'q'si *(n.)* **maxim**
**ጥንቁቕ** ẗnquq̈ *(adj.)* **chary**
**ጥቑብ** tqub *(adj.)* **reticent**

**ጥቂው** ẗquw ***(adj.)* proficient**
**ጥቃ** ẗqa ***(adj.)* adjacent**
**ጥቓንጥቓ** tqaneteqa' ***(adj.)* contiguous**
**ጥበብ** tbeb ***(n. )* wisdom**
**ጥበብ ስእሊ** tbeb seli ***(n.)* photography**
**ጥበብ** ẗbeb ***(n.)* art**
**ጥበበኛ** tbebegna ***(adj.)* tactful**
**ጥበበኛ** tbebenya ***(n.)* craftsman**
**ጥብቂ** tbki ***(adj.)* thorough**
**ጥብቀት** ẗbqet ***(n.)* attachment**
**ጥብቂ** ẗbqi ***(adj.)* strict**
**ጥብቂ ሰብ** ẗbqi seb ***(n. )* stickler**
**ጥብቂ** ẗbqi ***(adj.)* austere**
**ጥብጥብ በለ** tbtb bele ***(v. i)* drip**
**ጥብጥታ** tbtbta ***(n.)* tap**
**ጥብጠባ** ẗbẗeba ***(adj.)* spanking**
**ጥቡቕ** tbuk ***(adj.)* tenacious**
**ጥቡቅ ርክብ** tbuq rkb ***(n.)* rapport**
**ጥሩምባ** trumba ***(n.)* trumpet**
**ጥሩምባ** ṭrumba ***(n. )* horn**
**ጥሩምባ** ẗrumba ***(n.)* bugle**
**ጥሮታ** trota ***(n.)* pension**
**ጥሮተኛ** trotena ***(n.)* pensioner**
**ጥርጣረ** trtare ***(n.)* distrust**
**ጥርጣረ** trtare ***(n.)* doubt**
**ጥርጣረ** ẗr'ẗare ***(n.)* suspicion**
**ጥርዛዊ** trzawi ***(adj.)* peaky**
**ዝለዓለ ነጥቢ** zle'äle neẗbi ***(n. )* peak**
**ወሰን ዓንኬል** wesen 'änkeel ***(n. )* rim**
**ጥርዚ** ṭrzi ***(n. )* verge**
**ጥርዝያ** ẗrzya ***(n.)* banishment**
**ጥንሲ** ẗnsi ***(n.)* pregnancy**
**ጥንስቲ** ẗnsti ***(adj.)* pregnant**
**ጥንታዊ** tntawi ***(adj.)* primeval**
**ወደባት** wedebat ***(adj.)* aboriginal**
**ጥንታዊ** ẗntawi ***(n.)* antique**
**ጥንታዊ** ẗntawi ***(adj.)* ancient**
**ጥንታዊ** ẗntawi ***(adj.)* archaic**
**ጥንቲ** ẗnti ***(n.)* antiquity**
**ጦብሎቕ በሃሊ** ẗobloq̈ behali ***(n.)* interloper**
**ጦፍታ** ẗofta ***(n.)* fillip**
**ጥንቁቅ** tenquq ***(adj.)* cautious**
**ጥሙይ** temuy ***(adj.)* hungry**
**ጥዕና አእምሮ** t'ena a'emro ***(n.)* sanity**
**ጥዑም ግዜ** ṭ'üm gzee ***(n. )* heyday**
**ጥዑይ** ṭ'üy ***(adj. )* healthy**
**ጥንካረ** tenkara ***(n.)* tenacity**
**ጥንካሬ** tenkara ***(n.)* toughness**
**ጥራጥረ** teraterre ***(n.)* cereal**
**ጥማር** ẗmar ***(n.)* bunch**
**ጥሜት** ẗmeet ***(n.)* starvation**
**ጥምቀት** ẗmqet ***(n.)* baptism**
**ጥምረት** tmret ***(n.)* cohesion**
**ጥሙይ** tmuy ***(adj.)* skimp**
**ጥምየት** ṭmyet ***(n.)* hunger**
**ጥንቢ ክንቲት** tnbi kntit ***(n.)* shuttlecock**
**ጥንካረ** ẗnkare ***(n.)* stringency**
**ጥንቆላ** tnkola ***(n.)* tarot**
**ጥንቃቓዊ** ẗnqaq̈awi ***(adj.)* precautionary**
**ጥንቃቐ** ẗnqaq̈e ***(n.)* precaution**
**ጥንቃቔ ዘይፈልጥ** tnqaqhie zeyfelt ***(adj.)* imprudent**
**ጥንቅልዕሽው** ẗnql'ëshew ***(n.)* somersault**
**ጥንቆላ** tnqola ***(n. )* witchcraft**
**ጥንቆላ** tnqola ***(n.)* witchery**
**ጥንቆላ** ẗnqola ***(n.)* sorcery**
**ስቱር** stur ***(adj.)* discreet**
**ንጥንቁቕን ትኽክልን** nẗnquq̈n tḱkln ***(adj.)* meticulous**
**ጥንቁቕ** ẗnquq̈ ***(adj.)* alert**

ጥንቁቕ ïnquq̈ *(adj.)* **attentive**
ጥንቁቕ ïnquq̈ *(adj.)* **painstaking**
ጥንቁቕ ïnquq̈ *(adj.)* **prudential**
ጥንቁቕ ţnquq̈ *(adj.)* **vigilant**
ጥልቀት ïlqet *(n.)* **anti-climax**
ጥልቀት ኣልቦነት ïlqet albonet *(n.)* **superficiality**
ጥልቂ ïlqi *(adj.)* **abstruse**
ጥልቁይ t'lquy *(adj.)* **soggy**
ጥልቁይ ïlquy *(adj.)* **sopping**
ጥማር timar *(n.)* **ticket**
ጥንቁቅ tinkuq *(n.)* **combination**
ጥሪት trit *(n. )* **property**
ጥቕላል tklal *(adj.)* **exact**
ጥልፊ tlfi *(n.)* **embroidery**
ሪካሞ rikamo *(n. )* **sampler**
ሳላሚ salami *(n. )* **motif**
ጥልመት ïlmet *(n.)* **betrayal**
ጥሑል ïhul *(adj.)* **sunken**
ጥሕሰት thset *(n.)* **infringement**
ጥፈሻ ïfesha *(n.)* **bankruptcy**
ጥፉሽ ïfush *(adj.)* **bankrupt**
ጥፉሽ ïfush *(adj.)* **broke**

## ጬ

ጨቆነ čeqone *(v.)* **oppress**
ጸቃጢ xeq̈aïi *(adj.)* **oppressive**
ጨቋኒ čeqwani *(n.)* **oppressor**
ጨና chena *(n.)* **odour**
ጨንፈር ĉenfer *(n. )* **offshoot**
ጫፋቱ ተደራረበ chafatu tederarebe *(v.)* **overlap**
ጭቆና cheqona *(n.)* **oppression**
መወዳእታ meweda'ëta *(n. )* **end**
ጫፍ čaf *(n.)* **acme**
ጫፍ čaf *(n)* **apex**
ጫፍ ብርዒ čaf br'ï *(n.)* **nib**
ጫፍ čaf *(n.)* **brim**
ጫሕጫሕ ኣበለ čaȟčaȟ 'abele *(n.)* **jingle**
ጫካ čaka *(n.)* **jungle**
ጫማ ĉama *(n.)* **shoe**
ጫቍት čaqwit *(n. )* **nestling**
ጫዉጫዉታ ĉawĉawta *(n.)* **din**
ጭበጣ ĉbeta *(n. )* **shrinkage**
ጭቡጥ čbuť *(n.)* **concrete**
ጫፍ ccaf *(n.)* **climax**
ጭፍራ ከዋኽብቲ ccfra ke'wakib'ti *(n.)* **constellation**
ጩቕ በለ cchuq' bel'le *(v.)* **chirp**
ጭልታ cclta *(n.)* **clink**
ጨዳድ cdade *(n.)* **cleft**
ጨዓይ ጸጉሪ ዘለዎ ĉe'äy xeguri zelewo *(adj.)* **blonde**
ጨብጨባ čebčeba *(n.)* **applause**
ጨበጠ čebeťe *(v.)* **compress**
ጨብረቅረቅ ĉebreqreq *(n.)* **ripple**
ጨካን ĉekan *(adj.)* **ferocious**
ኣረመን 'aremen *(n.)* **fiend**
ጨካን ĉekan *(adj.)* **ruthless**
ጨካን čekan *(adj.)* **cruel**
ጨካን ፍጥረት čekan fťret *(n.)* **harpy**
ጨካን čekan *(n.)* **behemoth**
ጨለ čele *(adj.)* **adroit**
ጨማደደ ĉemadede *(v.)* **rumple**
ጨናዊ ĉenawi *(adj.)* **funky**
ጨነወ ĉenewe *(v.)* **reek**
ጨንፈር ĉenfer *(n.)* **ramification**
ጨንፈር ሕክምና ህጻናት čenfer ȟkmna hxanat *(n.)* **paediatrics**
ጨንፈር čenfer *(n.)* **branch**
ጨቓዊት čeq̈awit *(n.)* **brood**
ጨቅጨቀ čeqčeqe *(v.t. )* **nag**
ጨራዕራዕ በለ ĉera'ëraë bele *(v.)* **sizzle**

ጨረር ĉerer *(n.)* **ray**
ጨረርታ ĉererta *(n.)* **radiation**
ጨርሐ ĉerĥe *(v.)* **exclaim**
ጨርቂ ĉerqi *(n.)* **rag**
ጨርቂ ሽንቲ ĉerqi shnti *(n.)* **diaper**
ጨወየ çewey *(v.)* **kidnap**
ጨወየ čeweye *(v.t.)* **abduct**
ጭፍራ čfra *(n.)* **fleet**
ሕዳግ ĥdag *(n.)* **ledge**
ጫፍ čaf *(n.)* **tip**
ዝለዓለ ነጥቢ zle'äle neẗbi *(n. )* **zenith**
ጫፍ ch'af *(n.)* **summit**
ጫሕገረ chaĥgere *(adj.)* **streaky**
ጫካ chaka *(n. )* **woodland**
ጪካ ዝተሸፈነ ገቦ chaka ztexefene gebo *(n.)* **wold**
ጭቡጥ ch'buẗ *(adj.)* **substantive**
ምጭባጥ mčbaẗ *(v.)* **clasp**
ጨበጠ chebeẗe *(v.)* **squeeze**
ዓትዓተ 'ät'äte *(v.)* **grip**
ጨጫፍ chechaf *(n.)* **periphery**
ቸኮላታ checolata *(n.)* **chocolate**
ጨደደ chedede *(v.)* **cleave**
ጨደረ che-dere *(n.)* **howl**
ጨፋለቀ chefaleqe *(v.)* **mangle**
ጨፍለቐ chefleqhe *(v.)* **squash**
ጨጓር čheguar *(adj. )* **hairy**
ጨጉሪ ኣምበሳ ወይ ፈረስ cheguri ambesa wey feres *(n. )* **mane**
ጭሕሚ ድሙ chehmi *(n. )* **whisker**
ኣረመናዊ 'aremenawi *(adj.)* **savage**
ንቒጽ nüqux *(adj.)* **stark**
ጨካን chekan *(adj.)* **uncharitable**
ጨካን çhekan *(adj. )* **heartless**
ጨካን ኣምባ ገነን chekan ambagenen *(n. )* **tyrant**
ጨለ chele *(adv.)* **well**
ጨምዳድ chemdad *(adj.)* **wizened**
ጨና chena *(n.)* **perfume**
ጨና ምልካይ chena mlkay *(adv. )* **perfume**
ጨነወ chenewe *(v.)* **stink**
ጨንፈር chenfer *(n.)* **sprig**
ጨረት cheret *(n.)* **tick**
ጨርቃ ጨርቂ cherka cherki *(n)* **textile**
ጨው chew *(n.)* **salt**
ጨዋም chewam *(adj.)* **saline**
ጨዋም chewam *(adj.)* **salty**
ጨዋምነት chewamnet *(n.)* **salinity**
ጭሕጋር čĥgar *(n.)* **comma**
ጭጋረት chgaret *(n.)* **livery**
ጭጋረት chgaret *(n.)* **species**
ጨሓጋገረ chhagagere *(v.)* **scrabble**
ጭሕጋር ch'ĥgar *(n.)* **streak**
ጭፍጨፋ chif'chefa *(n.)* **carnage**
ጭኮንበሳ chikonbesa *(n.)* **cheetah**
ጭቃ chiqa *(n.)* **clay**
ጭካነኣዊ chkane-awi *(adj. )* **heinous**
ጭከና chkena *(n.)* **savagery**
ጭሕሚ čĥmi *(n.)* **beard**
ጭንጫ ch'ncha *(adj.)* **stony**
ጭንቀት chnqet *(n.)* **stress**
ጭንቂ chnqi *(n.)* **woe**
ጭንቂ ዝመልኦ chnqi zmelo *(adj.)* **woeful**
ጭኑቕ chnuq *(adj.)* **strained**
ኣጨናቒ ačenaqi *(adj.)* **worrisome**
ጭሖሎ čĥolo *(n.)* **bowl**
ጨቊኑ chqinu *(v.)* **tyrannize**
ጭራ chra *(n. )* **tail**
ጭራም chram *(n.)* **piece**
ጭርቃን chrqan *(n.)* **parody**
ጭሩ chru *(n.)* **wagtail**

ጭሩ ገበላ chru gebela *(n.)* **sparrow**
ጩቅ በለ chuqk' bele *(n.)* **cheep**
ጩራ chu-ra *(n. )* **girder**
ጭከነ čkane *(adv.)* **cruelty**
ጭንጫ ĉnĉa *(n.)* **detritus**
ጭንፋር ቀርኒ čnfar qerni *(n.)* **antler**
ኛኽ ምበል ňak mbal *(n.)* **fuss**
ምሽቓል mshq̈al *(n.)* **anxiety**
ጭንቂ ĉnqi *(n.)* **distress**
ጭንቁራዕ ĉnqura'ë *(n. )* **frog**
ጫፍ çaf *(n.)* **vertex**
ጨካን ĉekan *(adj.)* **evil**
ጭፍራ çfra *(n. )* **horde**
ጭፉን ĉfun *(n.)* **fanatic**
ጨንገር ምድ'ቓል çhenger mdq̈al *(n.)* **graft**
ጨወየ cheweye *(v.)* **hijack**
ጭኑቕ ĉnuq *(adj.)* **febrile**
ጭራሮ በረድ çraro bered *(n.)* **icicle**
ጭቃ čqa *(n.)* **bailiff**
ሓመዳይ[ንሕብሪ] ዝተደናገረ ȟamedaynȟbri ztedenagere *(n. )* **mud**
ጭራምዑት čram'ut *(n.)* **appendix**
ጭራዋጣ ĉrawaẗa *(n.)* **fiddle**
ችርችራ ĉrĉera *(n. )* **retail**
ጭርጭርታ cr'crta *(n.)* **trill**
ጭረት čret *(n.)* **apostrophe**
ጭርሖ ĉrȟo *(n. )* **slogan**
ጭርሖ čr̈ȟo *(n. )* **motto**
ጭርታ črta *(n.)* **aperture**
ጩራ ĉura *(n. )* **radius**
ልዙብ lzub *(adj.)* **genteel**
ጭዋ ĉ'wa *(adj.)* **decent**
ጭዋዳ čwada *(n. )* **muscle**
ጭዋዳዊ čwadawi *(adj.)* **muscular**
ጭውነት ĉ'wnet *(n.)* **decency**
ጭውያ čwya *(n.)* **abduction**
ጭብጨባ ĉbĉeba *(n.)* **ovation**
ጭንቀት chenqet *(n.)* **obsession**
ጭከነ abi wenjel *(n.)* **outrage**

# ጰ

ጲጵታ p̈ipta *(n.)* **bleep**
ጳጳስ ṕapas *(n. )* **pope**
ጲራቅሊጦስ peeraqlitos *(n.)* **whit**
ጵጵስና ppsna *(n.)* **papacy**

# ጸ / ፀ

ጸላዕላዕ tsela'ela'e *(adj.)* **sunny**
ጸዕዳ xaeda *(adj.)* **white**
ጸዕደወ xa'ëdewe *(v.)* **blanch**
ጸዕቂ xa'ëqi *(n.)* **congestion**
ጸዕረኛ xa'ëreňa *(adj.)* **assiduous**
ጸላም-ዓይኒ tselam'äyni *(n. )* **liver**
ጸህያይ xahyay *(n.)* **weed**
ጸጸ xaxe *(n.)* **ant**
ጸጸ መጺጽ xaxe mexix *(adj.)* **antacid**
ጽባቐ xbaq̈ *(n.)* **prettiness**
ጽባቐ ጽሕፈት xbaq̈e xȟfet *(n.)* **calligraphy**
ጽባቐኣዊ xbaq̈e'awi *(adj.)* **aesthetic**
ጽብቕቲ xbq̈ti *(n.)* **belle**
ፅቡቕ xbuq *(adj.)* **fine**
ጽዱይ xduy *(adj.)* **aseptic**
ጽድያዊ xdyawi *(adj.)* **vernal**
ጸዓደ xe'äde *(v.)* **assert**
ፀዓረ xe'äre *(v.)* **endeavour**
ፀባ xeba *(n.)* **milk**
ፀባ መሰል xeba mesel *(adj.)* **milky**
ፀባይ xebay *(n.)* **character**

ፀብሒ xebhi *(n.)* **chutney**
ፀቢብ xebib *(adj.)* **narrow**
መሳፍሒ ዘይብሉ mesafĥi zeyblu *(adj.)* **poky**
ፀብለልታ xeblelta *(n.)* **excellence**
ናይ ተጻባጻቢ ሞያ nay texabaxabi moya *(n.)* **accountancy**
ጸብጻብ xebxab *(n.)* **audit**
ፀብፃቢ xebxabi *(n.)* **correspondent**
ፅምብል xeembil *(n.)* **ceremony**
ፀፍዐ xef'ë *(v.)* **swat**
ፀፍዒ xef'ï *(n.)* **flurry**
ፀፊሕ xefiĥ *(adj.)* **flat**
ጸፊሕ ሸሓኒ xefiĥ sheĥani *(n.)* **platter**
ፀገም xegem *(n.)* **mishap**
ፀገነ xegene *(v.)* **mend**
ፀጉሩ ረገፈ xeguru regefe *(v.)* **moult**
ጸሓፊ xeḥafi *(n.)* **writer**
ፀሓፊ ኖቬል xeĥafi noveela *(n. )* **novelist**
ጸሓፊ ቲያትር xeĥafi tyatr *(n.)* **playwright**
ጽዕነት xëinet *(n.)* **pack**
ፀላኢ xela'i *(n.)* **enemy**
ፀላኢ xela'i *(n.)* **foe**
ፀላም xelam *(n. )* **negress**
ጸልአ xel'e *(v.)* **abominate**
ጸለቑ xeleq̈wu *(v.)* **abscond**
ጸለወ xelewe *(v.)* **affect**
ፀሊም xelim *(n.)* **negro**
ጸሊም መዝገብ xelim mezgeb *(n.)* **blacklist**
ፀሊም ሞሉስኮ xelim molusko *(n.)* **mussel**
ጸሊም ጸጉሪ xelim xeguri *(n.)* **brunette**
ጸሊም xelim *(adj.)* **black**
ጸሎት xelot *(n.)* **prayer**
ጸመቈ xemeq̈we *(v.)* **wring**
ጸመቈ xemeq̈we *(v.)* **brew**
ጸምሪ xemri *(n.)* **fleece**
ጸምሪ xemri *(n.)* **fur**
ፀንበረ xenbere *(v.)* **annex**
ጸንዐ xene *(v.)* **persist**
ጸንዐ xen'ë *(v.i)* **abide**
ፅዕነት x'ënet *(n.)* **cargo**
ጸቕጢ xeq̈iṫu *(n.)* **pressure**
ጸቕጣዊ xeq̈ṫawi *(v.)* **pressurize**
ጸረ xere *(n.)* **anti**
ጸረ ባልዕ xere ble *(n. )* **pesticide**
ጸረ-ጓና ኣካል xere gwana 'akal *(n.)* **antibody**
ጸረ-ሕንዚ xere ĥnzi *(n.)* **antidote**
ጸረ-ምቅፀፃል xere mqxxal *(n.)* **antioxidant**
ጸረበ xerebe *(v.)* **whittle**
ጸረ-ማሕበራዊ xeremaĥberawi *(adj.)* **antisocial**
ጸረ-ነፍሳት xerenefsat *(n.)* **antibiotic**
ጸረ-ቃንዛ xereqanza *(n.)* **analgesic**
ጸረ-ረኽሲ xerereќsi *(adj.)* **antiseptic**
ጽረጉ xerigu *(v.)* **pave**
ጸቓጡ xeṫiṫu *(v.)* **press**
ፅዋዕ xewaee *(n.)* **chalice**
ጸወታ xeweta *(v.i. )* **play**
ጸጸር xexer *(n. )* **pebble**
ጸህያይ ባሕሪ xahyay baḥri *(n. )* **wrack**
ጸጋማይ ገጽ xegamay gex *(n.)* **verso**
ጸሓፈ xeḥafe *(v.)* **write**
ጸንሐ xenḥe *(v.)* **wait**
ጽሕፈት xḥfet *(n.)* **writing**
ጽን በሃሊ xn behali *(adj.)* **wakeful**
ጽቡቕ tsebuq̈ *(adj.)* **good**
ጽኪ tseki *(n. )* **gland**
ጽርግያ tsergya *(n.)* **highway**
ጽፍዒት xf'it *(v.)* **whack**

ፅፉፍ xfuf *(adj.)* **natty**
ፅፉፍ xfuf *(adj.)* **neat**
ፅግዕ xg'ë *(n.)* **mumps**
ጽገ ዕንባባ xge ënbaba *(n.)* **pollen**
ጽግዕተኛ xg'ëteña *(adj.)* **ancillary**
ፅሕዲ xĥdi *(n.)* **fir**
ፅሕዲ ሊባኖስ xhdi libanos *(n.)* **cedar**
ፅሕዲ ቆጵሮስ xĥdi qopros *(n.)* **cypress**
ፅሕፍቶ xĥfto *(n.)* **fate**
ጽሕፍቶ xĥfto *(n.)* **predestination**
ፅሕጊ xĥgi *(n.)* **fibre**
ጺጽ በለ xix bele *(v.)* **wheeze**
ጽላል xlal *(n.)* **parasol**
ጽልኣት xl'at *(n.)* **aversion**
ጽልኢ xl'i *(n.)* **animosity**
ፅልኢ xl'i *(n.)* **enmity**
ፅሉል xlul *(adj.)* **crazy**
ፅልዋ xlwa *(n.)* **ambit**
ፅማቝ xmaq̈wu *(n.)* **juice**
ጽምብላሊዕ xmblali'ë *(n.)* **butterfly**
ፅምዳዊ xmdawi *(adj.)* **binary**
ጽምደ-ሰልፋዊ xmdeselfawi *(adj.)* **bipartisan**
ጽምደ-ትኹረታዊ xmdetḱuretawi *(adj.)* **bifocal**
ፅምዲ xmdi *(n.)* **couple**
ጽምዲ xmdi *(n.)* **pair**
ፅምዲት xmdit *(n.)* **couplet**
ጽምሉው xmluw *(adj.)* **pale**
ፅመራ xmra *(n.)* **synthesis**
ፅንዓት xn'at *(n.)* **consolidation**
ፅንበራ xnbera *(n.)* **annexation**
ፅንብል xnbl *(n.)* **fete**
ፅንበራ x'nera *(n.)* **merger**
ፅንፈኛ xnfenya *(n.)* **extremist**
ጽኑዕ xnue *(adj.)* **persistent**
ፅኑዕ ክትትል xnu'e kt'tl *(n.)* **surveillance**
ዘይውዳእ zeywda'è *(adj.)* **abiding**
ፅንፅሕለ xnxĥle *(n.)* **flint**
ፆታ ኣልቦ xota 'albo *(adj.)* **asexual**
ጽዖታዊ x'ötawi *(adj.)* **callous**
ፅርግያ ተሽከርከርቲ xrgya teshkerkerti *(n.)* **motorway**
ጽዋ xwa *(n.)* **anecdote**
ፅውፅዋይ xwxway *(n.)* **fable**
ፅውፅዋይ xwxway *(n.)* **myth**
ጽያቕ xyaq̈ *(v.)* **blur**
ፅዩፍ xyuf *(adj.)* **abhorrent**
ጽዩፍ xyuf *(adj.)* **vulgar**
ፀጥ ዝበለ ነገር set zbele neger *(adj.)* **tranquil**
ፀጥታ setta *(n.)* **tranquillity**
ፃድቅ tsadk *(n.)* **saint**
ፃድቃዊ tsadkawi *(adj.)* **saintly**
ፃዕዳ ሽጉርቲ tsa-e-da sh-gur-ti *(n.)* **garlic**
ሕፍሰት ȟfset *(n.)* **density**
ፃዕቂ tsa'ëqi *(n.)* **intensity**
ፃዕራም tsa'eram *(adj.)* **industrious**
ጻዕረኛ xa'ëreña *(adj.)* **studious**
ፃውዒት ዝርዝር ሽም tsaw'ït zrzr šm *(adj.)* **sanitary**
ፅባሕ tsbah *(adv.)* **tomorrow**
ፍሕሹው fĥshuw *(adj.)* **pleasant**
ጽቡቕ tsbuq *(adj.)* **twee**
ንፕሮግራም nprogram *(v.)* **download**
ፀዓነ tse'anew *(v.)* **download**
ፀዓቐ tse'äqe *(v.)* **intensify**
ፀዓረ tseare *(v.i.)* **toil**
ፀዓረ tse'äre *(v.)* **strive**
ፀቢብ መተሓላልፎ tsebib meteȟalalfo *(n.)* **stricture**

ዝርዝር ጸብጻብ zrzr xebxab *(n.)* **recital**
ፀብፃብ tsebtsab *(n. )* **record**
ፀብፃብ ሃበ tsebtsab habe *(v.)* **report**
ፀብፃብ ዜና tsebtsab zena *(n.)* **reportage**
ጸዳል tsedal *(v.)* **gleam**
ፀፍዐ tsef'ë *(v.t. )* **slap**
ጸፍዒ tsef'i *(n.)* **squall**
ጸጋ tsega *(n.)* **grace**
ፀጋም tsegam *(n.)* **left**
ጸግዒ tseg'e *(n. )* **tutelage**
ዘይምቻው zeymchaw *(n.)* **discomfort**
ጸቢብ xebib *(n.)* **strait**
ሰኪዕት seki'ët *(n. )* **toils**
ጸገሙ አካፈለ tsegemu 'akafele *(v.)* **unburden**
ፀገነ tsegene *(v.)* **refit**
ፀገነ tsegene *(v.)* **repair**
ጸጓር tseguar *(adj. )* **hirsute**
ጸጉሪ tseguri *(n.)* **hair**
ፀሓፋይ tsehafay *(n.)* **scribe**
ጸሓፊ tsehafe *(n.)* **secretary**
ፀሓፊ tsehafi *(n.)* **clerk**
ፀሓፊ ተዋስኦ tsehafi tewas'o *(n.)* **dramatist**
ፀሓታተረ tsehatatere *(v.)* **scribble**
ፀሓይ tse'ḧay *(n.)* **sun**
ፀሓይ ተፀልወ tse'ḧay tetselwe *(v.)* **sun**
ፀሓያማ tse'ḧayama *(n.)* **effort**
ፃዕሪ xa'ëri *(n.)* **menstruation**
ፃግን xag'n *(n.)* **cornea**
ፃዕዳ አይኒ xa'ëda ayni *(n.)* **tingle**
ፅላል tselal *(n. )* **umbrella**
ፀላም ኸብዲ tselam kebdi *(n.)* **coriander**
ፃቅዳ xaqda *(n.)* **iris**
ፀልአ tsel'e *(v.)* **detest**
ፀልአ tsel'e *(v.)* **dislike**
ጸልአ tsel'e *(v.t. )* **hate**
ጽልኢ tsel-ei *(n.)* **hostility**
ፅልኢ ሓደሽቲ ሰባት tselei hdeshti sebat *(n.)* **xenophobia**
ፀለመ tseleme *(n.)* **defamation**
ፀለቅ tseleq *(n.)* **ransom**
ፀሊም tselim *(adj.)* **stygian**
ጸሊም እምኒ tselim 'èmni *(n.)* **granite**
ፀሊም ሊላዊ tselim lilawi *(n.)* **indigo**
ፅልም ዝበለ tselm zebele *(n.)* **umber**
ፀልማት tselmat *(n.)* **darkness**
ጽልሙት tselmut *(adj.)* **gloomy**
ፀሎት tselot *(n.)* **invocation**
ጽሉእ tselu'è *(adj. )* **hateful**
ፀማም tsemam *(adj.)* **deaf**
ፅምብል በዓል tse-m-bel be-al *(n.)* **gala**
ፀረ ምንግስቲ tse-mengsti *(n.)* **insurgent**
ፀንበረ tsenber *(v.)* **combine**
ፀንበረ tsenbere *(v.)* **conflate**
ኣእተወ 'a'ètewe *(v.)* **subsume**
ፅዕነት ts'ënet *(n.)* **shipment**
ፀንሐ tsenhe *(v.)* **remain**
ጸንሐ tsenḧe *(v.)* **stay**
ጽንጽያ tsentseya *(n.)* **gnat**
ጸቕጢ-ደም ምቅናስ tseqti dem mqnas *(n.)* **hypotension**
ጸቕጢ-ደም ምውሳክ tseqti dem mwsak *(n.)* **hypertension**
ፀራቢ tserabi *(n.)* **carpenter**
ቀራጺ qeraxi *(n.)* **sculptor**
ፀረ ዕፈና tsere ë'fena *(n.)* **decongestant**

ፀረ ለዉጢ tsere lewuti ***(adj.)* conservative**
ጸረ ቃንዛ tsere qanza ***(n.)* painkiller**
ፀረ_ባልዕ tsere-bal'e ***(n.)* insecticide**
ፀረበ tserebe ***(v.)* sculpt**
ፀረፈ tserefe ***(v.t. )* insult**
ፀረገ ንጡፍ tserege ntuf ***(adj.)* radioactive**
ፀርፊ tserfi ***(n.)* invective**
ፀጥ ዝበለ tset zbele ***(adj.)* silent**
ፀጥታ tsetta ***(n.)* silence**
ጸዋግ tsewag ***(adj.)* stern**
ፀዋግ ገፅ tsewag getse ***(n. )* scowl**
ጸዋር tsewar ***(n.)* stoic**
ፀዉዐ tsew'e ***(v.)* summon**
ፀወዐ tsewe'ë ***(v.)* invite**
ፀየቐ tseyeqe ***(v.)* deface**
ጸየቐ tseyqhe ***(v.t. )* stain**
ፅፍፈት tsffet ***(n. )* quality**
ፈጣን ንጡፍ fetan nťuf ***(adj.)* dapper**
እሩም 'èrum ***(adj.)* suave**
ፅገሬዳ tsgereda ***(n.)* rose**
ፅገሬዳዊ tsgeredawi ***(adj.)* rosy**
ተጸጋዒ texega'ï ***(n.)* dependant**
ፅግዕተኛ tsg'ëtegna ***(n.)* protectorate**
ፅግዕተኛነት tsg'ëtegnanet ***(n.)* dependency**
ትሽዓተ tshäte ***(adj. & n.)* nine**
ፅሑፈት ኢድ tshfet 'id ***(n. )* script**
ፅሕፍቶ ts'ĥfto ***(n.)* destiny**
ፅሑፍ tshuf ***(n.)* text**
ፅያፍ tzyaf ***(n.)* gaffe**
ፅፍሪ txefri ***(n.)* claw**
ፅርበት tsirbet ***(n.)* carpentry**
ጺጽ በለ tsi-tse bele ***(v.i)* hiss**
ፅኪ ጉዕጉዕቲ tski gu'egu'eti ***(n.)* thyroid**
ፅላል tslal ***(n.)* shade**
ፅላል ዘለዎ tslal zelewo ***(adj.)* shady**
ፅላሎት መሳሊ tslalo mesali ***(adj.)* shadowy**
ፅላሎት tslalot ***(n.)* shadow**
ፅላሎት tslalot ***(n.)* silhouette**
ፅላኣት tsleat ***(n.)* repugnance**
ዘይተፈታውነት zeytefetawnet ***(n.)* disfavour**
ፅልኢ tsl'i ***(n.)* disgust**
ፅልኢ tsl'i ***(n.)* distaste**
ጽልሙት tslmut ***(adj.)* sombre**
ፅሉል tslul ***(n. )* psychopath**
ፅማቕ ፅሑፍ tsmaq tsĥuf ***(n. )* precis**
ፅምደ ዜማ tsmde zema ***(n.)* duet**
ፅምዲ tsmdi ***(n.)* duo**
ፅምኢ tsm'i ***(n.)* thirst**
ፅምሉው tsmluw ***(adj.)* sallow**
ፅሙእ tsmu'e ***(adj.)* thirsty**
ባድም badm ***(adj.)* desolate**
ብሕቱው bĥtuw ***(n.)* seclusion**
ብሕት'ነት bĥtnet ***(n.)* solitude**
ወሳኒነት wesaninet ***(v. t)* determination**
ውሳነ ብይን wsane byn ***(n.)* resolution**
ጽንዓት ts'n'ät ***(n.)* steadiness**
ጽንሰ-ሓሳባዊ tsnsehasabawi ***(adj.)* hypothetical**
ጽንኩር xnkur ***(adj.)* severe**
ጉልቡት gulbut ***(adj.)* stalwart**
ጽኑዕ tsnu'e ***(adj.)* steady**
ነቕ ዘይብል neq̈ zeybl ***(adj.)* resolute**
ፅኑዕ ምኽን tsnu'ë mkwan ***(n. )* rigour**
ጽኑዕ tsnu'ë ***(adj.)* steadfast**
ፅኑዕነት tsnu'enet ***(n.)* severity**
ፆታ tsota ***(n.)* sex**

ፆታ ዘይበሉ tsota zeybelu ***(adj.)* unisex**
ፆታዊ tsotawi ***(adj.)* sexual**
ፆታዊ ኣድልዎ tsotawi 'adlwo ***(n.)* sexism**
ፆታውነት tsotawnet ***(n. )* sexuality**
ጽቐጥቅጥ tsqtqt ***(n.)* throng**
ፅርበ እምኒ መቃብር tsrbe 'emni meqabr ***(n.)* sarcophagus**
ፅርግያ tsrgya ***(n.)* road**
ፅሩይ tsruy ***(adj.)* tidy**
ጥስጠሳ tstesa ***(n.)* saturation**
ፁብቕ tsubuqh ***(adj.)* luxuriant**
ፁሉል tsulul ***(adj.)* mad**
ፁሉል tsulul ***(n. )* maniac**
ፅዑቕ ts'üq ***(adj.)* dense**
ፅዑቕ ts'üq ***(adj.)* intensive**
ፁሩይ tsury ***(adj.)* immaculate**
ፅቡቕ ድልየት tzbuq dlyet ***(n. )* goodwill**
ፀጋምተኛ tzegamtegna ***(n.)* leftist**
ፀገም tzegem ***(n.)* masochism**
ፀሓፊ ታሪኽ tzehafi tarik ***(n.)* historian**
ፀንበረ tzenbere ***(v.)* fuse**
ፅዕነት tz'ënet ***(n.)* freight**
ፀዋግ tzewag ***(adj.)* grim**
ፅላለ tzlale ***(n. )* mania**
ፅልዋ tzlwa ***(n. )* leverage**
ፅምኢ tzm'i ***(n.)* lust**
ፅሙድ tzmud ***(adj. )* hooked**
ፅሟቅ ለሚን tzmwaq lemin ***(n.)* lemonade**
ፆታ tzota ***(n.)* gender**
ጹረት tsuret ***(n.)* octroi**
ፅልኣት tsl'at ***(n.)* odium**

## ፈ

ፈላሚ felami ***(n.)* origin**
ፊትንፊት fitnfit ***(n.)* obverse**
ፋል fal ***(n.)* omen**
ፍልልይ flly ***(n. )* odds**
ፋብሪካ fabrika ***(n.)* factory**
ፋዱስ fadus ***(n. )* noon**
ፋእሚ fa'emi ***(n. )* skein**
ፋሓም fahäme ***(n.)* charcoal**
ፋሕፋሒ fah̆fah̆i ***(adj.)* abrasive**
ፋሕፍሐ fahfhe ***(v.)* scrub**
ፋሕፍሐ fah̑fh̑e ***(v.)* rub**
ሓግሓገ h̆agh̆age ***(v.)* scrape**
ሓንጠጠ h̆antĕtĕ ***(v.t.)* scratch**
ፋጅ faj ***(n.)* fudge**
ፋጅዮ fajyo ***(n.)* beech**
ፋክስ faks ***(n.)* fax**
ፋክቱር faktur ***(n.)* invoice**
ፋሉላዊ falulawi ***(n.)* anarchist**
ፋሉልነት falulnet ***(n.)* anarchism**
ሰማፎሮ semaforo ***(n.)* beacon**
ሽግ shg ***(n. )* torch**
ፋንጋይ fangay ***(n. )* fungus**
ፋንጣ fanẗa ***(n.)* grasshopper**
ፋኑስ fanus ***(n. )* lamp**
ፋኑስ fanus ***(n. )* lantern**
ፋርዳ farda ***(n.)* singleton**
ፋረንሃይት farenhayt ***(n.)* Fahrenheit**
ፋርኬታ farkeeta ***(n.)* fork**
ፋስ fas ***(n. )* hatchet**
ፋስ fas ***(n.)* axe**
ፋሽስትነት fashstnet ***(n.)* fascism**
ፋሽያ fashya ***(n.)* fascia**
ፋጻ faxa ***(n.)* whistle**
ፋይል fayl ***(n.)* file**
ፋይቶት faytot ***(n.)* courtesan**
ፍድፋድ fdfud ***(v.t.)* abundant**

**ፈጨጭ በለ** fečeĉ bele ***(v.)*** **fizz**
**ፈደየ** fedeye ***(v.)*** **acquit**
**ገንዘብ መለሰ** genzeb melese ***(v.)*** **repay**
**ፈድፈደ** fedfede ***(v.i.)*** **abound**
**ፌስታዊ አኼባ** feestawi 'aḱeeba ***(n.)*** **jamboree**
**ፈሓረ** fehare ***(v.)*** **delve**
**ፈኸም በለ** fekhem bele ***(v.)*** **smoulder**
**ፈኩስ ቢራ** fekwis bira ***(n.)*** **lager**
**ፈላሳይ** felasay ***(n.)*** **migrant**
**ፈላስፋ** felasfa ***(n.)*** **sophist**
**ፈላሲ** felasi ***(n. )*** **monk**
**ፈላሲት** felasit ***(n.)*** **nun**
**ፈላጥ** felaẗ ***(n.)*** **geek**
**ፈላጥ** felaẗ ***(n.)*** **nerd**
**ፈላጥ** felat' ***(adj.)*** **conversant**
**ፈለኽለኽ በለ** felekhlekh ***(v.)*** **squirm**
**ፈለማ** felema ***(adj. & n.)*** **first**
**ፈለሰ** felese ***(v.)*** **immigrate**
**ፈለሰ** felese ***(v.)*** **migrate**
**ፈለጠ** felete ***(v.i. )*** **recognize**
**ፈለጥኩ በሃሊ** feletku bhali ***(adj.)*** **pedantic**
**ነጸለ** nexele ***(v.)*** **detach**
**ፈለየ** feleye ***(v. t)*** **distinguish**
**መለሰ** melese ***(v.)*** **refund**
**ኣግለለ** 'aglele ***(v.)*** **segregate**
ዝተኸፋፈለ zteḱefafele ***(v.)*** **separate**
**ፈለየ** feleye ***(v.)*** **thresh**
**ፈልፋሊ** felfali ***(n.)*** **font**
**ፈልፋሊት** felfalit ***(v.)*** **spring**
**ፈልፈለ** felfele ***(v.)*** **incubate**
**ፈልሐ** felḧe ***(v.i.)*** **boil**
**ፍእምቶ ኣሰናዳዊ** f'emto asenadawi ***(n.)*** **blurb**
**ፈንጨጨ** fencheche ***(v.)*** **splay**
**ዕጀባ** 'ëjeba ***(n.)*** **convoy**
**ፈነወ** fenewe ***(v.)*** **emit**
**ጸልአ** xel'e ***(v.)*** **loathe**
**ፈንፈነ** fenfene ***(v.)*** **abhor**
**ፈንጊ** fengi ***(n.)*** **faction**
**ፈንቀለ** fenqele ***(v.)*** **dislodge**
**ፈንጠጋር** fenẗegar ***(adj.)*** **bizarre**
**ፈንጠዝያ** fentezya ***(n.)*** **spree**
**ሃሰየት** haseyet ***(n.)*** **euphoria**
**ፈንጠዝያ** fenţezya ***(n. )*** **wassail**
**ፈንጠዝያ** fenẗezya ***(n.)*** **binge**
**ፈንጢስካ ምእታው** fenẗiska m'ètaw ***(n.)*** **irruption**
**ፈንፀሐ** fentseḧe ***(v.)*** **split**
**ፈቓድ** feqad ***(n.)*** **franchise**
**ብቕዓት** bq'ät ***(n.)*** **warrant**
**ስምምዕ** smm'ë ***(n.)*** **consent**
**ፈቃር** feqar ***(adj.)*** **affectionate**
**ህኑን** hnun ***(adj.)*** **fond**
**ፈቀደ** feqede ***(v.t.)*** **consent**
**ፈቀደ** feqede ***(v.)*** **let**
**ፈቐደ** feq̈ede ***(v.)*** **allow**
**ፈራዲ** feradi ***(n.)*** **arbiter**
**ፈራዶ** ferado ***(n.)*** **judiciary**
**ነባሮ** nebaro ***(n. )*** **jury**
**ዘፍርህ** zefrh ***(adj.)*** **fearful**
**ሃድአ** had'e ***(adj.)*** **meek**
**ብዘይ -ዓንዲሕቖ** bzey-'ändiḧq̈o ***(adj.)*** **spineless**
**ፈራሕነት** ferahnet ***(n.)*** **timidity**
**ፈራሚ** ferami ***(n. )*** **signatory**
**ፈራረሰ** ferarese ***(v.)*** **crumble**
**ፈራዪ** ferayi ***(adj.)*** **prolific**
**ፈረደ** ferede ***(v.)*** **adjudicate**
**ፈረደ** ferede ***(v.)*** **convict**
**ፈረመ** fereme ***(n.)*** **undersigned**
**ፈረቐ** fereq̈e ***(v.)*** **halve**
**ፈረስ** feres ***(n. )*** **horse**

ፈረስ ጋለቢ feres galabi *(adj.)* **equestrian**

ፈረሰኛ ወተሃደር fereseňa wetehader *(n.)* **knight**

ፈረሰኛ feresenya *(adj.)* **cavalier**

ፈርፈረ ferfere *(v.t)* **grate**

ፈርሀ ግብረ-ሰዶመኛ ferhe gbresedomeňa *(n.)* **homophobia**

ፈርሎንግ ferlonga *(n. )* **furlong**

ፈርን fern *(n.)* **fern**

ፈሳሲ fesasi *(n.)* **fluid**

ፈሳሲ fesasi *(n.)* **liquid**

ፈሳሲ ኮላ fesasi kone *(n. )* **mucilage**

ፈሳዊ fesawi *(adj.)* **flatulent**

ፈሰመ feseme *(v.)* **discolour**

ፈሰሰ fesese *(v.i)* **flow**

ፈስፋስ fesfas *(n.)* **sluggard**

ፈሲሕ fesiȟ *(v.)* **swanky**

ፈታላይ fetalay *(n. )* **spinner**

ፍጡን fťun *(adj.)* **nimble**

ቀዝሓዊ qezȟawi *(adj.)* **nippy**

ሓራቕ ȟaraq̈ *(adj.)* **snappy**

ፈጣን feťan *(adj.)* **speedy**

ፈጣን ጎደና feťan godena *(n.)* **speedway**

ፈታናይ fetanay *(n.)* **Trier**

ፈጣሪ fetari *(n.)* **creator**

ፈጣሪ fetari *(n.)* **innovator**

ፈታተሐ fetatȟe *(v.)* **dismantle**

ፈታው መጽሓፍ fetaw mexȟaf *(n.)* **bibliophile**

ፈታዊ ሃገር fetawi hager *(n. )* **nationalist**

መርመራ mermera *(n.)* **exam**

ፈተና fetena *(n.)* **test**

ፈተ'ነ fetene *(v.)* **attempt**

ብድሆ bdho *(n.)* **challenge**

ምኮራ mkora *(n.)* **experiment**

ኣቐዲሙ ረኣየ 'aq̈edimu re'aye *(n.)* **preview**

ምሕዳስ mȟdas *(n.)* **innovation**

ንምትላል ፈጠረ nmtlal feťere *(n. )* **trump**

ፈጠራ feťera *(n.)* **concoction**

ፈጠረ fetere *(v.)* **create**

ለቐቐ leq̈eq̈e *(v.)* **unleash**

ፈትሐ fet'ȟe *(v.)* **decipher**

ፈትሐ fetȟe *(v.)* **solve**

ፈንጢሑ ተንተነ feti'ȟu tentene *(v.)* **deconstruct**

ፈትሊ fetli *(n.)* **yarn**

ፈትሊ ሽምዓ fetli shm'a *(n.)* **wick**

ፈፀጋ ዓይኒ fetsega äynj *(n.)* **sty**

ፈፀጋ fetzega *(n.)* **freckle**

ፈዋሳይ fewasay *(n)* **quack**

ፈዋሲ fewasi *(adj.)* **medicinal**

ፈወሰ fewese *(v. t.)* **cure**

ፈውሲ fewsi *(n.)* **remedy**

ፈውሲ ዓሻ fewsi äsha *(n.)* **nostrum**

ፈፃሚ fexami *(n.)* **executive**

ፈፀጋ fexega *(n.)* **acne**

ፈጸጋ fexega *(n.)* **pimple**

ፈጸመ fexeme *(v.)* **commit**

ረሸነ reshene *(v.)* **execute**

ዛዘመ zazeme *(v.)* **accomplish**

መል'አ mel'e *(v.)* **consummate**

ኣጸቢቑ ዘይበሰለ 'axebiq̈u zeybesele *(adj.)* **sodden**

ነዋሚ newami *(adj.)* **torpid**

ፈዘዘ fezeze *(v.)* **glaze**

ፍግረት fgret *(n.)* **erosion**

ፍሕፍሕ fȟfȟ *(n. )* **friction**

ፍሒኛ fȟinya *(n.)* **balloon**

ፍሒሩ ኣውጽአ fhiru awts'a *(v.)* **unearth**

ፍሕኛ fȟňa *(n.)* **bladder**

ፍሕኛ fȟnyawi *(n.)* **cyst**

ፍሕኛዊ fḧnyawi *(adj.)* **cystic**
ፍሕሶ fḧso *(n.)* **cord**
ፍሕሶ ጸምሪ fhso tsemri *(n.)* **worsted**
ፊደል fidel *(n.)* **alphabet**
ብናይ ፊደላት ተርታ bnay fidelat terta *(adj.)* **alphabetical**
ፊደላዊ fidelawi *(adj.)* **literal**
ፌደራላዊ fiederalawi *(adj.)* **federal**
ፈደረሽን fiedereshn *(n.)* **federation**
ፌንግ ሽዊ fieng shwi *(n.)* **feng shui**
ፊፍ በለ fif bele *(v.)* **sniffle**
ፊሕታ fiḧta *(n.)* **boom**
ፊልሚ filmi *(n.)* **film**
ፊልሚ filmi *(n.)* **movies**
ፊሎሎጅየኛ filolojgna *(n.)* **philologist**
ፊሎሎጅያዊ filolojyawi *(adj.)* **philological**
ፊኖክዮ finokyo *(n.)* **fennel**
ፊንታ finta *(n.)* **vagary**
ፊርማ firma *(n. )* **signature**
ፊስቶ fiseto *(n.)* **cask**
ፊተውራሪ fitewrari *(n.)* **spearhead**
ፊዚክስ fizkis *(n.)* **physics**
ፊዝዮተራፒ fizyoterapi *(n.)* **physiotherapy**
ፍኩስ ጽፍዒት fkus xfeit *(v.)* **pat**
ፍላቅ flaq *(adj.)* **derivative**
ፍላጻ flaxa *(n.)* **arrow**
ፍልፍል fl'fl *(n. )* **spa**
ፍልሖ flho *(n.)* **termite**
ፍሊልታ flilta *(n. )* **jet**
ፍሊት flit *(n.)* **aerosol**
ፍልልይ flly *(n.)* **distinction**
ምልውዋጥ mlwwaẗ *(n.)* **variation**
ፍሎራይድ florayd *(n.)* **fluoride**
ፍልቀት flqet *(n.)* **evolution**
ፍልቀተ-ቃል flqeteqal *(n.)* **etymology**

ፍልሰት flset *(n.)* **migration**
ፍልስፍና flsfna *(n.)* **philosophy**
ፍልስፍናዊ flsfnawi *(adj.)* **philosophical**
ፍልጠት flẗet *(n.)* **mastery**
ፍሉ flu *(n.)* **flu**
ፍሉጥ flut *(adj.)* **renowned**
ዘየማትእ ሓቂ zeyemat'è ḧaqi *(n.)* **truism**
ዝተፈልየ ztefelye *(adj.)* **different**
ዝተቖራረጸ zteq̈orarexe *(adj.)* **discrete**
ፍሉይ fluy *(adj.)* **especial**
ዘይተለምደ zeytelemde *(adj.)* **extraordinary**
ዓጃበዊ 'äĵabawi *(adj.)* **remarkable**
ፍሉይ fluy *(adj.)* **special**
ዝተፈልየ ztefelye *(adj.)* **unique**
ልውጥ lwẗ *(n.)* **variant**
ፍሉይ fluy *(adj.)* **particular**
ናይ ፍላይ nay flay *(adj.)* **peculiar**
ፍሉይ ግዳሰ fluy gdase *(n.)* **hobby**
ፍሉይ ክእለት fluy k'elet *(n.)* **forte**
ውሕልነት wḧlnet *(n.)* **specialization**
ፍሉይ ክእለት አጥረየ fluy k'elet aẗreye *(v.)* **specialize**
ፍሉይ ጠባይ fluy ṭebay *(n.)* **idiosyncrasy**
ፍሉይ ፆታዊ fluy tzotawi *(adj. )* **heterosexual**
ፍሉይነት fluynet *(n.)* **speciality**
ፍልየት flyet *(n.)* **detachment**
ፍንጫል fnchal *(n.)* **splinter**
ፍንጫል ምእመናን fn'chal m'emenan *(n.)* **sect**
ፍንጪ fnči *(n.)* **cue**
ፍንጭልጫል fnĉlĉal *(n.)* **shrapnel**
ፊነክስ fneks *(n.)* **phoenix**
ፍንፈና fnfena *(n.)* **abhorrence**

ፍንፉን fnfun *(adj.)* **loathsome**
ፍዳ fda *(n.)* **vengeance**
ፈላሲ felasi *(n.)* **immigrant**
ፈለጠ feleṭe *(v.)* **know**
ፈታው ኩናት fetaw kunat *(adj.)* **warlike**
ፈታው ምቾት fetaw mchot *(n.)* **voluptuary**
ፈታው መግቢ fetaw megbi *(n.)* **gourmand**
ፈተነ fetene *(n.)* **venture**
ፍልልይ flly *(n.)* **variance**
ፍልሰት flset *(n.)* **immigration**
ፍልጠት flṭet *(n. )* **knowledge**
ፈኩስ ግመ fokis gme *(n.)* **haze**
ፍቓደኛ fq̈adeña *(n.)* **volunteer**
ፍጥነት fṭnet *(n. )* **velocity**
ፍንጉፅ fnguts *(adj.)* **deviant**
ፎልዮ folyo *(n.)* **folio**
ፎቅ foq *(n.)* **tower**
ፎረፎር forefor *(n.)* **dandruff**
ፎርኖ forno *(n. )* **toaster**
ፎጣ fota *(n.)* **towel**
ፍቶ ኮፒ foto kopi *(n.)* **photocopy**
ፎቶ ኮፒ foto kopi *(n.)* **photostat**
ፍቭያ fovya *(n.)* **phobia**
ፎዝፌት fozfeyet *(n. )* **phosphate**
ፍቓድ fqad *(n.)* **permission**
ፍቓድ fqad *(v.)* **will**
ፍቓደኛ fq̈adeṅa *(adj.)* **willing**
ፍቓድ ዘይብሉ fqad zeyblu *(adj.)* **unwarranted**
ፍቓደኛ fqadegna *(adj.)* **willing**
ፍቓድ ኣምላኽ fq̈d amlak *(n.)* **providence**
ፍቓድ fqhad *(n.)* **licence**
ፍቕሪ fqhri *(n.)* **love**
ፍቖድኡ fq̈odeu *(adj.)* **ubiquitous**
ፍቕራዊ fqrawi *(n.)* **paramour**
ፍቅራዊ fqrawi *(adj.)* **romantic**
ፍቕራዊ fq̈rawi *(adj.)* **amorous**
ፍቕሪ fqri *(n.)* **devotion**
ፍቅሪ ሃገር fqri hager *(n. )* **nationalism**
ፍቕሪ ክምስርት ፈተነ fqri kmsrt fetene *(v.)* **woo**
ፍቕሪ መግለጺ ቃል fqri meglexi qal *(n.)* **endearment**
ፍቑር fq̈ur *(adj.)* **beloved**
ፍራስ fras *(n. )* **wreckage**
ፍርዳዊ frdawi *(adj.)* **judicial**
ከም ገበነኛ ምፍራድ kem gebeneṅa mfrad *(n.)* **conviction**
ፍርዲ frdi *(n. )* **judgement**
ፍርዲ frdi *(n.)* **ruling**
ፍርዲ frdi *(n.)* **verdict**
ፍረ fre *(n.)* **fruit**
ፈረየ fereye *(n.)* **seed**
ፍረ ዓካት fre 'äkat *(n. )* **kernel**
ፍረ ካስታኖ fre kastano *(n.)* **conker**
ፍረ ነገር fre neger *(n.)* **essence**
ፍረ ነገር fre neger *(n.)* **gist**
ፍረ ነብሲ frenebsi *(n.)* **testicle**
ፍረ ነብሲ frenebsi *(n.)* **testis**
ፍርሓት frḧat *(n.)* **cowardice**
ፍርሃታዊ frhatawi *(adj.)* **reverential**
ምፍርራሕ mfrraḧ *(n.)* **threat**
ጭንቀት čnqet *(n.)* **dismay**
ፈርሀ ferhe *(n.)* **fear**
መሰንበዲ mesenbedi *(n.)* **fright**
ፍርሒ frḥi *(n. )* **horror**
ፍሪጅ frij *(n.)* **refrigerator**
ፍሪቅሪቅ ዝብል friqriq bele *(adj.)* **fizzy**
ፍርናሽ frnash *(n.)* **mattress**
ፍርናሽ frnash *(n.)* **pad**
ጉዝጓዝ guzgwaz *(v.)* **padding**
ፍርናሽ ሓሰር frnash haser *(n.)* **pallet**

ፍርቀ ክቢ frqe kebi *(n.)* **semicircle**
ፍርቀ ኽረምቲ frqe ḱremti *(adj.)* **midsummer**
ፍርቀ ለይቲ frqe leyti *(n.)* **midnight**
ፍርቀ መዓልቲ frqe me'älti *(n.)* **midday**
ፍርቂ frqi *(adj.)* **mid**
ፍርቁ frqu *(adv. )* **partly**
ፍርሰት frset *(n.)* **nullification**
ፍርስራስ frsras *(n.)* **debris**
ፍርትት ዝብል frtt zbl *(adj.)* **friable**
ፍሩስ frus *(adj.)* **null**
ፍሩሽካ frushka *(n.)* **fodder**
ፍርያት fryat *(n. )* **product**
ፍርያት ግጥሚ fryat gẗmi *(n. )* **poetry**
ፍሰሃ fseha *(n.)* **ecstasy**
ፍሰሃ fseha *(n.)* **felicity**
ፍሰት fset *(n.)* **creek**
ፍስሃ fsha *(n. )* **pleasure**
ፍሽኽታ fshḱta *(v.)* **grin**
ፍሹል fshul *(adj.)* **abortive**
ፍሽለት fšlet *(n.)* **refutation**
ፍሱሕ fsuh *(adj.)* **jaunty**
ፍታሕ ftaȟ *(n.)* **solution**
ፍታሕ ሃበ ftaĥ habe *(v.)* **resolve**
ፍትሕ ft'ĥ *(n.)* **divorce**
ፍትሓዊ ft'ĥawi *(adj.)* **dispassionate**
ፍትሒ ftĥi *(n.)* **equity**
ፍትሒ ftȟi *(n.)* **impartiality**
ፍትሒ ftȟi *(n.)* **justice**
ፍጥነት ftnet *(n.)* **pace**
ፍጥነት fẗnet *(n.)* **speed**
ፍትነት ማሽን መዐቀኒ ftnet mashn me'eqeni *(n.)* **tachometer**
ፍጥረት ftret *(n.)* **creature**
ፍጻመ ftsame *(n. )* **happening**
ፍፁም ftsum *(adj.)* **sheer**
ፍፁም ለወጠ ftṣum lewete *(v.)* **revolutionize**
ፍትወት ftwet *(n.)* **penchant**
ፍትወት ftwet *(n.)* **affection**
ፍትወተ ስጋ ftwete sga *(n.)* **sensuality**
ፍፁም ftzum *(adj.)* **implicit**
ፉል ful *(n.)* **peanut**
ፉሉይ fuluy *(adj.)* **inimitable**
ፉርዳ furda *(n.)* **bay**
ፉት በለ fut bele *(v.)* **sip**
ፍወሳ ሕማም ኣእምሮ fwesa ḧmam aèmro *(n.)* **psychotherapy**
ፍፃመ fxame *(n.)* **episode**
ፍጻሜ fxamee *(n.)* **event**
ምርሻን mrshan *(n.)* **execution**
ፍጻሜ fxamee *(n.)* **accomplishment**
ፍጹም fxum *(adj.)* **categorical**
ምሉ'እ mlu'è *(adj.)* **perfect**
ኣውቶክራት 'awtokrat *(adj.)* **autocrat**
ዘዋርድ zeward *(adj.)* **abject**
ፍፁም መላኪ fxum melaki *(adj.)* **absolute**
ፍጹምነት fxumnet *(n.)* **perfection**
ፍንፉን fnfun *(adj.)* **odious**
ፎርኖ forno *(n.)* **oven**

# T

ፐንጉን pengyun *(n.)* **penguin**
ፐፐሮኒ peperoni *(n.)* **pepper**
ፑርጋቶርዮ purgatoryo *(n.)* **purgatory**
ፒንሳ pinsa *(n.)* **pliers**
ፒራሚድ piramid *(n. )* **pyramid**
ፒሳ pisa *(n.)* **pizza**
ፒስቶን piston *(n. )* **piston**

ፒያኖ piyano *(n.)* **piano**
ዋልታ-ምድሪ waltamdri *(n. )* **pole**
ፖሎ palo *(n.)* **polo**
ፓንኬክ pankek *(n.)* **pancake**
ፓንታሎኒ pantaloni *(n. )* **pantaloons**
ፓፓጋሎ papagalo *(n.)* **parrot**
ፓራመተር parameter *(n.)* **parameter**
ፓርላማዊ parlamawi *(adj.)* **parliamentary**
ፓርላማ parlma *(n. )* **parliament**
ፓሮ paro *(n.)* **leek**
ፓስፖርት pasport *(n.)* **passport**
ፓይ pay *(n.)* **pie**
ፓይሎት paylot *(n.)* **pilot**
መራሕ ነፋሪት meraḧ nefarit *(n.)* **aviator**
ፔርሙዝ permuz *(n.)* **thermos**
ፕላኔት planiet *(n.)* **planet**
ፕላተሌት planiet *(n.)* **platelet**
ፕላስቲክ plastik *(n.)* **plastic**
ፕራላይን pralayn *(n.)* **praline**
ፕራንያ pranya *(n.)* **pram**
ፕሬዝደንት presdent *(n.)* **president**
ፕሬዝደንታዊ presdentawi *(adj.)* **presidential**
ፕሪዝም prizm *(n.)* **prism**
ፕሮፌሰር profieser *(n.)* **professor**
ፕሮጀክቶር proĵecter *(n.)* **projector**
ፕሮስተይት prosteyt *(n.)* **prostate**
ፕሮቲን protin *(n. )* **protein**
ፕላንተይን planteyn *(n. )* **plantain**
ፖድካስት podkast *(n.)* **podcast**
ፖለቲከኛ poletikegna *(n.)* **statesman**
ፖለቲከኛ poletikeňa *(n.)* **politician**
ፖለቲቻዊ ጥርናፈ poletikeňawi ẗrnafe *(n.)* **polity**
ፖለቲክስ poletiks *(n.)* **politics**
ፖሊግራፍ poligraf *(n.)* **polygraph**
ፖሊስ polis *(n. )* **police**
ፖሊስ polis *(n. )* **policeman**
ፖሊሳዊ ምርመራ polisawi mrmera *(n.)* **inquisition**
ፖለቲካዊ polotikawi *(adj.)* **political**
ፖርኖግራፊ pornografi *(n.)* **pornography**
ፖስታ posta *(n.)* **mail**
ፖስጣ ቤት posẗa biet *(n.)* **post office**
ፖስተር poster *(n. )* **poster**
ፖፕላር potlar *(n. )* **poplar**